A SENSE OF THE SACRED

The Virgin Mary Enthroned from the Ghent Altarpiece
Jan van Eyck (c. 1390–1441)
Cathedral of St. Bavo, Ghent, Belgium

©Scala/Art Resource, New York

JAMES MONTI

A SENSE OF THE SACRED

Roman Catholic Worship in the Middle Ages

IGNATIUS PRESS   SAN FRANCISCO

Nihil Obstat: Monsignor Francis J. McAree, S.T.D.

Imprimatur: † The Most Reverend Dennis J. Sullivan
Vicar General of the Archbishop of New York
November 27, 2012

The *Nihil Obstat* and *Imprimatur* are the official declaration that this book is free from doctrinal and moral error. There are no implications contained therein that those who have granted the *Nihil Obstat* and *Imprimatur* agree with the content, opinion or statements expressed.

Cover illustration by Stephen Dudro

Cover design by Riz Boncan Marsella

ISBN 978-1-58617-283-1
Library of Congress Control Number 2011930698
Printed in the United States of America ∞

To Our Lady of Good Counsel,
that through her loving intercession and her example of obedience,
we may attain an authentic liturgical renewal
and restore the sense of the sacred
by following the path of humble obedience to the Successor of Saint Peter.

Contents

Acknowledgments

I wish to express my gratitude to the staff of the Corrigan Memorial Library of Saint Joseph's Seminary in Yonkers, New York, for making available to me their outstanding collection of books and periodicals. I am especially grateful both to them and to the staff of the Irvington Public Library in Irvington, New York, for obtaining numerous inter-library loans of books and journal articles essential to the completion of this work. I also want to thank the staff of the Vatican Library (the Biblioteca Apostolica Vaticana) and, in particular, Sister Catherine M. Clarke, F.S.E., formerly of the library, for graciously providing the page reproductions I needed for my research from two sixteenth-century Spanish missals (those of Palencia and Seville) in the library's Barberini Collection. I am deeply grateful to Father Luke Sweeney, vocations director of the Archdiocese of New York, and to Mrs. Catherine Kolpak, managing editor of the periodical for which I write, *Magnificat*, for having contacted the Vatican Library on my behalf in 2006 and 2007 respectively, as well as for obtaining for me a number of books recently published in Rome and Spain pertaining to liturgical history. I am likewise grateful to both of them for their invaluable assistance in helping me to contact many of the publishers whose works are quoted in the present book. Finally, I wish to thank in a special manner Gail Gavin for her highly professional, dedicated, and patient copy editing in preparing my manuscript for publication.

Credits

The author gratefully acknowledges the following publishers and institutions for granting permission to quote from and translate excerpts from their publications or from documents in their digital collections.

Brepols Publishers, Turnhout, Belgium, for granting permission to quote from and translate excerpts from the following Brepols publications:

Brière, Maurice; Louis Mariès, S.J.; and B.-Ch. Mercier, O.S.B., eds. *Hippolyte de Rome sur les Bénédictions d'Isaac, de Jacob et de Moïse*. Patrologia orientalis 27, fasc. 1–2. Paris, Firmin-Didot, 1954.

Chibnall, Marjorie, ed. and trans. *The Ecclesiastical History of Orderic Vitalis*. Vol. 4, *Books VII and VIII*. Oxford Medieval Texts. Oxford: Clarendon, 1973. © Oxford University Press.

Costello Publishing Company, Northport, New York. Excerpts from *Vatican Council II*, vol. 1, *The Conciliar and Post Conciliar Documents*, edited by Rev. Austin Flannery, O.P., copyright 2007, Costello Publishing Company, Inc., Northport, N.Y., are used by permission of the publisher, all rights reserved. No part of these excerpts may be reproduced, stored in a retrieval system, or transmitted in any form or by any means—electronic, mechanical, photocopying, recording, or otherwise—without express permission of Costello Publishing Company, Inc.

Davril, A., O.S.B., and T. M. Thibodeau, eds. *Guillelmi Duranti: Rationale divinorum officiorum I–IV*. Corpus Christianorum: Continuatio mediaevalis 140. Turnhout, Belgium: Brepols, 1995.

———, eds. *Guillelmi Duranti: Rationale divinorum officiorum V–VI*. Corpus Christianorum: Continuatio mediaevalis 140a. Turnhout, Belgium: Brepols, 1998.

———, eds. *Guillelmi Duranti: Rationale divinorum officiorum VII–VIII*. Corpus Christianorum: Continuatio mediaevalis 140b. Turnhout, Belgium: Brepols, 2000.

Dessain, C. S., ed. *The Letters and Diaries of John Henry Newman*. Vol. 11, *Littlemore to Rome, October 1845 to December 1846*. London: Thomas Nelson and Sons, 1961. © Oxford University Press.

Diercks, G. F., ed. *Sancti Cypriani episcopi epistularium*. Corpus Christianorum: Series Latina 3b. Sancti Cypriani episcopi opera, pt. 3, 1. Turnhout, Belgium: Brepols, 1994.

Douteil, Heribertus, C.S.Sp., ed. *Iohannis Beleth: Summa de ecclesiasticis officiis*. Corpus Christianorum: Continuatio mediaevalis 41a. Turnhout, Belgium: Brepols, 1976.

Dumas, A., O.S.B., ed. *Liber sacramentorum Gellonensis.* Corpus Christianorum: Series Latina 159. Turnhout, Belgium: Brepols, 1981.

Franceschini, A., and R. Weber, eds. *Itinerarium Egeriae.* In *Itineraria et Alia geographia.* Corpus Christianorum: Series Latina 175. Turnhout, Belgium: Brepols, 1965.

Frere, Walter Howard, ed. *The Use of Sarum.* 2 vols. Cambridge, England: Cambridge University Press, 1898–1901. © Oxford University Press.

Haacke, Hrabanus, O.S.B., ed. *Ruperti Tuitiensis: Liber de divinis officiis* Corpus Christianorum: Continuatio mediaevalis 7. Turnhout, Belgium: Brepols, 1967.

Jugie, Martin, ed. and trans. *Homélies mariales byzantines: Textes grecs édités et traduits en latin.* Vol. 2. Patrologia orientalis 19, fasc. 3. Paris: Firmin-Didot, 1925.

Knowles, David, and Christopher N. L. Brooke, eds. and trans. *The Monastic Constitutions of Lanfranc.* Rev. ed. Oxford Medieval Texts. Oxford: Clarendon, 2002. © Oxford University Press.

Lawson, Christopher M., ed. *Sancti Isidori episcopi Hispalensis: De ecclesiasticis officiis.* Corpus Christianorum: Series Latina 113. Turnhout, Belgium: Brepols, 1989.

Legg, John Wickham, ed. *The Sarum Missal, Edited from Three Early Manuscripts.* Oxford: Clarendon, 1916. © Oxford University Press.

Maskell, William, ed. *Monumenta ritualia ecclesiae Anglicanae.* 3 vols. Oxford: Clarendon, 1882. © Oxford University Press.

Munier, C., ed. *Concilia Galliae, A. 314–A. 506.* Corpus Christianorum: Series Latina 148. Turnhout, Belgium: Brepols, 1963.

Oxford University Press, Oxford, England. Excerpts from the following publications have been quoted and translated by permission of Oxford University Press.

Renoux, Athanase, ed. and trans. *Le codex Arménien Jérusalem 121.* Vol. 2, *Edition comparée du texte et de deux autres manuscrits.* Patrologia orientalis 36, fasc. 2. Turnhout, Belgium: Brepols, 1971.

Young, Karl. *The Drama of the Medieval Church.* 2 vols. Oxford: Clarendon, 1933. © Oxford University Press.

The author likewise gratefully acknowledges the following publishers, institutions, and individuals for granting permission to quote from and translate excerpts from their publications or documents in their collections, which are listed in full in the footnotes and the bibliography:

Aarhus University Press, Aarhus, Denmark

Academic Press Fribourg (Editions Universitaires Fribourg), Universite de Fribourg, Fribourg, Switzerland

Akademiai Kiadó, Budapest, Hungary

Akademische Druck—u. Verlagsanstalt (ADEVA), Graz, Austria

Aschendorff Verlag, Munster, Germany

Bayerische Staatsbibliothek, Munich, Germany

Biblioteca Apostolica Vaticana, Vatican City

Biblioteca Nacional de España, Madrid, Spain

Biblioteka Narodowa (National Library of Poland), Warsaw, Poland

Credits

Cantus, University of Waterloo, Waterloo, Ontario, Canada (http://cantusdatabase.org)

The Catholic University of America Press, Washington, D.C.

Centro Liturgico Vincenziano, Rome

Church Music Association of America, Richmond, Virginia

CNRS Editions (Editions du Centre National de la Recherche Scientifique), Paris

Continuum International Publishing Group, London

Deutsches Historisches Institut in Rom, Rome

The Dominican Council, English Province of the Order of Preachers, Oxford, England

Father Vicente Dura Garrigues, S.J., Provincial, Company of Jesus, Province of Aragon, Valencia, Spain (permission to quote from the work of Blessed Juan Bautista Ferreres Boluda, S.J., *Historia del misal romano* [Barcelona; Eugenio Subirana, 1929])

Editions Beauchesne, Paris, France

Les Editions du Cerf, Paris

Edizioni Orientalia Christiana, Pontificio Istituto Orientale, Rome

Facultat de Teologia de Catalunya, Barcelona, Spain

The Governing Board of the School of Celtic Studies of the Dublin Institute for Advanced Studies, Dublin, Ireland

De Gruyter (Walter de Gruyter GmbH and Co.), Berlin and Munich, Germany

Heffers (W. Heffer and Sons), Cambridge, England

Henry Bradshaw Society, London and Cambridge, England

Institut de Droit Canonique, Bibliotheque, Universite de Strasbourg, Strasbourg, France

Institut Historique Belge de Rome, Rome and Louvain

The John Paul II Catholic University of Lublin, Lublin, Poland

Librairie Droz, Geneva, Switzerland

Libreria Editrice Vaticana, Vatican City

Gerard Lukken, Tilburg, Netherlands (permission to quote from a publication of Kok Pharos Publishing House, Kampen, Netherlands, co-edited by him)

Monumenta Germaniae Historica, Munich, Germany

Osterreichische Akademie der Wissenschaften (Austrian Academy of Sciences), Vienna, Austria

Pauline Books and Media, Boston, Massachusetts

Penn State Press, University Park, Pennsylvania

Pontifical Institute of Medieval Studies, Toronto, Canada

Publicacions de L'Abadia de Montserrat, Barcelona, Spain

Random House Archive and Library, Rushden, England

Revue d'Histoire Ecclesiastique, Louvain, Belgium

Roman Catholic Books, Fort Collins, Colorado

St. Paul's Publishing, London

Graham Salter, London—www.LionelSalter.co.uk (permission for excerpt from Lionel Salter's translation of Richard Wagner's *Parsifal*—translation © Lionel Salter)

Dr. Andrea Schmidt, editor, Corpus scriptorum Christianorum orientalium series, Université Catholique de Louvain, Louvain, Belgium

Franz Schmitt Verlag, Siegburg, Germany

Societas Historiae Ecclesiasticae Fennica (The Finnish Society of Church History), Helsinki, Finland

Societat Catalana d'Estudis Liturgics, Institut d'Estudis Catalans, Barcelona, Spain

SPCK Publishing, London

Speculum, Boston, Massachusetts

Franz Steiner Verlag GmbH, Stuttgart, Germany

Stiiftsbibliothek St. Gallen, St. Gallen, Switzerland

TAN Books/Saint Benedict Press, Charlotte, North Carolina

Universitat de València, Biblioteca Historica, Valencia, Spain

Verlag Herder GmbH, Freiburg im Breisgau, Germany

Vita e Pensiero, Universita Cattolica del Sacro Cuore, Milan, Italy

Yale University Press, New Haven, Connecticut

Abbreviations

BELS	Bibliotheca "Ephemerides Liturgicae", subsidia
BIHBR	Bibliothèque de l'Institut Historique Belge de Rome
CCCM	Corpus Christianorum: Continuatio mediaevalis
CCSL	Corpus Christianorum: Series Latina
CSCO	Corpus scriptorum Christianorum orientalium
CSEL	Corpus scriptorum ecclesiasticorum Latinorum
EL	*Ephemerides Liturgicae*
HBS	Henry Bradshaw Society
JTS	*Journal of Theological Studies*
MLCT	Monumenta liturgica Concilii Tridentini
MSIL	Monumenta studia instrumenta liturgica
PG	Patrologia Graeca
PL	Patrologia Latina
REDSMF	Rerum ecclesiasticarum documenta, series maior: Fontes
SC	Sources chrétiennes
SF	Spicilegium Friburgense
SSLED	Spicilegium sacrum Lovaniense: Etudes et documents
ST	Studi e testi

Introduction

> To see this immortal King face-to-face, the Church at present is preparing herself; and while she celebrates her temporal feasts here, she contemplates the festive and eternal joys of her native land, where her Spouse is praised by angelic instruments. And all the saints, continually celebrating the day of great festivity that the Lord has made, cease not to praise with nuptial songs the immortal Bridegroom, beautiful in form before the sons of men, who in his gratuitous mercy has chosen the Church for himself.
>
> *Mystical Mirror of the Church*, 1160–1165[1]

When Moses ascended Mount Sinai to investigate the mysterious burning bush that he had sighted on its slopes, he heard the voice of God commanding him, "Put off the shoes from thy feet; for the place whereon thou standest is holy ground" (Ex 3:5). The Lord had drawn near to converse with his servant, but it was needful that Moses should respond to his Creator's love and mercy with reverence and awe. In the Incarnation, God humbled himself to become man, to walk among men, and to die for man, but he did not will for men to lose sight of his divinity: on Mount Tabor, he revealed himself in majesty, moving Peter, John, and James to prostrate themselves in reverence and awe. This sense of the sacred, which is indeed a living perception of the infinite goodness, holiness, and omnipotence of God, the Church has inherited. It is in fact an expression of love for the infinitely good God, a disposition of the heart and soul conferred with the seventh gift of the Holy Spirit—the fear of the Lord.

The Church expresses her sense of the sacred supremely through the liturgy. For in the liturgy, it is Christ himself, the Priest of the New Covenant in his own blood, who offers the Church's praises to God the Father, in the Holy Spirit, at our altars, through his ordained ministers, with the participation of the faithful. Hence, because both he to whom the Church's praises are offered and he by whom those praises are offered are infinitely sacred, the words and actions with

---

[1] *Speculum ecclesiae*, attributed to Pseudo-Hugh of Saint Victor, chap. 1, PL 177, col. 338.

which the Church worships the Almighty need to express the sacred, to be permeated with the sacred: "Every liturgical celebration, because it is an action of Christ the Priest and of his Body, which is the Church, is a sacred action surpassing all others."[2]

When after two centuries of persecution the Church emerged from the catacombs, delivered from the shadow of Roman paganism, she was at last free to celebrate her public worship, the liturgy, truly in public. As the celebration of the Eucharist and the other sacraments moved from behind the closed doors of private homes and into the great basilicas, the Church began to express how very much the ineffable gifts of God meant to her through more expansive liturgical texts and actions. The pilgrim journey of the faithful toward the longed-for heavenly Jerusalem could now be manifested in great liturgical processions under the vaults of vast sunlit churches and through the city streets of a Christianized civilization. As the Church's numbers swelled with the gradual conversion of Europe, these newly won children of the Church offered the finest gifts of their respective cultures to the worship of God, laying at the feet of their Savior the gold, frankincense, and myrrh of great art, architecture, music, and literature. The largely anonymous authors of the medieval additions to, and modifications of, the liturgy expanded upon the work of their patristic ancestors, amplifying the meaning of the sacraments through the composition of new prayer texts, hymns, and rubrics, expressing in greater detail and depth the truths of the faith with the eyes of an artist, the ears of a musician, and the eloquence of a poet. Their work belonged not to themselves but to the Church they were endeavoring to serve. By incorporating their compositions into the liturgy, the Church made their words her own.

Catholic worship has always been characterized by a balance between unchanging elements preserving the continuity of the ages and elements that according to the mind of the Church have changed over the centuries as a manifestation of the Church's ever-deepening understanding of the faith. In medieval liturgy we find preserved so many of the textual treasures of the early sacramentaries, the Leonine, Gelasian, and Gregorian books of Rome. Rather than dispensing with these ancient liturgical masterpieces, the medieval liturgists simply built upon them, adorning the time-honored prayers with fittingly solemn liturgical actions to give them visual expression and adding further texts inspired by the Church's growing theological patrimony, drawn from generation upon generation of saints and scholars.

Strangely enough, the ceremonies of medieval liturgy are among the most underappreciated treasures of our Catholic heritage. While

---

[2] Second Vatican Council, *Sacrosanctum concilium* (December 4, 1963), chap. 1, no. 7, in Austin Flannery, O.P., ed., *Vatican Council II: The Conciliar and Post Conciliar Documents* (Northport, N.Y.: Costello, 1975), 5.

many rightly admire the artistic achievements of the Middle Ages, the great rites of worship for which so many works of medieval art were created have been largely forgotten. In this regard, the famed twentieth-century liturgical scholar Monsignor Michel Andrieu astutely observed, "Many have written, and learnedly, upon the architecture of our cathedrals and our old churches, but rarely has it been asked what took place in the interior of these edifices, and why our ancestors had built at such great expense. [The cathedral] has been considered only a frame of stone, as if, having in itself its reason to be, it was always a simple void." [3]

Far more troubling, however, has been the vilification of medieval liturgy by those intent upon ridding Catholic worship of its medieval inheritance. Building upon the seemingly noble premise of advocating a total return to the pristine liturgical forms of the early Church in the apostolic age, and creating for this purpose a somewhat romanticized and unrealistic picture of what the early liturgy was like, drawn from fragmentary sources, they proceed to condemn the liturgical developments of the Middle Ages and the Baroque era that followed it, criticizing these as a corruption and a distortion of what had come before. They fail to consider what a loss it would be to the Church if all the theological developments and spirituality of the Middle Ages and the Baroque era were similarly cast aside under the pretext of adhering in an exclusive manner to the theology and spirituality of the patristic age. To cite just a few examples, we would lose the brilliant insights of Saint Thomas Aquinas, Saint Bonaventure, and Saint Alphonsus Liguori, as well as the ascetic wisdom of Saint Bernard, Saint Francis of Assisi, Saint Teresa of Avila, and Saint Francis de Sales. Our Holy Father, Pope Benedict XVI, masterfully addressed this issue in his 2000 work *The Spirit of the Liturgy*:

> As I see it, the problem with a large part of modern liturgiology is that it tends to recognize only antiquity as a source, and therefore normative, and to regard everything developed later, in the Middle Ages and through the Council of Trent, as decadent. And so one ends up with dubious reconstructions of the most ancient practice, fluctuating criteria, and never-ending suggestions for reform, which lead ultimately to the disintegration of the liturgy that has evolved in a living way. On the other hand, it is important and necessary to see that we cannot take as our norm the ancient in itself and as such, nor must we automatically write off later developments as alien to the original form of the liturgy. There can be a thoroughly living kind of development in which a seed at the origin ripens and bears fruit. [4]

---

[3] Michel Andrieu, ed., *Les Ordines Romani du haut moyen âge*, vol. 2, SSLED 23 (Louvain, Belgium: "Spicilegium sacrum Lovaniense" Administration, 1948), xii.

[4] Benedict XVI [Joseph Ratzinger], *The Spirit of the Liturgy* (San Francisco: Ignatius Press, 2000), 82.

There is all the more reason to reassess the liturgy of the Middle Ages and the Baroque era in view of the sad fact that much of the misinterpretation of the liturgical renewal of Vatican II has been based on the false assumption that postconciliar worship must be purged of all that is medieval or Baroque if it is to fulfill the intentions of the Council. According to this faulty line of reasoning, a particular liturgical practice or church furnishing of medieval or Baroque origin is considered discredited a priori because it reflects the supposedly exaggerated and unscriptural medieval and Baroque emphases upon transubstantiation, the physical sufferings of Christ in his Passion, the divinity of Christ, the intercessory roles of the Blessed Virgin Mary and the saints, etc. In reality, the liturgical texts of the Middle Ages are permeated with quotations and paraphrases from and allusions to the Old and New Testaments, revealing an amazingly sophisticated familiarity with and understanding of the Scriptures and patristic teachings on the part of the medieval liturgists.

The unfamiliarity of many with medieval liturgical rites has sadly made it possible for blatant falsifications to circulate freely. For example, we hear the practice of kneeling during the liturgy derisively described as a custom borrowed from medieval feudalism, an attribution that seems calculated to evoke the highly negative image of an oppressed serf cowering on his knees before his despotic master. Even a cursory examination of the Scriptures would demonstrate that kneeling, and the most humbling posture of all, prostration, are *biblical* postures of worship, found in the Old and New Testaments alike (for example, 3 Kings 8:54 and Phil 2:10). Kneeling is in fact a sublime act of love and thanksgiving offered to a loving and merciful Creator.

It is the author's belief that the best way with which to refute such inaccurate and condemnatory characterizations of the medieval liturgy is to present the evidence of the ceremonies themselves, their prayers, hymns, and rubrics, cast in the light of the beautiful, deeply spiritual, and profound explanations that medieval liturgical commentators have offered for the words and actions of Catholic worship. We have assembled a wide range of ceremonies, encompassing the seven sacraments, the major feasts of the liturgical year (Christmas, Ash Wednesday, Holy Week, Corpus Christi, etc.), and special liturgical rites (the coronation of a pope, canonizations, the consecration of virgins, funerals, blessings of expectant mothers and their unborn babies, etc.). Rites from countries across western and central Europe have been utilized, including those from Germany, France, England, Italy, Switzerland, Austria, Hungary, Poland, Finland, and Portugal. We have particularly drawn examples from the liturgical texts of late medieval Spain, which until now have received relatively little attention from liturgical scholars. It is also the author's intention to offer in a subsequent book a comparable overview of the great treasures of "Baroque" liturgy, the liturgy as imparted following the Council of Trent (1545–1563) and promulgated over the two centuries that ensued.

During the Middle Ages, many ecclesiastical scholars composed treatises to explain the words and actions of the liturgy. The most notable of these scholars are the Frankish bishop Amalarius of Metz (+c. 850); Lothario of Segni, who became Pope Innocent III (+1216); and William Durandus of Mende (+1296). They offer what are largely "allegorical" or "mystical" interpretations of the sacred rites, interpretations that move beyond literal and "functional" explanations of the ceremonies to set them more deeply and profoundly in the overreaching drama of man's salvation. Seeing each liturgical action of the priest, acting *in persona Christi*, as sacred, these theologians sought to associate every action with a particular mystery of the faith, especially those of the Incarnation, life, Passion, death, and Resurrection of Christ. In doing so, they were expressing the fundamental truth that the entire liturgical life of the Church ultimately flows from the life of Christ, and principally from his salvific sacrifice on the Cross. The medieval liturgical commentators are in effect offering a contemplative approach to the liturgy, providing a meditative schema to fix the mind upon Christ and to fill one's thoughts with Christ as the sacred rites are celebrated. Like the liturgy of the Middle Ages, so too the writings of medieval liturgists have been the subject of much criticism. It is hoped that the synthesis of their insights to be presented in the pages to follow will lead to a renewed appreciation of their contributions to our Catholic heritage.

Although we will be drawing from a wide range of medieval liturgical commentators, it is in fact to William Durandus, the thirteenth-century prelate of the Roman Curia and bishop of Mende, France, that we will most often turn in this work to consider his profound reflections upon the sacred liturgy, encompassed in his encyclopedic liturgical commentary, the *Rationale divinorum officiorum*. Yet Durandus was not only a liturgical commentator; he was the compiler of two liturgical texts that have exercised a far-reaching influence upon the course of the Roman Rite liturgy. Many of the liturgical rites in the pontifical he produced, most notably the ordination and confirmation rites, were later to be incorporated virtually unchanged into the *Pontificale Romanum* of 1595–1596, which became the norm for the entire Roman Rite. The Mass directions provided by him in a book of instructions he composed for his own diocese of Mende, France, at the end of the thirteenth century ultimately shaped the rubrics of the 1570 *Missale Romanum* of Pope Saint Pius V. His postconsecration rubrics reveal that the Real Presence of Christ in the Eucharist was uppermost in his thoughts, likewise inspiring him to compose several devotional prayers to Christ in the Blessed Sacrament for the clergy and the laity.

While there are many features of medieval and Baroque liturgy to command our attention, it is the profound sense of the sacred permeating these rites that so urgently needs to be renewed in our own time. One of the major misinterpretations of the liturgical renewal of the Second Vatican Council has been the idea that Catholic worship somehow needs to be desacralized, secularized, and politicized in order to make it relevant to contemporary society. Hence it will be a major objective of the present work to convince the reader that the sense of the sacred is essential to the liturgy, a dimension inherited from the liturgy of the Old Testament and rooted in the teachings of the Church Fathers.

In the "Liturgical Movement" that preceded the liturgical renewal of the Second Vatican Council, there was a pronounced emphasis upon the rediscovery of the rites of the Church's early centuries. In an analogous manner the current discussion of a "reform of the reform" (i.e., a genuine implementation of the Vatican II and post–Vatican II documents and liturgical books) would benefit from a rediscovery of the rites of the Church's later centuries. Just as a knowledge of the surviving liturgical texts of the early Church is invaluable in revealing to us Catholic worship in the great "age of the martyrs" following the apostolic age, so too would the faithful benefit from a deeper knowledge of the liturgical texts that developed centuries later as the fruit of the Church's deepened understanding and unfolding of the great mysteries of the faith. It is thus hoped that the present work can serve as a source book in discussing the proposed "reform of the reform".

The medieval liturgists, as well as the Baroque era liturgists who followed in their footsteps, possessed an extraordinary gift for vividly and beautifully expressing the mysteries of the faith through the words and actions of the liturgy. Hence, while the Church has seen fit to revise her rites for the present age, our participation in the current rites will certainly be enhanced and deepened through reflection upon the expressive ceremonies of the past. An appropriate presentation of the older texts can serve as a form of "spiritual reading" in preparing ourselves for the sacraments as they are now administered. For just as the life of the Church in our own time is enriched by the writings of the saints and of the Church Fathers and doctors of earlier ages, so too can the Church draw inspiration from a renewed knowledge of the particular rites with which those who have come before us celebrated the sacraments and the liturgical year. It is not enough merely to preserve medieval liturgical manuscripts and early printed missals on the shelves of university libraries—the treasures they contain deserve to be translated and published so that they can inspire future generations of Catholics as they have inspired Catholics in the past.

All of the medieval liturgical texts presented as well as all of the medieval writings quoted (except for those of Saint Thomas Aquinas, Saint Ignatius of Loyola, Blessed Raymond Lull, and the Byzantine writer Nicholas Cabasilas; a ninth-century Gaelic-language treatise on the Mass; and the Middle English *Ancren Riwle*) have been translated by the author from the original Latin or, in a few instances, from a vernacular original. The intent has been to give truly literal translations so as to convey unaltered the meaning of the original texts. For those desiring to consult the original Latin, ample footnotes and bibliographical references are provided. Insofar as the principal edition of the Bible used in medieval liturgy was the Latin Vulgate, originally translated by Saint Jerome but revised by later scholars,[5] the author has utilized for all scriptural citations the principal English translation of the Vulgate, the Douay-Rheims Bible.[6] When in the liturgical texts scriptural verses have been employed unaltered as antiphons or in the texts of prayers, the author has generally chosen to utilize verbatim the Douay-Rheims translations of these verses. When possible, information on the antiquity of the particular prayer texts utilized in a given medieval rite is provided either in the discussion of the rite or in the accompanying footnotes. In citing the medieval liturgical texts known as the Roman *Ordines*, the author has utilized the liturgical scholar Monsignor Michel Andrieu's numbering of the individual texts (which differs almost entirely from Dom Jean Mabillon's older numbering of Roman *Ordines* in volume 78 of the Patrologia Latina series).

In quotations from the medieval liturgical books, the words of all prayer and hymn texts are italicized to distinguish them from the rubrics. In regard to prayer endings, medieval liturgical books usually give only the incipit (i.e., the first few words) of the particular ending to be used (e.g., "*Through Christ our Lord*"). Unfortunately, the incipit is sometimes insufficiently specific to allow a definite identification of which ending is to be utilized, even after considering the indications given by the wording of the prayer (e.g., which Person of the Holy Trinity is addressed). Moreover, insofar as it would be needlessly repetitive to give these standard endings for each and every prayer in the present work, we have provided prayer endings only when it seemed helpful in appreciating the overall content of a particular prayer and when the proper formula could actually be determined.

The work is arranged in three sections, the first of which presents the seven sacraments, beginning with the Mass, the supreme act of Catholic worship; the second section encompasses the major celebrations of the liturgical year; and the third examines a wide range of special liturgical rites. As a preface to all that follows, we shall begin in chapter 1 with an overview of the characteristic features of medieval liturgy.

The funeral rites of Blessed Pope John Paul II and the ensuing election and elevation rites of Pope Benedict XVI in April 2005 brought before the eyes of the whole world a number of centuries-old ceremonies

---

[5] Aryeh Graboïs, "Bible", in Joseph Strayer, ed., *Dictionary of the Middle Ages* (New York: Charles Scribner's Sons, 1982), 2:211.

[6] *The Holy Bible, Translated from the Latin Vulgate* [Douay-Rheims Version] (Baltimore, 1899; repr. Rockford, Ill.: TAN Books, 1971).

and practices of the papal liturgy that have survived at least partially intact amid innumerable liturgical changes following the Second Vatican Council. Among the most enduring images are those of the processional transfer of the body of Pope John Paul II, resting upon a bier borne by eight pallbearers, from the Apostolic Palace to the Basilica of Saint Peter on April 4, to the haunting, chanted accompaniment of the *Miserere* and the Litany of the Saints. Nearly three weeks later, on April 24, millions watched as the newly elected pope Benedict XVI humbly walked in solemn procession through the vast nave of the Basilica of Saint Peter and out into the Square of Saint Peter to begin his installation Mass, with the chanting of the majestic *Exaudi Christe* accompanying his measured steps. The moving public response to these rites serves to demonstrate the enduring value of the stately ceremonial splendor of medieval and Baroque liturgy. It is the author's hope that the present work on the splendors of the medieval liturgy will further contribute to the rediscovery of these liturgical treasures of our faith.

Holiness becometh thy house, O Lord, unto length of days.

Psalm 92:5

I   The Medieval Liturgy: An Overview

> The Church's liturgy may, therefore, be considered as a sacred poem, in the framing of which both heaven and earth have taken part, and by which our humanity, redeemed by the blood of the Lamb without spot, rises on the wings of the Spirit even unto the throne of God Himself.
>
> Blessed Ildefonso Schuster (+1954)[1]

In a famous painting of the Flemish master Rogier van der Weyden (+1464), an altar triptych known as *The Seven Sacraments*, we see the interior of a medieval cathedral permeated with the sacramental life of Catholic worship. In the left panel, depicting the left side of the church's nave, a priest in the foreground baptizes an infant, while further back a bishop confirms a boy and a priest hears confessions. In the right panel, the ordination of a priest, the marriage of a young couple, and the sacramental anointing of a dying man are correspondingly set amid the gothic arches lining the right side of the church. In the middle panel, the artist directs our gaze down the center of the vaulted nave, toward the high altar, where a priest celebrating Mass elevates the Host after the consecration. But in the immediate foreground, Weyden has placed a central scene that visually dominates the entire triptych—we see Christ hanging on a cross that towers nearly to the ceiling, surrounded by the mourning figures of the Blessed Virgin Mary, Saint John, Saint Mary Magdalene, Mary of Cleophas, and Salome. The theological message is clear—the entire sacramental and liturgical life of the Church flows from the sacrifice of Calvary, the sacrifice that is daily re-presented in the Mass. Yet Weyden's masterpiece also expresses visually what the English convert and cardinal Blessed John Henry Newman (+1890) was to say four centuries later regarding Catholic worship:

> I never knew what worship was, an as objective fact, till I entered the Catholic Church, and was partaker in its offices of devotion.... A

[1] Blessed Ildefonso Schuster, *The Sacramentary (Liber sacramentorum): Historical and Liturgical Notes on the Roman Missal* (London: Burns, Oates and Washbourne, 1924–1930), 1:3. Reproduced by permission of Continuum International Publishing Group, London.

Catholic cathedral is a sort of world, every one going about his own business, but that business is a religious one; groups of worshippers, and solitary ones—kneeling, standing—some at shrines, some at altars—hearing Mass and communicating—currents of worshippers intercepting and passing by each other—altar after altar lit up for worship, like stars in the firmament—or the bell giving notice of what is going on in parts you do not see—and all the while the canons in the choir going through matins and lauds, and at the end of it the incense rolling up from the high altar, and all this in one of the most wonderful buildings in the world and every day.[2]

The medieval liturgy fulfilled in a quite literal way the counsel of Psalm 112 (verse 3), "From the rising of the sun unto the going down of the same, the name of the Lord is worthy of praise." In cathedrals and monastic churches across medieval Europe, the day was punctuated from beginning to end by the regular rhythm of the seven "hours" (scheduled portions) of the Divine Office, with the morning climaxing in the celebration of Mass. While the exact times of these services varied from place to place, the following schedule based upon Benedictine customs[3] is fairly representative:

Matins: 2:00–2:30 A.M.

Lauds: 4:30–5:00 A.M.

Prime: 6:00 A.M.

Terce: 9:00 A.M.

Mass: always in the morning[4] (often celebrated more than once)

Sext: 12:00 noon

None: 4:00 P.M.

Vespers: 4:30 P.M.

Compline: 6:00 P.M.

---

[2] Blessed John Henry Newman to Henry Wilberforce, September 24–26, 1846, in C. S. Dessain, ed., *The Letters and Diaries of John Henry Newman*, vol. 11, *Littlemore to Rome, October 1845 to December 1846* (London: Thomas Nelson and Sons, 1961), 253 (quoted by permission of Oxford University Press—© Oxford University Press).

[3] We follow here the summary of the daily offices given in Karl Young, *The Drama of the Medieval Church* (Oxford: Clarendon, 1933), 1:74.

[4] The two exceptions to this norm were Christmas Day, when the first Mass of this solemnity took place in the night, at or after midnight, and Holy Saturday, when the Mass of the Easter Vigil began in the afternoon or the early evening, although this latter exception virtually disappeared toward the end of the Middle Ages as the Easter Vigil was shifted into the morning hours of Holy Saturday.

The voluminous corpus of texts that filled the seven "hours" of the Divine Office each day serves to demonstrate how very deeply the medieval Church immersed herself in the Scriptures, for the greater part of the Divine Office was taken from the Psalms and other biblical texts; even the antiphons and responsories were more often than not simply direct quotations or paraphrases of Scripture verses. The intent of offering to God a continual sacrifice of praise from dawn to dusk and through the night is reflected in the explanation given by the Church doctor Saint Peter Damian (+1072) regarding the Church's daily recitation of the *Magnificat* (Lk 1:46–55) during the office of Vespers:

> Not unfittingly is the canticle of the Blessed Mother of God also joined to the evening office. For with the day of the former age, as it were, already long spent, namely at the approach of that evening twilight of the world, now that she [had] conceived in the blossom of her fruitful womb the light of the eternal Word, she spontaneously broke into an utterance of divine praise, saying, "*My soul doth magnify the Lord*" (Lk 1:46). Therefore, in likeness to her who is the Mother of Christ, the whole universal Church also, who is certainly the mother of Christians, and who carries in her soul that very light, the gift that [Mary] carried in her womb, now at the waning of day, magnifies God with worthy praise; and her joyful spirit, giving thanks for benefits conferred, exults in her saving God.[5]

The Divine Office progressively developed from the days of the early Church through the Middle Ages. By the end of the tenth century (or perhaps as early as the ninth century), and particularly from the twelfth century onward, the various books used to recite the requisite Psalms and other scriptural texts of the daily office, as well as the accompanying antiphons, responsories, hymns, and homiletic and hagiographic readings, were being merged into a single volume, the breviary, a unification of monastic origin.[6] The thirteenth-century *Breviary according to the Use of the Roman Curia*, embodying the office practices of the Roman liturgy,[7] became a model for the Divine Office elsewhere after it was adopted for use by the newly founded Franciscan Order.[8] The modest modifications made to the curial text by the Franciscans were in turn embraced by the Holy See; this revised breviary subsequently shaped the Divine Office throughout western Christendom.[9] We have not in the present volume devoted a separate chapter

---

[5] Saint Peter Damian, *Opuscula* 10, chap. 4, PL 145, col. 226.

[6] Stephen J. P. Van Dijk, O.F.M., and Joan Hazelden Walker, *The Origins of the Modern Roman Liturgy: The Liturgy of the Papal Court and the Franciscan Order in the Thirteenth Century* (Westminster, Md.: Newman; London: Darton, Longman and Todd, 1960), 32–35.

[7] Ibid., 91–176.

[8] Ibid., 179–237.

[9] Fernand Cabrol, "Breviary", in *The Catholic Encyclopedia* (New York: Appleton, 1907–1912), 2:774.

to the Divine Office in the Middle Ages, but several distinctive ceremonies utilized in the celebration of the office on certain feasts will be presented; moreover, it is the author's intent in his planned future work on the Baroque era liturgy to examine the definitive codification of the Divine Office achieved in the 1568 *Breviarium Romanum* and the solemn rite for the public recitation of the office given in the 1600 *Caeremoniale episcoporum*.

The Holy Eucharist in Medieval Christendom

Through the ages, the Church has not changed her teachings, but she has developed increasingly clear and comprehensive ways of expressing and explaining the doctrines of the faith, inspired by an ever deepening and broadening understanding of the full ramifications of mankind's redemption. It is only natural that such "development of doctrine" should be mirrored in the Church's liturgy. Thus, if as the Middle Ages progressed the Church celebrated the Eucharist with increasing solemnity and ceremony, and found further ways of drawing spiritual nourishment from the Sacrament through a burgeoning worship of the Eucharist outside the immediate context of Mass, it simply reflected her heightened comprehension of the inestimable gift she had received at the Last Supper, Christ's gift of his very self. Moreover, contrary to the often-repeated accusation that medieval Catholic devotion to the Blessed Virgin Mary and the saints eclipsed the worship of Christ, the profound sense of the sacred with which the medieval Church enveloped the Mass and the reserved Eucharist demonstrates a truly Christocentric faith.

Over the course of the Middle Ages, the liturgical rites of the Mass underwent significant developments. In the following chapter, we will be examining in great detail the medieval celebration of Mass. Hence we offer here only some preliminary observations. The single most important text of the Roman Rite Mass at the threshold of the Middle Ages was the seventh- to eighth-century Gregorian Sacramentary. In the ninth century, a redaction of this Roman text was prepared for use throughout the Frankish empire by the abbot Saint Benedict of Aniane (+821), who supplemented the original with an appendix containing additions for the use of churches in medieval Gaul (France and Germany). This "Aniane" adaptation of the Gregorian Sacramentary ultimately became the prototype for Mass texts throughout medieval Europe.[10] Succeeding centuries brought further significant additions to the prayers and rubrics of the Mass, many of which had arisen and had entered the Roman Court's Ordinary of the Mass (the unchanging portion of the Mass, excluding whatever changes according to the particular feast day) by the first quarter of the thirteenth century,[11]

---

[10] Cyrille Vogel, *Medieval Liturgy: An Introduction to the Sources*, rev. William Storey and Niels Krogh Rasmussen, O.P. (Washington, D.C.: Pastoral Press, 1986), 85–89, 104–105.

[11] See Father Stephen Van Dijk's reconstruction of what he entitles the "Order of the Mass according to the Use of the Roman Church (Court)", dated before 1227 and drawn from various sources, in Stephen J. P. Van Dijk, O.F.M., and Joan Hazelden Walker, eds.,

with other notable additions entering the Roman liturgical books in the late fifteenth century. The sheer breadth of the medieval Church's contributions to the Eucharistic liturgy can be readily grasped from the following table comparing the prayer texts of the eighth-century Roman Rite Ordinary with the prayer texts and major post-eighth-century additions to the rubrics found in the 1502 Roman Rite Mass *Ordo* of the papal master of ceremonies John Burckard (supplemented by information from the earliest printed missal of Rome, the 1474 *Missale Romanum*):

Eighth-century Roman Rite[12]	1502 *Ordo missae*/1474 *Missale Romanum*[13]
Entrance Rite:	Entrance Rite:
	Judica me
	Confiteor
Kyrie	*Kyrie*
Gloria	*Gloria*
Gospel:	Gospel:
Alleluia	*Alleluia*
	Nicene Creed
Offertory:	Offertory:
(no specified prayer texts)	*Suscipe, sancte Pater*
	Deus, qui humanae
	Offerimus tibi Domine
	In spiritu humilitatis
	Veni Sanctificator
	Per intercessionem . . . Michaelis
	Incensum istud a te benedictum
	Dirigatur Domine oratio mea
	Accendat in nobis Dominus ignem
	Lavabo inter innocentes manus
	Suscipe, sancte Trinitas
	Orate fratres
	Suscipiat Dominus sacrificium

The Ordinal of the Papal Court from Innocent III to Boniface VIII and Related Documents, SF 22 (Fribourg, Switzerland: The University Press, 1975), 495–526.

[12] Mass *Ordo* from the eighth-century *Hadrianum* redaction of the Gregorian Sacramentary, in Jean Deshusses, ed., *Le sacramentaire grégorien: Ses principales formes d'après les plus anciens manuscrits*, vol. 1, 2nd ed., SF 16 (Fribourg, Switzerland: Editions Universitaires Fribourg, 1979), nos. 2–20, pp. 85–92, supplemented by additions from Roman *Ordo* 1 (c. 700–750) and Roman *Ordo* 4 (*Ordo* of Saint Amand, c. 760–770), in Michel Andrieu, ed., *Les Ordines Romani du haut moyen âge*, vol. 2, SSLED 23 (Louvain, Belgium: "Spicilegium sacrum Lovaniense" Administration, 1948), 80–108, 157–170.

[13] *Ordo missae* of John Burckard, 1502 edition, in John Wickham Legg, ed., *Tracts on the Mass*, HBS 27 (London: Henry Bradshaw Society, 1904), 135–170, supplemented by additions from the 1474 *Missale Romanum*, in Robert Lippe, ed., *Missale Romanum: Mediolani, 1474*; vol. 1, *Text*, HBS 17 (London: Henry Bradshaw Society, 1899), 200–201.

Preface:	Preface:
Sursum corda	*Sursum corda*
Sanctus	*Sanctus*
Canon:	Canon:
Te igitur (with repeated crosses)	*Te igitur* (with repeated crosses)
	Elevation after consecration
	Genuflection of celebrant,
	kneeling of others
Per ipsum with elevation	*Per ipsum* with elevation,
	genuflection
Communion Rite:	Communion Rite:
Pater noster	*Pater noster*
Libera nos	*Libera nos* with genuflection
Pax Domini	*Pax Domini*
Fiat commixtio et consecratio	*Fiat commixtio et consecratio*
	Genuflection
Agnus Dei (twice)	*Agnus Dei* (thrice)
	Dominus Jesu Christe, qui dixisti
Pax tecum	*Pax tecum*
	Domine Jesu Christe, Fili Dei vivi
	Perceptio corporis et sanguinis
	Genuflection
	Panem celestem accipiam
	Domine non sum dignus
Corpus Domini nostri Jesu	*Corpus Domini nostri Jesu Christi*
Christi prosit tibi[14]	*custodiat*
	Quid retribuam Domino with
	genuflection
	Sanguis Domini nostri Jesu Christi
	custodiat
Quod ore sumpsimus, Domine[15]	*Quod ore sumpsimus, Domine*
	Corpus tuum, Domine, quod sumpsi

---

[14] The eighth-century liturgical books provide no formula for the moment of Holy Communion, but a late eighth-century biography of Pope Saint Gregory the Great (+604) tells of the pontiff administering Holy Communion at Mass with the words "*May the Body of our Lord Jesus Christ avail you unto the remission of all your sins, and eternal life*" (Paul the Deacon, *Sancti Gregorii magni vita*, chap. 25, PL 75, col. 52). This formula can validly be seen as an antecedent to the later formula, "*Corpus Domini nostri Jesu Christi custodiat . . .*" ("*May the Body of our Lord Jesus Christ preserve your soul unto eternal life. Amen.*").

[15] This oration, although not mentioned in the Ordinary of the Gregorian Sacramentary, is included among ten orations entitled "Prayers after Communion" added in the seventh or eighth century to a Milan, Italy, manuscript of the sixth-century Leonine Sacramentary of Rome; text in Leo Cunibert Mohlberg, O.S.B.; Leo Eizenhöfer, O.S.B.; and Petrus Siffrin, O.S.B., eds., *Sacramentarium Veronense*, REDSMF 1 (Rome: Herder, 1956), no. 1378, p. 179.

Concluding Rites:	Concluding Rites:
Ite missa est	*Ite missa est*
	Placeat tibi sancta Trinitas
	Benedicat vos . . . Pa + ter . . .
	(final blessing)
	Last Gospel: John 1:1–14
	Trium puerorum
	Benedicite (Dan 3:52–88, 56)

Modifications of the liturgy in the Middle Ages always took place in tandem with a scrupulous preservation of the inherited features and texts of the ancient liturgical books. This "continuity of the ages" is well represented not only in the unchanging elements of the Ordinary of the Mass shown in the above comparison between the eighth-century liturgy and the sixteenth-century liturgy, but also in the texts proper to particular days of the liturgical calendar. By the ninth century, the Mass antiphonary of the Roman Rite, that is, the collection of Mass antiphons, versicles, and other chants assigned to specific days of the liturgical year (the Introit, the Gradual, the Lenten Tract, the *Alleluia* verse, the Offertory, and the Communion), had taken on a fixed and stable content that passed with minimal changes into the universally promulgated *Missale Romanum* of 1570.[16] Likewise, the prayers proper to the Masses of particular liturgical days (the Collect, the Secret, and the Postcommunion) in the 1570 *Missale Romanum* are virtually the same as those given seven centuries earlier for the same liturgical days in the ninth-century Aniane adaptation of the Gregorian Sacramentary.[17] As for the Scripture readings of the Roman Rite Mass, there appeared in the late eighth century the *Comes* of Murbach, a lectionary of the French-Alsatian abbey of Murbach, which, as a Frankish adaptation of earlier Roman lectionaries, established the temporal cycle of readings (the readings for the liturgical seasons and feast days from Advent and Christmas to Pentecost and the weeks thereafter, excluding saints' days) that was to pass essentially unchanged into the 1570 *Missale Romanum*.[18]

Just as Saint Benedict of Aniane had incorporated distinctively Frankish liturgical practices into his edition of the Gregorian Sacramentary, so too dioceses across medieval Europe added to the basic template of

---

[16] Vogel, *Medieval Liturgy*, 358–360. Vogel lists six early redactions of the Roman Mass antiphonary, beginning with the *Cantatorium* of Monza, Italy (eighth century). For the text of the latter, see René-Jean Hésbert, ed., *Antiphonale missarum sextuplex* (Brussels, 1935; repr., Rome: Herder, 1967), 1–196.

[17] Vogel, *Medieval Liturgy*, 104–105.

[18] Ibid., 347, 354–355. For the text of the *Comes* of Murbach, see D. A. Wilmart, "Le *Comes* de Murbach", *Revue Bénédictine* 30 (1913): 35–54. For the readings of the temporal cycle in the 1570 *Missale romanum*, see Manlio Sodi and Achille Maria Triacca, eds., *Missale Romanum: Editio princeps (1570)*, facsimile ed., MLCT 2 (Vatican City: Libreria Editrice Vaticana, © 1998), 58–291, 353–444 (new pagination).

the Gregorian text local adaptations. Thus in England the Sarum (i.e., Salisbury) and York rites arose as variants of the Roman Rite, bearing the names of the dioceses where they originated. The author has found in examining the texts of many medieval diocesan rites that they exhibit a remarkable fidelity to the texts of Rome while interweaving fitting local liturgical practices. In Spain, the ancient local usage known as the Mozarabic Rite gradually gave way to the Roman Rite as imported from France, with the changeover beginning in the northeastern region of Catalonia in the ninth century[19] and arriving in the north central kingdom of Castile during the eleventh century.[20] But as the Middle Ages progressed, the Roman Rite in Spain acquired local character- istics and customs, including some retentions of Mozarabic texts or practices, as well as newer additions of a distinctly Spanish nature. Customs often differed from one Spanish diocese to another, or from region to region (such as from Catalonia to Castile). As was the case elsewhere, the late medieval missals of Spain were given titles reflect- ing their local content; for example, a 1534 missal for the Spanish archdiocese of Seville bears the title *Missal of Divine Things according to the Custom of our Church of Seville.*[21] As we have already stated in the introduction, many examples in the chapters to follow will be drawn from the late medieval liturgical texts of Spain, including the partic- ularly beautiful Spanish ceremonies of Holy Week. Religious orders also developed their own distinctive liturgical practices, as we shall see from numerous examples to be presented in the following pages.

At the outset of the medieval era, the priest celebrating Mass was regularly assisted at the altar by a deacon and a subdeacon. But by the ninth century, a simpler manner of celebrating Mass (traceable to the sixth century) had become fairly commonplace, known as Low Mass (or private Mass), in which the priest would celebrate without the assistance of a deacon and subdeacon.[22] The original, more elaborate, form of celebration came to be reserved for more solemn occasions and acquired the appellation High Mass (or solemn Mass). It is to the rubrics for High Mass that we will turn in the next chapter, for they exemplify the ritual splendor with which the medieval Church offered adoration to God.

The custom of having the priest always recite *every* word of the Mass from beginning to end not only at Low Mass but also at High Mass, requiring him to repeat to himself even the words assigned to

---

[19] Richard Donovan, C.S.B., *The Liturgical Drama in Medieval Spain* (Toronto: Pontifical Institute of Medieval Studies, 1958), 26–27.

[20] Ibid., 21–25.

[21] *Missale divinorum secundum consuetudinem alme ecclesie Hispalensis* (Seville: Joannes Varela, 1534); Latin text provided to the author of the present work by the Biblioteca Apostolica Vaticana, Vatican City (shelf mark Stamp. Barb. B. X. 4).

[22] Josef Jungmann, S.J., *The Mass of the Roman Rite: Its Origins and Development* (New York: Benziger Bros., 1951–1955), 1:212–233; Vogel, *Medieval Liturgy,* 156–158; Adrian Fortescue, "Mass, Liturgy of the", in *Catholic Encyclopedia* (1907–1912), 9:797.

others, such as the Introit sung by the choir and the Gospel chanted by the deacon, had begun to develop by the twelfth century.[23] This practice can be understood as manifesting that the Mass *in its entirety* is celebrated and offered to God the Father by Christ himself through the priest acting *in persona Christi*. As for the often-repeated criticism that the medieval Church placed too exclusive an emphasis upon the unique role of the priest in the celebration of the sacred liturgy, it should be noted that this emphasis stems from the very nature of our redemption. For the priest at the altar, through whom Christ re-presents his perfect sacrifice of Calvary, images our Savior as the "*one* mediator of God and men" (1 Tim 2:5; emphasis added), who *alone* "entered once into the holies" (Heb 9:12) to offer his own precious blood for our salvation, just as in the Old Testament Moses ascended Mount Sinai *alone* to converse with God on behalf of the Israelites (Ex 34:1–32), and the high priest entered the Holy of Holies *alone* to pray and offer sacrifices for the people of Israel (Lev 16:1–17).

Developments in the celebration of the Mass were paralleled by a deepening comprehension of the full implications of the Eucharist. In a medieval biography of the Italian-born abbot Saint Victorian (+558) written probably in the eighth century, we find what constitutes the earliest extant, *explicit* account of prayer before the reserved Eucharist outside of Mass. After describing Victorian's devotion in celebrating Mass as a hermit-priest living in northeast Spain (prior to his becoming an abbot sometime between 522 and 531), the biographer tells of a chapel Victorian built adjoining his hermitage, "far off from every loud noise of the world", and how he spent his time there: "In this [chapel], more frequently and fervently, he poured forth his prayers before that indescribable Sacrament of divine goodness and commended to God the health of the whole Church; and in this holy exercise he consumed almost the entire day."[24] This account lends credence to the extraordinary claim of the Spanish city of Lugo that perpetual adoration of the Eucharist has existed in the city since the late sixth century.[25] While the subject of *personal* prayer before the

---

[23] An early form of this practice appears about 1140 in the *Ordo officiorum* of Rome's cathedral church of Saint John Lateran, a liturgical book compiled by Bernardo Cardinal di Porto (+1176); text in Ludwig Fischer, ed., *Bernhardi cardinalis et Lateranensis ecclesiae prioris Ordo officiorum ecclesiae Lateranensis*, Historische Forschungen und Quellen 2–3 (Munich: Dr. F. P. Datterer, 1916), 80–81.

[24] *Vita sancti Victoriani abbatis*, chap. 2, in John van Bolland et al., eds., *Acta sanctorum* (Antwerp, Belgium, 1643–; repr., Paris: Victor Palmé, 1863–1940), January, 2:22: "In hoc quo magis erat ab omni mundi strepitu remotum, hoc frequentius ac ferventius coram inenarrabili illo divinae pietatis Sacramento vota fundabat, totiusque salutem Ecclesiae Deo commendabat; atque in hac sancta exercitatione totum pene diem insumebat."

[25] See the examination of the evidence regarding Lugo in my work coauthored with Father Benedict J. Groeschel, C.F.R., *In the Presence of Our Lord: The History, Theology and Psychology of Eucharistic Devotion* (Huntington, Ind.: Our Sunday Visitor, 1997), 193–198. See also Amador López Valcárcel, "Lucus Augusti, locus sacramenti: El culto eucaristico en Lugo; Notas para su historia", *El Progreso*, June 8, 1969, repr. in Excma. Diputación Provincial

reserved Eucharist[26] does not fall within the province of our present subject matter—the public liturgical rites of the Middle Ages—public, communal forms of adoration of the reserved Eucharist do appear repeatedly in the medieval liturgy, as we shall later see in numerous examples to be presented from the ceremonies of Holy Week, Corpus Christi, and the bringing of Viaticum to the ill.

The medieval liturgy has often been criticized on the basis of a supposed lack of active lay participation in the sacred rites, most notably the infrequency of lay reception of Holy Communion. While we do not deny that this infrequency of Communion was in and of itself unfortunate, it needs to be understood in the context within which it arose. Such reticence was inspired not by lay ambivalence toward the liturgy but rather by a profound sense of the greatness of the Sacrament. The faithful who received Holy Communion only once a year, en masse at Easter,[27] would have brought with them to the altar a heightened appreciation of the magnitude of what they were about to do—an appreciation heightened by the sheer infrequency with which they partook of this privilege. Their awe for the Sacrament stemmed in large part from Saint Paul's admonition regarding Holy Communion, "For he that eateth and drinketh unworthily, eateth and drinketh judgment to himself, not discerning the body of the Lord" (1 Cor 11:29). In a 1995 essay, the scholar Charles Caspers argued quite convincingly that late medieval lay spirituality was in fact deeply Eucharistic, perceiving the Eucharist as "the most important sacrament" that nourished the Christian soul and deepened its union with Christ so as to bring it safely to eternal salvation.[28] Hence, understanding that Holy Communion constituted an intimate encounter with the living God, the medieval laity approached it with circumspection and prepared for its reception with great care. Caspers concludes, "We now understand why the men and women of faith availed themselves of sacramental Communion so rarely in that era. They did this out of caution, not out of indifference. Spiritual union with Christ by means of Communion was counted as the highest goal after which people could strive in earthly life."[29]

---

de Lugo, ed., *Historias luguesas* (Lugo, Spain: Imp. de la Excma. Diputación Provincial de Lugo, 1975), 40–45.

[26] The history of Eucharistic adoration is presented in my above-cited work coauthored with Father Groeschel, *In the Presence of Our Lord*, 178–285.

[27] The Fourth Lateran Council of 1215 decreed that all of the faithful had to receive Holy Communion at least once a year, at Easter; see Fourth Lateran Council, chap. 21, in J. D. Mansi, ed., *Sacrorum conciliorum nova et amplissima collectio*, vol. 22 (Florence and Venice, 1778; repr. Paris: Hubert Welter, 1903), cols. 1007, 1010 (Latin text), 1008–1009 (Greek text).

[28] Charles Caspers, "The Western Church during the Late Middle Ages: *Augenkommunion* or Popular Mysticism?", in Charles Caspers, Gerard Lukken, and Gerard Rouwhorst, eds., *Bread of Heaven: Customs and Practices Surrounding Holy Communion: Essays in the History of Liturgy and Culture*, Liturgia condenda 3 (Kampen, Netherlands: Kok Pharos, 1995), 88.

[29] Ibid., 94.

In regard to the wider issue of lay participation in the medieval liturgy, we would offer here one modest observation. It is a mistake to define active participation purely in terms of external actions when the matter under consideration is by its nature inherently spiritual, embodying invisible realities. One leading scholar of the Byzantine liturgy has made this same point, observing that "active participation" in the liturgy should be defined on a deeper level as the spiritual ascent of the mind to heavenly mysteries, by which "the contemplation of liturgical rites leads the soul to the spiritual, mystical realities of the invisible world."[30] We see this in the great events of redemption. In his Gospel account of the crucifixion, Saint John, when speaking of the Blessed Virgin Mary, tells us not that she spoke or "did" anything on Golgotha but simply that she "stood by the cross of Jesus" (Jn 19:25). Yet can anyone doubt the depth of her interior participation in the sacrifice of Calvary, as she pondered within her heart this mystery that pierced her soul with a sword? Hence, is it not unjust to characterize a medieval layman's devout and attentive presence at a liturgical rite as anything other than a genuine form of "active participation"? The famous maxim of the English poet John Milton seems applicable here: "They also serve who only stand and wait."[31]

The Beauty of Structured Worship

It is the universal experience of mankind that order imparts beauty to the works of creation, giving them recognizable forms, symmetry, and identifiable characteristics. Even the public ceremonies of secular governments, such as state funerals, draw their power to stir those present from the measured, solemn, and uniform actions of the participants. In an analogous manner, the medieval Church beautified the liturgy through the gradual codification of rites, an ordering of prayers and rubrics that engendered solemnity and profoundly deepened the sense of the sacred that befits acts of divine worship. The English martyr Saint Thomas More (+1535) testifies to the value of beautiful and well-ordered liturgical rites in his monumental apologetic work, *The Confutation of Tyndale's Answer*: "Good folk find this indeed, that when they be at the divine service in the church, the more devoutly that they see such godly ceremonies observed, and the more solemnity that they see therein, the more devotion feel they themselves therewith in their own souls."[32]

The medieval Church imparted order to the liturgy through the compilation of increasingly comprehensive and well-arranged liturgical

---

[30] Robert F. Taft, S.J., *The Precommunion Rites*, vol. 5 of *A History of the Liturgy of St. John Chrysostom*, Orientalia Christiana analecta 261 (Rome: Pontificio Istituto Orientale, 2000), 492.

[31] John Milton, "On His Blindness", verse 14.

[32] Saint Thomas More, *The Confutation of Tyndale's Answer*, ed. Louis Schuster et al., vol. 8 of the *The Complete Works of St. Thomas More* (New Haven: Yale University Press, 1973), bk. 2, p. 161.

books. This period saw from the ninth century onward the emergence of the *missalis plenarius*, later known simply as the missal, a liturgical book that ultimately brought together all the prayers, Scripture readings, and essential rubrics for the daily celebration of Mass.[33] In the ninth and tenth centuries, the volumes known as pontificals arose to provide bishops with all the special rites proper to their office.[34] By the twelfth century, parish priests were being given a single-volume manual for fulfilling their liturgical duties apart from Mass and the Divine Office, a volume known as a ritual, comprising the prayers and rubrics for the priestly celebration of the sacraments, processions, and blessing rites.[35] The preparation of all these volumes was itself considered a holy endeavor, as evinced by the opening words of many such books, including the following preamble to the 1499 missal of Jaén, Spain: "In the name of the indivisible Trinity, the Father, the Son, and the Holy Spirit, and of the spotless Blessed Virgin Mary, and of all the hierarchy, [here] begins the missal according to the manner and custom of the holy Church of Jaén." [36]

The amplification of the sense of the sacred in Catholic worship through the development of richly imaged and solemnly ordered liturgical ceremonies, replete with expressive and poetic prayer texts, grew in earnest from the tenth century onward, heralded by the compilation of the liturgical book known as the Romano-Germanic Pontifical. Believed to have been composed in Mainz, Germany, at the Benedictine monastery of Saint Alban sometime around 950–962,[37] the Romano-Germanic Pontifical stands as one of the most important milestones in the history of medieval liturgy. This book, embodying a wide range of liturgical ceremonies, very soon arrived in Rome during the reign of the German emperor Otto I (936–973) and became the norm for the Roman liturgy until it was superseded by later pontificals, which nonetheless retained much of what it contained. The Romano-Germanic Pontifical was likewise disseminated across medieval Europe.[38] In the pages to follow, we will be presenting several rites from this masterpiece of the medieval liturgy.

The enhancement of the liturgy through the implementation of well-composed rubrics can be seen by way of example in the directions for the bishop's blessing of the people that William Durandus (+1296) provided in the pontifical that he compiled as bishop for his own diocese of Mende, France, around 1294. These rubrics ably give outward

---

[33] Vogel, *Medieval Liturgy*, 105–106.

[34] Ibid., 225–230.

[35] Ibid., 262.

[36] *Missale Giennense / Manuale continens ordinem ad celebrandum ecclesiastica sacramenta* [*Missale secundum movem et consuetudinem sancte ecclesie Gienensis*] (Seville: Meinhardus Ungut and Stanislaus Polonus, 1499), fol. 1r.

[37] Vogel, *Medieval Liturgy*, 232–233.

[38] Ibid., 238–239.

expression to the invisible bestowal of grace with actions incorporating the ancient symbolism of the four ends of the earth to manifest the solicitude of God in extending his blessing to each and every one of the faithful present:

> But when they shall have come to that place, *And may the blessing of* [*almighty*] *God*, etc., then the subdeacon kneels, lest he should impede the view of the people; and the bishop, in saying, *And may the blessing of almighty God, the Father*, makes the sign of the cross over the people waiting on the south side of the church. But in saying, *and the Son*, he makes it before himself over the people situated on the western side. And in saying, *and the Holy Spirit*, he makes it on the northern side. Which having been done and said, he brings back his hands and forearms as before. But having said those words, *descend upon you and remain always* [*with you*], he now joins his hands before his face, and thus with hands joined, he turns back by the right side toward the altar.[39]

The medieval codification of liturgical rites also served to guarantee the validity and authenticity of the sacramental celebrations. The concern for validity was not invented by scholastic theologians; we find it expressed far earlier in a ninth-century Gaelic-language treatise on the Mass accompanying the text of Ireland's Stowe Missal, which refers to the words of consecration in the middle of the Roman Canon as the "perilous prayer", implying thereby that these words were crucial to the Eucharistic sacrifice.[40] Even earlier, the sixth-century *Preface of Gildas on Penance*, a penitential document of Wales, mandates a penance of three days or three fasts for any priest who "erring has changed anything of the words where 'danger' is written";[41] the seventh-century Irish *Penitential of Cummean* repeats this injunction almost verbatim but is more explicit, identifying the words in question as the "words of the sacred things", that is, the words of consecration.[42] In the twelfth century, Lothario of Segni, who became Pope Innocent III in 1198, discusses the liturgical requirements for valid consecration of the Eucharist in his treatise *De sacro altaris mysterio*.[43] By the late fifteenth and early sixteenth centuries, detailed instructions regarding the various possible "defects" in the celebration of Mass were being

---

[39] Text in Michel Andrieu, ed., *Le pontifical romain au moyen-âge*, vol. 3, *Le pontifical de Guillaume Durand*, ST 88 (Vatican City: Biblioteca Apostolica Vaticana, 1940), 655.

[40] Text as translated by George Warner, in George Warner, ed., *The Stowe Missal*, vol. 2, *Printed Text*, HBS 32 (London: Henry Bradshaw Society, 1915), 37 (Gaelic text), 40 (English translation).

[41] *Preface of Gildas on Penance*, no. 20; Latin text in Ludwig Bieler, ed. and trans., *The Irish Penitentials*, Scriptores Latini Hiberniae 5 (Dublin: Dublin Institute for Advanced Studies, 1963), 62. Latin texts in Bieler quoted and translated by permission of the Governing Board of the School of Celtic Studies of the Dublin Institute for Advanced Studies.

[42] *Penitential of Cummean*, chap. 9, no. 9; Latin text in Bieler, *Irish Penitentials*, 126.

[43] Innocent III, *De sacro altaris mysterio*, bk. 2, chap. 4, PL 217, cols. 851–884.

placed in missals, including the 1474 Franciscan *Missal according to the Custom of the Roman Curia*; the 1493 *Missale Romanum*; the Spanish missals of Valencia (1492), Vich (1496), and Palma de Majorca (1506); and virtually every edition of the Sarum Missal of Salisbury, England, from 1487 to 1557.[44] These directives served to apply in a practical manner what the Church taught about the Eucharist. In 1439 the Council of Florence defined the "form" of the Eucharist as "the words of the Savior, with which he confected this Sacrament", by which words the priest, uttering them *in persona Christi*, confects the Sacrament; the council defined the "matter" of the Sacrament as wheaten bread and "wine from the vine, to which before the consecration very little water ought to be added".[45] The importance of theological and liturgical clarity regarding the words of consecration is highlighted in the declaration of the French theologian William of Auxerre (+1231) that the transubstantiation of the Host is accomplished at the very moment when the priest completes the pronouncement of the words *"Hoc est enim Corpus meum"* (*"For this is my Body"*).[46]

The medieval Church rendered the sacrament of penance more accessible for regular penitents (i.e., those not guilty of grave crimes) by uniting into a single rite the confession of sins and the priestly absolution of one's sins. Instead of withholding absolution until after the penitent had completed the penance assigned for his sins, as had previously been the case, absolution was now granted immediately after the penitent's confession, albeit with the requirement that the penitent had to complete the assigned penance afterward. In addition, the medieval Church bore a heightened witness to the mercy of God by dispelling the notion formerly circulated among early Christians that those who after baptism had committed very grave sins should be given no more than one opportunity to return (by public penance) to communion with the Church (in other words, those who fell a second

---

[44] See Gabriel Seguí i Trobat, ed., *El missal mallorquí de 1506: Estudi i edició segons l'exemplar de la Biblioteca Bartomeu March,* Col·lectània Sant Pacià 79 (Barcelona: Centre d'Estudis Teològics de Mallorca, 2003), 219–232, plus footnote on 219 regarding the 1474 Franciscan missal; for the 1493 *Missale Romanum,* see the *Preparatio sacerdotis* included in several late medieval editions of the *Missale Romanum,* beginning with the 1493 edition, printed in Legg, *Tracts on the Mass,* xxiv–xxv, 114–117; for the Valencia missal, see Blessed Juan Bautista Ferreres Boluda, S.J., *Historia del misal romano* (Barcelona: Eugenio Subirana, 1929), xci; for the Vich missal, see Francesc Xavier Altés i Aguiló, ed., *Missale Vicense, 1496,* facsimile ed., Biblioteca litúrgica catalana 3 (Barcelona: Institut d'Estudis Catalans, 2001), temporal, fols. 191v–192v; and for the Sarum Missal, see Francis H. Dickinson, ed., *Missale ad usum insignis et praeclarae ecclesiae Sarum* (Burntisland, Scotland: E. Prelo de Pitsligo, 1861–1883), cols. 647–656.

[45] *Decree for the Armenians* (November 22, 1439), in J.D. Mansi, ed., *Sacrorum conciliorum nova et amplissima collectio,* vol. 31 (Florence and Venice, 1798; repr., Paris: Hubert Welter, 1906), cols. 1056–1057.

[46] William of Auxerre, *Summa aurea,* bk. 4, tract 7, chap. 2, in Jean Ribaillier, ed., *Magistri Guillelmi Altissiodorensis: Summa aurea; Liber quartus,* Spicilegium Bonaventurianum 19 (Paris: Editions du Centre National de la Recherche Scientifique; Rome: Editiones Collegii S. Bonaventurae ad Claras Aquas, 1985), 148.

time were to be denied reconciliation with the Church even if they repented).[47] Thus the medieval Church made the sacrament of penance readily repeatable in keeping with Christ's teaching that forgiveness should be granted "seventy times seven times" (Mt 18:22).

The medieval Church sought to sanctify and sacralize the formerly pagan world that had now become Christian Europe through liturgical rites that entrusted and consecrated to God every dimension of human existence. In essence, the Church endeavored to permeate the outside world of her sons and daughters with the fragrance of the sacred that filled her sanctuaries. As the Middle Ages progressed, rites for the blessing of objects used in ordinary life, from plant seeds and household wine to farm fields and ships, multiplied and grew more elaborate. Special blessings were provided for those of the laity with particular duties, or in special need, such as expectant mothers and their unborn babies, and knights in the service of the Church or state. Rites of extraordinary solemnity and majesty were formulated for the coronation and enthronement of the kings and queens of a Christianized Europe. Although considerations of space in selecting which rites to present in the present work have precluded us from including any examples of medieval monarchial coronations,[48] we shall examine at length the most important coronation rite of all, that of the successors of Saint Peter, the papal elevation rite, along with the antecedent ceremonies for the election of a new pontiff.

The magnificent gothic cathedrals and churches built for the liturgical rites of medieval Europe were themselves the subject of what became by far the longest and most complex of the Church's ceremonies—the rite of consecrating a new church. The tenth-century Romano-Germanic Pontifical provides an impressive rendering of this consecratory rite[49] that was further developed by William Durandus in his late thirteenth-century pontifical.[50] We shall reserve our exploration of this important ceremony for our future work on the Baroque era liturgy, in which we intend to examine the rite of dedicating a new church given in the 1595–1596 *Pontificale Romanum*, which closely corresponds to the medieval dedication rite of Durandus. In the present work, we simply note here that the medieval liturgical commentators speak of this

---

[47] See Bernhard Poschmann, *Penance and the Anointing of the Sick*, Herder History of Dogma (New York: Herder and Herder, 1968), 26–35, 104–108, and Pierre-Marie Gy, "Penance and Reconciliation", in Aimé-Georges Martimort, ed., *The Church at Prayer: An Introduction to the Liturgy*, vol. 3, *The Sacraments* (Collegeville, Minn.: Liturgical Press, 1988), 102.

[48] Liturgical rites for the coronations of emperors, empresses, kings, and queens are provided by William Durandus in his late thirteenth-century pontifical (c. 1294); see Andrieu, *Pontifical romain au moyen-âge*, 3:427–446. For further coronation texts, see Edmond Martène, *De antiquis ecclesiae ritibus* (Venice: Johannes Baptista Novelli, 1763–1764), bk. 2, chaps. 9–10, 2:204–237.

[49] Text in Cyrille Vogel and Reinhard Elze, eds., *Le pontifical romano-germanique du dixième siècle*, vol. 1, ST 226 (Vatican City: Biblioteca Apostolica Vaticana, 1963), 124–148.

[50] Text in Andrieu, *Pontifical romain au moyen-âge*, 3:455–478.

multistaged solemn blessing of a newly constructed House of God as an analogy for the three-staged infusion of the theological virtues into the Christian soul,[51] a comparison traceable to Saint Augustine (+430).[52] As Durandus explains in his commentary, the *Rationale divinorum officiorum*, "The church being dedicated is the soul being sanctified", with the visible church edifice representing the invisible temple of God, the human soul, built on faith, lifted upward by hope, and perfected by love.[53]

In any comprehensive assessment of medieval liturgy, the issue of intelligibility inevitably arises—did the laity understand what they were seeing and hearing, and did they understand texts spoken in Latin, a language different from that which they spoke in everyday life? In examining, selecting, and translating a wide range of medieval liturgical texts for the present work, the author has been struck time and again by the seemingly pedagogical content of many of the liturgical prayers, suggesting that the authors of these texts, in addition to seeking the most suitable vocabulary with which to praise, thank, and supplicate the Almighty in a given rite or sacrament, also intended to catechize listeners in the theological meaning of the particular rite or sacrament. While it is true that many of the prayers were originally composed at a time when Latin *was* the vernacular language of Romanized Europe, others are certainly of later origin. Perhaps the timeworn assumption that the medieval laity knew nothing of Latin needs to be reassessed. In a 1930 study of the Latin hymns of medieval England, the American scholar Ruth Ellis Messenger points out that Latin was frequently employed in popular songs, including the street songs of troubadours, and that in medieval poetry and drama Latin words or phrases were often freely intermingled with the vernacular.[54] She concludes, "It is highly probable that more of the actual Latin words were understood than is popularly supposed, from the twelfth century to the close of the Middle Ages."[55] Moreover, there is copious evidence for the vernacular instruction of the laity in at least the essentials of the liturgical rites through sermons and vernacular writings, as well as the visual catechesis provided by dramatic liturgical actions and by ecclesiastical art. As early as 747, the Second Council of Clovesho, England, enjoined priests to instruct the people in the vernacular about the meaning of the

---

[51] Lee Bowen, "The Tropology of Medieval Dedication Rites", *Speculum* 16 (1941): 469–470.

[52] Saint Augustine, *Sermones de tempore*, sermon 336, PL 38, col. 1475.

[53] William Durandus of Mende, *Rationale divinorum officiorum*, bk. 1, chap. 6, no. 7, in A. Davril, O.S.B., and T. M. Thibodeau, eds., *Guillelmi Duranti: Rationale divinorum officiorum I–IV*, CCCM 140 (Turnhout, Belgium: Brepols, 1995), 67. Hereafter cited as Durandus, *Rationale* (CCCM 140).

[54] Ruth Ellis Messenger, *Ethical Teachings in the Latin Hymns of Medieval England* (New York: Columbia University Press, 1930), 20–23.

[55] Ibid., 20.

Mass.[56] Medieval vernacular treatises on the liturgy include the *Interpretation and Virtues of the Mass*[57] and the *Meritae missae* authored by the fifteenth-century English poet John Lydgate (+c. 1450).[58]

It is impossible within the present work to address all the issues that have been raised by various commentators in assessing the liturgy of the medieval Church. Our focus here will be to present and explain the actual texts of the medieval rites and the insights of medieval liturgists, so that they can be judged on their own merits rather than be seen only through the filtered light of current interpretations.

In our introduction, we summarized the underlying principles of the great medieval liturgical commentators, most notably Amalarius of Metz, Pope Innocent III, and William Durandus, focusing upon their distinctively allegorical explanations of the sacred rites. Such allegorical interpretations of the liturgy can be seen as motivated by the intent of making *every* action in the course of a liturgical ceremony a conscious act of worship, so that the entire rite from beginning to end may be offered in its *totality* as a prayer and sacrifice to God. Thus actions that might seem to the modern mind as purely functional—for example, the requisite movements of the clergy or transferals of liturgical furnishings from one place to another during a given rite—became for medieval liturgists further occasions for man to direct his heart and soul to the praise and contemplation of the Creator. Such a disposition follows logically from Saint Paul's admonition, "All whatsoever you do in word or in work, do all in the name of the Lord Jesus Christ" (Col 3:17).

It should also be borne in mind that there has long existed in the East a comparable tradition of allegorically interpreting the actions of the Mass.[59] Writing in the late fourth century, the Eastern bishop and ecclesiastical writer Theodore of Mopsuestia (c. 350–428) links the succeeding portions of the Eucharistic liturgy to the events of the Passion, death, and Resurrection of Christ: "Through the priest we picture Christ our Lord in our mind, as through him we see the One who saved us and delivered us by the sacrifice of Himself. . . . We must also think of Christ being at one time led and brought to His Passion, and at another time stretched on the altar to be sacrificed for us . . . and He draws nigh unto us by His apparition, and announces resurrection to us through our

A Contemplative Perception of the Liturgy

---

[56] Second Council of Clovesho (747), canon 10, in J. D. Mansi, ed., *Sacrorum conciliorum nova et amplissima collectio*, vol. 12 (Florence and Venice, 1766; repr., Paris: Hubert Welter, 1901), col. 398.

[57] Text in Henry Noble MacCracken, ed., *The Minor Poems of John Lydgate*, pt. 1, Early English Text Society, extra series, 107 (London: Early English Text Society, 1911), 87–115.

[58] Text in T. F. Simmons, ed., *The Lay Folks' Mass Book*, Early English Text Society, original series, 71 (London: Early English Text Society, 1879), appendix, 148–154.

[59] See Robert F. Taft, S.J., *The Great Entrance: A History of the Transfer of Gifts and Other Preanaphoral Rites of the Liturgy of St. John Chrysostom*, vol. 2 of *A History of the Liturgy of St. John Chrysostom*, Orientalia Christiana analecta 200 (Rome: Pontificio Istituto Orientale, 1978), 7–8, 62–63; Taft, *Precommunion Rites*, 490–495.

communion with Him." [60] The interpretation of the various prayers and actions of the Eucharistic liturgy as corresponding symbolically to the different events in the life of Christ was to become widespread in the East, promulgated by such authors as the fourteenth-century Byzantine writer Nicholas Cabasilas, who in his *Commentary on the Divine Liturgy* (c. 1350) observes, "Indeed, it is the whole scheme of the work of redemption which is signified in the psalms and readings, as in all the actions of the priest throughout the liturgy." [61] Cabasilas explains that this symbolism does not replace the literal meaning of the prayers, readings, and rites of the liturgy; rather, it serves as a meditative overlay that focuses the mind undistractedly upon the divine mysteries in preparation for Holy Communion. [62]

The medieval liturgical commentators saw their task as a spiritual quest to understand the rites of divine worship as God willed for them to be perceived; this effort of faith seeking understanding was often expressed by such scholars in the virtual "statements of purpose" with which their treatises begin or conclude. Thus William Durandus explains at the outset of his massive treatise, the *Rationale divinorum officiorum*:

> I, William of the holy Church of Mende, the said bishop by the patience of God alone, knocking, shall knock at the door, if by chance the Key of David would vouchsafe to open, that the King may introduce me into the wine cellar in which the heavenly model may be shown to me that was shown to Moses on the mountain; to what extent from the individual things and ornaments that exist in the ecclesiastical offices, I may succeed in making known clearly and openly what they should signify and represent, to examine and state the reasons, by him who makes the tongues of infants eloquent [cf. Wis 10:21], the Spirit of whom breathes where he will [cf. Jn 3:8], dividing to everyone according as he will [cf. 1 Cor 12:11], to the praise of the Holy Trinity. [63]

While it is most certainly true, as the Church has defined, that all seven of the sacraments were divinely instituted by Christ, [64] the explicit

---

[60] Theodore of Mopsuestia, *Liber de baptizandos*, chap. 5; English translation in A. Mingana, ed. and trans., *Commentary of Theodore of Mopsuestia on the Lord's Prayer and on the Sacraments of Baptism and the Eucharist*, Woodbrooke Studies 6 (Cambridge: W. Heffer and Sons, 1933), 85, 112; see also 86–88. A similar interpretation is given a century later by the Syrian theologian Narsai of Nisibis (+502); see Narsai's homilies 17 and 21 in R. H. Connelly, trans., *The Liturgical Homilies of Narsai*, Texts and Studies 8, no. 1 (Cambridge, England: Cambridge University Press, 1909), 3–4, 55–56.

[61] English translation in Nicholas Cabasilas, *A Commentary on the Divine Liturgy*, trans. J. M. Hussey and P. A. McNulty (London: SPCK, 1983), chap. 1, p. 26. For the original Greek text, see PG 150, cols. 369, 372.

[62] Cabasilas, *Commentary on the Divine Liturgy*, chap. 1, pp. 26–30; Greek text in PG 150, cols. 369–376.

[63] Durandus, *Rationale* (CCCM 140), "Prohemium", no. 1, pp. 3–4.

[64] Council of Trent, session 7, March 3, 1547, *De sacramentis*, canon 1, in H. J. Schroeder, O.P., *Canons and Decrees of the Council of Trent: Original Text with English Translation* (Saint Louis, Mo.: B. Herder, 1955), 51, 329.

demarcation and enumeration of the seven sacraments as distinct by their very nature from other rites of the Church, and the theological quantification of how the sacraments differed from other blessings or consecration rites, took time to emerge, finally becoming established in the early twelfth century, when the seven sacraments were expressly identified in a sermon of the German bishop Saint Otto of Bamberg (episcopate, 1100–1139).[65] Yet long before this, the medieval Church, preserving and building upon the rites she had inherited from the patristic era, had undertaken the development of magnificent and theologically rich ceremonies for the conferral of all the sacraments. These rites are the subject of the first section of the present work, beginning in the chapter to follow with the heart of the medieval liturgy, the holy sacrifice of the Mass.

---

[65] Saint Otto of Bamberg, *Sermo ad Pomeranos*, PL 173, cols. 1557–1560.

Main Altar in the Capilla del Condestable 1523–32.
Diego de Silee (1495–1563) with Felipe Vignari
Cathedral, Burgos, Spain

PART ONE

THE SACRAMENTS

These seven sacraments, therefore, which for your sake it is pleasing to enumerate again, that is, baptism, confirmation, unction of the infirm, the Eucharist, the reconciliation of the lapsed, marriage, and orders, the heavenly Bridegroom has vouchsafed to entrust to you his Church and Bride through us his groomsmen as a wedding gift of his true love. Wherefore observe, love, and venerate the same sacraments with every honor and reverence; teach them to your children, that they may keep them in memory, and diligently observe them for all generations. Behold, from all these you have the Church, the priest, and whatever things are necessary for us.

Saint Otto of Bamberg, bishop (+1139)

Sermo ad Pomeranos, PL 173, col. 1560.

2   The Mass

May my soul, O Lord, perceive the sweetness of your most beautiful presence
and the sentries of your holy angels round about me. For mindful of your
venerable Passion, I approach your altar, although a sinner, that from your
gifts I may offer to you the sacrifice that you instituted and commanded to be
offered to your majesty, in commemoration of you, and for our salvation.

Priests' prayer before Mass, 1502[1]

Medieval liturgists saw in the Mass an epitome of the history of salvation and of the life of Christ, most especially his sacred Passion.
This arose from the very nature of the Mass as the re-presentation of
the sacrifice of Calvary. As Saint Thomas Aquinas (+1274) observes,
the Mass is "performed with greater solemnity than the other sacraments" because "the whole mystery of our salvation is comprised in
this sacrament."[2] In seeking apt analogies to help the clergy and laity
alike to grasp the cosmic dimensions of what takes place in each and
every celebration of the Mass, medieval liturgists drew powerful images
from the Scriptures. Foremost among these were the key moments in
the life of Christ, from his Incarnation and birth to his death, Resurrection, and Ascension. The incorporation of these events into the
explanation of the prayers and rites of the Mass was no baseless flight
of fancy. Indeed, the memory of these events is expressly evoked by
certain portions of the actual liturgical texts. But in addition to seeing
the Mass in the context of the life of Christ, many medieval liturgists
presented another striking allegorical image for the Mass, one likewise
drawn from the Scriptures: that of the celebration of Mass as a holy
battle of good against evil, and particularly of Christ, in his priest,
conquering the devil.[3] The basis for this analogy lies in the fact that
in the Scriptures mankind's salvation is repeatedly depicted as a battle,
an analogy epitomized in the first verse of the early medieval hymn of

---

[1] Excerpt, from the *Ordo missae* of John Burckard, 1502 edition, in John Wickham Legg,
ed., *Tracts on the Mass*, HBS 27 (London: Henry Bradshaw Society, 1904), 128.

[2] Saint Thomas Aquinas, *Summa theologica: First Complete American Edition in Three Volumes*, trans. Fathers of the English Dominican Province (New York: Benziger Brothers,
1948), pt. III, q. 83, art. 4, 2:2517.

[3] See, for example, Sicard of Cremona, *Mitrale*, bk. 3, chap. 9, PL 213, col. 144.

the holy Cross composed by Saint Venantius Fortunatus (+605), *Pange lingua gloriosi* (also known as *Crux fidelis*):

> *Sing my tongue the victory*
> *of the glorious battle,*
> *and about the trophy of the Cross,*
> *tell the triumph noble;*
> *how the Redeemer of the world,*
> *immolated, has conquered.*[4]

In the Book of Revelation, Saint John describes seeing Christ as the King of Kings, mounted on a white horse, in a blood-stained garment, leading the armies of Heaven into battle against Satan and his cohort (Rev 19:11–21). Saint Paul describes the Christian life in terms of fighting the good fight (1 Tim 6:12; 2 Tim 4:7) as "a good soldier of Jesus Christ" (2 Tim 2:3), having put on "the armor of God", so as to be able "to stand against the deceits of the devil" with the "breast-plate of justice", the "shield of faith", the "helmet of salvation", and the "sword of the Spirit" (Eph 6:11–17). The Old Testament likewise contributed to this analogy, most especially one of the key prefigurations of the Paschal mystery—Israel's crossing of the Red Sea (Ex 14:1–31). The Egyptian charioteers, symbolizing the hosts of hell, abandoned their pursuit of the Israelites across the opened sea upon realizing that "the Lord fighteth for them against us" (Ex 14:25).

Medieval liturgists came to see the vesting of the priest in preparation for Mass as an outward image of the "armor of God" described by Saint Paul, the armor of the virtues with which a priest needed to array his soul for the worthy and fruitful celebration of the Eucharist. Thus Sicard of Cremona (+1215) observes: "The priest going to do battle against the spiritual evils in the heavens is clothed in sacred vestments as if in arms.... Thus armed for all things, he proceeds to the altar."[5] Sicard explains this mystical battle image as twofold, applicable both to Christ as Head of his Mystical Body, the Church, and to the members of his Mystical Body: "It [the battle] is represented in the Head, because Christ, fighting with the devil, conquered him and despoiled hell; it is represented in the members, because we are assailed, not only by the world, but also by the flesh and by the devil."[6]

Medieval missals provided various prayers and other texts to assist a priest in preparing his heart and mind for the celebration of Mass. The 1496 missal of Vich, Spain, gives a meditation for the priest to read before Mass (entitled "Preparation of the Priest for Offering the Sacrifice"), admonishing the celebrant to ponder the magnitude of

---

[4] The Latin text of this hymn can be found in numerous sources, such as Matthew Britt, *The Hymns of the Breviary and the Missal* (New York: Benziger Bros., 1922), 126–128.

[5] Sicard of Cremona, *Mitrale*, bk. 3, chap. 9, PL 213, col. 145.

[6] Ibid., col. 144.

what he is about to do as constituting a re-presentation of the sacrifice that *"alone saves the soul from eternal death"*: *"For who of the faithful should be able to have a doubt, in the very hour of immolation, the heavens to be opened at the voice of the priest, in that mystery of Jesus Christ the choirs of angels to be present, the depths to be united to the heights, earthly things to be joined to heavenly things, and from things visible and invisible to be made one?"* [7]

A late medieval printed missal of England's Sarum Rite, dating from about 1489, has the priest prepare for Mass by invoking the Holy Spirit. During his vesting, he recites the Pentecost Sequence, *Veni Creator Spiritus* (*"Come, Creator Spirit"*). He then says the versicle and response *"Send forth thy Spirit . . . And thou shalt renew the face of the earth."* The prayer that follows is a plea for the grace of a purified heart: *"O God, to whom every heart lies open, every desire is uttered, and to whom no secret lies hidden, purify through the infusion of the Holy Spirit the thoughts of our hearts, that we may be worthy to love you completely and praise you worthily. Through . . ."* [8] The intention of coming to the altar with a pure heart is a common one, likewise reflected in the priest's prayer for putting on the chasuble found in a thirteenth-century abbot's ritual for the French-Alsatian abby of Morbach: *"Clothe me in the vestment of humility and chastity, and grant to me protection against the enemy plotter, that with a pure heart and a chaste body I may be worthy to praise your holy name. Through Christ . . ."* [9]

In an early fifteenth-century missal of Toul, France (c. 1409–1436), the intention of a pure mind for the fitting celebration of Mass is expressed in the prayer accompanying the priest's washing of his hands before Mass: *"Grant to our senses, almighty God, that just as outwardly the stains of the hands are cleansed, so interiorly may the defilements of our minds be purified by you, and may the advancements of the holy virtues flourish in us. Through Christ . . ."* [10] The other preparatory prayers from this same missal for the assumption of the different vestments generally utilize the physical characteristics of each vestment as an analogy for a particular virtue or grace requisite for the fruitful celebration of the Sacrament. Thus, for the amice, which during the Middle Ages was temporarily placed over the head until the priest reached the altar, where he folded it back onto his shoulders, the accompanying vesting prayer speaks of faith as an overshadowing protection: *"Overshadow, O Lord, my head in the shade of your holy faith, and expel from me the clouds of ignorance."* The prayers for the other vestments follow. For the alb: *"Clothe me, O Lord, in the robe of salvation, and encompass me with the*

---

[7] Text in Francesc Xavier Altés i Aguiló, ed., *Missale Vicense, 1496*, facsimile ed., Biblioteca litúrgica catalana 3 (Barcelona: Institut d'Estudis Catalans, 2001), temporal, fol. 169r.

[8] Text in Edmond Martène, *De antiquis ecclesiae ritibus* (Venice: Johannes Baptista Novelli, 1763–1764), bk. 1, chap. 4, art. 12, *ordo 35*, 1:239.

[9] Ibid., *ordo 32*, p. 235.

[10] Ibid., *ordo 31*, p. 234.

breastplate of fortitude. Through Christ . . ." For the cincture: *"Gird in me, O Lord, the custody of my mind, lest my mind be puffed up with the spirit of elation and pride."* For the maniple: *"Give me, O Lord, a right perception and a pure speech, that I may be able to fulfill your praise."* For the stole: *"Encompass my neck, O Lord, in the stole of innocence, and purify my mind from every corruption of sin."* For the chasuble: *"Clothe me, O Lord, in the vesture of humility, charity, and peace, that protected on all sides with the virtues, I may be able to resist the vices and enemies of soul and body. Through Christ . . ."* [11]

The vestments were also interpreted as mystically representing the vesture of Christ in his Passion, a comparison made by the Franciscan William of Melitona (+1260) and the Dominican cardinal Hugh of Saint-Cher (+1263).[12] The 1506 missal of Palma de Majorca, Spain, provides a short poem to remind the priest that he should recall the Passion imagery of his vestments before undertaking the celebration of Mass:

O you, whichever priest you are, who would wish to chant the Mass:
be totally mindful, and think over with your whole mind,
what manner of battles Christ suffered for you.
With head veiled, let the amice signify to you the derision of him.
Mark in the linen vesture, that he was mocked in white.
The cincture, stole, maniple represent his bonds.
May you recognize in the chasuble that the purple [robe] is signified.
Remember the place of Calvary while you proceed to the altar.
And may you contemplate Christ, as he proceeded to his dying.
And certainly, in piously recalling all these things thus, beat your breast. [13]

The thirteenth-century statutes of the Carthusian Order instruct the priest to say an Our Father kneeling at the altar step before preparing for Mass.[14] In Spain and Portugal, there was a widespread custom for the priest to invoke the intercession of the Blessed Virgin Mary in his preparation to approach the altar. Hence in the 1500 *Missale mixtum* of Spain's cardinal Francisco Ximenes de Cisneros (+1517), a liturgical book combining ancient Mozarabic Rite texts with borrowings from the late fifteenth-century archdiocesan missal of Toledo, and intended for the revival of the Mozarabic Rite, the priest calls upon the Blessed Virgin after washing his hands in the sacristy but before putting on his vestments:

---

[11] Ibid.

[12] Josef Jungmann, S.J., *The Mass of the Roman Rite: Its Origins and Development* (New York: Benziger Bros., 1951–1955), 1:112, footnote.

[13] Text in Gabriel Seguí i Trobat, ed., *El missal mallorqui de 1506: Estudi i edició segons l'exemplar de la Biblioteca Bartomeu March*, Col·lectània Sant Pacià 79 (Barcelona: Facultat de Teologia de Catalunya, Centre d'Estudis Teològics de Mallorca, 2003), 207.

[14] Martène, *De antiquis ecclesiae ritibus*, bk. 1, chap. 4, art. 12, *ordo* 25, 1:227.

Afterward he should kneel before his vestments; and he should say four Hail Marys. And from his innermost heart he should commend himself to the glorious Virgin Mary, that he may offer that mystery acceptably to God the Father, and the Son, and the Holy Spirit, and that he may have her in this sacrifice as a mediatrix and helper. Then he should fortify himself with the sign of the cross, and over each vestment he should say: *In the name of the Father, + and of the Son, and of the Holy Spirit. Amen.*[15]

For the laity, the Church provided a public liturgical rite of preparation for Mass on Sundays and feast days: the aspersion procession, by which the faithful awaiting Mass were blessed with holy water to the accompaniment of either the penitential chant *Asperges me* or the Easter chant *Vidi aquam*. This rite we shall examine separately in an excursus at the end of the present chapter.

The Mass Begins: The Entrance, the Introit, the Penitential Rite, the *Gloria*, and the Collect

As our primary example of the medieval Mass, we have chosen the Mass *Ordo* of England's Sarum Rite, a diocesan variant of the Roman Rite, as given in an early printed edition of the Sarum Missal dating from about the year 1489.[16] To simplify the citations of this text, we will hereafter refer to it as the "1489 Sarum Missal", even though its date is only an approximation. We shall follow the rubrics as they would have been carried out for High Mass, in which the priest is assisted by a deacon and a subdeacon. Where necessary, additional information about the Sarum Rite Mass is taken from other Sarum liturgical books. Although the Sarum Rite originally developed as the liturgical usage of one particular diocese, that of Salisbury, it was subsequently adopted by other English dioceses, spreading across most of southern England, including London, as well as Ireland and Scotland, by the end of the fifteenth century.[17] This, therefore, is the Mass as the people of pre-Reformation Catholic England, Ireland, and Scotland knew it, the Mass that Saint Thomas More attended daily and that Saint John Fisher celebrated daily.

By way of comparison, we have also drawn examples of particular portions of the Mass from the Roman Rite liturgical books of Rome itself, as well as from diocesan liturgical books utilized elsewhere in medieval Europe. For these additional examples, we have repeatedly utilized a book of instructions that the bishop and liturgist William Durandus of Mende (+1296) composed for his own diocese of Mende,

---

[15] *Missale mixtum secundum regulam beati Isidori dictum Mozarabes*, PL 85, col. 523. Similar rubrics appear in the 1499 missal of Jaén, Spain, and in the 1558 missal of Portugal's Braga Rite; see respectively *Missale Giennense / Manuale continens ordinem ad celebrandum ecclesiastica sacramenta* [*Missale secundum morem et consuetudinem sancte ecclesie Gienensis*] (Seville: Meinard Ungut and Stanislao Polono, 1499), fol. 94v, and Archdale King, *Liturgies of the Primatial Sees*, Rites of Western Christendom 3 (London: Longmans, Green, 1957), 253–254.

[16] Text in Martène, *De antiquis ecclesiae ritibus*, bk. 1, chap. 4, art. 12, *ordo* 35, 1:239–241.

[17] Archdale King, *Liturgies of the Past* (Milwaukee: Bruce, 1959), 285–300.

France, around the year 1294,[18] as well as the 1502 edition of a 1498 work, the *Ordo servandus per sacerdotem in celebratione misse* (Order to be observed by a priest in the celebration of Mass), a Roman Rite *Ordo missae* composed by the papal master of ceremonies John Burckard.[19] The magnificent corpus of Mass rubrics given at the beginning of the 1570 *Missale Romanum* of Pope Saint Pius V, known as the *Ritus servandus in celebratione missarum* (Rite to be observed in the celebration of Masses),[20] is a direct descendant of these two earlier texts.

In the 1489 Sarum Missal, the priest after completing the private preparatory prayers proceeds to say (while still in the sacristy) the introductory verse "*I will go unto the altar of God; to God, who gives joy to my youth*" (Ps 42:4) followed by the complete Psalm 42 (*Judica me, Deus*). To the psalm and verse he adds an Our Father and a Hail Mary before setting forth from the sacristy to begin the Mass.[21] Recited at the beginning of Mass from the ninth century onward,[22] Psalm 42 and its verse, "*I will go unto the altar of God*", here said in the sacristy but recited at the altar step in the Roman Rite and elsewhere, together serve as a prelude to the penitential rite of the Mass. Sicard of Cremona sees this psalm (especially its first verse) as a plea on the celebrant's part "to be separated from the wicked", lest he succumb to temptation in their company.[23] Durandus considers the psalm as a petition "to be liberated from temptation, and illuminated by grace", so that "liberated from the unjust man", the priest "may go worthily to the altar of God".[24] The psalm's fourth verse, "*I will go unto the altar of God*", which is used as the psalm's antiphon, is

---

[18] Text in J. Berthelé, "Les instructions et constitutions de Guillaume Durand le Spéculateur", in *Academie des Sciences et Lettres de Montpellier: Mémoires de la Section des Lettres*, 2nd series, vol. 3 (Montpellier, 1900–1907), especially 54–77 (*De officio missae*), and 79–80 (devotional prayers for Mass). This work of Durandus is based in part upon the liturgical text of Rome known as the Ceremonial of a Cardinal Bishop (c. 1280), ascribed to Latino Cardinal Malabranca (+1294); text in Marc Dykmans, S.J., ed., *Le cérémonial papal de la fin du moyen âge à la Renaissance*, vol. 1, BIHBR 24 (Brussels and Rome: Institut Historique Belge de Rome, 1977), 220–263.

[19] Text of 1502 edition in Legg, *Tracts on the Mass*, 126–171. Regarding the original 1498 edition of this *Ordo missae* of John Burckard, see Marc Dykmans, S.J., ed., *L'oeuvre de Patrizi Piccolomini, ou Le cérémonial papal de la première Renaissance*, vol. 1, ST 293 (Vatican City: Biblioteca Apostolica Vaticana, 1980), 95*, and Manlio Sodi and Achille Maria Triacca, eds., *Missale Romanum: Editio princeps (1570)*, facsimile ed., MLCT 2 (Vatican City: Libreria Editrice Vaticana, © 1998), editors' introduction, xviii–xix.

[20] Text in Sodi and Triacca, *Missale Romanum: Editio princeps (1570)*, 9–22 (new pagination).

[21] Martène, *De antiquis ecclesiae ritibus*, bk. 1, chap. 4, art. 12, *ordo* 35, 1:239. It is believed that in the Sarum Rite these prayers must have been said in the sacristy, even though the rubrics are silent on this point. See Blessed Juan Bautista Ferreres Boluda, S.J., *Historia del misal romano* (Barcelona: Eugenio Subirana, 1929), 74, and F. Thomas Bergh, "Sarum Rite", in *The Catholic Encyclopedia* (New York: Appleton, 1907–1912), 13:480.

[22] Mario Righetti, *Manuale di storia liturgica* (Milan: Editrice Ancora, 1949–1955), 3:159.

[23] Sicard of Cremona, *Mitrale*, bk. 3, chap. 2, PL 213, cols. 94–95.

[24] William Durandus of Mende, *Rationale divinorum officiorum*, bk. 4, chap. 7, no. 1, in A. Davril, O.S.B., and T. M. Thibodeau, eds., *Guillelmi Duranti: Rationale divinorum officiorum*

according to Sicard an expression of the priest's joy that in advancing to the altar, he is going in desire to the invisible altar of the sanctuary of Heaven.[25]

The order of clerics in the Sarum entrance procession is given in a supplemental liturgical book, the Sarum Customary, dating from the late fourteenth century: "first, the candle bearers, the two walking together, then the thurifer, after him the subdeacon, then the deacon, and after him the priest, the deacon and subdeacon being vested in chasubles ... but not keeping their hands outside the chasuble in the manner of a priest; whereas the other ministers, as the candle bearers, the thurifer, and the acolytes, appearing in albs with amices."[26]

The introductory rites of the Mass are likened by the medieval liturgists to the first coming of Christ into the world through the Incarnation. The priest represents Christ, for he is by virtue of the sacrament of holy orders an *alter Christus* who in approaching the altar is going to exercise the priestly office of Christ by offering the sacrifice of the New Covenant in the Mass. The priest's emergence from the sacristy is seen as symbolic of Christ coming forth from his Father in Heaven, and from the womb of the Blessed Virgin Mary, to enter the world "as a bridegroom coming out of his bride chamber" (Ps 18:6).[27] The priest, having clothed himself in sacred vestments just as Christ clothed himself in "the flesh of our humanity", comes to the altar just as Christ came to his people to save them.[28] In the entrance procession the two lit candles borne by the acolytes are seen as representing the Old Testament prophets and the Law of Moses that preceded the New Testament, which is represented by the Gospel book.[29] The acolyte carrying the smoking thurible symbolizes mankind imploring God for the salvation of the world.[30] The deacon and subdeacon assisting the priest are seen as two of the patriarchs closest to the time of Christ's birth, who prepare the way of the Lord.[31] Durandus identifies the subdeacon who carries the Gospel book with Saint John the Baptist, who began preaching the Gospel injunction of repentance in preparation for the preaching of Christ.[32] According to Amalarius of Metz (+c. 850), the celebrant walks behind the Gospel book, not ahead of it, so

I–IV, CCCM 140 (Turnhout, Belgium: Brepols, 1995), 282. Hereafter cited as Durandus, *Rationale* (CCCM 140).

[25] Sicard of Cremona, *Mitrale*, bk. 3, chap. 2, PL 213, col. 95.

[26] Text in Walter Howard Frere, ed., *The Use of Sarum* (Cambridge, England: Cambridge University Press, 1898–1901), 1:62–63.

[27] Pseudo-Hugh of Saint Victor, *Speculum*, chap. 7, PL 177, col. 357; Sicard of Cremona, *Mitrale*, bk. 3, chap. 2, PL 213, col. 92.

[28] Durandus, *Rationale* (CCCM 140), bk. 4, chap. 11, no. 2, p. 292.

[29] Pseudo-Hugh of Saint Victor, *Speculum*, chap. 7, PL 177, col. 357.

[30] Ibid.

[31] Ibid.

[32] Durandus, *Rationale* (CCCM 140), bk. 4, chap. 6, no. 3, p. 272.

as to symbolize the precept of Christ, "If any man will come after me, let him deny himself, and take up his cross, and follow me" (Mt 16:24).[33]

The carrying of a processional cross in the entrance procession is not mentioned in the Sarum Missal, but this usage can readily be inferred from scattered references to such crosses in other fourteenth- and fifteenth-century liturgical manuscripts of the Sarum Rite.[34] The general practice across medieval Europe was for a processional cross to be carried at or close to the front of the entrance procession at more solemn Masses;[35] in the thirteenth-century Pontifical of the Roman Curia, the processional cross is listed first among the objects to be carried in the entrance procession.[36] In a late fourteenth-century supplement to a papal book of ceremonies known as the Long Ceremonial, the front of the entrance procession is described thus: "First, one from the acolytes goes before, carrying the cross erect; the chaplains indeed follow, carrying candlesticks with lighted candles, whom one other acolyte follows with a thurible and incense. Finally comes the subdeacon vested in a tunic, carrying before his chest the book of the Gospels with the maniple of the pope laid over it."[37] Over two centuries later, the Roman Rite *Caeremoniale episcoporum* of 1600 was to specify for episcopal Masses the carrying of the cross between two acolytes with lit candles, ahead of all others in the procession, except the thurifer, who alone preceded the crossbearer.[38]

The crucifix (as distinct from a plain cross) was being used in some liturgical functions by the tenth century.[39] By the thirteenth to the fourteenth century, most processional crosses were crucifixes;[40] a rubric in a late fourteenth-century consuetudinary of the Sarum Rite clearly indicates that the processional cross used was a crucifix.[41] In the fourteenth-century *Liber ordinarius* of Essen, Germany, there is a rubric

---

[33] Amalarius of Metz, *Liber officialis*, bk. 3, chap. 5, no. 12, in John Michael Hanssens, ed., *Amalarii episcopi: Opera liturgica omnia*, vol. 2, ST 139 (Vatican City: Biblioteca Apostolica Vaticana, 1948), 275.

[34] The processional cross is mentioned in the late fourteenth-century Sarum Customary and again in the fifteenth-century Sarum Customary (Frere, *Use of Sarum*, 1:41, 73, 129, 157, 160).

[35] Herbert Thurston, S.J., "Cross and Crucifix, The, III: The Cross and Crucifix in Liturgy", in *Catholic Encyclopedia* (1907–1912), 4:533.

[36] Text in Michel Andrieu, ed., *Le pontifical romain au moyen-âge*, vol. 2, *Le pontifical de la Curie romaine au XIIIᵉ siècle*, ST 87 (Vatican City: Biblioteca Apostolica Vaticana, 1940), 457–458.

[37] Text in Marc Dykmans, S.J., ed., *Le cérémonial papal de la fin du moyen âge à la Renaissance*, vol. 3, BIHBR 26 (Brussels and Rome: Institut Historique Belge de Rome, 1983), 316.

[38] Text in Achille Maria Triacca and Manlio Sodi, eds., *Caeremoniale episcoporum: Editio princeps (1600)*, facsimile ed., MLCT 4 (Vatican City: Libreria Editrice Vaticana, © 2000), bk. 2, chap. 8, p. 165 (new pagination).

[39] The tenth-century Romano-Germanic Pontifical explicitly mentions the veneration of a crucifix during the Palm Sunday procession; see Cyrille Vogel and Reinhard Elze, eds., *Le pontifical romano-germanique du dixième siècle*, vol. 2, ST 227 (Vatican City: Biblioteca Apostolica Vaticana, 1963), 47–48.

[40] Thurston, "Cross and Crucifix", 533.

[41] Frere, *Use of Sarum*, 1:129.

directing that in all processions the cross should be carried with "the face of the image of the cross", that is, the face of the crucified Christ, "turned toward the people".[42] In explaining the carrying of a cross at the head of the entrance procession, Pope Innocent III (+1216) cites the second verse of Psalm 67: "Let God arise, and let his enemies be scattered: and let them that hate him flee from before his face." Hence the crucifix scatters the enemies of Christ, who "flee from before his face".[43] Durandus develops Innocent's explanation further, citing the opening words of the hymn *Vexilla Regis*, "*The standards of the King go forth* . . ." As the "royal standard", the Cross is "a sign of the victory of Christ . . . by which the demons have been conquered"; hence, at the sight of the Cross, demons flee in terror.[44] Moreover, both Pope Innocent III and Durandus see the setting ahead of the processional cross as a reminder of Saint Paul's admonition that we are to glory only in the Cross of Christ (Gal 5:14).[45]

As the priest and the assisting ministers proceed from the sacristy to the bottom step of the altar, the choir sings the Introit, a chant consisting of an antiphon followed by a psalm verse (or in some cases, a verse from elsewhere in the Scriptures), then the Glory Be to the Father, concluding with a repetition of the antiphon.[46] In the Sarum Rite there is an additional repetition of the antiphon between the psalm verse and the Glory Be.[47] The whole text served as an entrance song. This chant, the text of which would vary according to the particular Sunday or feast day, was considered as symbolic of the prayer, praises, and sighs offered to God by the prophets and holy ones of the Old Testament expressing their yearning for the coming of the Messiah.[48] Sicard of Cremona takes this analogy a step further. Describing the Introit as representative of "the praise of the Church of the Jews", he associates the Introit antiphon with the praise offered by the patriarchs (e.g., Abraham), the psalm verse with the praises of the prophets (e.g., Isaiah), and the Glory Be with the praises of the Apostles.[49]

Usually, the Introit antiphon, as well as the Introit verse, would be taken from the Psalms. Such Introits were classified as "regular". Some Introits, however, classified as "irregular", utilized nonscriptural antiphons so as to express in an explicit and poetic manner the mystery of

---

[42] Text in Franz Arens, ed., *Der Liber ordinarius der Essener Stiftskirche* (Paderborn, Germany: Albert Pape, 1908), 9.

[43] Innocent III, *De sacro altaris mysterio*, bk. 2, chap. 12, PL 217, col. 805.

[44] Durandus, *Rationale* (CCCM 140), bk. 4, chap. 6, no. 18, p. 279.

[45] Innocent III, *De sacro altaris mysterio*, bk. 2, chap. 12, PL 217, col. 805; Durandus, *Rationale* (CCCM 140), bk. 4, chap. 6, no. 18, p. 279.

[46] Adrian Fortescue, "Introit", in *Catholic Encyclopedia* (1907–1912), 8:81–82. For examples of Introits utilizing Scripture verses other than those from the Psalms, see the table of Sunday Introits in Jungmann, *Mass of the Roman Rite*, 1:331.

[47] Martène, *De antiquis ecclesiae ritibus*, bk. 1, chap. 4, art. 12, *ordo* 35, 1:239.

[48] Pseudo-Hugh of Saint Victor, *Speculum*, chap. 7, PL 177, col. 356.

[49] Sicard of Cremona, *Mitrale*, bk. 3, chap. 2, PL 213, col. 94.

the particular feast day being celebrated.[50] As an especially beautiful example of an irregular Introit, we offer the following from a set of Mass texts for the feast of the Immaculate Conception composed by the protonotary apostolic Leonard de Nogarolis and approved for use by Pope Sixtus IV in 1476.[51] This particular Mass is found in numerous editions of the *Missale Romanum* from 1481 through 1561[52] and was introduced elsewhere, including in eastern Spain, appearing in the 1496 missal of Vich (given as the second of two Masses for the feast), the 1506 missal of Palma de Majorca, and the 1529 missal of Tarazona.[53] The Introit verse, *Egredimini et videte*, an adaptation from the Song of Solomon (2:14), is quoted here from the earliest printed missal containing this Mass, the 1477 *Missal according to the Use of the Roman Curia*: "*Come forth and see, O daughters of Zion, your Queen, whom the stars of morning praise, at whose beauty sun and moon wonder, and all the children of God rejoice. Verse: May she show her face; may her voice sound in our ears. For her speech is sweet and her face exceedingly beautiful.*"[54]

Upon arriving before the altar step, the priest stands in the middle, with the assisting deacon on his right and the subdeacon on his left. The celebrant now recites the *Confiteor*, a component of the Mass traceable to the ninth century,[55] prefaced by the opening verse of Psalm 117: "*Give praise to the Lord, for he is good: for his mercy endureth forever.*"[56] In the Old Testament, this verse was sung by the priests assembled for the dedication of the Temple of Solomon; as soon as it was chanted, the glory of the Lord in the form of a cloud filled the Temple (2 Par 5:13). The Sarum form of the *Confiteor*, shorter than that of the Roman Rite,[57] follows: "*I confess to God, to blessed Mary, to all the saints, and to you: I have sinned exceedingly in thought, in word, and in deed, by my fault. I beseech holy Mary, all the saints of God, and you to pray*

[50] Jungmann, *Mass of the Roman Rite*, 1:329.

[51] Altés i Aguiló, *Missale Vicense, 1496*, introduction, 82–83.

[52] Robert Lippe, ed., *Missale Romanum: Mediolani, 1474*, vol. 2, *A Collation with Other Editions Printed before 1570*, HBS 33 (London: Henry Bradshaw Society, 1907), 165–166 (complete text of December 8 Mass); Seguí i Trobat, *Missal mallorquí de 1506*, 459, footnote.

[53] See respectively Altés i Aguiló, *Missale Vicense, 1496*, sanctoral, fol. 80v; Seguí i Trobat, *Missal Mallorquí de 1506*, 459; *Missale secundum ritum ac consuetudinem insignis ecclesiae Tirasonensis* (Saragossa, Spain: Jorge Coci, 1529; digitized text, Bayerische Staatsbibliothek, Munich, n.d.), fols. 274v–275v.

[54] *Missale secundum consuetudinem Curie Romane* (Naples, Italy: Matthias Moravus, 1477; digitized text, Bayerische Staatsbibliothek, Munich, n.d.), fol. 157v.

[55] An early form of the *Confiteor* appears in a sacramentary of Amiens, France (second half of the ninth century), quoted in Jungmann, *Mass of the Roman Rite*, 1:299. The particular text of the *Confiteor* that entered the liturgical books of Rome and became universal with the promulgation of the 1570 *Missale Romanum* is traceable to an eleventh-century Benedictine manuscript of Volturno, Italy, the Codex Chigi (manuscript: Vatican City, Biblioteca Apostolica Vaticana, Codex Chigi D V 77); see Martenè, *De antiquis ecclesiae ritibus*, bk. 1, chap. 4, art. 12, *ordo* 12, 1:205.

[56] Martène, *De antiquis ecclesiae ritibus*, bk. 1, chap. 4, art. 12, *ordo* 35, 1:239.

[57] The complete text of the Roman Rite *Confiteor* is given on p. 576 of the present work.

for me." It is recited first by the celebrant alone, after which the assisting clerics respond, "*May almighty God have mercy on you, and forgive you all your sins, free you from all evil, preserve and confirm you in good, and bring you to eternal life*" (priest: "*Amen*"). The parts are now reversed, with the assisting clerics reciting the *Confiteor* and the celebrant responding to them, "*May almighty God have mercy on you*", etc. The priest then concludes the penitential rite, saying, "*May the almighty and merciful Lord grant you the absolution and remission of all your sins, time of true penitence, and emendation of life, grace, and the consolation of the Holy Spirit*" (ministers: "*Amen*").[58]

Sicard of Cremona sets the *Confiteor* in the context of the allegory of the Mass as a holy battle of the priest against the devil. Thus, in reciting the *Confiteor*, the priest, having armed himself in the sacred vestments, in effect renounces Satan and thwarts him by humbly accusing himself of his own sins.[59] Pope Innocent III notes the significance of the priest reciting the *Confiteor* by himself before the others assisting do, observing that the just man in his speech is the "first accuser of himself" (Prov 18:17).[60] The Sarum Missal says nothing as to any change of posture by the celebrant during the *Confiteor*, but the universal tradition was for the priest to remain bowed while saying it and to strike his breast thrice at the words "*by my fault, by my fault, by my most grievous fault*".[61] Pope Innocent III explains that the striking of the heart is done in imitation of the example of the publican in Christ's parable of the two men at prayer in the Temple (Lk 18:9–14). By imitating this publican who beat his breast while praying, "O God, be merciful to me a sinner" (verse 13), we shall be enabled to return to our home justified in the eyes of God, as he did.[62]

The Sarum Rite specifies the sign of peace at two points during the Mass, the first of which follows the penitential rite, with the celebrant offering the sign of peace to the assisting deacon and subdeacon. Since the thirteenth century it had become the norm in England to utilize for this purpose the pax board, an ornamented tablet of wood, ivory, or metal with a picture of Christ or a saint.[63] The priest would kiss the pax board and then give it to the deacon to kiss, and afterward the subdeacon. The celebrant presented the pax board with the words "*Accept the kiss of peace and love, that you may be fitting in the sacred ministry of the altar of the Lord.*"[64] The conferral of a sign of peace near the beginning of Mass existed in twelfth-century Rome, as mentioned

---

[58] Martène, *De antiquis ecclesiae ritibus*, bk. 1, chap. 4, art. 12, *ordo* 35, 1:239.

[59] Sicard of Cremona, *Mitrale*, bk. 3, chap. 2, PL 213, col. 145.

[60] Innocent III, *De sacro altaris mysterio*, bk. 2, chap. 13, PL 217, col. 806.

[61] These actions during the *Confiteor* are specified in the late thirteenth-century *Instructions* of Durandus (Berthelé, "Instructions et constitutions de Guillaume Durand", 56).

[62] Innocent III, *De sacro altaris mysterio*, bk. 2, chap. 13, PL 217, col. 806.

[63] Jungmann, *Mass of the Roman Rite*, 2:328–329.

[64] Martène, *De antiquis ecclesiae ritibus*, bk. 1, chap. 4, art. 12, *ordo* 35, 1:239.

by Pope Innocent III, who explains it as an expression of the peace that Christ's first coming brought, as prophesied in Psalm 71 (verse 7): "In his days shall justice spring up, and abundance of peace, till the moon be taken away."[65] The placing of the sign of peace immediately after the penitential rite in the Sarum liturgy suggests in this context that it is likewise an expression of the peace and reconciliation brought by the confession and forgiveness of sins.

Following the sign of peace, the candle bearers who accompanied the celebrant from the sacristy now set down their candlesticks upon the first altar step.[66] The candles lit for Mass are seen as symbolic of the Holy Spirit, by whose outpouring the consecration takes place; the candlelight is also a sign of joy, the eternal happiness that the sacrifice of the Mass imparts.[67] The placing of at least one lit candle on each side of the altar is seen by Pope Innocent III as evocative of the Christmas mystery: the candlelight symbolizes the joy of both the Jews and the Gentiles at the birth of Christ, the two peoples represented by the placement of the candles at the two sides of the altar:

> The light of the candlesticks is the faith of the people. For to the Jewish people the prophet says [Is 60:1]: "Arise, be enlightened, O Jerusalem; for thy light is come, and the glory of the Lord is risen upon thee." But to the Gentile people the Apostle says [Eph 5:8]: "For you were heretofore darkness, but now light in the Lord." For also, at the birth of Christ, a new star appeared to the Magi.[68]

The candles derive this meaning from what stands between them at the center of the altar: "Between the two candlesticks on the altar the cross is placed in the middle, for between the two peoples Christ appears, the Mediator in the Church, the Cornerstone [cf. 1 Pet 2:7], 'who hath made both one' [Eph 2:14], to whom came the shepherds from Judea, and the Magi from the East."[69]

We return now to the Sarum Missal rubrics. The celebrant ascends to the altar at its middle. Bowing with his hands joined, he says in a low voice, "*Remove from us, we beseech you, O Lord, all our iniquities, that we may be worthy to enter unto the Holy of Holies with pure minds.*"[70] This first profound bow of the celebrant during the Mass, according to Durandus, expresses Christ's humbling himself to become man in the Incarnation.[71] In the Roman Rite, this bow accompanies the

[65] Innocent III, *De sacro altaris mysterio*, bk. 2, chap. 15, PL 217, col. 807.

[66] Martène, *De antiquis ecclesiae ritibus*, bk. 1, chap. 4, art. 12, *ordo* 35, 1:239.

[67] Honorius of Autun, *Gemma animae*, bk. 1, chap. 118, PL 172, col. 583. Regarding the role of the Holy Spirit in the consecration, see *Catechism of the Catholic Church*, English ed. (Vatican City: Libreria Editrice Vaticana, © 1994; Washington, D.C.: United States Catholic Conference, 1994), nos. 1104–1106, p. 287.

[68] Innocent III, *De sacro altaris mysterio*, bk. 2, chap. 21, PL 217, col. 811.

[69] Ibid.

[70] Martène, *De antiquis ecclesiae ritibus*, bk. 1, chap. 4, art. 12, *ordo* 35, 1:239.

[71] Durandus, *Rationale* (CCCM 140), bk. 4, chap. 7, no. 1, p. 282.

Confiteor at the foot of the altar; here it accompanies the ancient Collect *"Remove from us"* (*Aufer a nobis*, a prayer traceable to the sixth-century Leonine Sacramentary),[72] the words of which appropriately reflect the transition that the priest makes in passing from the outer world into the sanctuary, here identified as the *"Holy of Holies"*.[73] The prayer thus evokes the imagery of the innermost sanctuary of the ancient Temple of Solomon, the Holy of Holies, as an analogy for the action of the priest at the altar, especially in the Canon, an analogy that appears repeatedly in the Mass commentaries of the medieval liturgists, as we shall see. In this prayer the theme of coming to the altar with a purified heart and mind returns. In the above-cited early fifteenth-century missal of Toul, France, the above oration is preceded by a private devotional prayer addressed to Christ and said by the priest as he ascends to the altar, further amplifying the aspiration of approaching the altar with a humble and contrite heart:

> *Before the sight of your divine majesty, O Lord, I, guilty, stand near, who presume to invoke your holy name; have mercy on me, O Lord, a sinful man; forgive your unworthy priest, by whose hands this oblation is seen to be offered. . . . May you not enter into judgment with your servant. . . . Remember, O Lord, that I am flesh. . . . I am not worthy, Lord Jesus Christ, that I should be living. But you who do not will the death of the sinner, grant unto me forgiveness in my constituted flesh, that through the labors of penance I may be worthy thoroughly to enjoy life eternal in Heaven, through you, Jesus Christ, who with the Father . . .*[74]

Rising from his bow, the celebrant kisses the altar.[75] Pope Innocent III explains this kiss as signifying that in coming to earth Christ "joined himself in marriage to the holy Church".[76] The priest now makes the sign of the cross on his face with the traditional formula, *"In the name of the Father . . ."*[77] The making of the sign of the cross with these words at some point during the introductory rites of the Mass has existed since the fourteenth century.[78] As to the manner in which the sign of the cross is usually made (whether during Mass or on other occasions), Pope Innocent III observes that it is made with three fingers (of the right hand) to symbolize the invocation of the Trinity that accompanies it; the downward motion of the hand (from the forehead to the breast) symbolizes Christ descending from Heaven to earth, whereas the motion of the hand from the left shoulder to the

---

[72] Text in Leo Cunibert Mohlberg, O.S.B.; Leo Eizenhöfer, O.S.B.; and Petrus Siffrin, O.S.B., eds., *Sacramentarium Veronense,* REDSMF 1 (Rome: Herder, 1956), no. 985, p. 126.

[73] See François Amiot, *History of the Mass*, Twentieth Century Encyclopedia of Catholicism 110 (New York: Hawthorn Books, 1959), 33.

[74] Martène, *De antiquis ecclesiae ritibus*, bk. 1, chap. 4, art. 12, *ordo* 31, 1:234.

[75] Ibid., *ordo* 35, p. 239.

[76] Innocent III, *De sacro altaris mysterio*, bk. 2, chap. 15, PL 217, col. 807.

[77] Martène, *De antiquis ecclesiae ritibus*, bk. 1, chap. 4, art. 12, *ordo* 35, 1:239.

[78] Jungmann, *Mass of the Roman Rite*, 1:296; Amiot, *History of the Mass*, 32.

right symbolizes mankind's passing from misery to glory, just as Christ passed "from death to life" and "from hell to Paradise".[79] Recall that in his account of the Last Judgment Christ speaks of the condemned as being to his left, while those saved are to his right (Mt 25:31–33); hence the passage of the hand from left to right can be seen as representing our passage from condemnation to salvation.

The first incensation of the Mass now follows:

> Then the deacon should place incense in the thurible, and should say before to the priest, *Bless*. And the priest should say: *O Lord. May this incense be blessed by him, in whose honor it shall be burned, in the name of the Father*, etc. Then the deacon, handing over the thurible to him, should kiss his hand; and the priest himself should cense the middle of the altar, and each side of the altar: first on the right, secondly on the left side, and for a while in the middle. Then the priest himself should be censed by the deacon, and afterward the priest should kiss the text [i.e., the Gospel book] in the custody of the subdeacon.[80]

This particular incensation Pope Innocent III sees as representing Christ's prayers for the Church.[81] In the seventeenth century, the Barnabite liturgist Father Bartolommeo Gavanti (+1638) was to integrate this explanation into the schema of the Incarnation-focused interpretation of the early portion of the Mass by proposing that this incensation represents the prayers that Christ offered for us as an unborn child in the womb of the Blessed Virgin Mary.[82] As for the vessels used for this and every incensation, Durandus likens the thurible to the heart of man; the fire by which it is lit, to the fervor of devotion; and the smoking clouds of incense, to man's prayers carried to God.[83] The incense boat is seen as denoting "that by prayer, which the incense signifies, we should be diligent to navigate from the great and broad sea of this world to the celestial fatherland".[84] Amalarius explains the kissing of the Gospel book as representing the reconciliation willed by God between the Jews and the Gentiles—a reminder that "we should love those who had been put asunder from us."[85] Insofar as the altar symbolizes the altar of the Temple of Jerusalem, the leaving of the Gospel book on the altar until it is taken up for the readings is explained as symbolizing that the Gospel came forth from Jerusalem, as prophesied

---

[79] Innocent III, *De sacro altaris mysterio*, bk. 2, chap. 45, PL 217, col. 825.

[80] Martène, *De antiquis ecclesiae ritibus*, bk. 1, chap. 4, art. 12, *ordo* 35, 1:239.

[81] Innocent III, *De sacro altaris mysterio*, bk. 2, chap. 16, PL 217, col. 807.

[82] Bartolommeo Gavanti, *Thesaurus sacrorum rituum* (1628), in Bartolommeo Gavanti and Cajetan Merati, *Thesaurus sacrorum rituum* (Rome: Typographia Vaticana, 1736–1738), 1:722.

[83] Durandus, *Rationale* (CCCM 140), bk. 4, chap. 8, no. 3, p. 286.

[84] Ibid.

[85] Amalarius of Metz, *Liber officialis*, bk. 3, chap. 5, no. 30, in Hanssens, *Amalarii episcopi: Opera liturgica omnia*, 2:281.

by Isaiah (Is 2:3): "The law has come forth ... and the word of the Lord from Jerusalem."[86]

After this incensation, the celebrant and the assisting deacon and subdeacon take their places at the right side of the altar, where the celebrant now repeats the entire Introit begun earlier by the choir. During the Glory Be to the Father at the end of the Introit, the priest and the other ministers return in procession to the center of the altar: "first the two torchbearers walking together, then the thurifers, the subdeacon behind, then the deacon, after him the priest".[87] Although, inexplicably, the various texts of the Sarum Missal do not expressly state when during the Mass the *Kyrie* is sung, a late fourteenth-century instruction for choir rectors found in both the Sarum Customary and the Sarum Consuetudinary implies that the *Kyrie* is chanted at this point, after the final repetition of the Introit and just before the *Gloria*.[88] Moreover, the *Kyrie* always precedes the *Gloria* in other medieval Roman Rite texts. In keeping with the schema that likens the first part of the Mass to the first coming of Christ, Pope Innocent III interprets the *Kyrie* as a response to the advent of the Messiah, when the fullness of time had come, the time spoken of by the Psalmist: "Thou shalt arise and have mercy on Sion; for it is time to have mercy on it" (Ps 101:14). In chanting the *Kyrie*, the choir is pleading, in the words of Isaiah, "O Lord, have mercy on us; for we have waited for thee" (33:2). With the threefold repetition of each of the three verses of the *Kyrie*, thus asking for mercy nine times, the *Kyrie* can be seen as a plea for forgiveness of nine forms of sin (original, mortal, and venial sins; sins of thought, word, and deed; sins of frailty, ignorance, and malice). The three verses each repeated thrice also remind us that in sinning we sin against all three Persons of the Blessed Trinity.[89]

Throughout medieval Europe, the chanting of the *Kyrie* was embellished with the addition of expansive verses to each of the nine original invocations, a transformation of the text known as troping that first arose in the ninth century and became commonplace thereafter. Over 150 such troped renderings of the *Kyrie* are known to have been composed.[90] The following example (a variant of the *Lux et origo* troped *Kyrie* from Rome), found in numerous editions of the Sarum Missal, was assigned in the Sarum liturgy to feasts of the holy Cross:

> *O Light and Origin of the supreme light, God, have mercy.*
> *At whose command all things ever exist, have mercy.*
> *You who alone are able to have mercy, have mercy on us.*

---

[86] Ibid., no. 31.

[87] Martène, *De antiquis ecclesiae ritibus*, bk. 1, chap. 4, art. 12, *ordo* 35, 1:239.

[88] Frere, *Use of Sarum*, 1:38.

[89] Innocent III, *De sacro altaris mysterio*, bk. 2, chap. 19, PL 217, col. 809.

[90] Jungmann, *Mass of the Roman Rite*, 1:344.

Redeemer of men and their salvation, graciously have mercy on us.

By the Cross you have redeemed us from eternal death; we beseech you, have mercy.

You who are the Word of the Father, Source of goodness, Light of truth, have mercy.

O Paraclete, Holy Spirit, God, have mercy on us.

Our Medicine and Mercy, have mercy.

O Trinity and holy Unity, have mercy on us always.[91]

The priest now intones the *Gloria:* "*Glory to God in the highest.*"[92] This hymn, beginning as it does with the words sung by the angels at the birth of Christ (Lk 2:14), expresses the joy of men and angels wrought by Christ's birth, joy that the Good Shepherd has come to seek out the lost sheep.[93] The *Gloria* also manifests that he who is venerated in Heaven by the angels is venerated on earth by men.[94] It is likewise an expression of hope on the part of the Church.[95] Like the *Kyrie,* the *Gloria* from the ninth century onward was sometimes embellished with troping phrases inserted after certain verses;[96] one particularly widespread version of the troped *Gloria,* assigned to Marian feast days in the Sarum Rite and elsewhere, utilized insertions that added a Marian theme to the hymn.[97]

After beginning the *Gloria,* the celebrant returns to the right side with the other ministers following him.[98] This standing at the right side of the altar by the celebrant in the early part of the Mass, up to the reading of the Epistle, was seen as representative of Christ coming first to the Jews before the pagan Gentiles.[99]

The recitation of the *Collect* for the Mass of the day follows: "Having made the sign of the cross on his face, the priest should turn himself to the people, and having raised his arms a little, and with joined hands, he should say in this manner: *The Lord be with you.* And the choir should answer under the same tone. And again he should return to the altar, and should say in this manner: *Let us pray . . .* Then is said the prayer."[100] Durandus explains that the opening prayer of the Mass is called the Collect because in this prayer the priest, who acts as an ambassador to God on behalf of the people, "collects and encloses into one" the petitions of all the faithful so as to present

---

[91] Text in Francis H. Dickinson, ed., *Missale ad usum insignis et praeclarae ecclesiae Sarum* (Burntisland, Scotland: E. Prelo de Pitsligo, 1861–1883), cols. 931*–932*.

[92] Martène, *De antiquis ecclesiae ritibus,* bk. 1, chap. 4, art. 12, *ordo* 35, 1:240.

[93] Innocent III, *De sacro altaris mysterio,* bk. 2, chap. 20, PL 217, col. 810.

[94] Durandus, *Rationale* (CCCM 140), bk. 4, chap. 13, no. 3, p. 299.

[95] Ibid.

[96] Jungmann, *Mass of the Roman Rite,* 1:359.

[97] Dickinson, *Missale ad usum . . . Sarum,* cols. 585–586.

[98] Martène, *De antiquis ecclesiae ritibus,* bk. 1, chap. 4, art. 12, *ordo* 35, 1:240.

[99] Durandus, *Rationale* (CCCM 140), bk. 4, chap. 11, no. 2, p. 292.

[100] Martène, *De antiquis ecclesiae ritibus,* bk. 1, chap. 4, art. 12, *ordo* 35, 1:240.

them to God.[101] Evoking an image from the Book of Revelation, Pope Innocent III likens the Collect of the Mass to the sweet cloud of incense, offered by an angel, that ascends in the sight of God (Rev 8:3–4). Addressed usually to the Father, the Collect customarily ends with the formula "*Through our Lord Jesus Christ*", in accordance with Christ's promise that the Father will give us whatever we ask of him in Christ's name (Jn 15:16).[102] In keeping with the ancient tradition of reverence for the holy name of Jesus, Durandus in his diocesan *Instructions* directs the priest to bow his head whenever during the Mass the name of Jesus, or the name of Mary, is spoken.[103]

Pope Innocent III explains the priest's raising and extending of his hands for the recitation of the Collect as paralleling Moses' prayer for the Israelites in their battle with Amalec,[104] as recounted in the Book of Exodus (Ex 17:10–13):

> Josue did as Moses had spoken, and he fought against Amalec; but Moses, and Aaron, and Hur went up upon the top of the hill. And when Moses lifted up his hands, Israel overcame; but if he let them down a little, Amalec overcame ... and Aaron and Hur stayed up his hands on both sides. And it came to pass that his hands were not weary until sunset. And Josue put Amalec and his people to flight, by the edge of the sword.

Seeing this raising of Moses' hands in prayer as a prefiguration of Christ's extension of his hands on the Cross, Pope Innocent III fully develops the symbolism of this priestly posture:

> By reason of this, therefore, the priest extends his hands in the Mass when he prays. For also Christ, when he expanded his hands on the Cross, prayed for his persecutors, and said [Lk 23:34], "Father, forgive them, for they know not what they do", morally instructing that Christ is always prepared to receive penitents, according to what he promised [Jn 6:37]: "And him that cometh to me, I will not cast out." But when the true Moses—that is, Christ—elevates his hands, that is, extends his help and support, Israel—that is, the Church—conquers. For [Rom 8:31], "If God be for us, who is against us?" ... And thus with Josue the leader—that is, Christ the Leader—Israel puts Amalec and his people to flight—that is, the Church overcomes the devil and his host of demons in the face of the sword—that is, by the power of prayer. For the Word of God is indeed a sword [cf. Eph 6:17; Heb 4:12].[105]

---

[101] Durandus, *Rationale* (CCCM 140), bk. 4, chap. 15, no. 13, p. 315.

[102] Innocent III, *De sacro altaris mysterio*, bk. 2, chap. 26, PL 217, col. 813.

[103] Berthelé, "Instructions et constitutions de Guillaume Durand", 59, 79.

[104] Innocent III, *De sacro altaris mysterio*, bk. 2, chap. 28, PL 217, col. 815.

[105] Ibid.

Applying the Psalmist's words *"Let my prayer be directed as incense in thy sight; the lifting up of my hands, as evening sacrifice"* (Ps 140:2) to the lifting of Christ's hands on the Cross, Durandus repeats Pope Innocent's interpretation likening the priest's raising of his hands for the Collect to Christ on the Cross and the prayer of Moses against Amalec. But he also compares this sacerdotal action to Solomon's raising of his hands before the altar of the Lord, in the sight of the assembly of Israel, to pray for the people (3 Kings 8:22), and to Christ lifting his hands to bless the Apostles as he ascended to Heaven (Lk 24:50–51).[106]

The Liturgy of the Word: The Epistle, the Gradual, the *Alleluia*, the Sequence, the Gospel, and the Creed

The reading of the Epistle signifies the preaching of Saint John the Baptist in preparation for the Lord's preaching, which is represented by the Gospel.[107] Hence the Epistle precedes the Gospel just as the preaching of John the Baptist preceded the preaching of Christ; the Epistle likewise signifies the Old Testament Law and the prophets that preceded the coming of the Lord.[108] The Epistle is read on the right side of the church, the side symbolizing the Jews, because Christ came first to the people of Israel.[109] The *Gradual* that follows the Epistle is the medieval equivalent of the responsorial psalm in the *Novus ordo* Mass of Pope Paul VI, but it consists of just two scriptural verses, usually from the Psalms; in some instances, other biblical passages or even nonscriptural texts are utilized.[110] The first verse is identified as the Gradual itself, whereas the second is considered to be the Gradual verse.[111] It is immediately followed by the pre-Gospel *Alleluia*—the singing of the word *Alleluia* with a verse, usually but not always scriptural.[112] According to Durandus, the singing of the Gradual after the Epistle signifies that after hearing the Word of God we should respond by acting upon it.[113] Again, the Gradual itself signifies the conversion of the Jews; the Gradual verse, the conversion of the Gentiles; the *Alleluia* that follows, the joy of both peoples in their common faith, with the Sequence before the Gospel serving as a song of victory.[114] The *Alleluia* expresses angelic joy, "the joy of angels and men rejoicing in eternal felicity", that joy which "eye hath not seen, nor ear heard" (1 Cor 2:9).[115] The Tract, which takes the place of the *Alleluia* during the penitential season of Lent, consisting of a prolonged series of psalm verses, up to as much as an entire psalm,[116] represents the

---

[106] Durandus, *Rationale* (CCCM 140), bk. 4, chap. 15, no. 18, p. 318.
[107] Sicard of Cremona, *Mitrale*, bk. 3, chap. 3, PL 213, col. 103; also bk. 3, chap. 9, col. 146.
[108] Durandus, *Rationale* (CCCM 140), bk. 4, chap. 16, no. 3, p. 319.
[109] Ibid., no. 2.
[110] Adrian Fortescue, "Gradual", in *Catholic Encyclopedia* (1907–1912) 6:715–716.
[111] Jungmann, *Mass of the Roman Rite*, 1:427.
[112] Ibid., 429, 434; Fortescue, "Gradual", 716.
[113] Durandus, *Rationale* (CCCM 140), bk. 4, chap. 19, no. 1, p. 326.
[114] Ibid.
[115] Ibid., chap. 20, nos. 1–3, pp. 330–331.
[116] Jungmann, *Mass of the Roman Rite*, 1:430, 434.

hardships and sorrows of this present life, in likeness to the prolonged tribulation of the Israelites suffering under the Babylonian captivity, sitting beside the rivers of Babylon and weeping (Ps 136:1–2), a captivity that is a figure of captivity under the devil.[117]

The 1489 Sarum Missal lacks detailed rubrics regarding the Epistle, the Gradual, and the *Alleluia*, as well as the Gospel, but ample instructions are provided for these in a supplementary liturgical book of the Sarum Rite, the Sarum Customary of the late fourteenth century. As the priest begins the Collect (or the last Collect if more than one is said), the subdeacon advances through the middle of the choir to enter the pulpit. While he reads the Epistle, two choirboys in surplices go to the choir step, where they bow to the altar. After the subdeacon completes the Epistle, the choirboys enter the pulpit to begin the chanting of the Gradual together with its verse. During the Gradual, two clerics of the choir, having vested in silk copes, should proceed through the middle of the choir toward the pulpit. Upon completing the Gradual verse, the two choirboys begin again the Gradual itself, which is now sung through to its end by the choir. Exiting the pulpit, the choirboys go again to the choir step, bowing as before. The two older choristers now sing from the pulpit the *Alleluia*, after which they likewise go to the choir step and bow there.[118]

To illustrate the medieval Gradual and *Alleluia* verse, we again quote from the late medieval Mass of the Immaculate Conception of Leonard de Nogarolis as it appears in the 1477 *Missal according to the Use of the Roman Curia*. As with the Introit from this Mass, both the Gradual (*Qualis est dilecta*) and the *Alleluia* verse (*Veni, Regina nostra*) are adapted from the Song of Solomon (5:9–10; 5:1):

> *Tell, what manner of one is our most dearly beloved, what manner of one is the Mother of the Lord, what manner of one and how great should she be, the sister and spouse of Christ? Verse: Our beloved is immaculate, resplendent as the rising dawn.*
>
> *Alleluia. Verse: Come, our Queen; come, O Lady, into the garden of fragrance, aromatic above all others.*[119]

In the Sarum liturgy, as in much of northern Europe, Sequences were used extensively, being sung between the *Alleluia* and the Gospel. In content, each Sequence (also known as a Prose) constituted a hymnlike, poetic exposition of the subject of a particular feast or votive Mass. Durandus describes the Sequence as "a canticle of exultation", manifesting that the saints shall receive "a twofold robe of glory", the twofold garment of body and soul both glorified.[120] The corpus of

---

[117] Durandus, *Rationale* (CCCM 140), bk. 4, chap. 21, nos. 1, 5–6, pp. 334–336.

[118] Frere, *Use of Sarum*, 1:68–71.

[119] *Missale secundum consuetudinem Curie Romane* (1477), fol. 157v.

[120] Durandus, *Rationale* (CCCM 140), bk. 4, chap. 22, no. ·1, p. 337.

medieval Sequences is vast, with some missals providing over seventy for various occasions;[121] four such texts are still used in the Roman liturgy (*Victimae paschali*, for Easter Sunday and its octave; *Veni Creator Spiritus*, for Pentecost Sunday; *Lauda Sion*, for Corpus Christi; *Stabat Mater*, for the memorial of Our Lady of Sorrows). In our discussion of the Christmas liturgy, we will be presenting the complete text of a Sequence for Christmas midnight Mass. Here we give the opening lines of a Sequence for the First Sunday after Easter from the 1498 missal of Saragossa, Spain:

> *Christ has risen with triumph;*
> *now from the Lamb is made the Lion,*
> *in solemn victory.*
> *By his death, he conquered death;*
> *he opened the bolt of its gate*
> *by the grace of his death.*
> *Here is the Lamb who hung upon the Cross*
> *and redeemed the entire flock of sheep.*[122]

The Sarum Customary states that at Masses celebrated by the bishop, on days when there is a Sequence, all the ministers in the choir, excluding the deacon and subdeacon who assist the bishop, come forward to sing the Sequence.[123]

In the Sarum Rite as elsewhere, the Gospel is read on the left side of the altar,[124] which is seen by Durandus as symbolizing Christ's declaration that he came to call not the just but sinners (Mt 9:13).[125] To understand the reasoning underlying the mystical interpretation of the two sides of the altar, it is necessary to recall again Christ's account of the Last Judgment in the Gospel of Saint Matthew (Mt 25:31–46): the just are placed to the right of Christ's judgment seat, while the wicked are placed to the left. Hence the Gospel is on the "sinners' side" of the altar (the left), for Christ proclaimed the Gospel for the conversion of sinners. The Sarum Customary's highly detailed rubrics for the reading of the Gospel follow:

> And while the *Alleluia*, the Sequence, or the Tract is sung, the deacon, before he approaches for pronouncing the Gospel, should cense the middle of the altar only.... Then he takes the text [the Gospel book], and humbling himself to the priest standing before the altar, his face turned toward the south thus, saying without a sign, *Graciously*

---

[121] Jungmann, *Mass of the Roman Rite*, 1:437.

[122] *Missale secundum morem ecclesie Cesaraugustane* (Saragossa: Paul Hurus, 1498), temporal, fol. 186r.

[123] Frere, *Use of Sarum*, 1:74.

[124] 1489 Sarum Missal, in Martène, *De antiquis ecclesiae ritibus*, bk. 1, chap. 4, art. 12, *ordo* 35, 1:240.

[125] Durandus, *Rationale* (CCCM 140), bk. 4, chap. 23, no. 1, p. 339.

grant, O Lord, to bless, the priest responding, *May the Lord be in your heart and on your lips for pronouncing the holy Gospel of God, in the name of the Father, and of the Son, and of the Holy Spirit. [Amen.]* And thus the deacon proceeds through the middle of the choir, solemnly carrying the text itself upon his left hand. He approaches the pulpit, with the thurifer and candle bearers preceding.... And if the feast shall have been a duplex feast, the cross should precede, which shall be to the right in reading the Gospel, the face of the crucifix being turned toward him reading.... And when [the deacon] shall have come to the place of reading, the subdeacon takes the very text, and while the Gospel is read, he should hold the text, to the left of the deacon, nearly opposite him, the candle bearers assisting the deacon, one to the right, the other to the left, turned toward him; the thurifer should stand behind the deacon, turned toward him. And always the Gospel at Mass should be read facing north.... But when [the deacon] shall have begun the Gospel, after *The Lord be with you,* he should make the sign of the cross upon the book, then on his forehead and afterward on his chest with his thumb.... The Gospel having been read, the book should be kissed, and the subdeacon approaching should offer [the deacon] the text to be kissed to his right. Also, in returning the text, the deacon carries it before his own chest to the altar.[126]

In the above rubrics, the Gospel book is taken from the altar, which is seen to signify the Gospel going forth from Jerusalem.[127] Meanwhile, incense is prepared for the censing of the Gospel book; the symbolism of the thurible as representing the human heart burning with fervor[128] is beautifully utilized in a prayer that Durandus provides in his book of diocesan instructions (c. 1294) for the celebrant to say when he adds incense to the thurible prior to the Gospel: "*May the Lord kindle our hearts and bodies with the fragrance of heavenly inspiration for hearing and accomplishing the precepts of his Gospel.*" [129]

The deacon's reception of a blessing before going to read the Gospel signifies Christ's sending forth of his Apostles to preach the Gospel.[130] The ascent of the deacon into the ambo (the lectern for the Gospel) represents Christ's ascending the mount to preach the Sermon on the Mount (Mt 5:1–2), as well as Moses' ascent of Mount Sinai to receive the two tablets of the Ten Commandments (Ex 24:1–2, 9, 12–15).[131] The two candles carried before the deacon as he goes to the ambo to read the Gospel represent the Mosaic Law and the prophets

---

[126] Frere, *Use of Sarum,* 1:72–74.

[127] Innocent III, *De sacro altaris mysterio,* bk. 2, chap. 39, PL 217, col. 822.

[128] Durandus, *Rationale* (CCCM 140), bk. 4, chap. 8, no. 3, p. 286.

[129] Durandus, *Instructions,* in Berthelé, "Instructions et constitutions de Guillaume Durand", 62.

[130] Sicard of Cremona, *Mitrale,* bk. 3, chap. 4, PL 213, col. 106.

[131] Ibid.

of the Old Testament, the mysteries of which are illuminated and understood by the light of the Gospel.[132] The carrying of the processional cross before the deacon as he goes to read the Gospel is explained by Durandus as signifying that Christ Crucified ought to be preached from the pulpit and that those preaching the Gospel ought to follow Christ Crucified, in accordance with Christ's words to Saint Peter, "Follow me" (Jn 21:19); it is also a reminder that he who looks upon Christ on the Cross is by faith healed of the ancient serpent's bite.[133]

For the deacon's signing of his forehead, lips, and heart with the sign of the cross before reading the Gospel, Pope Innocent III proposes that the deacon pray silently to himself, "*I am not ashamed of the Cross of Christ, but I believe in the heart what I preach with the mouth.*"[134] Sicard of Cremona observes that the first cross is made upon the forehead, "the seat of modesty and shame", to testify that we are not ashamed of Christ Crucified.[135] Durandus explains the second cross, made upon the lips, as signifying that "our speech ought to be from the words of the Gospel"; the third cross, made upon the heart, symbolizes that "the words of the Gospel ought to strike us in the heart and mind."[136] Durandus adds that this triple signing, performed by all in attendance as well as the deacon, protects the listeners with the Cross, that they may hear the Gospel unimpeded by the devil.[137] The deacon's incensation, signing with the cross, and kissing of the Gospel book Sicard of Cremona sees as a manifestation of the Gospel book's dignity as "the Book of God ... the Book of the Crucified".[138] All stand for the Gospel, signaling a readiness to do battle for the Christian faith, and the Gospel's directing of our minds upward to the love of heavenly things.[139] In the Sarum Rite, following the Gospel, and after the beginning of the Creed, the Gospel book is carried to the celebrating priest to be kissed by him.[140]

The recitation of the Nicene Creed after the Gospel (following the homily) expresses the Church's faith in what the Gospel proclaims.[141] In late medieval editions of the Sarum Missal, the rubrics for the Creed direct the choir to bow toward the altar during the words "*and was made incarnate by the Holy Spirit from the Virgin Mary, and was made man; for us also he was crucified under Pontius Pilate*" and at the end, during the concluding words, "*and the life of the world to come. Amen.*"[142]

---

[132] Ibid., col. 107.

[133] Durandus, *Rationale* (CCCM 140), bk. 4, chap. 24, no. 16, p. 348.

[134] Innocent III, *De sacro altaris mysterio*, bk. 2, chap. 43, PL 217, col. 824.

[135] Sicard of Cremona, *Mitrale*, bk. 3, chap. 4, PL 213, col. 109.

[136] Durandus, *Rationale* (CCCM 140), bk. 4, chap. 24, no. 28, p. 353.

[137] Ibid.

[138] Sicard of Cremona, *Mitrale*, bk. 3, chap. 4, PL 213, col. 110.

[139] Durandus, *Rationale* (CCCM 140), bk. 4, chap. 24, no. 23, p. 351.

[140] Dickinson, *Missale ad usum ... Sarum*, col. 593.

[141] Durandus, *Rationale* (CCCM 140), bk. 4, chap. 25, no. 1, pp. 360–361.

[142] Dickinson, *Missale ad usum ... Sarum*, cols. 587, 591–592.

Elsewhere the practice was for all to kneel during the words "*and was made incarnate by the Holy Spirit from the Virgin Mary, and was made man*", as specified in the 1488 *Caeremoniale Romanum* of the papal master of ceremonies Patrizio Piccolomini.[143] The observance of an act of reverence to mark the Creed's words proclaiming the Incarnation, a custom traceable to the eleventh century,[144] is explained by Sicard of Cremona as an expression of our adoration of Christ for having become man and for having suffered crucifixion for us.[145] In the thirteenth-century statutes of the Carthusian Order, the monks are instructed to prostrate themselves and kiss the ground during the words "*and was made man*", while the celebrating priest (who remains standing) kisses the altar, and the assisting deacon kneels.[146]

The Offertory

The Offertory begins with the singing of an antiphon, likewise named the Offertory, a verse specific to the particular liturgical day[147] and often but not always of scriptural origin.[148] Durandus observes that just as the reading of the Gospel is an expression of the preaching of Christ, and the recitation of the Creed is an expression of faith, so too the Offertory portion of the Mass is an expression of the praise of God. Hence the Offertory chant constitutes a "sacrifice of praise" in the spirit of the Psalmist's words (Ps 26:6), "I have offered up in his tabernacle a sacrifice of jubilation; I will sing, and recite a psalm to the Lord."[149] Durandus also cites from the Old Testament the singing that accompanied the offering of holocausts on the occasion of the purification and restoration of the Temple of Solomon under King Ezechias (2 Par 29:27).[150] To illustrate the Offertory chant, we provide the following, *Ortus conclusus*, rich with the imagery of the Song of Solomon, from the aforementioned late medieval Mass of the Immaculate Conception composed by Leonard de Nogarolis, taken here from the 1477 *Missal according to the Use of the Roman Curia*: "*You, O Mary, are an enclosed garden, a sealed fountain, a Paradise; your hands dripped myrrh, and your effusions have made the heavens bedewed with sweetness, when you were fashioned by the hand of the Lord, O Mother of so great a God. Alleluia.*"[151]

---

[143] Text in Marc Dykmans, S.J., ed., *L'oeuvre de Patrizi Piccolomini, ou Le cérémonial papal de la première Renaissance*, vol. 2, ST 294 (Vatican City: Biblioteca Apostolica Vaticana, 1982), 266, 306.

[144] Jungmann, *Mass of the Roman Rite*, 1:465–466, footnote.

[145] Sicard of Cremona, *Mitrale*, bk. 3, chap. 4, PL 213, col. 113.

[146] "Of the Office of the Priest, the Deacon, and the Subdeacon", from the statutes of the Carthusian Order, thirteenth century, in Martène, *De antiquis ecclesiae ritibus*, bk. 1, chap. 4, art. 12, *ordo* 25, 1:227.

[147] Dickinson, *Missale ad usum ... Sarum*, col. 593.

[148] Adrian Fortescue, "Offertory", in *Catholic Encyclopedia* (1907–1912), 11:218.

[149] Durandus, *Rationale* (CCCM 140), bk. 4, chap. 27, no. 2, p. 374; see also Innocent III, *De sacro altaris mysterio*, bk. 2, chap. 53, PL 217, col. 831.

[150] Durandus, *Rationale* (CCCM 140), bk. 4, chap. 27, no. 2, p. 375.

[151] *Missale secundum consuetudinem Curie Romane* (1477), fol. 157v.

Upon the conclusion of the Offertory chant, the Offertory prayers that followed it would customarily be said in silence—a silence that Pope Innocent III interprets as symbolic of Christ's withdrawal "into a country near the desert, unto a city that is called Ephrem" as the chief priests and Pharisees were plotting to put him to death (Jn 11:47–54).[152] The Sarum Offertory rite closely resembles that of the Dominican Order's medieval liturgical rite, both having a "single oblation" of the host and chalice together instead of the separate offerings of the host and the chalice in the Roman Rite.[153] The Sarum text provides a prayer for the conjoined offering of the host and chalice similar to that for the offering of the host in the Roman Rite[154] (traceable to the eleventh century)[155] but differing in several aspects; rather than being addressed to the Father alone as in the Roman Rite, the Sarum prayer is addressed to the Trinity (exhibiting similarities with another of the Roman Rite's prayers said near the end of the Offertory, also addressed to the Trinity):[156]

> The deacon should present the chalice with the paten and the sacrifice to the priest and should kiss his hand both times. [The priest], however, receiving the chalice from him, should carefully place it in its due place upon the middle of the altar, and having momentarily bowed, he should elevate the chalice with both hands, offering the sacrifice to the Lord, saying this prayer:
>
> Prayer: *Accept, O Holy Trinity, this oblation, which I, an unworthy sinner, offer in honor of you, of Blessed Mary, and of all your saints, for my sins and offenses, and for the salvation of the living and the repose of all the dead. In the name of the Father, and of the Son, and of the Holy Spirit. May this new sacrifice be acceptable to almighty God.*[157]

In the above text, there is specified a kiss of the celebrant's hands when the deacon presents to him the unconsecrated host and chalice. This gesture needs to be understood properly, not as some exaggerated act of deference to the celebrant but rather in the manner explained by Durandus—this kiss is a sign of peace, designating that "every service

---

[152] Innocent III, *De sacro altaris mysterio*, bk. 2, chap. 54, PL 217, col. 831.

[153] For the relevant Dominican rubrics in the *Missale minorum altarium*, a liturgical text of the Dominican Order dating from 1256, see Francis Guerrini, O.P., ed., *Ordinarium juxta ritum sacri ordinis Fratrum Praedicatorum*, with the authorization of Louis Theissling, O.P. (Rome: Collegium Angelicum, 1921), 239. For an explanation of the Dominican Offertory rubrics, see William Bonniwell, O.P., *A History of the Dominican Liturgy* (New York: Joseph Wagner, 1944), 185–187.

[154] 1474 *Missale Romanum*, in Robert Lippe, ed., *Missale Romanum: Mediolani, 1474*, vol. 1, *Text*, HBS 17 (London: Henry Bradshaw Society, 1899), 200.

[155] Righetti, *Manuale di storia liturgica*, 3:269, footnote.

[156] *Suscipe sancta Trinitas . . . ob memoriam passionis . . .*, from the 1474 *Missale Romanum*, in Lippe, *Missale Romanum*, 1:201.

[157] Martène, *De antiquis ecclesiae ritibus*, bk. 1, chap. 4, art. 12, *ordo 35*, 1:240.

and every reverence exhibited to God ought to proceed from the fervor of charity and love."[158]

In the Sarum Rite, the infusion of wine and water into the chalice takes place ahead of the Offertory, immediately before the Gospel, when it is carried out by the deacon; prior to infusing the water, he asks the celebrant to bless it, and the latter, in blessing the water, says, "*May it be blessed by him, from whose side went out blood and water. In the name of the Father, and of the Son, and of the Holy Spirit. Amen.*"[159] By contrast, in the Roman Rite the infusion of wine and water into the chalice takes place during the Offertory, immediately before the offering of the chalice, as specified in the 1488 *Caeremoniale Romanum* of Piccolomini.[160] Durandus explains the adding of a bit of water to the wine in the chalice as symbolizing the union of Christ (represented by the unconsecrated wine) with the faithful (represented by the water). The commingling of the wine and the water in the chalice represents the indissolubility of this union between Christ and his people. Durandus also sees the unconsecrated wine as representing the blood of Christ (which it will actually become at the consecration later in the Mass), which is inseparable from the salvation of souls (represented by the water) that the blood of Christ has wrought. Finally, Durandus likens the wine and water to the divine nature and the human nature of Christ respectively, with their commingling in the chalice symbolizing the union of Christ's two natures in one Person.[161]

Durandus draws these comparisons from a fundamental view of the wine and water as imaging the blood and water from the side of Christ on the Cross,[162] an analogy explicitly evoked in the above-cited Sarum Rite blessing of the water. In the early fifteenth-century missal of Toul, France, this symbolism is likewise expressed in the prayer accompanying the infusion of the water into the wine within the chalice: "*From the side of Jesus Christ went out blood and water together; and in his honor may this mingling be made holy and immaculate, in the name of the Father, and of the Son, and of the Holy Spirit.*"[163]

Following the conjoined offering of the host and chalice, the Sarum text specifies the subsequent arrangement and disposition of the *oblata* and the sacred vessels and cloths upon the altar: "The prayer having been said, [the celebrant] should put back the chalice, and cover it with the corporals, and carefully place the bread upon the corporals before the chalice, containing the wine and water, and should kiss the paten, and put it back upon the altar to the right, under the corporals,

---

[158] Durandus, *Rationale* (CCCM 140), bk. 4, chap. 30, no. 22, p. 388.

[159] Dickinson, *Missale ad usum . . . Sarum*, col. 587; Frere, *Use of Sarum*, 1:71.

[160] Dykmans, *Oeuvre de Patrizi Piccolomini*, 2:267–268, 308.

[161] Durandus, *Rationale* (CCCM 140), bk. 4, chap. 30, no. 19, pp. 386–387.

[162] Ibid., 387.

[163] Missal of Toul, France, c. 1409–1436, in Martène, *De antiquis ecclesiae ritibus*, bk. 1, chap. 4, art. 12, *ordo* 31, 1:234.

covering it a little." [164] The "corporals" mentioned here, consisting of the linen corporal itself, and the corporal for covering the chalice, known as the pall, were earlier brought to the altar by the deacon shortly before the Gospel. [165] The unfolding and spreading of the corporal on the altar and the placement of the pall, folded, upon the chalice, are interpreted within the particular context of the Mass as a re-presentation of the sacrifice of Calvary. Hence the two cloths are seen as symbolic of the burial cloths of Christ: the corporal spread upon the altar symbolizes the Lord's shroud, and the pall on the chalice represents the *sudarium* with which his head was wrapped. [166] This symbolism has ancient roots, stemming from a decision mentioned in an early sixth-century redaction of the *Liber pontificalis*, a book of papal biographies, which attributes it, perhaps erroneously, to Pope Saint Sylvester I (314–335): "He constituted that the sacrifice of the altar ought not to be celebrated on either silk or dyed cloth but only on earth-begotten linen, since the body of our Lord Jesus Christ was buried in a pure linen shroud." [167] This understanding of linen as the cloth found worthy to wrap the body of Christ in the tomb explains why in the medieval and Baroque liturgies we see the consecrated Host being placed on the linen corporal as if it were as fitting a material as gold or silver. [168]

The placing of the host or hosts between the chalice and the priest standing before the altar is understood as expressing Christ's role as the one Mediator between God and man (1 Tim 2:5), with the unconsecrated host (destined later in the Mass to become the real Body of Christ) here symbolizing Christ, placed between the priest, symbolizing the Father, and the chalice, containing in addition to the unconsecrated wine a drop of water, understood as representing the people. [169] The kissing of the paten at this point of the Mass is specific to the Sarum Rite. The partial concealment of the paten under the edge of the corporal and its subsequent removal from the altar by the deacon (who in turn entrusts it to the subdeacon at the beginning of the Preface) are intended to represent the fleeing and hiding of the Apostles during the Passion—during the offering of the sacrifice of Calvary (which the Mass re-presents)—the fleeing prophesied by Christ after the Last Supper: "All you shall be scandalized in me this night.

---

[164] Martène, *De antiquis ecclesiae ritibus*, bk. 1, chap. 4, art. 12, *ordo* 35, 1:240.

[165] Frere, *Use of Sarum*, 1:71.

[166] Innocent III, *De sacro altaris mysterio*, bk. 2, chap. 56, PL 217, col. 832; Durandus, *Rationale* (CCCM 140), bk. 4, chap. 29, no. 4, p. 379; see also Saint Thomas Aquinas, *Summa theologica*, pt. III, q. 83, art. 3, reply obj. 7, 2:2517.

[167] From the account of the life of Pope Saint Sylvester I in the *Liber pontificalis*; text in Louis Duchesne, ed., *Le Liber pontificalis: Texte, introduction et commentaire* (Paris: Ernest Thorin, 1886–1892), 1:171.

[168] See, for example, the 1502 Roman Rite *Ordo missae* of John Burckard, in Legg, *Tracts on the Mass*, 156.

[169] Durandus, *Rationale* (CCCM 140), bk. 4, chap. 30, no. 23, p. 389.

For it is written: I will strike the shepherd, and the sheep of the flock shall be dispersed" (Mt 26:31). Part of the paten is left exposed, symbolizing that neither the Blessed Virgin Mary nor the Apostle Saint John fled or hid from Christ on Calvary.[170]

The Offertory incensation now follows, as described in the Sarum text:

> He [the priest] should take the thurible from the deacon and should cense the oblation: namely thrice, besides making the sign of the cross, and round about, and from each side of the chalice and oblation; then he should place it [the thurible] between himself and the altar. And while he censes, he should say: *May my prayer be directed, O Lord, even as incense in the sight of your majesty.* Afterward the priest himself should be censed by the deacon alone; and the subdeacon should bring him the text [Gospel book] to be kissed; then the acolyte should cense the choir, beginning with the rectors of the choir.... The boy [acolyte] himself should bow to them, censing the clerics one at a time, the subdeacon following him with the text to be kissed by all.[171]

This incensation, according to Pope Innocent III and Durandus, represents the anointing of Christ's feet given by Mary, the sister of Martha, six days before the Pasch, with "a pound of ointment of right spikenard" so that "the house was filled with the odor of the ointment" (Jn 12:3).[172] Durandus likens the priest censing the altar to the angel in the Book of Revelation who stands near the altar of the sanctuary of Heaven with a golden thurible in his hand, the burning incense of which ascends before God (Rev 8:3–4). The priest censing the altar thereby resembles Christ, who, for us, on the altar of the Cross, offered to the Father his immaculate body, "filled with the fire of the Holy Spirit in sweetness of odor". The censer is swung crosswise over the host and chalice, "that both with the sign of the cross and the sacrifice of incense the wickedness of diabolic deception may be removed, and may flee". This crosswise swinging of the censer also serves to testify that the fragrant incense of the prayers of the saints is "propagated by the ardor of charity from the Passion of the Lord", whereas the circular swing of the thurible symbolizes the crown of glory to which the prayers of the saints rising to God the Father serve to advance us. The triple nature of the incensation signifies the three times that Saint Mary Magdalene brought ointment to anoint the body of Christ: in the house of Simon the Pharisee (Lk 7:37–50); in Bethany (Jn 12:3–8; Mt 26:6–13); and on Easter Sunday, going to the tomb of Christ

---

[170] Ibid., no. 29, p. 391.

[171] Martène, *De antiquis ecclesiae ritibus*, bk. 1, chap. 4, art. 12, ordo 35, 1:240.

[172] Innocent III, *De sacro altaris mysterio*, bk. 2, chap. 57, PL 217, col. 832; Durandus, *Rationale* (CCCM 140), bk. 4, chap. 31, no. 1, p. 395.

(Mk 16:1; Lk 23:56—24:1, 10).[173] Here again, as with the earlier in-censation of the altar, the thurible itself symbolizes the human heart: "The incense of devotion is to be burned in the thurible of the heart with the fire of charity, that it may send out the odor of sweetness, that namely both we and our oblation may be a good odor unto God [cf. 2 Cor 2:15]."[174]

The washing of the priest's hands during the Offertory is likened by Pope Innocent III to the washing of the hands and feet that in the Old Testament Aaron and his sons were required to carry out when they went into the Tabernacle of the Testimony and approached the altar to offer incense (Ex 30:18–20). Hence all the more should the celebrant of the sacrifice of the New Covenant cleanse his hands for the offering of the pure, holy, and immaculate Host of the Eucharist. Moreover, this exterior washing testifies that the priest preparing to consecrate the Eucharist should cleanse his conscience with the tears of penitence.[175] In the Sarum Rite this penitential symbolism is expressed in the prayer accompanying the ablution: "*Purify me, O Lord, from all uncleanness of my heart and body, that [being] pure I may be able to accomplish the holy work of the Lord.*"[176] The concluding rites and prayers of the Offertory follow:

> Then [the celebrant] should turn himself, and standing before the altar, with both his head and his body bowed, his hands joined, he should say the prayer:
>
> *In a spirit of humility, and with a contrite heart, may we be accepted by you, O Lord; and may our sacrifice be so rendered in your sight, that it may be accepted by you this day and be pleasing to you, O Lord my God.*
>
> And raising himself up, he should kiss the altar to the right of the oblation; and giving the blessing over the sacrifice, afterward he should sign himself, saying: *In the name of the Father, and of the Son*, etc.
>
> Then the priest should turn himself to the people and in a silent voice say:
>
> *Pray, brothers and sisters, for me, that my sacrifice and yours equally may be fitting to the Lord our God.*
>
> Response of the clergy privately:
>
> *May the grace of the Holy Spirit illuminate your heart and your lips, that the Lord may accept this sacrifice of praise from your hands worthily for our sins and offenses.*
>
> ... And having turned back to the altar, the priest should say the secret prayers.[177]

---

[173] Durandus, *Rationale* (CCCM 140), bk. 4, chap. 31, nos. 1–3, pp. 395–396.

[174] Ibid., no. 3, p. 396.

[175] Innocent III, *De sacro altaris mysterio*, bk. 2, chap. 55, PL 217, col. 831.

[176] Martène, *De antiquis ecclesiae ritibus*, bk. 1, chap. 4, art. 12, *ordo* 35, 1:240. In the Roman Rite, the ablution is accompanied by the recitation of Psalm 25:6–12; see the 1474 *Missale Romanum*, in Lippe, *Missale Romanum*, 1:201.

[177] Martène, *De antiquis ecclesiae ritibus*, bk. 1, chap. 4, art. 12, *ordo* 35, 1:240.

The bow of the priest before the altar here denotes Christ's humbling himself to become man and die for us on the Cross, as well as his humbling and lowering himself to wash the Apostles' feet at the Last Supper.[178] The prayer "*In a spirit of humility*" (*In spiritu humilitatis*) is a variant of that found in the Roman Missal,[179] an oration that dates from the ninth century[180] and is based upon Daniel 3:39–40: "In a contrite heart and humble spirit let us be accepted.... So let our sacrifice be made in thy sight this day, that it may please thee." The priest's invitation to the faithful, "*Pray, brothers and sisters*", is a variant of the *Orate fratres* of the Roman Missal,[181] traceable to the eighth century.[182] The response is different from that of the Roman Rite. The Sarum text's use of the phrase "brothers and sisters" (*fratres et sorores*) in place of the single word "brethren" (*fratres*) in the Roman Rite's *Orate fratres* demonstrates that the expression "brethren" was understood to embrace both men and women; the terms "brethren" and "brothers and sisters" were in this context interchangeable.

In the Mass rubrics of Durandus' *Instructions* for his diocese of Mende, the priest is enjoined while reciting a concluding Offertory prayer, "turned toward the altar ... standing before the middle of the altar", to direct his gaze toward a crucifix there;[183] in this rubric we see an early antecedent to the directions in the 1570 *Missale Romanum* instructing the celebrant at various points during the Mass to look upon the altar crucifix.[184]

The Sarum text provides for an altered Offertory rite at Requiem Masses. Hence, after washing his hands, the priest proceeds thus:

> Immediately the priest should begin with joined hands at the middle of the altar, turned toward the altar, saying: *We offer sacrifices and prayers to you, O Lord*. And the choir with singing should respond: *Accept them for those souls whose memorial we celebrate this day; make them, O Lord, pass from death to life*. And meanwhile the priest should say: *In a spirit of humility* ... Then immediately he should say, turned toward the people, in a silent voice: *Pray, brothers and sisters, for the faithful departed*. Response of the clergy with singing: *Eternal rest grant unto them, O Lord; and let perpetual light shine upon them, as you once promised to Abraham and to his offspring*.[185]

The recitation of the prayer known as the Secret, so named because it is recited silently, brings the Offertory to its conclusion. Like the

---

[178] Durandus, *Rationale* (CCCM 140), bk. 4, chap. 32, no. 1, p. 397.

[179] 1474 *Missale Romanum*, in Lippe, *Missale Romanum*, 1:200.

[180] Righetti, *Manuale di storia liturgica*, 3:271.

[181] 1474 *Missale Romanum*, in Lippe, *Missale Romanum*, 1:201.

[182] Jungmann, *Mass of the Roman Rite*, 2:82–85.

[183] Berthelé, "Instructions et constitutions de Guillaume Durand", 67.

[184] *Ritus servandus in celebratione missarum*, in Sodi and Triacca, *Missale Romanum: Editio princeps (1570)*, 9–15, 19 (new pagination).

[185] Martène, *De antiquis ecclesiae ritibus*, bk. 1, chap. 4, art. 12, *ordo* 35, 1:240.

Collect at the beginning of the Mass, the Secret is particular to the feast day or liturgical occasion for which the Mass is celebrated. On days with multiple commemorations (e.g., multiple saints' feasts) the Sarum Rite would allow up to seven Secrets to be recited conjointly.[186]

Entering the Holy of Holies: The Preface, the Roman Canon, and the Consecration

The Preface constitutes a summons to the faithful to prepare their minds reverently for the approaching consecration of the Eucharist as the priest prepares himself for the consecration.[187] It represents the assembling of men and angels to sing "the praises of the King".[188] The priest's words to the faithful, "*Sursum corda*" ("*Lift up your hearts*"), introducing the Preface, constitute an invitation for the people to accompany the priest in spirit as he mystically enters the Cenacle to celebrate the Eucharistic sacrifice instituted at the Last Supper.[189] This versicle also admonishes the people to make themselves attentive to heavenly things and to banish all earthly and bodily thoughts.[190] It also invites us to imitate the woman who anointed Christ's head on the eve of his Passion (Mk 14: 3) by "lifting our hearts over his head" to pour out the pure, precious nard of professing the divinity of Christ "with the ointment of Catholic confession".[191] While praying during the Preface that his own heart may be freed from earthly cares, the priest calls upon the faithful to give thanks for the grace of having one's heart lifted from worldly thoughts and up to God, saying, "*Let us give thanks to the Lord our God.*"[192] In the 1502 Mass *Ordo* of the papal master of ceremonies John Burckard, these latter words are accompanied by a rubric directing the priest to "bow his head to God", an instruction that appears eight times over the course of the Mass in the Burckard text,[193] visually manifesting that the priest facing the altar, facing east, is seen as facing God.

The main body of the Preface is a text that varies according to the particular liturgical day or occasion and is taken from a corpus of Preface texts contained in the missal—eleven are provided in the medieval Sarum Rite (for Christmas, Epiphany, Lent, Easter, the Ascension, Pentecost, the Holy Trinity, the Holy Cross, the Blessed Virgin Mary, Apostles and Evangelists, and daily Mass when no feast is observed).[194] The Preface culminates in the great hymn of praise, the *Sanctus*. The

---

[186] Ibid.

[187] Durandus, *Rationale* (CCCM 140), bk. 4, chap. 33, no. 3, p. 401.

[188] Ibid., no. 2.

[189] Amalarius of Metz, *Liber officialis*, bk. 3, chap. 21, no. 4, in Hanssens, *Amalarii episcopi: Opera liturgica omnia*, 2:324–325; Pseudo-Hildebert of Tours, *Liber de expositione missae*, PL 171, col. 1160; Sicard of Cremona, *Mitrale*, bk. 3, chap. 6, PL 213, col. 122.

[190] 1540 *Missale Romanum*, rubrics of the Ordinary of the Mass, in Lippe, *Missale Romanum*, 2:104.

[191] Sicard of Cremona, *Mitrale*, bk. 3, chap. 6, PL 213, col. 122.

[192] Amalarius of Metz, *Liber officialis*, bk. 3, chap. 21, no. 4, in Hanssens, *Amalarii episcopi: Opera liturgica omnia*, 2:325.

[193] Legg, *Tracts on the Mass*, 153; see also 152, 155, 156, 165, and 167.

[194] Dickinson, *Missale ad usum ... Sarum*, cols. 596–610.

first portion of the *Sanctus* is taken almost verbatim from the acclamation of the seraphim around the throne of God as recorded by Isaiah: "Holy, holy, holy, the Lord God of hosts, all the earth is full of his
glory" (Is 6:3). The beginning of the *Sanctus* also resembles the praise
offered by the four living creatures around the throne of the Lamb in
the Book of Revelation: "Holy, holy, holy, Lord God Almighty" (Rev
4:8). Amalarius of Metz explains the triple repetition of the word "holy"
as signifying the three Persons of the Trinity, with the singular form
of "holy" (in the Latin, *sanctus* rather than *sancti*) indicating the one
Godhead.[195] The second half of the *Sanctus* is a direct quotation of
the praises offered to Christ by those who welcomed him into Jerusalem on Palm Sunday and is, in fact, interpreted to represent this
occasion:[196] "Blessed is he that cometh in the name of the Lord:
Hosanna in the highest" (Mt 21:9). Here we see the conjoining of the
angels' praises in the first half of the *Sanctus* with the praises of men in
the second half, as noted by Durandus. In the angels' portion of the
Sanctus the mystery of the Trinity is acclaimed, while in mankind's
portion of the hymn, the mystery of the Incarnation, of Christ as true
God and true man, is acclaimed.[197] Hence, in the *Sanctus* Heaven is
wedded to earth in divine worship, as Durandus explains: "Whereupon rightly do we sing the canticles of the angels in the Church, for
we firmly believe the things of earth to be united to heavenly things
by this sacrifice; and therefore we cry out to be saved with them on
high." [198]

In the Sarum Rite text, immediately after the Preface is introduced
with the verse "*Lift up your hearts*", the deacon takes the paten and
entrusts it to the subdeacon, who wraps it and keeps it until after the
Canon.[199] This action serves the same symbolic purpose as the earlier
concealment of the paten under the corporal, representing the Apostles hiding themselves in fear during the Passion,[200] but it also represents the hiddenness of Christ's divinity during his life on earth.[201]

In the printed editions of the Sarum Missal, the priest is instructed
to raise his arms momentarily as he begins the *Sanctus*, then to join
his hands up to the words "*in the name of the Lord*", at which point he
is to make the sign of the cross across his face.[202] Durandus explains
this sign of the cross, accompanying the phrase "*Blessed is he who comes
in the name of the Lord*", as signifying that "by the Cross Christ has

[195] Amalarius of Metz, *Canonis missae interpretatio*, nos. 19–20, in John Michael Hanssens, ed., *Amalarii episcopi: Opera liturgica omnia*, vol. 1, ST 138 (Vatican City: Biblioteca
Apostolica Vaticana, 1948), 302.

[196] Sicard of Cremona, *Mitrale*, bk. 3, chap. 6, PL 213, col. 123.

[197] Durandus, *Rationale* (CCCM 140), bk. 4, chap. 34, no. 2, p. 410.

[198] Ibid.

[199] Martène, *De antiquis ecclesiae ritibus*, bk. 1, chap. 4, art. 12, *ordo* 35, 1:240.

[200] Durandus, *Rationale* (CCCM 140), bk. 4, chap. 30, no. 29, p. 391.

[201] Ibid., no. 30.

[202] Dickinson, *Missale ad usum ... Sarum*, col. 610.

triumphed and makes us triumph." [203] A rubric in the thirteenth-century Sarum Missal directs the priest during the *Sanctus* to kiss the crucifix,[204] evidently the image of the crucifix rendered within the missal itself, which customarily accompanied the *Te igitur*, the opening words of the Roman Canon following the *Sanctus*. These images we will later explain in regard to the Roman Canon. The *Sanctus* is another Mass text that was sometimes troped with special additions to the basic text; fifteen such renderings of the *Sanctus* are given in a late thirteenth-century manuscript of the Sarum Missal.[205]

Following the conclusion of the *Sanctus*, there is silence. The priest now begins the silent recitation of the Roman Canon (Eucharistic Prayer I in the *Novus ordo* of Pope Paul VI), a text at least as ancient as the fourth century,[206] in which the consecration will take place. As Florus of Lyons (+c. 860) explains:

> All din of words ceasing, the intention is directed to God alone, and with the devotion of hearts, with the prayers and desires of all united to him, the priest begins to bring forth the prayer by which the mystery of the Body and Blood of the Lord is consecrated. For thus it is proper that in that hour of such sacred and divine action, with the whole mind by the grace of God separated from earthly thoughts, and the Church with the priest and the priest with the Church in spiritual desire, he should enter into the celestial and eternal sanctuary of God.[207]

In the above text, Florus ends by alluding to the sanctuary of Heaven, which, as the Letter to the Hebrews explains, was prefigured by the Old Testament sanctuary (Heb 9:2–4): "For there was a tabernacle made the first, wherein were the candlesticks, and the table, and the setting forth of loaves, which is called the holy. And after the second veil, the tabernacle, which is called the holy of holies: having a golden censer, and the ark of the testament covered about on every part with gold." Noting that only the high priest could enter the Holy of Holies (Heb 9:7), the Letter to the Hebrews explains that "Christ, being come as high priest of the good things, by a greater and more perfect tabernacle not made with hand, . . . by his own blood, entered once into

---

[203] Durandus, *Rationale* (CCCM 140), bk. 4, chap. 34, no. 7, p. 412.

[204] Text in John Wickham Legg, ed., *The Sarum Missal, Edited from Three Early Manuscripts* (Oxford: Clarendon, 1916), 220.

[205] Ibid., 540–543.

[206] Excerpts from the Roman Canon appear in the *De sacramentis* of Saint Ambrose (bk. 4, chaps. 5, 6). See Anton Hänggi and Irmgard Pahl, eds., *Prex Eucharistica: Textus e variis liturgiis antiquioiribus selecti*, SF 12 (Fribourg, Switzerland: Editions Universitaires Fribourg, 1968), 421–422. The earliest complete text of the Roman Canon appears in the eighth-century *Hadrianum* redaction of the Gregorian Sacramentary of Rome: see Jean Deshusses, ed., *Le sacramentaire grégorien: Ses principales formes d'après les plus anciens manuscrits*, vol. 1, 2nd ed., SF 16 (Fribourg, Switzerland: Editions Universitaires Fribourg, 1979), nos. 5–16, pp. 87–91.

[207] Florus of Lyons, *De expositione missae*, no. 42, PL 119, col. 43.

the holies, having obtained eternal salvation" (Heb 9:11–12). The medieval liturgists saw the words and actions of the priest during the Roman Canon as re-presenting the sacrifice that the high priest's entry into the Holy of Holies prefigured and that Christ accomplished on Calvary and offered in the sanctuary of Heaven. Saint Ivo of Chartres (+1115), Hildebert of Tours (+1133), Sicard of Cremona, and Durandus all liken the priest's recitation of the Roman Canon to the Old Testament image of the entrance of the high priest into the Holy of Holies.[208]

The division of the ancient sanctuary of the Ark of the Covenant into two parts—that is, the outer Holy Place and the inner, more sacred Holy of Holies (Ex 26:31–33; Heb 9:2–4)—is applied by Durandus to the Mass to delineate the unique character of the Roman Canon as the "inner sanctum" of the Eucharistic liturgy: "Truly, long ago the Temple was divided in two parts, with the veil interposed. The first part was called the Holy, but the inner, the Holy of Holies. Whatever therefore in the office of the Mass is done before the Secret [i.e., the Roman Canon] is as it were in the first habitation; but what is done in the Secret is within the Holy of Holies."[209] This view of the unique and supremely sacred character of the Roman Canon serves to explain why in the Middle Ages the Canon was believed to possess a particular power and efficacy against the devil, as we shall later see in our presentation of medieval rites for protection from storms (chapter 22). A spirit of reverence for the sacredness of the Roman Canon also inspired vigilance regarding its faithful recitation, as evinced by the extra-large print used for the words of the Canon in some medieval missals, such as that of Vich, Spain (1496)[210]—a visible manifestation of a priest's duties in this regard.

The priest alone recites the Roman Canon, Durandus notes, in likeness to Christ, who at the outset of his Passion withdrew to pray alone in Gethsemane (Mt 26:36, 39, 42, 44).[211] The recitation of the Canon by the priest alone follows from his acting *in persona Christi*, as an *alter Christus*; thus, the priest acts alone in the Canon insomuch as Christ alone offered himself on the Cross and in the heavenly sanctuary, as was prefigured in the Old Covenant: when "one priest entered the Holy of Holies [cf. Heb 9:7], all the people stood outside, and he who entered alone the interior of the veil offered the sacrifice for the people standing outside" (Florus of Lyons).[212] It is within this context

---

[208] Saint Ivo of Chartres, *Sermon 5*, PL 162, col. 554; Hildebert of Tours, *Versus de mysterio missae*, PL 171, cols. 1184–1185; Sicard of Cremona, *Mitrale*, bk. 3, chap. 6, PL 213, col. 125; Durandus, *Rationale* (CCCM 140), bk. 4, chap. 1, no. 13, and chap. 35, no. 10, pp. 243, 416.

[209] Durandus, *Rationale* (CCCM 140), bk. 4, chap. 1, no. 13, p. 243.

[210] Altés i Aguiló, *Missale Vicense, 1496*, temporal, unnum. fols. 183r–187v (sig. &1r–&5v).

[211] Durandus, *Rationale* (CCCM 140), bk. 4, chap. 35, no. 1, p. 414.

[212] Florus of Lyons, *De expositione missae*, no. 4, PL 119, col. 18.

of Christ offering himself for us, once for all, alone on the Cross, that the "sequestering" of the priest from the people during the Canon (in particular) must be viewed. It in no way implies "aloofness" from the faithful, as some modern liturgical authors have wrongly insinuated; rather, it images Christ taking upon himself the sins of the whole world. The medieval priest was by no means "aloof" from the people. He baptized their children and presided over their marriages. He came to their homes to anoint the dying and bring them Holy Communion, and when they died, he accompanied them to the grave. The medieval understanding of the priest's recitation of the Canon as an action carried out not in isolation from but rather on behalf of all the people is expressed explicitly in a prayer that the missal of Avila, Spain (1510), enjoins the priest to say privately, "bowed before the altar with hands joined in supplication", just before beginning the Canon:

> *O Lord, open my mouth to bless your holy, worthy, and glorious name; cleanse my heart from all vain, diverse, and wicked thoughts, that in my conduct I may be worthy to be heard favorably praying for the people whom you have chosen for yourself, you granting, our God, who in perfect trinity live and reign, God, through all ages of ages. By the sign of the Cross, our God, deliver us from our enemies. In the name of the Father, and of the Son, and of the Holy Spirit. Amen.*[213]

Hence, just as the high priest prayed within the Holy of Holies on behalf of the whole people of Israel, so too the priest alone at the altar, reciting the Canon, prays on behalf of all the faithful.

In the above-mentioned missal of Avila, the priest begins the Canon itself while "bowing deeply", with hands joined,[214] a bow that is likewise specified for the Sarum Rite;[215] a bow of the head is specified in the Roman Rite rubrics of the 1502 *Ordo* of John Burckard.[216] Durandus interprets this bow as signifying the humility of Christ in his Passion and the reverence with which the priest beginning the Canon approaches the mystery of the Cross.[217]

The priest's silent recitation of the Canon is likened by Sicard of Cremona to the Old Testament high priest's withdrawal into the Holy of Holies.[218] But it is explained in other ways as well. Amalarius observes that by this quiet prayer, the Church, speaking through the priest, imitates the Old Testament example of Anna (cf. 1 Kings 1:13), "who entreated God not with clamorous petition, but silently and modestly

---

[213] *Missale Abulense* (Salamanca, Spain: Juan de Porras, 1510), sig. t1r. Virtually the same prayer appears immediately before the Canon in a fourteenth-century missal of Gerona, Spain (Ferreres Boluda, *Historia del misal romano*, xxxv, 146).

[214] *Missale Abulense* (1510), sig. t1r.

[215] Dickinson, *Missale ad usum . . . Sarum*, col. 610; Frere, *Use of Sarum*, 1:80.

[216] Text in Legg, *Tracts on the Mass*, 154.

[217] Durandus, *Rationale* (CCCM 140), bk. 4, chap. 36, no. 5, p. 419.

[218] Sicard of Cremona, *Mitrale*, bk. 3, chap. 6, PL 213, col. 125.

within the hiding places of her heart", speaking "not with the voice, but with the heart".[219] This explanation is repeated by other liturgists, including Durandus[220] and Pope Innocent III.[221] The latter author, however, primarily interprets the silent recitation of the Canon as symbolic of Christ hiding himself after having been received into Jerusalem by the joyful multitude on Palm Sunday (Jn 12:36); this withdrawal into silent solitude by Christ before his Passion is to be imitated by the priest in the Canon:

> Therefore, this private silence represents that hiding place of Christ, in which, the tumult of words ceasing, attentive devotion is directed to God alone.
>
> Then indeed ought the priest to enter into the chamber of his heart and, the door of the senses having been shut, pray to God the Father, not in much speaking ... but "from a pure heart, and a good conscience, and an unfeigned faith" [1 Tim 1:5].[222]

The connection that Pope Innocent makes between the silent recitation of the Canon and the Lord's Passion is taken further by Durandus, who sees the prayers of the Canon as symbolizing the continual prayers that Christ offered throughout his Passion, "privately and alone", from the Last Supper to Calvary. Hence, just as Christ prayed "privately and alone" in his Passion, so too the prayers of the Canon are recited silently.[223]

Pope Innocent III observes that in the Roman Canon "the memory of the Passion is contemplated",[224] so that while the words of the Canon pertain to the consecration of the Eucharist, the outward signs made during the Canon call to mind the events of Holy Week.[225] Saint Ivo of Chartres notes that just as the high priest of the Old Covenant entered the Holy of Holies with the blood of goats and calves, and as Christ entered the heavenly sanctuary with his own blood (Heb 9:11–12), so should the priest enter the "Holy of Holies" of the Canon bearing in his mind the remembrance of the Passion of Christ.[226] Building upon this comparison, Durandus adds that in the Canon the celebrant enters the Holy of Holies with the Blood of Christ.[227] The opportunity to provide the priest celebrating Mass with a visual reminder of this dimension of the Canon arose from the fact that the first letter of the first word of the Canon is *T* ("*Te igitur ...*"). The resemblance

---

[219] Amalarius of Metz, *Liber officialis*, bk. 3, chap. 23, no. 11, in Hanssens, *Amalarii episcopi: Opera liturgica omnia*, 1:332.

[220] Durandus, *Rationale* (CCCM 140), bk. 4, chap. 35, no. 4, p. 415.

[221] Innocent III, *De sacro altaris mysterio*, bk. 3, chap. 1, PL 217, cols. 839–840.

[222] Ibid., col. 839.

[223] Durandus, *Rationale* (CCCM 140), bk. 4, chap. 35, no. 3, pp. 414–415.

[224] Innocent III, *De sacro altarus mysterio*, bk. 3, chap. 2, PL 217, col. 840.

[225] Ibid., bk. 5, chap. 2, col. 888.

[226] Saint Ivo of Chartres, *Sermon* 5, PL 162, col. 554.

[227] Durandus, *Rationale* (CCCM 140), bk. 4, chap. 36, no. 5, pp. 419–420.

of the letter *T* to a cross inspired the transformation of this letter into an artistic depiction of Christ's crucifixion at the beginning of the Roman Canon in medieval missal manuscripts, a tradition that continued when the first printed missals were introduced in the late fifteenth century (and endured into the twentieth century). These crucifixion images prefacing the Canon were already commonplace by the end of the twelfth century, as evinced by the testimony of Pope Innocent III, who notes, "The image of Christ is depicted, that not only the understanding of letters but also the sight of a picture may inspire the remembrance of the Passion of the Lord."[228] Sicard of Cremona likewise explains these pre-Canon crucifixion images as provided in order that "the Passion that is represented may be infused in the eyes of the heart"—"fastened upon the eyes of the priest's heart".[229] Sicard adds that it was the custom for the celebrant to kiss the crucifixion image in the missal before proceeding with the recitation of the Canon,[230] a custom that as we have already seen was observed, at least for a time, in the Sarum Rite.[231]

The 1489 Sarum Missal enjoins that all the choristers are to prostrate themselves from the beginning of the Roman Canon until after the Our Father, which follows the Canon.[232] This prostration throughout the Canon would have carried the same significance as the bowed posture in which the faithful were enjoined to remain during the Canon in the twelfth- and thirteenth-century commentaries of Pseudo-Hildebert of Tours and Sicard of Cremona respectively. These authors explain that the faithful bow during the Canon so as to worship the divine majesty with the angels, and the Incarnation of the Lord with their fellow men.[233] It is highly likely that the "bow" of which these authors speak was in fact a kneeling posture, or at least a bow made while kneeling, for the practice of kneeling throughout the Roman Canon had been introduced centuries earlier, as we shall later see in our discussion of the posture of the faithful during the consecration.

In the Sarum Rite, as the priest begins to say the Roman Canon, he kisses the altar to the right of the host and chalice while saying the phrase *"that you may accept and bless"* (*"uti accepta habeas et benedicas"*),[234] a gesture that according to Durandus expresses reverence for the mystery of the Passion that the Canon embodies.[235] The celebrant then makes the sign of the cross three times while saying the words *"these gifts, these offerings, these holy, unblemished sacrifices"* (*"haec do + na,*

---

[228] Innocent III, *De sacro altaris mysterio*, bk. 3, chap. 2, PL 217, col. 840.

[229] Sicard of Cremona, *Mitrale*, bk. 3, chap. 6, PL 213, cols. 124, 125.

[230] Ibid., col. 124.

[231] Sarum Missal, thirteenth century, in Legg, *Sarum Missal*, 220.

[232] Martène, *De antiquis ecclesiae ritibus*, bk. 1, chap. 4, art. 12, *ordo* 35, 1:241.

[233] Pseudo-Hildebert of Tours, *Liber de expositione missae*, PL 171, col. 1161; Sicard of Cremona, *Mitrale*, bk. 3, chap. 6, PL 213, col. 124.

[234] Dickinson, *Missale ad usum . . . Sarum*, col. 613.

[235] Durandus, *Rationale* (CCCM 140), bk. 4, chap. 36, no. 6, p. 420.

haec mu + nera, haec san + cta sacrificia illibata").[236] Pope Innocent III explains this triple signing as symbolizing the three ways in which Christ was delivered to death in his Passion. He was delivered by his Father as a gift ("God so loved the world, as to give his only begotten Son" [Jn 3:16]); he was delivered by Judas as an offering in exchange for the thirty silver pieces ("[Judas Iscariot] said to them: What will you give me, and I will deliver him unto you? But they appointed him thirty pieces of silver" [Mt 26:15]); and he was delivered as an unblemished sacrifice by the chief priests and Pharisees ("Caiaphas, being the high priest that year, said to them: '... Neither do you consider that it is expedient for you that one man should die for the people" [Jn 11:49–50]).[237] This same explanation is reiterated by Durandus and Saint Thomas Aquinas.[238] The plural is used—"*gifts ... offerings ... sacrifices*"—because the Eucharist is to be consecrated under the two species of bread and wine.[239]

In the first two sections of the Roman Canon, those beginning with the words "*Te igitur*" ("*You, therefore*") and "*Memento Domine*" ("*Be mindful, O Lord*") respectively, the priest prays for the Church, the pope, the local bishop, the monarch, and all the faithful, with a remembrance of particular individuals in the priest's intentions for the Mass. Drawing on the imagery of the high priest of the Old Covenant, Saint Ivo of Chartres notes that just as the high priest, having entered the Holy of Holies, prayed for himself and his own family (Lev 16:6), and Christ, on the threshold of his Passion, prayed at the Last Supper for himself ("Father, ... glorify thy Son" [Jn 17:1]) and for his disciples ("Holy Father, keep them in thy name whom thou hast given me" [Jn 17:11]), so too does the priest within the "Holy of Holies" of the Canon pray for the pope, the Church, and those in public office.[240] Making the same comparison, Hildebert of Tours adds that in offering this portion of the Canon the priest is following the example of Christ, who in offering himself in the heavenly sanctuary "always acts for the people, the Lord for the servant, the Shepherd for the sheep".[241] As for the priest praying also on his own behalf and that of his family, in likeness to the high priest's petitions in this regard, most of the printed editions of the Sarum Missal insert the following rubric following the opening words of

---

[236] All the signs of the cross made during the Roman Canon are indicated by cross symbols in the text. Such markings in the Canon appear as early as the eighth century in the *Hadrianum* redaction of the Gregorian Sacramentary; see Deshusses, *Sacramentaire grégorien*, nos. 5, 9, 11, 15, 1:87–89, 91. For these cross markings in the Sarum Missal texts, see Dickinson, *Missale ad usum ... Sarum*, cols. 613–619.

[237] Innocent III, *De sacro altaris mysterio*, bk. 3, chap. 3, PL 217, col. 841.

[238] Durandus, *Rationale* (CCCM 140), bk. 4, chap. 36, nos. 7–8, p. 420; Saint Thomas Aquinas, *Summa theologica*, pt. III, q. 83, art. 5, reply obj. 3, 2:2521.

[239] Innocent III, *De sacro altaris mysterio*, bk. 3, chap. 3, PL 217, col. 842.

[240] Saint Ivo of Chartres, *Sermon* 5, PL 162, col. 554.

[241] Hildebert of Tours, *Versus de mysterio missae*, PL 171, col. 1185.

the *Memento Domine*, "*Be mindful, O Lord, of your servants and maid-servants* [Name] *and* [Name]":

> In this prayer, order ought to be observed according to the order of charity. Five times the priest prays: first for himself; second, for his father and mother, namely his bodily and his spiritual parents; third, for his special friends, his parishioners and others; fourth, for all present; fifth, for all the Christian people; and here the priest can commend all his friends to God. I advise, however, that he should not linger overmuch thereon, first by reason of the distraction of the heart, then by reason of the inroads that can be made by demons, and by reason of other dangers.[242]

In the third section of the Canon, beginning with the words "*Communicantes et memoriam venerantes*" ("*Uniting with, and venerating the memory*"), the priest commemorates the communion of saints and beseeches God that the Church on earth may partake of the merits that the saints have won by their lives on earth and that their prayers in Heaven continue to obtain for those in this world. This naming of saints and martyrs in the Canon, including the twelve Apostles, was foreshadowed, according to Saint Ivo of Chartres, by the high priest's breastplate, which bore on twelve stones the names of the twelve patriarchs of the tribes of Israel (Ex 28:15–21).[243] Moreover, just as the high priest, taking coals from the altar of holocausts, after having offered the calf on the Day of Atonement, would fill a thurible with these coals so as to offer incense to the Lord in the Holy of Holies (Lev 16:11–13)—a foreshadowing of Christ entering the heavenly sanctuary with the thurible of his body, filled with "every good odor of the virtues"—so too the priest celebrating Mass brings into the inner sanctum of the Canon the living coals of the saints, who "both glow with divine love in themselves and are zealous by their example to make others from the [spiritually] dead alive [with divine love]".[244]

In the next two sections of the Canon, beginning with the words "*Hanc igitur oblationem*" ("*Therefore this oblation*") and "*Quam oblationem*" ("*Which oblation*") respectively, the celebrant prays that God the Father may accept and bless the gifts (of unconsecrated bread and wine) on the altar that are soon to be consecrated. The 1489 Sarum Missal directs that at the words "*Therefore this oblation*" the priest "should look upon the host with great veneration"; he should again look upon the host with the words "*Which oblation*".[245]

During the section of the Canon beginning with "*Which oblation*", five more signs of the cross are to be made over the gifts; all such

---

[242] Dickinson, *Missale ad usum ... Sarum*, col. 614.

[243] Saint Ivo of Chartres, *Sermon* 5, PL 162, col. 555.

[244] Ibid., cols. 554–555; see also Hildebert of Tours, *Versus de mysterio missae*, PL 171, col. 1185.

[245] Martène, *De antiquis ecclesiae ritibus*, bk. 1, chap. 4, art. 12, *ordo* 35, 1:240.

crosses throughout the Canon, whether they are made before or after the consecration, are ultimately intended "to commemorate the death of the Lord".[246] In the traditional orientation of churches, the altar and sanctuary would be situated so that the celebrant would face east while standing at the altar facing it. Saint Ivo of Chartres utilizes this fact to draw a further parallel between the actions of the Old Covenant's high priest in the Holy of Holies and the priest in the Canon. Just as the high priest facing eastward toward the Propitiatory (Mercy Seat) in the Holy of Holies sprinkled it with the blood of the immolated calf and goat, prefiguring the blood "sprinkled" by Christ in his Passion, facing eastward on the Cross (according to tradition), toward his heavenly Father, so too the priest praying the Canon "imitates under the sacred mysteries, as it were under the veil [of the Holy of Holies], this sprinkling of the blood of Christ, as often as turned toward the east he signs with the same sign of the cross the very sacraments, whence the Savior has come to us".[247]

The five signs of the cross in the aforementioned section *"Which oblation"* are made within the phrases *"blessed, approved, ratified"* (three crosses: *"bene + dictam, ascrip + tam, ra + tam"*) and *"that it may be made for us the Body and Blood of your most beloved Son"* (two crosses: *"cor + pus et san + guis"*).[248] Saint Thomas Aquinas explains the first three crosses as symbolizing Judas' selling of Christ to (1) the priests, (2) the scribes, and (3) the Pharisees for a threefold price, that is, thirty silver pieces. The two further crosses represent the betrayer (Judas) and he who was betrayed and sold (Christ).[249] It may seem surprising to the reader that medieval liturgists would see fit to give such prominence to Judas' odious betrayal of his Master within the sacrosanct confines of the Roman Canon. The answer lies in the fact that it was through Judas' betrayal that the salvific oblation of our Savior on the Cross was accomplished.

We come now to the summit of the Roman Canon—the consecration, beginning with the consecration of the Host, as given in the 1489 Sarum Missal. The actions that accompany the text serve to amplify the words spoken:

> Here the priest should raise his hands and join them; and afterward he should wipe clean his fingers, and should elevate the host, saying: *Who on the day before he suffered took bread into his sacred and venerable hands, and having raised his eyes to Heaven,* (Here he should raise his eyes:) *to you, O God, his almighty Father,* (Here he should incline himself and afterward raise himself a little, saying:) *giving thanks to you, he*

---

[246] Saint Ivo of Chartres, *Sermon 5*, PL 162, col. 556.

[247] Ibid.

[248] Dickinson, *Missale ad usum . . . Sarum*, cols. 615–616.

[249] Saint Thomas Aquinas, *Summa theologica*, pt. III, q. 83, art. 5, reply obj. 3, 2:2521–2522; see also Innocent III, *De sacro altaris mysterio*, bk. 3, chap. 12, PL 217, cols. 850–851.

blessed it, broke it, (Here he should touch the host:) *and gave it to his disciples, saying: Take and eat of this, all of you: For this is my Body.* And these words ought to be spoken with one breath, and under one pronouncement, with no pausing interposed. After these words, he should elevate it above his forehead, that it may be able to be seen by the people, and reverently he should put it back before the chalice in the manner of a cross made by means of the same.[250]

The directions in the above rubrics as to how the priest should pronounce the words of consecration manifest a vigilance in this regard likewise found in the *Instructions* of Durandus, which speak of the celebrant "bringing forth devoutly and very distinctly the individual words of the consecration, frequently looking at the book, however much he may know them to the end in his mind".[251] Although not mentioned in the Sarum rubrics above, the actual text of the Canon in the Sarum Rite, as in the Roman Rite, specifies that a sign of the cross should be made over the host at the word "blessed" in the phrase *"he blessed it, broke it"* (*"bene + dixit, fregit"*). During the consecration of the chalice, there will be a second sign of the cross at the same point in the phrase *"he blessed it, and gave it to his disciples"* (*"bene + dixit, deditque discipulis suis"*).[252] These two signs of the cross were interpreted by Sicard of Cremona as representing the two "walls", that is, the two peoples—Jews and Gentiles—that Christ the "Cornerstone" has joined together (Eph 2:11–22).[253] Saint Thomas Aquinas saw these two signs of the cross as expressing the prefiguration of the Passion at the Last Supper.[254]

The assertion of the Canon text that before consecrating the Eucharist at the Last Supper Christ elevated his eyes to his Father in Heaven, an action imitated by the priest, is for Durandus a reminder that at the outset of all our actions we should first direct the gaze of our mind's eye to God.[255] The Sarum rubrics are not specific as to precisely how the priest is to hold the host during the consecration, but Durandus in his *Instructions* directs the celebrant to hold the host with the thumbs and index fingers of both his hands, making the sign of the cross at the word *benedixit* over the host with his right hand.[256] In his 1502 Roman Rite *Ordo* John Burckard adds that when there is a vessel

[250] Martène, *De antiquis ecclesiae ritibus*, bk. 1, chap. 4, art. 12, *ordo* 35, 1:240–241.

[251] Berthelé, "Instructions et constitutions de Guillaume Durand", 69. The liturgical text of Rome known as the Ceremonial of a Cardinal Bishop (c. 1280), ascribed to Latino Cardinal Malabranca (+1294), similarly stresses that the priest should pronounce the words of consecration with clarity and devotion; text in Dykmans, *Cérémonial papal de la fin du moyen âge à la Renaissance*, 1:247.

[252] Dickinson, *Missale ad usum ... Sarum*, cols. 616, 617.

[253] Sicard of Cremona, *Mitrale*, bk. 3, chap. 6, PL 213, col. 126.

[254] Saint Thomas Aquinas, *Summa theologica*, pt. III, q. 83, art. 5, reply obj. 3, 2:2522.

[255] Durandus, *Rationale* (CCCM 140), bk. 4, chap. 41, no. 12, p. 445.

[256] Berthelé, "Instructions et constitutions de Guillaume Durand", 69. Durandus has clearly derived these specifications from Latino Cardinal Malabranca's Ceremonial of a

containing additional hosts to be consecrated, the priest should uncover it before saying, "*For this is my Body*."[257]

The significance of the elevation of the Host following the consecration, a practice traceable to the early thirteenth century,[258] is amply explained by Durandus:

> Those words having been said, "[*For*] *this is my Body*", the priest elevates the Body of Christ ... first, that all present may see it, and beseech what contributes to salvation, according to that said [Jn 12:32], "And I, if I be lifted up from the earth, will draw all things to myself." Secondly, for noting that there is no other worthy sacrifice; on the contrary, it is above all sacrifices. Third, the exaltation of the Eucharist in the hand of the priest signifies Christ the True Bread, exalted by the prophets in the Scriptures, when namely they prophesized his Incarnation; whence Isaiah [Is 7:14], "Behold a virgin shall conceive [and bear a son, and his name shall be called Emmanuel]." ... Fourth, it signifies the Resurrection.[259]

In the medieval liturgists' allegorical schema of the Mass, the elevation of the Host at the consecration was also seen as evoking in an anticipatory sense the image of Christ elevated on the Cross.[260] In discussing the consecration, the late medieval theologian and liturgical commentator Gabriel Biel (+1495) invites the faithful contemplating the elevated Host to recall the exhibiting of Christ in his Passion and on the Cross:

> And each of the faithful at the elevation and showing of this vivifying Sacrament is able to meditate in remembering the opprobrious showing of Christ, when, after the scourging and bruises of his body ... Pilate presented him ... and pointed him out with a contemptible voice, saying [Jn 19:5], "Behold the Man", and again [Jn 19:14], "Behold your king."
>
> Furthermore, at the elevation of the Sacrament he should ponder the elevation of Christ on the ignominious gibbet of the Cross, hung between evildoers and thieves, after considering the contemptibly impious

---

Cardinal Bishop (c. 1280); see Dykmans, *Cérémonial papal de la fin du moyen âge à la Renaissance*, 1:247.

[257] Text in Legg, *Tracts on the Mass*, 156.

[258] This elevation is first mentioned in a synodal decree of Paris dated before 1215 and attributed, at least formerly, to Bishop Odo of Sully (1196–1208); see V. L. Kennedy, C.S.B., "The Date of the Parisian Decree on the Elevation of the Host", *Mediaeval Studies* 8 (1948): 87–96. For the original decree, see *Synodicae constitutiones*, chap. 8, no. 28, in J. D. Mansi, ed., *Sacrorum conciliorum nova et amplissima collectio*, vol. 22 (Florence and Venice, 1778; repr., Paris: Hubert Welter, 1903), col. 682.

[259] Durandus, *Rationale* (CCCM 140), bk. 4, chap. 41, no. 51, pp. 461–462.

[260] See, for example, Radulphus Ardens (+1215): "When, therefore, the priest elevates the Host ..., it represents the elevation of Christ on the Cross" (*Sermon 47*, PL 155, col. 1836). See also Gavanti, *Thesaurus sacrorum rituum* (1628), in Gavanti and Merati, *Thesaurus sacrorum rituum*, 1:724.

mockeries and insults he endured. And thus for the contumelies, reproaches, and blasphemies, [each of the faithful] should devote the reverence of *latria* in adoring, thinking how much he underwent, and should bow down to give him thanks.[261]

In most of the late medieval Mass texts of the Sarum Rite, the priest is directed to bow toward the Host after pronouncing the words of consecration;[262] similarly, the missal of Avila, Spain (1510), speaks of the celebrant *adoring* "the Body of the Lord" with "a moderate bow" prior to elevating the Host.[263] But in the liturgical books of Rome, beginning with the 1485 *Pontificalis liber* (the edition of the *Pontificale Romanum* compiled by two papal masters of ceremonies, Patrizio Piccolomini and John Burckard), the celebrant is directed to genuflect at this point in the Mass.[264] In the 1502 edition of John Burckard's *Ordo* of the Mass (first published in 1498), the priest is enjoined to genuflect twice following the consecration, first before elevating the Host and then again after setting it down.[265] The earliest known reference to the genuflection of the celebrant following the consecration dates from the second half of the fourteenth century, appearing in a book regarding the proper celebration of the Mass, the *Secreta sacerdotum* of the Viennese theologian Henry of Langenstein (Henry of Hesse, c. 1325–1397): "Some make three elevations. For the words of the consecration having been completed, they lift up the Host to the height of a palm [of a hand], and rest their raised hands upon the altar, and then genuflect; and again they lift up the Host over the head, and rising up from their genuflection, they elevate the Sacrament a third time."[266] There is evidence that by the early 1500s priests celebrating Mass were in at least some cases genuflecting after the consecration even when the rubrics of the particular missals they were using prescribed only a bow. In a Mass commentary published in

---

[261] Gabriel Biel, *Exposition of the Canon of the Mass*, lesson 50, in Heiko Oberman and William Courtenay, eds., *Gabrielis Biel: Canonis misse expositio*, vol. 2, Veröffentlichungen des Instituts für europäische Geschichte Mainz 32 (Wiesbaden, Germany: Franz Steiner Verlag, 1965), 281.

[262] Dickinson, *Missale ad usum . . . Sarum*, col. 617; Frere, *Use of Sarum*, 1:80.

[263] *Missale Abulense* (1510), sig. t1v.

[264] Text in Manlio Sodi, ed., *Il "Pontificalis liber" di Agostino Patrizi Piccolomini e Giovanni Burcardo (1485)*, facsimile ed., MSIL 43 (Vatican City: Libreria Editrice Vaticana, © 2006), 567 (new pagination).

[265] Legg, *Tracts on the Mass*, 156. The idea of having the priest adore the newly consecrated Eucharist both before and after the elevation was not unique to John Burckard's *Ordo missae*. A rubric immediately following the words of consecration in a missal of Halberstadt, Germany (c. 1498), tells the priest, "With bowing adore before the elevation and after"; see *Missale Halberstatense* (Strasbourg, France: Johann Grüninger, c. 1498; digitized text, Bayerische Staatsbibliothek, Munich, 2009), ordinary, unnum. fol. 19v (the ordinary begins after fol. 126v of the temporal).

[266] Henry of Langenstein, *Secreta sacerdotum* (Nürnberg, Germany: Georg Stuchs, c. 1497; digitized text, Bayerische Staatsbibliothek, Munich, 2009), sig. A4r ("Qualiter Hostia debet elevari").

1505, John Bechoffen, an Augustinian theologian, urges priests to genuflect to the newly consecrated Sacrament even when not required by the rubrics to do so; Bechoffen provides a beautiful and compelling explanation of the practice:

> And thus where it is prescribed to bow reverently, it is well of the celebrant of the Mass to supplicate his Creator and Savior on his knees with the utmost devotion, reverence, and honor, to glorify him on his knees. And this for recognizing himself to be earth and dust in consideration of so great a God with all possible humility and reverence, by which means these outward things are signs of interior things; and the Creator himself ought to be honored and praised by his creature for the benefit of having been able to have known him.... Therefore, they are to be put to shame if perchance they should turn lukewarm, or more so, haughty and arrogant, who on this occasion do not fear with an erect neck scarcely to bend one knee to their Creator, Savior, and awesome Judge, for it is written: "Whosoever shall glorify me, him will I glorify: but they that despise me, shall be despised" (1 Kings 2:30).[267]

There is one piece of artistic evidence to suggest that the earliest instance of a celebrant kneeling to the consecrated Host during the Mass considerably predates the recorded references to this practice. A stained-glass window dating from about the year 1220 in Canterbury Cathedral depicts the English archbishop and martyr Saint Thomas Becket (1118–1170) genuflecting in his vestments as he celebrates Mass.[268] Setting aside the question as to whether the early thirteenth-century artist who designed this window was accurately depicting liturgical practices in Saint Thomas Becket's day, his work certainly demonstrates that such a practice must have been known in his own age, well over a century before Henry of Langenstein's testimony. It is also in the thirteenth century, around the year 1294, that we find the text of a private act of adoration for the priest to recite to himself immediately after the elevation of the Host. The text was composed by Durandus, who includes it with the Mass rubrics in his diocesan *Instructions*. The prayer is highly significant in that the Eucharist is *directly* addressed as Christ himself, true God and true man:

> Which words [of consecration] having been said, he [the celebrant] first, with a moderate bow and reverent devotion, adores the sacred Body of the Lord. And afterward he reverently elevates it on high so that it should be able to be seen and adored by the people; and then he reposes it in its place, his hands reverently joined, bowing to it

---

[267] John Bechoffen, *Quadruplex missalis expositio* (Basel, Switzerland: Michael Furter, 1505; digitized text, Bayerische Staatsbibliothek, Munich, 2007), sig. D2v–D3r.

[268] Jonathan Keates and Angelo Hornak, *Canterbury Cathedral* (Florence: Scala Books / Philip Wilson, 1980), 35.

and saying, if he should wish: *Hail, Light of the world, Word of the Father, true Host, living Flesh, entire Godhead, true Man.*[269]

In a very similar vein, a missal of Valencia, Spain, dating from around the year 1400, provides an expansive series of invocations (including the ancient threefold invocation used in the Good Friday liturgy, the Trisagion) for the priest to offer in silent adoration as he elevates the Host immediately after the consecration:

> The following prayers should be said at the elevation of the Body of Christ: *I adore you, Lord Jesus Christ, Son of the living God, Savior of the world, who by your most sacred Passion have redeemed the world, whom I believe to be very truly here under these species. You are Christ, the Son of the living God, who has come into this world. You are my Lord and my God, living and true; Savior of the world, save me, who by your Cross and Resurrection have redeemed me. Help me, my God.* [In Greek:] *Holy God, Holy Mighty One, Holy Immortal One;* [In Latin:] *Holy God, Holy Mighty One, Holy Immortal One, have mercy on us.*[270]

The kneeling of the assisting clergy together with the faithful during the consecration appears to have arisen by the end of the eighth century, judging from a careful reading of one liturgical document of this period. A Frankish text known as Roman *Ordo* 17, dating from about 790, directs that during the Preface the assisting priests are to "bow their faces to the earth".[271] At the *Sanctus*, "the deacons and the clergy bow again with all the people";[272] the use of the word "again" (*iterum*) in this rubric indicates that the second bow is like the first, with the face "to the earth". Another rubric adds that "the priests and the deacons or subdeacons remain bowed" until nearly the end of the Roman Canon;[273] from this it is clear that during the consecration they are to remain with "their faces to the earth". But does the expression "their faces to the earth" really indicate the lowering of the face toward the ground in a kneeling posture, or does it simply mean the bowing of the head in a standing position? The answer is revealed by another rubric in the text that speaks of the subdeacons *rising* shortly before the end of the Roman Canon.[274] Clearly they cannot be said to rise if they are already in a standing position. Thus it can be concluded that Roman *Ordo* 17 provides the earliest evidence for the practice of kneeling during the consecration. A few decades later, a ninth-century Gaelic-language treatise on the Mass

---

[269] Berthelé, "Instructions et constitutions de Guillaume Durand", 69.

[270] Missal of Valencia, Spain, c. 1400, quoted in Ferreres Boluda, *Historia del misal romano*, 154.

[271] Text in Michel Andrieu, ed., *Les Ordines Romani du haut moyen âge*, vol. 3, SSLED 24 (Louvain, Belgium: "Spicilegium sacrum Lovaniense" Administration, 1951), 181.

[272] Ibid.

[273] Ibid., 182.

[274] Ibid.

accompanying the text of Ireland's Stowe Missal expressly states that the people are to kneel for the words of consecration: "When is sung, '*Jesus took bread*,' the priest bows himself down thrice ... and the people kneel." [275]

The papal ceremonial of Pope Blessed Gregory X (+1276), dating from about the year 1273, provides detailed instructions as to how the clerics assisting in the sanctuary are to venerate the Eucharist at the elevation following the consecration:

> And at Mass similarly we ought to remain kneeling in prayer before the Epistle, and after the *Sanctus* having been sung, all the way to the elevation of the Body of Christ. But at the elevation of the Body of Christ, when a little beforehand they ought to rise, they prostrate themselves to the earth and reverently adore, falling on their faces; and thus prostrate they should remain all the way to *Through all ages of ages*, before the *Lamb of God*. [276]

According to the directions for High Mass given in the mid-thirteenth-century Humbert Codex of the Dominican Order (as found in a British Museum copy, dated to about 1263), the deacon and subdeacon are both to kneel for the consecration, with the deacon kneeling at the celebrant's right, continually incensing the newly consecrated Sacrament, and the subdeacon kneeling at the priest's left; two acolytes hold lit candles for the consecration on each side, one kneeling beside the deacon and the other beside the subdeacon. [277] The earlier-cited Augustinian theologian John Bechoffen explains that candles and torches are lit for the consecration so as to enkindle the hearts of those present, that "they may be more devoutly and fervently inflamed to prepare themselves for reverently and most devoutly adoring him who is the radiance of the eternal light and the consuming fire that is never extinguished." [278] An *Ordinarium* of the Carmelite Order compiled by the Carmelites' German provincial Sibert de Beka, dating from about 1312, stations the thurifer (an acolyte with incense) directly behind the priest, where on his knees he incenses the Eucharist at the elevation, taking care not to make the fumes so dense that the visibility of the Sacrament is impeded. [279] The 1568 *Missale Pallantinum* of Palencia, Spain, directs that during the Mass, from the consecration onward, all the ministers of the altar are to genuflect "all the way to the earth" whenever

---

[275] Text as translated by George Warner, in George Warner, ed., *The Stowe Missal*, vol. 2, *Printed Text*, HBS 32 (London: Henry Bradshaw Society, 1915), 37 (Gaelic text), 40 (English translation).

[276] Ceremonial of Pope Blessed Gregory X, in Dykmans, *Cérémonial papal de la fin du moyen âge à la Renaissance*, 1:188.

[277] Manuscript: London, British Museum, Add. MS 23935, in Legg, *Tracts on the Mass*, 80. The incensation did not take place at every High Mass but only on certain days.

[278] John Bechoffen, *Quadruplex missalis expositio*, sig. D3r.

[279] Text in Benedict Zimmerman, ed., *Ordinaire de l'ordre de Notre-Dame du Mont-Carmel*, Bibliothèque liturgique 13 (Paris: Alphonse Picard et Fils, 1910), 80–81.

they approach or depart from the altar.[280] The phrase "all the way to the earth" (*usque ad terram*), also used in the Palencia missal to describe the celebrant's genuflection after the consecration,[281] may indicate a double genuflection (the bending of both knees), an observance that is specified for the celebrant of Mass from the consecration onward in a 1548 ceremonial issued for Portugal's Rite of Braga by Archbishop Manuel de Sousa.[282]

The kneeling of the congregation for the elevation of the consecrated Host and later the chalice, as well as various other gestures of the faithful at the moment of elevation, are ably explained by Gabriel Biel (moreover, his comments on kneeling effectively provide a rationale for the genuflection of the celebrant to the Host):

> Similarly, he [the worshiper] should adore with exterior *latria*, with a fitting posture of the body at the elevation of the Sacrament, to signify the internal faith and reverence with which, as with an interior act, he should worship God himself, the Creator and Lord of all things. And that just as at his crucifixion he was shamefully disturbed, blasphemed, [and] mocked by the unbelieving with words and disordered exterior motions of the head and members, so conversely in the sacred office of the Mass (in which the commemoration of his Passion is expressed) he should be honored by the faithful with the exterior posture of the body.
>
> Accordingly, the faithful ought humbly to bend with heads uncovered to Christ in the Sacrament that is shown, whose head, tormented by a thousand wounds with the sharp points of thorns for the expiation of our sins, was in the hour of death most sorrowfully but most lovingly bent toward us. For with a bowed head he delivered his spirit.
>
> They ought to bend their knees to the earth, humbling themselves to him who emptied himself, taking the form of a servant, "becoming obedient" to the Father "unto death, even to the death of the cross" [Phil 2:8].
>
> And even as the most impudent dogs, [the unbelieving], in derision bending the knee, blasphemed the Eternal Wisdom of God the Father, saying: "Hail, king of the Jews" [Mt 27:29], and again, "If he be the king of Israel, let him now come down from the cross" [Mt 27:42], and other things of this kind, so on the contrary [the faithful], bending their knees, should inwardly humble themselves in the heart, adoring and uttering that saying of blessed Anselm:[283] "*I*

---

[280] *Missale Pallantinum* (Palencia, Spain: Sebastian Martinez, 1568), fol. 357r. The Latin text of this missal has been graciously provided to the author by the Biblioteca Apostolica Vaticana, Vatican City (shelf mark Stamp. Barb. B. X. 1).

[281] Ibid., fol. 353v.

[282] *Ceremonial da missa* (Lisbon: Germano Galharde, 1548; digitized text, Biblioteca Nacional Digital, Biblioteca Nacional de Portugal, 2009), fols. 12v–13r, 14v, 15v, 16r, 17v.

[283] Gabriel Biel here paraphrases from the prayers of Saint Anselm of Canterbury (PL 158, cols. 889–927).

adore you, Christ the King of Israel, Light of the nations, Sovereign of the kings of the earth, Lord Sabaoth, mightiest Almighty Power of God." And they ought to join their hands devoutly, against the very cruel fury of the Jews and Gentiles, extending their hands in wickedly slapping, striking, and crucifying. . . .

And they ought to beat their breasts, in memory of the fearful wound of the Lord's heart opened by the soldier's lance, whence blood and water flowed forth together in the washing and redemption of sins.

They ought also to beat [their breasts] in confession of the praise of God. . . . Thus devoutly conducting themselves in adoration of Christ in the Sacrament, they shall receive manifold grace and very great fruit.[284]

Durandus, in his diocesan *Instructions*, provides the following act of adoration for the faithful to say privately at the elevation of the Host:

Furthermore, when the Body of Christ is shown to the people between the hands of the priest to be adored thus, reverently kneeling, they should say: *O most precious Body of Christ, true God and true man, who are the Price and Reward, the Salvation, King, and Light of the world, whom every creature together justly praises and blesses, to you I devoutly commend my body and soul, suppliantly and earnestly beseeching that to me and all my relatives, my parents, friends, and benefactors, you may vouchsafe to grant spiritual and temporal peace, joy also, and all things opportune for health of soul and body, moreover the heart, time, and opportunity to repent and serve you worthily and laudably, and [may vouchsafe] to protect us from shame, want, and sudden death, and from every adversity of mind and body, and also to have mercy upon us and all the faithful, both the living and the dead.*[285]

The practice of ringing a bell for the elevation of the Host and later the chalice is explained by Durandus in his *Rationale divinorum officiorum*:

And also at the elevation of both [the Host and the chalice], the small handbell is rung, for in the Old Testament also, the Levites sounded the silver trumpets for the time of the sacrifice, that at the sound of them the people, forewarned, would have been prepared for adoring the Lord. And on account of the same reason, the small handbell is rung when the Body of Christ is carried to the infirm.[286]

The consecration of the chalice follows, as given in the 1489 Sarum Missal:

And then [the priest] should uncover the chalice, and should hold it between his hands, not separating the thumb from the index finger,

[284] Gabriel Biel, *Exposition of the Canon of the Mass*, lesson 50, in Oberman and Courtenay, *Gabrielis Biel: Canonis misse expositio*, 2:281–282.

[285] Berthelé, "Instructions et constitutions de Guillaume Durand", 79–80.

[286] Durandus, *Rationale* (CCCM 140), bk. 4, chap. 41, no. 53, p. 462.

except while he is giving the blessing only, saying thus: *In a similar manner, after they had supped, and taking this honorable chalice into his sacred and venerable hands, likewise to Thee* (Here he should incline himself, saying:) *giving thanks, he blessed + it, and gave it to his disciples, saying: Take and drink of it, all of you.* Here the priest should elevate the chalice a short space, saying thus: *For this is the chalice of my Blood of the new and eternal covenant, the mystery of faith, which shall be shed for you and for the many in remission of sins.* Here he should elevate the chalice up to his chest, or above his head, saying: *As often as you will have done these things, do them in memory of me.* Here he should put back the chalice.[287]

The instruction in the above text that the priest should not separate the thumb from the index finger is explained by Saint Thomas Aquinas as a matter of "reverence for the Sacrament" in that since the celebrant has held the consecrated Host with these fingers, he needs to hold them together "so that if any particle cling to the fingers, it may not be scattered".[288]

For this elevation of the chalice, a practice traceable to the second half of the thirteenth century,[289] Durandus in his diocesan *Instructions* provides for the priest a second private act of adoration that follows the consecration of the Precious Blood. After the words "*in remission of sins*", the priest, having set down the chalice, "reverently bowing, adores" before devoutly elevating the chalice on high so that the people may see and adore the Sacrament. Then "he carefully reposes it [the chalice] in its place, saying: *As often as you will have done these things*, etc.; and having put it down, with joined hands, reverently bowed, he adores, saying, if he should wish: *Hail, Blood of Christ, which was shed for the redemption of mankind.*"[290] Again, Durandus gives a corresponding act of adoration for the faithful to recite privately: "When the chalice with the Blood of Christ is shown to the people to be adored, they should say thus: *O most precious Blood of Christ, poured out on the altar of the Cross for our redemption, may you be blessed unto ages of ages; and by the might of your power, cleanse well the defilement of my sins.*"[291] In the 1502 Roman Rite *Ordo* of John Burckard, the priest is instructed to genuflect twice following the consecration of the chalice as he did with the Host, both before elevating the chalice and after setting it down.[292]

---

[287] Martène, *De antiquis ecclesiae ritibus*, bk. 1, chap. 4, art. 12, *ordo* 35, 1:241.

[288] Saint Thomas Aquinas, *Summa theologica*, pt. III, q. 83, art. 5, reply obj. 5, 2:2522.

[289] A 1262 statute of the Canons of Rome's Basilica of Saint Mary Major refers to the elevation of the "Blood of Christ". See Dykmans, *Cérémonial papal de la fin du moyen âge à la Renaissance*, 1:123.

[290] Berthelé, "Instructions et constitutions de Guillaume Durand", 69.

[291] Ibid., 80.

[292] Legg, *Tracts on the Mass*, 157.

Amalarius sees in the entire second half of the Roman Canon, beginning with the words *"And wherefore we your servants, O Lord, mindful"* (*"Unde et memores, Domine, nos tui servi"*), an image of Christ on the Cross: the altar represents the Cross itself, with the Host resting on the altar corresponding to Christ's crucified body spread upon the Cross, and the chalice beside the Host corresponding to the blood and water that flowed forth from his pierced side.[293] The Sarum rubrics, perhaps with this analogy in mind, direct the priest following the consecration to extend his arms in the manner of a cross[294] as he resumes the recitation of the Roman Canon, beginning with the words *"And wherefore we your servants"* (*"Unde et memores"*).[295] Durandus explains this action as representing the extension of Christ's hands upon the Cross.[296] During the words *"a pure Host, a holy Host, an immaculate Host, the holy Bread of eternal life, and the Chalice of everlasting salvation"*, the celebrant makes the sign of the cross five times: three times over the Host and chalice together, then once over the Host alone, then once over the chalice alone (*"hostiam pu + ram, hostiam san + ctam, hostiam immacu + latam, pa + nem sanctum vitae aeternae, et cali + cem salutis perpetuae"*).[297] Interpreting the whole second half of the Roman Canon as denoting the Passion of Christ in a manner similar to Amalarius, Pope Innocent III draws upon the imagery of the dove in the cleft of the rock in the Song of Solomon (2:14) to identify these five signs of the cross as representing the five wounds of Christ on the Cross, "those clefts of the living rock, in which resides the immaculate dove [i.e., the Church] fruitfully building her nest".[298]

The portion of the Canon beginning with the words *"Suppliant, we beseech you"* (*"Supplices te rogamus"*) is accompanied by a series of actions common to the Roman and Sarum rites[299] that Pope Innocent III sees as symbolic of events in the Garden of Gethsemane. Thus the priest bends forward in a bowed posture to represent Christ prostrating himself in prayer during his agony in the garden (Mt 26:39; Lk 22:41). Following the words in the Canon *"from this participation of the altar"* (*"ex hac altaris participatione"*), the priest raises himself from his inclined position and kisses the altar to the right of the Host and

[293] Amalarius of Metz, *Liber officialis*, bk. 4, chap. 47, nos. 1–2, in Hanssens, *Amalarii episcopi: Opera liturgica omnia*, 2:542–543.

[294] This posture following the consecration is not found in the Roman Rite texts, but it is found in the 1510 missal of Avila (*Missale Abulense*, sig. t1v) and at a slightly later point during the Canon in Durandus' *Instructions* (Berthelé, "Instructions et constitutions de Guillaume Durand", 70).

[295] 1489 Sarum Missal, in Martène, *De antiquis ecclesiae ritibus*, bk. 1, chap. 4, art. 12, ordo 35, 1:241.

[296] Durandus, *Rationale* (CCCM 140), bk. 4, chap. 43, no. 3, pp. 480–481.

[297] Dickinson, *Missale ad usum ... Sarum*, cols. 617–618.

[298] Innocent III, *De sacro altaris mysterio*, bk. 5, chap. 1, PL 217, col. 887.

[299] 1489 Sarum Missal, in Martène, *De antiquis ecclesiae ritibus*, bk. 1, chap. 4, art. 12, ordo 35, 1:241; 1502 Roman Rite *Ordo missae* of John Burckard, in Legg, *Tracts on the Mass*, 158–159.

chalice, a gesture symbolizing the kiss of betrayal that Judas gave to Christ in Gethsemane (Mt 26:49; Lk 22:47–48). A series of three crosses follow during the words *"that as many of us as . . . shall have partaken of the most holy Body [cor + pus] and Blood [sangui + nem] of your Son may be filled with every heavenly blessing [bene + dictione] and grace"*, recalling the three times that Christ in his agony prayed to his Father (Mt 26:39, 42, 44). The first of these crosses is made over the Host, the Body of Christ, to denote the sweat that appeared upon the Lord's body as he prayed in Gethsemane (Lk 22:44). The second cross is made over the Precious Blood in the chalice to denote that this sweat was bloody (Lk 22:44). The third cross is made on the priest's face to recall that Christ prostrated himself upon his face in Gethsemane (Mt 26:39).[300]

Regarding the first of the above series of gestures, the bending forward of the priest, the rubrics for the Sarum Rite (and for other rites) specify that the priest, while in this bowed posture, should keep his hands crossed before his chest.[301] Durandus interprets the two crossed hands as symbolizing the two forms of good works, those of the active life and those of the contemplative life.[302]

With the words *"Be mindful also, O Lord"* (*"Memento etiam, Domine"*), the priest begins the portion of the Roman Canon in which the faithful departed are prayed for. The Sarum text of the Canon differs here from the Roman Rite text in that the word "souls" (*animarum*) is added: *"Be mindful also, O Lord, of the souls of your servants and maidservants"* (*"Memento . . . animarum famulorum famularumque tuarum"*).[303] The 1502 Roman Rite *Ordo* of John Burckard instructs the celebrant at this point to fix his gaze upon the newly consecrated Eucharist lying on the altar as he thinks upon those of the faithful departed for whom he is offering the Mass.[304]

At the words in the Canon *"To us, also sinners"* (*"Nobis quoque peccatoribus"*), the priest strikes his breast.[305] Durandus explains this gesture as recalling the contrition of the good thief crucified with Christ (Lk 23:40–42), the contrite confession of faith made by the centurion upon witnessing the death of Christ ("Indeed this was the Son of God" [Mt 27:54]), and the contrition of the crowd that, after seeing the darkness and the earthquake accompanying the Savior's death, returned to their homes striking their breasts (Lk 23:48).[306] The three signs of the cross made during the words *"[you] sanctify, vivify, bless"* (*"sancti + ficas, vivi + ficas, bene + dicas"*)[307] are explained variously as

---

[300] Innocent III, *De sacro altaris mysterio*, bk. 5, chap. 4, PL 217, col. 890.

[301] Martène, *De antiquis ecclesiae ritibus*, bk. 1, chap. 4, art. 12, *ordo* 35, 1:241.

[302] Durandus, *Rationale* (CCCM 140), bk. 4, chap. 44, no. 4, p. 488.

[303] Dickinson, *Missale ad usum . . . Sarum*, col. 619.

[304] Legg, *Tracts on the Mass*, 158–159, 154.

[305] Dickinson, *Missale ad usum . . . Sarum*, col. 619.

[306] Durandus, *Rationale* (CCCM 140), bk. 4, chap. 46, nos. 1–2, p. 494.

[307] Martène, *De antiquis ecclesiae ritibus*, bk. 1, chap. 4, art. 12, *ordo* 35, 1:241.

representing the faith of the early Church in the Trinity;[308] the "third hour" of the day, spoken of in the Gospel of Saint Mark (Mk 15:25) as the hour when Christ was crucified;[309] the threefold shout of the crowd in Jerusalem for the death of Christ ("Crucify him . . ." [Lk 23:18, 21, 23]);[310] and the three prayers said by Christ on the Cross (Lk 23:34; Mt 27:46; Lk 23:46).[311]

In the Mass rubrics of his diocesan *Instructions*, Durandus specifies a further private act of adoration for the priest shortly before the conclusion of the Canon:

> The three aforesaid crosses during "sanctify", "vivify", etc., having been made accordingly, presently he [the priest] or the deacon shall have uncovered the chalice, and with hands joined, bowed a little, [the priest] adores the Body of the Lord, saying, if he should wish, *Hail, our King, Son of David, have mercy on us; blessed the womb that bore you and the breasts that suckled you,* or another [prayer], as it shall have been pleasing to him.[312]

At this same point in the Canon, the 1502 Roman Rite *Ordo* of John Burckard directs the priest to genuflect to the Sacrament.[313]

The actions accompanying the concluding doxology of the Canon, the *Per ipsum* ("*Through him . . . through all ages of ages*"), are described thus in the 1489 Sarum Missal:

> Here the priest should uncover the chalice and should make the sign of the cross with the Host five times: first, above the chalice from side to side [i.e., crosswise over the chalice]; second, level to the chalice [i.e., across the brim of the chalice]; third, farther down the chalice [i.e., crosswise between the side of the chalice and himself]; the fourth just as the first; the fifth in front of the chalice [i.e., crosswise between the brim of the chalice and himself]: *Through him +, and with him +, and in him +, to you, God the Father al + mighty, in the unity of the Holy + Spirit, be all honor and glory.*[314]

Pope Innocent III interprets the uncovering of the chalice—the removal of the corporal (i.e., the pall) from it—as symbolic of the rending of the veil of the Temple at the death of Christ (Mt 27:51).[315] Pope Innocent and Saint Thomas Aquinas identify the first three of the five crosses specified above (the three crosses accompanying "*Through him, and with him, and in him*") with the three hours that Christ hung on

---

[308] Durandus, *Rationale* (CCCM 140), bk. 4, chap. 46, no. 10, p. 497.

[309] Innocent III, *De sacro altaris mysterio*, bk. 5, chap. 14, PL 217, col. 896.

[310] Ibid.

[311] Saint Thomas Aquinas, *Summa theologica*, pt. III, q. 83, art. 5, reply obj. 3, 2:2522.

[312] Berthelé, "Instructions et constitutions de Guillaume Durand", 71.

[313] Legg, *Tracts on the Mass*, 159.

[314] Martène, *De antiquis ecclesiae ritibus*, bk. 1, chap. 4, art. 12, *ordo* 35, 1:241.

[315] Innocent III, *De sacro altaris mysterio*, bk. 5, chap. 11, PL 217, col. 895.

the Cross; the two further signs of the cross that follow are associated by these authors with the separation of the soul of Christ from his body at his death.[316] In tandem with the above-mentioned medieval belief that the Roman Canon as a whole was endowed with a singular efficacy in thwarting the devil, the concluding doxology of the Canon—the *Per ipsum*—was believed to possess a particular power to drive away demons, and even to bind Satan in hell, as will later be seen in the medieval rites for protection from storms (chapter 22).

Although it is not mentioned by the Sarum rubrics, there has existed since the seventh century an elevation of the Eucharist at some point during the concluding doxology of the Canon.[317] In the original form of this elevation, the celebrant would hold the Host aloft for the entire doxology, while the assisting deacon would hold aloft the chalice. Having likened the preceding reposition of the newly consecrated Eucharist upon the altar during the second half of the Canon to the spreading of the body of Christ upon the Cross, Amalarius here identifies the lifting of the Eucharist from the altar at the doxology with the taking down of Christ from the Cross and his burial in the sepulcher; the priest represents Nicodemus, and the deacon symbolizes Joseph of Arimathea.[318] By the time of Durandus (the thirteenth century), the rite had been reduced to a brief elevation of the Host and chalice during the words "*through all ages of ages*", but Durandus nonetheless upholds the association of the elevation with the deposition and burial of Christ, adding that the setting down of the Host and chalice upon the altar at the end of this elevation represents the lowering of the body of Christ into the tomb.[319] The covering of the chalice with the corporal (i.e., the pall) immediately after the elevation is identified by Durandus with the rolling of the stone across the entrance to Christ's tomb (Mt 27:60; an association also made by Pope Innocent III) and with the wrapping of the Lord's body in a clean linen shroud (Mt 27:59).[320] The precise manner of elevating the Host and chalice at the end of the doxology is given by Durandus in his *Instructions* for his diocese of Mende:

> Bringing the Host back over the mouth of the chalice, [the priest] holds it there with the thumbs and index fingers, and, the chalice having thus been elevated a little from the altar with both hands, he says, *through all ages of ages. Amen.* But in saying, *Let us pray. Admonished*

[316] Ibid., chap. 7, col. 894; Saint Thomas Aquinas, *Summa theologica*, pt. III, q. 83, art. 5, reply obj. 3, 2:2522.

[317] See Jungmann, *Mass of the Roman Rite*, 2:267.

[318] Amalarius of Metz, *Liber officialis*, bk. 3, chap. 26, nos. 9–10, in Hanssens, *Amalarii episcopi: Opera liturgica omnia*, 2:346–347.

[319] Durandus, *Rationale* (CCCM 140), bk. 4, chap. 46, nos. 21–22, pp. 502–503.

[320] Ibid., no. 23, p. 503; Innocent III, *De sacro altaris mysterio*, bk. 5, chap. 12, PL 217, col. 895.

by salutary precepts, etc., he sets back the chalice and Host in their places and, with hands joined, reverently bows to them; and afterward, either he or the deacon puts the corporal over the chalice.[321]

In the 1502 Roman Rite *Ordo* of John Burckard, this elevation is followed by another genuflection of the celebrant: "and genuflecting all the way to the ground, he venerates the Sacrament."[322]

Having introduced the Our Father (the *Pater noster*) with the words "*Admonished by salutary precepts . . . we venture to say*", the priest extends his hands for the recitation of the Lord's Prayer.[323] Amalarius sees this recitation of the Our Father as providing the transition between the portion of the Mass associated with the Passion of Christ and the ensuing portion associated with the Resurrection. The seven petitions contained in the Our Father evoke thoughts of the seventh day, Holy Saturday, during which Christ rested in the tomb. And just as on Holy Saturday the disciples would have prayed in their grief and fear for deliverance from evil, so now the Church prays vigilantly to be delivered from evil.[324]

Earlier in the Mass, the removal of the paten from the altar after the Offertory had symbolized the fleeing and hiding of the Apostles during the Passion of Christ. But now, at the Our Father, the subdeacon returns the paten to the deacon, who in turn after the Our Father presents it to the priest.[325] This returning of the paten represents the reception of the good news of the Resurrection, carried by the holy women to the Apostles on Easter Sunday.[326] Insomuch as the Our Father constitutes the beginning of the Communion rite of the Mass, in which the risen, glorified Body of Christ is received, the transition to the theme of the Resurrection for this portion of the Eucharistic liturgy is most appropriate. The first words that Christ spoke to the Apostles following His Resurrection were "Peace be to you" (Jn 20:19); hence it is fitting that in the 1489 Sarum Rite the paten is presented to the priest just before he pronounces the words "*Mercifully grant peace in our days*" (the concluding portion of the prayer *Libera nos*, "*Deliver us, we beseech you, O Lord*"):

Here the deacon should hand over the paten to the priest, kissing his hand, and the priest should kiss the paten. After this he should take it to the left eye, then to the right; thereafter he should make a cross

The Communion Rite: The Our Father, the Rite of Peace, the Communion Prayers, and Holy Communion

---

[321] Berthelé, "Instructions et constitutions de Guillaume Durand", 72.

[322] Legg, *Tracts on the Mass*, 159.

[323] Martène, *De antiquis ecclesiae ritibus*, bk. 1, chap. 4, art. 12, *ordo* 35, 1:241.

[324] Amalarius of Metz, *Liber officialis*, bk. 3, chap. 29, no. 7, in Hanssens, *Amalarii episcopi: Opera liturgica omnia*, 2:357.

[325] 1489 Sarum Missal, in Martène, *De antiquis ecclesiae ritibus*, bk. 1, chap. 4, art. 12, *ordo* 35, 1:241; Frere, *Use of Sarum*, 1:82 (late fourteenth-century customary).

[326] Durandus, *Rationale* (CCCM 140), bk. 4, chap. 50, no. 1, p. 522.

with the paten past his head. And then he should put it back in its place, saying: *Mercifully grant peace in our days . . . safe from every disorder.* Here he should uncover the chalice.[327]

According to Durandus, the kiss of the priest's hand signifies that the deacon wishes to partake in the Passion of Christ, and thereby partake in his kingdom, in accord with Saint Paul's words, "If we suffer, we shall also reign with him" (2 Tim 2:12). The kiss of the paten represents the homage of the holy women to the risen Christ ("But they came up and took hold of his feet, and adored him" [Mt 28:9]) and is moreover a plea for peace of soul and body.[328] By making the sign of the cross with the paten before his face, the priest fortifies himself to complete the Mass, but this action also signifies the holy women's seeking of the crucified Christ when they came to anoint His body on Easter morning, as reflected in the angel's words to them: "I know that you seek Jesus who was crucified" (Mt 28:5).[329] This latter interpretation of Durandus is clearly stressed by the Sarum Rite rubric calling for the priest to raise the paten to each eye before making the sign of the cross with it.

The fracture of the Host follows:

> Here [the celebrant] should uncover the chalice, and take the Body with a bow, transferring it within the concavity of the chalice, retaining it between the thumbs and index fingers; and he should break it in three parts while is said, *Through the same Jesus Christ, your Son, our Lord . . .* Here he should hold the two fractures in his left hand, and the third fracture in his right hand on top of the chalice, saying thus, *Through all ages of ages.*[330]

The priest then makes the sign of the cross three times within the chalice with the third portion of the Host, saying as he does so, "*May the peace of the Lord + be al + ways with + you*" (*Pax Domini*).[331] In the 1502 Roman Rite *Ordo* of John Burckard, the celebrant is directed to venerate the Eucharist with a genuflection before beginning the fracture of the Host.[332]

Pope Innocent III explains the removal of the corporal (i.e., the pall) from the chalice as signifying the rolling back of the stone from the Lord's tomb at his Resurrection.[333] The breaking of the Host calls to mind Christ's "breaking of the bread" before the two disciples in Emmaus, by which they recognized the risen Christ (cf. Lk 24:30–31,

---

[327] Martène, *De antiquis ecclesiae ritibus*, bk. 1, chap. 4, art. 12, *ordo* 35, 1:241.
[328] Durandus, *Rationale* (CCCM 140), bk. 4, chap. 50, no. 3, pp. 523–524.
[329] Ibid.
[330] Martène, *De antiquis ecclesiae ritibus*, bk. 1, chap. 4, art. 12, *ordo* 35, 1:241.
[331] Dickinson, *Missale ad usum . . . Sarum*, col. 622.
[332] Legg, *Tracts on the Mass*, 160.
[333] Innocent III, *De sacro altaris mysterio*, bk. 6, chap. 2, PL 217, col. 907.

35).[334] Saint Thomas Aquinas sees in the breaking of the Host an imaging of "the rending of Christ's body" in his Passion.[335] The three portions into which the Host has been fractured symbolize the three states of the members of the Mystical Body of Christ: (1) those who are in Heaven in both soul and body—Christ himself and the Blessed Virgin Mary; (2) those on earth; (3) those whose bodies rest in the grave but whose souls are in Heaven or Purgatory.[336]

The Mass continues with the Lamb of God—the *Agnus Dei*:

> At the Lamb of God that is to be said, the deacon and subdeacon should approach the priest, both to his right, the deacon nearer, the subdeacon further off, and they say privately, *Lamb of God* ... Here, [the priest] should deposit the said third part of the Host into the Sacrament of the Blood while making the sign of the cross, saying thus: *May this sacro + sanct mingling of the Body and Blood of our Lord Jesus Christ be made unto me, and unto all partaking of it, health of mind and body, and a salutary preparation to meriting and gaining life eternal. Through the same Christ ...*[337]

The diocesan *Instructions* of Durandus direct that while saying the *Agnus Dei* the celebrant should stand bowed slightly over the altar, with his hands joined, "reverently gazing upon the Eucharist",[338] a rubric manifesting that the *Agnus Dei* is addressed *directly* to Christ in the Sacrament. The 1502 Roman Rite *Ordo* of John Burckard instructs the priest to genuflect after immersing the third portion of the Host in the chalice, just before beginning the Lamb of God.[339]

The immersion of one portion of the Host into the Precious Blood denotes the reunion of the body and the soul of Christ at his Resurrection, according to Pope Innocent III.[340] The recitation of the Lamb of God at this point of the Mass is also fitted to the Easter motif, for just as earlier the priest's words "*May the peace of the Lord be always with you*" would have corresponded to Christ's first words to the Apostles on Easter Sunday, "*Peace be to you*" (Jn 20:19), so now the words "*Lamb of God, who take away the sins of the world*" correspond to the words Christ spoke shortly after his Easter greeting of peace: "Whose sins you shall forgive, they are forgiven them" (Jn 20:23).[341] Commenting upon the *Agnus Dei*, Florus of Lyons observes that just as Christ has taken away the sins of the world by giving his blood for us on the Cross, and by washing us with the waters of baptism made

---

[334] Ibid.

[335] Saint Thomas Aquinas, *Summa theologica*, pt. III, q. 83, art. 5, reply obj. 7, 2:2522.

[336] Ibid., reply obj. 7 and reply obj. 8, pp. 2522–2523.

[337] Martène, *De antiquis ecclesiae ritibus*, bk. 1, chap. 4, art. 12, ordo 35, 1:241.

[338] Berthelé, "Instructions et constitutions de Guillaume Durand", 73.

[339] Legg, *Tracts on the Mass*, 161.

[340] Innocent III, *De sacro altaris mysterio*, bk. 6, chap. 2, PL 217, col. 907.

[341] Ibid., chap. 4, col. 908.

efficacious by his sacred Passion, so also "he takes away the sins of the world, and washes us from our sins every day in his blood, when the remembrance of his same blessed Passion is unfolded at the altar." [342] Sicard of Cremona sees the Lamb of God as a petition that "by the mercy of the Lamb ... peace may be given to us, and his Body may be worthily consumed by us"; as for the transition in the *Agnus Dei* from the ending *"Have mercy on us"* to the ending *"Grant us peace"*, Sicard adds that with penitence and the remission of sins comes "the peace of God, of men, and of angels".[343]

The *Agnus Dei* is yet another Mass text that was sometimes troped with added phrases. In the Ordinary of the Mass from the various editions of the Sarum Missal, the standard threefold acclamation of the *Agnus Dei* is given;[344] but a late thirteenth-century manuscript of the Sarum Missal additionally provides over a dozen troped versions of the *Agnus Dei*, including the following fine example, rich with scriptural allusions (cf. Ps 44:2; 2 Tim 1:12; Song 3:1–4):

Lamb of God, my heart has uttered a good word;
I declare my works to the King. Have mercy on us.

Lamb of God, him whom I saw, whom I believed,
whom I loved. Have mercy on us.

Lamb of God, give the rewards of joys, give the rewards of graces, dissolve the
*   fetters of contention,*
bind fast the treaties of peace. Grant us peace. [345]

After the Lamb of God comes the sign of peace, which Sicard of Cremona also links to the Resurrection theme for this part of the Mass, seeing it as manifesting that by rising from the dead Christ has given peace to mankind.[346] In the Sarum Rite, before the sign of peace, the priest prays: *"Holy Lord, Father almighty, eternal God, grant me to partake of this most holy Body and Blood of your Son, our Lord Jesus Christ, so worthily that I may merit to receive through it the remission of all my sins, and be filled with your Holy Spirit, and have your peace; for you alone are God, and besides you there is no other, whose kingdom and glorious dominion endures unto ages of ages without end. Amen."* [347] The Sarum rite of peace follows, utilizing the pax board, as with the sign of peace at the beginning of the Sarum Mass. First, the priest kisses the corporals on the altar; then he kisses the top of the chalice. Giving the sign of peace to the assisting deacon, the celebrant says to him, *"Peace to you*

---

[342] Florus of Lyons, *De expositione missae*, no. 90, PL 119, col. 72.

[343] Sicard of Cremona, *Mitrale*, bk. 3, chap. 8, PL 213, col. 139.

[344] Dickinson, *Missale ad usum ... Sarum*, col. 623.

[345] Legg, *Sarum missal*, 546 (Latin text quoted and translated by permission of Oxford University Press).

[346] Sicard of Cremona, *Mitrale*, bk. 3, chap. 8, PL 213, col. 140.

[347] Martène, *De antiquis ecclesiae ritibus*, bk. 1, chap. 4, art. 12, *ordo* 35, 1:241.

and to the Church of God", after which the pax board is passed to the different ministers for them to kiss.[348]

In the missal of Avila (1510), the celebrant in the course of the rite of peace kisses the Host, an action explained by Durandus as denoting in a particular manner that "spiritual peace has been given to mankind by Christ":[349] "And holding the Body of Christ in his right hand over the chalice, while with his left hand he holds up the chalice, having bowed afterward, he says, *Lord Jesus Christ, who are the true peace and true concord,* [*make me make peace in this holy hour*]. And when he shall have said, *Make me make peace in this holy hour,* he raises himself up and kisses the Body of Christ that he holds in his right hand."[350] In Requiem Masses, the sign of peace is omitted, for as a rubric of the Avila missal observes, the souls in Purgatory suffer no disturbance of peace as we do on earth, in that they are no longer able to sin,[351] an explanation traceable to the *Rationale* of Durandus.[352]

In the 1489 Sarum Missal, after the rite of the pax board, the priest takes the Host, holding it with both hands, and begins a prayer (*Deus Pater, fons et origo totius bonitatis*) that, although addressed to God the Father, contains an intervening rubric implying that the act of adoration within the prayer is also addressed to Christ in the Sacrament:

> *God the Father, Fount and Source of all goodness, who, having drawn us with your mercy, willed your only-begotten* [*Son*] *to descend to the depths of the earth for us and to assume flesh, which I here hold in my hands,* (Here the priest should bow himself to the Host, saying:) *I adore you, I glorify you, and I praise you with the whole intention of my heart, and I pray that we your servants you may not indict but may forgive our sins, that we may be worthy to serve you alone, the living and true God, with a pure heart and a chaste body. Through the same Christ our Lord. Amen.*[353]

This prayer and its accompanying rubric appear in the Sarum liturgical books from the late fourteenth century onward.[354]

The priest continues with an oration to Christ (*Domine Jesu Christe, Fili Dei vivi*), found in both the Roman and Sarum missals, in which he asks to be delivered of all his sins and every evil, and to be faithful to the commandments, and never to be separated from Christ ("*Lord Jesus Christ, Son of the living God, who by the will of the Father*", etc.).[355]

---

[348] Ibid.

[349] Durandus, *Rationale* (CCCM 140), bk. 4, chap. 53, no. 1, p. 543.

[350] *Missale Abulense* (1510), sig. t2r.

[351] Ibid., sig. t2r–t2v.

[352] Durandus, *Rationale* (CCCM 140), bk. 4, chap. 53, no. 8, p. 546.

[353] Martène, *De antiquis ecclesiae ritibus*, bk. 1, chap. 4, art. 12, *ordo* 35, 1:241.

[354] Both the prayer and the rubric appear in the late fourteenth-century Sarum Customary (Frere, *Use of Sarum*, 1:86) and in printed editions of the Sarum Missal from 1487 to 1557 (Dickinson, *Missale ad usum ... Sarum*, col. 625).

[355] 1489 Sarum Missal, in Martène, *De antiquis ecclesiae ritibus*, bk. 1, chap. 4, art. 12, *ordo* 35, 1:241; 1474 *Missale Romanum*, in Lippe, *Missale Romanum*, 1:210.

As with the recitation of the Lamb of God earlier, here too Durandus in his *Instructions* reminds the priest that he is praying to Christ *in the Sacrament*, enjoining that the celebrant should be "reverently gazing upon the Eucharist" while saying this prayer.[356]

In an earlier manuscript text of the Sarum Missal from the thirteenth century, there follows a prayer (absent from the later printed missals) beseeching the Father to relieve the souls in Purgatory through the merits of the Mass being celebrated: "*We give thanks to you, God the Father almighty, entreating to be assisted by you, by virtue of the intercession of those already blessed; imploring also for those who are still in the purgative places, we immolate to you, O Father, your Son, that by this most holy sacrifice their pain may be shorter and lighter.*"[357]

Returning to the 1489 printed Sarum Missal, we find here two final prayers to Christ before the priest consumes the Host, the first of which is similar to but shorter than the pre-Communion prayer *Perceptio Corporis tui* of the Roman Missal:[358] "*May the Sacrament of your Body and Blood, Lord Jesus Christ, that I, although unworthy, receive, be to me not a judgment and condemnation but by your goodness be profitable to the salvation of my body and soul. Amen.*"[359] For the second of these prayers (*Ave in aeternum*), a text specifically of the Sarum Rite, the priest is instructed explicitly to address his prayer to the Eucharist:

> To the Body he should say with a humiliation before he should receive:
> *Hail forever, most holy Flesh of Christ, to me the supreme goodness before all things and above all things.*[360]

This prayer with its accompanying rubric can be found in the Sarum liturgical books from the late fourteenth century onward,[361] but the rubrical phrase *cum inclinatione*, "with a bow", given in the earlier texts, has been replaced with the phrase *cum humiliatione*, "with a humiliation", in the 1489 text above and in all the other printed editions of the Sarum Missal from 1487 onward. In this context "humiliation" usually means a genuflection.[362] Hence this Sarum usage would constitute the second earliest instance of a rubric directing the celebrant to genuflect to the Eucharist *during* the Mass, appearing only two years

---

[356] Berthelé, "Instructions et constitutions de Guillaume Durand", 74.

[357] Legg, *Sarum Missal*, 227 (Latin text quoted and translated by permission of Oxford University Press).

[358] 1474 *Missale Romanum*, in Lippe, *Missale Romanum*, 1:210.

[359] Martène, *De antiquis ecclesiae ritibus*, bk. 1, chap. 4, art. 12, *ordo* 35, 1:241.

[360] Ibid.

[361] Both the prayer and the rubric appear in the late fourteenth-century Sarum Customary (Frere, *Use of Sarum*, 1:86), the early fifteenth-century Sarum Missal (Ferreres Boluda, *Historia del misal romano*, 189), and printed editions of the Sarum Missal from 1487 to 1557 (Dickinson, *Missale ad usum . . . Sarum*, col. 626).

[362] A marginal note in the 1568 missal of Palencia, Spain, expressly identifies genuflections as *humiliationes*; see *Missale pallantinum* (1568), fol. 357r.

after the earlier-cited directions regarding the celebrant's genuflections in the 1485 *Pontificalis liber* of Rome.

The priest now takes up the Host to receive it, saying beforehand as he makes the sign of the cross with the Host, "*May the Body of our Lord Jesus Christ be to me, a sinner, the Way and the Life, in the name of the Father, and of the Son, and of the Holy Spirit. Amen.*"[363]

As can be seen above, the Sarum Rite does not utilize the well-known pre-Communion prayer of the Roman Rite, *Domine non sum dignus*, "*Lord, I am not worthy*" (first used in the twelfth century),[364] but it is found in the Communion rite of the aforementioned 1510 missal of Avila, which also instructs the priest to meditate before receiving:

> Thereupon he ought to meditate upon the Incarnation, the Passion, and the excellence of this Sacrament, saying, *I will receive the heavenly Bread* [*and invoke the name of the Lord*]. And afterward he says three times, *Lord, I am not worthy that you should enter* ... Which said, he raises himself up [from bowing] and takes Communion. And if any remnants of the Body of Christ are left on his fingers, he places them in the chalice.[365]

The meditation rubric in this Avila text is taken verbatim from the words of Durandus in his *Rationale*.[366] By the words "*I will receive the heavenly Bread*" ("*Panem celestem accipiam*", also found in the Roman Missal),[367] the priest reminds himself that he is about to receive "the bread of God ... which cometh down from heaven" (Jn 6:33), so as to motivate himself to receive the Eucharist "with greater reverence and devotion" (Durandus).[368] This reverence is expressed outwardly in the 1502 Roman Rite *Ordo* of John Burckard, which directs the priest to genuflect before saying, "*I will receive the heavenly Bread* ..."[369]

The prayer "*Lord, I am not worthy*" reminds the priest to receive with humility (Durandus).[370] That these words are addressed *directly* to Christ in the Sacrament is made clear by the rubrics of Durandus' *Instructions* for his diocese of Mende, in which the priest is told to hold the paten with the Host before him, "devoutly looking at the

---

[363] Martène, *De antiquis ecclesiae ritibus*, bk. 1, chap. 4, art. 12, *ordo* 35, 1:241. Regarding the Communion reception formula in the Roman Rite, see footnote 14 on p. 6 of the present work.

[364] The use of this verse as a separate pre-Communion prayer, with the phrase "my servant" from the scriptural original (Mt 8:8) changed to "*my soul*", appears in a twelfth-century missal of Norman France; see Jungmann, *Mass of the Roman Rite*, 2:355–356.

[365] *Missale Abulense* (1510), sig. t2v.

[366] Durandus, *Rationale* (CCCM 140), bk. 4, chap. 54, no. 10, p. 551.

[367] 1474 *Missale Romanum*, in Lippe, *Missale Romanum*, 1:211.

[368] Durandus, *Rationale* (CCCM 140), bk. 4, chap. 54, no. 10, p. 551.

[369] Legg, *Tracts on the Mass*, 163.

[370] Durandus, *Rationale* (CCCM 140), bk. 4, chap. 54, no. 10, p. 551.

very Body of Christ" as he says, "*Lord, I am not worthy ...*"[371] The Roman Rite usage of this prayer immediately before Holy Communion, one of many instances in the medieval Mass wherein the celebrant and the faithful are reminded that they are sinners, evokes not only the image of the centurion's protestation of unworthiness in receiving Christ, of which this prayer is virtually a direct quotation (cf. Mt 8:8), but also resembles the humble protestation of the prodigal son, "Father, I have sinned against heaven, and before thee, I am not now worthy to be called thy son" (Lk 15:21). The prodigal son's words were in fact used as a Communion prayer in a fifteenth-century missal of Evreux, France.[372] In this light we see the particular aptness of Durandus' comparison of the Mass to the banquet prepared for the prodigal son by his jubilant father upon his return home (Lk 15:23–24).[373]

For the Communion of the Precious Blood in the 1489 Sarum Missal, the priest prays again *to* the Sacrament before receiving it, saying "to the Blood with great devotion": "*Hail forever, heavenly Drink, to me the supreme goodness before all things and above all things.*"[374] As with the Sarum pre-Communion prayer "to the Body" of Christ, this prayer "to the Blood" of Christ is included with its rubric in the Sarum liturgical books from the late fourteenth century onward.[375] It is immediately followed by the prayer *Corporis et sanguinis tui, Domine Jesu Christe*: "*May the Body and Blood of our Lord Jesus Christ avail me, a sinner, for an everlasting remedy unto life eternal. Amen. In the name of the Father, and of the Son, and of the Holy Spirit. Amen.*"[376] After saying this prayer, the priest receives from the chalice. Although not expressly stated in the rubrics, it is evident that in the Sarum Rite, as in the Roman Rite, the priest would make the sign of the cross with the chalice before receiving the Precious Blood, for such an action is implied by the above words, "*In the name of the Father*", etc., and as we have already seen, the Sarum rubrics specify such a sign of the cross with the Host before the celebrant receives it. Moreover, in most of the late medieval printed editions of the Sarum Missal, there is a cross symbol inserted within the word *nomine* (name), which always indicates a signing with the cross.[377]

In the missal of Avila, as in the *Missale Romanum*, the priest says the prayer *Quid retribuam Domino*, consisting of two verses from Psalm 115 (verses 12–13) joined to a verse from Psalm 17 (verse 4), prior to the Communion of the chalice: "*What shall I render to the Lord, for all the*

---

[371] Berthelé, "Instructions et constitutions de Guillaume Durand", 74.

[372] Martène, *De antiquis ecclesiae ritibus*, bk. 1, chap. 4, art. 12, *ordo* 28, 1:232.

[373] Durandus, *Rationale* (CCCM 140), bk. 4, chap. 1, no. 1, p. 240.

[374] Martène, *De antiquis ecclesiae ritibus*, bk. 1, chap. 4, art. 12, *ordo* 35, 1:241.

[375] See Frere, *Use of Sarum*, 1:87 (late fourteenth-century Sarum Customary), Ferreres Boluda, *Historia del misal romano*, 189 (early fifteenth-century Sarum Missal), and Dickinson, *Missale ad usum ... Sarum*, col. 626 (printed editions of the Sarum Missal from 1487 to 1557).

[376] Martène, *De antiquis ecclesiae ritibus*, bk. 1, chap. 4, art. 12, *ordo* 35, 1:241.

[377] Dickinson, *Missale ad usum ... Sarum*, col. 626.

things that he hath rendered to me? I will take the chalice of salvation; and I will call upon the name of the Lord. Praising I will call upon the Lord; and I shall be saved from my enemies." [378] The 1502 Roman Rite *Ordo* of John Burckard instructs the priest to genuflect before saying, *"I will take the chalice of salvation . . ."* [379]

In the 1489 Sarum Missal, there is no indication as to when or how the celebrant administers Holy Communion to the other ministers or the congregants (if any will be receiving), but it is likely that the general Communion occurs at the same point as in the Roman Rite, that is, immediately after the priest's Communion of the chalice but before the purification of the celebrant's fingers, as specified in Burckard's 1502 *Ordo*.[380] The thirteenth-century statutes of the Carthusian Order do explicitly state the manner of receiving Holy Communion for the assisting deacon and for others: "The deacon going to communicate kneels at the altar step, where we all kneel, when either all or some of us communicate." [381] Kneeling for Holy Communion is likewise specified in a twelfth-century Cistercian book of customs[382] and in a Franciscan ceremonial dating from 1247 to 1251,[383] a practice that had already appeared by the eleventh century—if not considerably earlier. A customary for the French Benedictine abbey of Cluny compiled about 1075 by the monk Bernard speaks of a benchlike furnishing called a *reclinatorium* that would be placed in the sanctuary between two pillars, functioning as a kneeler or altar rail, where communicants would receive the Sacrament on their knees. When Holy Communion was to be administered, a linen cloth (a forerunner to what would become known as the Communion cloth) would be placed over the kneeler, and as each communicant received the Eucharist, a special platter called a *scutella*, an early form of the Communion plate, was held under the communicant's mouth to prevent the Host from falling.[384] Far earlier, Saint Augustine (+430) speaks of prostrating oneself to adore before receiving Holy Communion;[385] the *Regula coenobialis* of the Irish missionary monk Saint Columban (+615) prescribes a triple prostration prior to receiving the Eucharist.[386] A pre-Communion

---

[378] *Missale Abulense* (1510), sig. t2v; 1474 *Missale Romanum*, in Lippe, *Missale Romanum*, 1:211.

[379] Legg, *Tracts on the Mass*, 164.

[380] Ibid.

[381] Martène, *De antiquis ecclesiae ritibus*, bk. 1, chap. 4, art. 12, *ordo* 25, 1:228.

[382] *Usus antiquiores ordinis Cisterciensis*, pt. 2, chap. 58, PL 166, col. 1432.

[383] Text in Stephen J.P. Van Dijk, O.F.M., *Sources of the Modern Roman Liturgy: The Ordinals by Haymo of Faversham and Related Documents (1243–1307)*, Studia et documenta Franciscana 2 (Leiden, Netherlands: Brill, 1963), 2:358.

[384] *Ordo Cluniacensis*, pt. 1, chap. 35, in Marquard Herrgott, ed., *Vetus disciplina monastica* (Paris, 1726; repr., Siegburg, Germany: Franciscus Schmitt, 1999), 224–225.

[385] Saint Augustine, *Expositio in Ps. 98*, no. 9, PL 37, col. 1264.

[386] Felim O'Briain, O.F.M., "The Blessed Eucharist in Irish Liturgy and History", in *Studia eucharistica: DCC^i anni a condito festo sanctissimi Corporis Christi, 1246–1946* (Antwerp, Belgium: Uitgeverij Paul Brand, Bussum de Nederlandsche Boekhandel, 1946), 236.

genuflection had appeared in the liturgy of the East Syrian Rite by the sixth century.[387]

There is one piece of evidence suggesting that genuflection for the actual moment of receiving Holy Communion had appeared in at least a few places by the sixth century: the famous Evangelary (Gospel book) of Rossano, an illuminated manuscript of Byzantine origin preserved for centuries in the treasury of Italy's cathedral of Rossano, includes a depiction of the Apostles' reception of the Eucharist at the Last Supper. As several of the Apostles stand in line, waiting to receive Holy Communion, Christ, who is standing, gives the Eucharist to an Apostle who is bowing low and bending one knee to receive the Sacrament.[388] It seems highly likely that the artist chose to portray the Apostles' Communion in this way because he had seen the Eucharist received in this manner in his own age, the sixth century.

While the major medieval liturgical commentators do not discuss the posture of communicants, some do comment upon the reasons for the posture of kneeling in general. Honorius of Autun (+c. 1135) observes, "We with the Apostle say to God, 'I bow my knees to the Father of our Lord Jesus Christ' [Eph 3:14]."[389] Durandus states, "In church both knees are to be bent ... for to Christ every [knee] shall be bent [Phil 2:10]. Indeed, Solomon, praying for the people, fixed both his knees to the earth, and stretched his hands to heaven [1 Kings 8:54]."[390]

In the West, Holy Communion administered directly onto the tongue of the communicant (rather than into the communicant's hands), first appearing in seventh-century Gaul,[391] became a fairly established practice by the ninth century.[392] This manner of reception existed in the Byzantine East by the beginning of the fourth century.[393] Pope Saint Gregory the Great, in his *Dialogues*, relates that Pope Saint Agapitus I (+536) had administered Holy Communion in this way while in Greece.[394] For the laity in the West, Communion under one species

---

[387] Jungmann, *Mass of the Roman Rite*, 2:377.

[388] The particular image from the Evangelary of Rossano cited here is reproduced in Righetti, *Manuale di storia liturgica*, 3:457. Regarding the dating of this ancient text, see L. A. Jones, "Byzantine Art", in *New Catholic Encyclopedia*, 2nd ed. (Detroit: Thomson/Gale, 2003), 2:729.

[389] Honorius of Autun, *Gemma animae*, bk. 1, chap. 117, PL 172, cols. 582–583.

[390] Durandus, *Rationale divinorum officiorum*, bk. 5, chap. 2, no. 45, in A. Davril, O.S.B., and T.M. Thibodeau, eds., *Guillelmi Duranti: Rationale divinorum officiorum V–VI*, CCCM 140a (Turnhout, Belgium: Brepols, 1998), 35–36.

[391] Righetti, *Manuale di storia liturgica*, 3:424.

[392] *Statuta Bonifatii* (ninth century), statute 32, in J.D. Mansi, ed., *Sacrorum conciliorum nova et amplissima collectio*, vol. 12 (Florence and Venice, 1766; repr., Paris: Hubert Welter, 1901), col. 386; Council of Rouen (878), chap. 2, in J.D. Mansi, ed., *Sacrorum conciliorum nova et amplissima collectio*, vol. 10 (Florence and Venice, 1764; repr., Paris: Hubert Welter, 1901), cols. 1199–1200.

[393] Righetti, *Manuale di storia liturgica*, 3:424.

[394] Saint Gregory the Great, *Dialogues*, bk. 3, chap. 3, in Adalbert de Vogüé, ed., and Paul Antin, trans., *Grégoire le Grand: Dialogues*, vol. 2, *Livres I–III*, SC 260 (Paris: Cerf, 1979), 268–269 (Latin text with French translation).

had largely supplanted the earlier practice of Communion under both species by the end of the twelfth century.[395] By the thirteenth century, kneeling communicants were placing their hands beneath an oblong cloth for catching any particles of the Eucharist that might fall during the distribution of Holy Communion—the Communion cloth;[396] the aforementioned Franciscan ceremonial of 1247–1251 directs that two acolytes should hold the cloth (here described as a "pall") extended before the priest as he administers Holy Communion.[397] In rubrics for an ordination Mass, a liturgical text of Rome, the Ceremonial of a Cardinal Bishop (c. 1280), speaks of two clerics holding a cloth between the bishop and the newly ordained as they receive Holy Communion from him.[398]

Throughout the Middle Ages, the distribution of Holy Communion (under the species of bread) to other communicants at Mass was ordinarily reserved to priests and bishops,[399] a distinction with its roots in the early Church, as can be seen from a commentary of the Eastern bishop and ecclesiastical writer Theodore of Mopsuestia (c. 350–428):

> And the Seraph [Is 6:6] did not hold the live coal with his hand but with tongs. This vision demonstrates that the (faithful) should be afraid to draw nigh unto the Sacrament without an intermediary, and this is the priest, who, with his hand, gives you the Sacrament and says: "*The Body of Christ,*" while he himself does not believe that he is worthy to hold and give such things; but in the place of tongs he possesses the spiritual grace, which he received in his priesthood, and from which he acquired the confidence for giving such things.[400]

A particularly beautiful and highly detailed rite for the administration of Holy Communion, whether during Mass or, as was often the case, outside of Mass, is given in a liturgical manuscript dating from about the year 1263, a British Museum copy of the Dominican Order's mid-thirteenth-century Humbert Codex. The rite is provided in conjunction with rubrics for the celebration of High Mass in the Dominican Order.[401] The instructions for the Communion rite begin with directives regarding the proper reservation of the Eucharist in Dominican churches:

---

[395] Amiot, *History of the Mass*, 125.

[396] Jungmann, *Mass of the Roman Rite*, 2:375.

[397] Van Dijk, *Sources of the Modern Roman Liturgy*, 2:358.

[398] Ceremonial of a Cardinal Bishop, ascribed to Latino Cardinal Malabranca (+1294), in Dykmans, *Cérémonial papal de la fin du moyen âge à la Renaissance*, 1:258.

[399] Jungmann, *Mass of the Roman Rite*, 2:387, plus footnote.

[400] Theodore of Mopsuestia, *Liber de baptizandos*, chap. 5; English translation in A. Mingana, ed. and trans., *Commentary of Theodore of Mopsuestia on the Lord's Prayer and on the Sacraments of Baptism and the Eucharist*, Woodbrooke Studies 6 (Cambridge: W. Heffer and Sons, 1933), 119.

[401] Manuscript: London, British Museum, Add. MS 23935, in Legg, *Tracts on the Mass*, 84–87.

About sacred Communion and the manner of communicating in the convent, it is to be noted that for reserving sacred Communion, a becoming and fitting vessel ought to be kept to be set honorably upon the high altar, inside of which is to be kept a pyx of silver, ivory, or another precious material, within which, in a white and clean cloth, is to be reserved one consecrated Host, or more if they are reserved, yet not in great number. And also it should be seen to it that both the vessel and the aforesaid pyx be carefully made firm and be closed, lest in some case the aforesaid Hosts could fall or be removed.[402]

The text notes that on days when there will be a general Communion, an "exhortation" should be delivered to the religious community assembled for the daily chapter meeting in order that they might fittingly prepare themselves for the reception of the Sacrament. At the beginning of the actual Communion rite, all adore together and participate in a brief penitential rite before individually receiving:

When therefore the hour of communicating shall have approached, the deacon, with the candle bearers preceding him with tapers, should bring the aforesaid pyx with the Body of the Lord, opening the same upon the altar. And all the other friars should prostrate themselves adoring, except the priest celebrating, who alone should adore bowing.

But after a brief adoration, all should say, *I confess to God* ... And the priest should give the absolution, saying, *May almighty God have mercy on you* ..., the absolution also, etc.[403]

The distribution of Holy Communion follows. The manner of receiving the Sacrament is described first:

Afterward they should communicate. First, the ministers according to the order of their degree. Then the convent, beginning from the superiors. And the friars should come two by two. Last, the lay brothers....

But in the first place, when the ministers ought to communicate, two should approach from the friars standing in the choir, to whom the sacristan shall have signaled; and kneeling next to the priest on his right and his left, they should hold a clean and decent cloth[404] delivered by the sacristan, and extended between the priest and those communicating, from the priest all the way to those communicating, bringing it, moreover, under the chins of those communicating. But after all the ministers shall have been provided with Communion, the acolytes should hold the aforesaid cloth in the aforesaid manner, until all will have communicated. And when a friar shall approach for

---

[402] Ibid., 84–85.

[403] Ibid., 85.

[404] The word used in the original Latin, *mappula*, suggests that this was a relatively small cloth.

receiving Communion, he should not prostrate himself, nor kiss the ground or the foot of the priest, but kneeling upon the step in a fitting place, disposing himself with all the rest of his body erect, he should receive the Sacrament with fitting discipline and reverence, his mouth open neither exceedingly, nor a little, but moderately, guarding against the straying of his eyes, or the unusual disposition of his face.[405]

Instructions are then given as to how the priest is to distribute Holy Communion:

The priest should administer the reserved Hosts first. And when he administers each Host, he should take it with his right hand,[406] and the paten with his left hand, in putting it under the Host. And thus he should transfer [the Host] all the way to each friar communicating. And when he delivers it to him, he should say: *May the Body of our Lord Jesus Christ preserve you unto everlasting life. Amen.*[407]

After each friar receives Holy Communion, he goes to a deacon with an ablution chalice,[408] a chalice of *unconsecrated* wine (not the chalice used for the consecration of the Precious Blood), to ensure that every last particle of the Host is fully consumed:

The Sacrament having been received, the friar, bowing, should raise himself up. And the Host having been consumed, he should approach the wine, which is to be received standing, and in a moderate quantity for cleansing his mouth, lest any particle of the Host should remain between the teeth.... And [the deacon] ought to hold the foot of the chalice with a beautiful and fitting cloth with which the friars after the ablution of the mouth should also wipe their lips.[409]

Each of the friars makes a thanksgiving following Holy Communion: "But after a friar shall have communicated and shall have taken the wine, he can pray privately while the others communicate."[410]

To return now to our Sarum Rite text, the 1489 missal specifies that after the priest has received the Precious Blood from the chalice, he is to "say with devotion" in a bowed position the following prayer (*Gratias tibi ago, Domine . . . qui me refecisti*): "*I give you thanks, holy*

---

[405] Legg, *Tracts on the Mass*, 85–86.

[406] The use of the right hand to distribute Holy Communion is also specified in the liturgical text of Rome known as the Ceremonial of a Cardinal Bishop (c. 1280), ascribed to Latino Cardinal Malabranca (+1294); text in Dykmans, *Cérémonial papal de la fin du moyen âge à la Renaissance*, 1:258.

[407] Legg, *Tracts on the Mass*, 86.

[408] The giving of an ablution to communicants to ensure their consumption of all particles of the Host was fairly common in late medieval Europe; see Jungmann, *Mass of the Roman Rite*, 2:412–414.

[409] Legg, *Tracts on the Mass*, 86.

[410] Ibid.

Lord, Father almighty, eternal God, who have refreshed me from the most sacred Body and Blood of your Son, our Lord Jesus Christ, and I pray that this Sacrament of our salvation, of which I, an unworthy sinner, have partaken, may not come to me unto judgment, nor unto condemnation for my offenses, but unto the profit of my body and the salvation of my soul unto life eternal. Amen." [411] An earlier text of the Sarum Missal, dating from the beginning of the fifteenth century, adds to the rubrics for the above post-Communion prayer that in saying it the priest, bowing at the middle of the altar "with great veneration", should direct his gaze upon the cross—evidently a crucifix on or above the altar. [412] This instruction serves to remind the priest yet again to see in the Eucharist the sacrifice of Calvary.

Following the above prayer, the priest begins the ablutions of his fingers and of the chalice, which in the late medieval Sarum liturgy are very meticulous, out of deep reverence for even the smallest particles of the Host and every drop of the Precious Blood (similarly detailed ablution rubrics appear in Durandus' *Instructions*): [413]

> The priest should go to the right side of the altar with the chalice between his hands, his fingers still joined as before. And the subdeacon should approach and pour out into the chalice wine and water, and the priest should rinse his hands, lest any remnants of the Body or Blood should remain on the fingers or in the chalice.... After the first ablution or pouring forth is said this prayer: *What we have consumed with the mouth, O Lord, may we receive with a pure mind, that from a temporal gift it may be made unto us an everlasting remedy.* [414]
>
> Here he should wash his fingers in the concavity of the chalice with the wine poured by the subdeacon; which having been drunk, there should follow the prayer *May this Communion, O Lord, purify us from sin and make us to be partakers of the heavenly remedy.*
>
> After the partaking of the ablution, the priest should place the chalice upon the paten, lest if what remains should drip; and afterward, bowing himself, he should say: *Let us worship the sign of the Cross, by which we have partaken of the Sacrament of salvation.* Then he should wash his hands; the deacon meanwhile should fold together the corporals. The [priest's] hands having been washed, and the priest returning to the right side of the altar, the deacon should present the chalice to the mouth of the priest, if anything of the infusion shall have remained in it to be recovered. [415]

---

[411] 1489 Sarum Missal, in Martène, *De antiquis ecclesiae ritibus*, bk. 1, chap. 4, art. 12, *ordo* 35, 1:241.

[412] Early fifteenth-century Sarum Missal, quoted in Ferreres Boluda, *Historia del misal romano*, 189–190, 202.

[413] Berthelé, "Instructions et constitutions de Guillaume Durand", 75–76.

[414] This prayer, *Quod ore sumpsimus, Domine*, is also found in the Roman Rite; see the 1474 *Missale Romanum*, in Lippe, *Missale Romanum*, 1:211.

[415] Martène, *De antiquis ecclesiae ritibus*, bk. 1, chap. 4, art. 12, *ordo* 35, 1:241.

In the aforementioned early fifteenth-century manuscript of the Sarum Missal, predating the above text, the priest is instructed again to direct his gaze upon the cross when "with great veneration" he bows to recite the postablution antiphon, "*Let us worship the sign of the Cross . . .*"[416]

Pope Innocent III notes that the post-Communion ablution of the hands expresses symbolically the priest's humble acknowledgment of his unworthiness to have celebrated so great a sacrament—he recognizes that his hands, the hands of a corruptible mortal, are unworthy to have touched the sacred, incorruptible Body of Christ in the Sacrament. The priest has rightly celebrated according to his vocation, but he does not forget his unworthiness, in accordance with the Lord's admonition: "When you have done all these things that are commanded you, say: We are unprofitable servants" (Lk 17:10).[417] The antiphon regarding the Cross at the end of the Sarum ablution rite above serves as yet another affirmation of the Eucharist as a re-presentation of the sacrifice of Calvary.

Following the completion of the ablution, the Communion antiphon proper to the day or the particular Mass is recited by the celebrant and his ministers.[418] It is seen as symbolic of the Apostles' rejoicing at the Resurrection of Christ (cf. Jn 20:20).[419] This antiphon, comprising a verse often but not always taken from the Scriptures, was from the twelfth century onward recited *after* Holy Communion.[420] In this context it is explained by Rupert of Deutz (+c. 1129) as a thanksgiving offered after receiving "the Saving Food".[421] To illustrate the medieval Communion antiphon, we offer the following example from the 1498 missal of the Rite of Braga, Portugal, *Ave Regina caelorum*, used for the feast of the Immaculate Conception: "*Hail, Queen of the heavens, Mother of the King of angels. O Mother, flower of virgins, even as a rose or a lily, pour forth your prayers to your Son for the salvation of the faithful.*" [422] In the missal of Avila, immediately before saying the Communion antiphon, the priest prays in thanksgiving for Holy Communion the Canticle of Simeon, *Nunc dimittis:* "*Now thou dost dismiss thy servant, O Lord, according to thy word in peace; because my eyes have seen thy salvation, which thou hast prepared before the face of all peoples: a light to the revelation of the Gentiles, and the glory of thy people Israel*" (Lk 2:29–32).[423] These words are well suited to a post-Communion thanksgiving, for they express the finding of contentment

---

[416] Ferreres Boluda, *Historia del misal romano*, 203.

[417] Innocent III, *De sacro altaris mysterio*, bk. 6, chap. 8, PL 217, col. 910.

[418] 1489 Sarum Missal, in Martène, *De antiquis ecclesiae ritibus*, bk. 1, chap. 4, art. 12, *ordo* 35, 1:241.

[419] Innocent III, *De sacro altaris mysterio*, bk. 6, chap. 10, PL 217, col. 912.

[420] Adrian Fortescue, "Communion-Antiphon", in *Catholic Encyclopedia* (1907–1912), 4:170.

[421] Rupert of Deutz, *Liber de divinis officiis*, bk. 2, chap. 18, in Hrabanus Haacke, O.S.B., ed., *Ruperti Tuitiensis: Liber de divinis officiis*, CCCM 7 (Turnhout, Belgium: Brepols, 1967), 49. Hereafter cited as Rupert of Deutz, *Liber de divinis officiis* (CCCM 7).

[422] *Missale Bracarense* (Lisbon: Nicolaus de Saxonia, 1498), sig. z8v.

[423] *Missale Abulense* (1510), sig. t3r.

Concluding Rites of the Mass: The Postcommunion, the Final Blessing, and the Last Gospel

in Christ alone. The *Nunc dimittis* is also used as a thanksgiving prayer for Holy Communion in the Spanish missals of Valencia, circa 1400,[424] and Toledo, 1499.[425]

After the Communion antiphon, there follows in the Sarum Rite as in the Roman Rite the Postcommunion, a prayer proper to the day or the Mass, said by the priest at the right side of the altar: "Then, having made the sign of the cross on his face, the priest should turn himself to the people, and with his arms raised a little, and his hands joined, he should say: *The Lord be with you.* And once more turning himself back to the altar, he should say, *Let us pray*; then he should say the Postcommunion according to the number and order of the aforesaid prayer [Collect] before the Epistle."[426] Pope Innocent III considers the Postcommunion as symbolic of Christ's blessing of the Apostles at His Ascension (Lk 24:50–51: "And lifting up his hands, he blessed them.... Whilst he blessed them, he departed from them").[427] In the early part of the Mass, including for the opening Collect, the priest stood at the right side of the altar, which as we have already noted Durandus explains as imaging the preaching of the Gospel first to the Jews; the subsequent shift of the priest to the left side of the altar in turn represented the subsequent preaching of the Gospel to the Gentiles. Now, at the end of the Mass, the priest stands once more on the right side to say the Postcommunion. This is for Durandus a symbol of the renewed proclamation of the Gospel to the Jewish people that will lead them to embrace the Christian faith before the end of the world (as prophesied by Saint Paul in Romans 11:25–27).[428] In this context of the right side of the altar representing the Jews and the left side the Gentiles, Durandus adds that "the middle of the altar represents the faith of Christ, and God Himself, unto whom each people is united, brought back, and completed."[429]

Following the Postcommunion, the priest makes the sign of the cross on his forehead and, turning toward the people, says to them, "*The Lord be with you.*" The deacon then says, "*Let us bless the Lord.*"[430] The late fourteenth-century Sarum Customary adds that at these words the priest should turn back toward the altar,[431] for as Durandus observes, "He directs his face to the east and his mind to God."[432] The deacon

---

[424] Ferreres Boluda, *Historia del misal romano*, lxxxii.

[425] Juan Manuel Sierra López, "El misal Toledano de 1499: Una visión de su contenido en relación con el misal romano y el mozárabe", *EL* 119 (2005): 174.

[426] Martène, *De antiquis ecclesiae ritibus*, bk. 1, chap. 4, art. 12, *ordo* 35, 1:241.

[427] Innocent III, *De sacro altaris mysterio*, bk. 6, chap. 11, PL 217, col. 912.

[428] Durandus, *Rationale* (CCCM 140), bk. 4, chap. 57, no. 3, p. 556.

[429] Ibid.

[430] 1489 Sarum Missal, in Martène, *De antiquis ecclesiae ritibus*, bk. 1, chap. 4, art. 12, *ordo* 35, 1:241.

[431] Frere, *Use of Sarum*, 1:89.

[432] Durandus, *Rationale* (CCCM 140), bk. 4, chap. 57, no. 5, p. 558.

now solemnly announces the end of the Mass: "*Ite, missa est*" ("*Go, it is ended*").[433] This latter proclamation is seen by Pope Innocent III as corresponding to the angels' admonition to the Apostles after they had witnessed the Ascension of Christ and remained with their eyes gazing upward: "Ye men of Galilee, why stand you looking up to heaven? This Jesus who is taken up from you into heaven, shall so come, as you have seen him going into heaven" (Acts 1:11). The response, "*Thanks be to God*", in turn represents the Apostles' response of joy and praise to the Ascension: "And they adoring went back into Jerusalem with great joy. And they were always in the temple, praising and blessing God" (Lk 24:52–53).[434] Offering an additional explanation, Durandus sees the end of Mass as symbolic of the end of the world, with the words "*Go, it is ended*" representing "the freedom that shall be given to the just in their native land, where they shall ever bless God".[435]

In the 1489 Sarum Missal, the priest is directed to go to the center of the altar and, while bowed before it, to recite silently a prayer to the Holy Trinity also in the Roman Missal (*Placeat tibi sancta Trinitas* ["*May it be pleasing to you, O Holy Trinity*", etc.]).[436] In the Roman Rite, the priest kisses the altar immediately after completing this prayer, a gesture interpreted by Durandus as signifying the priest's assent to all that has transpired in the Mass "with the whole affection of his soul and body".[437] This gesture is lacking in the Sarum Rite; instead, the priest, immediately after completing the Trinity prayer, stands erect and, without turning, makes the sign of the cross to himself.[438] In the 1502 Roman Rite *Ordo* of John Burckard, the priest turns toward the people to give them a final blessing, making with his right hand the sign of the cross thrice over them, the first toward his left, the second looking forward, and the third to his right: "*May almighty God bless you, the Father [Pa + ter], and the Son [Fi + lius], and the Holy Spirit [Spiritus + Sanctus].*"[439] Durandus, who in his diocesan *Instructions* directs the priest to bless the people,[440] explains that this concluding blessing is deeply rooted in the traditions of the Old Testament. Aaron, after having offered holocausts at the altar, "stretching forth his hands to the people", blessed them (Lev 9:22). Moreover, upon emerging from the Tent of the Testimony, both Moses and Aaron blessed the people (Lev 9:23). At the end of his life, Moses gave his blessing

[433] 1489 Sarum Missal, in Martène, *De antiquis ecclesiae ritibus*, bk. 1, chap. 4, art. 12, *ordo* 35, 1:241.

[434] Innocent III, *De sacro altaris mysterio*, bk. 6, chap. 11, PL 217, col. 912.

[435] Durandus, *Rationale* (CCCM 140), bk. 4, chap. 57, no. 9, p. 560.

[436] Martène, *De antiquis ecclesiae ritibus*, bk. 1, chap. 4, art. 12, *ordo* 35, 1:241.

[437] Durandus, *Rationale* (CCCM 140), bk. 4, chap. 59, no. 8, p. 563.

[438] Martène, *De antiquis ecclesiae ritibus*, bk. 1, chap. 4, art. 12, *ordo* 35, 1:241.

[439] *Ordo missae* of John Burckard, in Legg, *Tracts on the Mass*, 166–167. There is also a final blessing of the people in the 1510 missal of Avila; see *Missale Abulense* (1510), sig. t3r.

[440] Berthelé, "Instructions et constitutions de Guillaume Durand", 77.

to the people of Israel (Deut 33:1–29). Jacob, at the end of his life, gave a blessing to each of his sons (Gen 49:28).[441] Durandus follows Pope Innocent III in asserting that the final blessing of the people at Mass corresponds to the sending forth of the Holy Spirit upon the Apostles at Pentecost.[442] John Bechoffen likens this concluding blessing to the "final benediction upon the elect who shall have persevered all the way to the end", which shall be imparted by Christ at the Last Judgment when He shall say to the just, "Come, ye blessed of my Father, possess you the kingdom prepared for you from the foundation of the world" (Mt 25:34).[443]

The 1489 Sarum Missal calls for the celebrant and the other ministers to depart in procession from the altar in the order by which they approached it at the beginning of the Mass, with each bowing to the altar before departing. The return to the sacristy is interpreted by Durandus as symbolic of Christ's Ascension, with the priest passing out of view into the sacristy just as Christ passed through the clouds and out of the view of His Apostles.[444] According to the Sarum rubrics, during the recessional procession to the sacristy, the priest recites the beginning of the Gospel of Saint John (Jn 1:1–14).[445] The earliest extant reference to the custom of reading the Gospel of Saint John at the end of Mass appears in the *Missale minorum altarium*, a liturgical text of the Dominican Order dating from 1256, which speaks of the priest reciting it as he removes his vestments, or afterward;[446] it is found soon afterward in the *Liber ordinarius* of the Monastery of Saint James in Liège, Belgium (c. 1285),[447] and in the *Ordinarium* of the Carmelite Order compiled by Sibert de Beka (c. 1312).[448] The rite in its fully developed form appears in an early fifteenth-century redaction of a book of customs for the Benedictine "Sagro Speco" monastery of Subiaco, Italy; the reading of the last Gospel follows the priest's blessing of the faithful:

> And the sign of the cross having been made, turning himself around and bowing deeply over the altar, he says, *May it please you, O Holy Trinity*; and the altar having been kissed, raising himself up, he says, *The Lord be with you*; he is answered, *And with your spirit.* [He says:] *The beginning of the holy Gospel according to John*; he is answered, *Glory to you, O Lord.* [He reads:] *In the beginning was the Word*, and a

---

[441] Durandus, *Rationale* (CCCM 140), bk. 4, chap. 59, no. 5, pp. 561–562.

[442] Ibid., no. 1, p. 560; Innocent III, *De sacro altaris mysterio*, bk. 6, chap. 14, PL 217, col. 914.

[443] John Bechoffen, *Quadruplex missalis expositio*, sig. H1r.

[444] Durandus, *Rationale* (CCCM 140), bk. 4, chap. 59, no. 8, p. 563.

[445] Martène, *De antiquis ecclesiae ritibus*, bk. 1, chap. 4, art. 12, *ordo* 35, 1:241.

[446] Text in Guerrini, *Ordinarium juxta ritum sacri ordinis Fratrum Praedicatorum*, 250.

[447] Text in Paul Volk, ed., *Der Liber ordinarius des Lütticher St. Jakobs-Klosters* (Münster, Germany: Aschendorff Verlag, 1923), 102.

[448] Zimmerman, *Ordinaire de l'ordre de Notre-Dame du Mont-Carmel*, 89.

genuflection having been made when he says, *And the Word was made flesh*, and with a reverence before the altar, as has been said earlier, he returns to the sacristy.[449]

This practice of reading the Gospel of Saint John at the end of Mass, likewise found in the aforementioned early fifteenth-century missal of Toul, France,[450] and in a 1481 Benedictine missal of Bamberg, Germany,[451] had entered the liturgy of Rome by 1485, when it is specified in the *Pontificalis liber* of Patrizio Piccolomini and John Burckard;[452] the genuflection during this reading appears in the rubrics of John Burckard's 1502 Roman Rite *Ordo*.[453] Durandus, although aware of the custom of reading this Gospel at the end of Mass, offers no explanation regarding it,[454] but the Augustinian John Bechoffen, in his Mass commentary of 1505, proposes that it serves to combat the devil, thwarting his efforts to harm us in soul and body and deprive us of union with God; he adds that the genuflection accompanying the words "*And the Word was made flesh*" is an act of thanksgiving for the Incarnation.[455] The postmedieval seventeenth-century liturgist Bartolommeo Gavanti sees this concluding Gospel as representing the Apostles' preaching of both the divinity of Christ and his Incarnation.[456] In the Middle Ages, the reading of the beginning of Saint John's Gospel was considered as conferring a blessing;[457] this may serve to explain its use at the end of Mass, as an adjunct to the blessing conferred upon the people by the priest. As we shall later see, this reading was used as a species of blessing in other medieval rites as well (at the end of some baptismal rites; in the Corpus Christi procession of Essen, Germany; and in rites invoking divine protection from storms).

Finally, in the sacristy, after having removed his vestments, the priest is instructed to recite the Canticle of the Three Young Men from the Book of Daniel, the *Benedicite* (Dan 3:52–88, 56: "*All ye works of the Lord, bless the Lord . . .*"), along with its accompanying antiphon, *Trium*

[449] Text in Joachim Angerer, O.Praem., ed., *Caeremoniae regularis observantiae sanctissimi patris nostri Benedicti ex ipsius regula sumptae, secundum quod in sacris locis, scilicet Specu et Monasterio Sublacensi practicantur*, Corpus consuetudinum monasticarum 11, pt. 1 (Siegburg, Germany: Franciscus Schmitt, 1985), 260. For the dating of this text (redaction "o"), see ibid., ccl–ccliii.

[450] Martène, *De antiquis ecclesiae ritibus*, bk. 1, chap. 4, art. 12, *ordo* 31, 1:235.

[451] *Missale Benedictinum* (Bamberg, Germany: Johann Sensenschmidt, 1481; digitized text, Bayerische Staatsbibliothek, Munich, 2008), fol. 151r.

[452] Sodi, "*Pontificalis liber*" *di Agostino Patrizi Piccolomini e Giovanni Burcardo (1485)*, 569 (new pagination).

[453] Legg, *Tracts on the Mass*, 168.

[454] Durandus, *Rationale* (CCCM 140), bk. 4, chap. 24, no. 5, p. 342.

[455] John Bechoffen, *Quadruplex missalis expositio*, sig. G2v.

[456] Gavanti, *Thesaurus sacrorum rituum* (1628), in Gavanti and Merati, *Thesaurus sacrorum rituum*, 1:727.

[457] Francesc Xavier Parés i Saltor, *L'ordinari d'Urgell de 1536*, Col·lectània Sant Pacià 74 (La Seu d'Urgell, Spain: Societat Cultural Urgel·litana / Facultat de Teologia da Catalunya, 2002), 201.

puerorum ("*Let us sing the hymn of the three young men*").[458] According to Durandus, this canticle is recited after Mass in order to give thanks to God for all his benefits, as it is he "whom we shall praise forever".[459] In the thirteenth-century statutes of the Carthusian Order, the priest after having removed his vestments kneels at the altar step to recite the Our Father.[460] The Mass in the 1496 missal of Vich, Spain, concludes on a Marian note, with the recitation of the *Salve Regina* and the following prayer, which is essentially the same as that said at the conclusion of the night office of Compline: "*Almighty eternal God, who prepared the body and soul of the glorious Virgin Mother Mary, that she might be worthy to be made a fitting habitation of your Son, your Holy Spirit cooperating: grant that, by the loving intercession of her in whose memory we rejoice, we may be delivered from present evils and dangers and be freed from sudden and eternal death. Through the same Christ our Lord. Amen.*"[461]

We conclude here with a prayer given in most of the late medieval printed editions of the Sarum Missal for the priest to recite privately after Mass:

> *Almighty eternal God, Protector of souls and Redeemer of the world: most mercifully behold me, your servant, prostrate before your majesty; and most lovingly behold this sacrifice that I have offered in honor of your name for the salvation of the faithful, both living and dead, and also for our sins and offenses. Your wrath turn away from me; grant unto me your grace and mercy; open to me the gate of Paradise, and from all evils powerfully deliver me; and forgive whatever I have committed by my own guilt. Thus make me in this world persevere in your precepts, that I may be made worthy to be joined to the flock of the elect, you granting, my God, whose blessed name, honor, and kingdom endure unto ages of ages. Amen.*[462]

Excursus: The Sunday Aspersion Procession

The procession is the way to the celestial fatherland. The holy water preceding is cleanliness of life: the lights, works of mercy, according to that said, "Let your loins be girt, and lamps burning in your hands" [Lk 12:35].

William Durandus of Mende (+1296)[463]

Just as the vesting prayers prepared the priest for the celebration of Mass, so too there was on Sundays and feast days a rite that served to prepare the people for their participation in the Eucharistic sacrifice—the aspersion rite, in which the faithful as well as the clergy and the

---

[458] 1489 Sarum Missal, in Martène, *De antiquis ecclesiae ritibus*, bk. 1, chap. 4, art. 12, *ordo* 35, 1:241. The celebrant's recitation of this canticle and its antiphon after Mass is also specified in the 1502 Roman Rite *Ordo missae* of John Burckard (Legg, *Tracts on the Mass*, 169–170).

[459] Durandus, *Rationale* (CCCM 140), bk. 4, chap. 59, no. 9, p. 563.

[460] Martène, *De antiquis ecclesiae ritibus*, bk. 1, chap. 4, art. 12, *ordo* 25, 1:228.

[461] Altés i Aguiló, *Missale Vicense, 1496*, temporal, fol. 191r.

[462] Dickinson, *Missale ad usum ... Sarum*, col. 639.

[463] Durandus, *Rationale* (CCCM 140), bk. 4, chap. 6, no. 17, p. 279.

altar were sprinkled with holy water by the celebrating priest. As early as the third century, there existed among Christians a custom of washing one's hands before praying, a practice mentioned by Tertullian (+223)[464] and inherited from Judaism (see, e.g., Ex 30:18–20). From the beginning, this action expressed outwardly the interior purification of the soul. By the fourth century, the practice of blessing the water for baptism was being applied to the devout use of water apart from this sacrament; thus the fourth-century *Euchology of Serapion of Thmuis* provides a blessing of oil and water.[465]

In an early sixth-century redaction of the *Liber pontificalis*, a book of papal biographies, there appears the first extant reference to the custom of "sprinkling" holy water. The text contains a statement not found in earlier editions of the *Liber pontificalis* asserting that Pope Saint Alexander I (121–132) introduced the practice of sprinkling holy water in the homes of the faithful; although the claim of an early second-century origin for the custom is considered apocryphal, the claim itself demonstrates that the sprinkling of holy water had been introduced by the sixth century.[466] A century later, the Gelasian Sacramentary of Rome provides a blessing entitled "Blessing of Water to be Sprinkled in the Home".[467] In addition to prayers for the exorcism and blessing of the water, the Gelasian ceremony also specifies the effusion of salt into the water (with prayers for the exorcism and blessing of the salt), a practice that became universal in the Middle Ages. The sacramentary indicates in a rubric that the holy water is to be sprinkled throughout the home with a branch of hyssop,[468] a practice clearly inspired by the Old Testament use of hyssop branches to sprinkle blood, water, and ashes in the purification of homes (Lev 14:51; Num 19:18; see also Ex 12:22). Hyssop is also mentioned in the ninth verse of the penitential Psalm 50: "Thou shalt sprinkle me with hyssop, and I shall be cleansed: thou shalt wash me, and I shall be whiter than snow." This verse would come to be utilized throughout medieval Europe as an antiphon for the Sunday aspersion rite.

Roughly contemporaneous with the Gelasian Sacramentary text is the series of prayers for the blessing of holy water and salt given in a liturgical book of Spain's Mozarabic Rite, the *Liber ordinum*, the contents of which are estimated to date from the fifth to the seventh

---

[464] Tertullian, *De oratione*, chap. 13, PL 1, col. 1271.

[465] *Sacramentarium Serapionis*, no. 17, in Francis Xavier Funk, ed., *Didascalia et Constitutiones apostolorum*, vol. 2, *Testimonia et scripturae propinquae* (Paderborn, Germany: Libraria Ferdinandi Schoeningh, 1905), 178–181 (Greek and Latin texts).

[466] Text in Duchesne, *Liber pontificalis*, 1:127. For the dating of this passage of the *Liber pontificalis*, see Righetti, *Manuale di storia liturgica*, 4:395–396.

[467] Text in Leo Cunibert Mohlberg, O.S.B.; Leo Eizenhöfer, O.S.B.; and Petrus Siffrin, O.S.B., eds., *Liber sacramentorum Romanae aeclesiae ordinis anni circuli (Sacramentarium Gelasianum)*, REDSMF 4 (Rome: Herder, 1960), nos. 1556–1565, pp. 224–227.

[468] Ibid., no. 1561, p. 226.

century. The title given to this ceremony in the *Liber ordinum* indicates that the blessing rite took place in front of the altar ("Order When Salt Is Placed before the Altar, Before It Should Be Exorcised").[469] Significantly, many of the prayers of this rite are individually preceded by the rubric *ad orientem*, instructing the priest to turn toward the east when God is being addressed, whereas the exorcisms of the water and salt are preceded by the words "*ad occidentem*" or "*contra occidentem*", directing the priest to face westward when he is commanding the devil to depart.[470]

It is in the ninth century that we begin to find the earliest direct references to a Sunday procession in the churches for the sprinkling of holy water upon the faithful. A directive included in a collection of capitular instructions dating from the reigns of the Holy Roman emperors Charlemagne and Louis the Pius (800–840) mandates that "every priest on Sunday should walk around his church together with the people, with the singing of psalms, and should carry blessed water with him."[471] By this time the blessing of holy water was becoming a regular prelude to Sunday Mass. Thus Pope Saint Leo IV (847–855) in a sermon instructs the priests, "On every Sunday, before Mass, make blessed water, whence the people and the places of the faithful may be sprinkled."[472] In France, the archbishop of Reims Hincmar echoes this papal mandate in his instruction of 852, *Chapters Given to Priests*, adding that the blessed water may also be brought home by the people to use in their own devotions:

> That on every Sunday each priest in his church before the solemnities of the Masses should make blessed water in a clean vessel, and with such appropriate functionality, out of which the people entering the church may be sprinkled, and they who shall have wished may take from it in their clean small vessels, and may sprinkle it through their homes and fields and vineyards, also over their livestock and over their fodder, as well as over both their foods and their drink.[473]

The antiphon most often chanted during the Sunday aspersion rite, the *Asperges me* ("*Thou shalt sprinkle me*"; verse 9 of Psalm 50, the *Miserere*), was used as early as the tenth century in the Romano-Germanic Pontifical, wherein it is assigned (together with the *Miserere*) to the aspersion with holy water of those receiving extreme

---

[469] Text in Marius Férotin, O.S.B., ed., *Le Liber ordinum en usage dans l'église wisigothique et mozarabe d'Espagne du cinquième au onzième siècle* (Paris, 1904), repr., ed. Anthony Ward, S.M., and Cuthbert Johnson, O.S.B., BELS 83 (Rome: Centro Liturgico Vincenziano, Edizioni Liturgiche, 1996), col. 11.

[470] Ibid., cols. 11–19.

[471] *Capitularium Karoli magni et Ludovici pii*, bk. 5, capitulary 372, in Mansi, *Sacrorum conciliorum nova et amplissima collectio*, vol. 17b (Paris: Hubert Welter, 1902), col. 903.

[472] Pope Saint Leo IV, *Homily*, no. 20, PL 115, col. 679.

[473] Hincmar of Reims, *Chapters Given to Priests*, chap. 5, PL 125, col. 774.

unction,[474] as well as to the sprinkling of holy water during the consecration of a church.[475] By the twelfth century, the *Asperges me* was being used for the Sunday aspersion procession on Sundays outside the Easter season, whereas the antiphon *Vidi aquam*, *"I saw water flowing forth from the right side of the Temple, alleluia"* (cf. Ez 47:1–2), was sung during this procession on the Sundays from Easter to Pentecost, as Rupert of Deutz attests.[476] This latter verse is seen as referring to the stream that flowed from the temple of Christ's body on the Cross, by which we are washed in baptism.[477]

We turn now to a fully developed example of the Sunday aspersion procession from the Sarum Rite of Salisbury, England, as drawn from a 1487 edition of the Sarum Missal[478] and the rubrics of the late fourteenth-century Sarum Consuetudinary.[479] The prayers are the same as those of the *Missale Romanum* of 1570.[480] The rubrics of the Sarum Consuetudinary direct the priest to stand in the middle of the sanctuary, facing the altar, vested in a silk cope (red in color, according to the rubrics of the Sarum Gradual, which adds that the priest is also vested in an alb and "the other priestly vestments").[481] With him are the deacon and the subdeacon, the latter carrying the Gospel book of Mass, as well as a thurifer, two candle bearers, and an acolyte carrying the cross, all vested in albs. Two other acolytes, vested in surplices, also assist the priest, one carrying the salt and water to be blessed, and the other holding the requisite liturgical book from which the priest will read the prayers for the blessing.[482] The priest begins by exorcising the salt:

> *I exorcise you, creature of salt, by the living + God, by the true + God, by the holy + God, by God who ordered you through the prophet Eliseus to be sent into the water, that the sterility of the water should be cured; that you, O salt, may become* (Here the priest should look at the salt) *exorcised, for the salvation of the believing, and be health of soul and body to all taking you, and every phantom and wickedness or craftiness of diabolical deception*

---

[474] Vogel and Elze, *Pontifical romano-germanique*, 2:258.

[475] Cyrille Vogel and Reinhard Elze, eds., *Le pontifical romano-germanique du dixième siècle*, vol. 1, ST 226 (Vatican City: Biblioteca Apostolica Vaticana, 1963), 84, 141.

[476] Rupert of Deutz, *Liber de divinis officiis* (CCCM 7), bk. 7, chap. 20, pp. 248–249. For two thirteenth-century examples of the use of the *Asperges me* in the aspersion rite, see the ritual of the Canons Regular of Coimbra, Portugal, and the *Ordinarium* of the Dominican Order, the latter dating from 1256; texts in Joaquim O. Bragança, "Ritual de Santa Crux de Coimbra: Porto, Biblioteca Municipal, ms. 858", *Didaskalia* 6 (1976): 150, and Guerrini, *Ordinarium juxta ritum sacri ordinis Fratrum Praedicatorum*, 149 (the latter, like Rupert of Deutz, specifies the antiphon *Vidi aquam* for the Easter season; ibid.).

[477] Rupert of Deutz, *Liber de divinis officiis* (CCCM 7), bk. 7, chap. 20, pp. 248–249.

[478] Text in Dickinson, *Missale ad usum . . . Sarum*, cols. 29**–33**.

[479] Text in Frere, *Use of Sarum*, 1:52–54.

[480] Sodi and Triacca, *Missale Romanum: Editio princeps (1570)*, 660–662 (new pagination).

[481] Sarum Gradual, quoted in Dickinson, *Missale ad usum . . . Sarum*, col. 29**, footnote.

[482] Frere, *Use of Sarum*, 1:52.

may flee and depart. Through him who is going to come to judge the living and the dead and the world by fire. Response: Amen.[483]

As for the symbolism of water and salt, the ninth-century archbishop of Mainz, Germany, and liturgist Blessed Rabanus Maurus (+856) explains:

> Salt and water are blessed for the different uses of the faithful, for infirm men, against the delusion of the enemy, for the health of livestock, for taking away illnesses.... Water cleanses from defilements, salt puts to flight corruption; water furnishes splendor, salt adds to uprightness; water signifies the draught of wisdom, and salt indicates the flavor of prudence ... that by the mouths of priests God himself may bless and by their sensible ministry divine power may invisibly effect the sacrament [or the sacramental].[484]

The reference in the salt exorcism to the prophet Eliseus evokes an Old Testament precedent for the infusion of salt into water. When told by the men of Jericho that the water of their city was unwholesome, rendering the land barren, Eliseus took salt and cast it into the spring that watered the city, declaring as he did so, "Thus saith the Lord: I have healed these waters, and there shall be no more in them death or barrenness"; the waters of Jericho were thereby cleansed (4 Kings 2:19–22). Citing this biblical incident, Durandus observes: "And if the barrenness of the water was healed by Eliseus with salt sprinkled, how much more does salt hallowed with divine prayers take away the barrenness of human things, and sanctify and purify those defiled, and multiply other good things, and avert the snares of the devil, and defend men from the subtleties of the phantom?"[485] The "hallowing" of the salt spoken of by Durandus is carried out in the Sarum aspersion ceremony with the following blessing recited by the priest immediately after the exorcism of the salt:

> *Your immense mercy, almighty eternal God, we humbly implore,* (Here the priest should look at the salt) *that this creature of salt, which you have given for the use of mankind, you may vouchsafe to bless + and sancti + fy with your goodness, that it may be health of mind and body to all taking it; that whatever shall have been touched or sprinkled with it may be devoid of every uncleanness and every attack of spiritual iniquity. Through our Lord Jesus Christ your Son, who with you lives and reigns in the unity of the Holy Spirit, God, through all ages of ages. Amen.*[486]

---

[483] Dickinson, *Missale ad usum ... Sarum*, col. 29**. This formula is traceable to the seventh-century Gelasian Sacramentary of Rome; see Mohlberg, Eizenhöfer, and Siffrin, *Liber sacramentorum,* no. 1559, p. 226.

[484] Blessed Rabanus Maurus, *De institutione clericorum,* bk. 2, chap. 53, PL 107, col. 367.

[485] Durandus, *Rationale* (CCCM 140), bk. 4, chap. 4, no. 2, p. 263.

[486] Dickinson, *Missale ad usum ... Sarum*, cols. 29**–30**. This prayer is traceable to Saint Benedict of Aniane's early ninth-century Frankish adaptation of Rome's Gregorian Sacramentary; text in Deshusses, *Sacramentaire grégorien,* no. 1452, 1:473.

The exorcism and blessing of the water follow:

> *I exorcise you, creature of water, in the name of God + the Father almighty, and in the name of Jesus + Christ his Son, our Lord, and in the power of the Holy + Spirit; that you, O water, may be made exorcised for driving away every power of the enemy; that you may be able to uproot and cast out the enemy himself with his apostate angels. Through the power of the same Jesus Christ our Lord, who is going to come and judge the living and the dead and the world by fire.* Response: *Amen.*

> *O God, who for the salvation of mankind have wrought all your greatest signs in the substance of water, mercifully attend to our invocations and impart to this element* (Here the priest should look at the water) *prepared with manifold purifications the power of your blessing, that your creature serving in your mysteries may obtain the effect of divine grace for casting off demons and casting out illnesses; that everything which this water shall have sprinkled in the homes or in the places of the faithful may be devoid of all uncleanness, freed from harm; may no pestilential spirit or corrupting air remain there; may all the deceits of the hidden enemy depart; and if there is anything that begrudges either the safety or the peace of the inhabitants, may it flee with the aspersion of this water, that freed from all attacks, their health may be protected by the invocation of your holy name. Through our Lord Jesus Christ your Son, who with you lives and reigns in the unity of the Holy Spirit, God, through all ages of ages.*[487]

Water, Blessed Rabanus Maurus explains, represents compunction, as intimated in the First Book of Kings: "They drew water, and poured it out before the Lord, and they fasted on that day, and they said there: We have sinned against the Lord" (1 Kings 7:6). Interpreting this verse, Rabanus observes, "From the depths of their hearts they brought forth compunction, and wept before God."[488] Implicit in this association of water with compunction is the symbolism of the sprinkling of water as an image of the washing away of sins. This symbolism is drawn from the sacrament of baptism, in which the effusion of water upon the candidate actually effects in the soul the washing away of sin. In explaining the Sunday aspersion rite, Rupert of Deutz notes that the sprinkling rite is intended as a "memorial of our baptism", reminding us "frequently to invoke the grace of the Divine Name upon us"; the rite is conducted on Sundays, for it is particularly on the eve of the greatest Sunday, Easter Sunday, that baptism is customarily administered and commemorated by the

---

[487] Dickinson, *Missale ad usum ... Sarum*, cols. 30**–31**. The exorcism formula is traceable to the eighth-century *Hadrianum* redaction of the Gregorian Sacramentary of Rome, and the blessing is traceable to the seventh-century Gelasian Sacramentary of Rome; see respectively Deshusses, *Sacramentaire grégorien*, no. 985, 1:336–337, and Mohlberg, Eizenhöfer, and Siffrin, *Liber sacramentorum*, no. 1556, p. 225.

[488] Blessed Rabanus Maurus, *Allegoriae in sacram scripturam*, "Aqua", PL 112, col. 860.

Church.[489] Durandus asserts that the Sunday aspersion rite is an efficacious sacramental, for the blessed water "sanctifies the people and
cleanses from venial sins", just as in the Old Testament the Israelites
were sanctified and purified through the sprinkling upon them of a
sacrificed heifer's ashes mingled with water (Num 19:9, 14–21; see
Heb 9:13–14).[490] Moreover, blessed water, having been exorcised, is
also endowed with the power to expel demons from the hearts of
the faithful and from their dwellings.[491]

The mingling of the salt with the water is interpreted by Durandus
as an image of how the faithful, represented by the water, are sanctified through the ministry of the priest who instructs them in the Word
of God, the priestly action being symbolized by the infusion of salt.[492]
Clearly Durandus has in mind Christ's words to his disciples, "You are
the salt of the earth" (Mt 5:13). The Sarum rubrics for the infusion of
the salt into the water follow:

> Here the priest should put salt into the water in the manner of a
> cross, saying thus, without a sign:
> *May the mingling of salt and water together be rendered, in the name of
> the Father, and of the Son, and of the Holy Spirit. Amen.*
> Verse: *The Lord be with you.*
> Response: *And with your spirit.*
> *Let us pray.*
> Prayer:
> *O God, Creator of invincible power, and unconquerable King of your domin-
> ion, and ever-glorious Conqueror, who repress the forces of hostile domina-
> tion, who overcome the ferocity of the roaring enemy, who overthrow the
> power of hostile iniquities: trembling and suppliant, we entreat and beseech
> you, O Lord, that you may worthily receive this* (Here he should look at
> the water mixed with salt) *creature of salt and water, mercifully glorify it,
> and sancti + fy it with the love of your goodness; that wherever it shall have
> been sprinkled, through the invocation of your holy name, every attack of the
> unclean spirit may be cast off, and the terror of the venomous serpent may be
> driven far away; and may the presence of the Holy Spirit vouchsafe to attend
> us, we entreating your mercy everywhere. Through our Lord Jesus Christ
> your Son, who with you lives and reigns in the unity of the Holy Spirit,
> God, through all ages of ages.* Choir: *Amen.*[493]

Honorius of Autun considers the sprinkling of blessed water upon the
people to be a representation of the salvific sprinkling of the blood of

---

[489] Rupert of Deutz, *Liber de divinis officiis* (CCCM 7), bk. 7, chap. 20, p. 248.

[490] Durandus, *Rationale* (CCCM 140), bk. 4, chap. 4, no. 2, p. 263.

[491] Ibid., no. 1.

[492] Ibid., no. 8, p. 266.

[493] Dickinson, *Missale ad usum ... Sarum*, cols. 31**–32**. This prayer is traceable to
Saint Benedict of Aniane's early ninth-century Frankish adaptation of Rome's Gregorian
Sacramentary; see Deshusses, *Sacramentaire grégorien*, no. 1455, 1:474–475.

Christ upon the faithful, as prefigured in the Old Testament by the lamb's blood that was sprinkled upon the Israelites' doorposts and lintels (Ex 12:22).[494] The Sarum rubrics for sprinkling the blessed water follow:

> The blessing of the salt and the water having been completed, the priest himself should approach the principal altar, and he should sprinkle all around himself. After the principal altar is sprinkled, the same priest sprinkles the ministers ordered thus, beginning from the acolyte [i.e., the crossbearer[495]]; then returning to the step of the choir, in the same place he should sprinkle the clerics.... After the sprinkling of the clerics, [the priest], standing in the sanctuary, should sprinkle the laity on each side.[496]

As indicated above, the sprinkling of the blessed water begins with the sprinkling of the high altar. Durandus explains that this is done out of "reverence of the Sacrament that is to be consecrated in that very place", so that the demons may be prevented from drawing near; moreover, he adds, since the altar symbolizes Christ, only one altar is sprinkled, insofar as there is only one Christ, one Savior alone who takes away the sins of the world.[497]

The chants accompanying the aspersion are specified in the Sarum Missal:

> While the blessed water is sprinkled, this antiphon should be sung [begun by the cantor[498]]:
> *You shall sprinkle me, O Lord, with hyssop, and I shall be cleansed; you shall wash me, and I shall be made whiter than snow.*
> Psalm [50]: *Have mercy on me, O God, according to your great mercy ...*
> [Antiphon:] *You shall sprinkle me ...*
> Verse [Ps 50:3]: *And according to the multitude of your tender mercies blot out my iniquity.*
> [Antiphon:] *You shall sprinkle me ...*
> Verse: *Glory be to the Father ... As it was ...*
> It should be repeated: *You shall wash me, and I shall be made whiter than snow.*
> ... The priest at the step of the choir should say the verse ...:
> *Show us, O Lord, your mercy.*
> Response: *And grant us your salvation.*
> A prayer follows....
> *Graciously hear us, O Lord, holy Father, almighty eternal God, and vouchsafe to send your holy angel from the heavens, that he may preserve, assist,*

---

[494] Honorius of Autun, *Gemma animae*, bk. 3, chap. 27, PL 172, col. 650.

[495] Sarum Gradual, quoted in Dickinson, *Missale ad usum ... Sarum*, col. 32**, footnote.

[496] Frere, *Use of Sarum*, 1:53–54.

[497] Durandus, *Rationale* (CCCM 140), bk. 4, chap. 4, no. 5, p. 265.

[498] Frere, *Use of Sarum*, 1:53.

protect, and defend all dwelling in this habitation, through Christ our Lord. It is answered: *Amen.*[499]

In the monastic churches of medieval Europe, Sunday aspersion processions were introduced at an early date; prayers to bless water and salt for aspersion are given in an eighth-century manuscript of the Swiss abbey of Saint Gall.[500] The Gellone Sacramentary, an eighth-century Frankish adaptation of the Gelasian Sacramentary of Rome, provides a series of prayers for the blessing of individual sites within a monastery complex, which together imply an outdoor procession preceding the Sunday High Mass;[501] although there is no explicit mention of holy water being used with these prayers, the placement of prayers for the blessing of water immediately before this sequence of orations strongly suggests that such was the case.[502] But the monastic aspersion rites differed from their counterparts in the parish churches in that the monastic procession passed not only through the church but also through various parts of the monastery, and even across the monastic grounds, before returning to the church.

The customary compiled about 1075 for the French Benedictine abbey of Cluny by the monk Bernard describes in great detail the aspersion procession that took place there on Sunday mornings. After blessing the water for the aspersion rite (as well as the salt mixed into it), the hebdomadarian (the priest assigned to preside over the Divine Office for the week) makes one circuit around the high altar, sprinkling the floor of the sanctuary with holy water. After sprinkling several side altars, he returns to sprinkle each of the monks. A crossbearer, and behind him, a brother carrying the holy water vessel, precede the priest as he makes his way through the "church of blessed Mary" and continues to the monastery's infirmary. There, holy water is sprinkled in each room. Afterward, the aspersion procession visits the dormitory, the refectory, the kitchen, and the pantry, with holy water sprinkled in every room. At each stop, the antiphon *Asperges me* is sung, and the priest recites a Collect as the brother carrying the holy water stands to his right and the crossbearer stands to his left. After returning

---

[499] Dickinson, *Missale ad usum ... Sarum*, cols. 32**–33**. The concluding prayer is traceable to the seventh-century Gelasian Sacramentary of Rome; see Mohlberg, Eizenhöfer, and Siffrin, *Liber sacramentorum*, no. 1558a, p. 225.

[500] Manuscript: Saint Gall Abbey, Switzerland, Stiftsbibliothek Sankt Gallen, MS Codex Sangallensis (Cod. Sang.) 193, eighth century, in Adolph Franz, *Die kirchlichen Benediktionen im Mittelalter* (Freiburg im Breisgau, Germany, 1909; repr. Graz, Austria: Akademische Druck—U. Verlagsanstalt, 1960), 1:155–158.

[501] Text in A. Dumas, O.S.B., ed., *Liber sacramentorum Gellonensis*, CCSL 159 (Turnhout, Belgium: Brepols, 1981), nos. 2859–2881, pp. 452–458. The identification of these prayers as orations for a Sunday outdoor procession is given in J. Evenou, "Processions, Pilgrimages, Popular Religion", in Aimé-Georges Martimort, ed., *The Church at Prayer: An Introduction to the Liturgy*, vol. 3, *The Sacraments* (Collegeville, Minn.: Liturgical Press, 1988), 248, footnote.

[502] Dumas, *Liber sacramentorum Gellonensis*, nos. 2857–2858, pp. 451–452.

to the church, the priest makes the final station of the procession before the church cross.[503]

A Sunday aspersion procession traversing a largely outdoor route is found in the fourteenth-century *Liber ordinarius* of Essen, Germany, a liturgical book for the quasi-monastic community of canons that staffed the city's collegiate church, in which an affiliated community of canonesses (women living a mitigated form of religious life) worshiped.[504] Following the blessing of salt and water (the prayers of which are the same as those of the Sarum Rite discussed above), the priest begins the aspersions by sprinkling not only the high altar but also the Blessed Sacrament: "The priest ... will sprinkle first the holy place of the Body of Christ, with an inclination of the head and a reverence; then the high altar, then the altar above the choir with a similar reverence."[505] Thereafter he sprinkles the canonesses in their choir stalls. He then exits the church briefly to sprinkle the nuns' dormitory before reentering the chapel to begin a procession across the monastery grounds, in which the canons accompany him, following a route around the perimeter of the cemetery, then through another church on the grounds, before returning back through the monastery building to the church where the procession began.[506] The chants sung along the way include the following two antiphons:

> *Sanctify us, O Lord, with the sign of the holy Cross, that it may be made for us an obstacle against the cruel arrow of our enemies; defend us, Lord, by the holy wood, and by the price of your righteous blood, with which you redeemed us.*[507]

> *Savior of the world, save us all; holy Mother of God, Mary ever Virgin, pray for us; with the prayers also of the saints; the Apostles; the martyrs and confessors; and the holy virgins, humbly we beseech that we may be delivered from all evils and be worthy to enjoy fully all good things now and always.*[508]

When passing the cemetery, the priest sprinkles it with holy water, and prayers are offered for the faithful departed, including Psalm 129, the *De profundis* ("*Out of the depths ...*").[509]

---

[503] *Ordo Cluniacensis*, pt. 1, chap. 45, in Herrgott, *Vetus disciplina monastica*, 234–236.

[504] Arens, *Liber ordinarius der Essener Stiftskirche*, 5–9.

[505] Ibid., 5–7 (quoted passage on 7).

[506] Ibid., 7–9.

[507] Ibid., 8. The antiphon *Sanctifica nos, Domine* is traceable to the early eleventh century, when it appears in an antiphonary of Monza, Italy; see René-Jean Hésbert, ed., *Corpus antiphonalium officii*, vol. 1, REDSMF 7 (Rome: Herder, 1963), 215.

[508] Arens, *Der Liber ordinarius der Essener Stiftskirche*, 8. The antiphon *Salvator mundi, salva nos omnes* is traceable to the early eleventh century, when it appears in the above-cited antiphonary of Monza, Italy; see Hésbert, *Corpus antiphonalium officii*, 1:287.

[509] Arens, *Liber ordinarius der Essener Stiftskirche*, 8–9.

3 Baptism

For this end is baptism conferred on a man, that being regenerated thereby, he may be incorporated in Christ, by becoming his member: wherefore it is written (Gal 3:27): As many of you as have been baptized in Christ, have put on Christ.

Saint Thomas Aquinas[1]

Like the Fathers of the early Church, medieval theologians and liturgists saw in the Old Testament multiple prefigurations of baptism, the sacrament that washes fallen man in the redeeming blood of Christ and brings him into the salvific embrace of Holy Mother Church. Saint Ivo of Chartres (+1115) observes that just as out of earth Adam was fashioned into the image of God by God, so too in baptism man has been remade into the image of God by Christ. And just as Eve was fashioned from the side of Adam, so too in baptism the Church is fashioned by means of the blood and "water of sanctification" from the pierced side of Christ.[2] Again, just as the "eight souls" of Noah and his family were delivered from the drowning flood by the sheltering enclosure of the wooden ark, so too the Church, by baptism, "not without the support of the saving wood" of the Cross, is delivered from the drowning "submersion of abounding temptations".[3] Moreover, just as a path through the Red Sea was opened to the Israelites fleeing servitude, pursued by their Egyptian enemies, when Moses struck the water with his staff, so too a safe path is opened to the people of God by baptism, the water of which is sanctified by the staff of Christ, the "health-giving wood" of the Cross. In reference to the Red Sea's attribute of "red", Ivo adds that baptism "reddens" those who receive it by consecrating them with the blood of Christ. He also sees in the drowning of the Egyptian charioteers that had pursued the Israelites into the Red Sea

---

[1] Saint Thomas Aquinas, *Summa theologica: First Complete American Edition in Three Volumes*, trans. Fathers of the English Dominican Province (New York: Benziger Brothers, 1948), pt. III, q. 68, art. 1, 2:2398.

[2] Saint Ivo of Chartres, *Sermon 1*, PL 162, col. 506.

[3] Ibid., cols. 506–507.

a foreshadowing of the blotting out of all past sins wrought by the waters of baptism.[4]

Saint Thomas Aquinas (+1274) explains that while the "washing with water" of the baptismal candidate and the accompanying words of the baptismal formula ("*I baptize you in the name of the Father, and of the Son, and of the Holy Spirit*") constitute respectively the only *essential* matter and form of the sacrament (as the Council of Florence was subsequently to define in 1439),[5] the other rites of the baptismal ceremony serve to inculcate in the faithful devotion and reverence for the sacrament, and to instruct them by outward signs about everything they should know concerning baptism. The accompanying prayers and blessings also serve to thwart the devil's attempts to counter the effects of the sacrament.[6]

The Baptismal Rite of Barcelona, Spain

We present here the baptismal rite from a Spanish liturgical book, the 1501 *Ordinarium* of Barcelona.[7] It contains a number of rubrics and texts unique to Spain, and particularly Catalonia. Nonetheless, many of its prayers and exorcism texts are traceable to the seventh-century Gelasian Sacramentary of Rome,[8] while other elements are drawn from later Roman liturgical books—some of the prayers and rubrics are those subsequently found in the two baptismal rites (one for adult catechumens, the other for infants) of the universally promulgated *Rituale Romanum* of 1614.[9] By way of comparison, we will also cite certain prayers and liturgical actions from the baptismal rite in a 1522 priest's manual for the diocese of Turku, Finland,[10] as well as particular rubrics from several other medieval baptism texts.

The Barcelona baptismal rite begins in front of the church's doors, where the godparents stand, holding the infant to be baptized in their arms, as the priest questions them in the vernacular about the child:

---

[4] Ibid., col. 507.

[5] "True and natural water" and the words "*I baptize you in the name of the Father, and of the Son, and of the Holy Spirit*" are defined respectively as the matter and form of baptism in the Florentine council's *Decree for the Armenians* (November 22, 1439); text in J. D. Mansi, ed., *Sacrorum conciliorum nova et amplissima collectio*, vol. 31 (Florence and Venice, 1798; repr., Paris: Hubert Welter, 1906), col. 1055. See also the 1566 *Roman Catechism* of the Council of Trent, pt. 2, "Baptism", in *Catechism of the Council of Trent for Parish Priests*, trans. John McHugh, O.P., and Charles Callan, O.P. (1923; repr., South Bend, Ind.: Marian Publications, 1972), 164–166.

[6] Saint Thomas Aquinas, *Summa theologica*, pt. III, q. 66, art. 10, 2:2389–2390.

[7] Text in Amadeu-J. Soberanas, ed., *Ordinarium sacramentorum Barchinonense, 1501*, facsimile ed., Biblioteca liturgica catalana 1 (Barcelona: Institut d'Estudis Catalans, 1991), fols. 13r–21r.

[8] For the Gelasian texts, see Leo Cunibert Mohlberg, O.S.B., et al., eds., *Liber sacramentorum Romanae aeclesiae ordinis anni circuli (Sacramentarium Gelasianum)*, REDSMF 4 (Rome: Herder, 1960), nos. 285–298, 598–616, pp. 42–46, 93–97.

[9] Text in Manlio Sodi and Juan Javier Flores Arcas, eds., *Rituale Romanum: Editio princeps (1614)*, facsimile ed., MLCT 5 (Vatican City: Libreria Editrice Vaticana, © 2004), 5–39 (original pagination).

[10] Text in Martti Parvio, ed., *Manuale seu exequiale Aboense, 1522*, facsimile ed., Suomen Kirkkohistoriallisen Seuran Toimituksia / Finska Kyrkohistoriska Samfundets Handlingar 115 (Helsinki: Societas Historiae Ecclesiasticae Fennica, 1980), fols. 3v–7v.

Is it a man or a woman? Response: *It is a man.*
What name will he be called? Response: [Name].
[Name], *what do you seek?* Response [by the godparents on behalf of the child]: *The faith of Christ.*
What will the faith of Christ grant you? Response: *Eternal life.*[11]

The priest now elaborates upon this answer of the godparents by reiterating in a paraphrased form the definition of eternal life that Christ gave at the Last Supper (Jn 17:3): "*This is eternal life: that you should know the one and true God, and him whom he sent, Jesus Christ. Who with him lives and reigns in the unity of the Holy Spirit, God, through all ages of ages*" (response: "*Amen.*")[12] This initial dialogue between the priest and the godparents, in the specific form we find it above, traceable to the eleventh century,[13] had become the norm across Catalonian Spain by the sixteenth century.[14]

The priest then blows three times upon the face of the infant, saying afterward, "*Depart, unclean spirit, in the name of the Holy Trinity, from this image of God.*"[15] Both Saint Ivo of Chartres (+1115) and William Durandus of Mende (+1296) follow Saint Augustine's interpretation of this action in explaining it as a kind of exorcism by which any demon heretofore oppressing the child is blown away, made to flee so as to give way to the coming of the Holy Spirit.[16]

The priest now imitates in a literal manner the action of Christ in healing the deaf-mute man (Mk 7:32–35). After placing his thumb, moistened with his own spittle, into the ears of the candidate, and likewise touching the candidate's tongue, the priest says, "*Ephphatha: that is, be opened. Ephphatha. In the odor of goodness: Ephphatha. But you, O devil, be driven away, for the judgment of God shall draw near.*"[17] Saint Ivo of Chartres explains this touching of the ears as symbolizing the

---

[11] Soberanas, *Ordinarium sacramentorum Barchinonense, 1501*, fol. 13r.

[12] Ibid.

[13] Francesc Xavier Parés i Saltor, *L'ordinari d'Urgell de 1536*, Col·lectània Sant Pacià 74 (La Seu d'Urgell, Spain: Societat Cultural Urgel·litana / Facultat de Teologia da Catalunya, 2002), 177–178.

[14] Adalberto Franquesa, "El ritual Tarraconense", in *Liturgica*, vol. 2, Scripta et documenta 10 (Barcelona: Publicacions de l'Abadia de Montserrat, 1958), 259–260.

[15] Soberanas, *Ordinarium sacramentorum Barchinonense, 1501*, fol. 13r. This adjuration is first found in the tenth-century Romano-Germanic Pontifical; see Cyrille Vogel and Reinhard Elze, eds., *Le pontifical romano-germanique du dixième siècle*, vol. 2, ST 227 (Vatican City: Biblioteca Apostolica Vaticana, 1963), 155.

[16] Saint Ivo of Chartres, *Sermon 1*, PL 162, col. 509; William Durandus of Mende, *Rationale divinorum officiorum*, bk. 6, chap. 83, no. 7, in A. Davril, O.S.B., and T.M. Thibodeau, eds., *Guillelmi Duranti: Rationale divinorum officiorum V–VI*, CCCM 140a (Turnhout, Belgium: Brepols, 1998), 416–417 (hereafter cited as Durandus, *Rationale* [CCCM 140a]); Saint Augustine, *De symbolo*, chap. 1, no. 2, PL 40, col. 628.

[17] Soberanas, *Ordinarium sacramentorum Barchinonense, 1501*, fol. 13r–13v. Although the use of this text is traceable to the seventh-century Gelasian Sacramentary of Rome (Mohlberg, Eizenhöfer, and Siffrin, *Liber sacramentorum*, no. 602, p. 94), the threefold repetition of the word *Ephphatha* is a distinctly Spanish addition (Parés i Saltor, *Ordinari d'Urgell de 1536*, 180).

opening of the "ears of the heart" to understanding the Word of God.[18] Similarly, Blessed Rabanus Maurus (+856) sees this action as an opening of the ears to "hearing the commandments of God".[19] The spittle itself is explained by Durandus as a symbol of the doctrines that have flowed forth to us "from the mouth of the Most High".[20] While the Barcelona rite completely imitates the action of Christ in specifying the touching of both the ears and the tongue, other baptism texts, such as that in the 1522 diocesan manual of Turku, Finland, substitute for the touching of the tongue a touching of the candidate's nostrils.[21] This action is seen symbolically to open the nostrils to "receiving the odor of the knowledge of God" (Rabanus Maurus).[22] It also symbolizes the imparting of discernment, that the soul may repel "the stench of sinful pleasures" (Ivo of Chartres).[23] Durandus develops more fully this concept of the imparting of discernment: "The nostrils are also touched, that they may receive divine power, by which they may discern good odor from bad, and may be able to separate sound doctrine from the stench of heretical wickedness." [24]

The account of the Last Judgment given by Christ in which the just are set at his right and the condemned on his left (Mt 25:31–46) led to an often-utilized symbolism associating that which is on the right with goodness and that which is on the left with evil. This directional imagery is drawn upon in the 1522 baptismal rite of Turku, Finland, in which the priest applying the spittle to the ears and nose of the child uses separate words for each ear: "To the right [ear], he should say: *Ephphatha; that is, be opened.* To the nostrils, he should say: *In the odor of goodness.* To the left [ear]: *But you, O devil, depart, for the judgment of God shall draw near.*" [25]

Returning to the Barcelona baptismal rite, we find following the touching of the ears and tongue a double signing of the child with the cross: "Here the priest with his thumb should make a cross on the forehead and the chest of the infant, saying: *Receive the sign of the cross both on the forehead + and on the heart +. Embrace the faith of heavenly precepts. Keep the divine precepts. Show yourself such in your actions, that you may be worthy to be made the Temple of God.*" [26] According to Saint Ivo of Chartres, this action draws upon the power of the cross as the emblem of Christ's exaltation and his conquest of Satan. For it is by

---

[18] Saint Ivo of Chartres, *Sermon 1*, PL 162, col. 509.

[19] Blessed Rabanus Maurus, *De clericorum institutione*, bk. 1, chap. 27, PL 107, col. 312.

[20] Durandus, *Rationale* (CCCM 140a), bk. 6, chap. 83, no. 10, p. 418.

[21] Parvio, *Manuale seu exequiale Aboense, 1522*, fol. 6v.

[22] Blessed Rabanus Maurus, *De clericorum institutione*, bk. 1, chap. 27, PL 107, col. 312.

[23] Saint Ivo of Chartres, *Sermon 1*, PL 162, col. 509.

[24] Durandus, *Rationale* (CCCM 140a), bk. 6, chap. 83, no. 10, p. 418.

[25] Parvio, *Manuale seu exequiale Aboense, 1522*, fol. 6v.

[26] Soberanas, *Ordinarium sacramentorum Barchinonense, 1501*, fol. 13v. This address is a shortened version of that from the seventh-century *Gelasian Sacramentary* of Rome (Mohlberg, Eizenhöfer, and Siffrin, *Liber sacramentorum*, no. 599, p. 93).

the power of the sign of the cross that "all our sacraments are also accomplished, and all the illusions of the devil are frustrated."[27] This power of the cross, Ivo adds, was prophesied by Habacuc, who foreshadowed the triumph of Christ nailed by his hands to the Cross in the words "Horns are in his hands; there is his strength hid" (Hab 3:4). By this particular prebaptismal signing of the cross, all the senses of the body are given protection. Furthermore, the signing of the forehead brings to mind the Old Testament episode of Ezechiel being commanded by God, "Mark Thau [a letter resembling a cross] upon the foreheads of the men that sigh, and mourn for all the abominations that are committed in the midst thereof" (Ez 9:4). From the perspective of viewing the forehead as in a sense the lintel of the soul, the crossing of the forehead is also reminiscent of the marking of the Israelites' homes on the lintels and doorposts with lambs' blood, a prefiguration of the blood of Christ on the Cross (Ex 12:7).[28] Moreover, Ivo likens all the different signs in the baptismal rite as a whole to the nourishment given to an unborn child in his mother's womb. The crosses made by the priest upon baptismal candidates are, as it were, made "upon the womb of Mother Church" as new Christians are "conceived" in her womb, that "Mother Church may deliver them joyful to Christ."[29]

The priest continues by reciting a series of three prayers for the child to be baptized,[30] the first of which is particularly rich in imagery:

> *Almighty everlasting God, Father of our Lord Jesus Christ, may you vouchsafe to look upon this your servant [Name] whom you have vouchsafed to call to the rudiments of the faith; expel from him all blindness of heart. Break asunder all the snares of Satan, in which he may have been bound. Open to him, O Lord, the door of your goodness. Initiated with the sign of your wisdom, may he not only be devoid of the stenches of all desires but also be devoted to you in your Church, rejoicing in the sweet odor of your precepts, and make progress from day to day, that, the remedy having been received, he may be made fit to accede to the grace of your baptism. Through the same Christ our Lord. Response: Amen.*[31]

---

[27] Saint Ivo of Chartres, *Sermon 1*, PL 162, col. 509.

[28] Ibid.

[29] Ibid.

[30] All three prayers are originally from the seventh-century Gelasian Sacramentary of Rome (Mohlberg, Eizenhöfer, and Siffrin, *Liber sacramentorum*, nos. 285–287, pp. 42–43).

[31] Soberanas, *Ordinarium sacramentorum Barchinonense, 1501*, fols. 13v–14r. Second prayer (fol. 14r): "*Mercifully hear our prayers, we beseech you, O Lord, and preserve this your elect in the strength of the Lord's Cross, with the impression of which we sign him +, that observing the principles of your glorious majesty by the safekeeping of your commands, he may merit to come to the glory of regeneration. Through Christ our Lord. Response: Amen.*" Third prayer (fol. 14r): "*O God, who, just as you are the Creator of mankind, so also are you its Restorer, be merciful to your adopted people, and number the offspring of the new progeny in the New Covenant, that what the sons of the promise have not been able to obtain by nature they may rejoice to have recovered by grace. Through Christ our Lord. Response: Amen.*"

Up until this point, the child, the godparents, and the priest have remained outside the doors of the church for the initial ceremonies of the baptismal rite. But now all enter the church as the priest addresses a dramatic invitation to the child, casting this entrance as a passage from darkness to light, from death to life:

> Here the priest should grasp the right hand of the infant or the god-father. And he should lead him into the church, saying thus:
>
> *Enter the temple of the living God, divested of the deception of darkness, and rejoicing, acknowledge yourself to have escaped the snares of death. May almighty God abide in your thoughts, who put together your human members and arranged the habitation of the divine Spirit. Fear therefore the heavenly commands. Await the coming of our only-begotten Savior, who was brought forth in virginal birth and was conceived by the infusion of the Holy Spirit, by whose light you are enlightened, by whose strength you are made strong, by whose sign you are signed on the forehead, that serving him, you may merit to come to the grace of baptism; who lives and reigns, God, through all ages of ages.* Response: *Amen.*[32]

The above invitation from the 1501 Barcelona *Ordinarium* is traceable to Spain's ancient Mozarabic Rite, appearing with almost-identical wording in the Mozarabic liturgical text known as the *Liber ordinum*, the contents of which are estimated to date from the fifth to the seventh century.[33] The accompanying action of taking the child through the doors of the church, unique to the liturgy of Catalonian Spain, is first mentioned in the eleventh century (in the *Missale parvum* of Vich and the monastic ritual of Santa Maria de La Grassa).[34]

The priest then takes a bit of salt, over which he has previously said a prayer of exorcism before the baptismal rite, and making the sign of the cross, places the salt in the mouth of the infant, saying, "*In the name of the Father + , and of the Son, and of the Holy Spirit. Amen. Receive the salt of wisdom favorably unto eternal life*" (response: "*Amen*").[35] The symbolism of this action is derived from salt's properties as both a preservative and a seasoning. Blessed Rabanus Maurus sees salt as representing wisdom, which preserves the soul from the stench and

---

[32] Ibid., fol. 14r–14v.

[33] Text in Marius Férotin, O.S.B., ed., *Le Liber ordinum en usage dans l'église wisigothique et mozarabe d'Espagne du cinquième au onzième siècle* (Paris, 1904), repr., ed. Anthony Ward, S.M., and Cuthbert Johnson, O.S.B., BELS 83 (Rome: Centro Liturgico Vincenziano, Edizioni Liturgiche, 1996), col. 26.

[34] Parés i Saltor, *Ordinari d'Urgell de 1536*, 183.

[35] Soberanas, *Ordinarium sacramentorum Barchinonense, 1501*, fol. 14v. This address is first found in the Gelasian Sacramentary (Mohlberg, Eizenhöfer, and Siffrin, *Liber sacramentorum*, no. 289, p. 43), but the particular wording in the Barcelona text more closely corresponds to that given in Saint Benedict of Aniane's early ninth-century Frankish adaptation of the Gregorian Sacramentary of Rome; see Jean Deshusses, ed., *Le sacramentaire grégorien: Ses principales formes d'après les plus anciens manuscrits*, vol. 1, 2nd ed., SF 16 (Fribourg, Switzerland: Editions Universitaires Fribourg, 1979), no. 1069, p. 373.

consuming worms of sin.[36] Durandus adds that the salt symbolizes the first lessons of faith, "without the seasoning of which every man is insipid".[37] The symbolic associations of salt are also developed in the prayer that follows the infusion of the salt:

> *God of our fathers, God of the universe, Author of truth, we humbly entreat you, that you may vouchsafe to look favorably upon this your servant* [Name] *and no longer permit him tasting this first nourishment of salt to hunger, that he may be purified by heavenly food, that he may always be a fervent soul, rejoicing in hope, serving always in your name. And lead him to the bath of new regeneration, that he may merit to obtain with your faithful the eternal rewards of your promises. Through Christ our Lord.* Response: *Amen.*[38]

The Barcelona rite continues with a distinctly Spanish addition[39] to the baptismal liturgy, utilizing an acclamation made popular in the Crusades:[40] "Here [the priest] should make three crosses with his thumb, first on the [infant's] forehead, second on the mouth, third on the chest, saying the following words: *Christ + conquers. Christ + reigns. Christ + commands. May Christ defend you from every evil.* Response: *Amen."*[41] This *Christus vincit* acclamation serves here as a form of exorcism; the *Christus vincit* has been used in Spanish exorcism rites since the eleventh century.[42]

The series of six prayers and admonitions that now follow all pertain to the rescuing of the child from the dominion of Satan. In the first of these, the priest prays that God will send his angel to protect the infant: "*God of Abraham, God of Isaac, God of Jacob, God who appeared to your servant Moses on Mount Sinai, and who led the sons of Israel out of the land of Egypt, assigning them the angel of your mercy, who guarded them day and night: we beseech you, O Lord, that you may vouchsafe to send your holy angel similarly to guard this your servant* [Name] *and lead him to the grace of your baptism. Through Christ our Lord.* Response: *Amen."*[43] Having prayed for an angel to watch over the child, the priest then confronts the devil threatening the infant and commands him to depart:

---

[36] Blessed Rabanus Maurus, *De clericorum institutione*, bk. 1, chap. 27, PL 107, col. 312.

[37] Durandus, *Rationale* (CCCM 140a), bk. 6, chap. 83, no. 9, p. 417.

[38] Soberanas, *Ordinarium sacramentorum Barchinonense, 1501*, fols. 14v–15r. This prayer is originally found in the Gelasian Sacramentary (Mohlberg, Eizenhöfer, and Siffrin, *Liber sacramentorum*, no. 290, p. 44).

[39] The triple signing with the cross and the accompanying acclamation were found in most of the nine sixteenth-century Spanish diocesan rituals consulted by Dom Franquesa for his article "Ritual Tarraconense" (p. 261).

[40] Ernst Kantorowicz, *Laudes Regiae: A Study in Liturgical Acclamations and Mediaeval Ruler Worship*, University of California Publications in History 33 (Berkeley, Calif.: University of California Press, 1946), 11.

[41] Soberanas, *Ordinarium sacramentorum Barchinonense, 1501*, fol. 15r.

[42] Parés i Saltor, *Ordinari d'Urgell de 1536*, 185–186.

[43] Soberanas, *Ordinarium sacramentorum Barchinonense, 1501*, fol. 15r; prayer originally in Gelasian Sacramentary (Mohlberg, Eizenhöfer, and Siffrin, *Liber sacramentorum*, no. 291, p. 44).

Therefore, accursed devil, recognize your sentence and give honor to the living and true God. Give honor to Jesus Christ his Son and the Holy Spirit, and depart from this servant of God [Name], for our God and Lord Jesus Christ has vouchsafed to call him to his holy grace and blessing, and the fount of baptism. And this holy sign of the cross + that we give on his forehead, may you, accursed devil, never dare to violate. Through the same Jesus Christ our Lord, who is going to come to judge the living and the dead and the world by fire. Amen.[44]

The prayer that follows the above adjuration is derived from the eighth-century *Hadrianum* edition of the Gregorian Sacramentary of Rome,[45] but from the eleventh century onward the oration is divided into two parts in the Barcelona rite and other texts of Catalonian Spain.[46] In the first portion of the prayer, the priest refers to the baptismal candidate by name: "*Immortal God, defense of all who petition [you], deliverance of suppliants, peace of those who entreat [you], life of the faithful, resurrection of the dead: I invoke you, O Lord, upon this your servant* [Name], *who, beseeching the gift of your baptism, longs to obtain by spiritual regeneration eternal grace. Through Christ our Lord*" (response: "*Amen.*")[47] The second part of the oration is preceded by a rubric traceable to the eleventh-century *Missale parvum* of Vich, Spain,[48] directing the priest to place his hand upon the child to be baptized as he prays:

Receive him, O Lord; for you have vouchsafed to say: Ask, and you shall receive. Seek, and you shall find. Knock, and it shall be opened to you [cf. Mt 7:7]. *Therefore, extend your recompense to him who asks, and open the door to him who knocks, that having obtained the eternal bless + ing of the heavenly bath, he may attain to the promises of your bounty. Through you, Jesus Christ, Son of the living God, who with the Father and the Holy Spirit live and reign, God, through all ages of ages.* Response: *Amen.*[49]

Again, the priest commands Satan to flee and give way to the coming of the Holy Spirit upon the baptismal candidate:

Hear, O reviled Satan, adjured by the name of the eternal God and his Son our Savior: depart with your hatred, conquered, trembling and groaning. May there be nothing in common to you with this servant of God, now pondering heavenly things, about to renounce you and your world and to attain blessed immortality. Give honor, therefore, to the Holy Spirit coming, descending from the supreme throne of Heaven, your deceptions having been overthrown, to make perfect the soul cleansed in the divine fount, that is, the temple and

---

[44] Soberanas, *Ordinarium sacramentorum Barchinonense, 1501,* fol. 15r–15v; originally in Gelasian Sacramentary (Mohlberg, Eizenhöfer, and Siffrin, *Liber sacramentorum,* no. 292, p. 44).

[45] Text in Deshusses, *Sacramentaire grégorien,* no. 1074, 1:374–375.

[46] Parés i Saltor, *Ordinari d'Urgell de 1536,* 187.

[47] Soberanas, *Ordinarium sacramentorum Barchinonense, 1501,* fol. 15v.

[48] Parés i Saltor, *Ordinari d'Urgell de 1536,* 187.

[49] Soberanas, *Ordinarium sacramentorum Barchinonense, 1501,* fols. 15v–16r.

dwelling place consecrated to God. And inwardly freed from all punishments of past sins, may this servant of God give thanks to the eternal God always and bless his holy name unto ages of ages. Response: *Amen.*[50]

The priest now formally exorcises whatever demon may be afflicting the child, pronouncing against the demon the following formula and making three times the sign of the cross. This adjuration invokes the manifestation of Christ's divinity in his walk upon the water (Mt 14:24–33; Jn 6:19–21): "*I exorcise you, unclean spirit, in the name of the Fa + ther, and of the Son + , and of the Holy + Spirit, that you may go out and depart from this servant of God* [Name]. *For he commands you, accursed damned one, he who walked on foot upon the sea and who stretched out his right hand to Peter sinking.*"[51] The earlier adjuration "*Therefore, accursed devil*" is here repeated as a further warning to the devil to leave the soon-to-be-baptized child in peace.[52]

In both the Barcelona baptismal rite and that found in the 1522 diocesan manual of Turku, Finland, certain portions of the rite differ according to whether the child to be baptized is a boy or a girl. All of the prayers we have thus far quoted from the Barcelona rite are for the baptism of a boy. In the above series of prayers and admonitions associated with the exorcism of the child to be baptized, several of these texts would be replaced with others when the child was a girl.[53] These alternate texts offer a range of biblical imagery comparable to but differing from that found in the texts for a male baptism. The 1522 manual of Turku, Finland, provides the following three texts in the exorcism portion of the baptismal rite for a female candidate (all three of which are traceable to the seventh-century Gelasian Sacramentary):

> *God of Heaven, God of earth, God of angels, God of archangels, God of prophets, God of Apostles, God of martyrs, God of confessors, God of virgins, God of all living well, God to whom every tongue confesses* [cf. Phil 2:11] *and every knee bows, of those that are in Heaven, on earth, and under the earth* [cf. Phil 2:10]: *I invoke you, O Lord, upon this your maidservant* [Name], *that you may vouchsafe to lead her to the grace of your baptism.*

> *God of Abraham, God of Isaac, God of Jacob, God who led the tribes of Israel out of Egyptian servitude and delivered Susanna from false accusation, and in the desert commanded through your servant Moses regarding the preservation of your commandments: suppliant, I entreat you, O Lord, that you may free this*

---

[50] Ibid., fol. 16r; originally in Gelasian Sacramentary (Mohlberg, Eizenhöfer, and Siffrin, *Liber sacramentorum*, no. 294, p. 45).

[51] Soberanas, *Ordinarium sacramentorum Barchinonense, 1501*, fol. 16r–16v; originally in Gelasian Sacramentary (Mohlberg, Eizenhöfer, and Siffrin, *Liber sacramentorum*, no. 296, p. 45).

[52] Soberanas, *Ordinarium sacramentorum Barchinonense, 1501*, fol. 16v.

[53] The Barcelona baptismal rite for females is given in Soberanas, *Ordinarium sacramentorum Barchinonense, 1501*, fols. 21r–30r. In the prayers common to both male and female baptisms, the pronouns referring to the child are changed from male to female in the texts for females.

your maidservant [Name] and may vouchsafe to lead her to the grace of your baptism.

I exorcise you, unclean spirit, by the Father, and the Son, and the Holy Spirit, that you may go out and depart from this maidservant of God [Name], for, O cursed one, damned and to be damned, he himself commands you, who opened the eyes of him born blind and raised up Lazarus, fetid [after] four days, from the tomb.[54]

In the Barcelona baptismal rite, the exorcism prayers are followed by a Gospel lection; this practice is a descendant of the prebaptismal "delivery" of the Gospels specified by the seventh-century Gelasian Sacramentary of Rome, in which four deacons, standing at the four corners of the altar, each with a Gospel book, read to the baptismal candidates the beginnings of each of the four Gospels (Mt 1:1–19; Mk 1:1–8; Lk 1:1–17; Jn 1:1–14).[55] Whereas medieval baptismal rites generally utilized the Gospel account of Christ blessing the children (Mt 19:13–15),[56] the passage read in the Barcelona rite is that of Christ declaring to his Father, "*Thou hast hid these things from the wise and prudent, and hast revealed them to little ones*" and concluding with the Savior's invitation "*Come to me, all you that labour, and are burdened. . . . Take up my yoke. . . . For my yoke is sweet . . .*" (Mt 11:25–30). The baptismal use of this Gospel lection is traceable to the prebaptismal Mass of exorcism in a late seventh-century liturgical text of Rome, Roman *Ordo* 11.[57] At the conclusion of the Gospel in the Barcelona baptismal rite, the priest makes with his thumb the sign of the cross on the child's forehead and chest, saying to him, "*By the word of the holy Gospel, may you possess the heavenly kingdom. Amen.*"[58] Clearly this

[54] Parvio, *Manuale seu exequiale Aboense, 1522*, fols. 5v–6r. All three of these prayers are traceable to the Gelasian Sacramentary, albeit the second is an expanded version of its Gelasian original (Mohlberg, Eizenhöfer, and Siffrin, *Liber sacramentorum*, nos. 293, 295, 297, pp. 44–45).

[55] Gelasian Sacramentary, in Mohlberg, Eizenhöfer, and Siffrin, *Liber sacramentorum*, nos. 299–309, pp. 46–48.

[56] Liturgical texts specifying this reading include the 1522 manual of Turku, Finland; the 1491 *Obsequiale Ratisponense* of Regensburg, Germany; the 1493 *Obsequiale Frisingense* of Freising, Germany; the 1496 *Obsequiale Salisburgense* of Salzburg, Austria; and a ritual of Mainz, Germany, dating from about 1400. See respectively Parvio, *Manuale seu exequiale Aboense, 1522*, fol. 6r–6v; *Obsequiale Ratisponense* (Nürnberg, Germany: Georg Stuchs, 1491; digitized text, Bayerische Staatsbibliothek, Munich, 2008), fol. 8v; *Obsequiale Frisingense* (Augsburg, Germany: Erhard Ratdolt, 1493; digitized text, Bayerische Staatsbibliothek, Munich, 2008), fol. 7r; *Obsequiale Salisburgense* (Nürnberg, Germany: Georg Stuchs, 1496; digitized text, Bayerische Staatsbibliothek, Munich, 2009), fol. 85r; Hermann Reifenberg, *Sakramente, Sakramentalien und Ritualien im Bistum Mainz: Seit dem Spätmittelalter*, vol. 1, Liturgiewissenschaftliche Quellen und Forschungen 53 (Münster, Germany: Aschendorff-sche Verlagsbuchhandlung, 1971), 185–186.

[57] Text in Michel Andrieu, ed., *Les Ordines Romani du haut moyen âge*, vol. 2, SSLED 23 (Louvain, Belgium: "Spicilegium sacrum Lovaniense" Administration, 1948), 425.

[58] Soberanas, *Ordinarium sacramentorum Barchinonense, 1501*, fols. 16v–17r. This signing of the child at the end of the Gospel in the baptism rite is also found in the 1536 *Ordinarium* of Urgel (La Seu d'Urgell), Spain; see Parés i Saltor, *Ordinari d'Urgell de 1536*, 188–189.

is an adaptation of the medieval Mass custom of signing oneself with the cross at the conclusion of the Gospel, a practice traceable to the ninth century.[59]

In the baptismal rite from the 1487 *Obsequiale Augustense* of Augsburg, Germany, which utilizes for the Gospel Saint Mark's account of Christ blessing the children (Mk 10:13–16), the priest symbolically reenacts the actions of Christ, touching the infant and making the sign of the cross upon the child at the words "*and laying his hands upon them, he blessed them*" (Mk 10:16).[60] A ritual of Vilna, Lithuania, from 1499 directs the priest to rest his hand upon the head of the child for the entire reading of Saint Matthew's account of Christ blessing the children (Mt 19:13–15).[61]

Following the Gospel in the Barcelona rite, the priest admonishes the godparents in the vernacular (in Barcelona, the Catalan language) on their duties to catechize the child: "*You, godfather and godmother, are obligated to teach to this infant the smaller Creed* [i.e., the Apostles' Creed], *in which are contained the articles of the Catholic faith, and the Our Father, which we shall now say for him.*"[62] The priest and godparents recite together in Latin the Apostles' Creed and the Our Father,[63] followed by a series of standard versicles and responses invoking divine protection for the child.[64] The priest then prays to God the Father with a prayer derived from the seventh-century Gelasian Sacramentary of Rome[65] but here divided into a series of versicles, each with the inserted response of "*Amen*", a modification that first arose in Catalonian Spain during the eleventh century:[66]

> *I entreat your eternal and most just mercy, O Lord, holy Father, almighty eternal God of light and truth, upon this your servant* [Name], *that you may vouchsafe to illuminate him in the light of your knowledge.* Response: *Amen.* Versicle: *Purify and sanc + tify him.* Response: *Amen.* Versicle: *Give him true knowledge.* Response: *Amen.* Versicle: *That he may be made worthy to accede to the grace of your baptism.* Response: *Amen.* Versicle: *May he keep a steadfast hope.* Response: *Amen.* Versicle: *An upright*

---

[59] This Mass custom is first found in Roman *Ordo* 5, a late ninth-century German Mass *ordo* based upon Roman usages; see Andrieu, *Ordines Romani du haut moyen âge*, 2:217.

[60] *Obsequiale Augustense* (Augsburg, Germany: Erhard Ratdolt, 1487; digitized text, Bayerische Staatsbibliothek, Munich, 2008), fol. 32r.

[61] *Agenda sive Exequiale divinorum sacramentorum*, ed. Martin, Canon of the Diocese of Vilna[, Lithuania] (Gdańsk, Poland: Conrad Bomgharten, 1499; digitized text, CBN Polona, National Digital Library, Biblioteka Narodowa, Warsaw, Poland, n.d.), sig. d8v.

[62] Soberanas, *Ordinarium sacramentorum Barchinonense, 1501*, fol. 17r. Other sixteenth-century rituals also provide a pastoral exhortation to the godparents at this point in the baptism rite (Parés i Saltor, *Ordinari d'Urgell de 1536*, 189).

[63] The recitation of the Nicene Creed and the Our Father are specified in the prebaptismal rite of the seventh-century Gelasian Sacramentary of Rome (Mohlberg, Eizenhöfer, and Siffrin, *Liber sacramentorum*, nos. 310–328, pp. 48–53).

[64] Soberanas, *Ordinarium sacramentorum Barchinonense, 1501*, fols. 17v–18r.

[65] Mohlberg, Eizenhöfer, and Siffrin, *Liber sacramentorum*, no. 298, pp. 45–46.

[66] Parés i Saltor, *Ordinari d'Urgell de 1536*, 191.

counsel. Response: *Amen.* Versicle: *A holy doctrine.* Response: *Amen.* Versicle: *That he may be fit to partake of the grace of your baptism. Through Christ our Lord.* Response: *Amen.*[67]

The priest now pronounces one final adjuration against Satan and against any other demon still menacing the child, invoking the power and authority of the Holy Spirit to drive the demon away:

> There is not hidden to you, Satan, punishments to threaten you, tortures to threaten you, the day of judgment to threaten you, and the day of eternal punishment, the day that is going to come like a flaming furnace, in which will be prepared eternal death for you and all your angels. And therefore, O one condemned for your wickedness and to be condemned, give honor to God living and true. Give honor to Jesus Christ his Son. Give honor to the Holy Spirit, the Paraclete, in whose name and power I command you, whoever you are, unclean spirit, that you may go out and depart from this servant of God [Name], whom this day our God and Lord Jesus Christ has vouchsafed to call to his holy grace and blessing + , and to the fount of baptism, with his gift, that he may be made his temple through the water of regeneration, in remission of all his sins. In the name of the same Jesus Christ our Lord, who is going to come to judge the living and the dead and the world by fire. Response: *Amen.*[68]

The Moment of Baptism Approaches

In preparation for the prebaptismal anointing and the actual baptism, the head, shoulders, and chest of the infant are now uncovered, and the child is brought to the baptismal fount by the godfather.[69] The priest then begins the set of questions known as the scrutinies, in which the godparents are asked to answer on behalf of the child. This examination, by which the child is asked (through his godparents) to renounce Satan and profess the Catholic faith, is characterized by Durandus as a preparation for the transformation of the soul from a habitation of demons to the "habitation of God", "that the empty house [of the soul] deserted by the ancient inhabitant [the devil] may be adorned with faith".[70] The priest begins the scrutinies with the renunciation of "the ancient inhabitant":

[Priest:] *Do you renounce Satan?* Response: *I renounce.*
Priest: *And all his pomps?* Response: *I renounce.*
Priest: *And all his works?* Response: *I renounce.*[71]

Before proceeding with the second series of scrutinies, the priest, using his thumb, anoints the infant with the oil of catechumens on the chest

---

[67] Soberanas, *Ordinarium sacramentorum Barchinonense, 1501,* fol. 18r–18v.

[68] Ibid., fol. 18v; originally in Gelasian Sacramentary (Mohlberg, Eizenhöfer, and Siffrin, *Liber sacramentorum,* no. 419, p. 67).

[69] Soberanas, *Ordinarium sacramentorum Barchinonense, 1501,* fol. 19r.

[70] Durandus, *Rationale* (CCCM 140a), bk. 6, chap. 83, no. 5, pp. 415–416.

[71] Soberanas, *Ordinarium sacramentorum Barchinonense, 1501,* fol. 19r; originally in Gelasian Sacramentary (Mohlberg, Eizenhöfer, and Siffrin, *Liber sacramentorum,* no. 421, p. 68).

and on the back between the shoulders, in each case making a cross with the oil. As he anoints the child, he says, "*And I anoint you with the oil of salvation in Jesus Christ our Lord unto life everlasting. Amen. And peace be with you.*"[72] This double anointing is rich in symbolic meanings. The placing of holy oil between the shoulders, a part of the body that has been traditionally associated with physical strength, was seen by Saint Ambrose (+397) as preparing the baptismal candidate for spiritual combat "as an athlete of Christ",[73] an interpretation repeated by Saint Thomas Aquinas.[74] Saint Ivo of Chartres sees the holy oil upon the chest as a spiritual breastplate defending the candidate from "the invisible enemy", and the anointing between the shoulders, where a man carries burdens on his back, as a symbol of fortitude conferred for "carrying the burden and heat of the day, as a good athlete".[75] Durandus considers the holy oil on the chest, over the heart, as preparing the heart to understand the Word of God.[76] Pope Innocent III provides the fullest explanation of the double anointing:

> For surely he to be baptized is anointed on the breast, that by the gift of the Holy Spirit he may cast off error and ignorance, and receive upright faith, for "the just man liveth by faith" [Rom 1:17]. And he to be baptized is also anointed between the shoulders, that by the grace of the Holy Spirit he may shake off negligence and sloth, and exercise sound action, for "faith without works is dead" [Jas 2:20], that by the sacrament of faith there may be cleanliness of thoughts in the heart, by the exercise of work, strength of labors on the shoulders.[77]

In the Barcelona rite, the second portion of the scrutinies, the portion that constitutes the adornment of the "habitation of God" with faith, as Durandus describes it,[78] now follows in the form of three questions. The candidate is asked to profess the Apostles' Creed in three parts, each part corresponding to each Person of the Holy Trinity ("[Name], *do you believe in God the Father almighty, Creator of Heaven and earth? . . . And do you believe in Jesus Christ, his only Son, our Lord, [who was] born and suffered? . . . And do you believe in the Holy Spirit, the*

---

[72] Soberanas, *Ordinarium sacramentorum Barchinonense, 1501*, fol. 19r. This formula first appears in a French ninth-century sacramentary from the Abbey of Saint Martin, Tours; see Jean Deshusses, ed., *Le sacramentaire grégorien: Le principales formes d'après les plus anciens manuscrits*, vol. 3, SF 28 (Fribourg, Switzerland: Editions Universitaires Fribourg, 1982), no. 3938, p. 98. The phrase "*And peace be with you*" is evidently a Catalonian addition to the text, found also in the baptismal rite of the 1536 *Ordinarium* of Urgel, Spain (Parés i Saltor, *Ordinari d'Urgell de 1536*, 193).

[73] Saint Ambrose, *De sacramentis*, bk. 1, chap. 2, PL 16, col. 419.

[74] Saint Thomas Aquinas, *Summa theologica*, pt. III, q. 66, art. 10, reply obj. no. 2, 2:2390.

[75] Saint Ivo of Chartres, *Sermon 1*, PL 162, col. 510.

[76] Durandus, *Rationale divinorum officiorum*, bk. 1, chap. 8, no. 8, in A. Davril, O.S.B., and T. M. Thibodeau, eds., *Guillelmi Duranti: Rationale divinorum officiorum I–IV*, CCCM 140 (Turnhout, Belgium: Brepols, 1995), 101. Hereafter cited as Durandus, *Rationale* (CCCM 140).

[77] Pope Innocent III, *Regestorum*, bk. 7 (year 1204), letter 3, PL 215, col. 285.

[78] Durandus, *Rationale* (CCCM 140a), bk. 6, chap. 83, no. 5, pp. 415–416.

holy Catholic Church, the communion of saints, the forgiveness of sins, the resurrection of the body, and life everlasting after death?"). To each of these questions, the godparents answer on behalf of the infant, *"I believe."* [79] In the baptismal rite from the 1499 diocesan manual of Jaén, Spain, the priest or bishop administering the sacrament is directed to hold the right hand of the infant while addressing these questions to him, and as his godparents answer for him. [80]

The priest now asks again the child's name, as he did at the beginning of the ceremony. Next, in what appears to be a distinctly Spanish feature of the Barcelona rite, the priest asks the candidate three times, "[Name], *do you will to be baptized?"*, to which the godparents respond for the child each time, *"I will."* [81] This threefold repetition of the question, likewise found in the 1499 manual of Jaén, Spain; [82] the 1536 *Ordinarium* of Urgel (La Seu d'Urgell), Spain; [83] and the 1568 *Manuale sacramentorum* of Mexico City, [84] is probably intended as an expression of the willingness to accept baptism in the name of each Person of the Holy Trinity, just as the actual baptismal formula is in the name of all three Persons of the Trinity. This interpretation is supported by evidence from the baptismal rite found in the 1518 ritual of Limoges, France. Although this latter source lacks the threefold repetition of the question found in the Spanish sources, it nonetheless expands the question so as to ask the candidate explicitly to accept baptism in the name of all three Persons of the Holy Trinity: *"Do you will to be baptized in the name of the Father, and of the Son, and of the Holy Spirit?"* [85] The threefold repetition of the question in the Barcelona rite may also be inspired by the threefold profession of love that Christ asked of Saint Peter on the shore of the Sea of Galilee after the Resurrection (Jn 21:15–17).

The actual conferral of the sacrament now follows. In the baptismal rite from the 1522 diocesan manual of Turku, Finland, the godparents are directed to state the name of the child before the priest proceeds with the baptism. [86] Durandus sees this practice as stemming from the Old Testament custom of giving an infant boy his name at his

---

[79] Soberanas, *Ordinarium sacramentorum Barchinonense, 1501*, fol. 19r–19v. This interrogatory profession of faith, like those in other late medieval baptism texts, constitutes an expanded version of the scrutinies found in the seventh-century Gelasian Sacramentary of Rome (Mohlberg, Eizenhöfer, and Siffrin, *Liber sacramentorum*, no. 449, p. 74).

[80] *Missale Giennense / Manuale continens ordinem ad celebrandum ecclesiastica sacramenta [Missale secundum morem et consuetudinem sancte ecclesie Gienensis]* (Seville: Meinard Ungut and Stanislao Polono, 1499), fol. 241v.

[81] Soberanas, *Ordinarium sacramentorum Barchinonense, 1501*, fol. 19v.

[82] *Missale Giennense / Manuale . . . sacramenta* (1499), fol. 241v.

[83] Parés i Saltor, *Ordinari d'Urgell de 1536*, 195.

[84] *Manuale sacramentorum, secundum usum almae ecclesiae mexicanae* (Mexico City: Petrus Ocharte, 1568), fol. 27v.

[85] Edmond Martène, *De antiquis ecclesiae ritibus* (Venice: Johannes Baptista Novelli, 1763–1764), bk. 1, chap. 1, art. 18, *ordo* 18, 1:78.

[86] Parvio, *Manuale seu exequiale Aboense, 1522*, fol. 7r.

circumcision, a rite that foreshadowed baptism.[87] In the Barcelona baptismal rite (as elsewhere), the baptism itself is threefold in form, with the priest pouring water over the head of the infant three times, corresponding to the naming of each of the three Persons of the Holy Trinity. While pouring the water, the priest says the complete baptismal formula, the wording of which is first found almost verbatim in the *Liber ordinum* of Spain's ancient Mozarabic Rite, the contents of which are estimated to date from the fifth to the seventh century;[88] the formula subsequently appears in the eighth-century *Hadrianum* redaction of Rome's Gregorian Sacramentary,[89] becoming universal in Western baptismal rites thereafter: "*And I baptize you, in the name of the Father, and of the Son, and of the Holy Spirit. Amen.*" The first pouring of water accompanies the words "*in the name of the Father*", the second pouring accompanies "*and of the Son*", and the third pouring accompanies "*and of the Holy Spirit*".[90] In the case of the 1522 baptismal rite of Turku, Finland, there is a threefold immersion of the child in the water of the fount rather than the pouring of water.[91]

The threefold application of water to the recipient of baptism, with the tripartite invocation of the Holy Trinity, is seen by Honorius of Autun (+c. 1135) as representing the restoration of the Trinitarian image of God within the soul that baptism accomplishes.[92] Durandus explains this triple effusion or immersion as also symbolizing the three days' burial of Christ,[93] a linkage inspired by Saint Paul's teaching that in baptism we are buried with Christ (Rom 6:3–4; Col 2:12). Moreover, the three washings or immersions can be seen as expressing the cleansing of the soul from sins of thought, of word, and of action.[94] Honorius views the threefold emergence of the baptismal candidate from the fount or from the poured water as signifying that by baptism we are raised from the dead with Christ, resurrected on the third day.[95]

In certain medieval texts of the baptismal rite, beginning with the Romano-Germanic Pontifical of the tenth century, the threefold immersion of the candidate is carried out by the priest in the form of a cross, that is, by lowering the child into the water in three different directions corresponding to the three upper points of the sign of the cross (the top of the cross and the two ends of its crossbeam). This can best be seen in the rubrics of a ritual of Mainz, Germany, dating from

---

[87] Durandus, *Rationale* (CCCM 140a), bk. 6, chap. 83, no. 13, p. 419.

[88] Férotin, *Liber ordinum*, col. 32.

[89] Deshusses, *Le sacramentaire grégorien*, no. 982, 1:336. This formula is also found in a letter of Pope Saint Zachary dating from 744 (*Epistle 7*, to Boniface, PL 89, col. 929).

[90] Soberanas, *Ordinarium sacramentorum Barchinonense, 1501*, fol. 19v.

[91] Parvio, *Manuale seu exequiale Aboense, 1522*, fol. 7r–7v.

[92] Honorius of Autun, *Gemma animae*, bk. 3, chap. 111, PL 172, cols. 672–673.

[93] Durandus, *Rationale* (CCCM 140a), bk. 6, chap. 83, no. 11, p. 419.

[94] Ibid., no. 12.

[95] Honorius of Autun, *Gemma animae*, bk. 3, chap. 111, PL 172. col. 673.

about 1400. It is evident that the priest faces east as he performs the baptism:

> And [the priest] shall dip him [the child] three times in this form of the cross, saying: *And I baptize you in the name of the Father* (with the head turned toward the east, the feet toward the west). And he should dip [him] a second time: *And of the Son* (and [with the head] toward the right, that is, toward the south). And he should dip [him] a third time: *And of the Holy Spirit* (the third time [with the head] toward the left, that is, toward the north).[96]

The directional sequence of east, south, and north respectively in the above rubrics is traceable to the tenth-century Romano-Germanic Pontifical.[97] The forming of a cross during the threefold application of water to the baptismal candidate is explained by Durandus as symbolizing that "he who is baptized is crucified to the world and affixed to the Cross of Christ."[98] A ritual of Vilna, Lithuania, from 1499 specifies that for all three immersions or pourings of water during the baptism the child's head is to face the east,[99] a practice reflecting the unique liturgical symbolism of this direction.

For all their preoccupation with the theological dimensions of the sacraments, medieval liturgists also recognized the need to address practical matters in their administration. Thus we find in the baptismal rite of the 1518 diocesan ritual of Limoges, France, a rubric advising the priest to keep in mind an infant's aversion to cold water as he confers the sacrament: "Yet that pouring [of water over the head of the infant] should be moderate, lest the tenderness of the infant be aggravated by the coldness of the water."[100]

The postbaptismal anointing (found in all medieval baptismal rites) signifies, according to Durandus, the espousal of the soul of the newly baptized to Christ, the Head of the Church.[101] Pope Innocent III and Saint Thomas Aquinas also see in this anointing of the head, the symbolic seat of human reasoning, a manifestation that the sacrament renders in the recipient a readiness to satisfy everyone who asks him to give a reason for his faith (cf. 1 Pet 3:15).[102] The words accompanying this anointing are virtually the same as those first found in the

---

[96] Quoted in Reifenberg, *Sakramente im Bistum Mainz* (vol. 1), 200, footnote. Similar directions appear in the baptismal rite given in a fifteenth-century manuscript from the Franciscan friary of Landshut, Germany, quoted in Bernhard Mattes, C.S.S.R., *Die Spendung der Sakramente nach den Freisinger Ritualien: Eine Untersuchung der handschriftlichen und gedruckten Quellen*, Münchener theologische Studien 34 (Munich: Max Hueber Verlag, 1967), 166, footnote.

[97] Vogel and Elze, *Pontifical romano-germanique*, 2:106.

[98] Durandus, *Rationale* (CCCM 140a), bk. 6, chap. 83, no. 12, p. 419.

[99] *Agenda sive exequiale divinorum sacramentorum* (1499), sig. e3r.

[100] Martène, *De antiquis ecclesiae ritibus*, bk. 1, art. 18, ordo 18, 1:78.

[101] Durandus, *Rationale* (CCCM 140), bk. 1, chap. 8, no. 9, p. 101.

[102] Saint Thomas Aquinas, *Summa theologica*, pt. III, q. 66, art. 10, reply obj. 2, 2:2390; Innocent III, *Regestorum*, bk. 7 (year 1204), letter 3, PL 215, col. 285.

seventh-century Gelasian Sacramentary of Rome:[103] "*May God, the almighty Father of our Lord Jesus Christ, who has regenerated you from water and the Holy Spirit, and who has granted you the remission of all your sins, himself anoint you with the chrism of salvation in the same Christ Jesus our Lord unto life eternal. Amen. And peace to you.*"[104]

Following the anointing, the priest wipes the chrism from the child's head, upon which he now places a "white garment" that in the original Latin of the Barcelona text is called a *capida*, a form of baptismal hood or veil traceable to the tenth-century Romano-Germanic Pontifical[105] and serving to symbolize the white robes given to the newly baptized in earlier times. This manner of baptismal garment became commonplace in late medieval Europe.[106] In the Barcelona rite, as the priest places the *capida* on the infant's head, he addresses the child: "*Receive the holy garment, the white garment, which you are to bear inviolate and preserve undefiled, that before the tribunal of our Lord Jesus Christ you may have eternal life. Amen. And peace to you.*"[107] This is a distinctively Catalonian version of the formula for presenting the white garment, expanded from that found in a twelfth-century missal of Huesca, Spain,[108] and ultimately derived from the earliest form of the garment presentation text given in the tenth-century Romano-Germanic Pontifical.[109]

The conferral of a white baptismal garment upon the newly baptized is explained by Blessed Rabanus Maurus (+856) as representing the "Christian innocence and purity" imparted by baptism after the soul has been cleansed of the "old stains" of sin, an innocence and purity that the recipient is expected to preserve spotless through "the practice of holy conduct" in readiness for the day when he shall be summoned before the "tribunal of Christ".[110] Saint Thomas Aquinas sees the white garment of baptism as "a sign of the glorious resurrection, unto which men are born again by baptism", as well as a reminder of the "purity of life" to which the recipient is thenceforth bound.[111]

---

[103] Mohlberg, Eizenhöfer, and Siffrin, *Liber sacramentorum*, no. 450, p. 74.

[104] Soberanas, *Ordinarium sacramentorum Barchinonense, 1501*, fol. 19v. The words "*And peace to you*" are an addition dating back to the tenth-century Romano-Germanic Pontifical; see Vogel and Elze, *Pontifical romano-germanique*, 2:163.

[105] Vogel and Elze, *Pontifical romano-germanique*, 2:107; see also Parés i Saltor, *Ordinari d'Urgell de 1536*, 198.

[106] Ritual of Mainz, Germany, c. 1400, quoted in Reifenberg, *Sakramente im Bistum Mainz*, 1:202, footnote; ritual of Augsburg, Germany, 1487 (*Obsequiale Augustense*), fol. 35r; ritual of Freising, Germany, 1493 (*Obsequiale Frisingense*), fol. 8v; ritual of Limoges, France, 1518, in Martène, *De antiquis ecclesiae ritibus*, bk. 1, chap. 1, art. 18, ordo 18, 1:78; missal of Orense, Spain, 1494 (*Missale secundum usum auriensis ecclesiae* [Monterrey, Spain: Gonzalo Rodriguez de la Passera and Juan de Porras, 1494; digitized text, Biblioteca Digital Hispánica, Biblioteca Nacional de España, Madrid, 2007]), fol. 95v.

[107] Soberanas, *Ordinarium sacramentorum Barchinonense, 1501*, fols. 19v–20r.

[108] Franquesa, "Ritual Tarraconense", 263, footnote.

[109] Vogel and Elze, *Pontifical romano-germanique*, 2:163.

[110] Blessed Rabanus Maurus, *De clericorum institutione*, bk. 1, chap. 29, PL 107, col. 313.

[111] Saint Thomas Aquinas, *Summa theologica*, pt. III, q. 66, art. 10, reply obj. 3, 2:2390.

Similarly, Durandus considers the baptismal robes, which he likens to the white robes given to the just in the Book of Revelation (Rev 6:11; see also Rev 7:9, 13–14), as a sign of "the future glorious resurrection of bodies and souls, and also the resurrection from sins".[112] He also mentions the practice in some places of bestowing "a certain round headdress" as the baptismal garment, indicating a custom similar to the baptismal hood or veil specified in the Barcelona rite. He explains this garment upon the head as representing "the crown of the kingdom of eternal life", to which the recipient is now entitled insofar as he is now "a member of Christ, who is King and Priest". Having thereby alluded to the Church's teaching that baptism confers upon all who receive it a share in both the kingship and the priesthood of Christ, Durandus takes the opportunity to clarify what is meant by this universal "priesthood" of the faithful, as distinguished from the unique priesthood of holy orders. The priestly function of the faithful is not that of being able to offer the Eucharist but rather that of being able to offer themselves as a living oblation to God:

> For indeed all Christians are called kings and priests, whence the Apostle Peter says: "But you are a chosen generation, a kingly priesthood" [1 Pet 2:9]. Kings, because they direct themselves and others; priests, because they offer themselves to the Lord, according to that [saying] of the Apostle [Paul]: "I beseech you therefore, brethren, by the mercy of God, that you present your bodies a living sacrifice" [Rom 12:1].[113]

The giving of a lit candle to the newly baptized after the conferral of the baptismal garment, although absent from the 1501 Barcelona baptismal rite, is specified in most medieval baptismal texts.[114] The anonymous tenth-century liturgist Pseudo-Alcuin tells of the newly baptized holding candles in their hands at the Easter Vigil,[115] just as Saint Ambrose had spoken of the "splendid lights of the neophytes" at the vigil five centuries earlier.[116] A formal ceremony to present the candle to the newly baptized, known as the Delivery of the Candle, is first found in the twelfth-century Roman Pontifical.[117] It appears in Spain at the same time, in the twelfth-century missal of Huesca.[118] In

---

[112] Durandus, *Rationale* (CCCM 140a), bk. 6, chap. 83, no. 16, pp. 420–421.

[113] Ibid., no. 15, p. 420.

[114] See the following liturgical texts: ritual of Limoges, France, 1518 (Martène, *De antiquis ecclesiae ritibus*, bk. 1, chap. 1, art. 18, *ordo* 18, 1:78); ritual of Salzburg, Austria, 1496 (*Obsequiale Salisburgense*), fol. 87v; and missal of Orense, Spain, 1494 (*Missale secundum usum Auriensis ecclesiae*), fol. 95v. In contrast to Barcelona, some other baptismal texts of Catalonian Spain dating from the first half of the sixteenth century do include the candle rite (Franquesa, "Ritual Tarraconense", 263; Parés i Saltor, *Ordinari d'Urgell de 1536*, 199).

[115] Pseudo-Alcuin, *Liber de divinis officiis*, chap. 19, PL 101, col. 1221.

[116] Saint Ambrose, *De lapsu virginis consecratae*, chap. 5, PL 16, col. 372.

[117] Text in Michel Andrieu, ed., *Le pontifical romain au moyen-âge*, vol. 1, *Le pontifical romain du XIIe siècle*, ST 86 (Vatican City: Biblioteca Apostolica Vaticana, 1938), 246.

[118] Franquesa, "Ritual Tarraconense", 263, footnote.

the 1522 ritual of Turku, Finland, the following words accompany the conferral of the candle, which is placed in the infant's hand: "*Receive this lamp burning and unspotted; preserve your baptism, that when the Lord shall have come to his nuptials you may be able to go to meet him together with his saints in the heavenly court, that you may have eternal life and live unto ages of ages. Amen.*" [119] Saint Ivo of Chartres sees the lit candle as an expression of Christ's teaching to "let your light shine before men, that they may see your good works, and glorify your Father who is in heaven" (Mt 5:16). It serves as a visual reminder that if he who has been baptized perseveres in virtue, he shall enter into the glory of Heaven in likeness to the wise virgins, who entered with their lamps still burning (Mt 25:1–13). [120] Durandus also utilizes the latter comparison to explain the lit candle given at baptism as symbolizing "the lights of the virtues and good works" with which the baptized should be prepared to meet Christ at his "nuptials" in the "celestial court". [121]

The Conclusion of the Baptismal Rite

For some of the medieval baptismal rites, such as the aforementioned rite of Turku, Finland, the presentation of the lit candle constitutes the end of the baptismal liturgy. But in others, including that of Barcelona, the rite concludes with a ceremony carried out at the altar. In the Barcelona rite, after the infant has been fully reclothed, and with the baptismal *capida* remaining on his head, he is carried by his godfather before the altar. [122] This simple procession appears to be a vestige of the procession that would have taken place with baptisms during the Easter Vigil as the newly baptized returned from the baptistery to the church proper for Easter Mass and Holy Communion. As baptisms increasingly took place apart from the Easter Vigil liturgy, a postbaptismal procession to the altar such as that found in the Barcelona rite would have filled the portion of the rite once occupied by the Easter Vigil Mass. [123] By the fourteenth century, such postbaptismal processions had appeared in various places, including Seville and Gerona, Spain. [124]

In the Barcelona rite, when the procession reaches the altar, the priest sprinkles the child and the others present with holy water, reciting during this aspersion the customary antiphon, *Asperges me* ("*Thou shalt sprinkle me*"), together with Psalm 66 ("*May God have mercy on us,*

---

[119] Parvio, *Manuale seu exequiale Aboense, 1522*, fol. 7v. This same formula, an expanded version of that originally found in the twelfth-century Roman Pontifical—as given in Andrieu, *Pontifical romain au moyen-âge*, 1:246—appears also in the 1494 missal of Orense, Spain, and in the 1518 ritual of Limoges, France; see respectively *Missale secundum usum Auriensis ecclesiae* (1494), fol. 95v, and Martène, *De antiquis ecclesiae ritibus*, bk. 1, chap. 1, art. 18, *ordo* 18, 1:78.

[120] Saint Ivo of Chartres, *Sermon 1*, PL 162, cols. 511–512.

[121] Durandus, *Rationale* (CCCM 140a), bk. 6, chap. 83, no. 22, p. 422.

[122] Soberanas, *Ordinarium sacramentorum Barchinonense, 1501*, fol. 20r.

[123] Parés i Saltor, *Ordinari d'Urgell de 1536*, 200.

[124] Ibid.

and bless us: may he cause the light of his countenance to shine upon us ...").[125] As early as the eighth century, there existed a sprinkling of holy water upon the faithful during the baptismal rite of the Easter Vigil as found in the Gellone Sacramentary, a Frankish adaptation of Rome's Gelasian Sacramentary.[126] A specifically *postbaptismal* sprinkling of holy water is thought to have arisen in Catalonian Spain by the early eleventh century, as inferred from a postbaptismal prayer for blessing water in the Pontifical of Roda (c. 1000).[127]

In the Barcelona rite, following the aspersion of holy water, and after several versicles and responses, the priest prays: "*Graciously hear us, holy Lord, Father almighty, eternal God, and may you vouchsafe to send your holy angel from Heaven, that he may preserve, sustain, protect, visit, and defend all the inhabitants or those assembling in this house of God. Through Christ our Lord*" (response: "*Amen*").[128] The priest next asks the godparents to tell him again the name of the child, after which he addresses the child by name to pronounce a blessing over him: "[Name], *may the Lord bless + you from Sion and preserve you. And may God sanctify you unto perfection, that your soul and mind and body may be kept blameless without accusation for the coming of our Lord Jesus Christ. Who lives and reigns ...*"[129] The priest then prays for the physical health of the infant: "*Almighty eternal God, we humbly entreat your majesty, that you may vouchsafe to regard your servant* [Name] *with serene glances; and to him whom you have given the sacrament of baptism, grant long-lived health. Through all ages of ages*" (response: "*Amen*").[130]

The priest next recites a Gospel reading, at the beginning of which he signs the forehead, the mouth, and the chest of the infant with the sign of the cross (the same triple signing of the cross that he makes upon himself when beginning the Gospel at Mass).[131] As he makes the crosses, he says to the child, "*May he who was born of the Virgin*

---

[125] Soberanas, *Ordinarium sacramentorum Barchinonense, 1501*, fol. 20r–20v. The same postbaptismal aspersion with the recitation of *Asperges me* and Psalm 66 can be found in a 1530 ritual of Tarragona, Spain (Franquesa, "Ritual Tarraconense", 264).

[126] See A. Dumas, O.S.B., ed., *Liber sacramentorum Gellonensis*, CCSL 159 (Turnhout, Belgium: Brepols, 1981), no. 705, p. 100.

[127] Parés i Saltor, *Ordinari d'Urgell de 1536*, 200.

[128] Soberanas, *Ordinarium sacramentorum Barchinonense, 1501*, fol. 20v. This oration, also used for the baptismal rite in the 1530 ritual of Tarragona, Spain (Franquesa, "Ritual Tarraconense", 264), is a shortened version of a prayer for sprinkling holy water in homes from the seventh-century Gelasian Sacramentary of Rome (Mohlberg, Eizenhöfer, and Siffrin, *Liber sacramentorum*, no. 1558, p. 225).

[129] Soberanas, *Ordinarium sacramentorum Barchinonense, 1501*, fol. 20v.

[130] Ibid., fols. 20v–21r.

[131] The making of a cross on the forehead by both the celebrant and the people immediately before the Gospel reading at Mass is first found in Roman *Ordo* 5, a late ninth-century liturgical text combining Roman and German usages; see Andrieu, *Ordines Romani du haut moyen âge*, 2:216. The signing of the forehead, the mouth, and the chest of the infant with the sign of the cross for the reading of the Gospel during the baptismal rite is also found in the 1487 *Obsequiale Augustense* of Augsburg, Germany (in this case for the prebaptismal Gospel reading); see *Obsequiale Augustense* (1487), fol. 32r.

succor you this day and always. Amen." [132] This same pre-Gospel invocation appears in the baptismal rite from the 1536 *Ordinarium* of Urgel, Spain, but with the added rubric that the priest is to place the tip of his stole upon the infant,[133] a practice observed in some other medieval baptismal rites during the earlier-mentioned prebaptismal reading of the Gospel (in particular, those of Regensburg, Germany, 1491; Freising, Germany, 1493; and Salzburg, Austria, 1496).[134] In Limoges, France, as in Urgel, this custom marked the postbaptismal Gospel reading, as can be seen in the 1518 diocesan ritual of Limoges: "Afterward, the godfather should take the child and present him to the priest at the altar or in another customary place; and the priest, with his stole placed upon the child's head in the manner of a cross, should recite the beginning of the holy Gospel according to John: *In the beginning was the Word, and the Word was with God, and the Word was God* ..." [135] Significantly, this will be the first time that the child will hear the Gospel as a baptized Christian. The postbaptismal Gospel reading was in fact considered a catechetical "delivery of the Gospel" to the newly baptized. It is also a vestige of the liturgical setting within which baptisms most often took place in earlier centuries, that is, during the Easter Vigil when the baptismal rite was immediately followed by Mass, with its Easter Gospel.[136]

In some places, such as Limoges (see the above-cited example) and Urgel (1536), the reading utilized was the beginning of Saint John's Gospel (Jn 1:1–14),[137] a text that in this context was considered a species of blessing, just as when it was daily read at the end of Mass.[138] In the Barcelona rite, the Gospel reading is from Saint Luke, chapter 11, verses 27–28, a passage concerning the motherhood of the Blessed Virgin Mary and the hearing and heeding of the Gospel: "*And it came to pass [while Jesus was speaking to the crowds], a certain woman from the crowd, lifting up her voice, said to him: Blessed is the womb that bore thee, and the paps that gave thee suck. But he said: Yea rather, blessed are they who hear the word of God, and keep it."* [139] The Limoges baptismal rite adds immediately after the Gospel reading a prayer for the protection of the child: "*Protect, O Lord, your servant with the provisions of your favor, and render him, trusting in the patronage of the Blessed Virgin Mary, secure from all enemies."* [140]

---

[132] Soberanas, *Ordinarium sacramentorum Barchinonense, 1501,* fol. 21r.

[133] Parés i Saltor, *Ordinari d'Urgell de 1536,* 200.

[134] See respectively the 1491 *Obsequiale Ratisponense* (fol. 8v), the 1493 *Obsequiale Frisingense* (fol. 7r), and the 1496 *Obsequiale Salisburgense* (fol. 85r).

[135] Martène, *De antiquis ecclesiae ritibus,* bk. 1, chap. 1, art. 18, *ordo* 18, 1:78.

[136] Parés i Saltor, *Ordinari d'Urgell de 1536,* 201.

[137] Martène, *De antiquis ecclesiae ritibus,* bk. 1, chap. 1, art. 18, *ordo* 18, 1:78; Parés i Saltor, *Ordinari d'Urgell de 1536,* 200–201.

[138] Parés i Saltor, *Ordinari d'Urgell de 1536,* 201.

[139] Soberanas, *Ordinarium sacramentorum Barchinonense, 1501,* fol. 21r.

[140] Martène, *De antiquis ecclesiae ritibus,* bk. 1, chap. 1, art. 18, *ordo* 18, 1:78.

In the Barcelona rite, following the Gospel reading, the godparents "present the infant with their offerings" to the priest.[141] In the 1536 *Ordinarium* of Urgel, Spain, the godparents are directed at this same point in the ceremony to kiss the priest's stole and offer him candles together with the other offerings—the candles would be used for Mass and for burning before the images of Mary and the saints, whereas the other offerings would be applied to the maintenance of the church.[142] The Barcelona text (as well as the Urgel text) then directs the priest to bless the godparents: "*May he bless + you, the Father and the Son in the unity of the Holy Spirit. Amen.*"[143] After this blessing, the priest takes from the infant's head the baptismal *capida* and accepts the offerings from the godparents, bringing the ceremony to a close.[144] In another Spanish ritual, that of Gerona, dating from 1550, the "presentation" rite following the Gospel at the end of the baptismal ceremony includes an additional action on the part of the priest. After the godparents present their offering, the priest "should take the [infant] boy and make him kiss the altar on each side, afterward in the middle", at the conclusion of which the priest returns the child to the arms of the godfather and removes the infant's baptismal *capida*.[145]

Some of the baptismal rites end with a rubric enjoining the priest to instruct the godparents regarding their obligations. At the end of the baptismal rite in the 1522 manual of Turku, Finland, there is a concluding rubric of this nature: "Then the priest should declare to the godparents that they should teach the child the Our Father and the Creed. Then he should say that the father and mother should preserve him from the danger of fire and water, and from other things of this kind up to the completed period of seven years."[146]

---

[141] Soberanas, *Ordinarium sacramentorum Barchinonense, 1501*, fol. 21r.

[142] Parés i Saltor, *Ordinari d'Urgell de 1536*, 201–202.

[143] Soberanas, *Ordinarium sacramentorum Barchinonense, 1501*, fol. 21r. For this blessing in the Urgel rite, see Parés i Saltor, *Ordinari d'Urgell de 1536*, 202.

[144] Soberanas, *Ordinarium sacramentorum Barchinonense, 1501*, fol. 21r.

[145] Ritual of Gerona, 1550, quoted in Franquesa, "Ritual Tarraconense", 265.

[146] Parvio, *Manuale seu exequiale Aboense, 1522*, fol. 7v.

4 Confirmation

The unction of confirmation is the nuptial garment.... The baptized are twice anointed with chrism: once by the priest at baptism, and on the head; second, by the bishop at confirmation, and on the forehead.... By the priest's unction their souls are espoused to Christ; by the bishop's confirmation they are endowed with the kingdom of Christ.

Honorius of Autun (+c. 1135)[1]

Saint Thomas Aquinas (+1274) explains that Christ instituted the sacrament of confirmation in an anticipatory manner, that is, by promising at the Last Supper the conferral of the Holy Spirit after his Ascension, telling the Apostles, "It is expedient to you that I go: for if I go not, the Paraclete will not come to you; but if I go, I will send him to you" (Jn 16:7; see also Jn 14:16–17).[2] Later, in the Acts of the Apostles, we find an early instance of the administration of this sacrament, which is described as distinct from baptism (Acts 8:14–17):

Now when the apostles, who were in Jerusalem, had heard that Samaria had received the word of God, they sent unto them Peter and John. Who, when they were come, prayed for them, that they might receive the Holy Ghost. For he was not as yet come upon any of them; but they were only baptized in the name of the Lord Jesus. Then they laid their hands upon them, and they received the Holy Ghost.

As for the purpose of confirmation, Saint Thomas Aquinas states that this sacrament imparts "spiritual growth bringing the soul to perfect strength".[3] In explaining how the action of the Holy Spirit in the sacrament of confirmation differs from that in baptism, William Durandus of Mende (+1296) observes that whereas in baptism the

---

[1] Excerpted from Honorius of Autun, *Gemma animae*, bk. 3, chaps. 113, 114, PL 172, col. 673.

[2] Saint Thomas Aquinas, *Summa theologica: First Complete American Edition in Three Volumes*, trans. Fathers of the English Dominican Province (New York: Benziger Brothers, 1948), pt. III, q. 72, art. 1, reply obj. 1, 2:2424.

[3] Saint Thomas Aquinas, *Summa contra gentiles*, bk. 4, chap. 58, in *The "Summa contra gentiles" of Saint Thomas Aquinas*, trans. English Dominican Fathers (New York: Benziger Brothers, 1923–1929), 4:221.

Holy Spirit confers the remission of sins, in confirmation "the Spirit himself is invited that he may come, and vouchsafe to descend into and inhabit the very home [i.e., the soul] he has sanctified, and be imparted at the invocation of the bishop."[4]

As early as the third century, the three most important actions in the conferral of confirmation—the anointing with chrism, the signing of the cross upon the forehead, and the imposition of hands—are mentioned by Saint Hippolytus of Rome (+c. 236)[5] and by Tertullian (+223), the latter of whom observes, "The flesh is anointed that the soul may be consecrated; the flesh is signed [with the cross] that the soul too may be protected; the flesh is overshadowed by the imposition of the hand that the soul may be illumined by the Spirit."[6] Although in the early centuries of the Church confirmation was usually conferred immediately after baptism within a single, larger liturgical ceremony—most often the Easter Vigil[7]—the administration of confirmation on an occasion separate from baptism had arisen in the West by the fifth century, when it is attested by Pope Innocent I (401–417).[8] By the ninth century, the rite of confirmation had expanded into a ceremony with multiple prayers, as found in the Sacramentary of Reichenau, a Frankish adaptation of the Gregorian Sacramentary of Rome compiled at the south German abbey of Reichenau.[9]

In the West, from the apostolic era onward, the bishop has always been considered the ordinary minister of confirmation.[10] Following the Fourth Lateran Council of 1215, confirmation was generally administered to children between four and seven years old.[11] In 1280, a synod for the archdiocese of Cologne, Germany, specified the age for confirmation to be seven or older, adding that any confirmation

---

[4] William Durandus of Mende, *Rationale divinorum officiorum*, bk. 6, chap. 84, no. 2, in A. Davril, O.S.B., and T. M. Thibodeau, eds., *Guillelmi Duranti: Rationale divinorum officiorum V–VI*, CCCM 140a (Turnhout, Belgium: Brepols, 1998), 430. Hereafter cited as Durandus, *Rationale* (CCCM 140a).

[5] Saint Hippolytus of Rome, *Apostolic Tradition*, chap. 16, in Francis Xavier Funk, ed., *Didascalia et Constitutiones apostolorum*, vol. 2, *Testimonia et scripturae propinquae* (Paderborn, Germany: Libraria Ferdinandi Schoeningh, 1905), 111.

[6] Tertullian, *De resurrectione carnis*, no. 8, translated by E. Evans, in Ernest Evans, ed. and trans., *Tertullian's Treatise on the Resurrection* (London: SPCK, 1960), 24 (Latin text), 25 (English translation).

[7] Such is the case in the seventh-century Gelasian Sacramentary of Rome; see Leo Cunibert Mohlberg, O.S.B., et al., eds., *Liber sacramentorum Romanae aeclesiae ordinis anni circuli (Sacramentarium Gelasianum)*, REDSMF 4 (Rome: Herder, 1960), nos. 449–452, p. 74.

[8] Pope Innocent I, *Epistle 25*, to Decentius of Gubbio, PL 20, col. 554. See also R. Cabié, "Christian Initiation", in Aimé-Georges Martimort, ed., *The Church at Prayer: An Introduction to the Liturgy*, vol. 3, *The Sacraments* (Collegeville, Minn.: Liturgical Press, 1988), 59.

[9] Sacramentary of Reichenau (excerpt), PL 138, cols. 957–959.

[10] Roger Béraudy, "L'initiation chrétienne", in Aimé-Georges Martimort, ed., *L'église en prière: Introduction à la liturgie* (Paris: Desclée, 1961), 558. See, for example, the testimony of Pope Innocent I (401–417) in his letter to Decentius of Gubbio (*Epistle 25*, PL 20, col. 554).

[11] Béraudy, "Initiation chrétienne", 559.

candidates who were ten or older should go to confession before being confirmed.[12] The custom of candidates taking an additional name at confirmation is ancient, being mentioned in the late sixth century by Saint Gregory of Tours (+594) in his account of the conversion of the Spanish prince and martyr Saint Hermenegild (+585).[13]

Rites of Confirmation in England and France

We present here concurrently two medieval confirmation rites, one from the Egbert Pontifical, a liturgical book of tenth-century England,[14] and the other, dating to about the year 1294, from the pontifical compiled for the French diocese of Mende by William Durandus.[15] The latter pontifical, including its confirmation rite, was subsequently incorporated with minimal alterations into the papal liturgy and spread elsewhere from the fourteenth century onward, recognized for its preeminent conformity to canon law and the liturgical traditions of Rome;[16] thereafter the Durandus confirmation rite served as the basis for the rite universally promulgated in the *Pontificale Romanum* of 1595–1596.[17]

It is evident from the rubrics of the Egbert Pontifical that the Egbert confirmation ceremony takes place immediately before a Mass that the candidates are to attend together.[18] While the Egbert text begins immediately with the first prayer of the rite, the Durandus text begins with a rubric specifying that the bishop, vested in an amice, a stole, and a white cope, with a miter upon his head, should deliver an introductory admonition; then, having washed his right thumb, he is to stand with his hands joined before his chest, his miter having been removed, as the candidates kneel before him, the hands of each joined before the chest.[19] Utilizing an invocation dating back to the ninth-century German Sacramentary of Reichenau,[20] the bishop now says, *"May the Holy Spirit come upon you and the power of the Most High preserve you from sins"* (response: *"Amen"*).[21]

---

[12] Synod of Cologne (1280), statutes, chap. 5, in J. D. Mansi, ed., *Sacrorum conciliorum nova et amplissima collectio*, vol. 24 (Florence and Venice, 1780; repr. Paris: Hubert Welter, 1903), col. 349.

[13] Saint Gregory of Tours, *Historia Francorum*, bk. 5, chap. 39, PL 71, col. 354.

[14] Text in H. M. J. Banting, ed., *Two Anglo-Saxon Pontificals (the Egbert and Sidney Sussex Pontificals)*, HBS 104 (London: Henry Bradshaw Society, 1989), 14–15.

[15] Text in Michel Andrieu, ed., *Le pontifical romain au moyen-âge*, vol. 3, *Le pontifical de Guillaume Durand*, ST 88 (Vatican City: Biblioteca Apostolica Vaticana, 1940), 333–335.

[16] See the editor's introduction, ibid., 15–20, and Marc Dykmans, S.J., *Le pontifical romain révisé au XVᵉ siècle*, ST 311 (Vatican City: Biblioteca Apostolica Vaticana, 1985), 9–10, 14.

[17] Text in Manlio Sodi and Achille Triacca, eds., *Pontificale Romanum: Editio princeps (1595–1596)*, facsimile ed., MLCT 1 (Vatican City: Libreria Editrice Vaticana, © 1997), 1–5 (original pagination).

[18] The rubrics speak of the candidates receiving a final blessing "at Mass after confirmation" and receiving Holy Communion following their confirmation (Banting, *Two Anglo-Saxon Pontificals*, 14–15).

[19] Andrieu, *Pontifical romain au moyen-âge*, 3:333.

[20] Sacramentary of Reichenau (excerpt), PL 138, col. 958.

[21] Andrieu, *Pontifical romain au moyen-âge*, 3:333.

The Egbert rite begins with the bishop reciting a prayer originally found in two early liturgical books of Rome, the seventh-century Gelasian Sacramentary[22] and the eighth-century *Hadrianum* redaction of the Gregorian Sacramentary,[23] beseeching the conferral of all seven gifts of the Holy Spirit:

> *Almighty eternal God, who have vouchsafed to regenerate this your servant from water and the Holy Spirit, and who have granted him the remission of all his sins, you, O Lord, send into him your sevenfold Holy Spirit, the Paraclete, from Heaven. Amen. Give him the spirit of wisdom and understanding. Amen. The spirit of counsel and fortitude. Amen. The spirit of knowledge and piety. Amen. Fill him with the spirit of the fear of God and of our Lord Jesus Christ and mercifully seal him with the sign of your holy Cross unto eternal life. Through the same Jesus Christ your Son, our Lord, who lives and reigns with you . . .*[24]

This same prayer (with some verbal differences) is utilized in the Durandus rite, with the added rubric that the bishop is to raise and extend his hands over the confirmation candidates for the recitation of this prayer.[25]

In the Egbert rite, the essential action that constitutes the "matter" of the sacrament follows: "Here [the bishop] ought to put the chrism on the forehead of each man and say: *Receive the sign of the holy Cross with the chrism of salvation in Christ Jesus unto eternal life. Amen.*"[26] The anointing with chrism, and the bishop's touching of the forehead in applying the chrism, an action serving as the requisite "imposition of hands" for confirmation, were in 1204 effectively identified by Pope Innocent III as constituting together the essential "matter" of this sacrament, for he defined confirmation as "the imposition of the [bishop's] hand in the course of the anointing of the forehead with chrism".[27] This explanation of the matter of confirmation was recently codified in the 1994 *Catechism of the Catholic Church*.[28] Saint Thomas Aquinas sees the chrism as a particularly suitable sign of the conferral of confirmation in that oil is a traditional biblical image of the grace of the Holy Spirit. The psalm verse "God, thy God, hath anointed thee with the oil of gladness above thy fellows" (Ps 44:8), understood as a prophecy of Christ,

---

[22] Mohlberg, Eizenhöfer, and Siffrin, *Liber sacramentorum*, no. 451, p. 74.

[23] Text in Jean Deshusses, ed., *Le sacramentaire grégorien: Ses principales formes d'après les plus anciens manuscrits*, vol. 1, 2nd ed., SF 16 (Fribourg, Switzerland: Editions Universitaires Fribourg, 1979), no. 376, p. 189.

[24] Banting, *Two Anglo-Saxon Pontificals*, 14.

[25] Andrieu, *Pontifical romain au moyen-âge*, 3:333–334.

[26] Banting, *Two Anglo-Saxon Pontificals*, 14.

[27] Pope Innocent III, *Regestorum*, bk. 7 (year 1204), letter 3, PL 215, col. 285.

[28] *Catechism of the Catholic Church*, English ed. (Vatican City: Libreria Editrice Vaticana, © 1994; Washington, D.C.: United States Catholic Conference, 1994), nos. 1300, 1320, pp. 329, 333.

testifies to Christ's having received in his humanity the fullness of the Holy Spirit. Thus the anointing in confirmation signifies the sacrament's conferral of the plenitude of the Holy Spirit.[29]

In the Egbert rite, the bishop's words when administering the chrism, "*Receive the sign of the holy Cross*", indicate that he inscribes with the oil a cross on the candidate's forehead. While the imparting of a cross in any sacramental anointing is always a visual reminder of the true Minister of every sacrament, Christ, who has redeemed us on the Cross, as Durandus observes,[30] Saint Thomas Aquinas notes that the cross made in the anointing of confirmation carries the added significance of testifying to the sacrament's conferral of "strength in the spiritual combat".[31] As the latter explains, the recipient of the sacrament, called to spiritual combat, is marked with the sign of Christ the King's victory in combat, the cross, just as soldiers are marked with the sign of the particular sovereign they are fighting under.[32] The cross is made appropriately on the forehead, the most conspicuous part of the body, where it serves as an overt manifestation of the recipient's identity both as a Christian and as a combatant for the cause of Christ, strengthened by this sacrament to overcome fear and shame, "that he may bravely confess the faith of Christ even in face of the enemies of that faith".[33]

According to Durandus, the chrism cross made prominently on the forehead serves to turn away "the destroying angel", just as he had been turned away from the Israelites' homes that had been marked on the lintels and doorposts with lambs' blood as a prefiguration of the Passion.[34] Moreover, the cross-marked forehead of the confirmed testifies to the more perfect following of Christ, the Lamb of God, that confirmation brings about, in conformity with Saint John's vision of the righteous gathered with "the Lamb" on Mount Sion, "having his name, and the name of his Father, written on their foreheads" (Rev 14:1).[35] Durandus also sees the marking of the forehead as rooted in Old Testament tradition, wherein the forehead of the high priest carried "the ineffable name of the Lord", as prescribed in the Book of Exodus: "Thou shalt make also a plate of the purest gold: wherein thou shalt grave with engraver's work, Holy to the Lord ... and it shall be upon the miter, hanging over the forehead of the high priest.... And the plate shall be always on his forehead" (Ex 28:36–38).[36]

---

[29] Saint Thomas Aquinas, *Summa theologica*, pt. III, q. 72, art. 2, 2:2425.

[30] Durandus, *Rationale* (CCCM 140a), bk. 6, chap. 84, no. 5, p. 432.

[31] Saint Thomas Aquinas, *Summa theologica*, pt. III, q. 72, art. 4, 2:2427.

[32] Ibid., art. 4 and art. 9, 2:2427, 2431.

[33] Ibid., art. 9, 2:2431.

[34] Durandus, *Rationale* (CCCM 140a), bk. 6, chap. 84, no. 5, pp. 432–433.

[35] Ibid., 433.

[36] Ibid.

Although the Egbert Pontifical makes no mention of the posture of the candidates as they are confirmed, the thirteenth-century Pontifical of Durandus indicates that each candidate kneels before the bishop for the anointing, presented by his sponsor,[37] likewise kneeling. After asking for the candidate's name, the bishop, seated upon a faldstool, dips his right thumb into the chrism and with his thumb makes the sign of the cross upon the candidate's forehead, saying as he does so, "[Name], *I mark you with the sign of the Cross and confirm you with the chrism of salvation, in the name + of the Father, and + of the Son, and of the Holy + Spirit, that you may be filled with the same Holy Spirit and may have eternal life*" (response: "*Amen*"). During the words "*In the name of the Father, and of the Son, and of the Holy Spirit*", the bishop makes with his hand the sign of the cross three times before the candidate's face.[38] The wording of this particular confirmation formula, first found in the twelfth-century *Pontificale Romanum* (albeit without the concluding clause),[39] was identified by Saint Thomas Aquinas as the "form" of the sacrament,[40] an identification subsequently defined by the Council of Florence in 1439.[41]

Immediately after the anointing with chrism, the bishop greets the newly confirmed candidate, welcomed, according to Durandus, as a "new man, who is worthy to be greeted according to the newness of life" (see Eph 4:24 and Rom 6:4).[42] In the tenth-century Egbert Pontifical this greeting takes the form of a pair of short versicles with corresponding responses ("*Peace be with you* ...").[43] In the Pontifical of Durandus the greeting is accompanied by a dramatic gesture: "And then [the bishop] gives him a blow lightly upon the cheek, saying: *Peace be with you.*"[44] The symbolic striking of the face, an action

---

[37] The custom of each confirmation candidate standing at the beginning of the confirmation rite with one foot resting upon the right foot of his sponsor (prior to kneeling before the bishop), traceable to the ninth-century German Sacramentary of Reichenau, subsequently appeared in the 1485 *Pontificalis liber* (the edition of the *Pontificale Romanum* compiled by two papal masters of ceremonies, Patrizio Piccolomini and John Burckard), and entered the 1595–1596 *Pontificale Romanum*. See respectively Sacramentary of Reichenau (excerpt), PL 138, col. 958; Manlio Sodi, ed., *Il "Pontificalis liber" di Agostino Patrizi Piccolomini e Giovanni Burcardo (1485)*, facsimile ed., MSIL 43 (Vatican City: Libreria Editrice Vaticana, © 2006), 8 (new pagination); and Sodi and Triacca, *Pontificale Romanum: Editio princeps (1595–1596)*, 2 (original pagination).

[38] Andrieu, *Pontifical romain au moyen-âge*, 3:334.

[39] Text in Michel Andrieu, ed., *Le pontifical romain au moyen-âge*, vol. 1, *Le pontifical romain du XIIᵉ siècle*, ST 86 (Vatican City: Biblioteca Apostolica Vaticana, 1938), 247.

[40] Saint Thomas Aquinas, *Summa theologica*, pt. III, q. 72, art. 4, 2:2426–2427.

[41] Council of Florence, *Decree for the Armenians* (November 22, 1439), in J.D. Mansi, ed., *Sacrorum conciliorum nova et amplissima collectio*, vol. 31 (Florence and Venice, 1798; repr., Paris and Leipzig: Hubert Welter, 1906), col. 1055. The words currently used and identified as the essential form of confirmation in the Roman Rite are different: "*Accipe signaculum doni Spiritus Sancti*"; see *Catechism of the Catholic Church*, English ed. (1994), nos. 1300, 1320, pp. 329, 333.

[42] Durandus, *Rationale* (CCCM 140a), bk. 6, chap. 84, no. 5, p. 432.

[43] Banting, *Two Anglo-Saxon Pontificals*, 14.

[44] Andrieu, *Pontifical romain au moyen-âge*, 3:334.

evidently added to the rite by Durandus himself,[45] is explained by him as bearing witness to the spiritual strength conferred by the sacrament upon the candidate, that, fortified to withstand the buffets of shame and disgrace in the eyes of the world for the sake of the Gospel, "he may no longer be ashamed to confess the name of Christ before anyone whatsoever."[46] The light slap is also intended to strike terror in any demon intent upon harming the newly confirmed candidate, "that he may flee and not dare to return", a connotation that Durandus notes is derived from the exorcism of a possessed monk that the father of Western monasticism, Saint Benedict (+c. 547), wrought by this means (as related by Pope Saint Gregory the Great in his *Dialogues*).[47]

Returning to the Egbert Pontifical, we find after the bishop's greeting to the candidates a series of prayers and blessings, beginning with the following: "*May God the Father, and the Son, and the Holy Spirit confirm you, that you may have life eternal, and unto ages of ages shall you live.*"[48] To this is added a blessing formula derived from Psalm 127 (verses 4–5): "*Behold, thus shall every man be blessed who fears the Lord. May the Lord bless you from Sion, that you may see the good things that are in Jerusalem all the days of your life. Peace be with you unto life eternal. Amen.*"[49] In the Durandus rite, after the anointing of the candidates, the bishop cleanses his thumb with a bread fragment or a piece of linen and some water as an antiphon from Psalm 67 (verses 29–30) is chanted: "*Confirm, O God, what you have wrought in us from your holy Temple that is in Jerusalem.*"[50]

In the Egbert rite, the bishop next prays for all the candidates:

> *O God, who gave your Apostles the Holy Spirit, and through them and their successors, willed him to be handed down to the other faithful, look mercifully upon the service of our humility, and grant that the Holy Spirit, coming into the hearts of these [male candidates] and these [female candidates], whose foreheads we have outlined and confirmed this day with the sign of the cross, may, by fittingly inhabiting them, make perfect the temple of his glory. Through the same Jesus Christ your Son, our Lord, who lives and reigns with you . . .*[51]

---

[45] Estanislau Llopart, "Les fórmules de la confirmació en el Pontifical romà," in *Liturgica*, vol. 2, Scripta et documenta 10 (Barcelona: Publicaciones de l'Abadia de Montserrat, 1958): 177.

[46] Durandus, *Rationale* (CCCM 140a), bk. 6, chap. 84, no. 8, p. 433.

[47] Ibid. Regarding Saint Benedict's exorcism of a possessed monk by means of a slap, see Pope Saint Gregory the Great, *Dialogues*, bk. 2, chap. 30, in Adalbert de Vogüé, ed., and Paul Antin, trans., *Grégoire le Grand: Dialogues*, vol. 2, *Livres I–III*, SC 260 (Paris: Cerf, 1979), 220–221 (Latin text with French translation).

[48] Banting, *Two Anglo-Saxon Pontificals*, 14.

[49] Ibid. This formula is also found in the ninth-century Sacramentary of Reichenau from southern Germany; see Sacramentary of Reichenau (excerpt), PL 138, col. 958.

[50] Andrieu, *Pontifical romain au moyen-âge*, 3:334.

[51] Banting, *Two Anglo-Saxon Pontificals*, 14–15. This prayer also appears in the ninth-century Sacramentary of Reichenau; see Sacramentary of Reichenau (excerpt), PL 138, col. 958.

The above prayer is followed by a rubric specifying the candidates' subsequent reception of Holy Communion.[52] In the Pontifical of Durandus, a rubric directs the bishop to say the above prayer standing with his hands folded before his chest, and with all the candidates "devoutly kneeling".[53] He then recites a final blessing derived from Psalm 127 (verses 4–5), the same as that used at an earlier point in the ceremony from the Egbert Pontifical, making the sign of the cross as he does so.[54] The Durandus rite ends with a series of instructions to be delivered by the bishop to the newly confirmed and their sponsors. It is only in these concluding rubrics that there is mention of a cloth band that has been tied around the head of each candidate at some point before the confirmation anointing,[55] which serves the purpose of absorbing the chrism running down from the forehead; the rubrics explain what is to be done with these cloths, moistened with the blessed oil:

> The bishop announces to the confirmed or crismated that in honor of the Holy Trinity they should bear the chrism cloths on their foreheads for the space of three days; and on the third day the priest shall wash their foreheads, and the chrism cloths upon their foreheads he will burn; or candles should be made from the chrism cloths for the use of the altar.
>
> To the male or female sponsors, however, he announces that they should instruct and train their godchildren in good actions and works, that they may flee evil things and do good things, and that they should teach them the Creed, the Our Father, [and] the Hail Mary, inasmuch as they have bound themselves with respect to this.[56]

The Egbert rite concludes after Holy Communion with a final episcopal blessing given to the newly confirmed at the end of Mass. For this blessing, two alternatives are provided by the pontifical, both of which warrant quoting in full:

> *May almighty God, who created all things from nothing, bless you and grant us in baptism and in confirmation the remission of all sins. Amen. And may he who gave the disciples the Holy Spirit in his fiery tongues illuminate our hearts in his own brightness and continually inflame them to the love of him. Amen. That, cleansed well of all vices and protected with his assistance from all adversities, you may be worthy to be made his temple. Amen. May he who created you preserve you from all imminent evils and defend you from all wickedness. Amen. Which [may] he himself [vouchsafe to grant, whose kingdom*

---

[52] Banting, *Two Anglo-Saxon Pontificals*, 15.

[53] Andrieu, *Pontifical romain au moyen-âge*, 3:334–335.

[54] Ibid., 335.

[55] A rubric of the 1595–1596 *Pontificale Romanum* indicates that the cloth is tied in place before the confirmation rite begins; text in Sodi and Triacca, *Pontificale Romanum: Editio princeps (1595–1596)*, 2 (original pagination).

[56] Andrieu, *Pontifical romain au moyen-âge*, 3:335.

and dominion endure without end, unto ages of ages]. Amen. [May] the blessing [of God, the Father, and the Son, and the Holy Spirit, and the peace of the Lord, be with you forever[57]*]. Amen.*[58]

Pour forth, we beseech you, O Lord, upon these your servants and maidservants your heavenly blessing, by which you have willed to deliver through us your priceless sevenfold Holy Spirit. And to the same grant the grace and gifts of the Holy Spirit. Amen. That whoever has been regenerated from water and the Holy Spirit may always be preserved by your protection. Amen. May there overflow in them charity poured forth by the Holy Spirit, which covers and conquers a whole multitude of sins. Amen. Protect these [men] and these [women] with divine protection, that all sins may vanish from them; and may they always strive to fulfill your precepts. Amen. May he graciously rest[59] *upon them who once rested upon the glorious*[60] *Apostles. Which [may] he himself [vouchsafe to grant . . .]. Amen. [May] the blessing [of God, the Father, and the Son, and the Holy Spirit, and the peace of the Lord, be with you forever*[61]*]. Amen.*[62]

---

[57] Insofar as the Egbert text provides only the incipit of this Trinitarian formula and of the formula preceding it (*"Which may he himself vouchsafe to grant"*), the rest of the wording is here supplied (in brackets) from Saint Benedict of Aniane's early ninth-century Frankish adaptation of the Gregorian Sacramentary of Rome; see Deshusses, *Sacramentaire grégorien*, no. 1738, 1:576 (conclusion of prayer).

[58] Banting, *Two Anglo-Saxon Pontificals*, 15. An earlier version of this blessing appears in a ninth-century addition to the eighth-century *Hadrianum* redaction of Rome's Gregorian Sacramentary preserved in an early ninth-century manuscript known as the Sacramentary of Hildoard of Cambrai (manuscript: Cambrai, France, Bibliothèque Municipale, codex 164); see Jean Deshusses, ed., *Le sacramentaire grégorien: Ses principales formes d'après les plus anciens manuscrits*, vol. 2, SF 24 (Fribourg, Switzerland: Editions Universitaires Fribourg, 1979), no. 3821, p. 358.

[59] The Latin of the Egbert text gives this verb in the future indicative tense, *requiescet*, but the context clearly calls for the present subjunctive tense, *requiescat*, as it is actually given in the text of this same prayer from the confirmation rite of the eleventh-century Sacramentary of Figeac, a liturgical book of Moissac, France; see Edmond Martène, *De antiquis ecclesiae ritibus* (Venice: Johannes Baptista Novelli, 1763–1764), bk. 1, chap. 2, art. 4, *ordo* 7, 1:94.

[60] In the Latin of the Egbert text, this adjective is given in the nominative singular declension (*gloriosus*), but it appears from the context that the correct rendering is the ablative plural (*gloriosis*), modifying the ablative plural noun *apostolis*, the rendering that is actually given in the text of this same prayer from the aforementioned Sacramentary of Figeac (Martène, *De antiquis ecclesiae ritibus*, bk. 1, chap. 2, art. 4, *ordo* 7, 1:94).

[61] As with the preceding prayer, the bracketed words of this prayer's conclusion are taken from Saint Benedict of Aniane's early ninth-century Frankish adaptation of the Gregorian Sacramentary of Rome; see Deshusses, *Sacramentaire grégorien*, no. 1738, 1:576 (conclusion of prayer).

[62] Banting, *Two Anglo-Saxon Pontificals*, 15. This prayer is also found in the confirmation rite of the aforementioned Sacramentary of Figeac (Martène, *De antiquis ecclesiae ritibus*, bk. 1, chap. 2, art. 4, *ordo* 7, 1:94).

5   The Sacrament of Penance

We beseech your majesty, O Lord, holy Father, almighty eternal God, who ever seek not the death but the life of sinners: regard the weeping of your servant prostrate before you, and turn his lamentation into the joy of your mercy; rend the sackcloth of his sins and clothe him in salutary gladness, that after the long famine of his roaming afar he may be satiated from your holy altars; having entered the chamber of the King, in His temple may he bless and exalt the name of your glory forever.

Penance rite for the sick, Italy, eleventh century[1]

Saint Thomas Aquinas (+1274) sees the sacrament of penance prefigured in the Book of Leviticus,[2] which states: "If any one sin through ignorance, and do one of those things which by the law of the Lord are forbidden, and being guilty of sin, understand his iniquity, he shall offer of the flocks a ram without blemish to the priest, according to the measure and estimation of the sin: and the priest shall pray for him, because he did it ignorantly: and it shall be forgiven him" (Lev 5:17–18). It is on Easter Sunday that Christ solemnly and expressly conferred upon the Apostles the power to forgive sins: "Receive ye the Holy Ghost. Whose sins you shall forgive, they are forgiven them; and whose sins you shall retain, they are retained" (Jn 20:22–23). Yet this conferral is implicitly promised by Christ earlier, during his public ministry, in his bestowal of the power of "binding" and "loosing" first and foremost upon Saint Peter (Mt 16:19), and then in a secondary manner upon all the Apostles (Mt 18:18). It is these latter two Scripture passages that explain why in the medieval rites for the

---

[1] Prayer excerpted from the penance rite of the "Order of the Sick or Dying" in an eleventh-century northern Italian ritual of pastoral rites (manuscript: Milan, Biblioteca Ambrosiana, codex T.27. Sup.), in C. Lambot, O.S.B., ed., *North Italian Services of the Eleventh Century: Recueil d'ordines du XIe siècle*, HBS 67 (London: Henry Bradshaw Society, 1931), 46. This prayer in its earliest form first appears in the seventh-century Gelasian Sacramentary of Rome; see Leo Cunibert Mohlberg, O.S.B., et al., eds., *Liber sacramentorum Romanae aeclesiae ordinis anni circuli (Sacramentarium Gelasianum)*, REDSMF 4 (Rome: Herder, 1960), no. 366, p. 59.

[2] Saint Thomas Aquinas, *Summa theologica: First Complete American Edition in Three Volumes*, trans. Fathers of the English Dominican Province (New York: Benziger Brothers, 1948), pt. III, q. 84, art. 7, 2:2535.

sacrament of penance the power to forgive sins is repeatedly spoken of as conferred through Saint Peter and the Apostles.

Saint Thomas Aquinas identifies the three requisite acts of the penitent—contrition, confession, and satisfaction[3]—as the "matter" of the sacrament of penance,[4] a judgment subsequently embraced by the Council of Florence in 1439[5] and the Council of Trent in 1551.[6] The "form" of the sacrament is identified by Saint Thomas and later defined by the councils of Florence and Trent as the priest's words of absolution, with the words *"Absolvo te"* ("*I absolve you*") defined at Trent as the *essential* phrase of the absolution formula.[7] The only valid ministers of the sacrament are priests and bishops, a demarcation expressly taught by Saint Ambrose (+397)[8] and Saint Thomas Aquinas[9] and likewise defined by the councils of Florence and Trent.[10]

The personal confession of one's sins to a priest or a bishop is ancient, being explicitly mentioned as early as the third century by the North African bishop and martyr Saint Cyprian (+258), who praises those who confess sins of thought: "Sorrowfully and honestly confessing this very thing before the priests of God, they make the confession of their conscience, set forth the burden of their soul, and seek a salutary remedy to their modest wounds, although small." [11] In the fourth century, the Eastern patriarch and Church doctor Saint Basil (+379), answering the question of whom a penitent should confess his sins to, declares, "In the confession of sins, the same order is to be observed that is applied in disclosing illnesses of the body. Accordingly, just as men do not lay open their bodily illnesses to all, nor to anyone, but to those who are skillful in the healing of them, so too the confession of sins ought to be made before those who can heal them." [12] In another passage Basil states, "It is necessary to confess sins to those to whom

---

[3] Satisfaction constitutes "the voluntary acceptance or endurance of the penance imposed by a confessor" (John Barton, *Penance and Absolution*, Twentieth Century Encyclopedia of Catholicism 51 [New York: Hawthorn Books, 1961], 81).

[4] Saint Thomas Aquinas, *Summa theologica*, pt. III, q. 84, art. 2, 2:2530.

[5] Council of Florence, *Decree for the Armenians* (November 22, 1439), in J.D. Mansi, ed., *Sacrorum conciliorum nova et amplissima collectio*, vol. 31 (Florence and Venice, 1798; repr., Paris: Hubert Welter, 1906), cols. 1057–1058.

[6] Council of Trent, session 14, November 25, 1551, *De poenitentia*, chap. 3, in H.J. Schroeder, O.P., *Canons and Decrees of the Council of Trent: Original Text with English Translation* (Saint Louis, Mo.: B. Herder, 1955), 90–91, 366–367.

[7] Saint Thomas Aquinas, *Summa theologica*, pt. III, q. 84, art. 3, reply obj. 3, 2:2531–2532; Council of Florence, *Decree for the Armenians*, in Mansi, *Sacrorum conciliorum nova et amplissima collectio*, vol. 31, col. 1058; Council of Trent, *De poenitentia*, chap. 3, in Schroeder, *Canons and Decrees of the Council of Trent*, 90, 366.

[8] Saint Ambrose, *De poenitentia*, bk. 1, chap. 2, no. 7, PL 16, col. 468.

[9] Saint Thomas Aquinas, *Summa theologica*, supplement, q. 8, art. 1, 3:2594.

[10] Council of Florence, *Decree for the Armenians*, in Mansi, *Sacrorum conciliorum nova et amplissima collectio*, vol. 31, col. 1058; Council of Trent, *De poenitentia*, canon 10, in Schroeder, *Canons and Decrees of the Council of Trent*, 103–104, 378.

[11] Saint Cyprian, *De lapsis*, chap. 28, PL 4, col. 488.

[12] Saint Basil, *Regulae brevius tractatae*, no. 229, PG 31, cols. 1235 (Latin), 1236 (Gréek).

the dispensation of the mysteries of God has been entrusted." [13] One of the finest summations of the sacrament of penance from these early centuries is given in a commentary of the Eastern bishop and ecclesiastical writer Theodore of Mopsuestia (c. 350–428):

> Since you are aware of these things, and also of the fact that because God greatly cares for us He gave us penitence and showed us the medicine of repentance, and established some men, who are the priests, as physicians of sins, so that if we receive in this world through them healing and forgiveness of sins, we shall be delivered from the judgment to come—it behooves us to draw nigh unto the priests with great confidence and to reveal our sins to them, and they, with all diligence, pain, and love ... will give healing to sinners. And they will not disclose the things that are not to be disclosed, but they will keep to themselves the things that have happened, as fits true and loving fathers, bound to safeguard the shame of their children while striving to heal their bodies. [14]

Note in the above words the emphasis upon keeping a penitent's confession secret. These early texts and others speak of confession not as a public act addressed to "the community" but as a personal attestation of one's sins given to a priest or bishop. [15] The requirement of atoning for one's sins in a manner prescribed by the Church is likewise affirmed in early references to the sacrament, including the following from a letter of Pope Saint Leo the Great (+461):

> The manifold mercy of God relieves human lapses, that not only through the grace of baptism but also through the medicine of penance the hope of eternal life may be restored, that he who has violated the gifts of regeneration, condemning himself by his own judgment, should come to the remission of his sins, in this manner, that by the safeguards ordained by divine goodness the forgiveness of God should be obtainable only by the supplications of priests. For the Mediator of God and men, the man Christ Jesus, delivered this power to the superiors of the Church, that to those confessing they also may assign the act of penance and admit the same, purified by salutary satisfaction, through the door of reconciliation to the communion of the sacraments. [16]

During the patristic era and the early Middle Ages, the actual moment of absolution (referred to as "reconciliation" in early texts) took place apart from confession in order to provide an interval for the penitent

---

[13] Ibid., no. 288, cols. 1283 (Latin), 1284 (Greek).

[14] Theodore of Mopsuestia, *Liber de baptizandos*, chap. 5; English translation in A. Mingana, ed. and trans., *Commentary of Theodore of Mopsuestia on the Lord's Prayer and on the Sacraments of Baptism and the Eucharist*, Woodbrooke Studies 6 (Cambridge: W. Heffer and Sons, 1933), 123.

[15] For further examples, see Joseph Pohle and Arthur Preuss, *The Sacraments: A Dogmatic Treatise* (Saint Louis: B. Herder, 1928–1931), 3:206–214.

[16] Saint Leo the Great, *Epistle 108*, PL 54, cols. 1011–1012.

to complete his penance; in other words, absolution was not granted until the prescribed penance was completed. In contrast to the confession of sins, the fulfillment of one's penance and the reception of absolution in the early Church took place in a public manner, at least for those guilty of the gravest sins.[17] Moreover, there was at this time a widespread belief that a penitent culpable of very grave sin should be admitted to this rite of public penance no more than once in his lifetime, a notion engendered in part by the second-century Christian work *The Shepherd of Hermas*.[18]

Provision was also made for the absolution of the dying; four such prayers of absolution appear in the seventh-century Gelasian Sacramentary of Rome under the section title "Reconciliation of Penitents at Death".[19] The importance of deathbed penance is succinctly stated in a sixth-century text of the Celtic Church of Ireland, the *Penitential of Finnian*: "There is to be no cessation in snatching prey away from the mouth of the lion or dragon—that is, from the mouth of the devil, who does not cease snatching away the prey of our souls—even if that prey must be pursued and striven for unto the utmost end of a man's life."[20]

Aside from public penance and deathbed penance, the frequency of sacramental confession for those guilty of lesser sins and the manner of their penance and absolution during this early period remain unresolved historical questions.[21] Convincing evidence that the reception of the sacrament was not limited to those with grave sins to confess is provided by the third-century writings of Saint Cyprian, who in one of his letters declares, "In case of minor sins, sinners should do penance in a just time and, according to the order of discipline, come to confession and, by the imposition of the hand of the bishop and of the clergy, receive the right of communion."[22]

---

[17] Mario Righetti, *Manuale di storia liturgica* (Milan: Editrice Ancora, 1949–1955), 4:127–138.

[18] *The Shepherd of Hermas*, vision 2, chap. 2, no. 5, in Francis X. Glimm, Joseph M.-F. Marique, S.J., and Gerald G. Walsh, S.J., trans., *The Apostolic Fathers*, Fathers of the Church 1 (New York: CIMA, 1947), 238. For a discussion of the early Christian idea of a "once-only" penance and the role of the *The Shepherd of Hermas* in propagating it, see Bernhard Poschmann, *Penance and the Anointing of the Sick*, Herder History of Dogma (New York: Herder and Herder, 1968), 26–35, 104–108.

[19] Texts in Mohlberg, Eizenhöfer, and Siffrin, *Liber sacramentorum*, nos. 364–367, pp. 58–59.

[20] Latin text in Ludwig Bieler, ed. and trans., *The Irish Penitentials*, Scriptores Latini Hiberniae 5 (Dublin: Dublin Institute for Advanced Studies, 1963), canon 34, p. 86. Latin texts in Bieler quoted and translated by permission of the Governing Board of the School of Celtic Studies of the Dublin Institute for Advanced Studies.

[21] Josef Jungmann, S.J., *The Early Liturgy to the Time of Gregory the Great*, Liturgical Studies 6 (Notre Dame, Ind.: University of Notre Dame Press, 1959), 247–248. Evidence for the existence of private penance in the third century, derived from the writings of Tertullian, Origen, and Saint Cyprian, is presented by the Jesuit scholar Father G. H. Joyce in his essay "Private Penance in the Early Church", *JTS* 42, 1st series (1941): 18–42. A detailed discussion of the patristic evidence is also given by Father Paul Galtier, S.J., in his work *De paenitentia: Tractatus dogmatico-historicus* (Rome: Pontificia Università Gregoriana, 1956), 232–260.

[22] Saint Cyprian, *Epistle 16*, no. 2, in G. F. Diercks, ed., *Sancti Cypriani episcopi epistularium*, CCSL 3b, Sancti Cypriani episcopi opera, pt. 3, 1 (Turnhout, Belgium: Brepols, 1994), 92. See also the earlier-quoted passage from Saint Cyprian's *De lapsis*.

Sixth-century evidence for the practice of private penance (the private confession of one's sins to a priest or bishop, followed by the private fulfillment of a penance assigned by the confessor and by public or private absolution), as distinguished from public penance, is provided by the aforementioned Irish text, the *Penitential of Finnian*, a manual instructing priests as to what particular penances should be imposed for various sins (proportional to their gravity), including lesser sins that clearly did not merit *public* penance:

> If anyone shall have sinned in word by oversight and immediately shall have repented, and he has not uttered any such by fixed intent, he ought to submit himself to penance but shall perform just one penitential fast. . . .
>
> If anyone of the clerics or ministers of God causes strife, he should do penance for a week with bread and water and salt, and beg forgiveness from his God and his neighbor with full confession and humility, and thus he can be reconciled to God and his neighbor.[23]

The text of the penitential explicitly speaks of private penance: "For we declare sins to be absolved in secret by penance and by a more diligent devotion of heart and body."[24] Another passage from the penitential directing that the penitent is to be "reconciled to the altar" demonstrates that the absolution spoken of is *priestly* absolution.[25] Some writers, discounting patristic evidence of private penance as inconclusive, have asserted that private penance actually originated in sixth-century Ireland,[26] but more recent scholarship has revealed the existence of private penance in sixth-century Gaul (France), independent of the subsequent arrival and influence of Irish monks in continental Europe.[27] The concurrent existence of this form of penance in two entirely separate regions suggests an earlier common source. It should also be noted that the *Penitential of Finnian*'s assignment of penances according to the gravity of the particular sin committed bears witness to a continuing tradition, well attested from the patristic era onward, distinguishing between grave and minor sins, between those sins that are deadly to the state of grace in the soul (mortal sins) and those that are not (venial sins).[28]

The seventh-century Gelasian Sacramentary of Rome specifies an Ash Wednesday rite for penitents to begin together their penances

---

[23] *Penitential of Finnian*, canons 4 and 5; Latin text in Bieler, *Irish Penitentials*, 74, 76. See also canon 29, p. 84.

[24] Ibid., canon 10, p. 76. See also Poschmann, *Penance and the Anointing of the Sick*, 125, 129–130.

[25] *Penitential of Finnian*, canon 6; Latin text in Bieler, *Irish Penitentials*, 76.

[26] Poschmann, *Penance and the Anointing of the Sick*, 124–125.

[27] Sarah Hamilton, *The Practice of Penance, 900–1050*, Royal Historical Society Studies in History, new series (Woodbridge, England: Boydell, 2001), 4.

[28] Numerous patristic references to the ranking of sins by their gravity are cited by Mario Righetti in his discussion of the history of penance; see Righetti, *Manuale di storia liturgica*, 4:120–121, 144–146.

and provides a solemn rite for absolving them together on Holy Thursday.[29] These public rites for penitents on Ash Wednesday and Holy Thursday spread across Christian Europe, leaving a permanent mark upon the Lenten liturgy from the tenth century onward in the Ash Wednesday imposition of ashes,[30] a sign of penitence for all the faithful borrowed from the rite of public penance. But as the rites of private penance flourished and came to be utilized for virtually all penitents in parallel with the Church's deepening theological understanding of the nature of sin, repentance, and the mercy of God toward sinners, the need for the public rites waned.

Evidence for the *repeated* reception of the sacrament of penance by individual penitents grows from the seventh century onward: a text attributed to the English archbishop Egbert of York (+766) attests that as far back as the pontificate of Pope Vitalian (657–672) English monastic clerics, as well as married laymen with their wives and children, had their own confessors (i.e., priests who regularly heard their confessions), to whom they would resort in preparation for Christmas.[31] The rule composed by Saint Chrodegang, bishop of Metz, France (742–766), for his cathedral clergy directs them and the lay paupers supported by the diocese to confess sacramentally twice a year.[32] A decree of an early ninth-century council convened in Bavaria enjoins the faithful to receive Holy Communion every three to four weeks after having prepared themselves by confession and penance, a directive implying the laity's reception of sacramental penance every three to four weeks.[33] An interpolated recension of the previously mentioned rule of Saint Chrodegang of Metz, dating from about 900, instructs the cathedral clergy to receive the sacrament of penance every Saturday, and the laity at least three times a year, adding that he who confesses more often does even better.[34] Thus, as the practice of the repeated reception of private penance came to prevail over public penance, the earlier concept of a once-only penance disappeared, giving way to a heightened ecclesial expression of God's mercy to all repentant sinners.[35]

---

[29] Texts in Mohlberg, Eizenhöfer, and Siffrin, *Liber sacramentorum,* nos. 78–83, 352–363, pp. 17–18, 56–58.

[30] The imposition of ashes upon all the faithful on Ash Wednesday is first found in the tenth-century Romano-Germanic Pontifical; see Cyrille Vogel and Reinhard Elze, eds., *Le pontifical romano-germanique du dixième siècle,* vol. 2, ST 227 (Vatican City: Biblioteca Apostolica Vaticana, 1963), 21–22.

[31] *Dialogue of Egbert,* archbishop of York (+766), quoted in Oscar D. Watkins, *A History of Penance* (London: Longmans, Green, 1920), 2:636–637 (Latin text).

[32] Saint Chrodegang of Metz, *Regula canonicorum* (original text), canons 14 and 34, PL 89, cols. 1104, 1118.

[33] *Capitula bavarica,* canon 6, in *Monumenta Germaniae historica: Capitula episcoporum,* vol. 3, ed. Rudolf Pokorny (Hanover, Germany: Hahn, 1995), 196.

[34] *Regula canonicorum* (interpolated text), canon 32, PL 89, col. 1072.

[35] See Righetti, *Manuale di storia liturgica,* 4: 171–172.

An early medieval penance rite bearing the title "The Manner of Hearing Confessions Handed Down from the Elder Fathers" is provided in a penitential of the French abbey of Fleury-sur-Loire dating from the period of 802–812.[36] The title, by referring to an inherited tradition, indicates that the rite significantly predates the text itself; we can thus assume it is at least as old as the eighth century.[37] The rubrics specify that the priest is first to instruct the penitent by giving him a synopsis of the history of salvation that ends with an exhortation on the need for the sacrament of penance:

Rites of Penance in Ninth-century France

It is fitting to exhort him according to the word of salvation and to give him an account of how the devil by his pride fell from the angelic dignity and afterward drove man out from Paradise. And hence Christ, for human salvation, came into the world through the womb of the Virgin, and after the Resurrection both conquered the devil and redeemed the world from sin and afterward through the Apostles bequeathed the grace of baptism, by which he has washed man from sin. And he who shall have sinned, if he has not done penance, would be sent into tormenting hell everlastingly. And he who shall give to the priests his confession after sins committed would obtain eternal rewards; or how [Christ] is going to come at the end of the world to judge the living and the dead and to render to everyone according to his works.[38]

The confessor then asks the penitent to profess his faith, and in particular, his faith in the efficacy of confession: "He asks him if he believes [in] the Resurrection, or all the latter things that have been said to him; or if he would have faith in obtaining forgiveness before the Lord by the priest's judgment of his confession. Because if he professes all these things, neither does he doubt life after death to be blessed in Paradise for the just or that fire is prepared in Gehenna for sinners."[39] The confessor next asks the penitent to confess his sins, after which the priest joins the penitent in a striking manifestation of contrition and penitence before the altar: "He asks him what he has done, why he fears. And when [the penitent] shall have given his entire confession, then the priest should prostrate himself with him before the altar; and those confessing [i.e., each penitent after confessing his sins] should recite the Psalms with sorrow, and if it can be done, with weeping." Remaining prostrate, the priest and penitent recite together the verses

---

[36] Manuscript: Florence, Biblioteca Mediceo-Laurenziana, MS Libri 82, c. 802–812, in Edmond Martène, *De antiquis ecclesiae ritibus* (Venice: Johannes Baptista Novelli, 1763–1764), bk. 1, chap. 6, art. 7, *ordo* 5, 1:281–282.

[37] See Adrien Nocent, "La pénitence dans les *Ordines* locaux transcrits dans le *De antiquis ecclesiae ritibus* d'Edmond Martène", in Giustino Farnedi, ed., *Paschale mysterium: Studi in memoria dell'Abate Prof. Salvatore Marsili (1910–1983)*, Studia Anselmiana 91, Analecta liturgica 10 (Rome: Pontificio Ateneo S. Anselmo, 1986), 124.

[38] Martène, *De antiquis ecclesiae ritibus*, bk. 1, chap. 6, art. 7, *ordo* 5, 1:281.

[39] Ibid.

"*Turn to me, O Lord, and deliver my soul*" (Ps 6:5) and "*Our help is in the name of the Lord*" (Ps 123:8). They then say Psalms 6 and 37 (both of which begin with the words "*O Lord, rebuke me not . . .*"), the opening verses of Psalm 50 (1–3: "*Have mercy on me, O God . . .*"), and the first five verses of Psalm 102 ("*Bless the Lord, O my soul . . .*"), followed by a verse from Psalm 78 (8): "*Remember not our former iniquities . . .*"[40]

The priest and the penitent now rise together. The priest declares to the penitent his judgment of the sins confessed. The penitent again prostrates himself, remaining thus as the priest commends him to God. The two say together the verse "*Confirm, O God, what you have wrought in us from your holy Temple that is in Jerusalem*" (cf. Ps 67:29–30). Afterward the penitent is given by the priest a penance "according to his guilt and his devotion, or according to his power". As with other penance rites from the early Middle Ages, absolution is not conferred within the penance rite itself but is deferred until a later date, when the penitent will have completed the assigned penance. The priest concludes the penance rite by saying to the penitent, "*The Lord keepeth thee from all evil*" (Ps 120:7).[41] This verse constitutes a prayer that the penitent may be preserved from sinning again in the future. Analogous to this is the conclusion of the confession rite in a 1499 combined missal and sacramental manual of the Spanish diocese of Jaén: the priest, after giving absolution, admonishes the penitent with the words that Christ addressed to the woman taken in adultery (Jn 8:11, slightly modified): "*Go in peace; and sin no more.*"[42]

A section entitled "Order of Private or Annual Penance" appears in a sacramentary of the Church of Saint Gatian in Tours, France, dating from the late ninth century.[43] The rite begins with the penitent bowing before the priest and then sitting opposite him. The priest examines the penitent's faith in the doctrines of the Trinity, the resurrection of the body, and the Last Judgment. He then asks the penitent, "*Are you willing to forgive all things in those who have sinned against you, that God may forgive all your sins also, himself saying, 'If you will not forgive men their sins, neither will your heavenly Father forgive you your sins'?*" (cf. Mt 6:15; Mk 11:26). The rubrics instruct the confessor to apply to the penitent the Lord's command that those seeking God's forgiveness must forgive: "If [the penitent] is willing to forgive, [the priest] should receive his confession and indicate to him his penance; if he is unwilling, he should not receive his confession."[44]

---

[40] Ibid.

[41] Ibid., 281–282.

[42] *Missale Giennense / Manuale continens Ordinem ad celebrandum ecclesiastica sacramenta* [*Missale secundum morem et consuetudinem sancte ecclesie Gienensis*] (Seville: Meinard Ungut and Stanislao Polono, 1499), fol. 262r.

[43] Manuscript: Paris, Bibliothèque Nationale, MS Nouv. acq. lat. 1589, late ninth century, in Martène, *De antiquis ecclesiae ritibus*, bk. 1, chap. 6, art. 7, *ordo* 4, 1:280–281.

[44] Ibid., 280.

The manner in which the penitent should confess his sins is next given. Note particularly how the priest is described as *"a go-between and intermediate between God and the sinner"*:

> Willing to forgive all things in those who have sinned against him, he should confess all his sins that he is able to remember. Which having been done, with his knees fixed upon the ground, and having rested upon them, remaining with his hands humbly stretched out, with a soft and sorrowing face looking at the priest, he should speak in these words:
>
> *Many indeed and innumerable are the other sins that I am unable to remember, in deeds, in words, and in thoughts, for all which things my wretched soul is grieved and meanwhile keenly tormented with repentance; and therefore, suppliant I entreat your counsel, or rather your judgment, who are an ordained man, a go-between and intermediate between God and the sinner, and I humbly implore that you may appear an intercessor for my selfsame sins.*
>
> Which having been said through, [the penitent] should totally prostrate himself on the ground and bring forth from his innermost heart groans and sighs or tears, according as God shall grant—certainly the priest should allow him to cast himself prostrate nearby for a while insofar as he shall have seen him remorseful by divine inspiration.[45]

The words of the penitent in the above passage constitute an early example of an *act of contrition*, manifested by the penitent's attestation of being "grieved and . . . tormented with repentance" out of remorse for his sins. Over seven centuries later, the recitation of an act of contrition became a universally mandated component of the rite of penance in the 1614 *Rituale Romanum*.[46]

The priest now gives his judgment upon the matter confessed and prescribes a penance: "Then the priest should order him to rise; and when he shall have stood upon his feet, with fear and humility [the penitent] should wait for the judgment of the priest; and the priest should indicate to him an abstinence or observance, minutely weighing the quality of the person, or the manner of guilt, the intention of the soul, and the health or weakness of the body." [47]

As with the Fleury-sur-Loire penance rite presented earlier, the Tours rite does not include the conferral of absolution, in virtue of its deferral until after the penitent's completion of his penance; there is in the text an implicit identification of Holy Thursday as the occasion when absolution would be given,[48] a common custom of the time.[49] However,

---

[45] Ibid., 280–281.

[46] Text in Manlio Sodi and Juan Javier Flores Arcas, eds., *Rituale Romanum: Editio princeps (1614)*, facsimile ed., MLCT 5 (Vatican City: Libreria Editrice Vaticana, © 2004), 41–42 (original pagination).

[47] Martène, *De antiquis ecclesiae ritibus*, bk. 1, chap. 6, art. 7, ordo 4, 1:281.

[48] Ibid., 280.

[49] Poschmann, *Penance and the Anointing of the Sick*, 144.

the Tours text explains that under certain circumstances the priest can absolve the penitent immediately (it does not specify what absolution formula should be used in such a case);[50] here we see the beginnings of what eventually became the norm—immediate absolution within the penance rite. Recent scholarship has suggested that the bringing together of confession and absolution into a single, unified rite had emerged elsewhere by the ninth century, judging from the penitential books of this period.[51] Foreseeing the risk of penitents failing to return a second time to receive absolution, the author of a statute in the tenth-century *Statuta Bonifatii*, a Germanic collection of ecclesiastical legislation, enjoins immediate absolution: "Every priest, immediately after having heard the confession of penitents, should see to it [that] each one be reconciled, a prayer having been offered."[52] From the eleventh century onward, the practice of bestowing absolution within the penance rite as an immediate sequel to the penitent's confession of his sins, rather than at some later date, became increasingly common.[53] It is found thus in three eleventh-century *ordines* for the administration of penance: one in a northern Italian ritual of pastoral rites,[54] another in a manuscript of Italian penitential books,[55] and the third in a cathedral pontifical of Arezzo, Italy.[56]

After hearing his penance, the penitent in the Tours rite prostrates himself, asking the priest's prayers, that he the penitent may receive discernment as to which virtue he particularly needs to make progress in.[57] The priest now offers a series of prayers over the prostrate penitent, beginning with a prayer for himself, that God may receive his supplications on behalf of the penitent. The prayer draws upon Ezechiel 18:23, "Is it my will that a sinner should die, saith the Lord God, and not that he should be converted from his ways, and live?":

> *O Lord, almighty God, be merciful to me, a sinner, that I may be able worthily to give you thanks, who by reason of your mercy have made unworthy*

---

[50] Martène, *De antiquis ecclesiae ritibus*, bk. 1, chap. 6, art. 7, *ordo* 4, 1:280.

[51] See Raymund Kottje, "Busspraxis und Bussritus", in Centro Italiano di Studi sull'Alto Medioevo, ed., *Segni e riti nella chiesa altomedievale occidentale, 11–17 Aprile 1985*, Settimane di Studio del Centro Italiano di Studi sull'Alto Medioevo 33 (Spoleto, Italy: Centro Italiano di Studi sull'Alto Medioevo, 1987), 1:391.

[52] *Statuta Bonifatii*, canon 31, in Mansi, *Sacrorum conciliorum nova et amplissima collectio*, vol. 12 (Florence and Venice, 1766; repr., Paris and Leipzig: Hubert Welter, 1901), col. 386.

[53] Barton, *Penance and Absolution*, 79.

[54] Manuscript: Milan, Biblioteca Ambrosiana, codex T.27. Sup., eleventh century, in Lambot, *North Italian Services of the Eleventh Century*, 35–42 (absolution, 40–41).

[55] Manuscript: Rome, Biblioteca Vallicelliana, codex B.58, eleventh century; text in Hermann Joseph Schmitz, ed., *Die Bussbücher und die Bussdisciplin der Kirche: Nach handschriftlichen Quellen dargestellt* (Mainz, Germany: Franz Kirchheim, 1883; Düsseldorf: L. Schwann, 1898), 1:776–779 (especially 777–778).

[56] Manuscript: Vatican City, Biblioteca Apostolica Vaticana, Codex Vaticanus latinus 4772, eleventh century; complete text in Schmitz, *Bussbücher und die Bussdisciplin der Kirche*, 2:403–407.

[57] Martène, *De antiquis ecclesiae ritibus*, bk. 1, chap. 6, art. 7, *ordo* 4, 1:281.

me, a minister of the priestly office, and have constituted me a poor and lowly mediator for the purpose of praying to and interceding with our Lord Jesus Christ for those sinning and turning back to penitence; and therefore, Ruler Lord, who will all men to be saved and to come to the knowledge of truth, who do not will the death of sinners but that they may be converted and live: receive my prayer, which I pour out before the sight of your clemency for your servants and maidservants, who have come to repentance. Through the same Jesus Christ your Son, our Lord . . .[58]

The priest then proceeds to four prayers for the penitent (the last two of which are first found in the seventh-century Gelasian Sacramentary of Rome).[59] These orations may have been given as four alternatives for the priest to choose from in praying for the particular penitent,[60] but the rubrics do not say whether this was in fact the case; hence all four prayers may have been said together:

May there be present, we beseech you, O Lord, to this your servant [Name] the salutary inspiration of your grace, that it may melt his heart in an abundance of tears; and thus by mortifying himself may he attain to allaying the motions of your wrath with fitting satisfaction. Through . . .

Enable, we beseech you, O Lord, this your servant to bear the continual observance of his purification in repenting; and that he may be able effectually to accomplish this, may the grace of your visitation both precede and follow. Through . . .

May your mercy guide this your servant, we beseech you, O Lord, and may all his sins be blotted out with swift forgiveness. Through . . .

Attend, we beseech you, O Lord, to our supplications, and may the mercy of your clemency not be far from this your servant; heal his wounds and pardon his sins, that, unseparated from you by any sins, he may be worthy ever to cleave to you, O Lord. Through . . .[61]

The priest enjoins the penitent to rise, while he himself rises from his seat. Then, "if it agrees with the place or the time", the priest and the penitent go into the church (following confession in a separate location, such as the rectory, a common practice until the eleventh century, when confession in church became the norm)[62] to recite together on their knees the seven penitential psalms, each of which is accompanied by versicles, the *Kyrie eleison* ("*Lord, have mercy*"), and a concluding prayer.[63] The custom of reciting Psalms 6, 31, 37, 50, 101,

[58] Ibid.

[59] For the Gelasian texts, see Mohlberg, Eizenhöfer, and Siffrin, *Liber sacramentorum*, nos. 79–80, p. 17.

[60] Nocent, "Pénitence dans les *Ordines* locaux", 125.

[61] Martène, *De antiquis ecclesiae ritibus*, bk. 1, chap. 6, art. 7, *ordo* 4, 1:281.

[62] Righetti, *Manuale di storia liturgica*, 4:212.

[63] Martène, *De antiquis ecclesiae ritibus*, bk. 1, chap. 6, art. 7, *ordo* 4, 1:281.

129, and 142 together as a penitential exercise can be traced back to sixth-century Celtic Christianity.[64] Following the last of the psalms, the priest ends the rite with a final prayer: "*O God, who made the morning jubilation of your sacred Resurrection known, when returning from the netherworld, you filled with joys the earth that you had left in darkness: we beseech the ineffable majesty of your power, that even as then you made the apostolic band rejoice in your sacred Resurrection, so may you vouchsafe to illuminate this your Church, entreating your mercy with hands outspread, in the splendor of celestial radiance. Through . . .*[65]

The Rite of Penance in Thirteenth-century Rome

The texts we have examined thus far date from the early medieval period. We now turn to a Roman example of the penance rite from the High Middle Ages, a rite entitled "Order for Giving Penance" found in the thirteenth-century Pontifical of the Roman Curia.[66] Although the text does not specify the vesture of the confessor, another thirteenth-century source, a statute of the 1279 Council of Westphalia, Germany, enjoins that a priest hearing confessions should wear a surplice (or a cloak) with a stole;[67] the confessor's wearing of a stole during the penance rite is mentioned as early as the eleventh century in the pontifical of Arezzo, Italy.[68] The penance ceremony in the Pontifical of the Roman Curia begins with a prayer that the priest offers for himself. Like the oration of this nature quoted earlier from the ninth-century Tours rite, this prayer utilizes Ezechiel 18:23 ("Is it my will that a sinner should die, saith the Lord God . . . ?"), but it culminates in a plea that the grace to sin no more may be imparted not only to the penitent but also to the confessor administering the sacrament: "*O Lord, almighty God, who do not wish the death of the sinner but that he may be converted and live, be merciful to me, a sinner, and receive my prayer, which I pour out before the sight of your clemency, that you may likewise divest both me and this [penitent] of all sins and bring it about that we may beware of sinning in the future. Through . . .*"[69] The priest then asks the penitent, "*Brother, for what reason have you come to this church?*" The penitent answers, "*I have come to do penance for my sins.*" The last words of Christ on the Cross are now recited by the penitent to express the commitment of his soul to the spiritual care of the priest, as Christ

---

[64] Righetti, *Manuale di storia liturgica*, 4:193.

[65] Martène, *De antiquis ecclesiae ritibus*, bk. 1, chap. 6, art. 7, *ordo* 4, 1:281.

[66] Text in Michel Andrieu, ed., *Le pontifical romain au moyen-âge*, vol. 2, *Le pontifical de la Curie romaine au XIIIᵉ siècle*, ST 87 (Vatican City: Biblioteca Apostolica Vaticana, 1940), 479–484.

[67] Council of Westphalia, Germany (1279), statute 15, in J. D. Mansi, ed., *Sacrorum conciliorum nova et amplissima collectio*, vol. 24 (Florence and Venice, 1780; repr., Paris and Leipzig: Hubert Welter, 1903), cols. 316–317.

[68] Schmitz, *Bussbücher und die Bussdisciplin der Kirche*, 2:406.

[69] Andrieu, *Pontifical romain au moyen-âge*, 2:479–480. This prayer is first found in the tenth-century Romano-Germanic Pontifical; see Vogel and Elze, *Pontifical romano-germanique*, 2:270.

delivered himself to his Father: "Then the sinner should rest his hands in the hands of the priest and say to God three times: *Into your hands, O Lord, I commend my spirit.*"[70]

The priest next recites Psalm 47, a text that instills confidence and expresses rejoicing in the goodness and mercy of God, which is accentuated by the use of the psalm's tenth verse as the antiphon: "*We have received thy mercy, O God, in the midst of thy temple.*" Following the recitation of the *Kyrie eleison*, the Our Father, and a series of standard versicles and responses ("*Save your servant*", etc.), the priest prays for the penitent, particularly that he may be delivered from temptations: "*O God, who make righteous the wicked and do not will the death of the sinner but that he may be converted and live, we humbly entreat your majesty, that you may graciously defend your servant, trustful of your mercy, with your divine assistance and preserve him with your unceasing protection, that he may serve you continually and never be separated from you by temptations. Through ...*"[71] The penitent now prostrates himself before the altar, and the priest recites the Litany of the Saints.[72] Following this and another recitation of the Our Father, the confessor says three more prayers, beseeching for the penitent forgiveness and amendment of life:

O God, to whom it is proper ever to have mercy and forbear, receive our supplication; and your servant, whom the bond of sins binds fast, remorseful with the inspiration to confession and penitence, and true emendation, and the indulgence of your goodness, may the mercy of your goodness absolve. Through ...[73]

Merciful God, loving God, God of forgiveness, God of goodness and peace, who for the love of men spread your hands on the Cross, who called the Canaanite and the publican to repentance, vouchsafe to convert your servant, who confesses his guilt before your sacred altar and acknowledges himself [to be] lowly, and begs for himself the forgiveness of all his crimes; and mercifully grant him time to repent, the merited fruits of repentance, and a penitentially fruitful end. Through ...[74]

O God, under whose eyes every heart trembles and all consciences become afraid, be merciful to the groans of your servant and of all men; heal the

---

[70] Andrieu, *Pontifical romain au moyen-âge*, 2:480.

[71] Ibid.; this prayer is first found in the Gellone Sacramentary, an eighth-century Frankish adaptation of the Gelasian Sacramentary of Rome; see A. Dumas, O.S.B., ed., *Liber sacramentorum Gellonensis*, CCSL 159 (Turnhout, Belgium: Brepols, 1981), no. 1860, p. 241.

[72] Andrieu, *Pontifical romain au moyen-âge*, 2:481.

[73] Ibid. This prayer is first found in a recension of the Romano-Germanic Pontifical of Mainz, Germany, adapted for use by the French diocese of Sees and dating from the second half of the eleventh century; manuscript: Paris, Bibliothèque Nationale, Codex Lat. 820 (Martène, *De antiquis ecclesiae ritibus*, bk. 1, chap. 6, art. 7, *ordo* 12, 1:288).

[74] Andrieu, *Pontifical romain au moyen-âge*, 2:481. This prayer first appears in an eleventh-century pontifical of Besançon, France; manuscript: Besançon, Bibliothèque Municipale, MS Z 174 (Martène, *De antiquis ecclesiae ritibus*, bk. 1, chap. 6, art. 7, *ordo* 13, 1:290).

infirmities of him and of all men, that, just as no one is free from sin, so may no one be dispossessed from forgiveness. Through . . .[75]

The priest next questions the penitent as to his faith and as to whether he harbors "anger or hatred toward anyone".[76] Hence here, as in the Tours rite examined earlier, the penitent's forgiveness of others is made a criterion for the sincerity of his confession. The confessor also questions the penitent to learn whether he has a firm purpose of amendment, including in the case of theft the intention of restoring or compensating for what was stolen. Having obtained from the penitent a promise to do all these things, the confessor admonishes him to confess his sins to God and to him the confessor.[77] In another thirteenth-century text, the book of instructions that William Durandus (+1296) composed as a bishop for his own diocese of Mende, France, around the year 1294, the parish priest is admonished to encourage the penitent as he undertakes the confession of his sins:

> The priest should diligently admonish and discretely induce the sinner that he should confess all his sins humbly, truly, entirely, simply, and faithfully; that he should not conceal any from shame or fear, showing him that he is going to speak not to man but to God, the Person of whom the priest himself represents; and that the priest himself is a sinner, and blessed Peter and Paul and Mary Magdalene were sinners, for it is a thing almost against nature that anyone would be without sin, and it is human to sin, but it is diabolic to persevere in sin.[78]

The importance of keeping a penitent's confession secret is already mentioned in the fifth century, not only by Theodore of Mopsuestia in the commentary of this Eastern bishop that we cited earlier, but also by Pope Saint Leo the Great (+461), who states, "It suffices for the guilt of consciences to be made known only to the priests in secret confession."[79] In 1215 the Fourth Lateran Council prescribed grave ecclesiastical punishments for those priests who violated the seal of confession by divulging a penitent's sins.[80] In this context, the placement of a grilled partition to screen the penitent from the sight of the confessor, in order to give the penitent anonymity in confessing his

---

[75] Andrieu, *Pontifical romain au moyen-âge*, 2:481. This prayer is first found in the seventh-century Gelasian Sacramentary of Rome (Mohlberg, Eizenhöfer, and Siffrin, *Liber sacramentorum,* no. 1360, p. 198).

[76] Andrieu, *Pontifical romain au moyen-âge*, 2:481.

[77] Ibid., 481–482.

[78] Text in J. Berthelé, "Les instructions et constitutions de Guillaume Durand le Spéculateur", in *Académie des Sciences et Lettres de Montpellier: Mémoires de la Section des Lettres,* 2nd series, vol. 3 (Montpellier, 1900–1907), 18.

[79] Saint Leo the Great, *Epistle 168,* PL 54, col. 1211.

[80] Fourth Lateran Council (1215), chap. 21, in J. D. Mansi, ed., *Sacrorum conciliorum nova et amplissima collectio,* vol. 22 (Florence and Venice, 1778; repr., Paris: Hubert Welter, 1903), cols. 1009 (Greek text), 1010 (Latin text).

sins, a practice that had appeared by the second half of the sixteenth century,[81] or perhaps earlier,[82] and was universally promulgated by the *Rituale Romanum* of 1614,[83] can be seen as a natural, "organic" development of the penance liturgy arising from the long-recognized need of keeping confessions secret.

The rubrics of the penance rite in the Pontifical of the Roman Curia direct the priest after hearing the penitent's confession to weigh the extenuating circumstances of the penitent's station of life (whether he is poor or rich, married or unmarried; his health and age; etc.) in determining a penance for him.[84] Before imposing the penance, the confessor is charged to impress upon the penitent the evil of his former sins while at the same time admonishing him that "he should not despair, because God is merciful and will still forgive him all his sins if he will have amended."[85] The priest prescribes the penance and then prays that God may absolve the penitent: "*Graciously hear our prayers, we humbly beseech you, O Lord, and show mercy to the sins of those confessing to you, that those whom the guilt of their conscience accuses, the indulgence of your mercy may absolve. Through . . .*"[86]

The pontifical provides three different formulas of absolution with which the penance rite concludes.[87] It is not altogether clear whether the priest was to choose only one of the formulas or whether he was to recite all three. Each formula mentions Saint Peter's reception of the power of binding and loosing:

---

[81] In 1577, as archbishop of Milan, Italy, Saint Charles Borromeo issued a directory governing church construction and furnishings for his archdiocese (*Instructionum fabricae et supellectilis ecclesiasticae*) in which he ordered the construction of two confessionals in each parish church, recommending that each confessional be built with two grilled openings, one on each side of the confessor between him and the penitent; see *Instructionum fabricae et supellectilis ecclesiasticae*, bk. 1, chap. 33, in Federico Borromeo, ed., *Acta ecclesiae Mediolanensis a s. Carolo cardinali s. Praxedis archiepiscopo condita* (Padua, Italy: Typus Seminarii Patavii, 1754), 1:498, 499.

[82] A fourteenth-century confessional for the Basilica of Saint Anthony in Padua, Italy, is constructed in the form of a booth enclosing the priest on three sides; outside each of the two opposite closed sides of the confessional is a kneeler, where a penitent can speak to the priest through a grilled opening. However, it is not clear whether the grilling is part of the original design or is a later addition. A photograph of this confessional is given in Edward Hanna, "Penance", in *The Catholic Encyclopedia* (New York: Appleton, 1907–1912), 11:622.

[83] Sodi and Flores Arcas, *Rituale Romanum: Editio princeps (1614)*, 41 (original pagination).

[84] Andrieu, *Pontifical romain au moyen-âge*, 2:482.

[85] Ibid., 482–483.

[86] Ibid., 483. The prayer in its earliest form is traceable to the seventh-century Gelasian Sacramentary of Rome (Mohlberg, Eizenhöfer, and Siffrin, *Liber sacramentorum*, no. 78, p. 17). Although this prayer asks for absolution, it is not an actual absolution formula, judging from its original use in the Gelasian Sacramentary as a prayer for those beginning the discipline of public penance on Ash Wednesday rather than its being said at the time of their reconciliation on Holy Thursday.

[87] In the Pontifical of the Roman Curia, there appears immediately after the section entitled "Order for Giving Penance" a separate section entitled "Order for Reconciling a Penitent", but there is no explanation in the text as to when or if this separate absolution rite was used in place of the absolution prayers with which the preceding rite of penance ends; see Andrieu, *Pontifical romain au moyen-âge*, 2:484–486.

May almighty God, who has given the power of binding and loosing to blessed Peter the Apostle and to the other Apostles, then to bishops and priests, himself absolve and liberate you completely from all your sins. Through . . .[88]

We absolve you, after the manner of blessed Peter the Apostle, to whom the power of binding and loosing has been granted by God, whose function although unworthy we nevertheless carry out in his name, albeit not by merit; and we pray that, as far as your accusation deserves and the remission of guilt belongs to us, almighty God may be the merciful absolver of all your sins. Who lives and reigns . . .[89]

By the authority of almighty God, may blessed Peter, key bearer of the heavenly kingdom, who has the power in Heaven and on earth of binding and loosing, whose function we carry out, although unworthily, yet with divine grace supporting, himself absolve you from all your sins. Through . . .[90]

Note that the second of the above formulas expresses the absolution with the indicative tense of the verb "absolve" ("*We absolve you*"), in contrast to the subjunctive tense used in the other two formulas ("*May almighty God . . . absolve and liberate you*"; "*may blessed Peter . . . absolve you*"). The use of the subjunctive tense in absolution formulas, which was the norm in the early Middle Ages, casts the absolution as a petition for absolution (a "deprecatory" formula), whereas the use of the indicative tense in absolution formulas, first found in tenth-century texts[91] and increasingly common from the eleventh century onward, expresses more directly the Church's God-given authority to forgive sins.[92] The absolution formula from one of the earliest extant penance rites to encompass confession and absolution within a single ritual, that of the eleventh-century cathedral pontifical of Arezzo, Italy, begins with a petition, in the subjunctive tense, that God may absolve the sinner, but it continues with a direct declaration of absolution in the indicative tense, cast in the first-person singular ("*I absolve you*"), manifesting thereby that the confessor himself possesses the power to forgive sins by virtue of his priesthood (by acting *in persona Christi*):[93]

---

[88] Andrieu, *Pontifical romain au moyen-âge*, 2:484. This prayer is earlier found in the twelfth-century Roman Pontifical; see Michel Andrieu, ed., *Le pontifical romain au moyen-âge*, vol. 1, *Le pontifical romain du XIIe siècle*, ST 86 (Vatican City: Biblioteca Apostolica Vaticana, 1938), 269.

[89] Andrieu, *Pontifical romain au moyen-âge*, 2:484. This formula is first found, albeit with significant differences, in the Benedictional of Archbishop Robert, a late tenth-century pontifical of Winchester, England; see Henry Austin Wilson, ed., *The Benedictional of Archbishop Robert*, HBS 24 (London: Henry Bradshaw Society, 1903), 57.

[90] Andrieu, *Pontifical romain au moyen-âge*, 2:484.

[91] See the absolution formula in the rite of visiting and anointing the sick from the tenth-century pontifical of Noyon, France, in Martène, *De antiquis ecclesiae ritibus*, bk. 1, chap. 7, art. 4, *ordo* 12, 1:317.

[92] Barton, *Penance and Absolution*, 93–94; Pohle and Preuss, *Sacraments*, 3:91–96.

[93] See Saint Thomas Aquinas, *Summa theologica*, pt. III, q. 22, art. 4, 2:2145: "Now Christ is the fountain-head of the priesthood. . . . The priest of the New Law works in his

Then the priest should tell him [the penitent] to rise and, by means of the stole in which he is vested, immediately grant remission to him, saying:

> *By this true and pure confession that you have just now made to me, although a sinner, a priest of Christ, may almighty God absolve you from all judgments that are owed you for your sins, according to the multitude of his*[94] *ancient mercies, and show mercy to and remit and blot out all your sins, and lead you to eternal life. Amen.*

> *And through the intercession of blessed Peter, Prince of the Apostles, to whom God delivered the power of binding and loosing, and through whom this same power has been given to the bishops and priests of Christ, and according to my ministry, I, a priest of Christ, absolve you from all judgments with which I have bound you for your sins, without, however, breaking your fasting and alms, and the prayers of the priests, just as I imposed upon you a little earlier; and if in this confession and penance you should die before you come to another confession, may Christ the Divine Son have mercy upon you, and may you remain absolved unto ages of ages. Amen.*[95]

It was to be an indicative formula, "*I absolve you . . .*", that the Council of Florence would later define in 1439 as henceforth the one valid form of absolution,[96] a decision solemnly reaffirmed by the Council of Trent in 1551.[97] The absolution text universally promulgated by the *Rituale Romanum* of 1614[98] appears to be an expanded and modified

---

person, according to 2 Cor 2:10: 'For what I have pardoned, if I have pardoned anything, for your sakes I have done it in the person of Christ.' " Regarding the absolution formula "*I absolve you*" and the priest's ministerial power to absolve sins, see ibid., pt. III, q. 84, art. 3, reply obj. 3, 2:2531–2532. A century earlier, the bishop and liturgist Stephen of Autun (+c. 1139) discusses the priest's identification with Christ in virtue of his ordination, observing with regard to the Eucharist, "The priest, going to celebrate the sacrosanct mystery that excels every sacrament, undertakes in himself the functions of his Head, namely Christ, whose member he is" (*De sacramento altaris*, chap. 10, PL 172, col. 1282; see also chap. 9, cols. 1280–1281). See also *Catechism of the Catholic Church*, English ed. (Vatican City: Libreria Editrice Vaticana, © 1994; Washington, D.C.: United States Catholic Conference, 1994), no. 1548, p. 387: "The priest, by virtue of the sacrament of Holy Orders, acts *in persona Christi Capitis* [in the Person of Christ the Head]."

[94] The original Latin has here the second-person pronoun *tuarum*, meaning "your", but the context clearly requires the third-person pronoun, in English "his", because the prayer addresses the penitent in the second person and invokes God in the third person with subjunctive verbs.

[95] Schmitz, *Bussbücher und die Bussdisciplin der Kirche*, 2:406.

[96] Council of Florence, *Decree for the Armenians* (November 22, 1439), in Mansi, *Sacrorum conciliorum nova et amplissima collectio*, vol. 31, col. 1058.

[97] Council of Trent, session 14, November 25, 1551, *De poenitentia*, canon 10, in Schroeder, *Canons and Decrees of the Council of Trent*, 103–104, 378.

[98] Text in Sodi and Flores Arcas, *Rituale Romanum: Editio princeps (1614)*, 43–44 (original pagination). An intermediate stage in the development of this absolution formula can be found in a penance rite dating from around 1400 recorded in a fifteenth-century recension (c. 1430) of John of Sion's fourteenth-century papal Long Ceremonial (manuscript: Venice, Biblioteca Marciana, Lat. 3, 14); see Marc Dykmans, S.J., ed., *Le cérémonial papal de la fin du moyen âge à la Renaissance*, vol. 3, BIHBR 26 (Brussels and Rome: Institut Historique Belge de Rome, 1983), 342.

descendant of the indicative absolution formula promulgated by the Synod of Nîmes, France, in 1284, the latter of which we give here: *"May the almighty Lord grant the forgiveness, absolution, and remission of all your sins; and I absolve you by the authority of our Lord Jesus Christ, and of the blessed Apostles Peter and Paul, and of the office entrusted to me, from those sins that you have confessed and from others forgotten."* [99] The Nîmes absolution formula is accompanied by a rubric instructing the priest to place his hand upon the head of the penitent while pronouncing the absolution, [100] a gesture traceable as a component of penance rites back to the third century, when it is mentioned by Saint Cyprian. [101] From this action, probably, arose the later practice of the confessor raising his right hand toward the penitent while reciting the absolution, as specified in the 1614 *Rituale Romanum*. [102] The placement of a grilled partition between the confessor and the penitent from the second half of the sixteenth century onward would have necessitated the change from a direct imposition of the priest's hand to a gesture of simply elevating his hand toward the penitent. The Paris bishop, theologian, and philosopher William of Auvergne (+1249) explains the placing of the priest's hand over the head of the penitent as signifying the presence of "the divine hand or power" to sanctify the penitent. [103]

At the conclusion of the penance rite in the eleventh-century pontifical of Arezzo, Italy, the priest instructs the penitent to venerate a crucifix, saying, *"Son, I now commend you to God and to this sign of the Cross of our Lord Jesus Christ."* The penitent then folds his hands to "offer himself at the feet of the crucifix" as the priest prays over him: *"By this sign of the health-giving Cross of our Lord Jesus Christ, and through the intercession of these and all the saints, may almighty God have mercy upon you and give you true humility [and] good perseverance, and forgive you all your sins, past, present, and future, and deliver you from the snare of the devil, and lead you to eternal life."* Telling the penitent, *"I now make the sign of the Cross of Christ against the devil and against all his temptations"*, the priest blesses him, making the sign of the cross with his hand as he pronounces a closing benediction before dismissing him with the words *"Son, go in peace."* [104]

---

[99] Synod of Nîmes (1284), "De paenitencia", in Mansi, *Sacrorum conciliorum nova et amplissima collectio*, vol. 24, col. 530. Virtually the same formula appears ten years later in the 1294 diocesan *Instructions* for Mende, France, composed by William Durandus; see Berthelé, "Instructions et constitutions de Guillaume Durand", 20–21.

[100] Synod of Nîmes (1284), "De paenitencia", in Mansi, *Sacrorum conciliorum nova et amplissima collectio*, vol. 24, col. 530. This rubric likewise appears in the diocesan *Instructions* of Durandus (Berthelé, "Instructions et constitutions de Guillaume Durand", 20).

[101] See the earlier-quoted passage from Saint Cyprian's *Epistle 16*, no. 2 (Diercks, *Sancti Cypriani episcopi epistularium*, 92).

[102] Sodi and Flores Arcas, *Rituale Romanum: Editio princeps (1614)*, 44 (original pagination).

[103] William of Auvergne [William of Paris], *De sacramento poenitentiae*, chap. 3, in *Guilielmi Alverni, episcopi Parisiensis ... Opera omnia* (Paris: Louis Billaine, 1674), 1:461.

[104] Schmitz, *Bussbücher und die Bussdisciplin der Kirche*, 2:406–407.

While in the Arezzo rite above we find the imagery of the Cross visually evoked *after* the penitent has received absolution, the sign of the cross was eventually to be incorporated into the act of absolution itself. Although not mentioned in the Pontifical of the Roman Curia or in the *Instructions* of Durandus, the priest's making of the sign of the cross while administering absolution, a practice that became a fixed part of the penance rite in the *Rituale Romanum* of 1614,[105] may have been introduced in some places by the thirteenth century, insofar as Saint Thomas Aquinas proposes it as a fitting accompaniment to absolution. He explains that such an action would signify that "sins are forgiven through the blood of Christ crucified."[106] He also proposes that the words for the sign of the cross ("*in the name of the Father, and of the Son, and of the Holy Spirit*") could be "suitably added" to the absolution formula,[107] an addition subsequently found in a penance rite dating from around 1400 recorded in a fifteenth-century recension (c. 1430) of John of Sion's fourteenth-century papal Long Ceremonial[108] and later promulgated in the 1614 *Rituale Romanum*.[109]

As a conclusion to our examination of the sacrament of penance in the Middle Ages, we offer here a prayer entitled "Prayer after Confession", composed for penitents to recite, as taken from the rite of "Confession of Sinners" given in a fourteenth-century missal of the Church of Saint Gatian, Tours, France:

> *Lord Jesus Christ, Son of the living God, who reign with the Father and the Holy Spirit: may you vouchsafe to grant me faith, hope, and charity; humility and chastity of mind and body; patience; true obedience; and the emendation of my actions. And for this that I have sinned in the day and in the night, O clement and merciful God, grant me also true forgiveness and the remission of my sins, that, you having mercy, we may be worthy to come to the glory of your kingdom, O Savior of the world, who with the Father and the Holy Spirit live and reign, God, through all ages of ages. Amen.*[110]

In a book of sacraments for the Austrian see of Salzburg dating from 1511, the rite of penance includes two prayers of absolution to reconcile to the Church those who had been excommunicated for their grave sins but were now repentant.[111] From the beginning, the Church has exercised the power of summoning to conversion those obstinately refusing to repent of their heresy or grave public sins by formally excluding them from any participation in the life of the Church. This

Excursus: Public Rites of Excommunication and Reconciliation of Excommunicates

---

[105] See Sodi and Flores Arcas, *Rituale Romanum: Editio princeps (1614)*, 44 (original pagination).

[106] Saint Thomas Aquinas, *Summa theologica*, pt. III, q. 84, art. 4, 2:2533.

[107] Ibid., art. 3, reply obj. 3, p. 2532.

[108] Manuscript: Venice, Biblioteca Marciana, Lat. 3, 14, in Dykmans, *Cérémonial papal de la fin du moyen âge à la Renaissance*, 3:342.

[109] Sodi and Flores Arcas, *Rituale Romanum: Editio princeps (1614)*, 44 (original pagination).

[110] Text in Martène, *De antiquis ecclesiae ritibus*, bk. 1, chap. 6, art. 7, *ordo* 18, 1:294.

[111] *Agenda secundum rubricam ecclesie cathedralis Saltzeburgensis* (Basel, Switzerland: Jacobus de Pfortzhein, 1511; digitized text, Bayerische Staatsbibliothek, Munich, 2007), fol. 96v.

power, known as excommunication, was instituted by Christ himself when he said of those refusing to be corrected by the Church, "And if he will not hear the church, let him be to thee as the heathen and publican" (Mt 18:17). Evidence of a particular rite of excommunication first appears in the sixth century: a decree of a synod at Tours, France, convened in 567 speaks of the recitation of Psalm 108 when excommunicating a malefactor.[112] By the early tenth century, there had emerged a fully developed and dramatic ceremony for public excommunication, the words and actions of which were consciously calculated to bring the excommunicated individual to conversion by warning him of the path to destruction he had chosen. The rubrics of Pope Blessed Gregory X's ceremonial (c. 1273), which describe the excommunication rite as a "maternal admonition and correction",[113] explain that these excommunications would be carried out particularly on Holy Thursday, Ascension Thursday, and the feast of the dedication of Rome's Church of the Twelve Apostles, in order that those excommunicated, "seeing themselves excluded from all the good things of such days, might more easily submit to the grace of reconciliation".[114]

The full rite, as given for the first time in the early tenth-century work *De ecclesiasticis disciplinis*, compiled by the abbot Regino of Prum (+915), begins with an introductory allocution, in which the bishop outlines the Church's teachings about excommunication, drawn from the Scriptures.[115] The rite climaxes with the bishop's pronunciation of the excommunication (*"We exclude him from the thresholds of Holy Mother Church in Heaven and on earth, and we determine him to be excommunicated and anathematized"*), which, however, is qualified by the all-important phrase *"unless he should repent"*.[116] The most dramatic action of the excommunication rite follows: "Twelve priests ought to stand around the bishop and hold burning candles in their hands, which at the conclusion of the anathema or excommunication they ought to cast down to the ground and trample with their feet."[117] In the ceremonial of Pope Blessed Gregory X, this action is explained as symbolizing that the grace of the Holy Spirit, represented by light, has been withdrawn from the excommunicated person.[118] The candle rite had probably arisen by the late ninth century, when an excommunication formula from a pontifical of Sens, France, concludes with the words *"Just as this light is extinguished in the eyes of men, so may their light*

---

[112] Council of Tours (567), canon 25, in Charles de Clercq, ed., *Concilia Galliae, A. 511–A. 695*, CCSL 148a (Turnhout, Belgium: Brepols, 1963), 192–193.

[113] Text in Marc Dykmans, S.J., ed., *Le cérémonial papal de la fin du moyen âge à la Renaissance*, vol. 1, BIHBR 24 (Brussels and Rome: Institut Historique Belge de Rome, 1977), 193.

[114] Ibid., 192.

[115] Regino of Prum, *De ecclesiasticis disciplinis*, bk. 2, nos. 407–408, PL 132, cols. 358–360.

[116] Ibid., no. 409, col. 360.

[117] Ibid.

[118] Dykmans, *Cérémonial papal de la fin du moyen âge à la Renaissance*, 1:192.

be extinguished forever." [119] Pope Gregory's ceremonial adds that at the end of the excommunication rite the church bells are rung in a discordant manner, noting that insofar as by the orderly ringing of the bells the faithful are gathered, so by the discordant ringing the unfaithful are scattered,[120] a contrast clearly inspired by the words of Christ, "He that gathereth not with me, scattereth" (Mt 12:30).

In the pages of the tenth-century Romano-Germanic Pontifical, as in other medieval pontificals, the rites of excommunication are immediately followed by their earnestly hoped-for, longed-for sequel, the rite of reconciliation of excommunicates.[121] The ceremony begins outside the front doors of the church, where the penitent goes before the bishop, who is surrounded by twelve priests; likewise present are those who had been harmed by the penitent's sins.[122] The penitent, having prostrated himself, "asks forgiveness, confesses his guilt, implores penance, and pledges surety about the future".[123] The bishop then takes the penitent by his right hand and leads him into the church to "restore to him Communion and Christian society".[124] The rite climaxes within the church, where the bishop absolves him of his excommunication, offering a series of prayers for his forgiveness, including the following:

O God of immense clemency and inestimable forgiveness, who have vouchsafed to repair the lapse of human frailty, accomplished by the odium of diabolic deception, with the most precious blood of your only-begotten Son, our Lord Jesus Christ, bend the ear of your mercy to our supplications, we beseech you; and this your servant, who, the author of death persuading, has not feared by sinning to depart from you, who are our true Life, and to set himself under the bond of anathema, behold with your serene countenance, returning by repentance; and vouchsafe to open the door of your mercy to his knocking, that you may restore him purified and absolved to the Body of your holy Church, the power of the Holy Spirit guiding, by the gift of whom the remission of all sins is conferred, with the intercession of all the saints and the Apostles, whose offices in binding and loosing sins we, although unworthy,

---

[119] The Sens Pontifical is preserved in a manuscript of Saint Petersburg, Russia (Publichnaja Biblioteca im M.E. Saltykova-Schedrina, codex Q.v.I, no. 35, late ninth century); the excommunication formula from this pontifical is printed in Lucas D'Achery, *Spicilegium, sive Collectio veterum aliquot scriptorum qui in Galliae bibliotecis delituerant* (Paris: Montalant, 1723), 3:320–321 (quote on 321).

[120] Dykmans, *Cérémonial papal de la fin du moyen âge à la Renaissance*, 1:192.

[121] Texts in Cyrille Vogel and Reinhard Elze, eds., *Le pontifical romano-germanique du dixième siècle*, vol. 1, ST 226 (Vatican City: Biblioteca Apostolica Vaticana, 1963), 308–317 (rites of excommunication), 317–321 (rite of reconciliation of excommunicates). This juxtaposition of the excommunication and reconciliation rites is likewise found in the 1485 *Pontificalis liber* (the edition of the *Pontificale Romanum* compiled by two papal masters of ceremonies, Patrizio Piccolomini and John Burckard); text in Manlio Sodi, ed., *Il "Pontificalis liber" di Agostino Patrizi Piccolomini e Giovanni Burcardo (1485)*, facsimile ed., MSIL 43 (Vatican City: Libreria Editrice Vaticana, © 2006), 514–523 (new pagination).

[122] Vogel and Elze, *Pontifical romano-germanique du dixième siècle*, 1:317.

[123] Ibid., 318.

[124] Ibid.

Part One: The Sacraments

perform in the priestly office; and him whom you in no way desire to die, according to your most truthful promise, the forgiveness of sins having been granted, may you lead to the ever green pastures of eternal life, joined to your flock; and all those defiled by the wickedness of the same sin, whether cooperating or consenting, nor less also conversing or eating or living with him, restore to salvation with the healing remedy of your grace, chastised and absolved. Through the same ... [125]

After several more prayers, the bishop sprinkles the penitent with holy water, incenses him, and ends the rite by saying to him, "*Arise, you who sleep, arise from the dead, and Christ will enlighten you.*" [126]

---

[125] Ibid., 319.
[126] Ibid., 319–321 (quote on 321).

6 Holy Orders

How great must be the excellence of the priestly office, by which the Passion of Christ is daily celebrated on the altar, and the guilty one, having turned from his sins, is reconciled to God.

Hugh of Saint Victor (+c. 1141)[1]

Saint Thomas Aquinas (+1274) begins his explanation of holy orders with the observation that God has willed to make himself known through his works of creation by giving them a certain likeness to himself, including a likeness to his ways of governing creation. Hence, in creation, there are higher things that serve to perfect lower things, thereby giving the beauty of order to the universe. God has likewise willed to impart this attribute of his to the Church: "Wherefore that this beauty might not be lacking to the Church, He established Order in her so that some should deliver the sacraments to others, being thus made like to God in their own way, as co-operating with God; even as in the natural body, some members act on others."[2] Saint Thomas adds that such a hierarchy of order in the Church does not enslave those governed, for "slavery consists in lording over others and employing them for one's own profit", whereas the ordained governing ministers of the Church "have to seek the salvation of their subjects and not their own profit".[3] He further defines the purpose of holy orders by its relation to the Eucharist: "The sacrament of Order is directed to the sacrament of the Eucharist, which is the sacrament of sacraments.... For just as temple, altar, vessels, and vestments need to be consecrated, so do the ministers who are ordained for the Eucharist; and this consecration is the sacrament of Order."[4]

Saint Ivo of Chartres (+1115) notes that while baptism enrolls all the faithful in the army of Christ, armed with spiritual arms to fight as privates in the "military camp of the Lord", the man who advances

---

[1] Hugh of Saint Victor, *De sacramentis*, bk. 2, pt. 3, chap. 12, PL 176, col. 429.

[2] Saint Thomas Aquinas, *Summa theologica: First Complete American Edition in Three Volumes*, trans. Fathers of the English Dominican Province (New York: Benziger Brothers, 1948), supplement, q. 34, art. 1, 3:2679.

[3] Ibid., reply obj. 1.

[4] Ibid., q. 37, art. 2, 3:2691.

to the sacrament of holy orders commits himself to a higher state of life requiring renunciation of the world and deep humility. It is a vocation that a man chooses not presumptuously, not for personal gain, but humbly, having been chosen by God, summoned to this higher state as in Christ's parable of the dinner guests: "Friend, go up higher" (Lk 14:10).[5]

The episcopate has always constituted the sacrament of holy orders in the fullest plenitude of its conferral, endowing the recipient with the power and authority "to ordain clerics, bless virgins, consecrate bishops, impose hands, dedicate churches, depose those to be degraded, celebrate synods, confect chrism, bless vestments and vessels", and "anoint with chrism on the forehead".[6] Second only to the episcopate is the order of priesthood, bestowing the power to celebrate and confect the Eucharist as well as to administer the sacraments of penance and extreme unction, whereas the diaconate, directed toward serving bishops and priests in the sacred liturgy, ranks third in degree of sacramental conferral. Ordination rites for the bestowal of these three "major" orders by the imposition of the bishop's hands are given in a third-century liturgical text, the *Apostolic Tradition* of Saint Hippolytus of Rome (+c. 236).[7] In addition to these orders that constituted the actual sacrament of ordination, there existed from the early centuries onward a series of lesser orders (until 1973),[8] conferred successively by the Church with solemn rites upon candidates advancing toward sacramental holy orders. As early as 251 Pope Cornelius mentions in descending order the degrees of subdeacon, acolyte, exorcist, lector, and doorkeeper,[9] the same series of lesser orders that is consistently found in the pontificals of Rome from the twelfth century onward.[10] The highest of these, the subdiaconate, came to be

---

[5] Saint Ivo of Chartres, *Sermon 2*, PL 162, col. 513.

[6] William Durandus of Mende (+1296), *Rationale divinorum officiorum*, bk. 2, chap. 11, no. 13, in A. Davril, O.S.B., and T.M. Thibodeau, eds., *Guillelmi Duranti: Rationale divinorum officiorum I–IV*, CCCM 140 (Turnhout, Belgium: Brepols, 1995), 175. Hereafter cited as Durandus, *Rationale* (CCCM 140).

[7] Saint Hippolytus of Rome, *Apostolic Tradition*, chaps. 1–3, in Francis Xavier Funk, ed., *Didascalia et Constitutiones Apostolorum*, vol. 2, *Testimonia et scripturae propinquae* (Paderborn, Germany: Libraria Ferdinandi Schoeningh, 1905), 98–99, 102–104.

[8] A 1972 apostolic letter of Pope Paul VI, *Ministeria qaedam*, the provisions of which went into effect on January 1, 1973, reduced the number of minor orders to two, those of lector and acolyte, and instructed that they be categorized as "ministries" rather than "minor orders"; see Pope Paul VI, *Ministeria qaedam* (August 15, 1972), in Austin Flannery, O.P., ed., *Vatican Council II: The Conciliar and Post Conciliar Documents* (Northport, N.Y.: Costello, 1975), 427–432 (especially 428–429).

[9] Letter of Pope Cornelius to Fabius of Antioch, in Eusebius of Caesarea, *Ecclesiastical History*, bk. 6, chap. 43, no. 11; text in Gustave Bardy, ed., *Eusèbe de Césarée: Histoire ecclésiastique*, vol. 2, *Livres V–VII*, SC 41 (Paris: Cerf, 1955), 156. In the early Middle Ages, all of these orders are also listed in one manuscript of the tenth-century Romano-Germanic Pontifical (Rome, Biblioteca Alessandrina, MS 173); text in Cyrille Vogel and Reinhard Elze, eds., *Le pontifical romano-germanique du dixième siècle*, vol. 1, ST 226 (Vatican City: Biblioteca Apostolica Vaticana, 1963), 12–13, plus footnotes.

[10] For the listing of the same orders in the twelfth-century Roman Pontifical, see Michel Andrieu, ed., *Le pontifical romain au moyen-âge*, vol. 1, *Le pontifical romain du XIIᵉ siècle*, ST

ranked with the priesthood and the diaconate as one of the "major orders" of ordination, as first attested by the Parisian theologian Peter Cantor (+1197) toward the end of the twelfth century,[11] even though its reception did not impart the sacrament of holy orders.[12]

It should be noted here that some medieval theologians, including Saint Thomas Aquinas, did not see the episcopate as a distinct sacramental order separate from the order of priesthood,[13] even though they unhesitatingly affirmed the higher sacramental powers and authority of the episcopate.[14] Nonetheless, Saint Thomas does concede that as a higher office of divine institution the episcopate could be considered an "order".[15] Other medieval theologians, including William of Auxerre (+1231),[16] Durandus de Saint-Pourçain (+1332),[17] and Peter de Palude (+1342),[18] fully upheld the Church's ancient tradition of identifying the episcopate as a true sacramental order in its own right. William of Auxerre argues that episcopal consecration imprints a sacramental character upon the soul and fulfills the definition of the sacrament of holy orders as "a sacred sign, by which spiritual power is conferred".[19] The bishop and liturgist William Durandus of Mende (+1296) expressly uses the word "sacrament" more than once in referring to episcopal consecration in his treatise *Rationale divinorum officiorum*.[20] Moreover, medieval ceremonies of episcopal consecration,

---

86 (Vatican City: Biblioteca Apostolica Vaticana, 1938), 125–129. For the thirteenth-century Pontifical of the Roman Curia, see Michel Andrieu, ed., *Le pontifical romain au moyen-âge*, vol. 2, *Le pontifical de la Curie romaine au XIIIᵉ siècle*, ST 87 (Vatican City: Biblioteca Apostolica Vaticana, 1940), 329–336. For the Roman Pontifical of 1485, see Manlio Sodi, ed., *Il "Pontificalis liber" di Agostino Patrizi Piccolomini e Giovanni Burcardo (1485)*, facsimile ed., MSIL 43 (Vatican City: Libreria Editrice Vaticana, © 2006), 19–36 (new pagination). For the Roman pontificals of 1497, 1520, and 1561, see Marc Dykmans, S.J., *Le pontifical romain révisé au XVᵉ siècle*, ST 311 (Vatican City: Biblioteca Apostolica Vaticana, 1985), 152. For the *Pontificale Romanum* of 1595–1596, see Manlio Sodi and Achille Triacca, eds., *Pontificale Romanum: Editio princeps (1595–1596)*, facsimile ed., MLCT 1 (Vatican City: Libreria Editrice Vaticana, © 1997), 19–40 (original pagination).

[11] See Peter Cantor (+1197), *Verbum abbreviatum*, chap. 60, PL 205, col. 184.

[12] William Fanning, "Subdeacon", in *The Catholic Encyclopedia* (New York: Appleton, 1907–1912), 14:320.

[13] Saint Thomas Aquinas, *Summa theologica*, supplement, q. 40, art. 5, 3:2704–2705.

[14] Ibid., art. 4, pp. 2703–2704.

[15] Ibid., art. 5, pp. 2704–2705.

[16] William of Auxerre, *Summa aurea*, bk. 4, tract 16, chap. 2, in Jean Ribaillier, ed., *Magistri Guillelmi Altissiodorensis: Summa aurea; Liber quartus*, Spicilegium Bonaventurianum 19 (Paris: Editions du Centre National de la Recherche Scientifique; Rome: Editiones Collegii S. Bonaventurae ad Claras Aquas, 1985), 371–373.

[17] Durandus de Saint-Pourçain, *In Petri Lombardi Sententias*, bk. 4, distinction 24, q. 6, no. 8; text in *D. Durandi a sancto Porciano, ord. Praed. et Meldensis, episcopi, in Petri Lombardi Sententias theologicas commentariorum libri IIII* (Venice: Guerraea, 1571), fol. 363v.

[18] Peter de Palude, *Liber quartus Sententiarum*, distinction 24, q. 7; text in *Petrus de Palude: In quartum Sententiarum* (Venice: Bonetus Locatellus, 1493), fols. 130v–131v.

[19] William of Auxerre, *Summa aurea*, bk. 4, tract 16, chap. 2, in Ribaillier, *Magistri Guillelmi Altissiodorensis: Summa aurea; Liber quartus*, 371–372 (© Editions du Centre National de la Recherche Scientifique, Paris).

[20] Durandus, *Rationale* (CCCM 140), bk. 1, chap. 8, no. 14, and bk. 2, chap. 11, no. 11, pp. 103, 174.

including the rite that Durandus compiled for his own diocese of Mende, France, certainly had the form and features of a sacramental ordination rite. In his apologetical work *De controversiis* (1581–1592), the Jesuit theologian, cardinal, and Church doctor Saint Robert Bellarmine (+1621) emphatically affirms the sacramentality of episcopal consecration as "most certain".[21] In 1947 Venerable Pope Pius XII effectively defined the identity of the episcopate as an order of the sacrament by solemnly defining which elements of the episcopal consecration rite constituted the "matter" and "form" of this degree of holy orders.[22] Hence the medieval episcopal consecration rite was truly a sacramental ordination rite, and it shall be presented as such in this chapter, after we begin by examining the medieval rite of ordination to the priesthood.

The Rite of Ordination to the Priesthood in Fourteenth-century Germany

The Old Testament contains numerous examples of the priestly office (Melchisedech, Aaron, etc.) that have always been understood to prefigure the priesthood of Christ and that of priests and bishops of the Church. As for prefigurations of the particular order of priesthood when considered apart from those distinctly foreshadowing the episcopate, Amalarius of Metz (+c. 850) sees the former prefigured in the sons of the high priest Aaron,[23] with the latter prefigured by Aaron himself.[24] Blessed Rabanus Maurus (+856) finds an Old Testament foreshadowing of the priesthood in the seventy elders that joined Moses and Aaron at the foot of Mount Sinai before Moses left them to ascend the mountain with Joshua (Ex 24:1–2, 9–15).[25] The bishop and liturgist Stephen of Autun (+c. 1139) utilizes this same comparison with the Mosaic elders to explain that priests are ordained to assist their bishops in directing and instructing "the flock of the Lord".[26]

The New Testament word for priest, *presbyteros* in Greek, *presbyter* in Latin, a term that also carries the meaning of elder, is explained by Honorius of Autun (+c. 1135) as indicating that Catholic priests are elders, "not in age, but in understanding".[27] In this regard, both Honorius and Hugh of Saint Victor (+c. 1141)[28] cite the Book of Wisdom

---

[21] Saint Robert Bellarmine, *De controversiis* 5 (*Of Extreme Unction, Order, and Matrimony*), bk. 2, chap. 5, in *S.R.E. cardinalis Roberti Bellarmini Politiani S.J.: Opera omnia* (Naples: C. Pedone Lauriel, 1872), 3:767–768.

[22] Venerable Pius XII, *Sacramentum ordinis* (apostolic constitution; November 30, 1947), nos. 4–5, excerpted in Benedictine Monks of Solesmes, eds., *Papal Teachings: The Liturgy* (Boston: Saint Paul Editions, 1962), 310–311. For the official Latin text, see *Sacramentum ordinis*, nos. 4–5, *Acta Apostolicae Sedis* 40 (1948): 6–7.

[23] Amalarius of Metz, *Liber officialis*, bk. 2, chap. 13, no. 1, in John Michael Hanssens, ed., *Amalarii episcopi: Opera liturgica omnia*, vol. 2, ST 139 (Vatican City: Biblioteca Apostolica Vaticana, 1948), 226.

[24] Ibid., chap. 14, no. 1, p. 233.

[25] Blessed Rabanus Maurus, *De clericorum institutione*, bk. 1, chap. 6, PL 107, col. 302.

[26] Stephen of Autun, *Tractatus de sacramento altaris*, chap. 9, PL 172, col. 1280.

[27] Honorius of Autun, *Gemma animae*, bk. 1, chap. 181, PL 172, col. 599.

[28] Hugh of Saint Victor, *De sacramentis*, bk. 2, pt. 3, chap. 12, PL 176, col. 428.

verse "For venerable old age is not that of long time, nor counted by the number of years: but the understanding of a man is grey hairs" (Wis 4:8). Honorius enumerates a priest's prerogatives and duties: to celebrate Mass, distribute Holy Communion, preach, baptize, absolve penitents, bless marriages, anoint the ill, bury the dead, pass judgments, and bless various objects, including water, candles, palms, ashes, and certain foods.[29] He notes that even the Latin word for priest, *sacerdos* (containing the words *sacer*, "sacred", and *dos*, "gift"), attests to the role of priests as givers of the sacred, for they give the Eucharist and other sacraments to the people.[30] By the exercise of his vocation, a priest shows the faithful the way "from the exile of this world to the native land of the celestial kingdom".[31]

We present here the priestly ordination rite from a fourteenth-century pontifical of the archdiocese of Mainz, Germany.[32] While this text has much in common with the medieval ordination rite of the late thirteenth-century Pontifical of Durandus,[33] the rite that with minimal changes ultimately passed into the universally promulgated 1595–1596 *Pontificale Romanum*,[34] the Mainz ceremony is also distinctive in many ways, making it a fine example of the numerous diocesan variants of the Roman Rite liturgy that flourished across medieval Europe. Not surprisingly, much of this fourteenth-century Mainz rite is derived from the ordination rite in the tenth-century Romano-Germanic Pontifical,[35] a text likewise compiled in Mainz[36] but that also embodies earlier traditions from Rome. The text in the fourteenth-century pontifical expands the rite considerably, especially through the chanting of several responsories relevant to the theme of priesthood.

The Mainz pontifical presents the priestly ordination rite as part of a Mass in which candidates to the seven degrees of holy orders (other than the episcopate) successively receive their respective orders from the bishop (the archbishop of Mainz), who is arrayed in all of his episcopal vestments. After the first Collect of the Mass, the bishop or another cleric reads a solemn declaration forbidding any unqualified candidates to receive holy orders. The bishop then pronounces a formula of absolution over the candidates.[37] An archdeacon (a cleric, usually a priest, who serves as

---

[29] Honorius of Autun, *Gemma animae*, bk. 1, chap. 181, PL 172, col. 599.

[30] Ibid., chap. 182.

[31] Ibid., chap. 181.

[32] Manuscript: Paris, Bibliothèque Nationale, MS Latin 948, in Edmond Martène, *De antiquis ecclesiae ritibus* (Venice: Johannes Baptista Novelli, 1763–1764), bk. 1, chap. 8, art. 11, *ordo* 16, 2:77–80.

[33] Text in Michel Andrieu, ed., *Le pontifical romain au moyen-âge*, vol. 3, *Le pontifical de Guillaume Durand*, ST 88 (Vatican City: Biblioteca Apostolica Vaticana, 1940), 364–373.

[34] Text in Sodi and Triacca, *Pontificale Romanum: Editio princeps (1595–1596)*, 53–75 (original pagination).

[35] Text in Vogel and Elze, *Le pontifical romano-germanique*, 1:28–37.

[36] Cyrille Vogel, *Medieval Liturgy: An Introduction to the Sources*, rev. William Storey and Niels Krogh Rasmussen, O.P. (Washington, D.C.: Pastoral Press, 1986), 232–233.

[37] Martène, *De antiquis ecclesiae ritibus*, bk. 1, chap. 8, art. 11, *ordo* 16, 2:77.

a high-ranking assistant to his bishop) now petitions the bishop: *"Reverend Father, Holy Mother Church asks for these suitable men to be consecrated to herself in orders by your paternity."* [38] The bishop replies: *"See that in their character, learning, and morals such persons should be introduced by you, yes indeed, such should be ordained by us in the house of the Lord, by whom the devil may be driven far away and the clergy may be enlarged by our God."* [39] After the archdeacon affirms the candidates' worthiness, the bishop answers: *"Our Lord God and Savior Jesus Christ assisting, we have elected these brethren to be advanced by us and, the grace of the [Holy] Spirit cooperating, consecrated by us. If, however, anyone has anything against them, before God and for the sake of God, he should boldly proceed forth and speak."* [40]

The four lowest degrees of holy orders, followed by the subdiaconate and lastly the diaconate, are all conferred before the Gospel, which is read by one of the newly ordained deacons. [41] The ceremony of priestly ordination takes place after the Gospel and the recitation of the Creed (in contrast to the placement of priestly ordination before the Gospel in the liturgical books of Rome). [42] The rite begins with the bishop calling upon the priestly ordination candidates to come forward, adding to this summons a declaration of a priest's duties: *"It is fitting for a priest to offer, to bless, to govern, to preach, and to baptize."* [43] The candidates, that is, the ordinands, are brought before the bishop two at a time. This echoes Christ's sending forth of the disciples two at a time to preach in his name (Mk 6:7). The bishop then inquires of the other clerics present about the character of the candidates: *"Are they worthy? . . . Are they just?"* The bishop next questions each candidate as to whether he wills to become a priest and about his intent to persevere in his vocation and to obey his bishop. Answering each of these three questions in the affirmative (*"I do"*), the candidate amplifies his third reply by promising to God and the saints that he will obey his bishop. The bishop thereupon commends him with the words, *"May God vouchsafe to bring your good and upright will to a perfection well pleasing to himself."* [44]

---

[38] Ibid. This formula is a greatly altered variant of the petition found in the tenth-century Romano-Germanic Pontifical; see Vogel and Elze, *Pontifical romano-germanique*, 1:210.

[39] Martène, *De antiquis ecclesiae ritibus*, bk. 1, chap. 8, art. 11, *ordo* 16, 2:78.

[40] Ibid. This formula is a variant of that first found in the tenth-century Romano-Germanic Pontifical; see Vogel and Elze, *Pontifical romano-germanique*, 1:21.

[41] Martène, *De antiquis ecclesiae ritibus*, bk. 1, chap. 8, art. 11, *ordo* 16, 2:78–79.

[42] See, for example, Roman *Ordo* 34, from the first half of the eighth century, in Michel Andrieu, ed., *Les Ordines Romani du haut moyen âge*, vol. 3, SSLED 24 (Louvain, Belgium: "Spicilegium sacrum Lovaniense" Administration, 1951), 606. See also the twelfth-century Roman Pontifical, in Andrieu, *Pontifical romain au moyen-âge*, 1:134, 137.

[43] Martène, *De antiquis ecclesiae ritibus*, bk. 1, chap. 8, art. 11, *ordo* 16, 2:77, 79. These words are first found in two manuscripts of the twelfth-century Roman Pontifical; see Andrieu, *Pontifical romain au moyen-âge*, 1:134, footnote.

[44] Martène, *De antiquis ecclesiae ritibus*, bk. 1, chap. 8, art. 11, *ordo* 16, 2:79. The wording of this examination is derived from the tenth-century Romano-Germanic Pontifical; see Vogel and Elze, *Pontifical romano-germanique*, 1:29–30.

We come now to the portion of the ordination rite encompassing the bishop's imposition of his hands upon the head of each candidate, the action that centuries later the Venerable Pope Pius XII was to define ex cathedra as "the matter and the sole matter" of this sacrament—the particular *action* that, together with the essential words of the priestly consecration formula pronounced by the bishop at a later point in the ordination rite, actually confers priesthood upon the candidate.[45] The imposition of hands in conferring the sacrament of holy orders is a practice dating from the apostolic age, expressly mentioned in the New Testament (Acts 6:6; 2 Tim 1:6). From the seventh century onward, it has been the custom to chant the Litany of the Saints in preparation for the imposition of hands, so as to invoke the assistance of the saints on behalf of those about to be ordained; the recitation of this litany, beginning with the words *Kyrie eleison*, is specified for the ordination rite of priests and deacons in the seventh-century Gelasian Sacramentary of Rome.[46] In Roman *Ordo* 34, a Roman liturgical document dating from the first half of the eighth century, the rubrics direct that both the ordaining celebrant—in this case the pope himself—and the candidate to be ordained to the priesthood or diaconate are to prostrate themselves for the litany.[47] The prostration of ordination candidates as they are prayed for in the litany became an established, visually dramatic, and deeply moving feature of ordination ceremonies thereafter.

Insofar as the Mainz rite of priestly ordination is situated within the context of a Mass for conferring multiple degrees of holy orders, the Litany of the Saints appears considerably earlier in the Mass, before the first of six readings, and prior to the conferral of the first of the seven orders, serving as a collective preparation for all of the candidates receiving their respective orders. However, it may have been the case that on those occasions when the only candidates were those for the priesthood the litany was transferred to the priestly ordination rite after the Gospel and the Creed; a comparable transferal of the litany to a position immediately preceding the conferral of priestly ordination is expressly mentioned in several manuscripts of the late thirteenth-century Pontifical of Durandus.[48] The Mainz text describes the chanting of the litany thus:

---

[45] Venerable Pius XII, *Sacramentum ordinis*, nos. 4–5, excerpted in Benedictine Monks of Solesmes, *Papal Teachings: Liturgy*, 310–311; Latin text in *Acta Apostolicae Sedis* 40 (1948): 6–7.

[46] Text in Leo Cunibert Mohlberg, O.S.B., et al., eds., *Liber sacramentorum Romanae aeclesiae ordinis anni circuli (Sacramentarium Gelasianum)*, REDSMF 4 (Rome: Herder, 1960), no. 142, p. 24.

[47] Andrieu, *Ordines Romani du haut moyen âge*, 3:605.

[48] Three manuscripts of the thirteenth-century Pontifical of Durandus specify the chanting of the litany in the priestly ordination rite when it has not been previously chanted during a preceding rite of holy orders for deacons or subdeacons; see Andrieu, *Pontifical romain au moyen-âge*, 3:367, footnote.

The bishop should incline forward over his seat, kneeling,[49] and the litany should be sung by two clerics, in the course of which the bishop rises in his place, and having turned toward the ordinands, holding his staff in his hand, he should say three times: *That you may vouchsafe to bless, sanctify, and consecrate these ordinands. We beseech you, hear us.* The bishop should repeat this three times,[50] and afterward the litany should be completed by those clerics: *That you may vouchsafe to preserve in your holy service our bishop and all the people entrusted to him. We beseech you . . .*

Meanwhile, the bishop should set himself over his seat [inclining and kneeling as before] all the way to the end of the litany. Which having been completed, he should sit upon his seat.[51]

In the Mainz rite of priestly ordination, following either the afore-mentioned examination of candidates or the litany as the case may be, the bishop now rises to intone an antiphon repeating the words of Christ that he spoke to his Apostles on Easter Sunday, conferring on them the Holy Spirit and the power to forgive sins (Jn 20:23): "*Receive ye the Holy Ghost: whose sins you shall forgive, they are forgiven them, alleluia.*"[52] Com-menting upon the recitation of these words in the ordination rite, Gil-bert of Tournai (+1284) compares the priestly power to absolve sins (or, in cases of impenitence, to refuse absolution), conferred by ordination, with the Old Testament priests' authority to render lepers clean or unclean (Lev 14).[53] As this antiphon is continued and repeated by the clergy, the bishop imposes his hands upon the head of each candidate.[54] In the ordi-nation rite from the late thirteenth-century Pontifical of Durandus, the imposition of hands is carried out in silence, without any accompany-ing words, in keeping with a long-standing and prevalent tradition in this regard that has continued to the present day.[55] But in the Mainz ordi-nation rite, there is a formula for the bishop to say as he imposes his hands on each ordinand, words that serve to remind the candidate of the action

---

[49] The bishop uses his seat like a prie-dieu to support himself in kneeling.

[50] The bishop's threefold repetition of this invocation during the litany is first found in the twelfth-century Roman Pontifical, which also directs the bishop to bless the candidates with the sign of the cross each of the three times he says these words; see Andrieu, *Pon-tifical romain au moyen-âge*, 1:131.

[51] Martène, *De antiquis ecclesiae ritibus*, bk. 1, chap. 8, art. 11, *ordo* 16, 2:78.

[52] Ibid., pp. 79–80; the complete text of the antiphon *Accipe Spiritum sanctum* is taken from René-Jean Hésbert, ed., *Corpus antiphonalium officii*, vol. 3, REDSMF 9 (Rome: Herder, 1968), no. 1234, p. 27. The use of these words in the priestly ordination rite is found earlier in one manuscript of the thirteenth-century Pontifical of the Roman Curia; see Andrieu, *Pontifical romain au moyen-âge*, 2:342, footnote.

[53] Gilbert of Tournai, *Tractatus de officio episcopi*, chap. 33, in Marguerin de la Bigne, ed., *Maxima bibliotheca veterum patrum, et antiquorum scriptorum ecclesiasticorum* (Lyons, France: Anis-sonios, 1677), 25:413.

[54] Martène, *De antiquis ecclesiae ritibus*, bk. 1, chap. 8, art. 11, *ordo* 16, 2:80.

[55] Pontifical of Durandus, in Andrieu, *Pontifical romain au moyen-âge*, 3:367. The impo-sition of hands is likewise conferred silently in the tenth-century Romano-Germanic Pon-tifical; see Vogel and Elze, *Pontifical romano-germanique*, 1:32.

of the Holy Spirit in this sacrament and of the importance of striving to sin no more, with the help of God: "*The Holy Spirit will come upon you; and may the power of the Most High preserve you without sin.*"[56] Amalarius of Metz notes that insofar as the hand is the principal human instrument of labor, its use in the conferral of ordination signifies the "works" of the Holy Spirit, with the individual fingers, distinct from one another, representing (albeit not by their number) the different gifts of the Holy Spirit; fittingly the hands are imposed upon the head, for the latter represents the human mind.[57] Commenting upon the imposition of hands that is common to both priestly and episcopal ordination rites, Durandus observes that this practice takes its origin from Isaac's blessing of his son Jacob (Gen 27:22–29) as well as from Moses' imposition of hands upon the head of Joshua in conferring upon him authority over the people (Deut 34:9).[58]

After the bishop imposes his hands on each candidate, the other assisting clergy repeat his action "in devotion".[59] The Mainz pontifical's use of the phrase "in devotion" to characterize this action of the assisting clergy serves as a reminder that it is only the bishop who possesses the power to confer holy orders. The assisting clergy impose their hands upon the ordinands not to administer the sacrament but rather to express their prayer that the Holy Spirit may be imparted upon those being ordained, as Amalarius observes;[60] it can also be seen as a public testimony of the clergy's fraternal acceptance of the ordinands into their ranks.[61]

The bishop then invites the congregation to pray for the ordinands, addressing the faithful in words dating back to the sixth-century Leonine Sacramentary of Rome:[62] "*Let us pray, dearly beloved, to God the Father almighty, that upon these his servants* [Name, Name, etc.], *whom he has elected to the office of the priesthood, he may multiply his heavenly gifts and that what they undertake by his graciousness they may obtain with his assistance*".[63] The deacon instructs all in attendance to kneel and afterward to rise. The bishop completes this supplication for the ordinands by reciting a Collect for priestly ordinations likewise traceable to the Leonine Sacramentary:[64] "*Graciously hear us, we beseech you, O Lord our*

[56] Martène, *De antiquis ecclesiae ritibus*, bk. 1, chap. 8, art. 11, *ordo* 16, 2:80.

[57] Amalarius of Metz, *Liber officialis*, bk. 2, chap. 12, nos. 11, 13, in Hanssens, *Amalarii episcopi: Opera liturgica omnia*, 2:225.

[58] Durandus, *Rationale* (CCCM 140), bk. 2, chap. 11, no. 10, pp. 173–174.

[59] Martène, *De antiquis ecclesiae ritibus*, bk. 1, chap. 8, art. 11, *ordo* 16, 2:80.

[60] Amalarius of Metz, *Liber officialis*, bk. 2, chap. 12, no. 13, in Hanssens, *Amalarii episcopi: Opera liturgica omnia*, 2:225.

[61] John Bligh, S.J., *Ordination to the Priesthood* (New York: Sheed and Ward, 1956), 95–96.

[62] Text in Leo Cunibert Mohlberg, O.S.B.; Leo Eizenhöfer, O.S.B.; and Petrus Siffrin, O.S.B., eds., *Sacramentarium Veronense*, REDSMF 1 (Rome: Herder, 1956), no. 952, p. 121.

[63] In his edition of the Mainz text, Martène provides only the incipit of this formula (*De antiquis ecclesiae ritibus*, bk. 1, chap. 8, art. 11, *ordo* 16, 2:80); the full text is here taken from the tenth-century Romano-Germanic Pontifical, in Vogel and Elze, *Pontifical romano-germanique*, 1:32.

[64] Mohlberg, Eizenhöfer, and Siffrin, *Sacramentarium Veronense*, no. 953, p. 121.

God, and impart upon these your servants [Name, Name, etc.] *the blessing of the Holy Spirit, and the strength of priestly grace, that they whom we offer to the glances of your mercy to be consecrated may obtain the unfailing largesse of your bounty. Through our Lord Jesus Christ your Son, who lives and reigns with you in the unity of the same Holy Spirit, God, through all ages of ages."* [65]

Raising his voice, the bishop now recites the consecratory prayer, a text that like the two preceding it dates back to the sixth-century Leonine Sacramentary of Rome[66] and that constitutes the "form" of the sacrament, that is, the words that together with the earlier action of imposing hands on the candidates efficaciously confer priestly ordination.[67] This text underwent virtually no verbal changes over the centuries. In presenting the consecratory prayer here, we have set in bold print the particular words within the prayer that Venerable Pope Pius XII defined ex cathedra as absolutely essential to the valid conferral of the sacrament.[68] While the Mainz rubrics do not specify the posture of the ordinands during the consecratory prayer, it is highly likely that they would have knelt, as the Pontifical of Durandus expressly states in this regard.[69] The prayer is cast in the form of a Preface (preceded by the usual prefatory versicles and responses: "*The Lord be with you ... Lift up your hearts ...*"):

It is truly fitting and just, right and salutary, for us always and everywhere to give you thanks, holy Lord, almighty Father, eternal God, Author of honors and Distributor of all dignities, by whom all things increase, by whom all things are made firm, in ever-increased augmentations for the betterment of rational nature, arranged by rank in their proper order. And wherefore the priestly degrees and the offices of the Levites have come into being, instituted with mystical rites, that while you set high priests over the people to govern them, you chose men of the next order, and of the secondary dignity, for the assistance of their company and labor. Thus in the desert, through the minds of seventy wise men, you propagated the spirit of Moses, with which useful assistants among the people he easily governed innumerable multitudes. Likewise you poured into Eleazar and Ithamar, the sons of Aaron, the profusion of their father's plenitude, that the ministry of priests should suffice for the salutary sacrifices and rites of a more frequent office. In this providence, O Lord, you have added companions, teachers of the faith, to the Apostles of

---

[65] In his edition of the Mainz text, Martène provides only the incipit of this prayer (*De antiquis ecclesiae ritibus*, bk. 1, chap. 8, art. 11, *ordo* 16, 2:80). The full text is here taken from the tenth-century Romano-Germanic Pontifical, in Vogel and Elze, *Pontifical romano-germanique*, 1:32.

[66] Mohlberg, Eizenhöfer, and Siffrin, *Sacramentarium Veronense*, no. 954, pp. 121–122.

[67] This text was defined ex cathedra as the form of the sacrament by Venerable Pope Pius XII in his 1947 apostolic constitution *Sacramentum ordinis*; see *Sacramentum ordinis*, no. 5, excerpted in Benedictine Monks of Solesmes, *Papal Teachings: Liturgy*, 310–311; Latin text in *Acta Apostolicae Sedis* 40 (1948): 7.

[68] Ibid., 311.

[69] Andrieu, *Pontifical romain au moyen-âge*, 3:367.

your Son, with which secondary preachers they have filled the whole world. Wherefore, grant, we beseech you, O Lord, to our weakness these assistants also; we who are weaker have the greater need of more of them. **Grant, we beseech you, O God, almighty Father, to these your servants** [Name, Name, etc.] **the dignity of the priesthood; renew in their inmost being the spirit of holiness, that they may obtain the gift of secondary ser-vice,**[70] **received from you, O God, and may teach the correction of morals by the example of their conduct.**[71] *May they be prudent coworkers of our order; may the pattern of total righteousness shine forth in them, that after rendering a good account of the stewardship entrusted to them, they may obtain the rewards of eternal beatitude. Through the same Jesus Christ your Son, our Lord . . .* Response: *Amen.*[72]

In the Mainz pontifical, following this prayer, the bishop approaches the ordinands, who are now priests, and intones a responsory taken from Christ's own words, speaking of the cross he gives his disciples as a yoke that is sweet and light and exhorting them to imitate his humil-ity and meekness (Mt 11:29–30).[73] The implication here is that the priesthood is the particular "yoke" that each ordinand is receiving from Christ in this sacrament—Christ will make it "sweet" and "light" for them—and they are likewise admonished to be humble and meek like their Master. While the chanting of this responsory is continued by the clergy, the identification of the priesthood as the "sweet yoke" of Christ is made explicit and is visually symbolized as the bishop turns the stole on each ordinand, moving it from the position desig-nating the diaconate (hung across only the left shoulder) to that des-ignating the priesthood (hung around the neck and over the front of both shoulders), saying as he does so, *"Receive the yoke of the Lord, for his yoke is sweet, and his burden light, in the name of the Lord. Amen."*[74]

---

[70] The priesthood is here called *"the gift of secondary service"* in that it constitutes the second-highest degree of holy orders, second only to the episcopate.

[71] In the original Latin, the words of the essential form are *"Da, quaesumus, omnipotens Pater, in hos famulos tuos presbyterii dignitatem, innova in visceribus eorum spiritum sanctitatis, ut acceptum a te, Deus, secundi meriti munus obtineant censuramque morum exemplo suae conversationis insinuent."*

[72] In his edition of the Mainz text, Martène provides only the incipit of this prayer (*De antiquis ecclesiae ritibus*, bk. 1, chap. 8, art. 11, *ordo* 16, 2:80). The full text is here taken from the tenth-century Romano-Germanic Pontifical; see Vogel and Elze, *Pontifical romano-germanique*, 1:33–34.

[73] Responsory: *"Take up my yoke upon you, says the Lord, and learn, because I am meek, and humble of heart; for my yoke is sweet and my burden light.* Verse: *And you shall find rest to your souls. For my yoke . . ."* Martène, *De antiquis ecclesiae ritibus*, bk. 1, chap. 8, art. 11, *ordo* 16, 2:80 (incipit only); complete text from René-Jean Hésbert, ed., *Corpus antiphonalium officii*, vol. 4, REDSMF 10 (Rome: Herder, 1970), no. 7770, p. 434. This responsory, *Tollite jugum*, is traceable to about 870, when it appears in the Antiphonary of Compiègne (France); see René-Jean Hésbert, ed., *Corpus antiphonalium officii*, vol. 1, REDSMF 7 (Rome: Herder, 1963), 48, 348.

[74] Martène, *De antiquis ecclesiae ritibus*, bk. 1, chap. 8, art. 11, *ordo* 16, 2:80. This rubric and the accompanying words are first found in the tenth-century Romano-Germanic Pon-tifical; see Vogel and Elze, *Pontifical romano-germanique*, 1:34.

According to Hugh of Saint Victor (+c. 1141), this shifting of the stole to a position over both shoulders symbolically "protects the right side and the left, that by this they [the newly ordained priests] may perceive themselves to be protected by the armor of righteousness to the right and to the left, that neither may adversity crush them, nor prosperity exalt them." [75] Saint Thomas Aquinas explains the positioning of the stole over both shoulders of a priest as manifesting that "he has received full power to dispense the sacraments, and not as the minister of another man, for which reason the stole reaches right down." [76] The interpretation of the stole itself as representing the yoke of Christ can be traced back to the ninth-century liturgist Amalarius of Metz. Insofar as the stole is first received by candidates for holy orders when they are ordained deacons, Amalarius discusses it in reference to the diaconate, but what he says of the stole's symbolism would likewise apply to its use by priests: "By the stole is signified the light and sweet burden, of which the Lord says, 'Take up my yoke upon you' (Mt 11:29), and in another place, 'For my yoke is sweet and my burden light' (Mt 11:30). By the yoke we perceive the Gospel.... The deacon himself should perceive in the stole superimposed on his neck the ministry of the Gospel." [77]

In the Mainz ordination rite, the bishop returns to the altar after the shifting of the stoles to offer a prayer for those upon whom he has imposed the priestly yoke of the Lord: "*O God, Author of eternal light, suppliant in prayer, we beseech your might, that you may accompany these your servants under your yoke and burden with the gift of your grace and uphold them amidst adversity always and everywhere. Through our Lord Jesus Christ ...*" (clergy: "*Amen.*") [78]

The bishop again steps toward the newly ordained priests while intoning a responsory admonishing them to be ready for the coming of the Lord, the text of which is drawn from Christ's words to his disciples in Luke 12:35–36 and Matthew 24:42: "*Let your loins be girt, and lamps burning in your hands, and you yourselves like to men who wait for their lord, when he shall return from the wedding. Verse: Watch ye therefore, because you know not what hour your Lord will come. And you yourselves ...*" [79] As

---

[75] Hugh of Saint Victor, *De sacramentis*, bk. 2, pt. 3, chap. 12, PL 176, col. 429; the same interpretation is given by Saint Ivo of Chartres (*Sermon 3*, PL 162, col. 525).

[76] Saint Thomas Aquinas, *Summa theologica*, supplement, q. 40, art. 7, 3:2706.

[77] Amalarius of Metz, *Liber officialis*, bk. 2, chap. 20, nos. 1–2, in Hanssens, *Amalarii episcopi: Opera liturgica omnia*, 2:242–243. This interpretation of the stole as the yoke of Christ is also given by the anonymous tenth-century author known as Pseudo-Alcuin (*Liber de divinis officiis*, chap. 39, PL 101, col. 1242).

[78] Martène, *De antiquis ecclesiae ritibus*, bk. 1, chap. 8, art. 11, *ordo 16*, 2:80. This prayer appears to be derived in part from an oration for the rite of consecration of an abbot (a rite entitled *Ordinatio abbatis*) in the tenth-century Romano-Germanic Pontifical; see Vogel and Elze, *Pontifical romano-germanique*, 1:68.

[79] Martène, *De antiquis ecclesiae ritibus*, bk. 1, chap. 8, art. 11, *ordo 16*, 2:80 (incipit only); the complete text of this responsory is taken from Hésbert, *Corpus antiphonalium officii*, no. 7675, 4:412. This responsory, *Sint lumbi vestri*, is traceable to the first half of the eleventh

the clergy continue the responsory, the bishop places over the neck of each of the newly ordained the distinctive priestly vestment, the chasuble. The solemn investiture of a newly ordained priest with the chasuble immediately after ordination dates back to the Angoulême Sacramentary of the late eighth century (a Frankish adaptation of Rome's Gelasian Sacramentary).[80] The words accompanying the imposition of the chasuble in the Mainz rite explain this vestment as symbolic of charity: "*In the name of the Holy Trinity, receive the priestly vesture, by which is understood charity; for God has power to augment in you charity and labor carried out in the name of the Lord. Amen.*"[81] This identification of the chasuble as symbolic of charity can be traced back to the anonymous tenth-century author known as Pseudo-Alcuin: "The chasuble, which is put over all the vestments, signifies charity, which excels the other virtues, of which the Apostle, in having commemorated certain virtues, says, 'But the greatest of these is charity' (1 Cor 13:13)."[82] Similarly, Saint Ivo of Chartres says of the chasuble: "Over all the vestments is superimposed the chasuble ... which, because it is the common vestment, signifies charity, which is superimposed over all the virtues, for the other virtues produce nothing profitable without it."[83] Undoubtedly this interpretation is also inspired by Saint Paul's injunction that man should clothe himself in the virtues, over all of which he should put on "charity, which is the bond of perfection" (Col 3:12–14). Durandus expands the explanation of his predecessors, observing that just as the chasuble is worn over and encloses all the other vestments, so too charity covers a multitude of sins (1 Pet 4:8) and contains within itself the Law and the prophets (Rom 13:10; see also Mt 5:17).[84] Saint Thomas Aquinas attributes the charity symbolism of the chasuble to the fact that priests consecrate "the sacrament of charity, namely the Eucharist".[85] In the ordination rite from a late tenth-century pontifical of Winchester, England (the so-called Benedictional of Archbishop Robert), the words with which the bishop clothes the new priest in the chasuble cast this vestment as a form of spiritual armor: "*Clad in this priestly garment, may you be worthy to be protected and*

---

century, when it appears in an antiphonary written at the Spanish monastery of Sant Sadurní de Tavèrnoles for use by the abbot Ponc at the court of King Sancho III of Navarre (Sancho the Great, 970–1033); manuscript: Toledo, Spain, Biblioteca Capitular, MS. 44.1, c. 1022, fol. 168v (as indicated by the Gregorian chant online database Cantus, http://cantusdatabase.org).

[80] Text in Patrick Saint-Roch, ed., *Liber sacramentorum Engolismensis*, CCSL 159c (Turnhout, Belgium: Brepols, 1987), no. 2093, p. 322.

[81] Martène, *De antiquis ecclesiae ritibus*, bk. 1, chap. 8, art. 11, ordo 16, 2:80. These words for the chasuble investiture, with some differences, are first found in the tenth-century Romano-Germanic Pontifical; see Vogel and Elze, *Pontifical romano-germanique*, 1:34.

[82] Pseudo-Alcuin, *Liber de divinis officiis*, chap. 39, PL 101, col. 1243.

[83] Saint Ivo of Chartres, *Sermon 3*, PL 162, col. 525.

[84] Durandus, *Rationale* (CCCM 140), bk. 3, chap. 7, no. 1, p. 195.

[85] Saint Thomas Aquinas, *Summa theologica*, supplement, q. 40, art. 7, 3:2706.

defended from all attacks of evil spirits."[86] This imagery accords well with the charity symbolism of the chasuble, for Saint Paul speaks of charity as a breastplate (1 Thess 5:8).

By the early thirteenth century, there had appeared in Rome a two-staged form of the imposition of the chasuble,[87] a practice not explicitly mentioned in the Mainz ordination text but implied by the instruction that the bishop is to place the chasuble "on the neck" of each ordinand.[88] This usage is fully described in the rubrics of the late thirteenth-century Pontifical of Durandus: "Afterward [the bishop] puts upon each one successively the chasuble as far as the shoulders, which each should keep folded together over the shoulders, hanging downward on the front side, [the bishop] saying to each: *Receive the priestly vestment, by which is understood charity.*"[89] Here the front side of the chasuble is fully unfurled, but the back side remains folded at the shoulders until nearly the end of the ordination rite, when it is likewise unfurled:

> The bishop imposes both hands upon the slightly bowed head of each one successively, saying to each: *Receive the Holy Spirit; whose sins you shall forgive, they are forgiven them; and whose [sins] you shall retain, they shall be retained* [cf. Jn 20:22–23]. Then, drawing and unfolding the chasuble, which each one has, folded together, over the shoulders, he successively clothes each with it—but such that the [new priest's] hands should always remain joined—saying to each: *May the Lord clothe you in the robe of innocence.*[90]

The underlying meaning of this two-staged vesting with the chasuble, which eventually became a universal practice, is not directly explained by Durandus either in his pontifical or in his *Rationale divinorum officiorum*; but a plausible explanation may be deduced from Durandus' comments on the symbolism of priestly vestments in the latter work. The front of the chasuble he sees as representing love toward God, and the back, love toward one's neighbor.[91] Citing this passage from Durandus, one twentieth-century scholar has noted that, significantly, the unfurling of the front side of the chasuble occurs within the portion of the ordination rite that stresses the priestly power of offering to God the sacrifice of the Mass, whereas the unfolding of the back of

---

[86] Text in Henry Austin Wilson, ed., *The Benedictional of Archbishop Robert*, HBS 24 (London: Henry Bradshaw Society, 1903), 124.

[87] The earliest reference to this practice, albeit brief, appears in the first recension of the Pontifical of the Roman Curia, the "alpha" recension, which is thought to date from the pontificate of Pope Innocent III (1198–1216). The text speaks of newly ordained cardinal priests being vested in a "chasuble folded over the shoulders"; see Andrieu, *Pontifical romain au moyen-âge*, 2:349, footnote.

[88] Martène, *De antiquis ecclesiae ritibus*, bk. 1, chap. 8, art. 11, *ordo* 16, 2:80.

[89] Andrieu, *Pontifical romain au moyen-âge*, 3:368.

[90] Ibid., 372.

[91] Durandus, *Rationale* (CCCM 140), bk. 3, chap. 7, no. 2, p. 195.

this vestment is carried out during the later portion of the rite, which stresses the priest's power and responsibility to preach to men and absolve their sins.[92] This reasoning, associating the front of the chasuble with the worship of God and the back with a priest's service to the faithful, follows from the rubrics of the medieval Mass, during which the front of the priest faces God at the altar *ad orientem*, whereas his back faces the people he serves.

After the imposition of the chasubles in the Mainz ordination rite, the bishop exhorts the congregation to be united with him in prayer for the newly ordained priests, reminding those in attendance that these men have been chosen to assist them in the salvation of their souls: "*May it be to us, brethren, a common prayer, that these who are chosen for the assistance and benefit of your salvation may obtain the blessing of the priesthood by the indulgence of the divine bounty, and that by the grace of the Holy Spirit they may preserve their priestly gifts with the law of the virtues, lest they be found unequal to their station.*"[93] This address, which dates back to the *Missale Francorum*, a Frankish liturgical book of the seventh to the eighth century,[94] is also found in the tenth-century Romano-Germanic Pontifical, in which it is identified as "Allocution to the People".[95] In both the Romano-Germanic Pontifical and the Mainz pontifical, it introduces the following prayer for the newly ordained priests, recited by the bishop:

> *O God, Author of all blessings, whose consecration is true, whose blessing is bountiful—you, O Lord, impart upon these your servants* [Name, Name, etc.], *whom we consecrate to the honor of the priesthood, the gift of your blessing, that by seriousness of deeds and correction of living they may prove themselves elders, instructed in these disciplines that Paul expounded to Titus and Timothy; that meditating on your law day and night, O omnipotent One, what they have read they may believe; what they have believed they may teach; what they have taught they may imitate; may they exhibit in themselves justice, constancy, mercy, fortitude; may they prove and confirm their admonition by their example and preserve the gifts of their ministry pure and undefiled; and by a spotless con-secration may they transform bread and wine into the Body and Blood of your Son for the worship of your people; and with a pure conscience, with true faith, filled with the Holy Spirit, may they, on the day of the just and eternal judg-ment of God, attain in inviolable charity to the perfect man, unto the measure of the age of the fullness of Christ* [cf. Eph 4:13]. *Through the same Jesus Christ your Son, our Lord . . .*[96]

---

[92] This explanation is offered by Father John Bligh, S.J., in his work *Ordination to the Priesthood*, 119.

[93] Martène, *De antiquis ecclesiae ritibus*, bk. 1, chap. 8, art. 11, *ordo* 16, 2:80.

[94] Text in Leo Cunibert Mohlberg, O.S.B., ed., *Missale Francorum*, REDSMF 2 (Rome: Herder, 1957), no. 31, p. 9.

[95] Vogel and Elze, *Pontifical romano-germanique* 1:34.

[96] In his transcription of the Mainz ordination rite, Martène provides only the incipit of this prayer (*De antiquis ecclesiae ritibus*, bk. 1, chap. 8, art. 11, *ordo* 16, 2:80). The full text

The Mainz pontifical directs that after the above prayer the bishop is to return to his seat, where water, a basin, and a towel are brought to him for the washing of his hands. The bishop then rises again, faces the altar, and kneels, intoning the verse *"Come, Holy Spirit"* (*"Veni Sancte Spiritus"*), which the clergy continues (*"fill the hearts of your faithful, and enkindle in them the fire of your love"*).[97] This verse is also used at the same point in the priestly ordination rite of the Pontifical of Durandus.[98]

Upon completion of the *Veni Sancte Spiritus*, the bishop rises from his knees and approaches the newly ordained priests; and having intoned the verse *"Mercifully impart your unction upon our minds"*, he begins to anoint each of the ordained on his hands with the holy oil known as the *oil of catechumens*. Each ordinand holds his two hands in an open position, side by side; this posture is inferred from the rubrics of the anointing that follow: "[The bishop] should first draw from the right thumb to the left [index finger] transversely; and afterward he should draw from the left thumb to the right [index finger]."[99] From these words it is clear that the bishop traces with the oil a "Saint Andrew's cross" on the palms of each priest's hands.[100] The anointing of a newly ordained priest's hands is believed to have arisen by the sixth century, when an implicit reference to the practice appears in a text of the English abbot Saint Gildas the Wise (+c. 570), who speaks of the blessing of a priest's hands as part of the ordination rite.[101] The earliest direct evidence of this observance is to be found in the Frankish *Missale Francorum* of the seventh to the eighth century, which provides two texts under the heading "Consecration of the Hands", both of which expressly speak of their anointing, with the second implying that the oil was applied in a crosswise manner (*"May they be anointed . . . making the image of the holy Cross of the Savior, our Lord Jesus Christ"*).[102]

Amalarius of Metz explains that priests' hands are anointed with holy oil that they may be "pure for offering sacrifices to God" and "generous for the other offices of piety", with the oil symbolic of

---

is here taken from the tenth-century Romano-Germanic Pontifical; see Vogel and Elze, *Pontifical romano-germanique*, 1:35.

[97] Martène, *De antiquis ecclesiae ritibus*, bk. 1, chap. 8, art. 11, *ordo* 16, 2:80. The complete text of this verse is here taken from Andrieu, *Pontifical romain au moyen-âge*, 3:369, footnote.

[98] Andrieu, *Pontifical romain au moyen-âge*, 3:369.

[99] Martène, *De antiquis ecclesiae ritibus*, bk. 1, chap. 8, art. 11, *ordo* 16, 2:80.

[100] The transverse anointing of the hands in holy orders is described as the tracing of the "cross of Saint Andrew" in an editor's footnote of Father Marc Dykmans, S.J., for his critical edition of the 1488 *Caeremoniale Romanum* of Patrizio Piccolomini, in *L'oeuvre de Patrizi Piccolomini, ou Le cérémonial papal de la première Renaissance*, vol. 1, ST 293 (Vatican City: Biblioteca Apostolica Vaticana, 1980), 63.

[101] Saint Gildas the Wise, *De excidio et conquestu Britanniae*, in *Monumenta Germaniae historica: Auctorum antiquissimorum*, vol. 13, ed. Theodore Mommsen (Berlin: Weidmann, 1898), 82.

[102] Mohlberg, *Missale Francorum*, nos. 33, 34, p. 10.

both "the grace of healing" and "the charity of love".[103] Gilbert of Tournai sees in this practice a parallel to the Mosaic rite for the consecration of Aaron and his sons in which the blood of a sacrificed ram was applied by Moses to the tips of their right ears, right thumbs, and right toes (Ex 29:20; see also Lev 8:24), with the ram's blood corresponding to the blood of Christ, which is signified by the tracing of a cross in the sacerdotal anointing.[104] Stephen of Autun (+c. 1139) sees the crosswise anointing as manifesting that the priest's hands "are conformed to the hands of Christ" and that the "extraordinary and saving miracle" of the consecration of the Eucharist, which takes place "within the hands of the priest", is wrought by the hands of Christ, for "with him, and through him, and in him the entire sacrifice is done."[105] The anointing prayer in the Mainz pontifical is a more developed descendant of the first of the two anointing texts from the earlier-cited *Missale Francorum*:[106] *"May you vouchsafe, O Lord, to consecrate and sanctify these hands through this anointing and our blessing, that whatever they shall consecrate may be consecrated, and whatever they shall bless may be blessed, and sanctified, in the name of our Lord Jesus Christ."*[107]

During the anointing of the hands, the Pentecost-octave sequence *Sancti Spiritus assit* (*"May the grace of the Holy Spirit attend you"*) is sung,[108] a hymn traceable to the end of the tenth century (first found in a manuscript of Einsiedeln, Switzerland). It speaks of the Holy Spirit inspiring the prophets and comforting the Apostles and of the Holy Spirit's cleansing of the heart, mind, and soul.[109] The antiphon with which the anointing begins is in fact a verse from this sequence and is repeated as a refrain after each verse. If the length of time needed to anoint all of the newly ordained priests requires it, the Pentecost hymn *Veni Creator Spiritus* is also sung,[110] a text that had begun to appear in priestly ordination rites by the end of the twelfth century.[111] The anointing concludes with a prayer of tenth-century

---

[103] Amalarius of Metz, *Liber officialis*, bk. 2, chap. 13, no. 1, in Hanssens, *Amalarii episcopi: Opera liturgica omnia*, 2:227.

[104] Gilbert of Tournai, *Tractatus de officio episcopi*, chap. 33, in de la Bigne, *Maxima bibliotheca veterum patrum*, 25:413.

[105] Stephen of Autun, *De sacramento altaris*, chap. 9, PL 172, col. 1281.

[106] For the *Missale Francorum* text of this prayer, see Mohlberg, *Missale Francorum*, no. 33, p. 10.

[107] Martène, *De antiquis ecclesiae ritibus*, bk. 1, chap. 8, art. 11, *ordo* 16, 2:80.

[108] Ibid.

[109] The complete text, as found in the 1531 Sarum Breviary of Salisbury, England, is in Francis Procter and Christopher Wordsworth, eds., *Breviarium ad usum insignis ecclesiae Sarum*, vol. 2 (Cambridge: Cambridge University Press, 1882), cols. 504–505. For the history of this hymn, see John Julian, *A Dictionary of Hymnology* (London: J. Murray, 1907), 993.

[110] Martène, *De antiquis ecclesiae ritibus*, bk. 1, chap. 8, art. 11, *ordo* 16, 2:80.

[111] The earliest use of this hymn in a priestly ordination rite is found in a late twelfth-century pontifical of Saint-Corneille de Compiègne, France (Martène, *De antiquis ecclesiae ritibus*, bk. 1, chap. 8, art. 11, *ordo* 7, 2:51). Its earliest use in Rome for this ceremony is found in the early thirteenth-century first recension ("alpha" recension) of the Pontifical of the Roman Curia; see Andrieu, *Pontifical romain au moyen-âge*, 2:346.

origin recited by the bishop: "*May the God and Father of our Lord Jesus Christ, who on this day has vouchsafed to elect you to the priestly dignity and who has anointed you with the unction of mystical firstfruits* [cf. Deut 26:1–10], *mercifully cleanse you well with the grace of the Holy Spirit and strengthen you with the fullness of spiritual benediction. Through the same Jesus Christ our Lord . . .*"[112]

The rite known as the tradition of the instruments[113] now follows. Having taken into his hands a chalice containing unconsecrated wine with a paten and an unconsecrated host over it, the bishop turns toward the new priests and intones a responsory from the Office of Pope Saint Gregory the Great, *Vere felicem praesulem*, which speaks of the ordained minister of God as he who confects the Eucharist for "*making strong the faith of the people*": "*Truly blessed protector, doctor of the true faith, by whose entreaty bread has received the form of Christ at his touch, converted to flesh without bloodshed, for making strong the faith of the people.* Verse [Ps 117:23]: *This is the Lord's doing; and it is wonderful in our eyes. For making strong . . .*"[114] The bishop's words to each new priest as he gives him the chalice and host remind him that he will be offering Mass for the assistance of both the living and the dead: "*Receive the power to offer sacrifice to God and to celebrate Mass, for both the living and the dead, in the name of the Lord. Amen.*"[115] This rite and its accompanying words are first found in the tenth-century Romano-Germanic Pontifical.[116] In the fourteenth-century Mainz ceremony, the prayer that follows the presentation of the chalice and host is derived from an oration for the rite of consecration of an abbot (a rite entitled *Ordinatio abbatis*) likewise found in the Romano-Germanic Pontifical;[117] the prayer has been modified and expanded to transform it into a supplication for newly ordained priests, that the celebration of Mass may bring about their own sanctification: "*O God, whom every power and dignity serves, give your servants the prosperous reward of their office and dignity, that in the confection of the sacred Body and precious Blood of your beloved Son they may love*

---

[112] Martène, *De antiquis ecclesiae ritibus*, bk. 1, chap. 8, art. 11, *ordo* 16, 2:80. This prayer is a greatly modified variant of that utilized for the anointing of a newly consecrated bishop's hands, the latter of which is first found in the tenth-century Romano-Germanic Pontifical; see Vogel and Elze, *Pontifical romano-germanique*, 1:220.

[113] Bligh, *Ordination to the Priesthood*, 136–137.

[114] Martène, *De antiquis ecclesiae ritibus*, bk. 1, chap. 8, art. 11, *ordo* 16, 2:80 (incipit only); the complete text of this responsory is taken from Hésbert, *Corpus antiphonalium officii*, no. 7844, 4:452. This responsory dates from the thirteenth century, when it appears in an office antiphonary of Rheinau (Switzerland); see René-Jean Hésbert, ed., *Corpus antiphonalium officii*, vol. 2, REDSMF 8 (Rome: Herder, 1965), 208. Regarding the objects presented by the bishop to the new priests for this rite, the Mainz rubrics explicitly mention only the chalice and the unconsecrated host, but the instruction that the chalice be "prepared for the sacrament" implies that it contains unconsecrated wine, and that the host is resting on a paten, in accord with the usual practice for this ceremony.

[115] Martène, *De antiquis ecclesiae ritibus*, bk. 1, chap. 8, art. 11, *ordo* 16, 2:80.

[116] Vogel and Elze, *Pontifical romano-germanique*, 1:35.

[117] Ibid., 68.

you above all things and fear you in all things and strive to be continually pleasing to you. Through ..." [118]

The conferral of the paten with an unconsecrated host and the chalice with unconsecrated wine into the hands of the ordinand was deemed so important a component of the ordination rite that some medieval theologians, most notably Saint Thomas Aquinas, considered it, rather than the imposition of hands, as the specific action in the rite of sacerdotal holy orders that conferred the priestly character upon the candidate and the power to celebrate the Eucharist. [119] This opinion, never a universal one, was ultimately superseded by Venerable Pope Pius XII's 1947 ex cathedra definition of the imposition of the bishop's hands as "the matter and the sole matter" of this sacrament. [120] The conferral of the chalice and host nonetheless serves as an important symbolic action that visually represents what the new priest actually received earlier in the ordination rite by the imposition of the bishop's hands—the power to confect the Eucharist. In discussing the tradition of the instruments, Gilbert of Tournai identifies the Old Testament practice of priests placing their hands upon the rams or calves to be sacrificed (Ex 29:10, 15, 19; Lev 3:2; 4:4) as a prefiguration of the Catholic priests' power to consecrate with their hands the Holy Eucharist. [121] Gilbert compares the ordination rite's conferral of the chalice and host to the Mosaic practice of placing miters upon Aaron and his sons during the rite of their priestly consecration (Ex 29:9). [122]

The bishop once again approaches the ordinands while intoning a responsory taken from Christ's conversation with Saint Peter at the Sea of Galilee following his Resurrection, as related in the Gospel of Saint John. As pastors of souls, the newly ordained priests are, like Peter, called to love Christ and are charged with feeding their sheep (Jn 21:17, 16, 15): *"Peter, lovest thou me? Lord, thou knowest that I love thee. Feed my sheep. Verse: Simon, son of John, lovest thou me more than these? Lord, thou knowest that I love thee. Feed ..."* [123] As the clergy continues the responsory, the bishop gives the sign of peace to the new priests one by one and humbly asks each of them to pray for him: *"Peace be with you, brother; pray for me."* [124] Addressing the ordinands,

---

[118] Martène, *De antiquis ecclesiae ritibus*, bk. 1, chap. 8, art. 11, *ordo* 16, 2:80.

[119] Saint Thomas Aquinas, *Summa theologica*, supplement, q. 37, art. 5, 3:2694–2695.

[120] Venerable Pius XII, *Sacramentum ordinis*, nos. 4–5, excerpted in Benedictine Monks of Solesmes, *Papal Teachings: Liturgy*, 310–311; Latin text in *Acta Apostolicae Sedis* 40 (1948): 6–7.

[121] Gilbert of Tournai, *Tractatus de officio episcopi*, chap. 33, in de la Bigne, *Maxima bibliotheca veterum patrum*, 25:413.

[122] Ibid.

[123] Martène, *De antiquis ecclesiae ritibus*, bk. 1, chap. 8, art. 11, *ordo* 16, 2:80 (incipit only); the complete text of this responsory is taken from Hésbert, *Corpus antiphonalium officii*, no. 7382, 4:345. This responsory, *Petre, amas me*, is traceable to 870, when it appears in the Antiphonary of Compiègne (France); see Hésbert, *Corpus antiphonalium officii*, 1:258.

[124] Martène, *De antiquis ecclesiae ritibus*, bk. 1, chap. 8, art. 11, *ordo* 16, 2:80. The giving of the sign of peace to the newly ordained is first found in the tenth-century Romano-Germanic Pontifical; see Vogel and Elze, *Pontifical romano-germanique*, 1:36.

the bishop then recites from the pontifical an exhortation on the priest-hood and its relationship with the episcopate that explains the reservation of certain greater powers to the bishop as essential to the preservation of concord within the Church:

> *The order of presbyters or priests took its beginning from the sons of Aaron, who were truly called priests in the Old Testament; these are now called presbyters. Indeed, a priest is called, as it were, a consecrated gift, or a sacred leader, or presbyters offering holy things, whereupon they are interpreted elders. For the Greeks call aged presbyters elders. We, however, say presbyters in merit and wisdom, not in age. To these therefore, as also to the bishop, is entrusted the dispensation of the mysteries of God. For they govern the churches of God, and in the confection of the Body and Blood of the Lord, and in the office of preaching, they are partakers with the bishop; but in this they differ, that certain greater and worthier things have been entrusted to bishops, lest the discipline of the Church, having protected concord, should dissolve and create scandals in many. Whereupon it befits priests, as also bishops, to be without sin and in the course of all things laudably to be devoted to the Lord.*[125]

After completing this exhortation, the bishop returns to the altar, where he blesses the new priests with a benediction traceable to the Angoulême Sacramentary,[126] a late eighth-century Frankish adaptation of Rome's Gelasian Sacramentary: "*May the blessing of God the Father +, and the Son +, and the Holy + Spirit, descend upon you, that you may be blessed in the priestly order and may offer appeasing sacrifices for the sins and offenses of the people to almighty God, to whom be honor and glory, through all ages of ages. Amen.*"[127] The bishop at his discretion can add at this point the responsory "*Bless, O Lord, this house, and all the inhabitants in it, and may there be in it health, humility.*"[128] The use of this responsory within the particular context of the ordination rite suggests that the term "*this house*" is seen here as referring to the cathedral or church where the ordination is taking place, or perhaps to the entire archdiocese of Mainz.

The bishop now resumes the ceremonies of the Mass, beginning with the Offertory. The new priests are positioned around the bishop, close enough that they may see the altar, in order to concelebrate with him, making the signs prescribed for the Roman Canon and the rest of the Mass in unison with him. After the Our Father and the prayer that follows it, "*Deliver us, we beseech you, O Lord*", but before the placing of the particle in the chalice and the *Agnus Dei*, the bishop

---

[125] Martène, *De antiquis ecclesiae ritibus*, bk. 1, chap. 8, art. 11, *ordo* 16, 2:80.

[126] Saint-Roch, *Liber sacramentorum Engolismensis*, no. 2093, p. 322.

[127] Martène, *De antiquis ecclesiae ritibus*, bk. 1, chap. 8, art. 11, *ordo* 16, 2:80.

[128] Ibid. This responsory, *Benedic, Domine, domum istam*, is traceable to about 870, when it appears in the Antiphonary of Compiègne (France); see Hésbert, *Corpus antiphonalium officii*, 1:376.

imparts upon the faithful present a solemn blessing dating from the early ninth century,[129] preceded by the deacon's invitation to the people:

> But before *And his peace* should be said, the deacon, having turned to the people, should say: *Humble yourselves for a blessing.* Clergy: *Thanks be to God.* The bishop, having put on his miter, holding his crosier in his hand, turned toward the people, should pronounce the blessing:
>
> *May Almighty God bless you with his mercy and impart upon you the understanding of the wisdom of salvation.* Clergy: *Amen.*
>
> Again, the bishop should say: *May he sustain you with the teachings of the Catholic faith and render you persevering in holy works.* Clergy: *Amen.*
>
> The bishop should say: *May he turn your steps from error and show you the way of peace and charity.* Clergy: *Amen.*
>
> Again, the bishop should say: *Which may he himself vouchsafe to grant, whose kingdom and dominion endure without end, unto ages of ages.* Clergy: *Amen.*
>
> The bishop should bless the people: *And may the blessing of almighty God, the Father, and the Son, and the Holy Spirit, descend and remain upon you.* Clergy: *Amen.*[130]

After the bishop has received Holy Communion, the new priests come forward to receive Communion from him two by two, which brings to mind yet again Christ's sending forth of his disciples two at a time (Mk 6:7). Before the new priests receive, they recite together the *Confiteor.*[131] Gilbert of Tournai sees the newly ordained priests' partaking of Holy Communion with their bishop as prefigured by the banquet of sacrificed ram's flesh and unleavened bread that Moses commanded Aaron and his sons to consume after he had consecrated them priests (Lev 8:31).[132]

Following Holy Communion and the recitation of the Communion antiphon, the bishop, having taken his miter and crosier, facing the new priests, admonishes them to learn the ceremonies of the Mass carefully before celebrating their first Mass by themselves, reminding them that the celebration of Mass is an awesome responsibility: "*Inasmuch as the thing that you are going to be celebrating is perilous enough, dearest brethren, I admonish you that you should learn diligently and decently from others, namely learned priests, the order of the entire Mass, and the consecration, and the fracture, and the Communion, before you should presume to sing the Mass.*"[133] The bishop then enjoins his newly ordained

---

[129] This blessing is first found in Saint Benedict of Aniane's early ninth-century Frankish adaptation of the Gregorian Sacramentary of Rome; see Jean Deshusses, ed., *Le sacramentaire grégorien: Ses principales formes d'après les plus anciens manuscrits*, vol. 1, 2nd ed., SF 16 (Fribourg, Switzerland: Editions Universitaires Fribourg, 1979), no. 1778, p. 594.

[130] Martène, *De antiquis ecclesiae ritibus*, bk. 1, chap. 8, art. 11, ordo 16, 2:80.

[131] Ibid.

[132] Gilbert of Tournai, *Tractatus de officio episcopi*, chap. 33, in de la Bigne, *Maxima bibliotheca veterum patrum*, 25:413.

[133] Martène, *De antiquis ecclesiae ritibus*, bk. 1, chap. 8, art. 11, ordo 16, 2:80. This admonition first appears in some pontificals of the twelfth century; see Luca Brandolini, C.M.,

clergy to say some Masses for him, in recognition of his own need for divine assistance and the prayers of his priests. The Mass is concluded in the usual manner, after which the bishop turns to the newly ordained one final time to intone a responsory addressed to them. This text, *Ite in orbem*, drawn from Christ's final words to his disciples before his Ascension, serves in effect as a mandate from the bishop to his new clergy, sending them forth into the Lord's vineyard to preach the Gospel, as Christ sent forth his Apostles (cf. Mk 16:15–17; Mt 28:19): "*Go into the whole world and preach, saying, Alleluia! He that believeth and is baptized, shall be saved, alleluia, alleluia, alleluia. Verse: In the name of the Father, and of the Son, and of the Holy Spirit . . .*"[134] Having begun the responsory, the bishop processes out from the choir, followed by the new priests, as the clergy continues the responsory. The concluding procession thereby takes on the character of a visual enactment of Christ's command, "*Go into the whole world and preach.*"

The Consecration of a Bishop in the Pontifical of Durandus

As we have noted earlier, the priestly order of the episcopacy is seen by medieval authors, including Amalarius of Metz, as prefigured in the Old Testament by the office of the high priest Aaron.[135] It is through episcopal consecration that the *plenitude* of holy orders is conferred. Regarding the episcopate, Saint Thomas Aquinas states:

> Just as the perfections of all natural things pre-exist in God as their exemplar, so was Christ the exemplar of all ecclesiastical offices. Wherefore each minister of the Church is, in some respect, a copy of Christ. . . . Yet he is higher who represents Christ according to a greater perfection. Now a priest represents Christ in that he fulfilled a certain ministry by himself, whereas a bishop represents him in that he instituted other ministers and founded the Church. Hence it belongs to a bishop to dedicate a thing to the divine offices, as establishing the divine worship after the manner of Christ. For this reason also a bishop is especially called the bridegroom of the Church even as Christ is.[136]

In the Middle Ages, a variety of Latin words were used in reference to bishops (beyond the literal term *episcopus*), including *speculator* (watchman), *antistes* (presiding officer), and *pontifex* (pontiff). Blessed Rabanus Maurus explains the characterization of a bishop as a watchman by

---

"L'evoluzione storica dei riti delle ordinazioni", *EL* 83 (1969): 86. Durandus utilizes it in his late thirteenth-century pontifical; see Andrieu, *Pontifical romain au moyen-âge*, 3:372–373.

[134] Martène, *De antiquis ecclesiae ritibus*, bk. 1, chap. 8, art. 11, *ordo* 16, 2:80 (incipit only); the complete text of this responsory is taken from Hésbert, *Corpus antiphonalium officii*, no. 7028, 4:257. This responsory is traceable to about 870, when it appears in the Antiphonary of Compiègne (France); see Hésbert, *Corpus antiphonalium officii*, 1:226.

[135] Amalarius of Metz, *Liber officialis*, bk. 2, chap. 14, no. 1, in Hanssens, *Amalarii episcopi: Opera liturgica omnia*, 2:233.

[136] Saint Thomas Aquinas, *Summa theologica*, supplement, q. 40, art. 4, reply obj. 3, 3:2704.

citing the following passage from the prophet Ezechiel (33:7–8): "So thou, O son of man, I have made thee a watchman to the house of Israel: therefore thou shalt hear the word from my mouth, and shalt tell it them from me. When I say to the wicked: O wicked man, thou shalt surely die: if thou dost not speak to warn the wicked man from his way, that wicked man shall die in his iniquity, but I will require his blood at thy hand." Rabanus interprets this passage in reference to the episcopacy as indicating that the bishop must watch over the lives and actions of his people and, when necessary, make known to them the iniquity of their deeds in order to bring them to conversion.[137] Honorius of Autun observes that just as watchmen are posted in high towers that they may watch vigilantly the approach of enemies and exhort the citizenry to resist the attackers, so too the bishop keeps watch "that he may strive to arm the people against the demon hosts and heresies". Honorius also compares a bishop to the custodian of a vineyard, "residing on high" to oversee "the vineyard of Christ" and to instruct the people placed under him. Dividing another Latin word used for bishops, *antistes*, into the two Latin terms *anti-*, a prefix meaning "against", and *stes*, a declined form of the verb *sto*, "to stand", Honorius comments that the bishop as shepherd is "to stand against heretics as against wolves and protect the sheep". The derivation of the Latin word *pontifex*, "pontiff", from the Latin word for "bridge", *pons*, leads Honorius to observe that "the life of a bishop ought to be a bridge for the people over the sea of the world to the native land of Paradise." Further, the bishop, by giving the faithful sound doctrine, makes a bridge to carry them safely over "the swamps of heresies" to the courts of everlasting life.[138]

In virtue of the sacramental powers and pastoral duties of bishops, the medieval rites of episcopal ordination were particularly elaborate. The finest example of these, which we will present here, is the episcopal consecration rite from the pontifical compiled by William Durandus for his own diocese of Mende, France, around the year 1294.[139] While the Durandus rite draws much of its content from the tenth-century Romano-Germanic Pontifical,[140] which in turn embodies earlier traditions from Rome and northern Europe, it also incorporates later texts and rubrics from the twelfth-century Roman Pontifical[141] and the thirteenth-century Pontifical of the Roman Curia,[142] as well as new texts and rubrics composed by Durandus himself. This consecration ceremony of Durandus' pontifical was later to pass with minimal changes into the universally promulgated *Pontificale Romanum*

---

[137] Blessed Rabanus Maurus, *De clericorum institutione*, bk. 1, chap. 5, PL 107, col. 301.

[138] Honorius of Autun, *Gemma animae*, bk. 1, chap. 183, PL 172, col. 600.

[139] Andrieu, *Pontifical romain au moyen-âge*, 3:374–393.

[140] Vogel and Elze, *Pontifical romano-germanique*, 1:199–226.

[141] Andrieu, *Pontifical romain au moyen-âge*, 1:138–152.

[142] Ibid., 2:351–368.

of 1595–1596.[143] Following our examination of the Durandus text, we will present as a further example a summary of the episcopal ordination ceremony found in the fourteenth-century Pontifical of Mainz, from which we have already derived the priestly ordination rite given earlier.

According to the Pontifical of Durandus, the consecration of a new bishop takes place on a Sunday, in keeping with a tradition dating back to the third century.[144] On the eve of the consecration, namely Saturday evening, there is a preparatory rite for the solemn presentation and examination of the episcopal candidate, a practice traceable to eighth-century Rome.[145] The bishop who will consecrate the episcopal candidate, in this case the metropolitan, the archbishop who heads the ecclesiastical province within which the future bishop will serve, sits on a faldstool in the vestibule of the church where the consecration will take place. In compliance with the ancient tradition from the third century onward that several bishops should participate in the consecration of a new bishop[146] (specifically three in number from the tenth century onward),[147] two suffragan bishops are also present, seated upon faldstools on either side of the archbishop; all three, vested in copes, have their miters and crosiers. An archdeacon (a cleric, usually a priest, who serves as a high-ranking assistant to his bishop), also vested in a cope, steps forward to address the archbishop, somewhat at a distance, kneeling and asking his blessing: "*Vouchsafe, Lord, to bless.*" The archbishop answers, "*May the Creator of the celestial court reign over and save us.*" The archdeacon rises, advances a short distance, and again kneels to ask the archbishop's blessing. This time the archbishop answers, "*May the Lord preserve, protect, and govern us.*" Once more the archdeacon advances, kneels, and asks for a blessing. The archbishop answers, "*The joys of Heaven may its Ruler give us.*"[148] This triple request for a blessing at the Saturday preparatory rite, traceable to the late tenth century,[149] is explained by Durandus in his *Rationale divinorum officiorum* as manifesting that the Holy Trinity presides over the episcopal consecration.[150]

---

[143] Text in Sodi and Triacca, *Pontificale Romanum: Editio princeps (1595–1596)*, 75–117 (original pagination).

[144] See the *Apostolic Tradition* of Saint Hippolytus of Rome (+c. 236), chap. 1, in Funk, *Didascalia et Constitutiones apostolorum*, 2:98.

[145] See Roman *Ordo* 34, a liturgical text of Rome from the first half of the eighth century, in Andrieu, *Ordines Romani du haut moyen âge*, 3:606–611.

[146] See the *Apostolic Tradition* of Saint Hippolytus of Rome, chap. 1, in Funk, *Didascalia et Constitutiones apostolorum*, 2:98.

[147] See Roman *Ordo* 35, a Roman-Frankish liturgical text dating from about 925, in Michel Andrieu, ed., *Les Ordines Romani du haut moyen âge*, vol. 4, SSLED 28 (Louvain, Belgium: "Spicilegium sacrum Lovaniense" Administration, 1956), 44.

[148] Andrieu, *Pontifical romain au moyen-âge*, 3:374–375.

[149] This threefold rite, with the same petitions and responses, is first found in Roman *Ordo* 35B, a late tenth-century Italian adaptation of the Romano-Germanic Pontifical; see Andrieu, *Ordines Romani du haut moyen âge*, 4:99.

[150] Durandus, *Rationale* (CCCM 140), bk. 2, chap. 11, no. 11, p. 174.

Holy Orders

181

The archbishop now questions the archdeacon about the episcopal candidate to be consecrated; their dialogue consists of several prescribed questions and answers traceable to eighth-century Rome:[151] "*My son, what do you ask?* The archdeacon answers: *That our God and Lord may grant us a pastor.* Question: *Do you have your [candidate]?* He answers: *We have.* Question: *Is he of the same church, or from another?* Response: *From the same [church].* Question: *What in him has been pleasing to you?* Response: *Sanctity, chastity, humility, kindness, and all things that are pleasing to God.*"[152]

The archdeacon then reads the canonical decree by which the cathedral chapter of the vacant see (the body of cathedral clerics who assist their bishop) formally requests from the archbishop of the ecclesiastical province the consecration of the candidate chosen for their diocese. This solemn petition, the wording of which (apart from the salutation) dates from the tenth century,[153] testifies to a bishop's role as the "bridegroom" of his diocese and the vigilant protector of his flock:

> *The chapter of the church of [Name] to the most reverend lord Father in Christ, [Name], distinguished with the dignity of the metropolitan see, [pledging] our submission of total devotion:*
>
> *We believe it not to be hidden to your highness that our church should not be widowed from her shepherd. . . . Wherefore, lest, with the shepherd absent, the Lord's flock should be open to the biting of treacherous wolves, and lest it should be made the prey of the evil plunderer, by a common vote and consent we have elected for bishop to us [Name], a priest of this church, a man indeed prudent, hospitable, adorned with morals, chaste, temperate, humble, pleasing to God in all things, whom we have taken care to send to your dignity, unanimously entreating and beseeching him to be ordained bishop for us by your majesty, that by the Lord Creator he may be able to govern and be advantageous as a fitting shepherd, and that under his holy direction we may be able always to fight for the Lord.*[154]

The salutation introducing the above text was modified by Durandus from its tenth-century original to indicate that the petitioner is the cathedral chapter rather than simply the "clergy and people" of the diocese, as the original had said; this change reflects the decision of

---

[151] These questions and answers first appear (with some differences) in Roman *Ordo* 34 (c. 700–750); see Andrieu, *Ordines Romani du haut moyen âge*, 3:608–609.

[152] Andrieu, *Pontifical romain au moyen-âge*, 3:375.

[153] The earliest text of this decree is preserved in the aforementioned late tenth-century Roman *Ordo* 35B of Italy; see Andrieu, *Ordines Romani du haut moyen âge*, 4:100. This earliest recension of the text is thought to date from the mid-tenth century or earlier; see Vogel, *Medieval Liturgy*, 176–177.

[154] Andrieu, *Pontifical romain au moyen-âge*, 3:375; the complete text of this decree is here taken from the twelfth-century Roman Pontifical, in Andrieu, *Pontifical romain au moyen-âge*, 1:139, collated with subsequent alterations in the Pontifical of the Roman Curia, from Andrieu, *Pontifical romain au moyen-âge*, 2:352, and the Pontifical of Durandus.

the Second Lateran Council in 1139 to reserve to a diocese's cathedral chapter the right of electing an episcopal successor.[155] Later in the Middle Ages, from the fourteenth century onward, the popes increasingly exercised their supreme authority over the selection of episcopal candidates, with the sovereign pontiff rather than the provincial archbishop (the metropolitan) confirming episcopal elections and increasingly reserving to himself the nomination of candidates.[156] This change is reflected in the text of the episcopal consecration rite in the 1485 *Pontificalis liber* (the edition of the *Pontificale Romanum* compiled by two papal masters of ceremonies, Patrizio Piccolomini and John Burckard), wherein the above-cited reading of a decree petitioning confirmation from the archbishop is replaced with the reading of an apostolic mandate, a document from the Holy See authorizing the consecration.[157] This change was universally promulgated in the 1595–1596 *Pontificale Romanum.*[158]

Following the reading of the decree in the Durandus rite, the archdeacon withdraws to prepare for the entrance of the episcopal candidate:

> Whereupon the candles having been lit, the candidate, still fasting, furnished with a cope or chasuble should it be the custom, is led processionally before the metropolitan, the canons of the church to which he has been elected preceding him, the archdeacon and the archpriest[159] of the metropolitan church on each side conducting him. And remaining suitably distant from him [the metropolitan], [the candidate] kneels, requesting his blessing and saying: *Graciously grant, Lord, to bless.* The metropolitan answers in the same tone with a lower voice: *May the grace of the Holy Spirit vouchsafe to illuminate our minds and hearts.*
>
> Then, rising and proceeding a little, [the candidate] again kneels, saying: *Vouchsafe, Lord, to bless.* Response: *May the Lord kindle the fire of his love in our hearts.*
>
> Rising again, and now approaching a little and kneeling, he says a third time: *Vouchsafe, Lord, to bless.* Response: *May the Lord guard your entering and going out.* Response: *Amen.*[160]

---

[155] A. Van Hove, "Bishop", in *Catholic Encyclopedia* (1907–1912), 2:583.

[156] F. Claeys Bouuaert, "Evêques", in R. Naz, ed., *Dictionnaire de droit canonique*, vol. 5 (Paris: Librairie Letouzey et Ané, 1953), col. 575.

[157] Text in Sodi, *"Pontificalis liber" di Agostino Patrizi Piccolomini e Giovanni Burcardo (1485),* 70 (new pagination). In his study of successive editions of the Roman Pontifical during the fifteenth century, Father Marc Dykmans, S.J., first finds this change in the 1485 pontifical; see his work, *Le pontifical romain révisé au XVe siècle,* 113.

[158] Sodi and Triacca, *Pontificale Romanum: Editio princeps (1595–1596),* 78–79 (original pagination).

[159] An archpriest serves as the head of one of the major churches within a diocese, assisting his bishop in this capacity; his office is ranked below that of an archdeacon.

[160] Andrieu, *Pontifical romain au moyen-âge,* 3:376. The episcopal candidate's threefold petition for a blessing at the Saturday rite is first found in the late tenth-century Roman *Ordo* 35B of Italy; see Andrieu, *Ordines Romani du haut moyen âge,* 4:100. The above-given

The archbishop examines the candidate so as to confirm his qualifications for the episcopate, utilizing a series of prescribed questions traceable in their earliest form to the first half of the eighth century.[161] After admonishing the candidate never to ordain to holy orders unworthy candidates and warning him that he must guard himself altogether from the vices of heresy and simony (the buying or selling of ecclesiastical offices), the archbishop tells the candidate: "*Therefore, because the recommendations of all agree upon you, today you shall abstain, and tomorrow, God assenting, you shall be consecrated.*"[162] He also assigns to the candidate a confessor to hear his confession.[163]

The candidate now prostrates himself, remaining thus as Psalm 67 is recited, "*Let God arise, and let his enemies be scattered . . .*", with an adaptation of the psalm's twenty-ninth and thirtieth verses serving as the antiphon: "*Confirm, O God, what you have wrought in us, from your holy temple that is in Jerusalem.*"[164] After two concluding prayers,[165] the candidate rises, and the archbishop imparts a solemn episcopal blessing to end the Saturday evening rite.[166]

On Sunday, around 9:30 A.M. ("around the middle of Terce"), the archbishop, clad in pontifical vestments as for Mass, advances to the altar in a procession with fellow bishops and the clergy in attendance. The episcopal candidate follows, vested in an alb or surplice, with an amice over his shoulders, and a stole, a belt, and a cope. He is accompanied by two bishops, one on each side. After the archbishop ("the consecrator") has taken his seat upon a faldstool before the altar, the two bishops accompanying the episcopal candidate ("the elect") present him:

---

wording of the consecrating bishop's responses for this blessing rite first appears in the twelfth-century Roman Pontifical; see Andrieu, *Pontifical romain au moyen-âge*, 1:140.

[161] The questions of this examination first appear in Roman *Ordo* 34, a Roman liturgical text from the first half of the eighth century; see Andrieu, *Ordines Romani du haut moyen âge*, 3:610.

[162] This concluding declaration, like the preceding examination, is traceable to Roman *Ordo* 34; see ibid., 611.

[163] Andrieu, *Pontifical romain au moyen-âge*, 3:376–377.

[164] This antiphon, *Confirma hoc, Deus*, is traceable to the Mass antiphonary of Rheinau (Switzerland, c. 800), in which it appears in a longer form as the Offertory chant for the Mass of Pentecost Sunday; see René-Jean Hésbert, ed., *Antiphonale missarum sextuplex* (Brussels, 1935; repr., Rome: Herder, 1967), 124.

[165] First prayer: "*Almighty eternal God, who alone work great wonders, extend over this your servant and over all the congregations entrusted to him the spirit of salutary grace, and pour upon him the dew of your perpetual blessing, that he may be truly pleasing to you. Through Christ our Lord*" (response: "*Amen*"). Second prayer: "*Our actions, we beseech you, O Lord, guide with your assisting and accompany with your helping, that our every prayer and work may always begin by you and, having been begun, be completed through you. Through Christ our Lord*" (response: "*Amen*"). See Andrieu, *Pontifical romain au moyen-age*, 3:377 (only the incipit for each prayer), 400–401 (complete texts of the two prayers). The first of these prayers is traceable to the seventh-century Gelasian Sacramentary of Rome; see Mohlberg, Eizenhöfer, and Siffrin, *Liber sacramentorum*, no. 1429, p. 207; the second dates back to the seventh-century Paduan redaction of Rome's Gregorian Sacramentary; see Deshusses, *Sacramentaire grégorien*, Paduan no. 169, 1:622.

[166] Andrieu, *Pontifical romain au moyen-âge*, 3:377.

Then the two escorting bishops, standing in the lower part of the church's choir behind the [other] bishops, keeping the elect in the middle facing the consecrator, bring him before him, saying in a high voice: *Reverend Father, Holy Mother Catholic Church asks that you would raise up this priest to the obligation of the episcopate.* And he consecrating says: *Do you know him to be worthy?* The bishops answer: *So much as human frailty allows us here, we know and believe him to be worthy.* The consecrator and the others respond: *Thanks be to God.*[167]

The candidate is now seated on a faldstool facing the archbishop.[168] As a final verification of the candidate's worthiness, the archbishop questions him with a lengthy doctrinal and moral examination, the wording of which dates back to the tenth-century Romano-Germanic Pontifical.[169] The inquiry regards the candidate's profession of the tenets of the Catholic faith (in this, similar to the profession required at baptism, but far more detailed) and his own moral fidelity in living according to the obligations of his state of life. This profession of faith includes a pledge of obedience to the pope and to the provincial primate under whom he will be serving; it is the only portion of the examination text that Durandus modified when incorporating it into his pontifical. We give here his rendering of the pledge; as bishop of the French diocese of Mende, he worded the formula specifically for the consecration rites of his successors in this see, which, until the nineteenth century, was under the primatial authority of the metropolitan see of Bourges:[170] "*Do you determine to promise faithfulness, subjection, and obedience, in accordance with canonical authority, to blessed Peter the Apostle, to whom the power of binding and loosing was given by God, and to his vicars the Roman pontiffs, and to me his minister of the holy Church of Bourges, and to my successors?*"[171] The candidate answers, "*I will.*" In the above formula, Durandus has amplified the bond of fidelity of the bishop elect to the pope and to his provincial primate by adding to the words of this formula given in the thirteenth-century Pontifical of the Roman Curia[172] the phrase "*obedience, in accordance with canonical authority*". The archbishop ends the examination with the words "*May this faith be increased in you unto true and eternal beatitude, most beloved brother in Christ.*"[173] The episcopal candidate, led forward now by the two bishops with him, kisses the hand of the archbishop as a visual expression of the fidelity he has pledged in the examination.[174]

---

[167] Ibid., 378.

[168] Ibid.

[169] Vogel and Elze, *Pontifical romano-germanique*, 1:200–204, 207–212.

[170] Georges Goyau, "Mende, Diocese of", in *Catholic Encyclopedia* (1907–1912), 10:180.

[171] Andrieu, *Pontifical romain au moyen-âge*, 3:379.

[172] See ibid., 2:356.

[173] Ibid., 3:379.

[174] Ibid., 379–380.

The archbishop, having risen and turned to face the altar, begins the Mass with the *Confiteor* as the candidate stands to his left. In the rubrics of his pontifical, Durandus explains that in Rome the Introit (here called the *Officium*) used at the episcopal ordination Mass is simply that assigned by the liturgical calendar to the particular day—it is not changed because of the ordination; elsewhere, some dioceses utilize the votive Mass of the Holy Spirit with its Introit, while still other dioceses use the following Introit specifically intended for the ordination Mass (from Ps 44:8, 18, 1): "*God has blessed you this day and has anointed you with the oil of gladness above your brothers. Be mindful of the name of the Lord your God. Verse: My heart has uttered a good word: I speak my works to the king. Glory be to the Father . . .*"[175]

During the Introit, the candidate is led by the two bishops with him behind the altar, where he is vested in a dalmatic, a chasuble, sandals, and all the pontifical vestments except for the miter, the episcopal ring, and the episcopal gloves. At the altar, the archbishop recites a special Collect for the episcopal consecration Mass, a prayer dating back to the eighth-century *Hadrianum* redaction of Rome's Gregorian Sacramentary:[176] "*Attend to our supplications, almighty God, that what is going to be administered by means of our lowliness may in effect be accomplished by your power. Through our Lord Jesus Christ . . .*"[177] To this is added the Collect for the particular day on the liturgical calendar. In Rome, the use of the third chapter of Saint Paul's First Letter to Timothy as the Epistle of the episcopal consecration Mass, a lection that describes the qualities of a good bishop, dates back to the first half of the eighth century, when it appears in Roman *Ordo* 34.[178] In the Pontifical of Durandus, the Epistle for this Mass consists of the first seven verses of 1 Timothy 3, to which is added one verse from Saint Paul's Letter to Titus (2:10).[179]

Following the recitation of the Gradual (Ps 49:14, 5),[180] the usual order of the Mass is interrupted in order to begin the rite of episcopal consecration before proceeding to the Gospel. The episcopal candidate is led by the two bishops escorting him to the step before the altar. The archbishop, seated again on the faldstool in front of the

---

[175] Ibid., 380. The earliest use of this Introit (*Benedixit te hodie*) for the episcopal consecration Mass is to be found in the Antiphonary of Senlis (France, c. 880); see Hésbert, *Antiphonale missarum sextuplex*, 171.

[176] Text in Deshusses, *Sacramentaire grégorien*, no. 21, 1:92.

[177] Andrieu, *Pontifical romain au moyen-âge*, 3:381, collated with the complete text of this prayer in the tenth-century Romano-Germanic Pontifical, from Vogel and Elze, *Pontifical romano-germanique*, 1:206.

[178] Andrieu, *Ordines Romani du haut moyen âge*, 3:612.

[179] Andrieu, *Pontifical romain au moyen-âge*, 3:380–381. This catena of verses from the First Letter to Timothy and the Letter to Titus is first found in the late tenth-century Roman *Ordo* 35B of Italy; see Andrieu, *Ordines Romani du haut moyen âge*, 4:104.

[180] The use of this Gradual (*Immola Deo*) in the episcopal consecration Mass is traceable to the Antiphonary of Senlis (France, c. 880); see Hésbert, *Antiphonale missarum sextuplex*, 171.

altar, facing the candidate, says, *"It is fitting for a bishop to judge, to interpret, to consecrate, to confirm, to ordain, to offer, and to baptize."* [181] The archbishop now stands and addresses those present in the following words, which date back to the seventh-century Gelasian Sacramentary of Rome: [182] *"Let us pray, O ones dearly beloved to us, that the providential goodness of almighty God may grant this man the bounty of his grace for the benefit of the Church. Through our Lord Jesus Christ . . .* (response: *"Amen"*). [183]

The archbishop, the episcopal candidate, and the two bishops assisting him, as well as the other bishops in attendance, all kneel down and lean forward over their faldstools. The rest of the clergy prostrate themselves on carpets. The Litany of the Saints, as used in the rite of holy orders for subdeacons, deacons, and priests, is now recited. Following the petition *"That you may make reasonable the homage of our service"*, the archbishop rises and, taking his crosier in his left hand, turns toward the episcopal candidate to bless him with the sign of the cross, saying, *"That you may vouchsafe to bless + this present elect. We beseech you, hear us."* A second time he says these words but with an addition: *"That you may vouchsafe to bless + and sancti + fy this present elect. We beseech you, hear us."* A third time he recites the petition, expanded further: *"That you may vouchsafe to bless + and sancti + fy and consecrate + this present elect. We beseech you, hear us."* As the archbishop imparts this threefold series of blessings, the other bishops, remaining in their places without rising, say the same words and bless the candidate in unison with the archbishop. The latter then returns to his kneeling posture, leaning forward over his faldstool, as the cantor resumes the litany with the petition *"That you may vouchsafe graciously to hear us."* [184]

Upon the conclusion of the litany, all rise. The archbishop ("the consecrator") stands before the altar, facing the choir, as the episcopal candidate kneels before him. A key rubric follows: "The consecrator opens the book of the Gospels, placing it upon the head and shoulders of him to be consecrated, and the two bishops support it, staying the book by its lower portion." [185] This visually impressive rite is ancient, appearing in a text of the late fifth century, the *Statuta ecclesiae antiqua*,

---

[181] Andrieu, *Pontifical romain au moyen-âge*, 3:381. This declaration first appears in the third recension of the Pontifical of the Roman Curia, the "gamma" recension, which is thought to date from the mid-thirteenth century; see Andrieu, *Pontifical romain au moyen-âge*, 2:358.

[182] Mohlberg, Eizenhöfer, and Siffrin, *Liber sacramentorum*, no. 766, p. 120.

[183] Andrieu, *Pontifical romain au moyen-âge*, 3:381.

[184] Ibid., 381–382. The complete texts of the individual litany petitions are taken from the subdeacons' ordination rite, ibid., 354. A twofold blessing of this nature, during the litany, is found in the twelfth-century Roman Pontifical; see ibid., 1:146. As early as the first half of the eighth century, Roman *Ordo* 34, a text of Rome, mentions a blessing of the episcopal candidate in connection with the litany, specifying that the pope is to bless the candidate following the litany's conclusion; see Andrieu, *Ordines Romani du haut moyen âge*, 3:613.

[185] Andrieu, *Pontifical romain au moyen-âge*, 3:382.

a collection of statutes thought to have been compiled at Marseilles, France, by the monk Gennadius: "When a bishop is ordained, two bishops should place and hold the book of the Gospels upon his neck."[186] The rite appears to stem from an even more ancient patristic exegesis of an Old Testament passage regarding the vestments for Aaron as high priest (Ex 28:9–10, 12): "And thou shalt take two onyx stones, and shalt grave on them the names of the children of Israel: Six names on one stone, and the other six on the other.... And thou shalt put them in both sides of the ephod.... And Aaron shall bear their names before the Lord upon both shoulders, for a remembrance." These two engraved stone tablets were mounted on the shoulder straps of the high priestly vestment, the ephod (which resembled a dalmatic, the deacon's vestment).[187] Alluding to this passage from Exodus, the third-century priest and martyr Saint Hippolytus of Rome describes Christ as "the Priest of God most high and invisible, who in the last times has taken upon himself the revelations and the truth, with the long robe [i.e., the ephod], bearing on his two shoulders the two Testaments—the 'Revelations' (the Law) [and] the 'Truth' (the Gospel)—so that he should appear the perfect Priest of the perfect Father".[188] Insofar as a bishop possesses the *plenitude* of the priesthood of Christ, the placement of a book of the Scriptures across the shoulders of the bishop-elect symbolically enacts Hippolytus' comparison, with the first portion of the book, representing the Old Testament, touching one shoulder, and the last portion, denoting the New Testament, touching the other.

The ninth-century liturgist Amalarius of Metz sees the imposition of the Gospel book as expressing the aspiration that God may "make firm" the Gospel in the heart of the new bishop, and as a reminder to the candidate that his episcopal consecration places him "yet more under the yoke of the Gospel" than he would otherwise have been.[189] In his *Rationale divinorum officiorum*, Durandus adds that this imposition of the Gospel book impresses upon the new bishop the "labor and obligation" that is now laid upon him, that is, to be "obedient to the Gospel" and "to carry the burden of the preaching of the Gospel".[190]

While the Gospel book is held in place on the candidate's shoulders, the archbishop "lays both hands upon his head, saying: *Receive*

---

[186] *Statuta ecclesiae antiqua*, canon 90, in C. Munier, ed., *Concilia Galliae, A. 314–A. 506*, CCSL 148 (Turnhout, Belgium: Brepols, 1963), 181.

[187] John Steinmueller and Kathryn Sullivan, R.S.C.J., eds., *Catholic Biblical Encyclopedia: Old Testament* (New York: Joseph F. Wagner, 1959), 324.

[188] Saint Hippolytus of Rome, *Benedictions of Moses*, "Levi", in Maurice Brière; Louis Mariès, S.J.; and B.-Ch. Mercier, O.S.B., eds., *Hippolyte de Rome sur les bénédictions d'Isaac, de Jacob et de Moïse*, Patrologia orientalis 27, fasc. 1–2 (Paris: Firmin-Didot, 1954), 144–145 (Armenian and Georgian texts with French translation).

[189] Amalarius of Metz, *Liber officialis*, bk. 2, chap. 12, no. 9, in Hanssens, *Amalarii episcopi: Opera liturgica omnia*, 2:235–236.

[190] Durandus, *Rationale* (CCCM 140), bk. 2, chap. 11, no. 8, p. 173.

the Holy Spirit."[191] As we have already seen in the rite of priestly ordination, the imposition of hands is an action dating back to the apostolic age; the accompanying formula, "*Receive the Holy Spirit*", comprising the words spoken by Christ as he conferred upon the Apostles the priestly power to absolve sins (Jn 20:22), was added to the hitherto-silent action by Durandus in his pontifical. Again, according to the solemn definition of Venerable Pope Pius XII, it is the imposition of hands, constituting "the matter and the sole matter" of the sacrament together with the essential words of the consecratory prayer recited at a later point in the episcopal ordination rite that actually confer the plenitude of holy orders, the episcopate.[192] The juxtaposition of the imposition of hands with the placing of the Gospel book on the episcopal candidate's shoulders dates back to the late fifth-century *Statuta ecclesiae antiqua*.[193] In both the *Statuta* and the Pontifical of Durandus, all of the other bishops present also impose hands upon the candidate (Pontifical: "And all the bishops do and say the same, so holding the book as the others successively").[194] In 1944, Pope Pius XII defined that the bishops who assist at an episcopal consecration, imposing hands and reciting the requisite prayers of the rite, must be considered "co-consecrators" who actually impart consecration together with the principal consecrating bishop.[195]

After all the bishops have imposed their hands upon the candidate, the archbishop kneels and prays: "*Listen favorably, O Lord, to our supplications and, with the horn of sacerdotal grace turned upon this your servant* [Name], *infuse into him the strength of your blessing. Through our Lord Jesus Christ . . .*"[196] In this prayer, traceable to the sixth-century Leonine Sacramentary of Rome,[197] the phrase "*horn of sacerdotal grace*" evokes the imagery of the horn of oil with which Samuel anointed David king of Israel and by which "the spirit of the Lord" came upon him (1 Kings 16:13).

Remaining on his knees, the archbishop now proceeds to the most important prayer of the episcopal consecration rite, which, like the consecratory prayer of priestly ordination, has the textual format of a Preface, preceded by the usual versicles and responses ("*The Lord be with you*"—"*And with your spirit*", etc.).[198] This consecratory prayer,

---

[191] Andrieu, *Pontifical romain au moyen-âge*, 3:382.

[192] Venerable Pius XII, *Sacramentum ordinis*, nos. 4–5, excerpted in Benedictine Monks of Solesmes, *Papal Teachings: Liturgy*, 310–311; Latin text in *Acta Apostolicae Sedis* 40 (1948): 6–7. Venerable Pope Pius XII defined the imposition of hands as "the matter and the sole matter" of the sacrament for all three degrees of holy orders: the episcopate, the priesthood, and the diaconate.

[193] Canon 90, in Munier, *Concilia Galliae*, 181.

[194] Andrieu, *Pontifical romain au moyen-âge*, 3:382.

[195] Venerable Pius XII, *Episcopalis consecrationis*, November 30, 1944, excerpted in Benedictine Monks of Solesmes, *Papal Teachings: Liturgy*, 297. For the official Latin text, see *Acta Apostolicae Sedis* 37 (1945): 132.

[196] Andrieu, *Pontifical romain au moyen-âge*, 3:382.

[197] Mohlberg, Eizenhöfer, and Siffrin, *Sacramentarium Veronense*, no. 946, p. 119.

[198] Andrieu, *Pontifical romain au moyen-âge*, 3:382–383.

dating back to the sixth-century Leonine Sacramentary of Rome,[199] constitutes the "form" of the sacrament for episcopal ordination, efficaciously imparting the sacrament together with the imposition of the consecrating bishop's hands preceding it.[200] Throughout the episcopal consecration prayer and the series of prayers and actions that follow it, the candidate remains on his knees with the Gospel book held upon his shoulders. Although the continuation of this posture after the imposition of hands is not explicitly mentioned in the Pontifical of Durandus, it is deducible from the rubrics of the twelfth-century Roman Pontifical, upon which that of Durandus is based. In fact, the twelfth-century Roman Pontifical,[201] the thirteenth-century Pontifical of the Roman Curia,[202] the 1595–1596 *Pontificale Romanum*,[203] and the fourteenth-century Pontifical of Mainz[204] all concur as to the moment when the Gospel book is removed—at the presentation of the Gospel book to the new bishop, which occurs somewhat later in the rite. For now, the candidate remains on his knees with the Gospel book astride his shoulders as the archbishop, with his hands folded before his chest, says the consecratory prayer, which is simultaneously recited in a lower voice by the two bishops holding the Gospel book.[205] In giving the text of this prayer below, we have set in bold print the particular words within the prayer that Venerable Pope Pius XII defined ex cathedra as essential to the valid ordination of a bishop:[206]

> *It is truly fitting and just, right and salutary, for us always and everywhere to give you thanks, holy Lord, Father almighty, eternal God, the Honor of all ranks that serve to your glory in sacred orders; O God, who instructing your servant Moses in the discourse of a secret, intimate friend, among other examples of heavenly worship, decreed also, concerning the form of sacerdotal apparel, that Aaron your elect be vested with mystical vesture during the holy rites, that the generations to come should receive a sense of understanding from the examples of former things, lest the learning of your doctrine should be wanting in any age; and whereas among the ancients the very form of these signs won reverence; among us, however, there were to be proofs of realities more certain than figurative allegories. For the garment of that earlier priesthood pertains to the adornment of our mind, and the distinction of vestments no longer commends to us the high priest's glory but the splendor of souls; for even those things that then pleased bodily vision called for those*

---

[199] Mohlberg, Eizenhöfer, and Siffrin, *Sacramentarium Veronense*, no. 947, p. 119.

[200] Venerable Pius XII, *Sacramentum ordinis*, no. 5, in Benedictine Monks of Solesmes, *Papal Teachings: Liturgy*, 311; Latin text in *Acta Apostolicae Sedis* 40 (1948): 7.

[201] Andrieu, *Pontifical romain au moyen-âge*, 1:150.

[202] Ibid., 2:363.

[203] Sodi and Triacca, *Pontificale Romanum: Editio princeps (1595–1596)*, 106 (original pagination).

[204] Martène, *De antiquis ecclesiae ritibus*, bk. 1, chap. 8, art. 11, ordo 16, 2:82.

[205] Andrieu, *Pontifical romain au moyen-âge*, 3:382–383.

[206] Venerable Pius XII, *Sacramentum ordinis*, no. 5, in Benedictine Monks of Solesmes, *Papal Teachings: Liturgy*, 311; Latin text in *Acta Apostolicae Sedis* 40 (1948): 7.

*things, rather, that were to be perceived in them. And therefore to this your servant, whom you have elected to the ministry of the supreme priesthood, may you grant this grace, we beseech you, O Lord, that everything that those robes in the brightness of gold, in the splendor of gems, and in the variety of manifold handiwork signified may shine forth in his actions and deeds. **Complete in your priest the summit of your mystery, and sanctify him, furnished with the ornaments of total glorification, in the dew of your heavenly unction.**[207]*

The archbishop now intones the Pentecost sequence, *Veni Sancte Spiritus* ("*Come, Holy Spirit*"), or, according to two variant manuscripts of Durandus' pontifical, the hymn *Veni Creator Spiritus*. As the sequence or hymn is continued, the archbishop rises and, using his right thumb, anoints with chrism the tonsure (shaved area) on the head of the new bishop, tracing the sign of the cross upon it (prior to the anointing there is tied around the perimeter of the new bishop's head a linen cloth twisted into a coil that serves to prevent the chrism from flowing downward onto his hair). As the archbishop applies the chrism, he says, "*May your head be anointed and consecrated with the celestial blessing in the pontifical order. In the name of the Fa + ther, and of the Son + , and of the Holy + Spirit.*" This formula is followed by the words "*Amen. Peace be with you. And with your spirit.*"[208] Although the Pontifical of Durandus does not indicate who is to say these concluding words, the tenth-century Romano-Germanic Pontifical, in which this formula first appears, identifies the "*Amen*" and the phrase "*And with your spirit*" as responses,[209] and hence they would have been said either by the new bishop or by the assisting clergy. The versicle "*Peace be with you*" was undoubtedly said by the consecrating bishop.[210]

Honorius of Autun (+c. 1135), in his *Gemma animae*, explains that just as on Pentecost Sunday "the Apostles were invisibly consecrated with oil by the Holy Spirit", so too are their successors fittingly anointed with sacred oil:

> Oil gives light to lamps and heals wounds. Thus the Holy Spirit gave the light of knowledge to the Apostles and has healed the wounds of sins. Therefore, bishops are anointed with oil, that they may be taught that they have received the Holy Spirit himself given to the Apostles, and that they should shine in life and doctrine before men and be diligent to heal them from their sins.[211]

---

[207] Andrieu, *Pontifical romain au moyen-âge*, 3:383. The full text of the prayer is here taken from the twelfth-century Roman Pontifical, ibid., 1:147.

[208] Ibid., 3:383.

[209] Vogel and Elze, *Pontifical romano-germanique*, 1:218.

[210] In the rubrics of his pontifical, Durandus mentions that in certain dioceses it was the custom for the other bishops present to replicate the anointing, just as they replicated the imposition of hands earlier; see Andrieu, *Pontifical romain au moyen-âge*, 3:383.

[211] Honorius of Autun, *Gemma animae*, bk. 1, chap. 189, PL 172, col. 602.

Gilbert of Tournai observes that just as Aaron was anointed by Moses
with a specially prepared oil of unction (Ex 30:23–25, 30, 31–32),
similarly chrism, the most sacred of Christian holy oils, is used for
the anointing of a new bishop.[212] According to Amalarius of Metz,
the bishop is anointed on the head to signify that just as Christ is
Head of the Church, so too a bishop is rendered through the grace
of his episcopal consecration and anointing head of the particular
diocese entrusted to him. And just as Christ governs and intercedes
for the whole Church, so also the bishop is charged with governing
and interceding for his own diocese.[213] Amalarius' ninth-century discussion of this subject, written about the year 825, constitutes the
earliest direct and explicit reference to the practice of anointing the
head of a new bishop. Later in the ninth century, the French bishop
Hincmar of Reims relates that at his own consecration in 845 the
consecrating bishop anointed him on the top of his head, tracing a
cross there with his right thumb after having dipped it in a vessel of
chrism. The cross was traced repeatedly in the course of the prayer
of episcopal consecration, "when they shall have come to the places
at which crosses have been marked";[214] Hincmar thereby indicates
the presence of cross symbols in the consecratory prayer text. This
latter detail points to the likely existence of the head unction a century earlier, for the text of the episcopal consecration prayer in the
eighth-century *Hadrianum* redaction of Rome's Gregorian Sacramentary contains cross symbols at three places in a portion of the prayer
that speaks of anointing.[215]

Although the linen cloth tied round about the new bishop's head is
intended to impede the downward flow of the chrism, the interior
graces represented by the chrism are intended to flow down upon his
entire soul and body. This imagery is beautifully expressed in a prayer
of the consecration rite that actually predates the earliest known references to the anointing of a newly ordained bishop's head: the text
appears originally in the sixth-century Leonine Sacramentary of Rome
as a second part of the earlier-cited episcopal consecration prayer.[216]
The Pontifical of Durandus utilizes a considerably expanded form of
the prayer traceable to the Frankish *Missale Francorum* of the seventh
to the eighth century.[217] From the tenth century onward, this oration
was used as a sequel to the anointing of the head.[218] In the Pontifical
of Durandus, the archbishop recites this prayer after the anointing and

[212] Gilbert of Tournai, *Tractatus de officio episcopi*, chap. 34, in de la Bigne, *Maxima bibliotheca veterum patrum*, 25:414.

[213] Amalarius of Metz, *Liber officialis*, bk. 2, chap. 14, nos. 6–7, in Hanssens, *Amalarii
episcopi: Opera liturgica omnia*, 2:234–235.

[214] Hincmar of Reims, *Epistle 29*, PL 126, col. 188.

[215] Deshusses, *Sacramentaire grégorien*, no. 23b, 1:93–94.

[216] Mohlberg, Eizenhöfer, and Siffrin, *Sacramentarium Veronense*, no. 947, pp. 119–120.

[217] Mohlberg, *Missale Francorum*, no. 40, p. 13.

[218] Vogel and Elze, *Pontifical romano-germanique*, 1:218–219.

the completion of the sequence *Veni Sancte Spiritus* (or after the hymn *Veni Creator Spiritus*):

> *May this [unction], O Lord, flow abundantly upon his head; may it run down to the edges of his face; may it descend upon the extremities of his whole body, that the power of your Spirit may both replenish his interior and cover round about his exterior. May there abound in him constancy of faith, purity of love, uprightness of peace. By your gift may his feet be beautiful unto preaching peace, unto preaching your good tidings. Give him, O Lord, the ministry of reconciliation in word and in deeds, in the power of signs and wonders. May his speech and preaching be not in eloquent words of human wisdom but with the evidence of the Spirit and of virtue. Give him, O Lord, the keys of the kingdom of Heaven, that he may employ, not glory in, the authority that you give for edification, not for destruction. May whatever he shall bind upon earth be bound also in Heaven and whatever he shall loose upon earth be loosed also in Heaven. Whose sins he shall withhold, may they be withheld, and whose sins he shall forgive, may you forgive. May he who shall bless him be filled with blessings and he who shall reproach him be reproached. May he be a faithful and prudent servant whom you have set, O Lord, over your household, that he may give them food in the opportune season [cf. Mt 24:45], and present every man perfect [cf. Col 1:28]. May he be diligent in solicitude, fervent in spirit. May he detest pride; may he love humility and never forsake it, overcome neither by praises nor by fear. May he not suppose the light darkness nor the darkness light. May he not call evil good nor good evil. May he be a debtor to the wise and not the foolish, that he may obtain fruit from the Source of all things. May you give him, Lord, the episcopal chair, to govern your Church and all the people. May you be to him authority; may you be to him strength; may you be to him steadfastness. May you multiply your blessing and grace upon him, that ever able by your bounty to beseech your mercy, he may be ever able by your grace to be devout. Through our Lord . . .*[219]

Following this prayer, the archbishop intones an antiphon that continues the motif of the anointing with chrism as a pouring forth of grace upon the entire soul and body of the new bishop: "*Like the precious ointment on the head, which ran down upon the beard, the beard of Aaron, which ran down to the hem of his garment, the Lord has commanded a blessing forever.*"[220] According to Gilbert of Tournai, this antiphon, from verses 2 and 3 of Psalm 132, manifests that, just as the oil with which Aaron was anointed upon his head ran down upon his beard and onward to the hem of his vestment, so too the grace conferred

---

[219] Andrieu, *Pontifical romain au moyen-âge*, 3:384 (incipit only); the remainder of the text is supplied from Vogel and Elze, *Pontifical romano-germanique*, 1:218–219.

[220] Andrieu, *Pontifical romain au moyen-âge*, 3:384. The use of this antiphon, *Unguentum in capite*, for episcopal consecration rites is traceable to the Antiphonary of Senlis (France, c. 880), in which it appears as the Communion chant in one of three different series of chants for episcopal consecration Masses; see Hésbert, *Antiphonale missarum sextuplex*, 169.

upon the new bishop through the anointing of his head flows down upon those under his authority, "first to his priests, then to the ill".[221] In the Pontifical of Durandus, this antiphon accompanies the recitation of Psalm 132 (*"Behold how good and how pleasant it is for brethren to dwell together in unity ..."*). After beginning the antiphon, the archbishop anoints with chrism the hands (held open, side by side) of the new bishop[222] by tracing across them transversely a diagonal sign of the cross (the cross of Saint Andrew) in the same manner as in priestly ordination. But whereas for priests the oil of catechumens is used to anoint the hands, for a bishop chrism is used instead.[223] During the anointing, the archbishop says:

> *May the God and Father of our Lord Jesus Christ, who willed you to be elevated to the dignity of the episcopate, himself anoint you with chrism and the liquid of mystical firstfruits and make you fruitful with the fullness of spiritual benediction, that whatever you shall bless may be blessed and whatever you shall sanctify may be sanctified, and the imposition of your consecrated hand or thumb may contribute to salvation. Through the same Jesus Christ ... Amen.*[224]

Following the completion of the anointing, both the archbishop and the new bishop wash the oil from their hands. The crosier for the new bishop is now brought by an acolyte to the archbishop to be blessed by him.[225] The bishop's use of a staff of authority, the crosier, is traceable to the fourth century,[226] although it can reasonably be argued that it dates back even further if one identifies it, as Durandus does, with the staff that Christ enjoined the Apostles to take with them when he sent them forth two by two (Mk 6:7–8).[227] The conferral of the crosier upon new bishops had arisen in the episcopal consecration rites of Spain by the first half of the seventh century, as attested by the Fourth Council of Toledo (633)[228] and Saint Isidore of Seville (+636);[229] by the mid-ninth century, this custom had appeared in France.[230]

---

[221] Gilbert of Tournai, *Tractatus de officio episcopi*, chap. 34, in de la Bigne, *Maxima bibliotheca veterum patrum*, 25:414.

[222] The anointing of a new bishop's hands is first found in the late eighth-century Angoulême Sacramentary, a Frankish adaptation of Rome's Gelasian Sacramentary (Saint-Roch, *Liber sacramentorum Engolismensis*, no. 2107, p. 325).

[223] Andrieu, *Pontifical romain au moyen-âge*, 3:384.

[224] Ibid., 385. This prayer first appears in the tenth-century Romano-Germanic Pontifical; see Vogel and Elze, *Pontifical romano-germanique*, 1:220.

[225] Andrieu, *Pontifical romain au moyen-âge*, 3:385.

[226] Polycarp Rado, O.S.B., *Enchiridion liturgicum* (Rome: Herder, 1961), 2:1468.

[227] Durandus, *Rationale* (CCCM 140), bk. 3, chap. 15, no. 1, pp. 214–215.

[228] Fourth Council of Toledo, canon 28, PL 84, col. 375.

[229] Saint Isidore of Seville, *De ecclesiasticis officiis*, bk. 2, chap. 5, no. 12, in Christopher M. Lawson, ed., *Sancti Isidori episcopi Hispalensis: De ecclesiasticis officiis*, CCSL 113 (Turnhout, Belgium: Brepols, 1989), 60.

[230] In a letter, Hincmar of Reims speaks of being given a crosier at his episcopal consecration in 845 (*Epistle 29*, PL 126, col. 188).

Durandus explains the crosier as comparable to the rod of Moses; for just as the latter represented the mission conferred upon Moses by God, so the crosier represents the doctrinal and disciplinary authority conferred upon a bishop by God, with which he is enabled to support the weak, sustain those wavering in their faith, and lead back those who have strayed from the flock.[231] Durandus is referring to the rod that Moses had with him when God revealed himself in the burning bush on Mount Sinai (Ex 4:2–4), the rod that God made miraculous and commanded Moses to take to Egypt: "And take this rod in thy hand, wherewith thou shalt do the signs" (Ex 4:17). Hence Moses returned to Egypt "carrying the rod of God in his hand" (Ex 4:20). The archbishop blesses the crosier with these words composed by Durandus for his pontifical: "*O God, Supporter of human weakness, bless + this crosier, and what is outwardly signified in it may it produce inwardly in the actions of this your servant, by the clemency of your mercy. Through Christ . . .*" (response: "*Amen*").[232] The archbishop then presents the crosier to the new bishop (who remains kneeling), saying: "*Receive the staff of the pastoral office; and may you be mercifully vehement in correcting vices, holding to judgment without anger, persuading the souls of hearers in fostering virtues, not neglecting censure in the tranquillity of sternness*" (response: "*Amen*").[233] The curved top end of the crosier, forming a hook in imitation of a shepherd's crook, is explained by Durandus as symbolizing the bishop's mission of drawing back to penitence those who have gone astray, just as a shepherd uses his staff to draw back the straying feet of the animals he is herding.[234]

The blessing and conferral of the episcopal ring now follow. The bestowal of a ring during the episcopal consecration rite can be traced back to the first half of the seventh century, when it is mentioned in Spain by both the Fourth Council of Toledo (633) and Saint Isidore of Seville (+636).[235] By the early tenth century, the episcopal ring had begun to take on the beautiful symbolism of nuptial imagery.[236] As the twelfth century liturgist Honorius of Autun explains, "The

---

[231] Durandus, *Rationale* (CCCM 140), bk. 3, chap. 15, nos. 1–2, pp. 214–215; see also bk. 1, chap. 8, no. 21, p. 107.

[232] Andrieu, *Pontifical romain au moyen-âge*, 3:385.

[233] Ibid. (incipit only). This formula first appears in the tenth-century Romano-Germanic Pontifical, from which the remainder of the text is here supplied, as given in Vogel and Elze, *Pontifical romano-germanique*, 1:222.

[234] Durandus, *Rationale* (CCCM 140), bk. 3, chap. 15, nos. 1–2, p. 215.

[235] Fourth Council of Toledo (633), canon 28, PL 84, col. 375; Saint Isidore of Seville, *De ecclesiasticis officiis*, bk. 2, chap. 5, no. 12, in Lawson, *Sancti Isidori episcopi Hispalensis: De ecclesiasticis officiis*, 60.

[236] See the texts for presenting and blessing the episcopal ring from the Pontifical of Aurillac (France), a liturgical book dating from the late ninth to the early tenth century, quoted in Antonio Santantoni, *L'ordinazione episcopale: Storia e teologia dei riti dell'ordinazione nelle antiche liturgie dell'occidente*, Studia Anselmiana 69, Analecta liturgica 2 (Rome: Editrice Anselmiana, 1976), 277.

bishop consequently bears a ring, that he may perceive himself the bridegroom of the Church, and, if it will have been necessary, lay down his life for her, like Christ." [237] In the application of this nuptial analogy to bishops, the bishop is seen particularly as the bridegroom of his own diocese.[238] After blessing the ring,[239] the archbishop puts it on the ring finger of the right hand of the new bishop; the particular hand and finger are not specified in the Pontifical of Durandus, but other sources, beginning with the testimony of Bishop Hincmar of Reims, who mentions imposition on the right hand, indicate a consistent tradition in this regard from the ninth century onward.[240] In giving the ring, the archbishop says, *"Receive the ring, that is, the sign of faithfulness, that you may preserve your Bride, namely the holy Church of God, spotless, adorned with unblemished faith"* (response: *"Amen"*).[241]

The Gospel book that was earlier laid open upon the shoulders of the new bishop, having been removed from his shoulders at or before this point,[242] is now presented to him by the archbishop as a sign of the new bishop's duty to instruct his flock in the faith. In giving the Gospel book, the archbishop says: *"Receive the Gospel, and go, preach to the people entrusted to you. For God has power to increase his grace unto you. Who lives and reigns. . . .* (response: *"Amen"*).[243] In some dioceses, according to Durandus, it was customary for the consecrating bishop to open the Gospel book held by the new bishop in the hope that the Scripture passage randomly selected in this manner might have a providential meaning for the new bishop.[244]

---

[237] Honorius of Autun, *Gemma animae*, bk. 1, chap. 216, PL 172, col. 609.

[238] Santantoni, *Ordinazione episcopale*, 162.

[239] Text of blessing: *"Creator and Defender of mankind, Giver of spiritual grace, Bestower of eternal salvation, you, O Lord, send out your bless + ing upon this ring, that he who shall go about adorned with this sacrosanct sign of faith, in the strength of heavenly protection, may advance himself to eternal salvation. Through Christ . . ."* (Andrieu, *Pontifical romain au moyen-âge*, 3:385–386). This prayer is first found (with minor differences) in the tenth-century Romano-Germanic Pontifical; see Vogel and Elze, *Pontifical romano-germanique*, 1:220–221.

[240] See Hincmar of Reims, *Epistle 29*, PL 126, col. 188; a rubric in the marriage rite of the twelfth-century pontifical of Lyre, France, in Martène, *De antiquis ecclesiae ritibus*, bk. 1, chap. 9, art. 5, *ordo* 3, 2:128; and the 1595–1596 *Pontificale Romanum*, in Sodi and Triacca, *Pontificale Romanum: Editio princeps (1595–1596)*, 105 (original pagination).

[241] Andrieu, *Pontifical romain au moyen-âge*, 3:386. This formula is first found in the late tenth-century Roman *Ordo* 35B of Italy; see Andrieu, *Ordines Romani du haut moyen âge*, 4:108.

[242] The twelfth-century Roman Pontifical, the thirteenth-century Pontifical of the Roman Curia, the fourteenth-century Pontifical of Mainz, and the 1595–1596 *Pontificale Romanum* all explicitly state that the book is removed from the shoulders immediately before it is presented to the new bishop, but the Pontifical of Durandus is silent on this point. See p. 189 of the present chapter.

[243] Andrieu, *Pontifical romain au moyen-âge*, 3:386 (incipit only); the remainder of the text is supplied ibid., 2:363. This prayer is traceable to a marginal notation in one manuscript of the tenth-century Romano-Germanic Pontifical; see Vogel and Elze, *Pontifical romano-germanique*, 1:222, footnote.

[244] Andrieu, *Pontifical romain au moyen-âge*, 3:386.

The new bishop now gives all the other bishops the sign of peace, beginning with the archbishop.[245] Then the *Alleluia* and its accompanying verse, which precede the Gospel of the episcopal consecration Mass, are sung. The *Alleluia* verse is taken from Psalm 44 (verse 3): "*Grace is poured abroad in thy lips; therefore hath God blessed thee for ever.*" During Lent, this is replaced by a Tract versicle from Psalm 20 (verses 3, 4): "*Thou hast given him his heart's desire, O Lord, and hast not withholden from him the will of his lips; thou hast set on his head a crown of precious stones.*"[246] During the *Alleluia* or Tract, the new bishop is led by the archdeacon into the vestibule or the sacristy, where his head is washed to remove the chrism from the earlier anointing. He then returns and takes his place with the other bishops. The Gospel reading that follows recounts Christ's sending forth of the twelve Apostles two by two to preach, heal the sick, and expel demons (Mk 6:6–13).[247]

At the Offertory, the new bishop presents as gifts two unconsecrated hosts, two amphoras of wine, and two lit candles.[248] This custom first appears, with certain differences, in the twelfth-century Roman Pontifical. The latter specifies that the newly consecrated bishop is to hold two lit candles, one in each hand, as the Gospel of the Mass is read (Mk 6:6–13) and as the Nicene Creed is chanted afterward. Then, for the Offertory, the new bishop carries to the archbishop the two lit candles, along with two unconsecrated hosts within a small cloth placed across his arms; an acolyte accompanying him carries a flask of wine, holding it over the two hosts as they proceed together. Following the presentation of these Offertory gifts, the new bishop joins the archbishop at the altar to concelebrate the Mass with him.[249] A comparable presentation of gifts is found in the priestly ordination Mass rubrics of this same twelfth-century pontifical[250] and the thirteenth-century Pontifical of the Roman Curia.[251] The use of two unconsecrated hosts (and in Durandus' pontifical, two flasks of wine) can be explained by the concelebration of the two bishops. The two candles *may* be inspired by the above-mentioned Gospel of the episcopal consecration Mass, which speaks of Christ sending forth his Apostles "two by two"

---

[245] Ibid. The exchange of a sign of peace following episcopal consecration is first found in Roman *Ordo* 34, from the first half of the eighth century; see Andrieu, *Ordines Romani du haut moyen âge*, 3:613.

[246] Andrieu, *Pontifical romain au moyen-âge*, 3:386. The *Alleluia* verse *Diffusa est* is first utilized as an episcopal consecration Mass text in the tenth-century Romano-Germanic Pontifical; the Tract *Desiderium anime* is traceable as an episcopal consecration Mass text to the Antiphonary of Senlis (France, c. 880). See respectively Vogel and Elze, *Pontifical romano-germanique*, 1:223, and Hésbert, *Antiphonale missarum sextuplex*, 171.

[247] Andrieu, *Pontifical romain au moyen-âge*, 3:387. This lection is first specified for the episcopal consecration Mass in the tenth-century Romano-Germanic Pontifical; see Vogel and Elze, *Pontifical romano-germanique*, 1:224.

[248] Andrieu, *Pontifical romain au moyen-âge*, 3:387.

[249] Ibid., 1:150–151.

[250] Ibid., 137.

[251] Ibid., 2:349.

(Mk 6:7), with the two candles thereby signifying that the new bishop has now joined the archbishop in apostolic service to Christ.

The Offertory antiphon, like most of the chants for the episcopal ordination Mass, is traceable to the late ninth century.[252] The Secret (known as the "Prayer over the Gifts" in the *Novus ordo* Mass of Pope Paul VI) at the conclusion of the Offertory is that assigned to the particular feast day of the liturgical calendar, to which is added a Secret proper to the episcopal consecration Mass. The latter oration is an ancient prayer ultimately derived from the sixth-century Leonine Sacramentary of Rome:[253] "*Accept, O Lord, the gifts that we offer you for this your servant* [the new bishop], *that you may mercifully preserve your gifts in the same. Through ...*" In reciting the Secret together with the archbishop, the new bishop, at the words "*this your servant*", instead refers to himself as "*me your pitiable servant*".[254] During the Roman Canon, the new bishop stands at the right side of the altar as a concelebrant to the archbishop, making the required signs in unison with him.[255] In the text of the Canon, a petition for the new bishop is inserted, an expanded version of the Canon insertion for episcopal consecration Masses first found in the Leonine Sacramentary (inserted after the words "*Therefore, this oblation of our service, as also of all your family*", that is, after "*Hanc igitur oblationem servitutis nostrae, sed et cunctae familiae tuae*").[256]

Following the Canon and the Our Father, immediately before the *Agnus Dei*, the deacon says to the congregation, "*Humble yourselves for a blessing*"; the archbishop now imparts a solemn blessing:

> *O God, to whom pertains the excellence of the priesthood, the victory of reigning, the discipline of the people, who on account of this put bishops in charge, that the clergy may have vigilance, the Church reverence, the faithful people protection, the poor nourishment: vouchsafe to gladden us in your celestial font, that the people may be able to draw water, your priest dispensing.* Response: *Amen.* [Archbishop:] *Grant him a norm of acting, a boldness of speaking, a temperance of living, a doctrine of admonishing.* Response: *Amen.* [Archbishop:] *And with your bishop employing zeal, approved by your people, may the shepherd be worthy to obtain grace, his flock healing.* [Response:] *Amen.* [Archbishop:] *Which may he himself vouchsafe to grant,*

---

[252] The Offertory *Benedic anima* is traceable as an episcopal consecration Mass text to the Antiphonary of Senlis (France, c. 880); see Hésbert, *Antiphonale missarum sextuplex*, 171.

[253] Mohlberg, Eizenhöfer, and Siffrin, *Sacramentarium Veronense*, no. 943, p. 119.

[254] Andrieu, *Pontifical romain au moyen-âge*, 3:387.

[255] Ibid.

[256] Text of insertion in the Pontifical of Durandus: "*Therefore, this oblation of our service, as also of all your family, which we offer to you also for this your servant, whom you have deemed worthy to advance to the order of the episcopate, we beseech you, O Lord, that appeased, you may accept and mercifully preserve in him your gifts, that what he has obtained by your divine bounty he may carry out in heavenly accomplishments; and may you order our days, etc.*" (ibid., 388). For the Leonine Sacramentary's version of this insertion, see Mohlberg, Eizenhöfer, and Siffrin, *Sacramentarium Veronense*, no. 944, p. 119.

whose government and dominion endure without end, unto ages of ages. Response: Amen. [Archbishop:] *And may the blessing of almighty God the Fa + ther, and the Son + , and the Holy + Spirit, descend upon you and remain always with you. Response: Amen.*[257]

After receiving Holy Communion, the archbishop administers the Sacrament (under the species of bread) to the new bishop (who receives standing at the side of the altar). The deacon then presents the chalice to the new bishop, who receives the Precious Blood from it.[258]

Following Holy Communion, an acolyte brings the miter for the new bishop to the archbishop, who now blesses it.[259] The earliest evidence for the use of the miter as one of the insignia of the episcopate dates from the eleventh century.[260] The conferral of the miter during the episcopal consecration rite is first mentioned in the twelfth-century Roman Pontifical.[261] However, it is Durandus who in the prayer he composed for the imposition of the miter imparts to this head vesture a rich symbolism drawn from the miter worn by the high priest Aaron (Ex 29:9; 39:26), likening the miter's twin peaks to the radiant light—"horns" of light, according to the Latin Vulgate text—that emanated from Moses' face after he had conversed with God on Mount Sinai (Ex 34:29–30, 35). We see these shafts of light depicted as two horns atop the head of Moses in the renowned statue of the patriarch sculpted by Michelangelo. Durandus adroitly makes of the miter a symbol of the bishop's role as a champion of truth called to do battle with the enemies of truth:

> *We place, O Lord, upon the head of this bishop and champion the helmet of your fortification and salvation, that with an honored countenance and a head armed with the horns of each Testament he may appear fearsome to the adversaries of truth and appear their mighty enemy, you bestowing upon him your grace, who adorned the face of your servant Moses, endowed by the company of your discourse with the horns of your most clear light and truth, and who ordered a tiara to be placed + upon the head of Aaron your high priest. Through Christ our Lord. Amen.*[262]

---

[257] Andrieu, *Pontifical romain au moyen-âge*, 3:388. This text, with the exception of the concluding words of blessing, is evidently an original composition of Durandus. The concluding formula ("*And may the blessing of almighty God ...*") is first found in the tenth-century Romano-Germanic Pontifical; see Vogel and Elze, *Pontifical romano-germanique*, 1:291. Prior to the tenth century, a precursor to this blessing formula, albeit with significant verbal differences, can be found in Saint Benedict of Aniane's early ninth-century Frankish adaptation of the Gregorian Sacramentary of Rome; see Deshusses, *Sacramentaire grégorien*, no. 1738, 1:576 (conclusion of prayer).

[258] Andrieu, *Pontifical romain au moyen-âge*, 3:388–389.

[259] Text of blessing: "*Lord God, Father almighty, whose goodness is renowned and whose power is immeasurable, by whom every excellent thing is given and every gift and ornament of total beauty is perfected, vouchsafe to bless + and sancti + fy this miter to be placed upon the head of this bishop your servant. Through Christ ...*" (ibid., 389).

[260] Santantoni, *Ordinazione episcopale*, 177–178.

[261] Andrieu, *Pontifical romain au moyen-âge*, 1:152.

[262] Ibid., 3:389.

The Communion antiphon is then recited, a text from the Scriptures expressing the need for priestly vocations (Mt 9:37–38): "*The harvest indeed is great, but the labourers are few; pray ye therefore the Lord of the harvest, that he send forth labourers into his harvest.*"[263] The Postcommunion prayer follows, beginning with the Postcommunion oration for the particular feast day, to which is added a Postcommunion prayer proper to the episcopal consecration Mass and traceable to the seventh-century Gelasian Sacramentary of Rome.[264]

The use of gloves as an episcopal vestment is thought to have originated in France during the ninth century.[265] The earliest reference to gloves in an episcopal consecration rite appears in the tenth-century Romano-Germanic Pontifical, which provides a prayer for conferring gloves upon the episcopal candidate as he is vested in preparation for his consecration.[266] In the Pontifical of Durandus, the imposition of the gloves is placed at the end of the consecration liturgy, where it is given a greater significance with special prayers composed by Durandus himself. After the concluding words of the Mass, "*Ite, missa est*" ("*Go, it is ended*") or "*Benedicamus Domino*" ("*Let us bless the Lord*"), have been said, but before the final blessing, an acolyte brings the gloves for the new bishop to the archbishop, who blesses them thus:

> *O omnipotent Creator, who have given man fashioned to your image hands endowed with the fingers of discernment, the organ, as it were, of judgment, for laboring virtuously, which you have commanded to be cut off without sin* [cf. Mt 5:30; 18:8], *that the soul may be worthily upheld in them* [cf. Ps 118:109] *and your mysteries worthily celebrated in them: vouchsafe to bless +* *and sancti + fy these coverings of the hands, that your mercy may furnish cleanliness of both heart and deed to whoever of your sacred ministers, the bishops, shall desire to cover his hands in them with humility. Through Christ our Lord. Amen.*[267]

After the archbishop sprinkles the gloves with holy water, he (or the acolyte) puts the gloves onto the hands of the new bishop. The words accompanying this action, composed by Durandus, utilize the Genesis account of Rebecca covering the hands of her son Jacob with animal skins, that he might assume the identity of his older brother, Esau,

---

[263] Ibid. The Communion chant *Messis quidem multa* is traceable as an episcopal consecration Mass text to the Antiphonary of Senlis (France, c. 880); see Hésbert, *Antiphonale missarum sextuplex*, 171.

[264] Text of the episcopal consecration Postcommunion prayer in the Pontifical of Durandus: "*We beseech you, O Lord, to work in us the full remedy of your mercy; and mercifully perfect us to be of such kind, and so sustain us, that we may be worthy to be pleasing to you in all things. Through . . .*" (Andrieu, *Pontifical romain au moyen-âge*, 3:390). For the earliest version of this prayer found in the Gelasian Sacramentary, see Mohlberg, Eizenhöfer, and Siffrin, *Liber sacramentorum*, no. 773, p. 122.

[265] Rado, *Enchiridion liturgicum*, 2:1475.

[266] Vogel and Elze, *Pontifical romano-germanique*, 1:214.

[267] Andrieu, *Pontifical romain au moyen-âge*, 3:390.

and thereby obtain in Esau's place the blessing of his blind father, Isaac, after offering him a dish of meat (Gen 27:1–29). The incident has traditionally been interpreted as a prefiguration of how those redeemed by Christ, having put on Christ (Gal 3:27) by their baptism, find favor with the heavenly Father. But here the identification of the bishop as an *alter Christus* is evoked in casting the gloves as symbolic of the bishop putting on the priestly identity of Christ (here referred to as *"the New Man ... from Heaven"* [see 1 Cor 15:47 and Eph 2:15]), offering the heavenly *"food and drink"* of the Eucharist as an acceptable sacrifice to the Father and thereby obtaining the Father's blessing:

> *Encompass, O Lord, the hands of this your minister in the cleanliness of the New Man who descended from Heaven, that just as your chosen one Jacob, with his hands covered by the pelts of young goats, obtained the paternal blessing with the food and drink most acceptably offered to his father, so also may he, by the saving sacrifice offered through his hands, merit to obtain the blessing of your grace. Through our Lord Jesus Christ your Son, who in the likeness of our sinful flesh offered his very self + to you for us. Response: Amen.*[268]

The concept of ceremonially enthroning a new bishop upon his *cathedra*, the chair that represents his office, is found by the late fourth century in the *Apostolic Constitutions*, a document thought to reflect the practices of Christian Syria.[269] In the episcopal consecration rite of Roman *Ordo* 34, a Roman liturgical text from the first half of the eighth century, the newly consecrated bishop is directed to take the seat of honor among his fellow bishops.[270] In the ninth century, the French bishop Hincmar of Reims relates that at the conclusion of the episcopal consecration Mass the new bishop is led to his own cathedral church to be enthroned upon his *cathedra*.[271] According to the Pontifical of Durandus, the enthronement takes place after the imposition of the gloves. The archbishop leads the new bishop to the episcopal throne, taking his right hand while another bishop takes his left hand. After the new bishop is seated on the *cathedra*, the archbishop, standing before him, intones the hymn of thanksgiving, *Te Deum*. As the schola of choristers continues the chant, the archbishop goes before the altar and remains there for the rest of the hymn. An antiphon from Psalm 88 follows,[272] after which the archbishop prays

---

[268] Ibid.

[269] *Apostolic Constitutions*, bk. 8, chap. 5, in Francis Xavier Funk, ed., *Didascalia et Constitutiones apostolorum*, vol. 1 (Paderborn, Germany: Libraria Ferdinandi Schoeningh, 1905), 476–477 (Greek and Latin texts).

[270] Andrieu, *Ordines Romani du haut moyen âge*, 3:613.

[271] Hincmar of Reims, *Epistle 29*, PL 126, col. 188.

[272] Text of antiphon *Firmetur manus* (Ps 88:14–15): "Let thy hand be strengthened, and thy right hand exalted; justice and judgment are the preparation of thy throne. Glory be ..." (Andrieu, *Pontifical romain au moyen-âge*, 3:391).

before the altar, utilizing an oration of ninth-century origin:[273] "*O God, Shepherd and Ruler of all the faithful, look favorably upon this your servant, whom you have willed to govern your Church; grant him, we beseech you, to do good by word and example to those whom he governs, that he together with the flock entrusted to him may attain to life eternal. Through Christ ...*" (response: "*Amen*").[274] The new bishop now imparts his first episcopal blessing:

> And then the consecrated one himself, standing, blesses solemnly the clergy and the people, saying in a high voice: Verse: *May the name of the Lord be blessed.* And saying this, he traces the sign of the cross with the thumb of his right hand upon his chest. Response: *Now and forever.* Verse: *Our help is in the name of the Lord.* And saying this, he makes the sign of the cross with two fingers before his face. Response: *Who made Heaven and earth.* [Consecrated one:] *May almighty God bless you, the Fa + ther, and the Son + , and the Holy + Spirit.* And saying this, he blesses the people on all sides.[275]

The Gospel book having been set upon the altar, the new bishop now approaches the altar, where he takes hold of the book with both hands to make a pledge of fidelity to the pope and to the archbishop, a pledge of obedience that he reads from a handwritten copy held or laid over the Gospel book. Ultimately descended from the promise of obedience given at Rome by the great archbishop and missionary of Germany Saint Boniface during his episcopal consecration in 722,[276] Durandus' text is an expanded variant of the pledge taken by new patriarchs of Jerusalem as found in the twelfth-century *Cartulaire* of the Church of the Holy Sepulcher[277] and is somewhat similar to the new bishops' pledge given in two twelfth-century Roman sources, the Roman Pontifical[278] and the *Liber censuum* (c. 1192).[279] Among other modifications, Durandus added to the wording an explicit promise of ecclesial obedience. Here again, as with the examination of the episcopal candidate at the outset of the consecration rite, Durandus inserts into the text the name of the French see of Bourges, which possessed primatial jurisdiction over his own see of Mende:

---

[273] This prayer is first found in the ninth-century French Sacramentary of Noyon; see Jean Deshusses, ed., *Le sacramentaire grégorien: Ses principales formes d'après les plus anciens manuscrits*, vol. 2, SF 24 (Fribourg, Switzerland: Editions Universitaires Fribourg, 1979), no. 1992, p. 69.

[274] Andrieu, *Pontifical romain au moyen-âge*, 3:391.

[275] Ibid.

[276] *Juramentum, quo s. Bonifacius se Gregorio II papae astrinxit*, PL 89, cols. 803–804.

[277] *Cartulaire de l'église du Saint Sepulcre*, no. 152, PL 155, col. 1237.

[278] Twelfth-century Roman Pontifical, in Andrieu, *Pontifical romain au moyen-âge*, 1:290–291.

[279] Text in Paul Fabre and Louis Duchesne, eds., *Le Liber censuum de l'église romaine*, vol. 1, fasc. 3, Bibliothèque des écoles françaises d'Athènes et de Rome, 2nd series, Registres des papes du XIIIᵉ siècle, 6 (Paris: Fontemoing, 1902), no. 147, p. 416.

I [Name], *the named bishop of* [Name of see], *promise in the sight of almighty God and of all the Church that from this hour, in the future, I shall be perpetually faithful and obedient to blessed* [Name of pope] *and to the holy Church of Bourges and to you my lord* [Name], *by the grace of God archbishop of the same Church, and to your successors entering canonically, as has been instituted by our holy fathers and observed by my predecessors, and as the ecclesiastical authority, and in particular that of the Roman pontiffs, recommends. I shall not take part in any deliberation or plot or misdeed to let you destroy life or limb or extort by evil fraud. I shall make known the counsel that you are going to entrust to me by yourself or by letters or by messenger, I knowing of none to your damnation. Summoned to a synod, I shall come, unless I will have been impeded by a canonical impediment. I shall honorably treat you and also your messengers and those of the Church of Bourges, whom I shall have recognized to be trustworthy, and shall assist them in their needs in proceeding, remaining, and returning. I shall certainly neither sell nor give out at my table possessions pertaining to the episcopate, nor shall I give them anew in fief or transfer them in any way against the law or custom of my church, unadvised by you or your successors. So help me God and these holy Gospels of God, with my seal hung, those present corroborating the aforesaid.*[280]

The rubrics of Durandus specifying that the pledge be in the new bishop's own handwriting and that it should be placed or held on or over the altar (specifically on or over the Gospel book upon the altar) are ultimately derived from the manner of Saint Boniface's pledge in 722, written in his own hand and delivered on the altar of the Basilica of Saint Peter. Boniface in his promise states that he has placed his pledge "over the most sacred body of Saint Peter",[281] that is, upon the altar over Saint Peter's tomb; thus the placement of a new bishop's handwritten promise on or over the high altar of the church where he is consecrated can be seen as a symbolic placement of his pledge over the body of Saint Peter, symbolizing his fidelity to the papacy.

At the end of the consecration rite, the *pallium* (when it has been granted to the new bishop by the Holy See) is presented to the new bishop by an archpriest of the Vatican.[282] Datable to the fourth century, this vestment of white wool, belonging by right to the popes in virtue of their Petrine office, has also been conferred by them as a privilege upon chosen prelates, particularly archbishops, to signify the plenitude of the episcopal office.[283] Over the centuries, the form of the pallium has varied widely; in the twelfth century (according to Pope Innocent III) it took the form of a narrow white cloth that circled the shoulders like a broad collar, with its two ends hanging

---

[280] Andrieu, *Pontifical romain au moyen-âge*, 3:392.

[281] *Juramentum, quo s. Bonifacius se Gregorio II papae astrinxit*, PL 89, col. 804.

[282] Andrieu, *Pontifical romain au moyen-âge*, 3:393.

[283] Joseph Braun, "Pallium", in *Catholic Encyclopedia* (1907–1912), 11:427–429.

downward, one over the chest and the other over the back. Woven into the white cloth were four purple crosses. The pallium was fastened to the vestments of the one wearing it with three jewel-topped gold pins affixed on the chest, the shoulder, and the back.[284] Some three centuries later, the 1488 *Caeremoniale Romanum* of the papal master of ceremonies Patrizio Piccolomini mentions the custom of shearing the wool for the pallium from two lambs presented annually by Rome's Monastery of Saint Agnes.[285] In the episcopal consecration rite of the Pontifical of Durandus, the Vatican archpriest takes the pallium from the altar and then confers it with the following words, which allude to the practice of placing a new pallium over the tomb of Saint Peter in Rome before sending it to the prelate who will wear it:[286] "*Receive the pallium taken from the body of blessed Peter, and in this pallium receive the plenitude of your office and the authority of celebrating councils and consecrating bishops.*"[287]

Pope Innocent III explains that the pallium is a sign of the discipline with which the archbishop who receives it is to govern both himself and those under his authority. The roughness of the wool signifies the firmness with which the prelate will need to chasten obstinate souls, whereas the wool's bright white color illustrates the kindness with which he is to treat penitent and humble souls. This wool, taken from the meek and gentle sheep, an image of vulnerability, also reminds the archbishop that he must imitate the Good Samaritan by taking a leading role in nursing the spiritual wounds of sinners. The four purple crosses stand for the virtues of justice, fortitude, prudence, and temperance. The three pins by which the pallium is fastened to the vestments denote compassion toward others, the faithful administration of one's office, and resolve in judgment. Each pin is pointed on one end but crowned with a jewel on the other end, signifying by the sharp point the shepherd's affliction in tending his sheep here on earth but denoting by the jeweled top the crown with which he will be rewarded in Heaven, where he will forever possess the Pearl of great price (Mt 13:45–46).[288]

While the episcopal consecration rite from the Pontifical of Durandus is surely the finest medieval rendering of this sacred ceremony, the episcopal ordination rite in the fourteenth-century German Pontifical of Mainz, from which we have already drawn the priestly ordination rite presented earlier, likewise deserves attention, for it contains several

The Consecration of Bishops in Fourteenth-century Germany

---

[284] Innocent III, *De sacro altaris mysterio*, bk. 1, chap. 43, PL 217, cols. 797, 798.

[285] Dykmans, *Oeuvre de Patrizi Piccolomini*, 1:174.

[286] This custom is prescribed in the aforementioned 1488 *Caeremoniale Romanum* of Piccolomini, which speaks of the pallium being left on the tomb of Saint Peter for an entire night (ibid.).

[287] Andrieu, *Pontifical romain au moyen-âge*, 3:393.

[288] Innocent III, *De sacro altaris mysterio*, bk. 1, chap. 43, PL 217, cols. 797–799.

notable features that distinguish it from the Durandus rite of a century earlier.[289] In the Mainz rite, the Sunday morning examination of the episcopal candidate by the consecrating bishop pauses at one point for a solemn pledge of fidelity to the pope and the provincial archbishop given by the candidate, resembling the pledge of fidelity found at the end of the Durandus consecration rite:

> The candidate, with two fingers of his right hand placed on the text of the Gospels, should take an oath and say:
>
> *And I* [Name], *bishop of* [Name of see], *determine to exhibit faithfulness and subjection to the holy Roman Church and to the lord* [Name], *supreme pontiff, to my lord* [Name] *of* [Name of primatial see] *my archbishop, and to their Catholic successors according to the doctrines of the holy Fathers; I shall receive the legate of the supreme pontiff and of the holy Roman Church with reverence and shall sustain him in his needs with counsel, assistance, and support, in good faith. Every two years I shall approach the holy Roman See in person, unless in my case it will have been dispensed with by the Roman pontiff, or else I will have been impeded by a just impediment. Called to a synod, I shall come. I shall preserve the goods of my church faithfully and recover and restore those dispersed. This I profess in these writings, and I determine to observe as much as human frailty allows, so help me God and these holy Gospels.*
>
> The consecrator should add:
>
> *All these and other good things may the Lord grant you, and may he preserve you and strengthen you in every good.*
>
> Those assisting should respond with him to be consecrated: *Amen.*[290]

During the anointing of the head, hands, and right thumb of the new bishop, the choir sings Psalm 44 with an antiphonal refrain (*Unxit te Dominus*) based upon the psalm's eighth verse: "*The Lord has anointed you with the oil of gladness above your fellows.*"[291] Psalm 44 is well suited to the occasion. Its verses speak of the king who is a champion of truth and justice, a prefiguration of Christ; similarly, the bishop, rendered by his priestly vocation an *alter Christus*, is called as shepherd of his flock to be a champion of truth, making the words of Psalm 44 applicable to his mission as well: "*Gird thy sword upon thy thigh. . . . Set out, proceed prosperously, and reign. Because of truth and meekness and justice: and thy right hand shall conduct thee wonderfully*" (Ps 44:4–5). Recall that the image of the bishop as a champion of truth was also evoked by Durandus in his prayer for the imposition of the miter.

The words for the anointing of the new bishop's hands differ from those in the Durandus text; the Mainz formula is in fact originally

---

[289] Text in Martène, *De antiquis ecclesiae ritibus*, bk. 1, chap. 8, art. 11, *ordo* 16, 2:81–82.
[290] Ibid., 81.
[291] Ibid.

found in the Frankish priestly ordination rite of the seventh- to eighth-century *Missale Francorum*[292] and is particularly beautiful:

> *May these hands be anointed from the sanctified oil and the chrism of holiness, as Samuel anointed David king and prophet; so may they be anointed and consecrated, in the name of the Father +, and the Son + , and the Holy + Spirit, making the sign of the holy Cross of our Savior Jesus Christ the Lord, who has redeemed us from death and has led us to the realms of Heaven; graciously hear us, loving Lord, Father almighty, eternal God, that what we ask we may mercifully obtain, in the name of the Lord. Amen.*[293]

This same prayer was later to appear in the episcopal consecration rite of the universally promulgated *Pontificale Romanum* of 1595–1596.[294] The Mainz rite adds a further anointing specifically for the right thumb of the new bishop.[295] This anointing of the thumb and the words accompanying it are traceable to the Romano-Germanic Pontifical;[296] the formula is the same as that used for the anointing of the entire hand in the Pontifical of Durandus.[297]

The prayer for the imposition of the episcopal gloves reflects the special function of a bishop's hands in administering the sacraments and sacramentals: "*We humbly beseech your immense mercy, almighty and most loving God, that just as the hands of this your servant are outwardly covered with these gloves, so may they be interiorly sprinkled with the dew of your blessing, that whatever things are to be blessed or consecrated by them may be blessed and consecrated by you. Through the same Jesus Christ our Lord ...*"[298] The words recited by the consecrating bishop for the imposition of the miter enjoin the new bishop that he must give his whole heart to God alone: "*I place this sign on your head, that you may admit none except your Creator himself for your beloved, in the name of the Lord. Amen.*"[299]

As mentioned previously, the Pontifical of Mainz expressly states the moment when the Gospel book that was placed on the episcopal candidate's shoulders earlier in the rite is to be removed from his shoulders; this is done immediately after the imposition of the miter, at which point the consecrating bishop takes the book and presents it to

---

[292] Mohlberg, *Missale Francorum*, no. 34, p. 10.

[293] Martène, *De antiquis ecclesiae ritibus*, bk. 1, chap. 8, art. 11, *ordo* 16, 2:82. In the Mainz pontifical, another anointing formula immediately follows this text, almost identical to the Mainz formula for anointing the hands of new priests, but it is unclear whether the latter formula was intended to be said in addition to the preceding formula or as an alternative text.

[294] Sodi and Triacca, *Pontificale Romanum: Editio princeps (1595–1596)*, 103–104 (original pagination).

[295] Martène, *De antiquis ecclesiae ritibus*, bk. 1, chap. 8, art. 11, *ordo* 16, 2:82.

[296] Vogel and Elze, *Pontifical romano-germanique*, 1:220.

[297] See p. 193 of the present chapter.

[298] Martène, *De antiquis ecclesiae ritibus*, bk. 1, chap. 8, art. 11, *ordo* 16, 2:82.

[299] Ibid.

the new bishop.[300] The words with which the consecrator and the assisting bishops offer the sign of peace to the newly consecrated bishop are nearly the same as those found in the priestly ordination rite of the Mainz pontifical: "*Peace to you, dearest brother; pray to God for me.*"[301]

The Gospel for the Mass is from the Last Supper discourse of Christ to his Apostles: "*If you love me, keep my commandments . . .*" (Jn 14:15ff.). For the Offertory, the original wording of the fourteenth-century Mainz manuscript calls for the new bishop himself to bring the Offertory gifts—two unconsecrated hosts, two flasks of wine, and two lit candles. But in the margin of the manuscript, a later writer has added a note calling for the family of the new bishop to carry these gifts, with the new bishop touching the gifts as they are taken by the clergy into the sanctuary.[302]

The Mass texts for the Mainz episcopal consecration Mass are those of the votive Mass of the Holy Spirit. Hence the Secret at the end of the Offertory is from the same: "*May this oblation, we beseech you, O Lord, cleanse the blemishes of our heart, that it may be made a worthy habitation of the Holy Spirit. Through our Lord Jesus Christ . . .*" To this is added the Secret proper to episcopal ordination Masses that Durandus likewise utilized in his consecration rite.[303]

Following the Roman Canon and the Our Father, there is a special rite of episcopal benediction similar to that found in the Mainz rite for the ordination of priests, and inserted at the same point preceding the *Agnus Dei* (where Durandus also inserts a blessing in his episcopal consecration rite). After the deacon announces the benediction by saying to the people, "*Humble yourselves for a blessing*", and the clergy answer, "*Thanks be to God*", the consecrating bishop turns toward the people; having assumed his miter and taken his crosier into his hand, he prays for the new bishop and also for the new bishop's mother and father, thereby adding a more personal dimension to the solemnities of the consecration rite. Addressing the new bishop, he says:

> *May the Lord bless you in the episcopal order, and protecting you even as he has willed to make you bishop over his people, so may he make you to be both [blessed] in the present age and a partaker of eternal blessedness.* Clergy: *Amen.*
>
> Consecrator: *May he make you to govern fruitfully the clergy and the people, whom he has willed under your rule and your governance, with his assistance, in temporal and spiritual matters, for a time of long duration.* Clergy: *Amen.*
>
> Consecrator: *That your parents, with the divine admonitions, being devoid of adversities, abounding in good works, [and] obedient in the faith to your*

---

[300] Ibid.

[301] Ibid.

[302] Ibid.

[303] Ibid. For the text of this same prayer in the Durandus rite, see p. 197 of the present chapter.

office, may both delight in the tranquillity of peace in the present age and be worthy to obtain a place in the company of the eternal citizens. Clergy: *Amen.*

Consecrator: *Which may he himself vouchsafe to grant, whose kingdom and dominion endure without end, unto ages of ages.* Clergy: *Amen.*[304]

Extending his right hand, the consecrating bishop imparts his blessing with a benediction formula traceable to the tenth-century Romano-Germanic Pontifical: "*May the blessing of almighty God, the Fa + ther, and the Son + , and the Holy + Spirit, descend upon you and remain with you forever.* Clergy: *Amen.* Consecrator: *And may his peace be always with you.*"[305]

The rubrics for the episcopal consecration rite in the Mainz pontifical end by noting that after Mass the new bishop, "clothed in white silk garments", should mount his horse and ride to his lodging "with great solemnity and character".[306] A comparable custom is found in the thirteenth-century Pontifical of the Roman Curia, which mentions that the new bishop blesses the people along the way as he rides from the church to his episcopal residence.[307] Although in his pontifical Durandus says nothing about this practice, he does state in his liturgical commentary, the *Rationale divinorum officiorum*, that the horse upon which a new bishop rides on the day of his consecration ought to be white or decked in white cloth. Durandus explains the symbolism of this by citing the Book of Revelation's description of the armies of Heaven as mounted on white horses and clothed in white linen, following Christ the King, who is himself mounted upon a white horse (Rev 19:11–16).[308] By associating the new bishop with the armies of Heaven who fight at the side of Christ against the devil (Rev 19:19), Durandus again evokes the imagery of the bishop as a "champion of truth" found in his episcopal consecration rite prayer for the imposition of the miter and implicit in the Mainz pontifical's use of Psalm 44

---

[304] Ibid. This text, with some differences, is first found in the tenth-century Romano-Germanic Pontifical; see Vogel and Elze, *Pontifical romano-germanique*, 1:225. The bracketed word "blessed" (*felicem*), absent from the Mainz text but present in the earlier Romano-Germanic Pontifical text, appears to be required by the context; its absence from the Mainz text may be a copyist's error.

[305] Martène, *De antiquis ecclesiae ritibus*, bk. 1, chap. 8, art. 11, *ordo* 16, 2:82. Insofar as Martène provides only the incipit of this blessing and of the accompanying versicle, the full text of the blessing is here taken from the tenth-century Romano-Germanic Pontifical, in Vogel and Elze, *Pontifical romano-germanique*, 1:291, modified to include a subsequent addition to the blessing as given in the late thirteenth-century Pontifical of Durandus, in Andrieu, *Pontifical romain au moyen-âge*, 3:655. Prior to the tenth century, a precursor to this blessing formula, albeit with significant verbal differences, can be found in Saint Benedict of Aniane's early ninth-century Frankish adaptation of the Gregorian Sacramentary of Rome; see Deshusses, *Sacramentaire grégorien*, no. 1738, 1:576 (conclusion of prayer). The full text of the versicle is taken from the Pontifical of Durandus, in Andrieu, *Pontifical romain au moyen-âge*, 3:573.

[306] Martène, *De antiquis ecclesiae ritibus*, bk. 1, chap. 8, art. 11, *ordo* 16, 2:82.

[307] Andrieu, *Pontifical romain au moyen-âge*, 2:368.

[308] Durandus, *Rationale* (CCCM 140), bk. 1, chap. 8, nos. 22–23, p. 107.

in the consecration rite. Durandus further explains the white horse or white-bedecked horse for the day of episcopal consecration as symbolic of the bodily purity and chastity required of prelates and all virtuous men.[309]

---

[309] Ibid., no. 23.

7 Matrimony

May the fragrance of your life be redolent as a white lily, that you may ever ascend in mind toward Heaven. . . . May the Lord of celestial glory and the King of all ages bless you. . . . The joy of children having also been conferred upon you, after a long life may he grant you the inhabitance of the heavenly mansions.

Nuptial rite, *Liber ordinum*, Spain, fifth to seventh century[1]

Of the sacrament of matrimony, Saint Thomas Aquinas (+1274) observes, "The joining of husband and wife by matrimony is the greatest of all joinings, since it is the joining of soul and body, wherefore it is called a conjugal union."[2] Elsewhere, he contrasts the object of matrimony with that of holy orders:

> There are those who propagate and safeguard the spiritual life, by a purely spiritual administration; to these corresponds the sacrament of orders; and there are those who propagate and safeguard the spiritual life by ministering to both body and soul; this is the object of matrimony in which husband and wife are joined together, in order to beget children, and bring them up in the fear of God.[3]

In keeping with the teaching of Pope Saint Nicholas I (+867) that valid Christian matrimony is effected solely by the mutual consent of the man and woman marrying,[4] the Church has consistently identified this mutual consent of the bridegroom and bride (the "marriage

---

[1] Excerpted from two nuptial prayers in Marius Férotin, O.S.B., ed., *Le Liber ordinum en usage dans l'église wisigothique et mozarabe d'Espagne du cinquième au onzième siècle* (Paris, 1904), repr., ed. Anthony Ward, S.M., and Cuthbert Johnson, O.S.B., BELS 83 (Rome: Centro Liturgico Vincenziano, Edizioni Liturgiche, 1996), cols. 436, 441 ("Manuscript B" text).

[2] Saint Thomas Aquinas, *Summa theologica: First Complete American Edition in Three Volumes*, trans. Fathers of the English Dominican Province (New York: Benziger Brothers, 1948), supplement, q. 44, art. 2, reply obj. 3, 3:2724.

[3] Saint Thomas Aquinas, *Summa contra gentiles*, bk. 4, chap. 58, in *The "Summa contra gentiles" of Saint Thomas Aquinas*, trans. English Dominican Fathers (New York: Benziger Brothers, 1923–1929), 4:221–222.

[4] Saint Nicholas I, *Response to the Bulgarians* (November 13, 866), chap. 3, in J. D. Mansi, ed., *Sacrorum conciliorum nova et amplissima collectio*, vol. 15 (Florence and Venice, 1770; repr., Paris: Hubert Welter, 1902), col. 403.

contract") as the essential matter and form of the sacrament and thus has taught that the man and woman mutually administer the sacrament to each other.[5] The Church has set the solemn consent of the marrying couple in a sacred liturgical setting, the wedding rite, in which the priest imparts to the couple the blessing of the Church and offers the Mass and other prayers for the sanctification of their union. Pope Nicholas explains that the nuptial blessing given by the priest is modeled upon the example of the first marriage of human history, that of Adam and Eve, for as the Book of Genesis relates, "And God blessed them, saying: Increase and multiply" (Gen 1:28). He adds that prayer likewise sanctified the marriage of Tobias and Sara, citing specifically the prayer of Tobias on their wedding night (Tob 8:4–10).[6] Although not expressly mentioned by Pope Nicholas, there is also in the Book of Tobias the prayer of Sara's father, Raguel (Tob 7:15), that can be said to prefigure the priest's blessing of a couple's marriage; Raguel's invocation was utilized in many medieval nuptial rites. In the sixteenth century, the Council of Trent imparted a heightened importance to the role of the priest in the marriage rite by declaring him to be the primary witness of the wedding, whose presence as a witness was defined as essential to the valid and licit reception of the sacrament.[7]

Hugh of Saint Victor (+c. 1141) explains that the sacrament of matrimony symbolizes the union between Christ and his Church,[8] as well as the individual union of God to each human soul, with the bridegroom symbolizing God and the bride representing the human soul.[9] The first of these two comparisons stems directly from the words of Saint Paul: "The husband is the head of the wife, as Christ is the head of the church.... Husbands, love your wives, as Christ also loved the church, and delivered himself up for it.... This is a great sacrament" (Eph 5:23, 25, 32). In the marriage liturgy, the Church is in a sense festively commemorating her own marriage to Christ. This is strikingly manifested in a unique custom found in a 1488 wedding ceremony from the diocese of Basel, Switzerland,[10] in which the rite of imparting the wedding ring includes the recitation of the words "*With his ring my Lord Jesus Christ has espoused me, and just as a bride he has*

---

[5] Joseph Pohle and Arthur Preuss, *The Sacraments: A Dogmatic Treatise* (Saint Louis: B. Herder, 1928–1931), 4:160, 166–167, 214–215. See, for example, the Council of Florence, *Decree for the Armenians* (November 22, 1439), in J.D. Mansi, ed., *Sacrorum conciliorum nova et amplissima collectio*, vol. 31 (Florence and Venice, 1798; repr. Paris and Leipzig: Hubert Welter, 1906), cols. 1058–1059.

[6] Saint Nicholas I, *Response to the Bulgarians*, chap. 3, in Mansi, *Sacrorum conciliorum nova et amplissima collectio*, vol. 15, cols. 402–403.

[7] Council of Trent, session 24, November 11, 1563, *De matrimonio*, chap. 1, in H.J. Schroeder, O.P., *Canons and Decrees of the Council of Trent: Original Text with English Translation* (Saint Louis, Mo.: B. Herder, 1955), 184, 455. See also Pohle and Preuss, *Sacraments*, 4:215.

[8] Hugh of Saint Victor, *De sacramentis*, bk. 2, pt. 11, chap. 3, PL 176, col. 482.

[9] Ibid., cols. 481, 482.

[10] The name of this city has also been given as Bale and Basle.

adorned me with a crown."[11] By incorporating into the nuptial rite this antiphon from the rite of consecrating virgins,[12] the compiler of the Basel ceremony was in effect casting the bridegroom as an earthly image of Christ the Divine Bridegroom, and the bride as the earthly image of Christ's mystical Bride, the Church.

Marriage, forming as it does a communion of persons beginning with the husband and wife, to whom children are added as the fruit of their love by the providence of God, has also been seen as symbolizing the unity of the three Persons of the Holy Trinity. As early as the fourth century, Saint Gregory Nazianzen (+390) makes reference to the ancient family of Adam, Eve, and their son Seth (Gen 4:25) as an analogy for explaining the Holy Trinity;[13] but it was not until the twentieth century, and in particular during the pontificate of Pope Blessed John Paul II, that the concept of family life as an image of the Holy Trinity reemerged in an explicit manner, appearing in the 1994 *Catechism of the Catholic Church*: "The Christian family is a communion of persons, a sign and image of the communion of the Father and the Son in the Holy Spirit."[14] Although this comparison does not appear in the writings of the major medieval theologians, the use of one or more texts from the votive Mass of the Holy Trinity at nuptial Masses did arise by the eleventh century[15] and continued in certain places until the promulgation of the 1570 *Missale Romanum* of Pope Saint Pius V, which provided a votive Mass exclusively for marriages, the "Mass for Bridegroom and Bride".[16] Additionally, the imposition of the wedding ring in medieval wedding rites was usually accompanied by a Trinitarian formula.

Through the texts and rubrics of the medieval nuptial rites, the Church sought to manifest the sacredness of matrimony as a sacrament. Thus in the French marriage rites from a pontifical of Meaux

---

[11] *Informatorium sacerdotum* (Basel, Switzerland, 1488), quoted in Jean-Baptiste Molin and Protais Mutembe, *Le rituel du mariage en France du XIIe au XVIe siècle*, Théologie historique 26 (Paris: Beauchesne, 1974), 174.

[12] This antiphon, *Anulo suo subarravit*, is used for the rite of consecrating virgins in the tenth-century Romano-Germanic Pontifical; see Cyrille Vogel and Reinhard Elze, eds., *Le pontifical romano-germanique du dixième siècle*, vol. 1, ST 226 (Vatican City: Biblioteca Apostolica Vaticana, 1963), 46.

[13] Saint Gregory Nazianzen, *Oration 31*, no. 11, PG 36, cols. 143–146 (Latin and Greek texts).

[14] *Catechism of the Catholic Church*, English ed. (Vatican City: Libreria Editrice Vaticana, © 1994; Washington, D.C.: United States Catholic Conference, 1994), no. 2205, p. 532. In his 1988 apostolic letter *Mulieris dignitatem*, Pope Blessed John Paul II describes marriage as mirroring in the world the "communion of love" of the three Persons of the Holy Trinity (*Mulieris dignitatem* [August 15, 1988], no. 7).

[15] Korbinian Ritzer, *Formen, Riten, und religiöses Brauchtum der Eheschliessung in den christlichen Kirchen des ersten Jahrtausends*, Liturgiewissenschaftliche Quellen und Forschungen 38 (Münster, Germany: Aschendorffsche Verlagsbuchhandlung, 1962), 189.

[16] Text in Manlio Sodi and Achille Maria Triacca, eds., *Missale Romanum: Editio princeps (1570)*, facsimile ed., MLCT 2 (Vatican City: Libreria Editrice Vaticana, © 1998), 636–638 (new pagination).

(c. 1280) and a ritual of the abbey of Saint-Maur-des-Fossés near Paris (second half of the thirteenth century), the bridegroom and bride, following the giving of their mutual consent, would be incensed by the priest.[17] In some marriage ceremonies, such as that of Urgel (La Seu d'Urgell), Spain (1536), reverence for the sacrament was manifested in the custom of sprinkling the couple with holy water at the outset of the nuptial rite as an outward sign of penitential purification, in preparation for the fruitful reception of matrimony.[18] As we shall see, this "sense of the sacred" in regard to marriage was expressed in numerous other ways as well.

In the medieval nuptial rites, the specific manner in which the couple expressed their mutual consent varied from place to place. The twelfth-century theologian Hugh of Saint Victor gives as examples of the words of consent the following formulas for the bridegroom and bride respectively: "*I take you for mine, and that henceforth you should be my wife, I your husband*"; "*I take you for mine, and that henceforth I should be your wife and you my husband.*"[19] From the twelfth century onward, such verbal consent was usually spoken in the vernacular rather than in Latin.[20] Thus the following familiar words of consent for the bridegroom to pronounce are given in English in the 1504 London edition of England's Sarum Missal: "*I* [Name] *take thee* [Name] *to my wedded wife, to have and to hold, for better, for worse, for richer, for poorer, in sickness and in health, till death us depart, and thereto I plight thee my troth.*"[21] In some rites, however, the mutual consent was expressed not through explicit verbal declarations of this nature *during* the nuptial rite but rather through the actions of the wedding ceremony (particularly the joining of the spouses' hands,[22] or the bestowal of the wedding ring). Such is the case with the text that we shall now present as our primary example of the medieval marriage rite, taken from the 1501 *Ordinarium* for the diocese of Barcelona, Spain.[23] It contains a number of rubrics and texts unique to Spain, and particularly Catalonia. Nonetheless, several of its key prayers are traceable to the Leonine and Gregorian sacramentaries of Rome. By way of comparison, we shall

---

[17] Manuscripts: Paris, Bibliothèque Nationale, Codex Lat. NA 1202 (c. 1280) and Codex Lat. 13317 (second half of thirteenth century), in Molin and Mutembe, *Rituel du mariage en France*, 297, 300.

[18] Francesc Xavier Parés i Saltor, *L'ordinari d'Urgell de 1536*, Col·lectània Sant Pacià 74 (La Seu d'Urgell, Spain: Societat Cultural Urgel·litana / Facultat de Teologia da Catalunya, 2002), 214.

[19] Hugh of Saint Victor, *De sacramentis*, bk. 2, pt. 11, chap. 5, PL 176, col. 488.

[20] Mark Searle and Kenneth Stevenson, eds., *Documents of the Marriage Liturgy* (Collegeville, Minn.: Liturgical Press, 1992), introduction, 12.

[21] Text in Francis H. Dickinson, ed., *Missale ad usum insignis et praeclarae ecclesiae Sarum* (Burntisland, Scotland: E. Prelo Pitsligo, 1861–1883), col. 831*.

[22] Molin and Mutembe, *Rituel du mariage en France*, 100–101, 302.

[23] Text in Amadeu-J. Soberanas, ed., *Ordinarium sacramentorum Barchinonense, 1501*, facsimile ed., Biblioteca liturgica catalana 1 (Barcelona: Institut d'Estudis Catalans, 1991), fols. 31v–38v.

afterward present excerpts from the nuptial rite found in a twelfth-century pontifical of Lyre, a monastery in the French diocese of Evreux.

In the 1501 Barcelona *Ordinarium* text there appears immediately before the nuptial liturgy a section entitled "Rite of Betrothal". This simple ceremony that takes place prior to the wedding does include explicit verbal declarations of consent by both the man and the woman intending to marry, yet here the words of consent are spoken not as a means of effecting the actual conferral of the sacrament but rather as a promise to marry in the future. Nonetheless, such a declaration in the presence of a priest would have provided verbal confirmation that both parties understood their subsequent participation in the ensuing nuptial rite to constitute mutual consent.[24] The priest first questions the couple under oath as to whether there are any canonical impediments to their marital union. Upon determining from their answers that there are no such impediments, the priest with his two hands takes and joins together the couple's right hands, a practice evidently derived from the Old Testament wedding of Tobias and Sara as related in the Book of Tobias, in which the father of Sara placed her right hand into that of Tobias (Tob 7:15–16). The priest then instructs the man to repeat after him these words of consent, which are said in the vernacular tongue of Barcelona, Catalan: "*I* [Name] *give my body to you* [Name] *as your faithful husband and take you as my faithful wife.*" Afterward, the priest turns to the woman and instructs her to repeat after him the words of consent, again in the vernacular: "*I* [Name] *give my body to you* [Name] *as your faithful wife and take you as my faithful husband.*" The priest then directs the couple to seal their mutual consent with a kiss, after which he concludes the betrothal rite by blessing them: "*As a confirmation of the present matrimony and of the faith that you have given, kiss, and may God give you his grace and bene + diction*" (response: "*Amen*").[25]

The Barcelona *Ordinarium* does not specify what time, if any, should elapse between the "betrothal rite" and the solemn wedding rite, but the text of the latter immediately follows the betrothal text and bears the title "Order or Rite of Celebrating Marriage". It begins with the presentation and blessing of two wedding rings, one for each spouse, mounted on a loaf of bread according to a local custom:

> First, the spouses should be seated before the altar on a kind of bench. And the woman [should be] to the left of the man. Then the priest should vest himself up to the chasuble, or without the chasuble he

---

[24] It appears that this declaration would have provided, albeit in an anticipatory manner, the verbal confirmation of the couple's mutual consent that Saint Thomas Aquinas asserts to be essential for a valid marriage (Saint Thomas Aquinas, *Summa theologica*, supplement, q. 45, art. 2, 3:2726).

[25] Soberanas, *Ordinarium sacramentorum Barchinonense, 1501*, fol. 31v.

should come to them. And the rings of the wedding gift having been fitted on top of the bread, the said bread should properly be held by the minister. Then the said spouses should come, and with them remaining on their knees before the priest, the priest should say to them: *Is it pleasing to you that these* arrhae *be blessed?* Response: *Yes, Father.*[26]

In the above text, the rings are referred to as the *arrhae*, the "pledges", a term that originally denoted a monetary wedding gift that a man would give to his prospective bride's family as a pledge of his intent to marry her.[27] The bestowal of such a monetary gift in the form of coins is found in some medieval nuptial rites,[28] but in other cases, such as the Barcelona rite, the wedding ring served as the *arrha*, the "pledge", in the wedding ceremony. The use of wedding rings as the *arrhae* is traceable to an ancient liturgical book of Spain's Mozarabic Rite known as the *Liber ordinum*, an eleventh-century compilation of older texts believed to date largely from the fifth to the seventh century.[29] In the 1501 Barcelona rite, the wedding rings are blessed by the priest with two prayers for the blessing of the *arrhae* originally found in the *Liber ordinum*;[30] the first likens the *arrhae* to the gifts that the servant of Abraham presented to Rebecca as he arranged for her to marry Abraham's son Isaac (Gen 24:22, 30, 47, 51–53):

> *O Lord God almighty, who ordered your servant Abraham to bind Isaac with Rebecca through the exchange of* arrhae *as an image of holy matrimony, that by the offering of gifts a multitude of children might come into being: we beseech your omnipotence, that you the Sanc + tifier may approve the offering of these gifts, which this your servant [Name] reserves to offer his beloved bride, that protected with your blessing and joined together by the bond of love, they may rejoice happily to be redeemed with your faithful. Through Christ our Lord. Response: Amen.*[31]

The second of the two blessings evokes the memory of several Old Testament marriages: "*Bless +, O Lord, these* arrhae, *which this day your servant [Name] delivers into the hand of your handmaid [Name], just as you blessed Abraham with Sara, Isaac with Rebecca, Jacob with Rachel. Bestow upon them, Lord, the grace of your blessing +. May they flourish like a rose planted in Jericho. And may they fear and adore the Lord Jesus Christ unto ages of ages. Amen.*"[32]

---

[26] Ibid., fols. 31v–32r.

[27] Searle and Stevenson, *Documents of the Marriage Liturgy*, 120–121.

[28] Molin and Mutembe, *Rituel du mariage en France*, 150 (various examples), plus 289–290 (nuptial rite from the twelfth-century missal of Bury Saint Edmunds, England).

[29] Férotin, *Liber ordinum*, cols. 434–436.

[30] First prayer: ibid., cols. 435–436 ("Manuscript B" text); second prayer: ibid., col. 435 ("Manuscript A" text).

[31] Soberanas, *Ordinarium sacramentorum Barchinonense, 1501*, fol. 32r.

[32] Ibid., fol. 32r–32v.

The bridegroom and the bride, still kneeling, now exchange wedding rings, guided and assisted by the priest.[33] The imparting of rings to both spouses was commonplace in Spain,[34] a practice traceable to the fifth- to seventh-century Mozarabic nuptial rites preserved in the aforementioned *Liber ordinum*.[35] In Poland also, two rings were imparted, but elsewhere in medieval Europe, it was usually the bride alone who received a ring.[36] Before being conferred, wedding rings would first be blessed, as they are in the Barcelona rite with the above-quoted prayers for blessing the *arrhae*. The earliest extant prayer that expressly mentions the wedding ring itself as the object to be blessed is found in the 856 nuptial rite for England's King Edilwulf and Judith of France as celebrated in France by Bishop Hincmar of Reims, a blessing that also explains the ring's symbolism: *"Receive the ring, the sign of faithfulness and love and the bond of conjugal union, inasmuch as man must not separate those God has joined. Who lives and reigns unto all ages of ages."* [37] A 1526 ritual of Senlis, France, explains further that the wedding ring "by its rotundity designates indissoluble union".[38] Describing the wedding ring as a "sign of love", William Durandus of Mende (+1296) expounds the symbolism of the different materials used for wedding rings in his time. He notes that some rings were made of iron with a mounted diamond, "for just as iron conquers all things, so love conquers all.... And just as a diamond is unbreakable, so love also is unconquerable, for love is strong as death"; other wedding rings were made of gold adorned with gems, "for just as gold surpasses other metals, so love surpasses all good things; and just as the gold is adorned with gems, so conjugal love is adorned with other virtues." [39]

By the twelfth century, the solemn bestowal of the wedding ring had become a complex rite with Trinitarian symbolism.[40] In Barcelona it was customary to place the wedding ring not on the left hand but on the right hand instead, a tradition that dates back to the aforementioned *Liber ordinum* of Spain.[41] The usage in this regard varied from place to place[42] until the placement of the ring on the left hand

[33] Ibid., fol. 32v.

[34] Molin and Mutembe, *Rituel du mariage en France*, 142, footnote.

[35] Férotin, *Liber ordinum*, cols. 434–435.

[36] Molin and Mutembe, *Rituel du Mariage en France*, 141–142.

[37] Text in Enzo Lodi, ed., *Enchiridion euchologicum fontium liturgicorum*, BELS 15 (Rome: Centro Liturgico Vincenziano, Edizioni Liturgiche, 1979), no. 2523, p. 1079.

[38] *Manuale* of Senlis, France (1526), quoted in Molin and Mutembe, *Rituel du mariage en France*, 172.

[39] William Durandus of Mende, *Rationale divinorum officiorum*, bk. 1, chap. 9, no. 11, in A. Davril, O.S.B., and T. M. Thibodeau, eds., *Guillelmi Duranti: Rationale divinorum officiorum I–IV*, CCCM 140 (Turnhout, Belgium: Brepols, 1995), 116–117.

[40] A ring-bestowal rite of this nature appears in the twelfth-century missal of Bury Saint Edmunds, England (Molin and Mutembe, *Rituel du mariage en France*, 290).

[41] Férotin, *Liber ordinum*, col. 435 ("Manuscript A" text).

[42] The right hand is specified in the nuptial rites of Bury Saint Edmunds, England (missal, twelfth century); Rouen, France (missal, thirteenth century); and Esztergom, Hungary

became prevalent in the seventeenth century.[43] Although there were certain places where the wedding ring was conferred upon the third finger (third from the thumb inclusive),[44] the Barcelona text follows the far-more-common practice of placing the ring on the fourth finger. This latter custom is first mentioned by the Spanish Church Father Saint Isidore of Seville (+636), who attributes it to the belief that there was a vein in the fourth finger that ran directly to the heart,[45] an idea dating back to the pagan Roman author Pliny the Elder (+79).[46] It is highly probable from the context that the mutual bestowal of wedding rings constituted the Barcelona nuptial rite's "marriage contract"—the essential expression of mutual consent that efficaciously wrought the actual conferral of the sacrament upon the couple. The Barcelona rubrics describe the ceremony thus, in which each ring is repeatedly shifted from one finger to another before being left on the fourth finger (we have added clarifications of the text in brackets):

> Here the priest should take one of the rings. And he should make the bridegroom take it in such a manner that he should hold it with three fingers [of his right hand]. And hereafter [the priest] should take the right hand of the bride, such that the priest with one hand should hold the right hand of the bridegroom, and with the other hold the right hand of the bride. And he should uphold the [right] hand of the bridegroom holding the ring, running [the ring] through the fingers [of the right hand] of the bride, placing the ring on the head of the thumb, [the priest] saying [to the bridegroom]:
>
> *You,* [Name], *say here* [i.e., repeat after him, with the ring on the thumb]: *In the name of the Father.* On the second finger: *And of the Son.* On the third: *And of the Holy Spirit.* On the fourth: *Amen.* On the fifth: *Peace be with me.* Repeating on the fourth [to which the ring is returned]: *Peace be with you* [i.e., to the bride]. And there the ring should be left.

(missal, fourteenth century). See Molin and Mutembe, *Rituel du mariage en France*, 290, 294 (Bury Saint Edmunds and Rouen), and Polycarp Radó, O.S.B., and Ladislaus Mezey, *Libri liturgici manuscripti bibliothecarum Hungariae et limitropharum regionum* (Budapest: Akadémiai Kiadó, 1973), 123 (Esztergom). The left hand is specified in a twelfth-century nuptial rite of Lyre, France, given later in this chapter (p. 228), as well as in the French wedding rites of Uzès (*Sacramentarium* [1500]), Autun (*Officiarium* [1503]), and Metz (*Manuale curatorum civitatis et diocesis Metensis* [1543]); see Molin and Mutembe, *Rituel du mariage en France*, 168, 318.

[43] The utilization of the left hand for the wedding ring was promulgated by the *Rituale Romanum* of 1614; see Manlio Sodi and Juan Javier Flores Arcas, eds., *Rituale Romanum: Editio princeps (1614)*, facsimile ed., MLCT 5 (Vatican City: Libreria Editrice Vaticana, © 2004), 139 (original pagination).

[44] French examples include Amiens, Soissons, and Paris; see Molin and Mutembe, *Rituel du mariage en France*, 167.

[45] Saint Isidore of Seville, *De ecclesiasticis officiis*, bk. 2, chap. 20, no. 8, in Christopher M. Lawson, ed., *Sancti Isidori episcopi Hispalensis: De ecclesiasticis officiis*, CCSL 113 (Turnhout, Belgium: Brepols, 1989), 92.

[46] Herbert Thurston, S.J., "Marriage, Ritual of", in *The Catholic Encyclopedia* (New York: Appleton, 1907–1912), 9:706.

Hereafter the priest should deliver the other ring to the bride. And the bride should act and speak to her bridegroom in the same manner and in the same words by the direction of the priest. This done, they should return to their place.[47]

In another Spanish marriage text, that of the 1494 missal of Orense (near Compostela), the groom receives his wedding ring first, placed on his hand by the priest rather than the bride (there is no indication as to which hand receives the ring):

[Blessed] water should be sprinkled upon the *arrhae* [i.e., wedding gifts] and the rings and the bystanders. And the priest should place the ring on the bridegroom's thumb, saying, *In the name of the Father.* And afterward on the index finger; and he should say, *And of the Son.* Then on the middle finger; and he should say, *And of the Holy Spirit.* And he should leave the ring on the bridegroom's fourth finger, saying, *Amen.*[48]

The placement of the ring on the hand of the bride is accompanied by an expansive rendering of the Trinitarian formula, followed by a declaration of consent:

Then, at the invitation of the priest, the bridegroom should take the bride's ring, the priest holding his hand over the bridegroom's hand, and the priest should say afterward in placing the ring on the bride's thumb, *In the name of the Father, who created the world.* And afterward on the index finger, *And of the Son, who redeemed the whole world.* Then on the middle, *And of the Holy Spirit, who illuminated the whole world.* And on the fourth finger, he should say, *Peace be with you. Amen.* And the bridegroom holding the ring accordingly, the bridegroom should say after the priest, naming his bride: *Bride, with this ring I espouse you, and with my body I honor you, and this gift I give you.*[49]

In the marriage rite of the 1499 manual of Jaén, Spain, the priest presents the rings to the bridegroom and bride respectively with an accompanying blessing reminding them that the married are also expected to practice the virtue of chastity: "*Bless + , O Lord, this ring, that the figure of it may preserve chastity.*"[50] In the Spanish missal of Avila (1510), the groom places his bride's ring on only one of her fingers, the fourth, on her left hand, making the sign of the cross with the

---

[47] Soberanas, *Ordinarium sacramentorum Barchinonense, 1501*, fol. 32v.

[48] *Missale secundum usum Auriensis ecclesiae* (Monterrey, Spain: Gonzalo Rodriguez de la Passera and Juan de Porras, 1494; digitized text, Biblioteca Digital Hispánica, Biblioteca Nacional de España, Madrid, 2007), first sig., 8v.

[49] Ibid.

[50] *Missale Giennense / Manuale continens ordinem ad celebrandum ecclesiastica sacramenta [Missale secundum morem et consuetudinem sancte ecclesie Gienensis]* (Seville: Meinard Ungut and Stanislao Polono, 1499), fol. 244r.

ring as he does so. After the bride has placed the other ring on the bridegroom's hand in the same manner, the bridegroom presents to the bride his wedding gifts—the *arrhae*, which in this case are distinct from the rings—before leading her into the church (in this and many other medieval nuptial rites, the beginning of the wedding takes place outside the front door of the church, after which the rest of the ceremony is celebrated inside the church):[51]

> Then the bridegroom should take into his hands from the hand of the priest the *arrhae* and give them to his bride, saying in the vernacular thus: [Name], *I give you these* arrhae *in token of matrimony, just as the Holy Mother Church of Rome orders.* Then they should enter the church, and the bridegroom should hold his bride by the hand; and he should place her at his left. And the priest should go to the other side, with the couple reciting the psalm *Blessed are all they that fear the Lord* [Ps 127].[52]

In the 1536 ritual of Urgel, Spain, the exchange of wedding rings is followed by an action resembling Eastern Rite marriage customs: "The priest should place leafy and green wreaths upon the heads of the spouses, and the spouses should give each other the kiss of peace."[53] In a twelfth-century missal of Bury Saint Edmunds, England, the bride, after receiving her wedding ring, kneels down before the bridegroom as a silent pledge on her part to observe Saint Paul's precept, "Wives, be subject to your husbands" (Col 3:18; see also Eph 5:24). Afterward the bride and groom, both carrying candles, follow the priest into the church as Psalm 127 is recited.[54] In the nuptial rite from the 1494 missal of Orense, Spain, the couple, after entering the church with lit candles to the accompaniment of Psalm 127, prostrate themselves before the entrance to the sanctuary as the priest asks the congregation to pray for them (a custom analogous to the ordination practice of reciting the Litany of the Saints for those to be ordained as they lie prostrate before the altar).[55]

In the marriage ceremony of the fourteenth-century missal of Esztergom, Hungary, there is only one ring, for the bride, which is laid upon a sacramentary to receive the benediction of the priest, who blesses it with two prayers, the second of which invokes the protection of the Holy Spirit for the bride who will wear the ring.[56] This prayer is in fact a nuptial adaptation of an oration first found in the *Missale Francorum* of seventh- to eighth-century France as a prayer for

---

[51] See, for example, the nuptial rite of Lyre, France, given later in this chapter (pp. 227–228).

[52] *Missale Abulense* (Salamanca, Spain: Juan de Porras, 1510), sig. D7r–D7v.

[53] Parés i Saltor, *Ordinari d'Urgell de 1536*, 215.

[54] Manuscript: Laon, France, Bibliothèque Municipale, MS 238 (twelfth century) in Molin and Mutembe, *Rituel du mariage en France*, 290.

[55] *Missale secundum usum Auriensis ecclesiae* (1494), first sig., 9r.

[56] Text in Radó and Mezey, *Libri liturgici manuscripti bibliothecarum Hungariae*, 123.

blessing wine and water used in consecrating new altars and churches;[57] the transformation of such a church consecration prayer into a prayer for a bride is most fitting in view of the symbolism of the church edifice as a representation of the universal Church, the mystical Bride of Christ: "*O Lord, you the Creator and Upholder of mankind, Giver of spiritual grace, Bestower of eternal salvation, send from Heaven the Holy Spirit your Paraclete upon this ring, that she who shall have borne it, armed with the strength of heavenly protection, may advance to salvation.*"[58] From the thirteenth century onward, the blessing of the wedding ring sometimes concluded with the aspersion of holy water upon the ring.[59] A fourteenth-century ritual from the Paris abbey of Saint-Victor directs that after blessing the ring the priest should sprinkle it with holy water and incense it, sprinkling and incensing the bridegroom and bride as well.[60]

Returning to the Barcelona rite, we find that immediately after the exchange of rings, the priest begins the celebration of Mass utilizing the prayers and antiphons proper to the Mass of the Holy Spirit,[61] a widespread custom for weddings in Catalonian Spain,[62] in contrast to the more common practice elsewhere of using texts from the Mass of the Holy Trinity.[63] The Epistle (1 Cor 6:15–20) provides Saint Paul's exposition on the sacredness of the human body as the temple of the Holy Spirit and the need to keep oneself pure and chaste. The use of this lection at nuptial Masses dates back to the seventh century, when it is specified in the most ancient Roman lectionary, the Capitulary of Würzburg.[64] The Gospel is that of Christ declaring to the Pharisees the indissolubility of marriage (Mk 10:1–9).[65] Saint Matthew's Gospel account of this same episode (Mt 19:3–6) has been used in nuptial Masses since the tenth century, when it appears, albeit in a longer

---

[57] Text in Leo Cunibert Mohlberg, O.S.B., ed., *Missale Francorum*, REDSMF 2 (Rome: Herder, 1957), no. 56, p. 17.

[58] Radó and Mezey, *Libri liturgici manuscripti bibliothecarum Hungariae*, 123.

[59] Molin and Mutembe, *Rituel du mariage en France*, 137.

[60] Manuscript: Paris, Bibliothèque Mazarine, MS 527, fourteenth century, ibid., 302.

[61] Soberanas, *Ordinarium sacramentorum Barchinonense, 1501*, fol. 32v.

[62] The Mass of the Holy Spirit is specified in the nuptial rites of Vich (1496), Saragossa (1498), Palma de Majorca (1506), Valencia (1527), Lérida (1532), Urgel (1536), and Gerona (1550). See respectively Francesc Xavier Altés i Aguiló, ed., *Missale Vicense, 1496*, facsimile ed., Biblioteca liturgica catalana 3 (Barcelona: Institut d'Estudis Catalans, 2001), sanctoral, fols. 109v–112r; *Missale secundum morem ecclesie Cesaraugustane* (Saragossa: Paul Hurus, 1498), sanctoral, fols. 18v–19v; Gabriel Seguí i Trobat, ed., *El missal mallorquí de 1506: Estudi i edició segons l'exemplar de la Biblioteca Bartomeu March*, Col·lectània Sant Pacià 79 (Barcelona: Facultat de Teologia de Catalunya, Centre d'Estudis Teològics de Mallorca, 2003), 533; Parés i Saltor, *Ordinari d'Urgell de 1536*, 218; and Adalberto Franquesa, "El ritual Tarraconense", in *Liturgica*, vol. 2, Scripta et documenta 10 (Barcelona: Publicaciones de l'Abadia de Montserrat, 1958), 270.

[63] Molin and Mutembe, *Rituel du mariage en France*, 207–208.

[64] Text of Capitulary of Würzburg, in Germain Morin, "Le plus ancien *Comes* ou lectionnaire de l'église romaine", *Revue Bénédictine* 27 (1910): 66.

[65] Soberanas, *Ordinarium sacramentorum Barchinonense, 1501*, fol. 32v.

form (Mt 19:1–6), in the wedding liturgy of the Romano-Germanic Pontifical.[66]

During the Mass of the Barcelona nuptial rite, both the *Gloria* and the Creed are said.[67] At the Offertory, the groom makes three separate presentations of gifts to the priest: first, "light" (evidently a lit candle), then bread, then wine (probably *not* the unconsecrated bread and wine for the confection of the Eucharist).[68] Immediately after him, the bride presents the same three separate offerings.[69] As a variant of this, the 1496 missal of Vich, Spain, specifies that during the reading of the Gospel and the recitation of the Creed, the bride and groom stand side by side before the altar, each holding a lit candle, which they jointly present at the Offertory, before jointly presenting the bread and wine.[70] Well before the medieval era, Saint Peter Chrysologus (+450) speaks of brides and bridegrooms carrying lit candles as a symbol of conjugal chastity.[71] At the end of the Offertory in the Barcelona rite, there are two Secrets (i.e., concluding prayers of the Offertory rite) specified, one from the Mass of the Holy Spirit, and the other proper to the nuptial Mass, which we quote here, an oration dating back to the sixth-century Leonine Sacramentary of Rome:[72] "*Accept, we beseech you, O Lord, the gifts offered for the sacred law of marriage, and be the Dispenser of that work of which you are the Bestower. Through our Lord Jesus Christ, your Son, who lives and reigns with you in the unity of the same Holy Spirit . . .*"[73]

In the Barcelona text, the nuptial blessing is conferred immediately before the priest administers Holy Communion to himself. The blessing rite begins with a practice traceable to the early seventh century, or perhaps even earlier, by which the joining together of the couple in the matrimonial bond is symbolically represented:

---

[66] Text in Cyrille Vogel and Reinhard Elze, eds., *Pontifical romano-germanique du dixième siècle*, vol. 2, ST 227 (Vatican City: Biblioteca Apostolica Vaticana, 1963), 415.

[67] Soberanas, *Ordinarium sacramentorum Barchinonense, 1501*, fols. 33r, 34v–35r. The inclusion of both the *Gloria* and the Creed in the nuptial Mass is also specified in the Catalonian Spanish rituals of Valencia (1527) and Urgel (1536); see Franquesa, "El ritual Tarraconense", 271, and Parés i Saltor, *Ordinari d'Urgell de 1536*, 218.

[68] Although it is unlikely that in most late medieval nuptial rites the couple would have presented to the priest the unconsecrated bread and wine for the celebration of Mass, there is a marriage rite from a 1543 ritual of Metz, France, in which the bridegroom and bride exchange their words of solemn consent when the priest places their joined hands over the bread and wine that they present at the Offertory, a custom analogous to the placing of the hand upon a Bible to take an oath in court. The wording of the bridegroom's formula of consent implies that the unconsecrated *oblata* for the Mass were used to solemnize the couple's consent in this manner. See the text from the 1543 *Manuale curatorum civitatis et diocesis Metensis* in Molin and Mutembe, *Rituel du mariage en France*, 317, plus the discussion of the text, 218.

[69] Soberanas, *Ordinarium sacramentorum Barchinonense, 1501*, fol. 35v.

[70] Altés i Aguiló, *Missale Vicense, 1496*, sanctoral, fol. 110r. The same instructions are given in the 1547 ritual of Vich; see Franquesa, "Ritual Tarraconense", 272.

[71] Saint Peter Chrysologus, *Sermon 22*, PL 52, col. 262.

[72] Text in Leo Cunibert Mohlberg, O.S.B.; Leo Eizenhöfer, O.S.B.; and Petrus Siffrin, O.S.B., eds., *Sacramentarium Veronense*, REDSMF 1 (Rome: Herder, 1956), no. 1106, p. 139.

[73] Soberanas, *Ordinarium sacramentorum Barchinonense, 1501*, fol. 35v.

Before [the priest] should begin communicating, he should turn himself [toward the congregation]. And the spouses should come before the altar, and the woman should stand to the left of the man. And [the spouses] having knelt, the priest should bind them with a certain stole, in such a manner that the said stole should go across the shoulders of the man and the head of the woman. And the knot having been made [with the two ends of the stole tied together in front of the couple],[74] he should say over them:

> *Receive the yoke of the Lord. For the yoke of the Lord is sweet and his burden light. + In the name of the Father, and of the Son, and of the Holy Spirit. Amen.*[75]

The bridegroom and bride will remain kneeling and bound together in this manner through the end of the Mass and the concluding nuptial prayers following it. The custom of tying the bride and groom together is first mentioned by the Spanish Church Father Saint Isidore of Seville (+636), who tells of a ribbon being wrapped around the couple "lest they should break asunder the conjugal joint of unity".[76] Similarly, the fifth- to seventh-century nuptial rites preserved in the *Liber ordinum* of Spain specify that the priest is to place over the head of the bride and the shoulders of the bridegroom a veil surmounted by a white and purple ribbon.[77] The joining together of the couple with the ribbon and veil is the dramatic visual counterpart to the description of marriage as a "holy knot" given by the sixteenth-century English martyr Saint Thomas More (+1535) in his voluminous apologetic work, *The Confutation of Tyndale's Answer.*[78]

The priest's words in the Barcelona text, "*Receive the yoke*", are the same as those in the priestly ordination rite (from the tenth century onward)[79] said by the bishop to each newly ordained priest as the bishop shifts the priest's stole from the position designating the diaconate to that designating the priesthood.[80] In the ordination rite these words express the new priest's reception of his God-given vocation to the priesthood; in the marriage rite they express the couple's reception of their God-given vocation to matrimony. In both cases the

---

[74] We have paraphrased this added explanation from the rubrics in a later 1569 edition of the Barcelona *Ordinarium*; see *Ordinarium Barcinonense* (Barcelona: Claudius Bornat, 1569; digitized text, Barcelona: Biblioteca de Catalunya, 2010), fol. 78v.

[75] Soberanas, *Ordinarium sacramentorum Barchinonense, 1501,* fols. 35v–36r.

[76] Saint Isidore of Seville, *De ecclesiasticis officiis,* bk. 2, chap. 20, no. 7, in Lawson, *Sancti Isidori episcopi Hispalensis: De ecclesiasticis officiis,* 92.

[77] Férotin, *Liber ordinum,* col. 436 ("Manuscript A" text; the veil and ribbon are also mentioned in "Manuscript B" but with less detail).

[78] Saint Thomas More, *The Confutation of Tyndale's Answer,* ed. Louis Schuster et al., vol. 8 of *The Complete Works of St. Thomas More* (New Haven: Yale University Press, 1973), bk. 1, p. 87.

[79] See the priestly ordination rite of the tenth-century Romano-Germanic Pontifical in Vogel and Elze, *Pontifical romano-germanique,* 1:34.

[80] See pp. 167–168 of the present work.

vocation received is symbolically imposed upon the shoulders of the recipients, with the stole around the priest's neck in the ordination rite and across the bridegroom's shoulders in the marriage rite. This underlines the meaning of the Lord's "yoke" as the cross that all are called to carry in their respective vocations. The concept of marriage as the yoke of the Lord had arisen by the fifth century, when it appears in a poem on matrimony composed by Saint Paulinus of Nola (+431): "Harmonious souls are united in chaste love, a celibate young man of Christ, a virginal young woman of God. O Christ our God, lead these matching doves to your bridles and govern their necks placed under your gentle yoke, for light is your yoke, O Christ, which a prompt will receives and love bears in your pleasant service.... May the Cross be to you a venerated yoke." [81]

Although the veil mentioned in the *Liber ordinum* is not used in the Barcelona rite, it is found in other Spanish marriage texts, one of which describes it as white and purple in color (Jaén, 1499). [82] Its specific use can be seen in the missal of Avila (1510): "Those marrying should be placed before the altar rail kneeling. The young woman should be at the left hand of the man, and the minister [i.e., an assisting acolyte] should veil them with a clean and decent veil, the man over the shoulders, the young woman over the head. And he should place over the veil a stole or the yoke of the Lord." [83] The arrangement of the veil, over the bride's head but not over that of the bridegroom, reflects Saint Paul's teaching regarding the veiling of women as a sign of a husband's headship over his wife in marriage (1 Cor 11:7, 10): "The man ought not to cover his head, because he is the image and glory of God; but the woman is the glory of man.... Therefore ought the woman to have a power over her head, because of the angels." The liturgical object referred to in the Avila text as "the yoke of the Lord" is the *jugalis*, a multicolored ribbon made specifically for the marriage ceremonies, first mentioned nine centuries earlier by Saint Isidore of Seville. Isidore describes the ribbon as intertwining the colors of white and purple (the same two colors specified for the ribbon in the *Liber ordinum* and specified for the marriage veil in the Jaén rite). He explains that the white color, by its brightness, signifies the "cleanliness of life" to which the couple is called, that is, the practice of conjugal chastity, attained through the observance of periods of continence in their marriage, as counseled by Saint Paul ("that you may give yourselves to prayer" [1 Cor 7:5]). Isidore identifies the purple of the ribbon, symbolizing the redness of blood, as a sign of the procreative conjugal dimension

---

[81] Excerpted from Saint Paulinus of Nola, *Poem 25*, in Wilhelm von Hartel, ed., *Sancti Pontii Meropii Paulini Nolani: Camina*, CSEL 30 (Vienna: Österreichischen Akademie der Wissenschaften, 1999), 238, 244.

[82] *Missale Giennense / Manuale ... sacramenta* (1499), fol. 245r.

[83] *Missale Abulense* (1510), sig. D8r.

of marriage (the "debt" of conjugal union, as Saint Paul describes it [1 Cor 7:3]).[84]

The *jugalis* ribbon of Spanish nuptial ceremonies is mentioned together with the marriage veil in an early twelfth-century manuscript of Urgel, the 1499 manual of Jaén, and a 1530 ritual of Tarragona, yet in these three cases, the ribbon is placed not over the veil but rather across the shoulders of both the bride and the groom.[85] This variant of the custom would have more overtly demonstrated that the bride as well as the groom was receiving this sacrament as "the yoke of the Lord", that she also had to carry her cross in her God-given vocation, and that she and her husband were to carry their crosses and the yoke of their shared vocation together. In yet another adaptation of the tradition of symbolically binding the couple together, the 1494 missal of Orense, Spain, specifies that after the priest has covered the kneeling spouses with a veil, he is to bind them together over the veil with a cincture, the cord that a priest ties about his waist in vesting for Mass.[86] The use in the marriage rite of a cincture, considered a symbol of chastity, was very likely intended to serve the same symbolic purpose as the white of the *jugalis* ribbon mentioned earlier—to remind the couple that the virtue of chastity is also required of those in the married state.

Outside of Spain, there were instances when the priest's stole was utilized in the marriage rite to manifest the Church's solemn recognition of the matrimonial bond. The *Obsequiale Brixinense* of 1493, a liturgical book of Brixen in the Austrian Tyrol (what is now Bressanone, Italy), directs the priest to take the right hands of the bridegroom and bride and join them together; after the bridegroom and the bride have each pronounced the words of matrimonial consent, the priest places his stole over their joined right hands and says, "*And I, by the authority of God, bind you together matrimonially,* [Name of bridegroom] *and* [Name of bride], *in the name of the Father, and of the Son, and of the Holy Spirit. Amen.*"[87]

In the Barcelona rite, as the couple remain kneeling before the altar, bound together by the stole placed across them, the priest says over them the following blessing, a prayer traceable to the sixth-century

---

[84] Saint Isidore of Seville, *De ecclesiasticis officiis*, bk. 2, chap. 20, no. 7, in Lawson, *Sancti Isidori episcopi Hispalensis: De ecclesiasticis officiis*, 92.

[85] The Urgel manuscript, a *Liber mysticus*, is in the library of the Spanish abbey of Montserrat (Biblioteca, MS 72, early twelfth century). The relevant passages from this and the Tarragona ritual are quoted in Franquesa, "Ritual Tarraconense", 272–273. For the Jaén manual, see *Missale Giennense / Manuale ... sacramenta* (1499), fol. 245r.

[86] *Missale secundum usum Auriensis ecclesiae* (1494), first sig., 9v.

[87] *Obsequiale Brixinense* (Augsburg, Germany: Erhard Ratdolt, 1493; digitized text, Bayerische Staatsbibliothek, Munich, 2009), fol. 44v. This same custom was observed in Passau, Germany (1514); see *Agenda sive Benedictionale de actibus ecclesie secundum chorum et observationem ecclesie Pataviensis* (Basel, Switzerland: Jacobus Pfortzensis, 1514; digitized text, Bayerische Staatsbibliothek, Munich, 2008), fol. 17v.

Leonine Sacramentary of Rome,[88] which highlights the procreative dimension of the sacrament: *"Be favorable, we beseech you, O Lord, to our supplications, and graciously assist with your precepts, by which you have established the propagation of mankind, that what is joined by you the Creator may be preserved by your assistance. Through our Lord Jesus Christ your Son ..."*[89] There follows a special blessing for the bride in the form of a Preface, expressing the consecration of the woman to her new vocation as a wife and future mother.[90] This prayer as a whole is traceable to the eighth-century *Hadrianum* redaction of Rome's Gregorian Sacramentary,[91] but some of the text (roughly the second half) dates back to the sixth century Leonine Sacramentary of Rome.[92] The offering of a consecratory prayer for the bride alone reflects the preeminent role she shall undertake in the life of the family as the bearer and nurturer of the couple's future children, a preeminence noted by Saint Thomas Aquinas.[93] After highlighting the symbolism of matrimony as an image of the union between Christ and his Church, the prayer asks of God that the bride may imitate the virtues of the women saints and the holy women of the Bible. It asks that the bride may be blessed with the gift of motherhood while at the same time preserving a *"purity worthy of reverence"*:

> *Truly it is fitting and just, right and salutary, for us always and everywhere to give you thanks, O Lord, holy Father, almighty eternal God, who made all things from nothing with the might of your power, who having set in order the beginnings of the universe, fashioned for man made to the image of God the help of woman, inseparable for that reason, that you have given the feminine body its beginning from the flesh of man, teaching that what it has pleased you to be made in unity may never be put asunder. O God, who have consecrated the marital union with so excellent a mystery, that you have represented in the covenant of marriage the mystery of Christ and the Church; O God, by whom woman is united to man, and society is principally established, given with that bless + ing that alone was taken away neither by the penalty of original sin nor by the sentence of the flood: look favorably upon this your maidservant [Name], who in the binding union of wedlock eagerly seeks to be defended with your protection. May there be in her the bond of love and peace; faithful and chaste, may she marry in Christ and remain an imitator of the women saints. May she be as lovable to her husband as Rachel, as wise as Rebecca, as long loved and faithful as Sara. May the author of*

---

[88] Mohlberg, Eizenhöfer, and Siffrin, *Sacramentarium Veronense*, no. 1109, p. 140.

[89] Soberanas, *Ordinarium sacramentorum Barchinonense, 1501*, fol. 36r.

[90] The consecratory nature of this prayer is noted by Father Herbert Thurston, S.J. (Thurston, "Marriage, Ritual of", 706–707).

[91] Text in Jean Deshusses, ed., *Le sacramentaire grégorien: Ses principales formes d'après les plus anciens manuscrits*, vol. 1, 2nd ed., SF 16 (Fribourg, Switzerland: Editions Universitaires Fribourg, 1979), no. 838a–838b, pp. 310–311.

[92] Mohlberg, Eizenhöfer, and Siffrin, *Sacramentarium Veronense*, no. 1110, p. 140.

[93] Saint Thomas Aquinas, *Summa theologica*, supplement, q. 44, art. 2, reply obj. 1, 3:2723.

transgression take possession of nothing in her on account of her deeds, and may she remain bound by the commands of faith; joined in one marriage bond, may she flee forbidden contacts; may she protect her weakness with the strength of discipline. May her modesty be serious, her purity worthy of reverence, instructed in heavenly doctrines. May she be fruitful in offspring, may she be tried and innocent, and may she come to the rest of the blessed and to the heavenly kingdom, and see her children's children up to the third and fourth generation, and come to desired old age. Through the same Jesus Christ your Son, our Lord, who lives and reigns with you in the unity of the Holy Spirit, God, through all ages of ages. Response: *Amen.*[94]

The priest then invites the congregation to pray with him for the couple; this invocation originated as a prayer first found in the seventh- to eighth-century Bobbio Missal (a liturgical book of French or north Italian origin):[95]

Let us pray, dearest brethren, to almighty God, who has vouchsafed to bestow offspring, the gifts of his bless + ing, for the multiplication of mankind, that he may preserve these his servants [Name] and [Name], whom he has preordained for marital union. May he give them peaceful minds, well-matched souls, mutual manners bound by charity; may they also have by his gift desired offspring, that like his gift, so may they obtain his blessing, that these his servants [Name] and [Name] may be devoted in all humility of heart to the same One by whom they firmly believe themselves to be redeemed and enriched, our Lord Jesus Christ granting, who with the Father and the Holy Spirit lives and reigns, God, unto ages of ages. Response: *Amen.*[96]

After reminding the couple that they should remain where they are (still kneeling and bound by the stole), the priest continues with Holy Communion and the conclusion of the Mass, which includes a Post-communion prayer traceable to the sixth-century Leonine Sacramentary of Rome:[97] "*We beseech you, almighty God, to accompany the ordinances of your providence with your merciful love, that those you join together in legitimate union you may preserve in long-lived peace. Through our Lord Jesus Christ, your Son . . .*"[98]

The ceremony that follows in the Barcelona marriage rite, a concluding nuptial blessing, begins with a prayer dating back to Spain's ancient Mozarabic Rite, the text first appearing in the fifth- to seventh-century contents of the *Liber ordinum*.[99] The priest asks God to bless

---

[94] Soberanas, *Ordinarium sacramentorum Barchinonense, 1501*, fols. 36r–37r.

[95] Text in A. Lowe, ed., *The Bobbio Missal: Text*, HBS 58 (London: Henry Bradshaw Society, 1920), no. 550, pp. 167–168.

[96] Soberanas, *Ordinarium sacramentorum Barchinonense, 1501*, fol. 37r–37v.

[97] Mohlberg, Eizenhöfer, and Siffrin, *Sacramentarium Veronense*, no. 1108, p. 140.

[98] Soberanas, *Ordinarium sacramentorum Barchinonense, 1501*, fols. 37v–38r.

[99] Férotin, *Liber ordinum*, col. 439 ("Manuscript B" text).

the couple with an indissoluble union of their hearts and with a joy
that will lead them to the joys of Heaven:

> The Mass finished and the [Mass] blessing having been given, the
> priest in an alb should turn himself to the newlyweds. And with
> them kneeling, the priest should say the following blessing:
>
> *Let us pray.*
>
> *May the Lord bless + you by the word of our mouth and join your hearts
> together in a perpetual bond of genuine love. May you prosper in an abun-
> dance of present things; may you be fittingly fruitful in children. May you
> rejoice eternally with your friends. May the Lord give to you everlasting gifts,
> and to your parents times happily extended, and at the end of all your days,
> eternal joys. Through Christ our Lord. Amen.*[100]

The above prayer is followed by another, known as the Raguel Prayer,
a blessing text based upon the invocation that the Old Testament father
Raguel said at the wedding of his daughter Sara to Tobias, as related
in the Book of Tobias (7:15): "And taking the right hand of his daughter, he [Raguel] gave it into the right hand of Tobias, saying: 'The
God of Abraham, and the God of Isaac, and the God of Jacob be with
you, and may he join you together, and fulfill his blessing in you.'"
The text of the Raguel Prayer in the Barcelona rite, first found as a
Christian nuptial invocation in the aforementioned Spanish *Liber ordinum*,[101] is essentially the same as the Old Testament original, albeit set
in a Christian context: "*In the name + of the Father, and of the Son, and
of the Holy Spirit. Amen. May the God of Abraham, and the God of Isaac,
and the God of Jacob be with you. May he bind you together and fulfill his
blessing in you through all ages of ages. Amen.*"[102] The accompanying
actions of the priest in reciting this invocation are also specified in the
Barcelona text, giving a further outward expression to the nuptial union
of the couple, blessed together by God:

> Here the priest, having made the sign of the cross, should extend his
> hands over the head of the man. And touching his head, he should
> say: *May the God of Abraham.* And afterward touching the head of the
> woman, he should say: [*And*] *the God of Isaac.* And afterward return-
> ing to the head of the man, he should say: [*And*] *the God of Jacob,* etc.
> Afterward he should repeat this same, beginning with the head of the
> woman [*May the God of Abraham*] and ending on the same. A third
> time he should do this same, beginning with the head of the man
> [*May the God of Abraham*] and ending on the same.[103]

---

[100] Soberanas, *Ordinarium sacramentorum Barchinonense, 1501,* fol. 38r.

[101] Férotin, *Liber ordinum,* col. 438 ("Manuscript A" text).

[102] Soberanas, *Ordinarium sacramentorum Barchinonense, 1501,* fol. 38r–38v.

[103] Ibid., fol. 38r.

The priest's alternating "imposition" of his hands over the heads of the bridegroom and bride is a distinctly Catalonian practice that had arisen by the fourteenth century.[104] Thus it is found in the Spanish wedding rites of Vich (missal, 1496), Palma de Majorca (missal, 1506), Tarragona (ritual, 1530), and Urgel (*Ordinarium,* 1536).[105]

The marriage rite having been concluded, the priest removes the stole that he had earlier placed across the couple and dismisses them with a final blessing: "*In the name + of the Father, and of the Son, and of the Holy Spirit. Amen. Go in peace. May God give you his grace and blessing. Amen.*"[106] The wedding rubrics from the 1487 *Obsequiale Augustense* of Augsburg, Germany, direct that at the end of the concluding blessing the priest is to sprinkle the kneeling couple with holy water.[107]

In the Tyrolean see of Brixen (now Bressanone, Italy), the custom of a final blessing for the newlyweds took a unique form, as prescribed in the *Obsequiale Brixinense* of 1493, inspired by the belief that the recitation of the Prologue of Saint John's Gospel (Jn 1:1–14) constituted a species of blessing. After the Mass, the bridegroom and bride would go to kneel together before the altar, where the priest would rest his book of rites, the *Obsequiale,* upon their heads and read from it the beginning of Saint John's Gospel. He would then recite three prayers for the couple and a fourth specifically for the bride before imparting upon them his priestly blessing with the sign of the cross.[108]

The Marriage Rite of Lyre, France

The marriage rite found in a twelfth-century pontifical of the French Benedictine monastery of Lyre, in the diocese of Evreux,[109] contains a number of beautiful prayers and rubrics that differ from the Barcelona rite we have already considered. The text begins with detailed instructions regarding the arrival of the wedding party before the doors of the church:

> Before all things, those who are to be united in wedlock should come to the doors of the church before the witness of very many; and the consent of both should be required by the priest. And a summation of the woman's dowry should be made, and dividing it in the middle, some money should be set aside for the poor. And then at length the woman should be given by her father or her friends, whom the man

---

[104] This practice is found in a fourteenth-century sacramentary of Elne, France, a region under Catalonian influence; see Kenneth Stevenson, *Nuptial Blessing: A Study of Christian Marriage Rites,* Alcuin Club Collections 64 (London: Alcuin Club / SPCK, 1982), 61.

[105] Altés i Aguiló, *Missale Vicense, 1496,* sanctoral, fol. 112r; Seguí i Trobat, *Missal mallorquí de 1506,* 534; Franquesa, "Ritual Tarraconense", 274–275; Parés i Saltor, *Ordinari d'Urgell de 1536,* 219.

[106] Soberanas, *Ordinarium sacramentorum Barchinonense, 1501,* fol. 38v.

[107] *Obsequiale Augustense* (Augsburg, Germany: Erhard Ratdolt, 1487; digitized text, Bayerische Staatsbibliothek, Munich, 2008), fols. 58r, 59r.

[108] *Obsequiale Brixinense* (1493), fol. 45v.

[109] Text in Edmond Martène, *De antiquis ecclesiae ritibus* (Venice: Johannes Baptista Novelli, 1763–1764), bk. 1, chap. 9, art. 5, *ordo* 3, 2:128–129.

should receive in the faith of God, protecting her both when healthy and when sick, as long as she shall have lived; and they should hold her by the right hand, the priest beginning in this way:

> *Command thy strength, O God; confirm, O God, what thou hast wrought in us . . .* [Ps 67:29–31]. *Glory be to the Father . . .*[110]

The priest blesses the ring with two prayers,[111] after which follows the complex rite of placing the wedding ring ultimately on the bride's left hand. The retention of the ring on the left hand is succinctly explained in the Lyre rubrics by way of contrast to the placement of the episcopal ring in the consecration rite for bishops:

> Here the bridegroom should take the ring, and together with the priest he puts it upon three fingers of the bride's right hand, saying at the first finger: *In the name of the Father.* At the second: *And of the Son.* At the third: *And of the Holy Spirit.* And likewise he should put the same ring upon one finger of the left hand; and there he should leave it, that henceforth she may bear it on the left hand, according to the difference from the episcopal station, in which the ring is to be borne publicly on the right hand in token of perfect and full chastity.[112]

The priest then says the Raguel Prayer from the Book of Tobias that we saw at the end of the Barcelona rite but without the special actions of the priest found in the Barcelona ceremony. This prayer is followed in the Lyre rite by a second blessing based upon that found in the Book of Numbers, taught to Moses by God for the blessing of the Israelites by Aaron and his sons (Num 6:22–26). In the Lyre rite the blessing begins with a Trinitarian preamble: "*May God the Father bless + you, Jesus Christ pro + tect you, the Holy Spirit en + lighten you, and the Lord show his face to you and have mercy on you. May he turn his face toward you, and give you peace, and enrich you with every spiritual bless + ing in remission of all your sins, that you may have eternal life and live unto ages of ages. Amen.*"[113]

The couple is now led into the church, and upon reaching what the text terms "the middle of the church"—presumably a point halfway up the center aisle of the nave—they prostrate themselves. The priest recites over them Psalm 127, which speaks of the blessings of marriage ("*thy wife as a fruitful vine . . . thy children as olive plants. . . .*

---

[110] Ibid., 128.

[111] First prayer: "*Creator and Defender of mankind, Giver of spiritual grace, Bestower of eternal salvation, you, O Lord, send your blessing upon this ring. Through . . .*" Second prayer: "*Bless, O Lord, this ring that we bless + in your holy name, that the betrothed one who will have borne it as a sign of faithfulness may continue in your peace, and persevere in the devoted purity of faithfulness, and live always in your love, and flourish, grow old, and be enriched unto length of days. Through Christ our Lord . . .*" (Ibid.)

[112] Ibid.

[113] Ibid. This formula also appears in a twelfth-century missal of Bayeaux, France (Molin and Mutembe, *Rituel du mariage en France*, 284, 322).

And mayst thou see thy children's children").[114] After this and several standard versicles, the priest says over the prostrate couple a series of five
blessings[115] embellished with Old Testament comparisons and phrases:

> *O God of Abraham, God of Isaac, God of Jacob, bless + this very young
> couple and sow the seed of eternal life in their souls, that whatever they have
> learned for their benefit, they may be eager to practice it. Through Jesus
> Christ your Son, the Recoverer of men, who lives with you in the unity of
> the Holy Spirit . . .*[116]

> *Behold, O Lord, and bless + from Heaven this concord; and just as you sent
> your holy angel Raphael to Tobias and to Sara the daughter of Raguel, so
> may you vouchsafe, O Lord, to send your bless + ing upon these young
> people, that they may persevere in your will, and continue in your safety, and
> live and grow old in your love, and be made worthy and also peaceful, and
> be enriched unto length of days. Through our Lord Jesus Christ . . .*[117]

> *Look mercifully, O Lord, upon this your servant and upon this your maid-
> servant, that they may receive a heavenly bless + ing in your name and may
> see their children's children safe unto the third and fourth generation, and
> persevere in your faithfulness always, and in the future come to the heavenly
> realms. Through our Lord Jesus Christ . . .*[118]

> *May Almighty God, who in his power joined in marriage our first parents
> Adam and Eve, himself sanctify and bless + your hearts and bodies, and may
> he bind you together in fellowship and the love of true love. Amen.*[119]

> *May the Lord bless + you with every blessing and make you worthy in his
> sight, and may the riches of his glory abound in you, and may he instruct
> you in the word of truth, that you may be worthy to please him equally in
> soul and body. Amen.*[120]

The couple now rises, and they are brought into the choir of the
church on the right side. When the bride and groom reach where
they are to remain for the Mass, the bride is placed to the right of the
bridegroom (in contrast to the placement in the Barcelona rite).[121]

---

[114] Martène, *De antiquis ecclesiae ritibus*, bk. 1, chap. 9, art. 5, *ordo* 3, 2:128.

[115] Ibid.

[116] This prayer first appears in the tenth-century English Pontifical of Egbert; text in
H. M. J. Banting, ed., *Two Anglo-Saxon Pontificals (the Egbert and Sidney Sussex Pontificals)*,
HBS 104 (London: Henry Bradshaw Society, 1989), 140.

[117] This prayer also appears in the twelfth-century missal of Bury Saint Edmunds, England
(Molin and Mutembe, *Rituel du mariage en France*, 290, 324).

[118] This prayer also appears in a twelfth-century pontifical of Ely, England (ibid., 324).

[119] This prayer also appears in the twelfth-century missal of Bury Saint Edmunds, England
(ibid., 290, 323–324).

[120] This prayer also appears in a twelfth-century ritual of Porquerolles, France (ibid.,
322).

[121] Martène, *De antiquis ecclesiae ritibus*, bk. 1, chap. 9, art. 5, *ordo* 3, 2:128.

In addition to what was done at Lyre, other special rites accompanied the couple's entrance into the church elsewhere in medieval France. The 1543 ritual of Metz specifies that upon entering the church the bride is to go before the altar alone, where she then kneels to pray, after which she is to kiss the side of the altar before taking her place for the nuptial Mass to follow.[122] A fifteenth-century ritual of Bordeaux directs that immediately before entering the church the bridegroom and bride should each venerate with a kiss a cross offered to them.[123] In the nuptial rite from a fourteenth-century ritual of Cambrai, the priest leads the couple by the hand into the church, saying as he does so, "*We shall go to the house of the Lord rejoicing.*"[124]

In the Lyre nuptial rite, the votive Mass of the Holy Trinity is celebrated,[125] the Mass most commonly used in medieval marriage rites. The readings, however, are specific to the nuptial Mass (1 Cor 6:15–20; Mt 19:3ff.), as is the second of two Secrets provided for the Offertory.[126] This Offertory oration is a modified version of a nuptial Mass prayer first found as a Collect in the seventh-century Gelasian Sacramentary of Rome[127] but ultimately derived from the special *Hanc igitur* insertion for the Roman Canon assigned to nuptial Masses in the sixth-century Leonine Sacramentary of Rome:[128] "*Attend, O Lord, to our supplications, and receive favorably and graciously this oblation, which we offer you on behalf of your servants, whom you have found worthy to bring to the state of maturity, and to the day of their wedding. Through . . .*"[129]

The bridegroom and bride again prostrate themselves for the entire Roman Canon: "After the *Sanctus* they should prostrate themselves in prayer, with a cloth extended over them, which four men should hold at the four sides."[130] This cloth, constituting a form of canopy, was commonly used in the wedding rites of northern France, where it was

---

[122] *Manuale curatorum civitatis et diocesis Metensis* (1543), in Molin and Mutembe, *Rituel du mariage en France*, 317.

[123] Manuscript: Bordeaux, France, Archives Diocésaines, MS Y 3, fifteenth century, cited ibid., 200; Stevenson, *Nuptial Blessing*, 61.

[124] Manuscript: Cambrai, France, Bibliothèque Municipale, MS 236, fourteenth century, in Molin and Mutembe, *Rituel du mariage en France*, 314.

[125] The chants for the Mass of the Holy Trinity are all traceable to the Antiphonary of Senlis (France, c. 880); see René-Jean Hésbert, ed., *Antiphonale missarum sextuplex* (Brussels, 1935; repr. Rome: Herder, 1967), 173.

[126] Martène, *De antiquis ecclesiae ritibus*, bk. 1, chap. 9, art. 5, *ordo* 3, 2:128. The text as transcribed by Dom Martène specifies only the opening verse of the Gospel reading; in medieval nuptial Masses, this lection would usually conclude with verse 6, but there are some French wedding rites, including those of Amiens, Reims, and Metz, in which the reading continues to verse 11 (Molin and Mutembe, *Rituel du mariage en France*, 213).

[127] Text in Leo Cunibert Mohlberg, O.S.B., et al., eds., *Liber sacramentorum Romanae aeclesiae ordinis anni circuli (Sacramentarium Gelasianum)*, REDSMF 4 (Rome: Herder, 1960), no. 1445, p. 208.

[128] Mohlberg, Eizenhöfer, and Siffrin, *Sacramentarium Veronense*, no. 1107, p. 139.

[129] Martène, *De antiquis ecclesiae ritibus*, bk. 1, chap. 9, art. 5, *ordo* 3, 2:128.

[130] Ibid.

known as the *poêle*.[131] Such canopies were used elsewhere, as in the nuptial rite of England's 1504 Sarum Missal, which directs four clerics vested in surplices to hold the cloth over the couple.[132] This cloth seems analogous to the canopy used in Jewish weddings, the *huppah*.[133] The *poêle* of the medieval French nuptial rites was often but not always white in color. The illuminated manuscript of a missal from 1300 depicts a *poêle* with alternating bands of red and white coloring; the *poêle* for a French nobleman's wedding in 1392 was made from green damask brocaded in gold.[134] A French ritual of Chartres dating from 1580 explains the *poêle* as signifying that the couple has been united by "legitimate and honorable love" and that they should steadfastly persevere in fidelity "under the same roof", considering all they have as shared in common.[135]

Before the sign of peace, the priest says over the prostrate couple the same two blessing prayers that in the Barcelona rite are said over the couple just before Holy Communion. The second of these is the special consecratory Preface devoted to the blessing of the bride.[136] At the conclusion of this latter blessing, the couple is directed to "rise from prayer", from their prostrate position, to receive from the priest the sign of peace (identified in the Lyre text as "the peace"):[137] "The bridegroom should receive the peace from the priest and pass it to the bride, kissing her, and neither he nor she [should pass it] to anyone else; but a cleric, after him, receiving the peace from the priest, should pass it to the others as is customary."[138] The thirteenth-century Dominican theologian William Pérault (+1271) observes that the sign of peace given by the bridegroom to his bride constitutes a solemn pledge of love to his wife, for it is given at Mass, "in the presence of the Body of the Lord".[139]

After the Mass, the priest blesses bread and wine to be shared by the bridegroom and bride in celebration of their wedding:

> Bread and wine in a small vessel should be blessed, and they should taste them in the name of the Lord.
> Blessing:
> *Let us pray.*
> *Bless, O Lord, this bread and this drink and this vessel, even as you blessed the five loaves in the desert and the six water jars in Cana of Galilee, that all tasting of it may be healthy and sober and blameless, O Savior of the*

[131] Molin and Mutembe, *Rituel du mariage en France*, 229, 231.
[132] Dickinson, *Missale ad usum insignis et praeclarae ecclesiae Sarum*, col. 839*.
[133] Stevenson, *Nuptial Blessing*, 8.
[134] Molin and Mutembe, *Rituel du mariage en France*, 229, 232.
[135] Ritual of Nicolas de Thou, Chartres, 1580, quoted ibid., 232.
[136] Martène, *De antiquis ecclesiae ritibus*, bk. 1, chap. 9, art. 5, *ordo* 3, 2:128–129.
[137] In the period from which the Lyre rite dates (twelfth century), the pax board (described on p. 33 of the present work) had not yet been introduced.
[138] Martène, *De antiquis ecclesiae ritibus*, bk. 1, chap. 9, art. 5, *ordo* 3, 2:129.
[139] William Pérault, *Summae virtutum, ac vitiorum*, vol. 1, *Summa aurea de virtutibus et vitiis* (Lyons, France: Antonius Vincentius, 1551; digitized text, Bayerische Staatsbibliothek, Munich, 2009), tome 1, pt. 2, tract 4, chap. 12, p. 391.

world, who live and reign with God the Father, in the unity of the Holy Spirit . . .[140]

A 1557 manual of Thérouanne, France, specifies that upon the conclusion of the nuptial Mass the newlywed couple should bring before the altar the candles they have held in their hands during the wedding rite, tracing a cross upon the altar and kissing it as they do so.[141] Many of the medieval marriage rites, including that of twelfth-century Lyre, provide a further ceremony for the newlyweds in which the priest comes to their new home after the nuptial Mass, either later in the day or in the evening, to bless their bridal chamber, the room they will share as husband and wife. It is likely that the practice drew its inspiration, at least in part, from the beautiful prayer said by Tobias and Sara on their wedding night, as related in the Book of Tobias (Tob 8:4–10):

> Then Tobias exhorted the virgin, and said to her: Sara, arise, and let us pray to God today, and tomorrow, and the next day; because for these three nights we are joined to God; and when the third night is over, we will be in our own wedlock. For we are the children of saints, and we must not be joined together like heathens that know not God. So they both arose, and prayed earnestly both together that health might be given them. And Tobias said: Lord God of our fathers, may the heavens and the earth, and the sea, and the fountains, and the rivers, and all thy creatures that are in them, bless thee. Thou madest Adam of the slime of the earth, and gavest him Eve for a helper. And now, Lord, thou knowest, that not for fleshly lust do I take my sister to wife, but only for the love of posterity, in which thy name may be blessed for ever and ever. Sara also said: Have mercy on us, O Lord, have mercy on us, and let us grow old both together in health.

The earliest extant Christian nuptial text to include a rite for blessing the bridal chamber of a newlywed couple is that found in the *Liber ordinum* of Spain, the contents of which date from the fifth to the seventh century.[142] The twelfth-century pontifical of Lyre specifies that the priest should come at night to the newlywed couple's home to impart his blessing:

> But at night, when [the bridegroom and bride] shall have come to their bed, the priest should approach and bless the bridal chamber, saying:

---

[140] Martène, *De antiquis ecclesiae ritibus*, bk. 1, chap. 9, art. 5, *ordo* 3, 2:129. Similarly, the twelfth-century nuptial rites in a pontifical of Avranches, France, and in the missal of Bury Saint Edmunds, England, include a blessing of wine (Molin and Mutembe, *Rituel du mariage en France*, 289, 291, 325).

[141] *Manuale* of Thérouanne, France, 1557, in Molin and Mutembe, *Rituel du mariage en France*, 222.

[142] Férotin, *Liber ordinum*, col. 433 ("Manuscript B" text).

Bless, O Lord, this bridal chamber and all dwelling in it, that they may continue in your peace, and persevere in your will, and live in your love, and grow old, and be enriched in length of days. Through our Lord Jesus Christ . . .

He should then confer a blessing over them, saying:

May God bless your bodies and your souls, and may he grant his blessing upon you even as he blessed Abraham, Isaac, and Jacob. Amen.

May the hand of the Lord be upon you, and may he send his holy angel, that he [the angel] may protect you all the days of your life. Amen.[143]

In the fourteenth-century missal of Esztergom, Hungary, the second of two prayers provided for the priest's blessing of the newlyweds' bridal chamber reminds the couple that in this room that they will share as husband and wife they are called above all else to serve God in their married vocation: "*Grant, we beseech you, O Lord, your bless + ing upon this young man and this young woman, that they may become your servants in this place and may continually serve you zealously. Through Christ our Lord. Amen.*"[144]

---

[143] Martène, *De antiquis ecclesiae ritibus*, bk. 1, chap. 9, art. 5, *ordo* 3, 2:129. The prayer in this rite, "*Bless, O Lord, this bridal chamber*" (*Benedic, Domine, thalamum istum*), predates the Lyre ceremony by at least two centuries, for it is also found in a tenth-century ritual of Durham, England (Molin and Mutembe, *Rituel du mariage en France*, 326).

[144] Text in Radó and Mezey, *Libri liturgici manuscripti bibliothecarum Hungariae*, 124. This prayer is a variant of an oration earlier found in the nuptial rite of the twelfth-century missal of Bury Saint Edmunds, England (Molin and Mutembe, *Rituel du mariage en France*, 290, 323).

8 Extreme Unction (Anointing of the Sick)

Almighty everlasting God, eternal salvation of the believing, graciously hear me, your unworthy servant, on behalf of your servant [Name], and give him true repentance, true fidelity. Deliver him, Lord, even as you vouchsafed to deliver Adam from hell; Peter from prison; Paul from chains; Thecla from beasts; Susanna from false accusation; the paralytic from his cot; Lazarus from the tomb; the people of Israel from the midst of the sea; Jonas from the belly of the whale; Lot from Sodom; the three youths Sidrach, Misach, and Abdenago from the furnace of burning fire; Daniel from the lions' den; David from the evil sword; [and] Mary Magdalen from seven demons; so may you vouchsafe to free him, Lord, from all his sins and from all his crimes.

Prayer from "Order for Visiting and Anointing the Sick",
Romano-Germanic Pontifical, tenth century[1]

In an early fifteenth-century Lenten instruction, the English priest John Drury, writing for his parish of Beccles, succinctly describes the sacrament of the anointing of the sick, known in the Middle Ages as *extreme unction*: "The last anointing alleviates both ghostly and bodily sickness, and strengthens the soul in his passing, and . . . furthers him greatly toward bliss."[2] Saint Thomas Aquinas (+1274) notes that extreme unction "prepares man for glory immediately, since it is given to those who are departing from this life".[3] The existence of this sacrament from the inception of the Church is clearly attested by the often-quoted words from the Letter of Saint James (Jas 5:14–15), "Is any man sick among you? Let him bring in the priests of the church, and let them pray over him, anointing him with oil in the name of the Lord. And the prayer of faith shall save the sick man; and the Lord

---

[1] Text in Cyrille Vogel and Reinhard Elze, eds., *Le pontifical romano-germanique du dix-ième siècle*, vol. 2, ST 227 (Vatican City: Biblioteca Apostolica Vaticana, 1963), 252.

[2] John Drury, "Tract on the Manner of Confession", in S. B. Meech, "John Drury and His English Writings", *Speculum* 9 (1934): 78 (original Middle English text). In this quotation, the spelling, punctuation, and word order of the original have been modernized.

[3] Saint Thomas Aquinas, *Summa theologica: First Complete American Edition in Three Volumes*, trans. Fathers of the English Dominican Province (New York: Benziger Brothers, 1948), supplement, q. 29, art. 1, reply obj. 2, 3:2665.

shall raise him up; and if he be in sins, they shall be forgiven him."
Further testimony to the administration of extreme unction in the
early Church is provided by a fourth-century prayer entitled "Prayer
for the Oil of the Sick", from the *Euchology of Serapion of Thmuis*, a
liturgical book of Christian Egypt:

> *We invoke you, who possess all power and strength, the Savior of all men,*
> *Father of our Lord and Savior Jesus Christ, and we pray, that you may send*
> *from Heaven your Son's power of healing upon this oil, that to those who are*
> *anointed with these your creatures or receive them, it may be made into a*
> *defense against every sickness and every infirmity, into a remedy against every*
> *demon, unto the expulsion of every unclean spirit, unto the warding off of*
> *every wicked spirit, unto the extirpation of every fever and chill and all*
> *weakness, unto good grace and the remission of sins, unto a remedy of life*
> *and salvation, unto health and soundness of soul and body and spirit, unto*
> *perfect health.* [4]

The anointing of the body with holy oil constitutes the essential
"matter" of the sacrament, as the Council of Trent was later to define
in 1551.[5] The suitability of oil for this sacred purpose is explained by
Saint Thomas Aquinas:

> The spiritual healing, which is given at the end of life, ought to be
> complete, since there is no other to follow; it ought also to be gentle,
> lest hope, of which the dying stand in utmost need, be shattered
> rather than fostered. Now oil has a softening effect, it penetrates to
> the very heart of a thing, and spreads over it. Hence, in both the
> foregoing respects, it is a suitable matter for this sacrament.[6]

The words accompanying the application of the holy oil were defined
by the Council of Trent as the "form" of the sacrament,[7] albeit the
particular wording of the anointing formula has varied over the centuries. The Council also defined that Christ himself instituted extreme
unction and that priests and bishops are the only valid ministers of this
sacrament.[8] It should be noted here that while there are no *direct* references to extreme unction in the Gospel accounts of the public ministry of Christ, the mention of the Apostles anointing the sick after
Christ had sent them out two by two, related in the Gospel of Saint

---

[4] *Sacramentarium Serapionis*, no. 29 (excerpt), in Francis Xavier Funk, ed., *Didascalia et Constitutiones apostolorum*, vol. 2, *Testimonia et scripturae propinquae* (Paderborn, Germany: Libraria Ferdinandi Schoeningh, 1905), 190–193 (Greek and Latin texts).

[5] Council of Trent, session 14, November 25, 1551, *De extrema unctione*, chap. 1, in H.J. Schroeder, O.P., *Canons and Decrees of the Council of Trent: Original Text with English Translation* (Saint Louis, Mo.: B. Herder, 1955), 100, 375.

[6] Saint Thomas Aquinas, *Summa theologica*, supplement, q. 29, art. 4, 3:2667.

[7] Council of Trent, session 14, November 25, 1551, *De extrema unctione*, chap. 1, in Schroeder, *Canons and Decrees of the Council of Trent*, 100, 375.

[8] Ibid., chaps. 1 and 3, pp. 99, 100–101, 375, 376.

Mark (6:13), was identified by the Council of Trent as an indirect reference to the sacrament.[9]

As for the specific liturgical rite by which extreme unction has been administered to the sick, a relatively brief unction ceremony is given in the ancient liturgical book of Spain's Mozarabic Rite known as the *Liber ordinum*, an eleventh-century compilation of older texts believed to date largely from the fifth to the seventh century. The *Liber ordinum* text directs the priest to anoint crosswise the head of the invalid and includes a prayer for the invalid's physical healing and the remission of his sins through the anointing.[10] In the seventh-century Gelasian Sacramentary of Rome, an anointing rite is not expressly mentioned, but the sacramentary does provide a series of four prayers to be said "over the infirm in the home" and four others for the "reconciliation of penitents at death".[11] By the ninth to the tenth century there had appeared in Carolingian France and Germany a fully developed liturgical rite for the administration of extreme unction, a long rite with multiple anointings, rich in prayers, psalms, antiphons, and versicles.[12] Under the inspiration of the Apostle Saint James' above-cited description of several priests coming together to pray over and anoint the sick man (Jas 5:14–15), it was also a common practice of the ninth- to tenth-century period for more than one priest to participate in the unction rite.[13] The sheer prolixity of these Carolingian unction rites manifested the depth of the Church's solicitude for the sick.

The need for an extreme unction rite that could be completed within a more practical time span subsequently led to the introduction of a considerably shorter ceremony.[14] A somewhat abbreviated unction rite is given in the *Liber tramitis* (formerly called the Customs of Farfa), a customary of the French Benedictine abbey of Cluny and dating from about 1043, which also simplifies the ceremony by prescribing only one priest (rather than several priests) for the administration of the

---

[9] Ibid., chap. 1, pp. 99, 375.

[10] Text in Marius Férotin, O.S.B., ed., *Le Liber ordinum en usage dans l'église wisigothique et mozarabe d'Espagne du cinquième au onzième siècle* (Paris, 1904), repr., ed. Anthony Ward, S.M., and Cuthbert Johnson, O.S.B., BELS 83 (Rome: Centro Liturgico Vincenziano, Edizioni Liturgiche, 1996), cols. 71–73.

[11] For the Gelasian texts, see Leo Cunibert Mohlberg, O.S.B., et al., eds., *Liber sacramentorum Romanae aeclesiae ordinis anni circuli (Sacramentarium Gelasianum)*, REDSMF 4 (Rome: Herder, 1960), nos. 1535–1538, pp. 221–222, and nos. 364–367, pp. 58–59.

[12] H. B. Porter, "The Origin of the Medieval Rite for Anointing the Sick or Dying", *JTS*, n.s., 7, no. 2 (October 1956): 214.

[13] Mario Righetti, *Manuale di storia liturgica* (Milan: Editrice Ancora, 1949–1955), 4:244. To cite one example, the unction rubrics of the tenth-century Romano-Germanic Pontifical repeatedly speak of "priests" rather than of a single priest arriving at the home of the infirm and performing the prescribed actions of the rite; see Vogel and Elze, *Pontifical romano-germanique*, 2:246, 258–260, 269.

[14] Antoine Chavasse, "Prières pour les malades et onction sacramentelle", in Aimé-Georges Martimort, ed., *L'église en prière: Introduction à la liturgie* (Paris: Desclée, 1961), 586.

sacrament.[15] The shortened unction rite that appeared in the thirteenth-century Pontifical of the Roman Curia, administered by one priest,[16] was subsequently disseminated by the Franciscan Order, beginning with the 1230 issuance of the friars' Regula Breviary, which provided the unction text in an *Ordo* appended to the breviary.[17] A modestly revised version of this unction rite, given in the Franciscans' 1260 Ritual for the Last Sacraments,[18] became the basis for the format of extreme unction universally promulgated in the *Rituale Romanum* of 1614.[19]

Commonly the administration of extreme unction was joined to the conferral of two other sacraments, penance and Holy Communion. At the end of this chapter we will provide an excursus on the bringing of the Eucharist to the sick, the Viaticum rite. As for the sacrament of penance, the rite entitled "Order for Anointing the Infirm" in the tenth-century Romano-Germanic Pontifical[20] advises that extreme unction should be preceded by confession: "Before the infirm should be anointed, he should wholly confess to God and at the same time to his priest all his sins and receive full reconciliation from him, that, with the boils of his sins the more cleanly opened by confession, the spiritual unction may more fittingly assist him in healing interiorly the hidden corruption of evils."[21] Further advice on how the priest should counsel the recipient of extreme unction is given at the end of the rubrics:

> Also, when you have come to the infirm, examine him particularly, and when he has confessed his sins, say to him that he should not despair of the forgiveness or the mercy of God, but he should firmly hold that he shall be saved, if he should die that very hour; only his intention should be such that, if he should live, what he has done he should amend by penitence and by fasting and alms and prayer, and no longer do the same. And say [to him] that by this intention he shall be able to be saved, even if he should die....

---

[15] *Liber tramitis* (formerly called the Customs of Farfa), bk. 2, chap. 54, in Bruno Albers, ed., *Consuetudines monasticae*, vol. 1, *Consuetudines Farfenses* (Stuttgart: Jos. Roth, Bibliopolae, 1900), 190–191.

[16] Text in Michel Andrieu, ed., *Le pontifical romain au moyen-âge*, vol. 2, *Le pontifical de la Curie romaine au XIIIe siècle*, ST 87 (Vatican City: Biblioteca Apostolica Vaticana, 1940), 486–492.

[17] The *Ordo fratrum minorum secundum consuetudinem romae ecclesiae*, included in the Regula Breviary that was issued at the Franciscans' general chapter of 1230, is discussed in Stephen J. P. Van Dijk, O.F.M., *Sources of the Modern Roman Liturgy: The Ordinals by Haymo of Faversham and Related Documents (1243–1307)*, Studia et documenta Franciscana 2 (Leiden, Netherlands: E.J. Brill, 1963), 1:135–137.

[18] Ritual for the Last Sacraments (1260), in Van Dijk, *Sources of the Modern Roman Liturgy*, 2:388–390 (text). See also the discussion of this text ibid., 1:134–137.

[19] Text in Manlio Sodi and Juan Javier Flores Arcas, eds., *Rituale Romanum: Editio princeps (1614)*, facsimile ed., MLCT 5 (Vatican City: Libreria Editrice Vaticana, © 2004), 59–63 (original pagination).

[20] Vogel and Elze, *Pontifical romano-germanique*, 2:258–270.

[21] Ibid., 258.

Say also that he should not fear to die, but he should unite his will with the will of God, that, even as it is pleasing to him [God], thus is it also pleasing to him [the infirm]. That if God wills that he should live, he should also be glad to live. Neither should he fear death on account of his wife, his children, his servants and maidservants, nor for anything, but he should place all things under the ordinance of God, for without him God is able to guide his family, both his wife and his children, because if he would have lived, he would not have been able to support them without the help of God.[22]

The Rite of Extreme Unction in Jaén, Spain

The rite that we shall present as our primary example of the medieval extreme unction liturgy, taken from a combined missal and sacramental manual issued for the Spanish diocese of Jaén in 1499, constitutes a late medieval illustration of the prolonged unction rite that had first developed in Carolingian Europe over six centuries earlier.[23] This Spanish text is largely composed of elements drawn from seventh- to tenth-century sources, particularly the seventh-century Gelasian Sacramentary of Rome and the tenth-century Romano-Germanic Pontifical.

The Jaén rite begins after the priest who is going to anoint the sick person has celebrated a Mass for him. Vested in an alb and stole and preceded by acolytes carrying the cross, holy water, and the holy oil (the "oil of the sick"), the priest proceeds to the home of the invalid. Upon arriving and entering, he says, "*Peace to this house and to all dwelling within it*",[24] an expanded form of the salutation that Christ taught to his disciples in sending them to preach (Mt 10:12; Lk 10:5–6). The priest now sprinkles the home with holy water while saying the antiphon *Asperges me* ("*Thou shalt sprinkle me*");[25] the aspersion of the invalid's dwelling at the outset of the extreme unction rite is found as early as the ninth century in the Pontifical of Saint Prudentius, a liturgical book of Troyes, France, which specifies that holy water "with the odor of incense" should be used for this sprinkling.[26] In the Jaén rite, the priest next recites an antiphon of tenth-century origin evoking the Passover imagery of the lambs' blood that was applied to the lintels and doorposts of the Israelites' homes to protect them from the plague striking the Egyptians' firstborn (Ex 12:7, 13, 22–23), prefiguring the Paschal mystery: "*Place, O Lord, the sign of salvation on these homes, that you may not allow the avenging angel to enter into the homes in which we live; from Heaven place your sign, O Lord, and protect us; then*

---

[22] Ibid., 270.

[23] *Missale Giennense / Manuale continens ordinem ad celebrandum ecclesiastica sacramenta* [*Missale secundum morem et consuetudinem sancte ecclesie Gienensis*] (Seville: Meinard Ungut and Stanislao Polono, 1499), fols. 249r–255r.

[24] Ibid., fol. 249r. This form of the versicle is first found as an extreme unction rite salutation in the tenth-century Romano-Germanic Pontifical; see Vogel and Elze, *Pontifical romano-germanique*, 2:246.

[25] *Missale Giennense / Manuale . . . sacramenta* (1499), fol. 249r.

[26] *Pontificale sancti Prudentii* (excerpt), PL 115, col. 1439.

there will be in us no plague to harm us." [27] After a brief series of versicles and responses, the priest then prays that God may send down his angel upon the invalid's home for the good of all dwelling or assembling within it.[28] This latter prayer, first found in the seventh-century Gelasian Sacramentary of Rome,[29] is in turn followed by three more originally from the Gelasian Sacramentary[30] in which the priest implores the forgiveness of the invalid's sins:

> *Hear, O Lord, our prayers, and show clemency for the sins of those confessing to thee, that those whom guilt of conscience accuses the pardon of thy mercy may absolve. Through Christ our Lord.*

> *Hearken, O Lord, to our supplications; let not the continued kindness of your mercy be absent from this your servant; heal his wounds and forgive his sins, that he may be worthy always to cling to you, Lord God, never separated from you by iniquities. Through Christ our Lord.*

> *O Lord our God, who are not vanquished by sin but are appeased by satisfaction for sin, we beseech you, look upon this your servant, who to you confesses to have grievously sinned; yours it is to give absolution of sins and to grant pardon to the sinning, who have said you prefer the repentance of sinners rather than their death; grant, O Lord, to this your servant, that he may observe vigils of penitence unto you and, with his deeds amended, rejoice to be granted everlasting joys by you. Through Christ our Lord.* [31]

The Jaén text says nothing about how the invalid's sickroom or home should be prepared beforehand for the priest's arrival, but in a contemporaneous text, a ritual of Châlons-sur-Marne, France (c. 1500), the rubrics specify that when the priest enters the house, "At least seven candles should be lit, which should burn through the entire office ..." [32] The Châlons ritual also directs that seven balls of cotton, "placed between two platters", should be provided, to be used later in the ceremony for wiping away the holy oil after the anointing of the invalid.[33]

---

[27] *Missale Giennense / Manuale ... sacramenta* (1499), fol. 249r. This antiphon is first found in the tenth-century Romano-Germanic Pontifical; see Cyrille Vogel and Reinhard Elze, eds., *Le pontifical romano-germanique du dixième siècle*, vol. 1, ST 226 (Vatican City: Biblioteca Apostolica Vaticana, 1963), 122.

[28] *Missale Giennense / Manuale ... sacramenta* (1499), fol. 249r–249v; prayer: "*Graciously hear us, holy Father, almighty eternal God, and vouchsafe to send your holy angel from Heaven, that he may preserve, sustain, protect, visit, and defend all living or assembling within this dwelling. Through Christ our Lord.*" This prayer subsequently appears in the universally promulgated extreme unction rite of the 1614 *Rituale Romanum*; see Sodi and Flores Arcas, *Rituale Romanum: Editio princeps* (1614), 60 (original pagination).

[29] Mohlberg, Eizenhöfer, and Siffrin, *Liber sacramentorum*, no. 1558, pp. 225–226.

[30] Ibid., nos. 78, 80, and 81, respectively, p. 17.

[31] *Missale Giennense / Manuale ... sacramenta* (1499), fol. 249v.

[32] Text in Edmond Martène, *De antiquis ecclesiae ritibus* (Venice: Johannes Baptista Novelli, 1763–1764), bk. 1, chap. 7, art. 4, *ordo* 30, 1:343.

[33] Ibid.

The theme of God's healing of the sick now comes to the fore with the recitation of the antiphon "*The Lord Jesus told his disciples: In my name expel demons; and impose hands upon the sick and they will recover.*" This verse is said together with Psalm 3, which expresses confidence in God amid afflictions: "*Many say to my soul: There is no salvation for him in his God. But thou, O Lord, art my protector, my glory, and the lifter up of my head*" (verses 3–4).[34]

The prayer that follows Psalm 3, an oration first found in the twelfth-century *Pontificale Romanum*,[35] quotes in full Saint James' account of the sacrament (Jas 5:14–15) in the course of pleading for the forgiveness and salvation of the invalid:

> *Almighty eternal God, who said through your blessed Apostle James, "Is any man sick among you? Let him bring in the priests of the Church; and let them pray for him, anointing him with holy oil in the name of the Lord. And the prayer of faith shall save the sick man; and the Lord shall raise him up; and if he be in sins, they shall be forgiven him*" [cf. Jas 5:14–15]: *we humbly beseech you, O Lord, that through the mystery[36] of our anointing and the gift of your holy mercy, this your servant may be worthy to obtain the forgiveness of his sins and attain to eternal life. Through Christ our Lord.*[37]

In words traceable to the seventh-century Gelasian Sacramentary,[38] the priest now humbly prays that his supplications in administering the sacrament may be acceptable to God: "*Attend, O Lord, to our supplications, and clemently hear me also, who foremost require your mercy, as him whom you have constituted the minister of this work not by an election of merit but by the gift of your grace; and give confidence of the fulfillment of your gift that he is to work in our ministry by your goodness. Who live and reign . . .*"[39]

The Jaén extreme unction rite includes the recitation of the seven penitential psalms with seven corresponding antiphons, the same antiphons that accompany these psalms in the rite entitled "Order for Visiting the Infirm" found in the twelfth-century *Pontificale Romanum* (albeit in a slightly different sequence).[40] In the Jaén text, the seven psalms are recited concurrently with the seven stages of anointing the invalid, such that each psalm serves as a prelude to the anointing of one particular part of the body. The first of the seven penitential psalms

---

[34] *Missale Giennense / Manuale . . . sacramenta* (1499), fol. 249v.

[35] Text in Michel Andrieu, ed., *Le pontifical romain au moyen-âge*, vol. 1, *Le pontifical romain du XIIᵉ siècle*, ST 86 (Vatican City: Biblioteca Apostolica Vaticana, 1938), 267.

[36] The use of the Latin word *mysterium* at this point in the Jaén text, instead of the term *ministerium* used in the twelfth-century *Pontificale Romanum*, is also found in the text of this prayer from the 1568 extreme unction rite of Mexico City; see *Manuale sacramentorum, secundum usum almae ecclesiae mexicanae* (Mexico City: Petrus Ocharte, 1568), fol. 75r.

[37] *Missale Giennense / Manuale . . . sacramenta* (1499), fol. 249v.

[38] Mohlberg, Eizenhöfer, and Siffrin, *Liber sacramentorum*, no. 356, p. 57.

[39] *Missale Giennense / Manuale . . . sacramenta* (1499), fols. 249v–250r.

[40] Andrieu, *Pontifical romain au moyen-âge*, 1:270.

to be said is Psalm 6, with its third verse as the source for the accompanying antiphon: "*Heal me, Lord, for my bones are troubled.*" As in the psalm recited earlier, so too in Psalm 6 grief gives way to hope in God: "*The Lord hath heard my supplication: the Lord hath received my prayer*" (Ps 6:10).[41]

The actual anointing of the invalid in the Jaén rite begins with the unction of the eyes. The priest is to apply the oil by tracing a cross, saying: "*By this holy anoint + ing and his most loving mercy, may God forgive you whatever you have sinned by vision. Amen.*"[42] This formula, traceable to the French Benedictine customary of Cluny known as the *Liber tramitis* (c. 1043),[43] and later universally promulgated in the *Rituale Romanum* of 1614,[44] reveals the reasoning behind the selection of the parts of the body to be anointed, as explained by Saint Thomas Aquinas:

> Since the remedy for sin should be applied where sin originates in us first, for that reason the places of the five senses are anointed; the eyes, to wit, on account of the sight, the ears on account of hearing, the nostrils on account of the smell, the mouth on account of the taste, the hands on account of the touch ... and the feet are anointed on account of the motive power of which they are the chief instrument.[45]

The anointing of at least five parts of the body representing the five senses had arisen by the ninth century, when it appears in a sacramentary of Essen, Germany:

> Certainly many priests anoint the infirm moreover on the five senses of the body, that is, on the eyebrows of the eyes, and on the ears from within, and on the point or the inside of the nostrils, and on the hands exteriorly, that is, on the outside [an anointing of the mouth is specified at an earlier point in the Essen extreme unction rite]. On all his members, therefore, [the priests] should make the cross out of the consecrated oil, saying, *In the name of the Father, and of the Son, and of the Holy Spirit.* Indeed, they should do this therefore that if some blemish of soul or body has adhered to the five senses it may be healed by this medicine.[46]

---

[41] *Missale Giennense / Manuale ... sacramenta* (1499), fol. 250r. The antiphon *Sana me, Domine* is earlier found not only in the twelfth-century *Pontificale Romanum* but also in the fifth- to seventh-century Spanish extreme unction rite of the *Liber ordinum* (Férotin, *Liber ordinum*, col. 71).

[42] *Missale Giennense / Manuale ... sacramenta* (1499), fol. 250r.

[43] *Liber tramitis*, bk. 2, chap. 54, in Albers, *Consuetudines monasticae*, 1:191.

[44] Sodi and Flores Arcas, *Rituale Romanum: Editio princeps* (1614), 60–61 (original pagination).

[45] Saint Thomas Aquinas, *Summa theologica*, supplement, q. 32, art. 6, 3:2677.

[46] Manuscript: Düsseldorf, Germany, Düsseldorf Landes- und Stadtbibliothek, MS D1, ninth century, in Jean Deshusses, ed., *Le sacramentaire grégorien: Ses principales formes d'après*

The anointing of *seven* parts of the body (eyes, ears, lips, nose, hands, loins, and feet) found in the Jaén rite had arisen by the eleventh century, when it appears in a customary of the French Benedictine monastery of Cluny compiled around 1080 by the abbot Saint Udalric of Zell (+1093);[47] it was this sevenfold anointing that was subsequently promulgated in the 1614 *Rituale Romanum* (albeit the anointing of the loins was often omitted).[48]

In addition to the anointings, early medieval extreme unction texts of the ninth to the eleventh century, including that of the tenth-century Romano-Germanic Pontifical, speak of an imposition of hands upon the invalid.[49] The observance of this practice declined in the later Middle Ages,[50] and it is absent from the 1614 *Rituale Romanum*.[51] But it does appear in some sixteenth-century extreme unction rites, including that of Liège, Belgium (1553),[52] and the Spanish rites of Barcelona (1501)[53] and La Seu d'Urgell (1536).[54] In the unction rite of the 1501 *Ordinarium* of Barcelona, the priest is directed after anointing the invalid to place his hands upon him and say:

les plus anciens manuscrits, vol. 3, SF 28 (Fribourg, Switzerland: Editions Universitaires Fribourg, 1982), 151.

[47] *Consuetudines Cluniacenses* of Saint Udalric of Zell, bk. 3, chap. 28, PL 149, col. 771.

[48] Sodi and Flores Arcas, *Rituale Romanum: Editio princeps* (1614), 60–61 (original pagination). A rubric of the 1614 *Rituale* explains that in administering the sacrament to women the anointing of the loins is always omitted and that it is not given to men who are too ill to be moved (ibid., 61). This anointing was entirely abrogated in the 1917 *Code of Canon Law* (1917 *Codex juris canonici*, canon 947, no. 2).

[49] For the Romano-Germanic Pontifical, see Vogel and Elze, *Pontifical romano-germanique*, 2:259. Rubrics for the imposition of hands are also found in the extreme unction rites of the ninth-century Sacramentary of Rodrad from the abbey of Corbie, France (a Frankish adaptation of the Gregorian Sacramentary of Rome) and the eleventh-century French Pontifical of Narbonne, a liturgical book exhibiting Spanish characteristics; see respectively the Sacramentary of Rodrad (manuscript: Paris, Bibliothèque Nationale, Codex Lat. 12050, c. 853), in Deshusses, *Sacramentaire grégorien*, 3:146, and Martène, *De antiquis ecclesiae ritibus*, bk. 1, chap. 7, art. 4, *ordo* 13, 1:320. Saint Possidius (+c. 440), in his biography of Saint Augustine (+430), speaks of the latter imposing hands upon the sick (*Vita Augustini*, chap. 27, PL 32, col. 56).

[50] There is no imposition of hands mentioned in the extreme unction rites of the Franciscans' Ritual for the Last Sacraments (1260); the Augustinian Canons' ritual of Beaulieu-lès-Mans, France (fourteenth century); the ritual of Châlons-sur-Marne, France (c. 1500); and the manual of Turku, Finland (1522). See respectively Van Dijk, *Sources of the Modern Roman Liturgy*, 2:388–390; Martène, *De antiquis ecclesiae ritibus*, bk. 1, chap. 7, art. 4, *ordo* 29 and *ordo* 33, 1:343–344; Martti Parvio, ed., *Manuale seu exequiale Aboense, 1522*, facsimile ed., Suomen Kirkkohistoriallisen Seuran Toimituksia / Finska Kyrkohistoriska Samfundets Handlingar 115 (Helsinki: Societas Historiae Ecclesiasticae Fennica, 1980), fols. 17v–22v.

[51] Sodi and Flores Arcas, *Rituale Romanum: Editio princeps* (1614), 59–63 (original pagination).

[52] Ritual of Liège, Belgium (1553), in Martène, *De antiquis ecclesiae ritibus*, bk. 1, chap. 7, art. 4, *ordo* 31, 1:344.

[53] *Ordinarium* of Barcelona (1501), in Amadeu-J. Soberanas, ed., *Ordinarium sacramentorum Barchinonense, 1501*, facsimile ed., Biblioteca liturgica catalana 1 (Barcelona: Institut d'Estudis Catalans, 1991), fol. 138r–138v.

[54] *Ordinarium* of La Seu d'Urgell, Spain (1536), in Francesc Xavier Parés i Saltor, *L'ordinari d'Urgell de 1536*, Col·lectània Sant Pacià 74 (La Seu d'Urgell, Spain: Societat Cultural Urgel·litana / Facultat de Teologia da Catalunya, 2002), 248.

Behold favorably, O Lord Savior, and confirm this imposition of our hands with the invocation of your name, that to this your servant whom we bless in supplication of your mercy, your celestial healing power may be present, that just as once the mother-in-law of your Apostle Peter rose at the touch of your hand, her fever fleeing, and therefore ministered to you, O Lord, so also may this your servant rise by the power of your name and your Spirit, made strong in body and at the same time made strong in spirit; may he perceive the blessings of this temporal life granted to him, that having been delivered, he may serve you; and if in the past he has committed anything wrongful, he may amend it by the path of good conduct and obtain that in the future he may be saved. Through you, O Jesus Christ, who with the Father and the Holy Spirit live and reign, God, through all ages of ages. Amen. [55]

The imposition of hands was universally promulgated centuries later in a 1925 revision of the extreme unction rite of the *Rituale Romanum*. [56]

Concern for the valid administration of the sacrament is expressed by a cautionary rubric in the Jaén text immediately preceding the anointing formula: "Then the priest should anoint him with the blessed oil, saying this prayer over the members individually. Note that just as in baptism you ought to immerse or sprinkle the candidate, saying, *I baptize you*, so you ought to apply the holy unction according to the form of the cross in saying the passage here. For in this formula the action of the sacrament is expressed." [57]

In the Jaén rite, each of the seven anointings of the body ends with a concluding prayer. The first of these, which follows the anointing of the eyes, an oration originally found in the eighth-century *Hadrianum* redaction of Rome's Gregorian Sacramentary, [58] recalls the Old Testament healing of King Ezechias, for whom Isaiah had obtained an extension of life by his prayers (4 Kings 20:1–11): "*O God, who granted to your servant King Ezechias fifteen years of life, so may your power also raise up this your servant from the bed of his sickness to health. Through Christ our Lord.*" [59]

---

[55] Soberanas, *Ordinarium sacramentorum Barchinonense, 1501*, fol. 138r–138v. This same prayer is found in the extreme unction rite of an eleventh-century northern Italian book of pastoral rites (manuscript: Milan, Biblioteca Ambrosiana, codex T.27. Sup.); text in C. Lambot, O.S.B., ed., *North Italian Services of the Eleventh Century: Recueil d'ordines du XIe siècle*, HBS 67 (London: Henry Bradshaw Society, 1931), 44.

[56] Aimé-Georges Martimort, "Prayer for the Sick and Sacramental Anointing", in Aimé-Georges Martimort, ed., *The Church at Prayer: An Introduction to the Liturgy*, vol. 3, *The Sacraments* (Collegeville, Minn.: Liturgical Press, 1988), 133. For the text of the 1925 revised rubric, see *Rituale Romanum, ordo . . . unctio infirmis*, no. 10, in *Collectio rituum: Pro dioecesibus Civitatum Foederatarum Americae Septentrionalis; Ritual Approved by the National Conference of Bishops of the United States of America* (New York: Benziger Bros., 1964), 176–177.

[57] *Missale Giennense / Manuale . . . sacramenta* (1499), fol. 250r.

[58] Text in Jean Deshusses, ed., *Sacramentaire grégorien: Ses principales formes d'après les plus anciens manuscrits*, vol. 1, 2nd ed., SF 16 (Fribourg, Switzerland: Editions Universitaires Fribourg, 1979), no. 987, p. 338.

[59] *Missale Giennense / Manuale . . . sacramenta* (1499), fol. 250r.

The antiphon for the psalm that follows—Psalm 31, the second penitential psalm—recalls the official from Capharnaum who came to Christ seeking the healing of his ill son (Jn 4:46–47): "*There was a certain ruler, whose son was sick at Capharnaum. When he had heard that Jesus had come into Galilee, he beseeched him to come down and heal his son.*" Psalm 31 speaks of the peace wrought by the confession of one's sins.[60]

The second anointing is of the ears: "*By this holy anoint + ing and his most loving mercy, may God forgive you whatever you have sinned by hearing. [Amen].*"[61] It is followed in turn by a prayer dating back to Saint Benedict of Aniane's early ninth-century Frankish adaptation of the Gregorian Sacramentary of Rome,[62] and later utilized in the 1614 *Rituale Romanum*,[63] that speaks of suffering as a means of purifying the soul: "*We beseech you, O Lord, behold your servant, wearied with the infirmity of his body, and revive the soul that you have created, that, cleansed well by chastisements, he may continually feel himself preserved by your healing power. Through Christ . . .*"[64]

The recitation of Psalm 37, the third penitential psalm, which declares, "*There is no health in my flesh*" (verses 4, 8), is accompanied by an antiphon that continues the Gospel account of the official of Capharnaum and the healing of his ill son (Jn 4:49–50): "*Lord, come down that you may heal my son before he should die. Jesus tells him, Go, your son lives.*"[65]

The words of the priest for the anointing of the mouth (lips) are basically the same as those said for the two previous anointings ("*By this holy anoint + ing and his most loving mercy, may God forgive you . . .*"), but in this case he asks that whatever sins the invalid has committed through the sense of taste may be forgiven.[66] With all of the remaining anointings, the same underlying formula is repeated, but the concluding phrase is reworded in each instance to ask forgiveness for sins committed by means of the particular sense or part of the body anointed. Following the anointing of the mouth, the priest offers a prayer traceable to the Gelasian Sacramentary of Rome:[67] "*O God, who ever reign over the holy work of your creation, incline your ear to our supplications; and being appeased, regard your servant wearied from the adverse health of his body; and visit him with your salutary favor, and furnish the medicine of your heavenly grace. Through . . .*"[68]

After the recitation of the fourth of the penitential psalms, Psalm 50 (the *Miserere*), with its antiphon, and the anointing of the nose,[69] another

---

[60] Ibid., fol. 250r–250v.

[61] Ibid., fol. 250v.

[62] Text in Deshusses, *Sacramentaire grégorien*, no. 1387, 1:454.

[63] Sodi and Flores Arcas, *Rituale Romanum: Editio princeps* (1614), 62 (original pagination).

[64] *Missale Giennense / Manuale . . . sacramenta* (1499), fol. 250v.

[65] Ibid., fols. 250v–251r.

[66] Ibid., fol. 251r.

[67] Mohlberg, Eizenhöfer, and Siffrin, *Liber sacramentorum*, no. 1535, p. 221.

[68] *Missale Giennense / Manuale . . . sacramenta* (1499), fol. 251r.

[69] Ibid., fol. 251r–251v. The antiphon accompanying the *Miserere* is based upon verses 3 and 19 of the psalm: "*A contrite and humbled heart, O God, you will not despise; but for the sake*

Gelasian prayer follows,[70] a petition for spiritual and physical healing reflecting the twofold power of the sacrament to restore both the soul and the body: "*O God, who have conferred upon mankind both the remedy of salvation and the bounties of eternal life, preserve in your servant the gifts of your virtues, and grant that he may experience your healing not only in body but also in soul. Through Christ . . .*"[71]

The fifth penitential psalm, Psalm 101, is said with an antiphon (*Domine, puer meus*) taken from the Gospel account of the Roman centurion who asked of Christ the healing of his servant (Mt 8:6–7): "*Lord, my servant lieth at home sick of the palsy, and is grievously tormented. Jesus saith to him: I will come and heal him.*"[72] The hands are now anointed,[73] after which the priest prays again for the restoration of the sick person's health with another oration derived from the Gelasian Sacramentary:[74] "*O God of heavenly powers, who drive away from human bodies every sickness and every infirmity by the power of your command: mercifully attend to this your servant, that with his infirmities driven away and his strengths of body restored, he may bless your holy name constantly in renewed health. Through Christ . . .*"[75]

The *De profundis*, Psalm 129, follows, the sixth of the penitential psalms, with the Roman centurion's humble response to Christ (Mt 8:8) as the antiphon: "*Lord, I am not worthy that thou shouldst enter under my roof; but only say the word, and my servant shall be healed.*"[76]

Following the anointing of the loins (the sixth of the anointings),[77] and another prayer of Gelasian origin[78] for the physical recovery of the invalid,[79] the seventh and last of the penitential psalms is recited, Psalm 142, a plea for divine mercy. The antiphon for the psalm, drawn from the Gospel of Saint Luke (*Cum sol autem*), tells of the many sick that were brought to Christ and healed by him at Capharnaum (Lk 4:40):

of your great mercy, have mercy on me, O God." This antiphon, *Cor contritum*, is also used with the *Miserere* in the extreme unction rite of the eleventh-century French Pontifical of Narbonne, a liturgical book exhibiting Spanish characteristics (Martène, *De antiquis ecclesiae ritibus*, bk. 1, chap. 7, art. 4, *ordo* 13, 1:320).

[70] Mohlberg, Eizenhöfer, and Siffrin, *Liber sacramentorum*, no. 1536, p. 221.

[71] *Missale Giennense / Manuale . . . sacramenta* (1499), fol. 251v.

[72] Ibid., fols. 251v–252r. This antiphon is also used in the extreme unction rite of the eleventh-century French Pontifical of Narbonne (Martène, *De antiquis ecclesiae ritibus*, bk. 1, chap. 7, art. 4, *ordo* 13, 1:321).

[73] *Missale Giennense / Manuale . . . sacramenta* (1499), fol. 252r.

[74] Mohlberg, Eizenhöfer, and Siffrin, *Liber sacramentorum*, no. 1537, p. 221.

[75] *Missale Giennense / Manuale . . . sacramenta* (1499), fol. 252r.

[76] Ibid. This antiphon, *Domine non sum dignus*, is also used in the extreme unction rite of the eleventh-century French Pontifical of Narbonne (Martène, *De antiquis ecclesiae ritibus*, bk. 1, chap. 7, art. 4, *ordo* 13, 1:321).

[77] *Missale Giennense / Manuale . . . sacramenta* (1499), fol. 252r.

[78] Mohlberg, Eizenhöfer, and Siffrin, *Liber sacramentorum*, no. 1538, pp. 221–222.

[79] Prayer: "*O Lord, holy Father, almighty eternal God, who uphold the frailty of our condition, that by the saving remedies of your goodness our bodies and members may be nourished: look favorably upon this your servant, that with every distress of bodily infirmity driven away, the grace of perfect health may be restored in him. Through . . .*" (*Missale Giennense / Manuale . . . sacramenta* [1499], fol. 252r.)

"And when the sun had set, all that had sick ones with various diseases brought them to Jesus, and they were healed." [80] The feet are now anointed, the seventh and last anointing.[81] The prayer that follows it, an oration traceable to the ninth-century Pontifical of Saint Prudentius (a liturgical book of Troyes, France),[82] serves at this point in the Jaén rite as a verbal summation of the preceding anointings of the different senses and portions of the body:

> *By this holy anointing and bless + ing may they* [the various senses and parts of the body] *be cleansed from every defilement and thought of sin; and may your hands be sancti + fied, and your mouth and heart, and your touch, smell, sight, hearing, and taste, and the deeds of your whole body and soul, that you may be made worthy to invoke the name of Christ; may the Lord restore to you the happiness of his salvation and uphold you in your original spirit; may he restore the Holy Spirit in your inmost parts, and may he not remove himself from you; but may the blessing of God the Father + almighty, and the Son + , and the Holy + Spirit, descend upon you, and flow out to the extremity of your entire body, descend to each side, and replenish and encompass you, and be always with you. Amen.*[83]

The joyful Psalm 66 is then said with an antiphon pleading for the healing of the invalid: *"Heal, O Lord, this infirm* [*man*]*; cure him with spiritual medicine, that having been returned to his previous health, he may render thanksgiving to you in the Church."* [84] The Jaén rite continues with a litany traceable to the tenth-century Romano-Germanic Pontifical[85] in which over fifty saints are invoked by name, and petitions specific to the spiritual needs of the invalid are offered, some of which are taken from the Psalms:

> . . . *Holy Trinity, one God. Have mercy on him.*
> *Holy Mary. Pray for him. . . .*
> *From every evil. Deliver him, O Lord.*
> *From the deceits of the devil. Deliver him, O Lord.*
> *From thy wrath. Deliver him, O Lord.*
> *From the torment of death. Deliver him, O Lord. . . .*
> *We sinners beseech thee, hear us.*
> *That thou mayest give us peace. We beseech thee, hear us.*
> *That thou mayest drive away evil thoughts from him. We beseech thee, hear us.*
> *That thou mayest grant him time for penitence. We beseech thee, hear us. . . .*
> Verse: *Wherefore convert him, O Lord.*
> Response: *And be merciful to thy servant.*

---

[80] Ibid., fol. 252r–252v.
[81] Ibid., fol. 252v.
[82] *Pontificale sancti Prudentii* (excerpt), PL 115, col. 1443.
[83] *Missale Giennense / Manuale . . . sacramenta* (1499), fol. 252v.
[84] Ibid.
[85] Vogel and Elze, *Pontifical romano-germanique*, 2:247–249.

Verse [cf. Ps 88:23]: *May the enemy effect nothing in him.*
Response [cf. Ps 88:23]: *And the son of iniquity not proceed to harm him.*
Verse [cf. Ps 40:3]: *May the Lord preserve him and give him life.*
Response [cf. Ps 40:3]: *And may he make him blessed upon the earth and not hand him over to the will of his enemies.*
Verse [cf. Ps 40:4]: *May the Lord help him on his bed of sorrow.*
Response [cf. Ps 40:4]: *Thou hast turned all his couch in his sickness.*[86]

The priest now prays that the Holy Spirit may sanctify and protect the invalid, offering another prayer derived from the ninth-century French Pontifical of Saint Prudentius:[87]

> *May the almighty and merciful God, who in the name of his only-begotten Son sent the Holy Spirit according to his promise to his disciples, pour forth upon you the sevenfold Paraclete from Heaven; may he fill you with the Spirit of counsel and fortitude, of understanding and wisdom, who destroys all rust of sins, that you may no longer be confounded by the errors of iniquity or frailty; but may he lead you into all truth of knowledge even as the same Son promised; may he protect you from the evil of all iniquity, and from the thought of mundane conversation or carnal impurity, and from the desire of an impure mind; and may he deliver you from all assaults or invasion of enemies visible and invisible, and bring you to the grace and glory of his kingdom, to whom honor, power, and dominion endure unto ages of ages. Amen.*[88]

The next prayer, originally found in the seventh-century Gelasian Sacramentary of Rome as part of the Holy Thursday rite for the public reconciliation of penitents,[89] serves in the Jaén rite as a further supplication for the spiritual and physical healing of the invalid, evoking the imagery of Christ laying his hand upon the sick to heal them and of the Good Shepherd seeking out and rescuing the lost sheep:

> *O God, most loving and merciful Restorer of mankind, who have redeemed man, cast down from immortality by the hatred of the devil, in the blood of your only-begotten Son: give life to this your servant whom you by no means desire to die, and lay claim to him snatched away, you who do not abandon him who wanders from the way; may the mournful sighs of this your servant stir your goodness to heal his wounds, we beseech you, O Lord; stretch out your health-giving hand to him lying ill; let not your Church be laid waste in any portion of her body, or your flock undergo loss, or the enemy rejoice in the punishment of your family, or a second death possess him regenerated in the saving water of baptism; to you, therefore, O Lord, we pour forth suppliant prayers in bewailing of heart; spare him confessing, that thus he may*

---

[86] Excerpted from *Missale Giennense / Manuale . . . sacramenta* (1499), fols. 252v–253v.
[87] *Pontificale sancti Prudentii* (excerpt), PL 115, col. 1443 (incipit only).
[88] *Missale Giennense / Manuale . . . sacramenta* (1499), fols. 253v–254r.
[89] Mohlberg, Eizenhöfer, and Siffrin, *Liber sacramentorum*, nos. 358–359, p. 57.

lament his sins in this mortal life, so that he may escape a sentence of eternal damnation in the day of dreadful judgment and not know that which terrifies in darkness, that which gnashes in flames; and thus having turned from the way of error to the way of justice, may he in no way be injured by wounds, but may that which your grace has conferred upon him, that which your mercy has reformed, be sound and undisturbed. Through . . .[90]

The Jaén text provides at this point in the rite a prayer for the absolution of the invalid's sins traceable to the tenth-century Romano-Germanic Pontifical:[91]

May the Lord Jesus Christ, who said to his disciples, "Whatsoever you shall bind upon earth, shall be bound also in Heaven" [Mt 18:18], of whose number, although unworthy, he has willed us to be, absolve you through our ministry from all your sins, whatever you have done negligently in thought, word, and action; and may he vouchsafe to bring you, absolved from the bonds of your sins, to the realms of Heaven. Who with the Father and the Holy Spirit lives and reigns unto ages of ages. Amen.[92]

The priest now recites a prayer that the Jaén rite inherited from Spain's ancient Mozarabic Rite, a rich and effusive text first found in the fifth- to seventh-century extreme unction ceremony of the Mozarabic *Liber ordinum:*[93]

Lord Jesus Christ, who are our Savior and our redemption, who are our true health and medicine, from whom all soundness and every remedy comes, who by the word of your Apostle instruct us that by touching the infirm with the liquid of oil we may entreat your mercy: look favorably from that wonderful summit [of Heaven][94] *upon this your servant, that the healing remedy of your grace may restore to health him chastised, whom sickness now bends toward death and whom infirmity now drags to the downfall of his strength; extinguish in him lust and the fires of fevers; crush the stings of sorrows and vices, dissolve the illness of mental torment and the tortures of the passions; restrain the tumor of pride; heal the threefold perils of the bowels, the inmost parts, and the marrows of thoughts; and obstructing the wounds of afflictions, assist him in physical and feverish dangers, and remove all the former passions; put together the structures of the flesh and the matter of blood, and mercifully grant him forgiveness of his sins; thus may your goodness continually preserve him, that his infirmity may lead neither to any corruption nor to perdition; but may this holy anointing of oil become for him the expulsion*

---

[90] *Missale Giennense / Manuale . . . sacramenta* (1499), fol. 254r.

[91] Vogel and Elze, *Pontifical romano-germanique*, 2:267–268.

[92] *Missale Giennense / Manuale . . . sacramenta* (1499), fol. 254r.

[93] Férotin, *Liber ordinum*, cols. 72–73.

[94] The phrase "*of Heaven*", absent from the Jaén text, is found in the *Liber ordinum* text of the prayer (Férotin, *Liber ordinum*, col. 72). It is inserted here to clarify the meaning of "*summit*".

of sickness and present feebleness, and the desired remission of all sins, O
Savior of the world. Who live and reign, God . . .[95]

Two more prayers for physical healing follow, the first[96] from the
seventh-century Gelasian Sacramentary[97] and the second from the tenth-
century Romano-Germanic Pontifical[98] (a prayer subsequently utilized in the universally promulgated extreme unction rite of the 1614
Rituale Romanum).[99] In the latter oration, the priest prays:

> *Holy Lord, almighty Father, eternal God, who by imparting to sick bodies
> the grace of your blessing preserve your handiwork in your manifold goodness:
> graciously assist at the invocation of your name, that with your right hand
> you may raise up this your servant, freed from illness and given to health;
> may you strengthen him with your power, uphold him with your might, and
> restore him to your Church and your holy altars, with every desired prosper-
> ity. Through . . .*[100]

The motifs of penance and the forgiveness of sins return with a
further prayer from the seventh-century Gelasian Sacramentary;[101] the
priest implores for the invalid that, "*the nuptial garment having been
received, he may be worthy to enter the royal banquet whence he had been
expelled.*"[102] The imagery here is taken from the parable of the wedding banquet for the king's son (Mt 22:2–14), and in particular, the
episode of the wedding guest who was not properly dressed for the
wedding (verses 11–13). The prayer that follows, another text from
the fifth- to seventh-century contents of Spain's *Liber ordinum*,[103] is a
petition for forgiveness, physical healing, and salvation: "*May God be
merciful with all your sins; and may he heal all your infirmities; and may he
redeem your life from the destruction of everlasting death; and may he accomplish your longing in all good things, who alone in perfect Trinity lives and
reigns, God, through all ages of ages. Amen.*"[104]

The next prayer, traceable to the tenth-century Romano-Germanic
Pontifical,[105] resembles in style the concluding portion of the famed
Celtic prayer of Saint Patrick (+461) known as "Saint Patrick's

---

[95] *Missale Giennense / Manuale . . . sacramenta* (1499), fol. 254r–254v.

[96] Ibid., fol. 254v: "*O Lord, holy Father, almighty God, who uphold the frailty of our condition . . .*" This prayer is a variant of the oration used earlier in the Jaén rite after the
anointing of the loins (ibid., fol. 252r).

[97] Mohlberg, Eizenhöfer, and Siffrin, *Liber sacramentorum,* no. 1538, pp. 221–222.

[98] Vogel and Elze, *Pontifical romano-germanique,* 2:266.

[99] Sodi and Flores Arcas, *Rituale Romanum: Editio princeps* (1614), 62 (original pagination).

[100] *Missale Giennense / Manuale . . . sacramenta* (1499), fol. 254v.

[101] Mohlberg, Eizenhöfer, and Siffrin, *Liber sacramentorum,* no. 365, p. 58.

[102] *Missale Giennense / Manuale . . . sacramenta* (1499), fol. 254v.

[103] Férotin, *Liber ordinum,* col. 73.

[104] *Missale Giennense / Manuale . . . sacramenta* (1499), fol. 254v.

[105] Vogel and Elze, *Pontifical romano-germanique,* 2:254.

Breastplate" (*Lorica of Saint Patrick*):[106] "*May the Lord Jesus Christ be with you that he may defend you; may he be within you that he may restore you; may he be around you that he may lead you; may he be over you that he may bless + you; may he be near you that he may deliver you. Who with the Father and the Holy Spirit lives and reigns, God ... Amen.*"[107] This is followed by a tripartite series of invocations, likewise derived from the tenth-century Romano-Germanic Pontifical[108] but with the distinctively Spanish interpolation of the word "Amen" at the end of each versicle:[109]

May the God of Heaven bless + you. Amen.
May Christ the Son of God sustain you. Amen.
May He make your body to be protected and preserved in his holy service. Amen.
May he illuminate your mind. Amen.
May he guard your understanding. Amen.
May he increase in you his grace to the perfection of your soul. Amen.
May he free you from every evil. Amen.
May his holy right hand defend you. Amen. Who always helps his saints.
May he himself vouchsafe to support and strengthen you, who in perfect Trinity lives and reigns, God, through ... Amen.

May God the Father bless + you. Amen.
May God the Son heal you. Amen.
May the Holy Spirit illuminate you. Amen.
May he preserve your body. Amen.
May he save your soul. Amen.
May he illuminate your heart. Amen.
May he direct your understanding. Amen.
And may he bring you to heavenly life, who, triune and one, lives and reigns unto ages of ages. Amen.

May God the Father, who in the beginning created all things, bless + you. Amen.
May he the Beginning, who came from his heavenly throne to redeem us, bless + you. Amen.
May the Holy Spirit, who in the form of a dove came to rest upon Christ in the Jordan River, bless + you. Amen.
May he in the Trinity sancti + fy and bless + you, whom we await for the

---

[106] An English translation of the *Lorica of Saint Patrick* is given in John Bernard and Robert Atkinson, eds., *The Irish Liber hymnorum*, vol. 2, *Translations and Notes*, HBS 14 (London: Henry Bradshaw Society, 1898), 49–51.

[107] *Missale Giennense / Manuale ... sacramenta* (1499), fol. 255r.

[108] Vogel and Elze, *Pontifical romano-germanique*, 2:254–255.

[109] Parés i Saltor, *Ordinari d'Urgell de 1536*, 249–250.

judgment to come, Jesus Christ our Lord, who lives and reigns unto ages of ages. Amen.[110]

The concluding prayer of the Jaén extreme unction rite is an oration traceable to an early eleventh-century penance rite of Gellone, France,[111] serving as a final absolution of the invalid: *"May almighty God, the Savior and Redeemer of mankind, who gave his Apostles the power of binding and loosing, himself vouchsafe to absolve you from all your sins; and as much as it is permitted to my frailty, himself assisting, may you be absolved before his face. Who lives and reigns unto ages of ages. Amen."* [112]

The text of the Jaén rite ends with the above prayer. But in the case of the extreme unction rite given in the ritual of Châlons-sur-Marne, France (c. 1500), there are concluding rubrics instructing the priest to make arrangements for the spiritual welfare of the invalid following his departure:

> Then the priest should take the cross, on which there ought to be depicted the image of Christ, and the image of the glorious Virgin Mary, and with it [the cross] he should sign the infirm man with the sign of the holy Cross, saying: *Bless.* Response: *The Lord.* [Priest:] *May the blessing of God the Father almighty, and the Son, and the Holy Spirit, descend + upon this infirm man and remain always. Amen.*
>
> The priest should present the cross to the infirm man and speak to him in making manifest the remembrance of the Passion of Christ our Lord and how he suffered for him and for the salvation of the whole world. Also, at the end, the infirm man ought to be sprinkled with blessed water, and also all present, that the demons may be expelled from the same place.... And it is to be noted that at the end some good and devout persons are to be led in to the sick for the purpose of visiting them, who should be profitable for the good disposition of the sick, always speaking to them sweetly and privately, relating the Passion of Christ and the articles of the faith, for their salvation; and [this should be done] likewise by the priest. The cross of Christ should be left close to the sick in a place where they would be able conveniently to look at it. Then the priest should withdraw to the church, and sign the people with the [vessel of] holy oil, and sprinkle them with blessed water, as is customary.[113]

The emphasis upon the use of a cross in the above rubrics was by no means unique to Châlons. The presentation of a cross to the ill and the dying became a common practice in the Church's late medieval rites of visiting the sick. As early as the eleventh century, the customary of the French Benedictine monastery of Cluny compiled around

---

[110] *Missale Giennense / Manuale . . . sacramenta* (1499), fol. 255r.

[111] Martène, *De antiquis ecclesiae ritibus*, bk. 1, chap. 6, art. 7, *ordo* 6, 1:283.

[112] *Missale Giennense / Manuale . . . sacramenta* (1499), fol. 255r.

[113] Martène, *De antiquis ecclesiae ritibus*, bk. 1, chap. 7, art. 4, *ordo* 30, 1:344.

1080 by Saint Udalric of Zell speaks of placing a cross before the face of an ill monk.[114] A thirteenth-century *Liber ordinarius* for the Abbey of Saint James in Liège, Belgium, provides an exhortation for the priest to address to the invalid when showing the cross to him: "*Behold the sign of the Passion of the Lord, which the Savior of the world endured because of you. Diligently take heed and behold the tokens of his Passion, referring the graces to him and placing your hope in him, who has vouchsafed to suffer such things for you.*"[115]

Excursus: The Viaticum Rite

The Church has always provided the Eucharist to the dying, the Viaticum, but it was in the Middle Ages that she gradually imparted to the Christian's final reception of the sacrament a ceremonial solemnity truly commensurate with the magnitude of this preparation for eternity. Roman *Ordo* 49, a liturgical text of France essentially Roman in content dating from the first half of the eighth century, explains the importance of this sacrament for a dying man, observing, "Communion shall be to him a defender and helper unto the resurrection of the just."[116] Toward the end of the eighth century, the beginnings of a prescribed rite for the administration of Holy Communion to the dying appear in the Phillipps Sacramentary (the *Liber sacramentorum Augustodunensis*) of northeastern France, a Frankish adaptation of the Gelasian Sacramentary of Rome: following the reading of the Passion of Saint John, the singing of Psalm 41 ("*As the hart panteth after the fountains of water; so my soul panteth after thee, O God . . .*"), and the recitation of a litany, the Eucharist is administered to the dying individual.[117]

By the tenth century, a solemn procession for bringing the Eucharist to the sick and the dying had emerged in the monasteries: the tenth-century *Regularis concordia*, a directory for England's monasteries attributed to Saint Ethelwold of Winchester (+984), speaks of the Blessed Sacrament being carried with incense in procession to the rooms of ill monks.[118] The French Benedictine customary of Cluny known as the *Liber tramitis* (c. 1043) directs that when the priest carrying the Viaticum enters the home of the invalid, all present should kneel before "the Body of the Lord", including the invalid himself, if he is able to do so.[119] Another customary of Cluny compiled about 1075 by the

---

[114] *Consuetudines Cluniacenses* of Saint Udalric of Zell, bk. 3, chap. 29, PL 149, col. 771.

[115] Text in Paul Volk, ed., *Der Liber ordinarius des Lütticher St. Jakobs-Klosters* (Münster, Germany: Aschendorff Verlag, 1923), 68.

[116] Text in Michel Andrieu, ed., *Les Ordines Romani du haut moyen âge*, vol. 4, SSLED 28 (Louvain, Belgium: "Spicilegium sacrum Lovaniense" Administration, 1956), 529.

[117] Text in O. Heiming, O.S.B., ed., *Liber sacramentorum Augustodunensis*, CCSL 159b (Turnhout, Belgium: Brepols, 1984), no. 1914, pp. 241–242.

[118] Text in Thomas Symons, trans., *Regularis concordia: The Monastic Agreement of the Monks and Nuns of the English Nation*, Medieval Classics (New York: Oxford University Press, 1953), chap. 12, no. 65, p. 64.

[119] *Liber tramitis*, bk. 2, chap. 54, in Albers, *Consuetudines monasticae*, 1:191.

monk Bernard adds that before the priest takes the Eucharist for the Viaticum from the high altar where it is reserved, he first incenses the Sacrament.[120] As for those whom the priest carrying the Viaticum passes in bringing the Sacrament from the church to the invalid's home, a synod for the archdiocese of Cologne, Germany, convened in 1280 declares: "Also, when the Body of the Lord is carried, the faithful before whom it is carried, if it can be done fittingly, should kneel [and] beat their breasts, and with head bowed, their hands joined and uplifted, they should adore reverently. But those on horseback should not refuse to descend from their horses to adore him who for us descended from Heaven."[121]

We present here the Viaticum rite given in a liturgical book of early colonial Mexico, the *Manuale sacramentorum* (Manual of the sacraments), published at Mexico City in 1568.[122] It is fairly representative of the Viaticum practices of late medieval Spain,[123] from which it is derived.

The Mexican text states that beforehand the priest should instruct those caring for the invalid to clean the house, furbishing the invalid's room with "good fragrances" and preparing there "a very small altar" furnished with several religious images and lit candles and suited to receive the Eucharistic vessel that the priest will bring, the *custodia*.[124] The church bells are rung—first a smaller bell and then a "greater bell", the latter tolled fifteen times—to summon "all the devout Christians" who can come to accompany the Eucharist to the invalid's home.[125] At the church, the majordomo of the parish's confraternity of the Blessed Sacrament distributes candles to those who will join the procession.[126]

The priest, vested in a surplice and stole, with a mantle or humeral veil over his shoulders, takes the Blessed Sacrament from the tabernacle (two Hosts, or more if several invalids are to receive Holy Communion) and, after placing the Eucharist within the *custodia* he will carry it in, sets out from the sanctuary, intoning the hymn of thanksgiving *Te Deum* as he does so. He brings with him a sack containing hyssop, a vessel of holy water, an empty chalice, and a paten. He also

---

[120] *Ordo Cluniacensis*, pt. 1, chap. 24, in Marquard Herrgott, ed., *Vetus disciplina monastica* (Paris, 1726; repr., Siegburg, Germany: Franciscus Schmitt, 1999), 191.

[121] Synod of Cologne (1280), statutes, chap. 7, in J. D. Mansi, ed., *Sacrorum conciliorum nova et amplissima collectio*, vol. 24 (Florence and Venice, 1780; repr., Paris: Hubert Welter, 1903), col. 352.

[122] *Manuale sacramentorum . . . ecclesiae mexicanae* (1568), fols. 67v–73r.

[123] For Spanish examples, see *Missale Giennense / Manuale . . . sacramenta* (1499), fols. 246v–249r (Jaén, 1499); and the *Ordinarium* of Barcelona (1501), in Soberanas, *Ordinarium sacramentorum Barchinonense, 1501*, fols. 117r–122v.

[124] *Manuale sacramentorum . . . ecclesiae mexicanae* (1568), fol. 67r–67v.

[125] Ibid., fol. 67v. The ringing of a bell before beginning the Viaticum procession is mentioned three centuries earlier in the Franciscans' 1260 Ritual for the Last Sacraments (Van Dijk, *Sources of the Modern Roman Liturgy*, 2:387).

[126] *Manuale sacramentorum . . . ecclesiae mexicanae* (1568), fol. 67v.

brings a small cross "in order that the sick may worship it", either enclosed with the Blessed Sacrament within the *custodia*, if there is room for it, or within the sack.[127] He is accompanied by the church sacristan, who assists him.[128]

In the procession from the church to the invalid's home, the priest carries the *custodia* under a canopy, preceded by another priest or a seminarian who carries a standard, evidently a banner of the Blessed Sacrament confraternity. The confraternity's majordomo, carrying a staff, directs the procession to ensure that a reverent decorum is maintained. The lay participants carry lit candles. Along the way, the Divine Office is recited, or the Office of the Blessed Virgin Mary, or the penitential psalms.[129]

Upon entering the invalid's home, the priest says, "*Peace to this house and to all dwelling within it.*" After setting the *custodia* upon the previously prepared temporary altar within the invalid's room, the priest takes the hyssop from his sack and sprinkles the invalid and all the others present with holy water, beginning a brief aspersion rite with the customary versicles and responses assigned to it: "*Thou shalt sprinkle me, O Lord, with hyssop, and I shall be cleansed . . .*"[130] Following a prayer for all the inhabitants of the home,[131] the priest prepares the invalid by asking him in Spanish, "*May God save you, brother. Do you have anything that should aggrieve your conscience, which through oversight you have failed to confess?*"[132] If the invalid replies in the affirmative, the priest now hears his confession. Otherwise, the priest directs the invalid to make an act of contrition as well as a profession of faith in question-and-answer form led by the priest.[133] The priest then asks, "*With this faith and belief, do you wish to worship the sign of the Cross, on which he [Christ] suffered his death and Passion?*" The invalid answers, "*Yes, I wish to*", at which point the priest offers him the cross he has brought so that he may venerate it with a kiss, the invalid saying in either Latin or the vernacular, "*We adore you, O Christ, and we bless*

---

[127] Ibid., fol. 68r.

[128] Ibid., fol. 71v.

[129] Ibid., fols. 67v–68r.

[130] Ibid., fol. 68r–68v. In the Viaticum rite from a twelfth-century ritual of Austria's Augustinian abbey of Saint Florian, when the priest arrives with the Eucharist, the invalid is not only sprinkled with holy water but also incensed; text in Adolph Franz, ed., *Das Rituale von St. Florian aus dem zwölften Jahrhundert* (Freiburg im Breisgau, Germany: Herder, 1904), 82.

[131] *Manuale sacramentorum . . . ecclesiae mexicanae* (1568), fol. 68v. This prayer (with minor differences) is also used in the 1499 Jaén extreme unction rite; see footnote 28 on p. 239 of the present chapter, which provides the complete text of the prayer.

[132] Ibid., fol. 68v.

[133] Ibid., fols. 68v–70v. The making of a profession of faith in question-and-answer form in preparation for the reception of Viaticum appears as early as the eleventh century in the rite entitled "Ordor of the Infirm" from a northern Italian book of pastoral rites (manuscript: Milan, Biblioteca Ambrosiana, codex T.27. Sup.); see Lambot, *North Italian Services of the Eleventh Century*, 46–47, plus 38.

you, for by your holy Cross you have redeemed the world."[134] A versicle, response, and prayer in honor of the Cross follow:

> Verse: *Through the sign of the Cross, from our enemies.*
> Response: *Deliver us, Lord our God.*[135]
> *Let us pray:* Prayer: *Graciously hear us, our saving God, and through the triumph of the holy Cross, defend us from all dangers. Through Christ our Lord. Amen.*[136]

The priest now goes to the temporary altar and takes a single Host from the *custodia*, placing it upon the paten he has brought. He then turns toward the invalid to "reveal the Body of our Redeemer" by "taking it in his hands with great reverence" while holding the paten directly under it, with a candle held before it.[137] Remaining thus, the priest asks the invalid in Spanish to profess his faith in the Eucharist:

> *Brother, you see here the Body of our Redeemer and Master Jesus Christ; you are to believe firmly that he is here in this Host as powerful and real as he is in Heaven.* [The invalid] should say: *Yes, I believe.* [Priest:] *Do you believe thus the same, that the priest on behalf of the sinner, as he is, saying those sacramental words, which our Lord Jesus Christ spoke on the Thursday of his Supper, when he instituted this most holy Sacrament, converts the bread into the Flesh and the wine into the Blood of our Lord Jesus Christ?* Response: *Yes, I believe.* [Priest:] *Do you believe all that which Holy Mother Church holds and believes?* Response: *Yes, I believe.* [Priest:] *Then do you agree that you should forgive all those who have wronged you?* Response: *Yes, I forgive* [*them*]. [Priest:] *And that you should ask forgiveness of those whom you have wronged?* Response: *Yes, I ask* [*it*].[138]

The invalid now beats his breast and prays three times in Spanish, "*My Lord Jesus Christ, I am not worthy that you should enter into my home; but by your most holy word my sins will be forgiven and my soul shall*

---

[134] *Manuale sacramentorum . . . ecclesiae mexicanae* (1568), fol. 70v. The kissing of a cross in the Viaticum rite is first mentioned in the French Benedictine customary of Cluny known as the *Liber tramitis* (c. 1043); see *Liber tramitis*, bk. 2, chap. 54, in Albers, *Consuetudines monasticae*, 1:191. The antiphon, "*We adore you, O Christ, and we bless you*"(*Adoramus te, Christe*), is first found as a text for the Office of the Exaltation of the Cross (September 14) in the Antiphonary of Compiègne (France, c. 870); see René-Jean Hésbert, ed., *Corpus antiphonalium officii*, vol. 1, REDSMF 7 (Rome: Herder, 1963), 304.

[135] The verse *Per signum crucis* is traceable to the Antiphonary of Compiègne (France, c. 870); see Hésbert, *Corpus antiphonalium officii*, 1:304.

[136] *Manuale sacramentorum . . . ecclesiae mexicanae* (1568), fol. 70v. The prayer in honor of the holy Cross, *Exaudi nos, Deus*, is earlier found in three Spanish sources (the 1499 missal of Jaén, the 1500 *Missale mixtum* of the Mozarabic Rite, and the missals of Toledo) as a private prayer for Mass, which is said by the priest when kissing the altar at the beginning of Mass. See respectively *Missale Giennense / Manuale . . . sacramenta* (1499), fol. 95v, and *Missale mixtum secundum regulam beati Isidori dictum Mozarabes*, PL 85, col. 527, plus editor's footnote in col. 526.

[137] *Manuale sacramentorum . . . ecclesiae mexicanae* (1568), fols. 70v–71r.

[138] Ibid., fol. 71r–71v.

be safe and sound."[139] The priest immediately gives him the Eucharist, saying, *"May the Body of our Lord Jesus Christ preserve your soul unto life eternal. Amen."*[140] Having put a small quantity of water in the empty chalice that was brought in the sack, the sacristan gives the water to the invalid. In cases when the invalid is impeded from receiving the Host, he adores the Host held by the priest, praying in Spanish, *"I adore you, O Body of my Lord and Savior Jesus Christ, and I bless you, who by your holy Cross have redeemed the world. Lord, save my soul."*[141] Following the invalid's Communion, and after a short series of versicles and responses concluding with a prayer for the remission of the invalid's sins,[142] the priest recites a Communion antiphon repeatedly found in late medieval Spanish Mass texts, the *Nunc dimittis* of Simeon (Lk 2:29–32): *"Now thou dost dismiss thy servant, O Lord, according to thy word in peace; because my eyes have seen thy salvation . . ."*[143] While saying this, the priest reposes the remaining Host or Hosts within the *custodia*. He then takes into his hands the *custodia* and says to the invalid in Spanish: *"Brother, give many thanks to God for the graces that you have received from his divine Majesty; may it be pleasing to his infinite mercy to give you that health, who knows what is most suitable for the safety and salvation of your soul."*[144]

The priest then asks the invalid if he is willing to receive afterward the sacrament of extreme unction, to which the invalid replies in the affirmative. The priest now returns to the church with the Blessed Sacrament in a procession ordered in the same manner as previously. Upon entering the church, the priest places the *custodia* on the altar. He then turns toward the people and tells them in Spanish:

> *All of you who have accompanied this most holy Sacrament have attained one of the seven works of corporal mercy, which is to visit the sick. Furthermore, you have gained many indulgences and remissions granted by the supreme pontiffs; you who have carried lit candles or have given alms for the wax of the most holy Sacrament gain them doubled. In order that you may be worthy to gain them more fittingly, as the most holy Sacrament is put in its customary place, you will recite three times the Our Father with the Hail Mary.*

---

[139] Ibid., fol. 71v. The use of this versicle in the Viaticum rite dates back to the thirteenth century, when it appears in its shorter and more common form in the Franciscans' 1260 Ritual for the Last Sacraments (Van Dijk, *Sources of the Modern Roman Liturgy*, 2:388).

[140] *Manuale sacramentorum . . . ecclesiae mexicanae* (1568), fol. 71v. This Communion formula, *Corpus Domini nostri Jesu Christi custodiat*, is a descendant of an earlier Communion formula from the eighth century; see footnote 14 on p. 6 of the present work.

[141] Ibid.

[142] Ibid., fols. 71v–72r; prayer: *"O God, to whom it is proper always to have mercy and forbear, receive our prayer, that he whom the bond of sins binds fast, the compassion of your goodness may release. Through Christ our Lord. Amen"* (fol. 72r). This prayer dates from the eleventh century; see footnote 73 on p. 147 of the present work.

[143] Ibid., fol. 72r. See the discussion of this antiphon on pp. 89–90 of the present work.

[144] Ibid.

The first will be for this infirm man whom we come to visit, that our Lord God may put him in those places where he may be more pleased with him.

The second will be for those who are in mortal sin, that our Lord God may remove them [their sins] from them and bring them to the state of true penitence.

The third will be for the souls of Purgatory and for graces for yourselves and for me, that our Lord, who has gathered us together into this holy temple, may gather us together into his holy glory.[145]

The priest now turns toward the altar, and taking the Blessed Sacrament enclosed within the *custodia*, he shows it to the people, "in order that they may adore it", before he reposes it in the tabernacle.[146]

---

[145] Ibid., fols. 72r–73r.
[146] Ibid., fol. 73r.

Cologne Cathedral. Interior with central nave. Gothic
Cologne, Germany

©Vanni/Art Resource, New York

PART TWO

SACRED TIME: THE LITURGICAL YEAR

Just as the Lord has punctuated the sky with stars, and the fields with flowers, and the years with seasons, so has he punctuated the seasons themselves with feast days, that by this distinction made from the daily services, the holy solemnities may lead slothful characters, at least after a time, willingly back to prayer, and idle minds may by these annual feasts make themselves ready for the Lord.

Saint Paulinus of Nola (+431)

From *Poem 27*, in Wilhelm von Hartel, ed., *Sancti Pontii Meropii Paulini Nolani: Carmina*, CSEL 30 (Vienna: Österreichischen Akademie der Wissenschaften, 1999), 266–267.

9 Christmas

Truly, the vigils that were kept by the shepherds on this night are divided into four, signifying namely the four laws, the first the natural law, the second the Mosaic, the third of the prophets, the fourth of the New Testament, during which [vigil the law] shone forth to the shepherds, that is, the ecclesiastical doctors. And we with the shepherds ought to keep watch, that we may be worthy to hear that most sweet harmony that was first sung on this night: *Gloria in excelsis Deo.*

Romano-Germanic Pontifical, tenth century[1]

The medieval liturgy of Christmas was intended to mark the transition from a pre-Christian world mired in the darkness of sin and death to a world illuminated and delivered from sin and death by the coming of Christ. William Durandus of Mende (+1296) sees a mystical significance in the celebration of Christmas on a calendar date near the end of the year. It brings to mind that Christ has come at the end of the ages. The feast occurs when astronomically the days are beginning to grow longer again after the shortest day of the year, the winter solstice, has passed. These progressively longer days following the day of Christ's birth symbolize that "those believing in him are called to the light of eternity."[2] Drawing on the tradition in his time that the first Christmas fell on a Sunday, Durandus compares this feast to the first day of the world, which was a Sunday, the first day of the week, observing that just as on the first day God proclaimed, "Let there be light", so too on Christmas Day Christ, "the dawn from on high", came to illuminate us.[3] Christ's birth in the night (as implied by the angels' announcement of the Savior's birth to the shepherds "keeping the night watches over their flock" [Lk 2:8]) is seen by Durandus as symbolizing that Christ has come with the intent of

---

[1] Text in Cyrille Vogel and Reinhard Elze, eds., *Le pontifical romano-germanique du dix-ième siècle*, vol. 2, ST 227 (Vatican City: Biblioteca Apostolica Vaticana, 1963), 2–3.

[2] William Durandus of Mende, *Rationale divinorum officiorum*, bk. 6, chap. 13, no. 2, in A. Davril, O.S.B., and T. M. Thibodeau, eds., *Guillelmi Duranti: Rationale divinorum officiorum V–VI*, CCCM 140a (Turnhout, Belgium: Brepols, 1998), p. 181. Hereafter cited as Durandus, *Rationale* (CCCM 140a).

[3] Ibid.

"illuminating our night", as prophesied by Isaiah: "The people that walked in darkness, have seen a great light; to them that dwelt in the region of the shadow of death, light is risen" (Is 9:2).[4]

The observances of December 25 as the anniversary of the Savior's birth, Christmas, and January 6 as that of the visit of the Magi to the Christ Child, the Epiphany, can both be traced back to the fourth century.[5] The earliest known attestations of a period of preparation for Christmas, the season of Advent, date from the fifth century.[6] The sense of joyful anticipation that characterized Christmas Eve in the Middle Ages is succinctly expressed in the Introit for the morning Mass of December 24 found in missals throughout medieval Europe, a verse that dates from the eighth century: "*Today you will know that the Lord shall come, and he shall save us; and tomorrow you shall see his glory.*"[7] Although the medieval Mass of December 24 contained no distinctive ceremonies, there was in association with the recitation of the Divine Office a simple but dramatic rite at the conclusion of the dawn "hour" of Prime. In keeping with the daily practice of reading at the end of Prime the Church's official roster of saints for the next day given in the martyrology, the announcement of December 25 was read at the conclusion of Prime on December 24. The wording of this solemn proclamation of the Christmas solemnity appeared in a considerably expanded form in the 1498 Martyrology of the Roman Curia (*Martyrologium secundum morem Romanae curiae*) compiled by the Augustinian friar Belinus of Padua:

> *In the 5,199th year from the creation of the world, when in the beginning God created Heaven and earth, which number of years was completed in that nearest following the month of March, the twentieth day of the same month, for on that day the world was created; but from the flood, the 2,957th year, which number was completed on the seventeenth of the following April; from the birth of Abram, the 2,015th year; from Moses and the going forth of the people of Israel from Egypt, the 1,510th year; from the destruction of Troy, the 1,179th year; from the anointing of David as king, the 1,032nd year; in the 193rd Olympiad; but from the first Olympiad, the 800th year; from the city of Rome being founded, the 752nd year; in the 63rd week, according to the prophecy of Daniel, namely in or around the 440th year, the 42nd year of the reign of Octavian; in the sixth age of the world, the gates having been*

---

[4] Ibid.

[5] Pierre Jounel, "The Year", in Aimé-Georges Martimort, ed., *The Church at Prayer: An Introduction to the Liturgy*, vol. 4, *The Liturgy and Time* (Collegeville, Minn.: Liturgical Press, 1986), 78–79.

[6] Mario Righetti, *Manuale di storia liturgica* (Milan: Editrice Ancora, 1949–1955), 2:39–40.

[7] This chant first appears in the Cantatorium of Monza (Italy, eighth century), albeit as a Gradual rather than an Introit; shortly afterward, it appears as an Introit in the Mass antiphonary of Mount Blandin (Belgium, c. 750–800). See René-Jean Hésbert, ed., *Antiphonale missarum sextuplex* (Brussels, 1935; repr., Rome: Herder, 1967), 12, from which the complete text of this Introit is here taken.

closed, with the entire world calmed in peace, Jesus Christ the eternal God, the Son of the eternal Father, willing to hallow the world by his most holy coming, having been conceived by the Holy Spirit, and nine months having passed after the conception—this is said in a high voice—*in Bethlehem of Judea is born of the Virgin Mary, having been made man*—this, however, [is said] higher and in the tone of the Passion—*the Nativity of our Lord Jesus Christ according to the flesh.*[8]

The above wording was later to pass with minor alterations into the universally promulgated *Martyrologium Romanum* of 1584.[9]

As for the actions accompanying the solemn announcement of Christmas at Prime on Christmas Eve, a twelfth-century ordinary for the French monastery of Saint-Jean-en-Vallée in Chartres states:

> On this day, from when the reader in the chapter shall have announced the feast of the Nativity of the Lord and shall have said, *Jesus Christ, the Son of God, is born in Bethlehem of Judea,* in memory of the humility of the Lord, we all prostrate together to the ground; whereas the reader, he having finished the versicle, prostrates with us. Then each says privately the psalms or prayers that it shall have pleased him [to say]. But when the lord abbot or the prior has risen, and some sign of rising shall have been given, we rise; but the reader continues the lection.[10]

This custom of an act of reverence marking the announcement of the Nativity is traceable to the tenth century, when it appears in the earliest redaction of the Benedictine customary of the French abbey of Cluny ("all fall on their faces")[11] and in the *Regularis Concordia* of England's Benedictine monasteries (which specifies a genuflection).[12] The rubrics of Cardinal Bernard of Porto's *Ordo* for Rome's Church of Saint John Lateran (c. 1140) explain the ceremony thus:

> And when the reader has announced the Nativity of the Lord, immediately with one accord we all prostrate ourselves to the earth, that with paces of love and longing hastening to meet him, we may humble ourselves with our whole heart and body, falling before God according to our own lowliness and insignificance, grateful and joyful. But

---

[8] Text quoted in Father John Baptist Sollerius' "Observationes" accompanying his 1745 edition of the Martyrology of Usuard in PL 124, col. 840.

[9] Text in Manlio Sodi and Roberto Fusco, eds., *Martyrologium Romanum: Editio princeps (1584),* facsimile ed., MLCT 6 (Vatican City: Libreria Editrice Vaticana, © 2005), 427–428 (new pagination).

[10] *Ordinarium* of Saint-Jean-en-Vallée, Chartres, France, twelfth century, in Edmond Martène, *De antiquis ecclesiae ritibus* (Venice: Johannes Baptista Novelli, 1763–1764), bk. 4, chap. 11, 3:31.

[11] Text in Kassius Hallinger, O.S.B., *Consuetudines Cluniacensium antiquiores cum redactionibus derivatis,* Corpus consuetudinum monasticarum 7, pt. 2 (Siegburg, Germany: Franciscus Schmitt, 1983), 27.

[12] Text in Thomas Symons, trans., *Regularis concordia: The Monastic Agreement of the Monks and Nuns of the English Nation,* Medieval Classics (New York: Oxford University Press, 1953), chap. 3, no. 31, p. 28.

having prostrated for prayer, let us bring to mind both our first creation and afterward our fall, or the pain and burden of sin, under which we were weighed down unto the infernal regions and those things to be shared in common with the demon of pride and disobedience, and also the punishments of transgression. And when for a little while, as devotion and reason shall have prescribed, we shall have prayed prostrate, the prelate assenting, we rise, and the reader should continue the rest.[13]

In the medieval liturgy, there were also instances of special Christmas Eve ceremonies at the approach of nightfall. The *Liber ordinarius*, a fourteenth-century liturgical book for the collegiate church and abbey of Essen, Germany, specifies that "on the night of the Nativity of the Lord", following the conclusion of the office of None (which was begun about three o'clock and thus would have concluded around or after four o'clock, close to sunset), the abbey's chaplain would exit the church with the abbess and several canonesses (women living a mitigated form of religious life) and proceed into the abbey's adjoining cemetery. Here the chaplain would lead those present in prayers for the faithful departed, including the psalm *De profundis* (Psalm 129) and the Our Father. The chaplain would conclude the rite with the following Collect traceable to the seventh-century Gelasian Sacramentary of Rome:[14] "*O God, in whose mercy the souls of the faithful are at rest, grant to all your servants and maidservants resting in Christ here and everywhere the forgiveness of their sins, that absolved from all guilt, they may rejoice with you without end. Amen.*"[15] This practice of praying for the faithful departed on Christmas Eve was to endure and spread beyond the cloister over the centuries that followed. In Austria, there still exists a custom of visiting the graves of one's family around sunset on December 24.

The above-cited *Liber ordinarius* of Essen also mentions an aspersion of holy water on the morning of Christmas Eve.[16] A 1489 liturgical book for the canons that staffed a monastic church in Münster, Germany, describes in greater detail a Christmas Eve aspersion rite that was carried out in the course of the evening office of Vespers. The Münster ceremony took the form of a visitation of the homes of the city's dignitaries, with the participants setting out from the church after beginning Vespers with the other canons: "The priest and clergy

---

[13] Text in Ludwig Fischer, ed., *Bernhardi cardinalis et Lateranensis ecclesiae prioris ordo officiorum ecclesiae Lateranensis*, Historische Forschungen und Quellen 2–3 (Munich: Dr. F. P. Datterer, 1916), 8–9.

[14] Text in Leo Cunibert Mohlberg, O.S.B., et al., eds., *Liber sacramentorum Romanae aeclesiae ordinis anni circuli (Sacramentarium Gelasianum)*, REDSMF 4 (Rome: Herder, 1960), no. 1680, p. 245.

[15] Text in Franz Arens, ed., *Der Liber ordinarius der Essener Stiftskirche* (Paderborn, Germany: Albert Pape, 1908), 22–23.

[16] Ibid., 22.

go out with blessed water in visiting the houses of the lords." As the aspersion procession makes its rounds, the Christmas hymn *A solis ortus cardine*, a composition of the fifth-century Christian poet Caelius Sedulius,[17] is sung:

> From the region of the rising of the sun
> unto the boundary of the earth,
> let us celebrate in song Christ the King,
> born of the Virgin Mary.
>
> The blessed Author of the world
> has put on a servile body;
> that delivering flesh with flesh,
> he might not lose those whom he has fashioned.
>
> The divine mercy enters
> the flesh of a chaste parent;
> the maiden's womb,
> which had not changed, secretly bears him.
>
> The home of a chaste heart
> suddenly becomes the temple of God;
> inviolate, not knowing man,
> she has conceived the Son in her womb.
>
> The Mother brings forth
> him whom Gabriel had foretold,
> whom John the Baptist, eagerly desiring,
> had perceived, enclosed in his mother's womb.
>
> She has borne him to lie on hay;
> the manger he has not shrunk from:
> and with a little milk has he been nourished,
> by whom a bird goes not hungry.
>
> The choir of heavenly ones rejoices,
> and the angels sing to God;
> and he manifestly becomes Shepherd to the shepherds,
> the Creator of all.
>
> O Jesus, to you be the glory,
> who were born of the Virgin,
> with the Father, and the dear Spirit,
> unto everlasting ages.[18]

---

[17] Matthew Britt, O.S.B., *The Hymns of the Breviary and Missal* (New York: Benziger Bros., 1922), 103.

[18] The Münster text gives only the incipit of this hymn. The complete text is here taken from the 1568 *Breviarium Romanum*, in Manlio Sodi and Achille Maria Triacca, eds., *Breviarium Romanum: Editio princeps (1568)*, facsimile ed., MLCT 3 (Vatican City: Libreria Editrice Vaticana, © 1999), 187 (new pagination).

The canons remaining in the church complete Vespers; then, after a period of silence, the bells announcing the night office of Compline are rung continuously until those in the aspersion procession return. The clergy thereupon begin Compline together.[19] The custom of sprinkling homes with holy water on Christmas Eve was to become an annual tradition for parish priests in certain regions of Germany, Switzerland, and northern Italy, and elsewhere in central Europe.[20]

Christmas Matins

The night office of Matins and the nocturnal first Mass of Christmas that followed it became two focal points for special liturgical actions commemorating the night of Christ's birth. On Christmas night, the customary Matins format of nine readings, read in three stages during the three "nocturns" of Matins, took on an added significance, with readings chosen to present the Nativity as the fulfillment of the Old Testament prophecies foretelling the coming of the Messiah. In this context, Durandus interprets the three nocturns of Christmas Matins as corresponding respectively to three ages in the history of salvation: the ancient first age of the Fathers "before the Law", that is, from Adam until just before Moses; the second age of the Fathers "under the Law" from Moses until the coming of Christ; and the third age, "the time of grace", brought by Christ.[21] Durandus adds that in certain places this symbolic identification would be visually expressed by the progressive removal of colored cloth hangings in the sanctuary—presumably frontals for the high altar. During the first nocturn, the outer hanging would be a black cloth, the age before Moses. For the second nocturn, this cloth is removed to reveal a white hanging, the age of the Mosaic Law. In turn, the latter is removed to reveal a red hanging for the third and final nocturn, the age of Christ.[22]

In certain places dramatic elements were appended to specific stages of the Christmas Matins rite. At the English cathedral of Exeter, just

---

[19] Text in Francis Schubert and Richard Stapper, eds., *Excerpta ex ordinariis Germanicis de summis anni ecclesiastici festivitatibus*, Opuscula et textus historiam ecclesiae eiusque vitam atque doctrinam illustrantia: Series liturgica, fasc. 7–8 (Münster, Germany: Aschendorff, 1936), 40.

[20] See *Sacramentale Ambrosianum* (Ambrosian Rite text; Milan, Italy, 1645), quoted in Martène, *De antiquis ecclesiae ritibus*, bk. 4, chap. 11, 3:32; *Rituale Frisingense* (Freising, Germany, 1673), 521–524, cited in Bernhard Mattes, C.S.S.R., *Die Spendung der Sakramente nach den Freisinger Ritualien: Eine Untersuchung der handschriftlichen und gedruckten Quellen*, Münchener theologische Studien 34 (Munich: Max Hueber Verlag, 1967), 62; *Rituale Romano-Curiense* (Chur, Switzerland, 1732), 90–93, cited in Hans Bissig, *Das Churer Rituale, 1503–1927: Geschichte der Agende-Feier der Sakramente*, Studia Friburgensia, neue Folge, 56 (Fribourg, Switzerland: Universitätsverlag Freiburg, 1979), 121; *Rituale Spirense* (Spire, Germany, 1748), 167–169, cited in Alois Lamott, *Das Speyerer Diözesanrituale von 1512 bis 1932: Seine Geschichte und seine Ordines zur Sakramentenliturgie*, Quellen und Abhandlungen zur mittelrheinischen Kirchengeschichte 5 (Speyer, Germany: Jaegerschen Buchdruckerei, 1961), 86; and *Manuale benedictionum* (Passau, Germany: Typis Ambrosii Ambrosi, 1845), 10–13.

[21] Durandus, *Rationale* (CCCM 140a), bk. 6, chap. 13, no. 6, p. 182.

[22] Ibid., no. 8, p. 183.

such an action is attached to the very first reading of Matins, as related in an ordinal of the cathedral dating from 1337:

> On this day and none other through the year, while the first lesson is read, toward the end, one boy in an alb and with an amice around his neck, his head bare, having a good and clear voice, going out from the place that is behind the high altar with a lit torch in his left hand, should come before the nearest step of the altar, and the first lesson having been recited, he should begin the responsory thus, having turned toward the choir in singing the first eight words,[23] *This day the King of Heaven has vouchsafed to be born for us of the Virgin,*[24] so that at that word, *King of Heaven,* he should elevate his right hand high toward Heaven; and at that word, *of the Virgin,* he should extend his hand toward the image of blessed Mary, turned toward the altar; and at that word, *has vouchsafed,* he shall genuflect to the ground; then the choir should continue (Response), *That lost man may be recalled to the heavenly realms. The host of angels rejoices, for eternal salvation has appeared to mankind.*[25] But in the interim, while the responsory is sung, immediately three other boys should come from the southern side, and three others from the northern [side], in the same vesture, to the step of the choir. And that first [boy] should descend to them, and together in the same place, having turned toward the choir, they sing together the verse [Lk 2:14]: *Glory to God in the highest, and on earth peace to men of good will.*[26] Which having been said, they should withdraw somberly in going through the middle of the choir out the western door.[27]

In other places, and Spain in particular, dramatic actions accompanied one of the other readings of Matins. One such ceremony, the Procession of Prophets, drew its inspiration from a sermon of the fifth or sixth century mistakenly attributed to Saint Augustine, the text of which was formerly used as a reading of the Christmas Matins rite.[28] The introductory portion of this sermon constitutes a penetrating meditation upon the significance of Christmas night, as can be seen in the following passage excerpted from the text as it appears in a 1533 office book of Valencia, Spain:

---

[23] In the original Latin, the responsory's opening phrase actually consists of nine words.

[24] This responsory is first found in the Antiphonary of Compiègne (France, c. 870); see René-Jean Hésbert, ed., *Corpus antiphonalium officii,* vol. 1, REDSMF 7 (Rome: Herder, 1963), 34.

[25] The complete text of this responsory is supplied from René-Jean Hésbert, ed., *Corpus antiphonalium officii,* vol. 4, REDSMF 10 (Rome: Herder, 1970), no. 6858, p. 216.

[26] This verse is first found in the Antiphonary of Compiègne (France, c. 870); see Hésbert, *Corpus antiphonalium officii,* 1:36.

[27] Text in J. N. Dalton, ed., *Ordinale Exoniense,* vol. 1, HBS 37 (London: Henry Bradshaw Society, 1909), 64.

[28] Karl Young, *The Drama of the Medieval Church* (Oxford: Clarendon Press, 1933), 2:125.

The words of the Apostle Paul are, "The night is passed, [and] the day is at hand" [Rom 13:12]. *Putting aside the works of darkness, put on yourselves the armor of light* [cf. Rom 13:12]. *Therefore, drive out the darkness of night; and with the darkness of sins driven away, may the ray of the true light shine in our hearts. . . . What have we done on this night? We have taken captive the captivator. What have we done on this night? We have shaken off the diabolical darkness from our hearts and have discovered the true light to be imbibed. What has come to pass on this night? True power coming: he has bound the strong one, that he may despoil him of his gear* [cf. Mt 12:29]. *What indeed has come to pass on this night? Pride has been uprooted; humility has been introduced. What has come to pass on this night? The prince of all vices has been driven out; the Origin of all good things has been received.*[29]

A fifteenth-century book of customs (*consueta*) for the cathedral of Palma on the Spanish island of Majorca specifies this sermon as the ninth reading for Christmas Matins; the rite of the Procession of Prophets begins immediately after the bishop of Palma reads the first portion of the pseudo-Augustinian text:

> At the ninth reading it is customary, if the most reverend lord bishop of Majorca does the office, when His Sovereignty shall have been at the Epistle book with his ministers and will say, *Be pleased, O Lord, to bless*, one prelate in his seat or a canon will respond in a high voice, *Pray for us, Father*, in the reading tone. And the lord bishop should say, *May holy Mary, Virgin of Virgins, intercede for us unto the Lord*. And the choir should say, *Amen.* . . . The superior bishop should proceed to the reading, *Amid afflictions and tribulations* . . .[30]

The bishop, after reading the beginning of the sermon, summons a priest chosen to assume the role of Saint Augustine, saying to him, "*Saint Augustine, examine the prophets, Saint Augustine.*" The priest, who is vested in a white mantle and has entered the pulpit where the Epistle for Mass is usually chanted, answers, "*I am present, Father.*" Again the bishop instructs him, "*Examine the prophets*", remaining silent afterward. The priest playing Saint Augustine now undertakes the "examination of the prophets according to his script".[31] The Palma liturgical book supplies no further details, but a complete text of just such an "examination of the prophets" is provided in the 1533 office book of Valencia cited earlier.[32] The Valencia text has Saint Augustine

---

[29] Excerpted from the sermon of Pseudo-Augustine assigned to Christmas Matins in the 1533 edition of the *Hores de la setmana sancta*, Valencia, Spain; text in Richard Donovan, C.S.B., *The Liturgical Drama in Medieval Spain* (Toronto: Pontifical Institute of Medieval Studies, 1958), 147.

[30] From the *Consueta de tempore* (Palma de Majorca, fifteenth century), in Donovan, *Liturgical Drama in Medieval Spain*, 121.

[31] Ibid.

[32] *Hores de la setmana sancta* (Valencia, 1533 ed.), in Donovan, *Liturgical Drama in Medieval Spain*, 148–153.

eliciting "responses" from thirteen figures of both the Old and New Testaments: from the Old Testament, Isaiah, Jeremiah, Daniel, David, Moses, Habacuc, Baruch, and Nebuchadnezzar, and from the New Testament, Zechariah, Elizabeth, Simeon, Saint John the Baptist, and Saint Peter. These responses constitute a catena of scriptural prophecies of and testimonies to the Messiah, as given in the middle portion of the pseudo-Augustinian sermon, ranging from Isaiah's prophecy that a virgin would conceive and bear a son to be called Emmanuel (Is 7:14) to Saint Peter's declaration of faith, "Thou art Christ, the Son of the living God" (Mt 16:16). It is apparent from the way this "dialogue" is arranged that other clerics apart from the reader chanted the words of the various biblical figures. Evidence from church inventories indicates that these speakers were to a certain extent costumed to represent the particular individuals whose words they were assigned to sing.[33]

Returning to the book of customs for the cathedral of Palma, we find a second dramatization toward the conclusion of the pseudo-Augustinian reading. A child "with the adornment of a beautiful maiden", representing one of the ancient pagan prophetesses known as Sibyls, would sing a text commonly referred to as the Sibylline Prophecy, which the real Saint Augustine quotes and interprets in his monumental work *The City of God*.[34] The earliest citation of this pagan prophecy in a Christian context appears in a work of the fourth-century Eastern bishop and ecclesiastical historian Eusebius of Caesarea (+c. 341), the *Oratio Constantini ad sanctorum coetum*, where it is attributed to the "Erythraean Sibyl" and is included in a catena of texts prophesying the coming of Christ.[35] The custom of repeating this "prophecy" was based on the belief that even among the pagans of old there was an expectation of a Messiah who would save the world. The relevance of the Sibylline Prophecy to the Christmas liturgy is most evident in the opening lines of the text, as transcribed by Saint Augustine:

The signal of the judgment moistens the earth with sweat.
From Heaven the King, coming through the ages, shall come,
    certainly
present in the flesh, that he may judge the earth.
Wherefore the unbelieving and the faithful shall see God,
on high with the saints, now at the very end of time.
Thus shall the souls that he judges be present with their flesh.[36]

---

[33] Donovan, *Liturgical Drama in Medieval Spain*, 123.

[34] Ibid., 121. For the relevant passage from Saint Augustine, see *De civitate Dei*, bk. 18, chap. 23, PL 41, cols. 579–581.

[35] Eusebius of Caesarea, *Oratio Constantini ad sanctorum coetum*, chap. 18, PG 20, cols. 1285–1290.

[36] Sibylline Prophecy, quoted in Saint Augustine, *De civitate Dei*, bk. 18, chap. 23, PL 41, col. 579.

Christmas Mass Throughout medieval Europe, the commemoration of the night of Christ's birth climaxed with the celebration of the first Mass of Christmas Day at midnight or in the late night hours afterward. It constitutes the first of three Mass liturgies for Christmas Day, each distinct from the others in the selection of readings, prayers, and antiphons. Durandus explains this tripartite offering of Masses in several ways. In a manner analogous to the three nocturns of Christmas Matins, the three Masses indicate the three ages of the Fathers whose peoples have been saved by the birth of Christ: those before the Mosaic Law, those under the Mosaic Law, and those after the Law had given way to Christ. Fittingly the first Mass takes place in total darkness, corresponding to the darkness of men's minds before God's revelations to Abraham and Moses. The second Mass, celebrated in the partial light of dawn, corresponds to the partial but incomplete knowledge of God given in the age of the Mosaic Law. The third Mass, celebrated in the bright, full light of day, and in accord with the Gospel reading assigned to it (Jn 1:1ff.), testifies to "the time of grace, in which the great Light descended from Heaven, which illuminates all men coming into this world" (cf. Jn 1:9).[37] But in addition to these comparisons, Durandus sees further symbolism in the three Masses of Christmas. The first brings to mind the "eternal generation" of Christ, that is, his being eternally begotten of the Father, a mystery completely hidden from human eyes and hence remembered appropriately at a Mass in the total darkness of night. Moreover, the Introit for this Mass (from Ps 2:7, 1) speaks specifically of the "eternal generation": "*The Lord hath said to me: thou art my Son, this day have I begotten thee . . .*" The second Mass, at dawn, testifies to the promise made by God in Old Testament times that he would send the Messiah, as intimated by the Introit assigned to this Mass, "*Light shall shine this day . . .*" It is celebrated in the dim light of dawn, just as the promise of the coming Messiah was delivered in the dim light of the age that preceded the coming of Christ. The third Mass bears witness to "the truth shown to us" as expressed in its Introit, "*A Child is born to us . . .*" And just as this truth was made fully manifest in the bright light of the New Testament, so too the third Mass is celebrated in the bright light of day.[38]

The juxtaposition of the first Mass of Christmas with the hour of midnight, or in the early hours following midnight, corresponds well to the prophecy in the Book of Wisdom regarding the birth of Christ, as Durandus explains:

> By that also [the Mass at midnight] is shown that the Bread that is daily sacrificed and eaten on the altar, namely Christ, was born in Bethlehem at midnight, and in this night just as Luke says, whence

---

[37] Durandus, *Rationale* (CCCM 140a), bk. 6, chap. 13, nos. 17, 21–22, pp. 187–189 (quote on 189).

[38] Ibid., no. 23, pp. 189–190.

Wisdom 18 [verses 14–15]: "For while all things were in quiet silence, and the night was in the midst of her course, thy mighty word leapt down from heaven from thy royal throne, as a fierce conqueror into the midst of the land of destruction." [39]

The medieval first Mass of Christmas, unlike the Mass liturgies of Holy Week, contained in and of itself no distinguishing external actions (such as a special procession) that would have visually set it apart from the celebration of High Mass for other solemnities. There were nonetheless cases of subtler additions to the customary framework of the Mass to give the nocturnal Christmas Mass a unique character. In many diocesan missals, the ancient tradition of utilizing two readings before the Gospel, one from the Old Testament and the second from the New Testament, was retained in the Christmas Masses. In the case of the first Mass, some missals contained a rubric directing that there should be no pause between the first reading (Is 9:2, 6, 7) and the second (Tit 2:11–15). Durandus explains this custom as signifying that "Christ is born for two peoples [Jews and Gentiles] to be bound together into one wall"; it also symbolizes that "by both Testaments the Nativity of Christ is preached harmoniously", for they are "the two cherubim who cover the Propitiatory" (cf. Ex 25:17–20).[40]

An additional "insertion" is found in the first Christmas Mass of the Sarum Rite, the rite of Salisbury, England. According to the Sarum Missal of 1494, the reading from Isaiah customarily assigned to this Mass (Is 9:2, 6, 7) was chanted one verse or phrase at a time by one cleric as a second cleric sang between each verse or phrase a beautiful peroration of that passage, called a trope, which elucidated its significance in the light of the Gospel. This troped rendering of the Isaiah reading is traceable to the Aquitaine region of France, where it appears for the first time in the eleventh century.[41] The reading begins and concludes with an antiphon. Taken as a whole, the text is imbued with the jubilant spirit of the famed *Exsultet* of the Easter Vigil and serves a comparable purpose in heralding the joy of the solemnity (in the text that follows, the troped additions to the Isaiah reading are given in italics):

I shall utter praises to God forever, who fashioned me with his right hand and redeemed me with the crimson blood of his Son on the Cross.

A reading of the prophet Isaiah, in which the bright Nativity of Christ is prophesied.
These things the Lord says:

---

[39] Ibid., chap. 12, no. 17, p. 187.
[40] Ibid., chap. 13, no. 20, p. 188.
[41] Eugenio Costa, "Tropes et séquences dans le cadre de la vie liturgique au moyen âge", pt. 1, *EL* 92 (1978): 301.

Father, Son, Holy Spirit, in whom all things have been established, the heavens and the depths.

The people that walked in darkness,

whom you created, whom the cunning enemy by deceit expelled from Paradise, and, taken captive, dragged with him to hell,

have seen a great light:

and to the shepherds at midnight an immense splendor has shone;

to them that dwelt in the region of the shadow of death, light

our eternal and true redemption,

is risen.

O wonderful Nativity;

For a child is born to us,

He shall be great, Jesus, Son of God,

and a son

of the supreme Father

is given to us,

so had it been prophesied from Heaven on high,

and the government is upon his shoulder:

that he may govern the skies and the land

and his name shall be called,

Messiah, Savior, Emmanuel, Saboath, Adonai,

Wonderful,

Root of David,

Counsellor,

of God the Father,

God

who created all things,

the Mighty,

destroying the worst dens of the abyss,

the Father of the world to come,

King omnipotent and governing all things,

the Prince of Peace

here and in eternity.

His empire shall be multiplied,

in Jerusalem, Judea, and Samaria,

and there shall be no end of peace:

through eternal ages

he shall sit upon the throne of David, and over his kingdom;

and there shall be no boundary to his kingdom;

to establish it

in the security of faith,

and strengthen it with judgment and with justice,

the Judge when he shall come to judge the ages.

from henceforth

glory, praise, and jubilation are due him

and for ever.

From the rising of the sun to its setting,
to the ends of the earth,
through the regions of Heaven,
let fitting praise to the Creator resound.
Let all things say Amen.[42]

The Office of Shepherds in Fourteenth-century France

The genre of liturgical composition known as the trope, seen above, and succinctly defined by the English medieval drama scholar Karl Young as "a verbal amplification of a passage in the authorized liturgy", in which the original liturgical text is embellished with an added "introduction, interpolation, or conclusion",[43] ultimately inspired the most dramatic liturgical rite of the medieval Christmas liturgy, the Office of Shepherds. Close to the year 900, the most prolific writer of tropes, Tutilo, a Benedictine monk of Switzerland's Saint Gall Abbey, composed a trope to preface the Introit to the third Mass of Christmas Day.[44] This trope was in turn superseded by another in the eleventh century composed for the same purpose, the text *Quem quaeritis in praesepe*, found in numerous liturgical manuscripts of eleventh-century France (Limoges, Nevers, and Moissac) and northern Italy (Mantua, Vercelli, Ivrea, and Novalesa).[45] We give here the version of this trope provided in an eleventh-century manuscript of Limoges, together with the Christmas Introit it amplifies:

> *Whom do you seek in the manger, O shepherds? Speak.*
>
> *The Savior Christ the Lord, the Infant wrapped in swaddling clothes, according to the angelic discourse.*
>
> *The little Child is present here with Mary his Mother, of whom the prophet Isaiah had once spoken in prophesying:*
>
> *Behold a virgin shall conceive and bear a Son; and going now, tell that he is born.*
>
> *Alleluia, alleluia! Now we truly perceive Christ born on earth, of which let all sing with the prophet, declaring:*
>
> [Introit:] *A Child is born to us, and a Son given to us; whose dominion is upon his shoulders; and his name shall be called the Angel of the great council.*[46]

By the twelfth century, the recitation of this trope had developed into an actual dramatization of the visit of the shepherds to the manger on Christmas night, with the use of this trope assigned to a new

---

[42] Text in Francis H. Dickinson, ed., *Missale ad usum insignis et praeclarae ecclesiae Sarum* (Burntisland, Scotland: E. Prelo de Pitsligo, 1861–1883); cols. 50–51.

[43] Young, *Drama of the Medieval Church*, 1:178 (quoted by permission of Oxford University Press).

[44] Ibid., 195.

[45] Ibid., 2:4, 6–8, 427 (Latin text quoted by permission of Oxford University Press).

[46] Quoted ibid., 4. The text of the Introit is here taken from an eleventh-century manuscript of Ivrea, Italy, quoted by Young (ibid., 6). (Latin text of trope and Introit quoted and translated by permission of Oxford University Press.)

position between Christmas Matins and the nocturnal first Mass of Christmas.[47] The earliest extant Office of Shepherds appears in a twelfth-century manuscript of Rouen, France.[48] In this city, the Christmas drama attained the high point of its development in the fourteenth century, as preserved in a Rouen ordinary of this latter period. Inserted between the end of Christmas Matins and the beginning of the first Christmas Mass, this Office of Shepherds also featured a further dramatized dialogue following the conclusion of Mass.[49] The rite begins following the singing of the *Te Deum* at the end of Matins, a manger having been prepared behind the altar, with images of the Blessed Virgin Mary and the Christ Child placed within it. A choirboy stationed "in a high position" before the choir, "in the likeness of the angel announcing the Nativity of the Lord", recites the following verse while five canons, assuming the roles of the shepherds, vested in tunics and amices, enter the choir through its western portal and proceed through the middle of the choir: "*Fear not; for, behold, I bring you good tidings of great joy, that shall be to all the people; for, this day, is born to you the Saviour of the world, in the city of David. And this shall be a sign unto you. You shall find the infant wrapped in swaddling clothes, and laid in a manger*" (cf. Lk 2:10–12).[50] The rubrics continue:

There should be several boys in the vaults of the church as angels, who should begin in a high voice [Lk 2:14]:

Glory to God in the highest; and on earth peace to men of good will.

Hearing this, the shepherds should approach the place in which the manger is prepared, singing this verse [the hymn *Pax in terris*]:

Peace on earth is announced,
in glory to the highest.
Earth is allied to Heaven,
grace mediating.

The Mediator, God, man,
descended unto his own,
that man the guilty one may ascend
to joys unbounded. Ah! Ah!

---

[47] Young, *Drama of the Medieval Church*, 2:9.

[48] Manuscript: Montpellier, France, Bibliothèque de la Faculté de Médecine, MS H. 304, twelfth century, ibid., 12–13.

[49] *Ordinarium ad usum cathedralis Rothomagensis* (manuscript: Rouen, France, Bibliothèque de la Ville, MS 384, fourteenth century); text in Young, *Drama of the Medieval Church*, 2:14–16. (Here and on the pages to follow, all passages from the Rouen *Ordinarium* as transcribed by Young are quoted and translated by permission of Oxford University Press—© Oxford University Press.)

[50] Ibid., 14. This Rouen text gives only the incipit of the choirboy's verse. Young provides the complete text of the verse from a thirteenth-century gradual of Rouen (ibid., 16). (Here and on the pages to follow, all passages from the Rouen gradual as transcribed by Young are quoted and translated by permission of Oxford University Press—© Oxford University Press.)

Let us go over; let us ponder
this announcement that has been made;
let us go over and perceive
what has been announced.

In Judea a Child wails,
this Child, the salvation of his people,
by which he portends himself waging war,
the ancient Upholder of the world.

Let us draw near, let us draw near
to the manger of the Lord,
and let us say,
Praise to the fruitful Virgin.[51]

The earlier-cited Christmas trope *Quem quaeritis in praesepe* is now recited in the form of a dialogue between the shepherds and two priests who symbolize the midwives that the *Protoevangelium of James*, a second-century apocryphal work, claims were present at the birth of Christ. The inclusion of these midwives in the medieval Office of Shepherds was undoubtedly inspired by their role in the *Protoevangelium* text as testators of the preservation of the Blessed Mother's virginity in child-birth.[52] The dialogue in the Rouen rite does in fact make direct reference to the perpetual virginity of Mary:

While [the shepherds] will have been entering, two priests from the greater seat, in dalmatics, as though midwives, who will have been near the manger, should say:
Whom do you seek in the manger, O shepherds? Speak.
The shepherds should respond:
The Savior Christ the Lord, the Infant wrapped in swaddling clothes, according to the angelic discourse.
Likewise the midwives, opening the curtain, should show the Child, saying:
The little Child is present here with Mary his Mother, of whom the prophet Isaiah had once spoken in prophesying.
Here they should show the Mother of the Child, saying:
Behold, a virgin shall conceive and bear a Son. And going forth, tell that he is born.[53]

---

[51] Ibid., 14. The fourteenth-century Rouen ordinary gives only the incipit of the hymn *Pax in terris*; Young provides the complete text of the hymn from the thirteenth-century gradual of Rouen (ibid., 16–17).

[52] *Protoevangelium of James*, chaps. 19–20, in Edgar Hennecke and Wilhelm Schneemelcher, eds., *New Testament Apocrypha* (Philadelphia: Westminster, 1963–1966), 1:384–385.

[53] The fourteenth-century Rouen Ordinary gives only the incipit of this chant; Young provides the complete text from a thirteenth-century gradual of Rouen (Young, *Drama of the Medieval Church*, 2:17).

Then, having seen him, having bowed their necks, they should adore the Child and should greet [them], saying:

Hail, excellent Virgin,
a Virgin remaining, you give birth to God,
begotten before time in the Heart of the Father.
Now let us adore him created from the flesh of his Mother.

Verse: O Mary, with your prayer,
purify the course of our sojourn from the mire of sin;
so dispose that your Son
may grant us to delight in his vision. [54]

Then they should turn themselves, returning to the choir and saying: *Alleluia, alleluia! Now we truly perceive Christ born on earth, of which let all sing with the prophet, declaring* [the Introit of the first Mass of Christmas immediately follows]. [55]

The Rouen text's casting of priests (specifically canons) in the role of the shepherds of Bethlehem accords well with medieval biblical interpretations of the Gospel account of the Nativity, which saw in the shepherds of the first Christmas a prefiguration of the ordained shepherds of the Church. Saint Bede's eighth-century presentation of this comparison in his commentary on the Gospel of Saint Luke[56] was developed further by the fourteenth-century Carthusian author Ludolph of Saxony (+1377) in his *Vita Jesu Christi*: "Mystically therefore, according to Bede, these shepherds of the flock signify the doctors and rectors of the souls of the faithful, who keep watch over the life of those put under them, lest they should sin, and keep vigils of the night over their flock, lest they should perish in the grips of the infernal wolves." [57]

The Rouen text indicates that the priests clothed as shepherds remain vested thus during the first Mass of Christmas that follows and are assigned a liturgical role: "The shepherds should direct the choir." The Mass, celebrated by the archbishop of Rouen if he is present, corresponds closely in content to the Christmas midnight Mass of Rome but with several notable additions. It begins with an Introit (drawn from Ps 2:7, 1) that has been assigned to this midnight Eucharistic liturgy since about 800:[58] "*The Lord hath said to me: Thou art my son, this day have I begotten thee. Why have the Gentiles raged, and the people*

---

[54] Young provides the complete text of this chant from a thirteenth-century gradual of Rouen (Young, *Drama of the Medieval Church*, 2:17).

[55] Young, *Drama of the Medieval Church*, 2:14–15.

[56] Saint Bede, *In Lucae evangelium expositio*, bk. 1, chap. 2, PL 92, col. 332.

[57] Ludolph of Saxony, *Vita Jesu Christi*, ed. Jean-Pierre Mabile and Jean-Jacques-Maria-Antoine Guerrin (Paris and Rome: Victor Palmé, 1865), pt. 1, chap. 9, p. 42.

[58] This chant appears in the Mass antiphonaries of Mount Blandin (Belgium, c. 750–800) and Rheinau (Switzerland, c. 800); see Hésbert, *Antiphonale missarum sextuplex*, 12.

devised vain things? Glory be to the Father . . ."[59] In the Rouen rite a troped version of the *Gloria* is sung by the shepherds, with the insertions, traceable to the tenth century,[60] added to the standard *Gloria* wording (in the text that follows, the troped additions to the *Gloria* are given in italics):

> Glory to God in the highest.
> *The Holy One whom the citizens of Heaven attend, crying out in praise.*
> And on earth peace to men of good will.
> *Which, the Word having been made flesh, the ministers of the Lord had promised to those of earth.*
> We praise you.
> *In whose praise the dark night watches press on.*
> We bless you.
> *By whom every holy thing and blessing is granted and increased.*
> We adore you.
> *The Almighty One, to be adored, worshiped, trembled at, venerated.*
> We glorify you.
> *As creating the creature, fashioning the image, molding the potter.*
> We give you thanks according to your great glory, O Lord God, King of Heaven, God the Father almighty.
> O Lord, the only-begotten Son, Jesus Christ, Lord God, Lamb of God, Son of the Father, you who take away the sins of the world, have mercy on us.
> You who take away the sins of the world, receive our supplication.
> You who sit at the right hand of the Father, have mercy on us.
> For you alone are the Holy One, you alone the Lord, you alone the Most High, Jesus Christ, with the Holy Spirit, in the glory of God the Father. Amen.[61]

The Collect, traceable to the seventh-century Paduan recension of Rome's Gregorian Sacramentary[62] as well as the Gelasian Sacramentary of Rome,[63] follows: "*O God, who have made this most holy night to*

---

[59] Young, *Drama of the Medieval Church*, 2:15 (incipit of Introit only). The complete text of this formula is here taken from Manlio Sodi and Achille Maria Triacca, eds., *Missale Romanum: Editio princeps (1570)*, facsimile ed., MLCT 2 (Vatican City: Libreria Editrice Vaticana, © 1998), 77 (new pagination).

[60] See Ulysse Chevalier, *Repertorium hymnologicum: Catalogue des chants, hymnes, proses, séquences, tropes en usage dans l'église latine depuis les origines jusqu'à nos jours*, vol. 2 (Louvain, Belgium: Polleunis and Ceuterick, 1897), no. 16268, p. 399.

[61] Young's transcription of the Rouen text gives only the incipit of the *Gloria* trope *Quem cives coelestes* (Young, *Drama of the Medieval Church*, 2:15); the complete text of this trope is here taken from a tropary (c. 935) of the Saint Gall Abbey, Switzerland (manuscript: Saint Gall, Stiftsbibliothek, MS Codex Sangallensis (Cod. Sang.) 484, pp. 232–234, digitized text, Stiftsbibliothek Sankt Gallen / Codices Electronici Sangallenses.

[62] Text in Jean Deshusses, ed., *Le sacramentaire grégorien: Ses principales formes d'après les plus anciens manuscrits*, vol. 1, 2nd ed., SF 16 (Fribourg, Switzerland: Editions Universitaires Fribourg, 1979), Paduan no. 327, p. 631.

[63] Mohlberg, Eizenhöfer, and Siffrin, *Liber sacramentorum*, no. 5, p. 7.

shine forth with the brightness of the true Light: grant, we beseech you, that as we have recognized the mysteries of his light on earth, we may also rejoice in his joys fully in Heaven. Who with you lives and reigns ..."[64] To this is added in the Rouen rite a second Collect, taken from the votive Mass of the Blessed Virgin Mary for the Christmas season, which illustrates that Christmas, in addition to being one of the principal solemnities of the Lord, can also be said to be one of the great Marian feasts in virtue of Mary's vocation as Mother of God: "*O God, who has granted the rewards of eternal salvation through the fruitful virginity of blessed Mary: grant, we beseech you, that we may feel her to intercede for us, through whom we have merited to receive the Author of life, our Lord Jesus Christ, your Son. Who with you lives and reigns ...*"[65]

As was the case in much of medieval Europe, the Rouen liturgy for Christmas night utilized both an Old Testament reading from the Book of Isaiah (Is 9:2, 6, 7), in this case read by one of the shepherds, and a lection from the Epistle of Saint Paul to Titus (Tit 2:11–15), read by a subdeacon, without any pause between the two readings,[66] in accordance with the aforementioned practice of beginning the second reading immediately after the first to symbolize the joining together of the Jews and the Gentiles wrought by Christ. The Titus lection has been used for the first Mass of Christmas in the Roman Rite since the seventh century,[67] with the Isaiah text appearing as a second reading from the late eighth century[68] until the sixteenth century.[69] Following these readings, two shepherds sing the Mass Gradual (an eighth-century text),[70] drawn from Psalm 109: "[Ps 109:3:] *With thee is the principality in the day of thy strength: in the brightness of the saints: from the womb before the day star I begot thee.* Verse [Ps 109:1]: *The Lord said to my Lord: Sit thou at my right hand: Until I make thy enemies thy footstool ...*"[71] In the Rouen rite, the *Alleluia* verse (dating from the eighth

---

[64] Young, *Drama of the Medieval Church*, 2:15 (incipit of Collect only). The complete text of this prayer is here taken from Sodi and Triacca, *Missale Romanum: Editio princeps (1570)*, 77 (new pagination).

[65] Young, *Drama of the Medieval Church*, 2:15 (incipit of Collect only). The complete text of this prayer is here taken from Sodi and Triacca, *Missale Romanum: Editio princeps (1570)*, 620 (new pagination).

[66] Young, *Drama of the Medieval Church*, 2:15.

[67] This reading is specified in the seventh-century *Comes* of Würzburg, a lectionary of Rome; see Germain Morin, "Le plus ancien *Comes* ou lectionnaire de l'église romaine", *Revue Bénédictine* 27 (1910): 46.

[68] The Isaiah lection is first specified in the *Comes* of Murbach, a late eighth-century lectionary of the French-Alsatian abbey of Murbach constituting a Frankish adaptation of earlier Roman lectionaries; see D. A. Wilmart, "Le *Comes* de Murbach", *Revue Bénédictine* 30 (1913): 35.

[69] In the *Missale Romanum* of 1570, the reading of the Isaiah lection was discontinued; see Sodi and Triacca, *Missale Romanum: Editio princeps (1570)*, 77 (new pagination).

[70] This Gradual first appears in the Cantatorium of Monza (Italy, eighth century); see Hésbert, *Antiphonale missarum sextuplex*, 12.

[71] Young, *Drama of the Medieval Church*, 2:15 (incipit only). Young provides the complete text of this chant from a thirteenth-century gradual of Rouen (ibid., 18).

century and drawn from Psalm 2:7),[72] sung by two other shepherds, is
followed by the chanting of the medieval Sequence *Nato canunt omnia*,
a text of tenth-century origin:[73]

> *All things sing to the Son, the holy hosts to the Lord, syllable by syllable*
> *dazzling the musical spirits. This sacred day on which are new joys, given*
> *plentifully to the world, and on this sublime night, glory has thundered in an*
> *angelic voice. And enormous lights have shone at midnight to the shepherds.*
> *While they warm their flocks, suddenly they receive divine admonitions. He*
> *who is born to the gracious Virgin exists before time. He is unmeasurable in*
> *Heaven, glory and peace on earth. So then the throng of Heaven exults in*
> *the highest, that the lofty frame of the sky should tremble with so great a*
> *song. And it resounds through all places, on this day in glory, rendered with*
> *a clear voice. Let all men resound to God born on earth; the cruelest powers*
> *of the enemy have been shattered, peace on earth restored. Let all things now*
> *be glad of him born before the beginning [of the world], who alone fashioned*
> *all things, who alone created all things. May he in his mercy remove all our*
> *sins.*[74]

The Gospel in the Rouen rite is Saint Luke's account of the Nativity
(Lk 2:1–14), as has been the case at the first Mass of Christmas since
the seventh century.[75] The Offertory chant, dating from about 800,
an adaptation of Psalm 95 (verses 11 and 13),[76] is likewise a universally
utilized text of the Roman Rite midnight Mass: "*Let Heaven rejoice and
the earth exult before the face of the Lord, for he comes.*"[77] The Rouen
rubrics also mention an Offertory presentation of certain unspecified
gifts that are received by and subsequently distributed among the
shepherds.[78]

---

[72] *Alleluia* verse: "*The Lord hath said to me: Thou art my son, this day have I begotten thee*"
(the complete text of this chant is here taken from Young, *Drama of the Medieval Church*,
2:18). This text is traceable as an *Alleluia* verse for Christmas Mass to the above-cited
Cantatorium of Monza (Italy, eighth century); see Hésbert, *Antiphonale missarum sextuplex*, 12.

[73] See Ulysse Chevalier, *Repertorium hymnologicum: Catalogue des chants, hymnes, proses,
séquences, tropes en usage dans l'église latine depuis les origines jusqu'à nos jours*, vol. 3 (Louvain,
Belgium: Polleunis and Ceuterick, 1904), no. 11890, p. 129. This Sequence is also found
in the 1498 missal of Saragossa, Spain; see *Missale secundum morem ecclesie Cesaraugustane*
(Saragossa: Paul Hurus, 1498), temporal, fol. 184r.

[74] Young, *Drama of the Medieval Church*, 2:15. Young provides the complete text of this
chant from a thirteenth-century gradual of Rouen (ibid., 18).

[75] This Gospel lection is specified in a seventh-century Roman source, the *Capitulare
evangeliorum*, part of the same manuscript as the aforementioned *Comes* of Würzburg; see
Germain Morin, "Liturgie et basiliques de Rome au milieu du VIIe siècle d'après les listes
d'évangiles de Würzburg", *Revue Bénédictine* 28 (1911): 297.

[76] This Offertory antiphon is traceable as a Christmas Mass text to the Mass antiphonaries of Mount Blandin (Belgium, c. 750–800) and Rheinau (Switzerland, c. 800); see
Hésbert, *Antiphonale missarum sextuplex*, 12.

[77] Young provides the complete text of this chant from a thirteenth-century gradual of
Rouen (Young, *Drama of the Medieval Church*, 2:18).

[78] Young, *Drama of the Medieval Church*, 2:15.

For the rest of the Mass, all but two of the remaining texts proper to the solemnity are those of the Roman Rite, including the first of two Secrets,[79] the Preface,[80] the *Communicantes* insertion for the Roman Canon,[81] the Communion chant,[82] and the first of two Postcommunion prayers.[83] The Rouen rite's second Secret is borrowed from an Advent Mass,[84] whereas the second Postcommunion is taken from the votive Mass of the Blessed Virgin Mary for the Christmas season (as was the case with the second Collect at the beginning of the Mass): "*May this Communion, O God, cleanse us from sin; and with blessed Mary, the Mother of God, interceding, may it make us to be partakers of the heavenly remedy. Through the same Jesus Christ, your Son, our Lord . . .*"[85]

---

[79] First Secret: "*May the oblation of this day's feast be acceptable to you, O Lord, we beseech you, that, your grace bestowing, through this sacrosanct transaction we may be found in the form of him in whom our substance is with you. Who with you . . .*" The complete text of this prayer is here taken from Sodi and Triacca, *Missale Romanum: Editio princeps (1570)*, 78 (new pagination). This prayer is traceable to two seventh-century Roman sources, the Gelasian Sacramentary and the Paduan recension of the Gregorian Sacramentary; see respectively Mohlberg, Eizenhöfer, and Siffrin, *Liber sacramentorum*, no. 830, p. 133, and Deshusses, *Sacramentaire grégorien*, Paduan no. 5, 1:609.

[80] Preface: "*. . . For by the mystery of the incarnate Word the new light of your glory has filled the eyes of our soul, that while visibly we perceive God, we may be carried off by this to invisible love. And therefore with angels and archangels . . .*" The complete text of this Preface is here taken from Sodi and Triacca, *Missale Romanum: Editio princeps (1570)*, 300 (new pagination). This text first appears in an eighth-century manuscript of Berlin (Berlin, MS Lat. Fol. 877), in Leo Cunibert Mohlberg, O.S.B., ed., *Missale Francorum*, REDSMF 2 (Rome: Herder, 1957), appendix, no. 170, p. 73.

[81] Canon insertion: "*Uniting with and celebrating this most holy night, in which the spotless virginity of blessed Mary brought forth to this world the Savior . . .*" The complete text of this formula is here taken from Sodi and Triacca, *Missale Romanum: Editio princeps (1570)*, 301 (new pagination). This insertion dates from the seventh century, when it is found at Rome in the Paduan recension of the Gregorian Sacramentary; see Deshusses, *Sacramentaire grégorien*, Paduan no. 7, 1:609.

[82] Communion: "*In the brightness of the saints, from the womb before the daystar I begot you*" (cf. Ps 109:3; the complete text of this chant is here taken from the thirteenth-century Rouen gradual as transcribed by Young, *Drama of the Medieval Church*, 2:18). As a Christmas Mass text, this antiphon dates from about 800, when it appears in the Mass antiphonaries of Mount Blandin (Belgium, c. 750–800) and Rheinau (Switzerland, c. 800); see Hésbert, *Antiphonale missarum sextuplex*, 14.

[83] First Postcommunion: "*Grant us, we beseech you, O Lord our God, that we who rejoice to celebrate the Nativity of our Lord Jesus Christ in his mysteries may by fitting lives be worthy to attain to his company. Who with you lives and reigns. . . .*" The complete text of this prayer is here taken from Sodi and Triacca, *Missale Romanum: Editio princeps (1570)*, 78 (new pagination). It is first found in the sixth-century Leonine Sacramentary of Rome; see Leo Cunibert Mohlberg, O.S.B.; Leo Eizenhöfer, O.S.B.; and Petrus Siffrin, O.S.B., eds., *Sacramentarium Veronense*, REDSMF 1 (Rome: Herder, 1956), no. 1242, p. 158.

[84] Second Secret: "*Having received our offerings and prayers, O Lord, we beseech you, may you both purify us for the heavenly mysteries and mercifully hear us. Through our Lord . . .*" The complete text of this prayer is here taken from Sodi and Triacca, *Missale Romanum: Editio princeps (1570)*, 68 (new pagination). This text is first found in the sixth-century Leonine Sacramentary of Rome; see Mohlberg, Eizenhöfer, and Siffrin, *Sacramentarium Veronense*, no. 1142, p. 142.

[85] Young, *Drama of the Medieval Church*, 2:15 (incipit only). The complete text of this prayer is here taken from Sodi and Triacca, *Missale Romanum: Editio princeps (1570)*, 621 (new pagination). It is a highly altered descendant of an oration from the sixth-century

Immediately after the Mass in the Rouen rite, there is a brief dialogue between the archbishop and the shepherds that leads directly into the office of Lauds for Christmas Day, in the course of which the shepherds are assigned to chant some of the liturgical texts:

> The Mass ended, the archbishop or another at the altar should say the versicle *Blessed is he who comes in the name of the Lord*. [Response:] *The Lord God, and he has given us light*.[86] [What follows is the office of Lauds:] *O God, [hearken] to my assistance. Glory be to the Father. As it was*, etc. *Alleluia*. The archbishop or another priest, having turned toward the shepherds, should say:
> *Whom have you seen, O shepherds? Speak. Announce to us who has appeared on earth.*
> The shepherds should respond (and they should complete the entire antiphon):
> *We have seen the Son and choirs of angels together praising the Lord, alleluia, alleluia.* [87]
> Then a certain one of the shepherds from the right side should begin the psalm *The Lord hath reigned* [Ps 92]. The antiphon [repeated]: *Whom have you seen, O shepherds? . . .* The shepherds should begin the other antiphons, each according to its order . . . and the shepherds should direct the choir.[88]

The office of Lauds is continued with a series of antiphons that have been used in the Christmas liturgy since the second half of the ninth century:[89]

> Antiphon: *The King the Mother has borne, to whom [is given] an eternal name, and having the joys of a mother together with the virginity of purity; neither has the like been seen before, nor [is there] to come another, alleluia.*
> Psalm [Ps 99]: *Sing joyfully to God . . .*
> Antiphon: *The angel says to the shepherds: I announce to you a great joy: for this day unto you has been born the Savior of the world, alleluia.*
> Psalm [Ps 62]: *O God, my God . . .*
> Antiphon: *There was with the angel a multitude of the heavenly army praising God and saying: Glory to God in the highest, and on earth peace to men of good will, alleluia.*

Leonine Sacramentary of Rome; see Mohlberg, Eizenhöfer, and Siffrin, *Sacramentarium Veronense*, nos. 878bis and 1131bis, pp. 111, 143.

[86] This text is first found as an office verse in the Antiphonary of Compiègne (France, c. 870); see Hésbert, *Corpus antiphonalium officii*, 1:36. The complete text of this versicle, *Benedictus qui venit*, is here taken from the Gregorian chant online database Cantus, http://cantusdatabase.org.

[87] This antiphon is first found in the above-cited Antiphonary of Compiègne (France, c. 870); see Hésbert, *Corpus antiphonalium officii*, 1:36. Young provides the complete text of *Quem vidistis, pastores* from a thirteenth-century gradual of Rouen (Young, *Drama of the Medieval Church*, 2:18).

[88] Young, *Drama of the Medieval Church*, 2:15.

[89] These four antiphons are first found in the Antiphonary of Compiègne (France, c. 870); see Hésbert, *Corpus antiphonalium officii*, 1:36.

Psalm [canticle; Dan 3:57–88]: *Blessed art thou, O Lord the God of our fathers . . .*

Antiphon: *This day a little child is born unto us, and he shall be called mighty God, alleluia, alleluia.*

Psalm [Ps 148]: *Praise ye the Lord from the heavens . . .*

Chapter reading [Is 9:2ff.]: *The people of the Gentiles . . .*[90]

The hymn *A solis ortus cardine*, cited earlier in our account of the Christmas Eve aspersion rite of Münster, is now sung. Following the recitation of the office verse, *"All the ends of the earth have seen"*,[91] and the Canticle of Zechariah with its antiphon, the concluding Collect of Christmas Lauds is said, a text traceable to the seventh-century Paduan redaction of Rome's Gregorian Sacramentary:[92] *"Grant, we beseech you, almighty God, that the new Nativity of your only-begotten Son may by his flesh deliver us, whom the old servitude holds under the yoke of sin. Through the same Jesus Christ your Son, our Lord, who with you lives and reigns in the unity of the Holy Spirit, God, through all ages of ages. Amen."*[93] Following the end of Lauds, the shepherds sing the trope *Verbum Patris hodie:*

> *This day the Word of the Father*
> *has proceeded from the Virgin;*
> *he comes to redeem us*
> *and has willed to return us to the celestial fatherland.*
> *Let the angelic hosts praise the Lord with joyful song.*
>
> Response: *An angel shining brightly*
> *proclaimed to the shepherds peace, the Herald of peace.*
> *You, O Shepherd of the Church,*
> *both guide and instruct your sons unto peace, then,*
> *thanks owed to you the Redeemer, with rejoicing.*[94]

Ascending into the pulpit, the shepherds then chant the antiphon *"Behold, all the things that were said of the Virgin Mary by the angel have*

---

[90] Young, *Drama of the Medieval Church*, 2:15. Young's transcription of the Rouen texts gives only the incipit of each of the four antiphons in this passage. The complete texts of these antiphons are here taken from the 1568 *Breviarium Romanum*, in Sodi and Triacca, *Breviarium Romanum: Editio princeps (1568)*, 187 (new pagination).

[91] This verse first appears in an eleventh-century antiphonary of Verona, Italy; see Hésbert, *Corpus antiphonalium officii*, 1:39. The complete text of this verse is here supplied from Hésbert, *Corpus antiphonalium officii*, no. 8242, 4:504.

[92] Deshusses, *Sacramentaire grégorien*, Paduan no. 17, 1:609.

[93] Young, *Drama of the Medieval Church*, 2:15–16. Young's transcription of the Rouen text gives only the incipit of this prayer, the complete text of which is here taken from Sodi and Triacca, *Missale Romanum: Editio princeps (1570)*, 80 (new pagination).

[94] Young, *Drama of the Medieval Church*, 2:16 (incipit only). Young provides the complete text of this chant from a thirteenth-century gradual of Rouen (ibid., 19).

been fulfilled." [95] The archbishop, or in his absence the presiding priest, now recites a verse that originated in the ninth century as an antiphon for the February 2 office of the Purification of the Blessed Virgin Mary (the Presentation of the Lord): *"After birth, O Virgin, you remained inviolate; Mother of God, intercede for us."* [96] The Rouen rite concludes with the Marian oration earlier utilized as the second Collect of midnight Mass. Following the closing versicle, *"Let us bless the Lord"*, said thrice, the second Mass of Christmas is begun.[97]

Liturgical dramatizations of the Nativity of Christ on Christmas night were not commonplace in medieval Europe, but they were by no means confined to Rouen. The medieval records of the cathedral of Valencia, Spain, testify to a magnificent scenography erected in the church for the Christmas drama enacted within its walls in conjunction with Christmas Matins. A massive scaffold was constructed, extending from near the pulpit in the sanctuary to the choir, upon which was mounted a model of the stable of Bethlehem, containing statues of the Christ Child, the Blessed Virgin Mary, and Saint Joseph, all three of which were lavishly clothed in garments made from rich fabrics. Around them were placed figures of angels, seraphim, and cherubim. Nearby on the same scaffold, a series of miniature castle turrets was constructed to represent the town of Bethlehem. On another part of the scaffold were placed splendidly garbed statues of the Old Testament prophets who had foretold the coming of Christ. There was also a contingent of twenty-five shepherds and shepherdesses, some of which were statues but others of which were costumed singers assigned to sing certain portions of the Christmas drama. The statue of the Blessed Virgin was framed behind by a sunburst of gilded wood rays, on the perimeter of which was represented a spread of clouds interspersed with twenty-eight large wax candles that illuminated the whole scene. In the choir, at a place separate from the scaffold, a representation of the tree of Paradise ("the tree of life" [Gen 2:9]) was erected, with statues of Adam and Eve beneath it and with a statue of the Infant Jesus suspended above it, ringed by seraphim. In the copula over the high altar was placed a canvas depicting Heaven, featuring the figure of God the Father. Along the balustrade that rimmed the copula, twenty-five boys costumed as angels stood holding lit candles. The canvas was made with an aperture that at the appointed moment opened, out of which emerged a wooden

---

[95] Ibid., 16 (incipit only). Young provides the complete text of this chant from a thirteenth-century gradual of Rouen (ibid., 19). This verse is first found in an early eleventh-century antiphonary of Monza, Italy; see Hésbert, *Corpus antiphonalium officii*, 1:39.

[96] This text is used for the office of February 2 in the Antiphonary of Compiègne (France, c. 870); see Hésbert, *Corpus antiphonalium officii*, 1:116. The complete text of this antiphon, *Post partum virgo*, is here taken from the Gregorian chant online database Cantus, http://cantusdatabase.org.

[97] Young, *Drama of the Medieval Church*, 2:16.

dove, covered with paper feathers, that was lowered all the way to the stable. As the dove reached the stable, a figure of an angel holding a lily was lowered while a chorister representing another angel sang. A choral dialogue ensued between the choir and a woman singer serving as the voice for the figure of the Blessed Virgin Mary in the stable.[98]

[98] Donovan, *Liturgical Drama in Medieval Spain,* 144–145.

IO The Feast of the Purification of the Blessed Virgin Mary, February 2 (The Presentation of the Lord)

Pope Sergius established that on the day of the Purification of holy Mary ... all the people, [singing] the litanies to be performed and [carrying] in their hands burning candles given by the bishop, should go forth through their churches with the priests or ministers of the Church in remembrance of the heavenly kingdom, because, according to the parable of the prudent virgins, all the elect, going on to meet the Bridegroom with the shining lamps of their good works, shall then enter with him unto the marriage feast of the celestial city.

Missale Bracarense, Rite of Braga, Portugal, 1498[1]

The liturgical commemoration of the presentation of Christ in the Temple appeared in the East by the end of the fourth century, when it is first mentioned by the Spanish pilgrim Egeria as one of the feasts she saw celebrated during her visit to Jerusalem around the year 382; in the Holy City the day was marked by a procession, a practice that was to become a permanent feature of the feast.[2] It was during the reign of the Byzantine emperor Marcian in the mid-fifth century (450–457) that the idea of using lights to celebrate the Presentation of the Lord was introduced by a Roman matron named Ikalia, who lived in Jerusalem. According to the sixth-century Palestinian monastic writer Cyril of Scythopolis, Ikalia, a woman of great holiness, "set the example of the use of candles for the first time in the procession" of this day.[3] The actual insertion of the feast of the Presentation into the

---

[1] *Missale Bracarense* (Lisbon: Nicolaus de Saxonia, 1498), sig. s3v.

[2] *Itinerarium Egeriae*, chap. 26, in Enzio Franceschini and Robert Weber, eds., *Itineria et Alia geographia*, CCCL 175 (Turnhout, Belgium: Brepols, 1965), 72.

[3] Cyril of Scythopolis, *Life of Saint Theodosius*, chap. 1; this passage is translated into English from the French translation of Cyril's biography in A.-J. Festugière, O.P., trans., *Les moines d'Orient*, vol. 3, pt. 3, *Les moines de Palestine* (Paris: Cerf, 1963), 58.

liturgy of Rome is attributed to Pope Sergius I (687–701);[4] Roman *Ordo* 20, a liturgical text of the late eighth century, describes a procession for the feast through the streets of Rome, in which the participants carried lit candles.[5] The earliest prayers for the blessing of candles on this day date from the tenth century, appearing in the Romano-Germanic Pontifical[6] and other texts of German origin.[7] The sprinkling of the candles with holy water is first mentioned in the aforesaid Romano-Germanic Pontifical; the incensation of the candles is first found in a monastic text of this same period, the *Regularis concordia*, compiled around 960 by the bishop Saint Ethelwold (+984) for the Benedictines of England.[8]

In the sixth century, the feast was given the Greek title of *Hypapante* (Meeting),[9] for in the words of a medieval liturgical book of Constantinople, the day commemorated "the Meeting of our great God and Savior Jesus Christ with Simeon the Just when the latter took him in his arms".[10] The manner of celebrating this day in the medieval West has often been criticized on the grounds that what was originally a feast focusing upon the Redeemer's presentation in the Temple was changed into a Marian feast, beginning with the title it was given from the seventh century onward as found in Rome's Gelasian Sacramentary,[11] the Purification of the Blessed Virgin Mary. Yet as we shall see in the texts to follow, the medieval prayers, antiphons, responsories, readings, and rubrics of the Purification embrace the mystery of our Lord's presentation in the Temple in its entirety. In keeping with the biblical narrative of the event, the Blessed Virgin does figure prominently in the medieval celebration of the feast, and rightly so, but certainly not in a disproportionate manner.

The imagery of candles on the feast of the Purification of Mary is drawn directly from the Gospel account of the event, in which Simeon

---

[4] This attribution appears in the *Liber pontificalis*; text in Louis Duchesne, ed., *Le Liber pontificalis: Texte, introduction et commentaire* (Paris: Ernest Thorin, 1886–1892), 1:376.

[5] Text in Michel Andrieu, ed., *Les Ordines Romani du haut moyen âge*, vol. 3, SSLED 24 (Louvain, Belgium: "Spicilegium sacrum Lovaniense" Administration, 1951), 235–236.

[6] Text in Cyrille Vogel and Reinhard Elze, eds., *Le pontifical romano-germanique du dixième siècle*, vol. 2, ST 227 (Vatican City: Biblioteca Apostolica Vaticana, 1963), 6–9.

[7] Texts in Adolph Franz, *Die kirchlichen Benediktionen im Mittelalter* (Freiburg im Breisgau, Germany, 1909; repr., Graz, Austria: Akademische Druck—U. Verlagsanstalt, 1960), 1:445–448.

[8] Text in Thomas Symons, trans., *Regularis concordia: The Monastic Agreement of the Monks and Nuns of the English Nation*, Medieval Classics (New York: Oxford University Press, 1953), chap. 3, no. 33, p. 31.

[9] Pierre Jounel, "The Year", in Aimé-Georges Martimort, ed., *The Church at Prayer: An Introduction to the Liturgy*, vol. 4, *The Liturgy and Time* (Collegeville, Minn.: Liturgical Press, 1986), 88.

[10] *Typicon of the Great Church* (ninth to tenth century), in Juan Mateos, ed., *Le Typicon de la Grande Eglise*, vol. 1, *Le cycle des douze mois*, Orientalia Christiana analecta 165 (Rome: Pont. Institutum Orientalium Studiorum, 1962), 220–221.

[11] The title is given as "Purification of Holy Mary"; see Leo Cunibert Mohlberg, O.S.B., et al., eds., *Liber sacramentorum Romanae aeclesiae ordinis anni circuli (Sacramentarium Gelasianum)*, REDSMF 4 (Rome: Herder, 1960), no. 829, p. 133.

describes Christ as a "light to the revelation of the Gentiles" (Lk 2:32). Honorius of Autun (+c. 1135) sees the lit candles of the feast as a symbol of Christ, "the Light of the saints", with the wax representing Christ's human nature, the wick the mortality of his human nature, and the flame representing his divinity. Honorius considers the day's procession as both a commemoration of Simeon and Anna going to meet the Christ Child and a reminder "that with the five wise virgins we should go forth to meet Christ the Bridegroom with the lighted lamps of good works" (Mt 25:10) and through Mary enter the marriage feast of the "heavenly city".[12] Honorius' contemporary Saint Bernard (+1153) notes the significance of the convention of walking two astride in the Purification procession (and in other religious processions), seeing in this a visible reminder of Christ sending out his disciples two by two (Lk 10:1), which itself was a sign of the bond of fraternal charity that Christ intended among his followers.[13] Drawing upon the key role of one's hands in carrying out occupations, Bernard interprets the candles in the hands of those in the procession as a symbol of the good works with which we must be occupied, lest we come before God empty-handed. The flames of the candles are a sign of the ardent love and the longing to please God that should accompany our good works, so that the Lord may find us ready with our lamps alight in our hands (Lk 12:35). Moreover, the flames of the candles are lit from a fire blessed by the presiding priest as a sign of the fire that Christ declared he had come to cast upon the earth (Lk 12:49).[14]

Two Fourteenth-century Rites for February 2

The candle-blessing rite of February 2 as given in the early fourteenth-century rubrics of a ceremonial for Cologne's Cathedral of Saint Peter[15] begins with an entrance procession in which a silver-gilded statue of the Blessed Virgin Mary is carried by two young nobles. The image is brought to the high altar, where it is then placed. Cologne's suffragan bishop, serving as celebrant, vested in a mantle, begins at the altar the prayers for the blessing of the candles. The first three are traceable to eleventh-century Germany:[16]

> *Lord Jesus Christ, the true Light, who illuminate every man coming into this world: pour forth your bless + ing upon these candles, and sancti + fy them with the light of your grace; and mercifully grant that just as these lights kindled with visible fire dispel the darkness of night, so may our hearts,*

---

[12] Honorius of Autun, *Gemma animae*, bk. 3, chap. 24, PL 172, col. 649.

[13] Saint Bernard, *De purificatione beatae Mariae*, Sermon 2, nos. 1–2, PL 183, col. 368.

[14] Ibid., no. 2, col. 369.

[15] Text in Gottfried Amberg, ed., *Ceremoniale Coloniense*, Studien zur Kölner Kirchengeschichte 17 (Siegburg, Germany: Franz Schmitt, 1982), 88, 90.

[16] All three of these prayers are found, with some differences, in an eleventh-century German manuscript transcribed by the sixteenth-century liturgist Melchior Hittorp (+1584); text in Franz, *Kirchlichen Benediktionen im Mittelalter*, 1:449–451.

illuminated with the invisible fire of the Holy Spirit, be free from the blind-ness of all sins, that with the eye of the mind purified, we may always be able to discern those things that are acceptable to you and beneficial for our salvation; that after the dark perils of this world we may be worthy to come to unfailing light. Through you, Jesus Christ, Savior of the world, the King of glory, who in perfect Trinity live and reign through all ages of ages. Amen.

O Lord Jesus Christ, who, appearing among men in the nature of our flesh, were presented by your parents in the Temple on this day, whom venerable, aged Simeon, illuminated by the Holy Spirit, took into his arms: grant, we beseech you, that illuminated and instructed by the grace of the same Holy Spirit, we may truly know you and faithfully love you. Who lives and reigns with God the Father in the unity of the Holy Spirit . . .

It is truly fitting and just, right and salutary, for us always and everywhere to give you thanks, holy Lord, Father omnipotent, eternal God, who com-manded Moses your servant to provide the purest liquid of oil for preparing the lights continually before your sight; graciously pour forth, we beseech you, the grace of your blessing upon these candles, that they may so administer light outwardly that, by you bestowing the light of your Spirit, it may not be wanting to our minds interiorly.[17]

These orations are followed by two further prayers in the Cologne text, both of which are derived from the tenth-century Romano-Germanic Pontifical:[18]

Lord God almighty, Creator of Heaven and earth, King of kings and Lord of rulers, graciously hear us your servants crying out and praying to you; we therefore beseech you, O Lord, holy Father, almighty eternal God, who cre-ated all things out of nothing, and by your command through the labor of bees have made this liquid to come forth for the finishing of candles, and who on this day also accomplished the expectation by prayer of the just Simeon, we humbly entreat you that you may vouchsafe to bless + and sanctify these candles for the use of men and for the health of their bodies and souls, whether on land or on the waters, through the invocation of your holy name and through the intercession of holy Mary, the Mother of your Son, whose feast is celebrated this day, and through the prayers of all the saints; and this your people, honorably carrying them in their hands with singing and praising, may you preserve with your governance and graciously hear their voices from your holy Heaven and your seat of majesty; and may you be merciful to all crying out to you, whom you have redeemed in the precious blood of your Son, who with you . . .

I bless you, O wax, in the name of God the Father almighty, and of his only-begotten Son, and of the Holy Spirit, the Paraclete, that you may bring

---

[17] Amberg, *Ceremoniale Coloniense*, 88.
[18] Vogel and Elze, *Pontifical romano-germanique*, 2:7.

about in all places the driving away of the devil and the expulsion of all his companions, the same holy and indivisible Trinity assisting, who in the essence of unity live . . .[19]

It is at this point in the Cologne ceremony that the symbolism of the candles of the Purification feast in regard to Simeon's prophecy of Christ as a "light to the revelation of the Gentiles" (Lk 2:32) is made explicit:

> The candles having been sprinkled and censed, the suffragan [bishop] personally kindles one of the blessed candles on the high altar and, holding it in his hand, sings, *A light to the revelation of the Gentiles*, the choir continuing the antiphon ["*and the glory of thy people Israel*"][20] and the psalm [Canticle of Simeon, Lk 2:29–32: "*Now thou dost dismiss thy servant, O Lord, according to thy word in peace . . .*"].[21]

The statue of the Blessed Virgin Mary is then taken from the altar and carried in a procession that exits the east end of the church and proceeds as far as the adjacent Church of Saint Mary of the Step before turning back toward the west, traversing the courtyard along the south side of the cathedral before reentering it. The reentry of the statue of Mary through the doors of the cathedral is accompanied by the singing of an antiphon of ninth-century origin, *Cum inducerent puerum*,[22] that calls to mind the entry of the Holy Family into the Temple of Jerusalem for the presentation of the Christ Child: "*When his parents brought in the Child Jesus, Simeon took him into his arms, and blessed God, and said: Now thou dost dismiss thy servant, O Lord, in peace*" (cf. Lk 2:27–29). The procession concludes with the singing of the thanksgiving hymn *Te Deum*, after which the Mass of the day is begun.[23]

In fourteenth-century Essen, Germany, the quasi-monastic community of canons that staffed the city's collegiate church also conducted an outdoor procession on the feast of the Purification of Mary, as described in the church's *Liber ordinarius* dating from this period.[24] Following the blessing of the candles and the lighting of all the tapers of the religious from the candle of the priest who will celebrate the Mass of the day, the canons (without the celebrant) proceed out of their collegiate church and across the city to the Church of Saint

---

[19] Amberg, *Ceremoniale Coloniense*, 88, 90.

[20] This antiphon is first found in the Antiphonary of Compiègne (France, c. 870); see René-Jean Hésbert, ed., *Corpus antiphonalium officii*, vol. 1, REDSMF 7 (Rome: Herder, 1963), 116. The complete text of this antiphon is here taken from René-Jean Hésbert, ed., *Corpus antiphonalium officii*, vol. 3, REDSMF 9 (Rome: Herder, 1968), no. 3645, p. 320.

[21] Amberg, *Ceremoniale Coloniense*, 90.

[22] This antiphon is first found in the Antiphonary of Compiègne (France, c. 870); see Hésbert, *Corpus antiphonalium officii*, 1:114, 116.

[23] Amberg, *Ceremoniale Coloniense*, 90.

[24] Text in Franz Arens, ed., *Der Liber ordinarius der Essener Stiftskirche* (Paderborn, Germany: Albert Pape, 1908), 32–35.

Gertrude, singing along the way the antiphon *Adorna thalamum*, derived from a hymn of the Byzantine liturgical poet Saint Cosmas of Jerusalem (+c. 781):[25] "*Adorn your bridal chamber, O Sion, and receive Christ the King; welcome Mary, who is the gate of Heaven, for she carries the glorious King of the new light. A virgin she remains, bringing in her hands the Son before the daystar, him whom Simeon, taking into his arms, prophesied to the peoples to be the Lord of life and death, and the Savior of the world.*"[26]

When the canons reach the Church of Saint Gertrude, two of them bring out of the church a gold statue of the Blessed Virgin Mary, with which they then lead the procession as the canons head back toward their monastery, singing the following responsory of ninth-century origin:[27] "*Rejoice, O Virgin Mary: you alone have destroyed all heresies, who believed in the words of the archangel Gabriel; while a virgin you bore God and man, and after birth a virgin inviolate you remained. Verse: We believe the archangel Gabriel to have spoken to you from Heaven; we believe your womb to have been made fruitful by the Holy Spirit.*"[28] The procession halts in a stone courtyard near the monastery, where the celebrant and the clerics assisting him, as well as Essen's community of canonesses (women living a mitigated form of religious life), have been awaiting the statue's arrival. Here the celebrant places a crown upon the head of the Blessed Virgin, intoning another Marian responsory (dating to the ninth century)[29] as he does so: "*Behold the miracle: the Mother of the Lord conceived, the Virgin not knowing male union. And remaining overwhelmed with a noble burden, Mary, joyful, perceives herself a mother, who is unacquainted with being a wife.*"[30] Before returning to the monastery for Mass, the canons sing another antiphon of eighth-century Eastern origin, *Ave gratia plena*, from a hymn of Saint Cosmas of Jerusalem:[31] "*Hail, full of grace, Virgin Mother of God, from you has truly arisen the Sun of justice, enlightening those who are in darkness; rejoice also, you elder just one* [i.e., Simeon], *bearing in your arms the Deliverer of our souls, giving us life and resurrection.*"[32]

---

[25] See Egon Wellesz, *Eastern Elements in Western Chant: Studies in the Early History of Ecclesiastical Music* (Copenhagen: Munksgaard, 1967), 61, note. In the West, this antiphon first appears in the Mass antiphonary of Mount Blandin (Belgium, c. 750–800); see René-Jean Hésbert, ed., *Antiphonale missarum sextuplex* (Brussels, 1935; repr., Rome: Herder, 1967), 38.

[26] Arens, *Liber ordinarius der Essener Stiftskirche*, 32–34 (antiphon on 33–34).

[27] This responsory first appears in the Antiphonary of Compiègne (France, c. 870); see Hésbert, *Corpus antiphonalium officii*, 1:116.

[28] Arens, *Liber ordinarius der Essener Stiftskirche*, 32, 34. The Essen text gives only the incipit of the responsory *Gaude Maria*. The complete text of this chant is here taken from René-Jean Hésbert, ed., *Corpus antiphonalium officii*, vol. 4, REDSMF 10 (Rome: Herder, 1970), no. 6759, p. 191.

[29] This responsory is a variant of that first found in the Antiphonary of Compiègne (France, c. 870); see Hésbert, *Corpus antiphonalium officii*, 1:116.

[30] Arens, *Liber ordinarius der Essener Stiftskirche*, 34.

[31] See Wellesz, *Eastern Elements in Western Chant*, 60–61. In the West, this antiphon first appears in the Mass antiphonary of Mount Blandin (Belgium, c. 750–800); see Hésbert, *Antiphonale missarum sextuplex*, 36.

[32] Arens, *Liber ordinarius der Essener Stiftskirche*, 34.

In his massive biblical commentary on the life of Christ, the Carthusian Ludolph of Saxony (+1377) enlarged the symbolism of the procession for the feast of the Purification of Mary, linking it with what transpired *after* the Blessed Virgin Mary had placed her divine Son in Simeon's arms and had received him back. Ludolph envisions the February 2 procession as a symbolic reenactment of the procession led by Joseph and Simeon in which Mary carried "Jesus the King" into the Temple, with the prophetess Anna at her side. All four, he notes, were filled with joy as they went together to present the Divine Infant in fulfillment of the Mosaic Law. In this latter procession, albeit a small one, people of essentially every state of life are represented: male and female, young and old, virgins, parents, and the widowed. And just as Mary and Simeon carried the Christ Child in their hands, those in the February 2 procession carry in their hands candles, symbols of Christ, which they bring to the altar and offer there, just as Christ was brought into the Temple to be presented to God the Father.[33] Moreover, Ludolph sees the candles of the feast as a symbol of both Christ and his blessed Mother:

> Mary inwardly and [outwardly] shone with the virtues. Wherefore she is also beautifully symbolized in the gold candlestick, which gave light in the Temple of the Lord to the people of Jerusalem, on top of which stood seven burning lamps, which seven symbolized the seven works of mercy, that is, Mary, who was the Queen of mercy and the Mother of goodness. This candlestick and this candle we honor, when on the feast of the Purification we carry lit candles. For Mary offered a candle to the Lord at her purification, when Simeon celebrated in song the Light to the revelation of the Gentiles; Christ the Son of Mary is a lit candle, by reason of the three things that are found in it, namely the wick, the fire, and the wax; and in Christ there are three things, namely the flesh, the soul, and the true divinity. This candle has been offered to the Lord for mankind, by which the night of our darkness has been illuminated.[34]

Ludolph develops further the symbolism of the candles' three elements of wax, wick, and fire. Just as the bee brings forth pure wax, he observes, so did the Virgin Mary bring forth the pure flesh of Christ, without corruption. And just as the wick is hidden in the wax, so was the soul of Christ hidden in his flesh. The representation of Christ's divinity by the flame hearkens back to Moses' declaration to the people of Israel that "the Lord thy God is a consuming fire" (Deut 4:24). Finally, the threefold nature of

**Other Rites for
February 2**

---

[33] Ludolph of Saxony, *Vita Jesu Christi*, ed. Jean-Pierre Mabile and Jean-Jacques-Maria-Antoine Guerrin (Paris and Rome: Victor Palmé, 1865), pt. 1, chap. 12, p. 60.

[34] Ibid., 56.

the candle as wax, wick, and fire can be seen as symbolic of the Holy Trinity.[35]

Nearly all of Ludolph's reflections upon the February 2 procession seem to be represented in the instructions for the feast of the Purification of Mary given in a document of the Guild of Saint Mary, Beverly, England, dating from 1388 or 1389:

> It is established that each year on the feast of the Purification of blessed Mary, beginning with this next feast of the Purification, all the brothers and sisters of the same guild should assemble in a determined decent place assigned to this, distant from the said church; and there a certain person from the guild shall be appointed who should be found more fitting to this, most nobly and decently clothed and adorned as the Virgin Queen after the fashion of the glorious Virgin Mary, having as it were her Son in her arms; and in that place there shall be two others resembling Joseph and Simeon; and there shall be two angels carrying a candlestick having the form of a harrow, and upon it twenty-four thick wax candles, with other large and thick lights preceding. And thus with every manner of melody and exultation, the said Virgin with her Son and Joseph and Simeon shall follow the said lights in procession toward the said church; and then all the sisters of the said guild shall immediately follow the said Virgin, and lastly all the brothers, each one of them having in his hand one candle of the weight of half a pound; and in the same place they shall go two by two in order with a sober and controlled step, processing thus to the said church. And when it [the procession] shall have arrived there, the said Virgin shall offer in that place her Son to Simeon near the high altar after the fashion of the Purification of the glorious Virgin Mary, and thus the individual sisters and brothers shall subsequently offer their wax candles with one denarius for every candle from his own property. And these things having been carried out with all solemnity accordingly, everyone shall return to his own property with joy.[36]

The intent of visually representing the events of the biblical presentation of the Savior in the Temple is likewise evident in the February 2 rite found in the 1487 *Obsequiale Augustense*, a liturgical book of Augsburg, Germany. Particular attention is given to Simeon, beginning with the recitation of the following antiphon (*Responsum accepit Symeon*) at a station just outside the front door of the church, beneath the porch:

---

[35] Ibid., 60.

[36] Text in Karl Young, "Dramatic Ceremonies of the Feast of the Purification", *Speculum* 5 (1930): 100.

Simeon received the response from the Holy Spirit, [that he was] not going to see death until he had seen Christ the Lord. And when they had brought the Child into the Temple, he took him into his arms, and blessed God, and said: Now thou dost dismiss thy servant, O Lord, in peace ... [cf. Lk 2:26–29].[37]

This antiphon having been finished, [the procession] enters into the church, where a certain worthier priest presents himself along the way, vested in a cope, holding in his arms before himself an image of the [Christ] Child upon a pillow, with two torchbearers standing around him, and stationing himself at a suitable place, that the whole procession may pass by him, which he afterward follows last. In entering the church, this antiphon is sung:

When his parents brought in the Child Jesus, Simeon took him into his arms, and blessed God, and said: Now thou dost dismiss thy servant, O Lord, in peace [cf. Lk 2:27–29].[38]

In the 1496 missal of Vich, Spain, we find among the prayers for the blessing of the candles on February 2 an oration borrowed from Spain's ancient Mozarabic Rite as given in the *Liber ordinum*, an eleventh-century compilation of older texts believed to date largely from the fifth to the seventh century, in which it was used as the blessing for the lamp at the beginning of the Easter Vigil.[39] The subsequent supplanting of the Mozarabic Rite with a Spanish form of the Roman Rite, beginning in the eleventh century, eliminated this prayer from the Spanish Easter Vigil, but it appears that an enterprising Spanish liturgist thought to salvage the beautiful oration by inserting it into the candle-blessing rite of the Purification of Mary, a feast that first reached Spain in the eleventh century.[40] In the Vich missal, the prayer is cast in the form of a Preface:

We give you thanks, O Lord our God, eternal God, Light unfailing, Light of the only Light, Source of light, Author of light, who created and illuminated the light of your angels, of thrones, dominations, principalities, and powers, and of all intellectual [beings], who created the light of your saints. May our souls be your lamps. May they be kindled by you and illuminated from you. May they shine with truth; may they burn with charity. May they

---

[37] This antiphon is traceable to the Mass antiphonary of Mount Blandin (Belgium, c. 750–800); see Hésbert, *Antiphonale missarum sextuplex*, 38.

[38] *Obsequiale Augustense* (Augsburg, Germany: Erhard Ratdolt, 1487; digitized text, Bayerische Staatsbibliothek, Munich, 2008), fol. 6v. Regarding the chant *Cum inducerent puerum*, see the use of this antiphon in the earlier-described Cologne rite (p. 289).

[39] For the original text in the *Liber ordinum*, see Marius Férotin, O.S.B., ed., *Le Liber ordinum en usage dans l'église wisigothique et mozarabe d'Espagne du cinquième au onzième siècle* (Paris, 1904), repr., ed. Anthony Ward, S.M., and Cuthbert Johnson, O.S.B., BELS 83 (Rome: Centro Liturgico Vincenziano, Edizioni Liturgiche, 1996), col. 209. The ceremony of light for the Easter Vigil in the *Liber ordinum* is described in chapter 15 of the present work (pp. 460–462).

[40] Mario Righetti, *Manuale di storia liturgica* (Milan: Editrice Ancora, 1949–1955), 2:94.

*shine and not become dark. May they burn and not turn to ashes. Bless +
this light, O Light; and because this [light] that we carry in our hands you
created, you gave, we therefore beseech you, O Lord, that even as by these
lights that we kindle we expel the night from this place, so also may you
expel from our hearts the darkness of all ignorance. May we be your dwelling
place, shining for you and shining in you. May we shine without sin. And
may we always worship you. May we be kindled in you, and not be extinguished. Through our Lord . . .*[41]

The insertion of this ancient Easter Vigil text into the Purification
liturgy also appeared in other Spanish liturgical books, including those
of Barcelona (twelfth century) and Saragossa (1498).[42] It is likewise
used for the candle-blessing rite of February 2 in the 1506 missal
of Palma de Majorca.[43] Following this prayer, the Palma rite continues with an evocation of the eschatological imagery of the lamps
lit to greet the Bridegroom in the parable of the ten virgins
(Mt 25:1–13):

> The blessing of the candles having indeed been completed, two boys
> holding lit candles in their hands should say the following antiphon:
> *Come and light, preparing your lamps; behold, the Bridegroom comes; go out
> to meet him.*[44] And the choir should repeat the said antiphon com-
> pletely. Which having been finished by the choir, the said boys should
> repeat the said antiphon for the third time in a high voice.[45]

As the Canticle of Simeon, *Nunc dimittis* (Lk 2:29–32), is sung three
times along with the antiphon "*A light to the revelation of the Gentiles,
and the glory of his people Israel*",[46] all those present light the candles
they have been given. An outdoor procession follows, and climaxes as
it returns to the church:

> And when they shall have been before the doors of the church, they
> should say this antiphon:[47] *Behold, Mary comes to the Temple with the
> Child Jesus, at whose entrance the sanctuary shines, and all the earth rejoices*

---

[41] Text in Francesc Xavier Altés i Aguiló, ed., *Missale Vicense, 1496*, facsimile ed., Biblioteca litúrgica catalana 3 (Barcelona: Institut d'Estudis Catalans, 2001), sanctoral, fols.
14v–15v.

[42] This prayer is used thus in a twelfth-century sacramentary of Barcelona and in the
1498 missal of Saragossa; see respectively Gabriel Seguí i Trobat, ed., *El missal mallorquí de
1506: Estudi i edició segons l'exemplar de la Biblioteca Bartomeu March*, Col·lectània Sant Pacià
79 (Barcelona: Facultat de Teologia de Catalunya, Centre d'Estudis Teològics de Mallorca,
2003), 364, notation; and *Missale secundum morem ecclesie Cesaraugustane* (Saragossa: Paul
Hurus, 1498), sanctoral, fols. 43v–44v (with textual differences).

[43] Seguí i Trobat, *Missal mallorquí de 1506*, 363–364.

[44] This antiphon is rare; it does not appear in any of the other sources consulted by the
author.

[45] Seguí i Trobat, *Missal mallorquí de 1506*, 364.

[46] See the use of this antiphon in the earlier-described Cologne rite (p. 289).

[47] This antiphon first appears as a Matins invitatory in an early eleventh-century antiphonary of Monza, Italy; see Hésbert, *Corpus antiphonalium officii*, 1:115.

in its King; with lamps lit, they have sung above, saying. And the choir should respond: *Blessed is the Lord who comes to his Temple.* Which having been finished, at the entrance of the church the precentors [leading choristers] should begin the office [the Introit of the Mass to follow], *We have received, O God, your mercy, in the midst of your Temple; as your name, O God, so also is your praise unto the ends of the earth; your right hand is filled with justice.*[48]

The readings assigned to the Mass for the feast of the Purification of Mary have remained essentially the same since the ninth century: the lection from the Book of Malachi, which prophesies the coming of the Lord to the Temple (Mal 3:1–4), first appears as a February 2 reading in the *Comes* of Alcuin (c. 800),[49] while the use of the Gospel recounting the presentation of the Infant Jesus (Lk 2:22–32) can be traced even further back, to fifth-century Jerusalem[50] and seventh-century Rome.[51] The prayers for this Mass (the Collect, the Secret, and the Postcommunion), first specified in the seventh-century Paduan redaction of Rome's Gregorian Sacramentary,[52] prevailed across medieval Europe and subsequently entered the *Missale Romanum* of 1570, as did the aforementioned readings.[53] Most of the chants for this Mass in the 1570 missal (namely the Introit, the Gradual, the Offertory, and the Communion) are traceable to the eighth century.[54]

We conclude this chapter with one final example of the beautiful prayers for the blessing of candles that have graced the feast of the Purification of Mary, the day of the Presentation of the Lord, over the centuries. The text is taken from the 1498 *Missale Bracarense* of Portugal's archdiocesan Rite of Braga; this benediction is traceable in its

[48] Seguí i Trobat, *Missal mallorquí de 1506*, 364.

[49] Text in G. Godu, "Epitres", in Fernand Cabrol and Henri Leclercq, eds., *Dictionnaire d'archéologie chrétienne et de liturgie* (Paris: Librairie Letouzey et Ané, 1907–1953), vol. 5, pt. 1, col. 302.

[50] The Armenian Lectionary, a liturgical book of early fifth-century Jerusalem, specifies the Gospel lection Luke 2:22–40 for this feast day; text in Athanase Renoux, ed. and trans., *Le codex arménien Jérusalem 121*, vol. 2, *Edition comparée du texte et de deux autres manuscrits*, Patrologia orientalis 36, fasc. 2 (Turnhout, Belgium: Brepols, 1971), no. 13, pp. 228–229.

[51] This Gospel lection is specified in the seventh-century Roman source known as the *Capitulare evangeliorum*, part of the same manuscript as the *Comes* of Würzburg; see Germain Morin, "Liturgie et basiliques de Rome au milieu du VIIᵉ siècle d'après les listes d'évangiles de Würzburg", *Revue Bénédictine* 28 (1911): 301–302.

[52] Text in Jean Deshusses, ed., *Le sacramentaire grégorien: Ses principales formes d'après les plus anciens manuscrits*, vol. 1, 2nd ed., SF 16 (Fribourg, Switzerland: Editions Universitaires Fribourg, 1979), Paduan nos. 104–106, p. 616.

[53] Text in Manlio Sodi and Achille Maria Triacca, eds., *Missale Romanum: Editio princeps (1570)*, facsimile ed., MLCT 2 (Vatican City: Libreria Editrice Vaticana, 1998), 467–469 (new pagination).

[54] The Introit is traceable to the Cantatorium of Monza (Italy, eighth century), albeit as a Gradual; it first appears as the Introit in the Mass antiphonary of Mount Blandin (Belgium, c. 750–800), in which the Offertory and the Communion are also found for the first time. The Gradual first appears in the Cantatorium of Monza. See Hésbert, *Antiphonale missarum sextuplex*, 38.

earliest form to eleventh-century France,[55] with the prayer subsequently entering the Braga liturgy in the twelfth century:[56]

Eternal God, fount and origin of all light, who have illuminated the world with the light of your glory in sending us your only-begotten Son through the womb of the spotless Virgin, and whom long before you promised by the oracles of your prophets [cf. Rom 1:2] was going to come in the end times; you sent the Light himself to the people sitting in darkness, and the Light everlasting has appeared to those walking in the land of the shadow of death [cf. Lk 1:79; Is 9:2]. We entreat you, therefore, that you may vouchsafe to bless + these candles prepared in your name with your benediction, with which you have removed us from the power of darkness into the light, and the kingdom of your most beloved Son, through whom light has appeared in the darkness to the upright in heart [cf. Ps 111:4], and the joy of eternal salvation; and who accomplished the expectation of Simeon the just, that he would not see death first before he had seen the same, his Christ, clothed in flesh, and saluted the Light of all the world; may you likewise fill us, we beseech you, with the light of your glory, that you may drive away from us all the darkness of infidelity. And just as on this day you dismissed your servant in peace, vouchsafe to govern us in the peace of your holy Church, that we may be worthy to enter the gate of eternal rest; that bathed in the rays of your true light, there on the day of judgment, joyful with the hymns of the choir of angels, we may be worthy to see the face of the everlasting Sun. Who with you lives and reigns in the unity of the Holy Spirit . . .[57]

[55] The prayer is first found in the French pontifical of Hugues de Salins, archbishop of Besancon (1031–1066); text in Edmond Martène, *De antiquis ecclesiae ritibus* (Venice: Johannes Baptista Novelli, 1763–1764), bk. 4, chap. 15, *ordo* 1, 3:46.

[56] In Portugal, this prayer first appears in a twelfth-century pontifical of Braga (manuscript: Porto, Portugal, Biblioteca Municipal, MS 1134); see Joaquim O. Bragança, "Ritual de Santa Cruz de Coimbra: Porto, Biblioteca Municipal, ms. 858", *Didaskalia*, 6 (1976): 158, footnote.

[57] *Missale Bracarense*, sig. s4v.

11   Ash Wednesday and Laetare Sunday

In every man's heart dwelling in [this] wretched vale of tears is needful to be found ghostly labor and travail in telling of his conscience this holy time of Lent, deputed and ordained to reformation of soul.

John Drury, English priest of Beccles, early fifteenth century[1]

The observance of Lent appeared in both the East and the West by the fourth century, attested in the East by Saint Athanasius (writing in 331)[2] and in the West by Saint Ambrose (in a homiletic text from c. 385).[3] In the late fourth century, Lent began on the Sunday six weeks prior to Easter Sunday, but by the early sixth century it had been expanded to begin four days earlier, on what ultimately came to be known as Ash Wednesday.[4] Across much of medieval Europe, this season was marked with a striking visual reminder of its penitential character: a curtain known as the Lenten veil would be hung in the church sanctuary, concealing the altar. This practice and the closely related Lenten custom of veiling the church's religious images are described in a thirteenth-century Swiss liturgical text for the city of Zurich, the *Liber ordinarius* of Konrad von Mure, a cantor of the cathedral (+1281):

> On Ash Wednesday, between the choir and the public altar, a veil is suspended under the arch of Saint Florian, which each day at the elevation of the Host is raised somewhat at its extremities by two scholars, by means of certain cords, that sight may be given to the people until the elevation should be completed. But on Sundays and feast days, from Vespers all the way to the end of the following day, the veil itself remains raised almost all the way to its middle portion by means of the aforesaid cords. But at the public Masses of Lent, the

Ash Wednesday

---

[1] John Drury, "Tract on the Manner of Confession"; original fifteenth-century Middle English text in Sanford Brown Meech, "John Drury and His English Writings", *Speculum* 9 (1934): 76. The author of the present work has modernized the spelling in this quotation.

[2] Saint Athanasius, *Third Festal Letter* (331), no. 6, PG 26, col. 1376.

[3] Saint Ambrose, *De Elia et jejunio*, chap. 10, no. 34, PL 14, col. 708.

[4] Pierre Jounel, "The Year", in Aimé-Georges Martimort, ed., *The Church at Prayer: An Introduction to the Liturgy*, vol. 4, *The Liturgy and Time* (Collegeville, Minn.: Liturgical Press, 1986), 67–68.

same veil ought not to be upheld with a suspension of this kind. Furthermore, all the crosses and images, both over the altars and on top of shafts and staffs, are veiled. And thus they should remain veiled all the way to the end of the office of the missal on Good Friday.[5]

Lenten veiling practices are traceable to the tenth century, when they appear for the first time in the earliest redaction of the Benedictine customary for the French abbey of Cluny, which calls for the hanging of a curtain before the high altar during Lent as well as the Lenten veiling of all the altars and the church cross.[6] In the Sarum Rite of Salisbury, England, the Lenten veil would appear in the sanctuary on the Saturday after Ash Wednesday, remaining there until the Mass on Wednesday of Holy Week, when, during the chanting of the Passion of Saint Luke, as the words relating the rending of the Temple veil (Lk 23:45) were sung, it was dramatically made to fall. Relics, crosses, and other religious images as well as the tabernacle were individually veiled with their own cloths from the Monday after Ash Wednesday until Easter Sunday.[7]

A fifteenth-century English pedagogical work known as *Dives and Pauper* explains that inasmuch as Lent represents (among other things) "the time of Adam's sin, for which we lost the sight of God's face, and God and the court of Heaven hid their faces from mankind, until the time of Christ's Passion", the religious images are veiled during this penitential season. The veiling likewise signifies that those in mortal sin cannot see the face of God or the saints in Heaven until they repent and confess their sins.[8] Similarly, the twelfth-century French liturgist Honorius of Autun (+c. 1135) observes: "This [the Lenten veil] is suspended by us for the veil between corporal things and spiritual things, by which Christ and that celestial fatherland are now concealed from us. Afterward ... the face of the Lord shall be revealed to us, and the celestial glory shall be uncovered."[9]

Honorius likens the Lenten curtain to the veil that divided the ancient sanctuary of the Ark of the Covenant and the Temple of Solomon into two parts, that is, the outer Holy Place and the inner, more sacred

---

[5] Text in Heidi Leuppi, *Der Liber ordinarius des Konrad von Mure: Die Gottesdienstordnung am Grossmünster in Zürich*, SF 37 (Fribourg, Switzerland: Universitätsverlag Freiburg, 1995), 225.

[6] Text in Kassius Hallinger, O.S.B., *Consuetudines Cluniacensium antiquiores cum redactionibus derivatis*, Corpus consuetudinum monasticarum 7, pt. 2 (Siegburg, Germany: Franciscus Schmitt, 1983), 53, 68.

[7] See the instructions of the Sarum Customary, dating from the late fourteenth century, in Walter Howard Frere, ed., *The Use of Sarum* (Cambridge: Cambridge University Press, 1898–1901), 1:138–139. A rubric specifying the dropping of the veil during the Mass on Wednesday of Holy Week is found in various printed editions of the Sarum Missal from 1487 to 1557; see Francis H. Dickinson, ed., *Missale ad usum insignis et praeclarae ecclesiae Sarum* (Burntisland, Scotland: E. Prelo de Pitsligo, 1861–1883), col. 294.

[8] Herbert Thurston, S.J., *Lent and Holy Week: Chapters on Catholic Observance and Ritual* (London: Longmans, Green, 1904), 102.

[9] Honorius of Autun, *Gemma animae*, bk. 3, chap. 46, PL 172, col. 657.

Holy of Holies (Ex 26:31–33; Heb 9:2–4). Just as the veil of old, a cloth of fine workmanship, screened the Holy of Holies from the sight of the people, so too the Lenten veil, wrought as "a painted Heaven adorned with shining gems in wonderful variety", conceals the Christian altar during the Lenten season.[10] Honorius also compares the Lenten curtain to the veil that Moses placed over his face, which had been made resplendent from conversation with God (Ex 34:33–35); just as Moses' face was thus concealed from the people, so too the Scriptures remain veiled in mystery until their meaning is revealed by the Passion and Resurrection of Christ.[11] In a similar vein, the author of a fifteenth-century English treatise composed for parish priests explains that the Lenten veil signifies the veiled biblical prophecies of the Passion that were not understood until the actual events of the Passion unfolded, as commemorated during Holy Week, when the altar is again "openly shown to all men" following the dropping of the veil.[12] This removal of the Lenten curtain during Holy Week is connected by Honorius to both the Passion and the Resurrection. In regard to the former, he observes: "In the Passion of Christ the veil of the Temple is rent, for by his death, Heaven and the book closed with seven seals (Rev 2) are opened to us."[13]

In consonance with Honorius' comparison, the usual occasion for the removal of the veil was, as we saw in the Sarum Rite, at the pronouncement of the words "*Velum templi scissum est*" ("*The veil of the temple was rent in the midst*" [Lk 23:45]), during Saint Luke's Passion on Wednesday of Holy Week. This unveiling was a widely observed custom traceable to the eleventh century, when it is mentioned in a liturgical text for Rouen, France, the *Liber de officiis ecclesiasticis* of Archbishop John of Avranches (episcopate, 1067–1079).[14] As for the linkage of the veil's removal to the Resurrection, Honorius explains: "At Easter the veil is removed, and the adornment of the altar is seen by all the people, for at the Resurrection all things shall be uncovered and revealed, when the blessed shall see the King of glory in his comeliness."[15] This association of the removal of the Lenten veil with the Resurrection may well have been the inspiration for another custom that developed from the tenth century onward, to which Honorius may be alluding, that of ceremonially unveiling the altar during the Easter Vigil or during the liturgical rites of Easter Day (a practice we shall examine in chapter 15).

In England, Lenten veils were usually white in color, embroidered with red crosses.[16] One sixteenth-century Englishman speaks of these

---

[10] Ibid., cols. 656–657.

[11] Ibid., col. 657.

[12] Text in Karl Young, "Instructions for Parish Priests", *Speculum* 11 (April 1936): 226.

[13] Honorius of Autun, *Gemma animae*, bk. 3, chap. 46, PL 172, col. 657.

[14] John of Avranches, *Liber de officiis ecclesiasticis*, PL 147, col. 48.

[15] Honorius of Autun, *Gemma animae*, bk. 3, chap. 46, PL 172, col. 657.

[16] For examples from Durham (1446) and Oxford (c. 1546), see Daniel Rock, *The Church of Our Fathers, as Seen in St. Osmund's Rite for the Cathedral of Salisbury*, vol. 3, pt. 2 (London: C. Dolman, 1853), 223.

curtains as also having on them scenes of the Passion, "that the mind should be fixed only on the Passion of Christ".[17] The cathedral of Gurk, Austria, possesses a Lenten cloth dating from 1458, a linen tapestry of nine hundred square feet decorated with one hundred scenes from the Old and New Testaments.[18]

On Ash Wednesday, the medieval Church embarked upon the great fast of Lent through the celebration of liturgical ceremonies commensurate with the spirit of this penitential season of preparation for the mysteries of Holy Week and Easter. Ash Wednesday's most distinctive rite, then as now, the imposition of ashes, first appearing as a sacramental for all the faithful to receive in the tenth-century Romano-Germanic Pontifical,[19] is explained by both Honorius of Autun and Sicard of Cremona as the visible calling to mind of "the day of our expulsion from Paradise" (Honorius), a public confession that "we who desired to be gods [Gen 3:5–6] are not gods from Heaven but men, and have our beginning from the earth" (Sicard). It is intended to impress upon our minds the words of God to fallen Adam, "*Dust thou art, and into dust thou shalt return*" (Gen 3:19), an admonition that is repeated as the ashes are administered.[20] The ceremony also draws inspiration from Job's confession of his human frailty, "*I am compared to dirt, and am likened to embers and ashes*" (Job 30:19).[21] Ash Wednesday prayers for the blessing of the ashes, as well as the formula for imposing the ashes, "*Remember, man, that you are dust, and unto dust you shall return*", an adaptation of the aforesaid Genesis verse, are found for the first time in the tenth-century Romano-Germanic Pontifical.[22] The significance of the ashes is richly expressed in a prayer of thirteenth-century origin for blessing the ashes utilized in the 1499 missal of Jaén, Spain:

> *Almighty everlasting God, who have mercy on all and hate nothing of those that you have made; who also, overlooking the sins of men because of their penitence, mercifully come to the aid of those crying out to the ears of your clemency: vouchsafe to bless + and sanctify these ashes, which by reason of holy religion and humility you have appointed [us] to carry upon our heads for our sins in the manner of the Ninivites; grant by the invocation of your holy name that all who shall have carried them upon their heads and today*

---

[17] This "Catholic" understanding of the Lenten curtain is related by an English Protestant otherwise hostile to the Church, Thomas Becon (1512–1567), quoted in Thurston, *Lent and Holy Week*, 104.

[18] Nigel J. Morgan, "Gurk Cathedral, 2: Painting", in Jane Turner, ed., *Dictionary of Art*, (New York: Oxford University Press, 1996), 13:858.

[19] Rubrics and prayers in Cyrille Vogel and Reinhard Elze, eds., *Le pontifical romano-germanique du dixième siècle*, vol. 2, ST 227 (Vatican City: Biblioteca Apostolica Vaticana, 1963), 21–22.

[20] Honorius of Autun, *Gemma animae*, bk. 3, chap. 43, PL 172, col. 655; Sicard of Cremona, *Mitrale*, bk. 6, chap. 4, PL 213, col. 255.

[21] Sicard of Cremona, *Mitrale*, bk. 6, chap. 4, PL 213, col. 255.

[22] Vogel and Elze, *Pontifical romano-germanique*, 2:21–22.

begin thus the holy fasts, unto beseeching your mercy, may be worthy to receive the forgiveness of all their sins from you, Lord Jesus Christ, that they may merit to attain worthily to the day of the resurrection with purified minds, and in the future, to everlasting and imperishable glory. Through our Lord Jesus Christ your Son . . .[23]

The Ash Wednesday rubrics in a thirteenth-century ritual for the Cistercians' Monastery of the Holy Cross in Coimbra, Portugal, direct that the ashes should be received "with great reverence and contrition of heart".[24] For centuries, the source of the ashes for Ash Wednesday has been the palms or other tree branches used in the Palm Sunday procession of the preceding year. This manner of obtaining the ashes is first mentioned in the Benedictine customary of Fructuaria, Italy (c. 1085), which specifies that on Ash Wednesday morning, before the hour of Terce (the office said around nine o'clock), the ashes are to be made by burning the olive branches that had been given to the celebrating priest at the previous year's Palm Sunday liturgy.[25] The practice appears in Rome about the year 1140 in the *Ordo officiorum* of the city's cathedral church of Saint John Lateran, a liturgical book compiled by Cardinal Bernard of Porto (+1176).[26] The sprinkling of holy water upon the ashes is first mentioned in the eleventh century, appearing in the *Liber tramitis*, a customary of the French Benedictine abbey of Cluny (c. 1043),[27] and in the customary composed by Archbishop Lanfranc for England's Canterbury Cathedral (c. 1077).[28] The incensation of the ashes is traceable to the twelfth century, when it is mentioned in a customary of the Italian monastery of Vallombrosa;[29] in the thirteenth century it is specified in both the *Liber ordinarius* of

---

[23] Text in *Missale Giennense / Manuale continens ordinem ad celebrandum ecclesiastica sacramenta* [*Missale secundum morem et consuetudinem sancte ecclesie Gienensis*] (Seville: Meinard Ungut and Stanislao Polono, 1499), fol. 23v. This prayer also appears in the Ash Wednesday rite found in the missal of Jaén's parent see, Toledo (1503–1518); see *Missale secundum consuetudinem almae ecclesiae Toletanae*, 1503–1518, vol. 2 (manuscript: Madrid, Biblioteca Nacional de España, MS 1541; digitized text, Biblioteca Digital Hispánica, Biblioteca Nacional de España, Madrid, 2007), fols. 40v–41r. This prayer is first found in a thirteenth-century Ordinary of the French see of Bayeux; text in Edmond Martène, *De antiquis ecclesiae ritibus* (Venice: Johannes Baptista Novelli, 1763–1764), bk. 4, chap. 17, ordo 6, 3:52–53.

[24] Text in Joaquim O. Bragança, "Ritual de Santa Cruz de Coimbra", *Didaskalia* 6 (1976): 162.

[25] *Consuetudines* of Fructuaria, Italy, bk. 1, chap. 33, in Bruno Albers, ed., *Consuetudines monasticae*, vol. 4, *Consuetudines Fructuarienses necnon Cystrensis in Anglia monasterii et congregationis Vallymbrosanae* (Monte Cassino, Italy: Typis Montis Casini, 1911), 33.

[26] Text in Ludwig Fischer, ed., *Bernhardi cardinalis et Lateranensis ecclesiae prioris Ordo officiorum ecclesiae Lateranensis*, Historische Forschungen und Quellen 2–3 (Munich: Dr. F. P. Datterer, 1916), 27.

[27] *Liber tramitis* (formerly called the Customs of Farfa), bk. 1, chap. 41, in Bruno Albers, ed., *Consuetudines monasticae*, vol. 1, *Consuetudines Farfenses* (Stuttgart: Jos. Roth, Bibliopolae, 1900), 31.

[28] Text in David Knowles and Christopher N. L. Brooke, eds. and trans., *The Monastic Constitutions of Lanfranc*, rev. ed., Oxford Medieval Texts (Oxford: Clarendon, 2002), chap. 19, pp. 28–29.

[29] Text in Hallinger, *Consuetudines Cluniacensium antiquiores*, 344.

Zurich, Switzerland,[30] and the *Ordo divinorum officiorum* of the Camaldolese Order (a liturgical text compiled about the year 1253).[31]

Medieval Ash Wednesday rites included a procession, which was seen as a representation of the Christian journey of life, by which "we strive to return to our country" (Sicard of Cremona), armed with the weapons of "humility, prayer, affliction" (Honorius of Autun) and the virtues (Sicard), so as "to do battle against the spirits of evil" that confront us on the way (Honorius).[32] William Durandus of Mende (+1296) describes the Ash Wednesday procession as a march to war against demons.[33]

At the Premonstratensian (Norbertine) abbey of Prémontré, France, the Ash Wednesday Mass, as recounted in a twelfth- to thirteenth-century ordinary of the monastery, would be preceded by the recitation of the seven penitential psalms. Before beginning the seventh and final psalm, the monks would remove their shoes, an Ash Wednesday practice explained by Sicard of Cremona as "representing the barrenness of Adam [Gen 3:7] and signifying that we lack the adornment of grace".[34] Meanwhile, the abbot sets a visible example of humility and contrition for his community by fully prostrating himself:

> The sacristans should spread carpets before the step of the sanctuary, where the abbot, midway between the deacon and the subdeacon, prostrates himself for the seven psalms, the other ministers leaning upon their seats. And the seven psalms having been said thus without the litany, the Collects follow, as they are contained in the missal, which the abbot, having prostrated himself, should say; afterward he should add the *Misereatur* ["*May almighty God have mercy on you and, with all your sins forgiven, lead you to eternal life*"] and the *Indulgentiam* ["*May the almighty and merciful Lord grant us the forgiveness, absolution, and remission of all our sins*"]. But the other brothers, kneeling meanwhile over their seats, should be bowing forward. After this, the prelate, rising, should bless the ashes.[35]

[30] Leuppi, *Liber ordinarius des Konrad von Mure*, 227.

[31] *Vetus Ordo divinorum officiorum* (compiled by Martin III), chap. 40, in John-Benedict Mittarelli and Anselm Costadoni, eds., *Annales Camaldulenses ordinis sancti Benedicti* (Venice: Monastery of Saint Michael of Muriano and John Baptist Pasquali, 1761), vol. 6, col. 116.

[32] Sicard of Cremona, *Mitrale*, bk. 6, chap. 4, PL 213, col. 255; Honorius of Autun, *Gemma animae*, bk. 3, chap. 43, PL 172, col. 655.

[33] William Durandus of Mende, *Rationale divinorum officiorum*, bk. 6, chap. 28, no. 17, in A. Davril, O.S.B., and T. M. Thibodeau, eds., *Guillelmi Duranti: Rationale divinorum officiorum V–VI*, CCCM 140a (Turnhout, Belgium: Brepols, 1998), 254.

[34] Sicard of Cremona, *Mitrale*, bk. 6, chap. 4, PL 213, col. 255.

[35] Text in P. F. Lefèvre, O.Praem., ed., *L'ordinaire de Prémontré d'après des manuscrits du XIIe et du XIIIe siècle*, Bibliothèque de la Revue d'Histoire Ecclésiastique 22 (Louvain, Belgium: Bureaux de la Revue, 1941), 48. The standard Mass formulas *Misereatur* and *Indulgentiam* are here supplied from the text of the 1570 *Missale Romanum* in Manlio Sodi and Achille Maria Triacca, eds., *Missale Romanum: Editio princeps (1570)*, facsimile ed., MLCT 2 (Vatican City: Libreria Editrice Vaticana, © 1998), 294 (new pagination).

The abbot now blesses the ashes with a Collect traceable to the tenth-century Romano-Germanic Pontifical[36] (and later used in the 1570 *Missale Romanum*),[37] sprinkling the ashes with holy water as he does so:

> *O God, who desire not the death of sinners but their repentance: most mercifully regard the frailty of our human condition; and these ashes, which by reason of fostering humility and obtaining forgiveness we intend to be put upon our heads, vouchsafe to bless + according to your goodness, that we who recognize ourselves to be ashes and by reason of the merit of our guilt to be turned back into ashes may be worthy to obtain the forgiveness of all our sins and the rewards mercifully promised in return to the repentant. Through Christ our Lord.*[38]

The hebdomadarian (that is, the priest assigned to lead the Divine Office in a given week) begins to sprinkle the assembled monks with holy water as the cantor intones the following antiphon derived from Psalm 68 (verse 17): "*Graciously hear us, O Lord, for loving is your compassion; regard us, O Lord, according to the multitude of your mercies.*"[39] As the aspersion of the monastic congregation continues, Psalm 68 is chanted in its entirety, a text both penitential and prophetic of the Savior's sufferings: "*Save me, O God, for the waters are come in even unto my soul. . . . My eyes have failed, whilst I hope in my God. They are multiplied above the hairs of my head, who hate me without cause . . .*" (verses 2, 4–5). Having earlier prostrated himself at the beginning of the rite, the abbot now sets a further example of humility by being the first to receive ashes upon his head:

> And all having been sprinkled by the hebdomadarian, presently the antiphon *Let us change* should be begun. And the abbot first, kneeling in that manner in which the rest [are to kneel], should receive the holy ashes from the prior or from the cantor priest; then standing upon the step, and having turned toward the choir, he [the abbot] should put the blessed ashes upon the heads [of the others] one at a time, beginning with the ministers of the altar, all kneeling to the ground.[40]

As the ashes are distributed to the intent, according to the rubrics, that all may be "admonished . . . to be mindful of their corruption",[41]

---

[36] Vogel and Elze, *Pontifical romano-germanique*, 2:22.

[37] This prayer is one of three orations utilized for the blessing of ashes in the Ash Wednesday rite of the 1570 *Missale Romanum*; see Sodi and Triacca, *Missale Romanum: Editio princeps (1570)*, 122 (new pagination).

[38] Lefèvre, *Ordinaire de Prémontré*, 48. The Prémontré text gives only the incipit of this blessing. The complete text of this prayer is here taken from Vogel and Elze, *Pontifical romano-germanique*, 2:22.

[39] Lefèvre, *Ordinaire de Premontre*, 48 (incipit only). This antiphon is traceable to the tenth-century Romano-Germanic Pontifical, from which the complete text is here taken (Vogel and Elze, *Pontifical romano-germanique*, 2:22).

[40] Lefevre, *Ordinaire de Prémontré*, 48.

[41] Ibid.

three antiphons are sung, the first two of which are traceable to the second half of the eighth century:[42]

> *Let us change our garb, unto ashes and sackcloth; let us fast and lament before the Lord, for he is very merciful to forgive our sins, our God* [cf. Joel 2:13].

> *Between the porch and the altar the priests, the Lord's ministers, shall cry out, and say: Spare, O Lord, spare your people; and smite not the mouths of those singing unto you, O Lord* [cf. Joel 2:17; Esther 13:17].[43]

After the brief antiphon "*Be forgiving, O Lord, to our sins*",[44] a responsory of ninth-century origin[45] follows: "*Let us amend for the better, who through ignorance have sinned, lest suddenly overtaken by the day of death, we should seek time for penance and not be able to find it. Attend, O Lord, and have mercy, for we have sinned against you. Verse: We have sinned with our fathers, we have acted unjustly, we have performed iniquity. Attend, O Lord . . .*"[46] The abbot concludes the ashes rite with an ancient prayer traceable to the sixth-century Leonine Sacramentary of Rome,[47] utilized in the Ash Wednesday liturgy from the seventh century[48] onward to the *Missale Romanum* of 1570,[49] an oration consonant with William Durandus' earlier-cited interpretation of the Ash Wednesday procession as a spiritual march into battle: "*Grant us, O Lord, to commence our services to the Christian army with holy fasts, that going forth to do battle against spiritual evils, we may be fortified with the supports of self-denial. Through . . .*"[50] Two monks now begin the recitation of the Litany of the Saints. When in the course of the litany the Blessed Virgin Mary

---

[42] These two antiphons (*Immutemur habitu* and *Iuxta vestibulum*) first appear in the Mass antiphonary of Mount Blandin (Belgium, c. 750–800); text in René-Jean Hésbert, ed., *Antiphonale missarum sextuplex* (Brussels, 1935; repr., Rome: Herder, 1967), 48.

[43] Lefèvre, *Ordinaire de Prémontré*, 48. The Prémontré text gives only the incipit for each of these antiphons. The complete texts are here taken from Sodi and Triacca, *Missale Romanum: Editio princeps (1570)*, 122 (new pagination).

[44] Lefèvre, *Ordinaire de Prémontré*, 48 (incipit only); the complete text of this antiphon is here taken from René-Jean Hésbert, ed., *Corpus antiphonalium officii*, vol. 3, pt. 1, REDSMF 9 (Rome: Herder, 1968), no. 4394, p. 416. This antiphon dates from the eleventh century, when it appears in the Italian antiphonaries of Verona and Ivrea; see René-Jean Hésbert, ed., *Corpus antiphonalium officii*, vol. 1, REDSMF 7 (Rome: Herder, 1963), 79, 99.

[45] This responsory is first found in the Antiphonary of Compiègne (France, c. 870); see Hésbert, *Corpus antiphonalium officii*, 1:136.

[46] Lefèvre, *Ordinaire de Prémontré*, 48 (incipit only). The complete text of this responsory is here taken from Rene-Jean Hésbert, ed., *Corpus antiphonalium officii*, vol. 4, REDSMF 10 (Rome: Herder, 1970), no. 6653, p. 167.

[47] Text in Leo Cunibert Mohlberg, O.S.B.; Leo Eizenhöfer, O.S.B.; and Petrus Siffrin, O.S.B., eds., *Sacramentarium Veronense*, REDSMF 1 (Rome: Herder, 1956), no. 207, p. 26.

[48] This prayer is specified as an Ash Wednesday oration in the seventh-century Paduan redaction of Rome's Gregorian Sacramentary; text in Jean Deshusses, ed., *Le sacramentaire grégorien: Ses principales formes d'après les plus anciens manuscrits*, vol. 1, 2nd ed., SF 16 (Fribourg, Switzerland: Editions Universitaires Fribourg, 1979), Paduan no. 127, p. 618.

[49] Sodi and Triacca, *Missale Romanum: Editio princeps (1570)*, 123 (new pagination).

[50] The Prémontré text provides only the incipit of this prayer (Lefèvre, *Ordinaire de Prémontré*, 48). The full text is here taken from the tenth-century Romano-Germanic Pontifical, in Vogel and Elze, *Pontifical romano-germanique*, 2:22.

is invoked (or else, upon the invocation of the abbey's patron saint), the religious community processes out of the church, led by the cross-bearer, with the abbot vested in a cope. The procession continues without stopping as the litany is chanted, returning back into the church before the end.[51] Regarding the monks' reentry into the choir, the Prémontré text notes, "We remain with our faces turned to the east until the litany should be completed."[52] The abbot and ministers immediately proceed to the sacristy to vest for the Mass that follows.[53]

Across medieval Europe, the Ash Wednesday Mass contained two distinctive features that were later preserved in the universally promulgated 1570 *Missale Romanum* of Pope Saint Pius V. The first of these regarded the recitation of the Tract before the Gospel, a text of eighth-century Frankish origin (based upon Psalm 102:10 and Psalm 78:8–9);[54] we quote it here as it appears in the *Missale Romanum* of 1570: "*O Lord, requite us not according to our sins that we have committed, nor according to our iniquities. Verse: Remember not our former iniquities; let your mercies speedily act before us, for we have become exceedingly poor. Verse: Help us, O God, our Savior, and for the glory of your name, O Lord, deliver us; and forgive us our sins, for your name's sake.*"[55] The rubrics of the twelfth- to thirteenth-century Prémontré rite specify that when the above verse "*Help us, O God*" ("*Adiuva nos, Deus*") is chanted, the monks are to bow toward the altar.[56] The demarcation of this verse became even more pronounced with the introduction of the practice of kneeling for this verse, an observance first found in the Franciscans' earliest ceremonial, dating from around 1244,[57] and appearing thereafter in an instruction from about 1300 appended to the early fourteenth-century papal ceremonial of Giacomo Cardinal Stefaneschi—the instruction speaks of the pope kneeling over a faldstool for the words

---

[51] Lefèvre, *Ordinaire de Prémontré*, 48–49.

[52] Ibid., 49.

[53] Ibid.

[54] See Josef Jungmann, S.J., *Die lateinischen Bussriten in ihrer geschichtlichen Entwicklung*, Forschungen zur Geschichte des innerkirchlichen Lebens 3–4 (Innsbruck, Austria: Druck und Verlag Fel. Rauch, 1932), 70–72, and Mario Righetti, *Manuale di storia liturgica* (Milan: Editrice Ancora, 1949–1955), 2:128–129. This Tract is specified for the Ash Wednesday Mass in the tenth-century Romano-Germanic Pontifical; see Vogel and Elze, *Pontifical romano-germanique*, 2:20.

[55] Sodi and Triacca, *Missale Romanum: Editio princeps (1570)*, 124 (new pagination). The wording of the first sentence of this Tract underwent a significant change over time: the phrase *facias nobis*, "*may you deal with us*", in the original text, regarding how God deals with us as sinners, was supplanted by *quae fecimus nos*, "*that we have committed*", referring instead to our guilt as sinners. For an example of the earlier wording, see the Rosslyn Missal, an Irish liturgical manuscript reflecting twelfth-century English liturgical practices (Hugh Jackson Lawlor, ed., *The Rosslyn Missal*, HBS 15 [London: Henry Bradshaw Society, 1899], 18).

[56] Lefèvre, *Ordinaire de Prémontré*, 49.

[57] *Ordo missalis* of the Franciscan superior general Haymo of Faversham, in Stephen J. P. Van Dijk, O.F.M., *Sources of the Modern Roman Liturgy: The Ordinals by Haymo of Faversham and Related Documents (1243–1307)*, Studia et documenta Franciscana 2 (Leiden, Netherlands: E. J. Brill, 1963), 2:343.

"Adiuva nos, Deus, salutaris noster." [58] This same Tract and the kneeling that accompanied it were repeated on the Mondays, Wednesdays, and Fridays of Lent up to Monday of Holy Week.[59]

The second distinctive action of the Ash Wednesday Mass would take place at the end of Mass, immediately before the final blessing. Although this action is not mentioned in the Prémontré text, it is found as a daily practice for the weekdays of Lent in other liturgical books, beginning with the seventh-century Paduan redaction of Rome's Gregorian Sacramentary.[60] The deacon assisting the celebrant declares, *"Humble your heads unto God."* [61] The priest then offers a prayer traceable to the Leonine Sacramentary of sixth-century Rome:[62] *"Mercifully regard, O Lord, those bending themselves to your majesty, that those who have been refreshed with your divine gift may ever be nourished with your celestial helps. Through our Lord . . ."* [63] The kneeling of the congregation for this Lenten "prayer over the people", in response to the deacon's declaration, was already an established custom in Rome by the mid-twelfth century, as attested about the year 1140 in the *Ordo officiorum* of Rome's Church of Saint John Lateran.[64] The earliest text to specify such a blessing "over the people" (*super populum*) on Lenten weekdays up to Wednesday of Holy Week, the seventh-century Paduan redaction of Rome's Gregorian Sacramentary, provides a different benediction formula for each day;[65] this cycle of Lenten blessings *super populum* from the Paduan text passed with very few changes into the 1570 *Missale Romanum*.[66]

The Mass lections for Ash Wednesday first given in the seventh-century *Comes* and *Capitulare evangeliorum* of Würzburg, a Roman liturgical manuscript, prevailed across medieval Europe, with the first reading taken from the second chapter of the Book of Joel (Joel 2:12–19) and the Gospel from the sixth chapter of Saint Matthew (Mt 6:16–21).[67]

---

[58] Text in Marc Dykmans, S.J., ed., *Le cérémonial papal de la fin du moyen âge à la Renaissance*, vol. 2, BIHBR 25 (Brussels and Rome: Institut Historique Belge de Rome, 1981), 469–470; for the date of this addendum to the ceremonial, see ibid., 237.

[59] See the Franciscan *Ordo missalis* of Haymo of Faversham (c. 1244), in Van Dijk, *Sources of the Modern Roman Liturgy*, 2:220–221, 343. These repetitions of the Tract and the kneeling that accompanied it later entered the *Missale Romanum* of 1570; see Sodi and Triacca, *Missale Romanum: Editio princeps (1570)*, 124 (new pagination).

[60] Deshusses, *Sacramentaire grégorien*, Paduan nos. 131–295, 1:618–629.

[61] The earliest text to specify this announcement by the deacon immediately before the Lenten blessing "over the people" is Roman *Ordo 22*, a Roman text of the late eighth century; see Michel Andrieu, ed., *Les Ordines Romani du haut moyen âge*, vol. 3, SSLED 24 (Louvain, Belgium: "Spicilegium sacrum Lovaniense" Administration, 1951), 260, from which the deacon's words are here taken.

[62] Mohlberg, Eizenhöfer, and Siffrin, *Sacramentarium Veronense*, no. 485, p. 64.

[63] Text from 1570 *Missale Romanum*, in Sodi and Triacca, *Missale Romanum: Editio princeps (1570)*, 125–126 (new pagination).

[64] Fischer, *Bernhardi cardinalis . . . Ordo officiorum ecclesiae Lateranensis*, 29, 37.

[65] Deshusses, *Sacramentaire grégorien*, Paduan nos. 131–295, 1:618–629.

[66] Sodi and Triacca, *Missale Romanum: Editio princeps (1570)*, 125–235 (new pagination).

[67] For the specification of these readings in the seventh-century Würzburg manuscript, see respectively Germain Morin, "Le plus ancien *Comes* ou lectionnaire de l'église romaine", *Revue Bénédictine* 27 (1910): 49 (Joel reading), and Germain Morin, "Liturgie et basiliques

The chants for the Ash Wednesday Mass (the Introit, the Gradual, the Tract, the Offertory, and the Communion), all traceable to the mid- or late eighth century,[68] as well as the prayers proper to this Mass (the Collect, the Secret, and the Postcommunion), found together for the first time in the seventh-century Paduan redaction of Rome's Gregorian Sacramentary,[69] likewise prevailed and subsequently entered the *Missale Romanum* of 1570 along with the aforesaid Scripture readings.[70] The assignment to this Mass of the Preface *Qui corporali jejunio* ("*It is truly fitting . . . to give you thanks . . . eternal God, who with corporal fasting suppress vices and elevate the soul . . .*"), also found in the 1570 *Missale Romanum*,[71] appears for the first time in the Ordinal of the Papal Court, a liturgical text from the pontificate of Pope Innocent III (1198–1216).[72]

In the papal liturgy, there arose the custom of adding to the ancient Collect, Secret, and Postcommunion of Ash Wednesday two more Collects, two more Secrets, and two more Postcommunions; these latter six prayers were also added to the Mass on each day of Lent until the fifth Sunday of Lent (the Sunday before Palm Sunday), known from the Middle Ages until 1969 as Passion Sunday (from Passion Sunday through Wednesday of Holy Week, a different set of prayers was added). Thus on Ash Wednesday three Collects, three Secrets, and three Postcommunions were recited. This practice is traceable to the Regula Missal, an early Franciscan liturgical book compiled around 1230 and modeled upon a lost papal missal from the pontificate of Pope Honorius III (1216–1227), which speaks of adding to the Collect of the day from Ash Wednesday to Passion Sunday the prayers *A cunctis nos* and *Omnipotens sempiterne Deus qui vivorum*.[73] Over a century later, the papal liturgical book known as the Long Ceremonial, attributed to John of Sion and dating from a little before 1342, mentions not only these three Collects but also the recitation of three Postcommunions.[74] The recitation of three Secrets was introduced by the mid-sixteenth century, when it appears in a 1543 edition of the *Missale*

---

de Rome au milieu du VIIe siècle d'après les listes d'évangiles de Würzburg", *Revue Bénédictine* 28 (1911): 302 (Gospel).

[68] All of these chants except the Tract appear for the first time in the Mass antiphonary of Mount Blandin (Belgium, c. 750–800); see Hésbert, *Antiphonale missarum sextuplex*, 48, 50. Regarding the eighth-century Frankish origin of the Tract, see the sources cited in note 54 above.

[69] Deshusses, *Sacramentaire grégorien*, Paduan nos. 128–130, 1:618.

[70] Sodi and Triacca, *Missale Romanum: Editio princeps (1570)*, 123–125 (new pagination).

[71] Ibid., 125, 303–305 (new pagination).

[72] Text in Stephen J. P. Van Dijk, O.F.M., and Joan Hazelden Walker, eds., *The Ordinal of the Papal Court from Innocent III to Boniface VIII and Related Documents*, SF 22 (Fribourg, Switzerland: The University Press, 1975), 175, 184.

[73] Text in ibid., 183.

[74] Text in Marc Dykmans, ed., *Le cérémonial papal de la fin du moyen âge à la Renaissance*, vol. 3, BIHBR 26 (Brussels and Rome: Institut Historique Belge de Rome, 1983), 191, 192, 194.

Romanum.[75] The use of three Collects, three Secrets, and three Post-communions from Ash Wednesday until Passion Sunday was universally promulgated in the *Missale Romanum* of 1570.[76] The texts of these added prayers focus upon the themes of protection from dangers to the soul and body and the intercession of the saints, as can be seen in the first of the two added Collects, *A cunctis nos*, a prayer composed by Pope Innocent III (+1216):[77] "*From all dangers of soul and body defend us, we beseech you, O Lord; and with the blessed and glorious Mother of God and ever-Virgin Mary interceding, with your blessed Apostles Peter and Paul, and blessed* [Saint's Name], *and all the saints, mercifully grant unto us safety and peace, that your Church may serve you in secure freedom, with all adversities and errors overthrown.*"[78]

Detailed instructions for the observance of Ash Wednesday are found in the fourteenth-century *Liber ordinarius* utilized by the quasi-monastic community of canons that staffed the collegiate church of Essen, Germany.[79] At dawn, the canons' hebdomadarian would deliver a sermon to a congregation comprising the church's two affiliated communities of canons and canonesses (women living a mitigated form of religious life). The rite of the blessing and distribution of ashes takes place later in the morning, after an early Mass and the midmorning office of Terce. Beginning the ceremony with the standard invocation, "*Our help is in the name of the Lord*", the presiding priest blesses the ashes with a benediction prayer derived from the tenth-century Romano-Germanic Pontifical,[80] and later used as one of three orations for the blessing of ashes in the 1570 *Missale Romanum*:[81]

> *Almighty eternal God, be sparing to those fearing you, merciful to those beseeching you; and vouchsafe to send your holy angel from Heaven, that he may bless and sanctify these ashes, in order that they may be a salutary remedy to all humbly imploring your holy name, and accusing themselves according to the consciousness of their sins, and deploring their crimes before the sight of your divine clemency, and also entreating suppliantly and earnestly your most serene majesty; grant also, according to the invocation of your most holy name, that all who shall have sprinkled them upon themselves for the remission of their sins may receive health of body and the protection of their souls. Through . . .*[82]

---

[75] See Robert Lippe, ed., *Missale Romanum: Mediolani, 1474*, vol. 2, *A Collation with Other Editions Printed before 1570*, HBS 33 (London: Henry Bradshaw Society, 1907), 34.

[76] Sodi and Triacca, *Missale Romanum: Editio princeps (1570)*, 123–125 (new pagination).

[77] See Van Dijk and Walker, *Ordinal of the Papal Court*, 152, footnote.

[78] Text from the 1570 *Missale Romanum*, in Sodi and Triacca, *Missale Romanum: Editio princeps (1570)*, 123 (new pagination).

[79] Text in Franz Arens, ed., *Der Liber ordinarius der Essener Stiftskirche* (Paderborn, Germany: Albert Pape, 1908), 36–38.

[80] Vogel and Elze, *Pontifical romano-germanique*, 2:21–22.

[81] Sodi and Triacca, *Missale Romanum: Editio princeps (1570)*, 121–122 (new pagination).

[82] Arens, *Liber ordinarius der Essener Stiftskirche*, 36 (incipit only). The complete text of this prayer is here taken from the tenth-century Romano-Germanic Pontifical, in Vogel and Elze, *Pontifical romano-germanique*, 2:21–22.

The priest now makes the sign of the cross over the ashes, saying as he does so, "*May the blessing of God the Father almighty, and the Son, and the Holy Spirit, descend upon these ashes and remain always. Amen.*"[83] He then sprinkles holy water upon the ashes, after which the antiphon "*Graciously hear us, O Lord*" is sung as in the earlier-described Pré-montré rite, together with a versicle from Psalm 68.[84] The distribution of ashes begins as the canons chant the above-cited antiphon "*Let us change our garb, unto ashes and sackcloth*":

> The priest, with the deacon carrying the ashes behind him, goes down to the religious community, by the step, being turned toward the choir of the canonesses in the course of smearing on the forehead of each of them a little from the ashes in the manner of a cross, beginning with those worthier and older and saying thus in smearing, in a lowered voice, and to each person: *Remember, man, that you are ashes, and unto ashes you shall return.*[85] Which having been done, he shall return to the altar and, kneeling, receive the ashes first from the other priest; then rising from his knees, he shall give them to the others, the deacon before, the subdeacon afterward, then to the other canons, and to the laity who are present. And it is to be noted that on the men the ashes shall be placed upon the head; on the women they shall be smeared on the forehead. . . .
>
> Thereupon the religious community shall sing the antiphon *Between the porch and the altar* while ashes are given to the clerics.[86]

The above rubrics specify that the ashes are to be applied in a cross-wise manner, a practice traceable to the eleventh century, when it appears in a manuscript of the eremitical monastery of Santa Croce in Fonte Avellana, Italy.[87] Although this usage is not mentioned in the liturgical texts of Rome, it is prescribed in a significant number of medieval liturgical books, including French texts from Chartres (twelfth century), Bayeux (thirteenth century), the Rouen monastery of Saint-Ouen (late thirteenth century), and Paris (fifteenth century),[88] as well

---

[83] Arens, *Liber ordinarius der Essener Stiftskirche*, 37. This blessing formula also appears in the Ash Wednesday rites of the 1499 missal of Jaén, Spain, and the missal of Jaén's parent see, Toledo (1503–1518); see respectively *Missale Giennense / Manuale . . . sacramenta* (1499), fol. 23v, and *Missale secundum consuetudinem almae ecclesiae Toletanae*, 1503–1518, vol. 2, fol. 41v.

[84] In place of the complete text of Psalm 68 that is sung with this antiphon in the Prémontré rite, only verse 2 of the psalm is sung, serving as a versicle.

[85] The Essen text uses the Latin word for ashes, *cinis*, in place of the Latin word for dust, *pulvis*.

[86] Arens, *Liber ordinarius der Essener Stiftskirche*, 37.

[87] *Primus codex Fontavellanensi* (excerpt), PL 151, col. 955. For the dating and identification of this text, see Blessed Juan Bautista Ferreres Boluda, S.J., *Historia del misal romano* (Barcelona: Eugenio Subirana, 1929), 246.

[88] See the *Ordinarium* of the canons regular, Monastery of Saint-Jean en Vallée, Chartres (manuscript: Paris, Bibliothèque Nationale, Codex Lat. 1794); the *Ordinarium* of Bayeux (manuscript: Bayeux, Bibliothèque Capitulaire, MS 121); the missal of Saint-Ouen, Rouen (manuscript: Rouen, Bibliothèque Municipale, MS A 459); and the missal of Paris (manuscript: Paris,

as in the printed missals of England's Sarum Rite from 1487 through 1557.[89] Continuing with the Essen rite, the priest, having completed the distribution of ashes, prays for divine mercy with a Collect traceable to the eighth-century *Hadrianum* redaction of Rome's Gregorian Sacramentary:[90] "*O God, who are justly angry and mercifully forgive, behold the tears of your afflicted people and mercifully avert the wrath of your indignation, which we justly deserve. Through Christ . . .*"[91]

A procession follows, exiting the collegiate church and proceeding around the monastery's cemetery, led by a cloth-veiled processional cross. Along the way are sung the earlier-quoted chants, *Emendemus in melius* ("*Let us amend for the better*") and *Iuxta vestibulum* ("*Between the porch and the altar*"). As the procession reenters the church, the clerics sing the responsory *Scindite corda*, a text traceable to the eleventh century:[92] "*Rend your hearts, and not your garments, and be converted to your Lord, for he is gracious and merciful. Verse: Turn back, everyone from his evil way, and from your very wicked thoughts. And be converted . . .*" (cf. Joel 2:13; Jer 25:5).[93] A responsory of twelfth-century origin from the Office of the Dead is also sung: "*We recognize, O Lord, that we have sinned; we beg forgiveness, which we do not deserve. Stretch out your hand to the fallen, O you who opened the gates of Paradise to the confessing thief. Verse: Our life sighs in sorrow and does not amend in deed; if you wait for us, we do not reform, and if you punish us, we do not endure it. Stretch out your hand . . .*"[94] The procession ends with a Collect dating back to the sixth-century Leonine Sacramentary of Rome:[95] "*Spare, O Lord, spare your people, that having been chastised by your merited blows, they may find relief in your mercy. Through Christ . . .*" The High Mass for the day follows.[96]

The Papal Blessing of the Golden Rose on Laetare Sunday

The Fourth Sunday of Lent, "Laetare Sunday", has traditionally been seen as a joyful stopping point on the Church's annual penitential

---

Bibliothèque Nationale, Codex Lat. 15280), in Martène, *De antiquis ecclesiae ritibus*, bk. 4, chap. 17, *ordo* 14, *ordo* 6, *ordo* 13, *ordo* 2, 3:56, 53, 56, 51, respectively.

[89] See Dickinson, *Missale ad usum . . . Sarum*, col. 134.

[90] Text in Deshusses, *Sacramentaire grégorien*, no. 843, 1:312.

[91] Arens, *Liber ordinarius der Essener Stiftskirche*, 37. This prayer is likewise used in the Ash Wednesday liturgy of England's Sarum Rite, as found in various printed editions of the Sarum Missal from 1487 to 1557; see Dickinson, *Missale ad usum . . . Sarum,* col. 134.

[92] This responsory appears in an eleventh-century antiphonary of Ivrea (Italy); see Hésbert, *Corpus antiphonalium officii*, 1:137.

[93] Arens, *Liber ordinarius der Essener Stiftskirche*, 37–38 (*Scindite corda* responsory on 38). The Essen text omits the responsory's verse; it is here taken from Hésbert, *Corpus antiphonalium officii*, no. 7626, 4:401.

[94] The Essen text provides only the incipit of this responsory (Arens, *Liber ordinarius der Essener Stiftskirche*, 38). The full text is here taken from Knud Ottosen, *The Responsories and Versicles of the Latin Office of the Dead* (Aarhus, Denmark: Aarhus University Press, 1993), 397, plus verse on 420. This responsory first appears in the twelfth-century antiphonary of Saint Denis (France); see Hésbert, *Corpus antiphonalium officii*, no. 6301, 4:77.

[95] Text in Mohlberg, Eizenhöfer, and Siffrin, eds., *Sacramentarium Veronense*, no. 509, p. 67.

[96] Arens, *Liber ordinarius der Essener Stiftskirche*, 38.

journey to Easter. Its title is taken from the first word of the Introit of the day's Mass, *Laetare* (Rejoice). It is this Introit that sets the tone for the day's liturgy: "*Rejoice, O Jerusalem, and gather together, all you who love her; rejoice with gladness, you who have been in sorrow . . .*" (cf. Is 66:10–11).[97] In a sermon about Laetare Sunday and the unique papal custom associated with it—the blessing of a molten-gold rose carried by the pontiff to the day's Mass—Pope Innocent III (+1216) observes that "this day represents charity after hatred, joy after sorrow, nourishment after hunger."[98] The custom of the golden rose had been introduced by the pontificate of Pope Leo IX (1049–1054), with the earliest extant reference to this handcrafted flower, one made from two ounces of the precious metal provided by a French convent near Colmar, dating from this period.[99] The earliest reference to the golden rose in the Laetare Sunday liturgy of Rome appears in the *Ordo* of Benedict, also known as the *Liber politicus* (c. 1140), which tells of the pontiff showing the rose to the people and explaining it in a homily.[100] The golden roses utilized over the centuries that followed featured an opening in which was placed sweet-smelling balsam and musk.[101] For Pope Innocent III, this brightly colored artificial rose with its balsam fragrance, imitating the qualities of a real rose that "delights in color, refreshes in odor, encourages in taste", represents "charity, in color; cheerfulness, in odor; [and] nourishment, in taste" corresponding to the aforementioned qualities of Laetare Sunday, "charity after hatred, joy after sorrow, nourishment after hunger".[102] But more important, the golden rose is a symbol of Christ himself:

> This flower signifies that Flower, who says of himself in the Canticles, "I am the flower of the field, and the lily of the valleys" [Song 2:1], and about whom the prophet says, "And there shall come forth a rod out of the root of Jesse, and a flower shall rise up out of his root" [Is 11:1]. Truly he is the Flower of flowers, because he is the Saint of saints, who before other flowers, that is, before other saints, in color gives delight to sight, for "thou art beautiful above the sons of men" [Ps 44:3], "on whom the angels desire to look" [1 Pet 1:12], who in fragrance gives refreshment to smell, for "thy breasts are better than wine, smelling sweet of the best ointments" [Song 1:1–2],

---

[97] The text of this Introit is here taken from the 1570 *Missale Romanum* (Sodi and Triacca, *Missale Romanum: Editio princeps (1570)*, 178 [new pagination]).

[98] Pope Innocent III, *Sermon 18*, PL 217, col. 394.

[99] See Paul Fabre and Louis Duchesne, eds., *Le Liber censuum de l'église romaine*, vol. 1, fasc. 2, Bibliothèque des écoles françaises d'Athènes et de Rome, 2nd series, Registres des papes du XIIIᵉ siècle, 6 (Paris: Fontemoing, 1901), 180, text and footnote.

[100] Text in Paul Fabre and Louis Duchesne, eds., *Le Liber censuum de l'église romaine*, vol. 2, fasc. 3, Bibliothèque des écoles françaises d'Athènes et de Rome, 2nd series, Registres des papes du XIIIᵉ siècle, 6 (Paris: Fontemoing, 1910), no. 36, p. 150.

[101] P. M. J. Rock, "Golden Rose", in *The Catholic Encyclopedia* (New York: Appleton, 1907–1912), 6:629.

[102] Innocent III, *Sermon 18*, PL 217, col. 394.

whom young maidens have loved [cf. Song 1:2], for they run after him to the odor of his ointments [cf. Song 1:3], who in flavor gives encouragement to taste, for the Bread that he gives is his flesh, for the life of the world [cf. Jn 6:52], having every delight and the sweetness of every taste [cf. Wis 16:20]. For this is he who, according to what you have heard in the Gospel, from five loaves and two fish fed five thousand men [cf. Jn 6:5–13].[103]

Pope Innocent III adds that "the porter of this flower is the vicar of the Savior, namely the Roman pontiff." [104] It would be over two centuries after Pope Innocent's time that prayers fully developing the mystical imagery of the rose would be added to the papal rose-blessing rite of Laetare Sunday. The prayers appear for the first time in the 1488 *Caeremoniale Romanum* of the papal master of ceremonies, Patrizi Piccolomini.[105] The ceremony, as given in this liturgical book, would begin before the Laetare Sunday Mass, in the "Hall of Vestments", the sacristy of the papal palace:

A small altar is prepared, and upon it two candlesticks; and the pontiff, vested in an amice, an alb, a cincture, a stole, a cope, and a miter, draws near to the altar itself and, with his miter put aside, says: *Our help is in the name of the Lord ... The Lord be with you ... Let us pray.*

O God, by whose word and power all things have been made, and by whose command all things are directed, who are the gladness and joy of all the faithful: we humbly beseech your majesty, that you may vouchsafe to bless and sanctify by your goodness this rose most pleasing in fragrance and appearance, which we carry in our hands on this day as a sign of spiritual gladness, that the people dedicated to you, led forth from the yoke of the Babylonian captivity by the grace of your only-begotten Son, who is the glory and exultation of his people Israel, may exhibit with sincere hearts the joy of that Jerusalem that is our mother above. And because your Church, to the honor of your name, this day rejoices and exults in this sign, may you, O Lord, grant her true and perfect joy and, accepting her devotion, forgive [her people's] sins, fill her with faith, favor [her people] with pardon, shelter her with mercy, destroy her adversity, [and] grant her all prosperity, that by the fruit of her good labor she may attain to the fragrance of the perfumes of that Flower who was mystically prophesied, brought forth from the root of Jesse, the Flower of the field and the Lily of the valleys, with whom may she rejoice with all the saints in heavenly glory without end, who with you lives and reigns in the unity of the Holy Spirit, God, through all ages of ages. Amen.

The prayer completed, he anoints with balsam the golden roses that are on the little branch itself [a cluster of golden roses on one

---

[103] Ibid., cols. 394–395.

[104] Ibid., col. 395.

[105] Text in Marc Dykmans, ed., *L'oeuvre de Patrizi Piccolomini, ou Le cérémonial papal de la premierè Renaissance*, vol. 1, ST 293 (Vatican City: Biblioteca Apostolica Vaticana, 1980), 131–133.

branch] and places upon it crushed musk, which things are administered to him by the sacristan; and finally he sprinkles the rose [cluster] with holy water and censes it with incense. Meanwhile, a cleric of the Apostolic Chamber holds the rose, which he then delivers into the hand of the cardinal deacon on [the pontiff's] right, and he [delivers it] into the hand of the pontiff, who, carrying the rose with his left hand and blessing with his right, advances to the chapel; and the cardinal deacons on each side [of him] elevate the fringes of his cope. When he comes to the faldstool, he gives the rose to the aforesaid deacon, who hands it over to the cleric of the chamber, and he places it upon the altar.[106]

It appears that almost from its inception the golden rose was destined to be presented afterward as a gift from the pope to a personage of his choosing. When in the spring of 1148 Pope Eugene III sent the golden rose as a gift to King Alfonso VII, monarch of the Spanish kingdom of Castile, he issued an accompanying letter to the king that provides further insights as to the underlying symbolism of this object:

> As a sign of our goodwill and grace toward you, the golden rose, which, as a sign of the Passion and Resurrection of our Lord Jesus Christ, on the Sunday which is called *Laetare, Jerusalem*, the Roman pontiff has been accustomed to carry every year, we provide to be transmitted to Your Serenity by our venerable brother [Pedro], the bishop of Segovia, that inspired by the remembrance of the same rose, you may be diligent to fill up "those things that are wanting of the sufferings of Christ" [Col 1:24] in your body, with the Lord's assistance, and, by his consoling clemency, be destined to attain to the glory of the resurrection.[107]

In the golden rose rite from the 1488 ceremonial of Piccolomini, the rose is presented by the pontiff to the personage he has selected for this honor following the papal Laetare Sunday Mass:

> The Mass having ended, the pontiff, having said a prayer before the altar, takes up the rose again, as above, and brings it to his chamber. And if he to whom he wishes to give it is present, he is summoned to his [the pontiff's] feet, and [the recipient] having knelt, he [the pontiff] gives the rose to him, saying:
>
> *Accept from the hands of us, who, although undeserving, hold the place of God on earth, this rose, by which is signified the joy of each Jerusalem, namely of the Church triumphant and [the Church] militant, by which is manifested to all the faithful of Christ the very Flower most beautiful that is the joy and crown of all the saints. Take this, most beloved son, who according to the world are noble, mighty, and endowed with abundant power, that*

---

[106] Ibid., 132.
[107] Eugene III, *Letter 296* (April 27, 1148), PL 180, col. 1346.

you may be made yet more illustrious with every virtue in Christ the Lord, like the rose planted by the brooks of bountiful waters [cf. Eccles 39:17]. *Which grace unto you out of his abounding clemency may he vouchsafe to grant, who is triune and one, unto ages of ages. Amen. In the name of the Father, and of the Son, and of the Holy Spirit. Amen.*[108]

---

[108] Dykmans, *Oeuvre de Patrizi Piccolomini,* 1:132–133.

12 Palm Sunday and Wednesday of Holy Week

Notable it is, and fitting for admiration, that, as if in the same interval, the Lord has created and recreated the world. For just as he, going to create man, and other things on account of man, began from Sunday, and having worked for six days, created man on the sixth day, and on the Sabbath ceased from all work, thus did he, going to recreate man, begin from Sunday, entering Jerusalem, and having entered on the individual days, redeemed him on the sixth day, suffering on the Cross, and on the Sabbath rested, sleeping in the sepulcher. Accordingly, just as on this first day he said, "Be light made" [Gen 1:3], beginning by light the work of creation, thus on this same day, with light, actually glory, he undertakes this work of his salubrious Passion.

Sicard of Cremona (+1215)[1]

The Procession of Palms

In his acclaimed work the *Spiritual Exercises*, the sixteenth-century Jesuit founder Saint Ignatius of Loyola (+1556) presents an unforgettable image, that of the "two standards", in which we see Christ as the "Leader of the good" in the midst of a vast plain stretching round about Jerusalem, taking a lowly stand, in stark contrast to the prince of darkness, Satan, who exults himself on a fiery throne in a plain encompassing Babylon.[2] Although not directly connected by Saint Ignatius to any particular episode from the Gospels, this scene corresponds well in essence to the medieval conception of Palm Sunday as the day on which Christ went forth to Jerusalem to battle Satan and vanquish his evil reign. It was in Saint Ignatius' native land of Spain nine centuries earlier that Saint Isidore, archbishop of Seville (+636), described Palm Sunday in precisely this way, observing: "For in the branches of palms was signified the victory, by which the Lord was going to conquer death by dying, and with the trophy of the Cross was going to triumph over the prince of death, the devil."[3]

---

[1] Sicard of Cremona, *Mitrale*, bk. 6, chap. 10, PL 213, col. 292.

[2] Text in Anthony Mottola, trans., *The Spiritual Exercises of St. Ignatius*, Image Books (Garden City, N.Y.: Doubleday, 1964), 75–76.

[3] Saint Isidore of Seville, *De ecclesiasticis officiis*, bk. 1, chap. 28, in Christopher M. Lawson, ed., *Sancti Isidori episcopi Hispalensis: De ecclesiasticis officiis*, CCSL 113 (Turnhout, Belgium: Brepols, 1989), 31.

The liturgical commentators of the Middle Ages saw Palm Sunday as the inauguration of the great undertaking of God to "recreate" the fallen world and fallen mankind by his redeeming Passion, paralleling his initial creation of the world and mankind. In the words of Rupert of Deutz (+c. 1129), "It is great and worthy of admiration that on Sunday, which is the first day, on which God began to be engaged in the creation of the world, the Savior enters into the labor of his Passion, and on the seventh day, having been engaged in our salvation throughout this week, which is called the 'Greater Week', he ceased and rested in the sepulcher." [4] Amalarius of Metz (+c. 850) sees Palm Sunday as the prelude to the pivotal moment in the history of the world, the sacrifice of Calvary: "For Christ deigned to come to Jerusalem on Palm Sunday and there expect the day of his immolation. Every previous immolation prefigured him; in him every immolation is consummated." [5]

Our earliest record of the Church's annual commemoration of Palm Sunday is that given by the Spanish pilgrim Egeria in the diary of her journey to the Holy Land, describing the ceremonies of Jerusalem as they existed about the year 382. She tells of a procession that set out from the Mount of Olives during the late afternoon of Palm Sunday: after a reading of Saint Matthew's Gospel account of Christ's entry into Jerusalem (from Matthew 21), the city's bishop and the people would head into the city, carrying palm and olive branches, with the Church of the Anastasis (the Church of the Holy Sepulcher) as their destination. [6] We subsequently find this procession in a more richly developed form in the ancient liturgical book of Jerusalem known as the Georgian Lectionary, the contents of which date from the fifth to the eighth century. The palms would be laid upon the altar at Vespers on the eve of Palm Sunday, remaining there overnight. On Palm Sunday morning, the day's rites would begin at nine o'clock with prayers, a psalm, and versicles, after which the priest would bless the palms and distribute them to the people. One of the manuscripts of the Georgian Lectionary also mentions an incensation "in the form of a cross" and the lighting of candles. Following a reading of Saint John's Gospel account of Christ's entry into Jerusalem (Jn 12:12–22), there was a procession to the Garden of Gethsemane, where Saint Luke's account of Christ's entry was then read (Lk 19:29–38). The procession continued to the site of the Probatic Pool within Jerusalem, where

---

[4] Rupert of Deutz, *Liber de divinis officiis*, bk. 5, chap. 9, in Hrabanus Haacke, O.S.B., ed., *Ruperti Tuitiensis: Liber de divinis officiis*, CCCM 7 (Turnhout, Belgium: Brepols, 1967), 158–159.

[5] Amalarius of Metz, *Liber officialis*, bk. 3, chap. 19, no. 10, in John Michael Hanssens, ed., *Amalarii episcopi: Opera liturgica omnia*, vol. 2, ST 139 (Vatican City: Biblioteca Apostolica Vaticana, 1948), 314.

[6] For the text, see A. Franceschini and R. Weber, eds., *Itinerarium Egeriae*, chap. 31, nos. 2–4, in *Itineraria et Alia geographia*, CCSL 175 (Turnhout, Belgium: Brepols, 1965), 77.

there was a reading of Saint Mark's account of Christ's entry (Mk 11:1–10). The procession advanced to what was then Jerusalem's principal church, the Martyrium (adjacent to the Church of the Anastasis), where the day's Mass was thereupon celebrated, in which the Gospel was Saint Matthew's account of the entry into Jerusalem (Mt 21:1–17).[7]

In the West, the procession of palms is first found in the ancient liturgical book of Spain's Mozarabic Rite, the *Liber ordinum*, an eleventh-century compilation of older texts believed to date largely from the fifth to the seventh century. The text speaks of the faithful gathering at one church, where "palms and branches" would be placed on the altar to be blessed by a bishop or priest; afterward, the people would go in procession with the singing of psalms to a second church, where Mass would be celebrated. The rite of blessing the palms consists of six prayers, the last of which is introduced by the deacon with the petition *"Let us pray that he [Christ] may mercifully vouchsafe to sanctify these branches of palms, willows, or olives with the right hand of his divinity."* In the benediction that follows, the bishop or priest prays:

> *Lord Jesus Christ, who [from] before the beginning of the world reign one with the Father and the Holy Spirit . . . , humbly we beseech your Majesty. . . . May you vouchsafe to bless and sanctify also these branches and flowers of palms, which you see brought within your church according to the custom of this feast day; defend from every evil and make pleasing to you your people also, who for love of your majesty, long to receive it [the branches] by the hand of our service.*[8]

The early spread of the palm procession elsewhere in Europe is attested by the Bobbio Missal, a seventh- to eighth-century liturgical book of French or north Italian origin, which provides a prayer for blessing palms, the text of which begins with the following explanation of Palm Sunday: *"Behold, this feast day, O Lord, is recollected, on which the foreknowing multitudes of children, taking cut tree branches, run to meet you in the triumph of your praise, namely crying out, 'Hosanna in the highest to the Son of David; blessed is he who comes in the name of the Lord'* [cf. Mt 21:9], *for which all the nations shall have perceived you both to have taken away victory from the world and to have won triumph over the devil."*[9]

Although as early as the seventh century we find the Sunday before Easter identified in two Roman sacramentaries as the "Sunday for the

---

[7] Michel Tarchnischvili, ed., *Le grand lectionnaire de l'église de Jérusalem (V^e–VIIIe siècle)*, vol. 1, CSCO 188–189 (Louvain, Belgium: Secrétariat du CorpusSCO, 1959); Georgian-language text: CSCO 188, nos. 576–594, pp. 100–105; Latin translation: CSCO 189, nos. 576–594, pp. 81–85.

[8] Text in Marius Férotin, O.S.B., ed., *Le Liber ordinum en usage dans l'église wisigothique et mozarabe d'Espagne du cinquième au onzième siècle* (Paris, 1904), repr., ed. Anthony Ward, S.M., and Cuthbert Johnson, O.S.B., BELS 83 (Rome: Centro Liturgico Vincenziano, Edizioni Liturgiche, 1996), cols. 178–184 (the petition and prayer quoted are on 182–183).

[9] Text in A. Lowe, ed., *The Bobbio Missal: Text*, HBS 58 (London: Henry Bradshaw Society, 1920), no. 558, p. 170.

Palms",[10] it is generally believed that the palm procession was first introduced into the liturgy of Rome, at least in the parish churches, toward the close of the tenth century, following the arrival in the city of a liturgical book containing the procession, the Romano-Germanic Pontifical, a text attributed to the Benedictine monastery of Saint Alban in Mainz, Germany, dating from around 950–962 and brought to Rome during the reign of the German emperor Otto I (936–973). The procession became an annual practice in the liturgy of the Basilica of Saint Peter when in 1026 Pope John XIX instructed a bishop delegated to oversee and celebrate the city's pontifical rites, "We have established that every year, on Palm Sunday, you should go out with a procession from the Church of Saint Mary *in Turri*[11] and, coming to the great altar of Saint Peter, celebrate Mass."[12]

A key motif of the medieval Palm Sunday procession was the concept that the Lord was spiritually present in the midst of the procession and that by means of the meditative principle of "composition of place" the participants in the Church's procession could place themselves in spirit among those who greeted Christ on the first Palm Sunday. This objective is expressly stated in the Palm Sunday rubrics of the Benedictine customary of Fructuaria, Italy, dating from about 1085:

> Then in all reverence all should stand, just as if the Lord himself were present; for if it were permitted to us to behold with our corporeal eyes, we would have seen ourselves going to meet the Son of God, which without doubt it befits us to believe [ourselves] to have done. For although he may not be seen corporally, nevertheless he whose interior eyes he [Christ] has opened is able to consider [himself] to have gone forth to meet our Lord Jesus Christ, who emptied himself for us by taking the form of a slave.[13]

In the fourth-century Palm Sunday rite of Jerusalem witnessed by Egeria, the presence of Christ in the procession was represented by the bishop: "And thus the bishop shall be led in that manner by which the

[10] The Sunday before Easter is identified as *Dominica in palmas de Passione Domini* in the Gelasian Sacramentary and as *Die Dominico ... ad palmas"* in the Paduan redaction of the Gregorian Sacramentary—see respectively Leo Cunibert Mohlberg, O.S.B., et al., eds., *Liber sacramentorum Romanae aeclesiae ordinis anni circuli (Sacramentarium Gelasianum)*, REDSMF 4 (Rome: Herder, 1960), no. 329, p. 53, and Jean Deshusses, ed., *Le sacramentaire grégorien: Ses principales formes d'après les plus anciens manuscrits*, vol. 1, 2nd ed., SF 16 (Fribourg, Switzerland: Editions Universitaires Fribourg, 1979), Paduan no. 281, p. 628.

[11] This small church, known as Saint Mary of the Tower in Pope John XIX's time, located in Rome's southwestern quadrant, the Trastevere district, is now known as the Church of the Madonna del Buon Viaggio; see Horace Mann, *The Lives of the Popes in the Early Middle Ages* (London: Kegan Paul, Trench, Trubner; Saint Louis: Herder, 1925), 5:236, note.

[12] John XIX, *Epistle 4*, to Peter of Silva Candida (1026), PL 141, col. 1130.

[13] *Consuetudines* of Fructuaria, Italy, bk. 1, chap. 44, in Bruno Albers, ed., *Consuetudines monasticae*, vol. 4, *Consuetudines Fructuarienses necnon Cystrensis in Anglia monasterii et congregationis Vallymbrosanae* (Monte Cassino, Italy: Typis Montis Casini, 1911), 45.

Lord was at that time led."[14] At Quedlinburg in tenth-century Germany, the bishop of Halberstadt on Palm Sunday would ride upon a donkey in procession to the Quedlinburg Abbey church as the people strewed branches before him. Upon arriving at the church, the bishop would celebrate Mass there.[15] The rubrics of Cardinal Bernard of Porto's *Ordo officiorum* for the canons regular of Rome's Church of Saint John Lateran, dating from about 1140, explain in this regard:

> The bishop, however, shall be last in the procession, supported by a priest and a deacon. But the procession having been ordered, the cantor begins the antiphons *Occurrunt turbae* and *Pueri Hebraeorum*,[16] and with all veneration, just as though accompanying the Lord himself, even as He says: ". . . I will walk among them; and I will be their God" [cf. 2 Cor 6:16], we proceed with singing all the way to the door of the church, just as though meeting him, whence it has been written, "Let us go to meet our Savior" [cf. Jn 12:13].[17]

The use of an image of Christ riding a donkey, known as the Palmesel, existed from the tenth century onward, with the earliest mention of this custom appearing in a biography of the bishop of Augsburg, Germany, Saint Ulric.[18] The Palmesel figure utilized in the fourteenth-century Palm Sunday procession of Essen, Germany, would be placed with the face of Christ turned eastward when it was set down in the city's collegiate church.[19] The practice of carrying the Gospel book to represent Christ in the Palm Sunday procession is mentioned by the tenth-century author known as Pseudo-Alcuin,[20] as well as in a Paris manuscript copy of the late twelfth-century text of Rome known as the *Liber censuum* (c. 1192).[21] In the palm procession from a twelfth-century customary of the Cistercian Order, an unveiled cross (probably a crucifix) would be carried, before which the monks would

---

[14] Franceschini and Weber, *Itinerarium Egeriae*, chap. 31, no. 3, in *Itineraria et Alia geographia*, 77.

[15] Georges Malherbe, "Le 'Palmezel'", *Bulletin Paroissial Liturgique* 14 (1932): 83.

[16] The texts of these two antiphons shall be presented later in this chapter (pp. 330–331).

[17] Text in Ludwig Fischer, ed., *Bernhardi cardinalis et Lateranensis ecclesiae prioris Ordo officiorum ecclesiae Lateranensis*, Historische Forschungen und Quellen 2–3 (Munich: Dr. F. P. Datterer, 1916), 43.

[18] *Vita s. Udalrici Augustani episcopi*, chap. 4, PL 135, col. 1019.

[19] See the *Liber ordinarius* of the collegiate church of Essen, Germany; text in Franz Arens, ed., *Der Liber ordinarius der Essener Stiftskirche* (Paderborn, Germany: Albert Pape, 1908), 44.

[20] Pseudo-Alcuin, *Liber de divinis officiis*, chap. 14, PL 101, col. 1201.

[21] All but one of the manuscripts of the *Liber censuum* lack rubrics for Palm Sunday. Thus this rubric is found only in a Paris manuscript copy of the *Liber censuum* utilized by the seventeenth-century liturgist Dom Jean Mabillon for his edition of the liturgical portion of the *Liber censuum* (what he refers to as Roman *Ordo* 12); PL 78, no. 18, col. 1071). Regarding the absence of this rubric from the other manuscripts, see Paul Fabre and Louis Duchesne, eds., *Le Liber censuum de l'église romaine*, vol. 1, fasc. 2, Bibliothèque des écoles françaises d'Athènes et de Rome, 2nd series, Registres des papes du XIIIᵉ siècle, 6 (Paris: Fontemoing, 1901), endnotes, 314–315.

subsequently prostrate themselves at the final station.[22] Yet by far, the most compelling means of placing the palm procession participants in the company of their Redeemer was achieved with the carrying of the Holy Eucharist in the procession, a practice of which we shall present a splendid example from England later in this chapter.

There was in unison with the thought of spiritually joining the Savior in entering the earthly Jerusalem the aspiration of accompanying him in his victorious entry into the celestial Jerusalem. As John Beleth (+1182) succinctly explains, on Palm Sunday "we make a great procession for the purpose of signifying that the Lord shall come to us and lead us to the eternal tabernacles."[23] Sicard of Cremona (+1215) develops this idea more fully. Utilizing a verse from the Book of Habacuc that speaks symbolically of horses and chariots ridden by God in his divine power, he masterfully explains Christ's entry into Jerusalem and the Church's annual Palm Sunday procession as a prefiguration of Christ's entry and that of redeemed mankind into the heavenly Jerusalem:

> "Who will ride upon thy horses: and thy chariots are salvation" [Hab 3:8]; by these, truly, you have indicated that, going to ascend to the Mount of Olives, that is, to the right hand of the Father, who is "the Father of mercies, and the God of all comfort" [2 Cor 1:3], sending the Apostles, who, binding and loosing with the power received the ass and the colt, that is, the Jewish people and the Gentile people, shall have absolved them from the burdens of their sins, and, mankind having been brought to you by faith, [you] sitting upon them (for the soul of the just man is the throne of God), in sitting upon them you would save them, and lead them into the celestial Jerusalem, the angels going to meet them with praises, with palms and olive branches, which are the insignia of peace and victory. In representation of this glorious reception of the Lord, the Church celebrates this day a procession with branches and flowers, bearing olive branches and palms in the hands.[24]

In a similar vein, William Durandus of Mende (+1296) observes, "He [Christ] sent [his disciples], I say, to ask for an ass and a colt, that is, the Jewish people and the Gentile people, that he might lead them into the celestial Jerusalem."[25] Yet ever present with this theme of the ultimate triumph of Christ there was in the medieval Palm Sunday rites the pervasive remembrance of the Savior's bitter Passion. At the

---

[22] *Usus antiquiores ordinis Cisterciensis*, pt. 1, chap. 17, PL 166, cols. 1397–1398.

[23] John Beleth, *Summa de ecclesiasticis officiis*, chap. 94, in Heribertus Douteil, C.S.Sp., ed., *Iohannis Beleth: Summa de ecclesiasticis officiis*, CCCM 41a (Turnhout, Belgium: Brepols, 1976), 166.

[24] Sicard of Cremona, *Mitrale*, bk. 6, chap. 10, PL 213, cols. 292–293.

[25] William Durandus of Mende, *Rationale divinorum officiorum*, bk. 6, chap. 67, no. 4, in A. Davril, O.S.B., and T.M. Thibodeau, eds., *Guillelmi Duranti: Rationale divinorum officiorum V–VI*, CCCM 140a (Turnhout, Belgium: Brepols, 1998), 322. Hereafter cited as Durandus, *Rationale* (CCCM 140a).

Spanish cathedral of Valencia, the day's liturgy (as it existed in 1494) would commence with the customary Sunday aspersion of the people, followed by a procession of the clergy with a cross, candles, incense, and holy water, in which the chants all anticipated the Passion of Christ,[26] beginning with this antiphon (cf. Lam 3:9–10): "*He hath shut up my ways; the hostile traitor has become to me even as the lion in hiding; he has filled and inebriated me with bitterness; O Lord, they have set stones before me and brought my life down into the chasm of death.*"[27]

As we have already seen, it was the arrival in Rome of the Romano-Germanic Pontifical from the German Benedictine monastery of Saint Alban in Mainz that is believed to have brought the procession of palms to the City of Peter in the third quarter of the tenth century. It is to this extraordinary text that we now turn to present the detailed rubrics and beautiful prayers it provides for the procession of palms. The pontifical, in fact, includes three different *ordines* for the palm procession. Here we shall examine the first and most highly developed of these.[28] The text provides twelve prayers for blessing palm and olive branches; four of these we shall present in full, and several others we shall summarize.

The Palm Sunday rite begins in a church outside the city gates shortly after eight o'clock in the morning, following the completion of the office of Terce. At a central location are placed palm branches, or olive branches, or branches of other trees, including flowering branches.[29] The custom of beginning the Palm Sunday rite at a church beyond the city walls or at least at a church apart from that where the procession would end was widespread in the Middle Ages. The reason for this practice is expressly stated in the 1493 *Obsequiale Brixinense*, a liturgical book of Brixen, in the Austrian Tyrol (what is now Bressanone, Italy): "The procession should be done outside the fortifications or gates, inasmuch as the children went outside the fortifications to meet the Lord coming from Bethany and entered Jerusalem with him."[30] The symbolism of this custom is explained further by Durandus:

> And therefore the Church on this day makes a procession corporally and spiritually. For the children went outside the city to meet the Lord from Bethany into Jerusalem; and we similarly ought [to go] outside the city, that is, outside the delights of the flesh, to go to

The Palm Sunday Procession of the Tenth-century Romano-Germanic Pontifical

---

[26] *Hores de la setmana sancta segons lo us del archibisbat de Valencia* (Valencia, Spain: Jacobi de Villa, 1494), fols. 31v–32r.

[27] Ibid., fol. 31v.

[28] Text in Cyrille Vogel and Reinhard Elze, eds., *Le pontifical romano-germanique du dixième siècle*, vol. 2, ST 227 (Vatican City: Biblioteca Apostolica Vaticana, 1963), 40–51.

[29] Ibid., 40.

[30] *Obsequiale Brixinense* (Augsburg, Germany: Erhard Ratdolt, 1493; digitized text, Bayerische Staatsbibliothek, Munich, 2009), fol. 10r.

meet him, even as the Apostle says: "Let us go forth therefore to him without the camp, bearing his reproach" [Heb 13:13].[31]

After an initial antiphon sung by the cantor, the celebrant offers an opening collect that speaks of the death of Christ as the cause of our hope.[32] A reading from the Book of Exodus follows (Ex 15:27—16:10), which tells of Moses leading the Israelites first to Elim, an oasis of seventy palm trees, and then across the Desert of Sin, where the people began to complain against Moses and Aaron. It ends with the promise of the manna from Heaven, with "the glory of the Lord ... in a cloud" appearing in the morning. Two cantors now sing from the pulpit the antiphon *Collegerunt pontifices*, which speaks of the decision of the chief priests and Pharisees to seek the death of Christ in accord with Caiphas' counsel that "one man should die for the people" (cf. Jn 11:47–49, 50, 53).[33] The account of Christ's triumphal entry into Jerusalem in the Gospel of Saint Mark (11:1–10) is read next, after which the bishop delivers a homily on the same subject.[34] Three of the aforementioned features, the Collect, the Exodus reading, and the responsory *Collegerunt pontifices*, were later to serve as the beginning of the Palm Sunday rite in the universally promulgated *Missale Romanum* of 1570 (the Gospel of Matthew 21:1–9 was used instead of Mark 11:1–10).[35]

The rite for the blessing of the palm, olive, or other tree branches begins with a brief Collect,[36] followed by an exorcism said over the branches, in which the celebrant prays that "every power of the adversary may be expelled" from the leafy and flowering branches he is about to bless. He also prays to the Father that the demons "may not follow the footsteps of those hastening to the grace of God".[37]

The first of the blessing prayers of the "leafy branches", including both palms and olive branches, draws upon the spiritual symbolism of the tree, originally created as a source of sustenance and which, even after the fall of man through the disobedient partaking of the fruit of the forbidden tree, was rendered a source of even greater blessings through the death of Christ upon the tree of the Cross. But among all the trees, the boughs of the olive tree and the fronds of the palm tree

---

[31] Durandus, *Rationale* (CCCM 140a), bk. 6, chap. 67, no. 2, p. 322.

[32] Vogel and Elze, *Pontifical romano-germanique*, 2:41.

[33] Ibid., 41–42 (full text of antiphon in note on 42). This antiphon first appears in the Mass chant portion of the Antiphonary of Compiègne (France, c. 870); text in René-Jean Hésbert, ed., *Antiphonale missarum sextuplex* (Brussels, 1935; repr. Rome: Herder, 1967), 223.

[34] Vogel and Elze, *Pontifical romano-germanique*, 2:42.

[35] Text in Manlio Sodi and Achille Maria Triacca, eds., *Missale Romanum: Editio Princeps (1570)*, facsimile ed., MLCT 2 (Vatican City: Libreria Editrice Vaticana, © 1998), 208–209 (new pagination).

[36] Collect: "*Look favorably upon us, almighty God, that what is administered by our office may be filled the more with the effect of your blessing. Through ...*" (Vogel and Elze, *Pontifical romano-germanique*, 2:42).

[37] Ibid.

carry a preeminent significance. The olive branches to be blessed are a reminder of the olive branch carried back to the ark of Noah by a dove, symbolizing the baptismal cleansing of the world's sins prefigured in the great flood and the peace restored to the world through the washing away of sins. The palms represent those strewn before Christ as he entered Jerusalem and thus testify to his mission of conquering sin and Satan by his sufferings. The palms also signify the joy of the saved entering into Heaven, and the olive branches with their oil-producing fruit symbolize the unction of God's mercy with which the souls of the saved are adorned:

> *O Lord, holy Father, almighty eternal God, Creator of the world, and wonderful Disposer of all creatures, who amid the very beginnings of the world, when you formed all things from nothing, also ordered the earth to produce all trees fruit-bearing and suitable to diverse employment, and later changed the curse of the forbidden tree into a blessing for us through the obedience of your only-begotten Son: bless + also these branches of various trees, among which especially the tree of the olive excels in richness all [others], by which also, when formerly the sins of the world were cleansed in the boundless flood, a dove bringing a branch of the same proclaimed peace on earth restored;[38] and likewise the innocent multitude, inspired by the Holy Spirit, running to meet our Lord Jesus Christ, your only-begotten Son, about to suffer for the salvation of the whole world, cutting off branches of palms and of this tree and strewing [them] in his footsteps, made [him] known as though [he were] already the Conqueror over the prince of death. We humbly entreat you, O Lord, that we who with annual devotion strive to look forward to the most sacred Passion of the same our Redeemer, may with him assisting, holding the palm of victory and inwardly shining brightly with the oil of mercy, be worthy to attain in his holy Resurrection the reward of life and the crown of immortality. Through the same . . .[39]*

The flowering branches among the boughs to be blessed serve as a source of imagery for another of the blessing prayers. The text begins by speaking of the fullness of revelation coming through the humility of Christ, manifested in the emptying of himself in his Passion. The varied, fragrant flowers to be blessed are seen as representing the good works with which the soul should be adorned in going forth to meet Christ in the heavenly Jerusalem:

> *Almighty eternal God, Flower of the world, Fragrance of goodness, and Origin of those being born, who made clear all things of the Law and the revelations of the prophets in the humility of your Son our Lord Jesus Christ, and who also made the devout multitude go forth with palm branches and*

---

[38] This passage regarding the dove is clearly borrowed from the Holy Thursday prayer for the consecration of chrism in the seventh-century Gelasian Sacramentary of Rome; see Mohlberg, Eizenhöfer, and Siffrin, *Liber sacramentorum*, nos. 386–388, p. 62.

[39] Vogel and Elze, *Pontifical romano-germanique*, 2:42–43.

mystical praises to meet him coming to Jerusalem on this day, look favorably upon the due service of your people and sanctify with your power the freshness of this creature, that just as the affection of this devotion of your first people was then pleasing to you, so may we also, celebrating these same [mysteries] through repeated seasons with senses purified in the truth of the confession of his name, bring you worthy homage, that flourishing with pious deeds as though with a variety of flowers, having put aside the burden of the flesh, we may be worthy to come with the fragrance of good works to the same your Son our Lord in the heavenly Jerusalem. Through the same . . .[40]

It should be added here that the custom of blessing flowers in addition to branches on Palm Sunday may have also been inspired by the mystical identification of Palm Sunday with the first day of the creation of the world, as mentioned by Honorius of Autun (+c. 1135). This is in fact the logical counterpart to the more frequently cited comparison of Good Friday with the sixth day of creation. Honorius notes that it is because of the sun, created on the first day of the world, that the earth flourishes with flowers and the forests with leafy branches.[41] In singling out these two particular "fruits" of sunlight in his comparison of the world's first day to Palm Sunday, it seems highly likely that Honorius was thinking of the blessing of flowers and branches on Palm Sunday.

Unlike any of the other prayers provided for the blessing of the palm and olive branches in the Romano-Germanic Pontifical, the following text is addressed to Christ rather than to God the Father. It speaks of Christ freely entering upon his Passion, in accord with his declaration, "I lay down my life, that I may take it again; no man taketh it away from me: but I lay it down of myself" (Jn 10:17–18). The Old Testament anointings of prophets and kings and of the memorial stone erected by Jacob at Bethel (Gen 28:18) are invoked in presenting the branches of the oil-producing olive as symbolic of the anointing of Christ himself, the Anointed of the Lord. The priest asks for the Lord's blessing upon the branches, that the faithful may take them up and follow their Savior and that Christ may remain in their hearts:

Almighty eternal Redeemer, who vouchsafed to descend from Heaven to earth and to come to the Passion of your own will, that you should free mankind with your precious blood, look favorably on the prayers of your Church and our supplications; for you, O Lord, humbly resting upon the back of a humble donkey, came willingly to the Passion for our redemption; and with multitudes of disciples eagerly going to meet you, the way was strewn with tree branches, and when, with the voice of praise of very many, the throngs came to meet you on Mount Olivet, resounding with one accord and saying, "Hosanna

---

[40] Ibid., 43.

[41] Honorius of Autun, *Gemma animae*, bk. 3, chap. 119, PL 172, col. 675.

to the son of David: Blessed is he that cometh in the name of the Lord"
[Mt 21:9], the way to you was covered with triumphal palms. Formerly you
guided Noah in the ark upon the waves of the flood and willed by the agency
of a dove to announce through an olive branch peace restored to the earth. As
also the patriarch Jacob, in the service of your glory, erecting a stone for a title,
poured on the highest point the oil of benediction from the branches of this
tree [cf. Gen 28:18], whence you have anointed your kings and prophets.
For you are Christ, the Son of God; the fruit of unction and of peace befits
you, in whose ineffable praise the Psalmist sang, saying: "God, thy God,
hath anointed thee with the oil of gladness above thy fellows" [Ps 44:8].
Wherefore humbly we entreat you, O Lord, that you may bless these tree
branches that your servants desire you to bless and glorify, and taking them in
their hands, to hasten in your course. Jerusalem, behold; meek King, you
have come, sitting upon an ass. Come therefore, we beseech you, and abide in
us and in our midst, that we may perceive you to come within our hearts.
And may you who restored us then by the Cross restore us, once again fallen,
by the same beatific Passion. Willingly receive the confession of our mouth
and the humiliation of our fasting, and grant us to have the fruit of verdancy,
so that watered with your rains, we may be worthy to please you with an
abundance of sweet fruits. And even as they went forth to meet you, having
gone forth with leafy tree branches, so may we, with you returning in your
Second Coming, be worthy to go to meet you with the palms of joyful victory,
O Savior of the world, who live and reign with the Father in the unity of the
Holy Spirit, God, through all ages of ages.[42]

A prayer in the form of a Preface follows, which draws out further
the symbolism of the olive branch, invoking the Old Testament episode of the widow whose generosity to the prophet Elias was rewarded
in the miraculous replenishment of her jar of oil (3 Kings 17:10–16).
The branch is seen moreover as an image of Christ himself, prophesied as the "tree which is planted near the running waters, which
shall bring forth its fruit, in due season" (Ps 1:3):

It is truly fitting ... to praise and bless you, O Lord, who among other
decrees of your wonders gave to Lamech the just offspring Noah [Gen 5:28–
29], to whom you gave foreknowledge through the Spirit to recognize the
future waters of the flood, whose ark Mother Church attests [to be] in like-
ness to our salvation, from which the dove of the Spirit, having been sent out
flying, brought back a fruitful olive shoot, which [dove] returning to him
Noah received rejoicing; for the unction of which branch Jacob your elect erected
a title, vowed a vow to the Lord, and poured oil from above. This gives
evidence of that bough of grace spreading from Heaven and filling again the
vessels of the people. This is the grace that also blessed the widow in her oil.
This gives evidence of that branch planted beside running waters, whose foli-
age does not wither, by which daily through the bath of baptism the Church

---

[42] Vogel and Elze, *Pontifical romano-germanique*, 2:44–45.

is begotten and our sins are blotted out. This is your exceedingly good plant-ing, O Lord, and you are the life and resurrection of the dead, who raised Lazarus [after] four days from the dead.[43]

Yet another of the blessing prayers provided, one that later entered the universally promulgated *Missale Romanum* of 1570,[44] speaks of Christ humbling himself before men in order to bring them back to the Father. It also utilizes the imagery of the crowds spreading their garments and palm branches before the feet of Christ as a symbol of the path we should prepare for Christ, and along which we should follow him:

> *O God, who sent your Son our Lord Jesus Christ into this world for our salvation, that he might lower himself unto us and recall us to you, for whom also, as he was coming to Jerusalem that he might fulfill the Scriptures, the most faithful crowd of the believing multitudes with devotion spread their garments with palm branches in his path: grant, we beseech you, that with the stone of offense and the rock of scandal removed we may prepare for him the way of faith, out of which our works may flourish in your presence with the branches of righteousness, that we may be worthy to follow his footsteps. Who with you lives . . .*[45]

The practices of sprinkling the palm branches with holy water and incensing them are both traceable to the tenth-century, with both actions specified in the tenth-century redaction of the Benedictine customary of Cluny, France,[46] as well as in the Benedictine *Regularis concordia* of England (c. 960)[47]—six centuries later, the aspersion and incensation of the palms entered the 1570 *Missale Romanum*.[48] In the Romano-Germanic Pontifical, only the aspersion is mentioned: the celebrant sprinkles the branches with holy water (which has previously been mixed with blessed salt), for which rite two further blessing prayers are provided, manifesting by their wording the function of the blessed branches as sacramentals that bring the protection of God wherever they are devoutly carried or placed. In the first oration (a text from the second half of the ninth century later used in the 1570 *Missale Romanum*), the celebrant prays that "*into whatever place they* [the branches] *shall have been brought in, all the inhabitants of that place may obtain your blessing, so that with every hostile illness driven away, your right hand may*

---

[43] Ibid., 45 (complete Preface on 45–46).

[44] Sodi and Triacca, *Missale Romanum: Editio princeps (1570)*, 211 (new pagination).

[45] Vogel and Elze, *Pontifical romano-germanique*, 2:46.

[46] Text in Kassius Hallinger, O.S.B., *Consuetudines Cluniacensium antiquiores cum redaction-ibus derivatis*, Corpus consuetudinum monasticarum 7, pt. 2 (Siegburg, Germany: Franciscus Schmitt, 1983), 63.

[47] Text in Thomas Symons, trans., *Regularis concordia: The Monastic Agreement of the Monks and Nuns of the English Nation*, Medieval Classics (New York: Oxford University Press, 1953), chap. 4, no. 36, p. 35.

[48] Sodi and Triacca, *Missale Romanum: Editio princeps (1570)*, 211 (new pagination).

protect those whom He [Christ] *has redeemed."* [49] In a similar vein, the second text asks for the sanctification of the very places where the branches shall be brought, so that *"every iniquity or illusion of demons may depart and your right hand may vouchsafe to protect us always."* [50] The celebrant then distributes the branches to the people, as the following antiphon of late ninth-century origin[51] is sung (a chant later used in the 1570 *Missale Romanum*):[52] *"Six days before the solemn Pasch, when the Lord came into the city Jerusalem, the children met him, and carried palm branches in their hands, and cried out with a loud voice, saying: Hosanna in the highest. Blessed are you who have come in the plenitude of your mercy. Hosanna in the highest."* [53]

In the rite of the Romano-Germanic Pontifical, as in other medieval Palm Sunday rites, it is the presiding bishop or priest who both blesses the palms and distributes them individually to the clergy and the faithful. In explaining this aspect of the Palm Sunday liturgy, Durandus begins by observing that on the first Palm Sunday, Christ neither blessed nor distributed the palms, for those carrying the branches "prefigured the triumph of Christ not yet completed but to be completed at the time of his Passion". By contrast, the Church in her liturgical commemoration of Palm Sunday "represents the triumph of Christ now completed". Hence, because Christ is now the Conqueror, and by his gifts of grace and sanctification the faithful share in his victory, "fittingly both the blessing and the distribution of branches ought to be fulfilled by the priest, who represents Christ." [54]

The custom of kneeling to receive the palms from the celebrant is first found in the Ordinal of the Papal Court, a text of the papal liturgy from the pontificate of Pope Innocent III (1198–1216);[55] this practice was later made universal in the *Caeremoniale episcoporum* of 1600.[56] In the Palm

---

[49] Vogel and Elze, *Pontifical romano-germanique*, 2:46. This prayer first appears in a sacramentary of Switzerland's Saint Gall Abbey dating from the second half of the ninth century, preserved in Oxford's Bodleian Library; see Jean Deshusses, ed., *Le sacramentaire grégorien: Ses principales formes d'après les plus anciens manuscrits*, vol. 3, SF 28 (Fribourg, Switzerland: Editions Universitaires Fribourg, 1982), no. 4328, p. 251. A truncated and modified version of this prayer entered the 1570 *Missale Romanum*; see Sodi and Triacca, *Missale Romanum: Editio princeps (1570)*, 210–211 (new pagination).

[50] Vogel and Elze, *Pontifical romano-germanique*, 2:46.

[51] This antiphon, *Ante sex dies*, is first mentioned in the late ninth-century pontifical of northern France formerly known as the Pontifical of Poitiers and in the Mass chant portion of the Antiphonary of Compiègne (France, c. 870); see respectively Aldo Martini, ed., *Il cosiddetto pontificale di Poitiers*, REDSMF 14 (Rome: Casa Editrice Herder, 1979), 85, and Hésbert, *Antiphonale missarum sextuplex*, 221.

[52] Sodi and Triacca, *Missale Romanum: Editio princeps (1570)*, 212 (new pagination).

[53] Vogel and Elze, *Pontifical romano-germanique*, 2:46.

[54] Durandus, *Rationale* (CCCM 140a), bk. 6, chap. 67, no. 11, p. 325.

[55] Text in Stephen J. P. Van Dijk, O.F.M., and Joan Hazelden Walker, eds., *The Ordinal of the Papal Court from Innocent III to Boniface VIII and Related Documents*, SF 22 (Fribourg, Switzerland: The University Press, 1975), 217.

[56] This text directs that the distribution of palms should be done in the same manner as that prescribed for the February 2 distribution of candles; see Achille Maria Triacca and Manlio Sodi, eds., *Caeremoniale episcoporum: Editio princeps (1600)*, facsimile ed., MLCT 4

Sunday rite from the missal of Avila, Spain, dating from 1510, the distribution of palms brings to the fore the medieval perception of the palm procession as a prefiguration of the entrance of the redeemed into the heavenly Jerusalem. The celebrating bishop or priest, after sprinkling with holy water and incensing the palms he has blessed (and after sprinkling the people with holy water in the usual Sunday *Asperges* rite), begins the distribution of palms by taking a palm branch in his hand, and as he stands on the bottom step of the altar, he intones the antiphon "*Palms were in the hands of the saints, and with a great cry they sang, 'Salvation to our Lord, sitting upon the throne, and to the Lamb.'*" The celebrant begins the antiphon three times, raising his voice higher each time, and the choir completes it thrice, as the palms are distributed to the clergy and the people.[57] This antiphon, also used for the palm distribution rite in a fourteenth-century missal of Vich, Spain,[58] is a paraphrase and evocation of Saint John's vision of the redeemed in the Book of Revelation (7:9–10): "After this I saw a great multitude, which no man could number, of all nations, and tribes, and peoples, and tongues, standing before the throne, and in sight of the Lamb, clothed with white robes, and palms in their hands. And they cried with a loud voice, saying: Salvation to our God, who sitteth upon the throne, and to the Lamb." This dimension of the palm procession brings to mind an episode from the life of Saint Clare of Assisi (+1253). Having resolved to consecrate her life to God, Clare went to the cathedral of Assisi on Palm Sunday 1212 to attend the liturgical rites of the day, dressed in her finest clothes, as she prepared in secret to become a bride of Christ. When the time came for the people to receive their palms from the bishop at the altar rail, Clare, overcome by shyness, could not bring herself to step forward for her palm. Taking notice of this, the bishop descended the sanctuary steps and went to Clare, giving her one of the palms, the branches that "signify the victory of Christ over death and the devil", as Durandus describes them.[59] This incident could be considered emblematic of her decision to become a Franciscan religious.[60]

In the Palm Sunday rite of the Romano-Germanic Pontifical, the procession of the day begins almost immediately after the distribution of palms. Following a prayer that all the faithful may imitate the innocence of those who had welcomed Christ into Jerusalem,[61] the clergy and the people set out together on a route from the originating church

---

(Vatican City: Libreria Editrice Vaticana, © 2000), bk. 2, chap. 21, p. 227 (new pagination); for the relevant February 2 rubrics, see ibid., bk. 2, chap. 16, p. 212 (new pagination).

[57] *Missale Abulense* (Salamanca, Spain: Juan de Porras, 1510), sig. g7r.

[58] Text in Jaime Villanueva, *Viage literario a las iglesias de España*, vol. 9, *Viage a Solsona, Ager y Urgel, 1806 y 1807* (Valencia, Spain: Imprenta de Oliveres, 1821), 205.

[59] Durandus, *Rationale* (CCCM 140a), bk. 6, chap. 67, no. 7, p. 324.

[60] *Vita sanctae Clarae Virginis*, in John van Bolland et al., eds., *Acta sanctorum* (Antwerp, Belgium, 1643–; repr., Paris: Victor Palmé, 1863–1940), August, 2:756.

[61] Vogel and Elze, *Pontifical romano-germanique*, 2:47. This prayer first appears in the above-cited sacramentary of Switzerland's Saint Gall Abbey (second half of the ninth century); see Deshusses, *Sacramentaire grégorien*, no. 4329, 3:251.

to the destination church within the city gates, where the Palm Sunday Mass is to be celebrated. Along the way, processional antiphons are sung, including the following chant of late ninth-century origin[62] (later used in the 1570 *Missale Romanum*):[63]

> *When the people had heard that Jesus was coming to Jerusalem, they took branches of palm trees and went out to meet him, and the children cried out, saying, This is he who has come for the salvation of the world. Here is our salvation and the redemption of Israel. How great is this One to whom thrones and dominations come. Fear not, daughter of Zion: behold, your King cometh, sitting on an ass's colt, as it is written. Hail, O King, Maker of the world, who have come to redeem us.*[64]

It should be noted here that the later-introduced invitation to begin the palm procession, "*Let us proceed in peace*", and the response, "*In the name of Christ. Amen*", are first found in a Palm Sunday context in the Long Ceremonial, a papal liturgical book attributed to John of Sion and dating from a little before 1342.[65] The Palm Sunday use of this versicle and response was universally promulgated in the *Rituale Romanum* of 1614.[66]

The fourth-century Spanish pilgrim Egeria relates that the Palm Sunday procession she witnessed in Jerusalem ended at the Church of the Anastasis with Vespers and a prayer said "at the Cross".[67] This concluding station before Jerusalem's relic of the True Cross may have been the inspiration for the station before the cross or crucifix found in many medieval Palm Sunday processions, beginning with that of the Romano-Germanic Pontifical. According to the latter, the procession makes one "station" along the route, stopping before a crucifix. The Gospel of Saint John states that as Christ approached Jerusalem, the people of the city "went forth to meet him" (Jn 12:13). Hence, the first leg of the procession, prior to the station of the cross, represented the multitudes going out to meet Christ. The subsequent

---

[62] This antiphon, *Cum audisset populus*, is first mentioned in the late ninth-century pontifical of northern France formerly known as the Pontifical of Poitiers and in the Mass chant portion of the Antiphonary of Compiègne (France, c. 870); see respectively Martini, *Cosiddetto pontificale di Poitiers*, 85, and Hésbert, *Antiphonale missarum sextuplex*, 221.

[63] Sodi and Triacca, *Missale Romanum: Editio princeps (1570)*, 212 (new pagination).

[64] Vogel and Elze, *Pontifical romano-germanique*, 2:47.

[65] Text in Marc Dykmans, ed., *Le cérémonial papal de la fin du moyen âge à la Renaissance*, vol. 3, BIHBR 26 (Brussels and Rome: Institut Historique Belge de Rome, 1983), 202. The Long Ceremonial gives the invitation as "*Let us proceed with peace.*" This was later modified to "*Let us proceed in peace*" in the 1488 *Caeremoniale Romanum* of the papal master of ceremonies Patrizio Piccolomini; see Marc Dykmans, ed., *L'oeuvre de Patrizi Piccolomini, ou Le cérémonial papal de la première Renaissance*, vol. 2, ST 294 (Vatican City: Biblioteca Apostolica Vaticana, 1982), 358.

[66] Text in Manlio Sodi and Juan Javier Flores Arcas, eds., *Rituale Romanum: Editio princeps (1614)*, facsimile ed., MLCT 5 (Vatican City: Libreria Editrice Vaticana, © 2004), 172 (original pagination).

[67] Franceschini and Weber, *Itinerarium Egeriae*, chap. 31, no. 4, in *Itineraria et Alia geographia*, 77.

330

station of the cross symbolizes the moment when the multitudes reached Christ, represented by the crucifix, and began to do him homage with their palms, strewn garments, and acclamations. Accordingly, the procession's arrival before the crucifix serves as an occasion for all to adore the Savior:

> But when they shall have come with palms to where the station of the holy cross is, the clergy and the people reverently stand by turns in their order. . . . And the lead choirboys standing in a suitable place, they should introduce the antiphon: *With shining palms, we prostrate ourselves before the Lord coming; let us all go to meet him, glorifying him with hymns and canticles and saying: Blessed be the Lord.* The schola on behalf of the people says in reply the antiphon: *The multitudes come to meet the Lord Redeemer with flowers and palms and give worthy homages to the triumphing Victor. The nations ever praise the Son of God, and in praise of Christ their voices resound through the clouds. Hosanna.*[68] Then the scholars in the vicinity of the cross, with a slow step, should come before it, and with all reverence casting their chasubles or copes upon the ground, prostrate, they should adore the crucifix, the clergy meanwhile singing the antiphon: *The children of the Hebrews cast their garments to the ground on the way and cried out, saying: Hosanna, Son of David. Blessed is he who comes in the name of the Lord.*[69]
>
> These withdrawing, immediately the lay choirboys should come from the other side, singing, *Lord, have mercy*; and following the banner that is carried before them, they should come before the cross and, nodding assent to a command, cast their palm branches upon the ground, prostrate, adoring the crucifix; and the clergy meanwhile sing the antiphon: *The children of the Hebrews cast their garments to the ground* . . .[70]

The antiphon *Pueri Hebraeorum vestimenta prosternebant* ("*The children of the Hebrews cast their garments to the ground*") in the text above, used in many medieval Palm Sunday rites, is explained by Durandus as signifying that "we ought to be children, that is, innocent, and we ought to be children of the Hebrews, that is, hastening past all earthly things or sins."[71] As for another of the above antiphons, *Occurrunt turbae* ("*The multitudes come to meet the Lord Redeemer with flowers and palms*"), Durandus observes that "we ought similarly to go to meet him [Christ] with the flowers of the virtues and the palms of victories; for palms

---

[68] This antiphon, *Occurunt turbae*, is first mentioned in the late ninth-century pontifical of northern France formerly known as the Pontifical of Poitiers (Martini, *Cosiddetto pontificale di Poitiers*, 87). It later entered the 1570 *Missale Romanum*; see Sodi and Triacca, *Missale Romanum: Editio princeps (1570)*, 212 (new pagination).

[69] This antiphon, *Pueri Hebraeorum vestimenta prosternebant*, is first mentioned in the late ninth-century pontifical of northern France formerly known as the Pontifical of Poitiers (Martini, *Cosiddetto pontificale di Poitiers*, 85).

[70] Vogel and Elze, *Pontifical romano-germanique*, 2:47–48.

[71] Durandus, *Rationale* (CCCM 140a), bk. 6, chap. 67, no. 2, p. 322.

signify victory, whence: 'The just shall flourish like the palm tree' [Ps 91:13]."[72]

The above-quoted passage from the Romano-Germanic Pontifical speaks of casting palms before the crucifix, a custom found in many medieval Palm Sunday rites, with some adding the tossing of palms toward the cross. This practice constitutes a reenactment of what Saint Matthew relates in his account of Christ's entry into Jerusalem: "Others cut boughs from the trees, and strewed them in the way" (Mt 21:8). Durandus explains further the symbolism of this gesture: "Truly, green branches are thrust before the cross and on the cross to indicate that we have all the freshness of the virtues from the Crucified; for Christ was the green branch, having in himself and us by him all the freshness of the virtues, whence he says: 'For if in the green wood they do these things, what shall be done in the dry?' [Lk 23:31]."[73]

Standing near the cross, the choirboys of the schola begin the famed Palm Sunday hymn of Saint Theodulph of Orléans (+821), *Gloria laus* ("*Glory, laud, and honor*"), which is addressed to Christ.[74] Given a prominent role in Palm Sunday processions throughout medieval Europe, choirboys represented not only the children that came to greet Christ on the first Palm Sunday but also, according to Durandus, the angels who greeted Christ when at his Ascension he triumphantly entered the celestial Jerusalem, Heaven.[75] The role of the crucifix as a symbol of Christ in the midst of those who entered Jerusalem with him is further indicated by the adult choristers of the schola bowing their heads to the crucifix as they sing the refrain "*Glory, laud, and honor be unto you, O Christ the King, Redeemer, to whom youthful virtue uttered a loving Hosanna.*"[76] Later in this chapter we shall present the full text of a ten-verse version of the *Gloria laus* used in the Palm Sunday liturgy of Palencia, Spain, the version of this hymn that was afterward universally promulgated in the *Missale Romanum* of 1570.[77]

The homage offered by all culminates in the prostration of the celebrant before the crucifix, as the rest of the clergy and the people prostrate themselves in unison with him:

> And then all the people strew flowers or leafy branches on each side, the clergy singing the antiphon: *With the angels and the children let us be found faithful, crying out to the Conqueror of death: Hosanna in the highest.*[78] These things having been finished accordingly, the bishop or priest should come before the cross, and having prostrated himself

---

[72] Ibid., no. 5, pp. 322–323.

[73] Ibid., no. 8, p. 324.

[74] Vogel and Elze, *Pontifical romano-germanique*, 2:48.

[75] Durandus, *Rationale* (CCCM 140a), bk. 6, chap. 67, no. 7, p. 323.

[76] Vogel and Elze, *Pontifical romano-germanique*, 2:48.

[77] Sodi and Triacca, *Missale Romanum: Editio princeps (1570)*, 213 (new pagination).

[78] This antiphon, *Cum angelis*, is first mentioned in the late ninth-century pontifical of northern France formerly known as the Pontifical of Poitiers (Martini, *Cosiddetto pontificale*

on the ground with all the people, he adores the crucifix, the clergy meanwhile singing the antiphon: *For it is written: I will strike the shepherd, and the sheep of the flock shall be dispersed, but after I shall be risen again, I will go before you into Galilee. There you shall see me, says the Lord* [cf. Mt 26:31–32].[79]

In the above text, the antiphon accompanying the celebrant's prostration imparts to this action the connotation that the prostrate bishop or priest, the shepherd of his flock, is an image of the Good Shepherd who humbled himself to lay down his life for his sheep. Over the centuries that followed, this symbolism was to be made more explicit. The Palm Sunday rubrics of a fifteenth-century missal of Salzburg, Austria, direct that after the cross has been unveiled to the strains of the sixth verse of the hymn *Vexilla Regis*, "O Cross, hail, our only hope", and the clergy and the faithful have prostrated themselves before the cross, the prostration of the celebrant is accompanied not only by the antiphon "*For it is written: I will strike the shepherd*" (*Scriptum est enim: Percutiam pastorem*) but also by actions that dramatize these words: "Then the archdeacon, standing near with a palm that he bears in his hand, should strike the prostrate bishop with a light blow; and when he shall have come to that place when is sung, *but after I shall be risen again*, the bishop should rise."[80] This same practice appears in the late medieval liturgical books of Freising, Germany (1493), and Brixen, in the Tyrol (1493).[81] In the Palm Sunday rite from a fifteenth-century missal of Bratislava, Slovenia, the words regarding the stricken Shepherd are dramatically applied to the crucifix as a symbol of Christ going to his Passion. The crucifix is then venerated in a manner similar to the veneration on Good Friday, concluding with the great holy Cross hymn of Christ's battle against Satan, *Pange lingua gloriosi*, also known as *Crux fidelis*:

Then the priest going to celebrate the Mass, kneeling before the cross, singing this following antiphon, striking the crucifix with a palm three times, should say: *For it is written: I will strike the shepherd* . . . Which having been completed, kneeling successively one by one before the cross, they should kiss it; the antiphon follows, *Hosanna, Son of David* . . . Afterward is sung the hymn: *O faithful Cross* [*Crux Fidelis*].[82]

---

di Poitiers, 87). It later entered the 1570 *Missale Romanum*; see Sodi and Triacca, *Missale Romanum: Editio princeps (1570)*, 212–213 (new pagination).

[79] Vogel and Elze, *Pontifical romano-germanique*, 2:48.

[80] Text in Polycarp Radó, O.S.B., and Ladislaus Mezey, *Libri liturgici manuscripti bibliothecarum Hungariae et limitropharum regionum* (Budapest: Akadémiai Kiadó, 1973), 181.

[81] See respectively *Obsequiale Frisingense* (Augsburg, Germany: Erhard Ratdolt, 1493; digitized text, Bayerische Staatsbibliothek, Munich, 2008), fol. 38r; *Obsequiale Brixinense* (1493), fol. 9v.

[82] Radó and Mezey, *Libri liturgici manuscripti bibliothecarum Hungariae*, 168–169. The same practice is found in the 1509 *Liber ordinarius* of Eger, Hungary; see László Dobszay, ed.,

In the Romano-Germanic Pontifical, the prayer that follows the prostration before the crucifix, an oration that later entered the universally promulgated *Missale Romanum* of 1570,[83] highlights the symbolism of the palms as emblems of Christ's victory over the devil while identifying the olive branches as tokens of the "spiritual unction" that the Passion brings to mankind:

> *O God, who by the wonderful disposition of your providence willed to show even from inanimate things the setting forth of our salvation, grant, we beseech you, that the devout hearts of your faithful may salutarily perceive what is mystically signified in the reality that [on] this day, inspired by celestial illumination, the crowd going forth to meet the Redeemer spread beneath his feet palm and olive branches. Accordingly, palm branches anticipate his triumphs over the prince of death, whereas the olive sprouts proclaim in a way his spiritual unction to have come. For already at that time, that blessed multitude of men perceived to be prefigured in human things how our Redeemer, suffering greatly for the life of the whole world, was going to do battle with the prince of death, and in dying to triumph the sooner. And submitting himself thus, he appointed such things, which in regard to him proclaimed both the triumphs of his victory and the abundance of his mercy. Wherefore as we also, with plentiful faith retaining both the reality and its signification, humbly beseech you, Lord, holy Father, almighty eternal God, through the same Jesus Christ our Lord, that in him and through him whose members you have willed us to be made, winning victory over the power of death, we may be worthy to be partakers of the glory of his resurrection. Who with you . . .*[84]

The crucifix is now taken up and carried with the banners at the head of the procession as it resumes its progress toward the gates of the city and the destination church within. The Romano-Germanic Pontifical provides a hymn for the procession, the *Magnum salutis gaudium*, that serves as a poetic reflection upon the themes of Palm Sunday:

> *O great joy of salvation!*
> *Let the whole world rejoice;*
> *Jesus, the Redeemer of the nations,*
> *has healed an infirm world.*
> The schola responding: *O great joy of salvation . . .*
>
> *Six days before the Pasch,*
> *he came into Bethany,*
> *where after three days*
> *he mercifully raised up Lazarus. Jesus, the Redeemer . . .*

Liber ordinarius Agriensis (1509), Musicalia Danubiana, subsidia, 1 (Budapest: Magyar Tudományos Akadémia Zenetudományi Intézet, 2000), 53, 174–175.

[83] Sodi and Triacca, *Missale Romanum: Editio princeps (1570)*, 211 (new pagination).

[84] Vogel and Elze, *Pontifical romano-germanique*, 2:49.

With pure nard Mary
anointed the blessed feet of the Lord,
washing them with her tears
and wiping them with her hair. O great joy of salvation . . .

After these things,
Jesus, the celestial Judge,
sat upon a colt, yoked together to an ass,
proceeding to glorious Jerusalem. Jesus, the Redeemer . . .

Oh, how wonderful the goodness,
the wonderful clemency of God:
the Creator of the world
vouchsafes to be made the rider of a donkey. O great joy of salvation . . .

Long ago the prophet foreknowing
prophesied by the gracious Spirit,
saying, Rejoice exceedingly, O daughter Sion,
and sing joyfully. Jesus, the Redeemer . . .

Fear not: behold, your King
shall come to you,
humble, merciful, patient,
sitting on a yoked colt. O great joy of salvation . . .

The young, very great multitude
had taken blooming branches, cut palms,
going forth to meet
the eternal King. Jesus, the Redeemer . . .

The assembly preceding and following,
filled with the Holy Spirit,
cried out, Hosanna in the highest
to the Son of David. O great joy of salvation . . .

Some covered the way
with their own loose garments,
and many with unsullied innocence
prepared the way for the Lord. Jesus, the Redeemer . . .

At whose entrance
the whole excited city trembled;
the beautiful Hebrew children
brought due praises. O great joy of salvation . . .

Therefore let us all run to meet
so great a Judge,
bearing palms of glory,
singing with a sober mind. Jesus, the Redeemer . . .

> *Honor, glory, dominion*
> *be to the one and only Trinity,*
> *to the Father, the Son, the Paraclete*
> *through infinite ages. O great joy of salvation* ...[85]

The above hymn is a composition of unknown authorship traceable to the ninth century.[86] The twelfth-century *Ordo* of Beroldus, a liturgical book of Italy's Ambrosian Rite of Milan, places the singing of the *Magnum salutis gaudium* at the beginning of the Palm Sunday liturgy, with the archbishop of Milan entering the city's Basilica of San Lorenzo at the words *"Behold, your King shall come to you, humble."*[87]

In the Palm Sunday rite of the Romano-Germanic Pontifical, the entrance of the procession through the city gates is cast as symbolizing the moment of Christ's entrance into Jerusalem through the singing of the responsory *Ingrediente Domino* (*"The Lord entering"*), a chant of late ninth-century origin[88] (later used in the 1570 *Missale Romanum*):[89]

> These things having been finished, when they shall have entered the gates of the city with all the people singing *Lord, have mercy*, the first [cantor] of the schola should introduce the responsory, *The Lord entering the Holy City, the children of the Hebrews, announcing the resurrection of life, with palm branches, cried out, Hosanna in the highest*, with all the clergy continuing together both the responsory and the verse, *And when they had heard that Jesus was coming to Jerusalem, they went out to meet him. With palm branches, they cried out, Hosanna in the highest* [cf. Jn 12:12–13].[90]

After passing through the city gates, the procession continues toward the destination church with the singing of antiphons from the office of Matins. The procession enters the church with the chanting of the antiphon *Coeperunt omnes turbae* (*"All the multitudes of those coming down, rejoicing, began to praise God with a loud voice for all that they had seen ..."*),[91] after which the celebrant concludes the rite with a Collect. The Mass of the day follows.[92]

---

[85] Ibid., 49–51.

[86] See Michel Andrieu, ed., *Les Ordines Romani du haut moyen âge*, vol. 5, SSLED 29 (Louvain, Belgium: "Spicilegium sacrum Lovaniense" Administration, 1961), 64.

[87] Text in Marcus Magistretti, ed., *Beroldus, sive Ecclesiae Ambrosianae Mediolanensis kalendarium et Ordines, saec. XII* (Milan: Joseph Giovanola, 1894), 96.

[88] This responsory is first mentioned in the late ninth-century pontifical of northern France formerly known as the Pontifical of Poitiers (Martini, *Cosiddetto pontificale di Poitiers*, 87).

[89] Sodi and Triacca, *Missale Romanum: Editio princeps (1570)*, 213 (new pagination).

[90] Vogel and Elze, *Pontifical romano-germanique*, 2:51. The pontifical provides only the incipit of the responsory *Ingrediente Domino* and its verse; the complete texts are here taken from *Obsequiale Brixinense* (1493), fol. 10r.

[91] This antiphon is first mentioned in the late ninth-century pontifical of northern France formerly known as the Pontifical of Poitiers and in the Mass chant portion of the Antiphonary of Compiègne (France, c. 870); see respectively Martini, *Cosiddetto pontificale di Poitiers*, 87, and Hésbert, *Antiphonale missarum sextuplex*, 221.

[92] Vogel and Elze, *Pontifical romano-germanique*, 2:51.

In the medieval Palm Sunday rites, the above-mentioned responsory *Ingrediente Domino* was to become universally assigned to the moment when the palm procession entered the destination church. Other texts were utilized as a prelude to the entrance. In many cases, the earlier-cited hymn of Saint Theodulph of Orléans, *Gloria laus*, would be sung by choristers within the destination church prior to the opening of the church door and the entrance of the procession. Thus the Palm Sunday rite of the twelfth-century Roman Pontifical specifies the closing of the doors of the destination church or of the gates of the city prior to the arrival of the procession before the church or the city walls, with two cantors from within singing the *Gloria laus*.[93] The drama of using the *Gloria laus* in this manner as a greeting to the approaching procession was enhanced with the custom of having those in the procession reply to each verse of the *Gloria laus* by chanting the refrain, a practice we find described in the 1568 *Missale Pallantinum* of Palencia, Spain:

> Then the procession returns to the place whence it went forth. But when it shall have arrived before the gates of the city, or before the closed doors of the church, the choir or cantors standing within sing these verses: *Glory, laud, and honor be unto you, O Christ the King, Redeemer, to whom youthful virtue uttered a loving Hosanna.* The priest and the ministers, and the other clerics standing outdoors, repeat the aforesaid verse, namely, *Glory, laud.* But the cantors, or the choir, continue the following verse; and at the end of each of those [verses] they who are outdoors respond as before, *Glory, laud.* And the cantors or the choir ought to be with their faces turned toward the procession, and the priest, and the ministers.

> Verse: *You are the King of Israel, the glorious offspring of David, the blessed King, who comes in the name of the Lord.* Response: *Glory . . .*
> Verse: *The entire celestial assemblage praises you in the highest, mortal man also, all things created, together.* Response: *Glory . . .*
> Verse: *The Hebrew people meet you with palms; with prayer, offering, hymns, behold, we attend unto you.* Response: *Glory . . .*
> Verse: *To you going to suffer, these proffered gifts of praise; to you reigning over us, behold, we make music.* Response: *Glory . . .*
> Verse: *These pleasing you, may our devotion be pleasing [to you], good King, merciful King, to whom all good things are pleasing.* Response: *Glory . . .*
> Verse: *The glory of your dear blood had gained these Hebrews; behold, your holy passage makes us Hebrews.* Response: *Glory . . .*
> Verse: *May you be a merciful rider, and we your donkey;*

---

[93] Text in Michel Andrieu, ed., *Le pontifical romain au moyen-âge*; vol. 1, *Le Pontifical Romain du XIIe siècle*, ST 86 (Vatican City: Biblioteca Apostolica Vaticana, 1938), 214.

may the venerable City of God receive us with you. Response: *Glory . . .*
Verse: *May we be covered with the golden splendor of the apostolic vesture,*
that, taught well by you, our congregation may bear that [splendor]. Response:
Glory . . .
Verse: *Thus may we cover our bodies with the shield of the soul,*
with which may there ever be for us a secure way to you. Response: *Glory*
. . .

Verse: *May there be for us a holy victory with palm branches,*
that thus by your ordinance we may sing to you victorious. Response: *Glory*
. . .[94]

According to Durandus, the chanting of the *Gloria laus* from behind
the closed church door or closed city gate "prefigures the assembly
and joy of the angels receiving Christ into Heaven after the Resurrection, which he merited to open to himself and those following
him by his most holy Passion." The door is closed, because fallen
mankind was hitherto barred from Heaven, but those outside come to
meet the Lord "that their ruin might be repaired". The angels within
welcome Christ and redeemed mankind accompanying him with a
"hymn of praise", which the *Gloria laus* represents.[95]

In some medieval Palm Sunday rites, particularly those of France
from the thirteenth century onward and those of late medieval Spain
and Portugal, the entrance of the procession into the destination church
or through the city gates would be prefaced by a dramatized recitation
of Psalm 23:7–10.[96] Thus we find it in the 1568 *Missale Pallantinum* of
Palencia, Spain (where it immediately follows the above-cited antiphonal singing of the *Gloria laus*):

---

[94] *Missale Pallantinum* (Palencia, Spain: Sebastian Martinez, 1568), fols. 72v–73r. Latin
text provided by Biblioteca Apostolica Vaticana, Vatican City (shelf mark Stamp. Barb.
B. X. 1).

[95] Durandus, *Rationale* (CCCM 140a), bk. 6, chap. 67, no. 7, p. 323.

[96] Dom Edmond Martène cites three thirteenth-century French texts as having this rite:
a customary (ritual) of the Church of Saint Martin in Tours (c. 1227), and the ordinaries
of Nantes (c. 1263) and Le Mans (late thirteenth century); see Edmond Martène, *De antiquis
ecclesiae ritibus* (Venice: Johannes Baptista Novelli, 1763–1764), bk. 4, chap. 20, no. 14, 3:72.
He also provides a complete text of this rite from another ordinary of Tours (c. 1400; ibid.,
bk. 4, chap. 20, *ordo* 4, 3:76). For Spanish examples from Jaén (1499), Segovia (1500), Avila
(1510), and Toledo (1503–1518), see respectively *Missale Giennense / Manuale continens ordinem
ad celebrandum ecclesiastica sacramenta [Missale secundum morem et consuetudinem sancte ecclesie
Gienensis]* (Seville: Meinard Ungut and Stanislao Polono, 1499), fol. 60r–60v; *Missale secundum consuetudinem Segobiensis ecclesie* (Venice: Johannes Emericus de Spira, 1500; digitized
text, Biblioteca Digital Hispánica, Biblioteca Nacional de España, Madrid, n.d.), fols. 60v–
61r; *Missale Abulense* (1510), sig. g8r; and *Missale secundum consuetudinem almae ecclesiae Toletanae*, 1503–1518, vol. 4 (manuscript: Madrid, Biblioteca Nacional de España, MS 1543;
digitized text, Biblioteca Digital Hispánica, Biblioteca Nacional de España, Madrid, 2007),
fols. 14v–16r. For Portuguese examples from Braga (1498) and Evora (1509), see respectively *Missale Bracarense* (Lisbon: Nicolaus de Saxonia, 1498), sig. g3r, and *Missale secundum
consuetudinem Elborensis ecclesie noviter impressum* (Lisbon: Germano Galharde, 1509; digitized
text, Biblioteca Nacional Digital, Biblioteca Nacional de Portugal, 2009), fol. 66r–66v.

Then the hebdomadarian priest,[97] having received the processional cross, sings: *Lift up your gates, O ye princes, and be lifted up, O eternal gates: and the King of Glory shall enter in.* With the summit of the staff of the cross, he strikes the door. And afterward the cantors who are within say: *Who is this King of Glory?* The priest responds: *The Lord who is strong and mighty.* And again, in a higher voice, the priest should say: *Lift up your gates, O ye princes, and be lifted up, O eternal gates: and the King of Glory shall enter in.* And a second time he strikes the door; and the cantors sing: *Who is this King of Glory?* The priest responds: *The Lord mighty in battle.* And a third time, in a still higher tone, the priest says: *Lift up your gates, O ye princes, and be lifted up, O eternal gates: and the King of Glory shall enter in.* The third time he strikes more firmly. The cantors as before say: *Who is this King of Glory?* Then the priest responds: *The Lord of hosts, he is the King of Glory.* And then the doors are opened, with great jubilation and pious devotion, and the procession enters. Then the cantor begins the responsory: *The Lord entering the Holy City . . .*[98]

The use of Psalm 23 for the Palm Sunday procession corresponds to the rite's symbolism connecting it with Christ's triumphal entry into the heavenly Jerusalem at his Ascension. In early fifth-century Jerusalem, this psalm was utilized for the liturgy of Ascension Thursday as found in the ancient liturgical book of the Holy City known as the Armenian Lectionary.[99] By the second half of the sixth century, the use of this psalm in the rite of consecrating new churches had arisen in the East: it was sung for the rededication of Constantinople's cathedral church of Hagia Sophia on December 24, 562, when the city's patriarch Eutychius arrived before the church.[100] In the West, the use of Psalm 23 for a church consecration rite is first found in a French text, Roman *Ordo* 41, dating from the second half of the eighth century, which also directs the bishop to strike the lintel of the church door with his crosier before entering.[101] By the middle of the ninth century, a threefold dialogue between the bishop striking upon the door and a cleric within the church, utilizing Psalm 23:7–10, had been added to the church consecration rite as found in the French sacramentary of Drogo of Metz (826–855).[102] It is this tripartite ceremony that subsequently entered the Palm Sunday liturgy in many places,

---

[97] The hebdomadarian is the priest assigned to lead the Divine Office for a given week.

[98] *Missale Pallantinum* (1568), fols. 73r–74r.

[99] Text in Athanase Renoux, ed. and trans., *Le codex arménien Jérusalem 121*, vol. 2, *Edition comparée du texte et de deux autres manuscrits*, Patrologia orientalis 36, fasc. 2 (Turnhout, Belgium: Brepols, 1971), no. 57, pp. 338–339.

[100] Quoted in Michel Andrieu, ed., *Les Ordines Romani du haut moyen âge*, vol. 4, SSLED 28 (Louvain, Belgium: "Spicilegium sacrum Lovaniense" Administration, 1956), 316.

[101] Text ibid., 340.

[102] The text of the church consecration rite from the sacramentary of Drogo of Metz (manuscript: Paris, Bibliothèque Nationale, Codex Lat. 9428) is given in Louis Duchesne, *Christian Worship: Its Origin and Evolution* (London: SPCK, 1910), 487–489.

including in the Palencia rite presented above. The symbolism given to this church dedication ceremony from its very inception, as explained in a late ninth-century commentary of Remigius of Auxerre (+c. 908), corresponds well to the Palm Sunday themes of Christ's arrival before the gates of Jerusalem to redeem mankind from sin and his arrival before the gates of the heavenly Jerusalem to open it to the redeemed. Evoking the identity of the bishop as an *alter Christus*,[103] Remigius observes:

> When, therefore, the bishop strikes the lintel of the future church three times with his staff, he shows that not only the power of Heaven but also of earth, and of hell, yield to him. Whence also, after the striking, the door is opened, namely because the adversary cannot resist his power of securing it unto himself. For the building itself, before the bishop should enter it, possesses the likeness of the people shut in by the bars of unknowing faithlessness, to whom the Lord came that he might lead forth all from darkness, he to whom the Father had said: "I will go before thee, and will humble the great ones of the earth: I will break in pieces the gates of brass, and will burst the bars of iron" (Is 45:2). And likewise, after other things the Father says to him: "That thou mightest say to them that are bound: Come forth: and to them that are in darkness: Shew yourselves" (Is 49:9); which also the Lord coming in the flesh accomplished by himself and does not cease to do all the way to the end of the world through his vicars.[104]

In the Palm Sunday rendering of this entrance rite, the identification of the celebrant knocking upon the door with Christ is explicitly stated in the rubrics of the 1543 missal of Bayonne, France: "The priest in the person of Christ should strike the door with the foot of the cross." [105] The use of this dialogue from Psalm 23 on Palm Sunday can also be seen in the context of Holy Week as an anticipation of Christ's descent into Sheol, following his death, to liberate the souls of the just barred from Heaven until his coming. In fact, the earliest casting of Psalm 23:7–10 as a dialogue between Christ and those within closed gates is found in an ancient apocryphal work, the *Gospel of Nicodemus*, dating from the second or third century: in this text, the voice of Christ is heard outside the barred gates of Sheol, commanding those inside, "Lift up your gates, O rulers." Satan and his fellow demons as well as Hades resist the Savior's entry in vain, and Christ, shattering the brass gates and iron bars of Sheol, enters to deliver the dead from Satan's power.[106]

---

[103] Remigius of Auxerre, *Tractatus de dedicatione ecclesiae*, PL 131, col. 847.

[104] Ibid., col. 848.

[105] Text in V. Dubarat, ed., *Le missel de Bayonne de 1543* (Pau, France: Leon Ribaut, 1901), 38.

[106] Text in Edgar Hennecke and Wilhelm Schneemelcher, eds., *New Testament Apocrypha* (Philadelphia: Westminster Press, 1963–1966), 1:473–474.

Although the dialogue from Psalm 23 was never incorporated into the Palm Sunday rites of Rome, the action of striking upon the closed door of the church was inserted into the papal Palm Sunday liturgy in the 1488 *Caeremoniale Romanum* of the master of ceremonies Patrizio Piccolomini[107] and was later universally promulgated in the *Caeremoniale episcoporum* of 1600 and the *Rituale Romanum* of 1614, which prescribe a single strike made by the subdeacon with the staff of the processional cross prior to the opening of the church door and the singing of *Ingrediente Domino*.[108]

Another element of the church consecration rite appears to have inspired a further addition to the Palm Sunday liturgy in Spain and Portugal. The Palm Sunday rubrics of a fourteenth-century missal of Vich, Spain, direct that before the door of the destination church is opened to receive the palm procession, the priest is to pray: "*Almighty eternal God, Creator and Guardian of the heavenly city of Jerusalem, protect this place with its inhabitants, that within it there may unceasingly be an abode of safety and peace.*"[109] This oration, traceable to an eleventh-century Benedictine sacramentary preserved in Barcelona, Spain,[110] also appears in the Palm Sunday rite of the 1498 missal of Braga, Portugal, where it is said by the bishop before the altar after the palm procession enters the church.[111] This prayer for the destination church being entered and the faithful who worship within it with its plea for peace corresponds to the petition "*Peace be unto this house and to all the inhabitants within it*", pronounced by the bishop in the church consecration rite immediately after entering the new church.[112]

Palm Sunday in the Sarum Rite of England

Over the course of the Middle Ages, the rites of Palm Sunday took on a wide variety of local characteristics. Perhaps the most moving examples are those in which the presence of Christ in the palm procession was expressed not merely by an image or symbol of Christ, such as the crucifix, or the Gospel book, or a "Palmesel" statue of Christ riding upon a donkey, but rather by the real, sacramental presence of Christ in the Blessed Sacrament. Such a practice, traceable to

---

[107] Dykmans, *Oeuvre de Patrizi Piccolomini*, 2:358.

[108] Triacca and Sodi, *Caeremoniale episcoporum: Editio princeps (1600)*, bk. 2, chap. 21, p. 229 (new pagination); Sodi and Flores Arcas, *Rituale Romanum: Editio princeps (1614)*, 173 (original pagination).

[109] Villanueva, *Viage literario a las iglesias de España*, 9:205.

[110] See Eugenio Moeller, Joannis Maria Clément, and Bertrandus Coppieters 'T Wallant, eds., *Corpus orationum*, vol. 6, CCSL 160e (Turnhout, Belgium: Brepols, 1995), no. 3787, pp. 39–40.

[111] *Missale Bracarense* (1498), sig. g3r.

[112] See, for example, the church consecration rite in the 1485 Roman Pontifical, the *Pontificalis liber*, in Manlio Sodi, ed., *Il "Pontificalis liber" di Agostino Patrizi Piccolomini e Giovanni Burcardo (1485)*, facsimile ed., MSIL 43 (Vatican City: Libreria Editrice Vaticana, © 2006), 265 (new pagination).

the eleventh century,[113] is consonant with the nature of the Eucharist as a memorial of the death of the Savior (cf. 1 Cor 11:26). A simple illustration of this is found in an early fourteenth-century ceremonial of Cologne, Germany, which prescribes a Eucharistic procession from the sacristy to the high altar in the cathedral after the procession of palms enters the church, immediately before High Mass.[114] In this case, the Eucharistic procession takes place as a short rite after the palm procession. But in England and northern France, the palm procession itself was in many cases celebrated as a magnificent Eucharistic procession. This latter tradition finds its most expansive development in the late medieval Sarum Rite of Salisbury, England, used across most of southern England as well as in Ireland and Scotland. For this ceremony, we turn to the late fifteenth-century printed Sarum Missal (c. 1489) that earlier served as our primary example of the medieval Ordinary of the Mass (see chapter 2).

The Sarum Palm Sunday rite[115] begins inside Salisbury Cathedral with the same Old Testament reading as in the earlier-described rite of the Romano-Germanic Pontifical (Ex 15:27ff.), but it is followed by a different Gospel account of Christ's entry into Jerusalem (Jn 12:12–19); the latter is read by the deacon "turned toward the east".[116] In the Sarum tradition, the vestment color for Palm Sunday is red, clearly representing the blood of Christ: "The Gospel having been finished, there should follow the blessing of flowers and branches by the priest upon the third step of the altar, clothed in a red silk cope, turned toward the south side, the flowers having been placed with the palms beforehand upon the altar for the clerics, but for others upon the altar step on the south side."[117] Among the prayers for blessing the palms in the Sarum ceremony is the oration *Deus qui dispersa congregas* ("O God, who gather the dispersed"), traceable perhaps to the eighth century[118] and later promulgated in the *Missale Romanum* of 1570.[119] Afterward, as the blessed branches are distributed, several clerics set out in

---

[113] The carrying of the Eucharist in the Palm Sunday procession appears in the customary composed by Archbishop Lanfranc for England's Canterbury Cathedral (c. 1077); text in David Knowles and Christopher N. L. Brooke, eds. and trans., *The Monastic Constitutions of Lanfranc*, rev. ed., Oxford Medieval Texts (Oxford: Clarendon, 2002), chap. 25, pp. 36–41.

[114] Text in Gottfried Amberg, ed., *Ceremoniale Coloniense*, Studien zur Kölner Kirchengeschichte 17 (Siegburg, Germany: Franz Schmitt, 1982), 112.

[115] Text in Martène, *De antiquis ecclesiae ritibus*, bk. 4, chap. 20, *ordo* 7, 3:76–77.

[116] Ibid., 76.

[117] Ibid., 77.

[118] A short phrase from this prayer appears in a November 751 letter of Pope Saint Zachary to Saint Boniface (*Letter 13*, PL 89, col. 949); see Germain Morin, "Notes et documents, 3: Une formule de la bénédiction des rameaux dans une lettre du pape Zacharie à saint Boniface", *Revue Bénédictine* 27 (1910): 401–402. The full text of the prayer appears for the first time as a ninth-century addition to the seventh-century Paduan redaction of the Gregorian Sacramentary of Rome; see Deshusses, *Sacramentaire grégorien*, no. 4334, 3:252.

[119] Sodi and Triacca, *Missale Romanum: Editio princeps (1570)*, 210–211 (new pagination).

a small procession separate from the main procession that will soon begin. Proceeding toward the first station at which the main procession will stop, a location just outside the cathedral on the north side of the church's eastern end, two of the clerics carry upon a bier a feretory, a portable shrine of the Blessed Sacrament, with the pyx enclosing the Eucharist suspended from the inside roof of the shrine. Various relics are also placed within the feretory. The bier is preceded by clerics carrying a lit lantern, an unveiled cross, and two banners.[120] A medieval chronicler's account of a Palm Sunday Eucharistic feretory for the English abbey of Saint Albans in Hertfordshire, donated by the abbot Simon (+1183), gives a sense of the richly symbolic ornamentation of these shrines:

> ... one extraordinary vessel, by way of a chest, the very attractive form of which corresponds with an ark; the top, however, is made narrower, rising by way of a bier, and it is encircled on all sides with raised circles, on which the history of the Passion of the Lord is symbolized with molten images, and throughout with beaten metal plates of solid density, thus, to wit, that it does not lack in bases or wooden supports.[121]

The use of an ark-shaped vessel to carry the Eucharist on Palm Sunday accords well with one of the symbolic associations of the palm procession identified by Durandus, who likens it to the Israelites' miraculous crossing of the Jordan River, with the Ark of the Covenant carried before them (Jos 3:1–17): "It recollects the procession of the children of Israel, who on this day crossed the Jordan with dry feet, and with triumph entered the land of promise."[122]

Following the distribution of palms in the Sarum Rite ceremony, the main procession, comprising the celebrant (in a red silk cope), the rest of the clergy, and the faithful, sets out for the first station, where it meets the Eucharistic procession, in commemoration of the people of Jerusalem going out to meet Christ as he approached the city.[123] At this station, Saint Matthew's Gospel account of Christ's triumphal entry (Mt 21:1–9) is read by a deacon, who faces north as he reads.[124] Christ in the Blessed Sacrament is now greeted with adoration. The worship accorded the Eucharist here and during the subsequent stations of the palm procession is aptly explained in the earlier-cited twelfth-century text from Saint Albans Abbey as intended

---

[120] Martène, *De antiquis ecclesiae ritibus*, bk. 4, chap. 20, *ordo* 7, 3:77.

[121] Matthew Paris (+1259), in Henry Thomas Riley, ed., *Chronica monasterii s. Albani: Gesta abbatum monasterii sancti Albani, a Thoma Walsingham ... compilata*, Rerum Britannicarum medii aevi scriptores 28, pt. 4 (London: Longmans, Green, Reader, and Dyer, 1867–1869), 1:191.

[122] Durandus, *Rationale* (CCCM 140a), bk. 6, chap. 67, no. 9, p. 324.

[123] Martène, *De antiquis ecclesiae ritibus*, bk. 4, chap. 20, *ordo* 7, 3:77.

[124] Ibid.

"that the faithful may see how much honor the most holy Body of
the Lord deserves, who in the selfsame time exposed himself to be
scourged, crucified, and buried."[125] In the Sarum ritual for the first
station, the choristers salute Christ in a series of versicles as the King
and Savior whom Zacharias prophesied would come to Sion riding
upon a donkey (Zach 9:9), as he who comes in garments reddened
in blood, having trodden the winepress of the Cross alone (Is 63:1–
3), and as the sinless Lamb of God who by his death has put death
itself to death:

> The Gospel having been completed, three clerics of the second rank,
> with their vesture unchanged, having turned toward the people, stand-
> ing before the great cross on its western side, should sing together
> the verse *Lo, your humble King comes to you, O Sion, mystical daughter,
> lowly, sitting upon beasts, whose coming the prophetic utterance has already
> prophesied.* But for the individual verses, the executor of the office
> [the celebrant], having turned toward the relics, should begin the
> antiphon *Hail, O you whom the people of the Hebrews attest [to be]
> Jesus, meeting you with palms, exclaiming words of greeting unto you,*
> which the choir should continue with a genuflection, kissing the
> ground. But the genuflection should be undertaken first by the office
> executor himself, with the choir. The clerics [sing] before the relics
> the verse *Lo, your humble King.* The senior [cleric] [sings] the anti-
> phon *Hail, O you whom,* which the choir, rising again, should con-
> tinue, *the people of the Hebrews attest* ... Likewise, the clerics, their
> position unchanged, should say before the relics the verse *This is he
> who comes from Edom, in dyed garments from Bosrah, beautiful in his
> raiment, walking with strength, not on horses of war or on exalted chariots.*
> Likewise, the senior [cleric], his position unchanged, should say, *Hail,
> O Light of the world.* The choir rising again continues, *King of kings,
> the glory of Heaven, with whom abides dominion, praise, and glory now
> and forever.* Likewise, the clerics before the relics, their position
> unchanged, should say the verse *This is he who as the innocent Lamb
> is handed over to death, the death of infernal death, devoured by death,
> giving life, as the blessed prophets once promised prophetically.* Likewise,
> the senior [cleric], his position unchanged, should say the antiphon
> *Hail, our Salvation.* The choir rising again continues, *our true Peace,
> Redemption, Strength, who of your own accord underwent the exactions of
> death for us.*[126]

---

[125] Quoted from Matthew Paris' description of the Saint Albans Palm Sunday procession, in Riley, *Chronica monasterii s. Albani,* 1:192.

[126] Martène, *De antiquis ecclesiae ritibus,* bk. 4, chap. 20, ordo 7, 3:77. Dom Martène
provides only the incipit of each antiphon in this passage; the complete texts are here taken
from John Wickham Legg's edition of the late thirteenth-century Sarum Missal, in which
all of these antiphons appear for the first time; see John Wickham Legg, ed., *The Sarum
Missal, Edited from Three Early Manuscripts* (Oxford: Clarendon, 1916), 95 (Latin text quoted
and translated by permission of Oxford University Press).

All now set out in a single procession accompanying the Blessed Sacrament (carried on the bier with the relics), proceeding toward the second station along an outdoor route around the east end of the cathedral:

> Then the procession should go to the place of the second station; and the bier with the small box of relics, together with the light in the lantern between the subdeacon and the thurible, should be brought with banners on each side, the cantor beginning the antiphon *Worthy are you, O Lord our God, to receive glory and honor.*[127] Here the second station should be done, namely by the south side of the church, where seven boys in a more prominent place should sing together the verse *Glory, laud, and honor be unto you, O Christ the King, Redeemer.*[128]

In the above rubrics, the antiphon *"Worthy are you, O Lord"* (*Dignus es Domine*) is used without any particular ceremony being attached to it; but in another medieval English liturgical text, a fifteenth-century manual for the archdiocese of York, this antiphon serves as the focal point for a brief rite of Eucharistic adoration in an otherwise non-Eucharistic Palm Sunday procession. The manual specifies that in the course of the palm procession a priest vested in an alb and a silk cope (a silver cope, according to a fifteenth-century missal for York Cathedral)[129] carries the Blessed Sacrament in a silver pyx out from the eastern end of the church as two deacons and two acolytes carry a canopy over the Sacrament and two clerics bear torches ahead of the Eucharist. When this Eucharistic procession reaches the outdoor station where the palm procession has paused, the priest serving as celebrant for the day's liturgy greets the Blessed Sacrament with a threefold recitation of the words *"Worthy are you, O Lord our God, to receive glory and honor"*, genuflecting each time. The choir then repeats his actions, chanting the same antiphon three times with three genuflections. The priest carrying the Eucharist then brings the Sacrament back into the church, going the same way by which he came.[130] A comparable salutation of Christ in the Blessed Sacrament during the Palm Sunday procession, with the antiphon *"Worthy are you"* and genuflections, appears in the French monastic customaries of Bec (c. 1300) and Lyre (c. 1400).[131]

---

[127] This antiphon is traceable to the late thirteenth-century Sarum Missal, from which the complete text is here taken; see Legg, *Sarum Missal*, 95 (Latin text quoted and translated by permission of Oxford University Press).

[128] Martène, *De antiquis ecclesiae ritibus*, bk. 4, chap. 20, *ordo* 7, 3:77.

[129] Manuscript: Cambridge, England, Sidney Sussex College, Cambridge University, missal of York, fifteenth century, in William George Henderson, ed., *Missale ad usum insignis ecclesiae Eboracensis*, vol. 1, Surtees Society Publications 59 (Durham, England: Andrews, 1874), 86–87 (text "D").

[130] Text in William George Henderson, ed., *Manuale et processionale ad usum insignis ecclesiae Eboracensis*, Surtees Society Publications 63 (Durham, England: Andrews, 1875), 149.

[131] For the Bec customary, see Edmond Martène, *De antiquis monachorum ritibus*, bk. 3, chap. 12, no. 15, in Martène, *De antiquis ecclesiae ritibus*, 4:120; for the Lyre customary, see ibid.

The Sarum Rite palm procession continues westward along the south side of the cathedral, heading for a third station before the western portal of the church. The station concludes with the lifting of the Eucharistic feretory over the lintel of the door through which the rest of the procession will reenter the cathedral, an action seemingly inspired by Christ's identification of himself as "the door of the sheep": "I am the door. By me, if any man enter in, he shall be saved" (Jn 10:7, 9). Moreover, it brings to mind the marking of the lintels of the Israelites' homes with the protecting blood of the unblemished lamb that prefigured Christ's saving blood shed on the Cross (Ex 12:7):

> This [second] station finished, the procession should go through the middle of the cloister on the right hand up to the western door of the church, singing the responsory: *The chief priests and the Pharisees gathered a council and said: "What do we, for this man performs many miracles? If we leave him thus, all will believe in him; lest perhaps the Romans should come and destroy our place and nation."* [132] Here the third station should be made, namely before the aforesaid door, where three clerics of higher rank, with their vesture unchanged, turned toward the people, should sing in the doorway itself the verse: *But one of them, Caiphas by name, as he would have been high priest that year, prophesied, saying: "It is expedient for you that one man should die for the people, and that the whole nation should not perish." From that day, therefore, they thought to kill him, saying, "Lest perhaps the Romans should come, and the Gentiles, and destroy our place and nation."*
>
> These things having been finished, they should enter the church through the same door, under the bier and the small box of relics lifted up transversely over the door, singing the responsory: *The Lord entering the Holy City* . . . [133]

In the above rubrics, the entry of the procession into the church is preceded simply by the chanting of one versicle. But in the Eucharistic Palm Sunday procession of the English see of Winchester, the entry through the city gate would be prefaced by a chanted dialogue, as recorded in a twelfth- to thirteenth-century gradual of Winchester. The palm procession, in which the Blessed Sacrament is carried on a bier, would divide into two groups prior to reaching the city gate. Before the gate, those in the group accompanying the city's bishop come to a stop a few yards away from the group accompanying the Blessed Sacrament. Two youths in the bishop's group then address the second retinue, asking them, "*Who is this?*" Those accompanying the Blessed Sacrament, described in the rubrics as speaking "just as

---

[132] This responsory, *Collegerunt pontifices*, is first mentioned in the late ninth-century pontifical of northern France formerly known as the Pontifical of Poitiers and in the Mass chant portion of the Antiphonary of Compiègne (France, c. 870); see respectively Martini, *Cosiddetto pontificale di Poitiers*, 85, and Hésbert, *Antiphonale missarum sextuplex*, 223.

[133] Martène, *De antiquis ecclesiae ritibus*, bk. 4, chap. 20, ordo 7, 3:77.

the disciples of Christ", reply: "*This is he who was going to come for the salvation of the people.*" The two youths in the bishop's retinue ask further, "*Of what manner is this one?*" The "disciples" respond, "*This is our salvation and Israel's redemption.*"[134]

In the Sarum Rite procession, the fourth and final station is made inside the cathedral, with veneration accorded to the unveiled crucifix at the entrance to the choir (evidently the rood screen crucifix), thereby incorporating the primary visual image of the Passion into the Sarum observances:

> Here should be made the fourth station before the cross within the church; and at the station itself the executor of the office should begin the antiphon *Hail,* with the cross now uncovered, and the choir with a genuflection should respond, kissing the ground, *our King, Son of David, Redeemer of the world, whom the prophets foretold to be the Savior coming to the house of Israel; for the Father sent you into the world to be a saving Victim, whom all the saints have awaited from the beginning of the world, and now* [*await*]. *Hosanna, O Son of David. Blessed is He who comes in the name of the Lord. Hosanna in the highest*; and the senior [cleric] should begin the antiphon thus three times, each time raising his voice; his genuflection should be made together with the choir; and after the third commencement, the choir should continue the same antiphon, remaining at the station itself; which [antiphon] having been finished, it [the choir] should enter the choir. All the crosses throughout the church should be uncovered until after Vespers.[135]

In the above text we see the dramatic use of the antiphon *Ave Rex noster,* a Palm Sunday chant traceable to the late tenth century[136] and usually assigned to the station before the cross. In the Sarum procession, as in the earlier-described tenth-century procession of the Romano-Germanic Pontifical, the cross would remain stationary as it was being venerated. But in the Spanish Palm Sunday rite of Seville (1534), the celebrating priest would take the crucifix into his hands and hold it for the threefold chanting of the *Ave Rex noster.*[137] The above-cited Sarum rubrics specify that the cross is to be unveiled prior to beginning the station before it and that the church's other crosses are to be

---

[134] Manuscript: Oxford, England, Bodleian Library, MS Rawlinson C. 892, fol. 47r; Latin text quoted in Karl Young, *The Drama of the Medieval Church* (Oxford: Clarendon, 1933), 1:92 (Latin text quoted and translated by permission of Oxford University Press).

[135] Martène, *De antiquis ecclesiae ritibus,* bk. 4, chap. 20, ordo 7, 3:77.

[136] This antiphon first appears in the Benedictine customary of Saint Vanne, Verdun, France (c. 990), in Bruno Albers, ed., *Consuetudines monasticae,* vol. 5, *Consuetudines monasteriorum Germaniae necnon s. Vitonis Virdunensis et Floriacensis abbatiae monumenta saeculi decimi continens* (Monte Cassino, Italy: Typis Societatis Editricis Castri Casini, 1912), 117.

[137] *Missale divinorum secundum consuetudinem alme ecclesie Hispalensis* (Seville, Spain: Joannes Varela, 1534), fol. 65r–65v. The Latin text of this missal has been graciously provided to the author by the Biblioteca Apostolica Vaticana, Vatican City (shelf mark Stamp. Barb. B. X. 4).

unveiled afterward. The unveiling of the crucifix or cross before or during the Palm Sunday procession in the medieval rites was likely intended to represent our Lord's open manifestation of himself in entering Jerusalem publicly on Palm Sunday after concealing himself for a time (Jn 8:59: "But Jesus hid himself, and went out of the temple"),[138] the latter concealment having been represented by the Roman custom (traceable to the twelfth century) of veiling crosses and crucifixes not from the beginning of Lent but rather from Passion Sunday onward, when the Gospel of John 8:46–59 was read.[139] In the Palm Sunday rite of the 1543 missal of Bayonne, France, the unveiling takes place in a most dramatic manner during the station before the cross and is clearly modeled upon the unveiling and veneration of the cross observed on Good Friday:

> And before they shall have come to the door of the church, the priest should begin the following antiphon, kneeling thrice, holding the cross in his hands, and with the uncovering of it, as is customary. In the first instance, he should uncover the right arm of the cross; in the second instance, the left; in the third instance, all the rest of the cross. Then with the cross a blessing should be rendered over the people; afterward it should be placed in an honorable place and be adored by the people. Antiphon: *Hail, our King, Son of David, Redeemer of the world . . .*[140]

The ringing of bells for the entry of the Palm Sunday procession into the destination church or through the city gates is found in numerous medieval texts, beginning in the tenth century with the Benedictine customaries of Cluny, France (tenth-century redaction),[141] and Einsiedeln, Switzerland (c. 984).[142] Many such texts also specify the ringing of the bells for the beginning of the procession. The customary composed by Archbishop Lanfranc for England's Canterbury Cathedral (c. 1077) directs that all the bells are to be rung when the procession

---

[138] This interpretation is given by Malherbe, "Le 'Palmezel'", 84.

[139] This practice is first mentioned in Cardinal Bernard of Porto's *Ordo officiorum* for the canons regular of Rome's Church of Saint John Lateran (c. 1140), which specifies the veiling of crosses after the Gospel of Passion Sunday; see Fischer, *Bernhardi cardinalis . . . Ordo officiorum ecclesiae Lateranensis*, 41. The 1488 *Caeremoniale Romanum* of the papal master of ceremonies Patrizio Piccolomini prescribes in addition to the veiling of the crosses the raising of a veil to conceal all the images on the altar, pulled into place with pulley-mounted cords by clerics of the papal chapel upon the pronouncement of the concluding words of the Passion Sunday Gospel, "But Jesus hid himself, and went out of the temple"; see Dykmans, *Oeuvre de Patrizi Piccolomini*, 2:354. The Passion Sunday veiling of crosses and images was universally promulgated in the *Caeremoniale episcoporum* of 1600; see Triacca and Sodi, *Caeremoniale episcoporum: Editio princeps (1600)*, bk. 2, chap. 20, pp. 225–226 (new pagination).

[140] Dubarat, *Missel de Bayonne de 1543*, 38. A similar threefold unveiling of a crucifix during the threefold singing of the *Ave Rex noster* appears earlier in the Palm Sunday rite from the fourteenth-century *Ordinarium canonorum regularum* of the Priory of Saint-Lô, a community of Augustinian canons regular in Rouen, France (PL 147, col. 167).

[141] Text in Hallinger, *Consuetudines Cluniacensium antiquiores*, 66.

[142] Text in Albers, *Consuetudines monasticae*, 5:89.

is exiting the choir of the church where the Palm Sunday rite begins. The "two greater bells" are rung as the procession enters the city and are continually sounded until the procession begins to enter the choir of the destination church, at which point the other bells are rung for Mass, and the "two greater bells" fall silent.[143] The custom of ringing all the bells as the procession enters the destination church appeared in Rome by the twelfth century.[144] In Rouen, France, where the Eucharist was carried in the city's principal Palm Sunday procession, the Priory of Saint-Lô, a community of Augustinian canons regular, would salute with bells the approach of the Blessed Sacrament to their quarter of the city: a fourteenth-century *Ordinarium* of the priory enjoins that as soon as the "cymbals" rung in the city's palm procession were heard at the priory, signaling that the procession was near, two of the priory's bells were to be rung "in honor of the Body of the Lord" as the procession entered and traversed the boundaries of the canons' parish.[145] A German *Ordinarium* for the city of Münster, dating from 1599 but probably preserving a medieval tradition in this regard, specifies that when the Palm Sunday procession is spotted from the bell tower of the cathedral church, the "great bells" are rung together continuously until the procession arrives before the cathedral's western doors, where a station is made before entering.[146]

The Mass of Palm Sunday

With the conclusion of the Palm Sunday procession, there was a stark and swift transition in the medieval rites from the joy of Christ's entry into Jerusalem to the solemn contemplation of the Passion pervading the Palm Sunday Mass. This transition was in some cases expressed through a change of vestments, as can be seen in the 1568 *Missale Pallantinum* of Palencia, Spain: "Then the priest and the ministers, taking off their white vestments in the sacristy, put on a black chasuble and dalmatics [respectively] and approach the altar, likewise covered with black ornaments, with the cross that has been placed on the altar also covered with a black veil." [147] Such a custom existed from the twelfth century, when it is mentioned in a Holy Week *ordo* of the Benedictine abbey of Monte Cassino, Italy, which calls for a change to purple vestments between the palm procession and the

---

[143] Knowles and Brooke, *The Monastic Constitutions of Lanfranc*, chap. 25, pp. 36, 38, 40 (Latin text quoted and translated by permission of Oxford University Press).

[144] Twelfth-century Roman Pontifical, in Andrieu, *Pontifical romain au moyen-âge*, 1:214; *Ordo* of Bernard of Porto for the Church of Saint John Lateran (c. 1140), in Fischer, *Bernhardi cardinalis . . . Ordo officiorum ecclesiae Lateranensis*, 43.

[145] *Ordinarium canonorum regularum*, for the Priory of Saint-Lô, Rouen, France (PL 147, col. 167).

[146] Text in Francis Schubert and Richard Stapper, eds., *Excerpta ex ordinariis Germanicis de summis anni ecclesiastici festivitatibus*, Opuscula et textus historiam ecclesiae eiusque vitam atque doctrinam illustrantia: Series liturgica, fasc. 7–8 (Münster, Germany: Aschendorff, 1936), 51, footnote.

[147] *Missale Pallantinum* (1568), fol. 74r.

Mass.[148] Durandus explains that the immediate progression from the victory motif of the procession to the suffering motif of the Mass is inherent to the commemoration of Christ's sacrifice, for we are both "glad of the fruit of the Passion" and "suffer because he has suffered for us"; we have reason both to rejoice "because of the love that he has shown us on the Cross" and to mourn "on account of our sins that are so many that it was therefore necessary for the Son of God to suffer".[149]

The Collect, the Secret, and the Postcommunion for the day's Mass were the same throughout late medieval Europe, the first two traceable to seventh-century Rome,[150] with the Postcommunion being added to the Palm Sunday Mass soon afterward in the eighth-century *Hadrianum* redaction of Rome's Gregorian Sacramentary.[151] The assignment of the Preface of the Holy Cross to this Mass appears for the first time in the Ordinal of the Papal Court, dating from the pontificate of Pope Innocent III (1198–1216).[152] The chants for this Mass (the Introit, the Gradual, the Tract, the Offertory, and the Communion), all of which are traceable to the eighth century,[153] were retained in the *Missale Romanum* of 1570 along with the aforementioned prayers.[154]

The Epistle for the Palm Sunday Mass, from the Letter of Saint Paul to the Philippians (Phil 2:5–11), first specified in the seventh-century Roman lectionary known as the *Comes* of Würzburg,[155] prevailed in medieval rites and entered the *Missale Romanum* of 1570.[156] The custom of a genuflection during this Epistle, when the words are read regarding the bending of every knee at the name of Jesus (*ut in nomine Jesu omne genu flectatur*), is first mentioned in a book of rites for cardinals and bishops composed in the early 1520s by the papal master of ceremonies and bishop Paride de Grassis (+1528).[157] This observance soon spread beyond Rome, appearing as a rubric in the 1568

---

[148] Text in Teodoro Leuterman, *Ordo Casinensis hebdomadae maioris (saec. XII)*, Miscellanea Cassinese 20 (Monte Cassino, Italy: Monte Cassino Abbey, 1941), 97.

[149] Durandus, *Rationale* (CCCM 140a), bk. 6, chap. 67, no. 11, p. 325.

[150] Both prayers are found in the Paduan redaction of the Gregorian Sacramentary; see Deshusses, *Sacramentaire grégorien*, Paduan nos. 281–282, 1:628.

[151] Deshusses, *Sacramentaire grégorien*, no. 314, 1:168.

[152] Text in Van Dijk and Walker, *The Ordinal of the Papal Court*, 218.

[153] The Introit, the Offertory, and the Communion first appear in the Mass antiphonary of Mount Blandin (Belgium, c. 750–800); the Gradual and the Tract first appear in the Cantatorium of Monza (Italy, eighth century); see Hésbert, *Antiphonale missarum sextuplex*, 86, 88.

[154] Sodi and Triacca, *Missale Romanum: Editio princeps (1570)*, 214–215, 221 (new pagination).

[155] Germain Morin, "Le plus ancien *Comes* ou lectionnaire de l'église romaine", *Revue Bénédictine* 27 (1910): 53–54.

[156] Sodi and Triacca, *Missale Romanum: Editio princeps (1570)*, 214 (new pagination).

[157] Paride de Grassis, *De caeremoniis cardinalium et episcoporum in eorum dioecesibus* (first published posthumously in 1564; Rome: Bernardinus Donangelus, 1587; digitized text, Bayerische Staatsbibliothek, Munich, 2009), bk. 2, chap. 44, p. 236.

350

Missale Pallantinum of Palencia, Spain.[158] Ultimately, the practice was universally promulgated through its appearance in the *Caeremoniale episcoporum* of 1600.[159] It may in fact be an adaptation of an earlier practice of kneeling for these same words during the Introit on Wednesday of Holy Week, an observance found in a thirteenth-century liturgical text of Zurich, Switzerland, the *Liber ordinarius* of Konrad von Mure, a cantor of the city's cathedral (+1281).[160]

We know from the sermons of Pope Saint Leo the Great (+461) that the practice of reading a Gospel account of the Passion on the Sunday before Easter had been established in Rome by the fifth century.[161] The specific use of Saint Matthew's Passion, first attested in the seventh-century Capitulary of Würzburg,[162] remained the norm throughout the Middle Ages and entered the *Missale Romanum* of 1570.[163] The significance of the Passion reading on Palm Sunday is explained by Sicard of Cremona:

> But the Passion is read during the Mass, for the Lord entering Jerusalem is explained by the chalice of his Passion, or because "mourning taketh hold of the end of joy" (Prov 14:13), and therefore, after the joy of the procession is added the reading of the Passion; or because the Lord in that exultation introduced the lamentation of destruction (cf. Lk 19:41–44); and because he said hanging on the Cross, "My God, my God, why hast thou forsaken me?" (Mt 27:46).[164]

In the medieval liturgy, the readings of the Gospel accounts of the Passion during Holy Week (on Palm Sunday, Tuesday, Wednesday, and Good Friday) were marked by a number of practices intended to set these readings in a context all their own, distinct from the Gospel readings for the rest of the liturgical year. In the early fifth century, the Church Father Saint Augustine (+430) speaks of the Passion being read "solemnly" on Good Friday.[165] During the Middle Ages, changes were made to the customary ceremonies for beginning the Gospel reading in order to express mourning for the sufferings and death of Christ related in the Passion narratives. The tenth-century

---

[158] *Missale Pallantinum* (1568), fol. 74r.

[159] Triacca and Sodi, *Caeremoniale episcoporum: Editio princeps (1600)*, bk. 2, chap. 21, p. 229 (new pagination).

[160] Text in Heidi Leuppi, *Der Liber ordinarius des Konrad von Mure: Die Gottesdienstordnung am Grossmünster in Zürich*, Spicilegium Friburgense: Texte zur Geschichte des kirchlichen Lebens 37 (Fribourg, Switzerland: Universitätsverlag Freiburg, 1995), 244.

[161] See particularly *Sermon 54* of Pope Saint Leo the Great, a homily delivered on the Sunday before Easter, at the conclusion of which Pope Leo states that the Passion will be "repeated" on Wednesday, thereby implying that the Passion had already been read on that Sunday (PL 54, col. 322).

[162] Text in Germain Morin, "Liturgie et basiliques de Rome au milieu du VIIᵉ siècle d'après les listes d'évangiles de Würzburg", *Revue Bénédictine* 28 (1911): 304.

[163] Sodi and Triacca, *Missale Romanum: Editio princeps (1570)*, 215–221 (new pagination).

[164] Sicard of Cremona, *Mitrale*, bk. 6, chap. 10, PL 213, col. 293.

[165] Saint Augustine, *Sermon 218*, no. 1, PL 38, col. 1084.

Romano-Germanic Pontifical directs that on Good Friday the Passion is to be read without the pre-Gospel salutation, *"The Lord be with you"*, and without incense being carried; for Palm Sunday, the text simply states that some omit the salutation from the Passion reading on this day as well (the incense omission is not mentioned).[166] An *ordo* of French origin thought to date from the late tenth century specifies for Good Friday the omission of lights as well as the omission of incense.[167] The Roman rubrics of the *Liber censuum* (c. 1192) for Good Friday add to these omissions the use of a stripped pulpit; this text also introduces a practice to delineate the portion of the Gospel preceding Christ's death from the concluding portion that follows his death: it directs that at the words *"Post haec autem rogavit Pilatum Joseph"* (Jn 19:38: *"And after these things, Joseph of Arimathea . . . besought Pilate"*), the use of incense for the Gospel should be resumed, that is, that incense should be brought to the pulpit as it is normally brought for beginning the Gospel.[168]

By the thirteenth century, all of the aforementioned omissions marked the Passion on Palm Sunday as well as on Good Friday, with Sicard of Cremona (+1215) adding the omission of the customary kiss of the Gospel book.[169] Both the Franciscan *Ordo missalis* of the friars' superior general Haymo of Faversham (c. 1244) and a missal of central Italy (c. 1250) specify the omission of the blessing that the deacon would normally receive from the celebrant before reading the Gospel; both of these texts add that the omissions of the blessing, the lights, and the incense should be observed at all of the Holy Week readings of the Passion (on Palm Sunday, Tuesday, Wednesday, and Good Friday).[170] Sicard, the Franciscan *Ordo*, and the Italian missal all speak of the resumption of the omitted practices when the portion of the Passion following Christ's death is read.[171] By the mid-fourteenth century, all of these omissions at the beginning of the Passion and their resumption before the end of the Passion, as well as the stripped pulpit for Good Friday, had become the norm

---

[166] Vogel and Elze, *Pontifical romano-germanique*, 2:87, 51, respectively.

[167] Roman *Ordo* 33, in Michel Andrieu, ed., *Les Ordines Romani du haut moyen âge*, vol. 3, SSLED 24 (Louvain, Belgium: "Spicilegium sacrum Lovaniense" Administration, 1951), 531.

[168] Text in Fabre and Duchesne, *Le Liber censuum de l'église romaine*, no. 29, vol. 1, fasc. 2, p. 296.

[169] Sicard of Cremona, *Mitrale*, bk. 6, chap. 10, PL 213, col. 294.

[170] See respectively the Franciscan *Ordo missalis* and the text known as the Lateran Missal in Stephen J. P. Van Dijk, O.F.M., *Sources of the Modern Roman Liturgy: The Ordinals by Haymo of Faversham and Related Documents (1243–1307)*, Studia et documenta Franciscana 2 (Leiden, Netherlands: E. J. Brill, 1963), 2:236, 240, and Shin-Ho Chang, ed., *Vetus missale Romanum monasticum Lateranense archivii basilicae Lateranensis, codex A65 (olim 65)*, MSIL 20 (Vatican City: Libreria Editrice Vaticana, 2002), 164.

[171] Sicard of Cremona, *Mitrale*, bk. 6, chap. 10, PL 213, col. 294; Van Dijk, *Sources of the Modern Roman Liturgy*, 2:136; Chang, *Vetus missale Romanum*, 164.

in the papal liturgy,[172] from which they later entered the universally promulgated *Missale Romanum* of 1570 and the *Caeremoniale episcoporum* of 1600.[173] The reading of the Passion in the Palm Sunday rite of the 1534 missal of Seville was marked by a unique practice: the sacristan would replace the incense usually used at the Gospel with a substance obviously symbolic of the death and burial of Christ: "He [the deacon] begins the Passion, which should be said without the blessing, and without the salutation, and without incense. However, in place of incense, on this day myrrh should be placed by the sacristan; and he should hold the cross, covered, near the deacon."[174]

According to Durandus, the deacon beginning the Passion omits the petition for a blessing because the Passion describes the taking away of him who is the Author of all blessings. The lights are omitted because the Passion announces the extinction by death of him who is the Light of the world, as well as the spiritual extinction of the disciples to whom he had said, "You are the light of the world" (Mt 5:14). The incense is omitted because in the Passion the Apostles' "fervor of devotion or prayer" grew tepid and was even extinguished. The salutation is omitted because of the duplicitous salutations offered to Christ by his enemies during his Passion.[175] The stripped pulpit represents Christ divested of his clothes on the naked Cross, as well as the nakedness of the innermost Holy of Holies in the Temple of Jerusalem, exposed by the rending of the Temple veil at the death of Christ.[176] The subsequent resumption of the use of lights, incense, etc., for the concluding portion of the Passion in which the events immediately following the death of Christ are related is explained by Durandus as a way of marking the consummation of the Savior's Passion and death.[177] We would add that this practice, particularly with regard to the resumption of lights, may have also been inspired by the return of daylight following the death of Christ, which is implied by the Gospel accounts of darkness from the sixth hour until the ninth hour, when Christ died (cf. Mt 27:45; Mk 15:33; Lk 23:44).

The marking of Gospel texts of the Passion with lettering to distinguish the words of Christ from the words of narration and from the words of other individuals (Judas, Caiphas, Pilate, etc.) can be traced back to

---

[172] See the papal ceremonial of Giacomo Cardinal Stefaneschi, dating from about 1325, in Marc Dykmans, ed., *Le cérémonial papal de la fin du moyen âge à la Renaissance*, vol. 2, BIHBR 25 (Brussels and Rome: Institut Historique Belge de Rome, 1981), 388–389; see also the Long Ceremonial of John of Sion, dating from a little before 1342, in Dykmans, *Cérémonial papal de la fin du moyen âge à la Renaissance*, 3:215, 216.

[173] Sodi and Triacca, *Missale Romanum: Editio princeps (1570)*, 215, 242 (new pagination); Triacca and Sodi, *Caeremoniale episcoporum: Editio princeps (1600)*, bk. 2, chap. 21, pp. 229–230 (new pagination).

[174] *Missale . . . ecclesie Hispalensis* (1534), fol. 66r.

[175] Durandus, *Rationale* (CCCM 140a), bk. 6, chap. 68, no. 5, p. 329.

[176] Ibid., chap. 77, no. 9, pp. 372–373.

[177] Ibid., chap. 68, no. 5, p. 329.

the seventh or the eighth century, when markings of this nature appear in the Bobbio Missal, a liturgical book of French or north Italian origin.[178] The purpose of these markings is explained by a monk of Switzerland's Saint Gall Abbey, Notker Balbulus (c. 840–912), who provides a table of "what the individual letters in superscription should signify to music", with the individual letters corresponding to particular tones of voice.[179] Numerous early medieval texts speak of only one deacon for the singing of the Passion.[180] The subsequent practice of dividing the reading of the Passion among multiple cantors, usually three in number, may have been introduced as early as the tenth century: a Benedictine missal of this period is thought to indicate such a division of parts.[181] The practice is explicitly mentioned for the first time in a Dominican text, the *Gros livre* of 1254.[182] A gradual for England's Sarum Rite dating from about 1300, the manuscript of which is preserved in Parma, Italy, distributes the parts of the Passion among five cantors, with an additional cantor assigned exclusively to the words spoken by Christ on the Cross.[183] The 1488 *Caeremoniale Romanum* of the papal master of ceremonies Patrizio Piccolomini is the earliest Roman document to specify three cantors for the chanting of the Passion on Palm Sunday and Good Friday,[184] a practice that was later universally promulgated in the *Caeremoniale episcoporum* of 1600.[185]

In regard to marking the moment of Christ's death in the Holy Week readings of the Passion, the earliest mention of such a practice, albeit for Good Friday only, appears in the twelfth-century *Ordo* of Beroldus for the Ambrosian Rite liturgy of Milan, Italy; it prescribes an extinction of the lights and a stripping of the altar at the moment of Christ's death in the Good Friday reading of the Passion (in the Ambrosian liturgy, Saint Matthew's Passion—at the words *"emisit spiritum"*, *"yielded up the ghost"* [Mt 27:50]).[186] The practice of kneeling out of reverence for the moment of Christ's death arose during or shortly before the thirteenth century, when it is mentioned in Geoffrey of Beaulieu's biography of Saint Louis IX of France (+1270):

> Similarly he [King Louis] perceived that in certain monasteries, when were pronounced *Inclinato capite emisit spiritum* [cf. Mt 27:50; Jn 19:30]

[178] Lowe, *Bobbio Missal: Text*, nos. 202–204, pp. 63–65.

[179] Notker Balbulus, *De musica*, PL 131, cols. 1171–1172.

[180] See, for example, Roman *Ordo* 31 (c. 850–900), in Andrieu, *Ordines Romani du haut moyen âge*, 3:497.

[181] Gerhard Römer, "Die Liturgie des Karfreitags", *Zeitschrift für Katholische Theologie* 77 (1955): 64.

[182] See Kurt Von Fischer, "Passion", *New Grove Dictionary of Music and Musicians* (Washington, D.C.: Grove's Dictionaries of Music, 1980), 14:277–278.

[183] Ibid., 278.

[184] Dykmans, *Oeuvre de Patrizi Piccolomini*, 2:359, 382.

[185] Triacca and Sodi, *Caeremoniale episcoporum: Editio princeps (1600)*, bk. 2, chaps. 21, 25, pp. 229–230, 245–246 (new pagination).

[186] Magistretti, *Beroldus, sive Ecclesiae Ambrosianae Mediolanensis ... ordines*, 106.

or *Expiravit* [Mk 15:37; Lk 23:46] during the four Passions, which [were read] during Holy Week, which is commonly called the Dolorous [Week], the religious community, devoutly kneeling and falling prostrate, applied themselves a little to prayer. Which also the devout king afterward made to be observed similarly in his chapel and in several churches. Whence also at his request, this pious custom was approved and established in the Order of Friars Preachers [the Dominican Order].[187]

This observance was subsequently mandated by a council of the French see of Paris held in 1261.[188] The *Ordinarium* of the Carmelite Order compiled by the Carmelites' German provincial Sibert de Beka, dating from around 1312, prescribes the same custom for the moment of Christ's death in all of the Passion readings of Holy Week, directing that the priest, the clerics assisting him, and the choir are all to prostrate themselves, "devoutly giving thanks to the Redeemer".[189] The Long Ceremonial, attributed to John of Sion and dating from a little before 1342, the earliest papal liturgical text to mention the practice, provides detailed directions in this regard for Saint Matthew's Passion on Palm Sunday:

> But when the [cardinal] deacon shall have said those words in the Passion, *Emisit spiritum*, immediately the pope and the cardinal deacon and all the others kneel to God, turned toward the altar, and they remain kneeling thus for the interval that the Our Father could be said once. Afterward they rise, and the said cardinal deacon continues the Passion in his [accustomed] manner.[190]

This custom spread elsewhere during the 1300s.[191] A century later, the above-cited Sarum Missal of Salisbury, England (c. 1489), specifies that the deacon reading the Passion, after pronouncing the words regarding Christ's death, should either bow or prostrate himself "toward the east" and recite privately an Our Father, a Hail Mary, and the Lord's

---

[187] Geoffrey of Beaulieu, *Vita sancti Ludovici Regis*, chap. 36 (alternately identified as chap. 6, nos. 55–56), in Bolland et al., *Acta sanctorum*, August, 5:554.

[188] Ibid., 555, endnotes.

[189] Text in Benedict Zimmerman, ed., *Ordinaire de l'ordre de Notre-Dame du Mont-Carmel*, Bibliothèque liturgique 13 (Paris: Alphonse Picard et Fils, 1910), 160.

[190] Dykmans, *Cérémonial papal de la fin du moyen âge à la Renaissance*, 3:205.

[191] See, for example, the early fourteenth-century ceremonial for the Cathedral of Saint Peter in Cologne, Germany (Amberg, *Ceremoniale Coloniense*, 136). Likewise, the rubrics of the late fourteenth-century ceremonial for the Benedictine "Sagro Speco" monastery of Subiaco, Italy, specify kneeling upon the pronouncement of the words "*Et inclinato capite emisit spiritum*" or their equivalent in the Passion readings during Holy Week; see Joachim Angerer, O.Praem., ed., *Caeremoniae regularis observantiae sanctissimi patris nostri Benedicti ex ipsius regula sumptae, secundum quod in sacris locis, scilicet Specu et Monasterio Sublacensi practicantur*, Corpus consuetudinum monasticarum 11, pt. 1 (Siegburg, Germany: Franciscus Schmitt, 1985), 86–87.

own words, "*Into your hands I commend my spirit*" (cf. Lk 23:46).[192] The 1568 *Missale Pallantinum* of Palencia, Spain, instructs the deacon at the moment of Christ's death to strike the Gospel book lightly with his right hand before kneeling to pray privately "some brief and devout prayer".[193] This hand action, which was repeated at all the Holy Week readings of the Passion[194] and was similarly observed in Seville (missal of 1534),[195] was probably intended to symbolize the convulsion of nature at the moment of the Lord's passing (the earthquake, the rending of the rocks, the opening of the graves, and the parting of the Temple veil, as recounted in Matthew 27:51–52). The genuflection for Christ's death during the four Passion readings of Holy Week was universally promulgated in the *Missale Romanum* of 1570.[196]

The tenth-century Romano-Germanic Pontifical specifies that the clergy and the laity are to hold their palm branches all the way to the end of the Palm Sunday Mass, a direction later repeated in the Ordinal of the Papal Court (from the pontificate of Pope Innocent III, 1198–1216).[197] The English Benedictine *Regularis concordia* (c. 960) and the Benedictine customary of Fructuaria, Italy (c. 1085), direct that the palms be held in the hands by those who have received them until the Offertory of the Palm Sunday Mass, when they are to be offered to the priest celebrating the Mass.[198] In the universally promulgated *Rituale Romanum* of 1614, the continued holding of palms during the Palm Sunday Mass (after the procession) is limited to the reading of the Passion.[199]

The custom of reading a Gospel account of the Passion on Wednesday of Holy Week had arisen in Rome by the fifth century, when it is mentioned by Pope Saint Leo the Great (+461).[200] The reading of the Passion of Saint Luke during the Mass of this day, first attested in the seventh-century Capitulary of Würzburg,[201] remained the norm throughout the Middle Ages and entered the *Missale Romanum* of

Wednesday of Holy Week

---

[192] 1489 *Sarum Missal*, in Martène, *De antiquis ecclesiae ritibus*, bk. 4, chap. 20, *ordo* 7, 3:77.

[193] *Missale Pallantinum* (1568), fol. 77r–77v.

[194] Ibid., fols. 81v (Saint Mark on Tuesday), 85v (Saint Luke on Wednesday), and 92r (Saint John on Good Friday).

[195] *Missale . . . ecclesie Hispalensis* (1534), fols. 69r (Palm Sunday), 73v (Tuesday), 77v (Wednesday), and 82v (Good Friday).

[196] Sodi and Triacca, *Missale Romanum: Editio princeps (1570)*, 220, 228, 235, 245 (new pagination).

[197] Van Dijk and Walker, *Ordinal of the Papal Court*, 218.

[198] Symons, *Regularis concordia*, chap. 4, no. 36, pp. 35–36; *Consuetudines* of Fructuaria, Italy, bk. 1, chap. 44, in Albers, *Consuetudines monasticae*, 4:47.

[199] Sodi and Flores Arcas, *Rituale Romanum: Editio princeps (1614)*, 174 (original pagination).

[200] Saint Leo the Great, *Sermon 54*, PL 54, col. 322.

[201] Morin, "Liturgie et basiliques de Rome", 304. The reading of Saint Mark's Passion on Tuesday of Holy Week arose later, in the tenth century; see Hermann Schmidt, S.J., *Hebdomada sancta* (Rome: Herder, 1956–1957), 2:673, 674.

1570.[202] The custom of unveiling the altar by withdrawing a curtain, usually the Lenten veil, during this reading, at the words "*Velum templi scissum est*" (Lk 23:45: "*The veil of the temple was rent in the midst*") can be traced back to the eleventh century, when it is mentioned in the *Liber de officiis ecclesiasticis* of John of Avranches, a liturgical text for Rouen, France,[203] as well as in the Benedictine customary of Fructuaria, Italy (c. 1085), which provides detailed directions in this regard:

> They should also put two curtains on a cord before the altar, namely on that [cord] on which it hangs through all of Lent; a slender cord should be fastened on both sides, that when the deacon shall have said at the Passion, *Velum templi scissum est*, there should be two brothers, one from one side of the church, the other from the other side outside the choir, and with each drawing his slender cord to himself the curtains should be parted from each other; but after Compline, they should be removed.[204]

We find this dramatic action also in the Holy Week rubrics of the 1568 *Missale Pallantinum* of Palencia, Spain, with the direction appearing immediately after the words in the Passion of Saint Luke regarding the rending of the Temple veil: "Which having been said, the veil that was hanging before the altar is dropped, and falls to the earth, and it does not hang there any longer."[205]

---

[202] Sodi and Triacca, *Missale Romanum: Editio princeps (1570)*, 230–235 (new pagination). The Tuesday reading of Saint Mark's Passion was also retained in the 1570 missal; see ibid., 223–228 (new pagination).

[203] John of Avranches, *Liber de officiis ecclesiasticis*, PL 147, col. 48.

[204] *Consuetudines* of Fructuaria, Italy, bk. 1, chap. 45, in Albers, *Consuetudines monasticae*, 4:48–49.

[205] *Missale Pallantinum* (1568), fol. 85v.

I3 Holy Thursday

Truly, Christ rising from the Supper is his coming from the seat of the Father; his laying aside his vesture is his emptying himself; his girding with a linen cloth is his taking the form of a slave; his putting water into a basin is his shedding his own blood; his washing the feet is his forgiving sins; his wiping dry with the linen cloth is his purifying us by faith in his Passion; his resuming his vesture is his rising from the dead and his putting on the glorious vesture of his flesh; his reclining is his ascending and sitting at the right hand of the Father.... His teaching the disciples is his sending them the Holy Spirit.

William Durandus of Mende (+1296)[1]

Tenebrae

The Church's celebration of the three days leading to Easter as a unique Triduum of liturgical rites commemorating the Passion, death, and Resurrection of Christ had developed by the fourth century.[2] This retracing of Christ's journey from suffering to glory came to be perceived as corresponding to the three days of Christ's burial, with the emphasis at the outset of the Triduum upon his Passion and death, in preparation for the joy of his Resurrection at the Triduum's conclusion. Before the end of the eighth century, there appeared the custom of silencing the church bells from Holy Thursday until the Easter Vigil (attested for the first time in Roman *Ordo 17*, c. 780–790).[3] Both Amalarius of Metz (+c. 850) and the tenth-century author known as Pseudo-Alcuin identify the Triduum of Holy Thursday, Good Friday, and Holy Saturday as a commemoration of the Savior's three days in the tomb.[4] William Durandus of Mende (+1296) states that for these

---

[1] William Durandus of Mende, *Rationale divinorum officiorum*, bk. 6, chap. 75, no. 7, in A. Davril, O.S.B., and T.M. Thibodeau, eds., *Guillelmi Duranti: Rationale divinorum officiorum V–VI*, CCCM 140a (Turnhout, Belgium: Brepols, 1998), 363–364. Hereafter cited as Durandus, *Rationale* (CCCM 140a).

[2] See Saint Ambrose (+397), *Letter 23*, nos. 12–13, PL 16, col. 1030. See also Saint Augustine (+430), *Letter 55*, no. 24, PL 33, col. 215.

[3] Text in Michel Andrieu, ed., *Les Ordines Romani du haut moyen âge*, vol. 3, SSLED 24 (Louvain, Belgium: "Spicilegium sacrum Lovaniense" Administration, 1951), 188.

[4] Amalarius of Metz, *Liber officialis*, bk. 1, chap. 12, nos. 32–33, and bk. 4, chap. 21, no. 8, in John Michael Hanssens, S.J., ed., *Amalarii episcopi: Opera liturgica omnia*, vol. 2, ST 139 (Vatican City: Biblioteca Apostolica Vaticana, 1948), 78–79, 470; Pseudo-Alcuin, *Liber de divinis officiis*, chap. 15, PL 101, col. 1202.

three days the Church celebrates the "funeral rites" of Christ.[5] He explains that although the three actual days of the Lord's entombment were from Good Friday to Easter Sunday, the Church's dedication of Easter night to the joyful celebration of the Resurrection necessitated a liturgical shift of the commemoration of the three days' entombment forward into Holy Thursday.[6] This inclusion of Holy Thursday provided a tangible means of representing the "three days and three nights" of entombment prophesied by Christ, as Amalarius observes:

> In the Triduum, the Lord rested in the tomb, according to the Gospel, which says: "For as Jonas was in the whale's belly three days and three nights: so shall the Son of man be in the heart of the earth three days and three nights" [Mt 12:40].... His three days' burial we recall to memory, which we do not recollect in celebrating unless the fifth [day] be joined with the sixth day and the seventh.... If according to Augustine the Resurrection was his glory, certainly his death and burial are His humiliation.... For three continuous days—that is, the fifth day, the sixth day, and the seventh—we celebrate his three days' burial.[7]

This understanding of the Triduum gave rise to the rite of the divine office known as Tenebrae (the Latin word for darkness). The earliest liturgical texts to describe a particularly solemnized form of the night offices of Matins and Lauds for the Triduum of Holy Thursday, Good Friday, and Holy Saturday date from the eighth century, specifying among other things the total omission of the *Gloria Patri* that is customarily added to the end of every psalm of the Divine Office throughout the rest of the liturgical year.[8] Yet evidence for the existence of such a rite two centuries earlier is to be found in the writings of the French bishop and ecclesiastical historian Saint Gregory of Tours (+594). He describes as a miracle a mysterious incident that took place at the Poitiers abbey of the Holy Cross on Good Friday in or close to the year 569, shortly after the monastery had received a relic of the True Cross: "On the sixth day before the Holy Pasch, when [the monks] were watching in vigils by night without light, around the third hour there appeared before the altar a small light in the form of a spark."[9] It is clear from the emphasis upon the lack of light and the conspicuousness of the tiny spark of miraculous light that the monks were

---

[5] Durandus, *Rationale* (CCCM 140a), bk. 6, chap. 72, no. 2, p. 336.

[6] Ibid., no. 1.

[7] Amalarius of Metz, *Liber officialis*, bk. 1, chap. 12, nos. 32–33, in Hanssens, *Amalarii episcopi: Opera liturgica omnia*, 2:78–79.

[8] See Roman *Ordo* 13a and Roman *Ordo* 23 (the latter of which specifies the omission of the *Gloria Patri*), both circa 700–750, in (respectively) Michel Andrieu, ed., *Les Ordines Romani du haut moyen âge*, vol. 2, SSLED 23 (Louvain, Belgium: "Spicilegium sacrum Lovaniense" Administration, 1948), 482–483, and Andrieu, *Ordines Romani du haut moyen âge*, 3:269.

[9] Saint Gregory of Tours, *Miraculorum liber de gloria martyrum*, bk. 1, chap. 5, PL 71, col. 709.

praying in total darkness, abstaining from the usual lighting for their nocturnal offices; this appears to be our earliest testimony to the symbolic withdrawal of light during the night offices of the Easter Triduum that came to characterize Tenebrae.[10] A fairly complete outline of the salient features of Tenebrae can be gleaned from the rubrics of an eleventh-century customary of the Monastery of Saint Paul in Rome:

> On the fifth day, the Supper of the Lord, and before the fifteen nocturns, on an instrument of wood before the altar, just as many candles should be lit as are the psalms to be assigned; and with the remaining thirty psalms, fifteen should be said silently before the nocturns. [Prayer:] Our Father ... This prayer having been said, the secretary should sound the bells, as is customary; which said bells sounding, after they shall have been rung, the hebdomadarian [the priest leading the Divine Office for the week] should begin the antiphon *Zeal for your house has consumed me*, and immediately one candle should be extinguished on one side, another thereafter; and thus should it be done in beginning all the psalms.... The first three lessons are read from the Lamentations of Jeremiah.[11]

The wooden candlestand referred to above as an "instrument of wood" may well have been in the shape of a pyramid, as was specified in another eleventh-century monastic customary, that of the Benedictine abbey of Saint-Bénigne in Dijon, France.[12] Such wooden candlestands (widely referred to as "hearses"), usually in a triangular form, became a universal feature of Tenebrae offices throughout medieval Europe. The successive extinction of candles described in the above text was explained two centuries earlier by Amalarius of Metz (+c. 850):

> By the present extinction is designated the extinction of joy, which is contemplated to be wrought in the hearts of the disciples of Christ while Christ slept in the sepulcher, or that extinction of joy that was wrought in the hearts of the Apostles after the handing over of the Lord, up until he went in to them with the doors closed, and showed them his hands and feet, and ate before them.[13]

Later commentators offered further explanations. Rupert of Deutz (+c. 1129) remarks that the extinguishing of the Tenebrae candles signifies collectively that "Christ having been crucified, there was darkness

---

[10] See A.J. MacGregor, *Fire and Light in the Western Triduum: Their Use at Tenebrae and at the Paschal Vigil*, Alcuin Club Collection 71 (Runcorn, England: Alcuin Club; Collegeville, Minn.: Liturgical Press, 1992), 10–11.

[11] Text in Edmond Martène, *De antiquis ecclesiae ritibus* (Venice: Johannes Baptista Novelli, 1763–1764), bk. 4, chap. 22, 3:124.

[12] Edmond Martène, *De antiquis monachorum ritibus*, bk. 3, chap. 12, no. 2, in Martène, *De antiquis ecclesiae ritibus*, 4:122.

[13] Amalarius of Metz, *Liber de ordine antiphonarii*, chap. 44, no. 4, in John Michael Hanssens, ed., *Amalarii episcopi: Opera liturgica omnia*, vol. 3, ST 140 (Vatican City: Biblioteca Apostolica Vaticana, 1950), 80.

over the land from the sixth hour up until the ninth hour" (cf. Mt 27:45); the individual extinguishing of each candle after each psalm represents the killing of the prophets who preceded Christ.[14] Adding a further dimension to the association made by Rupert of Deutz, Honorius of Autun (+c. 1135) notes that the three successive nights of extinguishing candles at Tenebrae symbolize the three hours of darkness while Christ hung on the Cross; moreover, the lights are also put out "because we lament the true Light extinguished in these days".[15] Similarly, Durandus sees in this practice a commemoration of the three nights that "the true Light slept in the sepulcher."[16]

The actual number of candles extinguished during Tenebrae varied from place to place, ranging from only five to as many as seventy-two.[17] The use of fifteen candles, which became universal in the *Breviarium Romanum* of 1568,[18] is traceable to the eleventh century, when it appears not only in the earlier-quoted customary of the Monastery of Saint Paul but also in France (Cluny, c. 1043, and Saint-Bénigne, Dijon),[19] with the practice reaching Spain by the mid-twelfth century.[20] This number of candles was interpreted by Durandus as representing the twelve Apostles and "the three Marys who followed the Lord".[21] The successive extinction of the candles, "not all together, but one after another", signifies that "the disciples departed from the Lord not together but gradually one after another."[22] The linking of the extinction of each candle to the completion of each psalm or canticle of Tenebrae symbolizes that in the context of this mournful office all the psalms and canticles end in grief, because "the true Sun has set, and our joy has been turned into mourning, according to that [passage]: 'The crown is fallen from our head, our dancing is turned into mourning' [Lam 5:16, 15]."[23] The custom of

---

[14] Rupert of Deutz, *Liber de divinis officiis*, bk. 5, chap. 26, in Hrabanus Haacke, O.S.B., ed., *Ruperti Tuitiensis: Liber de divinis officiis*, CCCM 7 (Turnhout, Belgium: Brepols, 1967), 180–181. Hereafter cited as Rupert of Deutz, *Liber de divinis officiis* (CCCM 7).

[15] Honorius of Autun, *Gemma animae*, bk. 3, chap. 87, PL 172, col. 665.

[16] Durandus, *Rationale* (CCCM 140a), bk. 6, chap. 72, no. 15, p. 341.

[17] MacGregor, *Fire and Light in the Western Triduum*, 54–66.

[18] Text in Manlio Sodi and Achille Maria Triacca, eds., *Breviarium Romanum: Editio princeps (1568)*, facsimile ed., MLCT 3 (Vatican City: Libreria Editrice Vaticana, © 1999), 376 (new pagination).

[19] *Liber Tramitis* (a customary of the Benedictine abbey of Cluny, formerly called the Customs of Farfa), bk. 1, chap. 54, in Bruno Albers, ed., *Consuetudines monasticae*, vol. 1, *Consuetudines Farfenses* (Stuttgart: Jos. Roth, Bibliopolae, 1900), 46; for the Abbey of Saint-Bénigne, see Martène, *De antiquis monachorum ritibus*, bk. 3, chap. 12, no. 2, in Martène, *De antiquis ecclesiae ritibus*, 4:122.

[20] A reference to fifteen candles for Tenebrae appears in a will for the Church of Saint Peter, Ager, Spain, dating from 1152; see Jaime Villanueva, *Viage literario a las iglesias de España*, vol. 9, *Viage a Solsona, Ager y Urgel, 1806 y 1807* (Valencia, Spain: Imprenta de Oliveres, 1821), 280.

[21] Durandus, *Rationale* (CCCM 140a), bk. 6, chap. 72, no. 18, p. 342.

[22] Ibid., no. 22, p. 343.

[23] Ibid., no. 23.

leaving one candle lit on the Tenebrae hearse is first attested in an eleventh-century breviary of York, England.[24] This candle is identified as symbolizing Christ by Hugh of Saint Victor (+c. 1141).[25] Within the context of the extinction of the other candles representing the desertion of the Apostles, the Carthusian writer Ludolph of Saxony (+1377) sees this solitary light as symbolizing the Blessed Virgin Mary, who alone remained faithful to Christ during the Passion.[26]

The eighth-century liturgical text Roman *Ordo* 26 (c. 750–775; composed for a parish near Rome) speaks of Tenebrae commencing in the night at two o'clock.[27] By the late fifteenth century, the hour of Tenebrae had in some places advanced into the late afternoon of the preceding day: a 1495 breviary of Limoges, France, indicates the beginning of Tenebrae at four o'clock in the afternoon (i.e., Holy Thursday Tenebrae would begin at four o'clock on Wednesday).[28] This practice was later promulgated in the 1600 *Caeremoniale episcoporum*.[29]

In discussing the responsories found in the Tenebrae offices, Amalarius observes that in addition to those taken directly from the Scriptures, some "were composed by the masters of the holy Roman Church, in which the sorrow of his [Christ's] handing over is frequented, and the sorrow of his crucifixion stirs the hearts of the faithful".[30] As for the singing of the Lamentations, Durandus explains that by the chanting of these words of Jeremiah in the Tenebrae offices "we lament the death and Passion of Christ our King."[31]

Jerusalem's most ancient liturgical book, the early fifth-century Armenian Lectionary, testifies to the celebration of Mass on Holy Thursday in the very place where the first Mass took place, the Cenacle of Mount Sion. Both the Epistle (1 Cor 11:23–32) and the Gospel (Mk 14:1–26) for this Jerusalem Mass recount the institution of the

The Mass and the Chrism Rite of Holy Thursday

---

[24] See Stephen Willoughby Lawley, ed., *Breviarium ad usum insignis ecclesie Eboracensis*, vol. 1, Surtees Society Publications 71 (Durham, England: Andrews, 1880), col. 382. For the dating of this text, see MacGregor, *Fire and Light in the Western Triduum*, 118.

[25] Hugh of Saint Victor, *Miscellanea*, bk. 7, title 40, PL 177, col. 889.

[26] Ludolph of Saxony, *Vita Jesu Christi*, ed. Jean-Pierre Mabile and Jean-Jacques-Maria-Antoine Guerrin (Paris and Rome: Victor Palmé, 1865), pt. 2, chap. 59, p. 615.

[27] Andrieu, *Ordines Romani du haut moyen âge*, 3:328.

[28] Martène, *De antiquis ecclesiae ritibus*, bk. 4, chap. 22, no. 1, 3:81. In quoting the Limoges rubric, Dom Martène does not identify his source, but it is known that in his research he consulted a 1495 breviary of Limoges; see Aimé-Georges Martimort, *La documentation liturgique de Dom Edmond Martène*, ST 279 (Vatican City: Biblioteca Apostolica Vaticana, 1978), no. 160, p. 131.

[29] Text in Achille Maria Triacca and Manlio Sodi, eds., *Caeremoniale episcoporum: Editio princeps (1600)*, facsimile ed., MLCT 4 (Vatican City: Libreria Editrice Vaticana, © 2000), bk. 2, chap. 22, p. 231 (new pagination).

[30] Amalarius of Metz, *Liber de ordine antiphonarii*, chap. 43, no. 5, in Hanssens, *Amalarii episcopi: Opera liturgica omnia*, 3:79.

[31] Durandus, *Rationale* (CCCM 140a), bk. 6, chap. 72, no. 11, p. 340.

Eucharist.[32] The earliest known Roman lectionary, the seventh-century *Comes* of Würzburg, specifies virtually the same Epistle for the Holy Thursday Mass (1 Cor 11:20–32),[33] a reading found universally in the medieval liturgical books and subsequently retained in the 1570 *Missale Romanum*.[34] The Holy Thursday Gospel in the latter (Jn 13:1–15), Christ's washing of the Apostles' feet,[35] was read at the Mass of this day in the West from the eighth century onward.[36] As for the prayers proper to the Holy Thursday Mass, the Collect, the Secret, and the Postcommunion, as well as the day's special insertions within the Roman Canon, uniformly the same across medieval Europe and preserved in the 1570 *Missale Romanum*,[37] are all traceable to seventh-century Rome.[38] The Mass chants, that is, the Introit, the Gradual, the Offertory, and the Communion, were universally used together for this solemnity from the late eighth century onward[39] and similarly entered the 1570 missal of Pope Saint Pius V,[40] as did the use on this day of the Preface of the Holy Cross, first mentioned as a Holy Thursday Preface in the Ordinal of the Papal Court, from the pontificate of Pope Innocent III (1198–1216).[41]

The custom of ringing bells during the singing of the *Gloria* at this Mass arose by the fifteenth century, when it is specified in both a missal of England's York Cathedral ("While [the *Gloria*] is sung, the bell array should be rung")[42] and in a French pontifical preserved (at

---

[32] Text in Athanase Renoux, ed. and trans., *Le codex arménien Jérusalem 121*, vol. 2, *Edition comparée du texte et de deux autres manuscrits*, Patrologia orientalis 36, fasc. 2 (Turnhout, Belgium: Brepols, 1971), no. 39, pp. 268–269.

[33] Text in Germain Morin, "Le plus ancien *Comes* ou lectionnaire de l'église romaine", *Revue Bénédictine* 27 (1910): 54.

[34] See Manlio Sodi and Achille Maria Triacca, eds., *Missale Romanum: Editio princeps (1570)*, facsimile ed., MLCT 2 (Vatican City: Libreria Editrice Vaticana, © 1998), 236 (new pagination).

[35] Ibid., 237 (new pagination).

[36] Herman Schmidt, S.J., *Hebdomada sancta* (Rome: Herder, 1956–1957) 2:674–675.

[37] Sodi and Triacca, *Missale Romanum: Editio princeps (1570)*, 236–238 (new pagination).

[38] See the Paduan redaction of the Gregorian Sacramentary in Jean Deshusses, ed., *Le sacramentaire grégorien: Ses principales formes d'après les plus anciens manuscrits*, vol. 1, 2nd ed., SF 16 (Fribourg, Switzerland: Editions Universitaires Fribourg, 1979), Paduan nos. 299, 300, 298, 296, and 301–302, respectively, p. 630. The Postcommunion actually predates the other prayers, appearing for the first time as a December oration in the sixth-century Leonine Sacramentary of Rome; see Leo Cunibert Mohlberg, O.S.B.; Leo Eizenhöfer, O.S.B.; and Petrus Siffrin, O.S.B., eds., *Sacramentarium Veronense*, REDSMF 1 (Rome: Herder, 1956), no. 1323, p. 169.

[39] These chants are all provided for Holy Thursday in the Mass antiphonary of Mount Blandin (Belgium, c. 750–800); the Gradual is also found, even earlier, in the Cantatorium of Monza (Italy, eighth century); see René-Jean Hésbert, ed., *Antiphonale missarum sextuplex* (Brussels, 1935; repr., Rome: Herder, 1967), 92, 94.

[40] Sodi and Triacca, *Missale Romanum: Editio princeps (1570)*, 236–238 (new pagination).

[41] Text in Stephen J. P. Van Dijk, O.F.M., and Joan Hazelden Walker, eds., *The Ordinal of the Papal Court from Innocent III to Boniface VIII and Related Documents*, SF 22 (Fribourg, Switzerland: The University Press, 1975), 218.

[42] Manuscript: Cambridge, England, Sidney Sussex College, Cambridge University, missal of York, fifteenth century, in William George Henderson, ed., *Missale ad usum insignis*

least formerly) in the sacristy of Rouen Cathedral ("While the *Gloria in excelsis* is sung, the entire bell array should sound, until it ends").[43] This practice, although absent from the original 1570 edition of the *Missale Romanum*,[44] was added almost immediately afterward in a 1574 edition of the same missal.[45] The custom of omitting from the Mass of this day the sign of peace, first attested in the seventh century[46] and serving as an expression of mourning for the traitorous kiss of Judas in Gethsemane,[47] corresponds with the theme of the Passion, with which the Mass begins in the Introit: "*It befits us now to glory in the Cross of our Lord Jesus Christ, in whom is our salvation, our life, and our resurrection, by whom we have been saved and delivered.*"[48] Durandus observes that the texts proper to the Holy Thursday Mass are a summary of the mystery of redemption, with the Cross commemorated in the Introit, the Eucharist in the Epistle, the death of Christ in the Gradual, the washing of the feet in the Gospel, and the Resurrection in the Offertory.[49]

The medieval liturgy of Holy Thursday included a dramatic and moving rite of reconciling public penitents, to which we have already referred, albeit briefly, in chapter 5; this reconciliation took place during Mass or as a separate ceremony before Mass. In the interest of addressing comprehensively other aspects of the Holy Thursday liturgy, we shall refrain from a detailed description of this particular rite, which has been widely discussed by other authors. The opening lines of the ancient allocution recited by the deacon to the bishop that became a permanent part of the Holy Thursday reconciliation rite throughout medieval Europe, a proclamation of seventh-century origin,[50] quoted here from the tenth-century Romano-Germanic Pontifical, will give the reader some sense of the rite's beauty:

---

ecclesiae Eboracensis, vol. 1, Surtees Society Publications 59 (Durham, England: Andrews, 1874), 96 (text "D").

[43] Text quoted by the seventeenth-century Benedictine liturgist Dom Nicolas-Hugues Menard (+1644) in his work on the Gregorian Sacramentary, reprinted in PL 78, col. 328. Dom Menard, who learned of this manuscript from a provost of Rouen Cathedral, describes it as composed for either Rouen or Reims (ibid., col. 327).

[44] Sodi and Triacca, *Missale Romanum: Editio princeps (1570)*, 236 (new pagination).

[45] 1574 *Missale Romanum*, in Robert Lippe, ed., *Missale Romanum: Mediolani, 1474*, vol. 2, *A Collation with Other Editions Printed before 1570*, HBS 33 (London: Henry Bradshaw Society, 1907), 72.

[46] See the seventh-century Gelasian Sacramentary of Rome, in Leo Cunibert Mohlberg, O.S.B., et al., eds., *Liber sacramentorum Romanae aeclesiae ordinis anni circuli (Sacramentarium Gelasianum)*, REDSMF 4 (Rome: Herder, 1960), no. 390, p. 63.

[47] See, for example, Pseudo-Alcuin, *Liber de divinis officiis*, chap. 16/17, PL 101, cols. 1203–1204.

[48] 1474 *Missale Romanum*, in Robert Lippe, ed., *Missale Romanum: Mediolani, 1474*, vol. 1, *Text*, HBS 17 (London: Henry Bradshaw Society, 1899), 156.

[49] Durandus, *Rationale* (CCCM 140a), bk. 6, chap. 75, no. 7, p. 363.

[50] This allocution appears for the first time in the seventh-century Gelasian Sacramentary of Rome; see Mohlberg, Eizenhöfer, and Siffrin, *Liber sacramentorum*, nos. 353–354, pp. 56–57.

Now is the acceptable time, O venerable bishop, the day of divine clemency and the salvation of man, in which death receives its ruin and eternal life takes its beginning, when a planting of new shoots is likewise to be made in the vineyard of the Lord Sabaoth, that the curse of the old may be cleared away. For although no time is devoid of the riches of God's goodness and mercy, now, however, the remission of sins through forgiveness is more bountiful, and the reclamation of those spiritually reborn abounds the more. Let us be increased by those reborn; by those returned, we flourish. Waters wash, tears wash. Henceforth there is gladness for the reclamation of those called; hence there is joy for the forgiveness of penitents.[51]

The celebration of rites to bless the holy oils for the administration of the sacraments is first attested in a third-century liturgical text, the *Apostolic Tradition* of Saint Hippolytus of Rome (+c. 236).[52] Originally carried out at the Easter Vigil, the blessing of the holy oils had become a regular feature of the Holy Thursday liturgy by the end of the fifth century, when its administration on this day is attested in the *Vita beati Sylvestri*, an apocryphal biography of the fourth-century pope Saint Sylvester I (314–335).[53] In seventh-century Rome, we find the blessing of the oils performed at the second of three Masses for Holy Thursday specified in the Gelasian Sacramentary, which provides prayers for the blessings of the oil of the sick, the chrism, and the oil of catechumens;[54] another Roman text, the Roman *Ordo in coena Domini*, dating from the first half of the seventh century, provides rubrics for the papal celebration of this rite.[55] The assignment of the blessing of chrism to Mass on Holy Thursday likewise appeared in the East, where it is first mentioned in an eighth-century *euchologion* (book of rites) known as the Codex Barberini, a liturgical text principally reflecting the observances of Byzantine Constantinople;[56] the Holy Thursday blessing of chrism is also attested in tenth-century Jerusalem, albeit in a rite separate from the Masses of the day.[57]

Here we summarize the Holy Thursday rite of blessing the holy oils as found in the tenth-century Romano-Germanic Pontifical; it is

---

[51] Text in Cyrille Vogel and Reinhard Elze, eds., *Le pontifical romano-germanique du dixième siècle*, vol. 2, ST 227 (Vatican City: Biblioteca Apostolica Vaticana, 1963), 59.

[52] *Apostolic Tradition*, chaps. 1, 16, in Francis Xavier Funk, ed., *Didascalia et Constitutiones apostolorum*, vol. 2, *Testimonia et scripturae propinquae* (Paderborn, Germany: Libraria Ferdinandi Schoeningh, 1905), 100–101, 109.

[53] Text of the passage from the *Vita beati Sylvestri* regarding Holy Thursday in Schmidt, *Hebdomada sancta*, 2:714.

[54] Mohlberg, Eizenhöfer, and Siffrin, *Liber sacramentorum*, nos. 375–390, pp. 60–63.

[55] Text in Antoine Chavasse, "A Rome, le Jeudi-saint, au VIIe siècle, d'après un vieil Ordo", *Revue d'Histoire Ecclésiastique* 50 (1955): 25–28.

[56] Manuscript: Vatican City, Biblioteca Apostolica Vaticana, Codex Barberini Gr. 336, in James Goar, O.P., *Euchologion sive Rituale Graecorum*, 2nd ed. (Venice, 1730; repr., Graz, Austria: Akademische Druck—U. Verlagsanstalt, 1960), 503.

[57] Text in A. Papadopoulos-Kerameus, ed., *Analekta hierosolymitikēs stachyologias*, vol. 2 (Saint Petersburg, Russia, 1894; repr., Brussels: Culture et Civilisation, 1963), 99–105.

this particular form of the rite that, with two additions made in the thirteenth century, was universally promulgated in the *Pontificale Romanum* of 1595–1596.[58] During the bishop's Holy Thursday Mass, the oil of the sick would be blessed shortly before the end of the Roman Canon, immediately before the words *"Per quem hec omnia Domine semper bona creas"* (*"Through whom always you, O Lord, create all these good things"*). As the archdeacon holds the ampule of holy oil before the bishop, the latter pronounces over the vessel first an exorcism and then an ancient prayer of blessing traceable to the seventh-century Gelasian Sacramentary of Rome,[59] after which the oil would be returned to its place and the bishop would continue with the Canon.[60]

Following the bishop's Holy Communion, but before the Communion of anyone else, the two other holy oils, the chrism and the oil of catechumens, are brought from the sacristy to the bishop in a solemn procession comprising an entourage of twelve priests with the singing of the hymn *O Redemptor sume carmen*:

> And the same [twelve] priests should be prepared, and with them the other clerics, in chasubles and solemn vestments. Then should go forth two acolytes, taking those two vessels that ought to be consecrated for the chrism and the oil of catechumens, enveloped with linens over the left shoulder, such that it may extend to the right shoulder, so that [the vessels] may be able to be held by suspension. And those priests and the aforesaid clerics should arrange themselves fittingly and in order, such that two acolytes with candlesticks and burning candles should walk first. Then should be borne the two crosses, and between them, at the middle, the chrismal oil. After them should be carried two thuribles with incense, and between them, at the middle, the oil of catechumens, as we mentioned earlier. Then should be carried the Gospel book, that every good thing may be accomplished. Afterward should follow two by two those twelve priests, witnesses and assistants of the same sacrosanct mystery of the chrism. But then should follow two boys singing in praise of the same mystery these verses corresponding to this: *Hear, O Judge of the dead, the only hope of mortals* ... And the choir should respond: *Receive, O Redeemer, the canticle that draws into one those singing.*[61]

---

[58] Text in Manlio Sodi and Achille Triacca, eds., *Pontificale Romanum: Editio princeps (1595–1596)*, facsimile ed., MLCT 1 (Vatican City: Libreria Editrice Vaticana, © 1997), 574–600 (original pagination).

[59] Mohlberg, Eizenhöfer, and Siffrin, *Liber sacramentorum*, no. 382, p. 61.

[60] Vogel and Elze, *Pontifical romano-germanique*, 2:70.

[61] Ibid., 71–72 (quoted passage on 72). The chrism hymn *O Redemptor, sume carmen temet concinentium* (*"Receive, O Redeemer, the canticle that draws into one those singing"*) is said to be a composition of Irish authorship, traceable to the ninth century; see Joseph Connelly, *Hymns of the Roman Liturgy* (Westminster, Md.: Newman, 1957), 87. The Latin word *temet* in the title verse of the hymn does not appear in any of the standard dictionaries or lexicons of Latin that the author was able to consult; the translation given here is thus

Those in the procession, upon arriving in the choir, stop and turn to face east. Upon the completion of the hymn, the archdeacon presents the ampule of chrism to the bishop, while a subdeacon brings forward a vessel of balsam, an aromatic substance that has been mixed into chrism at the Holy Thursday blessing rite since the eighth century.[62] Before continuing, the bishop instructs the people with a homily explaining the ceremony to them.[63] Then turning to the east, he blesses the balsam with one prayer; three centuries later William Durandus in his pontifical (c. 1294) would add to the rite two further blessings for the balsam.[64] After mixing the balsam into the chrism, the bishop breathes three times "in the manner of a cross" over the mouth of the ampule, an action that is then repeated by the twelve priests who accompanied the holy oils in the procession. The bishop next pronounces an exorcism over the chrism, followed by the consecratory prayer with which he actually blesses the oil, a text from the seventh-century Gelasian Sacramentary of Rome.[65] After the ampule has been temporarily unveiled, the newly consecrated chrism, considered symbolic of Christ, is "saluted" by the bishop, and then, after the ampule is covered again, it is saluted by the rest of the clergy.[66] The nature of this salutation is not explained, but the late thirteenth-century Pontifical of Durandus describes it as a threefold pronouncement of the words "*Hail, holy chrism*" by the bishop while bowing, after which he kisses the vessel.[67]

The ampule of the oil of catechumens is now brought forward and presented to the bishop, who pronounces over it an exorcism and a prayer of blessing, the texts of which are derived from the Gelasian Sacramentary.[68] The blessed oil is then saluted by the bishop and the clergy. The blessing rite concludes with the carrying of the chrism and the oil of catechumens back to the sacristy in a solemn procession ordered in the same manner as the earlier procession from the sacristy, after which the bishop continues with the distribution of Holy Communion.[69]

Honorius of Autun sees in the chrism procession imagery corresponding both to the Old Testament Exodus of Israel and to the New

---

based upon the assumption that *temet* is a variant spelling of the third-person singular present tense of the verb *tenere*. Father Connelly appears to make the same assumption in his rather free translation of the verse (ibid., 86).

[62] This infusion of balsam into the chrism is first mentioned in the Gellone Sacramentary, a Frankish adaptation of Rome's Gelasian Sacramentary; see A. Dumas, ed., *Liber sacramentorum Gellonensis*, CCSL 159 (Turnhout, Belgium: Brepols, 1981), no. 627, p. 84.

[63] The Romano-Germanic Pontifical provides the texts of two such sermons; see Vogel and Elze, *Pontifical romano-germanique*, 2:82–85.

[64] Text in Michel Andrieu, ed., *Le pontifical romain au moyen-âge*, vol. 3, *Le pontifical de Guillaume Durand*, ST 88 (Vatican City: Biblioteca Apostolica Vaticana, 1940), 576–577.

[65] Mohlberg, Eizenhöfer, and Siffrin, *Liber sacramentorum,* nos. 386–388, p. 62.

[66] Vogel and Elze, *Pontifical romano-germanique*, 2:73–75.

[67] Andrieu, *Pontifical romain au moyen-âge*, 3:578.

[68] Mohlberg, Eizenhöfer, and Siffrin, *Liber sacramentorum,* nos. 384, 389, pp. 61–63.

[69] Vogel and Elze, *Pontifical romano-germanique*, 2:75–76.

Testament manifestation of Christ. Regarding the first of these, he notes that the participants "imitate the going forward of the people of God, who in the figure of Christ and of the Church went through the desert". The acolytes who carry candles at the head of the procession represent the angel who bore the pillar of fire before the Israelites (Ex 13:21–22; 14:19–20; 23:20). He who carries the Gospel book symbolizes Moses with the book of the Law. The roles of the thurifers and crossbearers, filled by priests in the particular version of the chrism procession known to Honorius, correspond respectively to "Aaron with the priestly thurible" and to Christ with his Cross, prefigured by Joshua with the book of the Law (cf. Jos 1:8). The ampule of chrism corresponds to the urn filled with manna that was kept in the Ark of the Covenant, with the ark represented by the linen cloth veiling the ampule. The canopy carried over the holy oils is both the Tent of Meeting that sheltered the Ark of the Covenant and the shadow of the cloud that descended upon the tent when God spoke with Moses.[70]

As for the New Testament imagery in this procession, Honorius sees in the acolytes bearing candles before the holy oils a symbol of Saint John the Baptist, who was as it were "a lamp shining and burning before Christ". The canopy above is the bright cloud that overshadowed Christ in his Transfiguration. The chrism in the ampule is "the divinity in human flesh", and the linen cloth enveloping it is holy conduct. The ampule is covered and remains so until it reaches the altar, where it is unveiled, for Christ before his Passion was "hidden in the flesh", whereas on the altar of the Cross "the infirmity of his flesh stood open", and after his death, "his divinity shone forth openly." The bishop's salutation of the holy oils corresponds to the Apostle Saint Thomas touching the side of the risen Christ. The salutations offered to the chrism after it has again been covered represent the worship offered to Christ following his Ascension into Heaven.[71]

Sicard of Cremona (+1215) comments upon the symbolism of the paired objects in the procession as well as the significance of the retinue of twelve priests:

> The vessel with the oil signifies the humanity [of Christ] filled with the Holy Spirit; therefore, the two lights, the two crosses, and the two thuribles are the Law and the prophets that prophesied Christ to have suffered and nevertheless to be God. Then follows the Gospel book, for the Gospel following affirms what the Law and the prophets prophesied. Finally, twelve priests follow, two by two. Witnesses of the chrismal mystery, these are the two Apostles [i.e., the disciples sent two by two; Lk 10:1], coworkers appointed to the office of preaching, and witnesses of our Lord Jesus Christ. Their chant, namely

---

[70] Honorius of Autun, *Gemma animae*, bk. 3, chap. 83, PL 172, col. 664.

[71] Ibid., cols. 664–665.

O Redemptor, signifies the preaching and prayer of the Apostles. That the vessel is brought to the altar by every one of the [holy] orders intimates that the Lord in his body before his Passion filled the six offices of orders.[72]

The jar of manna kept within the Ark of the Covenant, which Honorius of Autun identifies with the ampule of chrism in the holy oils procession, was identified in quite a different way by the thirteenth-century Franciscan writer Salimbene de Adam (+c. 1288). He sees in the manna-filled urn a prefiguration of the reservation of the Blessed Sacrament.[73] Not surprisingly, some of the imagery and symbolism of the holy oils procession, a Holy Thursday rite confined largely to cathedral churches, was inherited by another procession of Holy Thursday that by the end of the Middle Ages was being observed in nearly every parish church—the procession to carry the Eucharist reserved for Good Friday to the place of its reposition. It is to this rite that we shall now turn.

The Eucharistic Procession and Reservation of Holy Thursday

The major liturgical commentators of the Middle Ages do not explain the significance of the Holy Thursday processional transfer of the Eucharist to be reserved for Good Friday; yet it is clear from even the most cursory examination of the medieval rites for this procession that the ceremony was imbued with rich symbolism in commemoration of the Passion of Christ. This centuries-old implicit understanding of the Holy Thursday procession to the repository has been most fully explained by Pope Benedict XVI and his predecessor, Pope Blessed John Paul II. Both pontiffs see the procession as a commemoration of Christ's journey from the Last Supper to Gethsemane and to the sufferings that were to culminate in his death on the Cross. Discussing in a 1995 homily the contrast between the jubilant Eucharistic procession of the feast of Corpus Christi and the solemn procession of Holy Thursday, Pope John Paul II says of the latter:

> This Eucharistic procession has a characteristic note: we pause beside Christ as the events of his Passion begin. We know, in fact, that the Last Supper was followed by the prayer in Gethsemane, by his arrest and trial, first before Annas and then before Caiaphas, high priest at the time. Thus on Holy Thursday we accompany Jesus on the way that leads him to the terrible hours of the Passion, a few hours before he was sentenced to death and crucifixion. In the Polish tradition the place of reposition for the Eucharist after the liturgy of the Lord's Supper is called "the dark chapel", because popular piety links it to

---

[72] Sicard of Cremona, *Mitrale*, bk. 6, chap. 12, PL 213, cols. 306–307.

[73] Salimbene de Adam, *Chronica*, anno 1250, in *Monumenta Germaniae historica: Scriptorum*, vol. 32, *Chronica fratris Salimbene de Adam, ordinis minorum*, ed. Oswald Holder-Egger (Hanover, Germany: Hahn, 1905–1913), 338.

the memory of the prison where our Lord Jesus spent the night between Thursday and Friday, a night certainly not of repose, but rather a further stage of physical and spiritual suffering.[74]

Prior to becoming pontiff, Pope Benedict XVI offered a very similar explanation in his 1985 book *Journey towards Easter*, drawn from a retreat he delivered in the presence of Pope John Paul II. He begins by describing Christ's journey from the Upper Room to the Garden of Olives, observing, "He went out into the night of Gethsemane, into the night of the Cross, the night of the tomb."[75] It is this journey, he explains, that the Holy Thursday procession recalls: "At the end of the liturgy of Holy Thursday the Church imitates Jesus' journey, carrying the Blessed Sacrament out of the tabernacle to a side chapel to represent the loneliness of Gethsemane, the loneliness of Jesus' mortal anguish. The faithful pray in the chapel, wanting to follow Jesus in the prayer of his loneliness so that it ceases to be loneliness."[76] In his first Corpus Christi homily as pontiff, Pope Benedict XVI reiterated this interpretation of the Holy Thursday procession, explaining:

> There is also a Eucharistic procession on Holy Thursday, when the Church repeats the exodus from the Upper Room to the Mount of Olives. . . .
>
> In the Holy Thursday procession, the Church accompanies Jesus to the Mount of Olives. It is the authentic desire of the Church in prayer to keep watch with Jesus, not to abandon him in the night of the world, on the night of betrayal, on the night of the indifference of many people. . . .
>
> The Holy Thursday procession accompanies Jesus in his solitude towards the *via crucis*.[77]

The seventh-century Gelasian Sacramentary of Rome is the earliest Western text to mention the reservation of the Eucharist from the Mass on Holy Thursday for a Holy Communion rite of the faithful on Good Friday.[78] This liturgical book, however, provides no specifics as to how the reservation was carried out. But in the eleventh century, beginning with the Benedictine monasteries of France, the transfer of the reserved Eucharist from the altar on Holy Thursday developed into a solemn procession that increasingly acquired a significance of its

---

[74] Pope Blessed John Paul II, Corpus Christi homily, June 15, 1995, *L'Osservatore Romano*, weekly edition in English, June 21, 1995, pp. 1–2.

[75] Pope Benedict XVI [Joseph Ratzinger], *Journey towards Easter: Retreat Given in the Vatican in the Presence of Pope John Paul II* (New York: Crossroad, 1987), 96. This edition is an English translation of the original text from 1985. (English translation © St. Paul's Publishing, London.)

[76] Ibid., 96–97.

[77] Benedict XVI, Corpus Christi homily, May 26, 2005, *L'Osservatore Romano*, weekly edition in English, June 1, 2005, p. 3.

[78] Mohlberg, et al., eds., *Liber Sacramentorum*, no. 390, p. 63.

own as both a remembrance of the going forth of Christ to his Passion and a testament to the Church's faith in his Real Presence in the Eucharist. It is on the eve of the eleventh century that we find the earliest reference to a specific requirement for the place of reposing the Blessed Sacrament on Holy Thursday, given in a Benedictine customary of the Abbey of Saint Vanne in Verdun, France, a text dating from about 990: "The Body only shall be reserved for the next day in a secure place, and with a light having been placed there also." [79] The earliest detailed instruction for the Holy Thursday transfer of the Eucharist to the place of reposition appears in a customary for the French Benedictine monastery of Gorze compiled by its abbot Sigibert of Gorze about the year 1030:

> After Mass, the deacon should come, and the secretary, and the lay brothers with candlesticks and a thurible; and they should take the chalice and the paten, which has the Body of the Lord, setting over it another paten, and they should envelop it in a very fine linen cloth, and they should repose it upon some altar, or in a very fine ark; and there should be a light before it all day and all night all the way to Matins. [80]

The directive in the above text regarding a light for the Sacrament is made more emphatic in a customary compiled about 1075 for the French Benedictine abbey of Cluny by the monk Bernard, which enjoins that the Holy Eucharist reserved from Holy Thursday to Good Friday is never to be left without lights, not even for one hour ("Nec una hora sine luminaribus manet"). [81] The significance of this usage is heightened by another rubric in the same text that states in regard to the Easter Triduum at Cluny, "During these three days there is no light in the church, except before the Body of Christ." [82] The insistence upon maintaining a perpetual light before the reserved Sacrament from Holy Thursday to Good Friday that we find in this and other subsequent texts of the Holy Thursday reservation rite (and later utilized for all forms of Eucharistic reservation) may well have been inspired by the ancient practice of Jerusalem regarding the Holy Sepulcher, within which a lamp was kept continuously alight night and day, as attested by the fourth-century Spanish pilgrim Egeria. [83]

---

[79] Text in Bruno Albers, ed., *Consuetudines monasticae*, vol. 5, *Consuetudines monasteriorum Germaniae necnon s. Vitonis Virdunensis et Floriacensis abbatiae monumenta saeculi decimi continens* (Monte Cassino, Italy: Typis Societatis Editricis Castri Casini, 1912), 120.

[80] *Consuetudines* of Sigibert, chap. 30, in Bruno Albers, ed., *Consuetudines monasticae*, vol. 2, *Consuetudines Cluniacenses antiquiores* (Monte Cassino, Italy: Typis Montis Casini, 1905), 93.

[81] *Ordo Cluniacensis*, pt. 1, chap. 67, in Marquard Herrgott, ed., *Vetus disciplina monastica* (Paris, 1726; repr., Siegburg, Germany: Franciscus Schmitt, 1999), 259.

[82] Ibid., pt. 2, chap. 15, p. 313.

[83] For the text, see A. Franceschini and R. Weber, eds., *Itinerarium Egeriae*, chap. 24, no. 4, in *Itineraria et Alia Geographia*, CCSL 175 (Turnhout, Belgium: Brepols, 1965), 68.

Another Cluny customary, that of the abbot Saint Udalric of Zell (compiled c. 1080), specifies for the Holy Thursday procession the placement of the Eucharist within a gold paten, enclosed between two gold plates that are in turn encompassed by two silver tablets normally used for the Gospel book; the text also prescribes the use of "very much incense" for the procession.[84] Archbishop John of Avranches, in his *Liber de officiis ecclesiasticis* for his see of Rouen, France (episcopate, 1067–1079), directs the use of the "most radiant linen cloths" for the adornment of the place where the Blessed Sacrament is to be reserved.[85] A missal of Rieux, France, thought to date from about 1100, is the earliest text to mention the carrying of a canopy over the Blessed Sacrament during the Holy Thursday procession to the place of repose. The canopy is described as a "very fine linen cloth" carried by several clerics. This text also mentions that while the Eucharist is being brought, the choir sings Vespers in the repository, providing the earliest evidence of prayer in the repository.[86]

In Rome, it is during the thirteenth century that we begin to find specific instructions for the Holy Thursday reservation of the Eucharist, as given in the Pontifical of the Roman Curia: a cardinal priest would carry the Eucharist to the "place prepared" in a pyx, with a canopy borne over the Sacrament, preceded by a processional cross and lights.[87] A canopy as well as a small bell are specified for the Holy Thursday procession in the pontifical that William Durandus prepared for his own diocese of Mende, France (c. 1294).[88] During the same century, a customary for the English diocese of Norwich dating from about 1260 prescribes the singing of a penitential psalm during the Holy Thursday Eucharistic procession and provides the earliest detailed account of how the place of reposition is to be adorned:

> The procession should depart with candles and a thurible, and the deacon with the chalice, and the bishop should follow, carrying with the utmost reverence the paten with the Body of the Lord, and the priest who shall be revested shall begin the psalm *Miserere mei Deus* [Ps 50]. The altar, however, to which they shall go forth, namely the altar of Saint Katherine, ought to be prepared in this manner. There shall be laid over it the purest linen cloth, and over it two napkins in a cross [crosswise]; over this the deacon shall place first the chalice. Then the bishop [shall place] before the chalice the paten with the Body, and the paten itself shall be covered with a certain very fine vessel that should be able to go around it entirely. The four ends of the two napkins shall be inverted

---

[84] *Consuetudines Cluniacenses* of Saint Udalric of Zell, bk. 1, chap. 12, PL 149, col. 659.

[85] John of Avranches, *Liber de officiis ecclesiasticis*, PL 147, col. 50.

[86] "Old Missal of the Bishop of Rieux", quoted by Jean Mabillon, in PL 78, col. 890.

[87] Michel Andrieu, ed., *Le pontifical romain au moyen-âge*, vol. 2, *Le pontifical de la Curie romaine au XIIIᵉ siècle*, ST 87 (Vatican City: Biblioteca Apostolica Vaticana, 1940), 463.

[88] Andrieu, *Pontifical romain au moyen-âge*, 3:580.

over these, covering all. And thus these things finally having been arranged, the priest shall offer incense over all these things. . . . All should return, a candlestand with a candle having been left continuously burning before the Body of the Lord.[89]

The fourteenth-century *Liber ordinarius* of the collegiate church and abbey of Essen, Germany, directs that the Host to be reserved for the Holy Communion of Good Friday is to be enfolded within a corporal that is then placed atop a chalice and covered with an inverted paten. The celebrant, upon lifting this chalice with the Host from the altar, intones the opening antiphon of Holy Thursday Vespers, *Calicem salutaris accipiam* ("*I will take the chalice of salvation*").[90] After the singing of Psalm 115, the priest, having intoned the antiphon a second time, departs with the Eucharist in a procession to the place of reposition, going forth "circumspectly and morosely" as he holds the stem of the chalice with one hand and rests the other hand over the inverted paten. Along the way, the Communion antiphon *Hoc Corpus* ("*This is my Body*"), a chant traceable to the second half of the eighth century,[91] is sung in a lowered voice. At the repository, all kneel as the Blessed Sacrament is placed in an "ark" (*archa*).[92] A fifteenth-century addition to the early fourteenth-century ceremonial of Cologne, Germany, also begins the reposition rite with the antiphon *Calicem salutaris*: the priest, having thrice incensed the Blessed Sacrament reserved in a chalice on the altar, takes the chalice into his hands and sings the *Calicem salutaris*, after which he recites with the deacon the entire office of Vespers before the Sacrament, subsequently incensing it again and taking it from the altar to the repository following the end of Vespers.[93]

A 1531 missal for the Monastery of Saint-Martin d'Ainay, near Lyons, France, directs that while the priest is carrying the Body of the Lord "with much honor" to the place of reposition, "the whole convent should kneel until it should be reposed."[94] Fourteenth-century texts from Olomouc, Czech Republic, and Cologne, Germany, speak of an aspersion of the repository with holy water.[95] The latter text also directs

---

[89] Text in J. B. L. Tolhurst, ed., *The Customary of Norwich*, HBS 82 (London: Henry Bradshaw Society, 1948), 84.

[90] This antiphon is traceable to about 870, when it appears in the Antiphonary of Compiègne (France); see René-Jean Hésbert, ed., *Corpus antiphonalium officii*, vol. 1, REDSMF 7 (Rome: Herder, 1963), 170.

[91] This chant first appears in the Mass antiphonary of Mount Blandin (Belgium, c. 750–800) as the Communion for the Fifth Sunday of Lent; see Hésbert, *Antiphonale missarum sextuplex*, 82. For the complete text of this antiphon, see the reposition rite of Palencia, Spain, given below, pp. 376–377.

[92] Text in Franz Arens, ed., *Der Liber ordinarius der Essener Stiftskirche* (Paderborn, Germany: Albert Pape, 1908), 48–49.

[93] Text in Gottfried Amberg, ed., *Ceremoniale Coloniense*, Studien zur Kölner Kirchengeschichte 17 (Siegburg, Germany: Franz Schmitt, 1982), 130, footnote.

[94] Martène, *De antiquis ecclesiae ritibus*, bk. 4, chap. 22, 3:125.

[95] See the Holy Thursday rubrics of a fourteenth-century missal of the collegiate church of Olomouc, Czech Republic, and the early fourteenth-century ceremonial of Cologne;

that a silver bell be rung "before the venerable Sacrament" in a sub-
dued manner during the procession to the repository.[96]

In the earliest detailed rubrics for the Holy Thursday Eucharistic
reservation rite, those of Sigibert for the French abbey of Gorze (c.
1031) quoted previously, there is already mention of bringing a chalice in the procession to the repository. At first this vessel was used
only for the infusion of the unconsecrated wine in the Good Friday
liturgy. But by the early fourteenth century, the custom had arisen of
placing the Host consecrated on Holy Thursday into the chalice rather
than on a paten, utilizing the chalice as if it were a pyx or ciborium
for bringing the Blessed Sacrament to the place of repose and reserving the Eucharist until Good Friday; the use of a chalice in this manner is indicated in the Carmelite *Ordinarium* compiled by the order's
German provincial Sibert de Beka, dating from about 1312.[97] This
practice soon entered the papal liturgy: the papal liturgical book known
as the Long Ceremonial, attributed to John of Sion and dating from a
little before 1342, directs that the reserved Sacrament is to be carried
in a chalice covered with a silk cloth to the place of reposition.[98] The
use of a monstrance-like Eucharistic vessel called a *custodia* for the
Holy Thursday reservation rite is specified in missals from Segovia,
Spain (1500), and Evora, Portugal (1509).[99]

The ceremonial of the papal master of ceremonies Pierre Ameil
(+1403; completed by Pierre Assalbit, 1435–1441), which refers to the
repository as the *Armariolum*, is evidently the earliest to specify the use
of a humeral veil for the procession; it also mentions "a large gold
chalice" specifically for the Holy Thursday reservation rite, in which
the Host is placed, and prescribes the placement of the paten over the
corporal covering the top of the chalice.[100]

From the pontificate of Pope John XXII (1316–1334) onward, the
pope himself sometimes carried the Eucharist in the processions to

texts in Polycarp Radó, O.S.B., and Ladislaus Mezey, *Libri liturgici manuscripti bibliothecarum
Hungariae et limitropharum regionum* (Budapest: Akadémiai Kiadó, 1973), 94, and Amberg,
Ceremoniale Coloniense, 130.

[96] Amberg, *Ceremoniale Coloniense*, 130.

[97] Text in Benedict Zimmerman, ed., *Ordinaire de l'ordre de Notre-Dame du Mont-Carmel*,
Bibliothèque liturgique 13 (Paris: Alphonse Picard et Fils, 1910), 164, 169. Although the Holy
Thursday rubrics of the Carmelite text are a bit vague as to whether the Eucharist was placed
within the chalice or over it on a paten (ibid., 164), a careful reading of the Good Friday rubrics
from the same text leaves little doubt that the Host for the Good Friday Communion rite
and the Hosts for Viaticum were reserved *within* the chalice (ibid., 169).

[98] Text in Marc Dykmans, S.J., ed., *Le cérémonial papal de la fin du moyen âge à la Renaissance*, vol. 3, BIHBR 26 (Brussels and Rome: Institut Historique Belge de Rome, 1983), 208.

[99] See respectively *Missale secundum consuetudinem Segobiensis ecclesie* (Venice: Johannes
Emericus de Spira, 1500; digitized text, Biblioteca Digital Hispanica, Biblioteca Nacional
de España, Madrid, n.d.), fol. 72v, and *Missale secundum consuetudinem Elborensis ecclesie noviter
impressum* (Lisbon: Germano Galharde, 1509; digitized text, Biblioteca Nacional Digital,
Biblioteca Nacional de Portugal, 2009), fols. 78v, 79v.

[100] Text in Marc Dykmans, S.J., ed., *Le cérémonial papal de la fin du moyen âge à la Renaissance*, vol. 4, BIHBR 27 (Brussels and Rome: Institut Historique Belge de Rome, 1985), 134–135.

and from the place of repose on Holy Thursday and Good Friday.[101] But it was Pope Sixtus IV (1471–1484), a Franciscan, who made this observance the norm, exhibiting in this regard a pronounced devotion to the Blessed Sacrament. On Holy Thursday 1476 he insisted upon carrying the Eucharist to the repository as eight assisting bishops bore the canopy over the Sacrament and twenty other clerics carried torches in the procession. The next day, he carried the Eucharist in the procession from the repository to the altar for the Good Friday liturgy.[102] Thereafter he decreed that the pope was to be the ordinary minister for the processional transfer of the Eucharist on Holy Thursday and Good Friday in the papal liturgy.[103] The papal master of ceremonies Patrizio Piccolomini, compiler of the 1488 *Caeremoniale Romanum*, credits Pope Sixtus with considerably expanding the ceremonial splendor of the processions to and from the repository, motivated by the consideration that it is "not possible for us to venerate our Savior with enough fitting praises".[104] The highly detailed rubrics for the papal Eucharistic processions of Holy Thursday and Good Friday in the 1488 ceremonial,[105] compiled only four years after Sixtus' death, formed the basis for the magnificent processions to and from the repository prescribed in the universally promulgated *Caeremoniale episcoporum* of 1600.[106] The Roman Diary of Jacobo Gherardi da Volterra, describing the papal Holy Thursday Mass of April 20, 1481, tells of Pope Sixtus IV carrying the Blessed Sacrament from the high altar to the "small chapel", where it would be placed in a "small silver ark" (*argentea arcula*) on the chapel's altar. In the procession, the ambassadors of several kings and princes carried the canopy over the Eucharist, which was borne by the pontiff as the assembled cardinals and bishops preceded him, each carrying a lit candle.[107]

---

[101] The ceremonial of Pierre Ameil lists several popes of the fourteenth century who carried the Host on Good Friday from the repository to the altar for the day's Mass of the Presanctified, beginning with Pope John XXII; see ibid., 152–153. The papal book of ceremonies known as the Long Ceremonial, dating from about 1340, is the first such book to mention that the pontiff (or a cardinal bishop) may carry the Eucharist in the Holy Thursday procession to the repository; see Dykmans, *Cérémonial papal de la fin du moyen âge à la Renaissance*, 3:208–209.

[102] This incident regarding Pope Sixtus IV is related in a marginal note added to a mid-fifteenth-century manuscript copy of a fourteenth-century papal book of ceremonies known as the Long Ceremonial; see Dykmans, *Cérémonial papal de la fin du moyen âge à la Renaissance*, 3:208, footnote.

[103] See the rubrics of the 1488 *Caeremoniale Romanum* of the papal master of ceremonies Patrizio Piccolomini in Marc Dykmans, S.J., ed., *L'oeuvre de Patrizi Piccolomini, ou Le cérémonial papal de la première Renaissance*, vol. 2, ST 294 (Vatican City: Biblioteca Apostolica Vaticana, 1982), 376–377.

[104] Ibid., 376 (quotation is Piccolomini's paraphrase of the sentiments of Pope Sixtus IV).

[105] Ibid., 368–371, 387–388.

[106] Triacca and Sodi, *Caeremoniale episcoporum: Editio princeps (1600)*, bk. 2, chaps. 23, 25, pp. 234–238, 248–250 (new pagination).

[107] Text in Enrico Carusi, ed., *Il diario romano di Jacopo Gherardi da Volterra*, Rerum Italicarum scriptores 23, pt. 3 (Castello, Italy: Tipi della Casa Editrice S. Lapi, 1904), 47.

The 1506 missal of Palma de Majorca, Spain, simply describes the Holy Thursday repository as "some good and beautiful place".[108] But in the book of rites for cardinals and bishops written in the early 1520s by the papal master of ceremonies and bishop Paride de Grassis (+1528), there are specifics regarding the arrangement of the repository: "And first of all, indeed, some chapel in the body of the church shall be adorned for the reposition of the Sacrament, as solemnly as it shall be possible ... and the altar there shall be adorned with a *capsula* [small coffer] upon it for the enclosure of the Sacrament."[109]

The use of the Passion Sunday Communion antiphon *Hoc Corpus* for the processional transfer of the Eucharist during the Easter Triduum is first mentioned (for Good Friday) in an eleventh-century customary of the eremitical monastery of Santa Croce, Fonte Avellano, Italy.[110] The use of this antiphon for the Holy Thursday procession, beginning in the fourteenth century, became by the sixteenth century common across much of late medieval Europe.[111] The singing of the Eucharistic hymn *Pange lingua*, rather than the *Hoc Corpus*, during this procession is traceable to the 1488 *Caeremoniale Romanum* of the papal master of ceremonies Patrizio Piccolomini.[112] The use of the *Pange lingua* for the Holy Thursday Eucharistic procession was subsequently made universal with the promulgation of the *Missale Romanum* of 1570.[113]

Earlier in this chapter, we cited Pope Benedict XVI's explanation of the journey of Christ from the Last Supper to the Garden of Olives, symbolically represented by the Holy Thursday Eucharistic procession, as a going forth not only into "the night of Gethsemane" but also a journey into "the night of the tomb". In medieval and Renaissance Spain, as well as in Italy, the Eucharistic procession and reposition of Holy Thursday became deeply identified with the defining moment of the Passion: the Savior's death and burial. In Spain, from the twelfth century onward, the repository increasingly came to be

---

[108] Text in Gabriel Seguí i Trobat, ed., *El missal mallorquí de 1506: Estudi i edició segons l'exemplar de la Biblioteca Bartomeu March*, Col·lectània sant pacià 79 (Barcelona: Facultat de Teologia de Catalunya, Centre d'Estudis Teològics de Mallorca, 2003), 287.

[109] Paride de Grassis, *De caeremoniis cardinalium et episcoporum in eorum dioecesibus* (Rome: Bernardinus Donangelus, 1587; digitized text, Bayerische Staatsbibliothek, Munich, 2009), bk. 2, chap. 46, p. 244.

[110] *Primus codex Fontavellanensi* (excerpt), PL 151, col. 882.

[111] Examples include Barking, England (late fourteenth-century ordinal); Hildesheim, Germany (1499 missal); and Seville, Spain (1534 missal); see respectively J. B. L. Tolhurst, ed., *The Ordinale and Customary of the Benedictine Nuns of Barking Abbey*, vol. 1, HBS 65 (London: Henry Bradshaw Society, 1927), 93; *Missale Hildensemense* (Nürnberg: Germany: Georg Stuchs, 1499; digitized text, Bayerische Staatsbibliothek, Munich, 2009), fol. 98r; and *Missale divinorum secundum consuetudinem alme ecclesie Hispalensis* (Seville, Spain: Joannes Varela, 1534; Latin text provided by Biblioteca Apostolica Vaticana, Vatican City [shelf mark Stamp. Barb. B. X. 4], fol. 79r. Other examples appear elsewhere in this chapter (Essen, Palencia, Jaén).

[112] Dykmans, *Oeuvre de Patrizi Piccolomini*, 2:370.

[113] Text in Sodi and Triacca, *Missale Romanum: Editio princeps (1570)*, 239 (new pagination).

known as the *monumento*, the tomb of Christ. Perhaps the finest example of the Spanish tradition in this regard is the majestic Holy Thursday procession prescribed in the rubrics of the 1568 missal of Palencia, the Latin text of which has been graciously provided to the author by the Vatican Library:

> The reservation of the Body of Christ until tomorrow follows accordingly, in a becoming and noble place prepared for this, which place the people call the *monumento*, with at least four from the leading men of the city, or from the principal clerics, holding the canopy aloft with four shafts, under which the Body of the Lord ought reverently to be carried away. The Communion of the Body and Blood of the Lord having been completed in the usual manner, and the Communion [verse] having been sung in the choir, namely *The Lord Jesus, after he had supper with his disciples, washed their feet*, etc., he who has celebrated the Mass, before he should say the Postcommunion, now takes the chalice, and washes it, and places within a pall and upon it the Body of Christ, namely, the other Host that he consecrated, that it may be reserved; placing over the chalice either the paten or the corporals or, preferably, some silver utensil with which the chalice should be covered, if it can be done; and it should be covered with a very fine cloth, most preferably of a black color, so that the entire chalice should remain veiled. But the Blood is not reserved to tomorrow. Holding then with two hands the chalice thus veiled, having turned toward the people, he shall begin the antiphon: *This is my Body*. But the cantors or the choir continue the same antiphon, repeating it as often as it will have been necessary. *Which shall be delivered for you; this is the chalice of the New Testament in my blood, says the Lord; do this whithersoever you eat it in my memory.* Meanwhile, the procession is arranged by the master of ceremonies, with the candle bearers preceding and some cleric bringing the processional cross. Then a certain cleric or noble layman carries the black standard of the church, adorned with a red cross, in the middle of the procession. And all the clerics, singing the antiphon *This is my Body*, go forth with candles kindled, their heads uncovered. The deacon and the subdeacon, however, support the arms of the priest carrying the Body of Christ, and two thurifers continually cense the Sacrament; but the porter, or someone else, continually casts down green grass or grain at the feet of the priest bringing the Sacrament from the altar all the way to the *monumento*. And approaching thus to the step of the *monumento*, the priest, the deacon, and the subdeacon, with two others from the principal priests, and the candle bearers and the thurifers, ascend to the place, where the ark has been placed; which opening, the priest places within it the chalice with the Eucharist upon the *ara* [an altar stone[114]] and the corporals, which ought to be there, with the aforesaid others watching; and there in the

---

[114] The Latin term *ara*, a wording meaning "altar", was also used to denote a small consecrated stone that served as a portable altar for celebrating Mass; it is this latter object

ark he places a book of the Old and New Testaments, or a missal, and a small cross, and a small hand bell, and an incense boat with incense, and some keys of the church, and cruets or flasks without the wine and water, all which things ought to be placed there beforehand by the sacristan; and then, the Sacrament having been censed, and a deep genuflection having been made, [the priest] carefully closes the ark, and with wax and a seal, he seals it; and the key should be given to the hebdomadarian, or someone from the principal clerics, or preferably the treasurer of the church, that he may carefully keep it until tomorrow. Then are lit very many candles, which ought to burn at all times before the *monumento* until tomorrow. Which having been completed, the priest, turning himself to the people, begins the antiphon of Vespers, *I will take the chalice of salvation*, and he who accompanies him the psalm, *I have believed* . . . [Ps 115]. And thus the procession should return to the choir, Vespers being sung.[115]

This ceremony has undoubtedly inherited in part the Exodus symbolism of the earlier-described chrism procession, including the imagery of the processional lights as the pillar of fire that went before the Israelites crossing the desert and that of the canopy as the cloud that overshadowed the Tent of Meeting. In the above rite, the strewing of greenery along the path of the procession would have called to mind Christ's identification of himself as the "green wood" when he spoke to the women lamenting him on the way to Calvary (Lk 23:27–31). Moreover, this action, resembling the strewing of palms before the Lord on Palm Sunday, would have also conveyed the Palm Sunday theme of Christ going triumphantly to his Passion. The explanation given by Durandus for the strewing of palms before the crucifix on Palm Sunday seems equally applicable to this Holy Thursday Eucharistic custom of medieval Spain: "Truly, green branches are thrust before the cross and upon the cross to indicate that we have all the freshness of the virtues from the Crucified; for Christ was the green branch, having in himself and us by him all the freshness of the virtues, whence he says: 'For if in the green wood they do these things, what shall be done in the dry?' [Lk 23:31]."[116]

After reaching the repository, the celebrant places into the *monumento* together with the Eucharist several liturgical objects: a Bible or a missal, a small bell, empty altar cruets, an incense boat, and a cross.

---

that is evidently specified here to serve as a fitting surface upon which to rest the reserved Sacrament; see the Segovia rite later in this chapter (p. 383).

[115] *Missale Pallantinum* (Palencia, Spain: Sebastian Martinez, 1568; Latin text provided by Biblioteca Apostolica Vaticana, Vatican City [shelf mark Stamp. Barb. B. X. 1]), fols. 87v–88v. A 1533 missal of Salamanca, Spain, directs the sacristan to place all the same liturgical objects into the "ark of the *monumento*" as the Palencia missal specifies; see *Missale ad usum alme ecclesie Salamanticensis* (Salamanca, Spain: Juan de Junta, 1533; digitized text, Universidad de Salamanca, Gredos Repositorio Documental, Salamanca, Spain, 2010), fol. 63r.

[116] Durandus, *Rationale* (CCCM 140a), bk. 6, chap. 67, no. 8, p. 324.

Although the rubrics give no reasons for the inclusion of these objects, we will venture to offer a plausible explanation based upon medieval principles of the allegorical interpretation of the liturgy. The placement of a bell in the *monumento* would have represented the traditional silencing of the bells during the Triduum, which, according to John Beleth (+1190), symbolizes the silencing of the preaching of the Apostles when in the hours of the Passion they deserted Christ. Beleth adds that the wooden clapper that sounds in place of the bells during the Triduum symbolizes Christ, who as the lone Preacher during the Passion cried out from the wood of the Cross, "Father, forgive them, for they know not what they do" (Lk 23:34).[117] The placement within the *monumento* of either a Bible or a missal, both of which contain the Gospels and Epistles written by the Apostles and disciples, could be explained as likewise symbolic of the "silence" of the Apostles and disciples during the Passion.[118] When a missal rather than a Bible was placed in the *monumento*, it would have carried the added significance of symbolizing the cessation of the celebration of Mass from after the Holy Thursday liturgy until the Easter Vigil, which is likewise intimated by the empty cruets. In this context, the aforementioned placement of a bell in the *monumento* would have additionally suggested the silencing of the "sacring bell" normally rung at the consecration of the Eucharist, in that there was to be no consecration again until the Easter Vigil. The incense in its incense boat would have represented the myrrh and aloes with which Nicodemus and Joseph of Arimathea buried Christ's body (Jn 19:38–40). The insertion of a cross, probably a crucifix, into the *monumento* would have served as a further sign of the burial of Christ at the conclusion of his three hours on the Cross. The affixing of a seal to the door of the *monumento* reenacted the sealing of Christ's tomb procured by the chief priests and Pharisees (Mt 27:66).[119]

It appears probable that underlying the symbolic association of the repository with the sepulcher of Christ was an intuitive perception of the repository as a kind of "mystic Gethsemane" where on Holy Thurs-

---

[117] John Beleth, *Summa de ecclesiasticis officiis*, chap. 100, in Heribertus Douteil, C.S.Sp., ed., *Iohannis Beleth: Summa de ecclesiasticis officiis*, CCCM 41a (Turnhout, Belgium: Brepols, 1976), 186. Hereafter cited as Beleth, *Summa de ecclesiasticis officiis* (CCCM 41a).

[118] This practice also appears in the Spanish missals of Valencia (1492), Segovia (1500), and Tarazona (1529); see respectively *Missale iuxta morem et consuetudinem sedis Valentiae* (Venice: Johann Hamman, 1492; digitized text, Biblioteca Digital Hispánica, Biblioteca Nacional de España, Madrid, n.d.), fol. 57r; *Missale secundum consuetudinem Segobiensis ecclesie* (1500), fol. 72v; and *Missale secundum ritum ac consuetudinem insignis Ecclesiae Tirasonensis* (Saragossa, Spain: Jorge Coci, 1529; digitized text, Bayerische Staatsbibliothek, Munich, n.d.), fol. 82r. Examples from Toledo and Jaén are cited later in this chapter (pp. 383–384).

[119] This practice of affixing a seal also appears in a 1499 missal of Tarragona, Spain; see *Missale secundum consuetudinem Ecclesiae Tarraconensis* (Tarragona, Spain: Johannes Rosenbach, 1499; digitized text, Biblioteca Virtual del Patrimonio Bibliográfico, Madrid, n.d.), fol. 86r. Examples from Toledo, Jaén, and Barcelona are cited later in this chapter (pp. 383–384, 386).

day the adorer could watch with Christ as Christ began his Passion in the Garden of Olives, the prelude to his death on Good Friday. Our Lord himself speaks of his Gethsemane agony as a sorrow "even unto death" (Mt 26:38). Moreover, insomuch as Christ at the Last Supper anticipated his own immolation on the Cross by offering the sacrifice of the Eucharist, it was not unreasonable for medieval liturgists and the faithful to see in the reservation of the Eucharist following the Mass of Holy Thursday a symbolic anticipation of the burial of the Lord that epitomized the totality of his immolation. There is also the Eucharistic exegesis of Saint Paul, who says of the Sacrament, "For as often as you shall eat this bread, and drink the chalice, you shall shew the death of the Lord, until he come" (1 Cor 11:26). Thus, when the medieval worshiper came to the repository, calling it the "sepulcher", he did not in any way think of Christ as "dead" in the tabernacle; rather, he came to adore and contemplate a loving God so merciful that he was willing to suffer even death and the tomb for our salvation.

The symbolic association of the Holy Thursday reservation of the Eucharist with the burial of Christ arose soon after the transfer of the Blessed Sacrament had developed into a solemn procession in the monasteries of eleventh-century France. The earliest reference to this symbolism appears in a sacramentary of probable monastic origin compiled in or near the French city of Albi and thought to date from about the year 1100: "In memory of his burial, the Body of the Lord is reserved from the fifth day [Holy Thursday] and consumed by the faithful on the sixth [Good Friday]." [120] It is shortly afterward that this symbolism of the Holy Thursday reposition first appears in Spain, in a will rediscovered over 650 years after its composition by a priest exploring the ecclesiastical archives of Catalonia in the early 1800s. Father Jaime Villanueva (+1824) found the document in the archives of the Church of Saint Peter in Ager, Spain. In this will dating from the year 1152, the viscount Gerald of Ager bequeaths his inheritance to the service of the church, making a specific provision for the annual adornment of the repository on Holy Thursday:

> Be it noted by all, both those present and those in the future, that I, Gerald, viscount of Ager, conscience-stricken by divine inspiration, give and circumscribe by my unconditional and sincere will unto the Lord God and the Church of Saint Peter all that tithed territory and government of my estate of Ager ... that has come to me from the gift conferred by my lord grandfather Ponce Gerald ... that they may be divided in this way, namely one portion for the sacred custody

---

[120] Extract from a lost sacramentary formerly in the archives of the cathedral chapter of Albi, recorded in the notes of the eighteenth-century French liturgist Pierre Lebrun (+1729) and quoted in Michel Andrieu, *Immixtio et consecratio: La consécration par contact dans les documents liturgiques du moyen âge*, Université de Strasbourg, Bibliothèque de l'Institut de Droit Canonique, 11 (Paris: A. Picard, 1924), 94.

of the said church, for one lamp to be illuminated perpetually in the chapel of the blessed Mary Magdalene, and for four suitable torches, which are to burn continually each year before the *monumentum* of the Body of Christ on the day of Holy Thursday, all the way until after the reception of the same.[121]

The use of the Latin term *monumentum* (in Spanish, *monumento*), thereby identifying the repository as "the sepulcher of the Body of Christ", constitutes a clear reference to the burial symbolism of the Holy Thursday reservation, and the earliest instance of the term by which the Holy Thursday repository later came to be known throughout Spain; the repository is referred to with the Latin term *monumentum* in the Spanish liturgical books of Toledo (1478), Valencia (1494), Orense (1494), Jaén (1499), Tarragona (1499), Valladolid (1499), Segovia (1500), Huesca (1505), Avila (1510), Seville (1565), Palencia (1568), and Barcelona (1569), as well as in a missal of Evora, Portugal (1509).[122] Equally significant in the above text is the provision to keep four torches continually burning in the repository. Here we find the beginnings of the tradition of illuminating the Holy Thursday repository with an abundance of lights. We see this practice developed further in the Holy Thursday rubrics of a fourteenth-century *consueta* (customary) for the Spanish diocese of Vich:

> Afterward the deacon should uncover the *Sancta* [the Eucharist], and the bishop should take from the *Oblata*, namely an intact consecrated Host. And it should be reserved in this way that the said consecrated Host is placed by the bishop or celebrant in a larger chalice with corporals, and in order that it shall be able to be done more

---

[121] Text in Villanueva, *Viage literario a las iglesias de España*, 9:279–280.

[122] See respectively *Missale mixtum secundum consuetudinem almae ecclesie Toletane* (1478; manuscript: Toledo, Spain, Toledo Cathedral, Library, MS Res. 2), fols. 155ff., 157ff., described in José Janini and Ramón Gonzálvez, *Catálogo de los manuscritos litúrgicos de la catedral de Toledo*, Publicaciones del IPIET, 3rd series, 11 (Toledo, Spain: Diputación Provincial, 1977), 260–261; *Hores de la setmana sancta segons lo us del archibisbat de Valencia* (Valencia, Spain: Jacobi de Villa, 1494), fol. 156r; *Missale secundum usum Auriensis ecclesiae* (Monterrey, Spain: Gonzalo Rodriguez de la Passera and Juan de Porras, 1494; digitized text, Biblioteca Digital Hispánica, Biblioteca Nacional de España, Madrid, n.d.), fol. 86r; *Missale Giennense / Manuale continens ordinem ad celebrandum ecclesiastica sacramenta* [*Missale secundum morem et consuetudinem sancte ecclesie Gienensis*] (Seville: Meinard Ungut and Stanislao Polono, 1499), fols. 74r–74v, 80v; *Missale secundum consuetudinem ecclesiae Tarraconensis* (1499), fols. 86r, 93v; *Missale secundum consuetudinem monachorum congregationis sancti Benedicti de Valladolid* (Montserrat, Spain: Johannes Luschner, 1499; digitized text, Biblioteca Virtual del Patrimonio Bibliográfico, Madrid, n.d.), fol. 84r; *Missale secundum consuetudinem Segobiensis ecclesie* (1500), fols. 72r–72v, 80v; *Missale Oscense*, 1505, quoted in Blessed Juan Bautista Ferreres Boluda, S.J., *Historia del misal romano* (Barcelona: Eugenio Subirana, 1929), 262; *Missale Abulense* (Salamanca, Spain: Juan de Porras, 1510), sig. i2v; *Missale divinorum secundum consuetudinem alme ecclesie Hispalensis* (Seville, Spain: Joannes Gotherius, 1565; digitized text, Fondos digitalizados de la Universidad de Sevilla, Seville, n.d.), fol. 99r; *Missale Pallantinum* (1568), fols. 87v–88v, 89r, 92r, 99r, 347v; *Ordinarium Barcinonense* (Barcelona: Claudius Bornat, 1569; digitized text, Biblioteca de Catalunya, Barcelona, 2010), fols. 142v–143r, 148v; and *Missale secundum consuetudinem Elborensis ecclesie* (1509), fols. 78v, 79v, 85v.

honorably, it should be transported with kindled lights in copious multitude under a canopy to its place prepared as befits it. And with the lights prominent in that very place, it should be reserved with great reverence.[123]

It is likely that the use of numerous lights in the repository was inspired in part by the association of the repository with the tomb of Christ, where candles and lamps have been used for centuries as a visual testament that Christ is risen and lives forever. According to the 1496 account of a pilgrim named Peter Rindfleisch visiting the Holy Land, the tomb of the Savior in Jerusalem's Church of the Holy Sepulcher was illuminated by forty lamps within the sepulcher, as well as by other lamps hanging around and above the tomb's exterior, and a number of large, tall candles beside the tomb that burned continuously throughout the day and night.[124] The practice of surrounding the reserved Eucharist with candles is enjoined in the Holy Thursday rubrics of a missal of Avila, Spain (1510). After directing that at Mass two hosts should be consecrated, "the one for communicating, and the other to be preserved in the *monumento*", the missal states:

> Then [the priest] should wash his hands and afterward repose the entire consecrated Host in a clearly empty chalice; and he should cover it with a corporal, and with the paten placed above. Then four of the honorable prebendaries [beneficed cathedral priests] should enter, coming forth in the choir; they should hold the silk canopy that is put over the priest, two boys also, with lit candles, and two others going before with censers and smoking incense. And the procession having been arranged, the bishop or priest, taking the chalice with the Body of Christ in his hands, thereupon brings it to the place fittingly prepared for this, singing with solemnity in a lowered voice the antiphon *This is my Body, which shall be delivered for you,* and the choir, in continuing the said antiphon to the end, saying thus, *which shall be delivered for you. This chalice is the new testament in my blood; this do ye for the commemoration of me.* Meanwhile, the bishop or priest should repose the chalice with the Body of Christ in the place prepared, ... and having faithfully closed the ark with the key, the priest should carry the key and carefully keep it until the next day; and he should return to the altar with his ministers, lights having been left all around the Body of Christ.[125]

---

[123] *Consueta*, fourteenth century, manuscript of the Archivo Capitular, Vich, quoted in Ferreres Boluda, *Historia del misal romano*, 284. These rubrics are repeated verbatim in a Vich *consueta* dating from 1413 (ibid.).

[124] Text quoted in Thomas Kamm, *Sein Grab wird herrlich sein: Heilige Gräber als Zeugen barocker Frömmigkeit* (Salzburg, Austria: PARC / Stiftung Heimathaus Traunstein, 2003), 58.

[125] *Missale Abulense* (1510), sig. i2v–i3r.

In the above text, we see an early instance of the use of *two* thuribles for the continuous incensation of the Blessed Sacrament during the procession, a practice that was later made universal in the rubrics of the *Caeremoniale episcoporum* of 1600.[126] The rubric prescribing the placement of the paten atop the corporal or pall with which the mouth of the chalice is covered, first found in the earlier-cited papal ceremonial of Pierre Ameil (+1403; completed by Pierre Assalbit, 1435–1441), is a symbolic action based upon the allegorical interpretation of these liturgical objects in medieval commentaries on the Mass, particularly that of Pope Innocent III, who explains, "Therefore, in this place the mouth of the chalice signifies the mouth of the tomb, from which the deacon shall remove the corporal, designating that the angel of the Lord rolled back the stone from the mouth of the tomb."[127] The paten placed atop the corporal covering the chalice represents the seal affixed to the tomb, as later explained by the Barnabite liturgist Father Bartolommeo Gavanti (+1638) in his commentary upon the Holy Thursday Eucharistic procession of the *Missale Romanum*.[128]

The entombment associations of the Holy Thursday repository stemmed in part from the fact that the Eucharist reserved there was to be received at the Good Friday liturgy, the primary occasion for commemorating the death of Christ in the Holy Week liturgy. A fourteenth-century *ordinarium* for the Priory of Saint-Lô, a community of Augustinian canons regular in Rouen, France, speaks of the Holy Communion of Good Friday as a memorial of the burial of Christ: "In memory of his burial, the Body of the Lord, reserved from Holy Thursday to Good Friday, is taken by the faithful." It is because of this burial symbolism, the text explains, that during the Good Friday liturgy a particle of the reserved Eucharist is deposited in a chalice of *unconsecrated* wine on the altar.[129] In other words, the particle of the Host is lowered into the chalice, traditionally seen as a symbol of the tomb of Christ, just as Christ's body was lowered into the tomb.

Insomuch as the Church began her three days' commemoration of the Lord's three days in the tomb on Holy Thursday, it would not have been so much of a stretch to identify the Holy Thursday Eucharistic procession at the outset of the Triduum of Christ's burial with the carrying of the Lord's body to the tomb. In fact, there was in the papal liturgy of Rome during the twelfth and thirteenth centuries a unique rite that implicitly associated the cessation of Mass during the Easter Triduum with the burial of Christ. On Holy Thursday, the upper portion (*mensa*) of the high altar at Rome's cathedral church of

---

[126] Triacca and Sodi, *Caeremoniale episcoporum: Editio princeps (1600)*, bk. 2, chap. 23, pp. 234, 236–238 (new pagination).

[127] Innocent III, *De sacro altaris mysterio*, bk. 6, chap. 2, PL 217, col. 907.

[128] Bartolommeo Gavanti, *Thesaurus sacrorum rituum* (1628), in Bartolommeo Gavanti and Cajetan Merati, *Thesaurus sacrorum rituum* (Rome: Typographia Vaticana, 1736–1738), 1:1031.

[129] *Ordinarium canonorum regularum*, PL 147, col. 175.

Saint John Lateran would be lifted off its base and be carried by several cardinal priests and deacons into the chapel of Saint Pancratius, where it was kept and guarded continually by the cathedral canons until its return to the Lateran for the Easter Vigil. Four seals were affixed to the chapel door, evoking the imagery of the sealed tomb of Christ, not unlike what we saw earlier in the Palencia rite of reposing the Eucharist.[130] Evidence of the influence of the Lateran rite upon subsequent Holy Thursday rites can be found in a missal of Segovia, Spain (1500): the *ara*, the portable altar stone that we previously saw employed in the Palencia rite, would be carried by the deacon during the Holy Thursday procession to the *monumento*, behind the cross and before the Eucharist, which is carried by the celebrant. Upon reaching the repository, the deacon sets the *ara* at the middle of the *monumento* and unfolds corporals upon it, after which the celebrant places the Eucharist on the corporals, with the cross placed beside the *monumento*. On Good Friday the *ara* would be carried back from the *monumento* to the high altar in the Eucharistic procession of the Mass of the Presanctified (the Good Friday rite of Holy Communion).[131]

By the second half of the fifteenth century, the Passion symbolism of the Holy Thursday Eucharistic reposition had been fully developed in the liturgy of Spain's primatial see of Toledo. In 1478, Toledo's archbishop Alonso Carillo issued a manuscript missal containing detailed rubrics for the Holy Thursday procession.[132] These rubrics were subsequently incorporated virtually verbatim into the 1499 missal of an adjacent suffragan diocese, that of Jaén (they likewise entered the 1500 *Missale mixtum* of Francisco Cardinal Ximenes de Cisneros, a liturgical book combining Spain's ancient Mozarabic Rite with the late medieval liturgy of Toledo),[133] and are clearly the antecedent to the ceremony of Palencia that we presented earlier. What follows is a full transcription of the rubrics as translated from the Jaén missal:

---

[130] This description is drawn from Cardinal Bernard of Porto's *Ordo officiorum* for the Church of Saint John Lateran (c. 1140); see Ludwig Fischer, ed., *Bernhardi cardinalis et Lateranensis ecclesiae prioris Ordo officiorum ecclesiae Lateranensis*, Historische Forschungen und Quellen 2–3 (Munich: Dr. F. P. Datterer, 1916), 50–51. It is also described in the thirteenth-century Pontifical of the Roman Curia; see Andrieu, *Pontifical romain au moyen-âge*, 2:459–460. See also the *Liber censuum* (c. 1192); text in Paul Fabre and Louis Duchesne, eds., *Le Liber censuum de l'église romaine*, vol. 1, fasc. 2, Bibliothèque des écoles françaises d'Athènes et de Rome, 2nd series, Registres des papes du XIIIᵉ siècle, 6 (Paris: Fontemoing, 1901), no. 24, pp. 294–295.

[131] *Missale secundum consuetudinem Segobiensis ecclesie* (1500), fols. 72v, 80v.

[132] *Missale mixtum secundum consuetudinem almae ecclesie Toletane*, 1478, Toledo Cathedral MS Res. 2, fol. 155ff, described in Janini and Gonzálvez, *Catálogo de los manuscritos litúrgicos de la catedral de Toledo*, 260. For an Internet-accessible edition of the Toledo rubrics, see *Missale secundum consuetudinem almae ecclesiae Toletanae*, 1503–1518, vol. 4 (manuscript: Madrid, Biblioteca Nacional de España, MS 1543; digitized text, Biblioteca Digital Hispánica, Biblioteca Nacional de España, Madrid, 2007), fols. 80v–82r (website: http://bibliotecadigitalhispanica.bne.es).

[133] *Missale mixtum secundum regulam beati Isidori dictum mozarabes*, PL 85, cols. 418–419.

And after the priest shall have communicated, he should take the chalice, thoroughly purified, and place within the chalice the pall with which the chalice is covered. And the priest should reverently take the Body of Christ and place it within the aforesaid pall in the chalice; then he should take another pall, with which he should cover the chalice. And he should place the paten of the chalice thereon and put [over] the aforesaid paten and chalice a beautiful chalice veil, with which chalice veil he should also cover the entire chalice. And he should put [the veil] over his shoulders and thus bring the Eucharist honorably to the *monumento* singing [the antiphon], *This is my Body*, the entire choir [singing] likewise and devoutly, with lights and incense preceding before the Eucharist. And one boy should bring a small bell, ringing it. And a veil or cloth [canopy] should be carried honorably over the Body of the Lord by four or six lords of the higher-born of the city, who should bear the cloth or veil. And thus [there should be] one of the church workers who from the exit of the choir should continually cast down green foliage beneath the feet of him bearing or bringing the Body of the Lord; and thus is it done on the other day [Good Friday] in returning the Body of the Lord from the *monumento* to the altar. And when he shall have come to the *monumento*, the bishop or priest, in his vestments, or in his absence another dignitary or an older canon of his choir, should ascend, the dean or the treasurer keeping his place. And having placed the Eucharist in the *monumento*, the bishop or priest ought to uncover the chalice and humbly show the consecrated Host to two such lords. And the chalice having been covered as before, and a cross, and a mixed missal or Bible, and a censer without coals, and an incense boat with incense, and a small bell having been placed in the said *monumento*, he should also incense reverently the *monumento* with the other censer. And with the utmost diligence it should be closed with two keys, and with red wax it should be sealed with two seals, which seals and keys the said two lords should keep. And there ought always to be a light before the sepulcher. And the *monumento* having been closed,[134] while the priest returns with his ministers to the altar, there should be a sounding for Vespers with wooden mallets.[135]

In the above text, we find among the items placed within the *monumento* an empty thurible. Insofar as the thurible was traditionally seen by medieval liturgists as a symbol of the body of Christ, the placement of the empty thurible within the *monumento* can be seen as a representation of Christ's body in death. The entrusting of the keys of the *monumento* to two civic authorities—two lords—would have

---

[134] In the Toledo missal, this phrase is worded, "The Lord having been buried, and the *monumento* having been closed ..." (*Missale secundum consuetudinem almae ecclesiae Toletanae*, 1503–1518, vol. 4, fol. 82r).

[135] *Missale Giennense / Manuale ... sacramenta* (1499), fol. 74r–74v.

represented the securing of Christ's tomb by both the Romans and the chief priests and Pharisees (Mt 27:62–66). This too is the likely reason for the use of *two* seals for closing the *monumento*.

A highly detailed description of a late medieval repository is given in a 1497 account of the Holy Thursday Eucharistic procession at the court of Duke Ercole I d'Este, of Ferrara, Italy. The author, Giovanni Sabadino degli Arienti, addresses his description to the Duke of Ferrara himself as a tribute in praise of the duke's participation in the Holy Week rites:

> Very early in the morning, you enter into your church established in the ducal hall, where is prepared a place adorned according to your providence to repose the Body of Christ in rich vessels of gold and of silver ingeniously wrought.... Then the hour having come, you return to the church, in which the Mass is celebrated with solemn order. After which celebration by the priest, first you light in the adorned sepulcher twenty-four torches of white wax, of which first Your Religious Excellency takes one therefrom, and the others your most nobly born, and the brothers, and your most worthy curial gentlemen, carrying them with the most holy pomp. Such a Sacrament is reposed in a gold vessel, which is placed in a sepulcher made with great ornament from figured wood boards on a porphyry stone, framed with gold and placed upon a certain rocky mountain with some herbs that seem [as if they had] sprouted upon it, and raised above, a canopy of the most splendid brocade of gold; and in the middle, where the canopy was entered, by that which I saw, it has two curtains of Spanish linen veils, and over the marble floor a large and beautiful carpet, a most beautiful work and of singular honor. And in front of the sides, outside of the canopy, there were first twelve candles of the best weight of three pounds each; they were lit, nor are they ever extinguished until the next day, when [the Sacrament] is taken away with similar spiritual and holy pomp. On this way that such a Sacrament is carried and reposed in the adorned sepulcher, the choristers, with solemn voice, do not cease from singing supplications and prophecies.[136]

The accentuation of the Passion theme in the Spanish and Italian Holy Thursday reposition rites was sometimes expressed also in the chants chosen to accompany the Eucharistic procession. In the *Hores de la setmana sancta*, a liturgical book for the cathedral of Valencia, Spain, dating from 1494, the responsory assigned to be sung "in a low, dignified voice" as the Blessed Sacrament is carried to the *monumento*

---

[136] Giovanni Sabadino degli Arienti, *De triumphis religionis*, in Werner L. Gundersheimer, ed., *Art and Life at the Court of Ercole I d'Este: The 'De triumphis religionis' of Giovanni Sabadino degli Arienti*, Travaux d'humanisme et Renaissance 127 (Geneva: Droz, 1972), 90–91.

presents the poignant image of the thorn-crowned Christ standing before Pilate: "*Jesus having come out from the Praetorium bearing the crown of thorns, the Jews then all cried out, Away with him, away with him, crucify him. Verse: Pilate says to them: Behold your King; and they cried out to him, saying, Away with him, away with him, crucify him.*" [137] A late fifteenth-century liturgical book of the Benedictines' Italian Cassinese Congregation specifies for the Holy Thursday procession to the repository the singing of a Good Friday text, *Cum autem venissem*, a chant expressing the grief of the Blessed Virgin associated with the medieval genre of Marian lamentations known as the *planctus Mariae*; the chant is intoned when the priest takes into his hands the Eucharist to begin the procession; the same verse will again be sung when the Blessed Sacrament is carried back from the repository on Good Friday: "*But when I had come to the place where my Son was going to be crucified, they stood him in the midst of all the people, and he having been despoiled of his clothes, they left his most sacred body stripped.*" [138] In the Cassinese Benedictine monasteries of sixteenth-century Venice, the *Improperia* (Reproaches) from the Good Friday veneration of the cross ("*My people, what have I done to you? . . .*") were sung during the Holy Thursday procession to the repository. [139] The 1569 *ordinarium* of Barcelona, Spain, assigns for the procession to the *monumento* the singing of a penitential psalm, Psalm 50, the *Miserere*. After the *monumento* chest is closed and locked, it is sealed with five seals of red wax "gum" in the shape of a cross. There is in this fivefold use of red wax a clear allusion to the five wounds of Christ. [140]

The rubrics of the 1534 missal of Seville, Spain, describe a Holy Thursday Eucharistic procession in which all the beneficed priests (prebendaries) of the city's cathedral participate, with the Blessed Sacrament carried under a canopy mounted upon "four silver scepters". [141] The use of four scepters as support poles for the canopy may have been intended to symbolize the four kingdoms of Spain that were ultimately united in 1512 under King Ferdinand V and Queen Isabella

---

[137] *Hores de la setmana sancta . . . Valencia*, fol. 134r–134v. The verse for this responsory is here supplied from Francesc Xavier Altés i Aguiló, ed., *Missale Vicense, 1496*, facsimile ed., Biblioteca litúrgica catalana 3 (Barcelona: Institut d'Estudis Catalans, 2001), temporal, fol. 90v.

[138] Claudio Bernardi, *La drammaturgia della settimana santa in Italia*, La città e lo spettacolo 2 (Milan: Vita e Pensiero, 1991), 179–180; the Latin text of *Cum autem venissem* is supplied from the *Liber sacerdotalis* of Alberto Castellani, O.P., first published in 1523, reprinted with a different title in 1555: *Sacerdotale iuxta s. Romane ecclesie et aliarum ecclesiarum* (Venice: Peter Bosellus, 1555; digitized text, Bayerische Staatsbibliothek, Munich, 2009), fols. 237v–238r (text with music). Insofar as the Cassinese text uses *venissem* ("I had come") rather than the Venetian text's *venissent* ("they had come"), the author has modified the translation in this instance to correspond to the Cassinese variant of the chant.

[139] John Bettley, "The Office of Holy Week at St. Mark's, Venice, in the Late 16th Century, and the Musical Contributions of Giovanni Croce", *Early Music* 22 (February 1994): 49.

[140] *Ordinarium Barcinonense* (1569), fols. 142v–143r.

[141] *Missale . . . ecclesie Hispalensis* (1534), fol. 79r–79v.

I (Aragon, Castile, León, and Navarre). In 1545 the Spanish craftsman Anton Florentin undertook the design and construction of a huge *monumento* for the Seville cathedral, a three-story wood and ironwork structure over one hundred feet high that took nine years to complete. This monument, erected near the west end of the cathedral, was white in color with gold and black gilding. The first story, where the Blessed Sacrament was placed, consisted of sixteen massive Ionic columns, with statues, twice life-size, depicting Abraham, Melchisedech, Moses, and Aaron as well as personifications of eternal life, human nature, the Old Law, and the law of grace, all mounted on pedestals inscribed with Scripture verses. The second story had eight columns with eight statues, including Saint Peter weeping over his denial of Christ, the high priest's servant who struck Christ in the face, the soldier who won the gamble for the robe of Christ at his crucifixion, and Isaac carrying the firewood with which he was to have been sacrificed by his father, Abraham. A smaller four-columned copula within this story featured a statue of Christ crowned with thorns, carrying with his right hand the Cross and with the other the orb of the world. The third story consisted of eight Corinthian columns surrounding a statue of Christ bound and scourged. A tall cross stood atop the structure (replaced in 1624 with a fourth story featuring a Calvary scene). The Seville *monumento* was adorned with a vast number of lights, as attested by a nineteenth-century author, who speaks of it being lit by 114 torches and 453 candles, making it a most striking sight amid the darkness that enveloped the huge cathedral on Holy Thursday night.[142] This *monumento* was used for Holy Week in the cathedral up until the mid-twentieth century.[143]

The ten-foot-high portable silver shrine within which the repository tabernacle enclosing the Blessed Sacrament was placed on the first story of the Saville *monumento*, a *custodia* completed by Juan de Arfe y Villafane in 1587,[144] is still used in Seville to carry the monstrance in the annual Corpus Christi procession. In 1774, a majestic golden urn was made in Rome by Luis Valadier to serve as the repository tabernacle within the *custodia*.[145] The construction and adornment of magnificent repositories such as that of Seville was inspired in part by a verse of Messianic prophecy from the Book of Isaiah: "His sepulchre shall be glorious" (Is 11:10); alluding to this verse, the Fourth Provincial Council of Milan, Italy, convened in 1576 by Milan's

---

[142] Jules Corblet, *Histoire dogmatique, liturgique et archéologique du sacrement de l'Eucharistie* (Paris: Société Générale de Librairie Catholique, 1885–1886), 1:539.

[143] Vicente Rus Herrera and Federico García de la Concha Delgado, *Leyendas, tradiciones y curiosidades historícas de la semana santa de Sevilla* (Seville: Editorial Castillejo, 1993), 133–135.

[144] María Jesús Sanz Serrano, *Juan de Arfe y Villafañe y la custodia de Sevilla*, Arte hispalense 17 (Seville: Excma. Diputación Provincial de Sevilla, 1978), 33–34, 70–71.

[145] Luis Martínez Montiel and Alfredo J. Morales, *The Cathedral of Seville* (London: Scala Publishers, 1999), 115, 116.

archbishop Saint Charles Borromeo, declared that the Holy Thursday "sepulcher", the repository, "ought to be decorated with precious adornment, even as Isaiah had prophesied it to be glorious".[146]

As we have already seen, early evidence of prayer before the reserved Sacrament on Holy Thursday is provided by a rubric dating from about 1100 in a missal of Rieux, France, that speaks of the recitation of Vespers in the repository. In the twelfth-century *Ordo* of Beroldus, of Milan's Ambrosian Rite, a Holy Thursday rubric states, "And the bishop goes into the sacristy, where he should instruct the subdeacons, that they should diligently guard the Sacrament of the Body and Blood of the Lord."[147] The text suggests that the subdeacons kept a watch before the Blessed Sacrament. Similarly, the pontifical that William Durandus prepared for his own diocese of Mende, France (c. 1294), directs that in the place where the Eucharist has been reserved on Holy Thursday the Sacrament should be "reverently guarded until the following day";[148] the wording implies that one or more watchers were to be present at all times in the place of reposition until the Sacrament was taken out for the Holy Communion of Good Friday.

There is circumstantial evidence of a continuous watch before the Blessed Sacrament from Holy Thursday to Good Friday in thirteenth-century Zara, Croatia, on the basis of two wills dating from 1214 and 1270 respectively, which mention a "prayer of forty hours" during Holy Week conducted by a confraternity called the Verberati at Zara's Church of Saint Sylvester; a reference in a diary entry from 1380 speaks of this forty-hour watch beginning on Holy Thursday evening and continuing until noon on Holy Saturday, with individuals taking one-hour turns. None of these references explicitly mention Eucharistic adoration, but the beginning of the watch on Holy Thursday night strongly suggests that it centered on the Eucharist that was reserved.[149]

In fifteenth-century Portugal, the young prince Saint Ferdinand (1402–1443) was accustomed to keep a continual day-and-night watch before the Blessed Sacrament from Holy Thursday to Easter[150]; clearly, this watch must have begun with prayer before the Blessed Sacrament in its place of repose on Holy Thursday. An instruction from a liturgical book of Esztergom, Hungary, dating from 1460–1464 speaks of a Holy Thursday visit to the "sepulcher", that is, the repository, in which

---

[146] Fourth Provincial Council of Milan (1576), "De ornatu, decore, ac nitore sacrorum locorum", in Federico Borromeo, ed., *Acta ecclesiae Mediolanensis a s. Carolo Cardinali s. praxedis archiepiscopo condita* (Padua, Italy: Typis Seminarii Pativii, 1754), 1:106.

[147] Text in Marcus Magistretti, ed., *Beroldus, sive Ecclesiae Ambrosianae Mediolanensis kalendarium et Ordines, saec. XII* (Milan: Joseph Giovanola, 1894), 104.

[148] Andrieu, *Pontifical romain au moyen-âge*, 3:580.

[149] Herbert Thurston, S.J., "Easter Sepulchre, or Altar of Repose?", *Month* 101 (April 1903): 404–406.

[150] Solange Corbin, *La déposition liturgique du Christ au Vendredi saint: Sa place dans l'histoire des rites et du théâtre religieux* (Paris: Société d'Editions "Les Belles Lettres"; Lisbon: Livraria Bertrand, 1960), 135, 259.

the visitors kneel while they silently recite Psalm 50 (the *Miserere*).[151] In Renaissance Italy, a confraternity known as the Company of the Most Holy Sacrament, founded in Genoa during the second half of the fifteenth century, is credited with having promulgated in an exceptional manner the Holy Thursday adoration of the Blessed Sacrament in the repository.[152] The earliest explicit reference to the practice of visiting the repositories of several different churches on Holy Thursday dates from 1529: an account of a miracle regarding a crucifix that occurred on Holy Thursday night of 1529 in Como, Italy, speaks of a confraternity going in procession through the city to visit seven repositories.[153]

The practice of a continual recitation of psalms before the repository arose in Spain by the mid-fifteenth century, as the Spanish ecclesiastical historian Father Jaime Villanueva found in examining the church archives of Vich, relating: "On April 5, 1463, Francisco Terrades, benefice of this church, instituted that twelve priests vested 'in the manner of the Apostles, who are accustomed to be vested in representations of the saints on the day of Corpus Christi', should assist at the *monumento* all of Holy Thursday, singing psalms 'all the way to the hour of communicating tomorrow'."[154] A fifteenth-century ceremonial for the Benedictines of Valladolid, Spain, enjoins that the *monumento* is never to lack the presence of monks throughout the day and nighttime hours; repeating this rubric, a customary for the Spanish Benedictine monastery of San Millan de Cogola instructs the prior to ensure the continual presence of monks before the *monumento*.[155] A book of rites for cardinals and bishops composed in the early 1520s by the papal master of ceremonies Paride de Grassis (+1528) calls for the selection of "some suitable attendants" to watch before the Blessed Sacrament so that it may be "guarded solemnly" and that "decorum and reverence" may be observed in the repository from Holy Thursday to Good Friday:

> When, however, the cardinal shall have first departed from the altar, if it should please him—two or three or four attendants having been summoned to him, those I have mentioned—he orders the Body of Jesus to be guarded. Those however present, surrounding the flanks

[151] *Epitome* of Esztergom, Hungary (1460–1464), in Radó and Mezey, *Libri liturgici manuscripti bibliothecarum hungariae*, 489.

[152] Bernardi, *La drammaturgia della settimana santa in Italia*, 340, footnote.

[153] Ibid., 302, footnote.

[154] Jaime Villanueva, *Viage literario a las iglesias de España*, vol. 6, *Viage á la iglesia de Vique, año 1806* (Valencia, Spain: Oliveres, 1821), 98.

[155] Ceremonial, Monastery of San Benito, Valladolid, Spain (manuscript 108, Girona: Biblioteca Publica del Estado en Girona, fifteenth century; digitized text, Biblioteca Virtual del Patrimonio Bibliográfico, Madrid, 2008), fols. 32v–33r. *Ceremonias y señales según el uso y costumbre de la religíon de nuestro glorioso padre sanct Benito, las quales son desta sancta casa de sanct Millán de la Cogolla* (manuscript, Madrid: Real Academia de la Historia, Codex 64, sixteenth to seventeenth century; digitized text, Biblioteca Virtual del Patrimonio Bibliográfico, Madrid, n.d.), chap. 28, fol. 72r.

of the altar to each side, guard the Body of Jesus up to the office of tomorrow, devoutly and reverently, for the honor of the Holy Sacrament.[156]

The 1568 missal of Palencia, Spain, in its Holy Thursday rubrics, refers to "the psalms of David, which from the custom of the Church of Palencia, today and the Friday following, are sung before the *monumento*", indicating an established tradition of Palencia's clergy keeping watch continually before the Blessed Sacrament in the repository from Holy Thursday to Good Friday; there were specific instructions for this vigil, which due to an unforeseen lack of space the editors of the 1568 missal were compelled to omit.[157]

The Mandatum

It is believed that the custom of a foot-washing rite specific to Holy Thursday in commemoration of Christ's washing of the Apostles' feet at the Last Supper originated in Jerusalem toward the end of the fifth century, appearing for the first time in the ancient liturgical book of Jerusalem known as the Georgian Lectionary, the contents of which date from the fifth to the eighth century. The Jerusalem rite, which took place after a reading of the Gospel account of the Last Supper foot washing and the departure of Judas (Jn 13:3–30), included the singing of three antiphonal texts, after which a recitation of the entire Psalter was begun.[158] The Georgian Lectionary supplies no details as to the participants in the Jerusalem *Mandatum*, but a later liturgical text of the Holy City, the tenth-century Typicon of the Anastasis, describes the rite in great detail, relating that the patriarch of Jerusalem would wash the feet of twelve clerics (one archbishop, two bishops, three priests, three deacons, and three subdeacons) in the very place where Christ had celebrated the Last Supper and had washed his disciples' feet, the Upper Room in Jerusalem's Church of Sion. Two lamps and four candlestands illuminated the room for this solemn occasion. The ceremony included an incensation of all present at the beginning of the rite.[159]

The earliest evidence of the Holy Thursday *Mandatum* in Constantinople appears in a seventh-century lectionary of the city, which assigns

---

[156] De Grassis, *De caeremoniis cardinalium et episcoporum in eorum dioecesibus* (1587), bk. 2, chap. 46, pp. 244, 248.

[157] *Missale Pallantinum* (1568), fols. 89r, 347v. There is a brief notice at the bottom of folio 347v explaining that these instructions and other items planned for the end of the missal were omitted for the sake of brevity but that they can be found in the "other greater missal edited by us" (an obvious reference to the 1567 Palencia missal, which is fifty folios longer than the 1568 edition).

[158] Michel Tarchnischvili, ed., *Le grand lectionnaire de l'église de Jérusalem (V^e–VIIIe siècle)*, CSCO 188–189, 204–205 (Louvain, Belgium: Secrétariat du CorpusSCO, 1959–1960); Georgian-language text: vol. 1, CSCO 188, nos. 640–641, p. 115, and vol. 2, CSCO 204, appendix 1, nos. 54–57, p. 124; Latin translation: vol. 1, CSCO 189, nos. 640–641, p. 92, and vol. 2, CSCO 205, appendix 1, nos. 54–57, pp. 100–101.

[159] Text in Papadopoulos-Kerameus, *Analekta hierosolymitikēs stachyologias*, 2:108–116.

the Gospel reading of John 13:12–17 to the "Washing of Feet" on the "Holy and Great Thursday".[160] The eighth-century *euchologion* of Constantinople known as the Codex Barberini provides three prayers for the *Mandatum*, one of which is an oration to bless the water for the foot washing.[161] The earliest Constantinople text to describe the participants in the *Mandatum*, the ninth- to tenth-century Typicon of the Great Church, tells of the city's patriarch washing the feet of twelve clerics (three archbishops, three priests, three deacons, and three subdeacons).[162]

In the West, the earliest instance of the Holy Thursday *Mandatum* that can be specifically dated appears in the Italian monastic rule known as the *Regula magistri*, a text from the first quarter of the sixth century,[163] which directs the abbot to wash the feet of the other monks.[164] The ancient liturgical book of Spain's Mozarabic Rite known as the *Liber ordinum*, an eleventh-century compilation of older texts believed to date largely from the fifth to the seventh century, specifies that the bishop, girded with a linen cloth, washes, dries, and kisses the feet of the clergy selected for this ceremony.[165] The custom of the *Mandatum* soon entered the papal liturgy: a papal text known as the Roman *Ordo in coena Domini*, dating from the first half of the seventh century, tells of the pope washing the feet of his chamberlains (attendants) on Holy Thursday.[166]

The use of an expansive series of chants for the *Mandatum* rite had arisen by the late ninth century, appearing in the pontifical of northern France formerly known as the Pontifical of Poitiers.[167] The Romano-Germanic Pontifical of the tenth century prescribes twenty-one antiphons, ten psalms, five prayers, several versicles, and two Gospel readings (from the Gospel of Saint John) for the Holy Thursday *Mandatum* rite, in which the bishop washes the feet of priests and other clerics.[168] The singing of a catena of antiphons, some

---

[160] Yvonne Burns, "The Lectionary of the Patriarch of Constantinople", *Studia Patristica* 15 (1984): 516–517, 520.

[161] Manuscript: Vatican City, Biblioteca Apostolica Vaticana, Codex Barberini Gr. 336, in Goar, *Euchologion sive rituale Graecorum*, 595.

[162] Text in Juan Mateos, S.J., ed., *Le Typicon de la grande église*, vol. 2, *Le cycle des fêtes mobiles*, Orientalia Christiana analecta 166 (Rome: Pont. Institutum Orientalium Studiorum, 1963), 72–75.

[163] For the dating of this document, see Pier Franco Beatrice, *La lavanda dei piedi: Contributo alla storia delle antiche liturgie cristiane*, BELS 28 (Rome: Centro Liturgico Vincenziano, Edizioni Liturgiche, 1983), 152.

[164] *Regula magistri*, chap. 53, PL 88, col. 1015.

[165] Text in Marius Férotin, ed., *Le Liber ordinum en usage dans l'église wisigothique et mozarabe d'Espagne du cinquième au onzième siècle* (Paris, 1904), repr., ed. Anthony Ward, S.M., and Cuthbert Johnson, O.S.B., BELS 83 (Rome: Centro Liturgico Vincenziano, Edizioni Liturgiche, 1996), cols. 192–193.

[166] Text in Chavasse, "A Rome, le Jeudi-saint, au VIIᵉ siècle, d'après un vieil Ordo", 28, 35.

[167] Text in Aldo Martini, ed., *Il cosiddetto pontificale di Poitiers*, REDSMF 14 (Rome: Casa Editrice Herder, 1979), 186–190.

[168] Vogel and Elze, *Pontifical romano-germanique*, 2:77–79.

about Christ washing the Apostles' feet, and others about charity, drawn from the Psalms, remained a universal feature of the *Mandatum* throughout the Middle Ages. The famed hymn *Ubi caritas et amor*, traceable to about the year 800 and first mentioned as a chant for the Holy Thursday *Mandatum* in an eleventh-century missal of Benevento, Italy,[169] later appeared as part of the *Mandatum* rite in the Franciscan *Ordo missalis* of the friars' superior general Haymo of Faversham (c. 1244),[170] from whence it entered the liturgy of Rome,[171] and was retained, along with five antiphons from the late ninth-century Pontifical of Poitiers, in the *Mandatum* rite of the 1570 *Missale Romanum*.[172]

By the tenth century, there had appeared in the monasteries a doubled form of the *Mandatum*, in which there would be on Holy Thursday two separate foot-washing ceremonies, one for paupers and the second for the monks themselves. Benedictine texts of this period, including those of Cluny, France (tenth century);[173] England (c. 960);[174] Einsiedeln, Switzerland (c. 984);[175] Gladbeck Abbey, Germany (late tenth century);[176] and Verdun, France (c. 990),[177] all specify these two *Mandatum* rites for Holy Thursday. The double *Mandatum* was introduced into the papal liturgy during the twelfth century, when it is mentioned for the first time in the Roman text known as the *Liber censuum*, dating from about 1192, which speaks of one *Mandatum* for twelve subdeacons and a second for thirteen paupers.[178] The second *Mandatum* disappeared from the papal liturgy in the early fourteenth century.[179] The *Mandatum* of the subdeacons continued until the papal *Mandatum* of paupers was revived and took the place of the subdeacons'

---

[169] Schmidt, *Hebdomada sancta*, 2:651, 766.

[170] Text in Stephen J. P. Van Dijk, O.F.M., *Sources of the Modern Roman Liturgy: The Ordinals by Haymo of Faversham and Related Documents (1243–1307)*, Studia et documenta Franciscana 2 (Leiden, Netherlands: E. J. Brill, 1963), 2:239–240.

[171] See the 1474 *Missale Romanum*, in Lippe, *Missale Romanum: Mediolani, 1474*, 1:160–161.

[172] Sodi and Triacca, *Missale Romanum: Editio Princeps (1570)*, 239–240 (new pagination).

[173] Tenth-century redaction of the customary of Cluny, France, in Kassius Hallinger, O.S.B., *Consuetudines Cluniacensium antiquiores cum redactionibus derivatis*, Corpus consuetudinum monasticarum 7, pt. 2 (Siegburg, Germany: Franciscus Schmitt, 1983), 79–84.

[174] *Regularis concordia*, in Thomas Symons, trans., *Regularis concordia: The Monastic Agreement of the Monks and Nuns of the English Nation*, Medieval Classics (New York: Oxford University Press, 1953), chap. 4, nos. 40, 42, pp. 39–41.

[175] Customary of Einsiedeln, Switzerland, in Albers, *Consuetudines monasticae*, 5: 91–92.

[176] See the so-called Customs of German Monasteries, actually a text attributed to Sandrat (+c. 984), abbot of Gladbeck Abbey, near Essen, Germany, in Albers, *Consuetudines monasticae*, 5:31, 33.

[177] Customary of the Abbey of Saint Vanne, Verdun, France, in Albers, *Consuetudines monasticae*, 5:120–121.

[178] Text in Fabre and Duchesne, *Le Liber censuum de l'église romaine*, vol. 1, fasc. 2, nos. 25, 27, pp. 295–296.

[179] See the papal ceremonial of Giacomo Cardinal Stefaneschi, dating from about 1325, in Marc Dykmans, ed., *Le cérémonial papal de la fin du moyen âge à la Renaissance*, vol. 2, BIHBR 25 (Brussels and Rome: Institut Historique Belge de Rome, 1981), 369–372.

Mandatum, as can be seen in the 1485 *Pontificalis liber* (*Pontificale Romanum*).[180]

In explaining the Holy Thursday *Mandatum* ceremony, the medieval liturgical commentators did not focus directly upon the details of the rite itself, because it was essentially a literal reenactment of Christ's actions at the Last Supper. Rather, they turned their attention to offering a mystical interpretation of Christ's actions, which in turn would have applied to the Church's annual re-presentation of those actions. Sicard of Cremona sees Christ's washing of the Apostles' feet as a symbolic expression of his Incarnation and Passion. Christ's rising from the table of the Cenacle represents his rising "from the banquet of eternal glory when he went forth from the repose of the Father" to descend to earth. His setting aside of his outer garments expresses his emptying of himself in becoming man. His girding of himself with a cloth symbolizes his assumption of the condition of a servant. He pours water into a basin and washes the Apostles' feet with that water, just as he pours out his blood to wash our actions, symbolized by the feet, for the remission of sins. Sicard adds, "Daily he washes our feet for us, when he intercedes for us."[181]

William Durandus interprets the actions of Christ at the Last Supper in an analogous manner but differs in certain respects. The cloth that Christ girds about his waist for the foot washing is for Durandus an expression of Christ's assumption of our human nature. Postulating as other authors do that the cloth was specifically a linen cloth, as was that used in the Holy Thursday *Mandatum* ceremony, Durandus interprets it as a symbol of Christ's "most pure humanity". He likens Christ's pouring of water into the basin to the pouring of grace into human hearts. The washing of the feet expresses Christ's love and humility but also represents the washing of man's affections. Christ's *Mandatum* also serves as a reminder that after the faithful have washed mortal sins from their souls—the washing that is indicated by Christ's instruction in regard to fasting, read on Ash Wednesday ("Wash thy face" [Mt 6:17])—they should wash the "dust" of venial sins from their feet, that is, their affections, as a final preparation for Holy Communion.[182]

Durandus notes that in addition to the primary symbolism of the Holy Thursday *Mandatum* rite as a reenactment of Christ's actions at the Last Supper, the ceremony also recollects the washing of Christ's own feet by the penitent woman (Lk 7:37–50), as reflected in an antiphon often sung during the rite, "*A certain woman who was a sinner in the city brought alabaster for anointing ...*"[183] This antiphon (*Mulier quae*

---

[180] Text in Manlio Sodi, ed., *Il "Pontificalis liber" di Agostino Patrizi Piccolomini e Giovanni Burcardo (1485)*, facsimile ed., MSIL 43 (Vatican City: Libreria Editrice Vaticana, © 2006), 480–482 (new pagination).

[181] Sicard of Cremona, *Mitrale*, bk. 6, chap. 12, PL 213, cols. 308–309.

[182] Durandus, *Rationale* (CCCM 140a), bk. 6, chap. 75, nos. 3–4, p. 362.

[183] Ibid., no. 4.

erat) and another recounting the same Gospel episode were used at *Mandatum* rites from the late ninth century to the fifteenth century.[184] Thus, in addition to representing Christ's sacrificial love for us, the Holy Thursday foot-washing ceremony serves also as an expression of loving contrition on the part of sinful man. We can deduce from this why there was a second *Mandatum* rite for paupers, insofar as the faithful are called upon to see Christ in the poor. Moreover, this further explains why men (and not women) were universally selected for the *Mandatum* rite, because in addition to representing the Apostles at the Last Supper, those whose feet are washed also represent Christ himself.

The antiphons of the Holy Thursday *Mandatum* rite that refer to the washing of the Lord's feet by the penitent woman, believed to be Saint Mary Magdalene, were underscored in the *Mandatum* of the early fourteenth-century ceremonial of Cologne, Germany, which directs a subdeacon to carry to the *Mandatum* the cathedral's relics of Mary Magdalene.[185] A suffragan bishop carries to the *Mandatum* a "staff of Saint Peter", presumably a staff believed to have been used by the Apostle, serving as a visual reminder of Saint Peter's key role at the Last Supper and his dialogue with Christ during the washing of the feet, commemorated in the antiphons.[186]

The imagery of Christ's actions at the Last Supper and those of the penitent woman who washed his feet are interwoven in the detailed instructions for the first of two Holy Thursday *Mandatum* rites in the 1498 missal of the archdiocesan rite of Braga, Portugal.[187] In this first *Mandatum*, the feet of paupers are washed:

> While Mass is being celebrated, those things that pertain to the *Mandatum* of the paupers should be prepared by the lay attendants: namely hot and cold water, and linen cloths for wiping dry the feet and hands; and seats should be prepared in front of the refectory where the paupers should sit, likewise [on] the porch before the church, where the religious community should sit; in the refectory, the tables on which the paupers should eat should be covered. And as many paupers should be brought into the cloister as there are elders; and they are stationed at their seats. But when the bishop shall have come into the cloister, together with the canons also, the paupers should be made ready in that place, the bishop sitting on the porch before the church together with the clergy, the others thereafter; and all should remove their shoes. And the cantor should begin the antiphon, *A new commandment I give unto you: That you love one another, as*

---

[184] See the late ninth-century pontifical of northern France formerly known as the Pontifical of Poitiers, in Martini, *Cosiddetto pontificale di Poitiers*, 190, and the 1474 *Missale Romanum*, in Lippe, *Missale Romanum: Mediolani, 1474*, 1:159–160.

[185] Amberg, *Ceremoniale Coloniense*, 130.

[186] Ibid.

[187] *Missale Bracarense* (Lisbon: Nicolaus de Saxonia, 1498), sig. i4r–i5r.

I have loved you, says the Lord [Jn 13:34]; Verse: *Blessed are the undefiled* ... [Ps 118:1], suitably prolonged and lengthened, however, with psalms in the meantime, until enough antiphons are said for this office. Then the bishop, since he is in the foremost order [of holy orders], should come in a surplice and bare feet through the porch with two clerics, similarly with him in surplices and bare feet. And having received a linen cloth, he should gird himself in the likeness of our Lord Jesus Christ, and after his example humbly and devoutly wash the feet of three paupers; he should wipe [their feet] clean with the linen cloth; with his hair also, just as that woman sinner, again and again he should wipe and kiss [their feet]. And likewise the religious community should fittingly come two by two; and they should wash the feet of each pauper, and wipe them with linen cloths and kiss them. And in that place the guardian of the church should be prepared, who should offer coins one at a time to each of the canons, which they should offer to the paupers, kissing the hand of each.[188]

At the conclusion of the foot washing, all the participating clerics wash their hands, and two acolytes bring water to the paupers so that they can also wash. The bishop and his clergy then serve a ceremonial banquet to their humble guests in the refectory.[189] Later in the day, after the altars have been stripped, there is a second *Mandatum* rite, in which the bishop washes the feet of his clergy:

But when it shall have been the hour of the *Mandatum*, the wood clapper should be struck. And the bishop, clothed in an alb, with the dean or the priests whom he himself shall have asked, should come into the cloister with all the clergy according to their set order. And all that shall pertain to the *Mandatum* should be prepared. In the chapter [chapter house] should be set in order the lectern where the Gospel is to be read, likewise the platform in the refectory where [the archdeacon] should read. The lord bishop himself should wash the feet of all, that it may be done according to the example of the Lord. And the cantor should recite the antiphon, *A new commandment I give unto you: That you love one another, as I have loved you, says the Lord* [Jn 13:34], and the other antiphons as they are contained in the book of the office. Meanwhile, the archdeacon should go into the church and be vested in a dalmatic and every vestment of his, and with him the subdeacon, vested in a tunic, carrying the [Gospel] text, and the acolytes a censer, and two torchbearers. And the *Mandatum* having been completed, the antiphon is begun, *God is charity: and he that abideth in charity, abideth in God, and God in him* [1 Jn 4:16]. Then the Our Father should be said, without *Lord, have mercy*, and without *The Lord be with you*. After this, *Blessed be the name of the Lord* should

[188] Ibid., sig. i4r.
[189] Ibid.

be said by the bishop. Response: *From this moment even unto eternity.
Our help is in the name of the Lord. Who made Heaven and earth. O
Lord, hear my prayer. And let my cry come unto you. The Lord be with you.
And with your spirit.*

    Prayer: *Let us pray. Look favorably, O Lord, we beseech you, upon the
offices of our service; and insofar as you vouchsafed to wash the feet of your
disciples, do not disdain the works of your hands, which you have commanded us to preserve, but grant that as here outward stains are washed away
by us, so may the interior sins of us all be washed away by you, which may
you yourself vouchsafe to grant: you who live and reign with God the Father.
Amen.*[190]

This second foot-washing rite is followed by a solemn reading of
the first two chapters of Saint John's account of the Last Supper
(Jn 13:1—14:31) in the cathedral's chapter house, with candles and
incense. When the archdeacon who reads this Gospel pronounces the
reading's final verse, "Arise, let us go hence" (Jn 14:31), all proceed
to the refectory, where the archdeacon reads the rest of Christ's Last
Supper discourse (Jn 15:1—17:26) after wine is ceremonially brought
to the bishop and his clergy, a custom clearly in memory of *the other
cup* at the Last Supper, not that of the Eucharist but rather the non-
Eucharistic cup of wine that Christ shared with his disciples at another
point during that evening in the Upper Room ("And having taken
the chalice, he gave thanks, and said: Take, and divide among you; for
I say to you, that I will not drink of the fruit of the vine, till the
kingdom of God come" [Lk 22:17–18]).[191] The reading of Saint John's
Gospel was a universal feature of medieval Holy Thursday *Mandatum*
rites. The *Liber ordinarius* of Zurich, Switzerland (thirteenth century),
directs that after the Gospel of the *Mandatum* rite the priest is to sprinkle those present with holy water as the versicles *Asperges me, Domine*
("*Thou shalt sprinkle me, O Lord*") and *Amplius lave me* ("*Wash me yet
more*") are said. He is then to incense those present as the versicle
Dirigatur Domine oratio mea ("*Let my prayer be directed as incense in thy
sight*") is said.[192] This incensation resembles that found at the beginning of the *Mandatum* rite in tenth-century Jerusalem's Typicon of the
Anastasis.[193]

    The element of contrition that the medieval *Mandatum* rites added
to the primary theme of recalling and following Christ's example of

[190] Ibid., sig. i4v. The concluding prayer, *Adesto, Domine, officiis*, is traceable to the tenth-
century Romano-Germanic Pontifical; see Vogel and Elze, *Pontifical romano-germanique*, 2:78–
79. It was retained in the *Mandatum* rite of the 1570 *Missale Romanum*; see Sodi and Triacca,
Missale Romanum: Editio princeps (1570), 240 (new pagination).

[191] *Missale Bracarense* (1498), sig. i4v–i5r.

[192] Text in Heidi Leuppi, *Der Liber ordinarius des Konrad von Mure: Die Gottesdienstordnung am Grossmünster in Zürich*, SF 37 (Fribourg, Switzerland: Universitätsverlag Freiburg,
1995), 249.

[193] Papadopoulos-Kerameus, *Analekta hierosolymitikēs stachyologias*, 2:108.

charity and humility was accentuated in the *Mandatum* of the 1499 missal of Jaén, Spain: the missal directs that as the bishop washes and kisses the feet of thirteen paupers, seated in a row on the bottom step of the cathedral's choir, the seven penitential psalms are to be sung.[194] One other notable detail of the Jaén rite is the instruction that the water for the foot washing should be "hot water with fragrant herbs", a direction identical to that given in the missal of Toledo, Spain (1503–1518),[195] and similar to that specified for the papal *Mandatum* in the 1485 *Pontificalis liber* and the 1488 *Caeremoniale Romanum*, which speak of "flowers and fragrant herbs" in the water for this rite.[196]

The Stripping and Washing of the Altars

The practice of stripping the altar cloths from the altars on Holy Thursday has existed from an early date: a Church council of Toledo, Spain, speaks of it as an established custom in 694 ("On the feast of the Lord's Supper ... the altars are customarily stripped in the usual manner").[197] The washing of the altars during the Easter Triduum is first mentioned by the Spanish bishop Saint Isidore of Seville (+636), who states that on Holy Thursday "the altars, walls, and floors of the church are washed, and the vessels that have been consecrated to the Lord are purified."[198] It is also in Spain, in the fifth- to seventh-century rubrics of the *Liber ordinum*, that we find our earliest description of a ceremonial stripping of the altars, indicating that the practice had symbolic associations almost from its inception:

> And with candles having been taken by twelve deacons, also making a brief pause, all advance, preceding the bishop, all the way to the altar. But when the altar shall have been surrounded by the clergy on every side, the bishop stands in the middle and sets forth this antiphon: *Behold, the hour cometh, that you shall be scattered, and shall leave me alone; but I am not alone, because the Father is with me. Have confidence, I have overcome the world* [cf. Jn 16:32–33].[199]

Psalm 108 is now sung, which prophesies the persecution of Christ in his Passion. The bishop then recites the antiphon "*My soul is exceedingly sorrowful, it is sorrowful even unto death; stay you here, and watch with me*" (cf. Mt 26:38). As this antiphon is said three times, the clergy strip the altar in three stages. Meanwhile, "all the lights set at the foot

---

[194] *Missale Giennense / Manuale ... sacramenta* (1499), fol. 72r–72v.

[195] *Missale secundum consuetudinem almae ecclesiae Toletanae*, 1503–1518, vol. 4, fol. 71v.

[196] *Missale Giennense/Manuale ... sacramenta* (1499), fol. 72v; Sodi, *"Pontificalis liber" di Agostino Patrizi Piccolomini e Giovanni Burcardo (1485)*, 480–481 (new pagination); Dykmans, *Oeuvre de Patrizi Piccolomini*, 2:373.

[197] Seventeenth Council of Toledo (694), canon 2, PL 84, col. 556.

[198] Saint Isidore of Seville, *De ecclesiasticis officiis*, bk. 1, chap. 29, in Christopher M. Lawson, ed., *Sancti Isidori, episcopi Hispalensis: De ecclesiasticis officiis*, CCSL 113 (Turnhout, Belgium: Brepols, 1989), 32.

[199] Férotin, *Liber ordinum*, col. 191.

of the altar"—presumably the twelve candles brought by the twelve deacons—are extinguished. The rite ends with a Collect recited silently by the bishop as he and all the clergy prostrate themselves before the altar.[200]

The liturgical text Roman *Ordo* 24 (c. 750–800) provides the earliest evidence of the Holy Thursday stripping of the altars in Rome.[201] By the tenth century, the custom of washing the altars on Holy Thursday had appeared in Constantinople[202] as well as in multiple locations across Europe. The *Regularis concordia* of the Benedictines of England (c. 960) speaks of a Holy Thursday washing of the altars with holy water performed by the priests and other clerics before Mass as the floors are washed by the other monks.[203] Three late tenth-century liturgical texts mention a Holy Thursday washing of the altars with both water and wine: the monastic customaries of Einsiedeln, Switzerland;[204] Gladbeck, Germany;[205] and Saint Vanne, Verdun, France, with the Verdun text prescribing for the first time the recitation of the responsory *Circumdederunt me* ("*Deceitful men have compassed me about*") during the stripping and washing of the high altar.[206]

The eleventh- to twelfth-century Benedictine *Ordo Casinensis hebdomadae maioris* of Italy's Monte Cassino Abbey specifies a Holy Thursday stripping of the altar carried out by two acolytes in black vestments.[207] By the mid-thirteenth century, the recitation of Psalm 21 with an antiphon derived from it, *Diviserunt vestimenta* ("*They parted my garments amongst them; and upon my vesture they cast lots*"; Ps 21:19), had been introduced as an accompaniment to the Holy Thursday stripping of the altars, appearing in the Franciscan *Ordo missalis* of Haymo of Faversham (c. 1244)[208] and in a missal of central Italy (c. 1250).[209] Another liturgical text of this period, an *ordo* of the Camaldolese Order (c. 1253), directs that after the sacristan, the deacon, and the subdeacon, vested in albs and barefoot, have stripped the altars while saying the aforesaid antiphon *Diviserunt vestimenta*, as well as seven psalms and

---

[200] Ibid., cols. 191–192.

[201] Andrieu, *Ordines Romani du haut moyen âge*, 3:295.

[202] The Typicon of the Great Church, a ninth- to tenth-century liturgical text for Constantinople's Hagia Sophia church, briefly mentions this observance; text in Mateos, *Typicon de la grande église*, 2:72–73.

[203] Symons, *Regularis concordia*, chap. 4, no. 40, pp. 38–39.

[204] Customary of Einsiedeln, Switzerland, in Albers, *Consuetudines monasticae*, 5:92.

[205] See the so-called Customs of German Monasteries, actually a text attributed to Sandrat (+c. 984), abbot of Gladbeck Abbey, near Essen, Germany, in Albers, *Consuetudines monasticae*, 5:31, 32–33.

[206] Customary of Saint Vanne, Verdun, France, in Albers, *Consuetudines monasticae*, 5:120.

[207] Text in Teodoro Leuterman, *Ordo Casinensis hebdomadae maioris (saec. XII)*, Miscellanea Cassinese 20 (Monte Cassino, Italy: Monte Cassino Abbey, 1941), 104.

[208] Text in Van Dijk, *Sources of the Modern Roman Liturgy*, 2:238.

[209] See the text known as the Lateran Missal in Shin-Ho Chang, ed., *Vetus missale Romanum monasticum Lateranense archivii basilicae Lateranensis, Codex A65 (olim 65)*, MSIL 20 (Vatican City: Libreria Editrice Vaticana, © 2002), 171.

the Litany of the Saints, they are to incense the altars and sprinkle them with holy water.²¹⁰

In addition to France and Germany, the Holy Thursday custom of washing the altars was observed in medieval Switzerland,²¹¹ Austria,²¹² Hungary,²¹³ and Poland.²¹⁴ The 1568 missal of Palencia, Spain, refers to its own Holy Thursday altar-washing rite as having "emanated to us from apostolic tradition".²¹⁵ Although there are no extant records of a *medieval* altar-washing rite in Rome, the introduction of an elaborate Holy Thursday altar-washing ceremony at the Basilica of Saint Peter in the seventeenth century, established by a 1635 decree, was repeatedly described as a restoration of a former custom, implying that the altar washing existed at an earlier time in Rome.²¹⁶ Late fifteenth-century Sarum Rite missals for the English see of Salisbury provide a highly developed rite for the washing of the altars with water and wine on Holy Thursday, with numerous responsories and verses sung during the ceremony.²¹⁷ A fifteenth-century manual for the English see of York contains a comparable rite.²¹⁸

In his explanation of the Holy Thursday stripping of the altars, Rupert of Deutz begins by invoking the traditional interpretation of the altar as a symbol of Christ. Hence the stripped altar brings to mind the stripping of Christ on Calvary: "The soldiers, therefore, when they

---

²¹⁰ *Vetus Ordo divinorum officiorum* (compiled by Abbot Martin III), chap. 47, in John-Benedict Mittarelli and Anselm Costadoni, eds., *Annales Camaldulenses ordinis sancti Benedicti*, vol. 6 (Venice: Monastery of Saint Michael of Muriano and John Baptist Pasquali, 1761), col. 127.

²¹¹ The thirteenth-century *Liber ordinarius* of Zurich mentions that in some churches the altars are washed with wine after they have been stripped on Holy Thursday (Leuppi, *Liber ordinarius des Konrad von Mure*, 248).

²¹² A fifteenth-century missal of Salzburg specifies a Holy Thursday washing of the altars, walls, and floors of the church, as well as the purification of "the sacred vessels of the Lord" (Radó and Mezey, *Libri liturgici manuscripti bibliothecarum Hungariae*, 181).

²¹³ The *Epitome* of Esztergom, Hungary (1460–1464), specifies that the bishop washes the stripped altars on Holy Thursday (Radó and Mezey, *Libri liturgici manuscripti bibliothecarum Hungariae*, 490).

²¹⁴ The Holy Thursday rubrics in a 1493 missal of Kraków, Poland, state that the altars are to be washed "according to the custom of each church" (*Missale Cracoviense* [Nürnberg, Germany: Georg Stuchs, 1493; digitized text, Bayerische Staatsbibliothek, Munich, 2009], fols. 82v–83r).

²¹⁵ *Missale Pallantinum* (1568), fol. 89r.

²¹⁶ The liturgical drama scholar Claudio Bernardi, citing an 1818 book by Francesco Cancellieri on the Holy Week ceremonies of the papal chapel, relates that the Holy Thursday ceremony of washing the altars in Saint Peter's Basilica was brought back into use in 1635 (Bernardi, *Drammaturgia della settimana santa in Italia*, 70). The author J.C. Battelli, in his 1702 book on the annual altar-washing ceremony at Saint Peter's Basilica, states that there was a 1635 decree that "newly ordered" the Vatican altar-washing rite; see Otto Nussbaum, "De altarium ablutione," *EL* 75 (1961): 106.

²¹⁷ Text in Francis H. Dickinson, ed., *Missale ad usum insignis et praeclarae ecclesiae Sarum* (Burntisland, Scotland: 1861–1883), cols. 308–310; in his footnotes, Dickinson supplies the texts of the responsories and versicles from a Sarum processional.

²¹⁸ Text in William George Henderson, ed., *Manuale et processionale ad usum insignis ecclesiae Eboracensis*, Surtees Society Publications 63 (Durham, England: Andrews, 1875), 152–156.

had crucified him, took his garments" (Jn 19:23).[219] Moreover, Rupert exhorts the faithful to see in the bare altar, despoiled of the beauty of its usual cloth adornments, a reminder of Isaiah's prophecy regarding the despoiling of Christ's beauty in his Passion: "We have seen him, and there was no sightliness, that we should be desirous of him: Despised, and the most abject of men, a man of sorrows, and acquainted with infirmity.... Surely he hath borne our infirmities and carried our sorrows" (Is 53:2–4).[220] Interpreting the altar cloths as symbolic of the Apostles, Honorius of Autun sees in their removal from the altar (identified with Christ) a representation of the Apostles' desertion and flight from Christ following his arrest in Gethsemane.[221]

Invoking Saint Paul's imagery of the soul as the temple of God (1 Cor 3:17), John of Avranches (+1079) interprets the altar-washing rite as symbolizing that, just as the altars (as well as the walls and floors) of the church are washed with holy water, so too the souls of the faithful ought to be cleansed by "sacred confession and a flood of tears".[222] We turn now to an example of this rite taken from a processional of the Dominican Order published in Seville, Spain, and dating from 1494.[223] The Holy Thursday context of this Dominican ceremony, a rite traceable to the order's *Ordinarium* of 1256,[224] is established immediately after the prior arrives at the high altar, as the first of ten responsories assigned to the rite is sung:

> The friars should assemble in the choir, the torchbearers preceding thus, and following after them those who bring the water and a broom [made from branches], then the subdeacon with a flask of wine and the deacon with the small book, which he ought to hold before the prior for the prayers to be said. The prelate should approach the major altar to be washed. And when he shall have arrived there, the cantor should begin in a moderate voice, in which the whole office ought to be done, the responsory *On Mount Olivet*, with its verse, and the religious community should continue ...
>
> *On Mount Olivet I prayed to the Father, "Father, if it be possible, let this chalice pass from me." The spirit indeed is willing, but the flesh weak. Thy will be done.* Verse: *Nevertheless not as I will, but as thou wilt. Thy will be done.*[225]

[219] Rupert of Deutz, *Liber de divinis officiis* (CCCM 7), bk. 5, chap. 30, pp. 183–184.

[220] Ibid.

[221] Honorius of Autun, *Gemma animae*, bk. 3, chap. 86, PL 172, col. 665.

[222] John of Avranches, *Liber de officiis ecclesiasticis*, PL 147, col. 50.

[223] *Liber processionum secundum ordinem Fratrum Praedicatorum* (Seville, Spain: Meinard Ungut and Stanislao Polono, 1494), sigs. b7r–c8v.

[224] Text in Francis Guerrini, O.P., ed. (with the authorization of Louis Theissling, O.P.), *Ordinarium juxta ritum sacri ordinis Fratrum Praedicatorum* (Rome: Collegium Angelicum, 1921), 167–168.

[225] *Liber processionum secundum ordinem Fratrum Praedicatorum* (1494), sig. b7r–b8r. The responsory *In monte Oliveti* is traceable to the Antiphonary of Compiègne (France, c. 870),

John Beleth, who sees the altar as an image of the "true altar" of the body of Christ, explains the use of wine and water for the Holy Thursday washing of the altars as representing respectively "the blood of our redemption and the water of redemption" with which Christ's body was "sprinkled" on the Cross when his side was pierced. The branches used in some altar-washing rites (but not in the Dominican ceremony) to wipe the altar are identified by Beleth with the scourges used to strike Christ, and the crown of thorns placed upon his head.[226] Similarly, Gilbert of Tournai (+1284) observes, "The altars are washed with wine and water, because from the side of Christ went forth the two sacraments, the blood of redemption and the water of washing, which are baptism and the Eucharist, by which the Church is cleansed."[227] Concurring with this interpretation of the altar-washing ceremony, William Durandus notes that it is by the blood and water from Christ's side that "mankind was washed." He then expands the ceremony's symbolism, adding that he also considers the water for the altar washing to be a symbol of the tears of the penitent woman (traditionally identified as Saint Mary Magdalene) who washed Christ's feet in the house of Simon the Pharisee (Lk 7:37–38); in this context, the wine represents the ointment with which she anointed the Savior's feet, and the branches used to wipe the altar symbolize her hair, with which she dried his feet.[228]

The rubrics of the Dominican processional specify the washing of each altar in the church:

> Then, while the first responsory *On Mount Olivet* is sung, he who brings the small pail should pour [some] of the water upon the great surface of the altar if it has been consecrated, or upon the surface of the portable altar, if the altar has not been consecrated. Which having been done, the prior, receiving the broom, should wash the altar with it. Then it should be wiped dry by the friar who brings the linen cloth. Afterward, the prior should return the broom to the friar. And having received the flask from the hand of the subdeacon, he should pour out the wine upon the altar in the manner of a cross. The responsory having been completed, the cantor should begin the antiphon of the saint or those saints in whose memory the altar has been built, and the religious community continues it; which having

---

in which it is utilized for the Holy Thursday office of Matins; see Hésbert, *Corpus antiphonalium officii*, 1:166.

[226] Beleth, *Summa de ecclesiasticis officiis* (CCCM 41a), chap. 104, p. 195. A 1487 missal for Amiens, France, specifies palm branches for the Holy Thursday altar-washing rite; see *Missale Ambianense* (Paris: Jean Du Pré, 1487; digitized text, Gallica Bibliothèque Numérique, Bibliothèque Nationale de France, Paris, n.d.), sig. h5v.

[227] Gilbert of Tournai, *Tractatus de officio episcopi*, chap. 44, in Marguerin de la Bigne, ed., *Maxima bibliotheca veterum patrum, et antiquorum scriptorum ecclesiasticorum* (Lyons, France: Anissonios, 1677), 25:418.

[228] Durandus, *Rationale* (CCCM 140a), bk. 6, chap. 76, nos. 5–6, pp. 367–368.

been completed, the torchbearers should recite the verse of that saint or those saints, the cantor continuing with them, and the prior [saying] the prayer. Then he should proceed to the other altars that are within the church.[229]

The Dominican processional provides the texts of ten responsories to be sung one at a time as the prior and those assisting him proceed from one altar to another. The processional adds that the rest of the religious community should also proceed from altar to altar when the size and arrangement of the church make this feasible. If the church has fewer than ten altars, the remaining responsories are omitted; if there are more than ten altars, the series of ten responsories is begun a second time, with the repetition of as many responsories as necessary to match the number of additional altars. These responsories summarize the opening scenes of the Passion at the Last Supper and in the Garden of Gethsemane:

> My soul is sorrowful even unto death; stay here and watch with me; now you shall see the multitude, which will encompass me. You shall take flight, and I shall go to be immolated for you. Verse: Behold, the hour shall draw near, and the Son of man shall be betrayed into the hands of sinners. You shall take flight . . .

> Behold, we have seen him having neither beauty nor comeliness; there is no sightliness in him; our sins he has carried, and he has suffered for us; but he was wounded for our iniquities, by whose bruises we are healed. Verse: Surely he has borne our iniquities and carried our sorrows. By whose bruises . . . Behold, we have seen him . . .

> My friend has betrayed me with the sign of a kiss: "Him whom I shall kiss, that is he, hold him fast"; he gave this wicked sign, who by a kiss fulfilled a homicide. This unhappy [man] has disregarded the price of blood and in the end has hung himself with a noose. Verse: The Son of man indeed goes, as it is written of him; but woe to that man by whom he shall be betrayed. This unhappy [man] . . .

> One of you shall betray me this day; woe to him by whom I shall be betrayed. It were better for him if he had not been born. Verse: He that dips his hand with me in the dish, he is going to betray me into the hands of sinners. It were better . . .

> I was as an innocent lamb; I was led to be immolated and knew it not; my enemies took counsel against me, saying, "Come, let us put wood on his bread and cut him off from the land of the living." Verse: All my enemies plotted evil things against me; they issued an evil word against me, saying, "Come . . ."

---

[229] Liber processionum secundum ordinem Fratrum Praedicatorum (1494), sig. b8r.

Could you not watch one hour with me, who professed to die for me? Or do you not see how Judas does not sleep but hastens to betray me to the Jews? Verse: Sleep now and take your rest; behold, he will draw near who will betray me. Or do you not see how Judas . . .

The elders of the people took counsel, that they might detain Jesus by deceit and slay him; with swords and clubs they went out as though to a robber. Verse: The chief priests, therefore, and the Pharisees, gathered a council. That they might detain Jesus . . .

The heavens revealed the iniquity of Judas, and the earth shall rise up against him, and his sin shall be manifest on the day of the Lord's wrath, with those who said to the Lord God, "Depart from us; we desire not the knowledge of your ways." Verse: He shall be kept for the day of perdition, and he shall be led to the day of punishment. With those . . .[230]

The processional instructs that regardless of the number of altars, the following responsory should always be sung for the last altar to be washed:

Deceitful men have compassed me about; without cause they have hewn me with scourges. But you, O Lord, my Defender, defend me. Verse: For tribulation is very near, and there is none to help me. But you . . .[231]

We conclude this chapter with the instructions regarding the observance of Holy Thursday night given by Cardinal Bernard of Porto in his *Ordo officiorum* for Rome's cathedral church of Saint John Lateran (c. 1140):

But they should remember in what manner the Lord Jesus lived out this night and what he suffered in it; namely, that having been betrayed immediately after the Supper, presented to the judge, and accused, now is he scourged, now crowned with thorns, now mocked, stricken with blows, smeared with spittle. Which night manifestly, because its entirety is expended in injuries to him, should by no means be passed by the faithful without contemplation of his Passion.[232]

---

[230] Ibid., sigs. b8r–c7v. All eight of these responsories are traceable to the Antiphonary of Compiègne (France, c. 870), in which they are utilized for the Holy Thursday office of Matins; see Hésbert, *Corpus antiphonalium officii,* 1:166, 168.

[231] *Liber processionum secundum ordinem Fratrum Praedicatorum* (1494), sig. c7v–c8v. The responsory *Circumdederunt me viri* is traceable to an early eleventh-century antiphonary of Monza, Italy, in which it is utilized for the office of Palm Sunday; see Hésbert, *Corpus antiphonalium officii,* 1:161.

[232] Fischer, *Bernhardi cardinalis . . . Ordo officiorum ecclesiae Lateranensis,* 54.

14 Good Friday

By the Passion of Christ the four elements are purified, and by the four arms of the Cross, the four quarters of the world are saved. It is for that reason that he is suspended between Heaven and earth, because by his Passion Heaven and earth are united, and the entire world is dedicated a temple to God in his blood.

Honorius of Autun (+c. 1135)[1]

It can be said without exaggeration that on Good Friday the entire medieval Christian world came to a standstill before the Cross and the Holy Sepulcher. The liturgical texts of this period testify to a shared longing to spend every hour of this solemnity with Christ crucified. This can best be seen in a rubric of Cardinal Bernard of Porto's *Ordo officiorum* for Rome's cathedral church of Saint John Lateran dating from about 1140:

> And because not one hour of this day is devoid of the Passion of Christ, its fitting remembrance by us for that purpose of meditation should run through the individual hours, such that this entire day we should continually remember and unceasingly meditate upon these things, when he would have borne the spittle, the reproaches, the blows, the slaps, the crown of thorns, the scourges, the Cross, the nails, the gall, the vinegar, the lance, and death.[2]

Benedictine customaries beginning in the tenth century prescribed the recitation of the entire Psalter from beginning to end on Good Friday, following the morning office of Prime,[3] a practice that by the

---

[1] Honorius of Autun, *Gemma animae*, bk. 3, chap. 90, PL 172, col. 667.

[2] Text in Ludwig Fischer, ed., *Bernhardi cardinalis et Lateranensis ecclesiae prioris Ordo officiorum ecclesiae Lateranensis*, Historische Forschungen und Quellen 2–3 (Munich: Dr. F. P. Datterer, 1916), 54–55. This same instruction, slightly reworded, appears two centuries later in the fourteenth-century *Ordinarium* of the Augustinian canons regular for their Priory of Saint-Lô in Rouen, France (PL 147, col. 173).

[3] This practice appears in the tenth-century redaction of the customary of Cluny, France; in the customary of the French abbey of Saint Vanne, Verdun (c. 990); and in the *Regularis concordia* of the Benedictines of England (c. 960), the last of which assigns this practice to all three days of the Easter Triduum. See respectively Kassius Hallinger, O.S.B., *Consuetudines Cluniacensium antiquiores cum redactionibus derivatis*, Corpus consuetudinum monasticarum 7, pt. 2 (Siegburg, Germany: Franciscus Schmitt, 1983), 88; Bruno Albers, ed., *Consuetudines*

404

thirteenth century was being observed by the popes and the Roman Curia.[4] The Benedictine customary of Fructuaria, Italy (c. 1085), after prescribing the Good Friday recitation of the Psalter, remarks that the monks should pray "with tears" in order that "he, who on this day vouchsafed to die for us, may mortify the vices in us and vivify the virtues."[5] As a penance, the Benedictines of tenth-century Europe also spent much or all of Good Friday barefoot,[6] a custom that by the twelfth century had spread to the laity.[7] At Italy's Benedictine abbey of Monte Cassino, the reading on Good Friday morning of the martyrology entry for the following day during the office of Prime, in anticipation of Holy Saturday, announced to the monks, "*Saturday: Our Lord rested in the sepulcher*", and was marked by a total prostration "to the earth" by all present.[8]

The practice of placing or unveiling a cross in the church on Good Friday *before* the actual liturgy of the day for the private devotion of those praying in the church is traceable to the tenth century, when it is mentioned in the earliest redaction of the Benedictine customary for the French abbey of Cluny.[9] A liturgical manual for the Polish diocese of Wrocław (Breslau), in a passage dating from 1448, specifies that after Matins of Good Friday, the cross (probably a crucifix), veiled in a black chasuble, is to be placed before the high altar on a carpet and over an altar cloth, with a single lit candle near it; one cleric is to keep watch before it.[10] The 1498 missal of Portugal's

---

monasticae, vol. 5, *Consuetudines monasteriorum Germaniae necnon s. Vitonis Virdunensis et Floriacensis abbatiae monumenta saeculi decimi continens* (Monte Cassino, Italy: Typis Societatis Editricis Castri Casini, 1912), 122; and Thomas Symons, trans., *Regularis concordia: The Monastic Agreement of the Monks and Nuns of the English Nation*, Medieval Classics (New York: Oxford University Press, 1953), chap. 4, no. 40, p. 38.

[4] The papal ceremonial of Pope Blessed Gregory X (c. 1273) specifies the recitation of the entire Psalter on Good Friday; text in Marc Dykmans, ed., *Le cérémonial papal de la fin du moyen âge à la Renaissance*, vol. 1, BIHBR 24 (Brussels and Rome: Institut Historique Belge de Rome, 1977), 194.

[5] *Consuetudines* of Fructuaria, Italy, bk. 1, chap. 47, in Bruno Albers, ed., *Consuetudines monasticae*, vol. 4, *Consuetudines Fructuarienses necnon Cystrensis in Anglia monasterii et congregationis Vallymbrosanae* (Monte Cassino, Italy: Typis Montis Casini, 1911), 59.

[6] This practice is prescribed in the tenth-century redaction of the customary of Cluny, France; in the *Regularis concordia* of the Benedictines of England (c. 960); and in the customary of the French abbey of Saint Vanne, Verdun (c. 990). See respectively Hallinger, *Consuetudines Cluniacensium antiquiores*, 87; Symons, *Regularis concordia*, chap. 4, no. 43, p. 41; and Albers, *Consuetudines monasticae*, 5:122.

[7] The eminent Benedictine liturgist Dom Edmond Martène (+1739) quotes a passage from the life of the twelfth-century abbot of Cava, Italy, Saint Constabilis (no. 16) in regard to the laity going barefoot on Good Friday; see Martène's work *De antiquis monachorum ritibus*, bk. 3, chap. 14, in Edmond Martène, *De antiquis ecclesiae ritibus* (Venice: Johannes Baptista Novelli, 1763–1764), 4:134.

[8] This rubric appears in the twelfth-century *Ordo Casinensis hebdomadae maioris* of Monte Cassino; text in Teodoro Leuterman, *Ordo Casinensis hebdomadae maioris (saec. XII)*, Miscellanea Cassinese 20 (Monte Cassino, Italy: Monte Cassino Abbey, 1941), 108.

[9] Hallinger, *Consuetudines Cluniacensium antiquiores*, 88.

[10] *Modus agendi in ecclesia Wratislaviensi* (portion of text dating from 1448), in Francis Schubert and Richard Stapper, eds., *Excerpta ex ordinariis Germanicis de summis anni ecclesiastici*

Rite of Braga prescribes that on Good Friday, at the "third hour" (nine o'clock in the morning), crosses are to be put in their respective places in the church, uncovered, so that they might be venerated by the people.[11]

The Romano-Germanic Pontifical of the tenth century states that on Good Friday "in the Roman Church all fire is extinguished on this day, at the sixth hour [noon], and rekindled at the ninth hour [three o'clock]";[12] this practice was likewise observed in certain other churches, according to William Durandus of Mende (+1296).[13] Commenting on this custom, the twelfth-century liturgist Honorius of Autun explains it as signifying the withdrawal of the sun's light from the sixth hour until the ninth hour on the first Good Friday.[14] The 1568 missal of Palencia, Spain, directs that no candles whatsoever are to be lit during the Good Friday liturgy (not even for the concluding portion of the Passion) until the Blessed Sacrament is brought from the *monumento* to the altar, at which point the altar candles are lit. As soon as the priest has received Holy Communion, the candles are again extinguished.[15]

The Liturgy of the Passion and the Veneration of the Cross

The Good Friday liturgy, from the eighth century onward, has always begun with a total prostration of the celebrant, a practice first attested in Roman *Ordo* 23 (c. 700–750).[16] The earliest extant Roman lectionary, the seventh-century Capitulary of Würzburg, prescribes the Good Friday Scripture readings that were to become the norm for the Good Friday liturgy throughout the Middle Ages: Hosea 6:1–6 for the first reading (a prophecy of the Resurrection), Exodus 12:1–11 (the Passover meal) for the second reading, and the Passion of Saint John for the Gospel (Jn 18:1—19:42).[17] From the eighth century onward, these readings have been accompanied by the same Gradual (*Domine audivi*, from Hab 3:1–3) and the same Tract (*Eripe me, Domine,*

---

festivitatibus, Opuscula et textus historiam ecclesiae eiusque vitam atque doctrinam illustrantia: Series liturgica, fasc. 7–8 (Münster, Germany: Aschendorff, 1936), 23.

[11] *Missale Bracarense* (Lisbon: Nicolaus de Saxonia, 1498), sig. i5r.

[12] Text in Cyrille Vogel and Reinhard Elze, eds., *Le pontifical romano-germanique du dixième siècle*, vol. 2, ST 227 (Vatican City: Biblioteca Apostolica Vaticana, 1963), 90.

[13] William Durandus of Mende, *Rationale divinorum officiorum*, bk. 6, chap. 77, no. 1, in A. Davril, O.S.B., and T. M. Thibodeau, eds., *Guillelmi Duranti: Rationale divinorum officiorum V–VI*, CCCM 140a (Turnhout, Belgium: Brepols, 1998), 369. Hereafter cited as Durandus, *Rationale* (CCCM 140a).

[14] Honorius of Autun, *Gemma animae*, bk. 3, chap. 94, PL 172, col. 667.

[15] *Missale Pallantinum* (Palencia, Spain: Sebastian Martinez, 1568; Latin text provided by Biblioteca Apostolica Vaticana, Vatican City [shelf mark Stamp. Barb. B. X. 1]), fols. 89r, 92r.

[16] Text in Michel Andrieu, ed., *Les Ordines Romani du haut moyen âge*, vol. 3, SSLED 24 (Louvain, Belgium: "Spicilegium sacrum Lovaniense" Administration, 1951), 271.

[17] For the Capitulary's Epistle list, see Germain Morin, "Le plus ancien *Comes* ou lectionnaire de l'église romaine", *Revue Bénédictine* 27 (1910): 54; for the Gospel list, see G. Morin, "Liturgie et basiliques de Rome au milieu du VIIe siècle d'après les listes d'évangiles de Würzburg", *Revue Bénédictine* 28 (1911): 304.

from Ps 139:2–10, 14),[18] which together with the aforesaid readings later entered the universally promulgated *Missale Romanum* of 1570.[19]

The use of two readings before the Gospel on this day, in contrast to the use of only one pre-Gospel lection on most of the days of the year in the medieval liturgy, is seen by John Beleth (+1182) as symbolizing that "Christ suffered for two peoples, namely the Hebrew and the Gentile."[20] One of the two readings is taken from the Law of the Old Covenant (the Exodus reading) and the other from the prophets (Hosea), Beleth notes, for "the Passion of Christ was prefigured by the Law and foretold by the prophets."[21] Of the symbolic actions associated with the reading of the Passion, we have already spoken at length in our Palm Sunday chapter (chapter 12). We would simply add here that from the ninth century onward, beginning with the Frankish liturgical document known as Roman *Ordo* 31, there was in many medieval Good Friday rites an additional dramatic gesture when in the course of Saint John's Gospel the words regarding the division of Christ's garments among the soldiers were read—"*They have parted my garments among them*" (Jn 19:24, citing Ps 21:19). At these words, two deacons, going to the altar, one to each side, would remove "in a thieving manner" two linen cloths covering the altar, each taking the cloth on his side.[22]

Of the solemn intercessions, the series of twelve petitions for the needs of the Church and the salvation of all men that have been a basic component of the Western Good Friday liturgy from the patristic era onward, Honorius of Autun explains: "The Passion having been read through, the prayers for all ranks are said, because Christ is crucified for all grades and peoples. The *Dominus vobiscum* ['*The Lord be with you*'], which is the priest's part, is suppressed, because this day our Priest is slain. At the individual prayers we genuflect, for we demonstrate all nations bending their knees to Christ."[23] It is evident that the wording of these petitions was established in the patristic era: a fifth-century text appended to a letter of Pope Celestine I (422–432) summarizes the petitions[24] with expressions that indicate that the writer knew the intercessions in the form that we first find them two centuries

---

[18] These two chants for Good Friday first appear in the Cantatorium of Monza (Italy, eighth century); see René-Jean Hésbert, ed., *Antiphonale missarum sextuplex* (Brussels, 1935; repr., Rome: Herder, 1967), 94, 96.

[19] Text in Manlio Sodi and Achille Maria Triacca, eds., *Missale Romanum: Editio princeps (1570)*, facsimile ed., MLCT 2 (Vatican City: Libreria Editrice Vaticana, © 1998), 240–246 (new pagination).

[20] John Beleth, *Summa de ecclesiasticis officiis*, chap. 98, in Heribertus Douteil, C.S.Sp., ed., *Iohannis Beleth: Summa de ecclesiasticis officiis*, CCCM 41a (Turnhout, Belgium: Brepols, 1976), 176.

[21] Ibid., 176–177.

[22] Roman *Ordo* 31, in Andrieu, *Ordines Romani du haut moyen âge*, 3:497.

[23] Honorius of Autun, *Gemma animae*, bk. 3, chap. 95, PL 172, col. 667.

[24] This addendum to Pope Celestine I's letter to the Gallic bishops is preserved by Peter the Deacon in his own *Letter 16* (written c. 519), no. 27, PL 65, col. 450.

later in the seventh-century Gelasian Sacramentary of Rome.[25] Hence the wording of these intercessions should be seen as a patristic feature of the Good Friday liturgy that the medieval liturgists left unaltered.[26]

William Durandus notes that in the Good Friday liturgy the unveiling of the cross comes after the intercessory prayers as a testament that prayer derives its effectiveness and its model from the Passion, during which Christ prayed on the Cross for both his friends and his enemies.[27] The Good Friday veneration of the cross first appeared in fourth-century Jerusalem, arising from the recovery of the wood of the True Cross in the Holy City. In what is our earliest extant account of the veneration, dating from about 382, the Spanish pilgrim Egeria relates that on Good Friday the wood of the True Cross would be removed from the silver casket in which it was kept, after which the bishop, taking hold of it with both of his hands, presented it to each of the faithful, who venerated it by bending down to touch it to their foreheads and their eyes before kissing it.[28] Unfortunately, neither Egeria nor the most ancient liturgical book of Jerusalem to record this Good Friday veneration, the early fifth-century Armenian Lectionary,[29] mentions what prayers, readings, or chants, if any, accompanied the veneration. We can, however, gain some insight as to how the faithful of the time understood this rite from the Church Father Saint Jerome's account of another female pilgrim, the widow Saint Paula, who came to the Holy Land about the year 385 and subsequently settled in Bethlehem. In a letter, he describes Paula's thoughts while venerating the Cross: "And having prostrated before the Cross, she would have

---

[25] Text in Leo Cunibert Mohlberg, O.S.B., et al., eds., *Liber sacramentorum Romanae aeclesiae ordinis anni circuli (Sacramentarium Gelasianum)*, REDSMF 4 (Rome: Herder, 1960), nos. 395–417, pp. 64–67.

[26] As for the often-discussed petition for the Jewish people, the language is largely taken from Saint Paul, a Jew who deeply loved his own people and his heritage, as he himself testifies (Rom 9:3–5; 11:1–4). Hence the Latin petition's pleas that "blindness" and the "veil" may be withdrawn from the hearts of the Jewish people with regard to belief in Christ are in fact Saint Paul's prayer for his own people's felicity: "But even until this day, when Moses is read, the veil is upon their heart. But when they shall be converted to the Lord, the veil shall be taken away" (2 Cor 3:15–16); "Blindness in part has happened in Israel, until the fulness of the Gentiles shall come in. And so all Israel should be saved" (Rom 11:25–26). The Latin adjective *perfidus* in the context of this petition simply means unbelieving, denoting that the petition is for Jews who do not believe in Christ; see John Oesterreicher, "*Pro perfidis Judaeis*", *Theological Studies* 8 (1947): 80–96. We have seen repeatedly in this work how the medieval liturgical commentators beautifully expressed the Church's longing for the day when Jews and Gentiles would be united in the joy of salvation. The Church, seeking to invite all men to belief in Christ the Savior, also invites the sons of Abraham, "to whom belongeth the adoption as of children, and the glory, and the testament, and the giving of the law and the service of God, and the promises" (Rom 9:4).

[27] Durandus, *Rationale* (CCCM 140a), bk. 6, chap. 77, no. 18, p. 377.

[28] For the Diary of Egeria, see A. Franceschini and R. Weber, eds., *Itinerarium Egeriae*, chap. 37, nos. 1–3, in *Itineraria et Alia geographica*, CCSL 175 (Turnhout, Belgium: Brepols, 1965), 80–81.

[29] Text in Athanase Renoux, ed. and trans., *Le codex Arménien Jérusalem 121*, vol. 2, *Edition comparée du texte et de deux autres manuscrits*, Patrologia orientalis 36, fasc. 2 (Turnhout, Belgium: Brepols, 1971), no. 43, p. 281.

discerned, as it were, the Lord hanging [on it]."[30] In other words, contact with the very Cross upon which Christ died directed the mind to Christ on the Cross.

The practice of presenting the relic of the True Cross for the veneration of the faithful on Good Friday soon disappeared in Jerusalem; the custom was evidently brought to an end by the temporary loss of the precious relic, which was stolen by Persian invaders in 614 and not recovered until 629.[31] Thereafter the Cross was venerated in another manner on Good Friday in the Holy City, providing evidence that the relic of the True Cross was seen liturgically as a symbol of Christ himself. In the ancient liturgical book of Jerusalem known as the Georgian Lectionary, the contents of which date from the fifth to the eighth century, there appears for the first time a Good Friday rite of "washing the Cross". That this ceremony constituted a symbolic "reenactment" of the washing of Christ's body for burial is made clear by the *ibakoj* chant sung during this rite: "*Joseph besought your body, O Savior, and placed it in his new tomb, for he perceived your Resurrection from the sepulcher, just as a going forth from your bridal chamber. Glory be to you, O Savior, who have broken the might of death and have opened the gates of Paradise to men.*"[32]

The transfer of portions of the True Cross to Rome and elsewhere led to the introduction of Good Friday rites for the veneration of the cross in western Europe; the ceremony appeared in Rome during the seventh century, as first attested in the Gelasian Sacramentary.[33] About the same time, the rite appeared in Spain, where it is found in the ancient liturgical book of Spain's Mozarabic Rite known as the *Liber ordinum*, an eleventh-century compilation of older texts believed to date largely from the fifth to the seventh century.[34] In this Spanish rite, the following verse would be sung as all came forward to kiss the Cross: "*Behold the glorious wood on which were once hung the members of Christ our Savior, redeeming the world. Prostrate [yourself] here, bringing forth all your prayers with weeping.*"[35] This verse is thematically quite similar to the antiphon that was to become a universal feature of the Good Friday veneration of the cross in the West, the *Ecce lignum crucis*,

---

[30] Saint Jerome, *Letter 108* (*Ad Eustochium virginem*, no. 9), PL 22, col. 884.

[31] Adrian Fortescue, "Jerusalem, II: From A.D. 71 to A.D. 1099", *The Catholic Encyclopedia* (New York: Appleton, 1907–1912), 8:359–360.

[32] Michel Tarchnischvili, ed., *Le grand lectionnaire de l'église de Jérusalem (V^e–VIIIe siècle)*, vols. 1–2, CSCO 188–189, 204–205 (Louvain, Belgium: Secrétariat du CorpusSCO, 1959–1960); Georgian-language text: vol. 1, CSCO 188, nos. 702–703, p. 132, and vol. 2, CSCO 204, appendix 1, nos. 161–167, pp. 142–143; Latin translation: vol. 1, CSCO 189, nos. 702–703, pp. 105–106, and vol. 2, CSCO 205, appendix 1, nos. 161–167, p. 115.

[33] Mohlberg, Eizenhöfer, and Siffrin, *Liber sacramentorum*, nos. 395, 418, pp. 64, 67.

[34] Text in Marius Férotin, O.S.B., ed., *Le Liber ordinum en usage dans l'église wisigothique et mozarabe d'Espagne du cinquième au onzième siècle* (Paris, 1904), repr., ed. Anthony Ward, S.M., and Cuthbert Johnson, O.S.B., BELS 83 (Rome: Centro Liturgico Vincenziano, Edizioni Liturgiche, 1996), cols. 194–200.

[35] Ibid., col. 194.

which appears for the first time in Roman *Ordo* 24, a liturgical text from the second half of the eighth century: "*Behold the wood of the Cross, on which hung the salvation of the world. Come, let us adore.*"[36]

The desire to bring the Good Friday rite of venerating the cross into churches that did not possess an actual relic of the True Cross led by the ninth century to the use of reproductions of the True Cross, as the ninth-century liturgical commentator Amalarius of Metz (+c. 850) explains:

> There have been certain ones wanting to say they themselves wished to venerate the same Cross on which the Lord was crucified. Would that it was possessed in all the churches! It would have been revered in merit before others. Yet although every church would not be able to have it, the virtue of the holy Cross is not wanting to them, in those crosses that have been made to the likeness of the Lord's Cross.[37]

Significantly, it is also Amalarius who attests that the *ultimate* object of the Good Friday veneration rite is not the *instrument* of salvation, the Cross in and of itself, but rather the Savior who hung upon it:

> The Cross of Christ [is] placed before me; in my mind I consider Christ, as it were, hanging upon it. The very words of our prayer demonstrate whom we should adore. . . . He whom I supplicate, him I adore; I am prostrated in body before the Cross, in mind before God; I venerate the Cross by which I have been redeemed, but I supplicate him who redeemed me.[38]

This Christocentric orientation of the Good Friday veneration of the cross is obvious in the earliest Western prayer texts to be composed for the ceremony. Thus we find the following oration, entitled "Prayer or Confession to the Lord Jesus before the Cross", for the rite of venerating the cross in a late ninth-century pontifical formerly known as the Pontifical of Poitiers but now recognized as a liturgical book of northern France:

> *I adore you, O Jesus Christ, eternal God, God of mercy, God of goodness and forgiveness. You, O Lord, who without beginning, remaining eternally with God the Father and the Holy Spirit, one, indivisible, and incomprehensible, you, O God, vouchsafed to be made man for us, assuming flesh from the Virgin Mary. . . .*
>
> *. . . I adore you, O Lord, coreigning with the Father in Heaven; I adore you suffering on the Cross for us. I adore you upholding the heavens and permitting your hands and feet to be fastened with nails on the Cross. I adore*

---

[36] Andrieu, *Ordines Romani du haut moyen âge*, 3:294.

[37] Amalarius of Metz, *Liber officialis*, bk. 1, chap. 14, no. 10, in John Michael Hanssens, S.J., ed., *Amalarii episcopi: Opera liturgica omnia*, vol. 2, ST 139 (Vatican City: Biblioteca Apostolica Vaticana, 1948), 102.

[38] Ibid., no. 8, pp. 101–102.

you crucified; I adore you dead and buried. I adore you hanging on the Cross and opening the gates of Paradise to the confessing thief. I adore you descending into hell, vanquishing the devil, destroying the kingdom of death....

... I adore the glorious mystery of your Passion. I adore the standard of your Cross, by which you willed to effect the ineffable mystery of our salvation.[39]

The Good Friday liturgy in the tenth-century Romano-Germanic Pontifical includes a prayer entitled "Prayer at the First Genuflection to the Cross of the Lord" for private recitation when venerating the cross with the first of three genuflections before it:

O Lord Jesus Christ, true God from true God, who for the redemption of mankind, deceived by serpentine persuasion, willed to illuminate a world entangled in errors and to undergo the ignominy of the Cross, that you might both conquer the gibbet by the gibbet and overcome the hereditary death of sin by your most powerful death: graciously hear me, wretched and unworthy, prostrate before the eyes of your most benign majesty, both adoring you and blessing your holy and fearsome name; and grant me to know you, praise you, and announce you with a pure heart; and by the standard of this holy Cross, to which I come this day, going to venerate it in your name, sanctify my soul and body, compass me about with the buckler of your faith, put upon me the helmet of salvation, gird me with the sword of the Spirit, that going to do battle against the most wicked enemy I may be fortified both with the help of your mercy and with the standard of your salutary Cross; and may all endowed with your holy name be secure from the attack of the treacherous enemy. Through you, O Jesus Christ, who live ...[40]

With prayers such as these appearing in the Good Friday liturgy within two to three centuries of the arrival of the cross veneration rite in the West, it becomes clear that the introduction into the veneration rite of a cross bearing the effigy of the crucified Christ upon it, a *crucifix*, was a natural, organic development arising inevitably from the Christocentric nature of this act of worship. There is, in fact, indirect evidence for the use of the crucifix in the Good Friday veneration rite during the tenth century, with direct evidence emerging from the first half of the eleventh century onward.

The most compelling tenth-century evidence for the use of a crucifix in the Good Friday liturgy appears in a Benedictine customary for the abbey of Saint Vanne, Verdun, France, dating from about 990. This text specifies that on Wednesday of Holy Week all the veils (Lenten veils) are to be removed except for those concealing the "Holy of Holies" (evidently the high altar) and "the crucifixes", which are to remain in place (presumably until Good Friday). The presence of multiple crucifixes in the abbey church during Holy Week makes it highly

---

[39] Text in Aldo Martini, ed., *Il cosiddetto pontificale di Poitiers*, REDSMF 14 (Rome: Casa Editrice Herder, 1979), 206.

[40] Vogel and Elze, *Pontifical romano-germanique*, 2:91.

likely that the cross venerated on Good Friday was in fact a crucifix.[41] It also appears likely that the Good Friday liturgy of the aforementioned tenth-century Romano-Germanic Pontifical utilized a crucifix, for the Palm Sunday rubrics of this pontifical speak directly of venerating a crucifix during the palm procession (see p. 330 of the present work). Notably, there is a large tenth-century wooden crucifix known as the Gero Cross, dating from about 975, preserved to the present day in Germany's Cologne Cathedral.[42]

The earliest *direct* evidence for the use of a crucifix rather than a plain cross in the Good Friday liturgy appears in the customary of Sigibert, abbot of the Benedictine monastery of Gorze, France, a text dating from about 1030. Although the word *crucifixus* is not used, the cross was undoubtedly a crucifix. In the rubrics for placing in the church ahead of time ("before Sext") the cross "that is to be adored", there is mention of hanging a "phylactery" (a small receptacle enclosing relics)[43] around the "neck" of the cross and that the "text of the Gospel" is to be placed "at the feet [*pedes*] on the right side".[44] The use of the Latin accusative plural, *pedes*, rather than the accusative singular, *pedem*, indicates the two feet of a corpus on the cross rather than the single "foot" of a plain cross. Moreover, the specification of the placement of the Gospel book on the right side of the cross was likely intended to call to mind the blood and water that flowed from the Savior's right side, suggesting that a corpus was on this cross, with the five wounds represented on it.

Other eleventh-century liturgical books attesting to the veneration of a crucifix on Good Friday include the Benedictine customaries of Canterbury, England (as composed by Lanfranc; c. 1077);[45] Fructuaria, Italy (c. 1085);[46] and Fontanelle, France,[47] as well as a Benedictine *ordinarium* for Raab, Hungary,[48] and a book of ecclesiastical offices for the French see of Rouen composed by Archbishop John of Avranches

---

[41] *Consuetudines* of Saint Vanne, Verdun, France, in Albers, *Consuetudines monasticae*, 5:117.

[42] Walter Schulten, *Cologne Cathedral* (Cologne: Greven Verlag, 1987), 19, 28.

[43] Regarding the "phylactery", see Hallinger, *Consuetudines Cluniacensium antiquiores*, 195. The practice of carrying relics in a receptacle hung from the neck is mentioned in the *Consuetudines Cluniacenses* of Saint Udalric of Zell, abbot of the French Benedictine monastery of Cluny (compiled c. 1080), bk. 1, chap. 21, PL 149, col. 670.

[44] *Consuetudines* of Sigibert, chap. 31, in Bruno Albers, ed., *Consuetudines monasticae*, vol. 2, *Consuetudines Cluniacenses antiquiores* (Monte Cassino, Italy: Typis Montis Casini, 1905), 96.

[45] *Consuetudines* of Lanfranc, in David Knowles and Christopher N. L. Brooke, eds. and trans., *The Monastic Constitutions of Lanfranc*, rev. ed., Oxford Medieval Texts (Oxford: Clarendon, 2002), chaps. 40–45, pp. 62–63.

[46] *Consuetudines* of Fructuaria, Italy, bk. 1, chap. 47, in Albers, *Consuetudines monasticae*, 4:60, 62.

[47] *Libro usum Beccensium* for the monastery of Fontanelle, France; Martène, *De antiquis monachorum ritibus*, bk. 3, chap. 14, no. 37, in Martène, *De antiquis ecclesiae ritibus*, 4:139.

[48] *Ordinarium* of the Benedictine cloister, Gjor [Raab], Hungary, in Walther Lipphardt, ed., *Lateinische Osterfeiern und Osterspiele*, Ausgaben deutscher Literatur des XV. bis XVIII. Jahrhunderts: Reihe Drama 5 (Berlin: Walter de Gruyter, 1975–1981), 2:686–687.

(+1079).[49] Moreover, there is indirect evidence that the famed French Benedictine abbey of Cluny was also using a crucifix for the Good Friday liturgy in the eleventh century.[50]

The practice of ceremonially carrying the cross through the church to the place where it is to be venerated is traceable to ninth-century France, appearing for the first time in the Frankish liturgical document known as Roman *Ordo* 31. The cross, carried by two acolytes, would be advanced in three stages toward the altar. At each station of this threefold advance, two cantors bowing before the cross would sing in Greek the ancient Eastern chant known as the Trisagion, a Trinitarian invocation traceable to the fifth century, which is then sung in Latin by the choir. There is a Syriac tradition that the Trisagion was sung by the seraphim as they hovered about Christ asleep in death on the Cross and resting in the tomb.[51] Following the completion of the Trisagion at the third and final station, the bishop would unveil the cross and begin the antiphon *Ecce lignum crucis*. The clergy would then chant Psalm 118, repeating the *Ecce lignum crucis* as an antiphon for the psalm.[52] This ninth-century liturgical text is the first to mention the Good Friday use of the Trisagion and the ceremonial unveiling of the cross, practices that were to spread throughout medieval Europe.

The unveiling of the cross from head to foot is thought to have been inspired in part by the well-known vision of the prophet Isaiah, who speaks of two seraphim veiling the Divinity: "I saw the Lord sitting upon a throne high and elevated. . . . Upon it stood the seraphims: the one had six wings, and the other had six wings: with two they covered his face, and with two they covered his feet" (Is 6:1–2).[53] In explaining this passage, Saint Jerome (+420) notes that some in his time identified the two seraphim as representing the Old and New Testaments of the Bible.[54] Such an interpretation may well have contributed to the medieval liturgists' perception of the Passion as an unveiling of the hitherto hidden meaning of the Scriptures, an unveiling

---

[49] John of Avranches, *Liber de officiis ecclesiasticis*, PL 147, col. 51.

[50] In a passage regarding Lent, the Cluny customary now known as the *Liber tramitis* (formerly called the Customs of Farfa), dating from about 1043, speaks of veiling the abbey church's "crucifixes" as well as its "very small crosses", implying that all or at least most of the church's larger crosses were crucifixes; it seems very likely that one of these crucifixes was used for the Good Friday veneration. See *Liber tramitis*, bk. 1, chap. 43, in Bruno Albers, ed., *Consuetudines monasticae*, vol. 1, *Consuetudines Farfenses* (Stuttgart: Jos. Roth, Bibliopolae, 1900), 33. The use of a crucifix is directly attested in a twelfth-century redaction of the Cluny customary, the *Redactio Galeatensis* (manuscript: Poppi, Italy, Biblioteca Communale 63); see Hallinger, *Consuetudines Cluniacensium antiquiores*, 90 (text "G").

[51] Antoine Gebran, *Il Venerdì santo nel rito Siro-Maronita*, BELS 136 (Rome: Centro Liturgico Vincenziano, Edizioni Liturgiche, 2006), 168.

[52] Text in Andrieu, *Ordines Romani du haut moyen âge*, 3:498.

[53] The association of the unveiling of the cross with this vision of Isaiah is discussed in Gian Paolo Ropa, "Il simbolismo medioevale della croce svelata", in Luigi Bettazzi, ed., *Miscellanea liturgica in onore di sua eminenza il cardinale Giacomo Lercaro*, vol. 2 (Rome: Desclée, 1967), 994–995.

[54] Saint Jerome, *On the Prophet Isaiah*, bk. 3, chap. 6, verses 2–3, PL 24, col. 95.

symbolized in the Good Friday unveiling of the cross.[55] The reference in Isaiah to the seraphim covering specifically the face and feet of God on his throne almost certainly inspired the particular manner of unveiling the crucifix found in the Good Friday rite of the 1364 ordinary of Strasbourg, France: in the first stage of this threefold unveiling, the veil is lifted to reveal only the feet of the crucifix, whereas in the second stage, it is lifted to the point of revealing the face and head of Christ, before the third stage, when the veil is entirely removed.[56]

Sicard of Cremona (+1215) likens the veil covering the cross to the veil that covered the face of Moses after conversing with God, and to the veil of the Temple of Solomon. The removal of the veil from the cross represents the rending of the Temple veil that signified the revelation of the sacraments and the doctrines of the Gospel, previously hidden under the letter of the Old Covenant but revealed in the Passion, a revelation to which Christ testified when before dying he said from the Cross, "It is consummated" (Jn 19:30). This is the same revelation that Christ gave verbally when on Easter Sunday he "uncovered the meaning of the Scriptures" to his disciples (cf. Lk 24:44–46). By this revelation "the standards of the King go forth" (*Vexilla Regis*).[57]

Describing the Cross as "the expectation of the patriarchs, the promise of the prophets",[58] Rupert of Deutz (+c. 1129) sees the unveiling of the crucifix as manifesting that Christ "reveals his face to us, that observing his glory we may be transformed into the same image from the glory of the Law to the glory of the Gospel just as by the Spirit of the Lord" (cf. 2 Cor 3:18).[59] In the above-cited Good Friday rite of the 1364 Strasbourg ordinary, the unveiling of "the face and head of the Crucified" is immediately preceded by the recitation of a verse from Psalm 66, "*May God have mercy on us, and bless us; may he cause the light of his countenance to shine upon us, and may he have mercy on us*" (Ps 66:2).[60] Significantly, Psalm 66 was used in many medieval rites of venerating the cross.

Most sources speak of the covering for the cross simply as a veil, but some prescribe the use of a particular liturgical cloth or even a priestly vestment. A late twelfth-century sacramentary of Vác, Hungary (1192–1195), directs that a chasuble be used;[61] the fourteenth-century *Liber ordinarius* of the collegiate church and abbey of Essen,

---

[55] Ropa, "Simbolismo medioevale della croce svelata", 973, 994–995.

[56] Text in Martène, *De antiquis ecclesiae ritibus*, bk. 4, chap. 23, 3:140. The same custom appears 140 years later in a 1505 ritual of Strasbourg: *Agenda, sive Exequiale sacramentorum* (Strasbourg, France: Prüss, 1505; digitized text, Bayerische Staatsbibliothek, Munich, n.d.), fol. 61r–61v.

[57] Sicard of Cremona, *Mitrale*, bk. 6, chap. 13, PL 213, cols. 318–319.

[58] Rupert of Deutz, *Liber de divinis officiis*, bk. 6, chap. 21, in Hrabanus Haacke, O.S.B., ed., *Ruperti Tuitiensis: Liber de divinis officiis*, CCCM 7 (Turnhout, Belgium: Brepols, 1967), 204. Hereafter cited as Rupert of Deutz, *Liber de divinis officiis* (CCCM 7).

[59] Ibid., chap. 20, p. 202.

[60] Martène, *De antiquis ecclesiae ritibus*, bk. 4, chap. 23, 3:140.

[61] Sacramentary of the cathedral of Vác, Hungary, adapted for monastic usage (contained in the Pray Codex), in Polycarp Radó, O.S.B., and Ladislaus Mezey, *Libri liturgici*

Germany, specifies an amice for veiling the crucifix.[62] A pall was used
for this purpose in the fourteenth-century Good Friday rites of Germany's Cologne Cathedral[63] and England's Barking Abbey (in the latter case, a red pall).[64] Some sources call for a black veil (Valencia,
Spain [1494]; Jaén, Spain [1499]; Toledo, Spain [1503–1518]);[65] the
1568 missal of Palencia, Spain, states that the cloth is to be either
black or violet.[66] Several texts mention the use of a staff for the unveiling, the earliest of which is the Benedictine customary of Einsiedeln,
Switzerland (c. 984), which directs the abbot to lift the veil from the
cross with a silver staff.[67]

By the end of the eleventh century, the chanting of the *Ecce lignum
crucis* had begun to take on a distinctly threefold form, with the triple
recitation of this antiphon appearing in the Benedictine customary of
Fructuaria, Italy (c. 1085).[68] It is shortly afterward that the practice of
unveiling the cross in three stages emerges in the twelfth-century *Roman
Pontifical*.[69] The Ordinal of the Papal Court, from the pontificate of
Pope Innocent III (1198–1216), developed the rite further, with three
separate stations for the three stages of the unveiling (to the right of
the altar, at the middle, and before the altar) as well as a prostration
for each stage.[70] This form of the unveiling, adopted by the Franciscans

manuscripti bibliothecarum Hungariae et limitropharum regionum (Budapest: Akadémiai Kiadó,
1973), 60.

[62] Text in Franz Arens, ed., *Der Liber ordinarius der Essener Stiftskirche* (Paderborn, Germany: Albert Pape, 1908), 51.

[63] Cologne, early fourteenth-century ceremonial, in Gottfried Amberg, ed., *Ceremoniale
Coloniense*, Studien zur Kölner Kirchengeschichte 17 (Siegburg, Germany: Franz Schmitt,
1982), 138.

[64] Late fourteenth-century ordinal of Barking Abbey, England, in J. B. L. Tolhurst, ed.,
The Ordinale and Customary of the Benedictine Nuns of Barking Abbey, vol. 1, HBS 65 (London: Henry Bradshaw Society, 1927), 98–99.

[65] See respectively *Hores de la setmana sancta segons lo us del archibisbat de Valencia* (Valencia, Spain: Jacobi de Villa, 1494), fol. 153r; *Missale Giennense / Manuale continens ordinem ad
celebrandum ecclesiastica sacramenta [Missale secundum morem et consuetudinem sancte ecclesie Gien-
ensis]* (Seville: Meinard Ungut and Stanislao Polono, 1499), fol. 79v; and *Missale secundum
consuetudinem almae ecclesiae Toletanae*, 1503–1518, vol. 4 (manuscript: Madrid, Biblioteca
Nacional de España, MS 1543; digitized text, Biblioteca Digital Hispánica, Biblioteca Nacional de España, Madrid, 2007), fol. 109v.

[66] *Missale Pallantinum* (1568), fol. 97r.

[67] *Consuetudines* of Einsiedeln, Switzerland, in Albers, *Consuetudines monasticae*, 5:94. The
Benedictine customary of Fructuaria, Italy, compiled around 1085 (bk. 1, chap. 47), specifies two staffs for the unveiling; see Albers, *Consuetudines monasticae*, 4:61. The *Officium
ecclesiasticum abbatum* of the English abbey of Evesham (c. 1250) directs that the abbot is
to use his abbatial staff for the unveiling of the crucifix; see Henry Austin Wilson, ed.,
Officium ecclesiasticum abbatum secundum usum Eveshamensis monasterii, HBS 6 (London: Henry
Bradshaw Society, 1893), cols. 88–89.

[68] *Consuetudines* of Fructuaria, Italy, bk. 1, chap. 47, in Albers, *Consuetudines monasticae*,
4:61–62.

[69] Text in Michel Andrieu, ed., *Le pontifical romain au moyen-âge*, vol. 1, *Le pontifical
romain du XIIᵉ siècle*, ST 86 (Vatican City: Biblioteca Apostolica Vaticana, 1938), 236.

[70] Text in Stephen J. P. Van Dijk, O.F.M., and Joan Hazelden Walker, eds., *The Ordinal
of the Papal Court from Innocent III to Boniface VIII and Related Documents*, SF 22 (Fribourg,
Switzerland: The University Press, 1975), 250–251.

in the mid-thirteenth century,[71] remained the norm in the papal liturgy thereafter (with changes only to the locations of the three stations) and entered the *Missale Romanum* of 1570.[72]

William Durandus, who as a prelate of the Roman Curia would have seen the three-staged unveiling of the cross in Rome and who prescribed this rite in the pontifical he compiled as bishop for his own diocese of Mende, France, around 1294,[73] interprets the three stages of the unveiling of the cross as representing the three times that Christ was mocked during his Passion. The first unveiling, revealing one arm of the cross while keeping the face of the crucifix veiled, symbolizes the mockery and blows to the face that Christ received while blindfolded in the court of the chief priest. The second unveiling, revealing the face of the crucifix, represents the mockery he received when he was crowned with thorns in the Praetorium. The third and final unveiling, completely uncovering the crucifix, symbolizes the mockery Christ received from passersby who, wagging their heads, blasphemed him as he hung stripped of his clothes on the Cross.[74] Durandus sees the complete unveiling of the cross as declaring "the victory of Christ" and as expressing that "all things that in the Law and the prophets had been obscure are uncovered and manifest in the Passion."[75]

The three stations at which the cross is progressively unveiled are interpreted by Durandus as symbolizing respectively the adoration given to Christ first by the Apostles and the other Jewish disciples (the station to the right of the altar), the proclamation of the Gospel to the nations by these disciples (the middle station at the altar), and the peaceful reign of Christ over his Church until the end of the world (the station at the foot of the altar). The acceptance of Christ by the "remnant of Israel" that shall come before the end of the world, bringing the Jews and the Gentiles together in one faith and in a common eternal destiny, is represented by the bearing away of the cross to a single location afterward.[76]

By the end of the ninth century, there had appeared in conjunction with the Trisagion in the Good Friday liturgy of France a series of three verses that would come to be known as the *Improperia* (Reproaches), in which Christ laments the ingratitude of sinful mankind, asking, "*My people, what have I done to you, or in what have I saddened you? Answer me.*" These verses borrow heavily from the Old

---

[71] Franciscan *Ordo missalis* of the friars' superior general Haymo of Faversham, c. 1244, in Stephen J. P. Van Dijk, O.F.M., *Sources of the Modern Roman Liturgy: The Ordinals by Haymo of Faversham and Related Documents (1243–1307)*, Studia et documenta Franciscana 2 (Leiden, Netherlands: E. J. Brill, 1963), 2:241–242.

[72] Sodi and Triacca, *Missale Romanum: Editio princeps (1570)*, 248–249 (new pagination).

[73] Text in Michel Andrieu, ed., *Le pontifical romain au moyen-âge*, vol. 3, *Le pontifical de Guillaume Durand*, ST 88 (Vatican City: Biblioteca Apostolica Vaticana, 1940), 584.

[74] Durandus, *Rationale* (CCCM 140a), bk. 6, chap. 77, nos. 16–17, pp. 376–377.

[75] Ibid., nos. 17, 19, p. 377.

[76] Ibid., no. 18.

Testament (Mic 6:3–4; Deut 8:2–3, 7; Is 5:4; Jer 2:21; Ps 68:22).[77]
They are also thought to be derived in part from the Good Friday
liturgy of Jerusalem: portions of the *Improperia* loosely correspond to
certain phrases within a series of twelve antiphons, *troparia*, utilized
in the Good Friday rites found in the Jerusalem liturgical book known
as the Georgian Lectionary, the contents of which date from the
fifth to the eighth century;[78] these Jerusalem *troparia*, thought to
have been authored by the city's patriarch Sophronius (c. 560–
638),[79] have become a permanent feature of the Byzantine Good
Friday liturgy.[80] The phraseology of two of the Jerusalem *troparia* is
traceable to the second century, when it is found in a Passion homily of the Church Father Saint Melito of Sardis (+190).[81] What is
believed to be the earliest indication of the existence of the *Improperia* in their Western form appears in the ancient liturgical book of
Spain's Mozarabic Rite known as the *Liber ordinum*, an eleventh-
century compilation of older texts thought to date largely from the
fifth to the seventh century: a rubric of the Good Friday liturgy
prescribes the singing of the verse *Populus meus*, the first words of
the first verse of the *Improperia*.[82] It is in the late ninth century that
the *Improperia* and the Trisagion begin to appear together in the Good
Friday liturgy, found thus in two French sources, the Antiphonary of
Senlis (France, c. 880)[83] and the liturgical book of northern France
formerly known as the Pontifical of Poitiers.[84] The introduction of
the *Improperia* into the cross veneration rite, like the introduction of
the crucifix that soon followed, accentuated the ceremony's focus
upon Christ crucified, for as a rubric of the 1498 Spanish missal of
Saragossa observes, the *Improperia* are sung "in the person of Christ
hanging on the wood".[85]

---

[77] Hermann Schmidt, S.J., *Hebdomada sancta* (Rome: Herder, 1956–1957), 2:794.

[78] See *troparia* 3 and 8, which contain phrases similar to those in the first and second
verses of the *Improperia* (Tarchnischvili, *Grand lectionnaire de l'église de Jérusalem*; Georgian-
language text; vol. 1, CSCO 188, nos. 668, 682, pp. 121, 126, and vol. 2, CSCO 204,
appendix 1, nos. 123, 139, pp. 136, 138; Latin translation: vol. 1, CSCO 189, nos. 668, 682,
pp. 97, 101, and vol. 2, CSCO 205, appendix 1, nos. 123, 139, pp. 109, 112).

[79] Sebastià Janeras, *Le Vendredi-saint dans la tradition liturgique byzantine: Structure et histoire
de ses offices*, Studia Anselmiana 99, Analecta liturgica 13 (Rome: Pontificio Ateneo S. Anselmo,
1988), 251, 258–259.

[80] Janeras (ibid., 249) provides a chart comparing the sequencing of the twelve *troparia*
in the current Byzantine liturgy (first column) with their order in the Georgian Lectionary
(second column).

[81] *Troparia* 7 and 8 exhibit this kinship with the Melito homily. See Egon Wellesz, "Melito's Homily on the Passion: An Investigation into the Sources of Byzantine Hymnography", *JTS* 44 (1943): 46–48.

[82] Férotin, *Liber ordinum*, col. 200.

[83] Hésbert, *Antiphonale missarum sextuplex*, 97.

[84] Martini, *Cosiddetto pontificale di Poitiers*, 192, 208.

[85] *Missale secundum morem ecclesie Cesaraugustane* (Saragossa, Spain: Paul Hurus, 1498),
temporal, fol. 97v. This same characterization of the singing of the *Improperia* appears seventy years later in the 1568 missal of Palencia, Spain; see *Missale Pallantinum* (1568), fol.
97r.

From the eleventh century onward, some Italian liturgical books, beginning with a text of Bologna, Italy,[86] add to the three first *Improperia* nine further verses, thereby enlarging the *Improperia* to twelve verses. Seven of these nine additional *Improperia* are based upon verses from a third-century Christian-authored portion of an ancient apocryphal work known as the Fourth Book of Esdras.[87] In the twelfth century, the expanded *Improperia* appear in the Good Friday liturgy of the Italian Benedictine abbey of Monte Cassino,[88] and in the thirteenth century, in the Franciscan *Ordo missalis* of the friars' superior general Haymo of Faversham (c. 1244)[89] as well as in a missal of central Italy.[90] Their use in the papal liturgy is first indicated in a redaction of the missal of Pope Honorius III dating from the third quarter of the thirteenth century.[91] They also appeared in the liturgical books of Padua[92] and Venice.[93] The long form of the *Improperia* seems not to have spread beyond Italy, except in the cases of the Franciscan friaries and those of the Augustinian Hermits,[94] until this

---

[86] Manuscript: Biblioteca Angelica, Rome, Codex Angelica 123, dated to between 1029 and 1039, cited in Gian Paolo Ropa, "Il preludio medioevale all' adorazione della croce nel Venerdì santo", in Luigi Bettazzi, ed., *Miscellanea liturgica in onore di sua eminenza il cardinale Giacomo Lercaro*, vol. 1 (Rome: Desclée, 1966), 645; see also 617, footnote, and 647, footnote.

[87] Jerome Gassner, O.S.B., "The 'Reproaches'", *Homiletic and Pastoral Review* 46 (February 1946): 326. The apocryphal Fourth Book of Esdras is largely of late first-century Jewish origin, but chapter 1, from which the additional *Improperia* are derived, is a third-century Christian addition to the text; see John Steinmueller, *A Companion to Scripture Studies*, vol. 1, *General Introduction to the Bible* (New York: Joseph F. Wagner; Houston: Lumen Christi Press, 1969), 132–133; Charles Souvay, "Esdras", *Catholic Encyclopedia* (1907–1912), 5:537–538.

[88] See the twelfth-century Holy Week *ordo* of Monte Cassino in Leuterman, *Ordo Casinensis hebdomadae maioris*, 111.

[89] Text in Van Dijk, *Sources of the Modern Roman Liturgy*, 2:242–243.

[90] *Vetus missale Romanum*, central Italy, c. 1250 (also known as the Lateran Missal); text in Shin-Ho Chang, ed., *Vetus missale Romanum monasticum Lateranense archivii basilicae Lateranensis, codex A65 (olim 65)*, MSIL 20 (Vatican City: Libreria Editrice Vaticana, © 2002), 176–177.

[91] The long version of the Good Friday *Improperia* is specified in a manuscript of the missal of Pope Honorius III (Rome, Archivio Santa Maria Maggiore, BB ii. 15); see Van Dijk and Walker, *The Ordinal of the Papal Court*, 256, footnote.

[92] See the Good Friday *Depositio* rite of the *Liber processionalis* for the cathedral of Padua, Italy (fourteenth to fifteenth century); text in Lipphardt, *Lateinische Osterfeiern und Osterspiele*, 2:588–589.

[93] See the Venetian Good Friday rite of veneration of the cross in the *Liber sacerdotalis* of Alberto Castellani, O.P., first published in 1523, reprinted with a different title in 1555: *Sacerdotale iuxta s. Romane ecclesie et aliarum ecclesiarum* (Venice: Peter Bosellus, 1555; digitized text, Bayerische Staatsbibliothek, Munich, 2009), fols. 228r–230r (text with music).

[94] A 1491 missal of the Augustinian hermits published in Nürnberg, Germany, gives the complete text of the long form of the *Improperia* for the Good Friday veneration of the cross; see *Missale ordinis Fratrum Eremitarum sancti Augustini de observantia* (Nürnberg, Germany: Fratres Ordinis Eremitarum Sancti Augustini / Georg Stuchs, 1491; digitized text, Bayerische Staatsbibliothek, Munich, 2009), fols. 80v–81r. Apart from the Augustinian and Franciscan liturgical books, the author was unable to find among the dozens of other medieval texts he consulted any examples of the long *Improperia* outside of Italy.

form was universally promulgated with the issuance of the 1570 *Missale Romanum.*[95]

In several Spanish liturgical books, including the 1568 missal of Palencia, a unique *Improperia* verse appears, taking the place of the second of the three original *Improperia*, from which it borrows some of its wording: "*I, indeed, conveyed you through the Red Sea and submerged Pharaoh before your eyes, for surely from his spoils I enriched you and led you through the desert for forty years; your garments are not blackened; I fed you with manna and brought you into an exceedingly good land; and you have prepared a cross for your Savior.*"[96] This verse, also found in the Spanish Good Friday rites of Vich (1496)[97] and Urgel (1536),[98] is at least as old as the thirteenth century, appearing in the thirteenth-century portion of a ritual from the Cistercians' Monastery of the Holy Cross in Coimbra, Portugal.[99]

In most of medieval Europe, the *Improperia* were sung during the solemn three-staged entrance procession of the cross, serving as a prelude to the unveiling of the cross; in the papal liturgy, however, beginning with the twelfth-century Roman Pontifical,[100] and in the Italian, Franciscan, and Augustinian Hermits' liturgical books that utilized the long form of the *Improperia*,[101] they were sung after the unveiling, as the clergy and laity came forward to venerate the cross individually; it was the latter arrangement that became universal with the issuance of the 1570 *Missale Romanum.*[102] As a lament uttered by Christ, the *Improperia* were usually sung by priests, in keeping with the priest's identity as an *alter Christus.* Most often, two priests were assigned to sing the verses together, a practice specified in numerous liturgical texts from the eleventh century onward.[103]

---

[95] Sodi and Triacca, *Missale Romanum: Editio princeps (1570)*, 249–250 (new pagination).

[96] *Missale Pallantinum* (1568), fol. 97r: "Ego quidem transvexi te per mare rubrum: et demersi Pharaonem coram oculis tuis: et de spoliis eius: ego namque ditavi te: et deduxi te per desertum quadraginta annis: vestimenta tua non sunt atrita: manna quoque cibavi te: et introduxi in terram satis optimam: et parasti crucem salvatori tuo."

[97] Missal of 1496, in Francesc Xavier Altés i Aguiló, ed., *Missale Vicense, 1496*, facsimile ed., Biblioteca litúrgica catalana 3 (Barcelona: Institut d'Estudis Catalans, 2001), temporal, fol. 89r.

[98] *Ordinarium* of 1536, described in Francesc Xavier Parés i Saltor, *L'ordinari d'Urgell de 1536*, Col·lectania Sant Pacià 74 (La Seu d'Urgell, Spain: Societat Cultural Urgel·litana / Facultat de Teologia da Catalunya, 2002), 119.

[99] Text in Joaquim O. Bragança, "Ritual de Santa Cruz de Coimbra: Porto, Biblioteca Municipal, ms. 858", *Didaskalia* 6 (1976): 144.

[100] Andrieu, *Pontifical romain au moyen-âge*, 1:236.

[101] *Vetus missale Romanum*, central Italy, c. 1250, in Chang, *Vetus missale Romanum*, 175–176; Franciscan *Ordo missalis* of Haymo of Faversham, c. 1244, in Van Dijk, *Sources of the Modern Roman Liturgy*, 2:241–242; *Missale ordinis fratrum eremitarum sancti Augustini de observantia* (1491), fols. 80v–81r.

[102] Sodi and Triacca, *Missale Romanum: Editio princeps (1570)*, 248–249 (new pagination).

[103] An early example can be found in the customary for the French Benedictine abbey of Cluny compiled by the monk Bernard, c. 1075; see the *Ordo Cluniacensis*, pt. 1, chap. 68, in Marquard Herrgott, ed., *Vetus disciplina monastica* (Paris, 1726; repr., Siegburg, Germany: Franciscus Schmitt, 1999), 316. See also Archbishop Lanfranc's customary for England's Canterbury Cathedral, c. 1077 (Knowles and Brooke, *The Monastic Constitutions of Lanfranc*,

Ninth-century texts of the Good Friday veneration rite speak of two acolytes as the bearers of the cross.[104] But from the eleventh century onward, numerous texts assign two priests to the carrying of the cross.[105] Durandus explains the two priests as representing the two natures, divine and human, of Christ.[106] A fifteenth-century manual of York, England, directs that two priests are to bear the cross on a pillow, following a path from the altar to the choir that has been laid with a carpet.[107] In the papal Good Friday rites, beginning with the twelfth-century Roman Pontifical, the cross has one bearer, the pope.[108] Similarly, the French missal of Bayonne (1543) assigns to the cross one priest only, flanked by two candle bearers and two thurifers.[109] The rubrics of the early fourteenth-century ceremonial of Cologne, Germany, direct that four priests are to carry the cross; the dean of the cathedral, who is the principal celebrant, stands at the head of the cross (its summit), where he is flanked by a deacon and a subdeacon to his right, with another deacon and another subdeacon to his left. Four other priests stand at the foot of the cross.[110]

The 1491 *Obsequiale Ratisponense*, a liturgical book of Regensburg, Germany, provides the principal celebrant of the Good Friday liturgy with an opportunity to prepare himself privately for the public rite of veneration of the cross. Before beginning the unveiling of the cross, the presiding priest goes to the veiled crucifix, barefoot, and kneeling before it, says Psalm 3 (*"Why, O Lord, are they multiplied that afflict me?"*) and several versicles and prayers, after which he sprinkles it with holy water and incenses it, and then proceeds with the carrying forth of the crucifix and the singing of the *Improperia*.[111]

60–61), and a late twelfth-century sacramentary of the Hungarian cathedral of Vác, adapted for monastic usage, found in Hungary's Pray Codex (Radó and Mezey, *Libri liturgici manuscripti bibliothecarum Hungariae*, 60).

[104] Roman *Ordo* 31, in Andrieu, *Ordines Romani du haut moyen âge*, 3:498; pontifical of northern France formerly known as the Pontifical of Poitiers (late ninth century), in Martini, *Cosiddetto pontificale di Poitiers*, 192–193.

[105] See Saint Udalric of Zell's customary for the French Benedictine monastery of Cluny, compiled around 1080 (bk. 1, chap. 13, PL 149, col. 661). Other texts specifying two priests include the *Consuetudines* of Lanfranc, Canterbury (c. 1077); the *Ordinarium* of Münster (1489); and the missals of Salzburg (fifteenth century), Salisbury (late fifteenth century), Jaén (1499), Avila (1510), Seville (1534), and Braga (1558).

[106] Durandus, *Rationale* (CCCM 140a), bk. 6, chap. 77, no. 13, p. 375.

[107] Text in William George Henderson, ed., *Manuale et processionale ad usum insignis ecclesiae Eboracensis*, Surtees Society Publications 63 (Durham, England: Andrews, 1875), 156.

[108] For the twelfth-century Roman Pontifical, see Andrieu, *Pontifical romain au moyen-âge*, 1:236.

[109] Text in V. Dubarat, ed., *Le missel de Bayonne de 1543* (Pau, France: Léon Ribaut, 1901), 43–44.

[110] Amberg, *Ceremoniale Coloniense*, 138, 140. The carrying of the cross by four priests is also found in a Benedictine *ordinarium* written around 1245 for the famous royal abbey of Saint Denis, a monastery located in the French village of the same name, near Paris; see Martène, *De antiquis monachorum ritibus*, bk. 3, chap. 14, no. 33, in Martène, *De antiquis ecclesiae ritibus*, 4:543, 545.

[111] *Obsequiale Ratisponense* (Nürnberg, Germany: Georg Stuchs, 1491; digitized text, Bayerische Staatsbibliothek, Munich, 2008), fol. 69v.

In an early printed book of the Spanish archdiocese of Valencia, the 1494 *Hores de la setmana sancta* (Hours of Holy Week), we find a particularly impressive example of the Good Friday veneration of the cross as it was celebrated in the city's cathedral in the late fifteenth century.[112] While possessing the same key elements as other medieval Good Friday veneration rites from elsewhere in Europe, the Valencia ceremony is distinguished by an unusual juxtaposition of the threefold unveiling of the cross with the singing of the *Improperia*. Nine other liturgical books of Spain among those studied, the missals of Orense (1494), Saragossa (1498), Tarragona (1499), Valladolid (1499), Segovia (1500), Avila (1510), Tarazona (1529), Seville (1534), and Palencia (1568),[113] also contain this juxtaposition, but it is absent from those of Toledo (1478), Vich (1496), Jaén (1499), and Palma de Majorca (1506),[114] suggesting that this form of the ceremony was widespread in Spain but not universal; the practice is traceable to the end of the twelfth century, when it appears for the first time, not in a Spanish text, but in a ritual of Soissons, France (c. 1185).[115] At whatever point in the Good Friday liturgy the verses of the *Improperia* are sung, they are always deeply moving. Durandus sees the *Improperia* (actually the *Improperia* joined to the Trisagion) as praising God symbolically in three languages; the words *Agois o Theos* are in Greek, the *Sanctus Deus* is in Latin, and the words of Christ, *"My people, what have I done to you?"*,

---

[112] *Hores de la setmana sancta ... Valencia* (1494), fols. 153r–156r.

[113] See respectively *Missale secundum usum Auriensis ecclesiae* (Monterrey, Spain: Gonzalo Rodriguez de la Passera and Juan de Porras, 1494; digitized text, Biblioteca Digital Hispanica, Biblioteca Nacional de España, Madrid, 2007), fols. 84v–85r; *Missale secundum morem ecclesie Cesaraugustane* (1498), temporal, fols. 97v–98r; *Missale secundum consuetudinem ecclesiae Tarraconensis* (Tarragona, Spain: Johannes Rosenbach, 1499; digitized text, Biblioteca Virtual del Patrimonio Bibliográfico, Madrid, n.d.), fol. 92r–92v; *Missale secundum consuetudinem monachorum congregationis sancti Benedicti de Valladolid* (Montserrat, Spain: Johannes Luschner, 1499; digitized text, Biblioteca Virtual del Patrimonio Bibliográfico, Madrid, n.d.), fol. 90r–90v; *Missale secundum consuetudinem Segobiensis ecclesie* (Venice: Johannes Emericus de Spira, 1500; digitized text, Biblioteca Digital Hispánica, Biblioteca Nacional de España, Madrid, 2007), fols. 78v–80r; *Missale Abulense* (Salamanca, Spain: Juan de Porras, 1510), sig. i7v–i8v; *Missale secundum ritum ac consuetudinem insignis ecclesiae Tirassonensis* (Sargossa: Jorge Coci, 1529; digitized text, Bayerische Staatsbibliothek, Munich, n.d.), fols. 90v–92r; *Missale divinorum secundum consuetudinem alme ecclesie Hispalensis* (Seville: Joannes Varela, 1534; Latin text provided by Biblioteca Apostolica Vaticana, Vatican City [shelf mark Stamp. Barb. B. X. 4]), fols. 85v–86r; and *Missale Pallantinum* (1568), fols. 97r–98r.

[114] *Missale mixtum secundum consuetudinem almae ecclesie Toletane*, 1478 (manuscript: Toledo, Spain, Toledo Cathedral, Library, MS Res. 2), fols. 157ff., described in José Janini and Ramón Gonzálvez, *Catálogo de los manuscritos liturgicos de la catedral de Toledo*, Publicaciones del IPIET, 3rd series, 11 (Toledo, Spain: Diputación Provincial, 1977), 260–261; Altés i Aguiló, *Missale Vicense, 1496*, temporal, fol. 89r; *Missale Giennense / Manuale ... sacramenta* (1499), fols. 79v–80r; Gabriel Seguí i Trobat, ed., *El missal mallorquí de 1506: Estudi i edició segons l'exemplar de la Biblioteca Bartomeu March*, Col·lectània Sant Pacià 79 (Barcelona: Facultat de Teologia de Catalunya, Centre d'Estudis Teològics de Mallorca, 2003), 289.

[115] The Good Friday rite from a late twelfth-century ritual of Soissons, France, has a multistaged processional unveiling of the crucifix during the singing of the *Improperia* with the Trisagion, preceding the *Ecce lignum crucis*, and thus corresponds to the format in many of the Spanish texts (Soissons text in Martène, *De antiquis ecclesiae ritibus*, bk. 4, chap. 23, 3:138).

although said in Latin, represent Hebrew (actually, Aramaic) as the language Christ would have spoken.[116] The Valencia ceremony begins at the door of the sacristy:

> And after [the bishop or priest] finishes saying the aforesaid prayers, two cantors, one a priest and the other a deacon, vested in copes of silk, should be at the door of the sacristy, who with reverence and humility hold the cross, covered with a fine black veil, and singing in the person of Jesus Christ crucified, say this verse: *My people, what have I done to you, or in what have I saddened you? Answer me. For with a mighty hand I led you out from the land of Egypt in great signs and glorious wonders; you have prepared a cross for your Savior.* And having finished saying the aforesaid verse, two boys standing before the altar say [in Greek]: *Holy God, Holy Mighty One, Holy Immortal One: have mercy on us.* And those of the choir, genuflecting with humility, respond [in Latin]: *Holy God, Holy Mighty One, Holy Immortal One: have mercy on us.* In entering, those who hold the cross shall uncover the left arm of the latter and sing the following verse: *For your Savior, who led you through the desert for forty years and who fed you with manna and brought you into an exceedingly good land, you have prepared a cross.* And the boys remaining at the altar shall repeat singing another time, *Holy God, Holy Mighty One, Holy Immortal One: have mercy on us.* And those of the choir, genuflecting with humility another time, respond: *Holy God, Holy Mighty One, Holy Immortal One: have mercy on us.* In the meantime, those who hold the cross shall uncover the other arm of the latter and, coming to the right side of the altar, sing the following verse: *What further ought I to have done for you and did not do? Indeed, I planted you [as] my most beautiful vine; and you have made me very bitter; for in my thirst you have given me a drink of vinegar mixed with gall; and you have pierced the side of your Savior with a lance.* And having finished the verse, the two boys who remain at the altar answer another time: *Holy God, Holy Mighty One, Holy Immortal One: have mercy on us.* And the choir, genuflecting, shall respond another time: *Holy God, Holy Mighty One, Holy Immortal One: have mercy on us.*[117]

For the third and total unveiling of the cross, the Valencia rite utilizes the verse almost universally associated with the unveiling of the cross in other medieval liturgical books, *"Behold the wood of the Cross"*. This verse is for Sicard of Cremona an invitation to behold the wood by which "the bitter waters" of the Law under the Old Covenant have become sweet (cf. Ex 15:25):[118]

> And afterward of this, those who hold the cross come to the middle of the altar, and uncovering that [cross] entirely, and lifting it as high

---

[116] Durandus, *Rationale* (CCCM 140a), bk. 6, chap. 77, no. 14, pp. 375–376.

[117] *Hores de la setmana sancta . . . Valencia* (1494), fol. 153r–153v.

[118] Sicard of Cremona, *Mitrale*, bk. 6, chap. 13, PL 213, cols. 318–319.

as they can, and turning the face toward the people, singing with a high voice they say: *Behold the wood of the Cross*. And the choir, making a genuflection, responds, singing: *Behold the wood of the Cross*. And another time, those who hold the cross, raising their voices more than the first time, say: *Behold the wood of the Cross*. And the choir, making a genuflection, similarly raising its voice, responds: *Behold the wood of the Cross*. And another time those who hold the cross, raising their voices more than the second time, say: *Behold the wood of the Cross*. And those of the choir, genuflecting, similarly raising their voices, say all of the following antiphon: *Behold the wood of the Cross, on which hung the salvation of the world; come, let us adore.*[119]

In the Valencia ceremony, as we have just seen, the three-staged unveiling of the cross is completed before beginning the chant *Ecce lignum crucis*. The more common practice by which the three stages of the unveiling take place in tandem with the threefold recitation of the *Ecce lignum crucis* can be seen in the rubrics of the 1488 *Caeremoniale Romanum* of the papal master of ceremonies Patrizio Piccolomini; the cross would be unveiled by the pope himself or by the cardinal serving as celebrant in the presence of the pope:

[The celebrant] proceeds to the rear [of the] Epistle side [of the altar] near the wall, and the deacon of the chapel takes the veiled cross from the altar and offers it to the celebrant, who, receiving it reverently, with his right hand uncovers the summit of the cross all the way to its crossbeam. Then with both hands elevating it to the height of his eyes, remaining thus, he sings alone in a low voice, *Behold the wood of the Cross*, his chaplain with a cope standing near to his left, holding the book. All then rise and uncover their heads. The master of ceremonies, the ministers, and all the chaplains of the celebrant near the altar continue, *On which hung the salvation of the world*. The cantors then finish, *Come, let us adore*. At which words, namely *Come, let us adore*, the pope and all the others, the celebrant excepted, should genuflect. Then the celebrant proceeds to the side of the altar itself, remaining on the same [Epistle] side; and he uncovers the right arm of the cross, and the head of the figure of the Crucified, and elevates it as before and sings a little higher just as earlier. To which it is answered and the knee bent as before. Third, the celebrant proceeds to the middle of the altar, and having turned toward the people, he uncovers the entire cross; and elevating it and singing higher, he does as before, and it is answered and the knee bent as earlier.[120]

---

[119] *Hores de la setmana sancta . . . Valencia* (1494), fols. 153v–154r.

[120] Text in Marc Dykmans, ed., *L'oeuvre de Patrizi Piccolomini, ou Le cérémonial papal de la première Renaissance*, vol. 2, ST 294 (Vatican City: Biblioteca Apostolica Vaticana, 1982), 384.

In the 1494 Good Friday rite of Valencia, the personal veneration of the cross by each of the clergy and laity immediately follows the *Ecce lignum crucis*:

> They shall place before the altar lengthwise a carpet, over which they shall put a beautiful cushion, and over those, fine blessed altar cloths. And here they shall place the cross, to which, with much humility and devotion, first shall come the bishop and the ministers of the altar, and afterward the people. And similarly there should be placed in the choir another cross in the aforesaid manner, which all the clergy shall come to worship. And at the adoration, the bishop or priest who stands at the altar should say the following prayer: *O Christ, who have undergone for us the ignominy of the Cross and of death, that you might drive out from us the power of death and free us with your precious blood, have mercy upon me, your most lowly servant, and grant me the forgiveness of all my sins; and deliver me, prostrate in prayer before your Cross, from all evils; and mercifully refresh me with your benefits. Who live and reign. Through all ages of ages. Amen.*[121]

The Valencia text does not describe the specific manner by which the clergy and the laity individually venerated the cross, but it would have almost certainly comprised at least one prostration as well as the kissing of the cross, as we find it in the rubrics of another Spanish liturgical book, the 1568 missal of Palencia:

> The prelate or priest, celebrating without a cope, with both feet bare, or at least with his shoes removed, receives the cross in his hands and, with the ministers following, proceeds with it somberly and devoutly, all the way to the couch prepared for this on the last step of the altar; and he places it there on the couch or on a clean cloth. And he having prostrated himself before the cross first, he adores, kissing it reverently, offering some oblation. But when he adores, he should say silently the following prayer: *Lord Jesus Christ, I adore you hanging on the Cross and bearing on your head the crown of thorns; I entreat you, that your own Cross may deliver me from the slaughtering angel. Lord Jesus Christ, I adore you wounded on the Cross, having tasted of the gall and the vinegar; I entreat you, that your wounds may be the remedy of my soul. Lord Jesus Christ, I adore you laid in the sepulcher; I entreat you, that your death may be my life. Lord Jesus Christ, I adore you going to come to the judgment and to judge the living and the dead; I entreat you, that in your holy coming you may not enter into judgment with me, an unworthy and miserable sinner, but may forgive me my sins according to your great mercy. Who live and reign, God, through all ages of ages. Amen.*[122]

---

[121] *Hores de la setmana sancta ... Valencia* (1494), fol. 154r–154v.

[122] *Missale Pallantinum* (1568), fol. 98v. (Latin text provided by Biblioteca Apostolica Vaticana, Vatican City.) The prayer recited here, *Domine Iesu Christe, adoro*, is a highly abbreviated form of an oration entitled "Holy Prayer to the Lord" first found in a ninth-century

Early Western texts of the veneration rite, including the eighth-century Roman *Ordo* 23 and the ninth-century Frankish Roman *Ordo* 31, mention a single prostration before the cross.[123] In the Good Friday rite of the late fourteenth-century Benedictine ordinal of England's Barking Abbey, there is likewise a single, total prostration before the crucifix, after which all five wounds of Christ on the cross are devoutly kissed.[124] The custom of prostrating three times before the cross is found from the tenth century onward.[125] The 1499 missal of Jaén, Spain, prescribes that worshipers are to genuflect before the crucifix three times, "kissing the ground with the utmost reverence and humility".[126] As Amalarius of Metz explains, the prostration before the cross is an expression of humility:

> On this day that the cross is kissed, he [Christ] was humbled unto the Father for us even unto death, death on a cross. If we ought to be imitators of his death, it is needful also to be humbled likewise. Whence let us prostrate before the cross, that constant humility of the soul may be demonstrated by the disposition of the body. We are not able to show the humility of the soul more than when the entire body is prostrated to the earth.[127]

According to the 1493 *Obsequiale Frisingense*, a liturgical book of Freising, Germany, those venerating the cross are to "kiss devoutly and humbly the wounds of the feet and side of the Crucified".[128] The 1494 missal of Eichstätt, Germany, provides five prayers to be said privately while kneeling after venerating the cross with a kiss; we give here the fourth prayer:

> *I beseech you, most merciful Lord Jesus Christ, by that extraordinary love with which you have loved mankind, when you, O celestial King, hung upon the Cross, with your deific flesh, with your most gentle soul, in your most sorrowful deed, with your senses troubled, your heart anguished, your body pierced with bloody wounds, your hands stretched, your veins extended, your mouth clamorous, with hoarse voice, your face pallid with the color of*

---

text of English composition, the Book of Cerne; text in A. B. Kuypers, ed., *The Prayer Book of Aedeluald the Bishop, Commonly Called the Book of Cerne* (Cambridge, England: Cambridge University Press, 1902), 114–117 (corresponding text, 116–117).

[123] Texts in Andrieu, *Ordines Romani du haut moyen âge*, 3:271, 498, respectively.

[124] Ordinal, Barking Abbey, England, in Tolhurst, *Ordinale . . . Barking Abbey*, 1:99.

[125] Tenth-century examples include the Romano-Germanic Pontifical, the Codex of Ratold for the French Benedictine abbey of Corbie, and the *Regularis concordia* of England's Benedictines (c. 960). See respectively Vogel and Elze, *Pontifical romano-germanique*, 2:91–92; *Codex Ratoldi* (excerpt), quoted by Dom Nicolas-Hugues Ménard (+1644) in his work on the Gregorian Sacramentary, reprinted in PL 78, col. 332; and Symons, *Regularis concordia*, chap. 4, nos. 44–45, pp. 43–44.

[126] *Missale Giennense / Manuale . . . sacramenta* (1499), fol. 80r.

[127] Amalarius of Metz, *Liber officialis*, bk. 1, chap. 14, nos. 5–6, in Hanssens, *Amalarii episcopi: Opera liturgica omnia*, 2:100–101.

[128] *Obsequiale Frisingense* (Augsburg, Germany: Erhard Ratdolt, 1493; digitized text, Bayerische Staatsbibliothek, Munich, 2008), fol. 39v.

death, with your eyes sorrowful, your throat groaning with yearnings of thirst, your head bowed with the parting of your deific body and soul, with the inception of the living fountain [from your side]. And so I beseech you, O most loving Lord Jesus Christ, in that love with which your most loving heart was rent on the Cross, that you may be readily forgiving to me over the multitude of my sins [and] vouchsafe to grant me a good and holy end to my life, as well as a most favored and joyful resurrection, for the sake of your great mercy, who with God the Father and the Holy Spirit live and reign through all ages of ages. Amen.[129]

In the 1494 Valencia rite, as the clergy and the faithful come forward to venerate the cross one by one, the choir sings a catena of antiphons and versicles of the holy Cross, dating for the most part from the sixth to the eleventh century, and drawn not only from the Good Friday office but from other sources as well, including texts associated with the May 3 and September 14 feasts of the holy Cross:[130]

During the time that the clergy and the people shall worship the cross, those of the choir shall sing the following antiphons. Antiphon: *Let us worship the sign of the Cross, through which we have obtained the promise of salvation, on which our Lord has weighed himself, as if on a balance, as our ransom, that by his life having been sold, death might be made captive, under which grievous fall the world was ruined. He has affixed his holy feet to the Cross; and against the mighty, the whole world has raised a mightier Conqueror. Yet this is more wondrous: that the Victor, who is not contained in the whole world, standing on one trunk, has accomplished his mission.*[131] Antiphon: *We worship your Cross, O Lord, and we praise and glorify your holy Resurrection; for behold, because of the Cross, joy has come into the whole world.*[132] Antiphon: *When the Maker of the world suffered the death of execution on a cross, crying out in a loud voice, he surrendered his spirit; and behold, the veil of the Temple was torn asunder; the tombs were opened; a great earthquake was wrought; for the world cried out at the death of the Son of God, unable to sustain itself. The side of the crucified Lord having then been opened by the soldier's lance, blood and water issued forth for the ransoming of our salvation.*[133] Antiphon: *O Cross, brighter [than] all the stars, renowned in the world, very lovely to men, holier to the*

---

[129] *Missale Eystetense* (Eichstätt, Germany: Michael Reyser, 1494; digitized text, Bayerische Staatsbibliothek, Munich, 2009), fol. 91r.

[130] *Hores de la setmana sancta . . . Valencia* (1494), fols. 154v–155v.

[131] *Adoremus crucis signaculum* is first found in the twelfth-century antiphonary of Saint-Maur-des-Fossés, France; see René-Jean Hésbert, ed., *Corpus antiphonalium officii*, vol. 2, REDSMF 8 (Rome: Herder, 1965), 557.

[132] *Crucem tuam* is believed to be of Byzantine origin (Schmidt, *Hebdomada sancta*, 2:793–794). As a Latin Rite text it is first found in the Mass chant portion of the Antiphonary of Compiègne (France, c. 870); see Hésbert, *Antiphonale missarum sextuplex*, 97.

[133] *Dum Fabricator mundi* is traceable to the late ninth-century pontifical of northern France formerly known as the Pontifical of Poitiers; see Martini, *Cosiddetto pontificale di Poitiers*, 193, 208.

whole world, who alone were worthy to bear the weight of the world; sweet the wood, sweet the nails, supporting sweet burdens; save this congregation present, gathered together continually in your praises. [134] Antiphon: *O Cross, admirable sign, on which our Lord, the Son of God, was hung for the burden of our sins. He has put to death the punishment of death, and his blood has been poured out for the ransom of our salvation.* [135] Antiphon: *O blessed Cross, who alone were worthy to bear the King and Lord of Heaven.* [136] Antiphon: *O venerable Cross, who alone were worthy to bear the King and Lord of Heaven.* [137] Antiphon: *We worship your Cross, O Lord, we contemplate your glorious Passion; have mercy on us, who suffered for us.* [138] Antiphon: *We glorify the tree of life, your Cross, O Lord; for by it death has been condemned; and by the selfsame the whole world has been illuminated; almighty Lord, glory to you.* [139] Antiphon: *Savior of the world, save us, who through your Cross and blood have redeemed us; help us, we entreat you, our God.* [140] Antiphon: *Save us, Christ our Savior, through the power of the Cross, you who saved Peter on the sea; have mercy on us.* [141] Antiphon: *The dear Cross shines, by which salvation has been restored to the world; the Cross has conquered, the Cross reigns, the Cross drives away every sin.* [142] Antiphon: *Sweet the wood, sweet the nails, sweet the burden they supported, they that were worthy to bear the ransom of this world.* [143] Antiphon: *Sanctify us, Lord, with the sign of the holy Cross, that it may be made in us an obstacle against the savage arrows of our enemies; defend us, Lord, by the sign of the Cross; and by the holy price of your blood, by which you have redeemed us.* Antiphon: *By the sign of the Cross, free us from our enemies, our God.* [144] Antiphon: *Faithful Cross, the one noble tree among all* [others]; *no forest brings forth* [one] *of such a kind, in flower, leaf, fruit. Sweet the wood, sweet the nails, sweet the burden they support.* [145] Antiphon:

---

[134] *O crux splendidior* is traceable to the above-cited late ninth-century pontifical of northern France (ibid., 208).

[135] *O crux admirabile signum* is first found as an antiphon in the above-cited late ninth-century pontifical of northern France (ibid., 193).

[136] *O crux benedicta quae sola* is first found in the Antiphonary of Compiègne (France, c. 870); see René-Jean Hésbert, ed., *Corpus antiphonalium officii*, vol. 1, REDSMF 7 (Rome: Herder, 1963), 302.

[137] *O crux veneranda* is evidently a variant of the preceding chant, *O crux benedicta quae sola.*

[138] *Tuam crucem adoramus* is first found in the above-cited Antiphonary of Compiègne (France, c. 870); see Hésbert, *Corpus antiphonalium officii*, 1:304.

[139] *Lignum vitae* is first found in the above-cited Antiphonary of Compiègne (ibid.).

[140] *Salvator mundi salva nos* is first found in the eleventh-century Antiphonary of Hartker (Saint Gall Abbey, Switzerland); see Hésbert, *Corpus antiphonalium officii*, 2:418.

[141] *Salva nos Christe Salvator per virtutem crucis* is first found in the Antiphonary of Compiègne (France, c. 870); see Hésbert, *Corpus antiphonalium officii*, 1:304.

[142] *Crux alma fulget* is first found in an early eleventh-century antiphonary of Monza, Italy (ibid., 213).

[143] *Dulce lignum, dulces clavas* is from the sixth-century hymn of Saint Venantius Fortunatus in honor of the holy Cross, *Pange lingua gloriosi.*

[144] *Per signum crucis de inimicis* is first found in the Antiphonary of Compiègne (France, c. 870); see Hésbert, *Corpus antiphonalium officii*, 1:304.

[145] *Crux fidelis* is from the above-cited hymn of Saint Venantius Fortunatus, *Pange lingua gloriosi.*

428

We adore you, O Christ, and we bless you; for by your Cross you have redeemed the world.[146] Antiphon: *Beauteous shining tree, adorned in the purple of the King; chosen from a worthy stock to touch such sacred members.*[147] Antiphon: *O Cross, green wood, for upon you hung the Redeemer of Israel; how sweet the wood, how sweet the nails, how sweet the burden they support. Oh, how precious is the wood, how beautiful the gem that bore and merited to support the Christ, by whom the whole world has been redeemed.*[148]

Among the antiphons in the above catena of chants is the deeply moving *Dum Fabricator mundi* ("*When the Maker of the world suffered death*"), one of the most beautiful pieces of Gregorian chant,[149] which, although absent from the papal liturgy (and hence absent from the 1570 *Missale Romanum*), was sung on Good Friday across much of medieval Europe. In the 1487 *Obsequiale Augustense* of Augsburg, Germany, and the 1514 *Agenda* of Passau, Germany, it is the first of the chants to be sung as the clergy and the laity come forward to venerate the cross.[150] This antiphon usually concluded with the sublime verse "*O wonderful Price, by whose weight the captivity of the world has been redeemed, the infernal gates of hell have been shattered, the gate of the kingdom has been opened to us.*"[151]

In the Valencia rite, the aforesaid catena of chants is followed by the awesome hymn of Saint Venantius Fortunatus (+c. 605), *Pange lingua gloriosi* ("*Sing, my tongue, the victory of the glorious battle,*" also known as *Crux fidelis*, and not to be confused with Saint Thomas Aquinas' Eucharistic hymn of the same name), that from the ninth century onward was sung during the Good Friday veneration of the cross[152] and remained a hymn of this rite in the universally promulgated *Missale*

---

[146] *Adoremus te Christe et benedicimus* is first found in the Antiphonary of Compiègne (France, c. 870); see Hésbert, *Corpus antiphonalium officii*, 1:304.

[147] *Arbora decora fulgida* is from the sixth-century hymn of Saint Venantius Fortunatus, *Vexilla Regis*.

[148] *O crux viride lignum* is first found as a responsory in an early eleventh-century antiphonary of Monza, Italy; see Hésbert, *Corpus antiphonalium officii*, 1:215.

[149] The beauty of this chant can be heard on a compact disc of Good Friday chants recorded by the Czech ensemble Schola Gregoriana Pragensis and the Boni Pueri (*Adoratio Crucis* [*Uctívání Kříže*—Devotion of the Cross], Supraphon, SU 3448-2-231, 2000).

[150] See respectively *Obsequiale Augustense* (Augsburg, Germany: Erhard Ratdolt, 1487; digitized text, Bayerische Staatsbibliothek, Munich, 2008), fol. 15v, and *Agenda sive Benedictionale de actibus ecclesie secundum chorum et observationem ecclesie Pataviensis* (Basel, Switzerland: Jacobus Pfortzensis, 1514; digitized text, Bayerische Staatsbibliothek, Munich, 2008), fols. 64r–65v.

[151] Text in Martin Gerbert, *Monumenta veteris liturgiae Alemannicae* (Sankt Blasien, Germany: Typis San-Blasianis, 1777–1779), 1:382.

[152] This hymn first appears as an accompaniment to the veneration rite in two ninth-century sources, the Frankish Roman *Ordo 31* and the liturgical book of northern France formerly known as the Pontifical of Poitiers (late ninth century); see respectively Andrieu, *Ordines Romani du haut moyen âge*, 3:498, and Martini, *Cosiddetto pontificale di Poitiers*, 193, 209–210.

Romanum of 1570.[153] The veneration of the cross concludes with a
further threefold showing of the totally unveiled crucifix to the
congregation:

> At the end they say the following antiphon: *Come, sons of Eve, come to
> the Son of Mary; behold how he hangs on the Cross, [his garments] split
> into four parts for thieves. What is there in him of sin? Truly nothing. Why,
> then, is he on the Cross, as if he were not the King of glory, the splendor and
> glory of Sion in beauty, its good, having conquered by love beyond measure?
> Even as [the Father] willed, so did he deliver his Son for his ungrateful
> servants; give thanks also to the Paraclete, one God. Hail, our King; you
> alone, obedient to the Father, having mercy on our errors, were led to the
> Cross, meek as a sheep to the slaughter. Glory to you; Hosanna, triumph,
> and victory to you; to you, the perfection of praise and the crown of honor.*[154]

And having finished the adoration of the cross, the priest with the deacon, elevating the former [i.e., the cross] on high, remaining before the
altar, says in a high voice, *Above all the trees of the cedars.*[155] And the choir
responds: *Above all the trees of the cedars.* And the priest and the deacon
do [this] another time, raising their voices more than the first [time] to
say: *Above all the trees of the cedars.* And the choir shall respond, continuing the same, intoning: *Above all the trees of the cedars.* And another
time they reply, the priest and the deacon raising their voices more than
the second time: *Above all the trees of the cedars.* And the choir, responding, should say all of the following antiphon: *Above all the trees of the cedars,
you alone [are] the loftiest, on which hung the Life of the world, on which Christ
triumphed and death conquered death forever.*[156]

As we have seen in the Valencia rite, the medieval Good Friday
liturgy inspired the use of a rich repertoire of antiphons, responsories,
and hymns. In the tenth-century Romano-Germanic Pontifical, a Marian dimension was added to the rite of venerating the cross through
the use of the responsory *Vadis Propitiator* ("*You go forth, O atoning
One*"), a text traceable to an acrostic composition of the Byzantine
hymnographer Saint Romanus the Melodist (+c. 560).[157] It is a lament

---

[153] Sodi and Triacca, *Missale Romanum: Editio princeps (1570)*, 250–251 (new pagination).

[154] This rare antiphon, *Venite filii Evae; venite ad filium Mariae*, also in the 1492 missal of
Valencia and in the almost identical Good Friday veneration rite from the 1498 missal of Saragossa, does not appear in any of the other sources or chant indexes consulted for this study.
See respectively *Missale iuxta morem et consuetudinem sedis Valentiae* (Venice: Johann Hamman,
1492; digitized text, Biblioteca Digital Hispánica, Biblioteca Nacional de España, Madrid,
2007), fol. 61v, and *Missale secundum morem ecclesie Cesaraugustane* (1498), temporal, fol. 99r.

[155] *Super omnia ligna* is first found in two French sources from the second half of the
ninth century, the Antiphonary of Compiègne (c. 870) and the pontifical of northern
France formerly known as the Pontifical of Poitiers; see respectively Hésbert, *Corpus antiphonalium officii*, 1:304, and Martini, *Cosiddetto pontificale di Poitiers*, 210.

[156] *Hores de la setmana sancta . . . Valencia* (1494), fols. 155v–156r.

[157] Anthony Ward, S.M., "Holy Week in the Ambrosian Liturgy", in Antony George
Kollamparampil, ed., *Hebdomadae sanctae celebratio: Conspectus historicus comparativus*, BELS
93 (Rome: Centro Liturgico Vincenziano, Edizioni Liturgiche, 1997), 200.

of the Blessed Virgin addressed to her Divine Son. The pontifical directs that the *Vadis Propitiator* be sung "in the name of Mary" while "saluting the cross": "*You go forth, O atoning One, to be immolated for all; Peter does not go to meet you, who said, 'I shall die for you.' Thomas has forsaken you, who cried out, saying, "Let us all die with him", and none of them but you alone are led away, who have preserved me immaculate, my Son and my God.*" [158] The 1496 missal of the Spanish see of Vich ends the Good Friday veneration of the cross with the antiphon known as the *Cum Rex gloriae*, a text ultimately derived from the final part of a sermon of an anonymous author known as Pseudo-Augustine.[159] It first appears as a Holy Week antiphon in a French antiphonary of the ninth to the tenth century, in which it is assigned to the procession of palms.[160] In the Vich missal, its use in the Good Friday liturgy in conjunction with the triumphant antiphon that we saw at the end of the Valencia rite, *Super omnia ligna* ("*Above all the trees*"), serves as a moving affirmation of what Christ's loving sacrifice has wrought:

> *When Christ the King of glory, going to wage war, entered hell, and the angelic choir commanded the gates of its rulers to lift up before his face, the choirs of saints who were held captive in death cried out with a mournful voice, "You have come, O Desired One, whom we have awaited in darkness, that you may lead forth this night those imprisoned by bars; our sighs have burned with love for you; our abundant laments have sought you; you have been made the hope of the hopeless, our bountiful consolation amid torments."* [161]

The Good Friday rite found in the 1534 missal of Seville, Spain, is unique in that those carrying the cross, representing Christ crucified, and those singing the Greek form of the Trisagion, representing fallen mankind in need of divine mercy, would set out from separate locations within the church and progressively advance in three stages toward each other and their common destination, the high altar. This rite would unfold within the vast reaches of Seville's sprawling gothic cathedral. Two priests, barefoot, bearing the crucifix covered with a linen veil, and stationed "in the place where the Body of Christ has been reposed" since Holy Thursday (the repository), begin to sing the *Improperia*, "*My people, what have I done to you, or in what have I saddened you? . . . You have prepared a cross for your Savior. Answer me.*" Responding to this haunting lament of the Savior emanating from the repository, the celebrating priest and the deacon and subdeacon assisting him, all

---

[158] Vogel and Elze, *Pontifical romano-germanique*, 2:90–91.

[159] Pseudo-Augustine, *Sermones supposititios*, sermon 160 (sermon *De tempore* 137), PL 39, cols. 2059–2061.

[160] Manuscript: Laon, France, Bibliothèque de Laon, Codex 239, in Abbaye Saint-Pierre, Solesmes, ed., *Antiphonale missarum sancti Gregorii, IXe–Xe siècle, Codex 239 de la Bibliothèque de Laon*, Paléographie musicale 10 (Solesmes, France, 1909; repr., Berne, Switzerland: H. Lang, 1971), 86.

[161] Altés i Aguiló, *Missale Vicense, 1496*, temporal, fol. 90r–90v.

barefoot, stationed behind the choir altar, reply with the Greek of the Trisagion, "*Holy God, Holy Mighty One, Holy Immortal One, have mercy on us.*" The cathedral choir, kneeling, repeats the Trisagion in Latin. Setting out from the repository, the two priests bearing the crucifix now carry it toward the cathedral's high altar, stopping before the first step, where the right arm of the crucifix is uncovered as they chant the next verse of the *Improperia*, "*For your Savior, who led you through the desert . . . you have prepared a cross.*" Advancing to the choir entrance, the celebrant, the deacon, and the subdeacon again respond in Greek, "*Holy God, . . . have mercy on us*", with the choir kneeling to repeat the Trisagion in Latin. The priests with the crucifix then ascend to one corner of the high altar, where the left arm of the crucifix is uncovered as they sing the third verse of the *Improperia*, "*What further ought I to have done for you, and did not do? . . . You have pierced the side of your Savior with a lance.*" The celebrant and his two ministers proceed to a position in front of the first step and the gate before the high altar and there plead again for mercy, "*Holy God, . . . have mercy on us*", their words once more repeated in Latin by the choir. The two priests now bring the crucifix to the middle of the high altar as the celebrant and his ministers ascend the altar steps to meet them there, the celebrant thereafter totally unveiling the crucifix and showing it to the people as he begins the *Ecce lignum crucis*.[162]

In the medieval liturgy, the unveiling of the cross constituted a visual expression of the Passion of Christ as a theophany, a revelation of the Divinity,[163] as Christ had foretold to the Pharisees: "When you shall have lifted up the Son of man, then shall you know, that I am he" (Jn 8:28). This perception of the unveiling as a symbolic theophany is implicit in a twelfth-century rubric for the Good Friday veneration rite at the French Benedictine abbey of Cluny: "Then those who carry the cross should put it in some more eminent place before the altar, uncovering it and exclaiming: *Behold the wood* . . . Immediately, this having been heard, seeing the holy crucifix, all should fall on their faces and adore."[164] Just as on Mount Tabor Christ was transfigured in a vesture of light, revealing his divine glory, so too on Mount Calvary Christ was transfigured in the vesture of his precious blood, revealing his divine love. The readings of the medieval Good Friday liturgy allude to this theophany. The first reading (Hos 6:1–6) says of the Lord, "His going forth is prepared as the morning light, and he will come to us as the early and the latter rain to the earth" (verse 3). The Gradual that follows this reading is taken from the Book of Habacuc (Hab 3:1–3), paraphrasing the third verse, the original wording of which declares, "God will come from the south, and the holy one from Mount

---

[162] *Missale . . . ecclesie Hispalensis* (1534), fols. 85v–87r.

[163] Ropa, "Simbolismo medioevale della croce svelata", 994–995, 1003–1005.

[164] See the twelfth-century redaction of the Cluny *Consuetudines*, the *Redactio Galeatensis*, in Hallinger, *Consuetudines Cluniacensium antiquiores*, 90 (text "G").

Pharan: His glory covered the heavens, and the earth is full of his praise." Although absent from the Good Friday Gradual, the complete Habacuc text includes further lines that suggest the theophany of the Savior on the Cross defeating death, sin, and Satan (Hab 3:4–5, 11, 13): "His brightness shall be as the light: horns are in his hands: There is his power hid: Death shall go before his face. And the devil shall go forth before his feet.... The sun and the moon stood still in their habitation, in the light of thy arrows, they shall go in the brightness of thy glittering spear.... Thou wentest forth for the salvation of thy people: for salvation with thy Christ." The medieval biblical exegete Haymon of Halberstadt (+853) believes that Habacuc's reference to "horns ... in his hands" prefigures the "standard and trophy of the Cross", on which the Savior's power was concealed but by which "he enlarged his reign."[165] Saint Bernard of Clairvaux (+1153) sees the "glittering spear" mentioned in this text as a prophetic reference to the lance that pierced the Savior's side on the Cross.[166]

In the Good Friday veneration of the cross found in a late fifteenth-century ceremonial of the diocese of Vienne, France,[167] the entire third chapter of the book of the prophet Habacuc, with all the above-cited verses, is recited after the total unveiling of the crucifix. The responsory assigned to accompany the Habacuc text relates Christ's comparison of his being lifted up on the Cross to Moses' mounting of the bronze serpent on a pole (Jn 3:14–15). The evocation of the episode of the bronze serpent is strikingly well suited to the veneration of the cross, for just as the Israelites were instructed to look upon the serpent so as to obtain from God the healing of their deadly snakebites (Num 21:8–9), so now the faithful are invited to look upon the image of their Savior affixed to the Cross for the healing of the wounds of sin. This imagery is vividly evoked in another French liturgical book, the 1543 missal of Bayonne, which directs the priest at the Good Friday liturgy to hold a serpent-shaped candlestick, with its candle lit at the beginning of the rite, during the reading of the Passion of Saint John and the intercessions.[168]

The rubrics of the late fifteenth-century Vienne ceremonial go beyond the sober relation of liturgical directions by expressly calling upon all to contemplate the love and mercy of Christ as the crucifix is shown to them; this devotional directive is actually borrowed almost verbatim from the Good Friday rubrics of Cardinal Bernard of Porto's *Ordo Officiorum* for Rome's Church of Saint John Lateran dating from about the year 1140.[169] The Vienne text states:

---

[165] Haymon of Halberstadt, *Enarrationes in Habacuc prophetam*, PL 117, col. 189.

[166] Saint Bernard of Clairvaux, *Meditatio in passionem et resurrectionem Domini*, chap. 8, PL 184, col. 754.

[167] Text in Martène, *De antiquis ecclesiae ritibus*, bk. 4, chap. 23, 3:139–140.

[168] Dubarat, *Missel de Bayonne de 1543*, 42.

[169] Fischer, *Bernhardi cardinalis ... Ordo officiorum ecclesiae Lateranensis*, 56.

Two deacons with the archdeacon, vested, coming near to the cantors, taking the selfsame cross from the hands of the same, uncover the entire [cross] in the same place—one to the right and the other to the left should hold it—to which all having turned, that presently they may contemplate the crucified Lord with his arms extended, inviting us to the embrace of his reconciliation, and hasten to that fount of goodness flowing from the side of the Lord hanging, open for the washing of the sinner, of those gazing upon him; how much they should be incited with the affection of devotion they ought to exhibit toward so great a favor. The archbishop and the ministers, on the side of the altar on which the Epistle is said, kneeling, and having prostrated [themselves] as often as the antiphon [*Ecce lignum crucis*] is begun, should adore God and kiss the earth, the others, however, [doing so] in the choir. The cantors, when they shall have handed over the cross to two deacons, should come before the altar, and in the same place, with another from the clerics holding the book before them, they should begin the responsory: *As Moses lifted up the serpent in the desert, so must the Son of man be lifted up; that whosoever believes in him, may not perish, but may have life everlasting.* Verse: *God sent not his Son into the world, to judge the world, but that the world may be saved by him* . . . [cf. Jn 3:14–15, 17]. Psalm [canticle]: *O Lord, I have heard thy hearing* [Hab 3:2–19]. The choir should respond, *And was afraid.* There should be repeated *As Moses*, without the psalm.[170]

In the Vienne rite, the veneration of the cross by each of the clergy and the religious individually takes place during the chanting of the responsory and the Habacuc canticle:

While *As Moses* is sung, the deacons holding the cross, and approaching the pedestal prepared before the altar, shall deposit the selfsame cross upon the pedestal, with the cantors emerging from the side of the choir near the pedestal, singing and repeating the aforesaid antiphons and responsories. The priest with the ministers, approaching the cross, having prostrated themselves upon the ground, should humbly and devoutly adore it, in such a way that the priest alone should say the three prayers only;[171] the ministers should listen very intently and, likewise rising, kiss the feet of the Lord. The brothers, however,

[170] Martène, *De antiquis ecclesiae ritibus*, bk. 4, chap. 23, 3:139. The Vienne ceremonial gives only the incipit of the responsory *Sicut Moyses*. The complete text is here taken from the *Breviarium Romanum* of 1568, in Manlio Sodi and Achille Maria Triacca, eds., *Breviarium Romanum: Editio princeps (1568)*, facsimile ed., MLCT 3 (Vatican City: Libreria Editrice Vaticana, © 1999), 771 (new pagination). This responsory first appears in a foureenth- or fifteenth-century antiphonary for the cathedral of Salamanca, Spain (manuscript: Salamanca Catedral-Archivo Musical, Codex 8, fol. 29v, as indicated by the Gregorian chant online database Cantus, http://cantusdatabase.org).

[171] These three orations would have been prayers of private devotion for this occasion, similar to those cited earlier in this chapter from the Romano-Germanic Pontifical and the 1494 missal of Eichstätt, Germany (pp. 411, 425–426).

proceeding two by two from the choir, first the elders, then those younger, approaching the cross and gazing at it, shall humbly prostrate themselves. And from the innermost intention of the heart they should briefly finish the prayer, in such a way that one of them should say one [prayer] only; the others should listen.[172]

The Vienne text again borrows a meditative passage from the Good Friday rubrics of Rome's Lateran *Ordo officiorum* of about 1140:[173] "Now, however, when they rise for the purpose of kissing the feet of the crucified Lord, [when] they return to the remembrance of that imprint of the nails and that mixture of blood with water, [then] what kind of love, and what kind of sweetness, and what manner of kisses ought they to confer, to be applied with an attentive mind, is more to be thought than to be spoken."[174]

The Mass of the Presanctified

Following the veneration of the cross, the medieval Good Friday liturgy climaxed with the processional return of the Eucharist to the altar and the reception of Holy Communion—in some places, a general Communion received by the clergy and the laity, in others, particularly Rome, from the thirteenth century onward, a Communion by the celebrant alone. The Holy Communion rite of Good Friday is a continuation of the ancient liturgical rite known as the Mass of the Presanctified, in which Scripture readings and prayers are followed by the solemn reception of the Eucharist that has been consecrated at a Mass prior to this nonconsecratory rite. As a liturgical form, the Mass of the Presanctified first appeared in Syria in the early sixth century (c. 515) and existed in Constantinople before 600.[175] The prohibition of the celebration of Mass on Good Friday, already the norm under Pope Innocent I (401–417),[176] permanently established the Western tradition of observing in place of Mass a nonconsecratory Mass of the Presanctified on this solemnity.

The seventh-century Gelasian Sacramentary of Rome is the earliest Western text to mention the bringing of the presanctified Eucharist to the altar for Holy Communion on Good Friday; it speaks of deacons (the number is unspecified) bringing the Body and Blood of the Lord, both reserved on Holy Thursday, to the altar from the sacristy.[177] Roman *Ordo* 24 (c. 750–800) is the earliest text to indicate reservation of the Eucharist under the one species of bread and the bringing to the altar of a chalice of unconsecrated wine; it is also the first text to assign two priests to the Good Friday transfer of

---

[172] Martène, *De antiquis ecclesiae ritibus*, bk. 4, chap. 23, 3:139.

[173] Fischer, *Bernhardi cardinalis . . . Ordo officiorum ecclesiae Lateranensis*, 57.

[174] Martène, *De antiquis ecclesiae ritibus*, bk. 4, chap. 23, 3:139.

[175] Janeras, *Vendredi-saint dans la tradition liturgique byzantine*, 372–373.

[176] Innocent I, *Letter 25*, no. 7 (chap. 4), PL 20, cols. 555–556.

[177] Mohlberg, Eizenhöfer, and Siffrin, *Liber sacramentorum*, no. 418, p. 67.

the Eucharist.[178] Amalarius of Metz (+c. 850) also mentions two priests for this rite.[179] In the late ninth-century liturgical book of northern France formerly known as the Pontifical of Poitiers, the two priests who carry the Eucharist to the altar are preceded by two candle bearers, constituting the earliest reference to lights for the Good Friday transfer of the Eucharist.[180]

During the eleventh century, the processional transfer of the reserved Sacrament from the place of reposition to the altar for the Good Friday Mass of the Presanctified acquired an ever-increasing solemnity, particularly in monasteries. As the Good Friday rubrics of an eleventh-century customary of Fonte Avellano, Italy, explain, the Eucharist should be carried with the utmost reverence, insofar as "in it is our entire salvation and redemption."[181] The *Liber tramitis* (formerly called the Customs of Farfa), a customary of the French Benedictine abbey of Cluny dating from about 1043, specifies that when during the Good Friday liturgy the deacon carrying the Blessed Sacrament from its place of reposition begins to proceed to the altar, accompanied by those carrying candles and incense, "immediately all should prostrate themselves on the earth"; after the Eucharist has been placed on the altar (evidently over the chalice carried with it in the procession), the presiding priest censes it.[182] A slightly later customary of Cluny (c. 1075) compiled by the monk Bernard of Cluny assigns a priest to carry the Eucharist and prescribes the use of silver candlesticks and a gold thurible "with an abundance of incense" for the procession; as the Blessed Sacrament is brought toward the altar, all rise and kneel.[183] The Benedictine customary of Lanfranc, archbishop of Canterbury, England, dating from about 1077, directs the priest to incense the Eucharist twice, first in the repository before the procession and then a second time after the Sacrament has been borne to the altar; during the procession, as the Blessed Sacrament approaches the altar, "all the brethren shall adore the Body of the Lord on their knees."[184]

A missal of Halberstadt, Germany (c. 1498), directs the priest, the deacon, and the subdeacon to go in procession to the repository (here identified as the *clausura*), led by thurifers and altar boys bearing candles; upon reaching the repository, all kneel, after which the priest

---

[178] Text in Andrieu, *Ordines Romani du haut moyen âge*, 3:294.

[179] Amalarius of Metz, *Liber officialis*, bk. 1, chap. 15, no. 1, in Hanssens, *Amalarii episcopi: Opera liturgica omnia*, 2:107.

[180] Martini, *Cosiddetto pontificale di Poitiers*, 191–192.

[181] From an eleventh-century manuscript of the eremitical monastery of Santa Croce, Fonte Avellano, Italy (*Primus codex Fontavellanensi* [excerpt], PL 151, col. 882).

[182] *Liber tramitis*, bk. 1, chap. 55, in Albers, *Consuetudines monasticae*, 1:53.

[183] *Ordo Cluniacensis*, pt. 1, chap. 68, in Herrgott, *Vetus disciplina monastica*, 260.

[184] Knowles and Brooke, *Monastic Constitutions of Lanfranc*, chaps. 40–45, p. 62 (Latin text quoted and translated by permission of Oxford University Press). Similarly, the fourteenth-century *Ordinarium* for the Augustinian priory of Saint-Lô in Rouen, France, directs that when on Good Friday the procession bringing the Eucharist nears the altar, "all should adore on bended knees the Body of the Lord" (PL 147, col. 175).

unlocks and opens the repository, incensing the Sacrament before taking it and bringing it to the altar in silence, "with great reverence".[185] A unique custom existed in Augsburg, Germany, as described in a missal from 1496: the Eucharist would be brought in procession, not after the veneration of the cross, but instead at the beginning of the cross veneration rite, when, as two priests carried in the crucifix, the deacon preceded them, bearing in a chalice the Eucharist under a small umbrella-shaped canopy (an *umbraculum*), after which the priests began the *Improperia*, "*My people, what have I done to you ... ?*"[186]

The burial associations of the preceding day's procession to the repository were carried through to this corresponding Eucharistic procession on the very day of the Lord's death. In the Good Friday rite as Rupert of Deutz knew it in the twelfth century, the Eucharist was brought back to the altar by two priests "to signify Joseph the Just from Arimathea and Nicodemus, who brought to be buried the body of Jesus sought from and conceded by Pilate."[187] Although in most medieval Good Friday texts the prevalent custom was for one cleric rather than two to carry the Blessed Sacrament to the altar, Rupert's identification of this liturgical action with the "funeral procession" of Joseph of Arimathea and Nicodemus to the tomb was intimated in other ways. In the Good Friday rubrics of the 1494 *Hores de la setmana sancta* of Valencia, Spain, the reservation of the Eucharist on Holy Thursday for Holy Communion on Good Friday is explained as representing Christ's subjecting himself to death and burial for the sake of our salvation: "The reason why [the priest] reserves the Body of the Lord from Holy Thursday and consumes it on Friday is because the body of our Redeemer God, Jesus Christ, was buried for the faithful."[188] This passage implies that the burial of Christ is symbolized not only by the Holy Thursday reposition of the Blessed Sacrament but also by the priest's Holy Communion on Good Friday. It is in fact a reiteration of the mystical interpretation of the Holy Communion of Good Friday proposed over a century earlier in a fourteenth-century *ordinarium* for the Priory of Saint-Lô, a community of Augustinian canons regular in Rouen, France: "In memory of his burial, the Body of the Lord, reserved from Holy Thursday to Good Friday, is taken by the faithful."[189] This association can best be understood in the light of a passage from the *Vita Jesu Christi* of the Carthusian writer Ludolph of Saxony (+1377), who likens the burial of Christ to the fitting reception of Holy Communion:

---

[185] *Missale Halberstatense* (Strasbourg, France: Johann Grüninger, c. 1498; digitized text, Bayerische Staatsbibliothek, Munich, 2009), fol. 70r.

[186] *Missale Augustanum* (Augsburg, Germany: Erhard Ratdolt, 1496; digitized text, Bayerische Staatsbibliothek, Munich, 2008), fol. 71v.

[187] Rupert of Deutz, *Liber de divinis officiis* (CCCM 7), bk. 6, chap. 23, p. 206.

[188] *Hores de la setmana sancta ... Valencia* (1494), fol. 156r–156v.

[189] *Ordinarium canonorum regularum*, Priory of Saint-Lô, Rouen, France, PL 147, col. 175.

Mystically, in the actions of Joseph [of Arimathea] and Nicodemus are signified several things required in us, if Christ is to be buried in our heart. For he communicating ought to be wrapped in linen cloths, by pure affection, and purity of conscience; for he wraps Jesus in a clean shroud, who receives him [Jesus] with a pure mind and a pure body, for it is fitting to receive the Body of Christ not only with a pure soul but also with a pure body. But it is necessary to wrap [him], for his mystery is closed and hidden. He [Jesus] ought also to be anointed with aromatic substances, by fervent devotion; for he wraps Jesus with myrrh and aloes, who lays up the Crucified in his heart with the bitterness of penance and compassion. But in the newness of the tomb it is denoted that the heart ought to be renewed by grace and purity and cleansed of every former way of sin before he should approach the Body of Christ, in which heart he also places him [Jesus] when he reflects continually about him, for it [the tomb] is called a *monumento*, as though admonishing the mind.... He also, with Christ buried in his heart, rolls a great stone to the entrance for an enclosure, who closes himself lest sin should be able to enter, and [being] diligent, places an obstacle against the recurring of sin—lest Christ should forsake him and abandon him—until he [Jesus] makes him rise from the dead.[190]

The above-cited *Hores de la setmana sancta* of Valencia gives the following rubrics for the Eucharistic procession of the Good Friday liturgy, in which the celebrant remains at the altar as all the other clergy and acolytes present form a cortege to accompany the Eucharist:

The priest should enter into the sacristy and divest himself of his cope and put on a chasuble. And vested with the ministers in white vestments, he should come to the altar, upon which they shall place a blessed white altar cloth, and upon that the corporals; and on the altar they shall light candles or tapers. And after this, with the priest remaining at the altar, the deacon with the ministers of the altar and all the clergy go to the sacristy or *monumento*[191] with a cross, candelabras, and a censer, and a canopy, for carrying the Body of the Lord, which should be returned to the altar and be carried by the deacon with that solemn veneration and devotion with which it [the Eucharist] was carried away [on Holy Thursday]. And from the *monumento* up to the altar, the Body of the Lord should be incensed continually by the subdeacon. And the deacon should sing in a low voice the following antiphon: *This is my Body, which shall be delivered for you* ...[192] And the priest standing at the altar shall take the Body of the

---

[190] Ludolph of Saxony, *Vita Jesu Christi*, ed. Jean-Pierre Mabile and Jean-Jacques-Maria-Antoine Guerrin (Paris and Rome: Victor Palmé, 1865), pt. 2, chap. 66, p. 682.

[191] This rubric indicates that the Blessed Sacrament could be reserved from Holy Thursday to Good Friday in either the sacristy or a separate repository, the *monumento* (sepulcher).

[192] This antiphon, *Hoc Corpus*, first discussed on p. 375, is discussed again later in the present chapter (p. 439).

Lord with great humility and reverence from the hands of the deacon.[193]

In the 1496 missal of Vich, Spain, the cortege for the Eucharist is even larger, including all the people in a candlelight procession to the repository: "[The priest] should go out from the sacristy with the ministers; and with the people with lights, in the manner of a procession, he should go to the place where the Body of Christ had been reserved." For the carrying of the Eucharist from the repository to the altar, the Vich missal specifies the singing of the same responsory that was used in the Holy Thursday procession of Valencia, evoking the moving image of Christ crowned with thorns: "*Jesus having come out from the Praetorium bearing the crown of thorns, the Jews then all cried out, Away with him, away with him, crucify him.* Verse: *Pilate says to them: Behold your King; and they cried out to him, saying, Away with him, away with him, crucify him.*"[194] Just as on Holy Thursday the burial symbolism of the reposition of the Eucharist was heightened in the rubrics of Archbishop Alonso Carillo's 1478 missal of Toledo, Spain, so too on Good Friday the Toledo rubrics for the return of the Blessed Sacrament to the altar continue in this vein.[195] Again, we quote the redaction of the Toledo rubrics found in the 1499 missal of the Spanish diocese of Jaén, which corresponds *verbatim* to the 1478 text of Toledo:

> And while the clergy and the people adore the cross, the priest with the ministers should go down to the sacristy and there put their shoes on; and the priest should take a black chasuble, and the deacon and the subdeacon [should take] black dalmatics, and come to the entrance of the major choir, with candles and a censer preceding. . . . The priest and his ministers, the clergy, and the people, with another black cross, and candles, and a censer without lit coals preceding the priest, should come in a procession made in silence all the way to the *monumento*; and when they shall have reached it, the priest should ascend to the *monumento* with the two lords who have the keys and the seals. And meanwhile, from lit coals the inside of the censer should be made ready. And the sepulcher having been opened, the priest should take from the incense that is inside and place it in the censer and immediately incense the Body of the Lord. Which having been done, he should uncover the chalice and show the consecrated Host privately and humbly to the said lords; and the chalice with the Body of the Lord having been covered, he reverently brings it with his amice as

[193] *Hores de la setmana sancta . . . Valencia* (1494), fol. 156r.

[194] Altés i Aguiló, *Missale Vicense, 1496,* temporal, fol. 90v.

[195] *Missale mixtum secundum consuetudinem almae ecclesie Toletane,* 1478 (manuscript: Toledo, Spain, Toledo Cathedral, Library, MS Res. 2), fols. 157ff., described in Janini and Gonzálvez, *Catálogo de los manuscritos litúrgicos de la catedral de Toledo,* 260–261. For an Internet-accessible edition of the Toledo rubrics, see *Missale secundum consuetudinem almae ecclesiae Toletanae,* 1503–1518, vol. 4, fols. 113r–115r (website: http://bibliotecadigitalhispanica.bne.es).

he carried it on the day before, with the ministers, namely the deacon [and] the subdeacon, assisting him, at times supporting him, that he may proceed more propitiously and securely with the Body of the Lord; and a silk veil [canopy] should be carried over the Body of Christ, as said earlier, by four or six noble lords of the city, the cross always preceding with candles and incense in the censer; and with [one] casting down green foliage as was said. And a certain prebendary from the elder ones clothed in white surplices should bring a black banner in the middle of the procession, that is to say, between the canons and the prebendaries; and thus in this order they should come to the major altar. When the deacon shall have arrived, he should spread out the corporals upon the altar. And the priest, with the greatest reverence, should place upon the altar the Body of Christ with the chalice in which it came; which having been set in place, he should go down to the altar step and there say the confession [i.e., the *Confiteor*]. Which having been done, he should go up to the altar and wash his hands; then he should reverently take the Body of Christ from the chalice and place it [the Eucharist] upon the altar at the foot of the chalice.[196]

It is in the Good Friday transfer of the Eucharist to the altar that we find the earliest use of the antiphon *Hoc Corpus* for the processions to and from the repository, a chant that, as we saw in chapter 13, had come to be used almost universally for the Holy Thursday Eucharistic procession by the end of the Middle Ages (until it was supplanted by Saint Thomas Aquinas' hymn *Pange lingua gloriosi*). On Good Friday, the *Hoc Corpus* first appears as a chant for the transfer of the Eucharist from the place of repose to the altar in an eleventh-century customary of the eremitical monastery of Santa Croce, Fonte Avellano, Italy.[197] This usage is found soon afterward, about the year 1140, in the Good Friday liturgy of the Augustinian canons regular of Rome's cathedral church of Saint John Lateran;[198] it subsequently spread to diocesan rites across much of medieval Europe, including those of Germany, Poland, France, Italy, Spain, and Portugal.[199]

Liturgical books of Hungary, beginning with a late twelfth-century sacramentary of Vác (1192–1195), specify the singing of the Holy

---

[196] *Missale Giennense / Manuale . . . sacramenta* (1499), fol. 80r–80v.

[197] *Primus codex Fontavellanensi* (excerpt), PL 151, col. 882.

[198] *Ordo* of Bernard of Porto, in Fischer, *Bernhardi cardinalis . . . Ordo officiorum ecclesiae Lateranensis*, 58.

[199] For examples, see the early fourteenth-century ceremonial of Cologne, Germany (Amberg, *Ceremoniale Coloniense*, 144); the missal of Kraków, Poland (1493; *Missale Cracoviense* [Nürnberg, Germany: Georg Stuchs, 1493; digitized text, Bayerische Staatsbibliothek, Munich, 2009], fol. 88r); the missal of Bayonne, France (1543; Dubarat, *Missel de Bayonne de 1543*, 44); the late thirteenth-century *Ordo officiorum* of Lucca, Italy (M. Giusti, "L'*Ordo officiorum* di Lucca", in *Miscellanea Giovanni Mercati*, vol. 2, *Letteratura medioevale*, ST 122 [Vatican City: Biblioteca Apostolica Vaticana, 1946], 546); the missal of Avila, Spain (1510; *Missale Abulense*, sig. k1r); and the missal of Braga, Portugal (1498; *Missale Bracarense*, sig. k1v).

Communion hymn *Laudes Omnipotens ferimus tibi* during the Good Friday processional transfer of the Eucharist to the altar,[200] a hymn composed by Ratpert (+c. 885), a Benedictine monk of Switzerland's Saint Gall Abbey:

Praises we bear unto you, O Omnipotent One,
worshiping the gifts of your incomparable Body and Blood.

Behold, O most holy Master, we approach your altar;
may you be merciful to your unworthy ones. Repeat: *Praises we bear . . .*

Be merciful, O Holy One; graciously absolve our sins,
that it may be permitted us
to appropriate your invincible holy things. Repeat: *Worshiping the gifts . . .*[201]

The Good Friday rubrics of a customary for Norwich, England (c. 1260), prescribe the singing of the penitential psalm *Miserere* (Psalm 50) as the bishop, assisted by two priests, carries the Eucharist from the repository to the altar.[202] A liturgical manual for the Polish diocese of Wrocław (Breslau), in a passage dating from 1448, directs that as two priests go to the sacristy and return with the Blessed Sacrament, accompanied by two candle bearers and two thurifers, the earlier-cited antiphon *Dum Fabricator mundi* ("*When the Maker of the world suffered death*") is sung.[203] The Good Friday rubrics of the 1536 *Ordinarium* of Urgel (La Seu d'Urgell), Spain, prescribe that after all have gone in silence to the *monumento* (the repository), Saint Thomas Aquinas' Eucharistic hymn *Pange lingua gloriosi* is sung as the Blessed Sacrament is carried in procession from the repository to the altar, with the *Hoc Corpus* sung following the placement of the Eucharist upon the altar.[204]

The earliest reference to the singing of Saint Venantius Fortunatus' majestic sixth-century hymn of the Cross *Vexilla Regis* during the Good Friday transfer of the Eucharist appears in a late fifteenth-century diary of papal events kept by the papal master of ceremonies John Burckard. On Good Friday, March 24, 1486, the *Vexilla Regis* was chanted as

---

[200] Sacramentary of the cathedral of Vác, Hungary, adapted for monastic usage (contained in the Pray Codex), and the 1484 missal of Esztergom, Hungary (*Missale Strigoniensi*), in Radó and Mezey, *Libri liturgici manuscripti bibliothecarum Hungariae*, 60, 33, respectively; the *Liber ordinarius* of Eger, Hungary, 1509, in László Dobszay, ed., *Liber ordinarius Agriensis (1509)*, Musicalia Danubiana, subsidia, 1 (Budapest: Magyar Tudományos Akadémia Zenetudományi Intézet, 2000), 59, 183.

[201] *Laudes Omnipotens ferimus tibi*, verses 1–3; for the complete nine-verse text, see PL 87, col. 40.

[202] Text in J. B. L. Tolhurst, ed., *The Customary of Norwich*, Henry Bradshaw Society 82 (London: Henry Bradshaw Society, 1948), 89.

[203] *Modus agendi in ecclesia Wratislaviensi* (portion of text dating from 1448), in Schubert and Stapper, *Excerpta ex ordinariis Germanicis*, 24.

[204] Parés i Saltor, *Ordinari d'Urgell de 1536*, 119–120.

Pope Innocent VIII carried the Eucharist to the altar.[205] Two years later, the singing of this hymn during the Good Friday Eucharistic procession is specified for the first time in a liturgical book, the 1488 *Caeremoniale Romanum* of another papal master of ceremonies, Patrizio Piccolomini.[206] The use of the *Vexilla Regis* for this ceremony was subsequently made universal with the promulgation of the *Missale Romanum* of Pope Saint Pius V in 1570.[207] Here we quote the opening verse:

> The standards of the King go forth,
> the mystery of the Cross shines,
> by which the Creator of flesh, in the flesh,
> is suspended on the gibbet.[208]

Among the most highly developed and splendid rubrics for the Good Friday Eucharistic procession from the repository to the high altar are those given in the 1568 *Missale Pallantinum* of Palencia, Spain, which are clearly descended from the earlier-cited Toledo rubrics of 1478:

The mystery of the Cross having been completed, and all things having been prepared just as yesterday, with the thurifers bringing thuribles with lit coals, and the procession having been arranged with extinguished candles, the priest, without a cope—as he has been up to this point and thus remains until the Body of Christ is placed on the altar, as shall be said below—and the ministers on each side go to the *monumento*, singing nothing; but approaching the step of the *monumento* in silence, the priest ascends with the ministers and with two others from the principal priests, and together they make a profound genuflection to the Sacrament. And the bolt [of the "ark", the repository tabernacle] having been unlocked and the seals opened, the priest privately shows them the Body of Christ placed in the chalice, and they adore it reverently; and with great reverence he covers the chalice, as it had been before. Meanwhile, all the clerics light their candles that they carry in their hands. Afterward, however, the priest puts [incense] in the thurible from the incense reserved there and censes the Sacrament; and bringing forth the chalice from the ark, and turning himself toward the people, having the chalice in his hands, he says, *This is my Body*. And the choir continues, as yesterday. And the ministers on each side support his arms; the standard [a black banner with a red cross] should also be brought, and the cloth [canopy], as on the preceding day, with the porter or some other minister

---

[205] John Burckard, *Diarium sive Rerum urbanarum commentarii (1483–1506)*, vol. 1, *1483–1492*, ed. L. Thuasne (Paris: Ernest Leroux, 1883), 184.

[206] *Caeremoniale Romanum*, 1488, in Dykmans, *Oeuvre de Patrizi Piccolomini*, 2:387.

[207] Sodi and Triacca, *Missale Romanum: Editio princeps (1570)*, 251 (new pagination).

[208] *Vexilla Regis*, verse 1, translated from the complete seven-verse text in Sodi and Triacca, *Breviarium Romanum: Editio princeps (1568)*, 354 (new pagination).

of the church casting down green grass or grain, as previously; and thus with singing, all proceed all the way to the altar. Then the deacon unfolds and extends the corporals upon the altar; and he moves the missal to the side of the altar, where the Gospel was customarily read; the celebrating priest, however, sets upon the altar the chalice, in which is brought the very Host hitherto placed within the chalice; and making a profound genuflection, he censes the Sacrament; after these things, he puts on a black chasuble in such a way that the back, folded behind, should extend only as far as his cincture. Then he puts wine with water in another chalice that the deacon offers to him, saying nothing.[209]

Following the arrival of the Eucharist upon the altar, the Good Friday liturgy concludes with an abbreviated form of the Communion Rite of the Mass that normally follows the end of the Roman Canon. Rupert of Deutz notes that by placing the processional return of the reserved Eucharist immediately before the priest's introduction of the Our Father, that is, before the words "*Oremus: praeceptis salutaribus moniti*" ("*Let us pray. Admonished by salutary precepts*"), an allegorical similitude is established between the Good Friday transfer of the Sacrament to the altar and the elevation of the Host and chalice from the altar for the concluding doxology of the Roman Canon, the *Per ipsum* ("*Through him, and with him, and in him . . . through all ages of ages*"). For just as the latter action has been explained (particularly by Amalarius of Metz) as symbolizing the taking away of Christ's body from the Cross,[210] so also the Good Friday procession symbolizes the carrying of Christ's body to the tomb.[211] This parallel is made explicit in the Good Friday rubrics of the early fourteenth-century ceremonial of Cologne, Germany, which direct that immediately before the priest introduces the Our Father—at the moment that corresponds to the *Per ipsum* elevation of the Mass—he is to elevate the Host slightly above the chalice, high enough that all may see it, "for the purpose of signifying that the Lord was lifted up on the Cross this day"; he then lays down the Host upon the corporal and covers the chalice, "which signifies the burial of the Lord, taken down from the Cross".[212]

A number of other liturgical books prescribe a similar action, albeit without explaining its symbolism. Thus the 1568 missal of Palencia, Spain, states:

> Then [the priest] raises himself, and reverently drawing out the Host from the chalice in which it had hitherto been placed, taking it with his right hand, over the cup of the other chalice, in which there is

---

[209] *Missale Pallantinum* (1568), fol. 99r–99v. The Latin text has been graciously provided to the author by the Biblioteca Apostolica Vaticana, Vatican City.

[210] See p. 74 above.

[211] Rupert of Deutz, *Liber de divinis officiis* (CCCM 7), bk. 6, chap. 23, p. 206.

[212] Amberg, *Ceremoniale Coloniense*, 146.

wine prepared with water, he elevates it (devoutly and somberly) in such a manner that it may be able to be seen and adored by those present, and the people; and at once when he elevates it, he says in a raised voice, just as it was accustomed to be done at other times, *Let us pray. Admonished by salutary precepts . . .*[213]

The Good Friday rubrics of the 1534 Seville missal direct the priest to turn toward the people and show them the Eucharist as he says, "*Let us pray. Admonished by salutary precepts . . .*"[214] The 1543 missal of Bayonne, France, defers the elevation to a later moment, specifying that during the recitation of the Our Father the priest should elevate the Eucharist with his right hand when he begins the phrase "*Give us this day our daily bread.*"[215]

Early medieval texts, including the seventh-century Gelasian Sacramentary of Rome, speak of a general Communion of all the faithful at the Good Friday liturgy,[216] a practice that persisted in some places to the end of the Middle Ages; thus the 1514 *Agenda* of Passau, Germany, directs that on this day "all should communicate with the fear of God and in silence."[217] In the thirteenth-century Pontifical of the Roman Curia, we find for the first time Holy Communion expressly limited to the celebrant alone,[218] an observance that gradually spread[219] and became the norm in the *Missale Romanum* of 1570.[220]

The *Depositio* Rite

In the preceding section, as well as in the previous chapter, we saw how certain portions of the medieval liturgical rites of Holy Thursday and Good Friday were associated *in an allegorical sense* with the burial of Christ. There was, however, one liturgical rite of Good Friday, celebrated across much of medieval Europe, that constituted an explicit liturgical commemoration of the Savior's interment in the tomb: the *Depositio* (Deposition). Such a rite mirrored the importance given to Christ's burial in the early Church as attested by the inclusion of this mystery among the fundamental articles of faith professed in both the

---

[213] *Missale Pallantinum* (1568), fol. 99v.

[214] *Missale . . . ecclesie Hispalensis* (1534), fol. 87r–87v.

[215] Dubarat, *Missel de Bayonne de 1543*, 45.

[216] Mohlberg, Eizenhöfer, and Siffrin, *Liber sacramentorum,* no. 418, p. 67.

[217] *Agenda sive Benedictionale de actibus ecclesie secundum chorum et observationem ecclesie Pataviensis* (1514), fol. 67r. A general Communion is also mentioned in the 1493 *Obsequiale Frisingense* of Freising, Germany; see *Obsequiale Frisingense* (1493), fol. 41r.

[218] Text in Michel Andrieu, ed., *Le pontifical romain au moyen-âge*, vol. 2, *Le pontifical de la Curie romaine au XIIIᵉ siècle*, ST 87 (Vatican City: Biblioteca Apostolica Vaticana, 1940), 469.

[219] The Good Friday reception of Holy Communion by the celebrant alone is indicated implicitly in the Franciscan *Ordo missalis* of Haymo of Faversham (c. 1244) and in the Carmelite *Ordinarium* of the order's German provincial Sibert de Beka (c. 1312); for the texts, see respectively Van Dijk, *Sources of the Modern Roman Liturgy*, 2:238, 244–245, and Benedict Zimmerman, ed., *Ordinaire de l'ordre de Notre-Dame du Mont-Carmel*, Bibliothèque liturgique 13 (Paris: Alphonse Picard et Fils, 1910), 164, 169–170.

[220] Sodi and Triacca, *Missale Romanum: Editio princeps (1570)*, 238, 251, 253 (new pagination).

Apostles' Creed and the Nicene Creed. Writing in the twelfth century, Saint Bernard (+1153) expressed his amazement at the enormous devotion to the sepulcher of Christ that he had witnessed in his own time.[221] It was this devotion that inspired the development of a separate Good Friday ceremony *totally* dedicated to the commemoration of the entombment of Christ, the *Depositio*, in which a crucifix, an image of Christ resting in death, or in some cases the Blessed Sacrament itself would be carried to a representation of the Savior's tomb and be symbolically "buried" there. Traceable in Europe to tenth-century Germany and England,[222] this ceremony may be a descendant of the rite of "washing the cross" in the Good Friday liturgy of fifth- to eighth-century Jerusalem, which we have already described (p. 409, above); as one scholar of the Byzantine liturgy has observed, this Jerusalem ceremony was "certainly a rite of burial".[223] As for the underlying purpose of the Good Friday *Depositio* rite, a 1438 declaration of Georg, bishop of Brixen in the Austrian Tyrol (what is now Bressanone, Italy), concerning the Good Friday erection of a representation of the Holy Sepulcher in Hall, Austria, provides a succinct explanation:

> Therefore, Holy Mother Church, commemorating the mystery of this Lord's Passion, and the most worthy insignia of the same, which was our redemption, the destruction of our death, and the regeneration of saving life, on the holy day of Good Friday, in memory of the death of the same Jesus Christ our Lord and the burial of this Lord, provides and establishes the sign of the vivifying Cross to be placed in the sepulcher, that in memory of him who was crucified and died for us we might adore with devout minds and continually contemplate his glorious Passion.[224]

A more expansive meditation upon devotion to Christ's burial is provided by the fourteenth-century Carthusian writer Ludolph of Saxony. He begins by noting that the visits of the faithful to the different churches and altars on Good Friday, as practiced in his time, represented the Good Friday visitation of the Savior's tomb made by the holy women (Mt 27:61; Mk 15:47; Lk 23:55). Stressing the women's attentive presence at the burial of Christ, and their loving devotion in remaining afterward, "sitting over against the sepulchre" (Mt 27:61),

---

[221] Saint Bernard, *De laude novae militiae*, chap. 11, no. 18, PL 182, col. 932.

[222] For tenth-century Germany, see the life of Saint Ulric, bishop of Augsburg (+973); *Vita s. Udalrici Augustani episcopi*, chap. 4, PL 135, cols. 1020–1021); for England, see the Benedictine *Regularis concordia* (c. 960), in Symons, *Regularis concordia*, chap. 4, no. 46, pp. 44–45. For a comprehensive study of the *Depositio* rite, see James Monti, *The Week of Salvation: History and Traditions of Holy Week* (Huntington, Ind.: Our Sunday Visitor, 1993), 267–285, 309–315.

[223] Sebastià Janeras, "La settimana santa nell'antica liturgia di Gerusalemme", in Kollamparampil, *Hebdomadae sanctae celebratio*, 44.

[224] Declaration of Bishop Georg of Brixen, March 16, 1438, in Lipphardt, *Lateinische Osterfeiern und Osterspiele*, 3:841.

Ludolph presents them as an example for all the faithful. In imitation of these women, he observes, "devout souls ought to contemplate diligently the mystery of the Passion of Christ" and "ought to be buried with Christ by compassion, that they may be worthy to be made partakers of his Resurrection."[225] He then invites the faithful to contemplate the Lord's interment:

> And therefore, wash with your tears his most sacred body sprinkled with his blood; and anoint him with the perfumes of holy prayer; and carry him with arms of charitable and humble toil; and bury him with the spices of good conduct and with good doctrines and examples, with much sighing and mourning and lamentation; and cover him under the ground of love and devotion in the shroud of your conscience and in chastity of mind, and in the *sudarium* [the facial cloth of Jesus in death] and labor of penitence; and you shall sit there close to him at the tomb, until you should see him rising from the dead.... May you bind his most beautiful, most loving, roseate wounds with the whitest, purest linen cloths of your thoughts and affections, until he should lead you to the joy of his Resurrection, adorned with wonderful gifts, and to the excellence of his Ascension, elevated above all the orders of Heaven.[226]

Ludolph's vivid reflection upon the entombment of Christ provides a fitting context for examining a particularly dramatic form of the *Depositio* ceremony found in a fourteenth- to fifteenth-century processional of the cathedral of Padua, Italy;[227] a very similar version of this rite was later to appear in the 1558 missal of the Portuguese see of Braga,[228] where it was subsequently preserved for centuries to come after Pope Saint Pius V gave Braga permission to retain its own distinctive missal and breviary following the issuance of the *Missale Romanum* of 1570. The Padua text begins with a description of the roles of the different participants in the procession that will follow, a procession that will exit the cathedral and afterward return to it:[229]

---

[225] Ludolph of Saxony, *Vita Jesu Christi*, pt. 2, chap. 66, pp. 683–684.

[226] Ibid., 684.

[227] Text from the *Liber processionalis* for the cathedral of Padua, Italy (fourteenth to fifteenth century), in Lipphardt, *Lateinische Osterfeiern und Osterspiele*, 2:585–590.

[228] Text of the 1558 *Missale Bracarense*, in Solange Corbin, *La déposition liturgique du Christ au Vendredi saint: Sa place dans l'histoire des rites et du théatre religieux* (Paris: Société d'Editions "Les belles lettres"; Lisbon: Livraria Bertrand, 1960), 261–262.

[229] Two scholars who have studied this text, Solange Corbin and Claudio Bernardi, assert that the procession journeyed from one church to another, but the author of the present work believes that the rubrics and chants simply indicate a procession that exited the cathedral and followed a prolonged course before reentering the cathedral for the conclusion of the rite. This was the practice with similar processions in Braga, Portugal, and in Venice. There are no references to two separate churches in the Padua rubrics. For the studies of the above-cited scholars, see respectively Corbin, *Déposition liturgique du Christ au Vendredi saint*, 37–39, and Claudio Bernardi, *La drammaturgia della settimana santa in Italia*, La città e lo spettacolo 2 (Milan: Vita e Pensiero, 1991), 194–196.

All the clerics should assemble in the cathedral church in the choir before the main altar, and there should be prepared a catafalque surmounted by a receptacle after the manner of a coffer or a turtledove,[230] fittingly covered with a cloth. And the Body of our Lord Jesus Christ should be reverently placed there. And four sextons, or attendants, should be clothed in albs and black chasubles,[231] supporting the aforesaid catafalque and carrying away reverently and devoutly the Body of the same Jesus Christ our Lord. Likewise, four priests should also be clothed in albs and dalmatics carrying the canopy; and a cleric clothed in a dalmatic or a black tunic should bring the cross, and another cleric, going to precede the cross, [is assigned with] beating the striker. And twelve clerics should be carrying torches, namely six preceding and six following the Body of our Lord Jesus Christ. And there should be four priests with thuribles to cense it, vested in albs.[232]

Before the procession sets out, two priests in front of the cathedral's high altar intone a series of laments expressing the Church's grief for her slain Bridegroom:

The Body of our Lord Jesus Christ having been prepared, two priests should stand erect, before the altar, with the others kneeling; and the first [two] begin the lamentations, namely:

Alas, alas, Lord, alas, alas, our Savior, we are become orphans without a father: our mothers are [as] widows [Lam 5:3].

The crown of our head has fallen. Woe to us! For we have sinned.

[They continue] as is marked below, making the appropriate gestures and motions. [Two] other [priests], however, respond, remaining on their knees:

The breath of our mouths, Christ our Lord,
has been taken captive for our sins.
The joy of our heart has vanished;
our singing is turned into lamentation.

Thereupon the other two [priests]—the first [two]—having also knelt, should remain [thus] and sing:

Forsaken is all happiness,
removed is the joy of the earth;
our life has grown faint in sorrow
and our years in groans.

---

[230] Dove-shaped vessels for reserving the Eucharist were common in the Middle Ages.

[231] According to the scholar of medieval Latin Albert Blaise, there existed a chasuble distinct from that of priests that was sometimes worn by lower-ranking clerics; see Albert Blaise, *Lexicon Latinitatis medii aevi*, CCCM (Turnhout, Belgium: Brepols, 1998), 693 (*planeta*).

[232] Lipphardt, *Lateinische Osterfeiern und Osterspiele*, 2:585–586.

Who will give water to our head
and to our eyes a fountain of tears?
And we shall lament day and night
our most merciful Lord.

Let us make bitter mourning
over the dearest Christ our Lord.
Let us put off our garments of joyfulness
and be covered in sackcloth and ashes.

Let us sit upon the ground and weep;
let not the pupils of our eyes be silent.
Let us cry out with our voice and tears:
Oh, oh, Lord.

Let fountains of tears flow from our eyes
over the slaughtered body of our Lord.
Let our hearts break into sighs
over so much wickedness of sin.

Indeed, the Lord of goodness,
alas, this day has been crucified.
And so with our head sunk to the ground
let us lament inconsolably.

And thus alternately two by two [they continue] up to the last song:

With the grief of a wounded heart . . .[233]

Afterward, four other priests rise. And the first two turn toward the people, stirring them with the motions of their hands unto the remembrance of the Passion of the Lord, saying:

Come, O faithful people,
to the memorial of the burial of the Lord.

The other two, also turning toward the people, say:

Come and let us wail before the Lord,
who has suffered for us, saying:

Thereafter the first two begin the *Improperia* [Reproaches], namely:

My people, what have I done to you, or in what have I saddened you? Answer me.
For I led you out from the land of Egypt; you have prepared a cross for your Savior . . .[234]

---

[233] The Padua text provides only the incipit of this chant.

[234] The Padua processional provides the complete text of the expanded twelve-verse version of the *Improperia* (Lipphardt, *Lateinische Osterfeiern und Osterspiele*, 2:588–589); we have given only the first verse here. The *Improperia* were discussed above (pp. 416–419).

448

And all rise, and the procession is begun in due order, following the lord archpriest, vested in a black cope. And thus for the whole procession they sing the aforesaid Reproaches, responding always, *My people*, up to the church.[235]

The Padua *Depositio* procession reenters the cathedral for the reposition of the Blessed Sacrament within a representation of the Holy Sepulcher erected for this ceremony:

Afterward, before the sepulcher, with the Body of our Lord Jesus Christ having been placed in the sepulcher by the lord archpriest, [there] is sung:

[Responsory:] *The Lord having been buried, the sepulcher was sealed, they rolling a stone to the door of the sepulcher, stationing soldiers, who watched over it.*
[Verse:] *Lest perhaps his disciples come and steal him away and say to the people: He has risen from the dead.*[236]

And meanwhile, the sepulcher is sealed by the lord archpriest. Which having been completed, the aforesaid priests sing, facing the people:

Reject not the sighs of the pupils of your eyes, O Savior.
In the shortest grave we hide you. Oh, oh, Lord!
O Sweetest Sweetness, quickly return to us.
Consider not of little matter, most amiable One, your sons fainting for you.
Anxious to see the King of glory, let us await you,
clothed in a white robe, the Prince of the courts of Heaven. Amen.

And then, with the aforesaid verses having been devoutly sung, finally is sung by two clerics facing [the people]:

They have set me in dark places. Response: *As they that be dead of old.*[237]

Afterward the archpriest, who placed the Body of our Lord Jesus Christ in the sepulcher, remaining on his knees in the same place, says without a sign this prayer:

Look down, we beseech you, O Lord, upon this your family, for which our Lord Jesus Christ did not hesitate to be delivered into the hands of wicked men and to undergo the torment of the Cross. Who lives and reigns with you in the unity . . .[238]

---

[235] Lipphardt, *Lateinische Osterfeiern und Osterspiele*, 2:586–589.

[236] This responsory, *Sepulto Domino*, the chant most widely used in medieval *Depositio* rites (based upon Mt 27:60, 64, 66), is first found in the Antiphonary of Compiègne (France, c. 870); see Hésbert, *Corpus antiphonalium officii*, 1:174.

[237] The versicle *Collocaverunt me* is traceable to the Antiphonary of Compiègne (France, c. 870); see ibid., 176.

[238] Lipphardt, *Lateinische Osterfeiern und Osterspiele*, 2:586–587, 589–590. The concluding prayer, *Respice quaesumus Domine super hanc familiam tuam*, is traceable to the seventh-century Paduan redaction of the Gregorian Sacramentary of Rome; text in Jean Deshusses, ed., *Le sacramentaire grégorien: Ses principales formes d'après les plus anciens manuscrits*, vol. 1,

The Padua text we have presented does not describe the symbolic sepulcher erected for the purpose of receiving the Eucharist at the end of the procession, but it was almost certainly adorned with numerous lights, as was generally the custom elsewhere for these representational sepulchers of Holy Week. In this they would have imitated the profusion of lights surrounding the true Holy Sepulcher of Jerusalem (see chapter 13). Evidence of Jerusalem's influence upon this Good Friday custom is also provided by a rubric in the *Depositio* rite of a fourteenth-century ordinal of Hereford, England, which directs that before closing the door of the Easter sepulcher a candle should be lit *within* it,[239] an observance probably inspired by the ancient Jerusalem practice of maintaining a perpetually burning lamp within the Holy Sepulcher.[240] The use of numerous lamps and candles around medieval Good Friday representations of the Holy Sepulcher would have also been drawn from medieval funeral practices, in which it was customary to surround the biers of the dead with such lights.[241] The number of lights was particularly copious for the funeral rites of kings and noblemen: at the 1406 funeral of Spain's King Henry III of Castile, one thousand candles of yellow wax were used, with twenty-six candles of white wax placed around the bier.[242] Hence the use of numerous lights for the Good Friday sepulcher constituted an act of homage to Christ as King of Kings. The lights of the Easter sepulcher were kept continuously lit until Easter: a liturgical directory for Mainz, Germany, from 1500 enjoins that the candles and lights around the sepulcher be kept burning "day and night."[243]

Easter sepulchers were either permanent stone structures or movable shrines that could be set in place for the Easter Triduum and be removed afterward. Among the latter, there is preserved in the Christian Museum of Esztergom, Hungary, a magnificent Easter sepulcher of gilded wood, built for the abbey church of Garamszenbenedek about

---

2nd ed., SF 16 (Fribourg, Switzerland: Editions Universitaires Fribourg, 1979), Paduan no. 295, p. 629. Lipphardt provides only the incipit of this prayer; the complete text is here taken from Sodi and Triacca, *Breviarium Romanum: Editio princeps (1568)*, 375 (new pagination).

[239] Text quoted in Edmund Bishop, "Holy Week Rites of Sarum, Hereford and Rouen Compared", in *Liturgica Historica: Papers on the Liturgy and Religious Life of the Western Church* (London: Oxford University Press, 1918), 295.

[240] For the reference to this practice in the Diary of Egeria (c. 382), see Franceschini and Weber, *Itinerarium Egeriae*, chap. 24, no. 4, in *Itineraria et Alia geographia*, 68.

[241] Neil C. Brooks, *The Sepulchre of Christ in Art and Liturgy, with Special Reference to the Liturgic Drama*, University of Illinois Studies in Language and Literature 7, no. 2 (Urbana, Ill.: University of Illinois, 1921), 73, 86; Pamela Sheingorn, *The Easter Sepulchre in England*, Early Drama, Art and Music Reference Series 5 (Kalamazoo, Mich.: Medieval Institute Publications, 1987), 28, 33, 35, 57–58.

[242] Antonio del Rocio Romero Abao, "Las fiestas de Sevilla en el siglo XV", in Centro de Estudios e Investigación de la Religiosidad Andaluza, ed., *Las fiestas de Sevilla en el siglo XV: Otros estudios*, CEIRA 2 (Madrid: Centro de Estudios e Investigación de la Religiosidad Andaluza / Deimos, 1991), 60–61.

[243] *Directorium missae aus dem Rhein-Main-Gebiet*, archdiocese of Mainz, Germany, 1500, in Lipphardt, *Lateinische Osterfeiern und Osterspiele*, 2:324.

the year 1485. This oblong shrine consists of a sarcophagus over which rises on slender columns a high-pitched gothic canopy; statues of the twelve Apostles line the sides of the structure, symbolizing their role as pillars of the Church. On Good Friday, the Blessed Sacrament and a statue of Christ resting in death would be brought to the sepulcher, where the Eucharist was mounted in a monstrance and the image of Christ was interred within the shrine.[244]

Easter sepulchers were usually adorned with rich cloth hangings: a liturgical manual for the Polish diocese of Wrocław (Breslau), in a passage dating from 1448, relates that the church's Easter sepulcher, prepared in a chapel under the bell tower, would be covered with two gold frontals and hung with gold curtains, with four lights placed around the sepulcher.[245] Cloths of red or crimson were frequently utilized.[246] The Good Friday rubrics of a liturgical book for the Netherland see of Utrecht (c. 1200) direct that after the cross (clearly a crucifix) has been placed in the Easter sepulcher, a "large pall with lions" is to be draped over the tomb, upon which are placed two candles, one at the head of the entombed crucifix and the other at its feet. The candles remain lit until Easter Sunday.[247] The lion imagery suggests the verse regarding Christ from the Book of Revelation, "Weep not; behold the lion of the tribe of Juda, the root of David, hath prevailed to open the book, and to loose the seven seals thereof" (Rev 5:5). The candles evoke what Saint Mary Magdalene saw when on Easter morning she stooped to look within the opened tomb of Christ: "And she saw two angels in white, sitting, one at the head, and one at the feet, where the body of Jesus had been laid" (Jn 20:12).

Permanent stone Easter sepulchers were commonplace in medieval England, with magnificent gothic examples preserved to the present day in the cathedrals of Lincoln (c. 1300) and Ely (late fifteenth century).[248] The stonework of an Easter sepulcher built into the wall of a medieval church in the English village of Berry-Pomeroy is lined with four carved shields emblazoned with symbols of the Passion as the "heraldry" of Christ.[249] This accords with the mysterious imagery

---

[244] Mária Prokopp, *Das heilige Grab von Garamszentbenedek im Christlichen Museum zu Esztergom* (Budapest: Corvina Kiadó, 1983), 9, 32–35, and passim; Pál Cséfalvay, ed., *Christian Museum, Esztergom* (Budapest: Corvina Books, 1993), 179. Other surviving examples of portable Easter sepulchers include a smaller coffin-sized wooden sepulcher for a Brigittine monastery of Mariager, Denmark, dating from about 1500; see Audrey Ekdahl Davidson, ed., *Holy Week and Easter Ceremonies and Dramas from Medieval Sweden*, Early Drama, Art and Music Monograph Series 13 (Kalamazoo, Mich.: Medieval Institute Publications, Western Michigan University, 1990), 112, and fig. 3.

[245] *Modus agendi in ecclesia Wratislaviensi* (portion of text dating from 1448), in Schubert and Stapper, *Excerpta ex ordinariis Germanicis*, 23, 24.

[246] Brooks, *Sepulchre of Christ in Art and Liturgy*, 79.

[247] *Liber ordinarius* of Utrecht, Netherlands (c. 1200), cited in Georges Malherbe, "La capsula des présanctifiés le Jeudi-saint", pt. 2, *Bulletin Paroissial Liturgique* 6 (1930): 90.

[248] Sheingorn, *Easter Sepulchre in England*, 103, 208–209, and figs. 37, 38, 53.

[249] Ibid., 28, 113.

of a late medieval English song believed to be inspired by the Easter sepulcher rite of Good Friday, the "Corpus Christi Carol" (traceable to c. 1504), which speaks allegorically of the crucified Christ as a slain, bleeding Knight, mourned by a weeping maiden, the Blessed Virgin, and lying upon a bed with hangings of "gold so red" within a hall hung "with purple and pall".[250]

In medieval *Depositio* rites that featured a statue of Christ resting in death or a crucifix, the interment of the statue or cross in the sepulcher was marked by additional symbolic actions. Thus, in fourteenth-century German liturgical books for the collegiate church and abbey of Essen and the Benedictine abbey of Fulda, the Good Friday rubrics specify that the figure of the crucified Christ (probably a crucifix in both cases) should be laid in the sepulcher with the head facing west.[251] This corresponds to the belief expressed six centuries earlier by Saint Bede (+735) that Christ was buried with his head toward the west.[252] Bede's belief is supported by the east-west orientation of the actual tomb couch of the original Holy Sepulcher, with the east end adjacent to the tomb's entrance; it is likely that the body would have been laid upon the burial couch with the head at the far end (the west end) and with the feet at the end adjoining the door (the east end).[253] In the *Depositio* rites, cloths were often used to represent the burial linens of Christ: the rubrics of a 1324 processional for the German see of Paderborn specify the spreading of a shroud within the Easter sepulcher, over which is placed the crucifix, the chest of which is then covered with a corporal, with a second shroud draped over the entire image.[254]

The use of a statue of Christ resting in death in some of the medieval *Depositio* ceremonies would have corresponded to the contemporaneous custom of carrying an effigy of a dead king in his funeral cortege, as was the case for the funeral rites of the French monarch Charles VII in 1461.[255] A fifteenth-century Augustinian breviary of

[250] This carol, also known as "Down in Yon Forest", first appears about the year 1504 in a manuscript compiled by an Englishman named Richard Hill; text in Percy Dearmer, Ralph Vaughan Williams, and Martin Shaw, eds., *The Oxford Book of Carols* (Oxford: Oxford University Press, Music Department, 1999), 134, footnote. The allusions to the Easter sepulcher in this carol are noted by Eamon Duffy in his work *The Stripping of the Altars: Traditional Religion in England, c. 1400–c. 1580* (New Haven: Yale University Press, 1992), 35–36.

[251] *Liber ordinarius*, Essen, Germany, fourteenth century, in Arens, *Liber ordinarius der Essener Stiftskirche*, 58; *Ordinarium* of the Benedictine priory of Johannesberg, Fulda, Germany, fourteenth century, in Lipphardt, *Lateinische Osterfeiern und Osterspiele*, 2:265.

[252] Saint Bede, *In Marci evangelium expositio*, bk. 4, chap. 16, PL 92, col. 295.

[253] For the east-west orientation of the Holy Sepulcher of Jerusalem, see Martin Biddle, *The Tomb of Christ* (Phoenix Mill, England: Sutton, 1999), 132, 134. A 1914 sketch of the theorized original form of the tomb indicates that the Savior's head would have rested upon the west end of the burial couch (ibid., 116, illustration).

[254] *Processionarius ecclesiae Paderbornensis*, 1324, in Lipphardt, *Lateinische Osterfeiern und Osterspiele*, 2:387.

[255] Notation added to a Book of Prime, Pontlevoy Abbey, France (manuscript: Blois, France, Bibliothèque Municipale, MS 44), in Martène, *De antiquis ecclesiae ritibus*, bk. 3, chap. 15, *ordo* 16, 2:404.

Wrocław (Breslau), Poland, directs that the image of Christ is to be carried on a bier to the Easter sepulcher by four of the senior religious.[256] At the Augustinian monastery of Polling, Germany (fifteenth to sixteenth century), where a statue of Christ in death, covered with a shroud, was carried to the sepulcher upon a bier resting on the shoulders of two priests, the interment would conclude with all the religious individually venerating the image: "And the brothers departing from the sepulcher, the image of Christ should be devoutly kissed by all before." [257]

In southern Europe (in particular, most of Italy and Spain), the *Depositio* developed toward the end of the Middle Ages not in the form of a liturgical rite but rather as an act of devotion organized by lay confraternities.[258] In Todi, Italy, the image of Christ was "laid in state" after being carried in procession by the Monte de la Pietà confraternity, according to an account dating from 1563:

> [The confraternity] went out from the aforementioned church, each with a lit torch of white wax in the hand, and carried with much devotion and reverence our dearest Savior, dead and tormented, in a casket adorned in gold brocade. For it caused great devotion, contrition, and weeping in the people, and with similar order the aforementioned procession continued through certain streets of the city, and, in the end, all of them returning to the temple of the glorious Saint Fortunatus, advocate and protector of his city; and in the choir was placed over a platform therein the aforementioned casket with the Savior, at a place made somewhat elevated, where all the people passed, men and women, offering and making various donations, at the service of the above-mentioned Monte de la Pietà.[259]

The origins of the devotional *Depositio* of the lay confraternities can be traced to fourteenth-century Assisi, Italy, where there arose a *Depositio* in which a crucifix with a removable corpus was used: the corpus, made with flexible limbs, would be taken down from the cross and be carried away in the *Depositio* procession. This custom is first mentioned in a collection of statutes for Assisi's Confraternity of Saint Stephen dating from 1327, which speaks of a Good Friday rite of "unnailing our Lord Jesus Christ".[260] The practice of "reenacting" the taking down of Christ's body from the Cross soon spread as far as

---

[256] *Breviarium des Augustiner-Ermitenstiftes Sagan*, Wrocław (Breslau), Poland, fifteenth century, in Lipphardt, *Lateinische Osterfeiern und Osterspiele*, 3:836.

[257] Augustinian *Ordinarium*, Polling, Germany, fifteenth to sixteenth century, in Lipphardt, *Lateinische Osterfeiern und Osterspiele*, 4:1161–1162.

[258] Corbin, *Déposition liturgique du Christ au Vendredi saint*, 22–23, 39, 113, 119, and passim.

[259] Text in Bernardi, *Drammaturgia della settimana santa in Italia*, 245.

[260] Text quoted in Arnaldo Fortini, "La settimana santa di Assisi", *Ecclesia* 17 (March 1958): 117–118. For the date of these statutes, see Bernardi, *Drammaturgia della settimana santa in Italia*, 206.

England's Barking Abbey (late fourteenth century),[261] Germany's Prüfening Abbey (fifteenth century),[262] and the Spanish island of Majorca (by 1456).[263]

In many medieval texts of the Good Friday *Depositio* rite, beginning with the tenth-century *Regularis concordia* of England's Benedictines (c. 960), there is mention of watchers remaining before the Easter sepulcher to keep vigil there until Easter Sunday.[264] Thus a late fourteenth-century breviary of Prague in the Czech Republic directs that after the *Depositio* rite concludes, "the canons, beginning with the seniors, or the vicars of the canons, two by two, sitting near the sepulcher, read their Psalters continuously until the Lauds visitation of the sepulcher" (on Easter morning).[265] Similarly, a 1530 *ordinarium* for a collegiate church in Halle, Germany, calls for eight priests vested in black copes to recite the Psalter (the entire Book of Psalms) "night and day" near the sepulcher, four on each side.[266] In Hungary, such a vigil was a widespread practice, appearing before the end of the eleventh century in a Benedictine *ordinarium* of Raab, which directs that after the Eucharist has been placed upon the chest of the crucifix in the Easter sepulcher, and the two have been covered with a linen altar cloth and a shroud, the custodians are to "watch this most sacred Body of the Lord, engaged in psalms and other prayers".[267] The recitation of the Psalter at the Easter sepulcher, adorned with "solemn hangings" and covered with a "sacred pall", is specified in the Good Friday rubrics of the 1493 missal of Kraków, Poland.[268] This prayer vigil corresponds to the medieval funeral custom of keeping a watch of continual psalmody and prayer beside the body of the deceased until his Requiem Mass and burial (see p. 601 below). A breviary of Mooseburg, Germany (1500), also associates the vigil at the Easter sepulcher with the ancient Christian belief that the Second Coming of Christ

---

[261] Tolhurst, *Ordinale . . . Barking Abbey*, 1:100.

[262] *Directorium chori* of Prüfening Abbey, Germany, in Brooks, *Sepulchre of Christ in Art and Liturgy*, 105.

[263] The earliest explicit reference to a Majorcan rite representing the descent from the Cross appears in a 1456 entry in the account books of the cathedral of Palma di Majorca; text in Gabriel Llompart, "El davallament de Mallorca, una paralitúrgia medieval", in Societat Catalana d'Estudis Litúrgics, *Miscel·lània liturgica catalana*, vol. 1 (Barcelona: Institut d'Estudis Catalans, 1978), 120.

[264] The *Regularis concordia* mentions a watch of psalms at the Easter sepulcher (Symons, *Regularis concordia*, chap. 4, no. 46, p. 45).

[265] Breviary of Prague, Czech Republic, late fourteenth century, in Lipphardt, *Lateinische Osterfeiern und Osterspiele*, 4:1191. Regarding the Easter morning "visitation of the sepulcher", the *Visitatio sepulchri* rite, see pp. 498–500 below.

[266] *Ordinarium* for the collegiate church "ad Velum aureum", Halle, Germany, 1530, in Lipphardt, *Lateinische Osterfeiern und Osterspiele*, 3:959.

[267] *Ordinarium* of the Benedictine cloister of Gjor (Raab), Hungary, end of the eleventh century, in Lipphardt, *Lateinische Osterfeiern und Osterspiele*, 2:687. For further Hungarian examples of the continuous recital of psalms at the Easter sepulcher, see Radó and Mezey, *Libri liturgici manuscripti bibliothecarum Hungariae*, 94, 159, 170.

[268] *Missale Cracoviense* (1493), fol. 88v.

would occur toward midnight of Easter Sunday (see pp. 457–458 of the present work).[269] An Augustinian breviary from Indersdorf, Austria, dating from 1496, specifies the placing of relics of the saints before the image of Christ in the sepulcher,[270] a practice perhaps intended to suggest that the saints pray with the faithful as mankind awaits the Second Coming of Christ and the raising of all the dead. The recitation of the Good Friday office of Vespers at the Easter sepulcher is mentioned in several liturgical books, including German texts from Regensburg (1491)[271] and Freising (1493)[272] and a 1493 ritual from Brixen in the Austrian Tyrol (what is now Bressanone, Italy).[273]

The placement of aloes and myrrh with Christ's body at his burial and the spices that the holy women intending to anoint his body brought on Easter morning were represented in the Good Friday *Depositio* rite of a fifteenth-century missal of Salzburg, Austria, which specifies the bringing of three thuribles with myrrh as well as incense for this ceremony, in which an "image of the Crucified" was carried to the sepulcher.[274] This usage may have been inspired by Eastern Good Friday practices: a fourteenth-century text regarding Egypt's Coptic Rite known as *The Lamps of the Darkness*, authored by Abu-l Barakat, relates that on Good Friday "the priests envelop the cross in a piece of fabric in representation of the burial of the body of our Lord, and one arranges fragrant plants and roses as a commemorative symbol of his embalming with perfumes."[275] One scholar of the Eastern liturgies believes that the ancient Good Friday cross-washing rite of Jerusalem may have included a perfuming of the Cross with fragrances.[276]

We conclude this discussion of the *Depositio* by presenting two excerpts from the beautiful Good Friday *Depositio* procession of Venice, Italy, as found in the 1523 *Liber sacerdotalis* of the Dominican father Alberto Castellani.[277] The Venice text is similar to the Padua ceremony presented earlier in that the Blessed Sacrament is carried on a bier covered in black silk, borne by four priests, with the *Improperia* sung. It differs from the Padua ceremony in its extensive use of selected

---

[269] *Breviarium Mosburgense* (1500); text in Karl Young, *The Drama of the Medieval Church* (Oxford: Clarendon Press, 1933), 1:141.

[270] Breviary of the Augustiner-Chorherrnstift, Indersdorf, Austria, 1496, in Lipphardt, *Lateinische Osterfeiern und Osterspiele*, 3:974.

[271] *Obsequiale Ratisponense* (1491), fol. 81v.

[272] *Obsequiale Frisingense* (1493), fol. 41r.

[273] *Obsequiale Brixinense* (Augsburg, Germany: Erhard Ratdolt, 1493; digitized text, Bayerische Staatsbibliothek, Munich, 2009), fol. 10v.

[274] Radó and Mezey, *Libri liturgici manuscripti bibliothecarum Hungariae*, 182–183.

[275] Abu-l Barakat, *The Lamps of the Darkness*, chap. 18, translated from the French translation of this passage in Emmanuel Lanne, O.S.B., "Textes et rites de la liturgie pascale dans l'ancienne église copte", *L'Orient Syrien* 6 (1961): 296. © Editions du Centre National de la Recherche Scientifique, Paris.

[276] Gebran, *Venerdì santo nel rito Siro-Maronita*, 37.

[277] Castellani, *Liber sacerdotalis* (Venice, 1523), as reprinted with a different title in 1555: *Sacerdotale iuxta s. Romane ecclesie et aliarum ecclesiarum* (1555), fols. 233r–240r (text with music).

responsories from the Holy Week liturgy to punctuate the different stages of the procession. The Venice procession was conducted on Good Friday afternoon at the Cathedral of Saint Mark, but the other churches of the city held the procession an hour after sunset, when according to a 1519 account, the streets were filled with so many lights that it "seemed day".[278] Anyone who has heard the mournful Holy Saturday responsory *Plange quasi virgo* ("*Lament like a virgin*") will readily appreciate its poignant use in this context:

The priest reverently receives the Sacrament from the altar; and holding it in his hands, standing, having turned toward the people, all the others having knelt, he begins the responsory *Lament* [*Plange*], with the others continuing:

Lament like a virgin, my people; wail, O shepherds, in ashes and sackcloth; for the great and exceedingly bitter day of the Lord has come. Two clerics should sing the verse: *Gird yourselves, you priests, and lament, you ministers of the altar; sprinkle yourselves with ashes. For . . .*[279]

The responsory having been completed with its verse and repetition, two priests, provided with stoles as above, standing before the Sacrament, with their faces turned toward the people, should sing the verse *My people* [from the *Improperia*], with all the others except him who performs the office having knelt, and with their faces turned toward the Sacrament:

My people, what have I done to you, or in what have I saddened you? Answer me. For I led you out from the land of Egypt; you have prepared a cross for your Savior.

The aforesaid verse having been said, the choir, having knelt as above, should sing:

Holy God, Holy Mighty One, Holy and Immortal One, have mercy on us.

This having been said, the priest should reverently place the Body of the Lord on the bier that the four priests mentioned earlier shall carry, or two where there is a paucity of priests, vested in albs, their heads covered with an amice;[280] and the responsory *Our Shepherd has departed* [*Recessit pastor noster*] having been begun, the procession proceeds in this order: first the acolytes with lit candles and a cross; thereafter the clerics, the younger ones preceding; lastly the two vested priests who sang *My people*. After them follows the bier with the

---

[278] John Bettley, "The Office of Holy Week at St. Mark's, Venice, in the late 16th Century, and the Musical Contributions of Giovanni Croce", *Early Music* 22 (February 1994): 49, 56–57 (endnote with quotation from the diary of the Venetian senator Marino Sanuto).

[279] *Plange quasi virgo* is first found in the Antiphonary of Compiègne (France, c. 870); see Hésbert, *Corpus antiphonalium officii*, 1:174.

[280] The covering of the head is a sign of mourning found in the Old Testament; see 2 Kings 15:30: "But David went up by the ascent of mount Olivet, going up and weeping, walking barefoot, and with his head covered."

Body of Christ carried by four or two, as above; and above the Sacrament a black canopy should be carried by some rather worthy persons. At the side should be two acolytes with thuribles, who shall continually cense around the Sacrament; lights and torches should be around it. Behind the bier, the priest follows with a chasuble, and the deacon and the subdeacon, and lastly the seculars, the greater ones preceding.... Responsory:

> Our Shepherd has departed, the Fount of living water, at whose passing the sun was darkened; but now he who has held captive the first man has himself been captured. This day our Savior has broken asunder death's gates and bars together. Verse: He has indeed destroyed the bolts of hell and has overthrown the powers of Satan. But now he who has held captive . . .[281]

Toward the end of the Venice rite, after the procession reaches its fourth and final station, stopping before the Easter sepulcher, the presiding priest takes the Eucharist from the bier and, turning toward the people, holds the Sacrament elevated as two kneeling clerics sing a series of verses, including the following evoking the image of the *Pietà*: "*But when they had taken down the body of Jesus from the Cross, they placed it on his Mother's lap in the midst of the women most bitterly lamenting, the most exceedingly afflicted Mother grieving over her Son.*" The priest blesses the people with the Eucharist before reposing it in the sepulcher.[282]

We shall end this chapter with the following passage, dating from about 1140, regarding the themes for meditation and prayer on Good Friday night as given in the rubrics of Bernard of Porto's *Ordo officiorum* for the canons regular of Rome's Church of Saint John Lateran:

> This night, however, the subject matter of meditating upon Christ should be this: namely his sepulchral rest, after he had borne so many things, and also, through his descent into hell, that great and ineffable joy, so long awaited and so suddenly bestowed, of those in misery whom, with the dominion of death having been taken captive, Christ led forth with him from the dead—that while [one's] mind is drawn by these reflections, he might in those very things sleep and rest in peace.[283]

---

[281] Castellani, *Sacerdotale iuxta s. Romane ecclesie et aliarum ecclesiarum* (1555), fols. 233r–235r (text with music). The responsory *Recessit Pastor noster* ("*Our Shepherd has departed*") is first found in the Antiphonary of Compiègne (France, c. 870); see Hésbert, *Corpus antiphonalium officii*, 1:174.

[282] Castellani, *Sacerdotale iuxta s. Romane ecclesie et aliarum ecclesiarum* (1555), fols. 237v–239r (text with music).

[283] Fischer, *Bernhardi cardinalis . . . Ordo officiorum ecclesiae Lateranensis*, 59.

15 Easter

On Saturday, after the deep night of sorrow, it is daylight to us after midday unto the height of joy and the imminent evening splendor of this night, in which Christ our true Sun rises as Victor from hell.... For what day is more extraordinary than this night? What solemnity is more excellent than this victory? ... This night is the death of death; it is the return of life, the light of grace, a cup of sweetness, a river of delights, a flood of peace, the attainment of fortitude, the praise of divine counsel. This night the oppressor has withdrawn, his tribute has ceased, the captives have returned, the faint have found relief, the rod of the persecutors has been shattered, the yoke of the dominators has rotted away. In the beauty of this night Paradise has bloomed anew, Heaven has been clad in royal purple, the angels robed in white, men made cheerful.... Christ the Lord has passed over from this world to the Father, from death to life, from dishonor to glory, from servitude to the kingdom, from contumelies to honor, from the billows of the world to the gate of Heaven, from the midst of thieves to enthronement with the Father. And we have passed over.... From twofold perdition we have passed over to the twofold salvation of body and soul, from the devil to God, from the enemy to the Father, from the tyrant, who is neither God nor man, to our King, who is God and man. We have passed over, I say, from darkness to light, from toil to rest, from lamentation to song ... from pain to glory.

Rupert of Deutz (+c. 1129)[1]

The Easter Vigil: An Overview

The rubrics for Holy Saturday in the late ninth-century pontifical of northern France formerly known as the Pontifical of Poitiers speak of an "apostolic tradition" that "at midnight, at the vigil of this most sacred night", Christ was "going to come to the judgment, according to what he says in the Gospel, 'And at midnight there was a cry made: Behold the Bridegroom cometh' [Mt 25:6]." The pontifical continues:

---

[1] Rupert of Deutz, *Liber de divinis officiis*, bk. 6, chaps. 24, 26, in Hrabanus Haacke, O.S.B., ed., *Ruperti Tuitiensis: Liber de divinis officiis*, CCCM 7 (Turnhout, Belgium: Brepols, 1967), 206–207, 208–209. Hereafter cited as Rupert of Deutz, *Liber de divinis officiis* (CCCM 7).

457

Yet indeed, even as it is passed on by the relation of truthful people, who in our time have come from Jerusalem, the faithful people, instructed there by this authority and tradition, converging into the church on the Saturday of the Paschal vigils, intent with all devotion and solicitude, wait for the hour designated in the Gospel with silence and fear, as if [they were] going to be selected by the Lord and, as it were, going to be hastened to his judgment. The clergy also, on that night, passing into the church with their bishop, await the foretold hour with fear and devotion.[2]

As we have noted in the previous chapter, this belief regarding the Second Coming of Christ and the Easter Vigil is traceable to the fourth century, when it is mentioned for the first time by the ecclesiastical writer Lactantius Firmianus (+320), who describes the vigil as a night of watching for "the coming of our God and King".[3] This belief, shared by Saint Jerome (+420)[4] and Saint Isidore of Seville (+636),[5] persisted into the Middle Ages, imparting to the Easter Vigil an Advent-like character of joyful anticipation on two levels: a memorial watch to await and prepare for the hour of the Lord's Resurrection, joined to the expectation of the Savior's ultimate return at the end of the world. In this context, the imagery of light that dominates the Easter Vigil liturgy can be seen as representing both the light of the risen Christ, the Light of the world (Jn 9:5), and the light of the lamps readied for the coming of the Divine Bridegroom at the end of time (cf. Mt 25:1–13), the latter seen particularly in the candles given to those baptized at the vigil.

From time immemorial, the Church has celebrated the anniversary of mankind's salvation with a liturgical rite that Saint Augustine (+430) called "the mother of all holy vigils".[6] The observance of an Easter vigil lasting until "cockcrow"—three o'clock in the morning—is attested around the year 150 in an apocryphal text known as the *Epistula apostolorum*.[7] Our earliest detailed record of the Easter Vigil liturgy appears in the most ancient liturgical book of Jerusalem, the Armenian Lectionary, dating from the early fifth century.[8] The Jerusalem vigil began

---

[2] Text in Aldo Martini, ed., *Il cosiddetto Pontificale di Poitiers*, REDSMF 14 (Rome: Casa Editrice Herder, 1979), 219.

[3] Lactantius Firmianus, *Divinarum institutionum*, bk. 7, chap. 19, in Samuel Brandt and George Laubmann, eds., *L. Caeli Firmiani Lactanti: Opera omnia*, pt. 1, *Divinae institutiones et Epitome divinarum institutionum*, CSEL 19 (Vienna: F. Tempsky, 1890), 645.

[4] Saint Jerome, *Commentary on the Gospel of Matthew*, bk. 4, chap. 25, vs. 6, PL 26, cols. 184–185.

[5] Saint Isidore of Seville, *Etymologiarum*, bk. 6, chap. 17, no. 12, PL 82, col. 248.

[6] Saint Augustine, *Sermon 219*, PL 38, col. 1088.

[7] Text in John Quasten, ed., *Monumenta Eucharistica et liturgica vetustissima*, pt. 1, Florilegium patristicum tam veteris quam medii aevi auctores complectens, fasc. 7, pt. 1 (Bonn, Germany: Peter Hanstein, 1935), 336–337.

[8] Text in Athanase Renoux, ed. and trans., *Le codex arménien Jérusalem 121*, vol. 2, *Edition comparee du texte et de deux autres manuscrits*, Patrologia orientalis 36, fasc. 2 (Turnhout, Belgium: Brepols, 1971), no. 44, pp. 294–311.

in the Church of the Anastasis—the Church of the Holy Sepulcher—with the singing of Psalm 112, chanted by the city's patriarch. This was followed by a lamp-lighting rite, a Paschal form of the ancient illumination rite known as the *lucernarium* with which early Christians began their liturgical vigils throughout the year. According to one manuscript of the Armenian Lectionary, one such lamp was lit; according to another manuscript, thought to represent a slightly later form of the Jerusalem rite, three lamps were lit. The Spanish pilgrim Egeria, describing in her diary the year-round *lucernarium* rite of Jerusalem as it existed around 382, relates that the source of the flame for this lighting was a lamp kept perpetually burning within the Holy Sepulcher itself, from which the bishop would bring forth the fire.[9] Following the lamp lighting, there was in the Jerusalem Easter Vigil a distribution of the light to candles held by the faithful. After the worshipers had proceeded to the adjacent Church of the Martyrium, the vigil continued with twelve Old Testament readings,[10] each (except the last) followed by a prayer for which all knelt. Although not directly mentioned by the Armenian Lectionary, it was evidently during these readings that baptism was administered by the patriarch, for the text speaks of him returning with "a great number of the newly baptized" at the end of the twelfth reading.[11] The Mass featured a Pauline Epistle (1 Cor 15:1–11) and Saint Matthew's Gospel account of the Resurrection (Mt 28:1–20). Afterward, a second Mass of the night was celebrated in the Church of the Anastasis, with a Gospel reading of Saint John's account of the Resurrection (Jn 20:1–18; in one manuscript, Jn 19:38—20:18).[12] A subsequent liturgical book of Jerusalem, the Georgian Lectionary, dating from the fifth to the eighth century, speaks of beginning the Easter Vigil with the preparation of three thuribles for a thrice-repeated procession around the Church of the Anastasis to the accompaniment of psalms, followed later by the blessing of a "new candle", the light of which was distributed to the people.[13]

In the West, the lighting of a Paschal candle at the Easter Vigil is attested from the fourth century onward, beginning with the mention of a hymn to the Paschal candle in a letter of Saint Jerome written in

---

[9] For the text, see A. Franceschini and R. Weber, eds., *Itinerarium Egeriae*, chap. 24, no. 4, in *Itineraria et Alia geographia*, CCSL 175 (Turnhout, Belgium: Brepols, 1965), 68.

[10] The readings were (1) Gen 1:1—3:24; (2) Gen 22:1–18; (3) Ex 12:1–24; (4) Jon 1:1—4:11; (5) Ex 14:24—15:21; (6) Is 60:1–13; (7) Job 38:2–28; (8) 4 Kings 2:1–22; (9) Jer 38:31–34; (10) Josh 1:1–9; (11) Ez 37:1–14; and (12) Dan 3:1–90; see Renoux, *Codex arménien Jérusalem 121*, no. 44, pp. 298–307.

[11] Ibid., 307. It is believed that this reference to numerous catechumens receiving baptism alludes to the large influx of Jews and pagans received into the Church in Jerusalem around A.D. 350 (ibid., notes).

[12] Renoux, *Codex arménien Jérusalem 121*, no. 44, pp. 308–311.

[13] Michel Tarchnischvili, ed., *Le grand lectionnaire de l'église de Jérusalem (V^e–VIIIe siècle)*, vol. 1, CSCO 188–189 (Louvain, Belgium: Secrétariat du CorpusSCO, 1959); Georgian-language text: CSCO 188, nos. 708–716, pp. 134–136; Latin translation: CSCO 189, nos. 708–716, pp. 107–109.

384 to the northern Italian deacon Praesidius.[14] An early fifth-century decree of Pope Zosimus (+418) authorized the blessing of the Paschal candle in parish churches.[15] There are no certain references to the use of the Paschal candle in the papal liturgy before the twelfth century, when it appears in the Roman Pontifical of this era: "The large candle that is to be blessed is placed on a candlestick before the altar."[16] Nonetheless, five centuries earlier, the lighting of such a candle in the suburban churches of Rome is attested in the seventh-century Gelasian Sacramentary.[17] Another Roman liturgical book of this period, Roman *Ordo* 11 (c. 650–700), tells of two large candles at the Easter Vigil described as each having "the stature of a man".[18] This pair of giant candles, evidently distinct from the Paschal candle, reappeared in various Easter Vigil texts over the centuries that followed, always described in the same manner, and are found as late as the fifteenth century in the rubrics of a missal for Salzburg, Austria.[19] It is the late ninth-century pontifical of northern France formerly known as the Pontifical of Poitiers that indicates their symbolism, stating that the candle to the right of the altar is engraved with the words "The angel sitting at the head", while the other, on the left side of the altar, bears the inscription "The angel sitting at the feet". The pontifical explains these to be "in the likeness of the two angels sitting together in the sepulcher of the Lord"—a clear reference to the angels that Saint Mary Magdalene saw "sitting, one at the head, and one at the feet, where the body of Jesus had been laid" (Jn 20:12).[20]

Our earliest extant description of the candle-lighting rite in the West appears in the Easter Vigil rubrics of the *Liber ordinum* of Spain's Mozarabic Rite, an eleventh-century compilation of older texts believed to date largely from the fifth to the seventh century. After the clergy and the faithful had assembled in the church, the bishop, seated, would distribute unlit candles to each of those present. He and the priests and deacons would then withdraw to the sacristy:

> And the doors or windows having been closed by veils, indeed that light may not be seen through a bit of the door, a rock [a stone for

[14] Saint Jerome, *Letter to Praesidius*, PL 30, cols. 182–183.

[15] For the reference to this decree in the collection of papal biographies known as the *Liber pontificalis*, see Louis Duchesne, ed., *Le Liber pontificalis: Texte, introduction et commentaire* (Paris: Ernest Thorin, 1886–1892), 1:225.

[16] Twelfth-century Roman Pontifical, in Michel Andrieu, ed., *Le pontifical romain au moyen-âge*, vol. 1, *Le pontifical romain au XIIe siècle*, ST 86 (Vatican City: Biblioteca Apostolica Vaticana, 1938), 239–241 (quoted passage on 240).

[17] Text in Leo Cunibert Mohlberg, O.S.B., et al., eds., *Liber sacramentorum Romanae aeclesiae ordinis anni circuli (Sacramentarium Gelasianum)*, REDSMF 4 (Rome: Herder, 1960), nos. 425–428, pp. 68–69.

[18] Text in Michel Andrieu, ed., *Les Ordines Romani du haut moyen âge*, vol. 2, SSLED 23 (Louvain, Belgium: "Spicilegium sacrum Lovaniense" Administration, 1948), 444.

[19] Text in Polycarp Radó, O.S.B., and Ladislaus Mezey, *Libri liturgici manuscripti bibliothecarum Hungariae et limitropharum regionum* (Budapest: Akadémiai Kiadó, 1973), 183.

[20] Martini, *Cosiddetto pontificale di Poitiers*, 215.

igniting the fire] is offered to the bishop by the sacristan, and a dish, and a striker of fire. And presently when he shall have stricken a fire with his hand, the tow [in the dish] is kindled, then a torch, [and] again, from it a lamp, [and] from this lamp also the [Paschal] candle. And, with no one kindling his own candle, the bishop approaches to bless the lamp, the deacon holding it, who is going to bless it afterward in the choir.[21]

The bishop now blesses the lamp with a Collect addressed to Christ as the *"Light unfailing"*, in the course of which he prays, *"Bless this light, O Light, for this [light] that we carry in our hands you created, you gave. And just as by these lights that we kindle we expel the night from this place, so also expel the darkness from our hearts."* [22] Another deacon then presents the Paschal candle to the bishop, who makes on the side of the candle— probably by inscription—the sign of the cross and the first and last letters of the Greek alphabet, alpha and omega, before blessing the candle with a second Collect. The bringing forth of the Easter light to the people follows:

[T]he bishop kindles his candle from the blessed candle, and the clergy enter into the sacristy secretly, that not even a bit of the door may be seen from the kindled lights. The priests and the deacons also kindle their wax candles from the blessed candle, and similarly all the clergy. And after all shall have been completely lit, the bishop stands near the door, and the deacon before him, holding the very candle that is going to be blessed afterward. And the veil of the door having been lifted, the bishop at once intones, *Thanks be to God.* And in this manner he is answered by all no more than three times. And afterward he intones this antiphon: *The true Light illuminates every man coming into this world.* Verse: *For it is by you, O Lord, the Fount of life, and in your light, [that] we shall see light. Glory and honor . . .* And after the *Glory*, before they should come to the choir . . ., the elders of the people also light from the blessed candle their wax candles. And thus one from another, the candles of all the people are illuminated.[23]

The ceremony would conclude with further blessing prayers for the lamp and the Paschal candle recited by the deacons in a manner corresponding to the deacon's proclamation of the *Exsultet* in the current Easter Vigil liturgy of the Roman Rite.[24] In the *Liber ordinum* lighting rite, we find a Western adaptation of the practices of Jerusalem. The

---

[21] Text in Marius Férotin, ed., *Le Liber ordinum en usage dans l'église wisigothique et mozarabe d'Espagne du cinquième au onzième siècle* (Paris, 1904), repr., ed. Anthony Ward and Cuthbert Johnson, BELS 83 (Rome: Centro Liturgico Vincenziano, Edizioni Liturgiche, 1996), col. 208.

[22] Ibid., cols. 208–209. An English translation of the complete text of this prayer is given on pp. 293–294 of the present work.

[23] Ibid., cols. 209–211.

[24] Ibid., cols. 211–215.

bishop's bringing forth of the Easter fire from within the sacristy was clearly modeled upon the bringing forth of light from the Holy Sepulcher by the patriarch of Jerusalem.[25] The custom of beginning the Easter fire in the sacristy was to endure until the end of the Middle Ages in certain churches of Spain and France.[26] In the bishop's versicles, "*Thanks be to God*" ("*Deo gratias*") and "*The true Light*" ("*Lumen verum*"), we see the antecedents to the threefold proclamation of *Lumen Christi* and *Deo gratias* that was later to arise in the Western Easter liturgy.

The use of a stone to kindle the Easter fire, seen in the above-cited *Liber ordinum* rite, is also found at an early date in Italy, appearing in a text for a church in the Roman suburbs, Roman *Ordo* 26 (c. 750–775).[27] Usually such flints were sparked by striking them with a piece of iron. Regarding this usage, William Durandus of Mende (+1296) notes that the stone represents Christ, the Rock and Cornerstone, who, having been struck on the Cross with the iron of the lance, poured forth upon us the Holy Spirit and emitted the fire of charity.[28] John Beleth (+1182) identifies the fire brought forth by the stricken stone as the "fire of the Holy Spirit".[29] The alternate practice of using a crystal to ignite the Easter fire by concentrating sunlight is implicitly mentioned for the first time by Ennodius of Pavia, a bishop of Italy (+521), who in each of the two *Praeconium paschale* texts that he composed for the blessing of the Paschal candle speaks of the candle's light as coming from the sky;[30] the use of a crystal or a lens to kindle a fire for this purpose is repeatedly mentioned in liturgical books from the late ninth century to the sixteenth century, beginning with the pontifical of northern France formerly known as the Pontifical of Poitiers.[31] John Beleth considers the crystal a symbol of "the most pure and brightest flesh of Christ", which like the crystal is "without

[25] This derivation is asserted by more than one scholar, including A. J. MacGregor; see his work *Fire and Light in the Western Triduum: Their Use at Tenebrae and at the Paschal Vigil*, Alcuin Club Collection 71 (Runcorn, England: Alcuin Club; Collegeville, Minn.: Liturgical Press, 1992), 151, 241, 487.

[26] Francesc Xavier Parés i Saltor, *L'ordinari d'Urgell de 1536*, Col·lectània Sant Pacià 74 (La Seu d'Urgell, Spain: Societat Cultural Urgel·litana / Facultat de Teologia da Catalunya, 2002), 145. For a Spanish example of this practice, see the 1498 missal of Saragossa (*Missale secundum morem ecclesie Cesaraugustane* [Saragossa: Paul Hurus, 1498]), temporal, fol. 99v; for a French example, see the 1543 missal of Bayonne, France (V. Dubarat, ed., *Le missel de Bayonne de 1543* [Pau, France: Léon Ribaut, 1901]), 46.

[27] Text in Michel Andrieu, ed., *Les Ordines Romani du haut moyen âge*, vol. 3, SSLED 24 (Louvain, Belgium: "Spicilegium sacrum Lovaniense" Administration, 1951), 325–326.

[28] William Durandus of Mende, *Rationale divinorum officiorum*, bk. 6, chap. 80, nos. 1, 2, in A. Davril, O.S.B., and T. M. Thibodeau, eds., *Guillelmi Duranti: Rationale divinorum officiorum V–VI*, CCCM 140a (Turnhout, Belgium: Brepols, 1998), 392, 393. Hereafter cited as Durandus, *Rationale* (CCCM 140a).

[29] John Beleth, *Summa de ecclesiasticis officiis*, chap. 107, in Heribertus Douteil, C.S.Sp., ed., *Iohannis Beleth: Summa de ecclesiasticis officiis*, CCCM 41a (Turnhout, Belgium: Brepols, 1976), 198. Hereafter cited as Beleth, *Summa de ecclesiasticis officiis* (CCCM 41a).

[30] Ennodius of Pavia, *Opuscula* 9 and 10, PL 63, cols. 259, 262.

[31] Martini, *Cosiddetto pontificale di Poitiers*, 138–139. This text states that either a crystal or a whetstone may be used to kindle the fire on the three days of the Easter Triduum.

blemish".[32] Durandus adds that the crystal is juxtaposed between the sun and the receptacle for the new fire in likeness to the role of Christ as "the Mediator between God and our infirmity", who, as he himself declared, came to cast fire upon the earth (Lk 12:49: "I am come to cast fire on the earth; and what will I, but that it be kindled?").[33]

In the papal liturgy of eighth-century Rome, the Easter fire was taken from three lights kindled on Holy Thursday. In a letter to the missionary of Germany Saint Boniface, Pope Saint Zachary (741–752) tells of three large oil lamps, lit during the Holy Thursday Chrism Mass at the Church of Saint John Lateran, which were kept alight in a secluded corner of the church until Holy Saturday, when the light for the Easter Vigil was kindled from them; the pontiff likens this to the perpetual lampstand outside the Holy of Holies, the inner sanctuary of the Ark of the Covenant (Ex 25:31–40; 27:20–21; Lev 24:1–4).[34] This practice was clearly intended to symbolize the three days of Christ, the Light of the world, in the tomb, ending in his Resurrection. From the twelfth century through the fifteenth century, papal liturgical books indicate the ignition of the Easter fire with a stone or a lens on Holy Saturday.[35] The stone became the sole means of ignition in the *Missale Romanum* of 1474[36] and in the universally promulgated *Missale Romanum* of 1570.[37]

The above-cited *Liber ordinum* of Spain speaks of a dish holding flammable tow as the receptacle in which to ignite the flame from the sparking of the stone. There is a tradition that the missionary of Ireland Saint Patrick (+461) introduced the practice of igniting a bonfire as the Easter fire, according to the memoirs of Saint Patrick's biographer Muirchu Maccu-Machtheni, written around the year 690: "Holy Patrick, therefore, celebrating the holy Pasch, kindled the blessed and exceedingly bright divine fire, which, shining brightly in the night, was seen by almost all living throughout the level ground of the plain."[38] At the very least, this passage certainly demonstrates the existence of this practice in late seventh-century Ireland. Most medieval liturgical

---

[32] Beleth, *Summa de ecclesiasticis officiis* (CCCM 41a), chap. 107, p. 198.

[33] Durandus, *Rationale* (CCCM 140a), bk. 6, chap. 80, no. 1, pp. 392–393.

[34] Saint Zachary, *Letter 13* (November 751), PL 89, col. 951.

[35] For the twelfth-century Roman Pontifical, see Andrieu, *Pontifical romain au moyen-âge*, 1:470; for the ceremonial of the papal master of ceremonies Pierre Ameil (+1403; completed by Pierre Assalbit, 1435–1441), see Marc Dykmans, S.J., ed., *Le cérémonial papal de la fin du moyen âge à la Renaissance*, vol. 4, BIHBR 27 (Brussels and Rome: Institut Historique Belge de Rome, 1985), 157.

[36] Text in Robert Lippe, ed., *Missale Romanum: Mediolani, 1474*, vol. 1, *Text*, HBS 17 (London: Henry Bradshaw Society, 1899), 174.

[37] Text in Manlio Sodi and Achille Maria Triacca, eds., *Missale Romanum: Editio princeps (1570)*, facsimile ed., MLCT 2 (Vatican City: Libreria Editrice Vaticana, © 1998), 253 (new pagination).

[38] Muirchu Maccu-Machtheni, *Memoirs of Saint Patrick, with Other Documents Relating to That Saint*, from the *Book of Armagh*, in Whitley Stokes, ed., *The Tripartite Life of Patrick*, Rerum Britannicarum medii aevi scriptores 89 (London: Eyre and Spottiswoode, 1887), 2:279.

texts, however, give no indication as to whether a fire of this size was utilized. The use of a bonfire is implied in one source, a 1531 missal for the Monastery of Saint-Martin d'Ainay, near Lyons, France, which in its rubrics for igniting a new fire on each of the three days of the Easter Triduum directs that after the staff-mounted candle has been lit from the fire in a cloister adjoining the refectory, the monks, while passing through the cloister on their way to the church, should pause to warm themselves at the fire.[39] The majority of medieval liturgical texts, beginning with Roman *Ordo* 26 (c. 750–775), indicate an outdoor location for the kindling of the Easter fire,[40] with some texts specifying the cloister.[41] Durandus explains the outdoor location of the Easter fire as representing the crucifixion of Christ outside Jerusalem, citing in this regard the Letter to the Hebrews: "Let us go forth therefore to him without the camp, bearing his reproach" (Heb 13:13).[42] Some churches chose an indoor location instead, such as before the high altar, an example of which we shall see later in this chapter.

It is in seventh-century Rome that we find two different systems of Old Testament readings for the Easter Vigil, one consisting of four readings, given in the Paduan redaction of the Gregorian Sacramentary,[43] and another comprising ten lections, specified in the Gelasian Sacramentary.[44] The practice of reading a total of twelve readings at the vigil, which we saw in Jerusalem, seems also to have existed in the West from an early date: the great monastic founder Saint Benedict (+c. 547) prescribes in his rule the recitation of twelve readings (distributed among three sets of four readings) for the vigil rites of all Sundays, and hence for the vigil of Easter Sunday.[45] A mid-seventh-century lectionary of Spain's Mozarabic Rite assigns twelve Old Testament readings to the Easter Vigil.[46] The series of twelve Old Testament readings specified for the Easter Vigil in Saint Benedict of Aniane's early ninth-century Frankish adaptation of Rome's Gregorian Sacramentary[47] later became the norm in Rome from the twelfth century

---

[39] Text in Edmond Martène, *De antiquis ecclesiae ritibus* (Venice: Johannes Baptista Novelli, 1763–1764), bk. 4, chap. 22, 3:125.

[40] Text in Andrieu, *Ordines Romani du haut moyen âge*, 3:325–326. For a survey of medieval practices in this regard, see MacGregor, *Fire and Light in the Western Triduum*, 187–198.

[41] See Archbishop Lanfranc's customary for Canterbury Cathedral (c. 1077) in David Knowles and Christopher N. L. Brooke, eds. and trans., *The Monastic Constitutions of Lanfranc*, rev. ed., Oxford Medieval Texts (Oxford: Clarendon, 2002), chaps. 46–49, pp. 66–67.

[42] Durandus, *Rationale* (CCCM 140a), bk. 6, chap. 80, no. 1, p. 393.

[43] Text in Jean Deshusses, ed., *Le sacramentaire grégorien: Ses principales formes d'après les plus anciens manuscrits*, vol. 1, 2nd ed., SF 16 (Fribourg, Switzerland: Editions Universitaires Fribourg, 1979), Paduan nos. 322–325, p. 631.

[44] Mohlberg, Eizenhöfer, and Siffrin, *Liber sacramentorum*, nos. 431–441, pp. 70–72.

[45] *Rule of Saint Benedict*, chap. 11, in Paul Delatte, *The Rule of Saint Benedict: A Commentary* (London: Burns, Oates, and Washbourne, 1921), 154–155.

[46] *Liber comicus* (c. 650), cited in Hermann Schmidt, S.J., *Hebdomada sancta* (Rome: Herder, 1956–1957), 2:478–479.

[47] Deshusses, *Sacramentaire grégorien*, nos. 1024–1047, 1:363–367.

onward.[48] In the papal liturgy, these twelve readings were repeated in Greek, such that each lection was heard in the two principal liturgical languages of the universal Church, Latin and Greek; this extraordinary practice did not disappear from the papal rubrics until the end of the fifteenth century.[49]

Saint Benedict of Aniane's system of twelve readings prevailed in Italy (central Italy, Lucca, Naples) and the Catalonian region of Spain (Vich, Urgel, Palma de Majorca), as well as in particular dioceses elsewhere (Salzburg, Austria; Besançon, France). It was embraced by some Benedictine abbeys (Gorze, Fructuaria, Monte Cassino) as well as by the Franciscan Order and the Augustinian Hermits. However, in the majority of medieval Easter Vigil rites, the system of four readings established in the seventh-century Paduan redaction of the Gregorian Sacramentary prevailed, with examples to be found in England (Salisbury, Exeter), Germany (Cologne, Bamberg, Essen, Augsburg, Regensburg, Passau), France (Soissons), Switzerland (Zurich), Spain (Avila, Palencia), Portugal (Braga), Hungary (Esztergom, Eger), Poland (Kraków), and the Czech Republic (Prague), as well as in some religious communities (Benedictines of Cluny and Cîteaux, and the Dominican Order). Five readings were used in Bayonne, France; in Freising and Eichstätt, Germany; in the Carmelite Order; and in some Spanish sees, as we shall later see.[50] In the end, it was Saint Benedict of Aniane's system of twelve readings that was universally promulgated in the 1570 *Missale Romanum* of Pope Saint Pius V.[51] Sicard of Cremona (+1215) sees the twelve readings as symbolizing that "the catechumens to be

---

[48] Twelve Old Testament readings are specified in both the *ordo* for the Church of Saint John Lateran compiled by Cardinal Bernard of Porto (c. 1140) and the Roman Ordo of Benedict, the *Liber politicus* (c. 1140), compiled for the canons of Saint Peter's Basilica; see respectively Ludwig Fischer, ed., *Bernhardi cardinalis et Lateranensis ecclesiae prioris Ordo officiorum ecclesiae Lateranensis*, Historische Forschungen und Quellen 2–3 (Munich: Dr. F. P. Datterer, 1916), 62, and the *Ordo* of Benedict, in Paul Fabre and Louis Duchesne, eds., *Le Liber censuum de l'église romaine*, vol. 2, fasc. 3, Bibliothèque des écoles françaises d'Athènes et de Rome, 2nd series, Registres des papes du XIIIe siècle, 6 (Paris: Fontemoing, 1910), no. 43, p. 151.

[49] This Latin-Greek arrangement for the Easter Vigil readings appears in the twelfth-century Roman Pontifical, the thirteenth-century Pontifical of the Roman Curia, the early fourteenth-century papal ceremonial of Giacomo Cardinal Stefaneschi (c. 1325), and the early fifteenth-century ceremonial of the papal master of ceremonies Pierre Ameil (+1403; completed by Pierre Assalbit, 1435–1441); see respectively Andrieu, *Pontifical romain au moyen-âge*, 1:241; Michel Andrieu, ed., *Le pontifical romain au moyen-âge*, vol. 2, *Le pontifical de la Curie romaine du XIIIe siècle*, ST 87 (Vatican City: Biblioteca Apostolica Vaticana, 1940), 472; Marc Dykmans, ed., *Le cérémonial papal de la fin du moyen âge à la Renaissance*, vol. 2, BIHBR 25 (Brussels and Rome: Institut Historique Belge de Rome, 1981), 395–396; and Dykmans, *Cérémonial papal de la fin du moyen âge à la Renaissance*, 4:159. There is no longer any mention of the practice in the 1488 papal ceremonial of Patrizio Piccolomini; see Marc Dykmans, S.J., ed., *L'oeuvre de Patrizi Piccolomini, ou Le cérémonial papal de la première Renaissance*, vol. 2, ST 294 (Vatican City: Biblioteca Apostolica Vaticana, 1982), 402.

[50] The liturgical books consulted in giving these statistics regarding the number of Easter Vigil readings in sees across medieval Europe are too numerous to cite here. These sources can readily be identified by consulting the bibliography at the end of the present work.

[51] Sodi and Triacca, *Missale Romanum: Editio princeps (1570)*, 265–278 (new pagination).

baptized [at the vigil] are instructed in the doctrine of the twelve Apostles." [52]

It would be remiss to begin our presentation of the medieval Easter Vigil liturgy without addressing the issue of the timing of the vigil on Holy Saturday. In the early Church, the Easter Vigil was a nearly all-night ceremony completed in the predawn hours of Easter Sunday. This arrangement, ideal in so many ways, was, however, not without its difficulties. As the heroic "age of the martyrs" gave way to more peaceful times, and the numbers of the faithful swelled, the Church saw the wisdom of modestly mitigating the demanding customs of earlier generations; we see this in the gradual tempering of the laws of fasting and abstinence that took place over the centuries. Similarly, from the seventh century onward, we see an incremental advancement of the hour for beginning the Easter Vigil. The vigil's extraordinary length, further prolonged by baptisms during the rite, made an earlier hour advantageous from a practical standpoint.

It should be noted that the first and lengthier portion of the Easter Vigil, featuring up to twelve Old Testament readings (doubled to twenty-four in Rome when they were read in both Latin and Greek), each accompanied by a Collect and a Tract, had a quasi-penitential character befitting the liturgical day of Holy Saturday as a time of watching beside the Lord's tomb, awaiting his Resurrection. To cite one example, we see this in the medieval Easter Vigil practice of omitting from each of the Old Testament readings the customary announcement of the biblical book's title, an omission traceable to the early ninth century [53] and corresponding to the omission of titles from the first and second readings of the Passion liturgy of Good Friday (traceable to the eleventh century). [54] When the vigil began in the afternoon, as was the case in the early Middle Ages, the vigil would have lasted long enough to defer the culminating "celebratory" portion of the vigil, the Mass of Easter, until nightfall. In fact, several texts from this period, including the late ninth-century pontifical of northern France formerly known as the Pontifical of Poitiers, speak of ensuring that the vigil Mass, beginning with the *Kyrie* and the *Gloria*, would not commence until eventide: "Care should be taken, however, with all solicitude, that the *Gloria in excelsis Deo* on this night not be begun earlier than a star should appear in the sky." [55]

---

[52] Sicard of Cremona, *Mitrale*, bk. 6, chap. 14, PL 213, col. 326.

[53] This omission is specified in the Easter Vigil rubrics of Roman *Ordo* 28 (c. 800); text in Andrieu, *Ordines Romani du haut moyen âge*, 3:404.

[54] This omission on Good Friday is first indicated in the customary of the French Benedictine monastery of Gorze compiled around 1030 by its abbot, Sigibert; for the text, see Bruno Albers, ed., *Consuetudines monasticae*, vol. 2, *Consuetudines Cluniacenses antiquiores* (Monte Cassino, Italy: Typis Montis Casini, 1905), chap. 31, p. 97. See also the twelfth-century Roman Pontifical, in Andrieu, *Pontifical romain au moyen-âge*, 1:235.

[55] Pontifical formerly known as the Pontifical of Poitiers, in Martini, *Cosiddetto pontificale di Poitiers*, 219.

An effort to restore the entire Easter Vigil to its ancient nocturnal setting was undertaken by Saint John Gualbert (+1073), founder of the Vallombrosan Order, a Benedictine congregation of Italy, as related by his biographer Blessed Andrew of Strumi (+1097): "Who in Tuscany other than he moved from the day to the night the annual and renowned office fittingly to be done on the night of the holy Resurrection? For with stealthy negligence and gathering gluttony this office was performed at None on Saturday, that is now rightly and worthily done in the holy night, this our father John beginning and establishing in our times."[56] Thus the Easter Vigil rubrics of the twelfth-century customary of Vallombrosa direct that the blessing of the Easter fire with which the vigil begins is to commence only when "the dusk of night shall have begun to appear."[57]

The continued advancement of the Easter Vigil into the morning hours of Holy Saturday during the later Middle Ages was driven in part by changes in the Lenten laws of fasting.[58] While the Church increasingly saw the need to allow the faithful to pause in their fasting by taking one or two small meals during the day (the meals now known as breakfast and lunch), the ancient tradition of abstaining from all food until after the reception of Holy Communion was nonetheless upheld; it would be several more centuries before the Church would contemplate the reduction of the Communion fast to one hour, as is now the case. Hence those intending to receive Holy Communion at the Easter Vigil when the Mass took place in the evening had to abstain from all nourishment throughout the day until well after nightfall. The commencement of the Easter Vigil in the morning made it possible for communicants to break their fast in the afternoon, following the conclusion of Mass. There was also the belief, traceable to the sixth century, that Mass, as the re-presentation of the sacrifice of Calvary, should take place in the daytime insofar as the crucifixion took place in the daytime.[59] Despite this overall trend, the tradition of beginning the Easter Vigil late enough to defer the vigil Mass until nightfall appears to have been preserved in some cases. The Holy Saturday rubrics of the 1498 missal for the Portuguese see of Braga state: "On this day, however, None should be sung more slowly [than] usual. And this is

---

[56] Blessed Andrew of Strumi, *Vita sancti Iohannis Gualberti*, no. 32, in *Monumenta Germaniae historica: Scriptorum*, vol. 30, pt. 2 (Leipzig: Karol Hiersemann, 1934), 1087.

[57] *Redactio Vallumbrosana*, in Kassius Hallinger, O.S.B., *Consuetudines Cluniacensium antiquiores cum redactionibus derivatis*, Corpus consuetudinum monasticarum 7, pt. 2 (Siegburg, Germany: Franciscus Schmitt, 1983), 354.

[58] An association between changes in the Lenten fast and the advancement of the Easter Vigil is proposed by Ambroise Verheul, "Le mystère du Samedi saint," *Questions Liturgiques* 65 (1984): 23–24.

[59] There is a passage dating from about A.D. 530 regarding the time for Mass in the biography of Pope Saint Telesphorus (142–154) given in the *Liber pontificalis*; see Duchesne, *Liber pontificalis*, 1:129. This idea is developed more fully by Amalarius of Metz (+c. 850); see his *Liber officialis*, bk. 3, chap. 42, nos. 1–2, in John Michael Hanssens, ed., *Amalarii episcopi: Opera liturgica omnia*, vol. 2, ST 139 (Vatican City: Biblioteca Apostolica Vaticana, 1948), 378–379.

to be observed such that the office should be drawn out, that the Mass may be said in the night."[60]

In a decree dated March 29, 1566, Pope Saint Pius V withdrew permission for celebrating Mass in the evening, thereby making the celebration of the Easter Vigil on Holy Saturday morning obligatory and universal;[61] this law was incorporated into the 1570 *Missale Romanum*.[62] The obvious disadvantages of this advancement of the Easter Vigil into an entirely daytime setting half a day removed from the first hour of Easter Sunday have been justifiably stressed by many, a situation that was definitively remedied by Venerable Pope Pius XII when in 1955 he mandated the return of the Easter Vigil to its original nocturnal setting.[63] It is, however, unfortunate that some critics of the medieval liturgy have assumed that the forward shift in the timing of the Easter Vigil betokened a fundamental collapse in the theological understanding of the Paschal mystery. A reasoned examination of the medieval Easter rites reveals quite the opposite—in the cathedrals and monasteries of medieval Europe, the hours of Holy Saturday and Easter Sunday were filled with liturgical rites encompassing the Paschal mystery in all its scriptural and theological dimensions. The rich complexity of the late medieval Easter Vigil, a ceremony that must have taken several hours to complete, the prayers, Scripture readings, and rubrics of which filled dozens of pages in medieval missals (over forty pages in the 1568 missal of Palencia, Spain), testify to a profound awareness of the centrality of the Easter solemnity in the liturgical life of the Church.

The Easter Vigil in Jaén, Spain (1499)

For a prime example of the medieval Easter Vigil, we turn now to the combined missal and sacramental manual issued in 1499 for the Spanish diocese of Jaén, a suffragan see of Toledo with a liturgical tradition clearly drawn from that of Toledo.[64] The Easter Vigil rubrics of the Jaén missal begin by instructing that in preparation for the vigil, the altars, previously stripped on Holy Thursday, should be adorned with

---

[60] *Missale Bracarense* (Lisbon: Nicolaus de Saxonia, 1498), sig. k2r.

[61] Saint Pius V, "Revocation of the Privilege Conceded to Anyone of Celebrating Masses in the Evening Time" (March 29, 1566), in Laertius Cherubini, ed., *Magnum bullarium Romanum*, vol. 2 (Lyons, France: Lawrence Arnaud et Peter Borde, 1673), 178.

[62] Sodi and Triacca, *Missale Romanum: Editio princeps (1570)*, 21 (new pagination).

[63] Venerable Pope Pius XII made this change mandatory through the promulgation of the revised *Ordo* of Holy Week in 1955; see Sacred Congregation of Rites, *Maxima redemptionis* (November 16, 1955), section 2, no. 9, *American Ecclesiastical Review* 134 (January 1956): 54–55.

[64] *Missale Giennense / Manuale continens ordinem ad celebrandum ecclesiastica sacramenta* [*Missale secundum morem et consuetudinem sancte ecclesie Gienensis*] (Seville: Meinard Ungut and Stanislao Polono, 1499), fols. 81r–94v. The Easter Vigil rubrics of Jaén closely correspond to those of Toledo; for the Toledo rubrics, see *Missale secundum consuetudinem almae ecclesiae Toletanae*, 1503–1518, vol. 4 (manuscript: Madrid, Biblioteca Nacional de España, MS 1543; digitized text, Biblioteca Digital Hispánica, Biblioteca Nacional de España, Madrid, 2007), fols. 117r–138r.

festive altar cloths. Durandus interprets this "reclothing" of the altars as a sign of the Resurrection, for "in the Resurrection, Christ, who is signified by the altar, was clothed in the robe of his body."[65] A fourteenth-century *ordinarium* for the Priory of Saint-Lô, a community of Augustinian canons regular in Rouen, France, directs that on Holy Saturday, after the hour of Sext (approximately noon), before the vigil, the altars should be reclothed and "all things should be most fittingly adorned" in order that this visible expression of "ineffable joy" might foster the interior preparation of the soul for the Easter solemnity.[66] The Jaén rubrics state:

> In the first place, the altars should be festively adorned with white decorations, namely with frontals and other decorations appointed for this; and they should be covered at once with other Lenten frontals, and with the gold retable [altarpiece] covered at the same time, that all ought to be concealed until they should reach the hour [during the vigil Mass] at which the priest should say, *Glory to God in the highest*. Which having been said, immediately the black frontals should be removed and the gold retable uncovered.[67]

The late tenth-century Benedictine customary of Einsiedeln, Switzerland (c. 984), calls for the decoration of the church on Holy Saturday with curtains, lamps, and candlestands, and the adornment of the altar with cloths, reliquaries, pyxes, and boxwood.[68] The *Liber tramitis*, a customary of the French Benedictine abbey of Cluny (c. 1043), directs that in preparation for the Easter Vigil all the walls of the church should be lined with linen and woolen curtains; the rubrics also mention the use of a crucifix adorned with gold and gems.[69] Another customary of Cluny compiled by the monk Bernard (c. 1075) relates that for the greater solemnities, including Easter, a massive triangular lampstand with 120 lamps was utilized as an adornment.[70] A ritual of Soissons, France (c. 1185), directs that "the entire church should be decorated with curtains and palls"; as for the altar, it states: "The sacrosanct altar should be adorned with its more solemn ornaments; it should be decorated entirely in gold and silver."[71]

---

[65] Durandus, *Rationale* (CCCM 140a), bk. 6, chap. 85, no. 1, p. 434.

[66] *Ordinarium cannorum regularum*, Priory of Saint-Lô, Rouen, France, PL 147, col. 175.

[67] *Missale Giennense / Manuale . . . sacramenta* (1499), fol. 81r–81v. Virtually identical rubrics appear in the Toledo missal; see *Missale secundum consuetudinem almae ecclesiae Toletanae*, 1503–1518, vol. 4, fol. 117r–117v.

[68] Text in Bruno Albers, ed., *Consuetudines monasticae*, vol. 5, *Consuetudines monasteriorum Germaniae necnon s. Vitonis Virdunensis et Floriacensis abbatiae monumenta saeculi decimi continens* (Monte Cassino, Italy: Typis Societatis Editricis Castri Casini, 1912), 95.

[69] *Liber tramitis* (formerly called the Customs of Farfa), bk. 1, chap. 56, in Bruno Albers, ed., *Consuetudines monasticae*, vol. 1, *Consuetudines Farfenses* (Stuttgart: Jos. Roth, Bibliopolae, 1900), 54.

[70] *Ordo Cluniacensis*, pt. 1, chap. 50, in Marquard Herrgott, ed., *Vetus disciplina monastica* (Paris, 1726; repr., Siegburg, Germany: Franciscus Schmitt, 1999), 244–245.

[71] Text in Martène, *De antiquis ecclesiae ritibus*, bk. 4, chap. 24, 3:161.

As noted earlier, the first portion of the Easter Vigil in the medieval rites clearly had a quasi-penitential character, manifested among other ways by the Lenten vestments that were worn up until the actual Mass of the vigil, when there was a change to festive vestments, a transitional action first mentioned in the early thirteenth-century Ordinal of the Papal Court.[72] Some medieval liturgical books, beginning with a tenth-century *ordo* for the French Benedictine abbey of Corbie,[73] as well as later texts from Germany,[74] Austria,[75] Spain,[76] and Finland,[77] even prescribe that the rite of blessing the Easter fire should begin with the recitation of the seven penitential psalms. The Easter Vigil rite of Jaén begins with a procession to the high altar, where the lighting of the Easter fire shall take place:

> The priest and the ministers should proceed to the sacristy and put on themselves black or indigo or violet vestments. . . . The priest with a cope and the ministers in dalmatics should go in procession to the major altar in this order. First should precede the serpent [a serpent-shaped candlestick] with an unlit candle of three branches that one boy shall carry. And after him another boy should bring the Paschal candle, and after the candle should be brought the cross, the torch-bearers going forth with candles before the cross; and on one side should come one boy bringing blessed water, and on the other side another should bring a silver plate with five resins of incense, which ought to be placed in the Paschal candle, and with incense for the purpose of censing. And after that should come a deacon with the Gospel book, and the priest with the missal; and when they shall have come to the altar, the sacristan should look after the instrument [a flint stone] and the candle for making the new light, and the candle to be kindled for the blessing.[78]

---

[72] Text in Stephen J. P. Van Dijk, O.F.M., and Joan Hazelden Walker, eds., *The Ordinal of the Papal Court from Innocent III to Boniface VIII and Related Documents*, SF 22 (Fribourg, Switzerland: The University Press, 1975), 263, 272.

[73] *Codex Ratoldi* (excerpt), quoted by Nicolas-Hugues Menard (+1644) in his work on the Gregorian Sacramentary, reprinted in PL 78, col. 336.

[74] Ritual of Mainz, c. 1400, quoted in Hermann Reifenberg, *Sakramente, Sakramentalien und Ritualien im Bistum Mainz: Seit dem Spätmittelalter*, vol. 1, Liturgiewissenschaftliche Quellen und Forschungen 53 (Münster, Germany: Aschendorffsche Verlagsbuchhandlung, 1971), 721, footnote; ritual of Würzburg, 1482, cited ibid., 728, footnote; ritual of Constance, 1482, in Alban Dold, ed., *Die Konstanzer Ritualientexte in ihrer Entwicklung von 1482–1721*, Liturgiegeschichtliche Quellen 5–6 (Münster, Germany: Aschendorffschen Verlagsbuchhandlung, 1923), 137.

[75] Ritual of the Augustinian monastery of Saint Florian, twelfth century; text in Adolph Franz, ed., *Das Rituale von St. Florian aus dem zwölften Jahrhundert* (Freiburg im Breisgau, Germany: Herder, 1904), 60; missal of Salzburg, fifteenth century, in Radó and Mezey, *Libri liturgici manuscripti bibliothecarum Hungariae*, 183.

[76] Missal of Avila, 1510 (*Missale Abulense* [Salamanca, Spain: Juan de Porras, 1510], sig. k2r).

[77] Manual of Turku, Finland, 1522, in Martti Parvio, ed., *Manuale seu exequiale Aboense, 1522*, facsimile ed., Suomen kirkkohistoriallisen seuran toimituksia / Finska kyrkohistoriska samfundets handlingar 115 (Helsinki: Societas Historiae Ecclesiasticae Fennica, 1980), fol. 52r.

[78] *Missale Giennense / Manuale . . . sacramenta* (1499), fol. 81v.

At the outset of the Jaén vigil, all the church's candles are unlit, having already been extinguished in the course of the Easter Triduum.[79] Rupert of Deutz considers the extinguished candles symbolic of all the prophets and just men slain from the time of Abel up to the time of Christ.[80] Honorius of Autun (+c. 1135) sees the extinguished lights as representing the observances of the Law of the Old Covenant put to rest by the death of Christ, making way for the "light of the New Law" revealed in his Resurrection.[81]

This "light of the New Law" is symbolized by the Easter fire kindled at the beginning of the Easter Vigil for the subsequent lighting of the Paschal candle and, in turn, the relighting of all the church's candles. The Paschal candle, as Durandus explains, represents Christ himself, "who illuminates us in the night of this world"; the wax symbolizes his body, the wick his soul, and the flame his divinity.[82] The Paschal candle is very large in stature compared with other candles— on its candlestand it was thirty-six feet tall at England's Salisbury Cathedral[83]—a characteristic explained by Rupert of Deutz as representing the greatness of Christ.[84] The custom of inscribing the year upon Paschal candles, a practice traceable to the eighth century,[85] is seen by Sicard of Cremona as a further testament to the identification of this candle with Christ, who is the "Ancient of days" (Dan 7:9).[86] Honorius sees in this practice a representation of the identity of Christ as the "acceptable year" spoken of by Isaiah in his prophecy of the coming of the Messiah (Is 61:2).[87] He adds that the twelve months of the year represent the twelve Apostles, and the individual days of the year all the faithful.[88] As we have already seen, the customs of inscribing or painting on the side of the candle a cross and the first and last

---

[79] "This day all the lights of the church should be unlit until when the hour should come that they be lighted" (ibid., fol. 82r).

[80] Rupert of Deutz, *Liber de divinis officiis* (CCCM 7), bk. 6, chap. 29, p. 211.

[81] Honorius of Autun, *Gemma animae*, bk. 3, chap. 100, PL 172, col. 668.

[82] Durandus, *Rationale* (CCCM 140a), bk. 6, chap. 80, no. 6, p. 396.

[83] Late medieval printed editions of the Sarum Missal expressly mention this size for the Paschal candle; see Francis H. Dickinson, ed., *Missale ad usum insignis et praeclarae ecclesiae Sarum* (Burntisland, Scotland: E. Prelo de Pitsligo, 1861–1883), col. 333.

[84] Rupert of Deutz, *Liber de divinis officiis* (CCCM 7), bk. 6, chap. 29, pp. 211–212.

[85] Writing in 725, the English ecclesiastical scholar Saint Bede tells of the monks from his abbey seeing in the Roman basilica of Saint Mary Major candles inscribed with the number of years since the Passion of Christ (*De temporum ratione*, chap. 47, PL 90, col. 494). Bede's reference to these candles in the plural, rather than to a single candle, implies that the tapers in question were the pair of large candles, essentially dual Paschal candles, found in early texts of the Easter Vigil of Rome, that are repeatedly described as "having the stature of a man" (see Roman *Ordo* 11, c. 650–700, in Andrieu, *Ordines Romani du haut moyen âge*, 2:444). The dating of candles from the year of the Passion was soon supplanted by the practice of inscribing the number of years from the Incarnation of Christ—the calendar year—first specified in the late ninth-century pontifical of northern France formerly known as the Pontifical of Poitiers (Martini, *Cosiddetto pontificale di Poitiers*, 215).

[86] Sicard of Cremona, *Mitrale*, bk. 6, chap. 14, PL 213, col. 323.

[87] Honorius of Autun, *Gemma animae*, bk. 3, chap. 102, PL 172, col. 668.

[88] Ibid.

letters of the Greek alphabet, alpha and omega, an evocation of Christ's words in the Book of Revelation, "I am Alpha and Omega, the beginning and the end" (Rev 1:8; cf. Rev 21:6; 22:13), are found for the first time in the Spanish *Liber ordinum*.[89] The use of the letters alpha and omega on the Paschal candle entered the liturgy of Rome in the twelfth century, appearing in both the Roman Pontifical[90] and Cardinal Bernard of Porto's *Ordo officiorum* for the Church of Saint John Lateran (c. 1140),[91] but disappeared in the thirteenth century.[92]

An eighth-century liturgical text, Roman *Ordo* 28, tells of the Paschal candle being lit directly from the Easter fire and carried afterward into the church, where it would be set upon a candlestand before the altar.[93] But in another text of the same century, Roman *Ordo* 26 (c. 750–775), we find an intermediary step added to the transferal of the Easter fire to the Paschal candle. After the fire was begun outside the church doors, a candle mounted on a reed would be lit from it and be carried by a junior bishop to the Paschal candle inside the church, which would then be lit with it.[94] This latter method of using a small candle to transfer the flame of the Easter fire to the Paschal candle was ultimately to prevail across medieval Europe. It has been suggested, not without reason, that the exceptionally large size and weight of the Paschal candle contributed to the introduction of a small candle that could be more easily borne in procession. However, it may also be that a concern to prevent any accidental extinction of the lighted Paschal candle, the Easter Vigil's premier symbol of the risen Christ, in the course of a procession from outdoors, where wind posed a threat, could have inspired the use of a lesser candle to bring the Easter fire to a Paschal candle securely pre-positioned within the church, where there was relatively little danger of extinction by the wind. The small candle was usually carried on a mounting, in some instances a reed, as was the case in the above-cited earliest mention of this candle in Roman *Ordo* 26. In some cases, as in Archbishop Lanfranc's Benedictine customary for England's Canterbury Cathedral (c. 1077), a spear (*hasta*) served as the mounting for the small candle of the lighting rite,[95] a usage that John of Avranches (archbishop of Rouen, France; +1079) sees as representing Christ on the Cross[96]—an association probably inspired by Christ's words, "And I, if I be lifted up from the earth, will draw all things to myself" (Jn 12:32).

---

[89] Férotin, *Liber ordinum*, cols. 209–210.

[90] Andrieu, *Pontifical romain au moyen-âge*, 1:240–241.

[91] Fischer, *Bernhardi cardinalis . . . Ordo officiorum ecclesiae Lateranensis*, 60.

[92] There is no mention of these insignia in the Easter Vigil rubrics of the thirteenth-century Pontifical of the Roman Curia; see Andrieu, *Pontifical romain au moyen-âge*, 2:470–471.

[93] Text in Andrieu, *Ordines Romani du haut moyen âge*, 3:403.

[94] Text ibid., 326, 329.

[95] Text in Knowles and Brooke, *The Monastic Constitutions of Lanfranc*, chaps. 46–49, p. 66 (Latin text quoted by permission of Oxford University Press).

[96] John of Avranches, *Liber de officiis ecclesiasticis*, PL 147, col. 49.

In the Jaén rite, the candle staff has a top fashioned in the shape of a serpent; the rubrics simply call the staff a "serpent".[97] The use of a serpent-shaped staff to carry one or more candles for the lighting of the Paschal candle is first mentioned in the rubrics of the late ninth-century pontifical of northern France formerly known as the Pontifical of Poitiers.[98] The symbolism of this form of the candle staff is explained by Durandus as drawn from the brazen serpent mounted on a pole by Moses, the sight of which brought healing to the snakebitten Israelites who gazed upon it (Num 21:8–9). Citing Christ's evocation of this Old Testament incident as a prefiguration of his being lifted upon the Cross (Jn 3:14), Durandus observes that the serpent-shaped candlestick of the Easter Vigil is carried and gazed upon "that the Passion of Christ may be remembered and by it we may be healed of the wounds of our sins, for the serpent on the staff is Christ on the gibbet."[99]

As we have already seen, our earliest extant account of the Easter fire rite from early fifth-century Jerusalem testifies to the lighting of a lantern rather than a Paschal candle. In the West, numerous texts, beginning with the fifth- to seventh-century rubrics of Spain's *Liber ordinum*, speak of a lantern being lit in addition to the Paschal candle.[100] By the eleventh century, the lantern was being used as a "backup" light for the staff-mounted candle, with both being kindled from the Easter fire and carried in procession to the Paschal candle; a rubric of the French Benedictine customary of Fleury (c. 1030) explains: "One of the youths, however, brings a candle in a lantern ... that its fire may be at hand, if that which is carried in the mouth of the serpent should be extinguished."[101]

In the eleventh century, the small candle for carrying the Easter fire began to take on a tripartite form, with three distinct candlesticks; serving a purpose similar to the lantern, the addition of two more candlesticks to the staff would have provided two "backup" flames in the event of the accidental extinction of one candlestick.[102] The use of a tripartite candle staff had its antecedents in the three lamps utilized for the Jerusalem Easter Vigil in the fifth century and the three oil lights mentioned by Pope Saint Zachary in the eighth century. A staff-mounted triple candle appears for the first time in an illustration accompanying an eleventh-century text of the Paschal candle chant, the *Exsultet* (an "*Exsultet* roll"), from Bari, Italy;[103] the triple candle is

---

[97] *Missale Giennense / Manuale ... sacramenta* (1499), fol. 81v.

[98] Martini, *Cosiddetto pontificale di Poitiers*, 215.

[99] Durandus, *Rationale* (CCCM 140a), bk. 6, chap. 89, no. 12, p. 467.

[100] Férotin, *Liber ordinum*, cols. 208–209.

[101] *Veteres consuetudines monasterii sancti Benedicti Floriacensis*, in Albers, *Consuetudines monasticae*, 5:143.

[102] Cardinal Bernard of Porto's *ordo* for the Roman church of Saint John Lateran expressly states this as the reason for multiple lights on the candle staff (Fischer, *Bernhardi cardinalis ... Ordo officiorum ecclesiae Lateranensis*, 61).

[103] MacGregor, *Fire and Light in the Western Triduum*, 273.

specified in a liturgical book for the first time in the twelfth-century Roman Pontifical.[104] It is the central stem of the three-branched candle, lit before the other two stems, that bears the light with which the considerably larger Paschal candle shall later be lit. Drawing upon the imagery of the bee as a producer of wax and the medieval belief that the mother bee virginally brings forth her offspring, Rupert of Deutz sees in the diminutive wax candle that is lit first a symbol of the Blessed Virgin Mary, who brought forth Christ in the flesh—"the honey in the wax".[105] The two other stems of the three-branched candle, lit from the fire of the central stem, are identified by Honorius of Autun as representing the prophets and the Apostles respectively, "illuminated by the Spirit of Christ".[106]

In the Jaén rite, it is a stone of flint that is used to ignite the Easter fire (as indicated by the prayer that follows below). The Jaén missal does not describe the fire but indicates that there were coals in it, for these coals are later placed in the thurible to be used for incensation at the vigil.[107] The priest blesses the fire with three prayers, the first of which is traceable to the tenth-century Romano-Germanic Pontifical:[108]

> *O God, who through your Son, namely the Cornerstone, conferred the fire of your light upon your faithful, sancti + fy this new light, profitable to our needs, produced from flint, and grant us thus through this Paschal feast to be inflamed with heavenly desires, that with pure minds we may be worthy to come to the feast of everlasting light. Through the same Christ our Lord. Amen.*[109]

The second prayer, traceable to the eighth-century Gellone Sacramentary (a Frankish adaptation of Rome's Gelasian Sacramentary)[110] and bearing a resemblance to the bishop's lamp benediction in the earlier-cited Easter Vigil rite of the Spanish *Liber ordinum*, is theorized to stem from a long-lost ancient prayer for the daily lamp-lighting rite in Jerusalem's Church of the Holy Sepulcher:[111]

> *Lord God, almighty Father, unfailing Light, who are the Creator of all lights, bless + this light to be carried by the faithful in honor of your name, that it may be sancti + fied and blessed + by you; and vouchsafe mercifully to grant*

---

[104] Andrieu, *Pontifical romain au moyen-âge*, 1:239.

[105] Rupert of Deutz, *Liber de divinis officiis* (CCCM 7), bk. 6, chap. 29, pp. 211–212.

[106] Honorius of Autun, *Gemma animae*, bk. 3, chap. 101, PL 172, col. 668.

[107] *Missale Giennense / Manuale ... sacramenta* (1499), fol. 82r.

[108] Romano-Germanic Pontifical, in Cyrille Vogel and Reinhard Elze, eds., *Le pontifical romano-germanique du dixième siècle*, vol. 2, ST 227 (Vatican City: Biblioteca Apostolica Vaticana, 1963), 57–58.

[109] *Missale Giennense / Manuale ... sacramenta* (1499), fol. 81v.

[110] Gellone Sacramentary, in A. Dumas, ed., *Liber sacramentorum Gellonensis*, CCSL 159 (Turnhout, Belgium: Brepols, 1981), no. 2848, p. 449. The Jaén missal contains a considerably altered form of this prayer.

[111] Kenneth Stevenson, "The Ceremonies of Light: Their Shape and Function in the Paschal Vigil Liturgy", *EL* 99 (1985): 181–182, footnote.

that it may be kindled and illuminated with the light of your brightness; and even as with the same fire you once illuminated your servant Moses, so illuminate our hearts and our senses, that we may be worthy to come to the vision of your eternal glory. Through . . .[112]

The third prayer appears for the first time in thirteenth-century English liturgical texts:[113] *"Holy Lord, almighty Father, eternal God, vouchsafe to bless + and sancti + fy this fire, which we [although] unworthy presume to bless + through the invocation of your only-begotten Son, our Lord Jesus Christ; and may you, most merciful One, sanctify [it] with your bless + ing and vouchsafe [it] to attain to the profit of mankind. Through the same Christ our Lord."*[114] The priest then blesses the five grains of incense to be inserted in the side of the Paschal candle with a prayer from the seventh-century Gelasian Sacramentary of Rome,[115] an oration that was originally composed as a blessing for the new fire, as is evident from the wording:

> *May the abundant outpouring of your bless + ing come, we beseech you, almighty God, upon this incense; and kindle, O invisible Regenerator, this brightness of the night, that the power of your majesty may not only illuminate the sacrifice that is offered on this night with the hidden admixture of your light but assist in whatever place [the light] shall have been carried forth from the rite of this benediction, the evil of diabolic deception having been expelled. Through . . .*
>
> *May the bless + ing of God the Father almighty, and the Son + , and the Holy + Spirit, descend and remain upon this light and this incense. Amen.*[116]

The Jaén rubrics do not give any specifics as to where the celebrant is to stand while blessing the Easter fire. In the Easter Vigil rubrics of the tenth-century Benedictine customary of Saint Vito, Verdun, France, the priest is instructed to face "not toward the north but toward the east" during the fire and candle-blessing rite;[117] similarly, the late fifteenth- and sixteenth-century editions of the Sarum Missal of Salisbury, England, all state in this regard: "The priest should stand close to the fire, turned toward the east."[118]

The new Easter fire—in the Jaén rubrics, the staff-mounted triple candle newly lit from the fire—as well as the incense grains are now

---

[112] *Missale Giennense / Manuale . . . sacramenta* (1499), fol. 81v.

[113] Ritual of Evesham Abbey, c. 1250, in Henry Austin Wilson, ed., *Officium ecclesiasticum abbatum secundum usum Eveshamensis monasterii,* HBS 6 (London: Henry Bradshaw Society, 1893), col. 81; Sarum Missal, Salisbury, late thirteenth century, in John Wickham Legg, ed., *The Sarum Missal, Edited from Three Early Manuscripts* (Oxford: Clarendon Press, 1916), 116.

[114] *Missale Giennense / Manuale . . . sacramenta* (1499), fol. 81v.

[115] Mohlberg, Eizenhöfer, and Siffrin, *Liber sacramentorum,* no. 429, pp. 69–70.

[116] *Missale Giennense / Manuale . . . sacramenta* (1499), fols. 81v–82r.

[117] Text in Albers, *Consuetudines monasticae,* 5:122.

[118] Dickinson, *Missale ad usum . . . Sarum,* col. 334.

sprinkled with holy water.[119] According to Durandus, this aspersion over the fire represents the blood and water that issued from the side of Christ on the Cross at the same moment that the "fire of charity" was cast forth from his side, when he, "the Rock", was stricken with the iron of the soldier's lance. Thus, just as the Easter fire is showered with holy water, so too the faithful, having been inflamed with the "fire of charity", are moistened with "the water of grace".[120] After live coals from the Easter fire are put into a thurible, the triple candle is censed.[121] Both the aspersion and the incensation of the Easter fire are specified for the first time in an eleventh-century customary of the Benedictine abbey of Saint-Bénigne in Dijon, France.[122]

In keeping with the joyful character of the hymn to the Paschal candle that he is about to sing, the deacon now changes temporarily into an Easter vestment. The assumption of a white dalmatic by the deacon exclusively for the chanting of the *Exsultet*, as an exception to the Lenten vestments worn by the clergy during the first part of the vigil, is first mentioned in a liturgical text of Rome, the Ceremonial of a Cardinal Bishop (c. 1280).[123] In the 1568 missal of Palencia, Spain, the rubrics direct the celebrant as well as the deacon to vest in white for the *Exsultet* but to change into red vestments at its conclusion, remaining thus until a second change into white vestments for the vigil Mass.[124] In the rubrics of the Jaén missal, the deacon's change of vesture is immediately followed by a description of the procession through the church with the triple candle and the as-yet-unlit Paschal candle:

> The deacon should remove his black dalmatic and take another [that is] white, and the three branches of the serpent candle should be lit from the new fire, and they should proceed to blessing the Paschal candle in this order that follows. First should precede the Paschal candle, and one acolyte with a censer; and immediately the subdeacon with the cross, the torchbearers with unlit candles preceding before the cross; also one acolyte clothed in a surplice, bringing the plate with the five grains of incense that ought to be placed in the Paschal candle. And after this proceeds the lector, bringing the serpent. And before the major altar, the deacon, holding the serpent in his right hand, should say in a high voice, *Light of Christ.* [Response:] *Thanks*

---

[119] *Missale Giennense / Manuale . . . sacramenta* (1499), fol. 82r.

[120] Durandus, *Rationale* (CCCM 140a), bk. 6, chap. 80, no. 2, p. 393.

[121] *Missale Giennense / Manuale . . . sacramenta* (1499), fol. 82r.

[122] Text in Martène, *De antiquis monachorum ritibus*, bk. 3, chap. 13, no. 34, in Martène, *De antiquis ecclesiae ritibus*, 4:126.

[123] For this text, ascribed to Latino Cardinal Malabranca (+1294), see Marc Dykmans, S.J., ed., *Le cérémonial papal de la fin du moyen âge à la Renaissance*, vol. 1, BIHBR 24 (Brussels and Rome: Institut Historique Belge de Rome, 1977), 225–226.

[124] *Missale Pallantinum* (Palencia, Spain: Sebastian Martinez, 1568; Latin text provided by Biblioteca Apostolica Vaticana, Vatican City [shelf mark Stamp. Barb. B. X. 1]), fols. 100v–101v, 109r, 120r, 342r–v.

be to God. And in this manner and order, it should be done in the middle of the church's crossing, he raising his voice somewhat higher. And the third time, they should come to the entrance of the choir and do in this way and order just as the other two times, raising the voice ever more strongly, with the choir, however, responding at each station, *Thanks be to God*.[125]

The versicle *Lumen Christi* ("*Light of Christ*"), with its corresponding response, *Deo gratias* ("*Thanks be to God*"), is mentioned for the first time in a monastic instruction of the eighth century, Roman *Ordo* 19 (c. 750–787), where it is used to announce the bringing of a light into the refectory when nightfall comes during the course of supper.[126] The threefold exclamation of the *Lumen Christi* first appears in the liturgy of the Easter Vigil at the end of the tenth century, when it is specified in the rubrics of an early missal from a Benedictine abbey of Italy's Abruzzi region (Biblioteca Apostolica Vaticana Latinus 4770)[127] and shortly afterward in a missal of the Italian Benedictine abbey of Benevento (c. 1000).[128] By the twelfth century, the threefold chant of the *Lumen Christi* had taken on a three-staged processional form, as described in a text of this period, the Benedictine customary of Vallombrosa, Italy: the deacon would sing the *Lumen Christi* for the first time as the procession approached the entrance of the church, a second time in a higher voice after entering the church, and a third time in an even higher voice upon coming before the altar.[129] In the papal ceremonial known as the Long Ceremonial, attributed to John of Sion and dating from shortly before 1342, we find for the first time a rubric directing the deacon who carries the triple candle to genuflect each of the three times he stops to sing the *Lumen Christi*.[130] In the 1488 *Caeremoniale Romanum* of the papal master of ceremonies Patrizio Piccolomini, the rite was further developed with the instruction that before the first *Lumen Christi* only one of the three candles should be lit; the

[125] *Missale Giennense / Manuale . . . sacramenta* (1499), fol. 82r.

[126] Roman *Ordo* 19, in Andrieu, *Ordines Romani du haut moyen âge*, 3:220.

[127] Manuscript: Vatican City, Biblioteca Apostolica Vaticana, Codex Vaticanus Latinus 4770 (a *missale plenarium*), fol. 92v, cited in Hallinger, *Consuetudines Cluniacensium antiquiores cum redactionibus derivatis*, 355, footnote. For the dating and provenance of this text, see Klaus Gamber, *Codices liturgici Latini antiquiores*, pt. 1, Spicilegii Friburgensis, subsidia, 1 (Fribourg, Switzerland: Universitätsverlag Freiburg, 1968), 531.

[128] Manuscript: Benevento, Italy, Biblioteca Capitolare, Codex VI 33, variously referred to as the *Missale Beneventanum* or the *Missale antiquum*; text in Sieghild Rehle, "Missale Beneventanum (Codex VI des Erzbischöflichen Archivs von Benevent)", *Sacris erudiri* 21 (1972–1973): 353.

[129] *Redactio Vallumbrosana*, in Hallinger, *Consuetudines Cluniacensium antiquiores*, 355. This practice also appears in Cardinal Bernard of Porto's *Ordo officiorum* for the Church of Saint John Lateran in Rome (c. 1140); see Fischer, *Bernhardi cardinalis . . . Ordo officiorum ecclesiae Lateranensis*, 61.

[130] Text in Marc Dykmans, S.J., ed., *Le cérémonial papal de la fin du moyen âge à la Renaissance*, vol. 3, BIHBR 26 (Brussels and Rome: Institut Historique Belge de Rome, 1983), 223–224.

second and third candles were to be lit at the second and third proc-
lamations of the *Lumen Christi* respectively.[131] The three genuflections
and the three-staged lighting of the triple candle were universally promulgated in the 1570 *Missale Romanum*.[132]

The rite of lighting the Paschal candle climaxes with the singing of
the *Exsultet*, a poetic text for blessing the Paschal candle widely believed
to have been composed by the Church Father Saint Ambrose (+397);
this attribution, although repeatedly challenged, has withstood the test
of time.[133] The earliest extant complete text of the *Exsultet* appears in
the *Missale Gothicum*, a Frankish liturgical book of the seventh to the
eighth century.[134] Its wider promulgation began with its use in Saint
Benedict of Aniane's early ninth-century Frankish adaptation of the
Gregorian Sacramentary of Rome.[135] The *Exsultet* was subsequently
brought to Rome itself in the tenth century with the arrival in the
city of the Romano-Germanic Pontifical[136] and appeared thereafter in
the Roman Pontifical of the twelfth century.[137]

Durandus sees the deacon who chants the *Exsultet* as representing
"the preacher of the Gospel", who, "enlightened by the luminous
grace of the Resurrection", ought to preach the praises of Christ, who
was "bodily extinguished for us in the violence of the Passion".[138] In
testimony to the gravity of this task given to the deacon, the rubrics
of the twelfth-century Holy Week *Ordo* of the Benedictine abbey of
Monte Cassino, Italy, state that before proceeding to the proclamation
of the *Lumen Christi* and the *Exsultet*, the deacon, while passing through
the middle of the choir, is to say privately to the other monks, with
his head bowed, *"Pray for me."* [139] In the Jaén missal, as well as in the
Spanish missals of Seville (1534) and Palencia (1568), the *Exsultet* is set
to a chant that differs markedly from the traditional Roman Rite melody for this text, with six prolonged melismas of rising and falling

---

[131] Text in Dykmans, *Oeuvre de Patrizi Piccolomini*, 2:400–401.

[132] Sodi and Triacca, *Missale Romanum: Editio princeps (1570)*, 254–255 (new pagination).

[133] See Bernard Capelle, O.S.B., "L'Exultet pascal: Oeuvre de Saint Ambroise", in *Miscellanea Giovanni Mercati*, vol. 1, *Bibbia-letteratura cristiana antica*, ST 121 (Vatican City: Biblioteca Apostolica Vaticana, 1946), 219–246. The belief that Saint Ambrose was the author
of the *Exsultet* is a centuries-old tradition, attested in the late thirteenth century by Durandus;
see the latter's *Rationale* (CCCM 140a), bk. 6, chap. 80, no. 2, p. 393.

[134] Text in Leo Cunibert Mohlberg, O.S.B., ed., *Missale Gothicum*, REDSMF 5 (Rome:
Herder, 1961), no. 225, pp. 59–61.

[135] Deshusses, *Sacramentaire grégorien*, nos. 1021–1022c, 1:360–363.

[136] Vogel and Elze, *Pontifical romano-germanique*, 2:97–99.

[137] Andrieu, *Pontifical romain au moyen-âge* 1:240. Although in this case the *Exsultet* is not
directly specified in the text, its use is indicated by passages quoted from it in the rubrics
of the pontifical.

[138] Durandus, *Rationale* (CCCM 140a), bk. 6, chap. 80, no. 3, p. 394.

[139] Text in Teodoro Leuterman, *Ordo Casinensis hebdomadae maioris (saec. XII)*, Miscellanea Cassinese 20 (Monte Cassino, Italy: Monte Cassino Abbey, 1941), 114. Similarly, the
rubrics of a fifteenth-century missal of Salzburg, Austria, state that the archdeacon, before
beginning the *Exsultet*, asks to be prayed for (Radó and Mezey, *Libri liturgici manuscripti
bibliothecarum Hungariae*, 183).

notes that occur in the opening verses (such as at the word *mysteria*).[140] The settings of the *Exsultet* in the Spanish missals of Saragossa (1498) and Avila (1510) feature thirteen and sixteen melismas respectively.[141] A ritual of Soissons, France (c. 1185), directs the choir to stand for the *Exsultet*.[142] In the Jaén rite, the deacon begins by censing the liturgical book from which he will sing the *Exsultet* (an incensation traceable to the twelfth-century Roman Pontifical[143] and retained in the *Missale Romanum* of 1570):[144]

> And when he shall have come to the pulpit, adorned and furnished, in which there ought to be the Gospel book, within which is the blessing of the Paschal candle, namely *Exsultet iam angelica*. First he should incense the book, then begin the blessing of the candle:
>
> *Now let the angelic multitude of Heaven rejoice, let the divine mysteries rejoice, and let the trumpet of salvation thunder for the victory of so great a King. Let the earth be glad, irradiated in the brightness of so great a light; and illuminated in the splendor of the eternal King, let all the earth perceive the darkness to have dispersed. And let Mother Church rejoice, adorned with the brightness of so great a light, and let this temple resound with the great voices of the peoples. Wherefore standing near you, dearest brethren, so near the wonderful brightness of this holy light, I beseech you, invoke together with me the mercy of almighty God. And may He who vouchsafed to include me, not by my merits, within the number of deacons perfect the praise of this candle by imparting the gift of his light. Through our Lord Jesus Christ . . .*[145]

The next portion of the *Exsultet*, in the form of a Preface (the opening words of which we omit here), addresses the prefiguration of Easter night in the parting of the Red Sea. This connection is expansively developed in the Easter Vigil commentary of Sicard of Cremona, who likens the lit Paschal candle to the pillars of cloud and fire that led the Israelites to safety. The pillar of cloud, like the wax column of the Paschal candle, is a figure of the human nature of Christ; the pillar of fire, like the flame of the Paschal candle, is a figure of Christ's divinity. Just as the pillars of cloud and fire gave the Israelites shade from the sun, protection from the devil, and illumination in the night, so too Christ, symbolized by the Paschal candle, "shades against the heat of vices, protects from the suggestions of demons", and

---

[140] Missals with this setting of the *Exsultet* include those of Seville (1534) and Palencia (1568); see respectively *Missale divinorum secundum consuetudinem alme ecclesie Hispalensis* (Seville: Joannes Varela, 1534; Latin text provided by Biblioteca Apostolica Vaticana, Vatican City [shelf mark Stamp. Barb. B.X.4]), fols. 88r–91v, and *Missale Pallantinum* (1568), fols. 101v–109r.

[141] Missal of Saragossa: *Missale secundum morem ecclesie Cesaraugustane* (1498), temporal, fols. 100r–107r; missal of Avila: *Missale Abulense* (1510), sig. k2r–k6r.

[142] Martène, *De antiquis ecclesiae ritibus*, bk. 4, chap. 24, 3:161.

[143] Andrieu, *Pontifical romain au moyen-âge*, 1:240.

[144] Sodi and Triacca, *Missale Romanum: Editio princeps (1570)*, 255 (new pagination).

[145] *Missale Giennense / Manuale . . . sacramenta* (1499), fols. 82r–83r.

"illuminates every man coming into this world [Jn 1:9], until he should lead them to the kingdom of Heaven."[146] In this context, the deacon chanting the *Exsultet*, according to Honorius of Autun, represents the angel who "carried" the pillars of cloud and fire before the Israelites.[147] The *Exsultet* continues:

> *It is truly fitting and just to proclaim with all the devotion of the heart and mind, and the service of the voice, the invisible God, the Father almighty, and his only-begotten Son our Lord Jesus Christ, who for us has paid the debt of Adam to the eternal Father and has wiped away the bond of the ancient punishment with his holy blood, and also the Holy Spirit, the Paraclete. For this is the Paschal feast, in which the true Lamb himself is slain, and the doorposts of the faithful are consecrated with his blood. This is the night, in which having first brought our fathers the sons of Israel out of Egypt, you made them to pass through the Red Sea dryshod. This therefore is the night that has purified the darkness of sins with the pillar of light. This is the night that today throughout the whole world restores to grace, unites in holiness, those believing in Christ, divided by the vices of the world and darkened by the darkness of sins. This is the night in which Christ rises from the dead the Victor, having destroyed the chains of death. For it availed us nothing to be born, if it had not availed us to be redeemed. O wonderful condescension of your goodness toward us; O inestimable love of charity, that to redeem a slave you handed over your Son. O surely necessary sin of Adam that was blotted out by the death of Christ; O happy fault that merited to have such a Redeemer, and so great. O blessed night that alone merited to know the time and the hour at which Christ rose from the dead. This is the night of which it is written, "And the night shall be light as the day" [Ps 138:12], "and night shall be my light in my pleasures" [Ps 138:11]. The holiness of this night, therefore, puts evil deeds to flight, washes away sins, and restores the innocence of the fallen, the happiness of the sorrowful. It puts hatreds to flight, establishes concord, and makes powers bow.[148]*

In the Jaén missal, a rubric at this point in the *Exsultet* states, "Here the five grains of incense are placed in the candle in the manner of a cross"; this action is tied to the words of the *Exsultet* that it immediately precedes, "*In the grace of this night, therefore, receive, holy Father, the evening sacrifice of this incense.*"[149] The custom of making a cross from incense grains on the side of the Paschal candle is first found in the rubrics of a tenth-century Benedictine *ordo* of Corbie, France;[150] several decades later, the customary compiled for the French Benedictine abbey of Gorze by its abbot Sigibert (c. 1030) specifies the use of five

---

[146] Sicard of Cremona, *Mitrale*, bk. 6, chap. 14, PL 213, col. 324.

[147] Honorius of Autun, *Gemma animae*, bk. 3, chap. 102, PL 172, col. 668.

[148] *Missale Giennense / Manuale . . . sacramenta* (1499), fols. 83r–84v.

[149] Ibid., fol. 84v.

[150] *Codex Ratoldi* (excerpt), as quoted by Dom Ménard and reprinted in PL 78, col. 336.

incense grains for this purpose.[151] The insertion of the incense grains as well as an incensation of the candle *during* the *Exsultet* are expressly mentioned for the first time in an eleventh-century customary of the Benedictine abbey of Saint-Bénigne in Dijon, France.[152]

Sicard of Cremona considers the bringing of the incense grains to the Paschal candle and their crosswise imposition upon it as symbolizing the holy women's bringing of spices to the tomb to anoint the body of Christ crucified.[153] This symbolism is implicit in the rubrics of the fourteenth-century *Liber ordinarius* of the collegiate church and abbey of Essen, Germany, which call for the insertion of myrrh as well as incense into the side of the Paschal candle.[154] Durandus adds to Sicard's interpretation by observing that the grains of incense, five in number to symbolize the five wounds that the body of Christ received on the Cross, likewise represent the "aromas" of the virtues that the Church offers to Christ as an expression of her devotion to him.[155] Moreover, the juxtaposition of the crosswise imposition of the incense grains with the words of the *Exsultet* that speak of this incense as an "evening sacrifice" offered to the Father testifies that the Passion of Christ corresponds to the "evening sacrifice of the Law" formerly offered under the Old Covenant. For just as the Psalmist speaks of the lifting up of his hands in prayer as an evening sacrifice to the Lord (Ps 140:2), so too Christ lifted up his hands on the Cross as he offered himself to the Father; furthermore, the sacrifice of the Cross was offered "in the evening of the world, that is, on the sixth day, and in the evening of the day".[156]

Following the insertion of the five grains of incense, the deacon continues: "*In the grace of this night, therefore, receive, holy Father, the evening sacrifice of this incense that your most holy Church, through the hands of your ministers, renders you in this solemn oblation of a candle from the labors of bees.*"[157] It is at this point in the *Exsultet* that the Jaén missal directs the Paschal candle to be lit.[158] The custom of lighting the Paschal candle at some moment during the *Exsultet* is first mentioned in the tenth-century *Ordo* for the French Benedictine abbey of Corbie.[159] Durandus sees the initial lighting of the Paschal candle after its blessing as representing "the

[151] *Consuetudines* of Sigibert, chap. 32, in Albers, *Consuetudines monasticae,* 2:99–100.

[152] Text in Martène, *De antiquis monachorum ritibus,* bk. 3, chap. 15, no. 7, in Martène, *De antiquis ecclesiae ritibus,* 4:142.

[153] Sicard of Cremona, *Mitrale,* bk. 6, chap. 14, PL 213, col. 323.

[154] Text in Franz Arens, ed., *Der Liber ordinarius der Essener Stiftskirche* (Paderborn, Germany: Albert Pape, 1908), 59.

[155] Durandus, *Rationale* (CCCM 140a), bk. 6, chap. 80, no. 9, p. 397.

[156] Ibid., no. 8, p. 397.

[157] *Missale Giennense / Manuale . . . sacramenta* (1499), fols. 84v–85r.

[158] Ibid., fol. 85r.

[159] *Codex Ratoldi* (excerpt), as quoted by Dom Ménard and reprinted in PL 78, col. 336. Both this text of Corbie and the 1570 *Missale Romanum* place the lighting of the Paschal candle one sentence later in the *Exsultet* than does the Jaén missal—at the words *rutilans ignis accendit* ("*the glowing fire kindles*"); see Sodi and Triacca, *Missale Romanum: Editio princeps (1570),* 262 (new pagination).

new doctrine of Christ", the doctrine of the New Testament, the new-ness of which was proclaimed by Christ himself when at the Last Supper he said to his disciples, "A new commandment I give unto you" (Jn 13:34).[160] Sicard of Cremona regards the kindling of the Pas-chal candle as representing the reunion of the soul of Christ with his body wrought by his divinity at the moment of the Resurrection.[161]

In the Jaén rite, the *Exsultet* resumes immediately after the lighting of the Paschal candle, but another pause follows soon afterward for the lighting of the church's other candles: "*But now we have known the praises of this pillar, which the glowing fire kindles to the honor of God.* Here should be lighted all the other lights of the church."[162] The kindling of other lights at this point in the *Exsultet* is traceable to the twelfth-century Roman Pontifical, which directs that seven lamps and two candlesticks should be lit at this moment in the chant.[163] Sicard of Cremona sees the lighting of all the church's candles from the new Easter fire as a visual representation of the Savior's declared intent "to cast fire on the earth" (Lk 12:49).[164] For Durandus, the distribution of the new Easter fire to all of the church's candles signifies that the "fire of the Holy Spirit" proceeds from Christ, symbolized by the Paschal candle, and that it is Christ who illuminates all the faithful.[165]

The words of the *Exsultet* that follow this general illumination speak of how the distribution of Christ's Easter light in no way diminishes it, "*which although it should be divided into parts of borrowed light, [it] has known no loss. It is sustained by the flowing wax that the mother bee has produced in the substance of this precious lamp.*"[166] The text of the *Exsultet* in the Jaén missal includes at this point a passage extolling the bee, the begetter of the wax, as a symbol of the Blessed Virgin Mary, from whose virginal womb was brought forth Christ, whose flesh is sym-bolized by the wax of the Paschal candle: "*O truly blessed and marvelous bee, whose sanctity neither male intercourse violates, nor breeding annuls, nor offspring destroys. Thus did the holy Mary conceive as a Virgin, give birth as a Virgin, and a Virgin she remained.*"[167] The above words, although absent from the 1474 and 1570 editions of the *Missale Romanum*, are traceable to the earliest extant text of the *Exsultet* in the seventh- to eighth-century *Missale Gothicum*[168] and are found in numerous medi-eval missals.[169] The *Exsultet* concludes:

---

[160] Durandus, *Rationale* (CCCM 140a), bk. 6, chap. 80, no. 7, p. 396.

[161] Sicard of Cremona, *Mitrale*, bk. 6, chap. 14, PL 213, col. 324.

[162] *Missale Giennense / Manuale . . . sacramenta* (1499), fol. 85r.

[163] Andrieu, *Pontifical romain au moyen-âge*, 1:240.

[164] Sicard of Cremona, *Mitrale*, bk. 6, chap. 14, PL 213, col. 324.

[165] Durandus, *Rationale* (CCCM 140a), bk. 6, chap. 80, no. 11, p. 398.

[166] *Missale Giennense / Manuale . . . sacramenta* (1499), fol. 85r.

[167] Ibid., fol. 85r–85v.

[168] Mohlberg, *Missale Gothicum*, no. 225, p. 61.

[169] Examples include the missals of Braga, Portugal (1498), and Bayonne, France (1543); see respectively *Missale Bracarense* (1498), sig. k3r, and Dubarat, *Missel de Bayonne de 1543*, 47.

O truly blessed night that despoiled the Egyptians [and] endowed the Hebrews, night in which heavenly things are wedded with those of earth. We therefore entreat you, O Lord, that this candle consecrated to the honor of your name may continue unfailing to destroy the darkness of this night. And having been received in the odor of sweetness, may it mingle with the lights of Heaven. May the morning star find its flames—he, I say, the Morning Star, who knows not setting; he who, having returned from the dead, has shone bright upon mankind. We therefore beseech you, O Lord, that you may vouchsafe to preserve us your servants, and all the clergy, and your most devout people together with our pope, and our king, and likewise our bishop in the peace of the times granted in these Paschal joys. Through our Lord Jesus Christ your Son, who lives and reigns with you in the unity of the Holy Spirit, God, through all ages of ages. Amen.[170]

Following the conclusion of the *Exsultet*, the deacon exchanges his festive white dalmatic for a black or indigo dalmatic corresponding to the black or indigo vestments worn by the rest of the clergy for this first portion of the Easter Vigil. The celebrating priest now recites a Collect (traceable to the seventh-century Gelasian Sacramentary of Rome)[171] asking of God "on this extraordinary night" the sanctification of all the clergy.[172] The 1568 missal of Palencia, Spain, directs that the celebrant, after exchanging his white cope for a red one, should kneel for the recitation of this prayer.[173]

The Old Testament readings follow, which in the case of the Jaén missal are five in number,[174] just as there are five in the Toledo missal of the period.[175] The Jaén selection of readings (Gen 1:1—2:2, the creation of the world; Ex 14:24—15:1, the crossing of the Red Sea; Is 4:1–6, a prophecy of deliverance by God; Is 54:17—55:11, a prophecy of baptism and the redemption of the nations; Deut 31:22–30, Moses' warning to the Israelites as they go to the Promised Land) is traceable to the tenth-century Romano-Germanic Pontifical;[176] the first four readings correspond to those of the seventh-century Paduan redaction of Rome's Gregorian Sacramentary.[177] In the Jaén rite, the first reading concludes with a Collect, while each of the other four readings concludes with both a Tract and a Collect, all of which are found together five centuries earlier in the Romano-Germanic Pontifical.[178] The four Tracts, based upon Old Testament passages (*Cantemus Domino*, Ex 15:1–3; *Vinea facta est*, Is 5:1–2, 7; *Attende caelum*, Deut 32:1–4;

---

[170] *Missale Giennense / Manuale . . . sacramenta* (1499), fols. 85v–86r.

[171] Mohlberg, Eizenhöfer, and Siffrin, *Liber sacramentorum*, no. 431, p. 70.

[172] *Missale Giennense / Manuale . . . sacramenta* (1499), fol. 86r–86v.

[173] *Missale Pallantinum* (1568), fol. 109r–109v.

[174] *Missale Giennense / Manuale . . . sacramenta* (1499), fols. 86v–88v.

[175] *Missale secundum consuetudinem almae ecclesiae Toletanae*, 1503–1518, vol. 4, fols. 122r–132r.

[176] Vogel and Elze, *Pontifical romano-germanique*, 2:100–101.

[177] Deshusses, *Sacramentaire grégorien*, Paduan nos. 322–325, 1:631.

[178] Vogel and Elze, *Pontifical romano-germanique*, 2:100–101.

Sicut cervus, Ps 41:2–4), all traceable as vigil texts to the eighth century,[179] were used at the Easter Vigil throughout medieval Europe, regardless of the number of Old Testament readings, and entered the *Missale Romanum* of 1570.[180] The 1570 missal also inherited the twelve Collects that Saint Benedict of Aniane had assigned to the set of twelve Old Testament readings for the vigil in his early ninth-century redaction of the Gregorian Sacramentary of Rome.[181] The fourth Tract, *Sicut cervus*, which always follows the final Old Testament reading in the medieval rites, serves to anticipate the baptismal focus of the ensuing portion of the Easter Vigil: "*As the hart panteth after the fountains of water, so my soul panteth after thee, O God.* [Verse:] *My soul hath thirsted after the strong living God; when shall I come and appear before the face of my God?* [Verse:] *My tears have been my bread day and night, whilst it is said daily: Where is their God?*"[182]

In continuity with the ancient tradition of administering the sacrament of baptism during the Easter Vigil, medieval liturgical books provide a rite for blessing the baptismal font that could be celebrated during the vigil even when there were no baptisms to be performed. For this portion of the Easter Vigil rite, we turn to a particularly detailed version of the ceremony given in another Spanish liturgical book, the Palencia missal of 1568. The celebrating priest goes in procession to the baptismal font, preceded by clerics carrying spear-mounted candles, regular candlesticks, the Paschal candle, thuribles, and a cross. Upon reaching the font, the priest or the deacon assisting him, facing the people, intones the Litany of the Saints with the *Kyrie eleison* ("*Lord, have mercy*"). Thereafter two priests or clerics, vested in red copes and holding scepters in their hands, continue the litany, with the choir responding to each verse. All kneel for the opening lines of the litany that address God and the Blessed Virgin directly; upon the completion of these verses, when the portion of the litany invoking the saints and angels begins, the faithful rise.[183] The litany of the Palencia vigil is unique in that it includes a blessing

---

[179] All four Tracts are specified for the Easter Vigil in the Cantatorium of Monza (Italy, eighth century) and in the Frankish-Roman Capitulary of Corbie, also known as the *Liber comitis* (c. 775); see respectively René-Jean Hésbert, ed., *Antiphonale missarum sextuplex* (Brussels, 1935; repr., Rome: Herder, 1967), 96, 98, and Walter Howard Frere, *Studies in Early Roman Liturgy*, vol. 3, *The Roman Epistle-Lectionary*, Alcuin Club Collections 32 (Oxford: Oxford University Press; London: Humphrey Milford, 1935), 9–10 (Latin text quoted by permission of Oxford University Press).

[180] Sodi and Triacca, *Missale Romanum: Editio princeps (1570)*, 271, 274, 276, 278 (new pagination).

[181] Ibid., 267, 269–276, 278 (new pagination). For the corresponding Collects in the Aniane redaction of the Gregorian Sacramentary, see Deshusses, *Sacramentaire grégorien*, nos. 1025, 1027, 1029, 1031, 1033, 1035, 1037, 1039, 1041, 1043, 1045, 1047, 1:363–367.

[182] The specific version of *Sicut cervus* given here is that found in the Jaén missal (*Missale Giennense / Manuale . . . sacramenta* [1499], fol. 88v). The second verse differs slightly from the usual text.

[183] *Missale Pallantinum* (1568), fol. 111v. (Latin text provided by Biblioteca Apostolica Vaticana, Vatican City.)

by the celebrant analogous to that found in the litany of ordination rites:

> Then the priest, or the bishop, if he himself carries out the office, even should he not celebrate, standing over the font with his miter and with his crosier in his left hand, in the same tone says:

> *That you may vouchsafe to bless + this water. We beseech you.*
> *That you may vouchsafe to bless + and sancti + fy this water. We beseech you.*
> *That you may vouchsafe to bless + , and sancti + fy, and conse + crate this water. We beseech you.*[184]

The tradition of a litany during the baptismal portion of the Easter Vigil dates back to the seventh century.[185] The customary for the French Benedictine abbey of Cluny compiled by the monk Bernard (c. 1075) directs that during the recitation of the Litany of the Saints at the Easter Vigil, as each individual saint or angel is invoked, those bearing the name of that particular saint or angel should at that moment bow.[186] The Easter Vigil rubrics of the Benedictine customary of Fructuaria, Italy (c. 1085), call for a threefold incensation when the archangels are invoked in the Litany of the Saints, with the first incensation at the naming of Saint Raphael, the second at the naming of Saint Michael, and the third at the naming of Saint Gabriel.[187]

In the Palencia rite, the litany is followed by the solemn blessing of the baptismal font with an ancient consecratory prayer cast in the form of a Preface, a text traceable to the seventh-century Gelasian Sacramentary of Rome[188] and retained in the *Missale Romanum* of 1570.[189] The celebrant, after beginning the blessing with several versicles, a Collect (also from the Gelasian Sacramentary),[190] and the customary introduction for all Prefaces ("*Lift up your hearts . . .*"),[191] continues:

> *Lord, holy Father, almighty eternal God, who with invisible power wonderfully work the effect of your sacraments, and although we be unworthy of carrying out such great mysteries, you, nevertheless, not bearing off the gifts of your grace, incline the ears of your mercy even to our prayers; O God, whose Spirit moved over the waters (during the very beginnings of the world), that the nature of the waters might receive the power of sanctification; O God,*

---

[184] Ibid., fols. 112v–113r.

[185] The seventh-century Gelasian Sacramentary of Rome speaks of a triple litany for this rite; see Mohlberg, Eizenhöfer, and Siffrin, *Liber sacramentorum*, no. 443, p. 72.

[186] *Ordo Cluniacensis*, pt. 2, chap. 18, in Herrgott, *Vetus disciplina monastica*, 318.

[187] *Consuetudines* of Fructuaria, Italy, bk. 1, chap. 48, in Bruno Albers, ed., *Consuetudines monasticae*, vol. 4, *Consuetudines Fructuarienses necnon Cystrensis in Anglia monasterii et congregationis Vallymbrosanae* (Monte Cassino, Italy: Typis Montis Casini, 1911), 67.

[188] Mohlberg, Eizenhöfer, and Siffrin, *Liber sacramentorum*, nos. 445–448, pp. 72–74.

[189] Sodi and Triacca, *Missale Romanum: Editio princeps (1570)*, 279–287 (new pagination).

[190] Mohlberg, Eizenhöfer, and Siffrin, *Liber sacramentorum*, no. 444, p. 72.

[191] *Missale Pallantinum* (1568), fol. 113r–113v.

who indicated the form of our regeneration in the very effusion of the flood, cleansing by waters the sins of a guilty world, that in the mystery of one and the same element there should be both the end to vices and the beginning of virtues; look, O Lord, upon the countenance of your Church, and multiply in her your regenerations, who gladden your city with the vigor of your abounding grace and open to all the earth the way to the font of baptism, with the nations returning [thenceforth], that by the power of your majesty she may obtain the grace of your only-begotten Son from the Holy Spirit,—Here with his hand [the celebrant] should touch the water, dividing it in the manner of a cross—*who makes this water fruitful in regenerating men, prepared with the hidden admixture of his divine power, that a heavenly progeny, conceived by his sanctification, may come forth from the immaculate womb of this divine font as a new and spiritually reborn creature*—Here the priest should touch the water with his hand—*and grace [as a] mother may bring forth to one and the same infancy all whom either gender in the flesh or age in time distinguishes. Therefore, may every unclean spirit henceforth depart far away, by you commanding this, O Lord; may all wickedness of diabolical deception be banished away. May the intervention of the hostile enemy have no place here, nor hover about lying in wait, nor creep up in hiding, nor corrupt by polluting.* Here he touches the water. *May this creature be holy and innocent, free from every assault of the enemy and cleansed by the banishment of all wickedness.* Here with his hand he should make in the water the sign of the cross. *May it be a living + font, regenerative + water, a purifying + stream, that all to be washed in this salubrious bath, with your Holy Spirit working in them, may obtain the pardon of perfect purification. Wherefore I bless + you, O creature of water, by the living + God, by the true + God, by the holy + God, by God who in the beginning separated you from the dry land with his word, whose Spirit moved over you, who made you to flow from the fountain of Paradise and commanded you to irrigate all the earth, dividing you into four rivers,*—Here he pours out water on four sides outside the font in the form of a cross, saying,

Gehon,

Tigris, + Euphrates,

Phison,[192]

who made you, bitter in the desert, to be drinkable, with sweetness given you, and brought you forth from the rock for a thirsty people. I bless + you by Jesus Christ, his only Son, our Lord, who in a wonderful sign of his power changed you into wine at Cana of Galilee; who with his feet walked upon you, and in you was baptized by John in the Jordan; who brought you forth together with blood from his side, and commanded his disciples that those believing should be baptized in you, saying, "Go, teach all nations, baptizing them in the name of the Father, and of the Son, and of the Holy Spirit"

---

[192] These four rivers are named in the Book of Genesis (Gen 2:10–14).

[cf. Mt 28:19]. Here the priest should change his voice to the tone of a reading, saying: *Look favorably upon us observing these precepts, O you, almighty, merciful God; may you, O gracious One, breathe,*—Here he should breathe upon the font and make with his breath the sign of the cross, repeating thrice the same words, *Look favorably upon us observing these precepts,* etc., ever in a higher tone; and each time he breathes upon the water. Then he should continue the blessing, saying, *you, upon these,* in the tone with which he had begun—*you, upon these simple waters with your bless + ed mouth, that beyond the natural cleansing that they are able to administer in washing bodies, they may also be efficacious in purifying souls.* Here he should put the Paschal candle into the water and say: *May the power of the Holy Spirit descend into the plenitude of this font and fill the entire substance of this water with the effect of regeneration.* Here he should raise the candle from the font and put several tiny drops of wax into the water, in the manner of a cross, saying in silence, *In the name of the Father, and of the Son, and of the Holy Spirit. Amen.* [He continues:] *Here may the stains of all sins be blotted out; here may nature be well cleansed of all its squalid former ways, fashioned unto your image and restored to the glory of its beginning, that every man, having entered upon this sacrament of regeneration, may be born again to a new infancy of true innocence. Through our Lord Jesus Christ your Son, who is going to come to judge the living and the dead and the world by fire.* Response: *Amen.* The blessing of the font having been completed, the sacristan should keep blessed water for the aspersion of the following day. And as many as shall have wished take from this water out of devotion, that their homes may have it for pious uses.[193]

Commenting on the various actions accompanying the above prayer, Durandus observes that the priest touches the water and divides it with the sign of the cross, that the Holy Spirit may make the baptismal water fruitful and expel Satan from it.[194] The fourfold pouring of water on the four sides of the font in conjunction with the naming of the four rivers of Paradise is explained by Durandus as symbolizing that "the grace of baptism should be extended to the four quarters of the world." [195] The plunging of the Paschal candle into the water of the font represents not only the coming of the Holy Spirit, descending upon the waters of the Jordan River in the form of a dove at Christ's baptism (Mt 3:16), but also the conferral of sanctification and regenerative power upon the waters of baptism wrought when the body of Christ, which the candle signifies, entered the waters of the Jordan at his baptism (Mk 1:9–10); this immersion of the candle likewise denotes the remission of sins obtained for us by the death of

---

[193] *Missale Pallantinum* (1568), fols. 113v–119v. (Latin text provided by Biblioteca Apostolica Vaticana, Vatican City.)

[194] Durandus, *Rationale* (CCCM 140a), bk. 6, chap. 82, no. 4, p. 409.

[195] Ibid., no. 8, p. 411.

Christ.[196] The priest breathes upon the font that Satan may be driven out, in fulfillment of Christ's words, "Now shall the prince of this world be cast out" (Jn 12:31).[197]

The blessing of the baptismal font was followed by the actual administration of baptism when there were candidates for the sacrament. As the conferral of baptism shortly after birth became almost universal in a largely Christianized Europe, the need to administer this sacrament during the Easter Vigil vastly declined in the Middle Ages, but even toward the end of the medieval era, some liturgical books still provided for cases of vigil baptisms.[198] Insofar as we have already discussed in full the medieval rite of baptism (chapter 3), we shall not repeat this subject here.

In the Italian city of Lucca, the return from the baptismal font became the occasion for a ceremony utilizing the "King of glory" verses of Psalm 23 that, as we have already seen, inspired several Holy Week rites. The late thirteenth-century *Ordo officiorum* of Lucca, in its rubrics for the Easter Vigil celebrated at the Church of Saint Reparata, relates that after the bishop and the clergy go out temporarily to the Church of Saint John for the vigil's baptismal rite, they return to the Church of Saint Reparata in procession, singing the Holy Week antiphon *Cum Rex gloriae* ("*When Christ the King of glory*"; complete text on p. 430 of the present work). Upon arriving before the door of the church, the bishop declares, "*Lift up your gates, O ye princes, and be ye lifted up, O eternal gates: and the King of Glory shall enter in.*" Thus begins the same threefold dialogue that we saw earlier in the Palencia Palm Sunday procession, with one within the closed door of the church asking thrice, "*Who is this King of Glory?*" When the bishop answers for the third time, "*The Lord of hosts, he is the King of Glory*", the door is opened, the bishop and the clergy enter, and the bells of Saint Reparata begin to toll, to which all the churches of the city reply by ringing their bells. The bishop proceeds to a cross suspended in the middle of the church and, halting before it, declares, "*Now Christ the Lord has risen.*" The choir answers, "*Thanks be to God.*" This proclamation and the response are repeated three times, with the bishop raising his voice higher each time. Then a cantor sings four times, "*Alleluia*", after which the bishop, immediately upon reaching the altar, intones in a high voice the *Gloria*.[199]

---

[196] Ibid., no. 10, p. 412.

[197] Ibid., no. 11, pp. 412–413.

[198] The rite of baptism is included in the Easter Vigil rubrics of the 1487 *Obsequiale Augustense* of Augsburg, Germany, and the 1536 *Ordinarium* of Urgel (La Seu d'Urgell), Spain; see respectively *Obsequiale Augustense* (Augsburg, Germany: Erhard Ratdolt, 1487; digitized text, Bayerische Staatsbibliothek, Munich, 2008), fols. 27r–35r; Parés i Saltor, *Ordinari d'Urgell de 1536*, 162–166.

[199] M. Giusti, "L'*Ordo officiorum* di Lucca", in *Miscellanea Giovanni Mercati*, vol. 2, *Letteratura medioevale*, ST 122 (Vatican City: Biblioteca Apostolica Vaticana, 1946), 547–548.

For the remainder of the Easter Vigil rite, we shall return to the 1499 missal of Jaén. The rubrics direct that after the blessing of the baptismal font concludes, the celebrating priest and those ministering to him withdraw into the sacristy to remove their "Lenten vestments" and take in their place white vestments.[200] Honorius of Autun sees the clergy's assumption of Easter vestments as a symbol of the catechumens' reception of their baptismal robes.[201] In a similar vein, Durandus considers the clergy's "precious and splendid" Easter vestments an image of the "garments of the virtues" with which the newly baptized are adorned.[202] In the Jaén rite, the candles of the high altar have remained unlit up to this point in the vigil (unlike the other church candles that were lit during the *Exsultet*). They are now lit to the accompaniment of the threefold proclamation of the command "*Accendite*" ("*Light!*"): "Two cantors should begin, *Accendite,* singing it three times, and raising their voice higher each time. And immediately the candles that are at the major altar should be lit. And the *Accendite* having been completed, the choir should begin the *Kirios* [i.e., "*Lord, have mercy; Christ, have mercy; Lord, have mercy*"] in their regular order."[203]

The chanting of the *Accendite* at the Easter Vigil, a custom traceable to the second half of the eighth century[204] and enduring in some places until the sixteenth century,[205] constituted a moment of particular jubilation. According to the rubrics of a twelfth-century pontifical of the French monastery of Saint-Germain-des-Prés, it was at this point during the vigil that the candles held by the newly baptized were lit.[206] But across much of medieval Europe, there was another moment during the vigil Mass, a moment shortly after the *Accendite,* that became even more pronounced as the symbolic point of transition from Lent to Easter: the singing of the *Gloria.* Durandus observes that in singing this hymn of the angels the choir rejoices with the angels that the Savior's Resurrection is at hand.[207] Moreover, in this particular context, the *Gloria* serves as a testament that those newly baptized on Easter night are given the peace announced by the angels in their *Gloria* on the night of Christ's birth; by their baptism the neophytes are enabled to sing with the angels.[208] In the Jaén vigil rite, the rubrics for the *Gloria* specify, "The priest should say solemnly,

---

[200] *Missale Giennense / Manuale . . . sacramenta* (1499), fol. 93v.

[201] Honorius of Autun, *Gemma animae,* bk. 3, chap. 118, PL 172, col. 674.

[202] Durandus, *Rationale* (CCCM 140a), bk. 6, chap. 85, no. 1, p. 434.

[203] *Missale Giennense / Manuale . . . sacramenta* (1499), fol. 93v.

[204] The *Accendite* is first mentioned in the Frankish-Roman document Roman *Ordo* 27 (c. 750–800); see Andrieu, *Ordines Romani du haut moyen âge,* 3:361.

[205] As late as 1543, the *Accendite* is found in the missal of Bayonne, France (Dubarat, *Missel de Bayonne de 1543,* 49).

[206] Martène, *De antiquis ecclesiae ritibus,* bk. 4, chap. 24, 3:160.

[207] Durandus, *Rationale* (CCCM 140a), bk. 6, chap. 85, no. 3, p. 435.

[208] Ibid.

Glory to God in the highest. And immediately all the bells should be rung, both the larger and the smaller; and the altars and the gold retables [altarpieces] with the black frontals should be uncovered, and all things should appear festive." [209]

The unveiling of the festive Easter frontal of the high altar, described above in conjunction with the *Gloria*, had its earliest antecedent in the aforementioned fifth- to seventh-century Easter lighting rite of the Spanish *Liber ordinum*, in which the bishop would emerge from the sacristy with the lighted Paschal candle after the veil before the sacristy door had been lifted. Toward the end of the tenth century, we find the earliest reference to an unveiling of the altar during the Easter Vigil in a customary of the Swiss Benedictine abbey of Einsiedeln (c. 984). The rubrics direct that the high altar, which has been lavishly decorated with altar cloths and other adornments before the vigil, is to be kept covered with linen cloths until the actual Mass of the Easter Vigil begins, at which time the cloths are removed. Following the conclusion of the vigil, the altar is again covered with linen cloths, which remain in place until they are removed once more for the first Vespers of Easter. After Vespers, for the third and final time the altar is covered with linen cloths, which are removed permanently when the Gospel is read during the night office of Matins. [210]

A century later, at the French Benedictine abbey of Cluny, there existed a somewhat similar custom for the night office of Matins on Easter Sunday and other major solemnities, as related by the monk Bernard in his customary for the abbey (c. 1075): "Also, the major altar should be adorned with three palls; and at the *Glory be* of the fourth responsory [of Matins] one of them is taken away, and another at the *Glory be* of the eighth, but the third after the pronouncement of the Gospel, when also the [altar] table and the remaining ornaments of the altar are uncovered." [211] Just such an unveiling of the high altar during the night office of Easter is described and explained by John Beleth (+1182), who relates that over the Easter frontal three other frontals would be hung—the outermost black, the second under it off-white, and the third underneath red. They were to be removed in succession: the black cloth after the first reading and responsory, the off-white cloth after the second reading and responsory, and the red cloth after the third reading and responsory, revealing at last the festive Easter frontal, which was sometimes gold colored. The removal of the black frontal signified the ending of the first phase of history, before the Mosaic Law. The off-white frontal's removal signaled the end of the age of the Mosaic Law. Lastly, the red frontal, representing the age

---

[209] *Missale Giennense / Manuale . . . sacramenta* (1499), fol. 93v. Virtually identical rubrics appear in the Toledo missal; see *Missale secundum consuetudinem almae ecclesiae Toletanae,* 1503–1518, vol. 4, fol. 133v.

[210] Albers, *Consuetudines monasticae,* 5:95.

[211] *Ordo Cluniacensis,* pt. 1, chap. 50, in Herrgott, *Vetus disciplina monastica,* 244.

of grace wrought by the Passion of Christ, was removed to signify that by the Passion "the gate to eternal glory lies open to us."[212]

By the end of the fifteenth century, the unveiling of the high altar had become a feature of the Easter Vigil liturgy in Spain.[213] In the Holy Saturday rubrics of the 1568 missal of Palencia, Spain, it is not a frontal but a large veil concealing the entire altar, comparable to the Lenten veil (described on pp. 297–300 of the present work), that is removed when the *Gloria* begins: "These things having been completed, the priest says, *Glory to God in the highest*. Which when it is said, the veil that is before the altar is taken away.... And all the bells, the larger and the smaller, both in the chapel and in the tower of the church, and in the church itself, and the organs, and all the musical instruments that shall have been in the church, are sounded."[214]

The custom of ringing the church bells at or shortly before the moment when the *Gloria* is begun during the Easter vigil is traceable to the eighth century, when it is mentioned for the first time in Roman *Ordo* 16 (c. 750–787): "When, however, they shall have rung the bell, they [the priests] with the deacons proceed from the sacristy, with lit candles [or] with thuribles . . . , and enter into the church, performing the litany. The litany, however, having been completed, the abbot or priest who celebrates the Masses begins, *Glory to God in the highest* . . ."[215] By the second half of the ninth century, the moment for beginning the pealing of the bells had shifted to the very moment when the *Gloria* begins, as stated in a rubric of Roman *Ordo* 31 (c. 850–900): "The litany having been completed, the bishop should say, *Glory to God in the highest*, and the bells should be rung."[216] In specifying this observance, a fifteenth-century customary for the Sarum Rite of Salisbury, England, explains: "Because this night of the Lord's Resurrection is illuminated by so great a light, rightfully should the angelic hymn *Gloria in excelsis* be most devoutly celebrated, inasmuch as those who were in the darkness of their sins return to the light of the virtues, and those whom the devil possessed, the Holy Spirit [now] inhabits."[217]

Several texts enjoin an act of reverent worship when the *Gloria* begins: the Benedictine customary of Gorze, France, compiled by Abbot Sigibert (c. 1030) directs the monks to kneel,[218] as does the fifteenth-century

---

[212] Beleth, *Summa de ecclesiasticis officiis* (CCCM 41a), chap. 115, p. 218.

[213] In addition to the 1499 Jaén missal, the 1500 *Missal mixtum* compiled by Cardinal Francisco Ximenes de Cisneros for the celebration of Spain's Mozarabic Rite in Toledo also specifies an unveiling of the altar at the *Gloria* (*Missale mixtum secundum regulam beati Isidori dictum mozarabes*, PL 85, col. 470).

[214] *Missale Pallantinum* (1568), fol. 120r. (Latin text provided by Biblioteca Apostolica Vaticana, Vatican City.)

[215] Text in Andrieu, *Ordines Romani du haut moyen âge*, 3:153.

[216] Text ibid., 504.

[217] Text in Walter Howard Frere, ed., *The Use of Sarum* (Cambridge: Cambridge University Press, 1898–1901), 1:151 (left column).

[218] *Consuetudines* of Sigibert, chap. 32, in Albers, *Consuetudines monasticae*, 2:101.

Sarum Customary, which adds that the choristers should also lay aside their black copes as the *Gloria* is begun.[219] The *Ordo divinorum officiorum* of the Camaldolese Order (c. 1253) specifies that when the priest intones "in a joyful voice" the words "*Glory to God in the highest*", all are to drop to their knees as they respond, "*And on earth peace to men*", continuing with the rest of the *Gloria*.[220] The Benedictine customary of Fructuaria, Italy (c. 1085), instructs the monks to prostrate themselves for the *Gloria*.[221]

The papal ceremonial known as the Long Ceremonial, attributed to John of Sion and dating from shortly before 1342, directs that after the conclusion of the Epistle the subdeacon who has read it bows toward the pope and, addressing him, sings, "*I announce unto you a great joy, alleluia.*" He then kisses the foot of the pontiff, after which the pope stands and the deacon sings, "*Alleluia.*" The pope then sings the *Alleluia* three times, raising his voice higher each time, with the choir repeating the *Alleluia* after him. Two cantors now sing the verse "*Give praise to the Lord, for he is good; for his mercy endureth for ever*" (Ps 117:1); the Tract and the Gospel follow.[222] This ceremony marks the moment when the word *Alleluia*, absent from the liturgy throughout the Lenten season, is heard again for the first time; the triple repetition of the *Alleluia* before the Easter Vigil Gospel, first mentioned in the twelfth-century Roman Pontifical,[223] was later retained in the *Missale Romanum* of 1570.[224] Commenting upon this singing of the *Alleluia* at the Easter Vigil, Durandus sees it as representing the song of the angels in Heaven, described as singing *Alleluia* in the Book of Revelation (19:1), who "glory on account of the baptized, delivered from servitude to the devil and converted to the faith"; this Hebrew word, he notes, is sung before the Latin of the Tract that follows it, for "the Hebrew language is the mother and noblest of all languages by reason of the authority of divine Scripture, Latin, however, as though a daughter, being lower." [225]

The Collect, the Secret, the Preface, and the special insertions within the Roman Canon for the Easter Vigil Mass were the same throughout late medieval Europe, all traceable to seventh-century Rome[226]

[219] Frere, *Use of Sarum*, 1:151 (left column).

[220] *Vetus ordo divinorum officiorum* (compiled by Abbot Martin III), chap. 49, in John-Benedict Mittarelli and Anselm Costadoni, eds., *Annales Camaldulenses ordinis sancti Benedicti* (Venice: Monastery of Saint Michael of Muriano and John Baptist Pasquali, 1761), vol. 6, col. 132.

[221] *Consuetudines* of Fructuaria, Italy, bk. 1, chap. 48, in Albers, *Consuetudines monasticae*, 4:68.

[222] Dykmans, *Cérémonial papal de la fin du moyen âge à la Renaissance*, 3:227.

[223] Andrieu, *Pontifical romain au moyen-âge*, 1:248.

[224] Sodi and Triacca, *Missale Romanum: Editio princeps (1570)*, 290 (new pagination).

[225] Durandus, *Rationale* (CCCM 140a), bk. 6, chap. 85, nos. 3, 4, pp. 436–437.

[226] All of these texts are found in both the Paduan redaction of the Gregorian Sacramentary of Rome and the Gelasian Sacramentary of Rome; see respectively Deshusses, *Sacramentaire grégorien*, Paduan nos. 327–331, 1:631; Mohlberg, Eizenhöfer, and Siffrin, *Liber sacramentorum*, nos. 454, 456, 458–460, pp. 75–76.

and all subsequently retained in the *Missale Romanum* of 1570,[227] as were the Gospel verse and the Tract, the latter two traceable as vigil chants to the eighth century.[228] The other Mass chants, namely those of the Offertory and Communion, were omitted on Easter night. The Epistle assigned to the Easter Vigil in the seventh-century Roman lectionary known as the *Comes* of Würzburg, from the Letter of Saint Paul to the Colossians (Col 3:1–4),[229] prevailed in the medieval rites. Similarly, Saint Matthew's account of the events of Easter morning (Mt 28:1–7), used in the Easter Vigil liturgy of fifth-century Jerusalem as recounted in the Armenian Lectionary (which we described earlier), served as the vigil's Gospel in the Roman liturgy from the seventh century onward.[230] The practice of omitting on this occasion the customary lit candles for the reading of the Gospel, an omission first mentioned in Roman *Ordo* 24 (c. 750–800), such that only incense would be brought for the reading, is explained in a rubric of Cardinal Bernard of Porto's *Ordo officiorum* for Rome's Church of Saint John Lateran (c. 1140) as signifying the circumstances with which Saint Matthew's Gospel account begins—that in the hearts of the holy women coming to anoint the body of Jesus, "the light of truth had not yet arisen, but while there was still darkness, they came to the tomb with spices."[231] Durandus also identifies the incense with the spices brought by the holy women.[232] The Easter Vigil rite from the Jaén missal, imitating a custom of Jaén's parent see, Toledo, found nowhere else, calls for a dramatic sign to mark the moment when the women first learn of the Resurrection: "The deacon should say the Gospel [Mt 28:1–7]; and there should be carried the censer, with incense for censing, and unlit candles; and when he shall have come to that part which says, *The Lord has risen indeed just as he said*, the aforesaid candles should be lighted."[233] A rubric identical to that above appears in the Toledo missal of this period.[234]

The 1568 missal of Palencia, Spain, concludes the Easter Vigil with the ringing of all the bells, followed by the celebration of Vespers.[235]

---

[227] Sodi and Triacca, *Missale Romanum: Editio princeps (1570)*, 290–292 (new pagination).

[228] These two chants (*Confitemini Domino* and *Laudate Dominum*) are first specified for the Easter Vigil Mass in the Cantatorium of Monza (Italy, eighth century); see Hésbert, *Antiphonale missarum sextuplex*, 98.

[229] Text in Germain Morin, "Le plus ancien *Comes* ou Lectionnaire de l'église romaine," *Revue Bénédictine* 27 (1910): 55.

[230] This Gospel is first listed for the Roman Rite Easter Vigil in the seventh-century Capitulary of Würzburg; see Germain Morin, "Liturgie et basiliques de Rome au milieu du VIIe siècle d'après les listes d'évangiles de Würzburg", *Revue Bénédictine* 28 (1911): 304.

[231] Fischer, *Bernhardi cardinalis ... Ordo officiorum ecclesiae Lateranensis*, 74. A modified form of this explanatory rubric appears in the 1498 *Missale Bracarense* of Braga, Portugal; see *Missale Bracarense* (1498), sig. k5r.

[232] Durandus, *Rationale* (CCCM 140a), bk. 6, chap. 85, no. 5, p. 438.

[233] *Missale Giennense / Manuale ... sacramenta* (1499), fol. 94r.

[234] See *Missale secundum consuetudinem almae ecclesiae Toletanae*, 1503–1518, vol. 4, fol. 135r.

[235] *Missale Pallantinum* (1568), fol. 121r.

The medieval practice of concluding the Easter Vigil Mass with a truncated form of Vespers immediately following Holy Communion appeared in the tenth century, when it is mentioned in the Romano-Germanic Pontifical.[236] This Vespers rite consisted only of an opening *Alleluia*, Psalm 116 (*Laudate Dominum, omnes gentes*), the *Magnificat* (the latter with an accompanying antiphon), and a Collect traceable to the Easter Vigil of seventh-century Rome.[237] Upon the Collect's conclusion, the closing versicle of Mass, "*Ite, missa est*" ("*Go, it is ended*"), would be pronounced, bringing the vigil liturgy to an end.[238] This fusion of Vespers with the end of the vigil Mass subsequently entered the *Missale Romanum* of 1570.[239]

Archbishop John of Avranches (+1079), in his *Liber de officiis ecclesiasticis* for the French see of Rouen, speaks of a custom where the faithful would bring the light of the new Easter fire back from the church to their own homes to kindle their lights.[240] Similarly, the twelfth-century pontifical of the French monastery of Saint-Germain-des-Prés enjoins that all lights in the homes should be extinguished beforehand in order that the light from the newly blessed Easter fire might be brought into every home.[241] John of Avranches sees this practice as showing mystically that the light of Christ's divinity, hidden in his flesh until the Passion but now shining forth in the Church by his Passion and Resurrection, and hence in the hearts of the faithful, resounds in the world through the profession of Christ's doctrine by the faithful.[242]

Easter Sunday

In the medieval liturgy of Easter Sunday (as distinguished from that of the Easter Vigil), there were no *universally* observed special ceremonies that would have outwardly distinguished this day's Mass and office from other days. Nonetheless, numerous dioceses and monasteries incorporated into their liturgical books local rites that visually represented and even dramatically reenacted the Gospel accounts of the first Easter Sunday. Two symbolic practices of this nature can be found in the papal liturgy of medieval Rome. The first of these evokes what is stated in the Gospel of Saint Luke—that Christ following his Resurrection appeared separately to Saint Peter before appearing to the other Apostles (Lk 24:34). A late twelfth-century text of Rome known as the *Liber censuum* (c. 1192) describes a rite at the Roman basilica of Saint Lawrence, better known as the Church of the Sancta Sanctorum, that

---

[236] Vogel and Elze, *Pontifical Romano-Germanique*, 2:111.

[237] For this Postcommunion from the Paduan redaction of the Gregorian Sacramentary of Rome (seventh century), see Deshusses, *Sacramentaire grégorien*, Paduan no. 332, 1:631.

[238] See the twelfth-century Roman Pontifical in Andrieu, *Pontifical romain au moyen-âge*, 1:249.

[239] Sodi and Triacca, *Missale Romanum: Editio princeps (1570)*, 293 (new pagination).

[240] John of Avranches, *Liber de officiis ecclesiasticis*, PL 147, col. 49.

[241] Martène, *De antiquis ecclesiae ritibus*, bk. 4, chap. 24, 3:160.

[242] John of Avranches, *Liber de officiis ecclesiasticis*, PL 147, col. 49.

the pope carried out before Mass on the morning of Easter Sunday, in which the Sancta Sanctorum's relic of the True Cross and its ancient icon of Christ, the *Acheiropita*, were both venerated by the pontiff:

> Rising, [the pope] enters to adore the Savior. He opens the image, [and] kisses the feet of the Savior, saying in a high voice three times, *The Lord has risen from the sepulcher*; and all answer him, *He who hung upon the wood for us, alleluia.*[243] Then the acolytes place the cross of the chapel upon the altar, and the lord pope worships it, after the kissing of the Savior, with all the others. He then returns to his seat and gives the peace [i.e., the sign of peace] to the archdeacon returning from the kiss of the feet of his [Christ's] image, saying, *The Lord has truly risen*; and he [the archdeacon] responds, *And he has appeared to Simon.*[244]

This custom, first mentioned in a slightly earlier liturgical text of Rome, the *Ordo* of Benedict, known also as the *Liber politicus* (c. 1140),[245] was continued into the fourteenth century, when it appears in the papal ceremonial of Cardinal Giacomo Stefaneschi (c. 1325),[246] but it fell into disuse when the place of papal residence shifted for several decades to Avignon, France. This observance was restored in an adapted form by Pope Blessed John Paul II in 2000.[247]

Another action of a symbolic nature in the medieval papal Mass of Easter Sunday is fully described in the rubrics of the 1488 *Caeremoniale Romanum* of the papal master of ceremonies Patrizio Piccolomini. Two clerics would be assigned to this silent representation during the portion of the Mass encompassing the Roman Canon:

> When the pope says *Through all ages of ages* before the Preface, or a little before, two younger cardinal deacons, besides those who assist the pope, or if deacons are lacking, two younger cardinal priests, come near to the altar, one at the right, the other at the left side of the altar; and standing on either side, the one gazes upon the face of the other, or as others propose, and better, they look toward the people, representing the two angels who appeared in white, watching the

---

[243] The versicle *Surrexit Dominus de sepulchro* is traceable to the Antiphonary of Compiègne (France, c. 870); see René-Jean Hésbert, ed., *Corpus antiphonalium officii*, vol. 1, REDSMF 7 (Rome: Herder, 1963), 180.

[244] Text in Paul Fabre and Louis Duchesne, eds., *Le Liber censuum de l'église romaine*, vol. 1, fasc. 2, Bibliothèque des écoles françaises d'Athènes et de Rome, 2nd series, Registres des papes du XIIIᵉ siècle, 6 (Paris: Fontemoing, 1901), no. 32, p. 297. The versicle *Surrexit Dominus vere* is traceable to the Mass antiphonary of Rheinau (Switzerland, c. 800), in which it appears as the *Alleluia* verse for the Fourth Sunday after Easter; see Hésbert, *Antiphonale missarum sextuplex*, 243.

[245] *Ordo* of Benedict, in Fabre and Duchesne, *Liber censuum de l'église romaine*, vol. 2, fasc. 3, no. 45, p. 152.

[246] Dykmans, *Cérémonial papal de la fin du moyen âge à la Renaissance*, 2:397–398.

[247] Pierro Marini, "Peter, Witness of the Resurrection: Historical and Liturgical Notes", Vatican News Services, April 23, 2000, http://www.vatican.va/news_services/liturgy/documents/ns_lit_doc_20000423_easter_en.html.

sepulcher of the Savior; which [two] ought to remain in the same place up to the *Lamb of God*. When the pope ascends to his throne, they then depart, returning to their place.[248]

The Long Ceremonial, attributed to John of Sion and dating from shortly before 1342, is the earliest papal text to describe this custom.[249] It appears to be a variant or derivation of an Easter office custom mentioned in the late thirteenth century by Durandus in which two cantors in surplices would be placed behind the altar to represent the two angels at the tomb.[250]

In diocesan and monastic rites that on Good Friday had commemorated the burial of Christ with one or another form of the *Depositio* rite, in which the Eucharist, or a crucifix or statue of Christ resting in death, or the Eucharist together with one of these images, had been placed in a symbolic sepulcher (the Easter sepulchre), there was on Easter Sunday morning a sequel to represent the Resurrection of Christ, the *Elevatio* ceremony, bringing to a triumphant conclusion the watch of prayer that had been maintained at the symbolic tomb since Good Friday. It was conducted as early as midnight of Easter Sunday.[251] The *Elevatio* rite observed in the cathedral of Esztergom, Hungary, as described in a liturgical book for the church dating from 1460–1464, would be conducted in the morning, "after the last homily". The church's choristers sing the following responsory (from Mk 16:1) as they accompany the bishop and the clerics assisting him in a procession to the Easter sepulcher, where the Blessed Sacrament and a small cross (probably a crucifix) have been reserved since Good Friday: "*When the Sabbath was past, Mary Magdalene, and Mary the mother of James, and Salome, brought sweet spices, that coming, they might anoint Jesus. Alleluia, alleluia.*"[252] As the assisting clerics stand near the sepulcher with lit candles, the bishop censes the Blessed Sacrament. He then takes out of the sepulcher the Eucharist and the cross to the accompaniment of the versicle "*The Lord has risen from the tomb, alleluia, he who hung upon the Cross for us.*" The bishop now symbolically reenacts the risen Christ's first revelation of himself to the frightened Apostles gathered in the locked Upper Room (Jn 20:19–20): "Then the lord bishop or curate, approaching the Body of Christ, holding it in his hand upon a paten, honorably and with the greatest reverence, should turn himself three times toward the people with the Body of

---

[248] Text in Dykmans, *Oeuvre de Patrizi Piccolomini*, 2:412–413.

[249] Dykmans, *Cérémonial papal de la fin du moyen âge à la Renaissance*, 3:163, 232.

[250] Durandus, *Rationale* (CCCM 140a), bk. 6, chap. 89, no. 15, pp. 470–471.

[251] See, for example, the *Elevatio* in the sixteenth-century Directory of the breviary and missal of Bamberg, Germany, in Walther Lipphardt, ed., *Lateinische Osterfeiern und Osterspiele*, Ausgaben deutscher Literatur des XV. bis XVIII. Jahrhunderts: Reihe drama 5 (Berlin: Walter de Gruyter, 1975–1981), 2:243–244.

[252] The responsory *Dum transisset sabbatum* is traceable to the Antiphonary of Compiègne (France, c. 870); see Hésbert, *Corpus antiphonalium officii*, 1:178.

Christ, singing, *Peace be with you*, with its *Alleluia*. The choir responds: *Do not fear, alleluia.*" The bishop, carrying the Eucharist, now goes in procession with the assisting clerics and the choristers back to the cathedral's choir as the hymn of thanksgiving *Te Deum* is sung.[253]

In Płock, Poland, according to a breviary of this diocese dating from 1520, the Easter morning procession of the clergy to the Easter sepulcher would be conducted in silence, with all carrying lit candles. But afterward, when the Blessed Sacrament had been brought forth from the sepulcher, it would be carried triumphantly in a monstrance three times around the church to the accompaniment of the continuous pealing of the "greater bells" and the singing of the Holy Week antiphon *Cum Rex gloriae*, in the course of which the priest carrying the monstrance would intone the antiphon's versicle, *Advenisti desiderabilis*: "*You have come, O desired One, whom we have awaited in darkness, that you may lead forth this night those imprisoned by bars; our sighs have burned with love for you; our abundant laments have sought you; you have been made the hope of the hopeless, our bountiful consolation amid torments.*"[254]

The rubrics for the Easter *Elevatio* rite in the 1487 *Obsequiale Augustense*, a liturgical book of Augsburg, Germany, direct that after the Eucharist and the crucifix have been taken out of the Easter sepulcher, they are to be carried in a procession through either the church's cloister or its cemetery, with the Eucharist borne ahead of the crucifix in a monstrance or a pyx. When routed through the cemetery, this procession would have brought to mind Christ's coming at the end of the world to raise the dead from their graves. Before the procession reenters the church, there is at the door a three-staged dialogue between the presiding bishop or priest in the procession and a youth behind the closed door, utilizing the words of Psalm 23 (verses 7–10) in the same manner that we saw this psalm used in the Palm Sunday procession of Palencia, Spain ("*Lift up your gates, O ye princes, and be ye lifted up, O eternal gates: and the King of Glory shall enter in . . .*"). The Easter version of this custom, as we find it here in the Augsburg rite, known as the "Harrowing of Hell", was specifically intended to represent Christ's descent into Sheol following his death to liberate the souls of the just who had been barred from Heaven until his coming.[255] In the Augsburg rite, after three knocks upon the door and the

---

[253] *Epitome* of Esztergom, Hungary, 1460–1464, in Radó and Mezey, *Libri liturgici manuscripti bibliothecarum Hungariae*, 490.

[254] *Breviarium Plocense* (1520), in Lipphardt, *Lateinische Osterfeiern und Osterspiele*, 2:623–624; as this source provides only the incipit of *Advenisti*, the complete versicle is here taken from the text of the antiphon *Cum Rex gloriae* in Karl Young, *The Drama of the Medieval Church* (Oxford: Clarendon Press, 1933), 1:151 (Latin text quoted and translated by permission of Oxford University Press). *Cum Rex gloriae* is discussed and presented in full on p. 430 of the present work.

[255] For more on the "Harrowing of Hell" Easter rites, see Young, *Drama of the Medieval Church*, 1:152–177, and James Monti, *The Week of Salvation: History and Traditions of Holy Week* (Huntington, Ind.: Our Sunday Visitor, 1993), 316–318, 395–396.

completion of the psalm verses, the door is opened and the procession enters the church. The crucifix is laid to rest before the high altar, where it is incensed. At the altar, the celebrant turns toward the people with the monstrance or pyx in his hands, showing them the Eucharist and singing thrice, each time in a higher voice, the one-verse hymn *O vere digna Hostia* ("*O truly worthy Victim, by whom the realms of hell are shattered, a captive people is redeemed, [and] the rewards of life are restored*").[256]

The 1493 *Obsequiale Frisingense* of Freising, Germany, provides a Paschal veneration of the cross in which the crucifix that has been ceremonially raised from the Easter sepulcher in the *Elevatio* rite is kissed by all the faithful, each of whom when venerating the cross says the versicle "*The Lord has risen; let us all rejoice.*"[257] This ceremony may possibly be a descendant of the papal veneration of the True Cross mentioned in the earlier-quoted Easter Sunday rubrics of the late twelfth-century *Liber censuum*.

Across most of central and northern Europe, and in some regions of southern Europe, Easter Sunday was also marked by a liturgical dramatization of the discovery of the empty tomb on the first Easter, a rite known as the *Visitatio sepulchri* (Visit of the sepulcher). These ceremonies, traceable to the tenth century,[258] have been widely discussed and documented as the highest expression of medieval drama.[259] We present here a single example, possessing the distinction of having been composed by a canonized saint, the Jesuit Francis Borgia (+1572). The work was composed in 1550, on the eve of the Council of Trent, for the royal monastery of Santa Clara in Borgia's own city of Gandía, Spain. It is evident from the contents of this liturgical drama that Francis Borgia must have consulted the text of Venice's *Visitatio sepulchri* given in a 1523 book of liturgical ceremonies, the *Liber sacerdotalis*, compiled by the Dominican priest Alberto Castellani.[260] Francis bestowed the institution of this Easter ceremony upon the monastery

---

[256] *Obsequiale Augustense* (1487), fols. 36r–38r. The chant *O vere digna Hostia* is at least as old as the twelfth century, when it appears in a Dutch antiphonary of the Church of Saint Mary in Utrecht (manuscript: Utrecht, Netherlands, Bibliotheek der Rijksuniversiteit, MS 406, fol. 101r, as indicated by the Gregorian chant online database Cantus, http://cantusdatabase.org. The Augsburg *Obsequiale* gives only the incipit of this hymn; the complete text is here taken from the Cantus online database.

[257] *Obsequiale Frisingense* (Augsburg, Germany: Erhard Ratdolt, 1493; digitized text, Bayerische Staatsbibliothek, Munich, 2008), fol. 49r.

[258] The earliest known example is that found in the Benedictine *Regularis concordia* of England (c. 960); see Thomas Symons, trans., *Regularis concordia: The Monastic Agreement of the Monks and Nuns of the English Nation*, Medieval Classics (New York: Oxford University Press, 1953), chap. 5, nos. 51–52, pp. 49–50.

[259] See the definitive discussion of the *Visitatio sepulchri* dramas in Young, *Drama of the Medieval Church*, 1:239–410, 576–683.

[260] See the *Liber sacerdotalis* of Alberto Castellani, O.P., first published in 1523, reprinted with a different title in 1555: *Sacerdotale iuxta s. Romane ecclesie et aliarum ecclesiarum* (Venice: Peter Bosellus, 1555; digitized text, Bayerische Staatsbibliothek, Munich, 2009), fols. 246r–248r (text with music).

as a parting gift before leaving for Rome.[261] The Monastery of Santa Clara had already possessed a papal privilege authorizing the religious to keep the Blessed Sacrament enshrined in a repository representing the tomb of Christ, the *monumento*, from the end of the Good Friday liturgy until the morning of Easter Sunday[262] (a custom widespread in other regions of Europe but rare in Spain). This *monumento* became the focal point of Francis Borgia's rite. The manuscript of his ceremony was destroyed amid the savage anti-Catholic violence of the Spanish Civil War (1936–1939),[263] but fortunately the complete text had been transcribed and published over three decades earlier, in 1902, by the Spanish scholar Mariano Baixauli.[264]

At five o'clock in the morning on Easter Sunday, the clergy of Gandía's cathedral and its collegiate church would go forth in procession to the monastery church of Santa Clara along streets decorated with myrtle, laurel, and other fragrant herbs. Along the way, the earlier-cited responsory *Dum transisset sabbatum* ("*When the Sabbath was past*") would be sung. The procession halts before the closed doors of Santa Clara's church, where two choirboys attired as angels, inside the church, sing to those outside, "*Whom do you seek in the sepulcher, O Christians?*"[265] The choir in the procession replies with a four-part polyphonic musical setting of the words "*Jesus of Nazareth, O citizens of Heaven.*" The two choirboy angels reply, "*He is not here; he has risen just as he had foretold. Go, announce that he has risen from the dead.*" The choir sings again, "*Jesus of Nazareth, O citizens of Heaven.*" The two angels now chant, "*Come and see the place where the Lord was placed.*" Once more the choir sings, "*Jesus of Nazareth, O citizens of Heaven.*" The presiding priest of the procession then takes a cross (probably the processional cross) and strikes the front door of the church three times with it. Following the third knock, the doors are opened and the procession enters the church. The choirboys sing again, "*Come and see the place where the Lord was placed*", with the choir replying yet again, "*Jesus of Nazareth, O citizens of Heaven.*"

Three children dressed to represent the three holy women Mary Magdalene, Mary the mother of James, and Mary of Salome, carrying in their hands silver ointment flasks and small embroidered cloths, now proceed to the top of the nine steps leading to the foot of the *monumento*, the Easter sepulcher from which the Blessed Sacrament has

---

[261] Richard Donovan, C.S.B., *The Liturgical Drama in Medieval Spain* (Toronto: Pontifical Institute of Medieval Studies, 1958), 139.

[262] Ibid.

[263] Ibid.

[264] See ibid., 139–141.

[265] This verse and the two that follow it constitute the trope known as *Quem quaeritis*, a chant traceable to the late ninth or early tenth century and thought to have been composed at Switzerland's Saint Gall Abbey by the Irish monk Tutilo; it served as the core text of the *Visitatio sepulchri* rite across medieval Europe. See Young, *Drama of the Medieval Church*, 1:201, 204–205.

quietly been taken to a different location prior to this ceremony. They are accompanied by two other individuals representing the Apostle Saint John and an angel, the latter wearing a crown and carrying a palm. After kneeling to pause in prayer before the now-empty shrine, the three Marys and Saint John sing, "*Who will roll away the stone from the tomb for us?*" One of the three Marys, the one on the right, then approaches the sepulcher and looks to both sides as if seeking something. Finding nothing, this first Mary makes gestures expressing wonder. Moving to the center in front of the sepulcher, she raises her hands toward Heaven and then joins them, making a profound reverence toward the sepulcher before returning to her place at the foot of the shrine. The Mary on the left side now comes forward and repeats the actions of the first. Finally the third Mary in the middle, Mary Magdalene, goes to search around the *monumento* and, drawing back the curtain covering the tomb, finds the shrine to be empty. The three Marys now turn to face the congregation as the Magdalene proclaims, "*Christ has risen.*" The choir answers, "*Thanks be to God.*" The Marys then descend three steps down from the top ninth step before the sepulcher, and the Magdalene sings again, but in a higher voice, "*Christ has risen.*" Once more the choir responds, "*Thanks be to God.*" The Marys descend another three steps, and the Magdalene sings a third time, in an even higher voice, "*Christ has risen.*" The choir answers, "*Alleluia, alleluia.*" The Blessed Sacrament that had been taken out and away from the *monumento* before the beginning of the *Visitatio sepulchri* ceremony is now brought forth in a triumphant procession that exits the church and follows a route along the streets lining the perimeter of the monastery grounds as the choir sings the Easter sequence, *Victimae paschali laudes.*[266] The procession then reenters the church, where the Blessed Sacrament is returned to the tabernacle at the high altar.[267]

In the Spanish archdiocese of Valencia, there arose a liturgical commemoration of the ancient tradition that Christ following his Resurrection appeared first to his Mother before revealing himself to the holy women and the Apostles. This commemoration was assigned to the First Sunday after Easter, the *Dominica in albis* (Sunday in white), the concluding day of the Easter octave. A Valencian missal dating from 1509 provides the complete texts for a Mass "of the first apparition of Christ to the Virgin", traceable to the fifteenth century. The Introit is cast as a declaration of the Blessed Virgin's joy: "*With twofold joy rejoice, O my sons, O faithful ones, alleluia. This day my Son has risen, alleluia. You beheld my Son rising. Rejoice again with me, for my Son rising has appeared first to me, alleluia, alleluia.*" In the Communion antiphon,

---

[266] This chant is attributed to the French priest Wipo (eleventh century); see H. T. Henry, "*Victimae paschali laudes immolent Christiani*", in *Catholic Encyclopedia* (New York: Appleton, 1907–1912), 15:407.

[267] Donovan, *Liturgical Drama in Medieval Spain*, 140–141.

Christ is presented as announcing the particular reason for his conferral of this privilege upon his Mother: "*It was just, O daughter, O my
Mother, that according to the multitude of sorrows in your heart that you
suffered in my Passion and death my sweet apparition and visitation should
have overwhelmed and gladdened you first, alleluia, alleluia.*"[268] The 1503
edition of the Valencia breviary provides a corresponding office for
this commemoration.[269] Although the Mass and office of the apparition of the risen Christ to his Mother do not appear to have spread
beyond Valencia and were discontinued before the end of the sixteenth century, there arose in Spain a related custom, first appearing
in Madrid in 1570, in which the visit of the risen Christ to the Blessed
Virgin was symbolically reenacted on Easter Sunday with statues of
Jesus and Mary, a devotion that came to be known as the *Encuentro*
(Meeting).[270]

[268] Introit and Communion texts quoted from *Missale iuxta ritum alme ecclesiae Valentine*
(Venice: Luca-Antonio Giunta, 1509), Biblioteca Històrica, Universitat de València, Valencia, shelf mark R-1/18 (digitized text, Biblioteca Virtual, Universitat de València, Valencia
n.d.), fols. 122v, 123v. This Mass is first found in a fifteenth-century missal of Valencia;
Manuscript: Valencia, Spain, Archivo Capitular, MS 59, cited in Blessed Juan Bautista Ferreres Boluda, S.J., *Historia del misal romano* (Barcelona, Spain: Eugenio Subirana, 1929), 294.

[269] Ferreres Boluda, *Historia del misal romano*, 294.

[270] Susan Verdi Webster, *Art and Ritual in Golden-Age Spain: Sevillian Confraternities and
the Processional Sculpture of Holy Week* (Princeton, N.J.: Princeton University Press, 1998),
237, endnote.

I6 The Corpus Christi Procession

> O most excellent Sacrament, oh to be adored, venerated, worshiped, glorified, magnified with extraordinary praises, exalted with worthy praises, honored with every effort, accompanied with devout homages, and clung to by faithful souls. O most noble memorial to be commemorated in the innermost heart, firmly bound in the soul, diligently kept in the depth of the heart, and recalled by earnest meditation and celebration.

> Pope Urban IV (+1265)[1]

When in 1264 Pope Urban IV instituted the solemnity of Corpus Christi for the universal Church, assigning it to the Thursday after Trinity Sunday, he made no mention of a procession for the feast, but his words certainly would have encouraged the introduction of such a festive custom for the day:

> On the Thursday itself [Corpus Christi] the devout multitudes of the faithful should lovingly run together to the churches because of this, and both the clergy and the people, rejoicing, should raise on high songs of praise. For then the hearts, and the prayers, the mouths and lips of all, should offer hymns of singular gladness; then let faith sing, hope dance, charity rejoice, devotion clap, the sanctuary rejoice, purity be delighted.[2]

In Cologne, Germany, the idea of a Corpus Christi procession arose almost immediately, recorded for the first time in the parish archives of the Church of Saint Gereon sometime between 1265 and 1277. Two such processions were held, one on the feast day itself and the second on the Sunday within the octave of the feast. The first procession followed a short course to the adjacent Church of Saint Christopher, while the second traveled further to the Church of Saint Quintinus:

---

[1] Pope Urban IV, *Transiturus* (September 8, 1264), in Laertius Cherubini, ed., *Magnum bullarium Romanum*, vol. 1 (Lyons, France: Lawrence Arnaud et Peter Borde, 1673), 147.
[2] Ibid.

Before Mass on the fifth day itself [Corpus Christi, on a Thursday], a solemn procession with purple choir mantles ought to be made around the cloister, with the Body of Christ being carried, and the head of the holy martyr [Saint Gereon], and the crown of Saint Helena, just as it befits a solemnity; and it is going to go to [the Church of] Saint Christopher with canticles and praises; in fact, on the next Sunday [it is also to be done] with the aforesaid solemnity and reverence, as has been said above, with a procession and the carrying of the relics around the cloister; and it is going to go to [the Church of] Saint Quintinus, that the Lord, because of the commemoration and reverencing of his most holy Body, may vouchsafe to turn away every evil both from us and from our church.[3]

In this, the earliest extant record of a Corpus Christi procession, we find the stated reason of the ceremony to be the invocation of divine protection against evil, an intention stemming from the long-standing tradition that over the centuries has inspired religious processions in times of natural or man-made calamities. Virtually contemporaneous with the institution of the Saint Gereon Corpus Christi processions is the mystical interpretation of religious processions offered by William Durandus of Mende (+1296). He saw processions as a symbol of the pilgrimage of the faithful to salvation and eternal life, prefigured in the journeys and processions of the Israelites recounted in the Old Testament:

In our processions is denoted our turning back to our fatherland, of which solemnity the flight of the people from Egypt is imitated in almost all things.

For just as that people was delivered by Moses from the minions of Pharaoh, so the people of God are liberated by Christ from the mouth of the lion.[4]

Durandus observes that both the carrying of the Ark of the Covenant into the Tent of Meeting by David (2 Kings 6:12–18) and the carrying of the ark into the Temple by Solomon, placed in the latter case under the wings of the Holy of Holies' two sculpted cherubim (3 Kings 8:1–7), in both instances to the accompaniment of hymns and canticles, serve as precedents for the processions of the New Covenant, echoing Christ's entrance into Heaven at his Ascension, to be adored by the angels and followed by faithful souls.[5]

---

[3] Text from the archives of the Church of Saint Gereon, Cologne, in Peter Browe, S.J., ed., *Textus antiqui de festo Corporis Christi*, Opuscula et textus historiam ecclesiae eiusque vitam atque doctrinam illustrantia: Series liturgica, fasc. 4 (Münster, Germany: Aschendorff, 1934), 45–46.

[4] William Durandus of Mende, *Rationale divinorum officiorum*, bk. 4, chap. 6, no. 15, in A. Davril, O.S.B., and T. M. Thibodeau, eds., *Guillelmi Duranti: Rationale divinorum officiorum I–IV*, CCCM 140 (Turnhout, Belgium: Brepols, 1995), 276–277. Hereafter cited as Durandus, *Rationale* (CCCM 140).

[5] Ibid., no. 16, p. 277.

In both of the Saint Gereon Corpus Christi processions we find the rite culminating in the entering of a destination church. Durandus sees such an ending to religious processions as likewise rich in symbolic meaning: "When we direct our course processionally to some church, then we approach as if to the land of promise. But when we enter the church singing, we arrive rejoicing as if reaching our native land."[6]

Corpus Christi processions arose elsewhere in Germany soon after the introduction of the Cologne procession, appearing at the Bavarian abbey of Benediktbeuern in 1286 and at Würzburg in 1298.[7] During the fourteenth century, Corpus Christi processions were introduced throughout western Europe. In the early part of the century, Germany continued to lead the way in the development of this ceremony. Around the year 1301, the custom of blessing those in attendance with the reserved Eucharist—benediction of the Blessed Sacrament—appeared for the first time in the Corpus Christi procession of the German Benedictine abbey of Hildesheim. According to the abbatial decree establishing this procession, the priest, vested in a red chasuble and holding the Blessed Sacrament in a pyx, would bless the people with the Eucharist before the Altar of the Holy Cross in the abbey chapel as the choir sang a versicle borrowed from the Good Friday liturgy, the concluding verse of the antiphon *Dum Fabricator mundi* ("*When the Maker of the world suffered death*"), doing so "with fitting bows and the bending of the knees, humbly prostrating themselves to the earth".[8] This verse, usually sung to a chant melody that soars at the words "*O wonderful Price*", speaks of him who became the price of our redemption by his sacrificial death on the Cross: "*O wonderful Price, by whose weight the captivity of the world has been redeemed, the infernal gates of hell have been shattered, the gate of the kingdom has been opened to us.*"[9]

Corpus Christi in Fourteenth-century Cologne, Germany

It is in Cologne, home of the earliest recorded Corpus Christi procession, that we find an exceptionally elaborate Corpus Christi rite in the early fourteenth-century rubrics of a ceremonial for the city's Cathedral of Saint Peter. To begin with, on each day of the Corpus Christi octave, there are two short processions within the cathedral itself in which the Blessed Sacrament is brought to the high altar, the first for

---

[6] Ibid., no. 15.

[7] Otto Nussbaum, *Die Aufbewahrung der Eucharistie*, Theophaneia 29 (Bonn, Germany: Hanstein, 1979), 155; Xaver Haimerl, *Das Prozessionswesen des bistums Bamberg im Mittelalter*, Münchener Studien zur historischen Theologie 14 (Munich: Verlag Kösel-Pustet, 1937), 33, footnote.

[8] Abbatial decree of Hildesheim Abbey, Germany, c. 1301, in Browe, *Textus antiqui de festo Corporis Christi*, 47.

[9] The Hildesheim text gives only the incipit of this versicle; the complete verse is here taken from Martin Gerbert, *Monumenta veteris liturgiae Alemannicae* (Sankt Blasien, Germany: Typis San-Blasianis, 1777–1779), 1:382.

the postmidnight office of Matins at the very beginning of the day, and the second for Vespers in the evening. On each occasion the congregation is blessed with the Eucharist:

> Throughout the octave [of Corpus Christi], before Matins and Vespers are begun, the venerable Sacrament is carried to the high altar by a deacon or canon priest clothed in a surplice and over it a cope, with two lit torches preceding and without the elder choristers, and with two other choristers with garnished wreaths upon their heads carrying two angel figures; and thus the venerable [Sacrament] with benediction having been set over the middle of the altar, the deacon or hebdomadarian,[10] having taken off his cope, should enter the choir.[11]

The two "angel figures" in this procession may well have been inspired by the two cherubim figures of the Holy of Holies in the Temple of Solomon that we mentioned earlier. The above rubrics say nothing about the form of the benediction, but we learn more in the instructions that the ceremonial provides for two further conferrals of benediction, one at the end of Vespers and the other at the end of High Mass, on each day of the Corpus Christi octave. In what follows we see the beginnings of the custom of preceding benediction with the concluding two verses (*Tantum ergo* and *Genitori, Genitoque*) of the Eucharistic hymn *Pange lingua* of Saint Thomas Aquinas (+1274); in this case only the final verse, *Genitori, Genitoque*, is utilized, and benediction is given during the singing of the verse rather than afterward:

> On each day during the octave, however, High Mass and Vespers having ended, the hebdomadarian, vested in a cope, stands before the altar facing west with the venerable Sacrament [as] the choir sings, *To the Father, and his only-begotten Son* [*Genitori, Genitoque*], up to this clause: *and blessing be* [*sit et benedictio*]; he shall then perform the benediction toward the west only; which having been done, he shall go into the sacristy, with the canons preceding, etc.[12]

Here we see the priest appointed to preside over the cathedral offices for the week, the hebdomadarian, raising from the altar the reserved Eucharist as glory is offered to the Holy Trinity, at the conclusion of which he faces west, toward the congregation, to give the benediction, which from other references in the Cologne text we know was made by tracing a cross. This early form of benediction, invoking the blessing and protection of God, has its Old Testament counterpart in the journey of Moses and the Israelites from Mount Sinai (Num 10:35–36): "And when the ark was lifted up, Moses said: Arise, O Lord, and

---

[10] A hebdomadarian is a priest assigned to lead the Divine Office for a given week.

[11] Text in Gottfried Amberg, ed., *Ceremoniale Coloniense*, Studien zur Kölner Kirchengeschichte 17 (Siegburg, Germany: Franz Schmitt, 1982), 208–210.

[12] Ibid., 210.

let thy enemies be scattered, and let them that hate thee, flee from before thy face. And when it was set down, he said: Return, O Lord, to the multitude of the host of Israel."

In addition to the daily Eucharistic processions inside Cologne's cathedral church, there was on the day of Corpus Christi itself an outdoor procession through the city's streets, carried out before High Mass at the cathedral. The procession, as described in the Cologne ceremonial, would begin by passing through the nave and out the newly constructed west end of the church:

> First, the seventh hour is struck. Sext having been sung, a procession with the venerable Sacrament is carried out only by our lords. The procession having been set in order, it goes out through the new end [of the cathedral] and returns through the same, with twelve torches preceding. At the head of the procession the chamberlain and the cantor shall follow the directors, the choristers [each] vested in an alb and over it a mantle, then the banner, then the deacon and the subdeacon together, vested in dalmatics, without the relics; after these, the senior chorister, with him sounding a bell; after this, the bell ringer, carrying a lamp with a lit candle set upon it; thirdly two choristers with [the images of] angels; lastly the bishop, or the deacon—or if neither of these shall have been present, the suffragan bishop, having been asked by a party of the cathedral chapter, or another in place of him—vested in an alb and a stole with a cope over them, carrying the venerable Sacrament, with two prelates from the more distinguished ones of our church leading him, vested in their surplices only. And thus going out of the choir, the procession passes through the door, which is on the prior's side, going through the new end.[13]

Turning left and southward, the procession would approach a gate known as the *Hachtpforte*, near a prison. Here the bishop pauses for the first benediction along the route, which is given to the prisoners. After passing through the *Hachtpforte* gate and onto one of Cologne's major east-west thoroughfares, the bishop stops again, giving at this point a four-way benediction, making a sign of the cross with the Eucharist toward each of the four cardinal points of the earth—first north, then east, then south, then west: "The crosses [with the Eucharist] should be made four times: first toward the way by which the procession came, another toward the new street, a third toward the street or church of Saint Lawrence, the fourth toward the church at the Garden of Mary."[14]

The four cardinal points, that is, the four ends of the earth, are mentioned repeatedly in the Scriptures. When God showed the Promised Land to Abraham, God declared to him: "Lift up thy eyes, and look from

---

[13] Ibid.

[14] Ibid., 210, 212.

the place wherein thou now art, to the north and to the south, to the east and to the west" (Gen 13:14). In like manner, Moses was told to view the Promised Land "to the west, and to the north, and to the south, and to the east" (Deut 3:27). The Temple of Solomon had a huge water basin for cleansing (the "brazen sea") mounted on twelve molten oxen, "of which three looked towards the north, and three towards the west, and three towards the south, and three towards the east" (3 Kings 7:25; see also 2 Par 4:4). In the Book of Revelation, the heavenly Jerusalem is described as having twelve gates situated so as to face the four cardinal points: "On the east, three gates: and on the north, three gates: and on the south, three gates: and on the west, three gates" (Rev 21:13). Thus the custom of directing a blessing toward the four cardinal points, a practice that was to appear in various forms in the liturgical rites of the Middles Ages, is rich in biblical meaning; it is particularly suggestive of Christ's invitation in the Gospel of Saint Luke summoning believers "from the east and the west, and the north and the south" to "sit down in the kingdom of God" (Lk 13:29).

The symbolism of the four cardinal points is also related to the imagery of the Cross, a comparison made as early as the fifth century by the bishop Saint Maximus of Turin (+c. 467): "Heaven itself has also been ordered in the figure of this sign [i.e., the Cross]. For while it is divided in four parts, that is, the east, and the west, and the south, and the north, it is bound together in four just like the corners of the Cross." [15] This comparison is further developed by the twelfth-century liturgist Honorius of Autun (+c. 1135): "By the four arms of the Cross, the four quarters of the world are saved." [16] Similarly, Durandus observes that "the figure of the Cross is divided in four … by reason of men whom [Christ] has drawn to himself from the four quarters of the world, according to that [pronouncement]: 'And I, if I be lifted up from the earth, will draw all things to myself' [Jn 12:32]." [17] Gilbert of Tournai (+1284) also sees the parallel between the four ends of the earth and the four ends of the Cross as representing the reconciliation wrought by Christ: "Not undeservedly is it called the vivifying Cross; for just as the first Adam, who had been the cause of perdition, had been scattered [in his descendants] throughout the four quarters of the world, so the second Adam, who is the cause of salvation, has bound together the four quarters of the world by the position of his body on the wood [i.e., the Cross]." [18]

---

[15] Saint Maximus of Turin, *Sermon 50*, PL 57, col. 342.

[16] Honorius of Autun, *Gemma animae*, bk. 3, chap. 90, PL 172, col. 667.

[17] Durandus, *Rationale divinorum officiorum*, bk. 5, chap. 2, no. 16, in A. Davril, O.S.B., and T. M. Thibodeau, eds., *Guillelmi Duranti: Rationale divinorum officiorum V–VI*, CCCM 140a (Turnhout, Belgium: Brepols, 1998), 21.

[18] Gilbert of Tournai, *Tractatus de officio episcopi*, chap. 47, in Marguerin de la Bigne, ed., *Maxima bibliotheca veterum patrum, et antiquorum scriptorum ecclesiasticorum* (Lyons, France: Anissonios, 1677), 25:419.

Heading west along a street bearing the amusing name of the Plump Hen, the Cologne procession pauses again at an intersection with an ancient north-south Roman road through the city. Here the bishop gives two blessings with the Eucharist, one southward toward the street of the Golden Pound, the other northward toward a gate on the Roman road, the Priests' Gate. The procession then turns north onto the Roman road and approaches the Priests' Gate. Before passing through the gate, the bishop gives another benediction and then proceeds to a major intersection beyond it. At this crossroads of Beverage Lane and Grease Street, the bishop again gives a four-way benediction, making the sign of the cross with the Sacrament first toward the south, then the west, then the north, and then the east. Heading eastward along Beverage Lane, the procession halts at another intersection near the Church of Saint Lupus. Here again, the bishop gives a four-way benediction (west, north, east, south). The procession then passes the Church of Mary at the Step immediately behind the east end of the cathedral and, turning westward, proceeds past the south side of the cathedral until it again reaches the *Hachtpforte* gate near the prison. Here benediction is given once more. The procession thereby completes a fairly rectangular circuit within the city, with the cathedral near the center of the rectangle.[19] Such a procession passing around all sides of a church is likened by Durandus to the Israelites' processions with the Ark of the Covenant round about the walls of Jericho (Jos 6:3–16).[20]

The Cologne procession reenters the cathedral through the same west end from which it emerged earlier. The Blessed Sacrament is now enthroned on the high altar as the antiphon *O sacrum convivium* ("*O sacred banquet*") is sung, one of the chants from the office that Saint Thomas Aquinas (+1274) composed for this solemnity:[21] "Entering through the new end, [the bishop] shall place the venerable Sacrament upon the high altar, with the entourage of those serving remaining in the choir of Saint Peter, singing in the same place the antiphon, *O sacred banquet, in which Christ is received, the memory of his Passion is recalled, the mind is filled with grace, and a pledge of future glory is given to us*. Which having been done, Mass is begun."[22] After Mass, the hymn *Pange lingua* is sung in its entirety, during the final verse of which a concluding benediction is given from the high altar (in the same manner that we saw earlier):

---

[19] Amberg, *Ceremoniale Coloniense*, 212.

[20] Durandus, *Rationale* (CCCM 140), bk. 4, chap. 6, nos. 15, 16, p. 277.

[21] This antiphon is first found in a late thirteenth-century manuscript of the Corpus Christi office—Paris, Bibliothèque Nationale, Codex Lat. 1143—that contains the version of this office authored by Saint Thomas Aquinas, named *Sacerdos in aeternum* from the incipit of its opening antiphon; see Barbara Walters, Vincent Corrigan, and Peter Ricketts, *The Feast of Corpus Christi* (University Park, Pa.: Pennsylvania State University Press, 2006), 303–304. Regarding the attribution of this version of the office to Saint Thomas Aquinas, see ibid., xviii, 63.

[22] Amberg, *Ceremoniale Coloniense*, 212.

[With the choir] continuing that [*Pange lingua*] all the way to the verse *To the Father, and his only-begotten Son*, etc., the [hebdomadarian] priest should then rise, with him holding the venerable Sacrament with each hand, standing before the high altar, until when the choir shall have come to this clause, *And blessing be*, with him giving the benediction; which having been done, the clergy enters the sacristy.[23]

Corpus Christi processions with long routes and multiple stations such as the above example from Cologne correspond well to another analogy that Durandus makes, likening a procession to the succession of journeys in the life of Christ:

In processions we also recall that Christ came from the bosom of the Father into the world, from the manger to the Temple, and from Bethany into Jerusalem, and from Jerusalem to the Mount [of Olives], desiring that we return from the world to our native land, and from one Church to the other, namely from the militant to the triumphant, following the Cross, that is, the footsteps of the Crucified, and crucifying ourselves with our sins and concupiscences, following also the footsteps of the saints [and] the precepts of the Gospels, and clothed in sacred garments, namely the breastplate of justice, the cincture of continence, the shield of faith, and the helmet of eternal salvation.[24]

Corpus Christi in Fourteenth-century Essen, Germany

Not far to the north of Cologne, the German city of Essen conducted a Eucharistic procession on the Friday within the Corpus Christi octave that set out across the countryside, passing through six villages along the way. The rubrics for this lengthy procession and for a shorter procession on the day of Corpus Christi are found in the *Liber ordinarius*, a fourteenth-century liturgical book for the quasi-monastic community of canons that staffed Essen's collegiate church, which they shared with an affiliated community of canonesses (women living a mitigated form of religious life). The shorter procession on Corpus Christi Day, tracing a rectangular course around the collegiate church, was held shortly before Mass. It would begin with a station before the high altar:

On the day of the Sacrament, Terce having been completed, a general procession is carried out around the cemetery with the Sacrament and three banners. And the first station is done thus: the priest and all the canons are vested in copes, the ministers in dalmatics. Then the priest, having taken the Sacrament with the pyx in his hands, the subdeacon with the lectionary, and three other canons with banners station themselves before the high altar, the priest

---

[23] Ibid.

[24] Durandus, *Rationale* (CCCM 140), bk. 4, chap. 6, no. 16, pp. 277–278.

with the Sacrament in the middle, and the banners and lectionary on either side, facing the people. The religious community [i.e., the canonesses] shall stand before the lower step [of the sanctuary] near the tomb of the founder. Then the religious community shall sing one antiphon of the day, or the hymn *Jesus, our Redemption,*[25] which having been completed, the priest [shall say] the Collect of the day.[26]

The procession exits the east end of the collegiate church (through the "red door") "with the banner bearers preceding, then the scholars, then the canons, then the ministers, then the priest with the Sacrament, and the religious community last, as is customary".[27] It follows a route along the perimeter of the religious community's cemetery, which surrounds the eastern end of the church. During the procession, a canopy is carried over the Blessed Sacrament: "And wherever the priest with the Sacrament shall have stood or gone, there four scholars shall hold and carry over him a canopy with four poles, upon which the canopy itself shall be firmly bound."[28] Along the way, the canons sing the Corpus Christi responsory *Homo quidam* (drawn from Lk 14:16–17; Prov 9:5), one of the chants from the Corpus Christi office of Saint Thomas Aquinas:[29] "*A certain man made a great supper, and he sent his servant at the hour of supper to say to them that were invited, that they should come, for all things are ready.* Verse: *Come, eat my bread, and drink the wine which I have mingled for you. For all things are ready.*"[30] The procession turns west and heads past the south sides of the collegiate church and the smaller Church of Saint John that stands in front of the west door of the collegiate church. It then turns north, passing in front of the west end of the Church of Saint John, after which it heads back eastward along the northern sides of the two churches. Finally the procession reenters the collegiate church, and the priest carrying the Eucharist again

---

[25] The hymn *Jesu, nostra Redemptio* dates back to before the mid-eleventh century, when it is mentioned as a chant for the office of Ascension Thursday in the *Liber tramitis* (formerly called the Customs of Farfa), a customary of the French Benedictine abbey of Cluny compiled around 1043; see *Liber tramitis*, bk. 1, chap. 69, in Bruno Albers, ed., *Consuetudines monasticae*, vol. 1: *Consuetudines Farfenses* (Stuttgart: Jos. Roth, Bibliopolae, 1900), 70.

[26] Text in Franz Arens, ed., *Der Liber Ordinarius der Essener Stiftskirche* (Paderborn, Germany: Albert Pape, 1908), 93.

[27] Ibid.

[28] Ibid.

[29] This responsory is from Saint Thomas Aquinas' version of the Corpus Christi office as preserved in the late thirteenth-century manuscript of the Bibliothèque Nationale, Paris, Codex Lat. 1143; see Walters, Corrigan, and Ricketts, *Feast of Corpus Christi*, 245–246.

[30] Arens, *Liber ordinarius der Essener Stiftskirche*, 93. The Essen text provides only the incipit of this responsory; the full text is here taken from the 1568 *Breviarium Romanum*, in Manlio Sodi and Achille Maria Triacca, eds., *Breviarium Romanum: Editio princeps (1568)*, facsimile ed., MLCT 3 (Vatican City: Libreria Editrice Vaticana, © 1999), 497 (new pagination).

comes to a halt before the high altar for a second and final station there, with the singing of the antiphon "*Oh, how sweet is your Spirit, O Lord*",[31] followed by another antiphon of the feast. The priest concludes the procession with the recitation of the Collect for the solemnity of Corpus Christi. Mass immediately follows.[32]

It is on the next day that Essen's major procession takes place:

> Friday, which is the next day of the Sacrament, the townspeople were accustomed to go about the countryside with the Sacrament of the Body of Christ; and one or two from the canons, whom they shall have asked, in surplices and a stole and also a cope, shall carry the Sacrament, with some older scholars from the school accompanying [them]; and they go out very early before sunrise.[33]

The rubrics for this procession say nothing as to what vessel was used to carry the Blessed Sacrament, but there is in the treasury of the present-day cathedral church of Essen a silver-gilded monstrance dating from the mid-fourteenth century adorned with the motif of the pelican, a traditional Eucharistic symbol of Christ nourishing his flock with his own precious blood. Dated to shortly before the writing of the Essen *Liber ordinarius*, this monstrance is likely to have been the vessel utilized.[34] The procession begins in the collegiate church, heading out through the "red door" at the church's eastern end. It then exits the city through the Kethwich Gate and travels for a short distance along the road toward the village of Kethwich before turning right onto a side road. The procession passes six villages along the way, with the clergy and the laity taking turns in singing. After winding past a linden tree orchard in Frohnhausen and through the village of Altendorf, the procession pauses in the village of Segerade for a reading of the beginning of Saint John's Gospel ("*In the beginning was the word . . .*"), followed by a threefold benediction with the Eucharist: "At the station [the priest] shall say thus, making three crosses over the people: *May the blessing of God the Father, and the Son, and the Holy Spirit descend upon you and remain forever. Amen.*"[35] The Essen rubrics also instruct the priest to give frequent blessings with the Eucharist to those who go to meet the procession and pay their homage to the Blessed Sacrament along the route: "On the way the priest shall frequently make the cross with the

---

[31] This antiphon, *O quam suavis*, is from Saint Thomas Aquinas' version of the Corpus Christi office as preserved in the late thirteenth-century manuscript of the Bibliothèque Nationale, Paris, Codex Lat. 1143; see Walters, Corrigan, and Ricketts, *Feast of Corpus Christi*, 248–250.

[32] Arens, *Liber Ordinarius der Essener Stiftskirche*, 93–94.

[33] Ibid., 94.

[34] Sabine Felbecker, *Die Prozession: Historische und systematische Untersuchungen zu einer liturgischen Ausdruckshandlung*, Münsteraner theologische Abhandlungen 39 (Altenberge, Germany: Oros Verlag, 1995), 247, footnote.

[35] Arens, *Liber ordinarius der Essener Stiftskirche*, 94–95 (quoted passage on 95).

Sacrament over the people coming anew and genuflecting to the Sacrament."[36]

When the procession reaches the convent of Stoppenberg, the nuns of this religious community join the procession, after which all come to a halt on the convent grounds, "under the trees", to hear a sermon preached by a friar selected for this occasion that concludes with an appeal for donations to the poor. Then, as the responsory *Verbum caro factum est* ("*The Word was made flesh.* Verse: *And dwelt among us*") is sung,[37] the procession resumes across the convent grounds, accompanied by the Stoppenberg nuns until it reaches the end of their land. Here there is a pause as the priest recites the Collect for the solemnity of Corpus Christi and administers benediction with the Eucharist. The procession now moves on to the village of Wisthoven, where again all halt for another recitation of the beginning of Saint John's Gospel and another threefold benediction. After passing through the village of Slangenberg and heading back toward Essen along Kethwich Road, the procession pauses "near the gardens outside the Kethwich Gate" for one more reading of the same Gospel lection and another threefold benediction.[38]

Reentering Essen through the Kethwich Gate, the procession, before returning to the collegiate church, passes through the adjacent Church of Saint John as the responsory *Immolabit haedum* is sung (based upon Ex 12:5–6, 8; 1 Cor 5:7–8): "*The multitude of the children of Israel shall sacrifice a kid on the evening of the Pasch. And they shall eat the flesh, and unleavened bread.* Verse: *Christ our Pasch is sacrificed: therefore let us feast with the unleavened bread of sincerity and truth. And they shall eat the flesh, and unleavened bread.*"[39] At the door of the collegiate church, the returning procession is met by a canon vested in a cope carrying a burning thurible, and with him the community of canonesses, who now join the procession for its concluding moments until the priest carrying the Eucharist arrives before the high altar, where he turns with the Sacrament toward the people. The canonesses station themselves near the front step of the sanctuary to sing an antiphon, after which the

---

[36] Ibid., 95.

[37] This responsory is first found in the Antiphonary of Compiègne (France, c. 870), in which it is utilized for the office of Christmas Day; see René-Jean Hésbert, ed., *Corpus antiphonalium officii*, vol. 1, REDSMF 7 (Rome: Herder, 1963), 36. The complete text of this responsory is here taken from René-Jean Hésbert, ed., *Corpus antiphonalium officii*, vol. 4, REDSMF 10 (Rome: Herder, 1970), no. 7838, p. 451. The use of this responsory in the Office of Corpus Christi can be found in a thirteenth-century Cistercian antiphonary preserved in Vienna, Austria (manuscript: Vienna, Osterreichische Nationalbibliothek, Musiksammlung, MS 1799, fols. 238v, 241r, as indicated by the Gregorian chant online database Cantus, http://cantusdatabase.org).

[38] Arens, *Liber ordinarius der Essener Stiftskirche*, 94–95.

[39] Ibid., 95. The Essen text provides only the incipit of this responsory; the full text is here taken from Sodi and Triacca, *Breviarium Romanum: Editio princeps (1568)*, 485 (new pagination). This particular version of the responsory *Immolabit haedum* is from Saint Thomas Aquinas' Corpus Christi office as preserved in the late thirteenth-century manuscript of the Bibliothèque Nationale, Paris, Codex Lat. 1143; see Walters, Corrigan, and Ricketts, *Feast of Corpus Christi*, 258–260.

priest recites one final time the Corpus Christi Collect and administers a final threefold benediction with the Blessed Sacrament.[40]

In fifteenth- and sixteenth-century Germany and Poland, and elsewhere in central Europe, the association of the four cardinal points with the carrying of the Gospel to peoples "from the east and the west, and the north and the south" (Lk 13:29) was made more explicit with the gradual introduction of the four-station Corpus Christi procession, in which the beginnings of all four Gospels were read, one at each station, each read facing a different cardinal point and followed by a benediction facing the same direction. The Polish cardinal and apologetics writer Stanislaus Hosius (Stanislaw Hozjusz; +1579) explains this practice: "But we observe in this our province, that in this procession [of Corpus Christi] the four beginnings of the Gospels are sung toward the four quarters of the world, that this Gospel of the Cross and death of Christ might be represented as having been preached openly in all quarters of the world by the Apostles and their successors."[41] This usage would have also been prompted by the medieval belief that the beginnings of the four Gospels possessed a singular efficacy in obtaining divine protection from storm damage and demonic attacks;[42] thus a rite for blessing a cross to be placed "over the harvest" from an eleventh-century ritual of Prüm, Germany, stipulates that after the cross is blessed, sprinkled with holy water, and censed, a Gospel book is to be opened four times to the beginnings of the four Gospels respectively, with the opened book laid down each time upon the cross, as if to sanctify it with these holy texts.[43]

The use of the beginnings of all four Gospel readings in a liturgical ceremony, and the indirect association of these readings with the four cardinal points, can be traced further back to the liturgy of seventh-century Rome as described in the Gelasian Sacramentary and Roman *Ordo* 11. In the Lenten rite of the Opening of the Ears (*Apertio Aurium*), a ceremony for catechumens preparing to receive their Easter baptism, four deacons would carry to the altar four separate Gospel books, each containing one of the four Gospels. The four books were placed on the four corners of the altar. Then, after a priest delivered an introductory homily regarding the Gospels, each deacon in turn would read to the catechumens the first page of the Gospel he had brought.[44]

---

[40] Arens, *Liber ordinarius der Essener Stiftskirche*, 95.

[41] Stanislaus Hosius, *Confessio Catholicae fidei Christiana*, chap. 8, in *D. Stanislai Hosii, S.R.E. cardinalis, maioris poenitentiarii, et episcopi Varmiensis: Opera omnia in duos divisa tomo*s (Cologne, Germany: Maternus Cholinus, 1584; digitized text, CBN Polona, National Digital Library, Biblioteka Narodowa, Warsaw, Poland, n.d.), 1:10.

[42] Adolph Franz, *Die kirchlichen Benediktionen im Mittelalter* (Freiburg im Breisgau, Germany, 1909; repr., Graz, Austria: Akademische Druck—U. Verlagsanstalt, 1960), 2:14, footnote.

[43] Manuscript: Munich, Bayerische Staatsbibliothek, MS Codex Latinus Monacensis (Clm) 100, ibid., 2:13–14.

[44] This ceremony formed part of the Third Scrutiny (one of seven scrutinies for the preparation of catechumens), conducted on Wednesday of the Fourth Week of Lent; Gelasian

The earliest reference to the four Gospels during the Corpus Christi procession dates from 1420, appearing in a document of Niemiec, Germany.[45] As for Poland, the earliest mention of the practice comes from the city of Płock in a notation written sometime between 1427 and 1439, added to the margins of an older liturgical book (a fourteenth-century ordinal of Płock).[46] The 1487 *Obsequiale Augustense* of Augsburg, Germany; a 1503 ritual for Chur, Switzerland; and a 1505 ritual of Strasbourg, France, provide the beginnings of the four Gospels specifically for the Corpus Christi procession.[47] The 1509 *Liber ordinarius* for the diocese of Eger, Hungary, directs that in the city's Corpus Christi procession there are to be four priests vested in "more solemn" dalmatics who are delegated to read the four beginnings of the four Gospels, the first three (those of Saints Matthew, Mark, and Luke respectively) at three separate churches along the procession route, and the fourth (that of Saint John) on the porch of Eger's cathedral when the procession returns there.[48] The linking of each Gospel reading with a different cardinal point is stated explicitly in the rubrics of a 1502 ritual (*Agenda*) for Naumburg, Germany, which refers to "the four beginnings of the Gospels with their own versicles and prayers, which are read to the four quarters of the world ... on the day of Corpus Christi, while a procession with the venerable Sacrament is conducted." [49] In early sixteenth-century Poland, the four-station Corpus Christi procession appears in the liturgical books of Płock (breviary of 1520), Gnesen (missal of 1523), and Poznań (ritual of 1533).[50] In the Poznań text, supplication for the faithful departed is expressed in the antiphon assigned to the procession's fourth station, a chant that borrows from the ancient Trinitarian prayer, the Trisagion: "*In midlife we are in death; what helper are we to seek, if not you, O Lord, who*

Sacramentary text in Leo Cunibert Mohlberg, O.S.B., et al., eds., *Liber sacramentorum Romanae aeclesiae ordinis anni circuli (Sacramentarium Gelasianum)*, REDSMF 4 (Rome: Herder, 1960), nos. 299–309, pp. 46–48; Roman *Ordo* 11, in Michel Andrieu, ed., *Les Ordines Romani du haut moyen âge*, vol. 2, SSLED 23 (Louvain, Belgium: "Spicilegium sacrum Lovaniense" Administration, 1948), 427–433.

[45] Zbigniew Zalewski, "Święto Bożego Ciała w Polsce do Wydania Rytuału Piotrkowskiego (1631 r.)", in *Studia z Dziejów Liturgii w Polsce*, vol. 1, Rozprawy Wydziału Teologiczno-Kanonicznego 33 (Lublin, Poland: Towarzystwo Naukowe, Katolickiego Uniwersytetu Lubelskiego, 1973), 138, plus footnote.

[46] Ibid., 137.

[47] See respectively *Obsequiale Augustense* (Augsburg, Germany: Erhard Ratdolt, 1487; digitized text, Bayerische Staatsbibliothek, Munich, 2008), fols. 92v–93r; Hans Bissig, *Das Churer Rituale, 1503–1927: Geschichte der Agende—Feier der Sakramente*, Studia Friburgensia, neue Folge, 56 (Fribourg, Switzerland: Universitätsverlag Freiburg, 1979), 46; and *Agenda, sive Exequiale sacramentorum* (Strasbourg, France: Prüss, 1505; digitized text, Bayerische Staatsbibliothek, Munich, n.d.), fol. 84r.

[48] Latin text and English translation in László Dobszay, ed., *Liber ordinarius Agriensis (1509)*, Musicalia Danubiana, subsidia, 1 (Budapest: Curis, 2000), 75, 202–203.

[49] *Agenda* of Naumburg, Germany, 1502, quoted in Peter Browe, S.J., *Die Verehrung der Eucharistie im Mittelalter* (Munich, 1933; repr., Rome: Herder, 1967), 109, footnote.

[50] Zalewski, "Święto Bożego Ciała w Polsce", 138.

are justly angry because of our sins? Holy God, holy mighty One, holy merciful Savior, be loving to the dead, lest you hand us over." [51]

In early sixteenth-century Krakόw, Poland, the four-station Corpus Christi procession had not yet been introduced, but the great importance given to the city's annual procession for this solemnity is evident from the fact that detailed rubrics for it are provided in the 1509 missal of Krakόw,[52] in contrast to the conventional practice of relegating the rubrics for this procession to a supplemental liturgical book (such as a ceremonial or a processional). Moreover, although there is only one benediction during the Krakόw procession, it is given not by the prelate assigned to carry the Eucharist but rather by the city's archbishop.

According to the 1509 Krakόw missal, the procession takes place after Mass, beginning outside the city as the prelate carrying the Blessed Sacrament elevates it, facing the people and intoning the earlier-cited antiphon *Homo quidam* ("*A certain man made a great supper*"). The procession then passes within Krakόw and advances to the Church of Saint Francis, entering it. As the earlier-cited antiphon *O sacrum convivium* ("*O sacred banquet*") is sung, the prelate carrying the Eucharist places it upon the altar. He then says the verse, *Panem caeli dedit* ("*He gave them bread from heaven*"), followed by the Corpus Christi Collect of Saint Thomas Aquinas, *Deus qui nobis sacramento* ("*O God, who under this wonderful Sacrament*"). Following the conclusion of the prayer, the archbishop (if he is present) takes the Eucharist and gives benediction to the people. After the archbishop places the Blessed Sacrament back upon the altar, the prelate who carried the Eucharist in the procession to the church now takes it up again and holds it before the people, intoning the next-to-last verse of the Corpus Christi Sequence of Saint Thomas Aquinas, *Lauda Sion* (verse 11: "*Behold, the Bread of angels*"). The other priests complete this verse and continue with the final stanza of *Lauda Sion* (verse 12: "*Good Shepherd, truly Bread, Jesus, have mercy on us ...*").[53] The procession resumes, leaving the Church of Saint Francis and proceeding to Krakόw's cathedral as several responsories are sung along the way, beginning with the earlier-cited *Immolabit haedum* ("*The multitude of the children of Israel*"). Seven other responsories are specified for the Krakόw procession:[54]

---

[51] *Agenda secundum cursum et rubricam ecclesie cathedralis Posnaniensis ad ritum metropolitane Gnesnensis*, 1533, quoted ibid., 139. The antiphon *Media vita* is traceable to the eleventh century, when it appears as a chant for the office of Compline in an antiphonary of Verona (Italy); see Hésbert, *Corpus antiphonalium officii*, 1:413.

[52] *Missale Cracoviense*, 1509, in Zalewski, "Święto Bożego Ciała w Polsce", 137, footnote.

[53] Ibid.

[54] All but one of these seven responsories (the sixth, *Discubuit Jesus*) are from Saint Thomas Aquinas' version of the Corpus Christi office as preserved in the late thirteenth-century manuscript of the Bibliothèque Nationale, Paris, Codex Lat. 1143; see Walters, Corrigan, and Ricketts, *Feast of Corpus Christi*, 261–262, 264–267, 272–273, 275–276, 286–287, 289–291, respectively.

You shall eat flesh, and you shall have your fill of bread. This is the bread, which the Lord hath given you to eat. Verse: Moses gave you not the true bread from heaven. This is the bread . . . [cf. Ex 16:12, 15; Jn 6:32].[55]

Elias beheld at his head a hearth cake, which rising he ate and drank. And he walked in the strength of that food unto the mount of God. Verse: If any man eat of this bread, he shall live for ever. And he walked . . . [cf. 3 Kings 19:6, 8; Jn 6:52].[56]

The bread that I will give is my flesh for the life of the world. The Jews therefore quarreled, saying: How can this man give us his flesh to eat? Verse: The people spoke against the Lord: Our soul now loatheth this very light food. How can this man . . . [cf. Jn 6:52–53; Num 21:5].[57]

Whilst they were at supper, Jesus took bread, and blessed, and broke, and gave to his disciples, and said: Take and eat. This is my Body. Verse: The men of my tabernacle have said: Who will give us of his flesh that we may be filled? Take and eat . . . [cf. Mt 26:26; Job 31:31].[58]

The living Father hath sent me, and I live by the Father. And he that eateth me, shall live by me. Verse: The Lord fed him with the bread of life and understanding. And he that eateth me . . . [cf. Jn 6:58].[59]

Jesus sat down, and his disciples with him, and said: With desire I have desired to eat this Pasch with you, before I suffer. [Verse:] *And taking bread, giving thanks he broke, and gave to them, saying: This is my Body. And having taken the chalice, giving thanks, he gave it to them, and said: This is my Blood. Glory be to the Father . . . Saying: This is my Body . . .* [cf. Lk 22:14–15, 19; Mk 14:23–24].[60]

---

[55] The full text of this responsory, *Commedetis*, is here taken from Sodi and Triacca, *Breviarium Romanum: Editio princeps (1568)*, 486 (new pagination).

[56] The full text of this responsory, *Respexit Helyas*, is here taken from Sodi and Triacca, *Breviarium Romanum: Editio princeps (1568)*, 486 (new pagination).

[57] The full text of this responsory, *Panis quem ego*, is here taken from the 1531 Sarum Breviary of Salisbury, England, in Francis Procter and Christopher Wordsworth, eds., *Breviarium ad usum insignis ecclesiae Sarum* (Cambridge: Cambridge University Press, 1879–1886), vol. 1, col. 1067.

[58] The full text of this responsory, *Cenantibus illis*, is here taken from Sodi and Triacca, *Breviarium Romanum: Editio princeps (1568)*, 486 (new pagination).

[59] The full text of this responsory, *Misit me*, is here taken from Sodi and Triacca, *Breviarium Romanum: Editio princeps (1568)*, 488 (new pagination).

[60] This responsory, *Discubuit Jesus*, is traceable to a fourteenth-century antiphonary of the Austrian abbey of Sankt Lambrecht in Steiermark (manuscript: Graz, Austria, Universitätsbibliothek, MS 29, fol. 186v, as indicated by the Gregorian chant online database Cantus, http://cantusdatabase.org). Zalewski gives only the incipit of this extremely rare responsory. It has taken the author of the present work nearly ten years to find the complete text. We provide here what we believe is the original text, which we were able to extract from a lengthened rendering of the responsory given in a sixteenth-century Lutheran manual of the Pomeranian duke Barnim XI from what is now Szczecin, Poland. Using information about the fourteenth-century Austrian text of this chant from the above-cited Cantus database, we were readily able to identify and delete what were clearly Protestant additions to the original Catholic text (the latter simply drawn from Lk 22:14–15, 19, and

We, being many, are one bread, one body, all that partake of one bread and of one chalice. Verse: *In thy sweetness, O God, thou hast provided for the poor, who make men of one mind to dwell in a house. All that partake . . .* [1 Cor 10:17; Ps 67:7, 11].[61]

As the procession nears the cathedral, the Corpus Christi antiphon *Melchisedech*, a characteristic feature of the Polish processions, is sung: "*Melchisedech, the king of Salem, bringing forth bread and wine, was indeed the chief priest of God; he blessed Abraham and said: Blessed be Abraham by God on high, who created Heaven and earth*" (cf. Gen 14:18).[62] The procession draws to a conclusion with the singing of the thanksgiving hymn *Te Deum* and the reposition of the Blessed Sacrament in "the accustomed place".[63]

We conclude this chapter with the ceremonies of Corpus Christi as they were celebrated by the Dominican Order, the religious congregation that gave the Church Saint Thomas Aquinas, author of the Corpus Christi office. A 1545 Dominican processional published in Venice prescribes for the friars a Corpus Christi procession with four stations, albeit without the fourfold conferral of benediction and the reading of four Gospels that we find in the German and Polish rites. The ceremony begins at the high altar, where, after all have knelt before the Blessed Sacrament, the prior rises and takes the Eucharist, enclosed within a pyx, into his hands. Turning toward the choir, he raises the pyx to the level of his face, at which point the choir begins the *Tantum ergo* (i.e., the last two verses of the *Pange lingua*). During the final verse, the prior gives benediction, making the sign of the cross with the Eucharist over the friars. Following the end of the hymn, the procession sets out into the cloister; a number of friars carry lit candles round about the Eucharist, borne by the prior, as the choir sings the first of three responsories from the Corpus Christi office, one for each of the first three stations.[64] The procession stops for the

Corpus Christi in a Dominican Friary (1545)

Mk 14:23–24). See Barnim XI, *Agenda, dat is, Ordninge der hilligen Kerckenempter unde Ceremonien wo sich de Parrherren, Seelsorgere unde Kerckendenere in erem Ampte holden Schölen* (Szczecin, Poland: Andreas Kellner, 1591; digitized text, Bayerische Staatsbibliothek, Munich, 2009), fols. 375v–377v.

[61] The full text of this responsory, *Unus panis*, is here taken from the 1531 Sarum Breviary of Salisbury, England, in Proctor and Wordsworth, *Breviarium ad usum insignis ecclesiae Sarum*, vol. 1, cols. 1071–1072.

[62] This antiphon, *Melchisedech rex Salem*, is believed to date from the second half of the thirteenth century as a component of one of the three earliest versions of the Corpus Christi office, the version named *Sapiencia aedificavit sibi* (from the incipit of its opening antiphon), preserved in a mid-fourteenth-century breviary of the Praemonstratensian abbey of Strahov, Prague, Czech Republic (manuscript: Prague, Strahov Abbey, MS D.E.I.7); see Walters, Corrigan, and Ricketts, *Feast of Corpus Christi*, 185, from which the complete text, given here, is taken. For the dating of the *Sapiencia aedificavit sibi* Corpus Christi office, see ibid., xviii, 58, 62–67, 74.

[63] Zalewski, "Święto Bożego Ciała w Polsce", 137, footnote.

[64] The responsories sung are *Respexit Helyas*, *Accepit Jesus calicem*, and *Unus panis*.

first station on one side of the rectangular cloister and then continues to the second station, on the opposite side. The third station is made within the outer portion of the friary's church, after which the prior carries the Eucharist to the high altar for the fourth and final station as the antiphon O *sacrum convivium* is sung.[65] The same processional provides separate rubrics for a public procession conducted by the Dominican friars, describing in detail the cortege accompanying the Blessed Sacrament:

> The procession goes forth, with holy water and two candle bearers preceding, and the crossbearer; and after them the *conversi* brothers and the youths who are not attired in sacred vestments; after them should proceed all the brothers who have been vested; and the priests and priors who are not vested follow them. Then proceed two thurifers with thuribles, and after them two other acolytes; lastly the prior with a silk cope, carrying in a fitting vessel the Body of Christ visibly elevated before his face, whom the deacon, to his right, and the subdeacon, to his left, should accompany, remaining slightly ahead of the prior. And over the Body of Christ an *umbella* [umbrella-shaped canopy] or baldachin should be carried by four distinguished scholars.[66]

---

[65] *Processionarium secundum ritum et morem Fratrum Predicatorum* (Venice: Luceantonius, 1545; digitized text, Bayerische Staatsbibliothek, Munich, 2009), fols. 41r–44v.

[66] Ibid., fol. 73v.

17 Processions of the Assumption (August 15) and All Souls' Day (November 2)

Dearest brethren, let us with prayers poured forth beseech the Lord, the Inhabitant of the virginal dwelling, the Bridegroom of the blessed bridal chamber, the Lord of the Tabernacle, the King of the Temple, who has conferred his own innocence upon his Mother, within whom the divinity deigned to become incarnate, whose soul, knowing nothing of the world, attentive only to prayers, preserved purity in her actions.

Prayer from the Mass of the Assumption,
Missale Gothicum, eighth century[1]

Processions Commemorating the Assumption of the Blessed Virgin Mary

The observance of a mid-August feast commemorating the Blessed Virgin Mary dates back to the early fifth century, when the ancient liturgical book of Jerusalem known as the Armenian Lectionary provides readings and an antiphon for a feast "of Mary, the Theotokos" (Mary, the Mother of God) on August 15.[2] Although the lectionary's title for the celebration makes no mention of the specific mystery commemorated by the feast, the assignment of the antiphon "*Arise, O Lord, into your resting place, you and the ark of your holiness*" (cf. Ps 131:8),[3] suggests that August 15 was from the beginning a memorial of the Blessed Virgin Mary's passage to eternal life.[4] The triumphal taking of the Ark of the Covenant into Sion of which the antiphon speaks appears to be utilized in this liturgical context as a metaphor for the Assumption, for, from the time of the Eastern Father Saint Athanasius of

---

[1] Text in Leo Cunibert Mohlberg, O.S.B., ed., *Missale Gothicum*, REDSMF 5 (Rome: Herder, 1961), no. 96, pp. 28–29.

[2] Text in Athanase Renoux, ed. and trans., *Le codex arménien Jérusalem 121*, vol. 2, *Edition comparée du texte et de deux autres manuscrits*, Patrologia orientalis 36, fasc. 2 (Turnhout, Belgium: Brepols, 1971), no. 64, pp. 354–357.

[3] Ibid., 354–355.

[4] Refuting a commonly held view that the observance of August 15 was originally a general Marian feast that later evolved into a memorial of the Assumption, Father Joseph Crehan, S.J., argues convincingly that this feast day was from its inception a commemoration of the Assumption through a carefully reasoned examination of patristic, liturgical, and archaeological evidence; see his article "The Assumption and the Jerusalem Liturgy", *Theological Studies* 30 (1969): 312–325.

Alexandria (+347) onward, the Ark of the Covenant was increasingly understood as a prefiguration of Mary.[5] The subsequent addition to Jerusalem's August 15 liturgy of an antiphon from Psalm 44 by the last quarter of the fifth century further testifies to the nature of the feast: "*Hearken, O daughter, and see, and incline thy ear; and forget thy people and thy father's house. And the king shall greatly desire thy beauty; for he is the Lord thy God, and him they shall adore*" (Ps 44:11–12). This antiphon, first mentioned in a homily of the Jerusalem priest Chrysippus (+479),[6] is assigned thereafter to August 15 together with a troparion that begins "*When you migrated*", in a later liturgical book of Jerusalem, the Georgian Lectionary, dating from the fifth to the eighth century, one manuscript of which uses the term "Assumption" in an apparent reference to August 15.[7]

It is the Syrian-born pope Sergius I (687–701) who is credited with instituting in Rome a procession on August 15 in honor of the "Dormition" of the Blessed Virgin.[8] Soon afterward, the feast was to receive the name by which we know it, the Assumption, in the eighth-century *Hadrianum* redaction of Rome's Gregorian Sacramentary.[9] Roman *Ordo 50*, a late tenth-century liturgical text of Rome, testifies to a simple dramatization of the mystery of the day: the famed *Acheiropita* image of Christ from the Basilica of Saint John Lateran would be carried by night in a torchlight procession to the Basilica of Saint Mary Major, where it was brought to the latter church's image of Mary known as the *Salus populi Romani* (Salvation of the Roman people), an action undoubtedly intended to represent the reunion of Mary with her Divine Son as she entered Heaven.[10]

During the Middle Ages, from the seventh century onward, and subsequently in the *Missale Romanum* of 1570, the Gospel assigned to the Mass of Assumption Day was that of Christ visiting the home of the sisters Martha and Mary (Lk 10:38–42).[11] The selection of this

---

[5] Ibid., 317–318, 322–325.

[6] Chrysippus of Jerusalem, "Oration on Holy Mary, the Mother of God", no. 2, in Martin Jugie, ed. and trans., *Homélies mariales byzantines: Textes grecs édités et traduits en latin*, vol. 2, Patrologia orientalis 19, fasc. 3 (Paris: Firmin-Didot, 1925), 338–339 (Greek text with Latin translation).

[7] Michel Tarchnischvili, ed., *Le grand lectionnaire de l'église de Jérusalem (V^e–VIIIe siècle)*, vol. 2, CSCO 204–205 (Louvain, Belgium: Secrétariat du CorpusSCO, 1960); Georgian-language text: CSCO 204, nos. 1148–1154, pp. 30–31, plus footnote to no. 1145, p. 30; Latin translation: CSCO 205, nos. 1148–1154, pp. 27–28, plus footnote to no. 1145, p. 27.

[8] This attribution is given in the *Liber pontificalis*; text in Louis Duchesne, ed., *Le Liber pontificalis: Texte, introduction et commentaire* (Paris: Ernest Thorin, 1886–1892), 1:376, 381.

[9] In this text, the feast bears the title "Assumption of Holy Mary"; see Jean Deshusses, ed., *Le sacramentaire grégorien: Ses principales formes d'après les plus anciens manuscrits*, vol. 1, 2nd ed., SF 16 (Fribourg, Switzerland: Editions Universitaires Fribourg, 1979), no. 661, p. 262.

[10] Text in Michel Andrieu, ed., *Les Ordines Romani du haut moyen âge*, vol. 5, SSLED 29 (Louvain, Belgium: "Spicilegium sacrum Lovaniense" Administration, 1961), 358–362.

[11] The specification of this Gospel lection for August 15 first appears in the seventh-century Roman source known as the *Capitulare evangeliorum*, part of the same manuscript as the lectionary called the *Comes* of Würzburg; see Germain Morin, "Liturgie et basiliques

reading is explained by William Durandus of Mende (+1296) as signifying that the Blessed Virgin Mary exemplified both the contemplative life, represented by the sister Mary, and the active life, represented
by the sister Martha. Just as Martha received Christ into her home
and served him, so too the Blessed Virgin Mary "most diligently fed
her Child, and carried him into Egypt, and earlier proved herself in
the active life in going to Elizabeth and serving her". And just as
Martha's sister Mary sat at Christ's feet to listen to him, similarly the
Blessed Virgin Mary engaged in the contemplative life, as indicated by
the testimony of the Gospel: "But Mary kept all these words, pondering them in her heart" (Lk 2:19; see also Lk 2:51).[12]

The processions conducted for the feast of the Assumption in Rome
and elsewhere across medieval Europe may have been inspired in part
by the ancient tradition that the Apostles brought the body of the
Blessed Virgin Mary in a funeral procession from her home to her
tomb, from which her body was assumed into Heaven three days later,
a tradition made popular through a widely circulated medieval book
of saints' lives, the *Golden Legend* of Jacobus de Voragine (+1298).[13]
This work quotes at length an eighth-century sermon of the eastern
Church Father Saint John of Damascus (+749), who describes the funeral
of Mary thus:

> What of those who stood around her most holy and sacred body?
> With love and reverence, with tears of exultation, they gathered about
> her, tending that divine and holy tabernacle with loving care.... The
> spotless body is wrapped in pure linen sheets, and the Queen is laid
> back upon her bed. Then bearing lights and sweet spices and singing
> hymns they make ready to go in procession before her.... When in
> this time the Ark of the Lord, borne on the shoulders of the Apos-
> tles, departed from Mount Sion to the heavenly abode of rest, it crossed
> over to it by way of an earthly tomb. And first it was taken through
> the midst of the city, like a bride in her beauty, but she is adorned in
> the unapproachable radiance of the Spirit, and thence it was borne to
> that most holy place, Gethsemane, angels overshadowing her with
> their wings, going before and with her and following after, together
> with the whole assembly of the Church.[14]

de Rome au milieu du VIIe siècle d'après les listes d'évangiles de Würzburg", *Revue Bénédictine* 28 (1911): 313. For the appearance of this reading in the *Missale Romanum* of 1570, see
Manlio Sodi and Achille Maria Triacca, eds., *Missale Romanum: Editio princeps (1570)*, facsimile ed., MLCT 2 (Vatican City: Libreria Editrice Vaticana, © 1998), 533 (new pagination).

[12] William Durandus of Mende, *Rationale divinorum officiorum*, bk. 7, chap. 24, nos. 6–7,
in A. Davril, O.S.B., and T.M. Thibodeau, eds., *Guillelmi Duranti: Rationale divinorum
officiorum VII–VIII*, CCCM 140b (Turnhout, Belgium: Brepols, 2000), 73–74. Hereafter
cited as Durandus, *Rationale* (CCCM 140b).

[13] Text in William Granger Ryan, trans., *Jacobus de Voragine: The Golden Legend; Readings on the Saints* (Princeton, N.J.: Princeton University Press, 1995), 2:91–92, 94–95.

[14] Saint John of Damascus, *Homily 2 on the Dormition of the Blessed Virgin Mary*, PG 96,
cols. 737–738, translated into English by M.F. Toal, in M.F. Toal, trans. and ed., *The*

John of Damascus' account is ultimately based upon an ancient apocryphal text known as the *Transitus Mariae* (Passage of Mary), which purports to relate the details of the death and bodily assumption of the Blessed Virgin Mary. Various versions of the *Transitus* exist in Coptic, Syriac, Latin, Greek, and Arabic;[15] internal evidence suggests a second-century origin for the *Transitus*.[16] The most ancient Latin rendering of the *Transitus* is an account formerly attributed to the Eastern Church Father Saint Melito of Sardis (+190) but now thought to be of sixth-century origin.[17] The moving imagery of the *Transitus* tradition, eloquently retold by Saint John of Damascus and promulgated by the *Golden Legend* of Jacobus de Voragine, would have filled the minds of the devout as they attended the Assumption Day processions of medieval Europe.

The fourteenth-century liturgical book of Essen, Germany, known as the *Liber ordinarius*, compiled for the quasi-monastic community of canons that staffed Essen's collegiate church, which they shared with an affiliated community of canonesses (women living a mitigated form of religious life), provides two processions for the Assumption: one for the feast day itself, confined to the grounds of the monastic community, and a second through the countryside conducted on the Sunday following the Assumption.[18] The procession of Assumption Day, in which a gold statue of the Blessed Virgin Mary is carried,[19] begins after an early Mass and the completion of the midmorning office of Terce:

> The aforesaid image [of Mary] shall be on the Gospel side of the high altar, placed on a bier and prepared for carrying. The priest and all the other canons shall be vested in copes, the ministers in dalmatics; three of which [ministers], with similar copes ..., having taken the banners, and the subdeacon with the lectionary shall stand before the high altar, with the banner of "the nails of the Lord" appearing always in the middle, facing the people; the priest and the other canons in their seats facing south; the two bearers of the image, namely two canons in copes, beside the image; the religious community [of

Sunday Sermons of the Great Fathers (Chicago, 1960–1963; repr., San Francisco: Ignatius Press, 2000), 4:432.

[15] Montague Rhodes James, *The Apocryphal New Testament* (Oxford: Clarendon, 1924), 194–227.

[16] See, for example, Hans Förster, ed., *Transitus Mariae: Beiträge zur koptischen Überlieferung*, Die griechischen christlichen Schriftsteller der ersten Jahrhunderte, new series, 14 (Berlin: Walter de Gruyter, 2006), 226–227.

[17] English translation of the Latin text in James, *Apocryphal New Testament*, 209–216. An Italian translation of this text is given in Luigi Moraldi, ed., *Apocrifi del Nuovo Testamento*, Classici delle religioni (Turin, Italy: Unione Tipografico-Editrice Torinese, 1971), 1:870–878.

[18] Texts in Franz Arens, ed., *Der Liber ordinarius der Essener Stiftskirche* (Paderborn, Germany: Albert Pape, 1908), 104–106.

[19] The liturgical scholar Franz Arens states that the Essen canons used their gold statue of the Blessed Virgin Mary for this procession; see his work *Der Liber ordinarius der Essener Stiftskirche und seine Bedeutung für die Liturgie, Geschichte und Topographie des ehemaligen Stiftes Essen*, Beiträge zur Geschichte von Stadt und Stift Essen (Essen, Germany: G. D. Baedeker, 1901), 60, 82.

women] before the sacristy of the Body of Christ facing north, or below near the sepulcher of blessed Alfrid. Then the religious community shall sing the antiphon *I am come into my garden, O my sister, my spouse, I gathered my myrrh with my aromatical spices* [cf. Song 6:1].[20]

After the priest recites the Collect of the day's Mass, the canons, the scholars, and the women religious set out in a procession that exits the church and files past the religious community's cemetery, led by the three standard-bearers with their banners, who immediately precede the image of the Blessed Virgin, carried by its two bearers. In going forth, the canons sing the particularly beautiful responsory *Vidi speciosam*, a text dating from the ninth century: "*I saw one beautiful as a dove, ascending from above the rivers of the waters, whose priceless fragrance was in her garments beyond measure. And like the days of spring, flowers of roses and the lilies of the valley encompassed her.* Verse: *Who is she that goeth up by the desert, as a pillar of smoke of aromatical spices, of myrrh and frankincense?* [cf. Song 3:6]. *And like the days of spring . . .*"[21] The responsory that follows, *Super salutem*, likewise from the ninth century, is sung by the canons as the procession heads back toward the church: "*Above prosperity and all beauty, you are beloved to the Lord and are worthy to be called Queen of the heavens; the choirs of angels rejoice, your consorts and fellow citizens.* Verse: *The gate of Paradise was closed to all by Eve and was opened again by the Virgin Mary. The choirs of angels rejoice . . .*"[22] After reentering the church, the procession concludes shortly before High Mass with a station at the Gospel side of the altar as the antiphon *Ave Regina*, a chant traceable to the twelfth century, is sung by the women religious: "*Hail, Queen of the heavens; hail, O Lady of the angels; hail, holy root, glorious Virgin, beautiful above all, from whom light has been born to the world; prevail, O exceedingly beauteous one, and ever supplicate Christ for us, alleluia.*"[23]

---

[20] Arens, *Liber ordinarius der Essener Stiftskirche*, 104. The Essen text gives only the incipit of the antiphon *Veni in ortum meum*; the complete text is here taken from René-Jean Hésbert, ed., *Corpus antiphonalium officii*, vol. 3, pt. 1, REDSMF 9 (Rome: Herder, 1968), no. 5325, p. 528. This antiphon is traceable to the eleventh century, when it is found in an antiphonary of Verona (Italy); see René-Jean Hésbert, *Corpus antiphonalium officii*, vol. 1, REDSMF 7 (Rome: Herder, 1963), 289.

[21] Arens, *Liber ordinarius der Essener Stiftskirche*, 104–105. The Essen text gives only the incipit of the responsory *Vidi speciosam*; the complete text is here taken from the *Breviarium Romanum* of 1568, in Manlio Sodi and Achille Maria Triacca, eds., *Breviarium Romanum: Editio princeps (1568)*, facsimile ed., MLCT 3 (Vatican City: Libreria Editrice Vaticana, © 1999), 853 (new pagination). This responsory first appears in the Antiphonary of Compiègne (France, c. 870); see Hésbert, *Corpus antiphonalium officii*, 1:284.

[22] Arens, *Liber ordinarius der Essener Stiftskirche*, 104–105. The Essen text gives only the incipit of the responsory *Super salutem*; the complete text is here taken from René-Jean Hésbert, ed., *Corpus antiphonalium officii*, vol. 4, REDSMF 10 (Rome: Herder, 1970), no. 7726, p. 424. This responsory first appears in the Antiphonary of Compiègne (France, c. 870); see Hésbert, *Corpus antiphonalium officii*, 1:284.

[23] Arens, *Liber ordinarius der Essener Stiftskirche*, 105. The Essen text gives only the incipit of the antiphon *Ave Regina*; the complete text is here taken from Hésbert, *Corpus antiphonalium officii*, vol. 3, pt. 1, no. 1542, p. 64. For the dating of this antiphon, see Matthew Britt, *The Hymns of the Breviary and Missal* (New York: Benziger Bros., 1922), 87.

The procession on the following Sunday takes place in the late morning after High Mass. A silver statue of the Blessed Virgin Mary is carried out of the collegiate church in a procession that exits the town and passes "through the rural areas", stopping at three or four stations along the way, with a sermon given at each station. As the procession circles the Church of Saint Gertrude, the responsory *Regnum mundi* is sung: "*The kingdom of this world and every adornment of the world I have disdained, for the sake of the love of my Lord Jesus Christ, whom I have seen, whom I have loved, in whom I have believed, whom I have prized. Verse: My heart hath uttered a good word; I speak my works to the king. Whom I have seen . . .*" (cf. Phil 3:7–8; 2 Tim 1:12; Ps 44:2).[24]

The earlier-cited responsory *Vidi speciosam*, sung during the Assumption Day procession of Essen and taken from the office of first Vespers for this feast, speaks of Mary as encompassed by "*flowers of roses and the lilies of the valley*". It is this association of the Blessed Virgin Mary with roses and lilies that Durandus believes is responsible for the medieval custom of collecting and blessing herbs on the feast of the Assumption, adding that "just as the thorn bore the rose, so Judea bore Mary." [25] In a similar vein, Sicard of Cremona (+1215) explains the blessing of herbs on Assumption Day by directly applying to the Blessed Virgin the verse from the Song of Solomon alluded to by Durandus, "As the lily among thorns, so is my love among the daughters" (Song 2:2).[26] There are, in fact, further aspects of the medieval liturgy of the Assumption that could additionally explain the selection of this feast as a fitting occasion for blessing plants. From the eleventh century to the *Missale Romanum* of 1570, the first reading for the Mass of the vigil of the Assumption (August 14) was a passage from the Book of Ecclesiasticus describing wisdom (Sir 24:23–31). The text's feminine personification of wisdom, which is filled with the vivid garden imagery of fragrant blossoms and ripening fruits, is used in this context to apply to the Blessed Virgin Mary:[27]

As the vine I have brought forth a pleasant odour: and my flowers are the fruit of honour and riches. I am the mother of fair love, and of

---

[24] Arens, *Liber ordinarius der Essener Stiftskirche*, 105–106. The Essen text gives only the incipit of the responsory *Regnum mundi*; the complete text is here taken from Hésbert, *Corpus antiphonalium officii*, vol. 4, no. 7524, p. 379. This responsory dates back to the eleventh century, when it appears in the Antiphonary of Hartker (Saint Gall Abbey, Switzerland); see René-Jean Hésbert, ed., *Corpus antiphonalium officii*, vol. 2, REDSMF 8 (Rome: Herder, 1965), 596.

[25] Durandus, *Rationale* (CCCM 140b), bk. 7, chap. 24, no. 10, p. 74.

[26] Sicard of Cremona, *Mitrale*, bk. 9, chap. 40, PL 213, col. 420.

[27] This reading is first specified for the Assumption vigil in an eleventh-century redaction of the customary of Cluny, a liturgical book of the French Benedictine abbey of Cluny; text in Kassius Hallinger, O.S.B., *Consuetudines Cluniacensium antiquiores cum redactionibus derivatis*, Corpus consuetudinum monasticarum 7, pt. 2 (Siegburg, Germany: Franciscus Schmitt, 1983), 121. For the specification of this reading in the 1570 *Missale Romanum*, see Sodi and Triacca, *Missale Romanum: Editio princeps (1570)*, 531 (new pagination).

fear, and of knowledge, and of holy hope. In me is all grace of the way and of the truth, in me is all hope of life and of virtue. Come over to me, all ye that desire me, and be filled with my fruits. For my spirit is sweet above honey, and my inheritance above honey and the honeycomb. My memory is unto everlasting generations.... They that explain me shall have life everlasting. (Ecclus 24:23–28, 31)

This evocation of plant symbolism is continued in the medieval Mass for Assumption Day, wherein another portion of the description of wisdom from the Book of Ecclesiasticus is utilized for the first reading (Ecclus 24:11–20), a text used in this way from the late eighth century onward[28] and retained in the *Missale Romanum* of 1570:[29] "I was exalted like a cedar in Libanus, and as a cypress tree on mount Sion. I was exalted like a palm tree in Cades, and as a rose plant in Jericho: as a fair olive tree in the plains, and as a plane tree by the water in the streets, was I exalted. I gave a sweet smell like cinnamon, and aromatical balm; I yielded a sweet odour like the best myrrh" (Ecclus 24:17–20).

The practice of blessing herbs on the feast of the Assumption had been introduced by the tenth century, when it appears in a liturgical manuscript of Germany.[30] Five centuries later, we find this tradition continued in a 1482 ritual of Konstanz, Germany, which provides three benediction prayers for blessing herbs on Assumption Day, the second of which is an expanded version of a prayer from the aforementioned tenth-century manuscript,[31] while the first and third prayers are traceable to the twelfth century:[32]

Holy Lord, almighty Father, who from the beginning made man to your image and formed Heaven and earth, the sun, and the moon, and the stars, and all things celestial and earthly: you, O Lord, have dominion over the power of the sea; you have control of the great abyss; you formed all the elements. May you vouchsafe to bless + and sanc + tify these creatures of herbs, just as you blessed the five loaves and two fish in the desert and fed the five thousand men; and vouchsafe to bless + and sancti + fy all who make use of them, that it may be to them health of soul and body, in the name of the Fa + ther, and the Son + , and the Holy + Spirit. And may you vouchsafe to expel from all men and sheep who shall have partaken of the

---

[28] This lection is first specified as a reading for the Mass of August 15 in the *Comes* of Murbach, a late eighth-century lectionary of the French-Alsatian abbey of Murbach constituting a Frankish adaptation of earlier Roman lectionaries; see D. A. Wilmart, "Le *Comes* de Murbach", *Revue Bénédictine* 30 (1913): 48.

[29] See Sodi and Triacca, *Missale Romanum: Editio princeps (1570)*, 532 (new pagination).

[30] Manuscript: Munich, Bayerische Staatsbibliothek, Codex Latinus Monacensis (Clm) 3851, in Adolph Franz, *Die kirchlichen Benediktionen im Mittelalter* (Freiburg im Breisgau, Germany, 1909; repr., Graz, Austria: Akademische Druck—U. Verlagsanstalt, 1960), 1:398–399.

[31] Ibid., 399.

[32] The first and third prayers appear in a twelfth-century monastic ritual of southwestern Germany (manuscript: Leipzig, Germany, Universitätsbibliothek, Codex Lipsiensis Paulinus 777), quoted in Franz, *Kirchlichen Benediktionen im Mittelalter*, 1:401, 400, respectively.

latter every corruption and every phantom of the devil, and every illness, and every pestilence and pain. Who in perfect Trinity live and reign, God . . . Amen.

Humbly, O holy Father, and relying upon prayers, we entreat your clemency, who have wonderfully created all things from nothing, and who have commanded the earth to bring forth diverse fruits, and have put in herbs various kinds of remedies for healing the bodies of men; may you vouchsafe in your goodness to bless + and sanc + tify these herbs of diverse kinds, that whoever on this solemnity of the venerable and holy Mary, Mother of God, is going to partake of them may receive health of both soul and body and, with the same blessed Mary ever Virgin interceding, be so salutarily glad in the use of them that they may be worthy to approach the gates of Paradise in the odor of your ointments, our Lord God Jesus Christ granting, who lives and reigns with you, God, through all [ages of ages]. Amen.

O God, who have furnished remedies for the needs of man with all kinds of herbs, bless with the right hand of your mercy this collection of herbs, that whoever having presented [himself] to your holy Church, weighed down with infirmity, shall have tasted anything from them may receive your gift of longed-for health, you granting. Through our Lord . . . [33]

The earlier-cited responsory *Vidi speciosam* ("*I saw one beautiful as a dove*") is now recited, the very text to which Durandus attributes the origin of the Assumption Day herb blessing. The priest ends the rite with a Collect dating back to the eighth-century *Hadrianum* edition of the Gregorian Sacramentary of Rome,[34] the prayer *Veneranda*, used for the Mass of Assumption Day throughout the Middle Ages (cited by Venerable Pope Pius XII in his 1950 apostolic constitution defining the dogma of the Assumption, *Munificentissimus Deus*):[35] "*May this venerable feast confer upon us the everlasting solace of this day, on which the holy Mother of God underwent temporal death yet was unable to be weighed down by the coils of death, who bore your Son our Lord, incarnate from her. Through the same Jesus Christ your Son, our Lord . . . Amen.*"[36] Subsequent editions of the Konstanz ritual, beginning with that published in 1502, conclude the Assumption Day blessing with the rubric "Afterward the herbs should be sprinkled and censed, and a procession should be made according to the custom of the church."[37] Thus Konstanz also observed the tradition of a procession on this day. Two other south German

---

[33] Text in Alban Dold, ed., *Die Konstanzer Ritualientexte in ihrer Entwicklung von 1482–1721*, Liturgiegeschichtliche Quellen 5–6 (Münster, Germany: Aschendorffschen Verlagsbuchhandlung, 1923), 151–152.

[34] Text in Deshusses, *Sacramentaire Gregorien*, no. 661, 1:262–263.

[35] Venerable Pius XII, *Munificentissimus Deus* (November 1, 1950), in *Apostolic Constitution of Pope Pius XII on the Assumption of the Blessed Virgin Mary*, trans. NCWC News Service (Staten Island, N.Y.: Daughters of Saint Paul, n.d.), no. 17, pp. 10–11.

[36] Dold, *Konstanzer Ritualientexte*, 152.

[37] Ibid., footnote.

liturgical books of the same period, the 1487 *Obsequiale Augustense* of Augsburg and the 1488 *Obsequiale Eystetense* of Eichstätt, also provide an Assumption Day rite of blessing herbs, likewise specifying the sprinkling of the herbs with holy water, their incensation, and a procession afterward.[38]

The specific focus of the feast of the Assumption upon the unique prerogative of the Blessed Virgin Mary in having not only her soul but also her body taken into Heaven, without undergoing any corruption, inspired representations of her bodily elevation to Heaven. Such is the case with the Assumption Day procession found in a liturgical text of the collegiate church of Halle, Germany (c. 1532). The rite follows the midafternoon office of None. Exiting the sacristy, a deacon and a cantor from the choir carry on a bier an image of the Blessed Virgin Mary, bringing it in front of the high altar as the church's provost (superior), two acolytes with candles and two others with thuribles precede them. Then, as all the bells of the church begin to peal, the deacon and the cantor set out with the image on its bier in a procession through the church and the adjacent cloister, led by a retinue of the clergy and the acolytes, as the earlier-quoted Assumption Day responsory *Vidi speciosam* ("*I saw one beautiful as a dove*") is sung:

> And the procession shall be ordered thus: first, the chamberlain shall precede, and two very small white damask banners shall be carried; afterward the choristers and the subcantor; again, two white damask banners; and the vicars and lords shall follow; again, two white banners; afterward, the boys with the candles; then those with the censers; [next,] the provost; lastly, the deacon and the cantor with the bier.[39]

After reentering the church, the procession halts before the front arch of the choir. The clergy and the acolytes stand before the arch in two parallel rows, facing east. Directly in front of the apex of the arch stands a throne covered in red samite, upon which is placed the statue of the Blessed Virgin. As soon as the image is enthroned, the candles near it are all lit. The image is flanked on each side by three acolytes: one with a thurible, one with a candlestick, and one with a white damask banner. The provost stands closest to the image. Two antiphons are now sung (*Tota pulchra* and *Assumpta est Maria*), the first of which is a catena of verses and phrases from the Song of Solomon (Song 4:7, 10–11; 2:10–13; 4:8):

---

[38] See respectively *Obsequiale Augustense* (Augsburg, Germany: Erhard Ratdolt, 1487; digitized text, Bayerische Staatsbibliothek, Munich, 2008), fol. 52r–52v, and *Obsequiale Eystetense* (Eichstätt, Germany: Michael Reyser, 1488; digitized text, Bayerische Staatsbibliothek, Munich, 2009), fols. 92r–93v.

[39] *Breviarius ecclesiae collegiatae Hallensis*, c. 1532, in Karl Young, *The Drama of the Medieval Church* (Oxford: Clarendon, 1933), 2:256. (Here and on the pages to follow, all passages from the *Breviarius* of Halle as transcribed by Young are quoted and translated by permission of Oxford University Press. Copyright Oxford University Press.)

528

You are all beautiful, my beloved, and there is no blemish in you; honey dripping from your lips, milk and honey under your tongue, the fragrance of your ointments over all aromas; for now the winter has passed, the rain has gone away and departed, the flowers have appeared, the flourishing vines have given forth their odor, and the voice of the turtledove is heard in our land; arise, make haste, my beloved; come from Libanus; come, you shall be crowned.[40]

Mary has been assumed into Heaven; the angels rejoice. Response: *Offering praise, they bless the Lord.*[41]

The Canticle of Zechariah (Lk 1:68–79, "*Blessed be the Lord God of Israel . . .*") is then sung to the accompaniment of the organ. As the concluding Glory Be to the Father is begun, the provost incenses the image of the Blessed Mother. Immediately before the words "*As it was in the beginning*", the deacon and the cantor harness the statue to cords from above, turning the face of the image toward the east as they do so. By means of the cords, the image is now raised upward toward the ceiling as flute players or pipers of the city, stationed above the choir arch, jubilantly serenade the Blessed Virgin together with the organ, continuing to play until the image disappears from sight. Meanwhile, two of the acolytes, having ascended to the porch over the choir arch, sing, "*Who is this who advances even as the sun, and beautiful like Jerusalem?*" The choir answers with a responsory (the chant *Ista est speciosa*): "*This is the most beautiful among the daughters of Jerusalem, even as you have seen her, filled with charity and love, amid [flower] beds and aromatic gardens.* [Verse:] *Hearken, in your comeliness and your beauty, go forth prosperously, and reign. Amid [flower] beds . . .*"[42] The subcantor then intones another antiphon of the feast: "*Today the Virgin Mary mounts the heavens; rejoice, for she reigns with Christ forever.*"[43] The provost says the verse "*You, O holy Mother of God, have been exalted*" (response: "*Above the choirs of angels, unto the celestial realms*"),[44]

---

[40] Ibid. This antiphon, *Tota pulchra*, is traceable to the early eleventh century, when it appears in an antiphonary of Monza, Italy; see Hésbert, *Corpus antiphonalium officii*, 1:282. The complete text, given here, is taken from Hésbert, *Corpus antiphonalium officii*, vol. 3, pt. 1, no. 5162, p. 508.

[41] Young, *Drama of the Medieval Church*, 2:256. The antiphon *Assumpta est Maria* first appears in the Antiphonary of Compiègne (France, c. 870); see Hésbert, *Corpus antiphonalium officii*, 1:286.

[42] Young, *Drama of the Medieval Church*, 2:256. The Halle text gives only the incipit of the responsory *Ista est speciosa*; the complete text is here taken from Hésbert, *Corpus antiphonalium officii*, no. 6994, 4:248. This responsory first appears in the Antiphonary of Compiègne (France, c. 870); see Hésbert, *Corpus antiphonalium officii*, 1:284.

[43] This antiphon, *Hodie Maria Virgo*, first appears in the Antiphonary of Compiègne (France, c. 870); see Hésbert, *Corpus antiphonalium officii*, 1:286.

[44] The Halle text gives only the incipit of this versicle, *Exaltata es*; the complete text is here taken from the Gregorian chant online database Cantus, http://cantusdatabase.org. This versicle is traceable to the late ninth century, when it appears in a combined gradual and antiphonary for the Cathedral of Sainte-Cécile, Albi, France, a liturgical book dating

followed by the earlier-quoted Collect of the Assumption Day Mass, *Veneranda* ("*May this venerable feast confer upon us*"), after which he and the other clerics return to the sacristy. The rite concludes with a sermon to the people.[45]

In the rubrics of a 1511 *consueta* (book of customs) for the Spanish cathedral of Palma de Majorca, the death scene of the Blessed Virgin Mary as described by Saint John of Damascus, whose account we cited earlier, is virtually recreated for the liturgical rites of Assumption Day. Shortly before the beginning of the predawn office of Lauds, in the section of the cathedral housing the tombs of the deceased canons, a statue of the Virgin Mother would be placed upon a bed that is draped with a cloth of yellow damask. At each of the four corners of the bed stands an iron candelabra, each of which is surmounted by four white candles. Twelve priests, vested to represent the Apostles, then enter and, seating themselves on benches beside the bed, recite Lauds together. The resemblance of this rite to a wake is unmistakable. In the morning, the same twelve priests, again vested as the Apostles, escort the image of the Blessed Mother through the church, with eleven of the Apostles serving as pallbearers, carrying the figure on its bed, as Saint John walks alone ahead of the bed, carrying a palm. The detail of the palm is traceable to the earliest Latin version of the ancient *Transitus Mariae*, in which an angel brings to the Blessed Virgin Mary before her death a palm branch from Heaven that the angel tells her is to be carried before her bier, a task subsequently fulfilled at her funeral by Saint John.[46] The Majorca "funeral procession" of Mary would be repeated at the evening office of Compline.[47]

The All Souls' Day Procession (November 2)

Sicard of Cremona (+1215) situates the significance of All Souls' Day within the context of the two days that precede it. While the eve of All Saints' Day is a "day of affliction", that is, a day of fasting recalling the "misery of the present life", and All Saints' Day itself is a "day of exultation" on which "we rejoice in the beatitude of the saints, rendering thanksgiving to the Lord", on All Souls' Day "we pray for those who are detained in Purgatory, obtaining for them by our prayers sometimes milder pain, sometimes complete absolution."[48] The designation of November 2 as a day of prayer for all the departed souls can be traced back to a monastic ordinance issued at the end of the tenth century by the abbot Saint Odilo (+1049)

from about 890 (manuscript: Albi, France, Bibliothèque Municipale Rochegude, MS 44, fol. 108r, as indicated by the Cantus online database).

[45] Young, *Drama of the Medieval Church*, 2:256.

[46] Pseudo-Melito of Sardis, *Transitus Mariae*, chaps. 3, 4, 11, in James, *Apocryphal New Testament*, 210–211, 213; Moraldi, *Apocrifi del Nuovo Testamento*, 1:871–872, 874–875 (Italian translation).

[47] Text in Richard Donovan, C.S.B., *The Liturgical Drama in Medieval Spain* (Toronto: Pontifical Institute of Medieval Studies, 1958), 137–138.

[48] Sicard of Cremona, *Mitrale*, bk. 9, chap. 50, PL 213, col. 424.

for his Benedictine congregation of Cluny, France. In this statute, Odilo observes that in addition to the established practice of commemorating all the saints on November 1, he deems it likewise fitting that "there should be conducted among us in a festive manner a commemoration of all the faithful departed, who have been from the beginning of the world all the way to the end"; thus he mandates that on November 2, Requiem Masses and the Office of the Dead should be offered for all the faithful departed.[49] Odilo in turn may have derived this custom from the recommendation of the ninth-century liturgist Amalarius of Metz that after the recitation of the office for All Saints' Day on November 1 the Office of the Dead should be said for the many who "pass from the present world" but "are not immediately joined to the saints".[50] Regarding this use of the Office of the Dead from the evening of November 1 through the end of November 2, Sicard of Cremona notes that it is begun at Vespers (on November 1), but it is not to be ended at Vespers (on November 2), for as he explains, "this office shall have an end" only "when the souls of those to be saved, freed from all pain, shall thoroughly enjoy eternal joy".[51]

The *Liber tramitis*, an eleventh-century customary of Saint Odilo's abbey of Cluny (c. 1043), provides rubrics for the liturgical observance of November 2, including a directive that for the Mass and the offices of the day twelve lit candles should be placed before the altar.[52] A book of customs for the Benedictine abbey of Saint Savin of Lavedan, near Tarbes, France, dating from about 1070, calls for "visiting the cemetery" on All Souls' Day,[53] the earliest indication of what would develop into the practice of conducting a procession on November 2. By the thirteenth century, the All Souls' Day procession had acquired a defined form, with multiple stations and specific chants and prayers to be sung and recited along the way. It is thus that we find it in a liturgical text of Zurich, Switzerland, the *Liber ordinarius* of Konrad von Mure, a cantor of the city's cathedral (+1281). The earliest of three different versions of Zurich's All Souls' Day procession given in this text can be dated to the period of

---

[49] *Statutum s. Odilonis de defunctis*, PL 142, col. 1037.

[50] Amalarius of Metz, *Liber de ordine antiphonarii*, chap. 65, in John Michael Hanssens, S.J., ed., *Amalarii episcopi: Opera liturgica omnia*, vol. 3, ST 140 (Vatican City: Biblioteca Apostolica Vaticana, 1950), 98.

[51] Sicard of Cremona, *Mitrale*, bk. 9, chap. 50, PL 213, col. 426.

[52] *Liber tramitis* (formerly called the Customs of Farfa), bk. 1, chap. 127, in Bruno Albers, ed., *Consuetudines monasticae*, vol. 1, *Consuetudines Farfenses* (Stuttgart: Jos. Roth, Bibliopolae, 1900), 124–125.

[53] *Consuetudines ecclesiarum abbatiae s. Savini Tarbiensis dioecesis subditarum*, quoted in Alfons Labudda, "Liturgia dnia Zadusznego w Polsce do Wydania Rytuału Piotrkowskiego w Świetle Ksiąg Liturgicznych: Studium historyczno-liturgiczne", in *Studia z dziejów liturgii w Polsce*, vol. 1, Rozprawy Wydziału Teologiczno-Kanonicznego 33 (Lublin, Poland: Towarzystwo Naukowe, Katolickiego Uniwersytetu Lubelskiego, 1973), 365–366, footnote.

1271–1278,[54] and it is this version that we present here. The procession takes place at the cathedral on the eve of November 2, immediately after the liturgical observance of All Saints' Day draws to a close with the completion of Vespers. The clerics and scholars set out from the choir of the cathedral and proceed through the nave after beginning the following responsory from the early eleventh century:[55]

> *Deliver me, O Lord, from eternal death on that fearful day, when the heavens and the earth are to be moved, when you shall come to judge the world by fire. [Verse:] I am made to tremble, and I fear, until the final judgment shall come, and the wrath to come. When the heavens ... [Verse:] That day, the day of wrath, of calamity and misery, the great day, exceedingly bitter. When you shall come ... [Verse:] Eternal rest grant unto them, O Lord. Deliver me ...[56]*

As the procession exits the nave through the main door of the cathedral and, turning right, heads toward the cemetery, a second responsory, of late ninth-century origin, is sung (based upon Job 10:20–21, 8):[57] "*The fewness of my days shall be finished shortly; send me, O Lord, outside, let me lament my sorrow a little, lest I go and not return, to the gloomy and hidden darkness of death. Verse: Thy hands have made me, and fashioned me wholly round about; and dost thou thus cast me down headlong on a sudden? Let me lament my sorrow ...*"[58] The procession halts at the gate of the cemetery, where the first of the procession's eleven stations is held.[59] Five psalms are recited: Psalm 114 ("*I have loved, because the Lord will hear the voice of my prayer ...*"), Psalm 119 ("*In my trouble I cried to the Lord ...*"), Psalm 120 ("*I have lifted up my eyes to the mountains ...*"), Psalm 129 ("*Out of the depths I have cried to thee, O Lord ...*"), and Psalm 137 ("*I will praise thee, O Lord ...*"). All of these psalms reiterate the theme of God mercifully answering supplications offered to him. A verse and an antiphon follow (from the late ninth

[54] Text in Heidi Leuppi, *Der Liber ordinarius des Konrad von Mure: Die Gottesdienstordnung am Grossmünster in Zürich*, SF 37 (Fribourg, Switzerland: Universitätsverlag Freiburg, 1995), 421–425; for the dating, see 496.

[55] This responsory, *Libera me, Domine, de morte aeterna*, also appears in an early eleventh-century antiphonary of Monza, Italy; see Hésbert, *Corpus antiphonalium officii*, 1:415.

[56] The Zurich *Liber ordinarius* gives only the incipit of this responsory; the complete text is here taken from the *Breviarium Romanum* of 1568, in Sodi and Triacca, *Breviarium Romanum: Editio princeps (1568)*, 1024 (new pagination). This responsory first appears in a ritual of Bobbio, Italy, dating from around 1000 (manuscript: Vatican City, Bibliotheca Apostolica Vaticana, Codex Vaticanus Latinus 5768); see Knud Ottosen, *The Responsories and Versicles of the Latin Office of the Dead* (Aarhus, Denmark: Aarhus University Press, 1993), 399.

[57] This responsory, *Paucitas dierum*, first appears in the Antiphonary of Compiègne (France, c. 870); see Hésbert, *Corpus antiphonalium officii*, 1:386.

[58] Leuppi, *Liber ordinarius des Konrad von Mure*, 421. The Zurich *Liber ordinarius* gives only the incipit of this responsory; the complete text is here taken from Ottosen, *Responsories and Versicles of the Latin Office of the Dead*, 400, 412.

[59] Leuppi, *Liber ordinarius des Konrad von Mure*, 421.

and early eleventh centuries respectively): "[Verse:] *The just shall be in everlasting remembrance* [Ps 111:7].[60] [Antiphon:] *All that the Father giveth to me shall come to me; and him that cometh to me, I will not cast out* [Jn 6:37]."[61] The *Magnificat* and the Our Father are then recited, after which the first station concludes with two prayers of early Roman origin (the second of which will be repeated at the end of all the other stations of the procession):

> *O God, by whose compassion the souls of the faithful are at rest, to all your servants and handmaids here and everywhere resting in Christ, graciously grant the forgiveness of their sins, that having been absolved from all guilt, they may rejoice with you without end. Through the same Jesus Christ . . .*

> *O God, Creator and Redeemer of all the faithful, grant to the souls of your servants and handmaids remission of all their sins, that the pardon that they have always desired they may obtain by our pious supplications. [You] who live and reign with God the Father. . .*[62]

The procession resumes, and another responsory of late ninth-century origin (drawn from Job 7:5–7) is sung along the way to the second station: "*My flesh is clothed with rottenness and the filth of dust, my skin is withered and drawn together. Remember, O Lord, that my life is but wind. Verse: My days have passed more swiftly than the web is cut by the weaver, and are consumed without any hope. Remember, O Lord . . .*"[63]

A soldier's tomb serves as the setting for the second station, which begins with the recitation of three more psalms: Psalm 5 ("*Give ear, O Lord, to my words. . . . In the morning thou shalt hear my voice . . .*"), Psalm 121 ("*I rejoiced at the things that were said to me: We shall go into the house of the Lord . . .*"), and Psalm 122 ("*To thee have I lifted up my eyes. . . .*

[60] The Zurich *Liber ordinarius* gives only the incipit of this verse, *In memoria aeterna*; the complete text is here taken from Hésbert, *Corpus antiphonalium officii*, no. 8096, 4:490. It first appears in the Antiphonary of Compiègne (France, c. 870); see Hésbert, *Corpus antiphonalium officii*, 1:296.

[61] The Zurich *Liber ordinarius* gives only the incipit of this antiphon, *Omne quod dat*; the complete text is here taken from Hésbert, *Corpus antiphonalium officii*, no. 4115, vol. 3, pt. 1, p. 381. It first appears in an early eleventh-century antiphonary of Monza, Italy; see Hésbert, *Corpus antiphonalium officii*, 1:415.

[62] Leuppi, *Liber ordinarius des Konrad von Mure*, 421. The Zurich *Liber ordinarius* gives only the incipit for each of these two Collects; the complete texts of the two prayers are here taken from Sodi and Triacca, *Missale Romanum: Editio princeps (1570)*, 658 and 649 respectively (new pagination). The first Collect is traceable to the seventh-century Gelasian Sacramentary of Rome, while the second is a variant of an oration first found in the sixth-century Leonine Sacramentary of Rome; see respectively Leo Cunibert Mohlberg, O.S.B., et al., eds., *Liber sacramentorum Romanae aeclesiae ordinis anni circuli (Sacramentarium Gelasianum)*, REDSMF 4 (Rome: Herder, 1960), no. 1680, p. 245, and Leo Cunibert Mohlberg, O.S.B.; Leo Eizenhöfer, O.S.B.; and Petrus Siffrin, O.S.B., eds., *Sacramentarium Veronense*, REDSMF 1 (Rome: Herder, 1956), no. 1150, p. 145.

[63] Leuppi, *Liber ordinarius des Konrad von Mure*, 421 (incipit only). The complete text of this responsory, *Induta est caro*, is here taken from Ottosen, *Responsories and Versicles of the Latin Office of the Dead*, 399, 407. It first appears in the Antiphonary of Compiègne (France, c. 870); see Hésbert, *Corpus antiphonalium officii*, 1:386.

Have mercy on us, O Lord, have mercy on us . . ."). After another prayer
for the dead from seventh-century Rome,[64] the second station ends
with the concluding prayer from the first station, "*O God, Creator and
Redeemer of all the faithful . . .*"[65]

The Zurich procession now sets out for the third station as a fourth
responsory is sung (a chant from the second half of the ninth century): "*I believe that my Redeemer liveth, and on the last day I shall rise out
of the earth. And in my flesh I shall see God my Savior. Verse: Whom I
myself shall see, and my eyes shall behold, and not another. And in my flesh
. . .*" (cf. Job 19:25–27).[66] The third, fourth, fifth, and sixth stations
steer the procession on a course that runs along the perimeter of the
cathedral, beginning under the porch on the north side, then passing
the west end, and continuing along the south side before turning left
to pass the church's east end.[67] It then enters an adjoining cloister for
the seventh station, which features the following prayer, dating from
about 850:[68] "*O God, Bestower of pardon and Lover of human salvation,
we beseech your mercy, that you may vouchsafe the brethren of our congregation, our relatives and benefactors, who have departed from this world, to attain
to the company of everlasting bliss, blessed Mary ever Virgin with all your
saints interceding. Through our Lord . . .*"[69]

The eighth station that follows is likewise in the cloister, after
which the procession reenters the cathedral through a north door.
Traversing the choir, the clerics and scholars halt at the church's
Altar of the Apostles for the ninth station.[70] As they advance to the
tenth station, the tomb of a former prior of the cathedral, they chant
a responsory from the early eleventh century: "*Deliver me, O Lord,
from the ways of hell, you who have shattered the gates of brass, and have
visited Sheol, and have given them light, that they might see you, who were
in the pains of darkness. Verse: Crying out and saying: You have come, our
Redeemer. Who were in the pains . . . Verse: Eternal rest grant unto them,*

---

[64] This prayer, *Deus indulgentiarum* (quoted in full later in this chapter as part of the All
Souls' Day rite of Płock, Poland; see p. 537), is first found in the seventh-century Gelasian
Sacramentary of Rome; see Mohlberg, Eizenhöfer, and Siffrin, *Liber sacramentorum*, no. 1692,
p. 246.

[65] Leuppi, *Liber ordinarius des Konrad von Mure*, 421.

[66] Ibid., 422 (incipit only). The complete text of this responsory, *Credo quod Redemptor*,
is here taken from Sodi and Triacca, *Breviarium Romanum: Editio princeps (1568)*, 1022 (new
pagination). It first appears in the Booklet of the Dead of the Palatine, from the second
half of the ninth century; see Ottosen, *Responsories and Versicles of the Latin Office of the
Dead*, 397.

[67] Leuppi, *Liber ordinarius des Konrad von Mure*, 422.

[68] This prayer appears in the mid-ninth-century sacramentaries of Reichenau, Germany,
and Modena, Italy; see Jean Deshusses, ed., *Le sacramentaire grégorien: Ses principales formes
d'après les plus anciens manuscrits*, vol. 2, SF 24 (Fribourg, Switzerland: Editions Universitaires Fribourg, 1979), no. 2862, p. 206.

[69] Leuppi, *Liber ordinarius des Konrad von Mure*, 422 (incipit only). The complete text of
this prayer is here taken from Sodi and Triacca, *Missale Romanum: Editio princeps (1570)*,
658 (new pagination).

[70] Leuppi, *Liber ordinarius des Konrad von Mure*, 422–423.

O Lord, and let perpetual light shine upon them. Who were in the pains . . ." (cf. Ps 106:16).[71]

During the final leg of the procession to the eleventh and last station, within the cathedral (near the Altar of Saints Pancras and Blase), the final responsory is sung, a chant likewise traceable to the early eleventh century: "*My Redeemer lives, and on the last day I shall rise, and my bones shall be restored anew, and in my flesh I shall see my Lord. Verse: Praise the Lord, O my soul; in my life I will praise the Lord, singing to my God as long as I shall be. And in my flesh . . .*" (cf. Job 19:25–26; Ps 145:2).[72]

The All Souls' Day processions of the medieval Church borrowed elements from the funeral liturgy, including the incensation and sprinkling with holy water of the graves of the faithful departed. Thus a directive for the All Souls' Day procession of Speyer, Germany, dating from 1304 specifies that "the priest who has celebrated the Mass, with all the ministers in the choir coming forth, should solemnly go around the cloister of the church with a cross, a censer, and blessed water" and "visit the tombs of the dead with the office suitable for this".[73] The tolling of bells for the faithful departed was also added to the liturgy of All Souls' Day: the *Liber tramitis* of the French Benedictine abbey of Cluny (c. 1043) calls for the ringing of all the church bells when Vespers of the Office of the Dead is begun on the eve of November 2.[74]

In Poland, the observance of a procession to the cemetery on All Souls' Day had been introduced by the fourteenth century, when it appears in an ordinal of the diocese of Płock.[75] By the sixteenth century, a fairly uniform format for the procession had spread across Poland, consisting of four stations at the cemetery, each of which was usually made facing one of the four cardinal points (north, east, south, west), followed by a fifth and final station in the church.[76] Some Polish liturgical books, including the 1502 breviary of Włocławek and the 1540 breviary of Gniezno, concluded the procession with the singing of the Marian chant *Salve Regina*.[77] An earlier breviary of Gniezno dating

[71] Ibid., 423 (incipit only). The complete text of this responsory, *Libera me, Domine, de viis*, is here taken from Sodi and Triacca, *Breviarium Romanum: Editio princeps (1568)*, 1024 (new pagination). It first appears in an early eleventh-century antiphonary of Monza, Italy; see Hésbert, *Corpus antiphonalium officii*, 1:413.

[72] Leuppi, *Liber ordinarius des Konrad von Mure*, 423 (incipit only). The complete text of this responsory, *Redemptor meus vivit*, is here taken from Ottosen, *Responsories and Versicles of the Latin Office of the Dead*, 400, 411. This chant first appears, albeit as an antiphon rather than as a responsory, in an early eleventh-century antiphonary of Monza, Italy; see Hésbert, *Corpus antiphonalium officii*, 1:415.

[73] Quoted in Labudda, "Liturgia dnia Zadusznego w Polsce", 358, footnote.

[74] *Liber tramitis*, bk. 1, chap. 127, in Albers, *Consuetudines monasticae*, 1:124.

[75] Labudda, "Liturgia dnia Zadusznego w Polsce", 358, 362.

[76] Ibid., 360–366, 368–369, 384.

[77] *Viaticum Vladislaviense* (1502) and *Breviarium seu viaticus alme ecclesie metropolitane Gnesnensis* (1540), quoted in Labudda, "Liturgia dnia Zadusznego w Polsce", 367, 368, footnotes; see also 380.

from 1504 mentions the All Souls' Eve custom of ringing all the bells "in commemoration of the souls".[78]

The All Souls' Day procession prescribed in a 1554 *Agenda* (ritual book) of Płock, Poland, is fairly typical of the Polish tradition for the November 2 commemoration; here we shall summarize the Płock rite, supplementing what the 1554 *Agenda* provides with further information drawn from a 1520 breviary of Płock.[79] The procession would be conducted twice, first on the eve of All Souls' Day—after Vespers on November 1—and again on the morning of All Souls' Day, shortly before High Mass: "A procession should be made, and the cross is brought without a banner; and the places of the dead should be sprinkled with blessed water." The rite begins in the church with the chanting of a responsory intoned by the rectors of the choir, the first of seven responsories for the procession, all except the last dating from the second half of the ninth century:[80] "*Absolve their souls, O Lord, from every fetter of their sins; let not the torment of death touch them, nor the chain of the guilty bind them, but let your mercy set them in a place of peace and light. Verse: And if, O Lord, there be sins in them, these having been deservedly punished, grant them the favors of your clemency. But let your mercy* ..."[81] Standing in the middle of the choir, the hebdomadarian (the priest assigned to lead the Divine Office for the week) begins the *Kyrie* ("*Lord, have mercy* ..."), followed by the Our Father, the Hail Mary, and the verse "*From the gate of hell, O Lord, deliver their souls.*"[82] He then prays for all the faithful departed with an oration from the Gelasian Sacramentary of seventh-century Rome:[83] "*We beseech you, O Lord, in your everlasting mercy to bestow your favor upon the souls of your servants and handmaids, that with their mortal bonds having been untied, eternal light may take hold of them.*

---

[78] *Breviarium Gnesnense*, 1504 (manuscript: Gniezno, Poland, Archiwum Archidiecezjalne w Gnieźnie, Zbiory d. Biblioteki Kapitulnej, MS 37), quoted in Labudda, "Liturgia dnia Zadusznego w Polsce", 368.

[79] *Agenda ecclesiae cathedralis Plocensis* (1554) and *Liber horarum canonicarum ecclesie Plocensis* (1520), in Labudda, "Liturgia dnia Zadusznego w Polsce", 363–365.

[80] The first responsory (*Absolve, Domine, animas eorum ab omni vinculo delictorum non eas tormentum* ...) and the five others that follow it in the Płock procession (*Domine, quando veneris; Heu mihi, Domine; Ne recorderis; Peccantem me cotidie; Credo quod Redemptor*) are traceable to the Booklet of the Dead of the Palatine, from the second half of the ninth century; see Ottosen, *Responsories and Versicles of the Latin Office of the Dead*, 397–400, 403, 405, 407, 417–418. For the dating of the final responsory, *Libera me, Domine, de morte aeterna*, see footnote 55, p. 531 above.

[81] Labudda, "Liturgia dnia Zadusznego w Polsce", 363 (incipit only). The complete text of this responsory (*Absolve, Domine, animas eorum ab omni vinculo delictorum non eas tormentum* ...) is here taken from the Gregorian chant online database Cantus, http://cantusdatabase.org.

[82] The complete text of this verse, *A porta inferi*, is here taken from the *Breviarium Romanum* of 1568, in Sodi and Triacca, *Breviarium Romanum: Editio princeps (1568)*, 1020 (new pagination). It first appears, albeit as an antiphon, in the Antiphonary of Compiègne (France, c. 870); see Hésbert, *Corpus antiphonalium officii*, 1:176.

[83] The prayer as it is found in the Płock All Souls' Day rite is a variant of an oration first found in the Gelasian Sacramentary of Rome; see Mohlberg, Eizenhöfer, and Siffrin, *Liber sacramentorum*, no. 1666, p. 243.

Through Christ our Lord. Amen."[84] The clergy, including the priests of the choir, now set out in procession, departing from the church as the second responsory is sung: "*Lord, when you shall come to judge the earth, where shall I hide from the face of your wrath, for I have sinned in my life? Verse: In my offenses I grow afraid, and I am ashamed before you. When you shall come to judge, be unwilling to condemn me. For I have sinned . . .*"[85]

Arriving at the cemetery, the procession halts for the first of four stations that, like the stations of Poland's Corpus Christi processions, face the four cardinal points of the compass. The first station, "toward the north", begins with the penitential psalm *De profundis*, Psalm 130, "*Out of the depths . . .*", accompanied by the antiphon "*Absolve, O Lord, the souls of all the faithful departed from every fetter of their sins*",[86] with the versicle "*Eternal rest grant unto them, O Lord, and let perpetual light shine upon them*"[87] said at the end of the psalm. A series of prayers and versicles follow, to be said at each of the four stations (including the *Kyrie eleison*, the Our Father, the Hail Mary, and the versicle "*I believe to see the good things of the Lord in the land of the living*").[88] The hebdomadarian concludes the station with a second Collect for the faithful departed: "*We beseech you, Lord, that to the souls of your servants and handmaids, whose day of commemoration we celebrate, you may vouchsafe to grant the fellowship of your saints and elect and impart unto them the everlasting dew of your mercy. Through Christ our Lord. Amen.*"[89]

The second station, directed "toward the east", begins with the third responsory: "*Alas for me, O Lord, for I have sinned exceedingly in my life; wretched, what shall I do? Where shall I flee, but to you my God? Have mercy on me when you shall come on the last day. [Verse:] My soul is exceedingly*

---

[84] Labudda, "Liturgia dnia Zadusznego w Polsce", 363.

[85] The Płock *Agenda* gives only the incipit of this responsory; the complete text of *Domine, quando veneris* is here taken from Ottosen, *Responsories and Versicles of the Latin Office of the Dead*, 398, 405.

[86] The Płock *Agenda* gives only the incipit of this antiphon, *Absolve, Domine, animas*; the complete text is here taken from Labudda, "Liturgia dnia Zadusznego w Polsce", 362. It is first found in the eleventh-century Antiphonary of Hartker (Saint Gall Abbey, Switzerland); see Hésbert, *Corpus antiphonalium officii*, 2:722.

[87] This versicle, *Requiem aeternam*, first appears as the opening words of the Introit for the Mass of the Dead in a ninth-century redaction of the Gregorian Sacramentary of Rome (manuscript: Vatican City, Biblioteca Apostolica Vaticana, Codex Vaticanus Latinus 14821), cited in Damien Sicard, *Le liturgie de la mort dans l'église latine des origines à la réforme carolingienne*, Liturgiewissenschaftliche Quellen und Forschungen 63 (Münster, Germany: Aschendorffsche Verlagsbuchhandlung, 1978), 187. For the ancient source of the wording of the funeral Introit, see footnote 57 on p. 602 below.

[88] Labudda, "Liturgia dnia Zadusznego w Polsce", 363–364. The full text of the versicle *Credo videre bona* (Ps 26:13) is taken from Labudda, 378. It is first found as a versicle in an early eleventh-century antiphonary of Monza, Italy; see Hésbert, *Corpus antiphonalium officii*, 1:413.

[89] Labudda, "Liturgia dnia Zadusznego w Polsce," 364. This prayer is a variant of an oration first found in the seventh-century *Gelasian Sacramentary* of Rome; see Mohlberg, Eizenhöfer, and Siffrin, *Liber sacramentorum*, no. 1691, p. 246.

troubled, but you, O Lord, succor me. Have mercy ...*[90]* After the aforementioned set of versicles and prayers from the first station is repeated,
the hebdomadarian offers another Collect derived from the seventh-
century Gelasian Sacramentary:*[91]* "*O God of indulgences, Lord, grant to your
faithful whose commemoration we celebrate a habitation of consolation, the beatitude of rest, the brightness of eternal light. Through Christ our Lord. Amen.*"*[92]*

The third station, facing the south, likewise has its own responsory
and Collect:

> [Responsory:] *Remember not my sins, O Lord, when you shall have come
> to judge the world by fire. Verse: Direct my way, O Lord my God, in your
> sight. When you shall have come ... Verse: Eternal rest grant unto them, O
> Lord ... When you shall have come ...*[93]

> [Collect:] *Almighty eternal God, who are never entreated without the hope
> of mercy, be merciful to the souls of your servants and handmaids, that they
> who have departed from this life in the confession of your name, you may
> cause to be added to the number of your saints. Through Christ our Lord.
> Amen.*[94]

All of the responsories for the Płock All Souls' Day procession are
borrowed from the Office of the Dead, including the following responsory for the fourth station ("toward the west"): "*Sinning daily, and not
repenting, the fear of death troubles me, for in hell there is no redemption.
Have mercy on me, O God, and save me. [Verse:] O God, in your name,
save me, and in your might deliver me. For in hell ...*"*[95]* The Collect for
the fourth station is a prayer we have already seen in the Zurich All
Souls' Day rite (the first Collect for Zurich's first station, "*O God, by
whose compassion the souls of the faithful are at rest ...*"). The procession
now reenters the church as the responsory "*I believe that my Redeemer
liveth*" is sung (*Credo quod Redemptor*, likewise seen earlier in the Zurich
procession), after which another Collect follows, a prayer of mid-
ninth-century origin:*[96]* "*O God, of whose mercy there is no measure,*

---

[90] The Płock *Agenda* gives only the incipit of this responsory; the complete text of *Heu
mihi, Domine* is here taken from Sodi and Triacca, *Breviarium Romanum: Editio princeps
(1568)*, 1023 (new pagination).

[91] Mohlberg, Eizenhöfer, and Siffrin, *Liber sacramentorum*, no. 1692, p. 246.

[92] Labudda, "Liturgia dnia Zadusznego w Polsce," 364. This prayer, *Deus indulgentiarum*,
was also used in the Zurich rite.

[93] The Płock *Agenda* gives only the incipit of this responsory; the complete text of *Ne
recorderis* is here taken from Sodi and Triacca, *Breviarium Romanum: Editio princeps (1568)*,
1023 (new pagination).

[94] Labudda, "Liturgia dnia Zadusznego w Polsce", 364. The Collect utilized here is first
found in the seventh-century Gelasian Sacramentary of Rome; see Mohlberg, Eizenhöfer,
and Siffrin, *Liber sacramentorum*, no. 1662, pp. 242–243.

[95] The Płock *Agenda* gives only the incipit of this responsory; the complete text of
Peccantem me cotidie is here taken from Sodi and Triacca, *Breviarium Romanum: Editio princeps (1568)*, 1023–1024 (new pagination).

[96] This prayer first appears in the mid-ninth-century sacramentaries of Reichenau, Germany, and Modena, Italy; see Deshusses, *Sacramentaire grégorien*, no. 2863, 2:206.

receive the prayers of our lowliness, and to the souls upon whom you have conferred the confession of your name, who have been commended by us to prayer, and whose friendship we enjoy through the giving of our assistance, grant the remission of all their sins. Through Christ our Lord. Amen." [97]

As the procession returns to the choir, the responsory *"Deliver me, O Lord, from eternal death"* is chanted (*Libera me, Domine, de morte aeterna*, seen earlier in the Zurich rite). After a series of versicles and prayers similar to those repeated at each of the four stations, the hebdomadarian prays, *"May they obtain a share in your blessed Resurrection and be worthy to possess eternal life in Heaven. Through you, O Jesus Christ, who live ..."* [98] Psalm 145 is now recited in a low voice: *"Praise the Lord, O my soul.... Blessed is he who hath the God of Jacob for his helper, whose hope is in the Lord his God.... The Lord lifteth up them that are cast down ..."* (verses 2, 5, 8). After two more versicles, the hebdomadarian offers a final Collect, the same prayer with which each station of the Zurich procession concluded (*"O God, Creator and Redeemer of all the faithful, grant to the souls of your servants and handmaids remission of all their sins ..."*). The Płock rite ends with the words *"May they rest in peace. Amen."* [99]

As a postscript to the above example, the All Souls' Day procession given in a 1578 *Agenda* (ritual book) of the Polish diocese of Gniezno apportions to the individual stations prayers for specific groups among the faithful departed. Hence, at the first station there are Collects for those in holy orders (first prayer) and for parents (second prayer); at the second station, a first Collect for relatives and a second one for benefactors; at the third station, a first Collect for the church's founders and a second for all those buried in the church and its cemetery; and at the fourth station, a single Collect for all the faithful departed. [100]

We conclude this chapter with a medieval responsory for the Office of the Dead, *Congregati sunt, Deus*, a text set to one of the most sublime chant melodies of the entire Gregorian repertoire but little known due to its absence from the *Breviarium Romanum* of 1568. The words and the music express the soul's longing for mercy and deliverance:

They have assembled, O God, to devour me, my deceivers, keeping evil records of what I have done. Thus do they clamor, saying, "God has forsaken him; pursue him and seize him; for there is no one to deliver him."

---

[97] Labudda, "Liturgia dnia Zadusznego w Polsce", 364.

[98] Ibid., 365. The Płock *Agenda* gives only the incipit of this prayer; the complete text is here taken from Jean Deshusses, ed., *Le sacramentaire grégorien: Ses principales formes d'après les plus anciens manuscrits*, vol. 3, SF 28 (Fribourg, Switzerland: Editions Universitaires Fribourg, 1982), no. 4072, p. 163. This prayer is traceable to the second half of the ninth century, when it appears in the French sacramentaries of Saint-Vaast, Arras, and Saint-Denis (ibid.).

[99] Labudda, "Liturgia dnia Zadusznego w Polsce", 365. Regarding the concluding versicle *Requiescant in pace*, said at the end of funeral Masses, see p. 606 of the present work.

[100] Labudda, "Liturgia dnia Zadusznego w Polsce", 379–380.

My God, be not far off from me; my God, look to my support; my God, hearken to my assistance. Verse: *Remember not the sins of my youth, O Lord, and turn not your face from me; for I am in trouble; answer me quickly, O Lord. My God, be not far off* . . .[101]

---

[101] Ottosen, *Responsories and Versicles of the Latin Office of the Dead*, 397, 407. An excellent performance of this rare chant is included on a compact disc of Good Friday chants recorded by the Czech ensemble Schola Gregoriana Pragensis and the Boni Pueri (*Adoratio Crucis* [*Uctívání Kříže*—Devotion of the Cross], Supraphon, SU 3448-2-231, 2000).

Book of Hours, use of Rome, end 14th century.
French and Latin, parchment
Illustration for the chapter on a requiem Mass, fol. 134
Russian National Library, St. Petersburg, Russia

PART III

OTHER RITES OF THE CHURCH

Just as by Christ coming the Old Law ceased and the new began, so also, the ancient ceremonies having been abolished, the new succeeded, through the traditions of the Apostles, which Dionysius, Ignatius, Clement, Anacletus, and the other holy martyrs, and the holy councils, teach us to be not by human invention but by the inspiration of the Holy Spirit, who has been given by Christ to his Church, that he may lead her into all truth; for our blessings and consecrations and exorcisms receive their power by the invocation of the Divine Name, holy Paul also bearing witness: "Every creature of God is good, which is sanctified by the Word of God and prayer" (cf. 1 Tim 4:4–5).

Liber obsequiorum ecclesiae Frisingensis, Freising, Germany, 1547

Preface, fol. 1v.

18 The Election, Installation, and Coronation of a Pope

"I announce to you a great joy. We have a pope. The most reverend doctor cardinal of Molfetta has been elected to supreme pontiff and has chosen for himself the name Innocent VIII." These things having been said, all the people cried out, the bells of the [Apostolic] Palace and the Basilica of Saint Peter were rung with great might, and the riflemen of the palace guard shot their loaded rifles without intermission in triumph.[1]

Diary of John Burckard
Papal Master of Ceremonies, 1484

It was in this manner that Francesco Cardinal Piccolomini (the future Pope Pius III) announced from a window of the Apostolic Palace in Rome the election of Pope Innocent VIII on August 29, 1484. The jubilant atmosphere that has marked the election and solemn installation of the popes down through the centuries found its supreme expression in the magnificent liturgical rites for the inauguration of a new pontificate that emerged during the Middle Ages. In this chapter we shall present these rites as they were celebrated in the late fifteenth century, beginning with the Papal conclave.

The Papal Conclave

From the earliest centuries of the Church, the selection of a successor to the See of Saint Peter has been wrought through an ecclesiastical election. During the first millennium, the makeup of the electorate varied, with the clergy of Rome always serving as electors, while in many cases the Roman laity also participated.[2] In 1059 Pope Nicholas II issued the first major decree regarding papal elections, *In nomine Domini*, in which the cardinal bishops were assigned the leading role in selecting a new pope. After assembling, the cardinal bishops were to deliberate and identify the worthiest candidates for the Petrine office. Thereafter the cardinal priests and cardinal deacons were to join them

---

[1] John Burckard, *Diarium sive Rerum Urbanarum commentarii (1483–1506)*, vol. 1, *1483–1492*, ed. L. Thuasne (Paris: Ernest Leroux, 1883), 62–63.

[2] William Fanning, "Papal Elections", in *The Catholic Encyclopedia* (New York: Appleton, 1907–1912), 11:456.

543

for the actual election. Following the vote of the convened College of Cardinals, the rest of the Roman clergy and the Roman laity were to be given an opportunity to voice their assent to the cardinals' chosen candidate.[3] The process was subsequently simplified when the right to vote in the papal election was limited exclusively to the cardinals, obviating the need to seek ratification from others of the clergy or the laity. It is believed that this change was enacted by Pope Innocent II in conjunction with the Second Lateran Council of 1139.[4] The Third Lateran Council of 1179 under Pope Alexander III mandated the requirement of at least a two-thirds majority for the election of a Roman pontiff.[5] The papal election procedure was given a more definitive form by Pope Blessed Gregory X in his apostolic constitution *Ubi periculum*, promulgated in conjunction with the Second Council of Lyons in 1274. It is in the provisions of this decree that we encounter the specific form of papal election that has become so familiar up to our own age, that of the conclave, the deliberation of the College of Cardinals behind closed and carefully locked doors.[6]

In the late thirteenth-century ceremonial of Pope Blessed Gregory X, there is a brief reference to the papal election procedure, followed by rubrics regarding the vesting of a newly elected pontiff and his reception of the papal ring; the homage rendered him by the cardinals, the other clergy, and the laity; prayers offered in thanksgiving for the pope's election; and the new pontiff's first blessing of the faithful.[7] A subsequent papal ceremonial, that of the papal master of ceremonies Giacomo Cardinal Stefaneschi, dating from about 1325, includes detailed instructions regarding the conclave proceedings themselves as well as the rites that immediately follow the election of a new pope.[8] But it is above all in the 1488 *Ceremoniale Romanum* of the papal master of ceremonies Patrizio Piccolomini that the liturgical ceremonies accompanying each stage of the conclave are expansively developed.[9]

---

[3] Nicholas II, *In nomine Domini* (April 1059), in *Monumenta Germaniae historica: Legum, sectio IV; Constitutiones et acta publica imperatorum et regum*, vol. 1, ed. Ludwig Weiland (Hanover, Germany: Hahn, 1893), 539–541. See also Fanning, "Papal Elections", 456, and Johannes Baptist Sagmuller, "Cardinal", in *Catholic Encyclopedia* (1907–1912), 3:335–336.

[4] See the editorial notes of Father H. J. Schroeder, O.P., in his work *Disciplinary Decrees of the General Councils: Text, Translation, and Commentary* (Saint Louis, Mo.: B. Herder, 1937), 196, 215, 334–335.

[5] Third Lateran Council (1179), canon 1, in J. D. Mansi, ed., *Sacrorum conciliorum nova et amplissima collectio*, vol. 22 (Florence and Venice, 1778; repr., Paris: Hubert Welter, 1903), cols. 217–218.

[6] The text of *Ubi periculum* is given as canon 2 of the Second Council of Lyons (1274); see J. D. Mansi, ed., *Sacrorum conciliorum nova et amplissima collectio*, vol. 24 (Venice, 1780; repr., Paris: Hubert Welter, 1903), cols. 81–86.

[7] Text in Marc Dykmans, S.J., ed., *Le cérémonial papal de la fin du moyen âge à la Renaissance*, vol. 1, BIHBR 24 (Brussels and Rome: Institut Historique Belge de Rome, 1977), 159–160.

[8] Text in Marc Dykmans, S.J., ed., *Le cérémonial papal de la fin du moyen âge à la Renaissance*, vol. 2, BIHBR 25 (Brussels and Rome: Institut Historique Belge de Rome, 1981), 257–269.

[9] Text in Marc Dykmans, S.J., ed., *L'oeuvre de Patrizi Piccolomini, ou Le cérémonial papal de la première Renaissance*, vol. 1, ST 293 (Vatican City: Biblioteca Apostolica Vaticana, 1980), 27–51.

On the tenth day following the death of the preceding pope, one day after the completion of nine days of Masses and prayers for the repose of the soul of the deceased pontiff, the members of the College of Cardinals attend together a votive Mass to prepare themselves for the task now at hand:

> The fathers should assemble in the Basilica of Saint Peter, or elsewhere, according to the need of a time and place, where the Mass of the Holy Spirit is celebrated by one from among them. And at the end, a sermon should be given by some prelate, or another learned man,[10] in which the fathers should be admonished that, with all personal feelings having been put aside, having before their eyes only God, they should take care to provide the holy Roman and universal Church with a fitting pastor.[11]

The custom of beginning a papal election with the Mass of the Holy Spirit is traceable to the late twelfth-century Roman text known as the *Liber censuum*, dating from about 1192.[12] The 1488 ceremonial of Piccolomini also prescribes that the cardinals should individually prepare their souls to discern the will of God: "It is seen necessary that, before the conclave should begin, all the fathers should confess their sins, and those who are not going to celebrate [Mass] should communicate, that they may be receptive to the grace of the Holy Spirit in such an exceedingly necessary thing to be accomplished."[13] Having been incorporated into the Church's canon law, the directives of Pope Blessed Gregory X's 1274 apostolic constitution *Ubi periculum* were still in effect when the 1488 ceremonial was compiled. Hence its instructions were still to be observed, including the following admonition regarding the spiritual participation of the rest of the Church's clergy and the laity in the deliberations of the conclave:

> We add to this by our sanction, that in all cities and other prominent places . . . each day, until a certain report shall have brought the truth of the decision of the Church herself, humble prayers are to be poured forth unto the Lord, he is to be implored with devout supplications in his presence, that he who makes concord in his lowly ones may so fashion in harmony the hearts of these same cardinals in electing, that from their unanimity a swift, harmonious, and beneficial decision

---

[10] The custom of a sermon at the end of this Mass is first mentioned in regard to the papal conclave of 1389 that elected Pope Boniface IX; see the ceremonial of the papal master of ceremonies Pierre Ameil (+1403; completed by Pierre Assalbit, 1435–1441), in Marc Dykmans, S.J., ed., *Le cérémonial papal de la fin du moyen âge à la Renaissance*, vol. 4, BIHBR 27 (Brussels and Rome: Institut Historique Belge de Rome, 1985), 232.

[11] Dykmans, *Oeuvre de Patrizi Piccolomini*, 1:36.

[12] *Liber censuum* (c. 1192), in Paul Fabre and Louis Duchesne, eds., *Le Liber censuum de l'église romaine*, vol. 1, fasc. 2, Bibliothèque des écoles françaises d'Athènes et de Rome, 2nd series, Registres des papes du XIIIᵉ siècle, 6 (Paris: Fontemoing, 1901), no. 77, p. 311.

[13] Dykmans, *Oeuvre de Patrizi Piccolomini*, 1:37–38.

may follow, as the salvation of souls demands and the profit of the entire world requires.[14]

Prior to the beginning of the conclave, the Vatican's Apostolic Palace is readied for the cardinals' assembly. The palace's Chapel of Saint Nicholas is to be used for all the liturgical rites and voting sessions during the conclave; temporary living quarters are created for the cardinals along the left side of the Sistine Chapel by means of linen or woolen curtains erected to partition the space into individual cubicles.[15] An earlier text, a late fourteenth-century supplement to John of Sion's mid-fourteenth-century Long Ceremonial of papal rites, adds the poignant detail that a crucifix, or an image of the Blessed Virgin Mary, or some other religious picture should be placed on the headboard of each cardinal's bed.[16] The great hall onto which both chapels open is walled off in the middle with a temporary partition, and its doors and windows are sealed with cement, hiding from view the northern part of the hall, through which the cardinals are able to pass from one chapel to the other sequestered from the outside world.[17] The ceremonial of the papal master of ceremonies Pierre Ameil (+1403; completed by Pierre Assalbit, 1435–1441) additionally specifies that the Blessed Sacrament should be present continually, with a lit candle near it, in the chapel where the conclave proceedings are to be conducted.[18]

In the 1488 ceremonial of Piccolomini, the formal inauguration of the conclave is marked by a solemn liturgical procession:

> The cleric of ceremonies should take the papal cross and precede, whom the cardinals—bishops, priests, deacons—should follow. The cardinals' lay attendants precede the cross, and immediately [before the cross] the singers chanting the hymn *Veni Creator Spiritus.* . . . After the cardinals, the prelates and other clerics of the Curia follow. The cardinals are with their dark cloaks [a vestment for the conclave known as the *crocea*].[19]

After all but the cardinals have been sent out of the Chapel of Saint Nicholas, the dean of the College of Cardinals reminds his brethren about the gravity of the decision they are about to make:

---

[14] Blessed Gregory X, *Ubi periculum* (Second Council of Lyons [1274], canon 2), in Mansi, *Sacrorum conciliorum nova et amplissima collectio*, vol. 24, col. 85.

[15] Dykmans, *Oeuvre de Patrizi Piccolomini*, 1:28.

[16] Manuscript: Vatican City, Biblioteca Apostolica Vaticana, Codex Vaticanus Barberinus Latinus 2651; text in Marc Dykmans, ed., *Le cérémonial papal de la fin du moyen âge à la Renaissance*, vol. 3, BIHBR 26 (Brussels and Rome: Institut Historique Belge de Rome, 1983), 274. It should be noted that this document is thought to have been compiled by François de Conzié, a chamberlain of the schismatic Avignon antipopes Clement VII (1378–1394) and Benedict XIII (1394–1428); nonetheless, the liturgical practices it describes are believed to correspond to those of the true popes, and its contents appear to have influenced subsequent papal ceremonials.

[17] Dykmans, *Oeuvre de Patrizi Piccolomini*, 1:28.

[18] Text in Dykmans, *Cérémonial papal de la fin du moyen âge à la Renaissance*, 4:228.

[19] Dykmans, *Oeuvre de Patrizi Piccolomini*, 1:36–37.

Then, with all others having been excluded, the first of the cardinal bishops [i.e., the dean] shall exhort the cardinals themselves in appropriate words that they should want to know the magnitude of the thing of which they are going to treat, of which nothing on earth can be more excellent. For they are going to elect the Vicar of Jesus Christ, the successor of Peter, the pastor of the Lord's flock, the key bearer of the heavenly court, and the prince and father of all Christians.... Accordingly, with all feelings of the heart dismissed, they should have before their eyes only the honor of God, the safety of the Christian republic, and the advantage of the Roman Church, and they should take care to elect such a one who would be worthy and know how to govern and be profitable to the Church of God.[20]

Each day of the conclave begins with morning Mass,[21] after which the one and only vote of the day is held. The ceremonial first describes the arrangement of the Chapel of Saint Nicholas for the actual vote:

When therefore they want to treat of the election, Mass having been heard, the lord cardinals alone remain in that chapel and sit upon stools prepared for them. Upon the altar rests an empty chalice and a paten; before the altar is placed a small table covered with a red cloth, and upon it a writing tablet and papyrus. Between it and the altar, near the table, are placed three stools, on the middle of which sits the first of the cardinal bishops, to the right the first of the cardinal priests, to the left the first of the cardinal deacons.[22]

The procedure for each cardinal to cast his vote follows:

Then, with all sitting down together at their places in the chapel, the first of the [cardinal] bishops approaches the altar with his ballot in his hand, and having knelt, he should pray for a little while. Then he rises, and the aforesaid ballot, which he first kisses, he places into the chalice, with the first of the deacons at the left side of the altar standing and elevating the paten with his hand. But these ballots that contain their votes, the most reverend lords are accustomed to write according to his direction, when it is pleasing to them, in this form: "I [Name], cardinal bishop of [Place], etc., elect to supreme pontiff the most reverend lord, my lord [Name and Title]."[23]

---

[20] Ibid., 38–39.

[21] The daily Mass of the conclave is first mentioned in the above-cited late fourteenth-century supplement to John of Sion's Long Ceremonial of papal rites (manuscript: Vatican City, Biblioteca Apostolica Vaticana, Codex Vaticanus Barberinus Latinus 2651), in Dykmans, *Cérémonial papal de la fin du moyen âge à la Renaissance*, 3:286. Regarding the origin of this document, see footnote 16 on p. 546.

[22] Dykmans, *Oeuvre de Patrizi Piccolomini*, 1:43.

[23] Ibid., 46.

When all of the cardinals have cast their votes, the dean of the College of Cardinals and the senior cardinal deacon carry out an open reading and a count of the ballots:

> Then the first of the [cardinal] bishops, taking the chalice from the altar together with the first of the deacons, sets it upon the aforesaid table. Then both he and the deacon sit, with the first of the priests, as we have said, sitting to the right. Sitting then, the first of the bishops, taking the chalice with his right hand and holding the paten firm with his left hand, turns over the chalice itself upon the paten, yet in such a way that nothing pours out; and lifting up the chalice again, he sets it as it was previously. Then, elevating the paten a little with his left hand, with two fingers of his right hand he openly draws out one ballot, which comes at hand by chance, and presents it to be read by the first of the deacons, who then opens it and, in a voice that can be heard by all, reads distinctly, *I* [Name], *cardinal of* [Place], *elect to supreme pontiff the most reverend lord, my lord* [Name and Title].
>
> ... All the ballots having been read through, and the votes of those electing having been transcribed, the three first [cardinals] count the votes, and in a high voice the deacon names those having several votes, saying: *The most reverend lord* [Name] *has ten votes, and the most reverend lord* [Name] *has eight votes.*[24]

If the vote is inconclusive, the conclave continues for another day, following the same format of morning Mass followed by a vote.[25] When at last one candidate has received the required two-thirds or more of the votes, the dean of the College of Cardinals announces to the assembled cardinals the elected candidate's name and asks him if he will accept elevation to the Petrine office. After the candidate has given his assent, the other cardinals rise to congratulate him. Then, removing from him the *crocea* (the aforementioned cloak worn by all of the cardinals during the conclave), they make him sit upon an ornamented seat placed in front of the cloth-covered table previously used for the ballot counting. After placing on his hand the fisherman's ring,[26] the cardinals ask by what name he wishes to be identified as pope.[27] This custom of elected pontiffs taking a new name began with Pope John XII in 955, in imitation of the name change of the first Vicar of Christ from Simon to Peter (cf. Mt 16:17–19).[28] Immediately the cardinals share their good news with the people of Rome:

---

[24] Ibid., 47–48.

[25] Ibid., 48.

[26] The imposition of the papal ring is first mentioned in the ceremonial of Pope Blessed Gregory X (c. 1273); see Dykmans, *Cérémonial papal de la fin du moyen âge à la Renaissance*, 1:159.

[27] Dykmans, *Oeuvre de Patrizi Piccolomini*, 1:49.

[28] Austin Dowling, "Conclave", in *Catholic Encyclopedia* (1907–1912), 4:194.

But meanwhile, the small window of the sacristy having been opened [the sacristy adjacent to the Chapel of Saint Nicholas],[29] at which the people awaiting [in the Courtyard of Marechal] can be seen, the first of the [cardinal] deacons brings forth the cross, shouting loudly: *I announce to you a great joy: we have a pope. The most reverend lord cardinal [Name] has been elected to supreme pontiff and has chosen for himself the name [Papal Name].*[30]

The tradition of a solemn public announcement of the election of a new pontiff is first mentioned in 1049, when the election of Bishop Bruno of Toul as Pope Leo IX was proclaimed to the clergy and the people of Rome with the words *"Blessed Peter has chosen the lord Bruno!"*[31] The formula *"I announce to you a great joy"* first appears in the papal ceremonial of Cardinal Stefaneschi (c. 1325).[32]

In the sacristy of the Chapel of Saint Nicholas, the new pope is now clothed for the first time in the vestments of his supreme office by the cardinal deacons. The pope is then led back into the church. Here the cardinals put over his other vestments a red cope and upon his head a jewel-studded golden miter.[33] The 1488 rubrics make no mention of a particular ceremony for vesting the new pontiff with the cope; but an earlier fifteenth-century text of papal rites directs that the cope is to be placed upon the pontiff's shoulders by the first cardinal deacon as he says to him, *"To the honor of almighty God, Father, Son, and Holy Spirit, of the blessed Apostles Peter and Paul, I invest you in the papacy of the Roman Church, that you may govern the city and the world."*[34] The tradition of the ceremonial imposition of a red cope upon the newly elected pontiff is traceable to the eleventh century,[35] with the above-quoted declaration of the cardinal deacon being added to the ceremony in the late thirteenth century.[36] Having seated the

---

[29] See Burckard, *Diarium sive Rerum Urbanarum commentarii*, 62, and Dykmans, *Oeuvre de Patrizi Piccolomini*, editor's introduction, 1:99*, footnote and image of Vatican floor plan.

[30] Dykmans, *Oeuvre de Patrizi Piccolomini*, 1:49.

[31] See the life of Pope Leo IX in the collection of papal biographies known as the *Liber pontificalis*; text in Louis Duchesne, ed., *Le Liber pontificalis: Texte, introduction et commentaire* (Paris: Ernest Thorin, 1886–1892), 2:355.

[32] Dykmans, *Cérémonial papal de la fin du moyen âge à la Renaissance*, 2:268–269.

[33] Dykmans, *Oeuvre de Patrizi Piccolomini*, 1:49–50.

[34] Manuscript: Vatican City, Biblioteca Apostolica Vaticana, Codex Vaticanus Ross. 719, quoted in Dykmans, *Cérémonial papal de la fin du moyen âge à la Renaissance*, 2:269, footnote.

[35] This custom is alluded to in an account of the 1049 election of Pope Leo IX and is explicitly mentioned in regard to the 1099 election of Pope Pascal II (see Duchesne, *Liber pontificalis*, 2:355, 296, respectively). The imposition of the red cope by one particular member of the College of Cardinals appears in the twelfth century, when it is first mentioned in an account of the 1124 election of Pope Honorius II (ibid., 327); the assignment of this task to the leading cardinal deacon of the college is specified in the late twelfth-century *Liber censuum* (c. 1192); see Fabre and Duchesne, *Liber censuum de l'église romaine*, vol. 1, fasc. 2, no. 77, p. 311.

[36] A verbal formula for imposing the cope first appears in the ceremonial of Pope Blessed Gregory X (c. 1273), in Dykmans, *Cérémonial papal de la fin du moyen âge à la Renaissance*, 1:159.

pope at the altar, the cardinals approach him one by one to offer him their homage, kissing his feet, his hand, and his face.[37] This private celebration by the College of Cardinals is immediately followed by the first public appearance of the new pontiff in the Basilica of Saint Peter:

> While these things are done, all the doors of the conclave are opened, the barriers and walls of the entrances and windows are cast down, and signs of joyfulness of every kind are brought forth. The new pontiff, with the cross[38] and the cardinals preceding, goes down to the Church of Saint Peter, and prostrate before the altar, without his miter, he should pray for a little while and give thanks to God and to the blessed Apostles. Then, rising, he is made by the cardinals to sit upon the altar with his miter, and the first of the [cardinal] bishops, having knelt, begins, *Te Deum laudamus*, which hymn the singers continue. Meanwhile, the cardinals again kiss the feet, hand, and face of the elected [pontiff] in the established order; which a fair number of other prelates and nobles do also.[39]

In the above rubrics, the custom of the new pontiff prostrating himself to pray before the high altar over Saint Peter's tomb (the Confession of Saint Peter) dates back to the ninth century.[40] The public homage of the cardinals and prelates and the singing of the *Te Deum laudamus* on this occasion are traceable to the papal election rubrics of the *Liber censuum* (c. 1192).[41] After the completion of the *Te Deum*, the leading cardinal bishop, standing at the left side of the altar, prays over the new pontiff, beginning with a series of versicles ("*Save, O Lord, your servant our elect. . . . Send him, O Lord, help from on high . . .*"). He then offers this Collect for the elect: "*Almighty eternal God, have mercy on your servant* [Name] *elected to supreme pontiff, and direct him according to your clemency in the way of eternal life, that, you granting, he may long for those things that are pleasing to you and accomplish them in all virtue. Through Christ our Lord. Amen.*"[42] The celebration climaxes and concludes with the new pontiff descending from the altar to impart

[37] Dykmans, *Oeuvre de Patrizi Piccolomini*, 1:50. The earliest reference to this private first offering of homage to the new pontiff by the College of Cardinals appears in the ceremonial of Pope Blessed Gregory X (c. 1273); see Dykmans, *Cérémonial papal de la fin du moyen âge à la Renaissance*, 1:159–160.

[38] The bearing of a cross, the "papal cross", before the newly elected pontiff is first mentioned in the ceremonial of Pope Blessed Gregory X (c. 1273); see Dykmans, *Cérémonial papal de la fin du moyen âge à la Renaissance*, 1:160.

[39] Dykmans, *Oeuvre de Patrizi Piccolomini*, 1:50.

[40] This prostration of the new pontiff before the basilica's Confession of Saint Peter is first mentioned in a ninth-century source, Roman *Ordo* 36; text in Michel Andrieu, ed., *Les Ordines Romani du haut moyen âge*, vol. 4, SSLED 28 (Louvain, Belgium: "Spicilegium sacrum Lovaniense" Administration, 1956), 203.

[41] Fabre and Duchesne, *Liber censuum de l'église romaine*, vol. 1, fasc. 2, no. 77, p. 311.

[42] Dykmans, *Oeuvre de Patrizi Piccolomini*, 1:50–51 (Collect on 51).

upon the people his first blessing as pope,[43] a tradition traceable to the late thirteenth-century ceremonial of Pope Blessed Gregory X.[44]

The election of a new pontiff has always been followed by a solemn public Eucharistic celebration, what is now referred to as the installation Mass. In the earlier centuries this Mass carried added importance in that during the rite one or more degrees of the sacrament of holy orders were conferred upon the pontifical candidate, who was often only a deacon or priest of Rome at the time of his election. However, from the late ninth century onward (beginning with the election of Pope Marinus I in 882), candidates for the papacy were increasingly selected not from the clergy of Rome but rather from the already-consecrated bishops of other dioceses, eliminating the need to carry out an episcopal consecration rite at the papal installation Mass.[45] The rite thereafter became primarily a solemn liturgical affirmation of the accession of the new pope to the Chair of Peter before the eyes of the entire Church, and, at one and the same time, a plea before the throne of God for the conferral of grace, wisdom, and divine assistance upon the new Vicar of Christ. For the medieval papal installation Mass and the rites that followed it, we turn again to the 1488 *Caeremoniale Romanum* of the papal master of ceremonies Patrizio Piccolomini.[46]

The Mass begins with a procession to the high altar of the Basilica of Saint Peter, supervised by a deacon wielding a staff, which sets out from the Chapel of Saint Gregory that adjoins the front end of the basilica's nave at its northeast corner. It briefly transverses the northwest corner of the basilica's front portico and then quickly turns right to enter a door opening upon the church's right nave, proceeding along the latter all the way to the north transept of the basilica. At the front of the procession are members of the papal household, followed by the noblemen and ambassadors present. These in turn are followed by the clergy of the Apostolic Chamber. Seven acolytes bearing candles, representing the seven ancient districts of Rome, and another carrying incense precede the core of the procession accompanying the pontiff. One subdeacon carries the papal cross, while two others, one of the Latin Rite and the other of the Byzantine Rite, carry Gospel books in the Latin and Greek languages respectively. Behind them is a Byzantine Rite deacon.[47] A large retinue of bishops, archbishops, cardinals, and abbots, followed by the three principal deacons to assist at

The Solemn Installation and Coronation of a Roman Pontiff

---

[43] Ibid., 51.

[44] Dykmans, *Cérémonial papal de la fin du moyen âge à la Renaissance*, 1:160.

[45] Francis Wasner, "De consecratione, inthronizatione, coronatione summi pontificis", pt. 2, *Apollinaris* 8 (1935): 251.

[46] Dykmans, *Oeuvre de Patrizi Piccolomini*, 1:69–71, 73–79.

[47] The Latin and Greek Gospel books, the Roman and Byzantine Rite subdeacons carrying them, and the Byzantine Rite deacon are first mentioned in the ceremonial of

Mass, and finally the papal master of ceremonies, precede the pope himself. The pontiff, vested in a cope, walks on foot under a canopy borne by eight noblemen or ambassadors as two deacons bear the fringes of his cope and the highest prince present in the city carries the cope's back end. Behind the canopy, the senior judge of the Roman Rota carries the pope's miter, which he is to provide to the pontiff at the various moments in the Mass that require it. The judge is accompanied by two personal attendants (chamberlains) of the pontiff, including the papal secretary.[48]

The course of the procession is punctuated by a dramatic threefold rite that serves to impress upon the new pontiff the vanity and transitory nature of earthly glory:

> Immediately before the pontiff, the master of ceremonies precedes with two shafts, carrying tow [a fibrous substance] upon one but a burning candle upon the other. And when the pontiff shall have exited the Chapel of Saint Gregory, the master of ceremonies, having turned to him, sets the tow on fire and, having genuflected, says in a high voice, *Holy Father, thus passes the glory of the world*, which he does three times, at equally divided intervals, before he should come to the chapel door.[49]

This remarkable ceremony, which first appeared in the papal installation rite at the beginning of the fifteenth century, can be traced back outside the installation rite to the twelfth century: in his work *Gemma animae*, Honorius of Autun (+c. 1135) describes this ceremony being observed in papal processions at Easter: "the Apostolicus [the Pope] then going forth at Easter, a candlestick is propped up out of the tow and over it [i.e., mounted atop the tow], which, kindled by the fire over it, is allowed to fall; but it is extinguished by the ministers or by the earth; and by this tow being reduced to ashes, he is warned [that] the glory of his adornment is likewise to be turned to ashes." [50] The tow-burning rite is first mentioned as part of the papal installation ceremony in a chronicle entry regarding the accession of Gregory XII to the papacy in 1406: "Before he would have come ... to the altar ... three times tow was set before him on staffs and set ablaze, and the cleric of the chapel said, *Thus, Holy Father, thus passes the glory of the world*." [51] Shortly after this time, probably around 1409, a rubric prescribing this observance was inserted into an early fifteenth-century transcription of the fourteenth-century papal ceremonial of Cardinal

---

Cardinal Stefaneschi (c. 1325); see Dykmans, *Cérémonial papal de la fin du moyen âge à la Renaissance*, 2:276.

[48] Dykmans, *Oeuvre de Patrizi Piccolomini*, 1:69–70.

[49] Ibid., 70.

[50] Honorius of Autun, *Gemma animae*, bk. 1, chap. 223, PL 172, cols. 611–612.

[51] Manuscript: Eichstätt, Germany, MS 292, quoted in Dykmans, *Cérémonial papal de la fin du moyen âge à la Renaissance*, 3:143, footnote.

Stefaneschi.[52] Rubrics prepared for the elevation of Martin V to the papacy in December 1417 at the cathedral of Konstanz, Germany, include the ceremony as an established part of the installation rite: "The Pope goes processionally toward the altar, making the sign of the cross continuously on each side; and while he proceeds to the altar a little bit further, on the way shall come to him one of the clerics, who shall carry a bit of tow over a small rod, which he burns there three times, also saying three times, *Holy Father, thus passes the glory of the world.*"[53] This instruction is followed by the comment that some recommended carrying out the tow-burning rite in front of the cathedral on the wooden scaffold upon which the papal throne would rest for the installation, visible to the people, and a "place of greater glory".[54] The intent of this recommendation was to accentuate the tow-burning rite's pedagogical lesson on the fleeting nature of temporal glory. This purpose is expressed more explicitly in the instructions for the tow-burning rite given in a fifteenth-century Vatican manuscript postdating the 1417 installation of Martin V: "Some think it to be better that such an action be done before the doors of the church in the presence of a multitude of people, where there is a place of greater glory and all may see the glory of the world [as] going to last for [only] a brief moment of time."[55]

The purpose of the tow-burning rite as a reminder of man's mortality and the transitory nature of earthly glory is likewise evident in the instructions of the 1488 Piccolomini ceremonial regarding what is to be done in the time of a pontiff's illness and subsequent death. In the preamble to these instructions, the text urges that the pope over the course of his pontificate "should diligently repeat in remembrance that prediction that amid the solemnities of his coronation is wont to be sung: *Holy Father, thus passes the glory of the world.*"[56]

The papal installation rubrics of the Piccolomini ceremonial direct that when the pontiff reaches the grating at the entrance to the Chapel of the Confession, which encloses the basilica's high altar, the last three cardinal priests in the retinue of cardinals are to approach the pope and greet him with the sign of peace. The pontiff then continues to a faldstool in front of the high altar, where, kneeling down, he pauses

---

[52] Inserted rubric: "When [the pope] approaches the high altar, tow on the tip of a rod or staff is kindled before the pope by one of the clerics or acolytes, [the latter] saying in a high voice, kneeling before the pope: *Holy Father, thus passes the glory of the world.* And the pope remains listening; and he advances for a little while, and again, in the same way, it is done three times"; text quoted in Dykmans, *Cérémonial papal de la fin du moyen âge à la Renaissance*, 3:143, footnote.

[53] Manuscript: Turin, Italy, Archives of the State of Turin, *Protocolli rossi*, 2, ibid., 464.

[54] Ibid.

[55] Manuscript: Vatican City, Biblioteca Apostolica Vaticana, Codex Vaticanus Barberinus Latinus 750, fol. 95v, in Bernhard Schimmelpfennig, *Die Zeremonienbücher der römischen Kurie im Mittelalter*, Bibliothek des Deutschen Historischen Instituts in Rom 40 (Tübingen, Germany: Max Niemeyer, 1973), 377.

[56] Dykmans, *Oeuvre de Patrizi Piccolomini*, 1:231.

to pray before beginning Mass.[57] Quite appropriately, the votive Mass of the Holy Spirit is utilized for this occasion, the prayers of which are added to the prayers for the Mass of the particular feast day on which the installation rite takes place.[58]

The liturgy proceeds as in other pontifical Masses until the completion of the *Kyrie* (*Lord, have mercy . . .*). Three bishops now step forward to recite a series of three prayers imploring the blessing of God, the gift of the Holy Spirit, and the bestowal of graces upon the new pontiff.[59] This nonsacramental "consecratory" rite takes place at the same point in the Mass that ordinations to holy orders were customarily performed. When in the earlier centuries of the medieval era the candidate chosen for the papacy was typically a cleric of the diocese of Rome who was not yet a bishop, the installation of the new pope included the elevation of the candidate to the plentitude of holy orders by consecration to the episcopate. The task of ordaining a new pontiff came to be the prerogative of the bishop of the Italian diocese of Ostia, who performed the consecration together with two other bishops from Albano and Porto respectively;[60] our earliest extant rubrics of a papal installation rite, those found in the *Liber diurnus* dating from about 625, speak of the bishops of Albano and Porto each reciting a prayer for the papal elect, after which the bishop of Ostia would carry out the sacramental consecration of the new pope.[61] However, as we noted earlier, from the late ninth century onward, candidates for the papacy were increasingly selected from the bishops of other dioceses, eliminating the need to carry out an episcopal consecration rite at the papal installation Mass. Nonetheless, the three bishops of Ostia, Albano, and Porto retained a key role in the ceremony, assigned the task of solemnly blessing the new pontiff with three benediction prayers, the texts of which are traceable to an eleventh-century manuscript of the Vatican Library.[62] The 1488 *Caeremoniale Romanum* of Piccolomini describes the blessing rite thus:

---

[57] Ibid., 70. The greeting given by the three cardinal priests and the kneeling of the new pontiff to pray before the high altar in preparation for the papal installation Mass are first mentioned in the rubrics for the installation of Pope Benedict XI in 1303 (manuscript: Toulouse, France, Bibliothèque Municipale, MS 67); text in Dykmans, *Cérémonial papal de la fin du moyen âge à la Renaissance*, 2:269–270. The latter practice, the prayer before the installation Mass, can be seen as derived from the earlier-described custom of the new pontiff prostrating himself before Saint Peter's altar to pray following his election, a tradition of ninth-century origin.

[58] Dykmans, *Oeuvre de Patrizi Piccolomini*, 1:74.

[59] Ibid., 71, 73.

[60] Bernhard Schimmelpfennig, "Coronation, Papal", in Joseph Strayer, ed., *Dictionary of the Middle Ages* (New York: Scribner's Sons, 1982), 3:603.

[61] Text of *Liber diurnus* quoted in Godehard Ebers, *Der Papst und die Römische Kurie*, vol. 1, *Wahl, Ordination und Krönung des Papstes*, Quellensammlung zur kirchlichen Rechtsgeschichte und zum Kirchenrecht 3 (Paderborn, Germany: Ferdinand Schöningh, 1916), 174.

[62] Wasner, "De consecratione, inthronizatione, coronatione summi pontificis", pt. 2, 260–261.

The confession having been made [at the end of the *Kyrie*], the pope immediately receives his miter and sits on the seat or faldstool prepared for him between the high throne and the altar, turning his face toward the altar itself.

And the three foremost bishops come up to the pontiff, and the younger [i.e., youngest] of them, standing by himself in between the two [others] without his miter over the pontiff [who is] standing without his miter, keeping his face before [the pontiff's] face, says the first prayer, namely: *O God, who do not disdain to be mindful wheresoever you are invoked with a devout mind, attend, we beseech you, to our invocations, and to this your servant [Name], whom the common judgment of your people has elected to the apostolic summit, impart the fullness of heavenly benediction, that he may perceive himself to have reached this summit by your bounty. Through . . .* The second cardinal bishop, likewise standing by himself in the middle, says immediately the second [prayer], namely: *Impart to our supplications, almighty God, the effect of your accustomed mercy, and fill this your servant [Name] with the grace of the Holy Spirit, that he who is put at the head of our churches in the ministry of your service may be strengthened by the steadfastness of your power. Through . . .* The third [bishop], the older [i.e., oldest], the foremost of the cardinal bishops, standing in the same place, [says] namely: *O God, who willed your Apostle Peter to possess primacy among the other fellow Apostles and placed upon him the burden of all Christianity, graciously regard, we beseech you, this your servant [Name], whom we eagerly elevate from a lowly seat to the exalted throne of the same Prince of the Apostles, that even as he is enriched with the benefits of so great a dignity, so may he be crowned with the merits of the virtues, that, with you assisting, he may worthily bear the burden of the ecclesiastical community and receive a just recompense from you, who are the beatitude of your [servants]. You who live . . .* [63]

The imposition of the pallium over the pontiff's chasuble follows. This cloth band of white wool decorated with six small black crosses, worn in a loop around the neck, with the two ends hanging downward over the chest and back respectively, serving as a symbol of the "plenitude of the pontifical office", is traceable to the fourth century.[64] The popes have always worn the pallium by right, in virtue of their Petrine office; it has been conferred on other prelates only as a special privilege granted to them by the pope. The above-cited text of the papal installation rite from the *Liber diurnus* (c. 625) assigns the imposition of the pallium upon the new pontiff to the same point in

---

[63] Dykmans, *Oeuvre de Patrizi Piccolomini*, 1:73. Father Dykmans provides only the incipit for each of these three prayers; the complete texts of the prayers are here taken from an account of the 1305 installation Mass of Pope Clement V (manuscript: Oxford, Bodleian Library, MS 901), in Dykmans, *Cérémonial papal de la fin du moyen âge à la Renaissance*, 2:289.

[64] Joseph Braun, "Pallium", in *Catholic Encyclopedia* (1907–1912), 11:427–428.

the papal installation Mass that it is found over eight centuries later in the 1488 *Caeremoniale Romanum* of Piccolomini—immediately before the enthronement of the pope, which in turn precedes the singing of the *Gloria*.[65] Utilizing a formula and rubrics traceable to the late twelfth-century *Liber censuum* (c. 1192),[66] the Piccolomini text states:

> The prayers having been said, the pope likewise approaches the altar without his miter. And the first of the deacons, with the second assisting, takes the pallium from the altar, puts it upon the pontiff, and says alone: *Receive the pallium, namely the plenitude of the pontifical office, to the honor of almighty God, the glorious Virgin Mary his Mother, the blessed Peter and Paul, and the holy Roman Church.* And he makes it firm with pins.[67]

The new pope now incenses the altar in the customary manner, after which, seated upon the pontifical throne, he receives homage from the cardinals and other prelates present as an outward pledge of their obedience to him.[68] The pontiff's ascent to the papal throne, the cathedra at the back of the sanctuary of the Basilica of Saint Peter, constitutes his "enthronement". This throne symbolized the one originally used by Saint Peter himself, which according to an ancient tradition has been preserved as a precious relic up to the present (with studies of the ancient chair lending credence to its authenticity).[69] The imagery of a bishop's chair, his cathedra, as a symbol of his authority, and particularly that of the Chair of Peter as a symbol of the unique Petrine authority, is extremely ancient. Around the year 200, we find Tertullian (+223) speaking of the preservation of the chairs used by the Apostles in various places, including Rome.[70] In the third-century poem *Adversus Marcionem*, composed by an unknown author identified as Pseudo-Tertullian, we find the earliest indication of the significance attached to the placing of a successor of Peter upon the Chair of Peter, in this case the first pope to succeed Peter, Pope Saint Linus: "On this chair, upon which Peter himself had sat, Rome the greatest

[65] *Liber diurnus*, quoted in Ebers, *Papst und die Römische Kurie*, 1:174; see also Francis Wasner, "De consecratione, inthronizatione, coronatione summi pontificis", pt. 1, *Apollinaris* 8 (1935): 97–98.

[66] Fabre and Duchesne, *Liber censuum de l'eglise romaine*, vol. 1, fasc. 2, no. 81, p. 312.

[67] Dykmans, *Oeuvre de Patrizi Piccolomini*, 1:74. Father Dykmans provides only the incipit of the pallium imposition formula; the complete text is here taken from an account of the 1305 installation Mass of Pope Clement V (manuscript: Oxford, Bodleian Library, MS 901), in Dykmans, *Cérémonial papal de la fin du moyen âge à la Renaissance*, 2:289.

[68] Dykmans, *Oeuvre de Patrizi Piccolomini*, 1:74. This additional act of homage by the cardinals is first mentioned in the rubrics of the 1303 installation Mass of Pope Benedict XI (manuscript: Toulouse, France, Bibliothèque Municipale, MS 67), in Dykmans, *Cérémonial papal de la fin du moyen âge à la Renaissance*, 2:271.

[69] Anton de Waal, "Chair of Peter", in *Catholic Encyclopedia* (1907–1912), 3:554; Wasner, "De consecratione, inthronizatione, coronatione summi pontificis", pt. 2, 272–273.

[70] Tertullian, *De praescriptionibus adversus haereticos*, chap. 36, PL 2, col. 49.

appointed Linus constituted to sit first."[71] For both popes and bishops, the image of the chair was especially associated with their teaching office, an association traceable to the Scriptures. Our Lord himself, in condemning the hypocritical actions of the scribes and Pharisees, nonetheless admonished the people to obey the valid teachings of the scribes and Pharisees because they "have sitten on the chair of Moses" (Mt 23:2). The concept of the "chair" of the teacher was so prevalent that Saint Augustine (+430) applied this image to the Teacher par excellence, Christ: "That Cross—it was his school. There the Master taught the thief. The wood of hanging has been made a chair of teaching."[72]

The Church considered the symbolism of the seat of Saint Peter so important that by the third century a feast had been introduced to remind the faithful of it—the feast of the Chair of Peter (February 22).[73] With the passage of time, the original, aging chair of Peter, revered as a precious relic, was withdrawn from use (probably out of concern for its preservation), and a new throne symbolizing Peter's chair came to be used by his successors. In the earliest text of the papal installation rite, that of the seventh-century *Liber diurnus* cited previously, we find the seating of the new pope on the pontifical throne as a ceremonial act that immediately follows his consecration to the episcopacy and his reception of the pallium and thus occurs immediately before the *Gloria* at the installation Mass.[74] When beginning in the late ninth century those elected to the papacy were increasingly bishops of other dioceses rather than lower-ranking Roman clerics who required episcopal consecration, the new pontiff's ascent to this throne took on even greater significance by representing, in a juridical sense, his actual assumption of Peter's office.[75] In 955 there was added to the papal enthronement rite the pontiff's assumption of a new name in his Petrine office;[76] it was in that year that Octavius, a Roman, took the name John XII.[77]

Later, in the twelfth century, the Third Lateran Council's decision to identify the election of a pope by two-thirds of the cardinalate as the juridical act that actually made a candidate the new Roman pontiff divested the enthronement of its formerly juridical significance.[78] Moreover, the growing importance of another component of the papal installation rite, the coronation (which we shall later discuss), also lessened somewhat the stress upon the enthronement, but the latter nonetheless remained an

[71] Pseudo-Tertullian, *Adversus Marcionem*, bk. 4, chap. 9, PL 2, col. 1077.

[72] Saint Augustine, *Sermon 234*, no. 2, PL 38, col. 1116.

[73] Wasner, "De consecratione, inthronizatione, coronatione summi pontificis", pt. 2, 272.

[74] *Liber diurnus*, quoted in Ebers, *Papst und die Römische Kurie*, 1:174; see also Wasner, "De consecratione, inthronizatione, coronatione summi pontificis", pt. 1, 97–98.

[75] Wasner, "De consecratione, inthronizatione, coronatione summi pontificis", pt. 2, 252.

[76] Schimmelpfennig, "Coronation, Papal", 604.

[77] J. P. Kirsch, "John XII, Pope", in *Catholic Encyclopedia* (1907–1912), 8:426.

[78] Schimmelpfennig, "Coronation, Papal", 604.

important part of the ceremony. As for the rite of homage that immediately follows the enthronement, this can be traced as far back as the elevation of Pope Formosus to the See of Peter in 891 (as recorded in a work entitled *Infensor et defensor*, authored by a Roman priest named Auxilius).[79] The 1488 *Caeremoniale Romanum* provides the following rubrics for the enthronement rite:

> The pallium having been received, the pontiff ascends without his miter to the altar, kisses it first and then the book of the Gospels, which the subdeacon offers him on the left side; he puts incense in the thurible, with the deacon of the Gospel offering him the incense boat; he censes the altar in the usual manner; and standing at the side of the altar, having received his miter, he is censed by the deacon. And he does not receive the deacons then with respect to the kiss, as at other times, but ascends to the high *cathedra* and sitting receives for the purpose of the reverence [an act of homage to the pope] all the cardinals and prelates prepared, the cardinals [prepared] with respect to the kiss of the foot, the hand, and the face, the others prepared with respect to the kiss of the foot and the hand.[80]

The pope now resumes the celebration of Mass: after repeating in his own voice the Introit and the *Kyrie* sung earlier by the choir, he intones the *Gloria*, upon the completion of which he recites the Collect of the day together with that of the votive Mass of the Holy Spirit. Silently he also recites "a prayer for himself", the Collect for episcopal consecration Masses: "*Attend to our supplications, almighty God, that what is going to be administered by means of our lowliness may in effect be accomplished by your power. Through our Lord Jesus Christ . . .*"[81]

After the pope sits, the first deacon, with a staff in his hand, and the subdeacons, judges, secretaries, and advocates go down from the high altar to the Confession of Saint Peter, where they arrange themselves in two rows flanking the Confession, with men of each ecclesiastical office represented in each flanking line.[82] They now begin the *Exaudi Christe*, also known as "the Lauds", a litany used in papal installation rites since the ninth century (when it is mentioned as part of the papal installation rite in Roman *Ordo* 36);[83] readers may recall the chanting of this same litany at the beginning of the installation Mass

[79] Wasner, "De consecratione, inthronizatione, coronatione summi pontificis", pt. 2, 258, 262.

[80] Dykmans, *Oeuvre de Patrizi Piccolomini*, 1:74.

[81] The 1488 ceremonial does not provide the text of this prayer (ibid.). It is here taken from the tenth-century Romano-Germanic Pontifical, in Cyrille Vogel and Reinhard Elze, eds., *Le pontifical romano-germanique du dixième siècle*, vol. 1, ST 226 (Vatican City: Biblioteca Apostolica Vaticana, 1963), 206. For the eighth-century origin of this prayer, see p. 185 of the present work.

[82] Dykmans, *Oeuvre de Patrizi Piccolomini*, 1:74-75.

[83] Roman *Ordo* 36, in Andrieu, *Ordines Romani du haut moyen âge*, 4:199, 204, 205.

of Pope Benedict XVI in April 2005 as the newly elected pontiff walked in procession through the vast nave of the Basilica of Saint Peter and out into the Square of Saint Peter. The Piccolomini rubrics state: "The first of the deacons begins alone in a high voice as though reading: *Graciously hear, O Christ*. The subdeacons, judges, secretaries, and advocates respond: *Our lord* [Name], *ordained by God supreme pontiff and universal pope in life*. And thus it is said by the first [a second time and] a third time, and it is answered by them as many times, and so forth." [84] The 1488 ceremonial does not provide the rest of the litany, but a complete text is given in the papal ceremonial of Cardinal Stefaneschi (c. 1325). Following the threefold recitation of the opening versicle given above, the first deacon continues, saying, "*Savior of the world*", to which the others respond, "*Assist him*." This invocation together with the response is said thrice. Twice the first deacon says, "*Holy Mary*", to which the others answer, "*Assist him*." The invocations to follow are each said and answered once:

Saint Michael. Response: *Assist him.*
Saint Gabriel. Response: *Assist him.*
Saint Raphael. Response: *Assist him.*
Saint John the Baptist. Response: *Assist him.*
Saint Peter. Response: *Assist him.*
Saint Paul. Response: *Assist him.*
Saint Andrew. Response: *Assist him.*
Saint James. Response: *Assist him.*
Saint John. Response: *Assist him.*
Saint Stephen. Response: *Assist him.*
Saint Lawrence. Response: *Assist him.*
Saint George. Response: *Assist him.*
Saint Leo. Response: *Assist him.*
Saint Gregory. Response: *Assist him.*
Saint Benedict. Response: *Assist him.*
Saint Basil. Response: *Assist him.*
Saint Saba. Response: *Assist him.*
Saint Agnes. Response: *Assist him.*
Saint Cecilia. Response: *Assist him.*
Saint Lucy. Response: *Assist him.*

In conclusion, the deacon says thrice, "*Lord, have mercy*", to which the others reply the first and second times, "*Lord, have mercy*"; the deacon is answered for the third time by all who are present for the Mass saying together, "*Lord, have mercy*." [85]

The Mass proceeds thereafter in the usual manner for a pontifical liturgy. By way of a slight digression, we note here that in the text

---

[84] Dykmans, *Oeuvre de Patrizi Piccolomini*, 1:75.

[85] Dykmans, *Cérémonial papal de la fin du moyen âge à la Renaissance*, 2:313–314.

of the papal installation Mass from the ceremonial of Cardinal Stefaneschi (c. 1325), the rubrics for the Gospel include a practice not
mentioned in any other papal liturgical text: when the deacon who
is to read the Gospel has signed his forehead, his lips, and his chest
in the customary manner before beginning the reading, he turns
toward the east to make a further sign of the cross over himself
before proceeding with the Gospel, and he repeats this action, again
toward the east, at the end of the reading.[86] Returning to the 1488
Piccolomini rite, we find that after the Mass the pope goes in procession together with all the cardinals and prelates to the front steps
of the basilica, where a throne mounted upon a platform has been
readied for the coronation of the new pontiff.[87] Our earliest evidence of a distinctive head covering for the pope dates from the
early eighth century, found in a biography of Pope Constantine (708–
715).[88] Originally the papal headpiece had taken the form of a white
cap,[89] but by the end of the eleventh century, this had been superseded by a papal tiara.[90] Pope Innocent III (+1216) found scriptural
precedents for the association of royal power with the priestly office
of the papacy, an association symbolized by the papal tiara. He quotes
a verse from Psalm 109: "Thou art a priest for ever according to the
order of Melchisedech" (Ps 109:4). As described in the Book of
Genesis, Melchisedech, one of the Old Testament types of Christ,
was both "king of Salem" and "the priest of the most high God",
"bringing forth bread and wine" (Gen 14:18). Pope Innocent also
cites Saint Peter's words "You are a chosen generation, a kingly priesthood" (1 Pet 2:9), observing that those chosen for the papacy should
hear these words as if addressed to them in particular. Pope Innocent
suggests a further royal dimension to the pontifical office in that the
pope is "vicar of him who is 'KING OF KINGS, AND LORD OF LORDS'
[Rev 19:16]."[91]

The earliest recorded ceremonial crowning of a new pontiff is that
found in a ninth-century liturgical text, Roman *Ordo* 36.[92] The distinctive three-tiered crown that would come to symbolize the papacy
is first mentioned in an inventory of the papal treasury dating from
1315 or 1316.[93] In the 1488 *Caeremoniale Romanum* it is the three-
tiered crown that is conferred upon the new pontiff:

---

[86] Ibid., 315.

[87] Dykmans, *Oeuvre de Patrizi Piccolomini*, 1:75.

[88] Francis Wasner, "De consecratione, inthronizatione, coronatione summi pontificis",
pt. 3, *Apollinaris* 8 (1935): 428.

[89] Joseph Braun, "Tiara", in *Catholic Encyclopedia* (1907–1912), 14:714.

[90] Mario Righetti, *Manuale di storia liturgica* (Milan: Editrice Ancora, 1949–1955), 4:332.

[91] Innocent III, *Sermon 7*, "On the Feast of Sylvester, Supreme Pontiff", PL 217, col.
481; see also his *Sermon 3*, "On the Consecration of a Pontiff", PL 217, col. 665.

[92] Andrieu, *Ordines Romani du haut moyen âge*, 4:205.

[93] Braun, "Tiara", 715.

The pontiff, having taken up again his gloves and rings with all his vestments in which he had celebrated [Mass], goes forth with all the cardinals, prelates, and officials, likewise vested as at the Mass, to the platform over the stairs of the basilica of the Prince of the Apostles, built from lumber and furnished; and there on the high throne prepared for him he sits.

And when all the prelates shall have assembled and the people shall have gone out from the basilica into the street, the deacon on the left removes the ordinary miter from the head of the pontiff, and the deacon on the right places upon the pontiff's head the tiara, which they call "the kingdom", a decorated triple crown, the people crying out, *Lord, have mercy*. And the deacon at the right in Latin, [the deacon] at the left, however, in the vernacular, make public the plenary indulgences.[94]

The three-tiered crown was variously interpreted to represent the diverse roles of the Roman pontiff. One such interpretation is found in the address that the papal master of ceremonies John Burckard (+1506) inserted into the above rite (after 1488), instructing the deacon on the right to say these words as he crowned the pope with the tiara: "*Receive the tiara adorned with three crowns; and may you perceive yourself to be a father to princes and kings, the rector of the world, and on earth the vicar of our Savior, to whom be honor and glory to ages of ages. Amen.*"[95] Burckard also adds a rubric specifying that after the crowning, the new pontiff is to give the people a solemn blessing.[96] Another insertion, of unknown origin and probably dating from about 1503 (judging from an apparent reference to Pope Julius II), adds the following series of verses to the coronation rite, elucidating the mystical significance of the ceremony, as well as a prayer immediately preceding the imposition of the three-tiered tiara that identifies the three roles of the pope as those of a "father, king, and ruler of all the faithful":

And when all the prelates shall have assembled and the people shall have gone out from the basilica into the street, the cantors sing the responsory, *A gold crown upon his head, stamped with the seal of holiness, the attainment of glory, honor, and strength*. Verse: *For you have preceded him with the blessings of sweetness. You have placed on his head a crown of precious stone. Stamped* ... Verse: *Glory be to the Father*, etc. *Stamped* ...[97] Then the first of the cardinal bishops standing to the left of the pope, with his head uncovered, says the Our Father, which he finishes privately. Meanwhile, the pope also rises, the miter for him

---

[94] Dykmans, *Oeuvre de Patrizi Piccolomini*, 1:75–76.

[95] Ibid., 76, footnote.

[96] Ibid. (footnote).

[97] This responsory, *Corona aurea*, from the Common of One Martyr, is first found in the Antiphonary of Compiègne (France, c. 870); see René-Jean Hésbert, ed., *Corpus antiphonalium officii*, vol. 1, REDSMF 7 (Rome: Herder, 1963), 264, 360.

having been removed previously, [remaining without his miter] up until the prayer that is to follow [is] said. The Our Father having been completed, the aforesaid first [of the cardinal bishops] says in a suitable voice the verse, *And lead us not into temptation.* Response: *But deliver us from evil.* Verse: *Let us sing to the Lord.* Response: *For he is gloriously exalted.* Verse: *Sound a trumpet at the new moon on the eminent day of your solemnity.* Verse: *Sing joyfully to God, all the earth.* Response: *Serve the Lord in joy.* Verse: *O Lord, hearken to my prayer.* Response: *And let my cry come unto you.* Verse: *The Lord be with you.* Response: *And with your spirit.* [Prayer:] *Let us pray. Almighty eternal God, honor of the priesthood and Creator of the kingdom, grant the grace of fruitfully governing your Church to your servant [Name] our pontiff, who by your mercy has been constituted and crowned father, king, and ruler of all the faithful, that all things may be governed well by your salutary providence. Through Christ our Lord ...* The deacon on the left removes the ordinary miter from the head of the pontiff, and the deacon on the right places upon the pontiff's head the tiara.[98]

In the fifth century, the installation rites of the popes took place at the cathedral church of Rome, the Basilica of Saint John Lateran.[99] The installation Mass was subsequently transferred to the Basilica of Saint Peter, the church where the chair representing the supreme pontiff's authority was enshrined; it was there that Saint Gregory the Great was elevated to the papacy in 590.[100] Despite this major change, the Lateran basilica and the palace adjoining it that served as the primary papal residence retained a key role in the installation of the popes. Each new pontiff was required to take possession of the Lateran basilica and palace as a further affirmation of his accession to the papacy, insofar as the Lateran is the cathedral church of the Bishop of Rome. By the twelfth century, there had arisen a solemn procession following the ceremonies at the Basilica of Saint Peter in which the new pope journeyed to the Lateran to take possession of it.[101] The procession was in part a borrowing from the coronation rites of the Holy Roman emperors that took place in Rome—after being crowned at the Basilica of Saint Peter, the new emperor would process to the Lateran, where a state banquet was conducted for him at the papal palace.[102] As the visible sovereign of the Church and as the temporal sovereign of the Papal States, a new pope was entitled to a comparable "royal progress" on the day that celebrated his elevation to the Throne of Peter. The procession would have also given those of Rome absent from the

[98] Dykmans, *Oeuvre de Patrizi Piccolomini*, 1:75–76, footnote.

[99] Schimmelpfennig, "Coronation, Papal", 603.

[100] Wasner, "De consecratione, inthronizatione, coronatione summi pontificis", pt. 1, 116.

[101] Schimmelpfennig, "Coronation, Papal", 604.

[102] Herbert Thurston, S.J., "Coronation", in *Catholic Encyclopedia* (1907–1912), 4:385.

ceremonies at the Basilica of Saint Peter the opportunity to greet the pontiff. Moreover, although not explicitly mentioned, this procession would have evoked the imagery of Christ riding triumphantly into Jerusalem to accomplish his salvific mission. By comparison, the triumphant journey of the new pontiff to the Lateran would have symbolized the undertaking of his own mission as Vicar of Christ.

In giving the instructions for the procession to the Lateran basilica, the 1488 *Caeremoniale Romanum* mentions that, in view of the advanced time of day following the prolonged rites at the Basilica of Saint Peter and due to the considerable length of the journey yet to be made to the Lateran, the pontiff, the cardinals, and the other prelates customarily pause for a refection before departing for the Lateran.[103] Afterward, all prepare for the procession. Standing ready to receive the pontiff is "a white harnessed horse, covered on the posterior with a crimson pall".[104] The tradition of a new pontiff going in procession on horseback following his installation Mass dates back to the ninth century,[105] with the details regarding the regalia of the horse appearing by the end of the thirteenth century.[106] The highest royal dignitaries present assist the pope in mounting:

> When the pope ascends his horse by the ladder … the greatest prince who is present, even if he should be a king or the emperor, holds the stirrup of the papal horse and then leads the horse somewhat by the bridle. If the emperor or king should be alone, namely, there is not another king present, he alone should lead the horse with his right hand. But if there should be another king, the greater should hold the bridle by the right, the other by the left. If there should be no kings, two worthier [princes] should lead the horse. And after the emperor, the king, or another great prince shall have led the horse somewhat, two other great nobles should substitute and be exchanged in their place.[107]

Along the way the pontiff, mounted thus, proceeds "under a canopy that eight great nobles or ambassadors carry".[108] The procession is led by the cardinals' valets, followed by a vast retinue comprising the personal attendants of the pope and the cardinals (including the pontiff's barber and tailor). In their midst, a white horse carries the ladder used

---

[103] Dykmans, *Oeuvre de Patrizi Piccolomini*, 1:76.

[104] Ibid., 79.

[105] See the ninth-century liturgical text Roman *Ordo* 36, in Andrieu, *Ordines Romani du haut moyen âge*, 4:204–205.

[106] The crimson pall covering the horse is first mentioned in the ceremonial of Pope Blessed Gregory X (c. 1273); see Dykmans, *Cérémonial papal de la fin du moyen âge à la Renaissance*, 1:172.

[107] Dykmans, *Oeuvre de Patrizi Piccolomini*, 1:79.

[108] Ibid. The papal ceremonial of Cardinal Stefaneschi (c. 1325) is the first text to mention a canopy being carried over the pontiff in this procession; see Dykmans, *Cérémonial papal de la fin du moyen âge à la Renaissance*, 2:282.

by the pope for mounting his horse; it is led by a groom clothed in red, "bearing the reins of the horse with his right hand, a red staff in his left".[109] A colorful contingent of standard-bearers follows:

> Twelve couriers of the pope follow this, also clothed in red garments, the equestrians carrying twelve red standards, two by two.[110] Thereafter, thirteen standard-bearers of the principal districts [of Rome] with their standards, then two couriers with standards of cherubim somewhat larger [than] the other standards; also in red garments, and all the equestrian standard-bearers.
>
> Then the standard-bearers of the Roman people with the standard and insignia of the Roman people. Then a white standard with a black cross, that the procurator of the order of blessed Mary of the Teutonics carries; the standard with the arms of the pope, which another great noble carries; the standard of the Church, likewise, another great noble carries; and finally the red standard of the order of Jerusalem with a white cross, which the procurator of this order carries. The latter five standard-bearers shall have horses barded and covered with silken cloth all the way to the horses' feet with their coats of arms. They themselves, however, in addition to a helmet, shall be armed, and in particular if a battle is going to be undertaken, with lanterns of silken cloth, likewise with their coat of arms; and each standard-bearer shall have four foot soldiers with lanterns of cotton fabric with the coats of arms of their lords.[111]

These in turn are followed by an array of riderless horses. Their number seems to suggest that they are intended to signify the spiritual participation of the twelve Apostles in this great celebration of the handing down of the apostolic succession in Rome: "After the standards proceed twelve white horses without riders, adorned with golden medallions and covered with crimson, which twelve grooms lead, clothed in red attire and carrying a red staff in the left hand."[112] The most distinguished Guest for the day's festivities now passes: Christ in the Blessed Sacrament, accompanied by his own retinue:

> Then [comes] the apostolic subdeacon with the papal cross, and his companions, vested as at Mass, and near the cross two master porters with their staffs. After these, twelve servants of the pope clothed in red attire—foot soldiers—carrying twelve lit torches before the Sacrament of the Body of Christ. Thereafter, two equestrian servants of

---

[109] Dykmans, *Oeuvre de Patrizi Piccolomini*, 1:77.

[110] The twelve red standards in this procession are first mentioned in the ceremonial of Pope Blessed Gregory X (c. 1273); see Dykmans, *Cérémonial papal de la fin du moyen âge à la Renaissance*, 1:173.

[111] Dykmans, *Oeuvre de Patrizi Piccolomini*, 1:77.

[112] Ibid., 78.

the sacristan, also clothed in red, carrying silver lanterns with light before the Sacrament.

And after them is led by the sacristan's servant—likewise clothed in red, and holding a staff in his left hand—a meek white horse, adorned just as the twelve others, carrying the Sacrament, having at the neck a small handbell ringing well. And overhead is borne a canopy with the arms of the pope and the Sacrament by Roman citizens, who change places with each other thirteen times, that every district may have its part. Immediately behind the Sacrament rides the sacristan on horseback, who, just as the other prelates, has his horse totally covered in cotton fabric, and he and all the others are clothed as at Mass with vestments and miters. The sacristan carries in his hand a white staff.[113]

The above-described carrying of the Blessed Sacrament in the procession of a newly elected pontiff from the Basilica of Saint Peter to the Lateran is not mentioned in any papal ceremonial prior to that of Piccolomini, but this custom is clearly derived from the practice of carrying the Blessed Sacrament in other papal processions and even on papal journeys, an observance that is thought to have arisen in the first half of the fourteenth century and existed until 1729.[114] Behind the Blessed Sacrament, the prelates who attended the earlier installation Mass serve as the immediate entourage of the new pontiff:

Next follow the prelates with covered horses, and they themselves with miter and cope: the nonresident abbots, bishops, archbishops, abbots of the city, the assisting bishops of the pope, the patriarchs— the deacons with dalmatics, the priests with chasubles, the cardinal bishops with copes. Then proceed the two assisting deacons of the pope, and midway between them the first deacon, if he himself has said the Gospel. The first of the deacons ought to carry a staff in his hand and order the whole procession and, it having been ordered, ride on horseback in his place.

Finally proceeds the supreme pontiff upon a white harnessed horse, covered on the posterior with a crimson pall, under a canopy that eight great nobles or ambassadors carry.[115]

Upon reaching the Lateran, the pope dismounts from his horse at the porch of the church, where he then kisses a cross brought to him by the prior of the canons regular of the Lateran, which is held to his lips by a cardinal deacon.[116] This custom, first mentioned in the papal installation rubrics of the ceremonial of Cardinal Stefaneschi (c. 1325),[117]

---

[113] Ibid.
[114] Righetti, *Manuale di storia liturgica*, 3:505–506.
[115] Dykmans, *Oeuvre de Patrizi Piccolomini*, 1:79.
[116] Ibid., 81–82.
[117] Dykmans, *Cérémonial papal de la fin du moyen âge à la Renaissance*, 2:283.

is clearly a papal version of the universal practice of solemnly greeting a visiting bishop or prelate upon his arrival by presenting to him a cross, which he in turn venerates with a kiss, an observance traceable to the pontifical of William Durandus of Mende (compiled c. 1294).[118]

Most of the ceremonial actions that follow in the 1488 Piccolomini rite date back to the late twelfth-century *Liber censuum* (c. 1192).[119] After the pontiff receives his miter, the canons lead him to the Lateran's ancient marble papal throne, the *stercoraria*, and have him sit upon it.[120] The cardinals come to the pontiff and "honorably elevate him", evidently lifting him slightly, as they recite the verse "*He raises up the needy from the earth and lifts up the poor out of the dunghill, that he may place him with princes, and possess the throne of glory*" (cf. Ps 112:7).[121] The pope then stands, and having taken up a fistful of coins from the chamberlain assisting him, he tosses them among the people as he repeats the words of Saint Peter to the lame man he was to heal in the name of Christ, "*Silver and gold I have none; but what I have, I give thee*" (Acts 3:6).[122] As the canons sing the thanksgiving hymn *Te Deum*, the pontiff enters the basilica and proceeds to a faldstool before the high altar, where he kneels to pray. Upon rising, the pope blesses the people, after which he takes his seat, and the canons pay homage to him as their new pastor by coming forward to kiss his feet.[123]

Further rites follow in the Lateran palace, the Chapel of Saint Sylvester, and the Sancta Sanctorum chapel,[124] including the presentation to the pontiff of several gifts, all of which are first mentioned and explained in the *Liber censuum* (c. 1192).[125] The 1488 Piccolomini rubrics state that the new pope is given a staff as a "sign of correction and governance", and the keys to the Lateran, representing the pontiff's "power of closing and opening, of binding and loosing".[126] He is

---

[118] Text in Michel Andrieu, ed., *Le pontifical romain au moyen-âge*, vol. 3, *Le pontifical de Guillaume Durand*, ST 88 (Vatican City: Biblioteca Apostolica Vaticana, 1940), 627.

[119] Fabre and Duchesne, *Liber censuum de l'église romaine*, vol. 1, fasc. 2, nos. 78–79, pp. 311–312.

[120] Dykmans, *Oeuvre de Patrizi Piccolomini*, 1:82.

[121] Ibid. The enthronement of the new pontiff upon the *stercoraria* and the association of Psalm 112:7 with this action are both first mentioned in the *Liber censuum*; see Fabre and Duchesne, *Liber censuum de l'église romaine*, vol. 1, fasc. 2, no. 78, p. 311. The actual recitation of the verse by the cardinals and their symbolic lifting of the pontiff to seat him on the *stercoraria* appear for the first time in the ceremonial of Pope Blessed Gregory X (c. 1273); see Dykmans, *Cérémonial papal de la fin du moyen âge à la Renaissance*, 1:177.

[122] Dykmans, *Oeuvre de Patrizi Piccolomini*, 1:82. This action, with these words, first appears in the *Liber censuum*; see Fabre and Duchesne, *Liber censuum de l'église romaine*, vol. 1, fasc. 2, no. 78, p. 311.

[123] Dykmans, *Oeuvre de Patrizi Piccolomini*, 1:82. The pope's prayer before the high altar of the Lateran, the pontifical blessing that follows it, and the act of homage by the Lateran canons are all first mentioned in the ceremonial of Pope Blessed Gregory X (c. 1273); see Dykmans, *Cérémonial papal de la fin du moyen âge à la Renaissance*, 1:177–178.

[124] Dykmans, *Oeuvre de Patrizi Piccolomini*, 1:82–84.

[125] Fabre and Duchesne, *Liber censuum de l'église romaine*, vol. 1, fasc. 2, no. 79, p. 312.

[126] Dykmans, *Oeuvre de Patrizi Piccolomini*, 1:83.

also girded with a red silken cincture on which hangs a burse of the same color and material containing twelve precious stones, scented with musk.[127] Regarding the symbolism of the cincture, the *Liber censuum* explains: "In the belt is signified the continence of chastity, in the burse the treasury, with which the paupers of Christ and widows should be supported. In the twelve figures [carved in precious stones] is signified the power of the twelve Apostles; musk is enclosed for perceiving odor, as the Apostle says: 'We are the good odour of Christ unto God' [2 Cor 2:15]." [128] It is highly likely that the use of precious stones to symbolize the Apostles was inspired by the Book of Revelation, in which the Apostles are symbolized by the twelve foundations supporting the wall of the heavenly Jerusalem, each of which was adorned with precious stones (Rev 21:19–20). In the 1488 Piccolomini rite, the papal installation ceremonies conclude with a great banquet.[129]

---

[127] Ibid.

[128] Fabre and Duchesne, *Liber Censuum de l'église romaine*, vol. 1, fasc. 2, no. 79, p. 312.

[129] Dykmans, *Oeuvre de Patrizi Piccolomini*, 1:84–91.

19 The Canonization of Saints

By the ceremonies of the Catholic Church, seen and heard and understood, men are inspired unto piety and inflamed to fervor.

Bishop Angelo Rocca (+1620)[1]

The concept of sainthood, the heroic imitation of Christ, is as ancient
as Christianity itself, inspired by Christ's invitation to be "perfect, as
also your heavenly Father is perfect" (Mt 5:48). The early Church,
certainly by the second century, venerated such heroism in the lives of
the martyrs and, by the fourth century, in those besides the martyrs
who had lived their faith with extraordinary devotion.[2] With the Church
threatened by heresies, the need arose to verify that those popularly
reputed as saints were true models of Christian perfection. Canonization, the Church's definitive recognition of a person's sainthood as
declared by the pope, gradually developed from the tenth century
onward, beginning with the first recorded canonization, that of the
German bishop Ulrich of Augsburg (+973), proclaimed a saint by Pope
John XV in 993. However, several more centuries were to pass before
there emerged a particular public ceremony for proclaiming a person's
canonization. The thirteenth-century Italian canonist and cardinal-
bishop Henry of Susa (+1271), often referred to as *Hostiensis* (because
he was bishop of Ostia),[3] provides the earliest extant outline of the
canonization rite as it existed in his time. The twelve steps for canonization that he lists in his work, *Lectures on the Decretals of Gregory IX*, include the assembling of the clergy and the laity for the
canonization ceremony in a particular church, adorned with cloth hangings and "many candles"; a sermon given by the pope in which he
asks for prayers that he may not err in his decision to canonize; an
ensuing prayer for this intention of divine guidance, said kneeling;
and the chanting of the *Veni Creator Spiritus*, after which the pope
makes his solemn pronouncement of the canonization decision. The

---

[1] Angelo Rocca, *De canonizatione sanctorum commentarius* (Rome: Guillelmus Facciottus,
1601; digitized text, Bayerische Staatsbibliothek, Munich, n.d.), 129.

[2] Camillus Beccari, "Beatification and Canonization", in *The Catholic Encyclopedia* (New
York: Appleton, 1907–1912), 2:364–365.

[3] A. Van Hove, "Henry of Segusio, Blessed", in *Catholic Encyclopedia* (1907–1912), 7:238.

Te Deum is then sung in thanksgiving, and the pope celebrates Mass in honor of the newly elevated saint.[4]

The earliest *detailed* records of a solemn liturgical rite for canonization date from the first quarter of the fourteenth century.[5] In the papal ceremonial compiled around 1325 by Cardinal Giacomo Stefaneschi (+1343), we find an account of the April 1317 ceremony for the canonization of the French bishop Saint Louis of Anjou (+1297), as well as details regarding the 1320 canonization of the English bishop Saint Thomas Cantelupe of Hereford (+1282).[6] In the last decade of the fourteenth century, the Augustinian bishop and papal master of ceremonies Pierre Ameil (+1403) compiled another ceremonial (subsequently completed by Pierre Assalbit, 1435–1441) which describes the liturgical rite in Rome for the 1391 canonization of Saint Bridget of Sweden (+1373).[7] While closely following the rite codified in the earlier ceremonial of Cardinal Stefaneschi, Ameil considerably enhanced the visual splendor of the canonization rite in several significant ways, including the lavish, celebrative adornment of the Basilica of Saint Peter for the day of canonization.[8] Over the century that followed, the rite of canonization changed little, becoming a stable component of the papal liturgy, with a fixed format of established rubrics and prayers to be utilized at every canonization. It is thus that we find it detailed in the *Caeremoniale Romanum* compiled by the papal master of ceremonies Patrizio Piccolomini, dating from 1488.[9]

In keeping with the canonization practices first related by the thirteenth-century canonist Henry of Susa, the ceremonial of Cardinal Stefaneschi, compiled at a time (c. 1325) when the popes were residing in Avignon, France, speaks of tapestries and "many lights" being placed in the Avignon church of Notre-Dame-des-Doms for the 1320 canonization of Saint Thomas Cantelupe of Hereford.[10] Such customs were continued and amplified when the popes subsequently returned to Rome. An eyewitness account of the 1391 canonization of Saint Bridget of Sweden given by a Brigittine monk, Lorenzo the Roman, tells of the splendid adornment of the Apostolic Palace for

---

[4] Henry of Susa [Hostiensis], *In III Decretalium* (Venice, 1581), fol. 172r–v, quoted in Marc Dykmans, S.J., ed., *Le cérémonial papal de la fin du moyen âge à la Renaissance*, vol. 2, BIHBR 25 (Brussels and Rome: Institut Historique Belge de Rome, 1981), 460–465 (italicized words), 226–227, 230–234.

[5] Ferdinando Dell'Oro, S.D.B., *Beatificazione e canonizzazione: "Excursus" storico-liturgico*, BELS 89 (Rome: Centro Liturgico Vincenziano, Edizioni Liturgiche, 1997), 42–44.

[6] Text in Dykmans, *Cérémonial papal de la fin du moyen âge à la Renaissance*, 2:458–466.

[7] Text in Marc Dykmans, S.J., ed., *Le cérémonial papal de la fin du moyen âge à la Renaissance*, vol. 4, BIHBR 27 (Brussels and Rome: Institut Historique Belge de Rome, 1985), 235–242.

[8] Dell'Oro, *Beatificazione e canonizzazione*, 63.

[9] Text in Marc Dykmans, S.J., ed., *L'oeuvre de Patrizi Piccolomini, ou Le cérémonial papal de la première Renaissance*, vol. 1, ST 293 (Vatican City: Biblioteca Apostolica Vaticana, 1980), 120–124.

[10] Dykmans, *Cérémonial papal de la fin du moyen âge à la Renaissance*, 2:464.

this occasion, as well as the festive heralding of the canonization on the night before the beginning of the ceremonies:

> On Friday also, at the time of Vespers ... the bells of Saint Peter began to be rung together with all the greater [bells] of all the dear city from the seventh hour continuously to the tenth of the evening; likewise, from the second hour after midnight they sound again up until after sunrise on Saturday. . . .
>
> For the [Apostolic] Palace was so adorned with splendid golden and purple hangings, and other resplendent decorations in fabric of various colors, that it would have insatiably captivated the minds and eyes of all; moreover, it shone, illuminated on every side with the kindled lights of candles everywhere, and it likewise wonderfully refreshed the souls of those visiting, overwhelmed with its fragrant scents.[11]

The rubrics for the canonization liturgy given in the 1488 *Caeremoniale Romanum* of Patrizio Piccolomini begin with detailed instructions for the decoration of the Vatican basilica:

> In the church is built a wooden platform of such breadth that upon it may be erected and prepared a chapel with an altar; credences; the pontifical throne; the seats of the cardinals assisting the pope, of the ambassadors, [and] of the prelates; and the places of all the ranks of the Roman Curia, to the likeness of the chapel of the Apostolic Palace from the grating and beyond, with respect to the pattern of the seats and the capacity. On the aforesaid platform are two papal thrones, one high at the left side, and the other shall be movable. It shall be ascended by a bridge to the platform with a small double door at the top and at the bottom. And the platform shall be adorned all around on the edges with plants and flowers and within with suitable cloths and tapestries.
>
> The church shall also be adorned, and there shall be hung throughout it the arms of the pontiff [and] of the Church, and the image of the one to be canonized, and also the arms of those procuring the canonization. A new canopy shall be made with the arms of the pontiff, of the procurators, and of those requesting the canonization and with the image of the saint, which ought to be hung above the altar where the pontiff shall celebrate. A large banner shall also be made with the image of the saint, which shall be carried before the religious, or those who are procuring the canonization; and it is placed near the door of the upper platform when the pontiff comes to the church. Torches should be placed all around in the church upon the

---

[11] Manuscript: Vatican City, Biblioteca Apostolica Vaticana, Codex Vaticanus Latinus 12229, in Dykmans, *Cérémonial papal de la fin du moyen âge à la Renaissance,* 4:277.

gallery, eighty or so in number, which should burn until the service is done.[12]

The large number of lights specified for the illumination of the interior of the Basilica of Saint Peter, a feature traceable to Cardinal Stefaneschi's ceremonial, became a regular characteristic of the canonization solemnities. Pierre Ameil's ceremonial states that eighty-six torches or candles were utilized for this purpose at the 1391 canonization of Saint Bridget.[13] In his account of this same canonization, Lorenzo the Roman mentions that during the night preceding the canonization five thousand lanterns were lit to illuminate the outside of the Vatican.[14] An account of the 1461 canonization Mass of Saint Catherine of Siena (+1380) speaks of "many lit torches amid the columns" within the basilica.[15] In addition to these "decorative" lights, many other candles and torches were required for distribution among those participating in the canonization procession and for various uses during the different parts of the canonization Mass. These are enumerated in the 1488 Piccolomini ceremonial:

> Wax should be prepared to be distributed: first for the pontiff, two white wax candles, of ten pounds each; for the cardinals, of four pounds. Also, for the elevation of the Sacrament, twelve torches of six pounds each. For the altar, seven wax candles, and two for the credence, of two pounds. Also, for the Offertory, two large wax candles of twelve pounds each, which the first cardinal offers. Also three wax candles of six pounds, which the three ambassadors or those appointed shall offer, with three cardinals. And all the aforesaid wax candles shall be white, besides the eighty torches of the church. Also, candles from ordinary wax of two pounds should be ordered for the prelates, the ambassadors, and the great nobles; for the officials and cantors, of one pound; for the others as it shall have seemed proper.[16]

In total, 108 candles and torches are listed in the above text, but the actual number of lights utilized for the canonization ceremony would have considerably exceeded this in that an unspecified number of candles were to be distributed to other participants in the canonization procession. A manuscript from 1487 (contemporaneous with the Piccolomini ceremonial), drawn up for the planned canonization of Saint

---

[12] Dykmans, *Oeuvre de Patrizi Piccolomini*, 1:120–121.

[13] Dykmans, *Cérémonial papal de la fin du moyen âge à la Renaissance*, 4:235; see also 240.

[14] Manuscript: Vatican City, Biblioteca Apostolica Vaticana, Codex Vaticanus Latinus 12229, in Dykmans, *Cérémonial papal de la fin du moyen âge à la Renaissance*, 4:276.

[15] Manuscript: Vatican City, Biblioteca Apostolica Vaticana, Codex Vaticanus Latinus 12348, in Dykmans, *Cérémonial papal de la fin du moyen âge à la Renaissance*, 4:282.

[16] Dykmans, *Oeuvre de Patrizi Piccolomini*, 1:121.

Frances of Rome (+1440)—a canonization that was subsequently post-
poned for over a century (not taking place until 1608)—speaks of a
total of over 1,350 candles for the entire ceremony.[17]

In the 1488 ceremonial of Piccolomini, as in the early fourteenth-
century ceremonial of Cardinal Stefaneschi, the canonization liturgy
begins with a procession of the pope into the Basilica of Saint Peter.
The rubrics for this procession in the 1488 text, given below, exhibit
the enhanced splendor that the rite had inherited from the late
fourteenth-century ceremonial of Pierre Ameil:

> It should also be made known to the clergy of the city that all should
> assemble processionally very early in the morning on the porch of
> the Church of Saint Peter.
>
> Accordingly, on the appointed day of the canonization, the pon-
> tiff, vested in a red cope and a miter of precious materials, with the
> cardinals, the prelates, and the officials vested, comes down proces-
> sionally to the church under a canopy. In the chamber of the vest-
> ment the wax candles are distributed, and they are carried by all lit.
> When, however, the pontiff shall have come to the porch of Saint
> Peter, he is received there by the clergy of the city vested proces-
> sionally. The pontiff enters the church and ascends to the platform
> with the prelates and the other officials. The clergy, however, stand
> around the platform.
>
> The prayer before the altar having been said, the pontiff ascends to
> the high throne and receives the vested cardinals and prelates for the
> reverence [an act of homage to the pope]. Which having been done,
> he descends and seats himself upon the other throne prepared before
> the altar, with his back turned toward the altar, where he renders a
> sermon recounting what are the deeds and the life and the miracles
> of the saint, summarily and in general. Finally he exhorts all that
> they should pour forth pious prayers to the Lord together with him,
> praying that [God] may not allow his Church to err in this matter.[18]

In the above text, the cardinals' greeting of the pope with a sign of
reverence, the papal homily on the virtues of the candidate for canonization, and the pontiff's call for prayer at its conclusion are all traceable to the ceremonial of Cardinal Stefaneschi.[19] The actual rite of
prayers in preparation for the formal enrollment of the candidate in
the catalogue of the saints, as given in the 1488 ceremonial, includes
the chanting of the hymn to the Holy Spirit, *Veni Creator Spiritus*, a
feature inherited from the Stefaneschi ceremonial,[20] but the 1488 text
is the first to specify for this rite the recitation of the Litany of the

---

[17] Manuscript: Vatican City, Biblioteca Apostolica Vaticana, Codex Vaticanus Latinus
5633, in Dykmans, *Cérémonial papal de la fin du moyen âge à la Renaissance*, 4:286–287.

[18] Dykmans, *Oeuvre de Patrizi Piccolomini*, 1:122.

[19] Dykmans, *Cérémonial papal de la fin du moyen âge à la Renaissance*, 2:464.

[20] Ibid., 458, 464.

Saints. As these prayers are offered for the intention of invoking the guidance of the Holy Spirit for the pope in making his decision to canonize the candidate, the candidate's name is not included in the litany, for at this point in the ceremony the candidate has not yet been proclaimed a saint:

> The pontiff then rises, his throne is removed, and he inclines forward upon the faldstool with his miter. The litany is sung by the cantors, and no mention is made of the one to be canonized, with all having knelt on the ground praying. The litany finished, the deacon on the right rises and, having turned to the people, says in a high voice, *Pray*. He again kneels, and all pray the longer. Thereupon the deacon on the left, rising in the same manner, says, *Rise*, and all rise. Then the pontiff, standing without his miter, begins in his own voice, *Veni Creator Spiritus*, and both he and all the others kneel for the first verse. The cantors continue the hymn, and the pontiff with his miter ascends to the high throne, and his miter having been removed, he awaits the end of the hymn. Which having ended, two cantors say the verse: *Send forth thy Spirit, and they shall be created*. And the others respond: *And thou shalt renew the face of the earth*. And the pontiff: *Let us pray. O God, who have taught the hearts of the faithful by the light of the Holy Spirit, grant us in the same Spirit to perceive right things and evermore to rejoice on account of his consolation. Through our Lord . . . in the unity of the same . . .*[21]

Following these prayers, as specified in the 1488 ceremonial, the petition for the candidate's canonization is solemnly announced to the pope (a practice first mentioned in a description of the canonization of Saint Bonaventure in 1482):[22] "Then the procurator of the cause immediately asks from the pontiff, in the procurator's name and in the name of the princes, etc., for the blessed [Name] to be pronounced and declared to be enrolled in the catalogue of the saints and that the

---

[21] Dykmans, *Oeuvre de Patrizi Piccolomini*, 1:122. The complete text of the Collect from the Mass of the Holy Spirit, *Deus, qui corda fidelium*, is here taken from Manlio Sodi and Achille Maria Triacca, eds., *Missale Romanum: Editio princeps (1570)*, facsimile ed., MLCT 2 (Vatican City: Libreria Editrice Vaticana, © 1998), 614 (new pagination). This Collect in its original form is traceable to the seventh-century Paduan redaction of the Gregorian Sacramentary of Rome; see Jean Deshusses, ed., *Le sacramentaire grégorien: Ses principales formes d'après les plus anciens manuscrits*, vol. 1, 2nd ed., SF 16 (Fribourg, Switzerland: Editions Universitaires Fribourg, 1979), Paduan no. 466, p. 642. The "modern" form of this Collect given above first appears in a Mass *ordo* of the papal court dating from before 1227; text in Stephen J. P. Van Dijk, O.F.M., and Joan Hazelden Walker, eds., *The Ordinal of the Papal Court from Innocent III to Boniface VIII and Related Documents*, SF 22 (Fribourg, Switzerland: The University Press, 1975), 496.

[22] Dell'Oro, *Beatificazione e canonizzazione*, 85. An account of the 1482 canonization of Saint Bonaventure appears in the Roman Diary of Jacobo Gherardi da Volterra; text in Enrico Carusi, ed., *Il diario romano di Jacopo Gherardi da Volterra*, Rerum Italicarum scriptores 23, pt. 3 (Castello, Italy: Tipi della Casa Editrice S. Lapi, 1904), 95–97.

saint be venerated by the faithful of Christ." [23] This rubric from the 1488 ceremonial does not provide any specific wording for this petitioning of the pope, but a document regarding the January 1485 canonization of Saint Leopold of Austria (+1136) prepared by the papal master of ceremonies John Burckard (+1506) includes just such a formula (added in the margins of the manuscript by Burckard): "*I, [Name], procurator, and in the procuratorial name of the most serene prince and lord master Frederick of the Romans, ever august emperor, urgently, more urgently, and most urgently beseech Your Holiness that the holy confessor Leopold, begotten of a noble family of Austria, be canonized and enrolled in the catalogue of the saints.*" [24]

The 1488 ceremonial gives the pope the option of prefacing his official proclamation of the candidate's sanctity with a formal proviso or disclaimer, known as a protestation, declaring that in canonizing the particular candidate he in no way intends his decision to supervene the teachings of the Church or to render dishonor to God. In the late fifteenth century, the canonization process had not yet attained its fullest stage of development, in which a formal papal canonization was universally considered an exercise of the charism of papal infallibility. The specific wording of the protestation is provided in the 1488 ceremonial: "*Before we should arrive at the pronouncement, we publicly protest in the presence of all of you present here that by this act of canonization we do not intend to do anything that would be against the faith or the Catholic Church or the honor of God.*" [25]

The solemn act of canonization immediately follows, the formula of which dates back to the ceremonial of Cardinal Stefaneschi (c. 1325). The eminent liturgical scholar who published the critical edition of the 1488 ceremonial we are using, Father Marc Dykmans, gives only the first words (the incipit) of the canonization formula, indicating in a footnote that the 1488 text simply repeats verbatim the Stefaneschi ceremonial's formula. [26] However, insofar as the Stefaneschi text contains two slightly different formulas (one for the 1317 canonization of Saint Louis of Anjou, and the other for the 1320 canonization of Saint Thomas Cantelupe), [27] we are uncertain as to which was used in the 1488 rite. We have therefore chosen to give here the formula from 1320:

> To the honor of almighty God, the Father and the Son and the Holy Spirit, and the exaltation of the Catholic faith, and the advancement of the Christian religion, by the authority of almighty God himself, the Father, and the

---

[23] Dykmans, *Oeuvre de Patrizi Piccolomini*, 1:122–123.

[24] Ibid., 241, footnote; see also Dell'Oro, *Beatificazione e Canonizzazione*, 89.

[25] Dykmans, *Oeuvre de Patrizi Piccolomini*, 1:123.

[26] Ibid., plus footnote. Father Dykmans cites both of the Stefaneschi formulas without indicating which of the two was used in 1488.

[27] Dykmans, *Cérémonial papal de la fin du moyen âge à la Renaissance*, 2:459, 465.

Son, and the Holy Spirit, of the blessed Apostles Peter and Paul, and ours, according to the counsel of our brothers, we determine and define [Name], of good memory, to be a saint and to be enrolled in the catalogue of the saints; and him we enroll in the catalogue of declared saints, establishing that his feast and office should be devoutly and solemnly celebrated by the universal Church each year [on such a day], [as for one confessor, if he should be a confessor, or as for one martyr, if he should be a martyr]. And if it shall have pleased the lord pope, he can add these words: *Furthermore, by the same authority, to all truly penitent and confessed who shall have devoutly come each year to the tomb of the same* [on such a day], [an indulgence of] *one year and forty days; but to those coming yearly to his tomb later than the octave days of the said feast we mercifully mitigate forty days from the penances imposed on them.*[28]

Immediately after the solemn proclamation of the new saint, the procurator of the saint's cause makes a formal request for the proto-notaries to give him a copy of the papal proclamation of canonization. If the pontiff has chosen to preface the canonization declaration with the optional protestation mentioned earlier, there is also at this point in the rite a formal request made by another procurator, the fiscal procurator, for a copy of the protestation. Both procurators also ask for the issuance of papal bulls regarding the two declarations.[29] Upon the completion of these paperwork formalities, the Church expresses her thanksgiving for the newly recognized saint with the chanting of the hymn *Te Deum*, an element of the rite also found in the canonization of Saint Louis of Anjou in 1317 (as mentioned in the papal ceremonial of Cardinal Stefaneschi, dating from about 1325).[30] This in turn is followed by the first official invocation of the new saint:

The pontiff rises without his miter and begins, *We praise you, O God* [the *Te Deum*], and the choir continues. The deacon on the right says at the end: *Pray for us, blessed* [Name of new saint]. The choir responds: *That we may be made worthy of the promises of Christ.* And the pontiff then says a prayer from the Common [office], suitable to the canonized saint, if one proper [to the saint] is not available, and concludes, *Through Christ our Lord.*[31]

The *Confiteor*, the act of contrition from the Ordinary of the Mass, is now recited by a deacon, with the name of the new saint inserted after the other saints mentioned in the *Confiteor*'s text, a custom traceable to the papal ceremonial of Cardinal Stefaneschi (c. 1325):[32]

---

[28] Ibid., 465.

[29] Dykmans, *Oeuvre de Patrizi Piccolomini*, 1:123.

[30] Dykmans, *Cérémonial papal de la fin du moyen âge à la Renaissance*, 2:459.

[31] Dykmans, *Oeuvre de Patrizi Piccolomini*, 1:123.

[32] Dykmans, *Cérémonial papal de la fin du moyen âge à la Renaissance*, 2:459, 466.

I confess to almighty God, to blessed Mary ever Virgin, to blessed Michael the archangel, to blessed John the Baptist, to the holy Apostles Peter and Paul, to [Name of new saint], to all the saints, and to you, brethren, that I have sinned exceedingly, in thought, in word, and in deed, by my fault, by my fault, by my most grievous fault. Therefore I beseech blessed Mary ever Virgin, blessed Michael the archangel, blessed John the Baptist, the holy Apostles Peter and Paul, [Name of new saint], all the saints, and you, brethren, to pray for me to the Lord our God.[33]

Following the *Confiteor,* the pope (without wearing his miter but with the papal cross near him) imparts a customary pontifical blessing (the formulas *Precibus et meritis* and *Indulgentiam*).[34] The 1488 ceremonial provides no further details, but it is highly likely that the practice of inserting the new saint's name into the benediction formula *Precibus et meritis* (in the same manner as with the *Confiteor*), specified in the papal ceremonial of Cardinal Stefaneschi (c. 1325),[35] was still being observed in the late fifteenth century:

> *By the prayers and merits of blessed Mary ever Virgin, blessed Michael the archangel, blessed John the Baptist, the holy Apostles Peter and Paul, [Name of new saint],*[36] *and all the saints, may almighty God have mercy on you and, with all your sins forgiven, bring you to eternal life. Amen. May the almighty and merciful Lord grant you forgiveness, absolution, and the remission of all your sins. Amen.*[37]

The pope now announces the indulgences he is granting on this occasion before beginning the midmorning office of Terce.[38] Following Terce, he celebrates Mass in commemoration of the new saint, during which another special rite for the canonization is carried out at the Offertory:

> While the Creed is sung, three superintendent cardinals go down to the lower door of the platform and arrange the Offertory. And at the preordained time, before the pope should wash his hands at his high throne, they come successively. And the first, that is, the cardinal

---

[33] Dykmans, *Oeuvre de Patrizi Piccolomini,* 1:123. The ceremonial gives only the incipit of the *Confiteor.* The complete text of the *Confiteor* (except for the canonization rite insertions) is here taken from the *Ordo missae* of the papal master of ceremonies John Burckard, 1502 edition, in John Wickham Legg, ed., *Tracts on the Mass,* HBS 27 (London: Henry Bradshaw Society, 1904), 136.

[34] Dykmans, *Oeuvre de Patrizi Piccolomini,* 1:123.

[35] Dykmans, *Cérémonial papal de la fin du moyen âge à la Renaissance,* 2:459, 466.

[36] The Stefaneschi ceremonial directs that the new saint should be mentioned "immediately after the Apostles" in the benediction formula *Precibus et meritis*; see ibid., 466.

[37] The complete text of this benediction (except for the canonization rite insertion) is taken from the 1485 *Pontificalis liber* (*Pontificale Romanum*), in Manlio Sodi, ed., *Il "Pontificalis liber" di Agostino Patrizi Piccolomini e Giovanni Burcardo (1485),* facsimile ed., MSIL 43 (Vatican City: Libreria Editrice Vaticana, © 2006), 563 (new pagination).

[38] Dykmans, *Oeuvre de Patrizi Piccolomini,* 1:123–124.

bishop, offers two large wax candles, and with him the first ambassador offers his wax candle and a small gilded basket with two turtledoves. Then the cardinal priest offers two large breads with maniples, and the second ambassador his wax candle and a small silver-plated basket with two white doves. Lastly the cardinal deacon offers two vessels of wine, and the third ambassador his wax candle and a small basket of diverse colors with various small birds. The cardinals kiss the knee of the supreme pontiff, the others his foot. The Mass is then continued, as at other times.[39]

The presentation of live birds, mentioned in the above rubrics, is traceable to the 1391 canonization of Saint Bridget of Sweden, as described in the papal ceremonial of Pierre Ameil (+1403), who is believed to have introduced the custom. In the 1391 ceremony two turtledoves and two white doves were presented in a single cage.[40] Lorenzo the Roman's account of Saint Bridget's canonization mentions that at a banquet following the canonization ceremony there was on one table a cage containing small birds.[41] The threefold presentation of turtledoves, white doves, and other birds in three separate cages during the Offertory of the canonization Mass, as specified in the 1488 papal ceremonial of Piccolomini, is first mentioned in an account of the 1461 canonization of Saint Catherine of Siena (+1380).[42] The latter source does not indicate the size or the species of the birds in the third cage but does state that they were four to six in number.

The medieval liturgical texts offer no explanation as to the specific symbolism of these birds within the canonization rite. It is likely that their use stemmed from the symbolic imagery of early Christian art, wherein birds, and doves in particular, were seen to represent the eternal bliss of Heaven and the souls of the faithful departed residing there, freed from the temporal bonds of their bodies.[43] Their significance within the context of the canonization liturgy is explained in full by the Augustinian scholar and Roman prefect Bishop Angelo Rocca (+1620) in his work *De canonizatione sanctorum commentarius*, published in 1601. Although this commentary was written after the close of the Middle Ages, it seems likely that Bishop Rocca's interpretations are based upon traditions predating his own era. Bishop Rocca begins by explaining the doves and turtledoves:

---

[39] Ibid., 124.

[40] Dykmans, *Cérémonial papal de la fin du moyen âge à la Renaissance*, 4:240. The canonization scholar Father Ferdinando Dell'Oro, S.D.B., attributes the introduction of this practice to Pierre Ameil (Dell'Oro, *Beatificazione e canonizzazione*, 67).

[41] Manuscript: Vatican City, Biblioteca Apostolica Vaticana, Codex Vaticanus Latinus 12229, cited in Dykmans, *Cérémonial papal de la fin du moyen âge à la Renaissance*, 4:60.

[42] Manuscript: Vatican City, Biblioteca Apostolica Vaticana, Codex Vaticanus Latinus 12348, in Dykmans, *Cérémonial papal de la fin du moyen âge à la Renaissance*, 4:282.

[43] Orazio Marucchi, *Manual of Christian Archeology* (Paterson, N.J.: St. Anthony Guild Press, 1949), 282–284.

The dove, which is devoid of bitterness, signifies the meekness of Christ the Lord, in whose mouth there was no deceit [cf. Is 53:9]. But the turtledove, ever moaning, suggests the sorrow of Christ in his Passion.... But inasmuch as the saints are imitators of Christ, in likeness to the saying of the blessed Apostle Paul, "Be ye followers of me, as I also am of Christ" [1 Cor 4:16], who is the Saint of saints, and the Maker of saints, on that account turtledoves and doves are offered at the Mass following the canonization of saints, because of those things to be intimated, in which the saints had imitated Christ the Lord.[44]

Bishop Rocca also cites the fact that doves and turtledoves mate once for life to explain a further dimension of their symbolism in the canonization rite:

The dove is not only an innocent bird but also a symbol of chastity and of the continence of widowhood, for one male has known only one female [i.e., doves mate for life; they never "remarry"]. Hence, in regard to sacred things, some thus take the oblation of doves, that with the law of stable marriage being kept to such a degree, we may likewise unite our soul to God unto persevering in firm steadfastness, just as to a spouse, and in particular to Christ the Bridegroom.... And thus it ought to be extraordinary to no one if turtledoves, and doves, especially white ones, which animals signify sincerity and purity in the saints canonized, should be offered in the canonization of saints, when those things that turtledoves and doves signify would apply so well to the saints, beloved to God.[45]

Bishop Rocca also observes that just as God was pleased to receive offerings of doves and turtledoves in the sacrifices of the Mosaic Law, creatures that can be seen as images of the virtues of chastity and simplicity, so does God welcome "the most chaste simplicity of the saints" as an oblation most pleasing to him.[46] Bishop Rocca adds that doves and turtledoves signify respectively the two principal forms of the Christian life seen in the saints; the active life, symbolized by doves, who tend to live in flocks, and the contemplative life, represented by turtledoves, who tend to roam in solitude.[47] The small birds also presented at the Offertory of the canonization Mass carry their own separate significance:

But those little birds of diverse kinds are offered and yet are determined to fly, for the purpose of intimating the flight of the saints at last into Heaven and signifying their celestial desires directed to God.

---

[44] Rocca, *De canonizatione sanctorum commentarius*, 130.
[45] Ibid., 131–132.
[46] Ibid., 132.
[47] Ibid.

For the saints, adorned with various kinds of virtues and gifts, and lifted up by pious desires and affections, are, in their seeking the things above, likened in a certain manner to the birds of Heaven, insofar as these inhabitants of earth, having been tested in both deed and desire, and forsaking the earth, ascend to Heaven.[48]

Drawing upon Pope Saint Gregory the Great's sixth-century interpretation of "the birds of the air" to which Christ refers in his parable of the mustard seed (Mt 13:32),[49] Bishop Rocca adds that the feathers of the birds represent the virtues with which holy souls "lift themselves up from earthly thought and prepare themselves for flight to Heaven".[50]

There is a twentieth-century anecdote regarding the canonization custom of presenting birds that bears repeating here. During the canonization Mass of Saints Gemma Galgani (+1903) and Euphrasia Pelletier (+1868) on Ascension Thursday of 1940, as the three birdcages were being carried away after the presentation, the birds spontaneously broke into song, bringing a smile to the face of Venerable Pope Pius XII and prompting a brief round of laughter among those near the pontiff.[51]

Most of the other details of the Offertory presentation of gifts specified in the 1488 *Caeremoniale Romanum* of Patrizio Piccolomini (the presentation of two large candles, two large breads, and two vessels of wine by three cardinals, mentioned in the passage quoted earlier) are traceable to the 1391 canonization rite of Saint Bridget in Ameil's ceremonial.[52] The three candles brought by the three ambassadors correspond to the six candles presented individually by five procurators and one advocate in the 1391 canonization rite.[53]

---

[48] Ibid., 132–133.

[49] See Saint Gregory the Great, *Moralium*, bk. 19, chap. 1, PL 76, col. 97.

[50] Rocca, *De canonizatione sanctorum commentarius*, 133.

[51] Gabriel Francis Powers, "Two New Saints: An Account of the Solemn Ceremony of Canonization of St. Euphrasia Pelletier and St. Gemma Galgani", *Sign* 19 (July 1940): 751.

[52] Dykmans, *Cérémonial papal de la fin du moyen âge à la Renaissance*, 4:239–240.

[53] Ibid., 240.

20 The Rite of Consecration of Virgins

Let us humbly supplicate the Lord, truly retaining chaste worship in incorrupt religion of inviolable nature, that he may strengthen this his handmaid, who has consecrated her holy, very great, and acceptable virginity to God, the counsel of holy men having been taken; may she persevere in her well-conceived resolution, that her virginity, which is likened to that of the Church and is assumed in similitude of the divine immolation, may obtain the supernatural gift of eternity. Through our Lord . . .

Missale Francorum, eighth century[1]

The state of consecrated virginity can be traced to the opening pages of the New Testament, where we find our Lady resolved to remain a virgin, a decision revealed by her question to the archangel Gabriel when he told her of her vocation to become the Mother of God: "How shall this be done, because I know not man?" (Lk 1:34). Christ in his public ministry advocated the state of celibacy (Mt 19:12), as did Saint Paul (1 Cor 7:8, 25–26, 32–35). We find among the martyrs of the first three centuries of the Church many women who had embraced the state of consecrated virginity, including Saints Cecilia, Agatha, and Agnes. By the fourth century, the conferral of a distinctive veil had already emerged as the premier outward symbol of a woman's total consecration of herself to God, as attested and so ably explained by Saint Ambrose (+397) in his treatise *De institutione virginis*:

> May this your maidservant, moved by the grace of virtue of this kind, stand near to your altars, not bearing her hallowed blond hair in a glowing red mound under a nuptial veil [the *flammeum*] but offering to be consecrated with the sacred veil that hair with which that woman of the Gospel holy Mary wiped dry the feet of Christ with solicitous devotion and filled the entire house with her ointment poured out.[2]

---

[1] Text in Leo Cunibert Mohlberg, O.S.B., ed., *Missale Francorum*, REDSMF 2 (Rome: Herder, 1957), no. 46, p. 14.

[2] Saint Ambrose, *De institutione virginis*, chap. 17, PL 16, col. 331.

Saint Ambrose likewise attests to a liturgical ceremony for the consecration of virgins, telling of just such a rite in Rome for the consecration of his sister Saint Marcellina, which was conducted by Pope Liberius at the Basilica of Saint Peter in 353. The consecration took place during a Mass; the pontiff blessed the maiden with a prayer of benediction and conferred upon her the veil representing her consecrated state.[3] The texts of two prayers for a rite of consecration of virgins are to be found in the earliest extant sacramentary, the sixth-century Leonine Sacramentary of Rome.[4] Over the centuries that followed, this rite was to develop in parallel with the closely related but separate rite of religious profession for women, exerting a significant influence upon the latter. In fact, for some religious congregations, particularly the Benedictines and the Carthusians, the rite of consecration of virgins served as one of the steps in becoming a fully professed nun. Thus a manuscript of the early 1500s from the Benedictine convent of Saint Mary in Winchester, England, provides a rite of consecration of virgins for the nuns of this religious community.[5]

For a highly developed rite of the consecration of virgins from the early Middle Ages, we turn now to the tenth-century Romano-Germanic Pontifical.[6] The maiden seeking consecration is presented to the bishop before Mass by her parents in a manner analogous to the giving of a daughter in matrimony. There is even the offering of a dowry. The bishop responds with the antiphon *Sum desponsata*, a text based upon words attributed to the virgin martyr Saint Agnes (+c. 304 or earlier) in the Latin *Acts* (account) of her martyrdom compiled around 420:[7]

> The parents present the virgin to the bishop with an offering, and he should receive her hand, wrapped in an altar cloth, [the bishop] saying with those standing nearby the antiphon *I am espoused to him whom the angels serve, whose splendor the sun and the moon admire.*
>
> A holy nun, a virgin, when she is presented to her bishop for consecration, should be brought in such fitting attire as is always the custom with those bound to [religious] profession and piety.[8]

---

[3] Saint Ambrose, *De virginibus*, bk. 3, chaps. 1, 4, PL 16, cols. 219–220, 224–225.

[4] For the Leonine Sacramentary, see Leo Cunibert Mohlberg, O.S.B.; Leo Eizenhöfer, O.S.B.; and Petrus Siffrin, O.S.B., eds., *Sacramentarium Veronense*, REDSMF 1 (Rome: Herder, 1956), nos. 1103–1104, pp. 138–139.

[5] Manuscript: Cambridge, England, Cambridge University Library, Folio Mm. 3.13, early sixteenth century; text in William Maskell, ed., *Monumenta ritualia ecclesiae Anglicanae* (Oxford: Clarendon, 1882), 3:333–359. For the Carthusian use of the rite of consecration of virgins, see the relevant rubrics quoted from a fourteenth-century Carthusian ritual in Edmond Martène, *De antiquis ecclesiae ritibus* (Venice: Johannes Baptista Novelli, 1763–1764), bk. 2, chap. 6, *ordo* 13, 2:197–198.

[6] Text in Cyrille Vogel and Reinhard Elze, eds., *Le pontifical romano-germanique du dixième siècle*, vol. 1, ST 226 (Vatican City: Biblioteca Apostolica Vaticana, 1963), 38–46.

[7] *Vita sanctae Agnetis* (Latin text), chap. 1, no. 3, in John van Bolland et al., eds., *Acta sanctorum* (Antwerp, Belgium, 1643–; repr., Paris: Victor Palmé, 1863–1940), January, 2:715.

[8] Vogel and Elze, *Pontifical romano-germanique*, 1:39.

In the pontifical that the bishop and liturgist William Durandus (+1296) compiled for his own diocese of Mende, France, around 1294, the ceremony for presenting the virgins to the bishop is more elaborate;[9] Durandus' entire consecration rite, it should be noted, was later retained, albeit with some modifications, in the universally promulgated *Pontificale Romanum* of 1595–1596.[10] The maidens assemble in a tent or a room outside the church proper. Within the church, Mass proceeds until immediately before the Gospel. The archpriest now goes before the entrance of the tent or room where the maidens are waiting and says to them, "*Wise virgins, prepare your lamps; behold, the Bridegroom comes, go out to meet him*" (cf. Mt 25:6).[11] Upon hearing his summons, the maidens light the candles given them and exit two by two, carrying their lit candles. The candles are in this context laden with biblical meaning, described by Durandus in his liturgical commentary the *Rationale divinorum officiorum* as representing the lamps of the wise virgins (Mt 25:1–13) and those burning lamps that all must have ready when Christ comes again in glory (Lk 12:35–37), as well as the light of good works that should shine before men (Mt 5:16).[12] The archpriest leads the maidens to a location in the western wing of the church, that is, in the nave outside the choir, yet close enough to the altar that the bishop, seated in the sanctuary, can see them.[13] This entrance into the church is explained by Durandus as a spiritual journey from the "darkness and deceptions of the present world . . . to the freedom, joy, and brightness of the heavenly kingdom and to the bridal chamber of the celestial King."[14] The maidens now kneel as the archpriest declares to the bishop, "*Reverend Father, our holy Mother the Catholic Church asks that you vouchsafe to bless and consecrate these virgins or nuns present and espouse them to our Lord Jesus Christ, Son of the supreme God.*"[15] After questioning the archpriest as to whether the candidates are worthy, and receiving an affirmative answer, the bishop says, "*With our Lord God and Savior Jesus Christ assisting* [*us*], *we have elected to consecrate and espouse to our Lord Jesus Christ these virgins present.*"[16]

---

[9] Michel Andrieu, ed., *Le pontifical romain au moyen-âge*, vol. 3, *Le pontifical de Guillaume Durand*, ST 88 (Vatican City: Biblioteca Apostolica Vaticana, 1940), 412–413.

[10] Text in Manlio Sodi and Achille Triacca, eds., *Pontificale Romanum: Editio princeps (1595–1596)*, facsimile ed., MLCT 1 (Vatican City: Libreria Editrice Vaticana, © 1997), 186–224 (original pagination). In the 1595–1596 rite, there is a ceremonial presentation of the breviary to each maiden (ibid., 222–223, original pagination), an observance not found in the rite of Durandus.

[11] Andrieu, *Pontifical romain au moyen-âge*, 3:412.

[12] William Durandus of Mende, *Rationale divinorum officiorum*, bk. 2, chap. 1, no. 40, in A. Davril, O.S.B., and T.M. Thibodeau, eds., *Guillelmi Duranti: Rationale divinorum officiorum I–IV*, CCCM 140 (Turnhout, Belgium: Brepols, 1995), 138. Hereafter cited as Durandus, *Rationale* (CCCM 140).

[13] Andrieu, *Pontifical romain au moyen-âge*, 3:412.

[14] Durandus, *Rationale* (CCCM 140), bk. 2, chap. 1, no. 40, p. 138.

[15] Andrieu, *Pontifical romain au moyen-âge*, 3:412.

[16] Ibid., 413.

What follows, as explained by Durandus himself, draws its inspiration from the invitation of the Bridegroom in the Song of Solomon, "Arise, make haste, my love, my dove, my beautiful one, and come. For winter is now past, the rain is over and gone.... Shew me thy face, let thy voice sound in my ears" (Song 2:10–14).[17] The bishop calls to the maidens, "*Come*", at the hearing of which the young women rise and advance to just outside the entrance of the choir. Here they kneel again. A second time, the bishop summons them: "*Come.*" The maidens answer, "*And now we follow*" and rising, proceed to the middle of the choir, where again they kneel. A third time the bishop summons them but in this instance with a complete verse adapted from Psalm 33 (verse 12): "*Come, come, come, daughters, hearken to me; I will teach you the fear of the Lord.*" The maidens stand and recite the following antiphon: "*And now we follow thee with all our heart, and we fear thee, and seek to see thy face; O Lord, put us not to confusion, but deal with us according to thy meekness, and according to the multitude of thy mercies*" (cf. Dan 3:41–42).[18] This threefold summoning of the maidens symbolizes their calling to embrace by their consecration the three evangelical counsels of poverty, chastity, and obedience.[19] The women now approach the bishop and prostrate themselves before him, each saying the antiphon "*Uphold me, O Lord, according to thy word, that no iniquity may have dominion over me*" (cf. Ps 118:116, 133).[20]

Let us now return to the tenth-century Romano-Germanic Pontifical for the rest of the consecration rite, beginning with the blessing of the maidens' habits and veils. After the maiden has been presented to the bishop and has expressed to him her assent to be consecrated, the habit and the veil to be worn by her after her consecration are brought before the altar to be blessed by the bishop publicly, "in the sight of all".[21] According to Durandus, the taking of new garments by a consecrated virgin expresses the putting on of the "new man ... created in justice and holiness and truth" spoken of by Saint Paul (Eph 4:24); white habits symbolize the need to remain pure and unblemished as brides of Christ, whereas a black habit "signifies the mortification of the flesh, for because Christ their Bridegroom has died for them, they ought also to die for him".[22]

The nuptial symbolism of the garments conferred upon consecrated virgins was later to be represented more directly in the rites of religious profession for women when beginning in the late seventeenth century certain religious congregations introduced the practice of clothing those taking their vows in wedding gowns for the first portion of the profession

[17] Durandus, *Rationale* (CCCM 140), bk. 2, chap. 1, no. 40, p. 138.

[18] Andrieu, *Pontifical romain au moyen-âge*, 3:413.

[19] Durandus, *Rationale* (CCCM 140), bk. 2, chap 1, no. 41, p. 138.

[20] Andrieu, *Pontifical romain au moyen-âge*, 3:413.

[21] Vogel and Elze, *Pontifical romano-germanique*, 1:39.

[22] Durandus, *Rationale* (CCCM 140), bk. 2, chap. 1, no. 42, p. 139.

ceremony.[23] In fact, such a practice has ancient roots. In an early treatise on consecrated virginity, the *Symposium of the Ten Virgins*, authored by Saint Methodius of Olympus (+c. 311), a virgin named Thecla sings to Christ, "For you, O King, I come in spotless garments"; elsewhere in the same text, the consecrated virgins are summoned to come to Christ "the Bridegroom" with lamps and clothed "in white dresses".[24] Later, in the correspondence of the twelfth-century abbess and mystic Saint Hildegard of Bingen (+1179), there is mention of the nuns of her Benedictine convent of Rupertsberg, Germany, dressing on feast days as brides in white dresses, with crowns of flowers upon their heads.[25] The previously mentioned rite of consecration of virgins in a manuscript of the early 1500s for the Benedictine convent of Saint Mary in Winchester, England, prescribes that for the first part of the ceremony the candidates are to enter "clothed all in white", carrying the habits and veils that they shall later receive over their right arms.[26] The tenth-century Romano-Germanic Pontifical provides three prayers for the blessing of the maiden's habit, all of which date from the eighth century:[27]

> *Eternal God, most faithful Promiser of good things, their most certain Fulfiller, who promised your faithful the garment of salvation and the apparel of eternal bliss, we humbly beseech your clemency, that you may mercifully bless these garments signifying humility of heart and contempt of the world, with which your maidservant is to be fashioned visibly in her holy resolution, that with you assisting, she may preserve the blessed habit of chastity that she shall have taken, you protecting her; and may you make her whom you clothe for a time in the garments of her venerable promise to be clothed in blessed immortality. Through . . .*

> *Lord God, Giver of all good virtues and abundant Imparter of all blessings, we entreat you, supported by prayers, that you may vouchsafe to bless and sanctify these garments, which your maidservant [Name] wills to put on as a sign of her avowal of religion, that among the rest of women she may be perceived to be dedicated to you. Through . . .*

---

[23] Giancarlo Rocca, "Vestizione: Dal cinquecento in poi", in Guerrino Pelliccia and Giancarlo Rocca, eds., *Dizionario degli istituti di perfezione* (Rome: Edizione Paoline, 1974–2003), vol. 9, cols. 1956–1957.

[24] Saint Methodius of Olympus, *Convivium decem virginum*, chap. 2, PG 18, cols. 207–208 (Latin and Greek).

[25] See Saint Hildegard of Bingen, *Letter 116*, PL 197, cols. 336–338.

[26] Manuscript: Cambridge, England, Cambridge University Library, Folio Mm. 3.13, in Maskell, *Monumenta ritualia ecclesiae Anglicanae*, 3:334 (Latin text quoted and translated by permission of Oxford University Press).

[27] The first prayer appears in a late seventh- or early eighth-century Frankish addition to the seventh-century Gelasian Sacramentary of Rome; text in Leo Cunibert Mohlberg, O.S.B., et al., eds., *Liber sacramentorum Romanae aeclesiae ordinis anni circuli (Sacramentarium Gelasianum)*, REDSMF 4 (Rome: Herder, 1960), no. 791, p. 126. The second and third prayers first appear in the Gellone Sacramentary, an eighth-century Frankish adaptation of Rome's Gelasian Sacramentary. Text in A. Dumas, ed., *Liber sacramentorum Gellonensis*, CCSL 159 (Turnhout, Belgium: Brepols, 1981), nos. 2605, 2606, p. 406.

Graciously hear our prayers, O Lord, and this garment, which your maid-servant [Name] herself earnestly begs to be covered in as a sign of the pre-serving of chastity, anoint with the rain of your most fruitful blessing, even as you anointed the border of Aaron's vestments with the blessing of the oint-ment flowing from the head onto the beard. And just as you have blessed the garments of all religious, pleasing to you in all respects, so also vouchsafe to bless this [garment], and grant, most merciful Father, that this garment may be to the aforesaid your maidservant [Name] a salutary protection, an avowal of religion, the commencement of sanctity, a mighty defense against all the darts of the enemy, that, if she is continent, she may receive the gifts of the sixtieth fruit,[28] and if a virgin, she may be enriched with the wealth of the hundredth gift, in each case persevering in continence. Through . . .[29]

The veil is blessed separately from the habit:

O God, Head of all the faithful and Savior of the whole body, sanctify with your right hand this covering of the veil, which your maidservant, by reason of your love and the love of your most blessed Mother, namely Mary ever Virgin, is going to put upon her head; and may your protection ever preserve undefiled in soul as well as in body that which is mystically expressed to be understood by it, that when she shall have come to the everlasting reward of the saints, she herself having also been made ready with the prudent virgins, you conducting [her], she may be worthy to enter the marriage of everlasting happiness. Through . . .[30]

The posture of total prostration has always been the ultimate visible expression of adoration and of one's humility and contrition before God. Tracing this practice back to Abraham (Gen 17:3) and the proph-ets, who prostrated themselves in adoration before God, Honorius of Autun (+c. 1135) observes that by prostrating the body upon the earth, man expresses his adoration of "Christ in the flesh", who "descended to the earth" and "put on flesh from the earth to wash us". It is a reminder that man, who before his fall had "stood with angels in Par-adise", has by sinning lowered himself into the mire and down to the level of the irrational beasts. Hence "we make our stomach to cleave to the earth, and our soul to the ground, that we may be worthy through Christ to rise from earthly desires."[31] The posture of pros-tration is thus well suited to the rite of religious consecration. In the consecration ceremony of the Romano-Germanic Pontifical, there are two prostrations, the first immediately following the blessing of the veil. By it the maiden expresses her total dependence upon God in keeping her resolution:

---

[28] This phrase appears to indicate that this blessing was also used separately from the rite of consecration of virgins for the conferral of the habit upon widows taking a vow of chastity.

[29] Vogel and Elze, *Pontifical romano-germanique*, 1:40.

[30] Ibid., 40–41.

[31] Honorius of Autun, *Gemma animae*, bk. 1, chap. 117, PL 172, col. 582.

Afterward, in the sight of the bishop and of the Church, she should humbly prostrate herself before the altar, saying this verse three times: *Uphold me, O Lord, according to thy word, and I shall live; and let me not be confounded in my expectation* [cf. Ps 118:116].[32]

The maiden now receives her habit (but not her veil, which she will receive later) and, withdrawing to put it on, returns afterward for Mass in her new vesture as a testament to her renunciation of the world and its ornaments for the love of Christ (Durandus):[33]

After these [things] the bishop should say: *Sister, take this garment in the name of the Lord.* And she should answer: *I take it in the name of the Father, and of the Son, and of the Holy Spirit.*

Then the bishop should give her the very garments of virginity, and he should make to be retained near him only the veil. The virgin herself, however, should go into the sacristy and put on herself the very garments blessed, and taking two burning candles into her hands, she should come before the altar; and the clergy introduces the Introit for the Mass. Whereupon after the Gospel, and she having prostrated, the litany having been said,[34] the bishop should bless her, with her head bowed before the altar, [the bishop] saying:

Look favorably, O Lord, upon this your maidservant [Name], *that her resolution of holy virginity, which, you inspiring, she has undertaken, she may preserve, you guiding* [her]. *Through . . .*[35]

The prayer *Deus castorum corporum* for solemnly consecrating the virgin to God follows, recited by the bishop in a high voice and taking the form of a Preface. The text is ancient, traceable to the sixth-century Leonine Sacramentary of Rome.[36] A convincing case has been made that Pope Saint Leo the Great (+461) is the author of this composition, the vocabulary and expressions of which are characteristic of Leo's known writings and homilies:[37]

O God, gracious Inhabitant of chaste bodies and Lover of uncorrupted souls, who thus in your Word, through whom all things have been made, restore human nature corrupted in the first men by the wile of the devil, that you may recall it not only to the innocence of our first beginning but also bring it to the experience of certain good things, which are to be had in the new

---

[32] Vogel and Elze, *Pontifical romano-germanique*, 1:41.

[33] Durandus, *Rationale* (CCCM 140), bk. 2, chap. 1, no. 43, p. 140.

[34] In the rite from the Pontifical of Durandus (c. 1294), the bishop at a certain point during the litany rises temporarily to bless the maidens while they remain prostrate; see Andrieu, *Pontifical romain au moyen-âge*, 3:414.

[35] Vogel and Elze, *Pontifical romano-germanique*, 1:41–42. The prayer *Respice, Domine, propitius super hanc famulam tuam*, is first found in a late seventh- or early eighth-century Frankish addition to the seventh-century Gelasian Sacramentary of Rome; see Mohlberg, Eizenhöfer, and Siffrin, *Liber sacramentorum*, no. 787, p. 124.

[36] Mohlberg, Eizenhöfer, and Siffrin, *Sacramentarium Veronense*, no. 1104, pp. 138–139.

[37] Odelia G. Harrison, O.S.B., "The Formulas *Ad virgines sacras*: A Study of the Sources", pt. 1, *EL* 66 (1952): 257–260.

world, and immediately advance it, still bound in the condition of mortals, to the likeness of angels: look upon this your maidservant [Name], *who, placing in your hand the resolution of her continence, offers her devotion to you, to whom she the selfsame has also taken a vow. For when would the soul encompassed in mortal flesh have prevailed over the law of nature, the liberty of license, the force of habit, and the goadings of age, unless you by her free will would have mercifully kindled this love of virginity, graciously nourished this eager desire in her heart,* [and] *supplied to her the strength? For by your grace poured forth upon all peoples, out of every nation that is under Heaven, unto the countless number of the stars, the adopted heirs of the New Testament, among other virtues that you have given to your sons begotten not by blood ties or by the will of the flesh but by your Spirit, this gift also has flowed from the fountain of your bounty into certain souls, that although no prohibitions have diminished the honor of marriage, and the original blessing has remained upon holy wedlock, nevertheless there have appeared loftier souls, who,* [although] *they would have been desirous of the sacrament, have spurned wedlock by the union of man and woman; nor have they imitated what is done in marriage but have highly esteemed what is signified by marriage. Blessed virginity has recognized her Author and, emulous of angelic purity, has vowed herself within his chamber, the bridal chamber of him who is likewise the Son of perpetual virginity, just as he is the Bridegroom of perpetual virginity. Therefore, to her imploring your help, O Lord, and desiring herself to be strengthened with the consecration of your blessing, impart the defense and guidance of your protection, lest the ancient enemy, who attacks more excellent endeavors with subtler deceits, creep by some carelessness of mind toward obscuring the palm of perfect continence and drag her away from the resolution of virgins insofar as it is also proper for her to be in the ways of marriage. May there be in her, O Lord, through the gift of your Spirit, prudent modesty, wise goodness, serious meekness, chaste freedom; may she glow in charity, and love nothing apart from you, live laudably, and not seek to be praised. May she glorify you in sanctity of body, you in purity of soul; may she fear you with love, serve you with love. May you be to her her honor, you her joy, you her will, you her solace in sadness, you her counsel in ambiguity, you her defense in injury, her patience in tribulation, her abundance in poverty, her nourishment in fasting, her medicine in infirmity. May she have all things in you, whom she desires to love over all things; and may she preserve what she has professed. Pleasing to the Searcher of hearts not in body but in soul, may she go over into the number of the wise maidens and persevere in enduring chastity, that she may await the heavenly Bridegroom with lamps kindled with the oil of preparation, not disturbed by the coming of the unexpected King but secure with light, and happily go to meet the choir of preceding virgins; and may she not be excluded with the foolish but freely enter the royal gate with the wise virgins, pleasing to the everlasting gentleness of your Lamb. Through the same Jesus Christ your Son, our Lord . . .*[38]

---

[38] Vogel and Elze, *Pontifical romano-germanique,* 1:42–43.

Following her consecration, the maiden receives her veil, the perennial outward symbol of consecrated virginity dating back to the early Church. Durandus sees the veil as a "sign of purity and future honor" and a symbol of the woman's renunciation of the world for the sake of Christ, by which she veils her senses from temptations. Resting over the virgin's head and shoulders, the veil manifests the humble submission of her will to obedience and testifies before men who see her that she is reserved exclusively for Christ as his eternal bride.[39] The Romano-Germanic Pontifical describes the veiling rite thus:

> The benediction having been completed, and she having publicly professed concerning the observance of the sacred veil at the examination of the bishop, the bishop should put the veil upon the head of the virgin herself, saying: *Receive the sacred veil, maiden, that you may bear it without blemish before the tribunal of our Lord Jesus Christ, to whom every knee is bent of those that are in Heaven, on earth, and under the earth* [cf. Phil 2:10]. Response: *Amen.*[40]
>
> Then the veiled one herself begins the antiphon *The Lord has clothed me in a robe woven from gold and has adorned me with immense jewels,*[41] with the other nuns who are present continuing. And if there shall have been several [maidens] veiled, the same antiphon should be begun by each separately as above.
>
> Prayer after [her] having taken the veil: *May the protection of your goodness preserve your maidservant, Lord, that her resolution of holy continence that, you inspiring, she has undertaken, she may preserve unharmed, you protecting [her]. Through . . .*
>
> The antiphon follows: *I am espoused to him whom the angels serve, whose splendor the sun and the moon admire.*[42]
>
> [Prayer:] *Grant, we beseech you, almighty God, that this your maidservant, who for the hope of eternal reward earnestly wishes to be consecrated to you, may persevere with full faithfulness and her entire soul in her holy resolution. May you, almighty Father, vouchsafe to sanctify and bless and preserve her forever. Grant her humility, chastity, obedience, charity, and a multitude of all good works. Give her, O Lord, for her works glory, for her purity reverence, for her chastity sanctity, that she may be able to attain to the merit of glory.*[43]

---

[39] Durandus, *Rationale* (CCCM 140), bk. 2, chap. 1, no. 44, p. 140.

[40] This prayer is traceable to an eighth-century Frankish liturgical book, the *Missale Francorum* (Mohlberg, *Missale Francorum*, no. 48, p. 15).

[41] This antiphon, *Induit me Dominus cyclade*, is based upon words attributed to the virgin martyr Saint Agnes in the Latin *Acts* of her martyrdom compiled around 420; see *Vita sanctae Agnetis* (Latin text), chap. 1, no. 3, in Bolland et al., *Acta sanctorum*, January, 2:715.

[42] This antiphon, *Sum desponsata*, is also utilized at the beginning of the Romano-Germanic Pontifical rite (see above p. 581).

[43] Vogel and Elze, *Pontifical romano-germanique*, 1:44.

Following another antiphon, "*He has placed a sign on my face, that I may admit no lover except him*",[44] the prayer known as the Blessing of Matthew the Apostle is said by the bishop over the newly consecrated virgin.[45] This oration, *Deus plasmator corporum*, is traceable to an account of uncertain authenticity, a biography of Saint Matthew found in several ninth-century manuscripts (but not earlier) that relates that while preaching the Gospel in Ethiopia the Apostle composed the prayer for an Ethiopian princess named Iphigenia, a Christian convert. Desiring to consecrate her virginity to God, the girl had sought to ward off a determined suitor seeking her hand in marriage by asking Matthew to consecrate her publicly and to veil her with the veil of married women so as to indicate that henceforth she belonged to Christ. The Apostle readily complied with her wish, spontaneously formulating this blessing for the occasion.[46] The prayer certainly predates the Romano-Germanic Pontifical, even if its alleged apostolic origin cannot be established:

> *O God, Maker of bodies, Infuser of souls, who spurn no age, refuse neither gender, [and] consider no condition unworthy of your grace but are equally to all Creator and Redeemer, cover about with the shield of your protection this your maidservant, whom out of the whole number of the flock you the Good Shepherd have vouchsafed to choose for preserving the crown of perpetual virginity and purity of soul, and prepare her for every work of virtue and glory, with wisdom teaching her, that overcoming the allurements of the flesh and declining lawful marriage, she may be worthy of the indissoluble union of your Son our Lord Jesus Christ. May you, O Lord, we beseech you, supply to this [maidservant] not bodily weapons but those of the spirit, mighty in virtue, that with you defending her senses and members, sin may not be able to dominate her in her body and soul; and with her longing to live under your grace, let not the guardian of the wicked and the enemy of the good prevail at all against her to lay claim to this your vessel now consecrated to your name. May the shower of your heavenly grace likewise extinguish every natural passion; may it truly kindle the light of perpetual chastity; may her chaste appearance not be exposed to scandals, nor may she unawares give occasion to carelessness of sinning. And may there be in her spotless virginity; and with her equally adorned and armed with sound faith, certain hope, [and] genuine charity, may virtue be furnished to such an extent, that with her soul prepared for continence, which overcomes all the figments and transitory things of the devil by despising them, she may strive after future things. May she prefer fasts to bodily feasts and place holy readings and prayers*

---

[44] Ibid. The antiphon *Posuit signum in faciem meam* is based upon words attributed to Saint Agnes in the Latin *Acts* of her martyrdom compiled around 420; see *Vita sanctae Agnetis* (Latin text), chap. 1, no. 3, in Bolland et al., *Acta sanctorum*, January, 2:715.

[45] Vogel and Elze, *Pontifical romano-germanique*, 1:45.

[46] *Acta sancti Matthaei apostoli et evangelistae*, chap. 2, nos. 16–21, in Bolland et al., *Acta sanctorum*, September, 6:223–224. See also Odelia G. Harrison, O.S.B., "The Formulas *Ad virgines sacras*: A Study of the Sources", pt. 2, *EL* 66 (1952): 352–354. Sister Odelia believes that there may be some truth to this account of the origin of the prayer.

before banquets and drinking parties, that nourished by prayers, filled with instructions, and enlightened by vigils, she may cultivate the fortification of virginal grace. Fortifying this your maidservant with these weapons of the virtues interiorly and exteriorly, grant her to complete unharmed the course of virginity. Through Christ our Lord. [47]

The consecrated maiden is now given a ring. Although the Romano-Germanic Pontifical does not specify on what hand or finger the ring should be placed, the right hand was the probable recipient of this symbolic wedding band. The right hand is singled out, albeit for an ornament other than a ring, in the *Acts* of the virgin martyr Saint Agnes, compiled about 420, which attribute to her these words regarding her consecration to Christ: "He has adorned my right hand with a priceless bracelet." [48] It is likely that there was an unbroken tradition regarding the right hand from the fifth century to the thirteenth century, when the first explicit references to the placement of the ring on the right hand begin to appear in liturgical books. [49] Durandus explains the ring of the consecrated virgin in the same manner that he explains the wedding ring of the nuptial rite. Placed on the fourth finger of the maiden's right hand (according to the rubrics of Durandus' own pontifical, c. 1294), [50] the finger that is traditionally said to have a vein running directly to the heart, the ring of consecrated virginity reminds those who receive it that they are bound "to love Christ their Spouse with all their heart and to cleave inseparably to him". [51] The ring's continuity as an unbroken circle, without beginning or end, is a further reminder that "they are espoused to Christ, who is the Alpha and the Omega, that is, the Beginning and the End." [52] In the Romano-Germanic Pontifical, the bishop confers the ring upon the consecrated maiden with these words: "*Receive the ring of faith, the signet of the Holy Spirit, that you may be called the bride of God, if you will faithfully be bound to him.*" [53] In his own pontifical, Durandus was to accentuate the nuptial symbolism of the virgin's ring by incorporating into the consecration rite the elaborate, multistaged imposition of the ring found in the medieval marriage rites of his time (as described earlier on pp. 215–217):

Then the bishop espouses them to Christ in this manner. For he takes the ring with his right hand, and with his left the virgin's right hand, saying:

[47] Vogel and Elze, *Pontifical romano-germanique*, 1:45.

[48] *Vita sanctae Agnetis* (Latin text), chap. 1, no. 3, in Bolland et al., *Acta sanctorum*, January, 2:715.

[49] Harrison, "Formulas *Ad virgines sacras*", pt. 2, 359–360.

[50] Andrieu, *Pontifical romain au moyen-âge*, 3:419.

[51] Durandus, *Rationale* (CCCM 140), bk. 2, chap. 1, no. 44, p. 140.

[52] Ibid.

[53] Vogel and Elze, *Pontifical romano-germanique*, 1:45.

I espouse you to Jesus Christ, Son of the supreme Father, that he may preserve you unharmed. Receive, therefore, the ring of faith, the signet of the Holy Spirit, that you may be called the bride of God, if you will serve him faithfully and purely. In the name of the Father, and of the Son, and of the Holy Spirit + . Response: *Amen.*

And saying, *In the name of the Father*, he puts it [the ring] a little on the thumb of the right hand. Then saying, *and of the Son*, he puts it a little on the index finger. But saying, *and of the Holy Spirit*, he puts it a little on the middle finger. And afterward he puts it and leaves it on the fourth finger.

Which having been done, the virgin—or two [virgins] together if there are several—sings this antiphon: *I am espoused to him whom the angels serve, whose splendor the sun and the moon admire.*[54]

In the rite of the Romano-Germanic Pontifical, a wreath (*torquis*) is now conferred on the head of the maiden,[55] constituting yet another instance of nuptial imagery in the consecration ceremony. In the marriage ceremonies of ancient Rome, the bride wore a wreath of flowers over her hair and under her red bridal veil.[56] The nuptial origin and symbolism of the wreath in the consecration rite are confirmed by the antiphon that is sung during the conferrals of the ring and the wreath: "*With his ring my Lord Jesus Christ has espoused me, and just as a bride He has adorned me with a crown.*"[57] The bridal connotations of the wreath are likewise expressed in the words with which the bishop confers this "crown" upon the consecrated virgin: "*Receive this sign of Christ on the head, that you may be made his wife and, if you shall have abided in him, be crowned forever.*"[58] In explaining the custom of "crowning" consecrated virgins, Durandus cites another antiphon (traceable to the second half of the ninth century)[59] from the office for the feast of the virgin martyr Saint Agnes, an antiphon that after the time of the Romano-Germanic Pontifical was added to the consecration rite itself: "*Come, bride of Christ, receive the crown that the Lord has prepared for you*

---

[54] Andrieu, *Pontifical romain au moyen-âge*, 3:419.

[55] Vogel and Elze, *Pontifical romano-germanique*, 1:45. The woodcuts accompanying the rite of consecration of virgins in the 1595–1596 *Pontificale Romanum* depict the consecrated women with wreaths upon their heads; see Sodi and Triacca, *Pontificale Romanum: Editio princeps (1595–1596)*, 214, 219, 221, 223 (original pagination).

[56] René Metz, "La couronne et l'anneau dans la consécration des vierges", *Revue des Sciences Religieuses* 28 (1954): 117.

[57] Vogel and Elze, *Pontifical romano-germanique*, 1:46. The portion of the antiphon *Anulo suo subarravit* regarding the ring is based upon words attributed to Saint Agnes in the Latin *Acts* of her martyrdom compiled around 420; see *Vita sanctae Agnetis* (Latin text), chap. 1, no. 3, in *Acta sanctorum*, January, 2:715.

[58] Vogel and Elze, *Pontifical romano-germanique*, 1:45.

[59] The antiphon *Veni sponsa Christi* is traceable to the Antiphonary of Compiègne (France, c. 870), in which it appears as a chant for the Office of One Virgin; see René-Jean Hésbert, ed., *Corpus antiphonalium officii*, vol. 1, REDSMF 7 (Rome: Herder, 1963), 370.

forever."[60] Durandus sees the crown (i.e., the wreath) as denoting that "when a virgin is espoused by consecration to the supreme King, she is made a queen, that is, [one] governing herself and others in virtues, whence Proverbs [1:9]: 'That grace may be added to thy head, and a chain of gold to thy neck.' "[61]

In the rite of the Romano-Germanic Pontifical, the bishop imparts a concluding blessing with a prayer of eighth-century origin,[62] in which he reminds the newly consecrated virgin of her unique fellowship with the Queen of virgins in vowing her chastity to God: "*May the Creator of Heaven and earth, God the Father almighty, bless you, [he] who deigns to choose you for the company of the holy Mother of our Lord Jesus Christ, that you may preserve intact and spotless the virginity that you have professed in the presence of the Lord and his angels, keep your resolution, love chastity, observe patience, and be worthy to receive the crown of virginity. Through . . .*"[63] Following the conclusion of the consecration rite, the Mass proceeds, resuming with the Offertory. The consecrated maiden temporally sets aside the two candles she has been holding to bring the Offertory "oblation" (unconsecrated hosts and wine) to the priest. Afterward, "taking the candles again, she should remain kneeling until she should communicate and Mass should be completed in its proper order."[64]

At the end of the Mass and consecration rite described in the above-cited manuscript of the early 1500s from the Benedictine convent of Saint Mary in Winchester, England, the abbess would pull down the veil of each newly consecrated virgin to conceal the maiden's face; they would remain thus for the next three days, receiving Holy Communion daily, observing absolute silence while devoting themselves to prayer. After the virgins receive Holy Communion on the third day, the abbess lifts up the veil of each, unveiling their faces; they then attend a votive "Mass of the Resurrection".[65] This triduum, clearly intended to link the virgins' consecration to the Passion, death, and Resurrection of Christ, manifests that those consecrating themselves

---

[60] This antiphon is used in the consecration rite of Durandus' own pontifical (c. 1294), from which the text is here taken; see Andrieu, *Pontifical romain au moyen-âge*, 3:420. It appears as part of the consecration rite for the first time in the thirteenth-century Pontifical of the Roman Curia; text in Michel Andrieu, ed., *Le pontifical romain au moyen-âge*, vol. 2, *Le pontifical de la Curie romaine au XIIIᵉ siècle*, ST 87 (Vatican City: Biblioteca Apostolica Vaticana, 1940), 417.

[61] Durandus, *Rationale* (CCCM 140), bk. 2, chap. 1, no. 44, p. 140.

[62] This prayer is traceable to an eighth-century Frankish liturgical book, the *Missale Francorum*; text in Mohlberg, *Missale Francorum*, no. 49, p. 16.

[63] Vogel and Elze, *Pontifical romano-germanique*, 1:46.

[64] Ibid.

[65] Manuscript: Cambridge, England, Cambridge University Library, Folio Mm. 3.13, in Maskell, *Monumenta ritualia ecclesiae Anglicanae*, 3:357–358 (Latin text quoted and translated by permission of Oxford University Press). The beginnings of this custom can be seen in the Pontifical of Durandus (c. 1294), which states that the newly consecrated virgins are to receive Holy Communion for three days after their consecration; see Andrieu, *Pontifical romain au moyen-âge*, 3:423.

to God have died to the world so as to live for Christ, in accord with
the words of Saint Paul: "For if we be dead with him, we shall live
also with him" (2 Tim 2:11).

2I   Funeral Rites

Go forth, Christian soul, from this world, in the name of God the almighty Father, who created you; in the name of Jesus Christ, the Son of the living God, who suffered for you; in the name of the Holy Spirit, who has been poured forth in you; in the name of the angels and the archangels; in the name of the thrones and dominations; in the name of the principalities and powers; in the name of the cherubim and seraphim; in the name of the patriarchs and prophets; in the name of the holy Apostles; in the name of the holy martyrs and confessors; in the name of the holy monks and hermits; in the name of the holy virgins and all the holy men and women saints of God; today may your place be in peace, and your habitation in holy Sion. Through Christ our Lord. Amen.

Proficiscere anima Christiana, from the "Order of
the Commendation of the Soul",
Pontifical of the Roman Curia, thirteenth century[1]

William Durandus of Mende (+1296) begins his discussion of the Church's funeral rite by relating what should be done for a man as the moment of his death nears (in addition to the administration of the sacraments). The Passion ought to be read to him, and a cross should be erected at his feet, that these may move him to greater compunction. He ought to be laid on the ground over ashes or straw as a reminder that he is dust and that unto dust he shall return. He should recline on his back, faceup, "that with his face ever upright he may gaze at Heaven".[2] It was by the eighth century that a specific rite had developed to assist the soul at the moment of death, the "Commendation of the Soul", a series of prayers offered by the priest at the dying man's deathbed, including the above-quoted prayer, *Proficiscere anima Christiana*, which first appears in the Gellone

---

[1] The text is here taken from Michel Andrieu, ed., *Le pontifical romain au moyen-âge*, vol. 2, *Le pontifical de la Curie romaine au XIIIᵉ siècle*, ST 87 (Vatican City: Biblioteca Apostolica Vaticana, 1940), 497.

[2] William Durandus of Mende, *Rationale divinorum officiorum*, bk. 7, chap. 35, no. 35, in A. Davril, O.S.B., and T.M. Thibodeau, eds., *Guillelmi Duranti: Rationale divinorum officiorum VII–VIII*, CCCM 140b (Turnhout, Belgium: Brepols, 2000), 97. Hereafter cited as Durandus, *Rationale* (CCCM 140b).

Sacramentary, an eighth-century Frankish adaptation of Rome's Gelasian Sacramentary.[3] The *Liber tramitis*, a customary for the French Benedictine abbey of Cluny dating from about 1043, directs that when it is evident that a monk is about to die, a wooden clapper (*tabula*) should be sounded; all of the monks who hear it, wherever they may be at the moment, should begin at once the recitation of the Nicene Creed. Immediately after the monk's death, all the bells are rung and the Office of the Dead is begun.[4] Durandus explains that the church bell should be tolled when a man dies in order that all those hearing the bell may be prompted to pray for him.[5] The death of a layman is indicated by a threefold ring, that of a woman by a twofold ring, and that of a cleric by a multiple ring corresponding to the degree of holy orders he has received (for example, seven for a priest).[6] The body ought to be washed as a sign that, just as the soul of the deceased is cleansed of sin before death by confession and contrition, so too shall his soul and body "obtain glorification and brightness on the day of judgment".[7]

Another customary for the French Benedictine abbey of Cluny, that of the monk Bernard, dating from about 1075, directs that the abbot or the prior should sprinkle the body with holy water and cense it. As the monks prepare the body for the funeral, a thurifer censes it continually.[8] The Christian funeral practice of incensing the body is of ancient origin: it is mentioned in the rubrics for the funerals of bishops and priests in the *Liber ordinum* of Spain's Mozarabic Rite, an eleventh-century compilation of older texts believed to date largely

---

[3] The Gellone Sacramentary provides a series of prayers under the heading "Prayers over the Dead, or the Commendation of the Soul", which includes the *Proficiscere anima Christiana*; see A. Dumas, ed., *Liber sacramentorum Gellonensis*, CCSL 159 (Turnhout, Belgium: Brepols, 1981), nos. 2892–2898, pp. 460–462 (text of *Proficiscere anima Christiana*: no. 2892, pp. 460–461). In the late eighth century we find for the first time a version of the commendation rite with rubrics and prayers specifically related to the moments immediately before and after a man's death; this appears in the Phillipps Sacramentary of northeastern France (the *Liber sacramentorum Augustodunensis*), another Frankish adaptation of Rome's Gelasian Sacramentary; commendation text in O. Heiming, ed., *Liber sacramentorum Augustodunensis*, CCSL 159b (Turnhout, Belgium: Brepols, 1984), no. 1914, pp. 241–242. It should be noted that the prayer *Proficiscere anima Christiana* later passed into the "Order of the Commendation of the Soul" in the *Breviarium Romanum* of 1568; text in Manlio Sodi and Achille Maria Triacca, eds., *Breviarium Romanum: Editio princeps (1568)*, facsimile ed., MLCT 3 (Vatican City: Libreria Editrice Vaticana, © 1999), 1030 (new pagination).

[4] *Liber tramitis* (formerly called the Customs of Farfa), bk. 2, chap. 56, in Bruno Albers, ed., *Consuetudines monasticae*, vol. 1, *Consuetudines Farfenses* (Stuttgart: Jos. Roth, Bibliopolae, 1900), 193.

[5] Durandus, *Rationale divinorum officiorum*, bk. 1, chap. 4, no. 13, in A. Davril, O.S.B., and T. M. Thibodeau, eds., *Guillelmi Duranti: Rationale divinorum officiorum I–IV*, CCCM 140 (Turnhout, Belgium: Brepols, 1995), 56. Hereafter cited as Durandus, *Rationale* (CCCM 140).

[6] Ibid.

[7] Durandus, *Rationale* (CCCM 140b), bk. 7, chap. 35, no. 36, p. 98.

[8] *Ordo Cluniacensis*, pt. 1, chap. 24, in Marquard Herrgott, ed., *Vetus disciplina monastica* (Paris, 1726; repr., Siegburg, Germany: Franciscus Schmitt, 1999), 194.

from the fifth to the seventh century.[9] Durandus explains that the incensation and aspersion of the body are carried out in order to keep away all "unclean spirits", that is, demons; he adds that the censing and sprinkling also function as "a sign of the society and the communion of the sacraments that they [the deceased] had with us while they lived".[10] Sicard of Cremona (+1215) sees the incensation of the body as expressing that prayers for the dead are profitable to them.[11]

Funeral Rites in a Sixteenth-century Ritual of Toulouse, France

The interment rite given in a sixteenth-century ritual of Toulouse, France, is rich in rubrical details regarding the conveying of the body from the home of the deceased to the church.[12] The rite begins with a procession of the parish priest and those assisting him from the church to the deceased man's home, during which the Gradual Psalms, Psalms 119 to 133, are chanted on behalf of the departed soul. This series of fifteen psalms is believed to have been recited by Jewish pilgrims as they advanced toward the holy city of Jerusalem for the great festivals.[13] This usage would fit well with the implicit symbolism of the funeral cortege as a representation of the soul's pilgrimage journey to the heavenly Jerusalem.[14] A similar comparison is made by Sicard of Cremona: noting that Psalm 64, sung of old to celebrate the end of the Israelites' Babylonian captivity, is used in the funeral rites of the Church (namely in the Office of the Dead),[15] he observes that just as the children of Israel returned from their captivity to the Promised Land, so too the faithful departed "set out from the misery of captivity unto eternal life".[16] The Toulouse rubrics state:

> The bells should be rung, that all may assemble. They having assembled, they should proceed two by two alternately chanting in a lowered voice the canticles of the Gradual [Psalms 119–133], without the Glory Be and without [the verse] *Eternal rest*, all the way to the place of the body, with the staff bearer and the choirboys preceding, who bring a staff, an upright cross, a thurible, and holy water. But

---

[9] Text in Marius Férotin, ed., *Le Liber ordinum en usage dans l'église wisigothique et mozarabe d'Espagne du cinquieme au onzième siècle* (Paris, 1904), repr., ed. Anthony Ward and Cuthbert Johnson, BELS 83 (Rome: Centro Liturgico Vincenziano, Edizioni Liturgiche, 1996), cols. 141–142, 146.

[10] Durandus, *Rationale* (CCCM 140b), bk. 7, chap. 35, no. 29, p. 96.

[11] Sicard of Cremona, *Mitrale*, bk. 9, chap. 50, PL 213, col. 428.

[12] Text in Edmond Martène, *De antiquis ecclesiae ritibus* (Venice: Johannes Baptista Novelli, 1763–1764), bk. 3, chap. 15, *ordo* 17, 2:404.

[13] John Corbett, "Gradual Psalms", in *The Catholic Encyclopedia* (New York: Appleton, 1907–1912), 6:718.

[14] See Damien Sicard, *Le liturgie de la mort dans l'église latine des origines à la réforme carolingienne*, Liturgiewissenschaftliche Quellen und Forschungen 63 (Münster, Germany: Aschendorffsche Verlagsbuchhandlung, 1978), 257.

[15] Psalm 64 is used as the second psalm of Lauds in the Office of the Dead; see the *Breviarium Romanum* of 1568, in Sodi and Triacca, *Breviarium Romanum: Editio princeps (1568)*, 1024 (new pagination).

[16] Sicard of Cremona, *Mitrale*, bk. 9, chap. 50, PL 213, col. 426.

when they shall have arrived at the place of the body, they should cease singing the aforesaid fifteen psalms; immediately the lord cantor or the hebdomadarian [the priest assigned to lead the Divine Office for the week] should vest himself in a stole and a cope of black color and hasten to the bier on which the body has been made ready to be brought; and the holy water and the thurible having been received [by him], he should sprinkle and cense it [the body], saying, *Lord, have mercy*, and the Our Father.[17]

The twelfth-century liturgist John Beleth (+1182) says of the arrival of the priest at the home of the deceased, "Pouring forth prayers for him to God, [the priest] ought to invoke and entreat the saints, that they might receive his soul and carry it away to that place of joy."[18] The customary of the monk Bernard for the French Benedictine abbey of Cluny (c. 1075) directs that before the procession to the church begins, the bier upon which the body shall be borne is to be sprinkled with holy water and censed.[19] The body, after it has been set upon the bier, is then placed at the entrance to the cloistered walkway (known as the Galilee), where the prior sprinkles it with holy water and censes it. The procession commences shortly thereafter.[20] The earlier customary of Cluny known as the *Liber tramitis* (c. 1043) specifies that two candlesticks, a crucifix, a thurible, and holy water should be brought for the procession to the church.[21]

The use of candles or torches in Christian funeral rites can be traced back to the third century; it became a widely accepted practice before A.D. 400.[22] The candles or torches carried in the funeral procession are explained by Saint John Chrysostom (+407) as a sign of spiritual victory over sin and death: "Now, tell me, what do the bright torches mean? Is it not that we conduct them [the dead] like athletes?"[23] The episcopal funeral rubrics of fifth- to seventh-century origin in the *Liber ordinum* of Spain's Mozarabic Rite speak of lights being carried before and behind the bishop's body as it is borne to the church and again when it is carried to the tomb.[24] Describing the funeral procession for bringing the deceased from his home to the church, the sixteenth-century ritual of Toulouse states, "The procession having been arranged; the lights

---

[17] Martène, *De antiquis ecclesiae ritibus*, bk. 3, chap. 15, *ordo* 17, 2:404.

[18] John Beleth, *Summa de ecclesiasticis officiis*, chap. 161, in Heribertus Douteil, C.S.Sp., ed., *Iohannis Beleth: Summa de ecclesiasticis officiis*, CCCM 41a (Turnhout, Belgium: Brepols, 1976), 317–318. Hereafter cited as Beleth, *Summa de ecclesiasticis officiis* (CCCM 41a).

[19] *Ordo Cluniacensis*, pt. 1, chap. 24, in Herrgott, *Vetus disciplina monastica*, 194.

[20] Ibid., chap. 34, p. 219.

[21] *Liber tramitis*, bk. 2, chap. 56, in Albers, *Consuetudines monasticae*, 1:193.

[22] Alfred Rush, *Death and Burial in Christian Antiquity*, Catholic University of America Studies in Christian Antiquity 1 (Washington, D.C.: Catholic University of America Press, 1941), 226.

[23] Saint John Chrysostom, *On the Epistle to the Hebrews, Chapter 2, Homily 4*, PG 43, col. 43 (Latin and Greek).

[24] Férotin, *Liber ordinum*, col. 142.

kindled; the cross with the candlesticks, the thurible, and the holy water preceding, the cantor shall begin the antiphon *To thee have I lifted up my soul. Come and deliver me; O Lord, to thee have I fled* [cf. Ps 24:1; 142:9],[25] and the other responsories, ... and thus having been set in order two by two, they should proceed to the church." [26] The carrying of one or more crosses in the funeral procession to the church had arisen by the late eighth century, when it appears in the rubrics of the Phillipps Sacramentary (the *Liber sacramentorum Augustodunensis*) of northeastern France, a Frankish adaptation of Rome's Gelasian Sacramentary.[27] The above-cited *Liber tramitis* of Cluny (c. 1043) specifies that during the funeral procession to the church the bells are to be rung and the responsory *Subvenite sancti Dei* should be sung.[28] This responsory, traceable to the aforementioned Phillipps Sacramentary of the late eighth century,[29] implores: "*Assist him, O saints of God; go to meet him, O angels of the Lord, taking up his soul, offering it in the sight of the Most High.* [Verse:] *May Christ, who has called you, receive you, and may the angels conduct you to the bosom of Abraham. Offering it ...*" [30]

The chanting of Psalm 50, the *Miserere* ("*Have mercy on me, O God ...*"), during the funeral procession to the church first appears in the Sacramentary of Rheinau (Rheinau 30), a text of northern French or Swiss origin dating from about 800.[31] As early as the tenth century, in the Office of the Dead, the *Miserere* was being paired with an antiphon derived from the psalm's tenth verse, namely "*The bones that have been humbled shall rejoice in the Lord*" ("*Exsultabunt Domino ossa humiliata*").[32] By the thirteenth century, we find this antiphon being sung at the moment when the body is set in place within the church to begin the wake.[33] The funeral rubrics of a 1545 processional of the

---

[25] The antiphon *Ad te levavi* is first found in the Antiphonary of Compiègne (France, c. 870); see René-Jean Hésbert, ed., *Corpus antiphonalium officii*, vol. 1, REDSMF 7 (Rome: Herder, 1963), 22. The complete text of the antiphon is here taken from René-Jean Hésbert, ed., *Corpus antiphonalium officii*, vol. 3, pt. 1, REDSMF 9 (Rome: Herder, 1968), no. 1255, p. 29.

[26] Martène, *De antiquis ecclesiae ritibus*, bk. 3, chap. 15, ordo 17, 2:404.

[27] Text in Heiming, *Liber sacramentorum Augustodunensis*, no. 1914, p. 242.

[28] *Liber tramitis*, bk. 2, chap. 56, in Albers, *Consuetudines monasticae*, 1:194.

[29] Heiming, *Liber sacramentorum Augustodunensis*, no. 1914, p. 242.

[30] The text of this responsory is here taken from the 1485 *Pontificalis liber* (*Pontificale Romanum*), in Manlio Sodi, ed., *Il "Pontificalis liber" di Agostino Patrizi Piccolomini e Giovanni Burcardo (1485)*, facsimile ed., MSIL 43 (Vatican City: Libreria Editrice Vaticana, © 2006), 582 (new pagination).

[31] Text in Anton Hänggi and Alfons Schönherr, eds., *Sacramentarium Rhenaugiense: Handschrift Rh 30 der Zentralbibliothek Zürich*, SF 15 (Fribourg, Switzerland: Universitätsverlag Freiburg, 1970), no. 1337, p. 274.

[32] The complete text of this antiphon is here taken from Hésbert, *Corpus antiphonalium officii*, vol. 3, pt. 1, no. 2810, p. 220. This antiphon, albeit with some verbal differences, first appears with the *Miserere* in the tenth-century Romano-Germanic Pontifical; see Cyrille Vogel and Reinhard Elze, eds., *Le pontifical romano-germanique du dixième siècle*, vol. 2, ST 227 (Vatican City: Biblioteca Apostolica Vaticana, 1963), 296.

[33] A thirteenth-century ritual from the Monastery of Saint-Eloi, Noyon, France (manuscript: Tours, France, Bibliothèque Municipale, MS 330), specifies the singing of *Exsultabunt*

Dominican Order published in Venice pair the *Exsultabunt* with the *Miserere* during the procession of the friars on their way to the church where the funeral is to be conducted.[34] The chanting of the *Exsultabunt Domino ossa* was eventually assigned to the beginning of the funeral procession to the church, accompanying the singing of the *Miserere*, as specified in the *Rituale Romanum* of 1614.[35] People around the globe witnessed the solemn beauty of this custom when on April 4, 2005, the *Exsultabunt Domino ossa* was chanted antiphonally with the *Miserere* during the processional transfer of the body of Pope Blessed John Paul II from the Apostolic Palace to the Basilica of Saint Peter, as prescribed in the rubrics of the most recent ceremonial book for papal funerals, the *Ordo exsequiarum Romani pontificis*, published in 2000.[36]

The arrival of the body at the church constituted an important moment in the medieval funeral liturgy. The rubrics of the Toulouse ritual state in this regard:

> Upon entering the church, however, they stop at that very place [the entrance]; and meanwhile, the celebrant, vested in a stole and a cope, sprinkles again the body of the deceased, saying, *Eternal rest grant unto them, O Lord, and let perpetual light shine upon them,*[37] and *From the gate of hell, O Lord, deliver their souls,*[38] and *Hearken, O Lord,* [*to my prayer.* Response: *And let my cry come unto you*].[39] Verse: *The Lord be with you.* [Response: *And with your spirit.*]
>
> Prayer: *Absolve, we beseech you, O Lord, the soul of your servant* [Name], *from every bond of sins, that having been raised up again in the glory of the Resurrection, he may return to life among your saints and elect. Through Christ our Lord.*[40]

Domino ossa as soon as the body has been set in place within the church, beginning the vigil for the deceased; a similar rubric appears in a ritual of the French abbey of Saint-Ouen, Rouen, a text thought to date from about 1300. See Martène, *De antiquis ecclesiae ritibus*, bk. 3, chap. 15, *ordo* 8 and *ordo* 13, 2:395–396 and 2:401, respectively.

[34] *Processionarium secundum ritum et morem Fratrum Predicatorum* (Venice: Luceantonius, 1545; digitized text, Bayerische Staatsbibliothek, Munich, 2009), fol. 141v.

[35] Text in Manlio Sodi and Juan Javier Flores Arcas, eds., *Rituale Romanum: Editio princeps (1614)*, facsimile ed., MLCT 5 (Vatican City: Libreria Editrice Vaticana, © 2004), 104 (original pagination).

[36] *Ordo exsequiarum Romani pontificis* (Vatican City: Officium de Liturgicis Celebrationibus Summi Pontificis, 2000), chap. 2, no. 73, pp. 91, 93, 95 (Latin text).

[37] This versicle, *Requiem aeternam*, first appears in the ninth century as the opening verse of the Introit for the Mass of the Dead; see the discussion of the Requiem Mass chants later in this chapter (p. 602). The complete text of the versicle is here taken from Martin Gerbert, *Monumenta veteris liturgiae Alemannicae* (Sankt Blasien, Germany: Typis San-Blasianis, 1777–1779), 1:400.

[38] Regarding the origin of the versicle *A porta inferi*, see p. 535 above.

[39] This widely used versicle, *Domine exaudi*, is traceable to the late tenth century, when it appears in an antiphonary from the Monastery of Saint Martial in Limoges, France (manuscript: Paris, Bibliothèque Nationale, Codex Lat. 1085, fol. 31v as indicated by the Gregorian chant online database Cantus, http://cantusdatabase.org).

[40] The Toulouse text gives only the incipit of the prayer *Absolve, quaesumus, Domine . . . respiret*; the complete text is here taken from the 1485 *Pontificalis liber* (Roman Pontifical), in Sodi, *"Pontificalis liber" di Agostino Patrizi Piccolomini e Giovanni Burcardo (1485)*, 585

Which having been said, they enter the church, and the cantors sing the antiphon [actually a responsory]: *If we have received good things at the hand of the Lord, why should we not also bear with evil things? The Lord gave, and the Lord hath taken away; as it hath pleased the Lord so is it done; blessed be the name of the Lord. Naked came I out of my mother's womb, and naked shall I return thither. The Lord gave . . .* [Job 2:10; 1:21].[41] Whereupon they entering into the choir, with the bier having been set in its prepared place and with lights having been placed everywhere around it, and the cross at the head, the immortal sacrifice should presently be offered for the soul of the deceased. Alms should also be distributed to the priests and the paupers while the deceased rests in the choir.[42]

The placing of candles or torches around the bier or casket of the deceased, mentioned in the above rubrics, is a practice almost as ancient as that of carrying lights in the funeral procession. The fourth-century ecclesiastical historian Eusebius of Caesarea (+c. 340) relates that the body of the Roman emperor Constantine I (+337) while lying in state was encompassed by lit candles mounted on candlesticks of gold.[43] The placement of a cross near the body at its place of temporary reposition in the church is traceable to the eleventh century, when it is mentioned in the French Benedictine *Liber tramitis* of Cluny (c. 1043), which directs that a crucifix should be placed at the head of the bier, with candlestands on either side, remaining thus until the body is taken to the grave.[44] The same text specifies that for the funeral of a bishop seven candlesticks should be placed at the head of the bier and seven at the feet.[45] As we saw earlier in our discussion of medieval burial customs imitated in the Good Friday rites commemorating the burial of Christ (see p. 449 above), and as we shall see later in our discussion of papal funeral customs, the number of candles or torches surrounding the bier of the dead was often much larger than the numbers mentioned here.

In many cases, the funeral Mass would begin immediately after the arrival of the body at the church. But when the Mass was deferred to

---

(new pagination). This prayer is traceable to the second half of the ninth century, when it is mentioned in the Booklet of the Dead of the Palatine (manuscript: Vatican City, Biblioteca Apostolica Vaticana, Codex Palatinus Latinus 550); text in Jerome Frank, O.S.B., "Der älteste erhaltene *ordo defunctorum* der römischen Liturgie und sein Fortleben in Totenagenden des frühen Mittelalters", *Archiv für Liturgie Wissenschaft* 7, pt. 2 (1962): 392.

[41] The responsory *Si bona suscepimus* in this form (i.e., with the verse *Nudus egressus*) is traceable to the eleventh century, when it is found in an antiphonary of Verona, Italy; see Hésbert, *Corpus antiphonalium officii*, 1:387, and René-Jean Hésbert, ed., *Corpus antiphonalium officii*, vol. 4, REDSMF 10 (Rome: Herder, 1970), no. 7647, p. 405.

[42] Martène, *De antiquis ecclesiae ritibus*, bk. 3, chap. 15, ordo 17, 2:404.

[43] Eusebius of Caesarea, *De vita Constantini*, bk. 4, chap. 66, PG 20, cols. 1221 (Greek), 1222 (Latin).

[44] *Liber tramitis*, bk. 2, chap. 56, in Albers, *Consuetudines monasticae*, 1:194.

[45] Ibid., chap. 61, p. 203.

the next day—a postponement made necessary if the funeral procession reached the church at a later hour, beyond the time for Mass—a
wake would begin following the arrival of the body, a custom established by the seventh century.[46] Thus the *Liber tramitis* of Cluny (c.
1043) states, "While it is day, all ought to sit beside the body and say
the Psalms."[47] As for the ensuing hours of the night, the *Liber tramitis*
calls for what we would describe today as a "sign-up sheet" for keeping a continual vigil through the night, with the recitation of the
Psalter and the Office of the Dead: "The *armarius* [sacristy archivist],
however, should put on a tablet the brothers by name, to regulate
who should make the first vigil, and the second ..."[48] The customary of Bernard of Cluny (c. 1075) speaks of a Cluniac practice of
keeping a candle continually burning before the monastery's chapter
house[49] through the night, until the clear light of daybreak, for as
long as the body remains unburied. The Psalter is recited continually,
with the monks saying it in shifts of three to five watches through the
night.[50] A comparable arrangement of successive watches, with monks
assigned by name on a tablet, appears in the twelfth-century customary of the Benedictine abbey of Vallombrosa, Italy, which directs that
"there should be two to four monks to sing the Psalms beside the
bier." When the time for the succeeding watch of the night comes,
one of the monks from the watch that is ending goes to the dormitory to wake the monks assigned to the next watch.[51]

The incensation of the body immediately before the funeral Mass is
first mentioned in the *Liber tramitis* of Cluny (c. 1043), which speaks
of a twofold incensation preceding the Mass in its rubrics for the funeral
of a bishop.[52] The Cluny customary of the monk Bernard (c. 1075)
specifies a single incensation before the funeral Mass, directing the
priest to perform a crosswise (cross-shaped) censing of the body.[53]

**The Funeral
Mass**

---

[46] An early biography of the French bishop of Noyon Saint Eloi (Eligius), recounting
the bishop's death in 660, speaks of the clergy and the people keeping an all-night vigil;
see *Vitae Eligii episcopi Noviomagensis*, bk. 2, chap. 37, in *Monumenta Germaniae historica:
Scriptorum rerum Merovingicarum*, vol. 4, *Passiones vitaeque sanctorum aevi Merovingici*, ed. Bruno
Krusch (Hanover, Germany: Hahn, 1902), 721. The episcopal funeral rubrics of fifth- to
seventh-century origin in the *Liber ordinum* of Spain's Mozarabic Rite prescribe the recitation of the Psalms over the bishop's body throughout the day and the night "without
intermission" until his funeral Mass is celebrated (Férotin, *Liber ordinum*, col. 142).

[47] *Liber tramitis*, bk. 2, chap. 56, in Albers, *Consuetudines monasticae*, 1:194.

[48] Ibid.

[49] The chapter house is a building adjoining the monastery in which certain functions
of the religious community are carried out, including meetings and the daily reading of
the martyrology.

[50] *Ordo Cluniacensis*, pt. 1, chap. 24, in Herrgott, *Vetus disciplina monastica*, 195.

[51] Text in Kassius Hallinger, O.S.B., *Consuetudines Cluniacensium antiquiores cum redactionibus derivatis*, Corpus consuetudinum monasticarum 7, pt. 2 (Siegburg, Germany: Franciscus Schmitt, 1983), 371.

[52] *Liber tramitis*, bk. 2, chap. 61, in Albers, *Consuetudines monasticae*, 1:203.

[53] *Ordo Cluniacensis*, pt. 1, chap. 24, in Herrgott, *Vetus disciplina monastica*, 196.

Nearly all of the prayers, chants, and readings proper to the medieval funeral Mass[54] were in use by the ninth century. The Collect and the Secret appear for the first time in a ninth-century French sacramentary from the Abbey of Saint Martin, Tours,[55] and the Postcommunion in its earliest form is first found in Saint Benedict of Aniane's early ninth-century Frankish adaptation of Rome's Gregorian Sacramentary.[56] Four of the Mass chants, that is, the Introit (*Requiem aeternam . . . caro veniet*), the Gradual (*Requiem aeternam . . . non timebit*), the Offertory (*Domine Jesu Christe Rex gloriae*), and the Communion (*Lux aeterna*), are traceable to a ninth-century redaction of the Gregorian Sacramentary of Rome;[57] the Tract (*Absolve Domine*) is first found in a missal of Hamburg, Germany (eleventh or twelfth century).[58] The well-known funeral sequence *Dies irae* is traceable to the twelfth century, when it appears in a manuscript of Naples, Italy.[59] Although the *Dies irae* may have originated as a devotional text, it soon entered the funeral liturgy, appearing as part of a Requiem Mass added around the middle of the thirteenth century to a Franciscan liturgical book dating from about 1238, the so-called Breviary of Saint Clare; the complete text of the *Dies irae* and its traditional musical setting are provided.[60] About a century later, the *Dies irae* is explicitly identified as the Sequence for funeral Masses in a fourteenth-century

---

[54] The complete series of texts proper to the medieval funeral Mass (except the *Dies irae*) can be found in the 1474 *Missale Romanum*; see Robert Lippe, ed., *Missale Romanum: Mediolani, 1474*, vol. 1, *Text*, HBS 17 (London: Henry Bradshaw Society, 1899), 483–486.

[55] Text in Jean Deshusses, ed., *Le sacramentaire grégorien: Ses principales formes d'après les plus anciens manuscrits*, vol. 2, SF 24 (Fribourg, Switzerland: Editions Universitaires Fribourg, 1979), nos. 2870–2871, p. 208.

[56] Text in Jean Deshusses, ed., *Le sacramentaire grégorien: Ses principales formes d'après les plus anciens manuscrits*, vol. 1, 2nd ed., SF 16 (Fribourg, Switzerland: Editions Universitaires Fribourg, 1979), no. 1429, p. 466. By the eleventh century, the phrase "*quae hodie de hoc saeculo migravit*" ("*who this day has departed from this world*") had been added to the prayer, appearing thus in the tenth- to eleventh-century Italian Sacramentary of Arezzo (Sicard, *Liturgie de la mort*, 186). It is this expanded version of the Postcommunion that entered the 1474 *Missale Romanum*; see Lippe, *Missale Romanum*, 1:486.

[57] Manuscript: Vatican City, Biblioteca Apostolica Vaticana, Codex Vaticanus Latinus 14821, ninth century, cited in Sicard, *Liturgie de la mort*, 187–188, 191. The wording of the Introit *Requiem aeternam* is derived from two verses in the third-century Christian-authored portion of an ancient apocryphal work known as the Fourth Book of Esdras (chap. 2, verses 34–35), the Jewish portion of which dates from the late first century; see John Steinmueller, *A Companion to Scripture Studies*, vol. 1, *General Introduction to the Bible* (New York: Joseph F. Wagner; Houston: Lumen Christi Press, 1969), 132–133, and Charles Souvay, "Esdras", in *Catholic Encyclopedia* (1907–1912), 5:537–538.

[58] Manuscript: Rome, Biblioteca Vallicelliana, Codex B 141, eleventh or twelfth century, cited in Sicard, *Liturgie de la mort*, 188.

[59] Manuscript: Naples, Italy, Biblioteca Nazionale, Codex VII-D-36, twelfth century, quoted in Enzo Lodi, ed., *Enchiridion euchologicum fontium liturgicorum*, BELS 15 (Rome: Centro Liturgico Vincenziano, Edizioni Liturgiche, 1979), no. 3319a, pp. 1657–1658 (including the editor's introduction on p. 1657).

[60] Manuscript: Assisi, Italy, Friary of San Damiano, Codex San Damiano, c. 1238. The Requiem Mass that includes the *Dies irae*, the second of two in the San Damiano manuscript, appears on fols. 262v–264r; see Stephen Aurelian Van Dijk, O.F.M., "The Breviary of Saint Clare", pt. 2, *Franciscan Studies* 8 (1948): 365.

Franciscan missal from northeastern Italy.[61] The assignment of the *Dies irae* to funeral Masses in the missals of Rome begins with the 1485 *Missale Romanum*.[62] Here we offer several verses from this renowned chant:

Day of wrath, that day
shall dissolve the world in ashes,
David bearing witness with the Sibyl.[63]

How great a trembling there shall be
when the Judge is going to come,
going to examine strictly ...

Death and nature shall be stunned
when the creature shall rise from the dead,
going to answer unto him judging ...

King of tremendous majesty,
who save freely those to be saved,
save me, O Font of Mercy.

Remember, O merciful Jesus,
that I am the reason for your life,
lest you should lose me that day ...

You who absolved Mary [Magdalene]
and heard favorably the thief:
unto me also you have given hope ...

Merciful Lord Jesus, give them rest.[64]

The Epistle (1 Thess 4:13–18) and the Gospel (Jn 11:21–27) are traceable as funeral Mass readings to the late eighth century.[65] All of these

---

[61] The *Dies irae* is specified as the "Prose", that is, Sequence, for the Mass of the Dead in a fourteenth-century Franciscan missal preserved in Verona, Italy (manuscript: Verona, Biblioteca Comunale, MS 573, fol. 189v); see Stephen J. P. Van Dijk, O.F.M., *Sources of the Modern Roman Liturgy: The Ordinals by Haymo of Faversham and Related Documents (1243–1307)*, Studia et documenta Franciscana 2 (Leiden, Netherlands: E. J. Brill, 1963), 1:207–208; 2:328, footnote (text "G").

[62] See Robert Lippe, ed., *Missale Romanum: Mediolani, 1474*, vol. 2, *A Collation with Other Editions Printed before 1570*, HBS 33 (London: Henry Bradshaw Society, 1907), 293.

[63] This refers to the Erythraean Sibyl, an ancient pagan prophetess to whom Saint Augustine, among others, attributed a prophecy circulated among the pagans that a king from Heaven would come to judge the world at the end of time—the Sibylline Prophecy (see p. 269 above).

[64] *Dies irae*, verses 1–2, 4, 8–9, 13, 18; the text is here taken from the 1570 *Missale Romanum*, in Manlio Sodi and Achille Maria Triacca, eds., *Missale Romanum: Editio princeps (1570)*, facsimile ed., MLCT 2 (Vatican City: Libreria Editrice Vaticana, © 1998), 649–650 (new pagination).

[65] These readings are among several listed for Masses of the Dead in the *Comes* of Murbach, a lectionary of the French-Alsatian abbey of Murbach constituting a Frankish adaptation of earlier Roman lectionaries; see D. A. Wilmart, "Le *Comes* de Murbach", *Revue Bénédictine* 30 (1913): 54.

prayers, chants, and readings were retained for the Requiem Mass in the 1570 *Missale Romanum* of Pope Saint Pius V.[66]

In two editions of the *Missale Romanum*, those of 1530 and 1540, a plea to the Blessed Virgin Mary on behalf of the dead is given immediately before the Gospel in the text of the Requiem Mass, described as a "prayer or sequence to blessed Mary for the dead". The wording reflects Mary's unique role as a cooperator in the salvation wrought by her Divine Son (hence we find an unusual application of the title "Key of David" to Mary, an appellation normally reserved for Christ):

> *O Mary, in your compassion come to the aid of those languishing in Purgatory, who are being purified in burning beyond measure and are tormented in great chastisement; you are the clear fountain, who have washed away sins. You heal all and reject no one. O Mary, stretch out your hand to the dead, who languish under continual pains. To you, O Mary, merciful one, the dead sigh, longing to be delivered from their pains, and to appear in your sight, and thoroughly to enjoy eternal joys. O Key of David, who open Heaven, O blessed one, succor those now in misery. O Mary, you assist those who are tortured by torments; lead them forth from the prison house. O law of the just, standard of believers, true salvation to those hoping in you, may there be devotion to you on behalf of the dead. O Mary, pray assiduously to your Son. O Mary, blessed by your merits, we beseech you, awaken the dead, and pardoning their sins, may you be for them the way to rest.[67]*

The late medieval theologian and liturgical commentator Gabriel Biel (+1495) relates an anecdote regarding Pope Pascal II (1099–1118) that bears repeating here. The pontiff, following the death of his nephew, offered in his own chapel five Masses for the repose of his nephew's soul. At the end of the fifth Mass, while Pascal was still at the altar, he saw at the apex of a window facing the altar a vision of the Blessed Virgin Mary drawing his nephew's soul out of Purgatory.[68]

As for the rubrics proper to the medieval funeral Mass, these did not prescribe additional ceremonies but rather a series of omissions from the usual order of the Mass observed on other occasions. By the beginning of the sixteenth century, the omitted rites and prayers included the *Gloria Patri* with which the entrance psalm *Judica me* was usually concluded, the incensation of the altar at the beginning of the Mass, the *Gloria in excelsis*, the *Alleluia*, the deacon's petition for the celebrant's blessing before reading the Gospel, the bringing of lights for the Gospel, the incensation of the Gospel book, the celebrant's kiss of the Gospel book, the Creed, the celebrant's blessing of the water to

---

[66] Sodi and Triacca, *Missale Romanum: Editio princeps (1570)*, 651–652 (new pagination).

[67] Text in Lippe, *Missale Romanum*, 2:293.

[68] Gabriel Biel, *Exposition of the Canon of the Mass*, lesson 57, in Heiko Oberman and William Courtenay, eds., *Gabrielis Biel: Canonis misse expositio*, vol. 2, Veröffentlichungen des Instituts für Europäische Geschichte Mainz 32 (Wiesbaden, Germany: Franz Steiner Verlag, 1965), 403.

be infused into the chalice, the Offertory incensation of those other than the celebrant, the subdeacon's holding of the paten behind the celebrant, the sign of peace, the striking of the breast during the *Agnus Dei*, and the final blessing.[69] All of these omissions passed into the *Missale Romanum* of 1570.[70] The omissions of the *Gloria in excelsis*, the *Alleluia*, the incensations, and the sign of peace date back to the ninth century, when they are mentioned by Amalarius of Metz (+c. 850).[71] Citing Leviticus 5:11, which states that frankincense should not be used for sacrifices offered in atonement for sin, Amalarius explains that similarly incensations are omitted (albeit not totally) from the funeral Mass because it is offered in atonement for the sins of the deceased.[72] Several of the omissions, particularly those regarding the Gospel and the sign of peace, resemble the omissions observed in the liturgy of Holy Week, and with good reason, for in explaining the omission of the sign of peace Amalarius notes that the funeral liturgy imitates the liturgical commemoration of the death of Christ.[73] Similarly, John Beleth sees the Office of the Dead as symbolizing the three days' entombment of Christ.[74]

In the medieval liturgy, the priest would silently apply the merits of the funeral Mass to the deceased when in the Roman Canon he reached the words "*Be mindful also, O Lord, of your servants and maidservants, who have preceded us with the sign of faith, and rest in the sleep of peace*" ("*Memento etiam, Domine . . .*"). Thus William Durandus, in the *Instructions* he composed for his diocese of Mende, France (c. 1294), directs that the celebrant after saying these words should "halt a short time, recollecting in his mind the dead for whom he especially intends to pray".[75]

The medieval funeral liturgy was also marked by two alterations to the usual texts of the Mass. In late medieval editions of the *Missale Romanum*, beginning with the 1497 edition, a modified version of the *Agnus Dei* is specified for Requiem Masses, in which the usual endings, "*Have mercy on us*" and "*Grant us peace*", are changed to "*Grant*

---

[69] This enumeration of the funeral Mass omissions is compiled from the rubrics of two liturgical books of Rome, the *Pontificalis liber* (*Pontificale Romanum*) of 1485 and the 1502 edition of the *Ordo missae* of the papal master of ceremonies John Burckard. For the texts, see respectively Sodi, "*Pontificalis liber*" di Agostino Patrizi Piccolomini e Giovanni Burcardo *(1485)*, 579–580 (new pagination), and John Wickham Legg, ed., *Tracts on the Mass*, HBS 27 (London: Henry Bradshaw Society, 1904), 138, 140, 145, 147, 148, 150, 161–162, 168.

[70] Sodi and Triacca, *Missale Romanum: Editio princeps (1570)*, 10, 12–13, 17–20 (new pagination).

[71] Amalarius of Metz, *Liber officialis*, bk. 3, chap. 44, no. 1, in John Michael Hanssens, ed., *Amalarii episcopi: Opera liturgica omnia*, vol. 2, ST 139 (Vatican City: Biblioteca Apostolica Vaticana, 1948), 381.

[72] Ibid.

[73] Ibid.

[74] Beleth, *Summa de ecclesiasticis officiis* (CCCM 41a), chap. 161, pp. 315–316.

[75] Text in J. Berthelé, "Les instructions et constitutions de Guillaume Durand le Spéculateur", in *Académie des Sciences et Lettres de Montpellier: Mémoires de la Section des Lettres*, 2nd series, vol. 3 (Montpellier, 1900–1907), 70–71.

them rest" and *"Grant them eternal rest"* respectively.[76] This funeral Mass modification of the *Agnus Dei* is traceable to the eleventh century, when it appears in a sacramentary of Soissons, France.[77] At the end of the Requiem Mass, the formulas *Ite, missa est* (*"Go, it is ended"*) and *Benedicamus Domino* (*"Let us bless the Lord"*) would be omitted and replaced with the verse *"Requiescant in pace"* (*"May they rest in peace"*),[78] a change traceable to the first half of the twelfth century.[79] Gabriel Biel explains these alterations to the *Agnus Dei* and the ending of the Mass as attesting that, in the case of Masses for the dead, "the fruit of the Mass" in its entirety from beginning to end is applied particularly to obtain for the deceased rest from his pains, that is, his deliverance from the sufferings of Purgatory.[80] It should be noted that the present custom of incensing the body during the Mass (at the Offertory) is generally absent from medieval rubrics, but it does appear in at least one text, the customary of the monk Bernard for the French Benedictine abbey of Cluny (c. 1075), which directs that during the funeral Mass the deacon is to cense the body in a crosswise (cross-shaped) manner, beginning from the head (the specific moment for this incensation is not indicated).[81]

The incensation of the body at the end of the funeral Mass is mentioned for the first time in the funeral rubrics of the French Benedictine *Liber tramitis* of Cluny (c. 1043), which prefaces this incensation with the prayer *Non intres in judicium* (*"Enter not into judgment"*);[82] this oration, traceable to the second half of the ninth century,[83] was to serve as a key text of the post-Requiem Mass rite of aspersion and incensation of the body that entered the *Rituale Romanum* of 1614.[84]

---

[76] For the appearance of this modified *Agnus Dei* in the 1497 Roman Missal, see *Missale Romanum* (Lyons, France: Michel Topié, 1497; digitized text, Bayerische Staatsbibliothek, Munich, 2009), unnum. fol. 97r (the text of the modified *Agnus Dei* is here taken from the 1497 edition). This same usage appears in editions of the *Missale Romanum* from 1505, 1509, 1543, 1558, and 1561; see Lippe, *Missale Romanum*, 2:113.

[77] Joseph Jungmann, S.J., *The Mass of the Roman Rite: Its Origins and Development* (New York: Benziger Bros., 1951–1955), 2:339. This modification is also mentioned by John Beleth (+1182); see his *Summa de ecclesiasticis officiis* (CCCM 41a), chap. 48, p. 84.

[78] The text is here taken from the 1502 edition of John Burckard's *Ordo missae* (Legg, *Tracts on the Mass*, 166).

[79] The ending *"Requiescant in pace"* is mentioned by Stephen of Baugé (+1139) in his work *Tractatus de sacramento altaris* (chap. 18, PL 172, col. 1303). It is also mentioned by John Beleth (+1182); see his *Summa de ecclesiasticis officiis* (CCCM 41a), chap. 49, p. 87.

[80] Gabriel Biel, *Exposition of the Canon of the Mass*, lessons 81, 89, in Heiko Oberman and William Courtenay, eds., *Gabrielis Biel: Canonis misse expositio*, vol. 4, Veröffentlichungen des Instituts für Europäische Geschichte Mainz 32 (Wiesbaden, Germany: Franz Steiner Verlag, 1967), 38, 179 (quoted phrase on 38).

[81] *Ordo Cluniacensis*, pt. 1, chap. 24, in Herrgott, *Vetus disciplina monastica*, 197.

[82] *Liber tramitis*, bk. 2, chaps. 56, 61, in Albers, *Consuetudines monasticae*, 1:195, 203.

[83] This prayer is first mentioned in the *Booklet of the Dead of the Palatine*, from the second half of the ninth century (Frank, "Älteste erhaltene *Ordo defunctorum* der römischen Liturgie", 392).

[84] Text in Sodi and Flores Arcas, *Rituale Romanum: Editio princeps (1614)*, 105 (original pagination).

The ceremony was known as the "absolution of the dead", not an absolution in the same sense as that given to the living in the sacrament of penance but rather a solemnized plea by the Church for the forgiveness of the faithful departed one's sins.[85] The rubrics of the Cluniac *Liber tramitis* state:

> The major Mass having been completed, the prior should sound the bell three times, that all may assemble, and receive candles from the secretary, and perform the service of the dead; and all should stand around the bier....
>
> Two brothers ... should exclaim, *Lord, have mercy....* The priest, who is the hebdomadarian, should be vested in an alb with a stole and say (prayer): *Enter not into judgment with your servant, O Lord, for no man shall be accounted righteous by you, unless the remission of all his sins be granted him by you. Therefore, we beseech you, let not your just sentence oppress him, whom the true supplication of Christian faith commends to you, but, your grace succoring him, may he be worthy to escape the judgment of punishment, who while he lived was adorned with the sign of the Holy Trinity. You who live ...*[86] This having been completed, he should take the thurible and cense the major altar only and the body.... A second time he should make fragrant the altar and the deceased, ... and [a third time] he should cense the altar and the bier.[87]

The Cluniac *Liber tramitis* speaks of tolling the bells for the procession to follow.[88] The twelfth-century customary of the Benedictine abbey of Vallombrosa, Italy, directs that all the bells are to be tolled from when the funeral procession leaves the church until it reaches the tomb.[89] As for the arrangement of those in the procession, the *Liber tramitis* of Cluny states, "All should proceed in order. In the first place the holy water, the cross, the incense, and the two candlesticks. The children follow with their teachers. Joined to them should be the *conversi* [brothers], ... then the others, two by two, just as those before them. At the end, the priest and those who carry the bier."[90]

In regard to the conveying of the body of the deceased to the grave, as well as the earlier procession of the body from the deceased person's home to the church, Durandus notes that it was the custom in

The Interment Rite of Turku, Finland (1522)

---

[85] Fernand Cabrol, "Absoute", in Fernand Cabrol and Henri Leclercq, eds., *Dictionnaire d'archéologie chrétienne et de liturgie* (Paris: Librairie Letouzey et Ané, 1907–1953), vol. 1, cols. 200–206.

[86] The *Liber tramitis* gives only the incipit of this prayer; the complete text is here taken from the thirteenth-century Pontifical of the Roman Curia, in Andrieu, *Pontifical romain au moyen-âge*, 2:506.

[87] *Liber tramitis*, bk. 2, chap. 56, in Albers, *Consuetudines monasticae*, 1:195.

[88] Ibid.

[89] Customary of Vallombrosa, Italy, in Hallinger, *Consuetudines Cluniacensium antiquiores*, 371.

[90] *Liber tramitis*, bk. 2, chap. 56, in Albers, *Consuetudines monasticae*, 1:195.

certain places to make three stops along the way of the procession. These three stations, he adds, can be explained in various ways: as a sign of the deceased man's faith in the Trinity or as a symbol of the three days Christ spent "in the heart of the earth" (Mt 12:40).[91] The rubrics for the rite of interment given in a 1522 manual for the Scandinavian diocese of Turku, Finland,[92] which we shall present here, make no mention of multiple stops for the procession to the tomb, but one stop does seem to be indicated. Two psalms are assigned to the procession, each of which is followed by a prayer recited by the priest. It is likely that the procession paused as the priest said the first prayer after the first of the two psalms and that the procession resumed as the second psalm was said; the second prayer was probably said when the procession reached the grave:

> The priest should bring the body to the sepulcher, and he with the clerics should recite the psalm in going to the sepulcher:
>
> Psalm [117]: *Give praise to the Lord, for he is good: for his mercy endureth for ever. . . . I shall not die, but live: and shall declare the works of the Lord . . .*
>
> Antiphon: *Open to me the gates of justice; and having entered into them, I will praise the Lord. This is the gate of the Lord; the just shall enter into it* [cf. Ps 117:19–20].[93]
>
> Prayer: *With the affection of holy remembrance, dearest brethren, we make a commemoration of our dear one, whom the Lord has taken from the temptations of this world; we implore the mercy of our God, that he [the Lord] may vouchsafe to forgive all his offenses of dangerous recklessness and give him a placid and peaceful dwelling, that with the pardon of full forgiveness having been granted to him, whatever he has sinned in this world by his own or another's fault, he [the Lord] may blot out and entirely wipe away in his ineffable mercy and goodness. Through Christ . . .*[94]
>
> Antiphon: *I shall enter into the place of the wonderful tabernacle, even to the house of God* [cf. Ps 41:5].[95]

---

[91] Durandus, *Rationale* (CCCM 140b), bk. 7, chap. 35, no. 37, pp. 98–99.

[92] Text in Martti Parvio, ed., *Manuale seu exequiale Aboense, 1522*, facsimile ed., Suomen kirkkohistoriallisen seuran toimituksia / Finska kyrkohistoriska samfundets handlingar 115 (Helsinki: Societas Historiae Ecclesiasticae Fennica, 1980), fols. 43v–49r.

[93] This antiphon, *Aperite mihi*, is traceable to the late eighth century, when it appears in the Phillipps Sacramentary (the *Liber sacramentorum Augustodunensis*) of northeastern France, a Frankish adaptation of Rome's Gelasian Sacramentary; text in Heiming, *Liber sacramentorum Augustodunensis*, no. 1914, p. 242.

[94] This prayer, *Piae recordationis affectu*, is a variant of the oration *Pio recordationis affectu*, the latter traceable to the seventh-century Gelasian Sacramentary of Rome; text in Leo Cunibert Mohlberg, O.S.B., et al., eds., *Liber sacramentorum Romanae aeclesiae ordinis anni circuli (Sacramentarium Gelasianum)*, REDSMF 4 (Rome: Herder, 1960), no. 1607, p. 234. The variant used in the Turku rite is likewise found in the Dominican processional of 1545; see *Processionarium secundum ritum et morem Fratrum Predicatorum* (1545), fols. 106v–107r. Regarding the influence of the Dominican liturgy upon the Turku rite, see Parvio, *Manuale seu exequiale Aboense, 1522*, editor's introduction, 201–202.

[95] This antiphon, *Ingrediar in locum*, is first found in the Sacramentary of Rheinau (Rheinau 30), a text of northern French or Swiss origin dating from about 800 that is considered

[Psalm 41:] *As the hart panteth after the fountains of water; so my soul panteth after thee, O God. . . . When shall I come and appear before the face of God? . . .*

Let us pray. [Prayer:] *We implore your mercy, almighty eternal God, who have vouchsafed to create man to your image, that you may receive the soul of your servant, whom you have willed this day to be delivered from human matters and have tenderly and gently summoned unto you. Let not the shades of death prevail over him, or the chaos and gloom of darkness envelop him, but, having been placed in the bosom of your patriarch Abraham, divested of every blot of sins, may he rejoice to have attained a place of light, of consolation, that when the day of judgment shall have come you may grant him to be raised up with your saints and elect. Through Christ . . .*[96]

As can be seen in the above passage from the Turku rite, some of the psalms and antiphons selected for medieval funeral ceremonies are in the first person, implying that the Church is addressing to God the supplications that the departed soul would offer if he were able to pray for himself. But insofar as the soul in Purgatory is unable to do this (although he can pray for others), the Church speaks on his behalf. This interpretation is borne out by the rubrics of the funeral rite for Roman priests in the thirteenth-century Pontifical of the Roman Curia: "These things having been done, the antiphon *Open to me the gates of justice* should be said in the person of the deceased. . . . Likewise the antiphon *I shall enter into the place of the wonderful tabernacle* should be said in the person of the same. . . . Also in the person of the same is said the antiphon *This is my rest for ever and ever* [Ps 131:14]."[97]

The aspersion and incensation of the body at the grave are first mentioned in a text from the second half of the ninth century known as the *Booklet of the Dead of the Palatine*.[98] The customary of the monk Bernard for the French Benedictine abbey of Cluny (c. 1075) prescribes that when the body arrives at the place of burial holy water should be continually sprinkled into the grave, which should also be censed.[99] The twelfth-century Benedictine customary of Vallombrosa,

---

to be a redaction of Rome's Gelasian Sacramentary; text in Hänggi and Schönherr, *Sacramentarium Rhenaugiense*, no. 1340, p. 275.

[96] Parvio, *Manuale seu exequiale Aboense, 1522*, fols. 43v–44v. The prayer *Obsecramus misericordiam tuam* ("*We implore your mercy, almighty eternal God*") is traceable to Saint Benedict of Aniane's early ninth-century Frankish adaptation of Rome's Gregorian Sacramentary; see Deshusses, *Sacramentaire grégorien*, no. 1409, 1:460–461.

[97] Text in Andrieu, *Pontifical romain au moyen-âge*, 2:509–510. A similar rubric appears as a fourteenth-century insertion into the text of a thirteenth-century *ordo* for the funerals of popes and cardinals; see Marc Dykmans, S.J., ed., *Le cérémonial papal de la fin du moyen âge à la Renaissance*, vol. 2, BIHBR 25 (Brussels and Rome: Institut Historique Belge de Rome, 1981), 506.

[98] Manuscript: Vatican City, Biblioteca Apostolica Vaticana, Codex Palatinus Latinus 550, second half of the ninth century; text in Frank, "Älteste erhaltene *Ordo defunctorum* der römischen Liturgie", 396.

[99] *Ordo Cluniacensis*, pt. 1, chap. 24, in Herrgott, *Vetus disciplina monastica*, 197.

Italy, directs that as the tomb is opened, sprinkled with holy water, and censed, a boy chorister sings the above-cited antiphon, "*Open to me the gates of justice.... This is the gate of the Lord; the just shall enter into it.*" [100] In the funeral rite of Turku, Finland, the ceremonies at the grave begin with a prayer for blessing the tomb traceable to a ritual of Bobbio, Italy (c. 1000): [101]

> [Prayer:] *We beseech you, O Lord our God, that you may vouchsafe to bless + and sanctify this sepulcher and the body being placed in it, that it may give repose to the soul resting within it and be a safeguard and rampart against the savage arrows of the enemy. Through ...*
>
> The prayer having been said, the priest should sprinkle the body with blessed water, the grave afterward. Then he should incense both and say over the corpse placed into the grave:
>
> Antiphon: *This is my rest for ever and ever; here will I dwell, for I have chosen it* [Ps 131:14]. [102]
>
> Psalm [131]: *O Lord, remember David, and all his meekness.... But upon him shall my sanctification flourish.*
>
> *Let us pray.* [Prayer:] *O God, in the presence of whom the spirits of the dead live and in whom the souls of the elect, with the burden of the flesh having been removed, rejoice in full happiness: grant to us beseeching you that the soul of your servant who has been devoid of the earthly vision of this light may become a partaker in the eternal consolation of that light. Let not the torment of death draw him, or the distress of [any] horrid apparition attach to him, or punishing dread torture him, or the tight chain of the guilty bind him fast; but with the pardon of all his sins having been granted to him, may he obtain the joys of desired rest promised in return. Through ...* [103]

The priest now pleads for the forgiveness of the deceased man's sins with an absolution (in the nonsacramental sense of the term explained earlier in this chapter), the text of which is traceable to the funeral rite of the twelfth-century Roman Pontifical: [104] "*May the Lord Jesus Christ, who gave blessed Peter his Apostle and his other disciples the permission of binding and loosing, himself absolve you from every bond of sins, and*

---

[100] Customary of Vallombrosa, Italy, in Hallinger, *Consuetudines Cluniacensium antiquiores*, 371.

[101] Sicard, *Liturgie de la mort*, 233.

[102] This antiphon, *Haec requies mea*, is traceable to the late ninth century, when it appears in the Sacramentary of Saint Denis, a liturgical book of the Abbey of Saint Denis, near Paris (c. 875); see Jean Deshusses, ed., *Le sacramentaire grégorien: Ses principales formes d'après les plus anciens manuscrits*, vol. 3, SF 28 (Fribourg, Switzerland: Editions Universitaires Fribourg, 1982), 174.

[103] Parvio, *Manuale seu exequiale Aboense, 1522*, fol. 45r–45v. The prayer *Deus apud quem mortuorum spiritus vivunt* ("O God, in the presence of whom the spirits of the dead live ...") is traceable to Saint Benedict of Aniane's early ninth-century Frankish adaptation of Rome's Gregorian Sacramentary; see Deshusses, *Sacramentaire grégorien*, no. 1410, 1:461.

[104] Text in Michel Andrieu, ed., *Le Pontifical romain au moyen-âge*, vol. 1, *Le pontifical romain du XIIᵉ siècle*, ST 86 (Vatican City: Biblioteca Apostolica Vaticana, 1938), 285. This pontifical refers to the prayer as an "absolution".

so much as it is permitted to my frailty, may you be absolved before the tribunal of our Lord Jesus Christ, and have eternal life, and live unto ages of ages." [105]

Durandus observes that the body should be laid in the grave with the head to the west and the feet to the east, [106] a funeral custom prescribed two centuries earlier in the customary of the monk Bernard for the French Benedictine abbey of Cluny (c. 1075). [107] This orientation of the body corresponds to what is believed to have been the position of Christ's body in his tomb, as indicated by the archaeology of Jerusalem's Holy Sepulcher and the testimony of Saint Bede (see p. 451). Durandus does not mention this similitude to the burial of Christ but explains the position of the body in the grave as corresponding to the posture assumed for prayer, in which the supplicant faces east. [108] This follows when we consider that if one were to stand erect upon rising from the specified west-east position, he would, upon rising, face east, the direction from which, it is believed, Christ shall come to raise the dead and judge the world at the end of time. Durandus also observes that this posture in the grave implies that the deceased "is willing that from the setting of the sun he may hasten to the rising of the sun, from the world to eternity". [109] He adds, "And in whatever place a Christian may be buried outside a cemetery, always the cross ought to be put near to his head for denoting him to have been a Christian, and because the devil exceedingly fears this sign and dreads to approach a place endowed with the mark of the cross." [110]

The Turku manual describes the interment of the body thus:

The prayer having been completed, [the body] should be sprinkled. The priest should say: *From the earth you have molded me and have clothed me in flesh, my Redeemer; Lord, raise me on the last day.* [111] And he should drop soil upon the body. The psalm follows, being read while the body is buried:

[Psalm 138:] *Lord, thou hast proved me, and known me. . . . And see if there be in me the way of iniquity: and lead me in the eternal way.*

Eternal rest grant unto him, O Lord, and let perpetual light shine upon him. [112]

---

[105] Parvio, *Manuale seu exequiale Aboense, 1522*, fols. 45v–46r.

[106] Durandus, *Rationale* (CCCM 140b), bk. 7, chap. 35, no. 39, p. 99.

[107] *Ordo Cluniacensis*, pt. 1, chap. 24, in Herrgott, *Vetus disciplina monastica*, 197.

[108] Durandus, *Rationale* (CCCM 140b), bk. 7, chap. 35, no. 39, p. 99.

[109] Ibid.

[110] Ibid.

[111] This chant, *De terra plasmasti*, is traceable to about 875, when it appears in a sacramentary of the Abbey of Saint Amand, a monastery of northern France (manuscript: Stockholm, Sweden, Royal Library, MS 136, dating from c. 870–875), and in the Sacramentary of Saint Denis, a liturgical book of the Abbey of Saint Denis, near Paris (c. 875); see respectively Sicard, *Liturgie de la mort*, 120, and Deshusses, *Sacramentaire grégorien*, 3:174.

[112] Parvio, *Manuale seu exequiale Aboense, 1522*, fol. 46r–46v.

The symbolic casting of a small portion of soil upon the body within the grave, an action performed by the officiating priest as indicated in the above rubrics, first appears in the customary of the monk Bernard for the French Benedictine abbey of Cluny (c. 1075); the latter directs that after the grave is covered with a wooden lid, the priest, using a spade, tosses a little soil upon it.[113] In the *Booklet of the Dead of the Palatine* from the second half of the ninth century, the filling of the grave with earth is accompanied by corresponding chants, beginning with the antiphon "*From the earth I was fashioned, and to the earth I have returned*" (*De terra sum formatus*).[114] A century later, in the German Sacramentary of Fulda (c. 975), the filling of the grave begins with the antiphon used in the Turku rite, "*From the earth you have molded me*" (*De terra plasmasti*), and continues with Psalm 138.[115] In a twelfth-century pontifical of Avranches, France, we find the latter antiphon said by the priest as he tosses soil thrice over the body,[116] an early example of the use of this antiphon with the symbolic tossing of soil by the priest seen nearly four centuries later in a 1505 ritual of Strasbourg, France,[117] and in the 1522 Turku rite. The antiphon is based upon words from the Book of Job: "Thy hands have made me, and fashioned me wholly round about.... Thou hast made me as the clay, and thou wilt bring me into dust again.... Thou hast clothed me with skin and flesh" (Job 10:8–9, 11).[118]

In a twelfth-century ritual of Austria's Augustinian abbey of Saint Florian, there arose a different tradition for the tossing of soil into the grave: the Saint Florian rubrics direct that when the priest begins the covering of the body with soil, he is to say, "*Take, O earth, what is yours; you are earth, and into earth you shall turn.*"[119] These words, clearly resembling the versicle of Ash Wednesday for the imposition of ashes, led to the development of an impressive observance in southern

[113] *Ordo Cluniacensis*, pt. 1, chap. 24, in Herrgott, *Vetus disciplina monastica*, 197.

[114] Manuscript: Vatican City, Biblioteca Apostolica Vaticana, Codex Palatinus Latinus 550, in Frank, "Älteste erhaltene *Ordo defunctorum* der römischen Liturgie", 396.

[115] Quoted in Jerome Frank, O.S.B., "Geschichte des Trierer Beerdigungsritus", *Archiv für Liturgie Wissenschaft* 4, pt. 2 (1956): 297, footnote. The assignment of *De terra plasmasti* and Psalm 138 to the filling of the grave is also found in an early fifteenth-century *Agenda* of the Confraternity of Saint John the Evangelist for the German cathedral of Trier (ibid., 291, and 297, footnote).

[116] Martène, *De antiquis ecclesiae ritibus*, bk. 3, chap. 15, ordo 5, 2:387.

[117] *Agenda, sive Exequiale sacramentorum* (Strasbourg, France: Prüss, 1505; digitized text, Bayerische Staatsbibliothek, Munich, n.d.), fol. 39v. The latter text specifies a threefold tossing of soil into the grave with the antiphon *De terra plasmasti*. The use of *De terra plasmasti* with the priest's tossing of soil over the body also appears in a fifteenth-century ritual preserved in the cathedral library of Cologne, Germany (manuscript: Cologne, Dombibliothek Köln, Domhandschrift Codex 1099 [digitized text, Codices Electronici Ecclesiae Coloniensis, Erzbischöfliche Diözesan- und Dombibliothek, and Universität zu Köln, Cologne, Germany, n.d.], fol. 36ar).

[118] Sicard, *Liturgie de la mort*, 124.

[119] Text in Adolph Franz, ed., *Das Rituale von St. Florian aus dem zwölften Jahrhundert* (Freiburg im Breisgau, Germany: Herder, 1904), 94.

Germany and the Austrian Tyrol, exemplified by the rubrics for the filling of the grave in the 1493 *Obsequiale* of Brixen (what is now Bressanone, Italy):

> Here the body should be put down into the sepulcher, and the priest should say, *Take, O earth, what is yours; let God take what is his. The body was formed from the earth; the spirit was breathed into it from above.* Then the priest should sprinkle it with blessed water and say, *May God moisten him with the dew of Heaven and refresh his soul.* From thence he should incense it and say, *May God nourish his soul with the fragrance of Heaven.* Which having been done, the priest with a spade should thrice cast earth over the body, saying thrice, *Remember, man, that you are dust, and unto dust you shall return.* Then the others bury [the body] as is customary.[120]

This same rite utilizing the Ash Wednesday versicle *"Remember, man"* appears in two south German texts of the same period, the 1487 *Obsequiale* of Augsburg[121] and the 1491 *Obsequiale* of Regensburg.[122]

The concluding portion of the Turku interment rite is permeated with the serene hope of eternal salvation. The priest offers the following two prayers, both traceable to the seventh-century Gelasian Sacramentary of Rome:[123]

> *Let us pray, dearest brethren, for the soul of our dear one, whom the Lord has vouchsafed to free from the bond of this world, whose small body is yielded this day to burial, that the goodness of God may vouchsafe to place him in the bosom of Abraham, Isaac, and Jacob; that when the day of judgment shall have come, with him having been placed among your saints and elect at your right side, he may be raised up, our Lord Jesus Christ granting, who lives and reigns with the Father and the Holy Spirit, God, through all ages of ages. Amen.[124]*

> *Fulfilling the debt of mankind, the office of the burial of the faithful, in the customary manner, we faithfully entreat God, to whom all things are alive, that this body of our dear one, buried by us in infirmity, may rise in the manner of his saints, that he may grant his soul to be joined to his saints and faithful ones, with whom may he be worthy fully to enjoy indescribable glory*

---

[120] *Obsequiale Brixinense* (Augsburg, Germany: Erhard Ratdolt, 1493; digitized text, Bayerische Staatsbibliothek, Munich, 2009), fol. 69r. The passage quoted here is from the *Obsequiale's* rite for the burial of prelates "and other great and powerful men"; the rite for the burial of ordinary laymen in the *Obsequiale* is virtually identical (ibid., fol. 59v).

[121] *Obsequiale Augustense* (Augsburg, Germany: Erhard Ratdolt, 1487; digitized text, Bayerische Staatsbibliothek, Munich, 2008), fol. 76r–76v.

[122] *Obsequiale Ratisponense* (Nürnberg, Germany: Georg Stuchs, 1491; digitized text, Bayerische Staatsbibliothek, Munich, 2008), fols. 39v–40r.

[123] Mohlberg, Eizenhöfer, and Siffrin, *Liber sacramentorum,* nos. 1620, 1623, pp. 236, 237, respectively.

[124] Parvio, *Manuale seu exequiale Aboense, 1522,* fols. 46v–47r.

and eternal happiness, our Lord Jesus Christ granting, who lives and reigns with the Father and the Holy Spirit, God, through all ages of ages. Amen.[125]

The cantor now sings the following antiphon, *Clementissime Domine*, a chant traceable to a late eleventh- or early twelfth-century antiphonary of the Benedictine convent of San Sisto in Rome:[126] "*Most merciful Lord, who on behalf of our misery endured the torture of death from the hands of the wicked, free his soul from the abyss of hell and release him from the infernal ministers, O merciful One, and blot out all his sins in perpetual oblivion; and may the angels bring him to the gate of Paradise and deliver him to your light, that while his body is delivered to dust, they may lead him to eternity. Lord, have mercy upon the sinner.*"[127] The priest then says, "*From the gate of hell.* [Response:] *O Lord, deliver his soul.* [Priest:] *I believe to see the good things of the Lord.* [Response:] *In the land of the living.* [Priest:] *May they rest in peace.*"[128] Utilizing a Scandinavian variant of a formula from the seventh-century Gelasian Sacramentary of Rome, the priest, praying for the repose of the deceased, invokes the intercession of the Blessed Virgin Mary and the saints, including two local saints of Scandinavia (Eric of Sweden and Henry of Uppsala), to which he adds the prayers of the departed one's family in attendance at his burial:

> *May the devout supplication of Mary, the holy Mother of God; and of your blessed Apostles Peter and Paul; and of the blessed martyrs Lawrence, Eric, and Henry; and of all the saints, and of the family present, give you satisfaction, O Lord our God, for the soul of your servant our brother, that he may obtain the pardon of all his sins, which we beseech you; suffer him not to be tormented in the flames of Gehenna, whom you have redeemed in the precious blood of your Son, our Lord Jesus Christ. Through . . .*[129]

The interment rite concludes on a joyful note with the recitation of Psalm 145: *Praise the Lord, O my soul. . . . The Lord lifteth up them that are cast down. . . . The Lord shall reign for ever: thy God, O Sion, unto generation and generation.*[130]

In southern Germany and the Austrian Tyrol, there existed an additional custom for the conclusion of the burial rite, as described in the rubrics of the 1493 *Obsequiale Brixinense* of Brixen in the Austrian Tyrol (what is now Bressanone, Italy). Before leaving the grave, the priest would take the spade he had used earlier for the ceremonial

---

[125] Ibid., fol. 48r.

[126] Manuscript: Rome, Biblioteca Vallicelliana, Codex C.5, late eleventh or early twelfth century, fol. 310r (as indicated by the Gregorian chant online database Cantus, http://cantusdatabase.org).

[127] Parvio, *Manuale seu exequiale Aboense, 1522*, fol. 48r–48v.

[128] Ibid., fol. 48v. Regarding the origin of the versicles *A porta inferi* and *Credo videre bona*, see pp. 535–536 above.

[129] Ibid., fols. 48v–49r. For the original formula in the Gelasian Sacramentary of Rome, see Mohlberg, Eizenhöfer, and Siffrin, *Liber sacramentorum*, no. 1659, p. 242.

[130] Parvio, *Manuale seu exequiale Aboense, 1522*, fol. 49r.

tossing of soil into the grave and would make the sign of the cross with it in three places over the sepulcher: first over the head of the deceased, then over his chest, and then over his feet. While making these three signs of the cross, the priest says, *"May the sign + of the Savior, our Lord Jesus + Christ, be signed + over you, who in this form redeemed you, lest he suffer the striking angel to enter forever. Peace be with you. In the name of the Father, and of the Son, and of the Holy Spirit. Amen."* The priest then adds, *"May your soul and the souls of all the faithful departed, through the great mercy of God, rest with Christ in peace. Amen."* [131] This same rite, albeit in a slightly simpler form, was also observed in the German sees of Augsburg (1487), Regensburg (1491), and Freising (1493), as well as in Salzburg, Austria (1511).[132]

Papal Funeral Rites

In view of the wide public response to the funeral rites of Pope Blessed John Paul II in April 2005, we shall conclude this chapter with an account of the papal funeral rites as they existed in the late fourteenth century, described in a ceremonial compiled by the papal master of ceremonies Pierre Ameil (+1403; completed by Pierre Assalbit, 1435–1441).[133] In the room where the pontiff has died, his body is clothed in red vestments and laid out upon a bier or bed with a mattress covered in red silk and overlaid with two cloth-of-gold sheets, with the coats of arms of the pope and the Church on a black or hyacinth-colored silk cloth round about the bier. The head of the pontiff rests upon a pillow covered in gold silk; at the opposite end of the bier, near the pope's feet, two of his skullcaps or hats are placed upon a second silk pillow with gold cords and silk tufts. Before the pontiff's body two large torches and a sufficient number of small candles are kept burning.[134] Thereafter the deceased pope is borne in a procession to the papal chapel, with at least twenty-five lit torches preceding the bier. After the procession reaches the chapel, the Office of the Dead is recited, and the body is sprinkled with holy water and censed. Mourners keep a continuous vigil through the night before the pontiff's body, as twenty-five torches burn before and around the bier.[135]

On the day of the funeral Mass, the body of the pope is carried in procession to the church where Mass is to be celebrated. There it is placed within a "castle of dolors" (an elaborate catafalque of

---

[131] *Obsequiale Brixinense* (1493), fols. 60r, 72r (quoted texts on 60r).

[132] *Obsequiale Augustense* (1487), fol. 77r; *Obsequiale Ratisponense* (1491), fol. 40r; *Obsequiale Frisingense* (Augsburg, Germany: Erhard Ratdolt, 1493; digitized text, Bayerische Staatsbibliothek, Munich, 2008), fol. 20v; *Agenda secundum rubricam ecclesie cathedralis Saltzeburgensis* (Basel, Switzerland: Jacobus de Pfortzhein, 1511; digitized text, Bayerische Staatsbibliothek, Munich, 2007), fol. 87v.

[133] Text in Marc Dykmans, S.J., ed., *Le cérémonial papal de la fin du moyen âge à la Renaissance*, vol. 4, BIHBR 27 (Brussels and Rome: Institut Historique Belge de Rome, 1985), 219–224.

[134] Ibid., 219–220.

[135] Ibid., 220, 222.

cloth-draped wood), with a torch at each of the four corners of this structure, and a fifth torch over the middle of the "castle". Additionally, two hundred torches as well as "an abundance of candles" are placed round about the castle of dolors, all of which are to be lit before Mass begins.[136] Following the Requiem Mass, which is celebrated by one of the cardinals, there takes place a special fourfold version of the funeral rite of aspersion, incensation, and absolution of the deceased,[137] a Roman practice traceable to the thirteenth-century Pontifical of the Roman Curia.[138] The ceremonial of Ameil does not provide detailed rubrics for this particular ceremony, but it would have been essentially the same as that utilized in the funeral rite of cardinals, which Ameil describes at length in one of his later additions to his ceremonial:

> The Mass having been completed, he who performs the office, his chasuble put aside, with his ministers, should approach with a thurible and blessed water near the head of the deceased outside the castle [of dolors], and he begins simply [i.e., without singing], with his miter put aside, *Enter not into judgment with your servant, O Lord* ...[139] The prayer having been said, actually completed, the cantors sing, *Assist him, O saints of God* ...[140] Which having been sung, he says, *Lord, have mercy*, and the body he censes and sprinkles with blessed water....
>
> Then four cardinal-priests approach, vested with copes and miters, [and] albs and stoles; and [the responsory] *Remember not my sins, O Lord, when you shall have come to judge the world by fire*[141] having been sung, the older [i.e., the oldest cardinal] says the prayer that is pleasing to him, after the Our Father, as before, and censes, etc. Afterward is sung [the responsory] *Remember me, O God, for my life is wind. Let not human sight look upon me.* [Verse:] *Out of the depths I have cried to thee, O Lord; Lord, hear my voice. Let not* ...[142]
>
> Which having been done, another cardinal, who is the next to last, in the same way censes and says another prayer.

---

[136] Ibid., 222.

[137] Ibid., 223–224.

[138] Andrieu, *Pontifical romain au moyen-âge*, 2:506–507.

[139] The complete text of the prayer *Non intres* is given earlier in this chapter (p. 607).

[140] The complete text of the responsory *Subvenite sancti Dei* is given earlier in this chapter (p. 598).

[141] The complete text of the responsory *Ne recorderis* is given on p. 537 of the present work. It first appears in a text from the second half of the ninth century, the aforementioned *Booklet of the Dead of the Palatine* (manuscript: Vatican City, Biblioteca Apostolica Vaticana, Codex Palatinus Latinus 550), in a portion of the text not included in the earlier-cited edition of Father Jerome Frank; see Knud Ottosen, *The Responsories and Versicles of the Latin Office of the Dead* (Aarhus, Denmark: Aarhus University Press, 1993), 399.

[142] The ceremonial of Ameil gives only the incipit of the responsory *Memento mei, Deus*; the complete text is here taken from Hésbert, *Corpus antiphonalium officii*, no. 7143, 4:286. This chant is first found in the Antiphonary of Compiègne (France, c. 870); see Hésbert, *Corpus antiphonalium officii*, 1:386.

Immediately thereafter another cardinal, who stands by the other side, who says the prayer in the next place, similarly censes, just as the others have done and said, also [saying] the prayer that is pleasing to him.

Then the last cardinal does likewise.

Which having been done, [the responsory] *Deliver me, O Lord, from eternal death*[143] is sung.

Which having been sung, he who performs the office censes similarly as before, etc., and says the last prayer, namely *Absolve, we beseech you, O Lord, the soul of your servant, that dead to the world, he may be alive to you; and whatever things he has committed in conduct on account of the frailty of human flesh, most mercifully blot out with the forgiveness of your clemency. Through* . . .[144]

Shortly before the April 8, 2005, funeral Mass of Pope Blessed John Paul II, a veil was placed over the pontiff's face prior to the closing of the coffin. Although there is no mention of this practice in the papal funeral rubrics of the ceremonial of Pierre Ameil, it is found in Ameil's instructions for the funeral of a cardinal, specified in reference to the vesting of the deceased prelate's body: "his face veiled with a veil of silk".[145] In the case of Pope John Paul II's burial, this practice is eloquently explained in the introductory locution with which the cardinal chamberlain (Eduardo Cardinal Martínez Somalo) began the rite, a locution taken from the most recent ceremonial book for papal funerals, the *Ordo exsequiarum Romani pontificis*, published in 2000 and first used for the funeral of Pope John Paul II: "*Reverently we shall cover the face of the deceased, supported by the hope of his being able to contemplate and delight in the face of the Father, in the company of the Blessed Virgin Mary and all the saints.*"[146] The spreading of a white silk veil over the pontiff's face[147] was preceded by the following prayer, said by the cardinal chamberlain:

Almighty eternal God, Lord of the living and the dead, we hope and believe the life of the supreme pontiff John Paul to be hidden in you now.

May his face, to which the light of this world has passed away, be perpetually illuminated with the true light that flows from you, its unfailing source.

---

[143] The complete text of the responsory *Libera me, Domine* is given on p. 531 of the present work.

[144] Additions to the ceremonial of Pierre Ameil, in Dykmans, *Cérémonial papal de la fin du moyen âge à la Renaissance*, 4:249–250. The final prayer, *Absolve, quaesumus, Domine* . . . *absterge*, first appears in the thirteenth-century Pontifical of the Roman Curia, from which the complete text of this oration is here taken; see Andrieu, *Pontifical romain au moyen-âge*, 2:504.

[145] Text in Dykmans, *Cérémonial papal de la fin du moyen âge à la Renaissance*, 4:247.

[146] Translated from the Latin text in *Ordo exsequiarum Romani pontificis*, chap. 2, no. 95, p. 135, © 2000 Libreria Editrice Vaticana.

[147] Ibid., no. 99, p. 137.

May his face, which has searched through your ways that he might show them to the Church, see your paternal face.

May his face, which departs from our sight, contemplate your beauty and commend his flock to you, the eternal Shepherd. Who lives and reigns through all ages of ages.[148]

---

[148] Ibid., no. 98, pp. 135, 137.

22 Blessings

Bless, O Lord, the entrance of our feet and this vessel of your servants, and bless the captain and those sailing with him, even as you vouchsafed to bless the ark of Noah, walking on the waves of the flood, and as you blessed Abraham, Isaac, and Jacob. Extend, O Lord, your right hand to your servants, even as you extended it to Peter walking upon the sea; give to them, O Lord, health of body and your mercy, and vouchsafe to bring them unharmed to the port of salvation.

From "Blessing of Ships and Small Boats"
in a ritual of central Italy, fifteenth century[1]

Prayers for the blessing of both persons and things, apart from the blessings imparted in the celebration of the sacraments, appeared at an early date in the history of the Church. These blessings were rooted in the practices of Christ himself while on earth. Thus, in regard to the blessing of persons, we read of Christ blessing children (Mk 10:16) and at his Ascension blessing the Apostles (Lk 24:50–51). The blessing of objects can be seen in Christ's blessings of the bread and fish with which he miraculously fed the multitudes on more than one occasion (Mt 14:19; Mk 6:41; 8:6–7; Lk 9:16). We have already noted in chapter 2 an early example of the Church's blessing of objects: the fourth-century blessing of oil and water from the *Euchology of Serapion of Thmuis* (p. 95). In chapter 20 we examined the Church's rite of blessing consecrated virgins that had emerged by the fourth century. Over the course of the centuries that followed, a wide range of blessing rites developed as the Church sought to sanctify all the vocations, labors, and activities of her children, in fulfillment of Saint Paul's admonition "Therefore, whether you eat or drink, or whatsoever else you do, do all to the glory of God" (1 Cor 10:31). From the innumerable examples that could be presented, we have chosen two regarding the blessing of persons: the blessing of unborn children and their mothers, and

---

[1] Manuscript: Vatican City, Biblioteca Apostolica Vaticana, Codex Vaticanus Barberinus Latinus 412, fifteenth century, in Adolph Franz, *Die kirchlichen Benediktionen im Mittelalter* (Freiburg im Breisgau, Germany, 1909; repr., Graz, Austria: Akademische Druck—U. Verlagsanstalt, 1960), 1:629 (complete rite on 628–629).

**The Blessing of
Unborn Children
in the Womb and
Their Mothers**

the blessing of knights. As for the blessing of things, we have chosen the rite of invoking the protection of God from the dangers of storms: a blessing of the clouds.

From the first century onward, the Church has consistently professed the personhood of unborn children, beginning with the categorical condemnation of abortion contained in the *Didache* ("You shall not kill an unborn child or murder a newborn infant").[2] This perennial belief led to the offering of prayers for the protection of unborn children and their mothers from the dangers that sometimes arise during pregnancy and childbirth. The fifth-century Syrian ecclesiastical historian Theodoret of Cyrrhus (c. 393–c. 457) provides early testimony to this, relating how his own life in the womb of his mother was saved by divine intervention. When after thirteen years of marriage Theodoret's mother was at last pregnant with her first child, having long hoped and prayed for a baby, she was threatened by the imminent danger of miscarriage in the fifth month of her pregnancy. The desperate mother thereupon sought spiritual assistance from the holy hermit Macedonius. Learning of her plight, the hermit blessed water and gave it to her, saying, "Drink this water, and you shall perceive the divine remedy." After drinking the blessed water, the mother was freed of the danger of miscarriage and bore her child to term, a boy who years later would recount the episode in his work the *Religious History*.[3] Over the centuries that followed, similar incidents were recorded in the annals of the saints. A woman suffering a difficult and very prolonged labor spanning several days was immediately brought to a safe delivery of her son after drinking water blessed and sent to her by the famed Cistercian abbot Saint Bernard of Clairvaux (+1153).[4] The Irish bishop Saint Malachy (+1148) similarly assisted another expectant mother in danger of losing her child during a difficult labor.[5]

Respect for the life and spiritual needs of the unborn child is manifested in the *Instructions* that the bishop and liturgist William Durandus (+1296) composed around 1294 for his diocese of Mende, France. He directs that if a woman dies during pregnancy, the unborn child within her womb should be baptized if the baby is still alive. Further, when in the course of delivering a child a midwife encounters the tragic case of a baby who cannot be fully delivered out of the womb, with only the head or some other major portion of the body emerging, she

---

[2] *Didache*, chap. 2, no. 2, in Francis X. Glimm, Joseph M.-F. Marique, S.J., and Gerald G. Walsh, S.J., trans., *The Apostolic Fathers*, Fathers of the Church 1 (New York: Cima, 1947), 172.

[3] Theodoret of Cyrrhus, *Religious History*, chap. 13, PG 82, cols. 1407–1410 (Greek text with Latin translation).

[4] *Vita prima* (biography of Saint Bernard), bk. 4, chap. 4, PL 185, col. 334.

[5] Saint Bernard, *Vita sanctae Malachiae*, chap. 6, in John van Bolland et al., eds., *Acta sanctorum* (Antwerp, Belgium, 1643–; repr., Paris: Victor Palmé, 1863–1940), November, vol. 2, pt. 1, 158.

is instructed to baptize the partially born child by pouring water over the baby's head or body while reciting the essential words of the sacrament, "*I baptize you, in the name of the Father, and of the Son, and of the Holy Spirit.*" [6]

The medieval Church came to provide to expectant mothers a regular and readily accessible means of seeking divine protection for their unborn children and themselves in the form of blessing rites that could be administered by parish priests. A tenth-century ritual from Mainz, Germany, contains the following simple blessing for a woman in labor: "*O God, who from the beginning made man and gave him a helpmate similar to himself, that they should increase and multiply upon the earth, grant your mercy to this your maidservant* [Name], *that she may bring forth favorably and without sorrow.*" [7] In this text, the unborn child is not directly mentioned but implicitly shares in the blessing bestowed upon his mother. In a far-more-developed blessing rite for pregnancy of fourteenth-century French origin, both the unborn child and his expectant mother are explicitly and repeatedly mentioned; this rite is found as a fourteenth-century addendum in six manuscripts of the late thirteenth-century pontifical that William Durandus had compiled for his diocese of Mende, France. In this French ceremony, the focus of the blessing is shifted to the child, as indicated by its very title: "Blessing of the Offspring in the Womb of a Mother"—that is, the blessing of an unborn child.[8] Three of the manuscripts containing this ceremony, including the earliest manuscript, provide an introductory rubric specifying that the bishop or priest giving the blessing should be vested in a stole and should stand facing the expectant mother, who is to remain kneeling and facing the altar.[9] The rite begins with a series of versicles and responses in which the priest prays for the mother and the child together:

Verse: *Save your handmaid and her child.*
Response: *Trusting in you, my God.*
Verse: *Be to them, O Lord, a tower of strength.*
Response: *In the face of the enemy.*
Verse: *May the enemy effect nothing in them.*
Response: *And the son of iniquity not proceed to harm them.*
Verse: *Send them, O Lord, help from on high.*
Response: *And from Sion defend them.*[10]

---

[6] Text in J. Berthelé, "Les instructions et constitutions de Guillaume Durand le Spéculateur", in *Académie des Sciences et Lettres de Montpellier: Memoires de la Section des Lettres*, 2nd series, vol. 3 (Montpellier, 1900–1907), 15.

[7] Manuscript: Vienna, Hofbibliothek, Codex Vindobonensis Palatinus 1888, tenth century, quoted in Franz, *Kirchlichen Benediktionen im Mittelalter*, 2:190.

[8] Text in Michel Andrieu, ed., *Le pontifical romain au moyen-âge*, vol. 3, *Le pontifical de Guillaume Durand*, ST 88 (Vatican City: Biblioteca Apostolica Vaticana, 1940), 678.

[9] Ibid., 679, footnote.

[10] Ibid., 679.

After reciting the Collect from the Mass of Trinity Sunday,[11] the priest offers a prayer for the present and future well-being of the unborn child:

> *Lord God, Creator of all things, mighty and fearsome, just and merciful, who alone are good and holy, King alone excelling, alone just, almighty, and eternal, you who liberate Israel from every evil, who have created all the fathers [and] the elect and have sanctified them with the gift of the Holy Spirit, manifestly Jeremiah, John the Baptist, and in particular the glorious Virgin in the womb after conception* [actually from conception, see footnote],[12] *beyond all passing of time, and others according to various degrees, before they were born in the usual manner: accept the sacrifice of a contrite heart, we beseech you, and the fervent desire of your afflicted maidservant humbly imploring for the preserving of her weak child, whom you have given her to conceive; and protect and sancti + fy your allotted possession with the immense blessing of your grace, and defend [him] from every deceit and injury of the cruel enemy, as well as from any cruel and wicked calamities, that with your hand delivering [him], he may come unharmed to the very happy light of the present life, and be continually devoted to you in all things, and be worthy finally to obtain everlasting life. Through Christ* . . .[13]

The priest now sprinkles the expectant mother with holy water and recites Psalm 66 ("*May God have mercy on us, and bless us* . . ."). After a further series of versicles and responses, the priest concludes the rite with a prayer for the mother and her child; the "dwelling" that the prayer refers to is undoubtedly the family's home, which would seem to indicate that the rite was sometimes performed within the home: "*Visit, we beseech you, O Lord, this entire dwelling, and drive far away from it and your maidservant present every snare of the enemy; and may your holy angels dwell in it, that they may preserve her and her child in peace. And may your blessing be ever upon them. Save them, almighty God, and grant your perpetual light to them. Through* . . ."[14]

The Blessing of a New Knight

The medieval transformation of the originally secular office of knight-hood into a vocation sanctified by the special blessings of the Church arose in parallel with the development of a rich tradition imparting to

---

[11] For this Collect, see the 1570 *Missale Romanum*, in Manlio Sodi and Achille Maria Triacca, eds., *Missale Romanum: Editio princeps (1570)*, facsimile ed., MLCT 2 (Vatican City: Libreria Editrice Vaticana, © 1998), 395 (new pagination).

[12] In the case of the Blessed Virgin Mary, according to the infallible doctrine of the Immaculate Conception, she was sanctified from the first moment of her conception (*Catechism of the Catholic Church*, English ed. [Vatican City: Libreria Editrice Vaticana, © 1994; Washington, D.C.: United States Catholic Conference, 1994], nos. 491–492, pp. 123–124). At the time that this prayer was composed, the doctrine of the Immaculate Conception had not yet been defined by the Church.

[13] Andrieu, *Pontifical romain au moyen-âge*, 3:679.

[14] Ibid., 680.

the image of the knight a deep religious symbolism, prompted in large part by the spiritual quest of the Crusades to recover the Holy Land. This symbolism had its Christian origin in Saint Paul's use of military imagery to explain the way of perfection as a spiritual battle against the devil (Eph 6:11–17). The imagery of knighthood figures prominently in the spirituality of Saint Francis of Assisi (+1226),[15] as well as in the allegorical legends of the Holy Grail. And as we have already seen, the priest celebrating Mass was viewed by medieval liturgists as going to the altar armored in his vestments to do battle with the devil (see pp. 23–24 above); thus, in his book on chivalry, Blessed Raymond Lull (+1316) calls the priest a "knight spiritual".[16]

In the context of this latter analogy, it is no surprise that the image of the noble and virtuous knight was utilized as a symbol of Christ himself, the Divine Knight. Hence the Third Order Dominican and mystic Saint Catherine of Siena (+1380) speaks of Christ as a knight who "on this field of battle ... has fought and vanquished the demons", with his scourged body as his coat of armor, the crown of thorns as his helmet, his nail-pierced hands as gauntlets, his nailed feet as spurs, and the lance that pierced his side as his sword.[17] In another letter, she addresses Christ thus: "O sweet and loving Knight, you regarded neither your death nor your life nor your humiliation.... Your death has destroyed our death. Love is the cause of it, you see."[18] Over a century earlier, a book written for English anchoresses known as the *Ancren Riwle* (early thirteenth century) similarly presents Christ as the Divine Knight, casting the knight's shield as a symbol of Christ's body stretched upon the Cross: "After the death of a valiant knight, men hang up his shield high in the church, to his memory. So is this shield, that is the crucifix, set up in the church, in such a place in which it may be soonest seen, thereby to remind us of Jesus Christ's knighthood, which he practiced on the cross."[19]

The medieval custom of a formal investiture rite for recruits to the knighthood emerged around the tenth century originally in the secular

---

[15] Johannes Jörgensen, *Saint Francis of Assisi: A Biography*, Image Books (Garden City, N.Y.: Doubleday, 1955), 30–31, 140–141, 195.

[16] Blessed Raymond Lull, *The Book of the Ordre of Chyvalry or Knyghthode: Westmynstre, William Caxton (1484)*, The English Experience 778 (Norwood, N.J.: Walter J. Johnson; Amsterdam: Theatrum Orbis Terrarum, 1976), sig. d6v (here and in all the quotations from Lull that follow we have modernized the spelling of Caxton's late fifteenth-century English translation). Lull also observes, "The office of priesthood and [that] of chivalry have great concordance" (ibid., sig. d7r).

[17] Saint Catherine of Siena, *Letter 260*, to the prisoners of Siena (March 26, 1377), in Niccolò Tommaseo and Piero Misciattelli, eds., *Le lettere di s. Caterina da Siena* (Siena, Italy: Libreria Editrice Giuntini e Bentivoglio, 1913–1922), 4:140.

[18] Saint Catherine of Siena, *Letter 204*, to Friar Bartolomeo Dominici, in Asciano (Lent 1376), in Tommaseo and Misciattelli, *Lettere di s. Caterina da Siena*, 3:239.

[19] *Ancren Riwle*, pt. 7, as rendered into modern English by James Morton, trans., *The Nun's Rule, Being the Ancren Riwle* (London: Chatto and Windus, 1924), 297–298 (passage quoted); for the complete knighthood analogy given in this text, see ibid., 294–298.

setting of a battlefield or the hall of a king or a noble. The earliest known feature of this ceremony was the girding of the sword upon the waist of the candidate.[20] The Christianization of this secular institution was already under way by the eleventh century, with several texts from this period attesting to the blessing of new knights[21] or the blessing of the ensigns they carried into battle.[22] Blessings for the weapons of knighthood arose even earlier: prayers for the blessing of a "sword newly girded on" appear in the tenth-century Romano-Germanic Pontifical.[23] Following the inauguration of the Crusades in 1095, knighthood was fully transformed into a distinctly Christian institution during the twelfth century.[24] This transformation reached its zenith in the founding of religious-military orders of knights, beginning in 1118 with the Templars, for whom Saint Bernard of Clairvaux composed both a monastic rule[25] and a discourse on knighthood.[26] In a book of private revelations, the Swedish widow, religious, and mystic Saint Bridget (+1373) tells of Christ describing to her the manner by which he wants men to be knighted—a religious ceremony in which they promise to defend the Catholic faith and to obey the Church's hierarchy, with the rite culminating in Holy Communion.[27]

The Christian meaning of knighthood is exemplified by the interpretation of this vocation that the aforementioned Spanish scholar and Third Order Franciscan Blessed Raymond Lull offers in his late thirteenth-century work *Le libre del orde de cauayleria* (The book of the order of chivalry); thus he says of the role of a knight, "The office of

[20] Robert Ackerman, "The Knighting Ceremonies in the Middle English Romances", *Speculum* 19 (1944): 288–289.

[21] Ibid., 291. The English-born monk and ecclesiastical historian Orderic Vitalis (+c. 1143) asserts that Lanfranc, the archbishop of Canterbury (+1089), knighted William the Conqueror's son Henry, the future English king Henry I, investing him with his coat of armor, placing his helmet upon his head, and girding him with the cincture of knighthood "in the name of the Lord"; see Orderic Vitalis, *Ecclesiastical History*, bk. 8, chap. 1, in Marjorie Chibnall, ed. and trans., *The Ecclesiastical History of Orderic Vitalis*, vol. 4, *Books VII and VIII*, Oxford Medieval Texts (Oxford: Clarendon, 1973), 120 (Latin text quoted and translated by permission of Oxford University Press). Another English ecclesiastical historian of the period, William of Malmesbury (+c. 1143), states in his work *De gestis regum Anglorum* (bk. 4, no. 305), that Lanfranc had knighted Henry's brother and predecessor on the English throne, William Rufus, who became King William II in 1087; text in William Stubbs, ed., *Willelmi Malmesbiriensis monachi: De gestis regum Anglorum, libri quinque; Historiae novellae, libri tres*, Rerum Britannicarum medii aevi scriptores 90 (London: Eyre and Spottiswoode, 1889), 2:360.

[22] Franz, *Kirchlichen Benediktionen im Mittelalter*, 2:289–290, 297.

[23] Text in Cyrille Vogel and Reinhard Elze, eds., *Le pontifical romano-germanique du dixième siècle*, vol. 2, ST 227 (Vatican City: Biblioteca Apostolica Vaticana, 1963), 379.

[24] Franz, *Kirchlichen Benediktionen im Mittelalter*, 2:289–290.

[25] The complete text of the *Regula militum Templariorum* is given in Lucas Holstenius, *Codex regularum monasticarum et canonicarum* (Augsburg, Germany, 1759; repr., Graz, Austria: Akademische Druck—U. Verlagsanstalt, 1957), 2:431–440.

[26] Saint Bernard, *De laude novae militiae*, PL 182, cols. 921–940.

[27] Saint Bridget of Sweden, *Revelations*, bk. 2, chap. 13; text (English translation) in Denis Searby, trans., *The Revelations of St. Birgitta of Sweden*, vol. 1, *Liber caelestis, Books I–III* (Oxford: Oxford University Press, 2006), 207–208.

a knight is to maintain and defend the holy Catholic faith."[28] He sees symbolism in everything a knight uses: his sword is shaped in likeness to the Cross of Christ, his spear represents truth, the head of the spear represents truth's strength over falsehood, and his helmet represents the modesty he must possess.[29] His horse symbolizes the "nobleness of courage", and the horse's saddle "surety of courage", which "makes a knight to be in the front of the battle".[30] The horse's head covering serves as a reminder that as the head of the horse is in front of the knight when riding, reason must precede all that a knight does, lest he use his arms without just cause.[31] Evidence from both historical records and medieval romances suggests that the age for the promotion of candidates, known as squires, to knighthood ranged largely from fifteen to twenty-one.[32] Raymond Lull enjoins squires to prepare themselves for knighthood by receiving the sacraments of penance and the Holy Eucharist; here we give Lull's words as they were rendered into late fifteenth-century English by the early printer William Caxton: "In the beginning that a squire ought to enter into the order of chivalry, it behooveth him that he confess himself of his defaults that he hath done against God and ought to receive chivalry in intention that in the same he serve our Lord God, which is glorious. And if he be clean out of sin, he ought to receive his Savior."[33]

The medieval definition of knights as defenders of the faith and of the holy sanctuaries of God stemmed from their role in the Crusades, both in the Holy Land, where Jerusalem's Church of the Holy Sepulcher had been virtually leveled in 1009 upon the command of the Egyptian caliph al-Hakim bi-Amr Allah,[34] and in Spain, where the pilgrimage shrine of Compostela had been destroyed by the Moors in 997.[35] The twelfth-century French poem *Chanson d'Antioch* tells of the dubbing of a knight (the conferral of knighthood) being carried out at the Holy Sepulcher of Christ in Jerusalem;[36] there are numerous historical instances of the conferral of knighthood at the Holy Sepulcher dating from the fourteenth and fifteenth centuries.[37] The famed commander of the First Crusade, Godfrey de Bouillon (+1100),

---

[28] Lull, *Book of the Ordre of Chyvalry or Knyghthode*, sig. b3v.

[29] Ibid., sigs. d7r–d8r, e2v.

[30] Ibid., sig. e2v and e2r, respectively.

[31] Ibid., sig. e3r.

[32] Jean Flori, "Les origines de l'adoubement chevaleresque: Etude des remises d'armes et du vocabulaire qui les exprime dans les sources historiques latines jusqu'au début du XIIIe siècle", *Traditio* 35 (1979): 214–215, 260–263; Karl Treis, *Die Formalitäten des Ritterschlags in der altfranzösischen Epik* (Berlin: Gustav Schade, 1887), 18–26, 115; Ackerman, "Knighting Ceremonies in the Middle English Romances", 296.

[33] Lull, *Book of the Ordre of Chyvalry or Knyghthode*, sig. d3v.

[34] Martin Biddle, *The Tomb of Christ* (Phoenix Mill, England: Sutton, 1999), 72–73.

[35] Donald Matthew, *Atlas of Medieval Europe* (New York: Facts on File, 1992), 71.

[36] Maurice Keen, *Chivalry* (New Haven: Yale University Press, 1984), 79.

[37] Walter Clifford Meller, *A Knight's Life in the Days of Chivalry* (London: T. Werner Laurie, 1924), 44; Keen, *Chivalry*, 78–79.

having been chosen against his will to be king of the re-Christianized Jerusalem, accepted only on the condition that he would never bear the title of king, preferring simply to be called "advocate of the Holy Sepulcher"; he refused to wear a crown out of deference to Christ, who had been given a crown of thorns in the Holy City.[38]

The medieval perception of the knight as a defender of "the sense of the sacred" shaped medieval legends of knighthood, particularly those of the Holy Grail, the chalice of the Last Supper. In Richard Wagner's 1882 music-drama *Parsifal*, an operatic adaptation of Wolfram von Essenbach's thirteenth-century epic of the same name (an opera so inherently Christian in content that Wagner's contemporary and erstwhile friend the atheist Friedrich Nietzsche bitterly denounced him for having prostrated himself at the foot of the Cross),[39] the innocent and chaste young knight Parsifal reveals to the Magdalene-like sinner Kundry his vocation to restore the holiness of the shrine of the Holy Grail and of its consecrated guardians, the Knights of the Holy Grail, by recovering from wicked hands the relic of the Holy Lance, the lance that had pierced the side of Christ, which had been stolen from the knights:

> The Savior's lament I hear there,
> the lament, ah! The lamentation
> from His profaned sanctuary:
> "Redeem Me, rescue Me
> from hands defiled by sin!"
> Thus rang the divine lament
> in terrible clarity in my soul.[40]

An early fourteenth-century manuscript of the thirteenth-century Pontifical of the Roman Curia contains a rite for the conferral of knighthood at the Basilica of Saint Peter in Rome that begins with the instruction that the knighthood candidate "ought to spend the night in prayers in the same basilica and remain in any of the chapels that he shall have regarded to have chosen".[41] The custom of candidates

---

[38] Louis Brehier, "Godfrey of Bouillon", in *The Catholic Encyclopedia* (New York: Appleton, 1907–1912), 6:625; M. Parisse, "Godefroy de Bouillon", in *Dictionnaire d'histoire et de géographie ecclésiastiques* (Paris: Letouzey et Ané, 1912–), vol. 21, cols. 389–390.

[39] The opera commentator Father Owen Lee, summarizing Nietzsche's angry reaction to *Parsifal*, tells of Nietzsche denouncing Wagner for having "sunk at the foot of the cross" in composing *Parsifal*; see M. Owen Lee, *The Operagoer's Guide: One Hundred Stories and Commentaries* (Portland, Ore.: Amadeus, 2001), 150.

[40] *Parsifal*, act 2, as translated into English by Lionel Salter, published in libretto booklet for *Richard Wagner: Parsifal*, Berliner Philharmoniker, conducted by Herbert Von Karajan, Deutsche Grammophon, 413 347-2, 1981, compact disc, p. 113. (Translation © Lionel Salter, www.LionelSalter.co.uk.)

[41] Manuscript: Vatican City, Biblioteca Apostolica Vaticana, Codex Vaticanus Latinus 4748 I, early fourteenth century; text in Michel Andrieu, ed., *Le pontifical romain au moyen-âge*, vol. 2, *Le pontifical de la Curie romaine au XIIIe siècle*, ST 87 (Vatican City: Biblioteca Apostolica Vaticana, 1940), 579.

preparing for their elevation to knighthood by spending the preceding night watching in prayer before the altar in a church or chapel had certainly arisen by the second half of the twelfth century, when this practice is mentioned in the earliest extant rendering of the legend of the Holy Grail, the French poet Chrétien de Troyes' epic *Perceval le Gallois* (also known as the *Comte del Graal*), written sometime between 1160 and Chrétien's death around 1181. In one passage Chrétien tells of a candidate on the eve of his knighting keeping watch in church, remaining continually on his knees throughout the night.[42] Not long afterward, the French ecclesiastical writer Helinand of Froidmont (+c. 1237), writing at the beginning of the thirteenth century, speaks of knighthood candidates in some places "keeping watch to conduct the entire preceding night in prayers, having the liberty neither of lying down nor of sitting".[43] In his late thirteenth-century book of knighthood, Raymond Lull describes the knighting vigil thus, as given in Caxton's English translation: "The squire ought to fast the night of the same feast in honor of the saint of whom the feast is made that day. And he ought to go to the church for to pray God, and ought to wake the night and be in his prayers, and ought to hear the Word of God."[44]

There were several possible sources for the custom of the night watch. Over the centuries, many devout monks and nuns engaged in all-night vigils in their monastic chapels, as attested in numerous accounts of medieval saints.[45] In the twelfth century, implicit references to adoration of the reserved Eucharist in the churches begin to multiply,[46] suggesting that the knights' prayer before the altar may have been specifically directed to the Sacrament reserved there. The nineteenth-century French historian Léon Gautier (+1897) proposed that the knighthood vigil stemmed from the Church's vigils of Easter and Pentecost, which served as a final preparation for those to be baptized on these two solemnities.[47] In view of the association of knighthood with the defense of the Holy Sepulcher, the knighthood vigil may have

---

[42] Chrétien de Troyes, *Perceval le Gallois*, line 10547, quoted and discussed in Treis, *Formalitaten des Ritterschlags in der altfranzosischen Epik*, 60–61. In his study, Karl Treis found the keeping of a night watch in church by knighthood candidates likewise mentioned in the French epics *Bueves de Commarchis*, *Garin le Loherain*, *Le mort de Garin le Loherain*, and *Jehan de Dammartin et Blonde of Oxford* (ibid., 60–62).

[43] Helinand de Froidmont, *De bono regime principis*, chap. 23, PL 212, col. 744.

[44] Lull, *Book of the Ordre of Chyvalry or Knyghthode*, sig. d3v–d4r.

[45] To cite but three of many examples, all-night vigils of prayer are mentioned in the lives of Saint Rusticula, a nun of Arles, France (+c. 632); Saint William of Gellone, a French monk (+812); and Saint Theobald, an Augustinian canon regular of Dorat, France (+1070). See respectively Bolland et al., *Acta sanctorum*, August, 2:660; May, 6:809; and November, 3:317.

[46] For twelfth-century developments regarding Eucharistic adoration, see my work coauthored with Father Benedict J. Groeschel, C.F.R., *In the Presence of Our Lord: The History, Theology and Psychology of Eucharistic Devotion* (Huntington, Ind.: Our Sunday Visitor, 1997), 202–205.

[47] Léon Gautier, *Chivalry* (New York: Crescent Books, 1989), 235.

also been inspired by the all-night watch before representations of the Holy Sepulcher that took place each year in many medieval churches on the night of Good Friday.[48]

The night watch served as a preparation for the knighting itself, which was carried out during a Mass the next day, usually on a Sunday morning. The Sunday most often chosen for this ceremony was Pentecost,[49] as was the case in the knighting of the future Duke of Anjou, France, Fulk IV le Rechin, in 1060,[50] but there were also some knightings on other Sundays and feast days, including Easter Sunday and Christmas Day.[51] An account of the 1213 French knighting of Almaric, the son of Simon of Montfort, tells of the candidate kneeling before the altar during Mass as two bishops girded him in the cincture of knighthood and intoned the hymn of the Holy Spirit, *Veni Creator Spiritus*.[52] After enjoining squires to have High Mass celebrated for their knightings, Raymond Lull describes the rite thus:

> And the squire ought to come before the altar, and offer to the priest, which holdeth the place of our Lord, to the honor of whom he must oblige and submit himself, to keep the honor of chivalry with all his power. In that same day ought to be made a sermon, in which should be recounted and declared the seven articles in which is founded the holy Catholic faith, the Ten Commandments and the seven sacraments of Holy Church, and the other things that appertain to the faith. And the squire ought much diligently to take heed and retain all these things.... The squire ought to kneel before the altar, and lift up to God his eyes corporeal and spiritual, and his hands to Heaven. And the knight [a senior knight] ought to gird him in sign of chastity, justice, and of charity with his sword. The knight ought to kiss the squire and to give him a palm, because that he be remembering of that which he receiveth and promiseth, and of the great charge.[53]

A complete knighting ceremony, entitled "Blessing of a New Knight", is found in the pontifical that William Durandus compiled around 1294 for his diocese of Mende, France; Durandus follows the norm of situating the rite within the framework of a Mass.[54] Most of the rite

---

[48] See pp. 453–454 above.

[49] Meller, *Knight's Life in the Days of Chivalry*, 44; Treis, *Formalitäten des Ritterschlags in der altfranzösischen Epik*, 48–49, 51; Ackerman, "Knighting Ceremonies in the Middle English Romances", 297.

[50] *Fragmentum historiae Andegavensis*, in Louis Halphen and René Poupardin, eds., *Chroniques des comtes d'Anjou et des seigneurs d'Amboise*, Collection de textes pour servir à l'étude et à l'enseignement de l'histoire 48 (Paris: Auguste Picard, 1913), 236.

[51] These two occasions are mentioned by Blessed Raymond Lull (*Book of the Ordre of Chyvalry or Knyghthode*, sig. d3v). See also Treis, *Formalitaten des Ritterschlags in der altfranzosischen Epik*, 48, 50–51.

[52] Peter Vallis Cernaius, *Historia Albigensium*, chap. 70, PL 213, col. 663.

[53] Lull, *Book of the Ordre of Chyvalry or Knyghthode*, sig. d4r, d5v.

[54] Andrieu, *Pontifical romain au moyen-âge*, 3:447–450.

focuses upon the investiture of the candidate with his sword, in accordance with the tradition of casting this action as the primary symbol of the conferral of knighthood. In the Pontifical of Durandus, the ceremony begins immediately before the Gospel. The sword to be presented to the candidate, having been laid upon the altar, is blessed by the bishop with two prayers:

> *Graciously hear our prayers, we beseech you, O Lord, and vouchsafe to bless with the right hand of your majesty this sword, with which this your servant earnestly wishes to be girded, that he may be enabled to be a defender of churches, widows, orphans, and all serving God, against the fury of the pagans; and may it be for him a terror and a dread to others laying snares, furnishing to him the rendering of just pursuit and just defense. Through Christ . . .*[55]

> *Bless + , holy Lord, almighty Father, eternal God, this sword, by the invocation of your holy name, and by the coming of Christ your Son, our Lord, and by the gift of the Holy Spirit, the Paraclete, that this your servant, who on this day is girded, your goodness granting, may trample underfoot the invisible enemies and, having obtained victory in every respect, ever remain unharmed. Through . . .*[56]

The practice of blessing swords dates from the tenth century, when the two above prayers appear for the first time in the Romano-Germanic Pontifical.[57] The custom of laying the sword on the altar for the blessing had been introduced by the twelfth century, as attested by the English-born bishop and scholar John of Salisbury (+1180), who speaks of "the sword having been placed and consecrated upon the altar".[58] The French-born churchman Peter de Blois (+c. 1208), who is thought to have been a pupil of John of Salisbury, sees this action as a visual reminder to the candidates of their obligations to the Church, explaining that "the recruits receive their swords from the altar, that they may profess themselves sons of the Church."[59]

Following the above prayers, the bishop, before proceeding with the conferral of the sword, blesses the other arms of the knight. The Pontifical of Durandus provides prayers for these blessings under a separate heading. Rather than give these orations here, we shall present as an early example of such blessings the prayer for the blessing of a knight's lance given in an eleventh-century pontifical (*Liber episcopalis*) of Cambrai, France. The text draws upon the scriptural imagery of Tubalcain, from the Book of Genesis, as the prototypical artisan (see Gen 4:22) in reference to the lance as a work of human hands, and of

---

[55] Ibid., 447.
[56] Ibid., 448.
[57] Vogel and Elze, *Pontifical romano-germanique*, 2:379.
[58] John of Salisbury, *Polycraticus*, bk. 6, chap. 10, PL 199, col. 602.
[59] Peter de Blois, *Letter 94*, to Archdeacon John, PL 207, col. 294.

the lance that served as an instrument of the Passion in opening Christ's side on Calvary (Jn 19:34):

> *O Lord God almighty, light and life of the workshop of the world, who by the hand of Tubalcain established the works of carpenter's tools for the use of men: mercifully regard the supplication of our office unto blessing this lance of the military equipment, you who for our salvation permitted the side of your Son, our Lord Jesus Christ, hanging upon the Cross, to be pierced by a soldier with a lance; and by the name of the same your Son vouchsafe to consecrate and bless it thus, that to him who shall have carried it, you may give the favorable token of your protection, even as you gave it to Gideon, Saul, King David also, that, sustained always by your supports, he may rejoice and be glad in you in all his successes.* [60]

In the Pontifical of Durandus, after the blessing of the arms, the knighting rite proceeds with the bishop's recitation of the three opening verses of Psalm 143: "*Blessed be the Lord my God, who teacheth my hands to fight, and my fingers to war. My mercy, and my refuge: my support, and my deliverer: My protector, and I have hoped in him.*" [61] The bishop then prays that the new knight may be a man of virtue who will use his sword in the defense of just causes but who will never use it unjustly:

> *Holy Lord, Father almighty, eternal God, who alone establish and rightly order all things, who, to restrain the malice of reprobates and uphold justice, permitted to men the use of the sword in their own lands by your salutary disposition and willed the military order to be instituted for the protection of the people, and who through blessed John [the Baptist], with soldiers coming to him in the desert, made it to be said that they should strike no one, but they should be content with their own wages [cf. Lk 3:14], we humbly beseech your clemency, O Lord, that just as you bestowed upon your servant David the power of vanquishing Goliath and made Judas Machabeus to triumph over the savagery of the nations not invoking your name, so also upon this your servant, who newly places his neck under the yoke of military service, may you shed heavenly goodness and bestow courage for the defense of the faith and justice, and an increase of faith, hope and charity, and likewise the fear of God, and love, humility, perseverance, obedience, and good patience, and rightly dispose all things in him, that he may harm no one unjustly with this sword or another and defend all just and upright things with it; and even as he is advanced from a lesser rank to the new honor of military service, so, putting aside the old man with his deeds, may he put on the new man [cf. Eph 4:22–24], that by his resolution he may rightly fear and worship you, shun company with the faithless, and extend his charity to*

---

[60] Manuscript: Cologne, Capitular Library, Codex 141, eleventh century, in Franz, *Kirchlichen Benediktionen im Mittelalter*, 2:295–296. This manuscript is described by Michel Andrieu, ed., *Les Ordines Romani du haut moyen âge*, vol. 1, SSLED 11 (Louvain, Belgium: "Spicilegium sacrum Lovaniense" Administration, 1931), 108, 112–113.

[61] Andrieu, *Pontifical romain au moyen-âge*, 3:448.

his neighbor, obey rightly in all things, and perform his office justly in all things. Through . . .[62]

The conferral of the sword upon the candidate follows. As we saw earlier, Blessed Raymund Lull describes the candidate's girding with the sword as a "sign of chastity, justice, and of charity".[63] The association of this action with chastity may well have arisen from a likening of the belt upon which the sword is hung to the cincture worn around the waist by priests and religious as a sign of chastity. The text of the pontifical continues:

After these things, the bishop takes the bare sword from the altar and places it in his [the candidate's] right hand, saying:
Receive this sword in the name of the Father, and of the Son, and of the Holy Spirit, and may you employ it for the defense of yourself and of the holy Church of God, and for the confutation of the enemies of the Cross of Christ, and of the Christian faith, and of the crown of the kingdom of France (or of such kind), and, so much as human frailty shall have suffered you, may you injure no one with it unjustly. Which may he vouchsafe to grant, who lives and reigns with the Father and the Holy Spirit through all ages of ages + . Response: *Amen.*
Then, with the sword having been placed in its sheath, he [the bishop] girds upon him the sword with its sheath and in girding [him] says: *Gird thy sword upon thy thigh, O thou most mighty* [cf. Ps 44:4], *in the name of our Lord Jesus Christ; and take heed that the saints conquered kingdoms not with the sword but by faith +* .
The sword having been girded accordingly, the new knight brings it forth from its sheath and manfully brandishes it unsheathed three times in his hand; and having wiped it upon his arm, he places it afterward back in its sheath.[64]

The "accolade" follows, a ceremonial tap popularly known as "dubbing". The ceremonial custom of lightly striking the new knight had arisen by the eleventh century as a tap delivered with the hand to the candidate's neck; during the twelfth century, there appeared in certain places the practice of tapping the new knight with a sword rather than a hand blow.[65] The late thirteenth-century Pontifical of Durandus identifies the dubbing simply as a light slap: "Endowing him with the military character, he [the bishop] gives him the kiss of peace, saying: *Be a peaceful knight, steadfast, faithful, and devoted to God +* . And afterward he gives him a slap lightly, saying: *May you be raised up from the sleep of evil and keep watch in the faith of Christ, and with a laudable reputation +* .

---

[62] Ibid., 448–449.

[63] Lull, *Book of the Ordre of Chyvalry or Knyghthode*, sig. d5v.

[64] Andrieu, *Pontifical romain au moyen-âge*, 3:449.

[65] Ackerman, "Knighting Ceremonies in the Middle English Romances", 302.

Amen."[66] The knight receives his spurs next: "Then the nobles stand-ing near put his spurs upon him, where this is the custom to be done, and the antiphon is sung: *Thou art beautiful above the sons of men; gird thy sword upon thy thigh, O thou most mighty* [Ps 44:3, 4]."[67] The bishop gives the new knight a final blessing before presenting to him the military standard under which he will fight: "*Almighty eternal God, upon this your servant* [Name], *who wishes to be girded about with an excellent sword, infuse the grace of your bless + ing and make him, trusting in the power of your right hand, to be armed with celestial defenses against all adversities,* [*that*] *in this world he may not be troubled by tempests of wars. Through* . . ."[68]

Blessings for Protection from Storms

The Old Testament contains numerous references to thunderstorms, lightning, and hail as manifestations of the glory, power, and majesty of God (Ps 17:10–15; Ps 76:17–19; Is 28:2; Jer 23:19; Ez 13:13; Nahum 1:3). In the Book of Job we find God speaking to Job from a storm cloud (Job 40:1), and the Canticle of the Three Young Men from the Book of Daniel includes the verse "O ye lightnings and clouds, bless the Lord: praise and exalt him above all forever" (Dan 3:73). In the New Testament, we find Christ comparing his Second Coming to the lightning that flashes from one side of the sky to the other (Mt 24:27), and when in the Book of Revelation the Temple of God opens, reveal-ing the Ark of the Covenant, there is lightning and "great hail" (Rev 11:19). In a sermon for Ascension Thursday, the Belgian-born bishop Ratherius of Verona (+974) stresses that storms are the handiwork of God, not the devil, asking, "How does he believe in God, who does not believe God to be the Creator of all things?"[69] The fall of man, however, has adversely affected nature in making the good things of God's creation capable of causing suffering and even death (cf. Rom 8:19–22). Hence, the medieval rites for protection from storms besought God to exercise his sovereignty over the storms that he himself had created, as he did in calming the storm on the Sea of Galilee (Mt 8:23–27), and at the same time invoked the Lord's protection from the mal-ice of Satan and his fellow demons, who from the fall of man onward have been agents of mankind's suffering. With the livelihoods of so many of her children dependent upon the fruitful harvesting of the land, the medieval Church, ever committed to the spiritual needs of the faithful, manifested her corresponding solicitude for the faithful's

---

[66] Andrieu, *Pontifical romain au moyen-âge*, 3:449–450.

[67] Ibid., 450. The antiphon *Speciosus forma* is a highly modified adaptation of a Christ-mas season antiphon of the same name, the latter traceable to the Antiphonary of Com-piègne (France, c. 870); see René-Jean Hésbert, ed., *Corpus antiphonalium officii*, vol. 1, REDSMF 7 (Rome: Herder, 1963), 60.

[68] Andrieu, *Pontifical romain au moyen-âge*, 3:450. This prayer is a variant of an oration from the rite of blessing a sword in the tenth-century Romano-Germanic Pontifical; see Vogel and Elze, *Pontifical romano-germanique*, 2:379.

[69] Ratherius of Verona, *Sermon 8*, "De ascensione Domini", PL 136, col. 739.

material needs through rites such as these, in which she "stormed Heaven" on their behalf.

The earliest known supplications for deliverance from storms in the Christian liturgy appear in two *Praeconium paschale* texts that Ennodius of Pavia (+521), a bishop of Italy, composed for the blessing of the Paschal candle at the Easter Vigil. In the first of these texts, a passage toward the end of the prayer beseeches God to make the wax from the Paschal candle, by his blessing, an instrument of his divine protection for those facing dangerous storms, serving as "an excellent refuge" and a "wall" against the devil.[70] It is clear from the wording of a comparable passage in the second of Ennodius' *Praeconium paschale* texts that small portions of the wax from the Paschal candle were at some point afterward distributed to the faithful to take home and keep as sacramentals for this purpose.[71] In the early sacramentaries, we find prayers from the seventh century onward for protection from lightning or storms, beginning with three such prayers regarding lightning in the Gelasian Sacramentary of Rome.[72]

It is in the tenth century that complete liturgical rites to invoke divine protection from storms begin to appear. One such ceremony from a tenth-century liturgical manuscript of Schaftlarn, Germany,[73] begins with a short litany of saints, followed by a series of verses invoking the protection of the Cross: "*May the Cross of Christ vouchsafe to be our consolation. May the Cross of Christ always be to us our salvation. O Cross of Christ, which we ever worship, vouchsafe always to be with us against all our enemies.*"[74] Further verses, the psalm *Miserere* (Psalm 50), and two exorcism formulas follow,[75] after which the priest adjures the storm clouds with the sign of the cross, which was considered to have a unique power in conquering demons:[76] "I sign you, O clouds, with the sign of the holy Cross and of the Passion of our Lord Jesus Christ, who lives and reigns.... I sign you, O clouds, with the sign of Christ, in the name of the Father, and of the Son, and of the Holy Spirit. I sign you. Holy, holy, holy, Lord, God of Sabaoth."[77] Psalm 147 is then recited, followed by the Our Father, the Creed, and an invocation utilizing the ancient Eastern chant known as the Trisagion that we saw earlier in the *Improperia* of the Good Friday liturgy (p. 422): "*Holy God, Holy Mighty One, Holy and Immortal One. [O Christ], you*

[70] Ennodius of Pavia, *Opusculum 9*, PL 63, col. 260.
[71] Ennodius of Pavia, *Opusculum 10*, PL 63, col. 262.
[72] Text in Leo Cunibert Mohlberg, O.S.B., et al., eds., *Liber sacramentorum Romanae aeclesiae ordinis anni circuli (Sacramentarium Gelasianum)*, REDSMF 4 (Rome: Herder, 1960), nos. 1566–1568, pp. 227–228.
[73] Manuscript: Munich, Bayerische Staatsbibliothek, Codex Latinus Monacensis (Clm) 17027, tenth century, in Franz, *Kirchlichen Benediktionen im Mittelalter*, 2:74–77.
[74] Ibid., 74.
[75] Ibid., 74–75.
[76] Regarding the sign of the cross, see Franz, *Kirchlichen Benediktionen im Mittelalter*, 2:54.
[77] Franz, *Kirchlichen Benediktionen im Mittelalter*, 2:76.

who take away the sins of the world, have mercy on us, who reign unto ages of ages." [78] A prayer follows, invoking the protection of Christ Crucified: *"O Christ Jesus, who hung on Golgotha, speak to the angel with the sword of slaying, that he may restrain his hand over these fields and that this wrath may cease, which has raged over this city* (or *this region)."* [79] After another exorcism formula, the rite concludes with the reading of Saint Matthew's Gospel narrative of the storm on the lake (Mt 8:23–27):

> *And behold a great tempest arose in the sea, so that the boat was covered with waves, but he was asleep. And they came to him, and awaked him, saying: Lord, save us, we perish. And Jesus saith to them: Why are you fearful, O ye of little faith? Then rising up he commanded the winds, and the sea, and there came a great calm. But the men wondered, saying: What manner of man is this, for the winds and the sea obey him?* [80]

The belief that the Cross of Christ afforded the faithful a special protection from the dangers of storms, reflected in the above rite, would have been bolstered by an incident in the life of the German nun Saint Gertrude of Helfta (+1302), as recounted in the book of her mystical experiences known as the *Herald of Divine Love*. Gertrude is described as experiencing an interior locution during a procession at her convent of Helfta held to invoke divine protection from a threatening storm. At the head of the procession, a crucifix was being carried, from which Gertrude interiorly heard these words: "Behold, with my army I come to you, going to entreat God the Father in this form by which I reconciled all human nature." Together with the locution, she experienced a vision of God the Father lifting up the crucifix in the clouds and speaking the words from Genesis, "This shall be a sign of the covenant between me and the earth" (Gen 9:13). [81] The image of the crucifix is seen here as a New Covenant sign of divine mercy and protection corresponding to the rainbow with which God promised Noah and all mankind never again to flood the whole world in a deluge.

A prayer entitled "Blessing against Lightning Bolts" from a thirteenth-century manuscript preserved in Munich utilizes as an invocation the title given to Christ on the Cross by Pilate: "Jesus of Nazareth, the King of the Jews" (Jn 19:19), called here the "triumphant title". It also uses the acclamation known as the *Christus vincit*, "Christ conquers, Christ reigns, Christ commands", [82] a text utilized in some

---

[78] Ibid.

[79] Ibid., 76–77 (quoted passage on 77).

[80] Ibid., 77.

[81] Saint Gertrude of Helfta, *The Herald of Divine Love*, bk. 3, chap. 31, no. 1, in Pierre Doyère, ed. and trans., *Gertrude d'Helfta: Oeuvres spirituelles*, vol. 3, *Le héraut, livre III*, SC 143 (Paris: Cerf, 1968), 164 (Latin text).

[82] Manuscript: Munich, Bayerische Staatsbibliothek, Codex Latinus Monacensis (Clm) 4616, thirteenth century, in Franz, *Kirchlichen Benediktionen im Mittelalter*, 2:87.

medieval exorcism rites from the eleventh century onward.[83] A manuscript ritual from 1511 likewise preserved in Munich provides a rite called "Blessings against Hailstones and Storms" that includes the following prayer beseeching Christ to bless the thunderclouds and send them away:

> *Lord Jesus Christ, who established Heaven and earth, and blessed the Jordan River, and willed to be baptized in it, vouchsafe to bless these clouds, which I see placed before me, that they may pass, that they may be made holy and blessed water, that the storm may fall in deserted places, that it may not harm other Christians or other harvests, in the power of the Holy Spirit and by the prayer of all the saints. Holy God, holy mighty One, holy immortal One. [O Christ], you who take away the sins of the world, have mercy on us. I sign you, O clouds, in the name of the Father, and of the Son, and of the Holy Spirit. Amen.*[84]

A fifteenth-century book of customs (*consueta*) for the archdiocese of Valencia, Spain, specifies that when "any storm, or thunders, lightnings, hail, or frightening air" threatens, one or more of the church bells should be tolled, with the number of bells rung dependent upon the severity of the storm.[85] This particular use of church bells had arisen by the late thirteenth century, when it is mentioned by William Durandus. He explains bell ringing at the approach of a storm as instilling terror in demons, who flee from the sound of the "trumpets of the eternal King", that is, church bells, thereby quieting the harmful effects of the storm. The tolling of the church bells also serves as a warning to those endangered by the storm that they should pray for protection.[86] Over four centuries later, the Spanish ecclesiastical writer Father Batholomé de las Casas, in a 1730 book on the subject of church bells, observes that insofar as bells are blessed objects, their peals— their voice, as it were—constitute in a sense a prayer that disperses the storms.[87]

Two fifteenth-century Austrian rituals, one from Haunsperg in the archdiocese of Salzburg (c. 1420), and the other from Wilhering, near Linz (1477), specify four readings for the storm protection rite: the

---

[83] See p. 110 above.

[84] Manuscript: Munich, Bayerische Staatsbibliothek, Codex Latinus Monacensis (Clm) 23059, 1511, in Franz, *Kirchlichen Benediktionen im Mittelalter*, 2:100.

[85] *Consueta*, Valencia, Spain, fifteenth century, quoted in Francesc Llop i Bayo, "Toques de campanas y otros rituales colectivos para alejar las tormentas", in Alfonso Esteban and Jean-Pierre Etienvre, eds., *Fiestas y liturgia: Actas del coloquio celebrado en la Casa de Velázquez, 12/14-XII-1985* [December 12–14, 1985], (Madrid: Casa de Velázquez, Universidad Complutense, 1988), 123–124.

[86] William Durandus of Mende, *Rationale Divinorum Officiorum*, bk. 1, chap. 4, no. 15, in A. Davril, O.S.B., and T. M. Thibodeau, eds., *Guillelmi Duranti: Rationale divinorum officiorum I–IV*, CCCM 140 (Turnhout, Belgium: Brepols, 1995), 57.

[87] Batholomé Casas, *Campanas sin vida, campanas con alma* (Valencia, 1730), cited in Llop i Bayo, "Toques de campanas y otros rituales", 124.

beginnings of the four Gospels, which we earlier saw used in the four-station Corpus Christi processions of late medieval Germany and Poland (chapter 16).[88] In the Wilhering text, the rubrics direct that each lection be read facing a different cardinal point: Matthew, to the east; Mark, toward the west; Luke, to the south; and John, toward the north.[89] The 1548 *Ordinarium* of Urgel, Spain, has a more varied selection of Gospel readings: to the west, Matthew 24:27–38 ("For as lightning cometh out of the east, and appeareth even into the west: so shall also the coming of the Son of man be ..."); to the south, Luke 1:26–38 (the Annunciation); to the north, Mark 16:14–20 (Christ appearing to the Apostles on Easter Sunday, and his Ascension); and to the east, John 1:1ff.[90]

A rite entitled "Order against Storms" in a manual of Burgos, Spain, dating from 1497 provides very detailed and dramatic rubrics for the storm protection rite, including an instruction reflecting the belief that the words of the Roman Canon possessed a singular power against the devil.[91] The Burgos rite begins thus:

> First, and before all things, the sacristan should look to the clouds and to the disposition of the storm, and when he shall have seen the storm to be stirred, immediately he should ring the cymbals. And the priest, with surplice and stole, should come to the sanctuary and uncover the altar, opening the corporals as if he were intending to say Mass, and he should place on the lectern at the Gospel side the mixed missal[92] opened at its section, where "*You, therefore*" [*Te igitur,* the first words of the Roman Canon] is, up to the words of consecration. And he should kindle the lights and the Paschal candle and open the tabernacle, where the Body of Christ is, but he should not withdraw the Body of Christ from the *custodia* or from the pyx ..., but he should only open the tabernacle, and it should be open thus, until the storm shall have been quieted.[93]

A ritual from Saint Gall, Switzerland, dating from about 1470, provides similar rubrics:

> When it shall have been evident that the clouds of Heaven threaten storms, and lightning bolts flash, and thunders are heard, the priest,

---

[88] Manuscripts: Munich, Bayerische Staatsbibliothek, Codex Latinus Monacensis (Clm) 23645, c. 1420 (Haunsperg); Wilhering, Austria, Cistercienserstift, Codex Wilheringensis 53 (Wilhering), 1477; texts in Franz, *Kirchlichen Benediktionen im Mittelalter,* 2:91–92 and 2:97, respectively.

[89] Manuscript: Wilhering, Austria, Cistercienserstift, Codex Wilheringensis 53, 1477, in Franz, *Kirchlichen Benediktionen im Mittelalter,* 2:97.

[90] *Ordinarium Urgellinum* (1548), cited in Franz, *Kirchlichen Benediktionen im Mittelalter,* 2:58.

[91] This belief regarding the words of the Roman Canon is explained later in this chapter (p. 637); see also Franz, *Kirchlichen Benediktionen im Mittelalter,* 2:70.

[92] Certain missals of late medieval Spain bear the title *Missale mixtum.*

[93] *Manuale ecclesie Burgensis* (1497), in Franz, *Kirchlichen Benediktionen im Mittelalter,* 2:104.

with an ecclesiastical stole put over his neck, should go forth with
the small exorcism book, standing on the porch to the major church
with a thurible of blessed incense, with a reliquary and also blessed
water, and the Paschal candle or the Purification candles [from the
feast of the Purification, February 2], and an *Agnus Dei*[94]—if he should
have one; and a stroke of the bells should be made, and the [Roman]
Canon should be spread out upon the altar, and a stole should be laid
over it in the manner of a cross.[95]

The belief in the efficacy of the words of the Roman Canon in driving away demons that we see in the two above texts is traceable to the
writings of the German Cistercian monk Caesarius von Heisterbach
(+1240). In his *Dialogue of Miracles*, he relates an incident of demonic
possession in which the demon admitted that the concluding words of
the Canon, "*Per ipsum, et cum ipso, et in ipso*" ("*Through him, and with
him, and in him*"), had the power of binding Satan in hell, saying while
pointing to these words in a missal, "Behold, these are those words by
which my master has been bound."[96] A rite for invoking protection
from storms found in a fifteenth-century Cistercian manuscript from
the vicinity of Salzburg, Austria, utilizes the concluding words of the
Canon in a prayer to bless the water of the storm so as to render it
free from Satan's influence, in likeness to the exorcism of water to be
used in baptism (the words taken from the Roman Canon are in bold):
"*Bless, O Lord, this creature of water **through Christ our Lord Jesus, by
whom you create, sanctify, bless, and grant us all these things; through
him, and with him, and in him be all honor and glory to you, O God,
almighty Father, in the unity of the Holy Spirit, unto ages of ages**.*"[97]

Returning to the rubrics of the Burgos rite, we find relics utilized
in a manner comparable to the way they were sometimes used in exorcism rites; the ceremony concludes with a prayer incorporating the
earlier-mentioned acclamation *Christus vincit*:

---

[94] An *Agnus Dei* is a disk of wax impressed with the image of a lamb representing Christ
as the Lamb of God. These were blessed by the pope and were distributed as sacramentals
on the Saturday after Easter Sunday; see Herbert Thurston, S.J., "Agnus Dei", in *Catholic
Encyclopedia* (1907–1912), 1:220. The symbolism of the wax *Agnus Dei* is explained by the
Frankish bishop and liturgist Amalarius of Metz (+c. 850), who observes, "The *Agni* that
the Romans make signify the Lamb made immaculate for us.... When we see the lamb of
wax, the Lamb prefigured and immolated in the Pasch is recalled" (*Liber officialis*, bk. 1,
chap. 17, nos. 1–2, in John Michael Hanssens, ed., *Amalarii episcopi: Opera liturgica omnia*,
vol. 2, ST 139 [Vatican City: Biblioteca Apostolica Vaticana, 1948], 110 [quoted passages in
no. 2]).

[95] Manuscript: Saint Gall Abbey, Switzerland, Stiftsbibliothek Sankt Gallen, MS. Codex
Sangallensis (Cod. Sang.) 692, c. 1470, quoted in Franz, *Kirchlichen Benediktionen im Mittelalter*, 2:70, footnote.

[96] Caesarius von Heisterbach, *Dialogus miraculorum* (Cologne: Johann Koelhoff der Ältere,
1481; digitized text, Bayerische Staatsbibliothek, Munich, 2009), distinction 5, chap. 13,
sig. n3r–n3v.

[97] Manuscript: Vienna, Hofbibliothek, Codex Vindobonensis Palatinus 1854, fifteenth
century, in Franz, *Kirchlichen Benediktionen im Mittelalter*, 2:90.

Then the priest should take the cross and the relics of the saints that he wishes to carry with him to exorcise the clouds, and before the Body of Christ he should say the psalm *In thee, O Lord, have I hoped ... [Psalm 30]*, the whole psalm. And afterward he should say: *Let us pray. O God, strength of those in battle and palm of the martyrs, turn to my assistance. O Lord, hasten to help me. Glory be to the Father ...*—three times. Afterward he should say the psalm *To thee, O Lord, have I lifted up my soul* [Psalm 24]. And when he shall have been at the place of exorcism, he should boldly keep back the clouds by showing the cross and saying: *Behold the Cross of the Lord; flee, O adverse factions, the Lion of the tribe of Judah has conquered, the Root of David, the Holy One,*[98] to the east, and the west, and the south, and the north.

[Prayer:] *Look favorably upon us, almighty God, Father and Holy Spirit; Christ lives, Christ conquers, Christ reigns, Christ commands; may Christ protect us from every evil, lightning, storm, and malignity of time; O Christ, Son of the living God, have mercy on us.*[99]

To conclude this chapter on medieval blessings, we present here a prayer from the rite of blessing pilgrims found in a liturgical book of Catalonian Spain, the 1501 *Ordinarium* of Barcelona:

O God, who preserved your servant Abraham, led forth from Ur of the Chaldeans, through all the ways of his travel, vouchsafe to preserve with the rampart of your protection these your servants (or your maidservants), voluntarily seeking to go on pilgrimage for the love of your name. Be to them, O Lord, on the battlefield a harbor of protection in shipwreck, a lodging place on the journey, a shade in the heat, a light in the darkness, a staff in slipperiness, joy in grief, consolation in sadness, security in adversity, caution in prosperity, that these your servants (or your maidservants), with you leading them, may both come untroubled to where they are traveling and return from there unharmed. Through our Lord Jesus Christ ...[100]

---

[98] This versicle is traceable to the eleventh century, when it appears in a manuscript of Tegernsee, Germany (Munich, Bayerische Staatsbibliothek, Codex Latinus Monacensis [Clm] 18372), from which the complete text of the versicle is here taken, as given in Franz, *Kirchlichen Benediktionen im Mittelalter*, 2:80.

[99] *Manuale ecclesie Burgensis* (1497), in Franz, *Kirchlichen Benediktionen im Mittelalter*, 2:104.

[100] Text in Amadeu-J. Soberanas, ed., *Ordinarium sacramentorum Barchinonense, 1501*, facsimile ed., Biblioteca litúrgica catalana 1 (Barcelona: Institut d'Estudis Catalans, 1991), fol. 106r–106v. For the complete rite of blessing pilgrims, see fols. 105v–107r. This prayer is traceable to the eleventh century, when it appears for the first time in a sacramentary of Vich, Spain (manuscript: Vich, Museu Episcopal, Codex 66); see Francesc Xavier Parés i Saltor, *L'ordinari d'Urgell de 1536*, Col·lectània Sant Pacià 74 (La Seu d'Urgell, Spain: Societat Cultural Urgel·litana / Facultat de Teologia da Catalunya, 2002), 131.

23 Conclusions

Lord Jesus Christ, most glorious Creator of the world, splendor of glory coequal and coeternal with the Father and the Holy Spirit, who vouchsafed to assume flesh from the immaculate Virgin and permitted your most glorious hands to be nailed to the gibbet of the Cross, that you might destroy the gates of hell and deliver mankind from death: have mercy on me, have mercy, over-whelmed by the burden of my sin, defiled by the blot of my iniquities. Do not forsake me, O most merciful Father, but vouchsafe to forgive me whatever impieties I have committed. Graciously hear me, prostrate before you to adore your most glorious Cross, that having been purified, I may be worthy to attend upon you in these sacred solemnities and be pleasing in your sight, and freed from all evils, I may ever be consoled by your assistance, through you, Jesus Christ, the Savior of the world. . .

Prayer for the veneration of the cross,
Good Friday, *Missale Eystetense*, 1494[1]

In the preceding pages, we have attempted to explore and understand that great and continual hymn of praise, supplication, and thanksgiving that rose from the vaulted churches and monastic chapels of medieval Europe and ascended to the throne of God—the medieval liturgy. Our examination of the medieval liturgical texts has shown them to be pervaded by the words and thoughts of the Sacred Scriptures and filled with prayers drawn from the earliest known liturgical books of the Western tradition. Clearly these medieval rites evince what the Second Vatican Council describes as the organic development of the liturgy: "Any new forms adapted should in some way grow organically from forms already existing".[2] Throughout this work, we have seen fit largely to let the medieval Church speak for herself through

---

[1] *Missale Eystetense* (Eichstätt, Germany: Michael Reyser, 1494; digitized text, Bayerische Staatsbibliothek, Munich, 2009), fol. 90v. This prayer in its earliest form is traceable to the late ninth-century pontifical of northern France formerly known as the Pontifical of Poitiers; see Aldo Martini, ed., *Il cosiddetto pontificale di Poitiers*, REDSMF 14 (Rome: Casa Editrice Herder, 1979), 207.

[2] Second Vatican Council, *Sacrosanctum concilium* (December 4, 1963), chap. 1, no. 23, in Austin Flannery, O.P., ed., *Vatican Council II: The Conciliar and Post Conciliar Documents* (Northport, N.Y.: Costello, 1975), 10.

the texts of these liturgical rites and the explanations offered by the theologians of medieval Christendom. Our intent has been to introduce into current-day discussions of the liturgy the wisdom of an earlier age—to give the reader what we hope has been a fairly complete and accurate picture of medieval worship. That picture reveals a liturgy filled with rich imagery testifying to invisible truths, a liturgy that was explained in its time so as to impart a sacred meaning to each and every action. The comments of the modern French historian Louis Chatellier regarding Catholic worship in the Baroque age are equally applicable to what we have seen in the medieval liturgy:

> Just as, by the force of their images, the Spiritual Exercises [of Saint Ignatius of Loyola] in a sense constrained whoever made them to follow in the footsteps of Christ, so the Mass described in this way was designed to lead the Christian to live with his Savior. Thus each act and each word had their value and meaning. Nothing was gratuitous. Carrying the book from one place to another had its significance, replying "Amen" and making the sign of the cross had the value of participation. The time, place, acts and words spoken all had a sacred character.[3]

The author of the present work hopes that negative presuppositions about the medieval liturgy will be changed by an authentic knowledge and understanding of the medieval rites. Donald Matthew, author of the *Atlas of Medieval Europe*, referring to the eighteenth-century English historian Edward Gibbons, says of the latter that in his writings he evinces "an intolerable condescension to the Middle Ages".[4] That same condescending attitude toward the medieval Church has all too often permeated modern liturgical studies. There has likewise been too much carelessness regarding the facts of history. As we hope the present work has shown, the facts of liturgical history are knowable, albeit in an imperfect and incomplete manner because much has been lost. Much remains yet to be discovered.

Knowledge of the medieval ceremonies can help us to understand on a deeper level the liturgical rites of the post–Vatican II era, the rites that our Holy Father Pope Benedict XVI has affirmed as constituting the "ordinary form" of the Roman Rite for the present,[5] the liturgy that he himself celebrates daily. But it is also to be hoped that the presentation of these medieval texts can contribute to a "reform of the reform", of which we spoke at the outset of this work. Indeed,

---

[3] Louis Chatellier, *The Europe of the Devout: The Catholic Reformation and the Formation of a New Society*, Past and Present Publications (Cambridge, England: Cambridge University Press; Paris: Editions de la Maison des Sciences de l'Homme, 1989), 40–41.

[4] Donald Matthew, *Atlas of Medieval Europe* (New York: Facts on File, 1992), 14.

[5] Pope Benedict XVI, in his letter accompanying *Summorum pontificum*, his July 7, 2007, decree widening the availabiliy of the preconciliar form of the Mass, states, "The Missal published by Paul VI and then republished in two subsequent editions by John Paul II, obviously is and continues to be the normal Form—the *Forma ordinaria*—of the Eucharistic Liturgy" (*L'Osservatore Romano*, weekly edition in English, July 11, 2007, p. 9).

the 2008 decision of the Holy Father to make reception of Holy Communion on the tongue, with the communicant in a kneeling posture, normative for all those receiving Communion from the pontiff at papal Masses is one of several indications that the implementation of a reform of the reform is already under way. Pope Benedict's 2007 *motu proprio* decree to expand the use of the "extraordinary form" of the Roman Rite Mass, the 1962 redaction of the 1570 Mass of Pope Saint Pius V,[6] certainly suggests that the Holy Father is inviting the Church to rediscover the liturgical treasures of her past and bring them to bear upon the present age. Less well known has been the Holy See's project, recently completed, to reprint in facsimile form the first editions of the Roman liturgical books that ensued from the Council of Trent, beginning with reprints of the 1595–1596 *Pontificale Romanum* in 1997 and the 1570 *Missale Romanum* in 1998. Before drawing our exploration of the medieval liturgy to a close, we shall offer the reader a few key considerations, drawn from what we have seen in the medieval rites of divine worship and addressing the liturgical issues of the present day.

We have all heard time and again Saint Mark's Gospel account of the exchange between Christ and the scribe who asked of him what is the greatest commandment (Mk 12:28–34):

A Commandment Forgotten

> And Jesus answered him: The first commandment of all is, Hear, O Israel: the Lord thy God is one God. And thou shalt love the Lord thy God, with thy whole heart, and with thy whole soul, and with thy whole mind, and with thy whole strength. This is the first commandment. And the second is like to it: Thou shalt love thy neighbour as thyself. There is no other commandment greater than these. (verses 29–31)

Certainly these words of our Lord teach us that there cannot be any genuine love of God without a genuine love of neighbor. This dimension of the Gospel passage is universally known. But there is another essential lesson to be learned from this passage—that there cannot be a genuine love of neighbor without a genuine love for God himself, a love that must take the first place in our lives, even as Christ has set the love of God as the *first* of his two great commandments of love. In modern times, there has been a tendency to emphasize the second of these commandments, the love of neighbor, to the extreme of virtually effacing and forgetting the first. There is in this the implication that love of neighbor is the one and only thing required of us and that there is no need to offer and address our love and adoration directly to God. Over sixteen centuries ago, the Eastern Church Father Saint Gregory of Nyssa (+c. 395) warned of this misrepresentation of the two great commandments, asking, "What solicitude of charity could

---

[6] Benedict XVI, *Summorum pontificum*, 8–9.

he sincerely and earnestly have for his brothers, who does not love God with his whole heart and with his whole soul?"[7]

But how, it may be asked, does this pertain to the sacred liturgy and to the medieval texts we have examined? In our own age, when some have deliberately sought to pervade the liturgy with the spirit of the world and treat it as merely a platform for airing heterodox theological opinions and secular causes before a captive audience, we need to learn from medieval Christendom that the liturgy is before all else an act of adoration humbly and reverently offered to the infinitely good and infinitely holy God of the universe, who in his unfathomable mercy became man and came to redeem us and now calls us to an eternity of happiness with him. Indeed, the liturgy is mankind's response of love to a loving God. Moreover, the medieval liturgical rites bear witness to the truth that "the Liturgy is not about us, but about God", as Pope Benedict XVI has observed.[8]

The very word "adoration" and everything it means need to be restored to their rightful place in liturgical theology. The Holy Father reminded the entire Church in his 2007 apostolic exhortation *Sacramentum caritatis* that the Mass is "the Church's supreme act of adoration"; regarding Holy Communion, he added, "Receiving the Eucharist means adoring him whom we receive."[9] Pope Benedict's words serve as a corrective to a certain contemporary mentality that considers the Real Presence as an undesirable distraction from the communal dimensions of the Eucharist. As the liturgical scholar Monsignor Klaus Gamber stated in his 1993 work *The Reform of the Roman Liturgy*, there needs to be a return to the Church's timeless theology of the liturgy, "when the purpose of the Mass is again seen as an act of adoration and glorification of God and of offering thanks for His blessings, for our salvation and for the promise of the heavenly life to come, and as the mystical reenactment of the Lord's sacrifice on the cross."[10]

The preeminence of the spirit of adoration in the Mass that pervaded medieval celebrations of this sacrament has also been undermined by the absurd assertion of some that the early Church did not see the Eucharist as Christ himself present on the altar but rather as a "thing-like gift" and that the medieval Church subsequently distorted Eucharistic theology by addressing and worshiping the Eucharist as Christ in his totality (body, blood, soul, and divinity). Commenting on this issue, Pope Benedict XVI explained in his 2000 book *The*

---

[7] Saint Gregory of Nyssa, *De instituto Christiano*, PG 46, cols. 299–300 (Greek text with Latin translation).

[8] Benedict XVI [Joseph Ratzinger], preface to Alcuin Reid, O.S.B., *The Organic Development of the Liturgy* (San Francisco: Ignatius Press, 2005), 13.

[9] Benedict XVI, *Sacramentum caritatis* (February 22, 2007), no. 66, *L'Osservatore Romano*, weekly edition in English, March 21, 2007, xii.

[10] Klaus Gamber, *The Reform of the Roman Liturgy: Its Problems and Background* (San Juan Capistrano, Calif.: Una Voce Press; Harrison, N.Y.: Foundation for Catholic Reform, 1993), 175 (© Roman Catholic Books, Fort Collins, Col.).

Spirit of the Liturgy, "Receiving the Eucharist does not mean eating a 'thing-like' gift.... No, there is a person-to-person exchange, a coming of the one into the other. The living Lord gives himself to me, enters into me, and invites me to surrender myself to him." [11] It was this recognition of the Eucharist as the living Christ, the second Person of the Blessed Trinity incarnate, present in his risen and glorified body, that moved the medieval Church to treat the Eucharist with the utmost reverence. Thus do we find an entire chapter devoted to instructions regarding the reverent handling of the Eucharist in the customary for the French Benedictine abbey of Cluny that the monk Bernard compiled around 1075, declaring at the beginning of the chapter, "Here it bears calling to mind, however, with what devotion and with what diligence should service be rendered with respect to the consecration of the Body and Blood of the Lord." [12] The devotion and diligence toward the Eucharist prescribed by Bernard's customary can be seen in his instruction regarding the pre-Communion fracture of the Host:

> The priest, taking it [the Host] with his middle fingers, places it upon the corporal at the foot of the chalice, and after he shall have broken the Host, he drops one particle into the chalice (as is the general custom), two upon the paten, and with the corporal covers both; beforehand, however, over the chalice itself, he rubs and shakes off his fingers, with which he has touched [the Host], lest by chance anything shall have adhered during the breaking of the Body of Christ; which [fingers] meanwhile closing with the utmost care, and joining his hands against his chest in the manner of the Cross, he turns himself first to the deacon. [13]

The *Ordinarium* of the Carmelite Order compiled by the order's German provincial Sibert de Beka, dating from around 1312, instructs the priest celebrating Mass that he should not even turn the pages of the missal with the fingers with which he is going to touch the Eucharist but instead leave the page-turning to the deacon assisting him at the altar. [14] Some may disdainfully regard such rubrics as symptomatic of an excessive and eccentric fastidiousness born of an exaggerated preoccupation with the Real Presence; but in reality, these rubrics testify to a living and unwavering faith that continually proclaims in the presence of the risen Christ, "It is the Lord" (Jn 20:7). As Venerable Pope Pius XII (+1958) has observed, our understanding of the Eucharist must be shaped (as it was in the Middle Ages) by a fundamental

---

[11] Benedict XVI [Joseph Cardinal Ratzinger], *The Spirit of the Liturgy* (San Francisco: Ignatius Press, 2000), 88–89.

[12] *Ordo Cluniacensis*, pt. 1, chap. 35, in Marquard Herrgott, ed., *Vetus disciplina monastica* (Paris, 1726; repr., Siegburg, Germany: Franciscus Schmitt, 1999), 220–227 (quoted passage on 220).

[13] Ibid., 223–224.

[14] Text in Benedict Zimmerman, ed., *Ordinaire de l'ordre de Notre-Dame du Mont-Carmel*, Bibliothèque liturgique 13 (Paris: Alphonse Picard et Fils, 1910), 80.

recognition of "the '*infinita, summa, divina Maiestas*' of Christ" (the infinite, supreme, divine Majesty of Christ).[15]

The antidevotional attitude toward the Eucharist on the part of some in our time is linked to a wider contemporary agenda that seeks to reduce Catholic worship to an abstraction totally devoid of any imagery that can speak to the human heart, a liturgy in which the senses are largely denied any meaningful participation. Such a mentality contradicts the very nature of the sacraments in which sensible signs (the pouring of water in baptism, the imposition of hands in holy orders, etc.) are made efficacious instruments in the conferral of the invisible gifts of God. It is this abstractionist mentality that has robbed us of our sense of communion with the citizens of Heaven by stripping images of the Blessed Virgin Mary and the saints from the sanctuaries and naves of our churches, turning them visually into empty voids; it is this mentality that has even barred the faithful from kissing the feet of their crucified Savior on Good Friday by opposing the use of crucifixes in the rite of venerating the cross. It is this mind-set that divests the sacred liturgy of all sensible beauty. By contrast, Pope Benedict XVI in his apostolic exhortation *Sacramentum caritatis* declares that beauty is essential to the celebration of the sacred liturgy:

> Like the rest of Christian Revelation, the liturgy is inherently linked to beauty: it is *veritatis splendor*. The liturgy is a radiant expression of the Paschal Mystery, in which Christ draws us to himself and calls us to communion.... The beauty of the liturgy is part of this mystery; it is a sublime expression of God's glory and, in a certain sense, a glimpse of heaven on earth.... Beauty, then, is not mere decoration, but rather an essential element of the liturgical action, since it is an attribute of God himself and his revelation.[16]

The need for beauty in the liturgy was discovered twelve centuries ago by a Benedictine monk who in his earlier years had been inclined to think otherwise, Saint Benedict of Aniane (+821). Benedict's medieval biographer tells how as a young monk the future abbot of the French monastery of Aniane had believed that the pursuit of evangelical poverty and simplicity in religious life precluded the use of precious materials and beautiful adornments in monastic celebrations of the liturgy. Thus, acting on this presupposition, he insisted upon using Eucharistic vessels made from wood, glass, or tin rather than silver and refused to wear chasubles sewn from silk.[17] But by 782, Benedict had undergone a profound change of view on this very point. In that year,

---

[15] Venerable Pius XII, "The Liturgical Movement: An Address of Pope Pius XII to the International Congress on Pastoral Liturgy" (September 22, 1956), *Pope Speaks* 3 (Winter 1956–1957): 285.

[16] Benedict XVI, *Sacramentum caritatis*, no. 35, p. viii.

[17] Ardone, *Vita Benedicti abbatis Anianensis et Indensis*, chap. 5, in *Monumenta Germaniae historica: Scriptorum*, vol. 15, pt. 1 (Leipzig, Germany: Karl W. Hiersemann, 1925), 204.

as abbot of Aniane, he began the construction of a new church and monastery for his religious community. Benedict sought to make the house of God beautiful in every way, adorning it with seven ornately fashioned candelabras, as well as seven hanging lamps before the high altar and a crown-shaped array of silver lamps within the choir. The church featured four altars, with the high altar symbolizing the one God and the three side altars representing the three Persons of the Blessed Trinity.[18] With great zeal, Benedict now sought out large silver chalices and other silver altar vessels as well as costly vestments for his monastery.[19] Aniane became a model for other monasteries,[20] and Benedict imparted to the universal Church a lasting legacy of liturgical beauty through his compilation of the "Aniane" adaptation of the Gregorian Sacramentary, the prototype for Mass texts throughout medieval Europe, as we have already observed.[21] Benedict's commitment to make the liturgy as beautiful and majestic as possible was inherited by the Benedictines of the tenth- to eleventh-century Cluniac reform, who with their magnificent liturgical rites helped to spread "the sense of the sacred" throughout medieval Christendom.

The medieval liturgy has been criticized for its frequent references to the sinfulness of man and its repeated pleas for divine mercy and forgiveness—indeed, such references do appear quite frequently in the texts we have examined. We are told by the critics that these medieval admissions of human guilt and frailty are too negative. But are they really? We need look only to our Lord's parable of the two men praying in the Temple to find the answer. It is the man with bowed head, calling himself a sinner and beseeching God's mercy, whom Christ says went home justified, whereas the other, filled with high self-esteem, that most prized of secularist "virtues", left the Temple unjustified (Lk 18:9–14). The recurrent humble pleas for God's mercy and forgiveness that permeate medieval liturgical rites are consonant with the way that our Lord himself has taught us to approach him: with a profound awareness of our sinfulness and a deep confidence in his mercy and love. Thus is it that a directory of instructions for the celebration of Mass in the 1568 missal of Palencia, Spain, begins with a rite of sacramental confession for a priest intending to celebrate Mass, in order that he might "purify his conscience". The missal provides the following prayer for the priest to say on his knees before confessing his sins:

> *Receive my confession, O my most merciful and clement Lord Jesus Christ, the only hope for the salvation of my soul, and give me, I beseech you, contrition of heart, and tears to my eyes, that day and night I may lament all*

---

[18] Ibid., chap. 17, pp. 205–206.
[19] Ibid., chap. 18, p. 207.
[20] Ibid., 206.
[21] See p. 4 above.

my negligences with humility and purity of heart. Let my prayer come before your sight, O Lord. If you shall be angry against me, whom shall I ask to help me? Who shall have mercy upon my sins? Remember, O Lord, that you called the Canaanite and the publican to penitence. You accepted the weeping of Peter. O Lord my God, receive my prayers. O good Jesus, Savior of the world, who gave yourself to death on a cross, that you might save sinners, look upon me, a wretched one invoking your name, and do not mark my iniquity, lest you should forget your goodness. For if because I have sinned you could have condemned me, because you are disposed to save me you have not sent me away. Therefore, spare me, my Savior, and have mercy upon my sinful soul. Loosen its bonds. Heal its wounds. I long for you, Lord Jesus Christ, I seek you, I desire you; show me your face, and I shall be saved. Send forth, O Lord, by the prayers of the immaculate Virgin your Mother and all your saints and elect, your light and your truth into my soul, that it may show me all my defects that it is necessary for me to confess in truth and may help me and teach me to reveal them completely and with due contrition. Who live and reign . . .[22]

Undoubtedly some will take exception to this prayer and other medieval expressions of penitence as too self-demeaning, but I believe that the court of Heaven judges otherwise. We need only recall the Psalmist's words: "A contrite and humbled heart, O God, thou wilt not despise" (Ps 50:19).

In *Sacramentum caritatis*, Pope Benedict XVI speaks of the importance of what he calls "the *ars celebrandi*, the art of proper celebration" in fostering "a sense of the sacred".[23] He is, of course, referring to the manner of celebrating the liturgy, a manner that *must* be determined by the approved rubrics of the universal Church. Much of the genius and beauty of medieval liturgy is to be found in rubrics that created a profound sense of solemnity, raising the heart and the soul to "the things that are above" (Col 3:1). In our time there have been instances in which the deliberate desacralization of the liturgy has taken the form of a contempt for the rubrics so flagrant that it gives the appearance of an effort to drag God from his throne. Alarmed by a comparable disdain for the precepts of the Church in his own time, the English martyr Saint Thomas More (+1535) likens those responsible to Judas the betrayer greeting Christ with a kiss in the Garden of Gethsemane: "In just this way is He kissed by those priests who consecrate the most holy body of Christ and then put to death Christ's members, Christian souls, by their false teaching and wicked example."[24]

---

[22] *Missale Pallantinum* (Palencia, Spain: Sebastian Martinez, 1568; Latin text provided by Biblioteca Apostolica Vaticana, Vatican City [shelf mark Stamp. Barb. B. X. 1]), fol. 348r.

[23] Benedict XVI, *Sacramentum caritatis*, nos. 38, 40, p. viii.

[24] Saint Thomas More, *De Tristitia Christi*, ed. and trans. Clarence H. Miller, vol. 14 of *Complete Works of St. Thomas More* (New Haven: Yale University Press, 1976), 390–391 (Latin text with English translation). The English translation of Clarence Miller is quoted here.

Those who have been intent upon filling the sanctuary of God with the spirit of the world would do well to heed our Savior's command to the merchants who had polluted the Temple with their secularism: "Take these things hence, and make not the house of my Father a house of traffic" (Jn 2:10).

The liturgy is not about "self-affirmation" or "empowerment". The faithful, when they enter their churches, are not looking for a mirror in which to see themselves or the world—they want to find the sacred, the transcendent; they want to find God. We need to discard the concept of conforming the liturgy to the transitory preoccupations of our own age and let it again be the timeless expression of our unchanging faith. Casting in a Christian context a thought from the writings of the ancient Roman orator Cicero, Pope Blessed John XXIII (+1963) observed, "Time destroys the inventions of public opinion; truth remains and grows ever stronger, and lives and lasts forever."[25]

The Keys of the Kingdom of Heaven

In the library of Saint John's College, Oxford, there is preserved the sole surviving copy of the 1502 *Processionale ad usum Sarum*, a book of liturgical chants for the Sarum Rite of late medieval England. On folio 75 of this text, toward the end of the *Exsultet*, the great hymn of the Easter Vigil, an unknown hand over four and a half centuries ago mutilated the parchment, scraping away with a knife the words *"patre nostro papa N."*, a reference to the reigning pontiff. A later hand attempted to undo the damage by writing the missing words over the scraped parchment, but the marring of the original is still visible.[26] The damaged parchment bears witness to the June 25, 1535, letter of King Henry VIII ordering the expurgation of all references to the pope from the liturgical books of England.[27] The monarch wanted to hold on to the Latin Mass, but he wanted it without the pope. For most of Tudor England, this severance of the Latin Mass from the papacy soon led to the end of the Latin Mass, replaced by the "liturgical projects" of the Reformation ideologue Thomas Cranmer. This unfortunate chapter of English history can serve as a cautionary tale—a warning of what can happen when the sacred liturgy is separated from its supreme guardian on earth, the Vicar of Christ.

---

[25] Blessed John XXIII, *Journal of a Soul* (New York: McGraw-Hill, 1965), 145 (reproduced by permission of Continuum International Publishing Group, London). Pope John's words freely paraphrase a passage from the *De natura deorum* of Cicero (bk. 2, chap. 2, no. 5; Latin text with English translation in H. Rackham, trans., *Cicero: De natura deorum; Academica* [London: William Heinemann; Cambridge, Mass.: Harvard University Press, 1961], 126–127).

[26] *Richard Pynson: Processionale ad usum Sarum, 1502*, facsimile ed., The Use of Sarum 1 (Clarabricken, Ireland: Boethius, 1980), editor's introduction, p. 3, plus text, fol. 75r.

[27] Henry VIII, circular letter of June 25, 1535, in John Strype, *Ecclesiastical Memorials Relating Chiefly to Religion, and the Reformation of It and the Emergencies of the Church of England, under King Henry VIII, King Edward VI, and Queen Mary I*, vol. 1, pt. 2 (Oxford: Clarendon, 1822), p. 210.

It can be inferred that our Holy Father Pope Benedict XVI has in various ways invited the Church to undertake a frank reassessment of the liturgical "reforms" enacted after the Second Vatican Council—his decision to make more widely available the pre–Vatican II "extraordinary form" of the Roman Rite Mass certainly seems to suggest this, especially when seen in the context of the concerns he had earlier voiced as a cardinal regarding the way in which certain postconciliar liturgical changes had been made.[28] Such a reassessment, by its very nature, would include an honest but reverent discussion of those particular changes that have proved to be unfortunate, in which centuries-old liturgical traditions, soundly rooted in the Church's Eucharistic and sacramental theology, were hastily cast aside by certain individuals entrusted with the task of preparing the revised liturgical books and the emendations that followed, sometimes on the basis of fleeting preoccupations of the 1960s and 1970s, sometimes on the basis of a failure to understand and respect the wisdom of our forefathers in the faith—especially the wisdom of medieval and Baroque Christianity.[29] Such a discussion, however, if it is to be spiritually fruitful, must take place always within the context of a filial adherence to the teaching and disciplinary authority of the supreme pontiff, and the recognition that the final decision as to what is to be changed or retained in the sacred liturgy rests solely with the Vicar of Christ. No one should dispute the authority of a reigning pontiff or that of his predecessors to promulgate a revised liturgical book or restore to use an earlier one.

In a Spanish sacramentary of Tortosa from the twelfth or early thirteenth century, we find a short summary of the history of the Ordinary of the Mass in which each of the components of the rite is attributed to the intervention of a particular pope. Thus Pope Saint Telesphorus (142–154) is credited with adding the *Gloria* to the Mass; Pope Saint Sixtus I (132–142) is credited with adding the *Sanctus*; and the popes Saint Clement I (90–100), Saint Leo the Great (440–461), and Saint Alexander I (121–132) are credited with contributing the *Te igitur*, *Hanc igitur*, and *Qui pridie* respectively to the text of the Roman

---

[28] Benedict XVI, *Spirit of the Liturgy*, 163, 165–166.

[29] A good example of an "honest but reverent discussion" regarding post–Vatican II liturgical texts can be seen in the liturgical scholar Father Anthony Ward's 2005 assessment of the postconciliar funeral liturgy; see his articles "Some Euchology of the 1969 'Ordo Exsequiarum'" and "Further Euchology of the 1969 'Ordo Exsequiarum'", published in the Roman journal *Ephemerides Liturgicae* (*EL* 119 [2005]: 3–51 and 201–254, respectively [especially 6–10, 39–42, 201, 228–230, 232–235, and 244–251]). Father Ward found evidence of Protestant source material having been used to shape certain portions of the postconciliar funeral rites. Observing that, unlike Catholic sources, such Protestant sources do not recognize the need of praying *for* the dead, he points out that there is a rich corpus of Catholic funeral texts from the past that could have been utilized instead (see 246–247). Father Pierre-Marie Gy, one of the compilers of the *Novus ordo* funeral rite, publicly admitted that some Anglican sources had been utilized in composing the new rite; see Pierre-Marie Gy, O.P., "Le nouveau ritual romain des funérailles", *La Maison-Dieu* 101 (1970): 30.

Canon.[30] Similar listings of the contributions of various popes to the Mass can be found in other medieval liturgical books,[31] as well as in Honorius of Autun's twelfth-century liturgical commentary the *Gemma animae*[32] and, three centuries earlier, in the *De rebus ecclesiasticis* of the German theologian Walafrid Strabo (+849).[33] Regardless of the historical accuracy of these attributions, they certainly testify to a medieval recognition of the popes as actively shaping and governing the development of the liturgy, with the authority to make changes or additions to the sacred rites. In the ninth century we find Pope Saint Leo IV (+855) stating in no uncertain terms the Petrine authority and primacy in liturgical matters. Firmly taking to task an abbot who had obstinately resisted the use of Gregorian chant in the liturgy, Pope Leo writes to the recalcitrant monk:

> A thing exceedingly unbelievable has sounded in our ears.... It is because you detest so greatly the sweetness of Gregory's chant, which he established and handed down with his tradition of singing and reciting in the Church, that you would dissent in all things by reasoning of this sort not only from this neighboring see but also from almost every Western Church, and certainly from all who with Latin voices give praise and offer their melodious tones to the eternal King....
>
> Just so, I beseech you surely to forsake dissenting from this Church, the supreme head of religion, of which none wants to dispossess himself, or from such aforesaid Churches, if you wholly love to have the peace and concord of the universal Church. For if, which we cannot believe, you have so greatly despised our doctrine and the tradition of our holy pontiff, that you would not follow our rite in all respects, in songs and readings, know that we shall cast you out from our communion; for it befits you salutarily to follow these things, which the Roman Church, mother of all and our teacher, does not spurn but desires and holds insolubly. Therefore we command you under the bringing forth of excommunication that in no way are you to celebrate otherwise what both holy Pope Gregory handed down and we hold, in the chanting and reading in the Churches, and you should cultivate and sing with all men unceasingly. For if, which we certainly do not believe, there shall have been any attempt by you in the present or the future to draw back or turn away in any way whatsoever to another tradition contrary to this, which we have commanded you to be celebrated, we shall order him to be alienated not only from the sacred Body and Blood of our Lord Jesus Christ but indeed

[30] Sacramentary of Tortosa (manuscript: Tortosa, Spain, Biblioteca Capitular, MS 34), quoted in Blessed Juan Bautista Ferreres Boluda, S.J., *Historia del misal romano* (Barcelona: Eugenio Subirana, 1929), 217–218.

[31] Ferreres Boluda, *Historia del misal romano*, 216, 218.

[32] Honorius of Autun, *Gemma animae*, bk. 1, chaps. 87–90, PL 172, cols. 572–574.

[33] Walafrid Strabo, *De rebus ecclesiasticis*, chaps. 21–23, PL 114, cols. 943–951.

by our authority and that of all our predecessors we [shall] condemn him to anathema enduring forever by reason of the audacity of his arrogance.[34]

Note that Pope Leo in this letter is commanding obedience to liturgical traditions that at the time were less than three centuries old, established not by the Apostles but rather by a predecessor of his, Pope Saint Gregory the Great (+604).

It is most unfortunate that in some recent discussions concerning the sacred liturgy there has arisen an increasingly antipapal rhetoric. In such instances the focus has been shifted away from a sincere quest to restore the sense of the sacred through an objective evaluation and comparison of past and present liturgical texts and rubrics—to explore whether a certain liturgical form may more effectively offer glory to God and contribute to the salvation and sanctification of souls than its modern or ancient counterpart. Instead, the discussion degenerates into a thinly veiled attack upon the papacy, with the allegation that the exercise of papal authority has thwarted authentic liturgy. But if the current crisis in the liturgy is to be resolved in a truly decisive and universal manner, there needs to be the recognition that the supreme pontiff can, if he so decides, exercise his Petrine authority to order an authentic restoration of the sacred liturgy that all must obey. Those who deny the jurisdiction of past popes in liturgical matters thereby deny the authority of the present pontiff to rectify or even reverse unfortunate decisions of the past.

The author would beg all to recall and contemplate prayerfully the infallible declaration of the First Vatican Council (1869–1870) that the Roman pontiff has "full and supreme power of jurisdiction in the universal Church, not only in things that pertain to faith and morals but also in those things that pertain to the discipline and government of the Church spread out through the entire world".[35] In his 1947 encyclical *Mediator Dei*, Venerable Pope Pius XII declared unequivocally, "The Sovereign Pontiff alone enjoys the right to recognize and establish any practice touching the worship of God, to introduce and approve new rites, as also to modify those he judges to require modification."[36] To reject a pope's authority to govern the specific prayers and rubrics of the liturgy is to invite a state of total liturgical anarchy in which the content of the rites is determined by personal, subjective judgments as to what constitutes an "authentic" liturgy. Whatever

---

[34] Saint Leo IV, *Letter 33*, to the abbot Honoratus, c. 852, in *Monumenta Germaniae historica: Epistolarum*, vol. 5; *Epistolae Karolini aevi III* (Berlin: Weidmann, 1899), 603–604.

[35] First Vatican Council, session 4, *Constitutio dogmatica I de ecclesia Christi* (July 18, 1870), chap. 3, translated from Henry Denzinger and John Baptist Umberg, S.J., eds., *Enchiridion symbolorum: Definitionum et declarationum de rebus fidei et morum*, ed. 21–23 (Freiburg im Breisgau, Germany: Herder, 1937), no. 1831, p. 505.

[36] Venerable Pius XII, *Mediator Dei* (November 20, 1947), no. 58, in *Encyclical Letter of Pope Pius XII on the Sacred Liturgy: Mediator Dei* (Boston: Saint Paul Editions, n.d.), 27 (Vatican Library translation).

proposals anyone may have for the future of the sacred liturgy, the decision whether to act upon such proposals must rest with the See of Peter. As the liturgical scholar László Dobszay has astutely observed, "Only the 'official' Church may *act*. What we do may later appear useful; but it bears fruit only after the Church embraces it and makes it her own." [37]

In approaching the liturgy, both to participate in it and to study it, humility is essential. We need the humility to bend our knees before our gracious and merciful God. We need the humility to obey the decisions of the supreme pontiff in his governance of the liturgy. Those involved in any future work of renewing, reforming, and restoring the liturgy need the humility to respect the texts of our forefathers. Let us place all our hopes and prayers for an authentic restoration of the sense of the sacred at the foot of the tabernacle, where (to borrow a term from one of the Spanish liturgical books) "His Sacramental Majesty" [38] dwells among us, "the king of ages, immortal, invisible, the only God" (1 Tim 1:17), he who is the "Alpha and Omega, the first and the last" (Rev 22:13), the "King of Kings and Lord of Lords" (cf. Rev 19:16). And let us end by invoking the ever-loving and gracious intercession of his immaculate and all-beautiful Virgin Mother, offering her our filial love in the words of a fifteenth-century text of the Carmelites' office for the feast of Our Lady of Mount Carmel:

> *O Mary, . . . O blessed Lady of Heaven, flower of virgins, Queen of those on earth, Empress of the dead, O lily of chastity, chamber of the continent; you, the banner of truth, the compendium of goodness, O rose of cleanliness; you, the royal purple of patience; you, the dawn of righteousness; you, the violet of beauty; O mirror of prudence, the foundation of fortitude; you, the book of temperance; you, the scale of rectitude; you, the unfailing hope of all; you, the brooch of faith; you, the consolation of the afflicted, the vessel of good things; you, the providence of the poor; you, the joy of the just; you, the praise and honor of women; you, the level gate of life; you, the school of virtue; you, the jewel of salvation; you, the pattern of morals; you, the health of the infirm; you, the open harbor of the shipwrecked; you, the full canopy of protection; you, the beginning of humility and the consummation of sanctity.* [39]

---

[37] László Dobszay, *The Bugnini-Liturgy and the Reform of the Reform*, Musicae sacrae meletemata 5 (Front Royal, Va.: Church Music Association of America / Catholic Church Music Associates, 2003), 217 (Emphasis in original).

[38] From a rubric for the Easter Sunday Eucharistic procession of the Mercedarian Order in their *Manual of Benedictions, Offices, Processions, and Holy Week*; see *Manual de bendiciones, oficios, procesiones, y semana santa con el oficio de sepultura . . . para el uso de los religiosos Descalzos de nuestra Señora de la Merced, redención de cautivos christianos* (Madrid: D. Joachin Ibarra, 1789), 131.

[39] Office of the feast of Our Lady of Mount Carmel, Matins, 2nd nocturn, lesson 6, in a manuscript of Cambridge, England, Cambridge University Library, 7, f. 6, 28 (fol. 5r–5v); text in Zimmerman, *Ordinaire de l'ordre de Notre-Dame du Mont-Carmel*, 326.

Bibliography

Abbaye Saint-Pierre, Solesmes, ed. *Antiphonale missarum sancti Gregorii, IXᵉ–Xᵉ siècle, Codex 239 de la Bibliothèque de Laon.* Paléographie musicale 10. Solesmes, France, 1909. Reprint, Berne, Switzerland: H. Lang, 1971.

Ackerman, Robert. "The Knighting Ceremonies in the Middle English Romances". *Speculum* 19 (1944): 285–313.

Agenda secundum rubricam ecclesie cathedralis Saltzeburgensis. Basel, Switzerland: Jacobus de Pfortzhein, 1511. Digitized text, Bayerische Staatsbibliothek, Munich, 2007.

Agenda sive Benedictionale de actibus ecclesiae secundum chorum et observationem ecclesie Pataviensis. Basel, Switzerland: Jacobus Pfortzensis, 1514. Digitized text, Bayerische Staatsbibliothek, Munich, 2008.

Agenda sive Exequiale divinorum sacramentorum. Edited by Martin, Canon of the Diocese of Vilna[, Lithuania]. Gdańsk, Poland: Conrad Bomgharten, 1499. Digitized text, CBN Polona, National Digital Library, Biblioteka Narodowa, Warsaw, Poland, n.d.

Agenda sive Exequiale sacramentorum. Strasbourg, France: Prüss, 1505. Digitized text, Bayerische Staatsbibliothek, Munich, n.d.

Albers, Bruno, ed. *Consuetudines monasticae.* Vol. 1, *Consuetudines Farfenses.* Stuttgart: Jos. Roth, Bibliopolae, 1900.

———, ed. *Consuetudines monasticae.* Vol. 2, *Consuetudines Cluniacenses antiquiores.* Monte Cassino, Italy: Typis Montis Casini, 1905.

———, ed. *Consuetudines monasticae.* Vol. 4, *Consuetudines Fructuarienses necnon Cystrensis in Anglia monasterii et congregationis Vallymbrosanae.* Monte Cassino, Italy: Typis Montis Casini, 1911.

———, ed. *Consuetudines monasticae.* Vol. 5, *Consuetudines monasteriorum Germaniae necnon s. Vitonis Virdunensis et Floriacensis abbatiae monumenta saeculi decimi continens.* Monte Cassino, Italy: Typis Societatis Editricis Castri Casini, 1912.

Altés i Aguiló, Francesc Xavier, ed. *Missale Vicense, 1496.* Facsimile ed. Biblioteca litúrgica catalana 3. Barcelona: Institut d'Estudis Catalans, 2001.

Amberg, Gottfried, ed. *Ceremoniale Coloniense.* Studien zur Kölner Kirchengeschichte 17. Siegburg, Germany: Franz Schmitt, 1982.

Amiot, François. *History of the Mass.* Twentieth Century Encyclopedia of Catholicism 110. New York: Hawthorn Books, 1959.

Andrieu, Michel. *Immixtio et consecratio: La consécration par contact dans les documents liturgiques du moyen âge.* Université de Strasbourg, Bibliothèque de l'Institut de Droit Canonique, 11. Paris: A. Picard, 1924.

———, ed. *Les Ordines Romani du haut moyen âge.* 5 vols. Spicilegium sacrum Lovaniense: Etudes et documents 11, 23, 24, 28, 29. Louvain, Belgium: "Spicilegium sacrum Lovaniense" Administration, 1931–1961.

————, ed. *Le pontifical romain au moyen-âge.* Vol. 1, *Le pontifical romain du XIIe siècle.* Studi e testi 86. Vatican City: Biblioteca Apostolica Vaticana, 1938.

————, ed. *Le pontifical romain au moyen-âge.* Vol. 2, *Le pontifical de la Curie romaine au XIIIe siècle.* Studi e testi 87. Vatican City: Biblioteca Apostolica Vaticana, 1940.

————, ed. *Le pontifical romain au moyen-âge.* Vol. 3, *Le pontifical de Guillaume Durand.* Studi e testi 88. Vatican City: Biblioteca Apostolica Vaticana, 1940.

Angerer, Joachim, O.Praem., ed. *Caeremoniae regularis observantiae sanctissimi patris nostri Benedicti ex ipsius regula sumptae, secundum quod in sacris locis, scilicet Specu et Monasterio Sublacensi practicantur.* Corpus consuetudinum monasticarum 11, pt. 1. Siegburg, Germany: Franciscus Schmitt, 1985.

Arens, Franz, ed. *Der Liber ordinarius der Essener Stiftskirche.* Paderborn, Germany: Albert Pape, 1908.

————. *Der Liber ordinarius der Essener Stiftskirche und seine Bedeutung für die Liturgie, Geschichte und Topographie des ehemaligen Stiftes Essen.* Beiträge zur Geschichte von Stadt und Stift Essen. Essen, Germany: G. D. Baedeker, 1901.

Banting, H. M. J., ed. *Two Anglo-Saxon Pontificals (the Egbert and Sidney Sussex Pontificals).* Henry Bradshaw Society 104. London: Henry Bradshaw Society, 1989.

Bardy, Gustav, ed. *Eusèbe de Césarée: Histoire ecclésiastique.* Vol. 2, *Livres V–VII.* Sources chrétiennes 41. Paris: Cerf, 1955.

Barnim XI. *Agenda, dat is, Ordninge der hilligen Kerckenempter unde Ceremonien wo sich de Parrherren, Seelsorgere unde Kerckendenere in erem Ampte holden Schölen.* Szczecin, Poland: Andreas Kellner, 1591. Digitized text, Bayerische Staatsbibliothek, Munich, 2009.

Barton, John. *Penance and Absolution.* Twentieth Century Encyclopedia of Catholicism 51. New York: Hawthorn Books, 1961.

Beatrice, Pier Franco. *La lavanda dei piedi: Contributo alla storia delle antiche liturgie cristiane.* Bibliotheca "Ephemerides Liturgicae", subsidia, 28. Rome: Centro Liturgico Vincenziano, Edizioni Liturgiche, 1983.

Beccari, Camillus. "Beatification and Canonization". In *Catholic Encyclopedia* (1907–1912), 2:364–369.

Bechoffen, John. *Quadruplex missalis expositio.* Basel, Switzerland: Michael Furter, 1505. Digitized text, Bayerische Staatsbibliothek, Munich, 2007.

Bellarmine, Saint Robert. *S.R.E. cardinalis Roberti Bellarmini Politiani S.J.: Opera omnia.* 8 vols. Naples: C. Pedone Lauriel, 1872.

Benedict XVI [Joseph Ratzinger]. Corpus Christi homily. May 26, 2005. *L'Osservatore Romano,* weekly edition in English, June 1, 2005, p. 3.

————. *Journey towards Easter: Retreat Given in the Vatican in the Presence of Pope John Paul II.* New York: Crossroad, 1987.

————. Preface to Alcuin Reid, O.S.B., *The Organic Development of the Liturgy.* San Francisco: Ignatius Press, 2005.

————. *Sacramentum caritatis.* February 22, 2007. *L'Osservatore Romano,* weekly edition in English, March 21, 2007, special insert.

————. *The Spirit of the Liturgy.* San Francisco: Ignatius Press, 2000.

————. *Summorum pontificum.* July 7, 2007. With accompanying letter. *L'Osservatore Romano,* weekly edition in English, July 11, 2007, pp. 8–9.

Benedictine Monks of Solesmes, eds. *Papal Teachings: The Liturgy.* Boston: Saint Paul Editions, 1962.

Béraudy, Roger. "L'initiation chrétienne". In Aimé-Georges Martimort, ed., *L'église en prière: Introduction à la liturgie,* 514–568. Paris: Desclée, 1961.

Bergh, F. Thomas. "Sarum Rite". In *Catholic Encyclopedia* (1907–1912), 13:479–481.

Bernard, John, and Robert Atkinson, eds. *The Irish Liber hymnorum*. Vol. 2, *Translations and Notes*. Henry Bradshaw Society 14. London: Henry Bradshaw Society, 1898.

Bernardi, Claudio. *La drammaturgia della settimana santa in Italia*. La città e lo spettacolo 2. Milan: Vita e Pensiero, 1991.

Berthelé, J. "Les instructions et constitutions de Guillaume Durand le Spéculateur". In *Académie des Sciences et Lettres de Montpellier: Mémoires de la Section des Lettres*, 2nd series, vol. 3 (Montpellier, 1900–1907), 1–148.

Bettley, John. "The Office of Holy Week at St. Mark's, Venice, in the late 16th Century, and the Musical Contributions of Giovanni Croce". *Early Music* 22 (February 1994): 45–60.

Biddle, Martin. *The Tomb of Christ*. Phoenix Mill, England: Sutton, 1999.

Bieler, Ludwig, ed. and trans. *The Irish Penitentials*. Scriptores Latini Hiberniae 5. Dublin: Dublin Institute for Advanced Studies, 1963.

Bishop, Edmund. "Holy Week Rites of Sarum, Hereford and Rouen Compared". In *Liturgica Historica: Papers on the Liturgy and Religious Life of the Western Church*, 276–300. London: Oxford University Press, 1918.

Bissig, Hans. *Das Churer Rituale, 1503–1927: Geschichte der Agende—Feier der Sakramente*. Studia Friburgensia, neue Folge, 56. Fribourg, Switzerland: Universitätsverlag Fribourg, 1979.

Blaise, Albert. *Lexicon Latinitatis medii aevi*. Corpus Christianorum: Continuatio mediaevalis. Turnhout, Belgium: Brepols, 1998.

Bligh, John, S.J. *Ordination to the Priesthood*. New York: Sheed and Ward, 1956.

Bolland, John van, et al., eds. *Acta sanctorum*. 68 vols. Antwerp, Belgium, 1643–. Reprint, Paris: Victor Palmé, 1863–1940.

Bonniwell, William, O.P. *A History of the Dominican Liturgy*. New York: Joseph Wagner, 1944.

Borromeo, Federico, ed. *Acta ecclesiae Mediolanensis a s. Carolo cardinali s. praxedis archiepiscopo condita*. 2 vols. Padua, Italy: Typus Seminarii Patavii, 1754.

Bowen, Lee. "The Tropology of Mediaeval Dedication Rites". *Speculum* 16 (1941): 469–479.

Bragança, Joaquim O. "Ritual de Santa Cruz de Coimbra: Porto, Biblioteca Municipal, ms. 858". *Didaskalia* 6 (1976): 123–210.

Brandolini, Luca, C.M. "L'evoluzione storica dei riti delle ordinazioni". *Ephemerides Liturgicae* 83 (1969): 67–87.

Brandt, Samuel, and George Laubmann, eds. *L. Caeli Firmiani Lactanti: Opera omnia*. Pt. 1, *Divinae institutiones et Epitome divinarum institutionum*. Corpus scriptorum ecclesiasticorum Latinorum 19. Vienna: F. Tempsky, 1890.

Braun, Joseph. "Pallium". In *Catholic Encyclopedia* (1907–1912), 11:427–429.

———. "Tiara". In *Catholic Encyclopedia* (1907–1912), 14:714–715.

Bréhier, Louis. "Godfrey of Bouillon". In *Catholic Encyclopedia* (1907–1912), 6:624–626.

Brière, Maurice; Louis Mariès, S.J.; and B.-Ch. Mercier, O.S.B., eds. *Hippolyte de Rome sur les Bénédictions d'Isaac, de Jacob et de Moïse*. Patrologia orientalis 27, fasc. 1–2. Paris: Firmin-Didot, 1954.

Britt, Matthew, O.S.B. *The Hymns of the Breviary and Missal*. New York: Benziger Bros., 1922.

Brooks, Neil C. *The Sepulchre of Christ in Art and Liturgy, with Special Reference to the Liturgic Drama*. University of Illinois Studies in Language and Literature 7, no. 2. Urbana, Ill.: University of Illinois, 1921.

Browe, Peter, S.J., ed. *Textus antiqui de festo Corporis Christi*. Opuscula et textus historiam ecclesiae eiusque vitam atque doctrinam illustrantia: Series liturgica, fasc. 4. Münster, Germany: Aschendorff, 1934.

———. *Die Verehrung der Eucharistie im Mittelalter*. Munich, 1933; Reprint, Rome: Herder, 1967.

Burckard, John. *Diarium sive Rerum urbanarum commentarii (1483–1506)*. Vol. 1, *1483–1492*. Edited by L. Thuasne. Paris: Ernest Leroux, 1883.

Burns, Yvonne. "The Lectionary of the Patriarch of Constantinople". *Studia Patristica* 15 (1984): 515–520.

Cabasilas, Nicholas. *A Commentary on the Divine Liturgy*. Translated by J. M. Hussey and P. A. McNulty. London: SPCK, 1983.

Cabié, Robert. "Christian Initiation". In Aimé-Georges Martimort, ed., *The Church at Prayer: An Introduction to the Liturgy*, vol. 3, *The Sacraments*, 11–100. Collegeville, Minn.: Liturgical Press, 1988.

Cabrol, Fernand. "Absoute". In Fernand Cabrol and Henri Leclercq, eds., *Dictionnaire d'archéologie chrétienne et de liturgie*, vol. 1, cols. 199–206. Paris: Librairie Letouzey et Ané, 1907–1953.

———. "Breviary". In *Catholic Encyclopedia* (1907–1912), 2:768–777.

Capelle, Bernard, O.S.B. "L'*Exultet* paschal: Oeuvre de Saint Ambroise". In *Miscellanea Giovanni Mercati*, vol. 1, *Bibbia-letteratura cristiana antica*, 219–246. Studi e testi 121. Vatican City: Biblioteca Apostolica Vaticana, 1946.

Carusi, Enrico, ed. *Il diario romano di Jacopo Gherardi da Volterra*. Rerum Italicarum scriptores 23, pt. 3. Castello, Italy: Tipi della Casa Editrice S. Lapi, 1904.

Caspers, Charles. "The Western Church during the Late Middle Ages: *Augenkommunion* or Popular Mysticism?" In Charles Caspers, Gerard Lukken, and Gerard Rouwhorst, eds., *Bread of Heaven: Customs and Practices Surrounding Holy Communion: Essays in the History of Liturgy and Culture*, 83–97. Liturgia condenda 3. Kampen, Netherlands: Kok Pharos, 1995.

Castellani, Alberto, O.P. *Sacerdotale iuxta s. Romane ecclesie et aliarum ecclesiarum*. Venice: Peter Bosellus, 1555. Digitized text, Bayerische Staatsbibliothek, Munich, 2009.

Catechism of the Catholic Church. English ed. Vatican City: Libreria Editrice Vaticana, © 1994; Washington, D.C.: United States Catholic Conference, 1994.

Catechism of the Council of Trent for Parish Priests. Translated by John McHugh, O.P., and Charles Callan, O.P. N.p., 1923. Reprint, South Bend, Ind.: Marian Publications, 1972.

The Catholic Encyclopedia. 15 vols. New York: Appleton, 1907–1912.

Ceremonial da missa [for the archdiocese of Braga, Portugal]. Lisbon: Germano Galharde, 1548. Digitized text, Biblioteca Nacional Digital, Biblioteca Nacional de Portugal, 2009.

Ceremonias y señales según el uso y costumbre de la religión de nuestro glorioso padre sanct Benito, las quales son desta sancta casa de sanct Millán de la Cogolla. Manuscript, Madrid: Real Academia de la Historia, Codex 64, sixteenth to seventeenth century. Digitized text, Biblioteca Virtual del Patrimonio Bibliográfico, Madrid, n.d.

Chang, Shin-Ho, ed. *Vetus missale Romanum monasticum Lateranense archivii basilicae Lateranensis, codex A65 (olim 65)*. Monumenta studia instrumenta liturgica 20. Vatican City: Libreria Editrice Vaticana, © 2002.

Chatellier, Louis. *The Europe of the Devout: The Catholic Reformation and the Formation of a New Society*. Past and Present Publications. Cambridge, England: Cambridge University Press; Paris: Editions de la Maison des Sciences de l'Homme, 1989.

Chavasse, Antoine. "A Rome, le Jeudi-saint, au VIIᵉ siècle, d'après un vieil Ordo". *Revue d'Histoire Ecclésiastique* 50 (1955): 21–35.

———. "Prières pour les malades et onction sacramentelle". In Aimé-Georges Martimort, ed., *L'église en prière: Introduction à la liturgie*, 580–594. Paris: Desclée, 1961.

Chevalier, Ulysse. *Repertorium hymnologicum: Catalogue des chants, hymnes, proses, séquences, tropes en usage dans l'église latine depuis les origines jusqu'à nos jours*. 3 vols. Louvain, Belgium: Lefever (vol. 1), Polleunis and Ceuterick (vols. 2–3), 1892–1904.

Chibnall, Marjorie, ed. and trans. *The Ecclesiastical History of Orderic Vitalis*. Vol. 4, *Books VII and VIII*. Oxford Medieval Texts. Oxford: Clarendon, 1973.

Claeys Bouuaert, F. "Evêques". In R. Naz, ed., *Dictionnaire de droit canonique*, vol. 5, cols. 569–589. Paris: Librairie Letouzey et Ané, 1953.

Collectio rituum: Pro dioecesibus Civitatum Foederatarum Americae Septentrionalis; Ritual Approved by the National Conference of Bishops of the United States of America. New York: Benziger Bros., 1964.

Cologne, Germany, manuscript: Dombibliothek Köln, Domhandschrift codex 1099. Ritual, fifteenth century. Codices Electronici Ecclesiae Coloniensis, Erzbischöfliche Diözesan- und Dombibliothek, and Universität zu Köln, Cologne, Germany.

Connelly, Joseph. *Hymns of the Roman Liturgy*. Westminster, Md.: Newman, 1957.

Connolly, R. H., trans. *The Liturgical Homilies of Narsai*. Texts and Studies 8, no. 1. Cambridge, England: Cambridge University Press, 1909.

Corbett, John. "Gradual Psalms". In *Catholic Encyclopedia* (1907–1912), 6:718.

Corbin, Solange. *La déposition liturgique du Christ au Vendredi saint: Sa place dans l'histoire des rites et du théâtre religieux*. Paris: Société d'Editions "Les belles lettres"; Lisbon: Livraria Bertrand, 1960.

Corblet, Jules. *Histoire dogmatique, liturgique et archéologique du sacrement de l'Eucharistie*. 2 vols. Paris: Société Générale de Librairie Catholique, 1885–1886.

Corpus Christianorum: Continuatio mediaevalis. Turnhout, Belgium: Brepols, 1966–.

Corpus Christianorum: Series Latina. Turnhout, Belgium: Brepols, 1953–.

Costa, Eugenio. "Tropes et séquences dans le cadre de la vie liturgique au moyen âge". Pts. 1–2. *Ephemerides Liturgicae* 92 (1978): 261–322, 440–471.

Crehan, Joseph, S.J. "The Assumption and the Jerusalem Liturgy". *Theological Studies* 30 (1969): 312–325.

Cséfalvay, Pál, ed. *Christian Museum, Esztergom*. Budapest: Corvina Books, 1993.

D'Achery, Lucas. *Spicilegium, sive Collectio veterum aliquot scriptorum qui in Galliae bibliothecis delituerant*. 3 vols. Paris: Montalant, 1723.

Dalton, J. N., ed. *Ordinale Exoniense*. 2 vols. Henry Bradshaw Society 37–38. London: Henry Bradshaw Society, 1909.

Davril, A., O.S.B., and T. M. Thibodeau, eds. *Guillelmi Duranti: Rationale divinorum officiorum*. 3 vols. Corpus Christianorum: Continuatio mediaevalis 140, 140a, 140b. Turnhout, Belgium: Brepols, 1995–2000.

Dearmer, Percy, Ralph Vaughan Williams, and Martin Shaw, eds. *The Oxford Book of Carols*. Oxford: Oxford University Press, Music Department, 1999.

De Clercq, Charles, ed. *Concilia Galliae, A. 511–A. 695*. Corpus Christianorum: Series Latina 148a. Turnhout, Belgium: Brepols, 1963.

De Grassis, Paride. *De caeremoniis cardinalium et episcoporum in eorum dioecesibus.* Rome: Bernardinus Donangelus, 1587. Digitized text, Bayerische Staatsbibliothek, Munich, 2009.

De la Bigne, Marguerin, ed. *Maxima bibliotheca veterum patrum, et antiquorum scriptorum ecclesiasticorum.* 28 vols. Lyons, France: Anissonios, 1677.

Delatte, Paul. *The Rule of Saint Benedict: A Commentary.* London: Burns, Oates, and Washbourne, 1921.

Dell'Oro, Ferdinando, S.D.B. *Beatificazione e canonizzazione: "Excursus" storico-liturgico.* Bibliotheca "Ephemerides Liturgicae", subsidia, 89. Rome: Centro Liturgico Vincenziano, Edizioni Liturgiche, 1997.

Denzinger, Henry, and John Baptist Umberg, S.J., eds. *Enchiridion symbolorum: Definitionum et declarationum de rebus fidei et morum.* Ed. 21–23. Freiburg im Breisgau, Germany: Herder, 1937.

Deshusses, Jean, ed. *Le sacramentaire grégorien: Ses principales formes d'après les plus anciens manuscrits.* 3 vols. Vol. 1, 2nd ed. Vols. 2–3, 1st ed. Spicilegium Friburgense 16, 24, 28. Fribourg, Switzerland: Editions Universitaires Fribourg, 1979–1982.

Dessain, C. S., ed. *The Letters and Diaries of John Henry Newman.* Vol. 11, *Littlemore to Rome, October 1845 to December 1846.* London: Thomas Nelson and Sons, 1961.

Dickinson, Francis H., ed. *Missale ad usum insignis et praeclarae ecclesiae Sarum.* Burntisland, Scotland: E. Prelo de Pitsligo, 1861–1883.

Diercks, G. F., ed. *Sancti Cypriani episcopi epistularium.* Corpus Christianorum: Series Latina 3b. Sancti Cypriani episcopi opera, pt. 3, 1. Turnhout, Belgium: Brepols, 1994.

Dobszay, László. *The Bugnini-Liturgy and the Reform of the Reform.* Musicae sacrae meletemata 5. Front Royal, Va.: Church Music Association of America / Catholic Church Music Associates, 2003.

————, ed. *Liber ordinarius Agriensis (1509).* Musicalia Danubiana, subsidia, 1. Budapest: Magyar Tudományos Akadémia Zenetudományi Intézet, 2000.

Dold, Alban, ed. *Die Konstanzer Ritualientexte in ihrer Entwicklung von 1482–1721.* Liturgiegeschichtliche Quellen 5–6. Münster, Germany: Aschendorffschen Verlagsbuchhandlung, 1923.

Donovan, Richard, C.S.B. *The Liturgical Drama in Medieval Spain.* Toronto: Pontifical Institute of Medieval Studies, 1958.

Douteil, Heribertus, C.S.Sp., ed. *Iohannis Beleth: Summa de ecclesiasticis officiis.* Corpus Christianorum: Continuatio mediaevalis 41a. Turnhout, Belgium: Brepols, 1976.

Dowling, Austin. "Conclave". In *Catholic Encyclopedia* (1907–1912), 4:192–195.

Doyère, Pierre, ed. and trans. *Gertrude d'Helfta: Oeuvres spirituelles.* Vol. 3, *Le héraut, livre III.* Sources chrétiennes 143. Paris: Cerf, 1968.

Dubarat, V., ed. *Le missel de Bayonne de 1543.* Pau, France: Léon Ribaut, 1901.

Duchesne, Louis. *Christian Worship: Its Origin and Evolution.* London: SPCK, 1910.

————, ed. *Le Liber pontificalis: Text, introduction et commentaire.* 2 vols. Paris: Ernest Thorin, 1886–1892.

Duffy, Eamon. *The Stripping of the Altars: Traditional Religion in England, c. 1400–c. 1580.* New Haven: Yale University Press, 1992.

Dumas, A., O.S.B., ed. *Liber sacramentorum Gellonensis.* Corpus Christianorum: Series Latina 159. Turnhout, Belgium: Brepols, 1981.

Durandus de Saint-Pourçain. *D. Durandi a sancto Porciano, ord. Praed. et Meldensis, episcopi, in Petri Lombardi Sententias theologicas commentariorum libri IIII.* Venice: Guerraea, 1571.

Dykmans, Marc, S.J., ed. *Le cérémonial papal de la fin du moyen âge à la Renaissance.* 4 vols. Bibliothèque de l'Institut Historique Belge de Rome 24–27. Brussels and Rome: Institut Historique Belge de Rome, 1977–1985.

———, ed. *L'oeuvre de Patrizi Piccolomini, ou Le cérémonial papal de la première Renaissance.* 2 vols. Studi e testi 293–294. Vatican City: Biblioteca Apostolica Vaticana, 1980–1982.

———. *Le pontifical romain révisé au XVe siècle.* Studi e testi 311. Vatican City: Biblioteca Apostolica Vaticana, 1985.

Ebers, Godehard. *Der Papst und die Römische Kurie.* Vol. 1, *Wahl, Ordination und Krönung des Papstes.* Quellensammlung zur kirchlichen Rechtsgeschichte und zum Kirchenrecht 3. Paderborn, Germany: Ferdinand Schöningh, 1916.

Ekdahl Davidson, Audrey, ed. *Holy Week and Easter Ceremonies and Drama from Medieval Sweden.* Early Drama, Art and Music Monograph Series 13. Kalamazoo, Mich.: Medieval Institute Publications, Western Michigan University, 1990.

Evans, Ernest, ed. and trans. *Tertullian's Treatise on the Resurrection.* London: SPCK, 1960.

Evenou, J. "Processions, Pilgrimages, Popular Religion". In Aimé-Georges Martimort, ed., *The Church at Prayer: An Introduction to the Liturgy,* vol. 3, *The Sacraments,* 241–262. Collegeville, Minn.: Liturgical Press, 1988.

Fabre, Paul, and Louis Duchesne, eds. *Le Liber censuum de l'église romaine.* 3 vols. in 6 fascicles. Bibliothèque des écoles françaises d'Athènes et de Rome, 2nd series, Registres des papes du XIIIe siècle, 6. Paris: Fontemoing, 1889–1910.

Fanning, William. "Papal Elections". In *Catholic Encyclopedia* (1907–1912), 11:456–457.

———. "Subdeacon". In *Catholic Encyclopedia* (1907–1912), 14:320–321.

Felbecker, Sabine. *Die Prozession: Historische und systematische Untersuchungen zu einer liturgischen Ausdruckshandlung.* Münsteraner theologische Abhandlungen 39. Altenberge, Germany: Oros Verlag, 1995.

Férotin, Marius, O.S.B., ed. *Le Liber ordinum en usage dans l'église wisigothique et mozarabe d'Espagne du cinquième au onzième siècle.* Paris, 1904. Reprint, ed. Anthony Ward, S.M., and Cuthbert Johnson, O.S.B. Bibliotheca "Ephemerides Liturgicae", subsidia, 83. Rome: Centro Liturgico Vincenziano, Edizioni Liturgiche, 1996.

Ferreres Boluda, Blessed Juan Bautista, S.J. *Historia del misal romano.* Barcelona: Eugenio Subirana, 1929.

Festugière, A.-J., O.P., trans. *Les moines d'Orient.* Vol. 3, pt. 3, *Les moines de Palestine.* Paris: Cerf, 1963.

Fischer, Ludwig, ed. *Bernhardi cardinalis et Lateranensis ecclesiae prioris Ordo officiorum ecclesiae Lateranensis.* Historische Forschungen und Quellen 2–3. Munich: Dr. F. P. Datterer, 1916.

Flannery, Austin, O.P., ed. *Vatican Council II: The Conciliar and Post Conciliar Documents.* Northport, N.Y.: Costello, 1975.

Flori, Jean. "Les origines de l'adoubement chevaleresque: Etude des remises d'armes et du vocabulaire qui les exprime dans les sources historiques latines jusqu'au début du XIIIe siècle". *Traditio* 35 (1979): 209–272.

Förster, Hans, ed. *Transitus Mariae: Beiträge zur koptischen Überlieferung.* Die Griechischen christlichen Schriftsteller der ersten Jahrhunderte, new series, 14. Berlin: Walter de Gruyter, 2006.

Fortescue, Adrian. "Communion-Antiphon". In *Catholic Encyclopedia* (1907–1912), 4:169–170.

———. "Gradual". In *Catholic Encyclopedia* (1907–1912), 6:715–718.

————. "Introit". In *Catholic Encyclopedia* (1907–1912), 8:81–82.

————. "Jerusalem, II: From A.D. 71 to A.D. 1099". In *Catholic Encyclopedia* (1907–1912), 8:355–361.

————. "Mass, Liturgy of the". In *Catholic Encyclopedia* (1907–1912), 9:790–800.

————. "Offertory". In *Catholic Encyclopedia* (1907–1912), 11:217–219.

Fortini, Arnaldo. "La settimana santa di Assisi". *Ecclesia* 17 (March 1958): 114–119.

Franceschini, A., and R. Weber, eds. *Itinerarium Egeriae*. In *Itineraria et Alia geographia*, 27–103. Corpus Christianorum: Series Latina 175. Turnhout, Belgium: Brepols, 1965.

Frank, Jerome, O.S.B. "Der älteste erhaltene *Ordo defunctorum* der römischen Liturgie und sein Fortleben in Totenagenden des frühen Mittelalters". *Archiv für Liturgie Wissenschaft* 7, pt. 2 (1962): 360–415.

————. "Geschichte des Trierer Beerdigungsritus". *Archiv für Liturgie Wissenschaft* 4, pt. 2 (1956): 279–315.

Franquesa, Adalberto. "El ritual Tarraconense". In *Liturgica*, 2:249–298. Scripta et documenta 10. Barcelona: Publicaciones de l'Abadia de Montserrat, 1958.

Franz, Adolph. *Die kirchlichen Benediktionen im Mittelalter*. 2 vols. Freiburg im Breisgau, Germany, 1909. Reprint, Graz, Austria: Akademische Druck—U. Verlagsanstalt, 1960.

————. *Das Rituale von St. Florian aus dem zwölften Jahrhundert*. Freiburg im Breisgau, Germany: Herder, 1904.

Frere, Walter Howard. *Studies in Early Roman Liturgy*. Vol. 3, *The Roman Epistle-Lectionary*. Alcuin Club Collections 32. Oxford: Oxford University Press; London: Humphrey Milford, 1935.

————, ed. *The Use of Sarum*. 2 vols. Cambridge, England: Cambridge University Press, 1898–1901.

Funk, Francis Xavier, ed. *Didascalia et Constitutiones apostolorum*. 2 vols. Paderborn, Germany: Libraria Ferdinandi Schoeningh, 1905.

Galtier, Paul, S.J. *De paenitentia: Tractatus dogmatico-historicus*. Rome: Pontificia Università Gregoriana, 1956.

Gamber, Klaus. *Codices liturgici Latini antiquiores*. Pt. 1. Spicilegii Friburgensis, subsidia, 1. Fribourg, Switzerland: Universitätsverlag Freiburg, 1968.

————. *The Reform of the Roman Liturgy: Its Problems and Background*. San Juan Capistrano, Calif.: Una Voce Press; Harrison, N.Y.: Foundation for Catholic Reform, 1993.

Gassner, Jerome, O.S.B. "The 'Reproaches'". *Homiletic and Pastoral Review* 46 (February 1946): 323–332.

Gautier, Léon. *Chivalry*. New York: Crescent Books, 1989.

Gavanti, Bartolommeo, and Cajetan Merati. *Thesaurus sacrorum rituum*. 2 vols. in 4 tomes. Rome: Typographia Vaticana, 1736–1738.

Gebran, Antoine. *Il Venerdì santo nel rito Siro-Maronita*. Bibliotheca "Ephemerides Liturgicae", subsidia, 136. Rome: Centro Liturgico Vincenziano, Edizioni Liturgiche, 2006.

Gerbert, Martin. *Monumenta veteris liturgiae Alemannicae*. 2 vols. Sankt Blasien, Germany: Typis San-Blasianis, 1777–1779.

Girona, Spain, manuscript: Biblioteca Pública del Estado en Girona, MS 108. Ceremonial, Monastery of San Benito, Valladolid, Spain, fifteenth century. Digitized text, Biblioteca Virtual del Patrimonio Bibliográfico, Madrid, 2008.

Giusti, M. "L'*Ordo officiorum* di Lucca". In *Miscellanea Giovanni Mercati*, vol. 2, *Letteratura medioevale*, 523–566. Studi e testi 122. Vatican City: Biblioteca Apostolica Vaticana, 1946.

Glimm, Francis X., Joseph M.-F. Marique, S.J., and Gerald G. Walsh, S.J., trans. *The Apostolic Fathers.* Fathers of the Church 1. New York: CIMA, 1947.

Goar, James, O.P. *Euchologion sive Rituale Graecorum.* 2nd ed. Venice, 1730. Reprint, Graz, Austria: Akademische Druck—U. Verlagsanstalt, 1960.

Godu, G. "Epîtres". In Fernand Cabrol and Henri Leclercq, eds., *Dictionnaire d'archéologie chrétienne et de liturgie,* vol. 5, pt. 1, cols. 245–344. Paris: Librairie Letouzey et Ané, 1907–1953.

Goyau, Georges. "Mende, Diocese of". In *Catholic Encyclopedia* (1907–1912), 10:180.

Graboïs, Aryeh. "Bible". In Joseph Strayer, ed., *Dictionary of the Middle Ages.* New York: Charles Scribner's Sons, 1982, 2:210–217.

Groeschel, Benedict, J., C.F.R., and James Monti. *In the Presence of Our Lord: The History, Theology, and Psychology of Eucharistic Devotion.* Huntington, Ind.: Our Sunday Visitor, 1997.

Guerrini, Francis, O.P., ed. *Ordinarium juxta ritum sacri ordinis Fratrum Praedicatorum.* With the authorization of Louis Theissling, O.P. Rome: Collegium Angelicum, 1921.

Gundersheimer, Werner L., ed. *Art and Life at the Court of Ercole I d'Este: The 'De triumphis religionis' of Giovanni Sabadino degli Arienti.* Travaux d'humanisme et Renaissance 127. Geneva: Droz, 1972.

Gy, Pierre-Marie, O.P. "Le nouveau rituel romain des funérailles". *La Maison-Dieu* 101 (1970): 15–32.

———. "Penance and Reconciliation". In Aimé-Georges Martimort, ed., *The Church at Prayer: An Introduction to the Liturgy,* vol. 3, *The Sacraments,* 101–115. Collegeville, Minn.: Liturgical Press, 1988.

Haacke, Hrabanus, O.S.B., ed. *Ruperti Tuitiensis: Liber de divinis officiis.* Corpus Christianorum: Continuatio mediaevalis 7. Turnhout, Belgium: Brepols, 1967.

Haimerl, Xaver. *Das Prozessionswesen des bistums Bamberg im Mittelalter.* Münchener Studien zur historischen Theologie 14. Munich: Verlag Kösel-Pustet, 1937.

Hallinger, Kassius, O.S.B. *Consuetudines Cluniacensium antiquiores cum redactionibus derivatis.* Corpus consuetudinum monasticarum 7, pt. 2. Siegburg, Germany: Franciscus Schmitt, 1983.

Halphen, Louis, and René Poupardin, eds. *Chroniques des comtes d'Anjou et des seigneurs d'Amboise.* Collection de textes pour servir à l'étude et à l'enseignement de l'histoire 48. Paris: Auguste Picard, 1913.

Hamilton, Sarah. *The Practice of Penance, 900–1050.* Royal Historical Society Studies in History, new series. Woodbridge, England: Boydell, 2001.

Hänggi, Anton, and Irmgard Pahl, eds. *Prex Eucharistica: Textus e variis liturgiis antiquioribus selecti.* Spicilegium Friburgense 12. Fribourg, Switzerland: Editions Universitaires Fribourg, 1968.

Hänggi, Anton, and Alfons Schönherr, eds. *Sacramentarium Rheinaugiense: Handschrift Rh 30 der Zentralbibliothek Zürich.* Spicilegium Friburgense 15. Fribourg, Switzerland: Universitätsverlag Freiburg, 1970.

Hanna, Edward. "Penance". In *Catholic Encyclopedia* (1907–1912), 11:618–635.

Hanssens, John Michael, S.J., ed. *Amalarii episcopi: Opera liturgica omnia.* 3 vols. Studi e testi 138–140. Vatican City: Biblioteca Apostolica Vaticana, 1948–1950.

Harrison, Odelia G., O.S.B. "The Formulas *Ad virgines sacras*: A Study of the Sources". Pts. 1–2. *Ephemerides Liturgicae* 66 (1952): 252–273, 352–366.

Hartel, Wilhelm von, ed. *Sancti Pontii Meropii Paulini Nolani: Carmina.* Corpus scriptorum ecclesiasticorum Latinorum 30. Vienna: Österreichischen Akademie der Wissenschaften, 1999.

Heiming, O., O.S.B., ed. *Liber sacramentorum Augustodunensis.* Corpus Christianorum: Series Latina 159b. Turnhout, Belgium: Brepols, 1984.

Henderson, William George, ed. *Manuale et processionale ad usum insignis ecclesiae Eboracensis.* Surtees Society Publications 63. Durham, England: Andrews, 1875.

————, ed. *Missale ad usum insignis ecclesiae Eboracensis.* Vol. 1. Surtees Society Publications 59. Durham, England: Andrews, 1874.

Hennecke, Edgar, and Wilhelm Schneemelcher, eds. *New Testament Apocrypha.* 2 vols. Philadelphia: Westminster, 1963–1966.

Henry, H. T. "*Victimae paschali laudes immolent Christiani*". In *Catholic Encyclopedia* (1907–1912), 15:407–408.

Henry of Langenstein. *Secreta sacerdotum.* Nürnberg, Germany: Georg Stuchs, c. 1497. Digitized text, Bayerische Staatsbibliothek, Munich, 2009.

Herrgott, Marquard, ed. *Vetus disciplina monastica.* Paris, 1726. Reprint, Siegburg, Germany: Franciscus Schmitt, 1999.

Hésbert, René-Jean, ed. *Antiphonale missarum sextuplex.* Brussels, 1935. Reprint, Rome: Herder, 1967.

————, ed. *Corpus antiphonalium officii.* 4 vols. Rerum ecclesiasticarum documenta, series maior: Fontes 7–10. Rome: Herder, 1963–1970.

Hores de la setmana sancta segons lo us del archibisbat de Valencia. Valencia, Spain: Jaime de Villa, 1494.

Holstenius, Lucas. *Codex regularum monasticarum et canonicarum.* 6 vols. in 3 tomes. Augsburg, Germany, 1759. Reprint, Graz, Austria: Akademische Druck—U. Verlagsanstalt, 1957.

The Holy Bible, Translated from the Latin Vulgate [Douay-Rheims Version]. Baltimore, 1899. Reprint, Rockford, Ill.: TAN Books, 1971.

Hosius, Stanislaus [Hozjusz, Stanislaw]. *D. Stanislai Hosii, S.R.E. cardinalis, maioris poenitentiarii, et episcopi Varmiensis: Opera omnia in duos divisa tomos.* 2 vols. Cologne, Germany: Maternus Cholinus, 1584. Digitized text, CBN Polona, National Digital Library, Biblioteka Narodowa, Warsaw, Poland, n.d.

James, Montague Rhodes. *The Apocryphal New Testament.* Oxford: Clarendon, 1924.

Janeras, Sebastià. "La settimana santa nell'antica liturgia di Gerusalemme". In Antony George Kollamparampil, ed., *Hebdomadae sanctae celebratio: Conspectus historicus comparativus,* 19–50. Bibliotheca "Ephemerides Liturgicae", subsidia, 93. Rome: Centro Liturgico Vincenziano, Edizioni Liturgiche, 1997.

————. *Le Vendredi-saint dans la tradition liturgique byzantine: Structure et histoire de ses offices.* Studia Anselmiana 99. Analecta liturgica 13. Rome: Pontificio Ateneo S. Anselmo, 1988.

Janini, José, and Ramón Gonzálvez. *Catálogo de los manuscritos litúrgicos de la catedral de Toledo.* Publicaciones del IPIET, 3rd series, 11. Toledo, Spain: Diputación Provincial, 1977.

John XXIII, Blessed. *Journal of a Soul.* New York: McGraw-Hill, 1965.

John Paul II, Blessed. Corpus Christi homily. June 15, 1995. *L'Osservatore Romano,* weekly edition in English, June 21, 1995, pp. 1–2.

Jones, L. A. "Byzantine Art". In *New Catholic Encyclopedia,* 2nd ed., 2:727–741. Detroit: Thomson/Gale, 2003.

Jörgensen, Johannes. *Saint Francis of Assisi: A Biography*. Image Books. Garden City, N.Y.: Doubleday, 1955.

Jounel, Pierre. "The Year". In Aimé-Georges Martimort, ed., *The Church at Prayer: An Introduction to the Liturgy*, vol. 4, *The Liturgy and Time*, 31–150. Collegeville, Minn.: Liturgical Press, 1986.

Joyce, G. H., S.J. "Private Penance in the Early Church". *Journal of Theological Studies* 42, 1st series (1941): 18–42.

Jugie, Martin, ed. and trans. *Homélies mariales byzantines: Textes grecs édités et traduits en latin*. Vol. 2. Patrologia orientalis 19, fasc. 3. Paris: Firmin-Didot, 1925.

Julian, John. *A Dictionary of Hymnology*. London: J. Murray, 1907.

Jungmann, Josef, S.J. *The Early Liturgy to the Time of Gregory the Great*. Liturgical Studies 6. Notre Dame, Ind.: University of Notre Dame Press, 1959.

―――. *Die lateinischen Bussriten in ihrer geschichtlichen Entwicklung*. Forschungen zur Geschichte des innerkirchlichen Lebens 3–4. Innsbruck, Austria: Druck und Verlag Fel. Rauch, 1932.

―――. *The Mass of the Roman Rite: Its Origins and Development*. 2 vols. New York: Benziger Bros., 1951–1955.

Kamm, Thomas. *Sein Grab wird herrlich sein: Heilige Gräber als Zeugen barocker Frömmigkeit*. Salzburg, Austria: PARC / Stiftung Heimathaus Traunstein, 2003.

Kantorowicz, Ernst. *Laudes Regiae: A Study in Liturgical Acclamations and Mediaeval Ruler Worship*. University of California Publications in History 33. Berkeley, Calif.: University of California Press, 1946.

Keates, Jonathan, and Angelo Hornak. *Canterbury Cathedral*. Florence: Scala Books / Philip Wilson, 1980.

Keen, Maurice. *Chivalry*. New Haven: Yale University Press, 1984.

Kennedy, V. L., C.S.B. "The Date of the Parisian Decree on the Elevation of the Host". *Mediaeval Studies* 8 (1948): 87–96.

King, Archdale. *Liturgies of the Past*. Milwaukee: Bruce, 1959.

―――. *Liturgies of the Primatial Sees*. Rites of Western Christendom 3. London: Longmans, Green, 1957.

Kirsch, J. P. "John XII, Pope". In *Catholic Encyclopedia* (1907–1912), 8:426–427.

Knowles, David, and Christopher N. L. Brooke, eds. and trans. *The Monastic Constitutions of Lanfranc*. Rev. ed. Oxford Medieval Texts. Oxford: Clarendon, 2002.

Kollamparampil, Antony George, ed. *Hebdomadae sanctae celebratio: Conspectus historicus comparativus*. Bibliotheca "Ephemerides Liturgicae", subsidia, 93. Rome: Centro Liturgico Vincenziano, Edizioni Liturgiche, 1997.

Kottje, Raymund. "Busspraxis und Bussritus". In Centro Italiano di Studi sull'Alto Medioevo, ed., *Segni e riti nella chiesa altomedievale occidentale, 11–17 Aprile 1985*, 1:369–395. Settimane di Studio del Centro Italiano di Studi sull'Alto Medioevo 33. Spoleto, Italy: Centro Italiano di Studi sull'Alto Medioevo, 1987.

Kuypers, A. B., ed. *The Prayer Book of Aedeluald the Bishop, Commonly Called the Book of Cerne*. Cambridge, England: Cambridge University Press, 1902.

Labudda, Alfons. "Liturgia dnia Zadusznego w Polsce do Wydania Rytuału Piotrkowskiego w Świetle Ksiąg Liturgicznych: Studium historyczno-liturgiczne". In *Studia z dziejów liturgii w Polsce*, 1:301–385. Rozprawy Wydziału Teologiczno-Kanonicznego 33. Lublin, Poland: Towarzystwo Naukowe, Katolickiego Uniwersytetu Lubelskiego, 1973.

Lambot, C., O.S.B., ed. *North Italian Services of the Eleventh Century: Recueil d'ordines du XIe siècle*. Henry Bradshaw Society 67. London: Henry Bradshaw Society, 1931.

Lamott, Alois. *Das Speyerer Diözesanrituale von 1512 bis 1932: Seine Geschichte und seine Ordines zur Sakramentenliturgie.* Quellen und Abhandlungen zur mittelrheinischen Kirchengeschichte 5. Speyer, Germany: Jaegerschen Buchdruckerei, 1961.

Lanne, Emmanuel, O.S.B. "Textes et rites de la liturgie pascale dans l'ancienne église copte". *L'Orient Syrien* 6 (1961): 279–300.

Lawley, Stephen Willoughby, ed. *Breviarium ad usum insignis ecclesie Eboracensis.* 2 vols. Surtees Society Publications 71, 75. Durham, England: Andrews, 1880–1883.

Lawlor, Hugh Jackson, ed. *The Rosslyn Missal.* Henry Bradshaw Society 15. London: Henry Bradshaw Society, 1899.

Lawson, Christopher M., ed. *Sancti Isidori episcopi Hispalensis: De ecclesiasticis officiis.* Corpus Christianorum: Series Latina 113. Turnhout, Belgium: Brepols, 1989.

Lee, M. Owen. *The Operagoer's Guide: One Hundred Stories and Commentaries.* Portland, Ore.: Amadeus, 2001.

Lefèvre, P. F., O.Praem., ed. *L'ordinaire de Prémontré d'après des manuscrits du XIIe et du XIIIe siècle.* Bibliothèque de la Revue d'Histoire Ecclésiastique 22. Louvain, Belgium: Bureaux de la Revue, 1941.

Legg, John Wickham, ed. *The Sarum Missal, Edited from Three Early Manuscripts.* Oxford: Clarendon, 1916.

———, ed. *Tracts on the Mass.* Henry Bradshaw Society 27. London: Henry Bradshaw Society, 1904.

Leuppi, Heidi. *Der Liber ordinarius des Konrad von Mure: Die Gottesdienstordnung am Grossmünster in Zürich.* Spicilegium Friburgense 37. Fribourg, Switzerland: Universitätsverlag Freiburg, 1995.

Leuterman, Teodoro. *Ordo Casinensis hebdomadae maioris (saec. XII).* Miscellanea Cassinese 20. Monte Cassino, Italy: Monte Cassino Abbey, 1941.

Liber obsequiorum ecclesiae Frisingensis. Ingolstadt, Germany: Weyssenhorn, 1547. Digitized text, Bayerische Staatsbibliothek, Munich, 2009.

Liber processionum secundum ordinem Fratrum Praedicatorum. Seville, Spain: Meinard Ungut and Stanislao Polono, 1494.

Lippe, Robert, ed. *Missale Romanum: Mediolani, 1474.* Vol. 1, *Text.* Henry Bradshaw Society 17. London: Henry Bradshaw Society, 1899.

———, ed. *Missale Romanum: Mediolani, 1474.* Vol. 2, *A Collation with Other Editions Printed before 1570.* Henry Bradshaw Society 33. London: Henry Bradshaw Society, 1907.

Lipphardt, Walther, ed. *Lateinische Osterfeiern und Osterspiele.* 6 vols. Ausgaben deutscher Literatur des XV. bis XVIII. Jahrhunderts: Reihe Drama 5. Berlin: Walter de Gruyter, 1975–1981.

Llompart, Gabriel. "El davallament de Mallorca, una paralitúrgia medieval". In Societat Catalana d'Estudis Litúrgics, *Miscel·lània litúrgica catalana,* 1:109–133. Barcelona: Institut d'Estudis Catalans, 1978.

Llop i Bayo, Francesc. "Toques de campanas y otros rituales colectivos para alejar las tormentas". In Alfonso Esteban and Jean-Pierre Etienvre, eds., *Fiestas y liturgia: Actas del coloquio celebrado en la Casa de Velázquez, 12/14-XII-1985* [December 12–14, 1985], 121–134. Madrid: Casa de Velázquez, Universidad Complutense, 1988.

Llopart, Estanislau. "Les fórmules de la confirmació en el Pontifical romà". In *Liturgica,* 2:121–180. Scripta et documenta 10 Barcelona: Publicaciones de l'Abadia de Montserrat, 1958.

Lodi, Enzo, ed. *Enchiridion euchologicum fontium liturgicorum*. Bibliotheca "Ephemerides Liturgicae", subsidia, 15. Rome: Centro Liturgico Vincenziano, Edizioni Liturgiche, 1979.

López Valcárcel, Amador. "Lucus Augusti, locus sacramenti: El culto eucaristico en Lugo; Notas para su historia". *El Progresso*, June 8, 1969. Reprinted in Excma. Diputación Provincial de Lugo, ed., *Historias luguesas*, 39–49. Lugo, Spain: Imp. de la Excma. Diputación Provincial de Lugo, 1975.

Lowe, A., ed. *The Bobbio Missal: Text*. Henry Bradshaw Society 58. London: Henry Bradshaw Society, 1920.

Ludolph of Saxony. *Vita Jesu Christi*. Edited by Jean-Pierre Mabile and Jean-Jacques-Maria-Antoine Guerrin. Paris and Rome: Victor Palmé, 1865.

Lull, Blessed Raymond. *The Book of the Ordre of Chyvalry or Knyghthode: Westmynstre, William Caxton (1484)*. The English Experience 778. Norwood, N.J.: Walter J. Johnson; Amsterdam: Theatrum Orbis Terrarum, 1976.

MacCracken, Henry Noble, ed. *The Minor Poems of John Lydgate*. Part 1. Early English Text Society, extra series, 107. London: Early English Text Society, 1911.

MacGregor, A.J. *Fire and Light in the Western Triduum: Their Use at Tenebrae and at the Paschal Vigil*. Alcuin Club Collection 71. Runcorn, England: Alcuin Club; Collegeville, Minn.: Liturgical Press, 1992.

Magistretti, Marcus, ed. *Beroldus, sive Ecclesiae Ambrosianae Mediolanensis kalendarium et Ordines, saec. XII*. Milan; Joseph Giovanola, 1894.

Malherbe, Georges. "La capsula des présanctifiés le Jeudi-saint". Pts. 1–2. *Bulletin Paroissial Liturgique* 12 (1930): 85–88, 89–96.

———. "Le 'Palmezel'". *Bulletin Paroissial Liturgique* 14 (1932): 81–90.

Mann, Horace. *The Lives of the Popes in the Early Middle Ages*. 18 vols. in 19 tomes. London: Kegan Paul, Trench, Trubner; Saint Louis: B. Herder, 1925–1932.

Mansi, J.D., ed. *Sacrorum conciliorum nova et amplissima collectio*. Florence and Venice, 1759–1798. Reprint ed. with continuation, edited by J.-B. Martin and L. Petit. 53 vols. in 60 tomes. Paris: Hubert Welter, 1901–1927.

Manual de bendiciones, oficios, procesiones, y semana santa con el oficio de sepultura ... para el uso de los religiosos Descalzos de nuestra Señora de la Merced, redención de cautivos christianos. Madrid: D. Joachin Ibarra, 1789.

Manuale benedictionum. Passau, Germany: Typis Ambrosii Ambrosi, 1845.

Manuale sacramentorum, secundum usum almae ecclesiae mexicanae. Mexico City: Petrus Ocharte, 1568.

Marini, Piero. "Peter, Witness of the Resurrection: Historical and Liturgical Notes". Vatican News Services, April 23, 2000. http://www.vatican.va/news_services/ liturgy/documents/ns_lit_doc_20000423_easter_en.html.

Martène, Edmond. *De antiquis ecclesiae ritibus*. 4 vols. Venice: Johannes Baptista Novelli, 1763–1764.

Martimort, Aimé-Georges. *La documentation liturgique de Dom Edmond Martène*. Studi e testi 279. Vatican City: Biblioteca Apostolica Vaticana, 1978.

———. "Prayer for the Sick and Sacramental Anointing". In Aimé-Georges Martimort, ed., *The Church at Prayer: An Introduction to the Liturgy*, vol. 3, *The Sacraments*, 117–137. Collegeville, Minn.: Liturgical Press, 1988.

Martínez Montiel, Luis, and Alfredo J. Morales. *The Cathedral of Seville*. London: Scala, 1999.

Martini, Aldo, ed. *Il cosiddetto pontificale di Poitiers*. Rerum ecclesiasticarum documenta, series maior: Fontes 14. Rome: Casa Editrice Herder, 1979.

Marucchi, Orazio. *Manual of Christian Archeology*. Paterson, N.J.: St. Anthony Guild Press, 1949.

Maskell, William, ed. *Monumenta ritualia ecclesiae Anglicanae*. 3 vols. Oxford: Clarendon, 1882.

Mateos, Juan, S.J., ed. *Le Typicon de la grande église*. 2 vols. Orientalia Christiana analecta 165–166. Rome: Pont. Institutum Orientalium Studiorum, 1962–1963.

Mattes, Bernhard, C.S.S.R. *Die Spendung der Sakramente nach den Freisinger Ritualien: Eine Untersuchung der handschriftlichen und gedruckten Quellen*. Münchener theologische Studien 34. Munich: Max Hueber Verlag, 1967.

Matthew, Donald. *Atlas of Medieval Europe*. New York: Facts on File, 1992.

Meech, Sanford Brown. "John Drury and His English Writings". *Speculum* 9 (1934): 70–83.

Meller, Walter Clifford. *A Knight's Life in the Days of Chivalry*. London: T. Werner Laurie, 1924.

Messenger, Ruth Ellis. *Ethical Teachings in the Latin Hymns of Medieval England*. New York: Columbia University Press, 1930.

Metz, René. "La couronne et l'anneau dans la consécration des vierges". *Revue des Sciences Religieuses* 28 (1954): 113–132.

Mingana, A., ed. and trans. *Commentary of Theodore of Mopsuestia on the Lord's Prayer and on the Sacraments of Baptism and the Eucharist*. Woodbrooke Studies 6. Cambridge: W. Heffer and Sons, 1933.

Missale Abulense [*Missale secundum consuetudinem cathedralis ecclesie civitatis Abulensis*]. Salamanca, Spain: Juan de Porras, 1510.

Missale ad usum alme ecclesie Salmanticensis. Salamanca, Spain: Juan de Junta, 1533. Digitized text, Universidad de Salamanca, Gredos Repositorio Documental, Salamanca, Spain, 2010.

Missale Ambianense. Paris: Jean du Pré, 1487. Digitized text, Gallica Bibliothèque Numérique, Bibliothèque Nationale de France, Paris, n.d.

Missale Augustanum. Augsburg, Germany: Erhard Ratdolt, 1496. Digitized text, Bayerische Staatsbibliothek, Munich, 2008.

Missale Bambergense. Bamberg, Germany: Johann Pfeyl, 1499. Digitized text, Bayerische Staatsbibliothek, Munich, 2008.

Missale Benedictinum Bamberg, Germany: Johann Sensenschmidt, 1481. Digitized text, Bayerische Staatsbibliothek, Munich, 2008.

Missale Bracarense. Lisbon: Nicolaus de Saxonia, 1498.

Missale Coloniense. Cologne, Germany: Heinrich Quentell, 1494. Digitized text, Bayerische Staatsbibliothek, Munich, 2009.

Missale Cracoviense. Nürnberg, Germany: Georg Stuchs, 1493. Digitized text, Bayerische Staatsbibliothek, Munich, 2009.

Missale divinorum secundum consuetudinem alme ecclesie Hispalensis. Seville: Joannes Varela, 1534. Biblioteca Apostolica Vaticana, Vatican City. Shelf mark Stamp. Barb. B. X. 4.

Missale divinorum secundum consuetudinem alme ecclesie Hispalensis. Seville: Joannes Gotherius, 1565. Digitized text, Fondos Digitalizados de la Universidad de Sevilla, Seville, n.d.

Missale Eystetense. Eichstätt, Germany: Michael Reyser, 1494. Digitized text, Bayerische Staatsbibliothek, Munich, 2009.

Missale Frisingense. Augsburg, Germany: Erhard Ratdolt, 1492. Digitized text, Bayerische Staatsbibliothek, Munich, 2009.

Missale Giennense / Manuale continens ordinem ad celebrandum ecclesiastica sacramenta [*Missale secundum morem et consuetudinem sancte ecclesie Gienensis*]. Seville: Meinard Ungut and Stanislao Polono, 1499.

Missale Halberstatense. Strasbourg, France: Johann Grüninger, c. 1498. Digitized text, Bayerische Staatsbibliothek, Munich, 2009.

Missale Hildensemense. Nürnberg, Germany: Georg Stuchs, 1499. Digitized text, Bayerische Staatsbibliothek, Munich, 2009.

Missale iuxta morem et consuetudinem sedis Valentiae. Venice: Johann Hamman, 1492. Digitized text, Biblioteca Digital Hispánica, Biblioteca Nacional de España, Madrid, 2007.

Missale iuxta ritum alme ecclesiae Valentine. Venice: Luca-Antonio Giunta, 1509. Biblioteca Històrica, Universitat de València, Valencia. Shelf mark R-1 / 18. Digitized text, Biblioteca Virtual, Universitat de València, Valencia, Spain, n.d.

Missale ordinis Fratrum Eremitarum sancti Augustini de observantia. Nürnberg, Germany: Fratres Ordinis Eremitarum Sancti Augustini / Georg Stuchs, 1491. Digitized text, Bayerische Staatsbibliothek, Munich, 2009.

Missale Pallantinum. Palencia, Spain: Sebastian Martinez, 1568. Biblioteca Apostolica Vaticana, Vatican City. Shelf mark Stamp. Barb. B. X. 1.

Missale Pataviense. Augsburg, Germany: Erhard Ratdolt, 1494. Digitized text, Bayerische Staatsbibliothek, Munich, 2009.

Missale Ratisbonense [*Missale Ratiponense*]. Regensburg, Germany: Johann Sensenschmidt and Johann Beckenhaub, 1485. Digitized text, Bayerische Staatsbibliothek, Munich, 2009.

Missale Romanum. Lyons, France: Michel Topié, 1497. Digitized text, Bayerische Staatsbibliothek, Munich, 2009.

Missale secundum consuetudinem almae ecclesiae Toletanae. 7 vols. Manuscript: Madrid, Biblioteca Nacional de España, MSS 1540–1546, dated 1503–1518. Digitized text, Biblioteca Digital Hispánica, Biblioteca Nacional de España, Madrid, 2007.

Missale secundum consuetudinem Curie Romane. Naples, Italy: Matthias Moravus, 1477. Digitized text, Bayerische Staatsbibliothek, Munich, n.d.

Missale secundum consuetudinem ecclesiae Tarraconensis. Tarragona, Spain: Johannes Rosenbach, 1499. Digitized text, Biblioteca Virtual del Patrimonio Bibliográfico, Madrid, n.d.

Missale secundum consuetudinem Elborensis ecclesie noviter impressum. Lisbon: Germano Galharde, 1509. Digitized text, Biblioteca Nacional Digital, Biblioteca Nacional de Portugal, 2009.

Missale secundum consuetudinem monachorum congregationis sancti Benedicti de Valladolid. Montserrat, Spain: Johannes Luschner, 1499. Digitized text, Biblioteca Virtual del Patrimonio Bibliográfico, Madrid, n.d.

Missale secundum consuetudinem Segobiensis ecclesie. Venice: Johannes Emericus de Spira, 1500. Digitized text, Biblioteca Digital Hispánica, Biblioteca Nacional de España, Madrid, 2007.

Missale secundum morem ecclesie Cesaraugustane. Saragossa: Paul Hurus, 1498.

Missale secundum ritum ac consuetudinem insignis ecclesiae Tirasonensis. Saragossa, Spain: Jorge Coci, 1529. Digitized text, Bayerische Staatsbibliothek, Munich, n.d.

Missale secundum usum Auriensis ecclesiae. Monterrey, Spain: Gonzalo Rodriguez de la Passera and Juan de Porras, 1494. Digitized text, Biblioteca Digital Hispánica, Biblioteca Nacional de España, Madrid, 2007.

Mittarelli, John-Benedict, and Anselm Costadoni, eds. *Annales Camaldulenses ordinis sancti Benedicti.* Vol. 6. Venice: Monastery of Saint Michael of Muriano and John Baptist Pasquali, 1761.

Moeller, Eugenius, Joannis Maria Clément, and Bertrandus Coppieters 'T Wallant, eds. *Corpus orationum.* Vol. 6. Corpus Christianorum: Series Latina 160e. Turnhout, Belgium: Brepols, 1995.

Mohlberg, Leo Cunibert, O.S.B., ed. *Missale Francorum.* Rerum ecclesiasticarum documenta, series maior: Fontes 2. Rome: Herder, 1957.

———, ed. *Missale Gothicum.* Rerum ecclesiasticarum documenta, series maior: Fontes 5. Rome: Herder, 1961.

Mohlberg, Leo Cunibert, O.S.B.; Leo Eizenhöfer, O.S.B.; and Petrus Siffrin, O.S.B., eds. *Liber sacramentorum Romanae aeclesiae ordinis anni circuli (Sacramentarium Gelasianum).* Rerum ecclesiasticarum documenta, series maior: Fontes 4. Rome: Herder, 1960.

———. *Sacramentarium Veronense.* Rerum ecclesiasticarum documenta, series maior: Fontes 1. Rome: Herder, 1956.

Molin, Jean-Baptiste, and Protais Mutembe. *Le rituel du mariage en France du XIIe au XVIe siècle.* Théologie historique 26. Paris: Beauchesne, 1974.

Monti, James. *The Week of Salvation: History and Traditions of Holy Week.* Huntington, Ind.: Our Sunday Visitor, 1993.

Monumenta Germaniae historica: Auctorum antiquissimorum. 15 vols. in 20 tomes. Berlin: Weidmann, 1877–1919.

Monumenta Germaniae historica: Capitula episcoporum. 4 vols. Hanover, Germany: Hahn, 1984–2005.

Monumenta Germaniae historica: Epistolarum. 8 vols. Berlin: Weidmann, 1891–1939.

Monumenta Germaniae historica: Legum, sectio IV; Constitutiones et acta publica imperatorum et regum. 9 vols. in 12 tomes. Hanover, Germany: Hahn, 1893–1927.

Monumenta Germaniae historica: Scriptorum. 32 vols. in 34 tomes. Hanover, Germany, 1826–1934. Reprint. Leipzig, Germany: Karl W. Hiersemann, 1925–1934.

Monumenta Germaniae historica: Scriptorum rerum Merovingicarum. 7 vols. in 8 tomes. Hanover, Germany: Hahn, 1888–1951.

Moraldi, Luigi, ed. *Apocrifi del Nuovo Testamento.* 2 vols. Classici delle religioni. Turin, Italy: Unione Tipografico-Editrice Torinese, 1971.

More, Saint Thomas. *The Confutation of Tyndale's Answer.* Edited by Louis Schuster, Richard Marius, James Lusardi, and Richard Schoeck. In 3 parts. Vol. 8 of *The Complete Works of St. Thomas More.* New Haven: Yale University Press, 1973.

———. *De Tristitia Christi.* Edited and translated by Clarence H. Miller. Vol. 14 of *The Complete Works of St. Thomas More.* New Haven: Yale University Press, 1976.

Morgan, Nigel, J. "Gurk Cathedral, 2: Painting". In Jane Turner, ed. *Dictionary of Art* (1996), 13:858. Grove. New York: Oxford University Press, 1996.

Morin, Germain. "Liturgie et basiliques de Rome au milieu du VIIe siècle d'après les listes d'évangiles de Würzburg". *Revue Bénédictine* 28 (1911): 296–330.

———. "Notes et documents, 3: Une formule de la bénédiction des rameaux dans une lettre du pape Zacharie à saint Boniface". *Revue Bénédictine* 27 (1910): 401–402.

———. "Le plus ancien *Comes* ou lectionnaire de l'église romaine". *Revue Bénédictine* 27 (1910): 41–74.

Morton, James, trans. *The Nun's Rule, Being the Ancren Riwle*. London: Chatto and Windus, 1924.

Mottola, Anthony, trans. *The Spiritual Exercises of St. Ignatius*. Image Books. Garden City, N.Y.: Doubleday, 1964.

Munier, C., ed. *Concilia Galliae, A. 314–A. 506*. Corpus Christianorum: Series Latina. 148. Turnhout, Belgium: Brepols, 1963.

Nocent, Adrien. "La pénitence dans les *Ordines* locaux transcrits dans le *De antiquis ecclesiae ritibus* d'Edmond Martène". In Giustino Farnedi, ed., *Paschale mysterium: Studi in memoria dell'Abate Prof. Salvatore Marsili (1910–1983)*, 115–138. Studia Anselmiana 91. Analecta Liturgica 10. Rome: Pontificio Ateneo S. Anselmo, 1986.

Nussbaum, Otto. "De altarium ablutione". *Ephemerides Liturgicae* 75 (1961): 105–116.

———. *Die Aufbewahrung der Eucharistie*. Theophaneia 29. Bonn, Germany: Hanstein, 1979.

Oberman, Heiko, and William Courtenay, eds. *Gabrielis Biel: Canonis misse expositio*. 5 vols. Veröffentlichungen des Instituts für Europäische Geschichte Mainz 32. Wiesbaden, Germany: Franz Steiner Verlag, 1963–1976.

O'Briain, Felim, O.F.M. "The Blessed Eucharist in Irish Liturgy and History". In *Studia Eucharistica: DCC^i anni a condito festo sanctissimi Corporis Christi, 1246–1946*, 216–245. Antwerp, Belgium: Uitgeverij Paul Brand, Bussum de Nederlandsche Boekhandel, 1946.

Obsequiale Augustense. Augsburg, Germany: Erhard Ratdolt, 1487. Digitized text, Bayerische Staatsbibliothek, Munich, 2008.

Obsequiale Brixinense. Augsburg, Germany: Erhard Ratdolt, 1493. Digitized text, Bayerische Staatsbibliothek, Munich, 2009.

Obsequiale Eystetense. Eichstätt, Germany: Michael Reyser, 1488. Digitized text, Bayerische Staatsbibliothek, Munich, 2009.

Obsequiale Frisingense. Augsburg, Germany: Erhard Ratdolt, 1493. Digitized text, Bayerische Staatsbibliothek, Munich, 2008.

Obsequiale Ratisponense. Nürnberg, Germany: Georg Stuchs, 1491. Digitized text, Bayerische Staatsbibliothek, Munich, 2008.

Obsequiale Salisburgense. Nürnberg, Germany: Georg Stuchs, 1496. Digitized text, Bayerische Staatsbibliothek, Munich, 2009.

Oesterreicher, John. "*Pro perfidis Judaeis*". *Theological Studies* 8 (1947): 80–96.

Ordinarium Barcinonense. Barcelona: Claudius Bornat, 1569. Digitized text, Biblioteca de Catalunya, Barcelona, 2010.

Ordo exsequiarum Romani pontificis. Vatican City: Officium de Liturgicis Celebrationibus Summi Pontificis, 2000.

Ottosen, Knud. *The Responsories and Versicles of the Latin Office of the Dead*. Aarhus, Denmark: Aarhus University Press, 1993.

Palude, Peter de. *Petrus de Palude: In quartum Sententiarum*. Venice: Bonetus Locatellus, 1493.

Pamelius [Jacques de Joigny de Pamèle]. *Liturgicon ecclesiae Latinae*. 2 vols. Cologne, Germany: Gervinus Calenius, 1571.

Papadopoulos-Kerameus, A., ed. *Analekta hierosolymitikēs stachyologias*. Vol. 2. Saint Petersburg, Russia, 1894. Reprint, Brussels: Culture et Civilisation, 1963.

Parés i Saltor, Francesc Xavier. *L'ordinari d'Urgell de 1536*. Col·lectània Sant Pacià 74. La Seu d'Urgell, Spain: Societat Cultural Urgel·litana / Facultat de Teologia da Catalunya, 2002.

Parisse, M. "Godefroy de Bouillon". In *Dictionnaire d'histoire et de géographie ecclésias-tiques*, vol. 21, cols. 388–391. Paris: Letouzey et Ané, 1912–.

Parvio, Martti, ed. *Manuale seu exequiale Aboense, 1522*. Facsimile ed. Suomen kirkko-historiallisen seuran toimituksia / Finska kyrkohistoriska samfundets handlingar 115. Helsinki: Societas Historiae Ecclesiasticae Fennica, 1980.

Patrologia Graeca. 161 vols. in 162 tomes. Paris: Jacques-Paul Migne, 1857–1887.

Patrologia Latina. 221 vols. Paris: Jacques-Paul Migne, 1844–1890.

Pérault, William. *Summae virtutum, ac vitiorum*. Vol. 1, *Summa aurea de virtutibus et vitiis*. Lyons, France: Antonius Vincentius, 1551. Digitized text, Bayerische Staats-bibliothek, Munich, 2009.

Pius V, Saint. "Revocation of the Privilege Conceded to Anyone of Celebrating Masses in the Evening Time". March 29, 1566. In Laertius Cherubini, ed., *Magnum bullar-ium Romanum*, 2:178. Lyons, France: Lawrence Arnaud et Peter Borde, 1673.

Pius XII, Venerable. *Episcopalis consecrationis*. November 30, 1944. *Acta Apostolicae Sedis* 37 (1945): 131–132.

———. "The Liturgical Movement: An Address of Pope Pius XII to the Inter-national Congress on Pastoral Liturgy". September 22, 1956. *Pope Speaks* 3 (Win-ter 1956–1957): 273–286.

———. *Mediator Dei*. November 20, 1947. In *Encyclical Letter of Pope Pius XII on the Sacred Liturgy: Mediator Dei*. Boston: Saint Paul Editions, n.d.

———. *Munificentissimus Deus*. November 1, 1950. In *Apostolic Constitution of Pope Pius XII on the Assumption of the Blessed Virgin Mary*. Translated by NCWC News Service. Staten Island, N.Y.: Daughters of Saint Paul, n.d.

———. *Sacramentum ordinis*. November 30, 1947. *Acta Apostolicae Sedis* 40 (1948): 5–7.

Pohle, Joseph, and Arthur Preuss. *The Sacraments: A Dogmatic Treatise*. 4 vols. Saint Louis: B. Herder, 1928–1931.

Porter, H.B. "The Origin of the Medieval Rite for Anointing the Sick or Dying". *Journal of Theological Studies*, new series, 7, no. 2 (October 1956): 211–225.

Poschmann, Bernhard. *Penance and the Anointing of the Sick*. Herder History of Dogma. New York: Herder and Herder, 1968.

Powers, Gabriel Francis. "Two New Saints: An Account of the Solemn Ceremony of Canonization of St. Euphrasia Pelletier and St. Gemma Galgani". *Sign* 19 (July 1940): 749–751.

Processionarium secundum ritum et morem Fratrum Predicatorum. Venice: Luceantonius, 1545. Digitized text, Bayerische Staatsbibliothek, Munich, 2009.

Procter, Francis, and Christopher Wordsworth, eds. *Breviarium ad usum insignis ecclesiae Sarum*. 3 vols. Cambridge: Cambridge University Press, 1879–1886.

Prokopp, Mária. *Das heilige Grab von Garamszentbenedek im Christlichen Museum zu Esztergom*. Budapest: Corvina Kiadó, 1983.

Quasten, John, ed. *Monumenta Eucharistica et liturgica vetustissima*. Pt. 1. Florilegium patristicum tam veteris quam medii aevi auctores complectens, fasc. 7, pt. 1. Bonn, Germany: Peter Hanstein, 1935.

Rackham, H., trans. *Cicero: De natura deorum; Academica*. London: William Heine-mann; Cambridge, Mass.: Harvard University Press, 1961.

Radó, Polycarp, O.S.B. *Enchiridion liturgicum*. 2 vols. Rome: Herder, 1961.

Radó, Polycarp, O.S.B., and Ladislaus Mezey. *Libri liturgici manuscripti bibliothecarum Hungariae et limitropharum regionum*. Budapest: Akadémiai Kiadó, 1973.

Rehle, Sieghild. "Missale Beneventanum (Codex VI 33 des Erzbischöflichen Archivs von Benevent)". *Sacris erudiri* 21 (1972–1973): 323–405.

Reifenberg, Hermann. *Sakramente, Sakramentalien und Ritualien im Bistum Mainz: Seit dem Spätmittelalter.* 2 vols. Liturgiewissenschaftliche Quellen und Forschungen 53–54. Münster, Germany: Aschendorffsche Verlagsbuchhandlung, 1971–1972.

Renoux, Athanase, ed. and trans. *Le codex Arménien Jérusalem 121.* Vol. 2, *Edition comparée du texte et de deux autres manuscrits.* Patrologia orientalis 36, fasc. 2. Turnhout, Belgium: Brepols, 1971.

Ribaillier, Jean, ed. *Magistri Guillelmi Altissiodorensis: Summa aurea; Liber quartus.* Spicilegium Bonaventurianum 19. Paris: Editions du Centre National de la Recherche Scientifique; Rome: Editiones Collegii S. Bonaventurae ad Claras Aquas, 1985.

Richard Pynson: Processionale ad usum Sarum, 1502. Facsimile ed. The Use of Sarum 1. Clarabricken, Ireland: Boethius, 1980.

Righetti, Mario. *Manuale di storia liturgica.* 4 vols. Milan: Editrice Ancora, 1949–1955.

Riley, Henry Thomas, ed. *Chronica monasterii s. Albani: Gesta abbatum monasterii sancti Albani, a Thoma Walsingham . . . compilata.* 3 vols. Rerum Britannicarum medii aevi scriptores 28, pt. 4. London: Longmans, Green, Reader, and Dyer, 1867–1869.

Ritzer, Korbinian. *Formen, Riten, und religiöses Brauchtum der Eheschliessung in den christlichen Kirchen des ersten Jahrtausends.* Liturgiewissenschaftliche Quellen und Forschungen 38. Münster, Germany: Aschendorffsche Verlagsbuchhandlung, 1962.

Rocca, Angelo. *De canonizatione sanctorum commentarius.* Rome: Guillelmus Facciottus, 1601. Digitized text, Bayerische Staatsbibliothek, Munich, n.d.

Rocca, Giancarlo. "Vestizione: Dal cinquecento in poi". In Guerrino Pelliccia and Giancarlo Rocca, eds., *Dizionario degli istituti di perfezione* (Rome: Edizione Paoline, 1974–2003), vol. 9, cols. 1956–1957.

Rock, Daniel. *The Church of Our Fathers, as Seen in St. Osmund's Rite for the Cathedral of Salisbury.* Vol. 3, pt. 2. London: C. Dolman, 1853.

Rock, P. M. J. "Golden Rose". In *Catholic Encyclopedia* (1907–1912), 6:629–630.

Römer, Gerhard. "Die Liturgie des Karfreitags". *Zeitschrift für Katholische Theologie* 77 (1955): 39–93.

Romero Abao, Antonio del Rocio. "Las fiestas de Sevilla en el siglo XV". In Centro de Estudios e Investigación de la Religiosidad Andaluza, ed., *Las fiestas de Sevilla en el siglo XV: Otros estudios*, 12–178. CEIRA 2. Madrid: Centro de Estudios e Investigación de la Religiosidad Andaluza / Deimos, 1991.

Ropa, Gian Paolo. "Il preludio medioevale all' adorazione della croce nel Venerdì santo". In Luigi Bettazzi, ed., *Miscellanea liturgica in onore di sua eminenza il cardinale Giacomo Lercaro*, 1:609–659. Rome: Desclée, 1966.

———. "Il simbolismo medioevale della croce svelata". In Luigi Bettazzi, ed., *Miscellanea liturgica in onore di sua eminenza il cardinale Giacomo Lercaro*, 2:957–1032. Rome: Desclée, 1967.

Rush, Alfred. *Death and Burial in Christian Antiquity.* Catholic University of America Studies in Christian Antiquity 1. Washington, D.C.: Catholic University of America Press, 1941.

Rus Herrera, Vicente, and Federico García de la Concha Delgado. *Leyendas, tradiciones y curiosidades históricas de la semana santa de Sevilla.* Seville: Editorial Castillejo, 1993.

Ryan, William Granger, trans. *Jacobus de Voragine: The Golden Legend; Readings on the Saints.* 2 vols. Princeton, N.J.: Princeton University Press, 1995.

Sacred Congregation of Rites. *Maxima redemptionis.* November 16, 1955. *American Ecclesiastical Review* 134 (January 1956): 51–55.

Sagmuller, Johannes Baptist. "Cardinal". In *Catholic Encyclopedia* (1907–1912), 3:333–341.

Saint Gall Abbey, Switzerland, manuscript: MS Codex Sangallensis (Cod. Sang.) 484. Tropary, c. 935. Stiftsbibliothek Sankt Gallen / Codices Electronici Sangallenses.

Saint-Roch, Patrick, ed. *Liber sacramentorum Engolismensis*. Corpus Christianorum: Series Latina 159c. Turnhout, Belgium: Brepols, 1987.

Santantoni, Antonio. *L'ordinazione episcopale: Storia e teologia dei riti dell'ordinazione nelle antiche liturgie dell'occidente*. Studia Anselmiana 69. Analecta Liturgica 2. Rome: Editrice Anselmiana, 1976.

Sanz Serrano, María Jesús. *Juan de Arfe y Villafañe y la custodia de Sevilla*. Arte hispalense 17. Seville: Excma. Diputación Provincial de Sevilla, 1978.

Schimmelpfennig, Bernhard. "Coronation, Papal". In Joseph Strayer, ed. *Dictionary of the Middle Ages*. New York: Charles Scribner's Sons, 1982, 3:602–605.

———. *Die Zeremonienbücher der Römischen Kurie im Mittelalter*. Bibliothek des Deutschen Historischen Instituts in Rom 40. Tübingen, Germany: Max Niemeyer, 1973.

Schmidt, Herman, S.J. *Hebdomada sancta*. 2 vols. Rome: Herder, 1956–1957.

Schmitz, Hermann Joseph, ed. *Die Bussbücher und die Bussdisciplin der Kirche: Nach handschriftlichen Quellen dargestellt*. 2 vols. Mainz, Germany: Franz Kirchheim, 1883; Düsseldorf: L. Schwann, 1898.

Schola Gregoriana Pragensis and Boni Pueri. *Adoratio Crucis* [*Uctívání Kříže—Devotion of the Cross*]. Supraphon, SU 3448-2-231, 2000, compact disc.

Schroeder, H.J., O.P., ed. *Canons and Decrees of the Council of Trent: Original Text with English Translation*. Saint Louis: B. Herder, 1955.

———, ed. *Disciplinary Decress of the General Councils: Text, Translation, and Commentary*. Saint Louis: B. Herder, 1937.

Schubert, Francis, and Richard Stapper, eds. *Excerpta ex ordinariis Germanicis de summis anni ecclesiastici festivitatibus*. Opuscula et textus historiam ecclesiae eiusque vitam atque doctrinam illustrantia: Series liturgica, fasc. 7–8. Münster, Germany: Aschendorff, 1936.

Schulten, Walter. *Cologne Cathedral*. Cologne: Greven Verlag, 1987.

Schuster, Blessed Ildefonso. *The Sacramentary (Liber sacramentorum): Historical and Liturgical Notes on the Roman Missal*. 5 vols. London: Burns, Oates and Washbourne, 1924–1930.

Searby, Denis, trans. *The Revelations of St. Birgitta of Sweden*. Vol. 1, *Liber caelestis, Books I–III*. Oxford: Oxford University Press, 2006.

Searle, Mark, and Kenneth Stevenson, eds. *Documents of the Marriage Liturgy*. Collegeville, Minn.: Liturgical Press, 1992.

Seguí i Trobat, Gabriel, ed. *El missal mallorquí de 1506: Estudi i edició segons l'exemplar de la Biblioteca Bartomeu March*. Col·lectània Sant Pacià 79. Barcelona: Facultat de Teologia de Catalunya, Centre d'Estudis Teològics de Mallorca, 2003.

Sheingorn, Pamela. *The Easter Sepulchre in England*. Early Drama, Art and Music Reference Series 5. Kalamazoo, Mich.: Medieval Institute Publications, 1987.

Sicard, Damien. *Le liturgie de la mort dans l'église latine des origines à la réforme carolingienne*. Liturgiewissenschaftliche Quellen und Forschungen 63. Münster, Germany: Aschendorffsche Verlagsbuchhandlung, 1978.

Sierra López, Juan Manuel. "El misal Toledano de 1499: Una visión de su contenido en relación con el misal romano y el mozárabe". *Ephemerides Liturgicae* 119 (2005): 151–199.

Simmons, T. F., ed. *The Lay Folks' Mass Book*. Early English Text Society, original series, 71. London: Early English Text Society, 1879.

Soberanas, Amadeu-J., ed. *Ordinarium sacramentorum Barchinonense, 1501.* Facsimile ed. Biblioteca litúrgica catalana 1. Barcelona: Institut d'Estudis Catalans, 1991.

Sodi, Manlio, ed. *Il "Pontificalis liber" di Agostino Patrizi Piccolomini e Giovanni Burcardo (1485).* Facsimile ed. Monumenta studia instrumenta liturgica 43. Vatican City: Libreria Editrice Vaticana, © 2006.

Sodi, Manlio, and Juan Javier Flores Arcas, eds. *Rituale Romanum: Editio princeps (1614).* Facsimile ed. Monumenta liturgica Concilii Tridentini 5. Vatican City: Libreria Editrice Vaticana, © 2004.

Sodi, Manlio, and Roberto Fusco, eds. *Martyrologium Romanum: Editio princeps (1584).* Facsimile ed. Monumenta liturgica Concilii Tridentini 6. Vatican City: Libreria Editrice Vaticana, © 2005.

Sodi, Manlio, and Achille Maria Triacca, eds. *Breviarium Romanum: Editio princeps (1568).* Facsimile ed. Monumenta liturgica Concilii Tridentini 3. Vatican City: Libreria Editrice Vaticana, © 1999.

―――, eds. *Missale Romanum: Editio princeps (1570).* Facsimile ed. Monumenta liturgica Concilii Tridentini 2. Vatican City: Libreria Editrice Vaticana, © 1998.

―――, eds. *Pontificale Romanum: Editio princeps (1595–1596).* Facsimile ed. Monumenta liturgica Concilii Tridentini 1. Vatican City: Libreria Editrice Vaticana, © 1997.

Souvay, Charles. "Esdras". In *Catholic Encyclopedia* (1907–1912), 5:535–538.

Steinmueller, John. *A Companion to Scripture Studies.* 3 vols. New York: Joseph F. Wagner; Houston: Lumen Christi Press, 1969.

Steinmueller, John, and Kathryn Sullivan, R.S.C.J., eds. *Catholic Biblical Encyclopedia: Old Testament.* New York: Joseph F. Wagner, 1959.

Stevenson, Kenneth. "The Ceremonies of Light: Their Shape and Function in the Paschal Vigil Liturgy". *Ephemerides Liturgicae* 99 (1985): 170–185.

―――. *Nuptial Blessing: A Study of Christian Marriage Rites.* Alcuin Club Collections 64. London: Alcuin Club / SPCK, 1982.

Stokes, Whitley, ed. *The Tripartite Life of Patrick, with Other Documents Relating to That Saint.* 2 vols. Rerum Britannicarum medii aevi scriptores 89. London: Eyre and Spottiswoode, 1887.

Strype, John. *Ecclesiastical Memorials Relating Chiefly to Religion, and the Reformation of It, and the Emergencies of the Church of England, under King Henry VIII, King Edward VI, and Queen Mary I.* Vol. 1, in 2 parts. Oxford: Clarendon, 1822.

Stubbs, William, ed. *Willelmi Malmesbiriensis monachi: De gestis regum Anglorum, libri quinque; Historiae novellae, libri tres.* 2 vols. Rerum Britannicarum medii aevi scriptores 90. London: Eyre and Spottiswoode, 1889.

Symons, Thomas, trans. *Regularis concordia: The Monastic Agreement of the Monks and Nuns of the English Nation.* Medieval Classics. New York: Oxford University Press, 1953.

Taft, Robert F., S.J. *The Great Entrance: A History of the Transfer of Gifts and Other Preanaphoral Rites of the Liturgy of St. John Chrysostom.* Vol. 2 of *A History of the Liturgy of St. John Chrysostom.* Orientalia Christiana analecta 200. Rome: Pontificio Istituto Orientale, 1978.

―――. *The Precommunion Rites.* Vol. 5 of *A History of the Liturgy of St. John Chrysostom.* Orientalia Christiana analecta 261. Rome: Pontificio Istituto Orientale, 2000.

Tarchnischvili, Michel, ed. *Le grand lectionnaire de l'église de Jérusalem (V^e–VIIIe siècle).* 4 vols. Corpus scriptorum Christianorum Orientalium 188, 204 (Georgian-language text), 189, 205 (Latin translation). Louvain, Belgium: Secrétariat du CorpusSCO, 1959–1960.

Thomas Aquinas, Saint. *The "Summa contra gentiles" of Saint Thomas Aquinas*. Translated by the English Dominican Fathers. 4 vols. in 5 tomes. New York: Benziger Brothers, 1923–1929.

———. *Summa theologica: First Complete American Edition in Three Volumes*. Translated by the Fathers of the English Dominican Province. 3 vols. New York: Benziger Brothers, 1948.

Thurston, Herbert, S.J. "Agnus Dei". In *Catholic Encyclopedia* (1907–1912), 1:220–221.

———. "Coronation". In *Catholic Encyclopedia* (1907–1912), 4:380–386.

———. "Cross and Crucifix, The, III: The Cross and Crucifix in Liturgy". In *Catholic Encyclopedia* (1907–1912), 4:533–539.

———. "Easter Sepulchre, or Altar of Repose?" *Month* 101 (April 1903): 404–414.

———. *Lent and Holy Week: Chapters on Catholic Observance and Ritual*. London: Longmans, Green, 1904.

———. "Marriage, Ritual of". In *Catholic Encyclopedia* (1907–1912), 9:703–707.

Toal, M. F., trans. and ed. *The Sunday Sermons of the Great Fathers*. 4 vols. Chicago, 1960–1963; Reprint, San Francisco: Ignatius Press, 2000.

Tolhurst, J. B. L., ed. *The Customary of Norwich*. Henry Bradshaw Society 82. London: Henry Bradshaw Society, 1948.

———, ed. *The Ordinale and Customary of the Benedictine Nuns of Barking Abbey*. Vol. 1. Henry Bradshaw Society 65. London: Henry Bradshaw Society, 1927.

Tommaseo, Niccolò, and Piero Misciattelli, eds. *Le lettere di s. Caterina da Siena*. 6 vols. Siena, Italy: Libreria Editrice Giuntini e Bentivoglio, 1913–1922.

Treis, Karl. *Die Formalitäten des Ritterschlags in der altfranzösischen Epik*. Berlin: Gustav Schade, 1887.

Triacca, Achille Maria, and Manlio Sodi, eds. *Caeremoniale episcoporum: Editio princeps (1600)*. Facsimile ed. Monumenta liturgica Concilii Tridentini 4. Vatican City: Libreria Editrice Vaticana, © 2000.

Urban IV. *Transiturus*. September 8, 1264. In Laertius Cherubini, ed., *Magnum bullarium Romanum*, vol. 1 (Lyons, France: Lawrence Arnaud et Peter Borde, 1673), 146–148.

Van Dijk, Stephen Aurelian, O.F.M. "The Breviary of Saint Clare". Pts. 1–2. *Franciscan Studies* 8 (1948): 25–46, 351–387.

Van Dijk, Stephen J. P., O.F.M. *Sources of the Modern Roman Liturgy: The Ordinals by Haymo of Faversham and Related Documents (1243–1307)*. 2 vols. Studia et documenta Franciscana 2. Leiden, Netherlands: E. J. Brill, 1963.

Van Dijk, Stephen J. P., O.F.M., and Joan Hazelden Walker, eds. *The Ordinal of the Papal Court from Innocent III to Boniface VIII and Related Documents*. Spicilegium Friburgense 22. Fribourg, Switzerland: The University Press, 1975.

———. *The Origins of the Modern Roman Liturgy: The Liturgy of the Papal Court and the Franciscan Order in the Thirteenth Century*. Westminster, Md.: Newman; London: Darton, Longman and Todd, 1960.

Van Hove, A. "Bishop". In *Catholic Encyclopedia* (1907–1912), 2:581–589.

———. "Henry of Segusio, Blessed". In *Catholic Encyclopedia* (1907–1912), 7:238.

Verheul, Ambroise. "Le mystère du Samedi saint". *Questions Liturgiques* 65 (1984): 19–38.

Villanueva, Jaime. *Viage literario a las iglesias de España*. Vol. 6, *Viage á la iglesia de Vique, año 1806*. Valencia, Spain: Oliveres, 1821.

———. *Viage literario a las iglesias de España*. Vol. 9, *Viage a Solsona, Ager y Urgel, 1806 y 1807*. Valencia, Spain: Oliveres, 1821.

Vogel, Cyrille. *Medieval Liturgy: An Introduction to the Sources*. Revised by William Storey and Niels Krogh Rasmussen, O.P. Washington, D.C: Pastoral Press, 1986.

Vogel, Cyrille, and Reinhard Elze, eds. *Le pontifical romano-germanique du dixième siècle*. 3 vols. Studi e testi 226, 227, 269. Vatican City: Biblioteca Apostolica Vaticana, 1963–1972.

Vogüé, Adalbert de, ed., and Paul Antin, trans. *Grégoire le Grand: Dialogues*. Vol. 2, *Livres I–III*. Sources chrétiennes 260. Paris: Cerf, 1979.

Volk, Paul, ed. *Der Liber ordinarius des Lütticher St. Jakobs-Klosters*. Münster, Germany: Aschendorff Verlag, 1923.

Von Fischer, Kurt. "Passion". In *New Grove Dictionary of Music and Musicians* (Washington, D.C.: Grove's Dictionaries of Music, 1980), 14:276–282.

Von Heisterbach, Caesarius. *Dialogus miraculorum*. Cologne, Germany: Johann Koelhoff der Ältere, 1481. Digitized text, Bayerische Staatsbibliothek, Munich, 2009.

Waal, Anton de. "Chair of Peter". In *Catholic Encyclopedia* (1907–1912), 3:551–554.

Wagner, Richard. *Parsifal*. English translation of Lionel Salter. Published in libretto booklet for *Richard Wagner: Parsifal*. Berliner Philharmoniker. Conducted by Herbert von Karajan. Deutsche Grammophon, 413 347–2, 1981, compact disc.

Walters, Barbara, Vincent Corrigan, and Peter Ricketts. *The Feast of Corpus Christi*. University Park, Pa.: Pennsylvania State University Press, 2006.

Ward, Anthony, S.M. "Further Euchology of the 1969 'Ordo Exsequiarum'". *Ephemerides Liturgicae* 119 (2005): 201–251.

———. "Holy Week in the Ambrosian Liturgy". In Antony George Kollamparampil, ed., *Hebdomadae sanctae celebratio: Conspectus historicus comparativus*, 187–235. Bibliotheca "Ephemerides Liturgicae", subsidia, 93. Rome: Centro Liturgico Vincenziano, Edizioni Liturgiche, 1997.

———. "Some Euchology of the 1969 'Ordo Exsequiarum'". *Ephemerides Liturgicae* 119 (2005): 3–51.

Warner, George, ed. *The Stowe Missal*. Vol. 2, *Printed Text*. Henry Bradshaw Society 32. London: Henry Bradshaw Society, 1915.

Wasner, Francis. "De consecratione, inthronizatione, coronatione summi pontificis". Pts. 1–3. *Apollinaris* 8 (1935): 86–125, 249–281, 428–439.

Watkins, Oscar D. *A History of Penance*. 2 vols. London: Longmans, Green, 1920.

Webster, Susan Verdi. *Art and Ritual in Golden-Age Spain: Sevillian Confraternities and the Processional Sculpture of Holy Week*. Princeton, N.J.: Princeton University Press, 1998.

Wellesz, Egon. *Eastern Elements in Western Chant: Studies in the Early History of Ecclesiastical Music*. Copenhagen: Munksgaard, 1967.

———. "Melito's Homily on the Passion: An Investigation into the Sources of Byzantine Hymnography". *Journal of Theological Studies* 44 (1943): 41–52.

William of Auvergne [William of Paris]. *Guilielmi Alverni, episcopi Parisiensis . . . Opera omnia*. 2 vols. Paris: Louis Billaine, 1674.

Wilmart, D. A. "Le *Comes* de Murbach". *Revue Bénédictine* 30 (1913): 25–69.

Wilson, Henry Austin, ed. *The Benedictional of Archbishop Robert*. Henry Bradshaw Society 24. London: Henry Bradshaw Society, 1903.

———, ed. *Officium ecclesiasticum abbatum secundum usum Eveshamensis monasterii*. Henry Bradshaw Society 6. London: Henry Bradshaw Society, 1893.

Young, Karl. *The Drama of the Medieval Church*. 2 vols. Oxford: Clarendon, 1933.

———. "Dramatic Ceremonies of the Feast of the Purification". *Speculum* 5 (1930): 97–102.

————. "Instructions for Parish Priests". *Speculum* 11 (April 1936): 224–231.

Zalewski, Zbigniew. "Święto Bożego Ciała w Polsce do Wydania Rytuału Piotrkowskiego (1631 r.)". In *Studia z Dziejów Liturgii w Polsce*, 1:95–161. Rozprawy Wydziału Teologiczno-Kanonicznego 33. Lublin, Poland: Towarzystwo Naukowe, Katolickiego Uniwersytetu Lubelskiego, 1973.

Zimmerman, Benedict, ed. *Ordinaire de l'ordre de Notre-Dame du Mont-Carmel*. Bibliothèque liturgique 13. Paris: Alphonse Picard et Fils, 1910.

Internet Websites Cited in Footnotes and Bibliography

Biblioteca Digital Hispánica, Biblioteca Nacional de España, Madrid. Digitized texts from the Biblioteca Nacional de España. Website: http://bibliotecadigitalhispanica.bne.es.

Biblioteca Nacional Digital, Biblioteca Nacional de Portugal. Digitized texts from the Biblioteca Nacional de Portugal. Website: http://purl.pt.

Biblioteca Virtual del Patrimonio Bibliográfico, Madrid. Digitized texts of books published in Spain or pertaining to Spanish history. Website: http://bvpb.mcu.es.

Cantus. Maintained at the University of Waterloo, Waterloo, Ontario, Canada. Online database of Gregorian chant indices of medieval liturgical manuscripts. Website: http://cantusdatabase.org.

CBN Polona, National Digital Library, Biblioteka Narodowa, Warsaw, Poland. Digitized texts of books published in Poland or pertaining to Polish history. Website: http://www.polona.pl/dlibra.

Codices Electronici Ecclesiae Coloniensis (CEEC), Erzbischöfliche Diözesan- und Dombibliothek, and Universität zu Köln, Cologne, Germany. Digitized texts of medieval manuscripts of Cologne. Website: http://www.ceec.uni-koeln.de.

Codices Electronici Sangallenses (CESG), Digital Abbey Library of Saint Gall, Switzerland. Website: http://www.cesg.unifr.ch/en.

Fondos Digitalizados de la Universidad de Sevilla, Seville. Digitized texts from the University of Seville. Website: http://fondosdigitales.us.es.

Gallica Bibliothèque Numérique, Bibliothèque Nationale de France, Paris. Digitized texts from the Bibliothèque Nationale de France. Website: http://gallica.bnf.fr.

Gateway Bayern, Bibliotheks Verbund Bayern, Germany. Online catalog of Bavarian libraries, with digitized copies of certain texts provided by Bayerische Staatsbibliothek, Munich. Website: http://opac.bib-bvb.de.

Vatican (Holy See), Vatican City: Website: http://www.vatican.va.

Index of Persons

Aaron, 228, 322, 367, 387, 585
  Holy Orders, 160, 166, 173, 175–178, 187, 189,
    191–192, 198
  the Mass, 39, 50, 91
Abdenago, 234
Abel, 471
Abraham, 270, 387, 408n26, 517, 585
  baptism, 110, 112
  blessings, 619, 638
  the Corpus Christi procession, 506–507
  funeral rites, 598, 609, 613
  the Mass, 31, 51
  matrimony, 214, 226, 229, 233
Adam, 104, 234, 480, 507
  Ash Wednesday, 298, 300, 302
  Christ as second, 507
  Christmas, 266, 283
  matrimony, 210–211, 229, 232
Adam, Salimbene de, 368
Agapitus I, Pope St., 84
Agatha, St., 580
Agnes, St., 203, 559, 580–581, 588n41, 589n44,
  590–591
Albano, bishop of, 554
Alcuin, 295
Alcuin, Pseudo-. See Pseudo-Alcuin
Alexander I, Pope St., 95, 648
Alexander III, Pope, 544
Alfonso VII of Castile, King, 313
Alfrid, 523
Almaric (son of Simon of Montfort), 628
Alphonsus Liguori, St., xix
Amalarius of Metz, xxi, 316, 467n59, 530, 605,
  637n94
  Good Friday, 410, 425, 435, 442
  Holy Orders, 160, 165, 168, 172–173, 178, 187,
    191
  Holy Thursday, 357–359, 361
  the Mass, 17, 29, 36, 56, 71, 74–75
Amalec, 39–40

Ambrose, St., 54n206, 136, 297, 478
  the Ambrosian Rite, 335, 353, 388
  baptism, 116, 121
  consecration of virgins, 580–581
Ameil, Pierre, 463n35, 465n49, 546, 569
  canonization of saints, 571–572, 577
  funeral rites, 615, 617
  Holy Thursday, 373–374, 382
Anacletus, Pope St., 541
Andrew, St., 172, 193, 559
Andrew of Strumi, Bl., 467
Andrieu, Michel, Msgr., xix, xxiii, 122n119,
  181n154, 207n305
  passim, 178–203 and throughout
Anna, 56–57, 287, 291
Annas, 368
Anselm of Canterbury, St., 68–69
Arens, Franz, 522n19
Arfe y Villafane, Juan de, 387
Assalbit, Pierre, 373, 382, 463n35, 465n49, 546,
  569, 615
Athanasius, St., 297, 519–520
Augustine, Pseudo-. See Pseudo-Augustine
Augustine, St., 16, 242n49, 350, 358, 382, 557,
  603n63
  baptism, 106
  Christmas, 267–269
  the Communion rite, 83
  Easter, 458
Auxilius (Roman priest), 558

Baixauli, Mariano, 499
Barakat, Abu-l, 454
Barberini, Francesco Cardinal (Codex Barberini),
  364, 391
Barnim XI (Pomeranian duke), 516n60
Baruch, 269
Basil, St., 136–137, 559
Battelli, J. C., 399n216
Beaulieu, Geoffrey of, 353–354